Japan

a Lonely Planet travel survival kit

Chris Taylor
Robert Strauss
Tony Wheeler

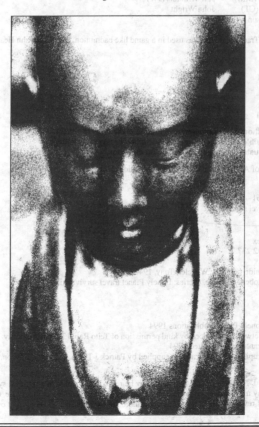

Japan

5th edition

Published by
Lonely Planet Publications
Head Office: PO Box 617, Hawthorn, Vic 3122, Australia
Branches: 155 Filbert St, Suite 251, Oakland, CA 94607, USA
                10 Barley Mow Passage, Chiswick, London W4 4PH, UK
                71 bis rue du Cardinal Lemoine, 75005 Paris, France

Printed by
SNP Printing Pte Ltd., Singapore

Script Typeset by
Yoko Speirs, Yukari Shuppan, Australia

Photographs by
Richard I'Anson (RI)   Tony Wheeler (TW)
Martin Moos (MM)   Jeff Williams (JW)
Chris Taylor (CT)   John Wright
Alex Thompson (AT)

Front cover: Traditional Hagoitas used in a game like badminton, (Dallas & John Heaton, Scoopix)

First Published
October 1981

This Edition
October 1994

**Although the authors and publisher have tried to make the information as
accurate as possible, they accept no responsibility for any loss, injury or
inconvenience sustained by any person using this book**.

National Library of Australia Cataloguing in Publication Data

Taylor, Chris, 1961–
    Japan – a travel survival kit.

    5th ed.
    Includes index.
    ISBN 0 86442 237 7.

    1. Japan – Guide-books. I. Wheeler, Tony, 1946 –
    II. Strauss, Robert. III. Title. (Series: Lonely Planet travel survival kit).

915.20449

text & maps © Lonely Planet Publications 1994
Tokyo Subway Network reproduced by kind permission of Teito Rapid Transit Authority
photos © photographers as indicated 1994
climate charts compiled from information supplied by Patrick J Tyson, © Patrick J Tyson, 1994

0544 650972

Chris Taylor
Chris Taylor spent his early years in England. He emigrated to Australia with his family in the '70s. After frittering away his youth in a variety of fruitless occupations, travelling and working on a useless BA, Chris joined Lonely Planet to work on the phrasebook series. He has since co-authored *China* and written the *Mandarin Chinese Phrasebook* and city guides for *Tokyo* and *Seoul*. He is currently somewhere in North-East Asia.

Robert Strauss
In the early '70s Robert Strauss took the overland route to Nepal and then studied, taught and edited in England, Germany, Portugal and Hong Kong. For Lonely Planet he has worked on travel survival kits to *China*, *Tibet*, *Brazil* and *Bolivia*. For Bradt Publications he wrote the *Trans-Siberian Rail Guide*. He has contributed photos and articles to other books, magazines and newspapers in the USA, Australia and Asia.

Tony Wheeler
Tony Wheeler was born in England but spent most of his youth overseas. He returned to England to do a university degree in engineering, worked as an automotive design engineer, returned to university to complete an MBA, then dropped out on the Asian overland trail with his wife Maureen. They've been travelling, writing and publishing guidebooks ever since, having set up Lonely Planet Publications in the mid-70s. Travel for the Wheelers is now considerably enlivened by their daughter Tashi and their son Kieran.

From Chris Taylor
In the course of traipsing from one end of Japan to another and writing up the results of all that traipsing, I have incurred a great many personal debts. A number of people deserve a special thank you, however. John Ashburne (and Akko of course) of *Kansai Time Out* put me up in their kitchen for a week and gave me a break from an endless run of youth hostels, ryokan and business

hotels – thanks for the company and all the tips. Murray White gave me the use of his Lamma Island woodland retreat when I needed it most. Fusako Sasaki (Paul says 'hello') looked after me in Osaka and pulled out the stops in sending me last-minute information. Hilary Sagar of Kodansha International did some much appreciated backroom maneuvering on my behalf – thanks Hilary.

In Tokyo, thanks to the *Tokyo Journal*

team, who will hopefully continue to turn a blind eye to my unashamed pilfering of their excellent coverage of the city. Thanks to Andrew Marshall and Abigail Haworth for the evenings out and putting up with my ramblings when I was at my exhausted worst. John 'I-hate-Kyūshū' Ravenscroft, erstwhile legendary Tokyo resident, should have got a thank you for the last edition of Japan. Well, here it is – thanks John. Another Tokyo thank you is due to Kibo, who always looks after me.

There were countless other travellers and Japan residents along the way who went out of their way to give me their views and tips on what to do. Thanks everyone. Thanks also to all the Japanese, who never failed to be courteous and help out the annoying *gaijin* with never-ending questions. Special thanks to the folks at the Kyoto and Tokyo TICs. No thanks to the assorted breweries of Japan.

This Book
The first three editions of this book were written by Ian L McQueen, a Canadian who has lived in Tokyo for many years. The fourth edition was rewritten by Chris Taylor, Robert Strauss and Tony Wheeler. Chris Taylor updated this edition.

From the Publisher
Producing a book like *Japan* is a collaborative effort requiring the talents and energies of many people. This edition was edited by Robert Flynn and designed and layed out by Valerie Tellini. The new and updated maps for this edition were produced by Chris Klep.

Adrienne Costanzo, Simone Calderwood and Ian Foletta helped with copy editing; Tom Smallman and Sharan Kaur, with the proofing; and Sharon Wertheim, with the indexing. Katie Purvis proofed the kanji script.

Thanks also to Keith Parker, who guided us through the complexities of the Japanese railway system; Peter Morris for the cartoons; Tamsin Wilson for the cover design; Dan Levin for the romaji fonts; and Margaret Jung and Rachel Black, who assisted Valerie with the art.

Thanks
A special thanks to those travellers who took the time and energy to write to us. These people's names appear on page 797.

Warning & Request
Things change – prices go up, schedules change, good places go bad and bad places go bankrupt – nothing stays the same. So if you find things better or worse, recently opened or long since closed, please write and tell us and help make the next edition even better.

Your letters will be used to help update future editions and, where possible, important changes will also be included in a Stop Press section in reprints.

We greatly appreciate all information that is sent to us by travellers. Back at Lonely Planet we employ a hard-working readers' letters team to sort through the many letters we receive. The best ones will be rewarded with a free copy of the next edition or another Lonely Planet guide if you prefer. We give away lots of books, but, unfortunately, not every letter/postcard receives one.

Contents

CENTRAL HONSHŪ 274

KANSAI REGION 348

Map Legend

BOUNDARIES

⋯⋯⋯⋯⋯⋯⋯⋯⋯ ⋯⋯⋯⋯⋯⋯⋯International Boundary

— — — — — — — ⋯⋯⋯⋯⋯⋯⋯Prefectural Boundary

ROUTES

⋯⋯⋯⋯⋯⋯⋯⋯⋯⋯⋯⋯⋯⋯⋯⋯⋯⋯⋯⋯Expressway

⋯⋯⋯⋯⋯⋯⋯⋯⋯⋯⋯⋯⋯⋯⋯⋯⋯⋯⋯⋯Highway

⋯⋯⋯⋯⋯⋯⋯⋯⋯⋯⋯⋯⋯⋯⋯⋯⋯⋯Major Road

— — — — — — ⋯⋯⋯⋯Unsealed Road or Track

+++++++++++++ ⋯⋯⋯⋯⋯⋯⋯⋯⋯JR Railway Line

⋯⋯⋯⋯⋯⋯⋯⋯⋯⋯⋯⋯⋯⋯⋯⋯⋯JR Shinkasen

+—+—+—+—+ ⋯⋯⋯⋯⋯⋯Private Railway Line

⋯⋯⋯⋯⋯⋯⋯⋯⋯⋯⋯⋯⋯⋯⋯⋯⋯⋯⋯⋯⋯Subway

⋯⋯⋯⋯⋯⋯⋯⋯⋯⋯⋯⋯⋯⋯⋯⋯⋯⋯⋯⋯⋯⋯⋯Tram

— — — — ⋯⋯⋯⋯⋯⋯⋯⋯⋯⋯⋯Walking Track

— — — — ⋯⋯⋯⋯⋯⋯⋯⋯⋯⋯⋯⋯⋯Bus Route

⋯⋯⋯⋯⋯⋯⋯⋯⋯⋯⋯⋯⋯⋯⋯⋯⋯⋯⋯Ferry Route

-+-+-+-+-+-+-+-+ ⋯⋯⋯⋯⋯Cable Car or Chairlift

AREA FEATURES

⋯⋯⋯⋯⋯⋯⋯⋯⋯⋯⋯Park, Gardens

⋯⋯⋯⋯⋯⋯⋯⋯⋯⋯⋯National Park

⋯⋯⋯⋯⋯⋯⋯⋯⋯⋯⋯Built-Up Area

⋯⋯⋯⋯⋯⋯⋯⋯⋯Pedestrian Mall

⋯⋯⋯⋯⋯⋯⋯⋯⋯⋯⋯⋯⋯⋯Market

× × × × × × ⋯⋯⋯⋯Shinto/Buddhist Cemetery

+ + + + + + ⋯⋯⋯⋯⋯⋯Christian Cemetery

⋯⋯⋯⋯⋯⋯⋯⋯⋯⋯⋯⋯⋯⋯⋯Reef

⋯⋯⋯⋯⋯⋯⋯⋯⋯⋯⋯⋯⋯Rocks

HYDROGRAPHIC FEATURES

⋯⋯⋯⋯⋯⋯⋯⋯⋯⋯⋯⋯⋯Coastline

⋯⋯⋯⋯⋯⋯⋯⋯⋯⋯River, Creek

— — — — ⋯⋯⋯Intermittent River or Creek

⋯⋯⋯⋯⋯Lake, Intermittent Lake

⋯⋯⋯⋯⋯⋯⋯⋯⋯⋯⋯⋯⋯⋯⋯Canal

⋯⋯⋯⋯⋯⋯⋯⋯⋯⋯⋯⋯⋯⋯⋯Swamp

SYMBOLS

✪ CAPITAL		⋯⋯⋯⋯⋯⋯⋯⋯National Capital
● CITY		⋯⋯⋯⋯⋯⋯⋯⋯⋯Major City
● City		⋯⋯⋯⋯⋯⋯⋯⋯⋯⋯⋯⋯City
● Town		⋯⋯⋯⋯⋯⋯⋯⋯⋯⋯⋯⋯Town
● Village		⋯⋯⋯⋯⋯⋯⋯⋯⋯⋯⋯Village
■		⋯⋯⋯⋯⋯⋯⋯⋯⋯Place to Stay
▼		⋯⋯⋯⋯⋯⋯⋯⋯⋯Place to Eat
✉	☎	⋯⋯⋯⋯⋯Post Office, Telephone
❶	⑤	⋯⋯⋯⋯Tourist Information, Bank
⬗	℗	⋯⋯⋯⋯⋯⋯Transport, Parking
🏛	⌂	⋯⋯⋯⋯Museum, Youth Hostel
⚏	⚹	Caravan Park, Camping Ground
†	🕂	† ⋯⋯⋯⋯⋯Church, Cathedral
𝍥	⚵	⋯⋯⋯Shinto Shrine, Mosque
⊥	⚌	Buddhist Temple, Hindu Temple
✿	⚴	⋯⋯⋯⋯⋯Synagogue, Stupa
⛽	↑	⋯⋯⋯Petrol Station, Golf Course

⊕	★	⋯⋯⋯Hospital, Police Station
✈	✝	⋯⋯⋯⋯⋯⋯Airport, Airfield
◪	✿	⋯⋯Swimming Pool, Gardens
❖	🐘	⋯⋯⋯Shopping Centre, Zoo
⚶	🎋	⋯Winery or Vineyard, Picnic Site
←	A25	One Way Street, Route Number
	∴	⋯⋯Archaeological Site or Ruins
🏛	▲	⋯⋯Stately Home, Monument
⚑	■	⋯⋯⋯⋯⋯⋯Castle, Tomb
⌒	⌂	⋯⋯⋯Cave, Hut or Chalet
▲	☼	⋯Mountain or Hill, Lookout
⚓	⚓	⋯⋯⋯Lighthouse, Shipwreck
)(	⚲	⋯⋯⋯⋯⋯⋯Pass, Spring
		⋯⋯⋯Ancient or City Wall
		⋯⋯Rapids, Waterfalls
		⋯Cliff or Escarpment, Tunnel
		⋯⋯⋯⋯Railway Station

Note: not all symbols displayed above appear in this book

BOUNDARIES

International Boundary
Protected Area Boundary

ROUTES

Expressway
Highway
Major Road
Unpaved Road or Track
Railway Line
JR Line
Private Highway Line
Subway
Tram
Walking Track
Bus Route
Ferry Route
Cable Car or Chairlift

AREA FEATURES

National Park
Built-Up Area
Pedestrian Mall
Market
Christian Cemetery
Beach

HYDROGRAPHIC FEATURES

Coastline
River, Creek
Intermittent River or Creek
Lake, Intermittent Lake
Canal

SYMBOLS

CAPITAL	National Capital		
CITY	State Capital		
City			
Town			
Village			
	Place to Stay		
	Place to Eat		
Post Office, Telephone			
Capital Information, Bank			
Transport, Parking			
Museum, Youth Hostel			
Camping Ground			
Church, Cathedral			
Islamic Shrine, Mosque			
Buddhist Temple, Hindu Temple			
Synagogue, Stupa			
Point of Interest, Golf Course			

Hospital, Police Station
Airport, Airfield
Swimming Pool, Gardens
Shopping Centre, Zoo
Winery, Picnic Site
One Way Street, Route Number
Archaeological Site or Ruin
Castle, Tomb, Monument
Lookout
Cave, Hut or Shelter
Mountain, Hill, Lookout
Lighthouse, Observatory
Pass, Spring
Ancient or City Wall
Rapids, Waterfalls
Cliff or Escarpment, Tunnel
Railway Station

Note: not all symbols displayed above appear in this book

Introduction

Contemporary Japan is a land of extremes. But then, arguably, it has always been that way. After being wracked by centuries of bloodshed and social upheaval as warlords struggled to gain control of the nation, the country was shut tight from 1600 to 1867 under a policy of *sakoku* or 'national seclusion'. The arrival of Commodore Perry's 'black ships' in 1853, set Japan's fastness a-jitter with speculation about the changing world outside its locked doors, and by 1868 the doors had been flung open, an emperor was restored to his throne and the Japanese rushed to greet an incoming tide of Western technology and ideas that would turn their traditional world upside down.

Today, after having their economy and country ravaged by WW II and having spec-

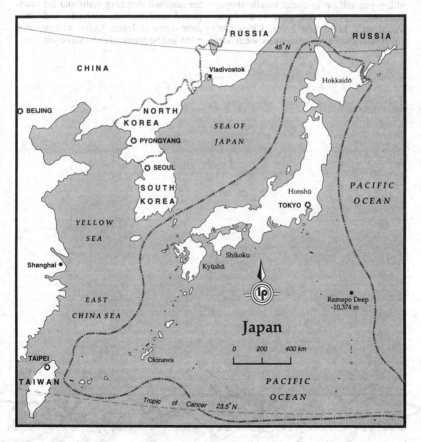

tacularly bounced back to become an economic superpower, it's surprising just how much of that traditional world still lingers. It's this, as much as anything else, that gives the visitor the sensation of having strayed into a land of startling opposites, a land where suburban sprawl gives way to the sensuous contours of a temple roof, where rustic red-lantern restaurants nestle in the shadow of the high-rise future.

The extremes never end. You could splurge your life savings on a week in Tokyo, but then again you could just as easily maintain a diet of youth hostels and country inns, filling yourself up in cheap noodle shops, and come away spending no more than you would on a holiday at home. Cities like Tokyo and Osaka can sometimes seem like congested, hi-tech visions of the future, but the national parks of Hokkaidō and the alps of central Honshū offer sparsely populated vistas that very few foreigners set their eyes on.

All this, perhaps, is to add to the mythology of Japan, a country which is the subject of more gullible and misguided musings than any other place in the world. The best way to approach Japan is by discarding your preconceptions. Somewhere between the elegant formality of Japanese manners and the candid, sometimes boisterous exchanges that take place over a few drinks, between the sanitised shopping malls and the unexpected rural festival, everyone finds their own vision of Japan. Come with an open mind and be prepared to be surprised.

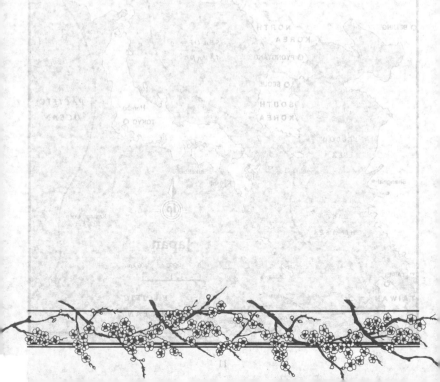

Facts about the Country

HISTORY
Prehistory

The origin of Japan's earliest inhabitants is obscure and uncertain. There was certainly emigration via land bridges that once connected Japan with Siberia and Korea, but it is also thought that seafaring migrants from Polynesia may have landed on Kyūshū and Okinawa. The truth is probably that the Japanese are a result of emigration from Siberia in the north, China and Korea to the west and perhaps Polynesian stock from the south.

The first recorded signs of civilisation in Japan are found in the Neolithic period around 10,000 BC. This is called the Jōmon (Cord Mark) period after the discovery of pottery fragments with cord marks. The people at this time lived as fishers, hunters and food-gatherers.

This period was gradually superseded by the Yayoi era, which dates from around 300 BC, and is named after the site where pottery fragments were found near modern Tokyo. The Yayoi people are considered to have had a strong connection with Korea and their most important developments were the wet cultivation of rice and the use of bronze and iron implements.

The period following the Yayoi era has been called the Kofun (Burial Mound) period by archaeologists who discovered thousands of grave mounds concentrated mostly in central and western Japan. Judging by their size and elaborate construction, these mounds must have required immense resources of labour. It seems likely that the custom of building these tombs was eclipsed by the arrival of Buddhism, which favoured cremation.

As more and more settlements banded together to defend their land, groups became larger until, by 300 AD, the Yamato Kingdom had loosely unified the nation through conquest or alliance. The Yamato leaders claimed descent from the sun goddess, Amaterasu, and introduced the title of emperor *(tennō)* around the 5th century.

Historical Periods	Date	Kanji Script
Jomon	10,000-300 BC	縄文時代
Yayoi	300 BC-300 AD	弥生時代
Kofun	300-710	古墳時代
Nara	710-794	奈良時代
Heian	794-1185	平安時代
Kamakura	1185-1333	鎌倉時代
Muromachi	1333-1576	室町時代
Azuchi-Momoyama	1576-1600	安土桃山時代
Edo	1600-1867	江戸時代
Meiji	1868-1912	明治
Taishō	1912-1926	大正
Shōwa	1926-1989	昭和
Heisei	1989 to the present	平成

Buddhism & Early Chinese Influence

In the mid-6th century, Buddhism was introduced from China via the Korean kingdom of Paekche. The decline of the Yamato court was halted by Prince Shōtoku (573-620), who set up a constitution and laid the guidelines for a centralised state headed by a single ruler. He also instituted Buddhism as a state religion.

Despite family feuds and coups d'état, subsequent rulers continued to reform the country's administration and laws. Previously, it had been the custom to avoid the pollution of imperial death by changing the site of the capital for each successive emperor, but in 710 this custom was altered and the capital was shifted to Nara, where it remained for the next 75 years.

During the Nara period (710-794) there was strong promotion of Buddhism, particularly under Emperor Shōmu, who ordered construction of the Tōdai-ji Temple and the casting of its Daibutsu (Great Buddha) as supreme guardian deity of the nation. Both the temple and its image of Buddha can still be seen in Nara.

Heian Period (794-1185) – Establishment of a Native Culture

By the end of the 8th century, the Buddhist clergy had become so politically meddlesome in Nara that Emperor Kammu decided to sever the ties between Buddhism and government by moving the capital. The site eventually chosen was Heian (modern-day Kyoto). Like Nara, this city was modelled on Chang-an (present-day Xi'an), the capital of the Tang dynasty in China, and it was to continue as the capital of Japan until 1868. It was a period that saw a great flourishing in the arts and important developments in religious thinking, as ideas and institutions imported from China were adapted to the needs of their new homeland.

Rivalry between Buddhism and Shintō, the traditional religion of Japan, was reduced by presenting Shintō deities as manifestations of Buddha. Religion was assigned a role separated from politics, and Japanese monks returning from China established two new sects, Tendai and Shingon, which became the mainstays of Japanese Buddhism.

With the conquest of the Ainu (Japan's original inhabitants) in the early 9th century, Japan's borders were extended to the tip of Northern Honshū. However, the emperors began to devote more time to leisure and scholarly pursuit and less time to government. This created an opening for a noble family called Fujiwara to capture important

---

Samurai

The prime duty of a samurai was to give faithful service to his feudal lord. In fact, the origin of the term samurai is closely linked to a word meaning 'to serve'. Over the centuries, the samurai established a code of conduct which came to be known as Bushidō (the Way of the Warrior). The components of this code were drawn from Confucianism, Shintō and Buddhism.

Confucianism required the samurai to show absolute loyalty to his lord; towards the oppressed he was expected to show benevolence and a belief in justice. Subterfuge was to be despised as were all commercial and financial transactions. A real samurai had endless endurance, total self-control, spoke only the truth and displayed no emotion. Since his honour was his life, disgrace and shame were to be avoided above all else and all insults were to be avenged.

From Buddhism, the samurai learnt the lesson that life is impermanent, a handy reason to face death with serenity. Shintō provided the samurai with patriotic beliefs in the divine status both of the emperor and of Japan, the abode of the gods.

Ritual suicide, (seppuku or harakiri), to which Japanese Buddhism conveniently turned a blind eye, was an accepted means to avoid dishonour. This grisly 'procedure' required the samurai to ritually disembowel himself before a helpful aide, who then drew his sword and lopped off the samurai's head. One reason for this ritual was the requirement that a samurai should never surrender but always go down fighting. Since surrender was considered a disgrace, prisoners received scant mercy. During WW II this attitude was reflected in Japanese treatment of prisoners of war – still a source of bitter memories for those involved.

In slack moments when he wasn't fighting, the samurai dressed simply but was easily recognisable by his triangular eboshi, a hat made from rigid black cloth.

The samurai's standard battle dress or armour (usually made of leather or lacquered steel) consisted of a breastplate, a similar covering for his back, a steel helmet with a visor and more body armour for his shoulders and lower body. Samurai weaponry – his pride and joy – included a bow and arrows (in a quiver), swords and a dagger – and he wasn't complete without his trusty steed.

Before entering the fray, a samurai was expected to be freshly washed and groomed and some even added a dash of perfume! The classic samurai battle took the form of duelling between individuals rather than the clashing of massed armies.

Not all samurai were good warriors adhering to their code of conduct: portrayals of samurai indulging in double-crossing, subterfuge or outright cowardice became popular themes in Japanese theatre. ■

court posts and become the chief power brokers, a role the family was able to maintain for several centuries.

The Heian period is considered the apogee of Japanese courtly elegance, but out in the provinces a new power was on the rise, that of the *samurai* or 'warrior class', which built up its own armed forces and readily turned to arms to defend its autonomy. Samurai families moved into the capital, where they muscled in on the court.

The corrupt Fujiwara were eventually eclipsed by the Taira clan, who ruled briefly before being ousted by the Minamoto family (also known as the Genji) at the battle of Dannoura (Shimonoseki) in 1185.

Kamakura Period (1185-1333) – Domination through Military Rule

After assuming the rank of *shōgun* (military leader), Minamoto Yoritomo set up his headquarters in Kamakura, while the emperor remained the nominal ruler in Kyoto. It was the beginning of a long period of feudal rule by successive samurai families. In fact this feudal system was effectively to linger on until imperial power was restored in 1868.

Yoritomo purged members of his own family who stood in his way, but after his death in 1199 (he fell from his horse), his wife's family (the Hōjō) eliminated all of Yoritomo's potential successors and became the true wielders of power behind the figureheads of shōguns and warrior lords.

During this era, the popularity of Buddhism spread to all levels of society. From the late 12th century, Japanese monks returning from China introduced a new sect, Zen, the austerity of which offered a particular appeal to the samurai class.

The Mongols, under Kublai Khan, reached Korea in 1259 and sent envoys to Japan seeking Japanese submission. In response, the envoys were expelled and the Mongols reacted by sending an invasion fleet which arrived near present-day Fukuoka in 1274. This first attack was only just repulsed with a little help from a typhoon. Further envoys from Kublai Khan were promptly beheaded as a sign that the

government of Japan was not interested in paying homage to the Mongols.

In 1281, the Mongols dispatched a huge army of over 100,000 soldiers to Japan for a second attempt at invasion. After an initial success, the Mongol fleet was almost completely destroyed by yet another typhoon. Ever since, this lucky typhoon has been known to the Japanese as the *kamikaze* (divine wind) – a name later given to the suicide pilots of WW II who vainly attempted to repulse another invasion.

Although the Kamakura government emerged victorious, it was unable to pay its soldiers and lost the support of the warrior class. Buddhist temples also put in a claim for prayer services intended to whip up the divine wind. Emperor Go-Daigo led an unsuccessful rebellion against the government and was exiled to the Oki Islands near Matsue, where he waited a year before trying again. The second attempt successfully toppled the government.

Emperor Go-Daigo

Muromachi Period (1336-1576) – Country at War

Emperor Go-Daigo refused to reward his warriors, favouring the aristocracy and priesthood instead. This led to the revolt of Takauji Ashikaga, who had previously changed sides to support Emperor Go-Daigo. Ashikaga defeated Go-Daigo at Kyoto and then installed a new emperor and appointed himself shōgun; the Ashikaga family later settled at Muromachi, a part of

Kyoto. Go-Daigo escaped to set up a rival court at Yoshino in a mountainous region near Nara. Rivalry between the two courts continued for 60 years until the Ashikaga made a promise (which was not kept) that the imperial lines would alternate.

The Ashikaga ruled with gradually diminishing effectiveness in a land slipping steadily into civil war and chaos. Despite this, there was a flourishing of those arts now considered typically Japanese such as landscape painting, classical Nō drama, flower arranging *(ikebana)* and the tea ceremony *(chanoyu)*. Many of Kyoto's famous gardens date from this period as do such well-known monuments as the Kinkaku-ji (Golden Temple) and Ginkaku-ji (Silver Temple). Formal trade relations were reopened with Ming China and Korea, although Japanese piracy remained a bone of contention between both sides.

The Ōnin War, which broke out in 1467, developed into a full-scale civil war and marked the rapid decline of the Ashikaga family. *Daimyō* (domain lords) and local leaders fought for power in bitter territorial disputes that were to last for a century. This period, from 1467 to around the start of the Momoyama period in 1576, is known as the Warring Sates period.

Momoyama Period (1576-1600) – Return to Unity

In 1568 Oda Nobunaga, the son of a daimyō, seized power from the imperial court in Kyoto and used his military genius to initiate a process of pacification and unification in central Japan. His efforts were cut short when he was betrayed by one of his own generals, Akechi Mitsuhide, in 1582. Under attack from Mitsuhide and seeing all was lost, he disembowelled himself in Kyoto's Honnō-ji Temple.

Nobunaga was succeeded by his ablest commander, Toyotomi Hideyoshi, who was reputedly the son of a farmer, although his origins are not clear. His diminutive size and pop-eyed features earned him the nickname of Saru-san (Mr Monkey). Hideyoshi extended unification so that by 1590 the

whole country was under his rule. He then became fascinated with grandiose schemes to invade China and Korea. The first invasion was repulsed in 1593 and the second was aborted on the death of Hideyoshi in 1598.

The arts of this period are noted for their boisterous use of colour and gold-leaf embellishment. There was also a vogue for building castles on a flamboyant scale; the most impressive example was Osaka Castle, which reputedly required three years of labour by up to 100,000 men.

The Christian Century (1543-1640)

In the mid-16th century, when the Europeans first made their appearance, there was little authority over foreign trade. The first Portuguese to be shipwrecked off southern Kyūshū in 1543 found a most appreciative Japanese reception for their skills in making firearms, which were soon spread throughout the region. The Jesuit missionary Francis Xavier arrived in Kagoshima in 1549 and was followed by more missionaries who quickly converted local lords keen to profit from foreign trade and assistance with military supplies. The new religion spread rapidly, gaining several hundred thousand converts, particularly in Nagasaki.

At first, Nobunaga saw the advantages of trading with Europeans and tolerated the arrival of Christianity as a counterbalance to Buddhism. Once Hideyoshi had assumed power, however, this tolerance gradually gave way to the suspicion of subversion by an alien religion which was deemed a threat to his rule. Edicts against Christianity were followed in 1597 by the crucifixion of 26 foreign priests and Japanese believers.

Proscription and persecution of Christianity continued under the Tokugawa government until it reached its peak in 1637 with the ferocious quelling by the authorities of the Christian-led Shimabara Rebellion. This brought the Christian century to an abrupt close, although the religion continued to be practised in secret until it was officially allowed to resurface at the end of the 19th century.

Top: Cherry blossoms (CT)
Middle: Shin-kyō Bridge, Nikkō (CT)
Bottom: Temple doors, Tokyo (CT)

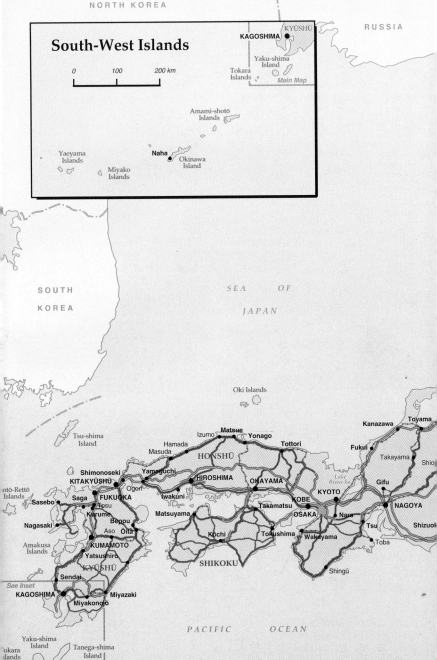

South-West Islands

0   100   200 km

NORTH KOREA

RUSSIA

KYŪSHŪ

KAGOSHIMA

Yaku-shima Island

Tokara Islands

Main Map

Amami-shotō Islands

Naha

Yaeyama Islands

Miyako Islands

Okinawa Island

SOUTH

KOREA

SEA   OF

JAPAN

Oki Islands

Tsu-shima Island

Kanazawa

Toyama

Izumo

Matsue

Yonago

Tottori

Fukui

Hamada

HONSHŪ

Takayama

Shio

Masuda

Yamaguchi

Shimonoseki

KITAKYŪSHŪ

HIROSHIMA

OKAYAMA

Lake Biwa-ko

Gifu

otō-Rettō Islands

Ogori

Iwakuni

KOBE

KYOTO

NAGOYA

Sasebo

Saga

FUKUOKA

Tosu

Matsuyama

Takamatsu

OSAKA

Nara

Tsu

Shizuok

Karume

Beppu

Nagasaki

Aso

Ōita

Kōchi

Tokushima

Wakayama

Toba

Amakusa Islands

KUMAMOTO

Yatsushiro

SHIKOKU

Shingū

See Inset

Sendai

KYŪSHŪ

KAGOSHIMA

Miyazaki

Miyakonojō

PACIFIC   OCEAN

Yaku-shima Island

Tanega-shima Island

Tokara Islands

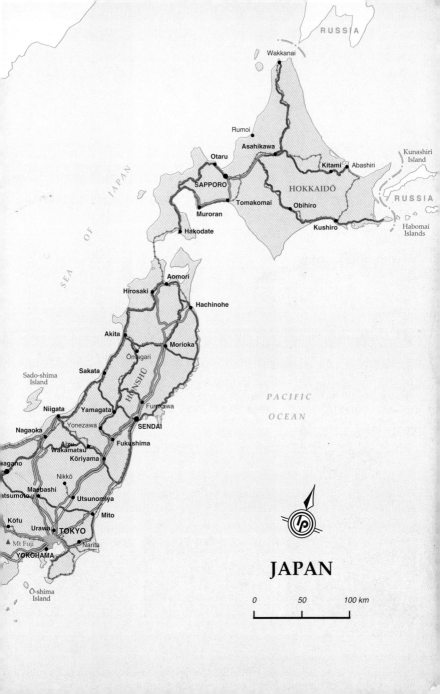

RUSSIA

Wakkanai

Rumoi

Asahikawa

Otaru

SAPPORO

Kitami • Abashiri

Kunashiri
Island

HOKKAIDŌ

Tomakomai

RUSSIA

Muroran

Obihiro

Hakodate

Kushiro

Habomai
Islands

SEA

OF

JAPAN

Aomori

Hirosaki

Hachinohe

Akita

Morioka

Ōmagari

Sakata

HONSHŪ

Sado-shima
Island

PACIFIC

Niigata

Yamagata

Furukawa

OCEAN

Nagaoka

Yonezawa

SENDAI

Aizu-
Wakamatsu

Fukushima

agano

Kōriyama

Nikkō

Maebashi

tsumoto

Utsunomiya

Kōfu

Mito

Urawa

TOKYO

Mt Fuji

Narita

YOKOHAMA

Ō-shima
Island

JAPAN

0   50   100 km

A	B	C
D	E	F
G	H	I

Patterns
A: Torii (CT)
B: Garden, Kyoto (CT)
C: Kasa (umbrella) (CT)
D: Cemetery (CT)
E: Akihabara, Tokyo (CT)
F: Stacked wood, Hida Folk Village, Takayama (C
G: Ginza, Tokyo (CT)
H: Abandoned bicycles, Fukuyama (TW)
I: Koinobori (carp banners) (TW)

Edo or Tokugawa Period (1600-1867) – Peace & Seclusion

The supporters of Hideyoshi's young heir, Toyotomi Hideyori, were defeated in 1600 by his former ally, Tokugawa Ieyasu, at the battle of Sekigahara. Ieyasu set up his field headquarters *(bakufu)* at Edo, now Tokyo, and assumed the title of shōgun; the emperor and court continued to exercise purely nominal authority in Kyoto.

A strict political regime was introduced. The Tokugawa family, besides retaining large estates, also took control of major cities, ports and mines; the remainder of the country was allocated to autonomous daimyō. In descending order of importance, society consisted of the nobility, who had nominal power; the daimyō and their warriors (samurai); the farmers; and at the bottom of the list, artisans and merchants. To ensure political security, the daimyō were required to make ceremonial visits to Edo every alternate year, and their wives and children were kept in permanent residence in Edo as virtual hostages of the government. The cost of this constant movement and the family ties in Edo made it difficult for the daimyō to remain anything but loyal. At the lower end of society, farmers were subject to a severe system of rules which dictated in minutest detail their food, clothing and housing. Social mobility from one class to another was blocked; social standing was determined by birth.

According to a standard parable frequently trotted out by Japanese to elucidate the unification of Japan, the characters of Oda Nobunaga, Toyotomi Hideyoshi and Tokugawa Ieyasu can be imaginatively compared by their techniques for tackling a cuckoo which refuses to sing. Nobunaga, noted for his ruthlessness, would make a generous offer: sing or die. Hideyoshi, revered for his pragmatism, would insist on *making* the cuckoo perform; Ieyasu, renowned for his shrewd patience, would coolly wait until the bird decided to sing.

In the modern Japanese business world, managers reputedly seek inspiration from this comparison when calculating their style of command in a company.

Under Tokugawa rule, Japan entered a period of national seclusion *(sakoku)*. Japanese were forbidden on pain of death to travel to or return from overseas or to trade abroad. Only the Dutch, Chinese and Koreans were allowed to remain and they were placed under strict supervision; the Dutch were confined to Dejima Island near Nagasaki and their contacts restricted to merchants and prostitutes.

The rigid emphasis of these times on submitting unquestioningly to rules of obedience and loyalty has lasted to the present day. One effect of strict rule during the Tokugawa period was to create an atmosphere of relative peace and security in which the arts excelled. There were great advances, for example, in *haiku* poetry, *bunraku* puppet plays and *kabuki* theatre. Weaving, pottery, ceramics and lacquerware became famous for their refined quality.

Perhaps the most bizarre ruler of this period was the fifth Tokugawa shōgun, Tokugawa Tsunayoshi, often referred to as the 'Dog Shōgun' because of his preoccupation with canine welfare. After a priest advised Tsunayoshi that he had failed to produce a male heir because of mistreating a dog in a previous life, he determined to make amends. Orders were issued for the construction of special dog pounds and the provision of quality dinners for dogs which were to be addressed in honorific language only. Anyone caught mistreating canines faced severe punishment.

By the turn of the 19th century, the Tokugawa government was facing stagnation and corruption. Famines and poverty among the peasants and samurai further weakened the system. Foreign ships started to probe Japan's isolation with increasing insistence and the Japanese soon realised that their outmoded defences were ineffectual. Russian contacts in the north were followed by British and American visits. In 1853, Commodore Matthew Perry of the US Navy arrived with a squadron of 'black ships' to demand the opening of Japan to trade. Other countries moved in to demand the opening of treaty ports and the relaxation of restrictions on trade barriers.

A surge of antigovernment feeling among the Japanese followed. The Tokugawa government was accused of failing to defend

Japan against foreigners and of neglecting the national reconstruction necessary for Japan to meet the West on equal terms. In 1867 the ruling shōgun, Keiki, resigned and the Emperor Meiji resumed control of state affairs.

Meiji Restoration (1868-1912) – Emergence from Isolation

The initial stages of this restoration were resisted in a state of virtual civil war. The abolition of the shogunate (military government) was followed by the surrender of the daimyō, whose lands were divided into the prefectures that exist today. Edo became Japan's new capital and was renamed Tokyo (Eastern Capital). The government became

Emperor Meiji

centralised again and Western-style ministries were appointed for specific tasks. A series of revolts by the samurai against the erosion of their status culminated in the Saigō Uprising, when they were finally beaten and stripped of their power.

Despite nationalist support for the emperor under the slogan of *sonnō-jōi* (revere the emperor, repel the barbarians), the new government soon realised it would have to meet the West on its own terms. Under the slogan *fukoku kyōhei* (rich country, strong military), the economy underwent a crash course in Westernisation and industrialisation. An influx of Western experts was encouraged and Japanese students were sent abroad to acquire expertise in modern technologies. In 1889, Japan created a Western-style constitution which, like the military revival, owed much to Prussian influences.

By the 1890s, government leaders were concerned by the spread of liberal Western ideas and encouraged a swing back to nationalism and traditional values.

Japan's growing confidence was demonstrated by the abolition of foreign treaty rights and by the ease with which it trounced China in the Sino-Japanese War (1894-5). The subsequent treaty recognised Korean independence and ceded Taiwan to Japan. Friction with Russia led to the Russo-Japanese War (1904-05), in which the Japanese army attacked the Russians in Manchuria and Korea. The Japanese navy stunned the Russians by inflicting a crushing defeat on their Baltic fleet at the battle of Tsu-shima Island. For the first time, the Japanese were able to consider that they had drawn level with the Western powers.

Industrialisation & Asian Dominance

On his death in 1912, the Emperor Meiji was succeeded by his son, Yoshihito, whose period of rule was named the Taishō era. The later stages of his life were dogged by ill-health that was probably attributable to meningitis.

When WW I broke out, Japan sided against Germany but did not become deeply involved in the conflict. While the Allies were occupied with war, the Japanese took the opportunity, through shipping and trade, to expand their economy at top speed. At the same time, a strong foothold was gained in China, thereby giving Japan a dominant position in Asia.

Social unrest led the government to pursue a more democratic, liberal line; the right to vote was extended and Japan joined the League of Nations in 1920. Under the influence of the *zaibatsu* (financial cliques of industrialists and bankers), a moderate and pacific foreign policy was followed.

Nationalism & the Pursuit of Empire

The Shōwa era commenced when Emperor Hirohito ascended to the throne in 1926. He had toured extensively in Europe, mixed with European nobility and developed a liking for the British lifestyle.

A rising tide of nationalism was quickened by the world economic depression that began in 1930. Popular unrest was marked by plots to overthrow the government and political assassinations. This led to a strong increase in the power of the militarists, who approved the invasion of Manchuria in 1931 and the installation of a Japanese puppet regime, Manchukuo. In 1933, Japan withdrew from the League of Nations and, in 1937, entered into full-scale hostilities against China.

As the leader of a new order for Asia, Japan signed a tripartite pact with Germany and Italy in 1940. The Japanese military leaders saw their main opponents to this new order for Asia, the so-called 'Greater East Asia Co-prosperity Sphere', in the USA.

World War II

When diplomatic attempts to gain US neutrality failed, the Japanese launched themselves into WW II with a surprise attack on Pearl Harbor on 7 December 1941.

At first, Japan scored rapid successes, pushing its battle fronts across to India, down to the fringes of Australia and out into the mid-Pacific. The Battle of Midway opened the US counterattack, puncturing Japanese naval superiority and turning the tide of the war against Japan. Exhausted by submarine blockade and aerial bombing, by 1945 Japan had been driven back on all fronts. In August of the same year, the declaration of war by the Soviet Union and the atomic bombs dropped by the USA on Hiroshima and Nagasaki proved to be the final straws: Emperor Hirohito announced unconditional surrender.

Having surrendered, Japan was occupied by Allied forces under the command of General MacArthur. The chief aim was a thorough reform of Japanese government through demilitarisation, the trial of war criminals and the weeding out of militarists or ultranationalists from the government. A new constitution was introduced which dismantled the political power of the emperor, who completely stunned his subjects by publicly renouncing any claim to divine origins. This left him with the status of a mere figurehead.

The occupation was terminated in 1952, although the island of Okinawa was only returned to Japan in 1972.

Postwar Reconstruction

At the end of the war, the Japanese economy was in ruins and inflation was rampant. A programme of recovery provided loans, restricted imports and encouraged capital investment and personal saving.

By the late '50s, trade was again flourishing and the economy continued to expand rapidly. From textiles and the manufacture of labour-intensive goods such as cameras, the Japanese 'economic miracle' has branched out into virtually every sector of economic activity. Economic recession and inflation surfaced in 1974 and again in 1980, mostly as a result of steep price hikes for imported oil on which Japan is dependent. In the early '90s, Japan, like other developed nations, struggled through a period of recession.

Emergence as an Economic Superpower & Political Strife

Despite these setbacks, Japan has become so

successful at selling overseas and producing massive trade surpluses that it has aroused resentment in competing nations, which face mounting import bills and unemployment. At present, Japan dominates such fields as electronics, robotics, computer technology, car production and banking – by the year 2000, it looks set to overtake the USA as the world's leading economy.

Postwar politics in Japan have been virtually monopolised by the conservatives, in particular (since 1955) by the Liberal Democratic Party (LDP). While LDP monopoly rule has been occasionally rocked by affairs such as the Lockheed corruption scandal, which tainted the office of Tanaka in the '70s, and the Recruit Cosmos affair of the '80s, which implicated the government of Prime Minister Takeshita in the acceptance of complimentary shares in return for favours, it was not until the early '90s, when a spate of scandals demonstrated the cosiness of the LDP and big business, that the voting public decided enough was enough. In 1993 an eight-party coalition government, led by a former Kumamoto governor, Morihiro Hosokawa, swept the LDP out of power after 40 years at the helm.

After a troubled few months in power, Hosokawa's term as prime minister was cut short in April 1994 when he was forced to resign amid further corruption allegations. Hosokawa left a fragile coalition of 'cleanup' political groupings in his wake and, as we went to press, many analysts were predicting the return to power of the LDP.

GEOGRAPHY

Japan is an island nation and, although much of its cultural heritage has been drawn from nearby Asian countries, its 'apartness' from the Asian mainland differentiates the Japanese from their neighbours. Both China and Korea are close enough to have been decisive influences, but at the same time they are too distant to have dominated Japan.

Japan has not always been physically isolated. At the end of the last ice age, around 10,000 years ago, the level of the sea rose enough to flood the land bridge connecting Japan with the mainland. Today, Japan consists of a chain of islands that rides the back of a 3000 km long arc of mountains along the eastern rim of the Asian continent. It stretches from around 25°N at the southern islands of Okinawa to 45°N at the northern end of Hokkaidō; cities at comparable latitudes would be Miami or Cairo in the south and Montreal or Milan in the north. Japan's total land area is 377,435 sq km, and more than 80% of it is mountainous.

Japan consists of some 1000 small islands and four major ones: Honshū (slightly larger than the UK), Hokkaidō, Kyūshū and Shikoku. Okinawa, the largest and most significant of Japan's many smaller islands, is about halfway along an archipelago that stretches form the western tip of Honshū almost all the way to Taiwan. It was far enough from the rest of Japan to have developed a culture that differs from that of the 'mainland' in many respects.

If Japanese culture has been influenced by isolation, it has equally been shaped by the country's mountainous topography. Many of the mountains are volcanic (more than 40 of which are presently active), thereby blessing the islands with numerous hot springs and spectacular scenery, and at the same time bringing the danger of frequent eruptions and intense seismic activity. Indeed, the rough and tumble of earthquakes, volcanic eruptions and tsunami (tidal waves), along with a monsoonal climate, has perhaps contributed to Japanese industriousness. The Japanese are used to rebuilding their world every 20 or 30 years.

Japan has the dubious distinction of being one of the most seismically active regions of the world. It is calculated that the country gets around 1000 earthquakes a year, most of them too small to notice without sophisticated seismic equipment. This seismic activity is particularly concentrated in the Kantō region, in which Tokyo is situated. Tokyo is on the receiving end of a monster tremor about every 60 years. The last biggie measured 8.2 on the Richter scale and occurred in 1923, so another big one is overdue.

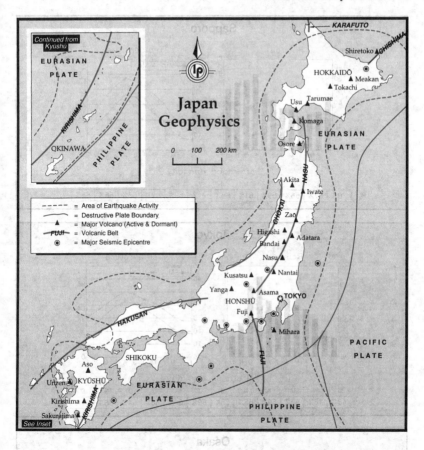

Japan Geophysics

0   100   200 km

= Area of Earthquake Activity
= Destructive Plate Boundary
▲ = Major Volcano (Active & Dormant)
FUJI = Volcanic Belt
◉ = Major Seismic Epicentre

CLIMATE

The combination of Japan's mountainous territory and the length of the archipelago (covering 22° of latitude) makes for a complex climate. There are big climatic differences between Hokkaidō in the north, which has short summers and long winters with heavy snowfalls, and the southern Ryūkyū Islands, which enjoy a subtropical climate. At the same time, Japan's proximity to the continental landmass also has significant climatic implications, producing a high degree of seasonal variation.

In the winter months (December to February), cold, dry air masses from Siberia move down over Japan, where they meet warmer, moister air masses from the Pacific. The resulting precipitation results in huge snowfalls on Japan's western side. The eastern side of Japan receives less snow but can still get very cold; Tokyo has colder average January temperatures than Reykjavik in Iceland, but snow, when it does fall on the capital, rarely lasts long.

The summer months (June to August) are dominated by warm, moist air currents from the Pacific, and produce high temperatures and humidity throughout most of Japan. In

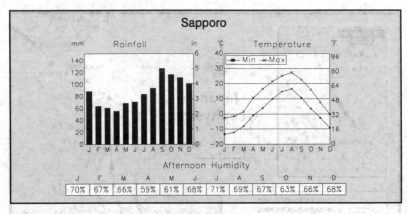

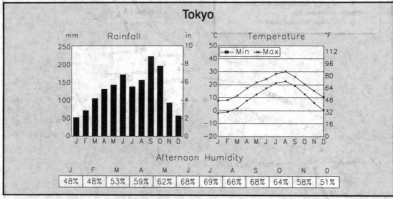

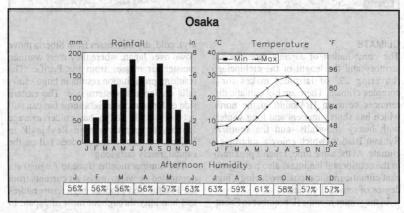

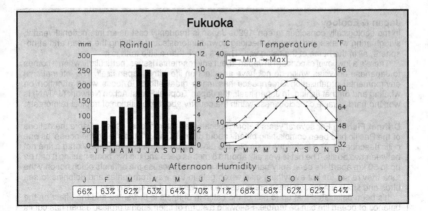

the early part of summer there is a rainy season lasting a few weeks that starts in the south and gradually works its way northwards. Further heavy rains can occur in late summer when the country is visited by typhoons bringing torrential rains and strong winds that can have devastating effects, particularly on coastal regions.

In contrast to the extremes of summer and winter, spring and autumn are comparatively mild. Rainfall is relatively low and the days are often clear.

FLORA & FAUNA

The latitudinal spread of the islands of Japan makes for a wide diversity of flora and fauna. The Ryūkyū and Ogasawara island groups in the far south are subtropical, and flora and fauna in this region is related to that found on the Malaysian peninsula. Mainland Japan (Honshū, Kyūshū and Shikoku), on the other hand, shows more similarities with Korea and China, while sub-arctic northern and central Hokkaidō has features of its own.

One thing to consider in terms of the flora of Japan is that what you see today as you travel around the country is not what Japanese saw hundreds of years ago. This is not just because much of Japan's natural landscape has succumbed to modern urban culture, but that much of Japan's flora is naturalised and not indigenous. It is thought that some 200 to 500 plant species have been introduced to Japan since the Neiji period (1858-1912), mainly from Europe but with the USA becoming a major source in recent years. Japanese gardens laid out in the Edo period and earlier represent a good opportunity to see native Japanese flora even if you aren't seeing it as it might have naturally flourished.

Much of Japan was once heavily forested. The cool-temperate zones of central and northern Honshū and southern Hokkaidō were home to broad-leaved deciduous forests and still are to a certain extent. Nevertheless, Japan's reckless flight into the embracing arms of modernity has led to the widescale deforestation of much of the country. Pollution and acid rain have also taken their toll. Fortunately, the sheer inaccessibility of much of Japan's mountainous topography has preserved areas of great natural beauty – in particular the alpine regions of central Honshū and the natural parks of Hokkaidō.

Japan's one-time conjunction with the Asian continent has led to the migration of animals from Korea and China, and the fauna of Japan has much in common with these regions, though there are species that are unique to Japan, such as the Japanese giant salamander and the Japanese macaque. In the

Japan & Ecology

In the ecologically conscious 'green' 1990s Japan is frequently cast as an international vandal, slaughtering whales and dolphins, hacking down rainforests and polluting the ocean and atmosphere, all in the name of the rising yen. There's more than a little truth to it.

There's a low level of concern in Japan about environmental issues, particularly when it comes to Japanese activities which do not have an effect on life within Japan itself. The international environmental organisation Greenpeace has made great efforts to focus world attention on whaling and driftnet fishing. In Japan itself, the Japan Tropical Forest Action Network (JATAN) is working hard to raise consciousness within the country about exploitation of tropical rainforests.

Driftnet Fishing For several years before it became an international *cause célèbre* the nations of the Pacific had been complaining bitterly about driftnet fishing, 'strip mining the ocean' as one critic described it. The technique is simple, the devastation dramatic – you simply drag a fine net between two boats. The net is typically about 15 metres deep and the two boats hauling it can be up to 50 km apart! It's been aptly named a 'wall of death' because the driftnets catch not only the tuna they're set for but everything else which gets in the way from turtles and dolphins to sea birds and sharks. Although these creatures are not wanted, they die anyway.

It's been calculated that up to half of the catch in driftnets is unwanted and the effect on the balance of ocean life can be terrible. Following a storm of international protest, Japan has cut its driftnet fleet by one-third although Taiwan, the other chief culprit, is still using driftnets. There have been accusations that Japanese aid to the tiny South Pacific nations most at risk from the depredation of driftnet fishing has been used as a lever to silence complaints.

Packaging One example of Japan's lack of environmental concern (which every visitor will soon be aware of) is the Japanese penchant for overpackaging. At a time when most Western nations are trying to cut back on packaging, in Japan it's full speed ahead to wrap things in the largest possible number of layers of paper, plastic and cardboard, all tied together with string and bows.

Rainforests Japan is the world's largest consumer of tropical rainforest timber. The terrible destruction wrought upon the rainforests of the Malaysian states of Sabah and Sarawak has principally been to supply Japan. Apart from the large-scale destruction of the forests (where minimal regeneration takes place), the logging also silts up rivers and kills fish.

Most of the logging activity is conducted by the big Japanese trading companies and 70% to 80% of the timber ends up as plywood, most of which is used for concrete formwork moulds and then destroyed. Rainforest and coastal mangrove forests have also been wiped out to supply Japanese woodchipping operations.

Recycling Recycling is a two sided coin in Japan. On one side, many household disposables, such as glass bottles, are efficiently recycled. On the other side, Japan is the throwaway society *par excellence*. The severe *shaken* vehicle inspection system encourages car owners to scrap their cars and buy new ones; cars more than a few years old are a rare sight on Japanese roads. There's little demand for second-hand goods and appliances, and consumer equipment is quickly scrapped to be replaced by the latest model. Stories abound of resident *gaijin* setting up house with Japanese throwaways. Around almost any big city railway station there will be tangled heaps of perfectly good bicycles, abandoned by their users.

Turtles Dolphins and whales are not the only creatures to fall prey to the Japanese economy. It's estimated that every year 30,000 hawksbill turtles, an endangered species, are killed to provide Japan with 30 tonnes of turtle shell.

Waribashi Japan's vast number of restaurants almost all provide their customers with disposable chopsticks or *waribashi*. Forests fall in order to supply these one-use only utensils.

Whales The international outcry against whaling has cut the whaling nations down to just three – Iceland, Norway and Japan. When the Japanese finally agreed to halt whaling they reserved the right to kill 300 minke whales a year for 'scientific research'. After they've been 'researched' they end up as restaurant whale meat. ∎

Ryūkyū island group, which has been separated from the mainland longer than the rest of Japan there are examples of fauna (for example the Iriomote cat) that are classified by experts as 'living fossils'.

Japan's largest carnivorous mammals are its bears. Two species are found in Japan – the *higuma* (brown hear) of Hokkaidō and the *tsukinowaguma* (Asiatic brown bear) of Honshū, Shikoku and Kyūshū. The brown bear can grow to a height of two metres and weigh up to 400 kg. The Asiatic brown bear is smaller at an average height of 1.4 metres and a weight of 200 kg.

The Japanese macaque is a medium-sized monkey that is found in Honshū, Shikoku and Kyūshū. They average around 60 cm in length and have a short tail. The last survey of their numbers was taken in 1962, at which time there were some 30,000. They are found in groups of 20 to 150 members.

National Parks

Japan has 28 national parks *kokuritsu kōen* and 55 quasi-national parks *kokutei kōen*. Ranging from the far south (Iriomote National Park is the southernmost of Japan's national parks) to the northern tip of Hokkaidō (Rishiri-Rebun-Sarobetsu National Park), the parks represent an effort to preserve as much as possible of Japan's natural environment. The parks are administered either directly (in the case of national parks) or indirectly (in the case of quasi-national parks) by the Environment Agency of the Prime Minister's Office.

The highest concentration of national parks and quasi-national parks is in the Tōhoku (Northern Honshū) and Hokkaidō regions, where population density is relatively low. But there are also national parks and quasi-national parks (Chichibu-Tama and Nikkō) within easy striking distance of Tokyo. The largest of Japan's national parks is the Inland Sea National Park (Seto Naikai Kokuritsu-Kōen), which extends some 400 km east to west, reaches a maximum width of 70 km and encompasses over 1000 islands.

GOVERNMENT

Japan's governmental system is more similar to the British parliamentary system than the American presidential one. Just as the British parliament has two houses, so the Japanese Diet has the lower House of Representatives and the upper House of Councillors. The party that controls the majority of seats in the Diet is the party in power and has the right to appoint the prime minister – usually the party's president. The prime minister then appoints his cabinet, which is usually entirely constituted of Diet members.

Like the UK's royal family, the emperor plays a ceremonial figurehead role but, perhaps even more than his British counterpart, he still commands a great deal of respect and deference. The emperor has a curious position in Japan. For centuries under the shogunate his role was purely symbolic. The Meiji Restoration 'restored' the emperor to real power, or at least it was supposed to. In fact it merely brought him out of the closet, dusted him off and gave him a new figurehead position. The close of WW II brought further changes when it was announced that the emperor was no longer divine; despite this, he still has enormous importance in Japan.

In terms of the mechanics of political power, until very recently, from its formation in 1955, the Liberal Democratic Party (LDP), the conservative party in Japanese politics, had been continuously in power, shaking off scandal after scandal, apparently invincible. By 1993, however, the scandals had become too much even for the Japanese, who seem to be the most forgiving voting public a corrupt political party could wish for, and the LDP was replaced by an eight-party coalition made up of LDP defectors (read reformers) and new clean-up-politics groupings.

Democracy Japanese-style has indeed been prone to scandals, matching all the regular influence-buying and favour-repaying scandals of Western democracies and managing to add a few local versions of its own. The Lockheed scandal of the '70s (in which the prime minister took large bribes to ensure that All Nippon Airways (ANA) bought Lockheed Tristar aircraft) was eclipsed by the Recruit Cosmos affair of the late '80s (in which all sorts of LDP politicians from the prime minister down accepted all sorts of bribes).

Obviously on a roll, the LDP was still shrugging off scandals into the early '90s. The situation reached a climax when Shin Kanemaru, the doyen of LDP back-room politics, was convicted of evading tax on stashed-away election funds amounting to over US$9 million.

The root of Japan's 'money politics' problem lies in Japan's so-called multi-seat constituency system, which compels members of the same party to fight each other for the same constituency, a situation that requires astronomical election funding. An associated problem is Japan's creaking bureaucracy. When business needs to get something done in hurry, the only way to bypass laborious bureaucratic procedure is to seek the assistance of a politician. Not surprisingly, the quickest way to a politician's heart is via his pocket.

Geographical, Political & Administrative Divisions

Japan is divided up into nine political regions (see map) and further subdivided into 47 smaller divisions. Prefectures or *ken* make up 43 of these divisions, and they are written as 'Okayama-ken' or 'Chiba-ken'. The remaining four are Hokkaidō, which is a *dō* (district); Tokyo-to, which is a *to* (metropolis); and Osaka-fu and Kyoto-fu, which are *fu* (urban prefectures). Each of the three city areas incorporates the named city but is otherwise similar in land area to a ken.

There are other traditional names for regions of the country. Thus, Chūgoku or Western Honshū, consists of the San-in or north coast region and the San-yō or south coast region. Other traditional names you may come across in tourist literature or other sources include Hokuriku (Fukui, Ishikawa and Toyama prefectures), Sanriku (Aomori, Iwate and Miyagi), Shin-etsu (Nagano and Niigata) and Tokai (Aichi, Gifu, Mie and

Shizuoka). In addition, the Tokyo area is often referred to as Kantō, while the area around Osaka is known as Kansai or Kinki.

ECONOMY

Japan is widely perceived as an economic powerhouse, utterly dominating world trade and with an enormous trade surplus that is being used to buy up industries and real estate in Western nations. Although that view has some truth, Japan's exports account for only 9% of its GNP (gross national product), a much smaller percentage than that of many European nations, such as the UK (18%) and Germany (27%). Also, despite the huge Japanese investments overseas, these are still much smaller than the foreign investments of many other Western nations. The UK has far more industrial investment in the USA than Japan, and the biggest foreign owners of real estate in the USA are not the Japanese but the Canadians.

The huge Japanese trade surpluses are chalked up not so much by massive exports as by a low level of imports. Japanese exports are highly visible – they're predominantly in consumer durables and their success in this field has made Japanese manufacturers (such as Honda, Suzuki, Sony, Sanyo, Toshiba and National) familiar names throughout the world. The major Japanese imports are oil and energy resources, which are used frugally. Despite the limited land available for agricultural use, the Japanese manage to supply a large part of their food requirements by highly efficient and intensive land use.

Japanese farming policy is a continuing stumbling block to trade negotiations. Although land use is highly efficient in terms of output to area, in terms of cost it is in fact highly inefficient. It's frequently cited that Japanese rice growers produce far more per hectare than rice growers in, say, Indonesia. That's quite correct, but if the Indonesians spent as much per hectare of rice paddy, they too would grow a lot more rice but at a much higher cost per kg.

The Japanese would save themselves a great deal of money by simply buying their

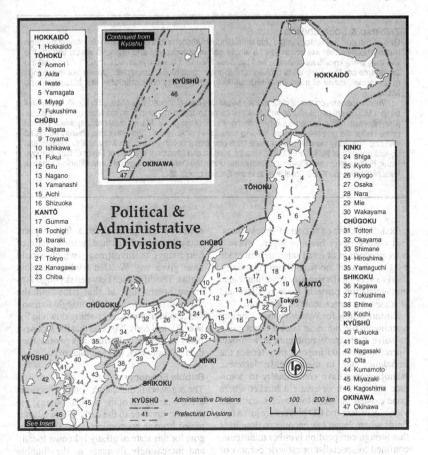

HOKKAIDŌ
1 Hokkaidō
TŌHOKU
2 Aomori
3 Akita
4 Iwate
5 Yamagata
6 Miyagi
7 Fukushima
CHŪBU
8 Niigata
9 Toyama
10 Ishikawa
11 Fukui
12 Gifu
13 Nagano
14 Yamanashi
15 Aichi
16 Shizuoka
KANTŌ
17 Gumma
18 Tochigi
19 Ibaraki
20 Saitama
21 Tokyo
22 Kanagawa
23 Chiba

Continued from Kyūshu

KINKI
24 Shiga
25 Kyoto
26 Hyogo
27 Osaka
28 Nara
29 Mie
30 Wakayama
CHŪGOKU
31 Tottori
32 Okayama
33 Shimane
34 Hiroshima
35 Yamaguchi
SHIKOKU
36 Kagawa
37 Tokushima
38 Ehime
39 Kochi
KYŪSHŪ
40 Fukuoka
41 Saga
42 Nagasaki
43 Oita
44 Kumamoto
45 Miyazaki
46 Kagoshima
OKINAWA
47 Okinawa

Political & Administrative Divisions

KYŪSHŪ = Administrative Divisions
41 = Prefectural Divisions

0   100   200 km

food overseas, but the system won't change for two reasons. One is that according to public sentiment, the nation should, as far as possible, be self-sufficient and not at the mercy of foreign countries, particularly when it comes to food. The other and possibly more important reason is the blunt fact that the LDP, the party that had ruled Japan for some 40 years until 1993, had its power base in the country. A particularly wet and cool summer in 1993 forced the present coalition government to agree to rice imports, but the government claims that this is not the thin end of the wedge, and that

Japan is still committed to supplying its own rice needs. This despite the fact that the present government was voted in on a platform of wide-scale reform.

The high-cost farmers are not the only component of the Japanese economy contributing to sky-high prices. The Japanese distribution and retail system also jacks up prices, making it even more difficult for foreign competitors to break in. Goods reach consumers via a layer cake of intermediaries, each taking their slice out of the final price. Even the final stage, the retailer, is inefficient and costly by Western standards. Whoever

Zaibatsu & Sōgō Shōsha

One of the curious factors in the Japanese industrial scene is the important role played by huge trading houses that are involved in a whole gamut of industrial and financial areas. Before the war they were known as *zaibatsu*, and because it was felt that they played a major role in pushing Japan into conflict, they were broken up into their constituent companies. Drawn like iron filings to a magnet, many of them have regrouped to form mighty conglomerates like Mitsubishi and Mitsui.

When Japanese consumers fill up their Mitsubishi cars (financed by a Mitsubishi bank), it may well be in a Mitsubishi petrol station with fuel that came to Japan in a ship from the Mitsubishi shipyards. Kirin beer and Nikon cameras are two other products of the group. Many household Japanese names come under the umbrella of these holding companies or *keiretsu*, often with cross shareholdings so that one company may be part of more than one major holding company. Mitsukoshi, Toshiba and Toyota are part of Mitsui; Fuji Bank, Hitachi, Nissan and Marubeni are part of Fuyo; C Itoh, Kangyo Bank, Fujitsu, Isuzu and Kawasaki Steel come under the Dai-Ichi banner; and Sanwa Bank, Daihatsu, Hitachi, Sharp and Kōbe Steel line up in the Sanwa group. ■

called the British 'a nation of shopkeepers' had clearly never been to Japan, where a huge proportion of retail sales are still made by tiny, hole-in-the-wall shops. Naturally, this is a very inefficient way of selling things but legislation protects these retailers and shackles any larger-scale competition.

Unfortunately for Western nations, simply opening up the Japanese market is not going to solve their trade problems at a stroke. Spending more on imports may reduce the imbalance but, in many fields, Japanese manufacturers have come totally to dominate the market, or create a market where none existed before. Motorcycles, cameras, video recorders and CD players are just a few fields where Japan has become so dominant that foreign competition is either minuscule, confined to specialist or esoteric corners of the market or simply nonexistent.

The belief in superlative Japanese efficiency and cautious Japanese investment policies are, however, just another example of the myths about how things work in Japan. In terms of output per hour, Japan is not really that efficient, it's certainly a long way behind comparable levels in the USA. The difference is that Japanese workers put in many more hours than their counterparts in other advanced economies.

Don't believe that Japanese companies are models of financial circumspection either. In the go-go days of the '60s when Japan's economy was growing at a frantic pace, many Japanese firms had gearing (ratio of borrowings to investment) which would have given any Western banker sleepless nights. The difference between sky-high Japanese borrowings at that time and the sky-high borrowings which brought so many Western entrepreneurs crashing down in the late '80s and early '90s was that the Japanese firms made their borrowings work, they didn't simply buy, sell and take over.

Bubble Economy

The big news is that Japan, long impervious to the vicissitudes of the world economy, got its come-uppance in the early 1990s when it reeled from an economic slump. The scapegoat for this state of affairs is known locally and increasingly overseas as the 'bubble economy'. Chances are you won't have been in the country any more than a couple of days before you come across the phrase, '...since the collapse of the bubble economy...' in a local newspaper.

What is this bubble economy? In essence it refers to the credit boom of the late 1980s in which Japanese companies enjoyed the combined fruits of escalating property values, a bullish stock market and low-interest borrowings. That the bubble had sprung a leak became apparent when the Tokyo stock market began its long slow slide in January 1990 (by October of that year it had lost 48% of its value). In 1991, Japanese banks, also hit by the fall in stock market values, could no longer afford to be so free with their money and raised interest rates. Capital became more expensive, and many speculative ventures initiated with cheap capital had to be cut back. On a consumer level, households hit by the rise in interest rates on their borrowings were forced to cut back on their spending.

In his book *Japan's Global Reach* (Arrow, 1992), Bill Emmott compared the puncturing of Japan's economic bubble to Ben Johnson's loss of his 100-metres gold medal in the 1988 Olympics after testing positive for anabolic steroids. As Emmott points out, without steroids Johnson is still fast; similarly, the Japanese economy, even artificially inflated by seemingly limitless reserves of cheap capital, is fundamentally strong and will, in time, bounce back.

The collapse of the bubble economy has provided Japan watchers with a steady diet of financial and political scandals. It has also brought with it unprecedented levels of bankruptcies, and graduating university students are currently confronted with an extremely competitive job market. Foreigners eyeing Japan as a possible place to work will find the job market at its leanest in some 20 years.

POPULATION
Japan has a population of around 123 million people (the seventh largest in the world), and, with 75% of it concentrated in urban centres, population density is extremely high. Areas such as the Tokyo-Yokohama-Kawasaki conurbation are so densely populated that they have almost ceased to be separate cities, running into each other and forming a huge urban sprawl, which, if considered as a whole, would constitute the world's largest city.

While this high urban population density is tough on the Japanese, it has the advantage of leaving other parts of the country reasonably sparsely populated. Travellers visiting Japan are still able to enjoy large national parks, mountainous regions and, in places like Hokkaidō, near wilderness.

The other notable feature of Japan's population is its ethnic and cultural homogeneity. This is particularly striking for visitors from the USA, Australia and other nations whose countries are host to populations of considerable

---

Imported Cars
Who says the Japanese don't import cars? It may be 'coals to Newcastle' and, compared to the local industry, the proportion of imported vehicles is indeed small, yet 5% of the Japanese market is still a lot of cars. BMW appears to be the most common imported nameplate. Spend long enough on Japanese expressways and you'll come away with the impression that every BMW comes complete with an 'ignore all speed limits' permit so drivers can imagine they're zooming down the autobahn to Munich. It's popularly rumoured that BMW make more money in Japan than they do in the USA.

Other German makes – Mercedes, Porsche – get a good show and you'll also see Saabs, plenty of Volvos, a few Fiats, quite a few hot Peugeot 205 GTis and a surprising number of Jaguars, Bentleys and Rolls-Royces. Believe it or not, the other major-selling European car is the good old British Mini. Minis have a huge cult following in Japan, which has developed to such an extent that more Minis are now sold in Japan than in the UK (sales almost match the combined sales in Japan of all US cars!). In a country where cars seem to be redesigned every six months, many of the Minis are sold as the 'Mini Thirty', with a notation on the side announcing that the design has barely altered since 1959.

All manner of oddities also find a market in Japan, although, no doubt, they're only brought out for a drive on the odd sunny Sunday. I saw a Ferrari Testa Rossa in Kyoto, and in Yamaguchi a flawless Lotus 7, complete with mini aero-screens and two samurai pilots in WW I leather flying helmets and aviator goggles.

Tony Wheeler

ethnic and cultural diversity. The Japanese have ensured that only a small number of foreigners settle in their country. Inhabitants of non-Japanese origin crept over the 1% mark for the first time in 1993. The vast majority of these are Koreans, but the new-comers who are pushing up the numbers of foreigners are largely foreign workers seeking a share in the economic miracle.

For outsiders, Koreans are an invisible minority. Indeed, even the Japanese them-selves have no way of knowing that someone is of Korean descent if he or she adopts a Japanese name. Nevertheless, Japanese-born Koreans, who in some cases speak no lan-guage other than Japanese, were only very recently released from the obligation to carry thumb-printed ID cards at all times, and still face discrimination in the work place and other aspects of their daily lives.

Other ethnic groupings include the Chinese and a wide cross section of foreign-ers hitching a ride on the Japanese economic juggernaut. Groups such as the Ainu have been reduced to very small numbers and are today found almost only in reservations on Hokkaidō.

PEOPLE

According to mythology, the origins of the Japanese people stretch back to a time when a pristine world was the playground of the gods. The Japanese themselves are, accord-ing to this scheme of things, divine in origin, being the issue of the sun goddess, Amaterasu Omikami. In terms more familiar to the scientific frame of mind, the Japanese are not a distinct race but belong to the Mongoloid group, like the Koreans and Han Chinese.

The Japanese probably arrived from Korea via a land bridge that connected Japan to the continent prior to the end of the last ice age, 10,000 years ago. At that time, Japan was already inhabited by the Caucasian Ainu people but they were gradually displaced by the invaders through a policy of active sup-pression and assimilation. Today there are only around 14,000 Ainu left, concentrated mainly in reservations on Hokkaidō.

Whatever the truth about their ancestry, the Japanese have developed a complex mythology concerning their origins and their uniqueness. To inhabitants of other parts of the globe, the Japanese curiosity about them-selves and their differences is, at times, nothing short of obsessional. Books written about the Japanese by foreign writers fre-quently become best sellers and the Japanese themselves contribute to the endless specu-lation with their own books. One of the more absurd theories gobbled up by a gullible Japanese public is the idea that the Japanese brain is unique. According to this theory, the 'Japanese brain' processes stimuli in the right hemisphere and is thus emotional and in harmony with nature, while the 'Western brain', with its left-hemisphere bias, is more rational and less harmonious. Where this leaves the rest of the world from Inuit to Zulus is not quite clear!

Theories like these, known as *nihonjinron* (theories about the Japanese), may to a large extent be a case of the public getting what it wants to hear – a recent example would be the huge sales of Ezra Vogel's book *Japan as Number One*. Clearly, however, this curios-ity also points to a certain anxiety among the Japanese, both about who they are and what their place in the world is. Some see this as one of the major sources of the energy of modern Japanese society. Eager for praise, the Japanese can't help but harbour a sneak-ing suspicion that somewhere people are sniggering behind their backs – an anxiety that only serves to goad them on to greater efforts.

Burakumin

Among the Japanese themselves, a tradi-tional class of outcastes, the *burakumin*, still retain a certain degree of their untouchabil-ity. Traditionally, the burakumin belonged to communities whose work, such as leather-craft, was unclean according to the principles of Japanese Buddhism. While the conditions of modern Japan have long since rendered the burakumin distinction obsolete, it contin-ues to exercise influence in such important aspects of Japanese social life as work and marriage. It is common knowledge, though it is rarely alluded to, that information about any given individual's possible burakumin origin is available to anyone (generally employers and prospective fathers-in-law) who is prepared to make certain discreet investigations. This is not a subject, however, that most Japanese feel happy about discussing with foreigners: they will often feign complete ignorance if the subject is raised.

Ainu

The indigenous population of Hokkaidō originally included a variety of ethnic groups, but they are now generally referred to collectively as Ainu. In Ainu language, the word 'Ainu' means man (male or human being). There is a possible link between the Ainu and the people known in ancient records as 'hairy people' who once lived in Tōhoku. Although there is a heavier growth of body hair and a tendency towards lighter skin colouring, the physical differences between Ainu and Japanese are slight; intermarriage has further reduced these differences.

From the Meiji period onwards, the Ainu rapidly lost out to a policy of colonisation and assimilation. The old ways of life based on hunting, fishing and plant gathering were replaced with a reliance on commercial fishing and agriculture. Their housing, dress and language gave way to the substitutes of Japanese culture.

During the '80s, the Ainu population was estimated to be around 25,000; almost half of this number lived in the Hidaka district, south-east of Sapporo. Intermarriage with Japanese has become so common, it's calculated that there are now probably less than 200 pure-blooded Ainu left.

Culturally, the Ainu have suffered a fate similar to the American Indians. The Ainu have made some efforts recently to rekindle pride in their culture, but the absence of a written language means that when the old folks die they also take with them a rich tradition of *yukar* or 'epic poems', folktales and songs. The Japanese still exercise racial discrimination against the Ainu (most of whom speak Japanese). The Ainu, however, lack the land or the finance to compete with the Japanese who have settled on Hokkaidō.

Japanese tourists seem comfortable at seeing the Ainu culture debased by pseudo 'Ainu villages' with Disneyland surroundings and souvenir shops selling tacky carvings. The old Ainu festivals and shamanic rites are 'acted' by listless, elderly Ainu. These tourist circuses can be intensely depressing – they are often combined with caged bears in zoos, a sight equally depressing, symbolic of the freedom lost by the Ainu.

If you want to see how the Ainu wish to portray themselves, make a point of visiting the Ainu Museum (not the souvenir shop ghetto) in Shiraoi, which has excellent displays and sells a catalogue sensitively compiled by the Shiraoi Institute for the Preservation of Ainu Culture, Wakakusa 2-3-4, Shiraoi, Hokkaidō 059-09.

Ageing Japan, Vacationing Japan

Foreign observers looking for signs of change in the Japanese economic powerhouse frequently focus their attention on the changing age make-up of the population. WW II left Japan with a very young population and, at that time, the average life span was also relatively short compared to advanced Western nations. A low birth rate and an average life span which is now the longest in the world is turning that age make-up right around. From being a nation of youngsters Japan is rapidly becoming a nation of oldsters. Other advanced nations are facing the same problem as the postwar baby boomers enter middle age, but nowhere is the change so dramatic as in Japan. Inevitably, such demographic change will have a major influence on the economy in coming decades.

Not only is the population ageing, it's also becoming, albeit rather slowly, less entranced with the Japanese workstyle, with its long working hours and short vacations. Japanese workers are becoming increasingly keen on enjoying their mighty yen in other ways than by acquiring new electronic gadgets. Still, although Japan's 16 annual leave days and 20 holidays (a total of 36) are not as good as the best Western European levels, they're nowhere near as bad as those in the USA. The Germans get 40 days of annual leave and holidays a year, the French 33.5, the British 33, and the downtrodden Americans just 23 miserable days. The Japanese are inclined not to take all their annual leave; on average they utilise only nine of the 16 days, but that's gradually changing.

EDUCATION

Among the many things that surprise visitors to Japan is the leniency with which very young children are treated. Volumes have been written on this subject and the general consensus would seem to be that the Japanese see the early years of childhood as a kind of blissful Eden, a period of gloriously spoiled dependency that prefaces the harsh socialisation of the Japanese education system.

At an age as young as three or four, however, the party is over: children then enter the nurseries that start preparing them for one of the most gruelling education systems in the world. Competition is fierce from the beginning, since getting into the right school can mean an important head start when it comes to the university exams. These exams, of legendary difficulty, are so demanding that any student preparing for them and getting more than four hours sleep a night, is said to have no hope of passing.

To help coach students through the exams, evening schools have sprung up and are often more successful in teaching the school curriculum than the schools themselves. Students who fail to gain entry to the university of their choice frequently spend one or two years repeating the final year of school and sitting the exams again. These students, known as *rōnin*, or 'masterless samurai', are in a kind of limbo between the school education system and the higher education system, the key to employment in Japan.

The intense pressure of this system derives in no small part from the fact that 12 years of education culminates in just two examinations that effectively determine the future of the examinee. One exam is sat by all Japanese final-year high school students on the same day; the other exam is specific to the university the student wishes to attend.

Once exams have been completed and a student gains a university place, it is time to let loose a little. University or college is considered a transitional stage between the world of education and employment, a stage in which one spends more time in drinking bouts with other students than in the halls of higher learning. In a sense the university years, for those who make it, are similar to the early years of childhood. All kinds of antics are looked upon indulgently as the excesses of youth. Some have seen a pattern in this – an alternation between extreme pressure and almost complete relaxation – which is mirrored in many aspects of Japanese social life.

As in other parts of the world, the Japanese education system processes male and female students differently. The top universities are dominated by male students, with many female students opting for two-year college courses, often in topics seen as useful training for family life, such as child psychology.

According to one traveller, the best way to gain an understanding of the Japanese education system is to visit a school:

I think it is a good idea to pay a visit to an elementary or high school. It will tell you a great deal about Japanese society and you might get a chance to tell the students about your own country. You'll be a hit! **Inge Nielsen**

ARTS

Here at the tail end of the 20th century, even the casual visitor to Japan has to reflect that one of the most remarkable qualities of the place is the way in which, more than any other non-European nation, it has adapted so successfully to the demands of the modern world. Unlike its huge continental neighbour, China – where modernity and tradition make for irascible bedfellows – Japan has taken the whole modern experience on board, synthesised it and made it uniquely Japanese.

There's something of a historical tradition at work in this. As a group of islands fairly distant from the continent, civilisation came to Japan later than it did to China and Korea, its nearest neighbours. Japan had a prehistoric culture, but the significant civilising influences – a writing system, laws, administrative codes, ethics, etc – were Chinese in origin and made their way to Japan from the 6th century via the Korean kingdom of Paekche.

While it is true that in the early stages of Chinese influence the institutions, arts and religion of Japan's powerful neighbour tended to eclipse earlier native traditions, by the early Heian period (794-1185), these influences began to be assimilated, allowing a truly native culture to emerge.

For the Japanese, the Heian period is considered the apogee of elegant courtly life. The high point of Heian arts was probably literary. The break with Chinese traditions can be seen in the development of the 31 syllable *waka* poem, precursor to the 17 syllable *haiku*, and in narrative epics like the *Genji Monogatari* (Tale of the Genji) by Murasaki Shikibu. In the visual arts the break with the Chinese landscape was in the development of *Yamato-e* (literally, 'Japanese painting') that depicted court scenes on folding screens.

The rise of a samurai class in the Kamakura and Muromachi periods, the patronage of Zen Buddhism, the austerities of which bolstered and enriched the military ethic, also had artistic and cultural implications. Importantly, Zen was the catalyst for art forms that are now thought of as distinctively Japanese: the tea ceremony, Japanese garden design, flower arrangement and Nō, a ritualised theatre that had its origins in Shintō and Buddhist elements.

In 1600, with the start of the Edo period, Japan closed its doors and embarked on a period of national seclusion. Despite the government's authoritarianism, it was a period of peace and prosperity, and when Commodore Perry demanded entry in 1853

the Japan he saw was very different from the Japan of two centuries earlier. The important change was the urbanisation that the long period of stability had allowed. Edo had a population of over one million. Despite their low status in the rigidly hierarchical social order of the day, a vast moneyed merchant class led to the development of a lively popular culture. Probably the most famous artistic achievement of this culture is the *ukiyo-e* or woodblock print.

From the Meiji Restoration, the impact of the West on Japanese culture has been nothing short of explosive. Nowhere in Asia can you find a people whose responses to the shifting tides of cultural change in the West have been as sophisticated as those of the Japanese. And from imitation the Japanese have quickly moved to innovation. In everything from film to fashion design, architecture to literature, Japanese artists have made unique international contributions.

Establishing just what constitutes 'Japanese style' is probably best left to the Japanese, but there are certain qualities that are hard to miss. Even something as commonplace as the Walkman, it has been argued, owes much to the culture that originally produced it. Like essentially Japanese forms such as the tea ceremony, the Walkman creates a personal, contemplative space for the individual. In most Japanese design, as in the arts, there is a particular attention to the utilisation of space.

Traditional Theatre

The two most famous Japanese theatrical traditions are *kabuki* and Nō. Both are fascinating, but without a great deal of prior study, don't expect to understand much of the proceedings. This is not a major problem as both forms work well on the level of spectacle. Even native Japanese speakers have difficulties understanding the archaic Japanese used in traditional theatre, so although you may have spent the last few years diligently working on your Japanese, it probably won't be much use to you. Fortunately, some theatres in Tokyo and Kyoto (the two places where you are most likely to see kabuki or

Nō) have programmes with a synopsis of the play in English, and headphones are sometimes available for a commentary in English.

The best source for details of performances is the Tourist Information Centre (TIC) in Tokyo or Kyoto. Some local publications such as *Tour Companion* in Kyoto and *Kansai Time Out* also publish theatre information. If you want to watch drama productions on TV in Tokyo, check the programme on channels 1 and 3. If you want to delve deeper into the subject the following publications may be useful:

The Kabuki Handbook by Aubrey & Giovanna Halford (Tuttle, New York, 1979)
The Nō Plays of Japan by Arthur Waley (Tuttle, Tokyo 1976)
A Guide to Nō by P G O'Neill (Hinoki Shōten, Tokyo & Kyoto, 1954)
A Guide to Kyōgen by Don Kenny (Hinoki Shōten, Tokyo & Kyoto, 1968)
The Bunraku Handbook by Shuzaburo Hironaga (Maison des Arts, Tokyo, 1976)

Kabuki The origins of kabuki lie in the early 17th century, when it was known as *kabuki odori*, which can be loosely translated as avant-garde dance. Its first exponent was a maiden of Izumo Taisha shrine who led a troupe of women dancers to raise funds for the shrine. It quickly caught on and was soon being performed with prostitutes in the lead roles. With performances plumbing ever greater depths of lewdness, the Tokugawa government banned women from the kabuki stage. The women were promptly replaced with attractive young men of no less availability. The exasperated authorities issued yet another decree, this time commanding that kabuki roles be taken by older men.

This move had a profound effect on kabuki. The roles played by these older male actors required greater artistry to be brought off credibly. The result was that, while remaining a popular art form that gave expression to popular themes, kabuki also metamorphosed into a serious art form, with the more famous of its practitioners becoming the stuff of which legends are made.

Kabuki is a theatre of spectacle, of larger-

than-life gestures, and as such employs opulent sets, a boom-crash orchestra, and a ramp through the audience that allows important actors to get the most mileage out of their melodramatically stylised entrances and exits. Initially, it featured plebeian versions of Nō classics but, as this displeased the Tokugawa government, kabuki was compelled to develop a canon of its own. It did so by drawing on disparate themes, both modern and historical. For the most part kabuki deals with feudal tragedies of divided loyalties, of the struggle between duty and inner feelings; the latter has produced a large body of work on the theme of love suicides.

One thing worth bearing in mind if you do get to see a kabuki performance is that, unlike the theatre of the West, kabuki is not a theatre in which the playwright is the applauded champion. The play is merely a vehicle for the genius of the actor; he is remembered long after the writer who put the words in his mouth is forgotten.

Kabuki Dancer

The main kabuki theatres in Japan are the Kabuki-za and National theatres in Tokyo, the Minami-za Theatre in Kyoto and the Shin Kabuki-za Theatre in Osaka. Rather than staying for the whole performance, you can also buy a *tachi-mi-seki* ('stand and watch') ticket for one act.

Nō Nō is an older form of theatre than kabuki, dating back some 600 years. It seems to have evolved as a cross-pollination between both indigenous Shintō-related dance and mime traditions, and dance forms that had their origins elsewhere in Asia. It was adopted as a courtly performing art, and in this capacity underwent numerous refinements. The result was an essentially religious theatre whose aesthetic codes were defined by the austerities, the minimalism of Zen. Unlike the spectacle of kabuki, the power of Nō lies in understatement. And in this respect – its use of masks as a mode of expression and the bleak emptiness of the sets, directing all attention to the performers – Nō has been a form of Japanese theatre that has fascinated Western artists searching for a more elementally powerful theatre in which to express themselves. Of these, perhaps the most famous is WB Yeats.

One of the most interesting aspects of Nō is the formalised structure of its plays. Two performers alone are vital to its presentation – the one who watches *(waki)* and the one who acts *(shite)*. Remembering that Nō is a theatre of masks, it is the role of the one who watches to, as it were, demask the one who acts. The reason is that the shite is not who he or she seems. Usually the shite is a ghost whose spirit has lingered on in a particular place because of some tragedy that took place in the past. The recognition, the demasking by the waki, gives way to the second act, in which the shite dances a re-enactment of the tragedy, and reveals his or her true identity.

Whether this is a kind of cathartic liberation or a sorrowful celebration of the lingering pain of the tragedy is partly dependent on whether the story is a happy one or

not. It also depends on how you interpret the sometimes quite bizarre but nevertheless spell-binding proceedings of the Nō performance.

For Nō, the main theatres are the National Nō Theatre and Ginza Nō Stage in Tokyo and the Kongō Nō Stage in Kyoto.

Kyōgen *Kyōgen* is a comic drama that evolved hand in hand with Nō. It originally served as an interlude, a little light relief within the more serious business of a Nō play, but came to stand on its own and is now more often performed separately between two different Nō plays. Unlike the heavily symbolic Nō, kyōgen draws on the real world for its subject matter and is acted in colloquial Japanese. The subjects of its satire are often samurai, depraved priests and faithless women – the performers are without masks and a chorus or chants are used.

Performances are often held in major Nō theatres such as the Ginza Nō Stage in Tokyo, Kongō Nō Stage in Kyoto and Osaka Nō Kaikan in Osaka.

Bunraku Like kabuki, *bunraku* developed in the Edo period. It is Japan's professional puppet theatre, using puppets that are a half to two-thirds life-size operated by three puppeteers. The puppeteers often make little attempt to hide their presence, which can seem obtrusive until you get used to concentrating on the puppets rather than their manipulators. A narrator tells the story and provides the voices for individual characters, while musical accompaniment is provided by the three-stringed *shamisen*.

For bunraku, the main theatres are the National Theatre in Tokyo, Gion Corner in Kyoto and the Asahiza Theatre and National Bunraku Theatre, both in Osaka.

Painting
The techniques and materials used in the early stages of Japanese painting owed much to Chinese influence. The introduction of Buddhism to Japan in the 6th century also provided Japanese painting with a role as a medium for religious instruction.

Towards the end of the Heian period, after contacts between Japan and China had dwindled, the emphasis on religious themes painted according to Chinese conventions gave way to a purely Japanese style of painting. Known as *yamato-e*, this style covered indigenous subjects and was frequently used in scroll paintings and on screens.

Ink paintings *(suiboku* or *sumi-e)* by Chinese Zen artists were introduced to Japan during the Muromachi period and copied by Japanese artists who produced hanging pictures *(kakemono)*, scrolls *(emaki)* and decorated screens and sliding doors.

During the Momoyama period, the rulers demonstrated their opulence and prestige by commissioning artists to use flamboyant colours and copious gold leaf. The most popular themes were those depicting Japanese nature (plants, trees and seasons) or characters from Chinese legends. The outstanding school of painting in this period was that of the Kanō family.

Western techniques of painting, including the use of oils, were introduced during the 16th century by the Jesuits. Japanese painters who combined Western and Japanese styles sometimes produced interesting results: portraits of Westerners thoughtfully included an oriental incline to the eyes.

The Edo period was marked by the enthusiastic patronage of a wide range of painting styles. The Kanō school continued to be in demand for the depiction of subjects connected with Confucianism, mythical Chinese creatures, or scenes from nature. The Tosa school, whose members followed the yamato-e style of painting, was kept busy with commissions from the nobility to paint scenes from the ancient classics of Japanese literature.

The Rimpa school not only absorbed the style of other schools (Chinese, Kanō and Tosa), but progressed beyond their conventions to produce strikingly original decorative painting. The works of art produced by a trio of outstanding artists from this school (Tawaraya Sōtatsu, Honami Kōetsu and Ogata Kōrin) ranks among the finest of this period.

Ukiyo-e Another genre of painting which developed at this time was the *ukiyo-e* (wood-block print). If there is one art form that Westerners instantly associate with Japan, this is it. The name ukiyo-e or 'pictures of the floating world' refers to the Buddhist metaphor for the transience of the human world. The subjects chosen by ukiyo-e artists were characters and scenes from the 'floating world' of the entertainment quarters of Edo (modern Tokyo), Kyoto and Osaka.

In the West, the vivid colours, novel composition and flowing lines of these prints caused great excitement, sparking a vogue which a French art critic dubbed 'Japonisme'. Ukiyo-e became a key influence on impressionist (for example, Toulouse-Lautrec, Manet and Degas) and postimpressionist artists.

Among the Japanese, however, the prints were hardly given more than passing consideration – millions were produced annually in Edo. They were cheap items, often thrown away or used as wrapping paper for pottery. For many years, the Japanese continued to be perplexed by the keen interest foreigners took in this art form which they considered of ephemeral value.

Since the '70s, Japanese collectors have returned to buy back their own prints and now account for about half of the market in these works. The biggest auctions of ukiyo-e are held not in Japan, but in New York and London. If you want to see the best and largest collection of ukiyo-e in the world, pay a visit to the Boston Museum of Fine Arts.

In 1987, Yasuda Fire & Marine Insurance bought Van Gogh's *Sunflowers* for US$39.9 million. More recently, Ryoei Saito (a Japanese business magnate) snapped up Van Gogh's *Portrait of Dr Gachet* for a cool US$82.5 million. Van Gogh, who only sold one of his paintings in his lifetime, shortly before his death approached his brother Theo to fund a business venture which he thought would solve his constant money problems. Van Gogh's proposal was to set himself up as a dealer in ukiyo-e!

The first prints of ukiyo-e were made in

black and white in the early 17th century; the technique for colour printing was only developed in the middle of the 18th century. The success of a publisher lay in close cooperation between the artist, engraver and printer through all stages of production.

The first stage required the artist *(eshi)* to draw a design on transparent paper and indicate the colouring needed. The engraver *(horishi)* then pasted the design face down on a block of cherry wood and carved out the lines of the design in relief. The printer *(surishi)* inked the block and took a proof.

Each colour required a separate block; it was up to the printer to use his skill to obtain accurate alignment and subtle colour effects that depended on the colour mixture and pressure applied.

The reputed founder of ukiyo-e is Iwa Matabei. The genre was later developed by Hishikawa Moronobu, who rose to fame with his illustrations for erotic tales. His wood-block prints of scenes from the entertainment district of Yoshiwara introduced the theme of *bijin-e* (paintings of beautiful women), which later became a standard

The Floating World

The Tokugawa era saw the flourishing of a culture that is referred to by the Japanese as *ukiyo* or the 'floating world'. The term itself derives from Buddhism and refers to the transient world of fleeting pleasures. By Edo times, however, the term had come to signify the burgeoning popular culture that was much in evidence in the sprawling pleasure districts of Japan's major towns.

The floating world, centred in pleasure districts like Edo's Yoshiwara, was a topsy-turvy kingdom, an inversion of all the usual social hierarchies that were held in place by the power of the Tokugawa Shogunate. Here, money counted for more than rank, actors and artists were the arbiters of style, and prostitutes elevated their art to a level such that their social and artistic accomplishments matched those of the ladies of noble families. Added to this was an element of spectacle. Both *kabuki* and *sumō*, with their ritualised visual opulence found large popular audiences in this period.

Many of the features of this floating world can still be seen in Japanese popular culture. Still, to get a glimpse of this world as it was in its heyday, it is best to turn to *ukiyo-e*, wood-block prints, or literally 'pictures from the floating world'. In keeping with the topsy-turvy world from which it issued, the ukiyo-e turned traditional Japanese graphic art upside down. For one, wood-block prints could be produced in quantity and made accessible to a large audience, and for another, ukiyo-e chose as its topics not Chinese-style landscapes and mannered court scenes but the people and scenes that filled the floating world. The ukiyo-e artist Utamarō, for example, depicted the lives of courtesans, sometimes depicting his subjects seminude, in a celebration of the female form. Other artists, such as Sharaku, turned their talents to depicting scenes from the kabuki theatre.

Ukiyo-e prints, ranging from around ¥5000 upwards, are readily available in Japan, and make excellent souvenirs. ■

subject. Early themes also covered scenes from the theatre (including the actors) and the erotic *shunga*. Kitagawa Utamaro is famed for his *bijin-e* which emphasise the erotic and sensual beauty of his subjects. All that is known about Tōshūsai Sharaku, a painting prodigy whose life is a mystery, is that he produced 145 superb portraits of kabuki actors between 1794 and 1795.

Towards the end of the Edo period, two painters produced outstanding works in this art genre. Katsushika Hokusai was a prolific artist who observed his fellow inhabitants of Edo (Tokyo) with a keen sense of humour. His most famous works include *manga* (cartoons), *Fugaku Sanjūrokkei* (Thirty-Six Views of Mt Fuji) and *Fugaku Hyakkei* (One Hundred Views of Mt Fuji). As Hokusai approached the end of his life – he died at the age of 89 – he delighted in signing his works with the pen name *gakyōrōjin* (literally, 'old man mad with painting').

Andō Hiroshige followed the lead of Hokusai and specialised in landscapes, although he also created splendid prints of plants and birds. His most celebrated works include *Tōkaidō Gojūsan-tsugi* (Fifty-Three Stations of the Tōkaidō); *Meisho Edo Hyakukei* (One Hundred Views of Famous Places in Edo); and *Omi Hakkei* (Eight Views of Omi) – Omi is now known as Lake Biwa-ko.

Modern Japanese Painting From the beginning of the Meiji Restoration, Japanese painting has been heavily influenced by Western trends. Despite an initial reaction against the Westernisation of local painting, Japanese painting has become increasingly internationalised, with modern Japanese painters making important contributions to all major artistic movements.

Irezumi Japanese *irezumi* or tattooing is widely considered the best of its kind. In feudal times, the authorities tattooed criminals, who then felt ashamed by the stigma of being 'branded'. In due course, those who had been tattooed exhibited a kind of defiant pride in their markings which they saw almost as a status symbol that set them apart from others in society.

Japanese tattoos, usually completed in blue and red natural dyes, often cover the whole body with amazingly intricate designs featuring auspicious animals, flowers, Buddhist deities or subjects drawn from Japanese folktales.

As a sop to foreign sensibilities, tattooing was banned during the Meiji era, but was promptly reinstated after the Prince of Wales (later to become the UK's King George V) took a liking to the art and had a rampant dragon inscribed on his arm in 1881.

Nowadays, many ordinary Japanese shun tattoos; it is a fair assumption that any Japanese you see flaunting tattoos are either Yakuza (Japanese Mafia types) or have connections with the shady side of society.

Music
Ancient Music *Gagaku* is the 'elegant' music of the Japanese imperial court which was derived from Chinese models. It flourished between the 8th and 12th centuries, then declined for several centuries until it became part of a revival of interest in national traditions during the Meiji period.

Court orchestras were divided into two sections with formally prescribed functions. The orchestra of the 'right' dressed in green, blue or yellow and played Korean music. The orchestra of the 'left' dressed in red and played Chinese, Indian or Japanese music. The repertoire of an orchestra included *kangen* (instrumental) pieces and *bugaku* (dance) pieces.

Nowadays, a gagaku ensemble usually consists of 16 players performing on drums and kettle drums; string instruments such as the *biwa* (lute) and *koto* (plucked zither); and wind instruments such as the *hichiriki* (Japanese oboe) and various types of flute.

Traditional Japanese Instruments There are several traditional Japanese instruments which continue to play a part in Japanese life, both publicly and privately. Some are used in orchestras or the theatre, while others are used for solo performances or mastered by young women to increase their chances in the marriage stakes.

The *shamisen* is a three-stringed instrument resembling a banjo with an extended neck. It was very popular during the Edo period, particularly in the entertainment districts of Osaka and Edo. It is still used as formal accompaniment in Japanese theatre (kabuki and bunraku), and the ability to perform on the shamisen remains one of the essential skills of a geisha.

The koto is a type of plucked zither with 13 strings. It was adapted from a Chinese instrument before the 8th century and the number of strings gradually increased from five to 13. Koto schools still operate, often catering to large numbers of young women.

The biwa, which resembles a lute, was also derived from a Chinese instrument and appeared in Japan in the 8th century. It was played by travelling musicians, often blind, who recited Buddhist sutras to the accompaniment of the instrument. During the Heian period, the biwa was used in court orchestras. In the succeeding Kamakura period, storytellers created a different style for the biwa to accompany tales from medieval war epics, the most famous of which are the *Tales of Heike*.

Although biwa ballads were in vogue during the 16th century, the instrument later fell out of favour. More recently, the composer Takemitsu Tōru has found a new niche for the biwa in a Western orchestra.

Modern Music Japan has the second-largest domestic record market in the world. More than any other nation in Asia, the Japanese have taken to Western music and you can meet fans of everything and everybody from Bach fugues to acid Jazz, from Ry Cooder to Iggy Pop. Even if you don't speak any Japanese, you can at least sit around with young Japanese and swap the names of bands you like.

Tokyo in particular is very much on the live-music circuit nowadays and is a good place to catch up with everything from symphonies to the latest indie bands. The best place to get information on who's going to be in town is *Tokyo Journal* in Tokyo and *Kansai Time Out* in the Kansai region.

An overwhelming feature of the local music scene is the *aidoru* or idol singer.

Contemporary Japanese Music

Recent years have seen something of a quiet revolution in Japanese popular music, the winds of change blowing in from far-flung Okinawa. No longer are the pop charts solely the domain of warbling *enka* has-beens, tuneless cutie *aidoru* bimbos and equally tuneless teenage pseudo-punks. Groups like the Rinken Band, Nenes, Champloose and soloist Kina Shoukichi have skilfully fused contemporary pop rhythms and melodies with the traditional sounds of their native island to produce crossover music that is both ethnic and danceable.

Nenes, for example, on their album *Ashibi* do a wicked version of Bob Marley's *No Woman No Cry* in Okinawan dialect! The success of such local musicians has made Naha a mecca for musicians from the mainland, much as Kyoto was for the blues two decades ago. (Kitajima Osamu was attempting much the same with rock and Nō 20 years ago in Kyoto, though sadly his weird and truly wonderful *Benzaiten* album, which I first mistook for David Byrne, is extremely rare and has never been released on CD in Japan – I got my copy in New York.)

The Japanese talent for imitation and improvement has rarely extended successfully into the realms of contemporary pop – with one notable exception. Orqesta de la Luz, a salsa band composed entirely of Japanese musicians, regularly plays to ecstatic hispanic audiences at stadium-sized venues across the USA and Latin America. When its latest CD went on sale at Tower Records in New York, the entire stock was sold out within three hours. In 1993 they became the first group ever to receive an award for Cultural Achievement from the United Nations.

For most Western listeners, homegrown bands singing in Japanese are almost universally mediocre. Shonen Knife have had considerable overseas success, and rumour has it that the girls are actually starting to learn to play.

Japanese reggae star Nahki is convincing as a would-be Jamaican both on stage and off. His live shows are fun, as are those of salaryman-turned-reggaeman Ranking Taxi. Sakamoto Ryuich and his reformed Yellow Magic Orchestra are worth checking out, as are occasional songs by the Southern All Stars, Tokyo Ska Paradise Orchestra, Yuming and teeny-bopper favourites Kome Kome Club. The latter's *Funk Fujiiyama* is a splendid parody of foreigners' stereotyped views of Japan: 'Everybody Samurai, Sushi, Geisha...Be-yoo-ti-ful Fujiyama...Ha! Ha! Ha!'

John Ashburne

Generally untalented, the popularity of idols is generated largely through media appearances and is centred on a cute, girl-next-door image – something akin to the Kylie phenomenon that swept the Western music scene in the early '90s.

But almost every Western musical form and trend has produced Japanese imitators. A visit to Tokyo's Yoyogi-kōen Park on a Sunday afternoon is as good an introduction to this aspect of the Japanese music scene as any. Stroll past the rockabilly kids and the Kiss lookalikes to the post-'70s punk crew; just down the road a little will be a group of '60s leftovers belting out some Creedence.

The predominance of imitation of Western styles is probably the main reason why very few Japanese acts have had any popularity in the West. Exceptions are performers like Kitarō, whose oriental synthesised sounds have had considerable success, and Sakamoto Ryūichi, a former member of Yellow Magic Orchestra. Still, no Japanese act has as yet been able to match the success of one Sakamoto Kyū, who made it to the top of the American hit parade in 1963 singing 'Sukiyaki'.

Little known in his own country, one musician who is held in high esteem by many Western musicians is Kina Shōkichi. He has been a major force in the popularisation of indigenous Okinawan music. His electric-traditional crossovers make for fascinating, often haunting listening. The Tsugaru-hantō Peninsula, at the tip of Tōhoku (Northern Honshū), has its own brand of music called Tsugaru-jamisen, which is a fun combination of racing banjos and wailing songs.

Literature

Murasaki Shikibu's *The Tale of the Genji*, translated by Edward Seidensticker, is the most famous classic of Japanese literature, and is available in paperback. It's a *very* long domestic drama of courtly intrigues and romances – strictly for the keen Japanophile.

The Narrow Road to the Deep North is a famous travel classic by the revered Japanese poet Matsuo Bashō. *Kokoro*, by Natsume Sōseki, is a modern classic depicting the conflict between old and new Japan in the mind and heart of an aged scholar. The modern and the traditional also clash in the lives of two couples in *Some Prefer Nettles* by Tanizaki Junichirō.

The Makioka Sisters by Tanizaki Junichirō (Berkley Windhover, 1957) is a famous family chronicle that has been likened to a modern-day *Tale of the Genji*. Ibuse Masuji's *Black Rain* (Kodansha, 1969) is a response to Japan's defeat in WW II. (Although made into a film in Japan, the book bears no relation to the Hollywood movie of the same name.)

Snow Country by Kawabata Yasunari is a famous story set in Japan's northern regions. Endō Shūsaku's *Silence* is a historical story of the plight of Japanese Christians following Tokugawa Ieyasu's unification of the country.

Mishima Yukio's *The Golden Pavilion* reconstructs the life of a novice monk who burned down Kyoto's Golden Temple in 1950. Although Mishima is probably the most controversial of Japan's modern writers and is considered unrepresentative of Japanese culture by many Japanese, his work still makes for very interesting reading. Abe Kōbō's *Woman of the Dunes* is a classic tale by one of Japan's more respected avant-garde writers.

Of course not all Japanese fiction can be classified as literature. Murakami Ryū's *Almost Transparent Blue* is strictly sex and drugs and was a blockbuster in the Japan of the '70s. Murakami Haruki is another bestselling author and his recent novel *A Wild Sheep Chase* is available in English.

It's surprising that more Western novelists haven't used Japan as a setting for their books, although James Clavell is an exception. His book *Shogun* has undoubtedly been a major influence on many people's perceptions of the country.

Guy Stanley's *A Death in Tokyo*, a reason-ably gripping whodunit set in and around Tokyo, manages to reveal a fair bit about life in Japan along the way. Probably the most interesting use of Japan as a fictional backdrop is in US science fiction writer William Gibson's 'cyberspace' novels where Japan becomes almost a metaphor for the future: Japanese settings, technology, customs, language and slang are all heavily featured. *Mona Lisa Overdrive* and *Necromancer* are good examples of his work.

Ikebana

Ikebana, the art of flower arranging, developed in the 15th century and can be grouped into four main styles: *rikka* (standing flowers); *nageire* (throwing-in); *shōkai* (living flowers); and *moribana* (heaped flowers). There are several thousand different schools at present, the top three of which are Ikenobō, Ōhara and Sōgetsu, but they share one aim: to arrange flowers to represent heaven, earth and humanity. Ikebana displays were originally part of the tea ceremony but can now be found in private homes – in the *tokonoma* (alcove for displays) – and even in large hotels.

Apart from its cultural associations, ikebana is also a lucrative business – its schools have millions of students, including many young women who view proficiency in the art as a means to improve their marriage prospects.

To find out more about courses for foreigners, contact Ikebana International (☎ 03-3293-8188), Ochanomizu Square Building, 1-6 Surugadai, Kanda, Chiyoda-ku, Tokyo. Some schools provide instruction in English; prices start around ¥3000 an hour.

Chanoyu

Also known as *chadō*, or 'the way of tea', the ritualised drinking of tea dates back to the to the Nara period, when it was used by meditating Buddhist monks to promote alertness. By the 14th century, it had developed into a highly elaborate and expensive pursuit for the aristocracy.

The turning point for the tea ceremony took place in the 16th century. Sen-no-

Rikkyū (1522-91) eschewed opulence and established a more elemental aesthetic, using utensils that echoed the irregularities of the natural world. Other tea masters took different approaches, and today the tea ceremony can be divided into three major schools.

The traditional setting for tea ceremony is a thatched teahouse in the setting of a landscaped garden. The preparation and drinking of the tea is conducted according to a highly stylised etiquette and the mental discipline involved was once an essential part of the training of a samurai warrior. Novices tend to find the proceedings fatiguing, and connoisseurs maintain that full appreciation of the art takes years of reflection.

For a demonstration of chanoyu in Tokyo or Kyoto ask for details at TIC or check with the large hotels; prices for a session start at ¥1000. A classic treatment of this subject, written with precision and devotion, is *The Book of Tea* (Dover Publications, New York, 1964) by Kakuzo Okakura.

Japanese Gardens

Japanese gardens aim to imitate nature as opposed to the Western emphasis on reforming it. However, Japanese gardening with its strong Chinese influences, still has common motifs and standard conventions for different styles.

Although the real mecca for Japanese garden enthusiasts has to be Kyoto (which has dozens of gardens to choose from), Japan's three best gardens are said to be Okayama's Kōraku-en, Kanazawa's Kenroku-en and Mito's Kairaku-en. Other cities with renowned gardens are Tokyo, Yokohama, Nagoya, Nara, Hiroshima, Takamatsu, Kumamoto and Kagoshima.

Full-scale Japanese gardens can be roughly categorised into three types: *tsukiyama* (hill garden), the dry landscape of *kare-sansui* (waterless stream garden) and *chaniwa* (tea garden).

The hill garden usually contains a hill combined with a pond and a stream with islands and bridges. You can view the garden by strolling along paths or contemplating it from an attached house. Examples of this type are the gardens of the Tenryū-ji Temple and Saihō-ji Temple, both in Kyoto.

The waterless stream garden features the dry landscape often associated with Zen meditation. The main elements are rocks and sand – furrows in a layer of sand suggest the ripples of the sea, and rocks suggest a waterfall. The Ryōan-ji Temple and Daitoku-ji Temple in Kyoto are representative of this type of garden.

The tea garden surrounds a teahouse and features stepping stones. The Kinkaku-ji Temple in Kyoto is a typical example.

Most gardens charge admission fees ranging from ¥150 to ¥500. Further information is given in a detailed leaflet entitled *Japanese Gardens*, published by the Japan National Tourist Organisation (JNTO), or you can contact TIC in Tokyo or Kyoto. For a thorough dig into Japanese gardens, try *The World of the Japanese Garden* (Weatherhill, Tokyo, 1968) by Lorraine Kuck.

The Japanese like to rank their gardens according to a traditional hit parade and patronise them accordingly, but many foreigners in search of peace and a break from hordes of people (who are presumably looking for the same thing!) opt to visit less famous gardens – preferably early in the morning or towards the end of the afternoon. Some technical knowledge about Japanese gardens is certainly an asset, but considerable pleasure and relaxation can be gained by simply wandering around and slowly absorbing the differences for investigation at a later date.

Bonsai

Bonsai, a skill imported from China during the Kamakura era (1192-1333), is the artificial dwarfing of trees or the miniaturisation of nature.

Bonsai trees are carefully clipped and their roots pruned to keep their dwarf dimensions. Some specimens have been handed down over generations and are extremely valuable. A related art is *bonkei* which is the technique of reproducing nature on a small tray using moss, clay, sand, etc.

TIC offices can provide further information on where to find or practice bonsai. Large hotels or department stores often have bonsai displays. Devotees of the art should make the 30 minute trip outside Tokyo to visit the Bonsai Village at Bonsai-machi, Omiya, Saitama.

Ceramics & Pottery

Ceramic art in Japan is usually considered to have started around the 13th century with the introduction of Chinese ceramic techniques and the founding of a kiln in 1242 at Seto (Aichi Prefecture) by Tōshirō. The Japanese term for pottery and porcelain, *setomono* (literally, 'things from Seto'), clearly derives from this ceramic centre which is still thriving.

During the following century, five more kilns were established: Tokoname, Shigaraki, Bizen, Echizen and Tamba. Together with Seto, these were known as the 'Six Ancient Kilns' and acquired a reputation for high-quality stoneware.

The popularity of the tea ceremony in the 16th century stimulated developments in ceramics. The great tea masters, Furuta Oribe and Sen-no-Rikyū, promoted production of exquisite Oribe and Shino wares in Gifu Prefecture. Hideyoshi, who thought nothing of smothering the walls of his tearoom with gold, encouraged the master potter Chōjiro to create works of art from clay found near Hideyoshi's palace. Chōjiro was allowed to embellish the tea bowls he created with the character *raku* (enjoyment). This was the beginning of Kyoto's famous *raku-yaki* style of pottery. Tea bowls became highly prized objects commanding stupendous prices. Even today, connoisseurs of the tradition of the tea ceremony are happy to shell out as much as US$30,000 for the right tea bowl.

Hideyoshi's invasion of Korea at the end of the 16th century was a military disaster, but it proved to be a boon to Japanese ceramics when captured Korean potters introduced Japan to the art of manufacturing porcelain. In 1598, a Korean master potter, Ri Sampei, built the first porcelain kiln at Arita in Kyūshū.

During the Edo period, many daimyō encouraged the founding of kilns and the production of superbly designed ceramic articles. The climbing kiln *(noborigama)* was widely used. Constructed on a slope, the kiln had as many as 20 chambers and the capability to achieve temperatures as high as 1400 °C.

During the Meiji period, ceramics waned in popularity, but were later included in a general revival of interest in *mingeihin* (folk arts) headed by Yanagi Sōetsu, who encouraged famous potters such as Kawai Kanjirō, Tomimoto Kenchiki and Hamada Shōji. The English potter Bernard Leach studied in Japan under Hamada Shōji and contributed to the folk-art revival. On his return to Cornwall in England, Leach maintained his interest in Japanese ceramics and promoted their appreciation in the West.

There are now over 100 pottery centres in Japan with large numbers of artisans producing everything from exclusive tea utensils to souvenir badgers *(tanuki)*. Department stores regularly organise exhibitions of ceramics. Master potters are highly revered and the government designates the finest as 'living national treasures'.

TIC's useful *Ceramic Art & Crafts in Japan* leaflet is published by JNTO and provides full details of pottery centres, kilns and pottery fairs in Japan. Well-known pottery centres include:

Arita porcelain, Arita, Kyūshū – Arita porcelain is still produced in the town where the first Japanese porcelain was made. In the mid-17th century, the Dutch East India Company exported these wares to Europe, where they were soon copied in ceramics factories such as those of the Germans (Meissen), the Dutch (Delft) and the English (Worcester). It is commonly known to Westerners as 'Imari' after the name of the port from which it was shipped. The Kakiemon style uses designs of birds and flowers in bright colours. Another popular style is executed in blue and white and incorporates scenes from legends and daily life.

Satsuma-yaki, Kagoshima, Kyūshū – The commonest style of this porcelain has a white, cloudy, cracked glaze enamelled with gold, red, green and blue.

Karatsu-yaki, Karatsu, Kyūshū – Karatsu, near Fukuoka in northern Kyūshū, produces tea ceremony utensils which are Korean in style and have a characteristic greyish, crackled glaze.

Hagi-yaki, Hagi, Honshū – The town of Hagi in Western Honshū is renowned for Hagi-yaki, a type of porcelain made with a pallid yellow or pinkish crackled glaze.

Bizen-yaki, Bizen, Honshū – The ancient ceramics centre of Bizen in Okayama Prefecture is famed for its chunky, unglazed bowls which turn red through oxidation. Bizen also produces roofing tiles.

Mashiko-yaki, Mashiko, Honshū – The town of Mashiko in Tochigi Prefecture, Northern Honshū, is renowned as a folk craft centre producing wares with a distinctive reddish glaze.

Mino-yaki, Toki, Honshū – From Toki in Gifu Prefecture in the Kansai district come pieces executed in the Oribe style which have a greenish glaze and are decorated with creatures and flowers; the Shino style, greatly prized by connoisseurs of tea utensils, employs a heavy white glaze.

Temmoku, Seto, Honshū – Seto city in Aichi Prefecture, Central Honshū, has a long tradition as a ceramics centre. The standard product is ash-glazed, heavy stoneware, but Seto also produces special ceramic wares such as *temmoku*, an ancient Chinese style which uses a brown and black glaze.

Kiyomizu-yaki, Kyoto, Honshū – The approach roads to the Kiyomizu-dera Temple in Kyoto are lined with shops selling Kiyomizu-yaki, a style of pottery which can be enamelled, blue-painted, or red-painted.

Kutani-yaki, Ishikawa, Honshū – The porcelain from Ishikawa Prefecture in Central Honshū is usually green or painted.

Cinema

At the time cinema first developed in the West, Japan was in the throes of the Meiji Restoration and was enthusiastically embracing everything associated with modernity. Motion pictures were first imported in 1896 and, in characteristic Japanese fashion, they were making their own by 1899. Until the advent of talkies, dialogue and general explanation of what was going on was provided by the *benshi*, a live commentator. This was necessary for foreign films but the benshi quickly became as important a part of the cinematic experience as the film itself.

At first, Japanese films were merely cinematic versions of traditional theatrical performances, but the Tokyo earthquake in 1923 prompted a split between period films or *jidaigeki* and new *gendaigeki* films, which followed modern themes. The more realistic storylines of the new films soon reflected back on the traditional films with the introduction of *shin jidaigeki* or 'new period films'. During this era, samurai themes became an enduring staple of Japanese cinema.

As the government became increasingly authoritarian in the years leading up to WW II, cinema was largely put to propaganda purposes. After the war, feudal films with their emphasis on blind loyalty and martial ability were banned by the Allied authorities but cinematic energy soon turned to new pursuits, including animated films, monster movies and comedies.

The '50s are generally thought to be the golden age of Japanese cinema. Directors like Akira Kurosawa led Japanese cinema onto the international stage when his *Rashōmon* (1950) took the top prize at the Venice Film Festival in 1951. Kurosawa continued his success and emerged as Japan's most influential director. His *Shichinin-no-Samurai* (Seven Samurai; 1954) gained the ultimate accolade when it was shamelessly ripped off by the Hollywood blockbuster *The Magnificent Seven*. Other Kurosawa classics include *Yōjimbō* (1961), the tale of a masterless samurai who single-handedly cleans up a small town bedevilled by two warring gangs, and *Ran* (1985), an epic historical film. Kurosawa still commands a high reputation among Western directors, though his recent films (he is now over 80) like *Yume* (Dreams; 1990) and *Madadoyo* (1993) have not been particularly well received in the West.

In the '70s and '80s Japanese cinema retreated before the onslaught of international movie making, in part because of the failure to develop new independent filmmaking companies in an era when big production companies were losing their clout worldwide. Recently, however, there have been a number of independently produced Japanese films which have had some art-house success in the West and serve as a good introduction, not just to Japanese cinema but to modern Japan itself.

Itami Jūzō's *Tampopo* (1985) is a wonderful comedy weaving vignettes on the themes of food and sex into a story about a Japanese noodle restaurant – 'Zen and the art of noodle making' as one critic described it. From the same director comes *Marusa-no-Onna* (A Taxing Woman; 1988), an amusing insight into taxation, Japanese style. The latter was so popular in Japan that it has spawned an equally amusing sequel: *A Taxing Woman 2*.

Donald Richie's *Japanese Cinema – An Introduction* (Oxford University Press, Hong Kong, 1990) is brief, but useful for the beginner.

CULTURE

Are the Japanese really different from the rest of us? As usual, the answer is 'yes...and no'. If the question is whether the Japanese possess characteristics that are theirs alone (a unique brain, singular features, etc) the answer is obviously 'no'. On the other hand, the sum total of the culturally conditioned aspects of the 'typical' Japanese character can only be found in Japan. In short, it is Japanese culture, not Japanese nature, that is unique.

Of course, all cultures are unique. It is possible to feel the shock of entering another world simply by flying from Hamburg to Paris, or by driving from California to Texas. The difference is one of degree. Adapting from one European culture to another is much simpler than adapting from a Western culture to one of those of the East. In the case of Japan, the differences are such that some fairly major shifts have to take place in Westerners' thinking if they are to make sense of the Japanese world.

The Group

One of the most widely disseminated ideas regarding the Japanese is the importance of the group over the individual. The image of loyal company workers bellowing out the company anthem and attending collective exercise sessions has become a motif that is almost as powerful as Mt Fuji in calling to mind the Land of the Rising Sun.

It's easy to fall into the spirit of these kinds of images and start seeing the business-suited crowds jostling on the Yamanote line as so many ant-like members of a collectivised society that has rigorously suppressed individual tendencies. If this starts to happen, it's useful to remember that in some senses the Japanese are no less individual than their Western counterparts. The Japanese are not robotic clones, they experience the same frustrations and joys as the average Westerner and, given the opportunity, many will complain about their work conditions, the way their boss treats them and so on, just as we do. The difference is, that while these individual concerns have a place, the principal Japanese orientation remains that of the group. The Japanese do not see their individual differences as defining.

For the Japanese, individuals have their rights and interests, but in the final analysis, these are subsumed under the interests of the group. Indeed the tension between group and individual interests and the inevitable sacrifices demanded of the latter has been a rich source of inspiration for Japanese art. The Japanese see the tension as one between *honne*, the individual's personal views, and *tatemae*, the views that are demanded by the individual's position in the group. The same difference is expressed in the terms *ninjō*, which translates loosely as 'human feelings' or, looser still, as the 'dictates of the heart', and *giri*, which is the individual's social obligations. Salaried workers who spend long hours at the office away from the families they love are giving priority to giri over ninjō.

The precedence of the group is so important that it cannot be stressed too much in understanding Japanese culture. Among other things, it gives rise to the important *uchi* (inside) and *soto* (outside) distinction. For the Japanese all things are either inside or outside. Relationships, for example, are generally restricted to those inside the groups to which they belong. Mr Satō, who works with Nissan, will have a social life comprised entirely of fellow Nissan workers and family. Mrs Satō, if she doesn't work (which is likely), will mix with members of the tea ceremony and jazz-ballet clubs to which she belongs.

The whole of Japanese social life is an intricate network of these inside-outside distinctions. Of course, this is hardly unique to Japan; it's just that in Japan being inside a group makes such special demands on the individual. Perhaps foreigners who have spent many years in Japan learning the language and who finally throw up their hands in despair, complaining 'you just can't get inside this culture', should remember that to be 'inside' in Japan is to surrender the self to the priorities of the group – and not many foreigners are willing or able to do that.

Men & Women
Japan may be a modern society in many respects, but don't expect the same level of equality between the genders that you have come to expect in your own country. As everything else in Japan, male-female roles and relationships are strictly codified. Although there's some evidence that this is

changing, it's definitely doing so at a much slower pace than it has done in the West. Part of the reason is that 'feminism' is a Western import and in a Japanese context tends to have a different resonance than it does in its culture of origin. Even the word 'feminist' has been co-opted so that a Japanese male can proudly proclaim himself a *femunisuto* when he means that he is the kind of man that treats a woman as a 'lady', in the Walter Raleigh sense.

Anyone who visits Japan will be struck by the fact that Japanese women are subordinate to men in public life. However, both sexes have their own spheres of influence, domains in which they wield power. Basically, women are *uchi-no* (of the inside) and men are *soto-no* (of the outside). That is, the woman's domain is the home, and there she will take care of all decisions related to the daily running of domestic affairs. The husband, on the other hand, while he may be the breadwinner, will still hand over his pay packet to his wife, who will then allocate the money according to domestic expenses and provide the husband with an allowance for his daily needs.

In public life, however, it is the men who rule supreme. In this world it is the role of women to listen, to cater to male needs and often to bear the brunt of men's frustrations. As any Western woman who tries hostessing will discover, women are expected to help men bear the burden of their public-life responsibilities not by offering advice – which would be presumptuous in the extreme – but by listening and making the appropriate sympathetic noises at the right moments.

Switch on a Japanese TV and you will see the same male-female dynamic at work. The male host invariably has a female shadow whose job it is to agree with everything he says, make astonished gasps at his erudition and to giggle politely behind a raised hand at his off-the-cuff witty remarks. These *sō desu* girls, as they're known, are a common feature of countless aspects of Japanese daily life. It's *de rigueur* for all companies to employ a bevy of nubile OLs, or 'office ladies', whose tasks include chiming a chorus of falsetto 'welcomes' to visitors, making cups of tea and generally adding a personal touch to an otherwise stolid male atmosphere.

Unfortunately, for many Japanese women, this is the sum of their job prospects. To make matters worse, it is considered that by the age of 25 they should be married, and in Japan married women are expected to resign from their work. This cut-off point of 25 years is a very serious one. Women who remain unmarried after this age are frequently alluded to as 'Christmas cake', this being a useless commodity after the 25th. By the time a woman is 26 or older, she will be regarded with suspicion by many men, who will wonder whether there isn't some flaw in her character that has prevented her from being swallowed up by the marriage market earlier.

Perhaps most disturbing for Western women visiting Japan is the way in which women feature in so much of the male-oriented mass culture. It's not so much a problem of women being depicted as sex objects, which most Western women would at least be accustomed to in their own countries, but the fact that in comic strips, magazines and movies, women are often shown as brutalised, passive victims in bizarre, sado-masochistic rites. Some disturbing conclusions could be drawn from much of the output of the Japanese media – at the very least it could be said that popular Japanese male sexuality has a very sadistic edge to it.

While these fantasies are disturbing, it is possible to take refuge in the thought that they *are* fantasies, and women are in fact a great deal safer in Japan than they are in other parts of the world. Harassment, when it does occur, is usually furtive, occurring in crowded areas such as trains; however, with direct confrontation, almost all Japanese men will be shamed into withdrawing the groping hand.

Work

Company life is very different for men and women. For men, it has traditionally meant a lifetime commitment that will take up far more of their waking hours than will their family. For women, company-life experience is liable to be limited to four or five years of answering the phone and offering tea to visitors before retreating to a life of domesticity. Women who return to work after marriage, and more and more are doing so, are likely to be involved in small-scale industry that provides none of the benefits available to most Japanese workers. The gap between average female earnings and average male earnings is greater in Japan than any comparable advanced nation.

For the Japanese themselves, the issue is a difficult one. After all, Japanese companies make such excessive demands on their workers that many Japanese women have no desire to share the responsibilities that are, at present, almost entirely undertaken by men. Company life for most men is a nonstop commitment from graduation to retirement. Even their annual two-week holidays are often forfeited because it would look like disloyalty to want to have a holiday from the company.

Peter Tasker, in his book *Inside Japan* (Penguin, 1987), points to the story of the Bureau for the Promotion of the Forty Hour Week; so enormous was their task of persuading Japanese corporations to change their work practices that members of the bureau were forced to put in long hours of overtime and weekend work. Before too long their efforts came to the attention of the authorities, who were unhesitating in praising them for their devotion to such a just cause!

The Japanese & Gaijin

As a foreign visitor to Japan, you are a *gaijin*, literally, an 'outside person'. Some foreigners insist (correctly in fact) that the term *gaikokujin* (literally, 'outside country person') is more polite than the contraction gaijin, but it's a small concession, and the expression gaijin is so widespread that you will be knocking your head against a brick wall trying to change it.

Away from the gaijin-infested big cities you will often be a sufficiently unusual sight to warrant being pointed out. It's not unusual to hear whispered exclamations of *gaijin da* ('it's a foreigner!') when you amble through less visited parts of rural Japan; even in suburban Tokyo, where gaijin are a dime a dozen, many school children are still unable to resist erupting into giggles at the sight of a foreign face.

Long-term visitors to Japan are prone to what has been called the 'Seidensticker syndrome', an ongoing love-hate relationship which frequently shifts sides. After being initially overwhelmed by Japanese courtesy, many foreigners, who feel that they have been in Japan long enough to deserve a more intimate footing with the culture, come to the conclusion that Japanese politeness and helpfulness mask a morbid ethnocentricity. Everybody has to deal with this in their own way, but fortunately for the short-term visitor, the polite and friendly nature of most contacts with the Japanese is likely to be the main impression.

The best advice to the visitor to Japan is to enjoy Japanese courtesy and leave its more sinister implications for long-term residents to fret over. Excessive politeness does have a distancing effect, but when you're lost in a crowded city the invariable polite offer of assistance is a godsend. And, whatever the long-timers say, most visitors to Japan come away with miracle stories of Japanese courtesy: the hitchhikers who are treated to lunch and taken kilometres off their host's original route to be deposited at their destination; the traveller who arrives too late at the bank to change money and, standing miserably outside the closed doors, is offered a loan by a passer-by.

Etiquette

One of the most enduring Western notions about Japan is that of Japanese courtesy and rigid social etiquette. With a little sensitivity, however, there is little chance of mortally offending anyone with your lack of social grace.

To be sure, many things are different: the

Japanese bow and indulge in a ritualised exchange of *meishi* (business cards) when they meet; they exchange their shoes for uncomfortable plastic slippers before entering the home; and social occasions involve sitting on the floor in positions that will put the legs of an ill-bred foreigner to sleep within five minutes. But, overall, most of the really complex aspects of Japanese social interaction are functions of the language and only pose problems for the advanced student who's trying to get as close to the culture as possible.

Sitting When socialising with the Japanese or visiting them in their homes, sitting on the floor for extended periods of time can be a real nightmare for many foreigners. Sit with your legs beneath you for as long as possible and then, if you *must* stretch your legs out, do so discreetly without pointing them in anyone's direction. Pointing your feet (the lowest part of the body, literally) at people, even inadvertently, is bad form throughout Asia.

Bowing When you meet Japanese, it's polite to bow slightly from the waist and incline your head. Actually, the rule is that the deepness of a Japanese bow depends on the status (relative to oneself) of the person to whom one is bowing. When A has higher status than B, it is important that B's bow is deeper than A's. As the bows take place simultaneously, it is often incumbent on B to give a quick, surreptitious glance in the direction of A's exalted presence to determine that his or her bow is indeed lower than A's. Fortunately, no-one expects foreigners to carry on like this, and nowadays, many Japanese have taken to shaking hands, though the bow is still the most important mark of respect.

Business Cards If you're going to be working in Japan, get some business cards made up: without them, you'll be a nobody. All introductions and meetings in Japan involve an exchange of business cards – handing out yours to the right people can make things happen; not having a card will definitely look very bad. Cards should be handed over, and accepted, with some ceremony, studied carefully and referred to often. It's polite to accept a card with two hands. Do not simply stuff a proffered card into your pocket. Also, never write anything on a card you are given.

Gift Giving Reciprocity is an integral part of Japanese culture, and the exchange of gifts, the return of one kindness with another, is an important part of Japanese daily life. If you visit somebody at their home, you should bring them a gift. It needn't be anything big – chocolates or flowers, much the same things that are used as gifts in the West, will do. Ideally, it is nice to bring something from your own country. Gifts used for cementing friendships and for paying off small obligations are usually small and unostentatious. Where money is given it is presented in an envelope.

As a foreigner, it's quite likely that people will sometimes want to give you gifts 'for your travels'. You may not be able to reciprocate in these situations. The polite thing to do is to refuse a couple of times when the gift is offered. The other party will probably keep pushing as long as you keep refusing. A couple of refusals are enough not to seem too grasping before making off with your spoils.

Gift giving is so important in Japan that it has become institutionalised in many aspects of Japanese social life. If, for example, you are invited to a wedding, you are expected to bring a 'gift' of at least ¥20,000 – consequently young Japanese with too many friends of a marriageable age can often have a very lean time if they all get married in the same year. One of the most notorious 'gifts', among foreign residents at least, is 'key money', the two months' rent that you must dole out to the owner of your new home. For many Westerners, this all seems like so much bribery; for the Japanese, these gift-giving rituals operate to show respect, to give face and to ensure smooth interpersonal relations.

Flattery What passes for flattery in the West is often perceived as quite natural in Japan. The Japanese recognise the importance of a bit of ego stroking and generally will never pass up the opportunity to praise each other in company. The foreigner who has made an effort to learn a few sentences of Japanese or to get by with chopsticks is likely to be regularly regaled with gasps of astonishment and unctuous praise. Don't feel anxious; the intent is not facetious, it's genuinely meant to make you feel good.

The correct response to praise is to decline it. Even if you do feel your dexterous manipulation of the chopsticks has reached a rarely achieved level of proficiency, the best response to exclamations of 'How skilful you are!' is to smile and say something like 'Not at all'. Importantly, don't forget to return a few compliments here and there – although there's no need to force yourself if it doesn't come naturally.

Directness One major difference between the Japanese and Westerners is that the Japanese do not make a virtue out of being direct. Indeed, directness is seen as vulgar; the Japanese prefer to resort to more vague strategies and to feel their way through a situation when dealing with others. The Japanese have a term for this that translates as 'stomach talk' – where both sides tentatively edge around an issue, feeling out the other's point of view until it is clear which direction negotiations can go. This can often result in what for many Westerners is a seemingly interminable toing and froing that only ever seems to yield ambiguous results. But don't be deceived, the Japanese can usually read the situation just as clearly as if both sides were clearly stating their interests.

Basically, when you're dealing with the Japanese, avoid direct statements that are likely to be perceived as confrontational. If someone ventures an opinion, however stupid it may seem, try not to crush it with a 'No, I disagree completely,' or something similar.

Go-Betweens The dislike of directness

among the Japanese gives rise to another interesting phenomenon that residents are likely to come into contact with: the go-between. When the Japanese do have to confront someone with something unpleasant, it is customary to find a disinterested third party to do so. For example, if a misunderstanding arose between you and your concierge, he/she might contact your employer who, in turn, would represent his/her interests to you.

The thing to do in situations like this is not to become angry at the person meddling in your private affairs but to remember that the Japanese do this not so much from timidity as from a sense of being too close to an issue to be able to deal with it sensibly. The mediator plays an important role in all kinds of difficult social situations, the most famous of these being the *o-miai* or marriage go-betweens.

Calls of Nature It's not unusual to find men urinating in crowded streets, and public toilets are occasionally unsegregated, but the public use of handkerchiefs for blowing your nose is definitely frowned upon. A Japanese student related with an air of genuine disgust how, on a train, he had seen a beautiful Western girl take a hankie from her handbag and blow her nose into it. 'How could such a beautiful girl have such bad manners?' he wondered. The polite thing to do if you have a cold in public is to keep sniffing (an admirable sign of self-restraint in Japanese eyes) until you can get to some private place to do your business.

Avoiding Offence
Japanese are generally remarkably tolerant when it comes to the curious ways of visiting gaijin, and there's little chance of committing any grave faux pas. There are certain situations however, where it is important to follow Japanese example. Shoes should always be removed, for example, when entering a Japanese home or entering a tatami room of any kind – Japanese will not make allowances for foreign customs in this case.

Bathing in Japan also conforms to fairly strict rules and you should follow them. Whether it's a Japanese-style bath or an onsen, remember that the actual washing takes place before entering the water. Showers or faucets are provided for this purpose. Baths and onsen are for soaking in after you have washed.

There are a number of points that are worth bearing in mind with regards to Japanese etiquette, though you are unlikely to seriously offend anyone if you forget to follow them. As in other parts of Asia, the respectful way to indicate for someone to approach you is by waving your fingers with the palm downwards – not beckoning with the fingers upwards, as we do in the West. As a Westerner you can offer your hand when you meet someone for the first time, though if you want to add a Japanese touch to the proceedings you can make a slight bow, which is the traditional Japanese greeting.

Japanese don't eat food in the street unless there are seats provided to do so. Ice creams are an exception to this rule. It's up to you whether you want to abide by this custom: no-one's going to be particularly upset if they see you wandering down the street munching on a Big Mac, but they might feel it's a little uncivilised.

Finally, the cardinal rule of dealing with people in Asian cultures applies equally in Japan: stay cool, don't express anger and keep smiling. When things aren't going your way, try a different tack and don't force anyone into a situation they can't back down from without a loss of face. The Japanese are much more amicable in this respect than the Chinese, say, but the smiling, friendly approach achieves much more than belligerence.

Meeting the Japanese
Your opportunities to meet the Japanese will depend a great deal on the way you travel. Obviously, anyone who is on a whirlwind tour of Japan, stopping in a different destination every night, is going to have far fewer opportunities to meet locals than the traveller who spends some months working in Tokyo

or Osaka and then a month or so seeing the country. Nevertheless, even for those with limited time schedules, meeting the Japanese is not impossible due to the thoughtful provision of such programmes as the home visit system (described later in this section).

One thing to consider is that the following pointers apply to fairly formal situations. If you take to hanging out in bars in Japan, you're likely to meet young Japanese people for whom little of the traditional etiquette applies. In informal settings (especially after a few drinks) young Japanese can be surprisingly forward in making contact. Generally all it takes is a smile and a nod to be brought into conversation.

Shyness Perhaps the most difficult aspect of getting to meet the Japanese is their almost chronic shyness. Young Japanese have generally been discouraged from taking individual initiative and consequently, visitors are much more likely to be surrounded by a gaggle of giggling school children chorusing 'haro' than having an interesting conversation with one or two Japanese. Many young Japanese will simply freeze in stunned and embarrassed silence if directly addressed by a foreigner. Unfortunately, the same applies to many adults if they have had little experience of gaijin.

Much of the Japanese shyness stems from the fear of making a mistake and somehow causing offence. The possibility of not responding appropriately often makes them extremely nervous in situations they've not been trained to deal with, such as a foreigner speaking to them in English or in halting Japanese. If you need to make casual contact with a Japanese, say, to ask directions, it is always best to appear calm and relaxed and smile as you talk.

I once had the experience of turning to a Japanese in frustration after wandering around Ikebukuro station looking for the north exit for what seemed an eternity, only to hear her screech in fear and scamper off. The harassed look on my face promised all kinds of potential communication problems that most Japanese would simply rather not deal with.

Tony Wheeler

Nowadays, particularly in the big cities, more and more Japanese are becoming accustomed to dealing with foreigners. The school system is using foreign teachers as assistants for teaching English and many students attend private English-language schools where they regularly have contact with gaijin. The result is that levels of foreign-language expertise and confidence in dealing with ambassadors from the outside world are on the rise in Japan.

Home Visit System The home visit system is publicised in JNTO pamphlets and gives visitors to some of Japan's larger cities the opportunity to visit a Japanese family in their home. Visits take place in the evening and, while dinner is usually not served, the hosts will often provide tea and sweets. It is polite to bring a small gift with you when you visit to show your appreciation of your hosts' thoughtfulness and hospitality.

Home visits can be organised in the following cities:

City	Telephone
Tokyo	☎ 03-3502-1461
Yokohama	☎ 045-641-4759
Kyoto	☎ 075-752-3511
Osaka	☎ 06-345-2189
Kōbe	☎ 078-303-1010
Nagoya	☎ 052-581-0100
Sapporo	☎ 011-211-3341
Okayama	☎ 086-222-0457
Hiroshima	☎ 082-247-9715
Fukuoka	☎ 092-733-2220
Nagasaki	☎ 0958-22-9690
Kuma-moto	☎ 096-328-2111
Kagoshima	☎ 0992-24-1111

Conversation Lounges The conversation lounge is a uniquely Japanese institution that gives members an opportunity to meet foreigners in an informal setting. Generally, Japanese pay a fee to participate for an evening, while foreigners are admitted free. The lounge is usually a coffee-shop setup, though occasionally, as in Mickey House in Tokyo, alcohol is served. Lounges are almost always an excellent place to meet and talk with Japanese people who have an interest in the world outside their own country. For more information about conversation lounges, check the English-language magazines and the Tokyo chapter of this book.

SPORT
Sumō

Sumō, Japanese wrestling, is a simple sport but a complicated ritual. The rules of the game are deceptively simple: the *higashi* (east) wrestler tries either to push his *nishi* (west) opponent out of the ring or unbalance him so that some part of his body other than his feet touch the ground. The 4.55 metre diameter ring *(dohyō)* is on a raised platform, much like a boxing ring, but there the similarity ends. Sumō matches do not go 10 rounds, they are brief and often spectacular and the ritual and build up to the brief encounter is just as important as the clash itself.

There are no weight classes in sumō; they're all big, and in lookalike Japan, sumō wrestlers certainly stand out. Gargantuan bulk is the order of the day and sumō wrestlers achieve their pigged-out look through diet (or lack of it from the weight-watcher's point of view). Large quantities of an especially fattening stew called *chankonabe* are supplemented with esoteric activities, such as masseurs who manipulate the wrestler's intestines so they can pack more food in.

Would-be sumō wrestlers, usually 15-year-olds from rural areas, traditionally join one of the 28 *heya* (stables) of wrestlers, often run by retired fighters, and work their way up through the ranks.

Sumō still retains traces of its connections to Shintō fertility rites, including the shrine-like roof which hangs over the ring and the referee or *gyōji* in his wizard-like outfit. It is said that the dagger worn by the referee was to allow him to commit instant seppuku if he made a bad refereeing decision! The wrestlers wear a *mawashi* with a broad leather belt; it's rather like a *fundoshi*, the traditional loincloth drawn between the buttocks. A good grasp on the belt is a favourite hold but there are 48 recognised holds and throws.

The pre-game preliminaries often last far longer than the actual struggle, as the opponents first hurl salt into the dohyō to purify it and then put great effort into psyching each other out with malevolent looks and baleful stares. A series of false starts often follows before two immovable objects finally collide with an earth-shaking wallop. Sometimes that initial collision is enough to tip one of them out of the ring but usually there's a brief interlude of pushing, shoving, lifting and tripping. Sometimes neither opponent is able to get a grip on the other and they stand there,

slapping at each other like two angry, and very overweight, infants.

Short though a sumō encounter may be, it can often be very exciting. In one match I saw a much smaller wrestler virtually lift up and hurl his enormous opponent out of the ring with such force that he, in turn, went flying out, right over the top of the defeated wrestler.

Tony Wheeler

The Tokyo sumō stables are in Ryōgoku, near the new Kokugikan sumō arena. Six major sumō tournaments *(basho)* are held each year: January (Tokyo – Kokugikan Stadium), March (Osaka – Furitsu Taiikaikan Gymnasium), May (Tokyo – Kokugikan Stadium), July (Nagoya – Aichi Kenritsu Taiikukan Gymnasium), September (Tokyo – Kokugikan Stadium) and November (Fukuoka – Kokusai Centre Sogo Hall).

At a basho, prices start at ¥1000 for a basic bench seat at the back, but if you can afford ¥7000 for a balcony seat, you will not only be closer to the action but will also be able to delve deep into the mysteries of the refreshment bag that comes with the ticket. Ringside seats are highly prized and virtually unobtainable unless you have inside contacts. Tune in to Far East Network (FEN) on 810 kHz for simultaneous radio coverage of the action in English. TV coverage is extensive and most of the English-language newspapers devote a section to sumō.

Each basho commences on the Sunday closest to the 10th of the month and lasts a fortnight, during which each wrestler competes in one bout a day. The big crowds arrive in the late afternoon to watch the top-ranking wrestlers; the earlier part of the day is reserved for the lower-ranking fighters.

If you want to see a sumō bout, but arrive in Japan at a time when no basho is being held, you can visit one of the sumō stables to watch training. JNTO publishes a leaflet entitled *Traditional Sports* which has a sumō section with full details of tournaments, purchase of tickets, visits to sumō stables and even a bibliography of books and magazines in English on the subject. Contact TIC for more information.

Wrestlers who reach the rank of *yokozuna* or 'grand champion' become celebrity figures in Japan. With the exception of several Hawaiians, very few foreigners have successfully made the big time in this sport. And what happens to a retired sumō wrestler? Well he loses weight, cuts his hair and returns to Japanese anonymity; many sumō wrestlers experience severe heart problems later in their lives.

Baseball

Sumō wrestling may be the most Japanese sporting activity, but baseball is Japan's number one sport both for spectators and participants. Baseball bounced into Japan in 1873 with a US teacher, Horace Wilson, who taught at Tokyo University. There have been professional teams since the 1930s and, just as in the USA, there are little-league teams, school teams, work teams and 'bunch of friends in the local park' teams. At the professional level, however, baseball is big business and the nightly televised games draw huge audiences.

Despite the similarity to American baseball – even many of the terms (double play, first base, home run) are carried straight over without translation – baseball has been cleverly altered to fit the Japanese mood. Read Robert Whiting's *You've Got to Have Wa* (Macmillan, New York, 1989) for the full story on baseball Japanese-style. Even the Japanese emphasis on the group over the individual has played its part in fitting baseball into the Japanese mould and *wa* means something like 'team spirit'.

Japanese professional baseball is divided into two leagues: Central and Pacific. Each league has six teams, which are usually given really original names such as Tigers or Giants (although the Hiroshima Carp do sound distinctly Japanese) and are mostly supported or owned by big businesses. Each team is allowed two gaijin players, usually Americans past their prime or facing some sort of contractual difficulty in the USA. They often have trouble adapting to the Japanese requirements that they be just another

J-League

The inauguration of Japan's professional soccer league, dubbed the J-League, heralds a revolution in the Japanese sportsworld unparalleled since the introduction of pro-baseball in the1950s. Suddenly Japan has gone soccer mad. Twelve teams from around the country, supported by corporations such as Matsushita, Kodak, Coca-Cola and Ford Japan, are cheered on by thousands of rabidly partisan supporters, chanting team songs and bearing team colours painted on their faces. In its first year, soccer has earned more from merchandising than baseball has in its 40 year history.

The runaway success of the sport is perhaps attributable to the fact that it has caught the imagination of Japan's increasingly leisure-minded youth. TV pundits and couch psychologists suggest that soccer reflects a fundamental change in Japanese attitudes – more fluid, less stylised and predictable than baseball, soccer allows players to express their individuality both on and off field. Soccer players in Japan sport the same dubious hairstyles as their foreign counterparts. Undoubtedly games are exciting, played at a frenetic pace, more in the style of South American than European football. Unlike, say, British League soccer, there is no possibility of a draw – if games are tied after 90 minutes, 30 minutes of extra time are played with the sudden death rule applying: the first team to score wins. Where extra time fails to bring a result, a penalty shoot-out is imposed.

Teams are allowed three foreign players each, and some outstanding players have been imported, a factor which will no doubt serve to raise the quality of soccer in Japan. Japan narrowly failed to qualify for the 1994 World Cup in the USA, but this seems to have done little to dampen local enthusiasm for the sport. Japan must be hot favourite to host the World Cup in 2002, when it comes to Asia for the first time.

John Ashburne

member of the team, not rock the boat and definitely not show up the local stars!

The season lasts from April to October and is followed by the Japan Series, a seven-match contest between the top two teams. In Tokyo, the centre of the baseball universe is Korakuen Stadium. Expect to pay around ¥700 for a basic seat.

The All-Japan High School Baseball Championship Tournaments, are taken very seriously in Japan. These are the major annual sporting events when the flower of youthful vitality goes on display. During August, when the summer tournament is in progress, baseball seems to be the only topic on everybody's mind.

Golf

In 1903 an intrepid English merchant named Arthur Groom set up the Kōbe Golf Club, Japan's first. More than 40 million Japanese now play the game, although golf is neither ritual like sumō nor sport like baseball: to most Japanese it's a combination of business and prestige. The golf course is another place where business contacts are made and culti-

vated so, for the upwardly mobile, the ability to play golf (and equally important to look like a real golfer) is a necessity. Since golf is expensive – anything requiring lots of real estate is expensive in Japan – playing golf also carries considerable prestige.

If you want to set foot on a green, a fat wallet and corporate clout are handy assets. Membership fees are rarely less than US$5000, can easily reach US$25,000 and often soar higher. Of course it is usually the company that takes out corporate membership and thus pays for its employees to go golfing. Green fees usually start at around US$100 a day. Real golf courses have recently prompted an environmental backlash as Japanese non-golfers have raised a storm of protest against more and more of the countryside being converted to golf courses.

For most Japanese, golf time is principally time spent on one of the multi-tiered driving ranges which are a familiar sight in almost any Japanese city. It's easy to spot their green nets, often perched like aviaries on the tops of high-rise buildings.

The prohibitive cost of golfing in Japan

means that it is often cheaper for Japanese to book a packaged golfing tour abroad, which explains the common sight at international airports of bevies of Japanese bent double under a huge bag of clubs. On the other hand, there seem to be plenty of Japanese carrying golf clubs to the fleshpots of Asia – it gives the right impression even if some might have a different intent.

Several years ago, foreigners were mystified to see young Japanese men outside sunbathing, but wearing gloves. The answer, of course, was that this resulted in the ultimate status symbol: suntanned arms and those lily-white hands which are the instantly recognisable and envied sign of a frequent golfer.

Tennis

Tennis was introduced to Japan in the late 19th century. A few years ago, it received a considerable boost in public esteem, particularly in the eyes of young women, when it was discovered that the Crown Prince Akihito (who has since succeeded his father to become emperor) met his bride-to-be on the tennis court.

Early this century, the Japanese came up with *nankyu*, a local adaptation which has its own rules and is only played as doubles using a soft rubber ball. International championships are held regularly and, for unfathomable reasons, the game is quite popular in Zaire.

Skiing

Skiing developed in Japan in the 1950s and there are now more than 300 ski resorts, many with high-standard runs and snow-making equipment. The majority of resorts are concentrated on the island of Honshū, where the crowds are huge, the vertical drops rarely more than 400 metres and all runs start at altitudes of less than 2000 metres. Snow cover in southern and eastern Honshū is generally adequate, but can be sparse and icy.

Skiers on Hokkaidō, however, can look forward to powder skiing that matches anything in the European Alps or North American Rockies. Niseko and Furano, two of Hokkaidō's best resorts, have excellent facilities (Niseko has 43 lifts) and neither suffers from extreme crowding.

JNTO's *Skiing in Japan* pamphlet covers 20 resorts on Honshū and Hokkaidō with travel information, ski season dates, accommodation details, resort facilities and costs. Japan Airlines offers special ski tour packages including air fares, transportation, meals and accommodation.

Skiing is normally possible from December to April, though the season can be shorter in some of Honshū's lower-altitude resorts. Akakura, which is within easy reach of Tokyo, is known for its deep snow that thaws quickly by the end of March. Shiga and Zao, on Honshū, are best for early April skiing. The best time for cross-country skiing is March or April, when the snow is firmer and deeper; January and February are often very cold and stormy.

Resort accommodation ranges from hostels to expensive hotels but is heavily booked during the ski season. Many resorts are sited at hot springs and double as *onsen* or bathing spas. Avoid weekends and holidays when lift lines are long and accommodation and transportation are heavily booked.

Lift passes cost ¥2600 to ¥4200 a day. Daily rental of skis, stocks and boots can cost up to ¥5000 but finding larger-size ski boots may be difficult. Equipment can only be hired at resorts and is usually old and of a low standard; advanced equipment for the more experienced skier is rare. Since clothing cannot be hired, and second-hand gear is very hard to find, it's advisable to bring your own equipment. For those with plenty of cash it is possible to buy it in Japan – many ski shops hold sales from September to November and package-deal bargains can be found with skis, bindings and stocks included. Tokyo's Jimbocho, Shinjuku, Shibuyu and Ikebukuro areas have good ski shops.

As well as downhill skiing, Japan also offers good terrain for cross-country skiing and touring, especially in the Hakodate region of Hokkaidō – a good way to get away from the crowds. The Japanese are very hospitable and foreigners are welcome to join in races and festivities organised by the local authorities. One of the most famous is the Sapporo Marathon cross-country ski race.

Martial Arts

Japan is renowned for its martial arts, many of which filtered through from China and were then adapted by the Japanese. During feudal times, these arts were highly valued by ruling families as a means of buttressing their power.

After WW II, martial arts were perceived as contributing to the aggressive stance which had led to hostilities and their teaching was discouraged. Within a decade, however, they had returned to favour and are now popular both in Japan and abroad.

For more information contact TIC or the associations listed in the Martial Arts section of Studying in Japan in the Facts for the Visitor chapter. JNTO also publishes a leaflet entitled *Traditional Sports – MG088*, which covers this subject.

Kendō *Kendō*, or the 'way of the sword', is the oldest of the martial arts and was favoured by the samurai to acquire skills in using swords as well as to develop mental poise. Today, it is practised with a bamboo stave and protective body armour, gauntlets and a face mask. The winner of a bout succeeds in landing blows to the face, arms, upper body or throat of an opponent.

Iaijutsu, the art of drawing a sword, is closely related to kendō. One of the few martial arts developed specifically for women was the art of wielding *naginata*, a type of halberd.

Karate Karate (literally, 'empty hands') may have originated in India, but was refined in China and travelled from there to Okinawa, where it took hold as a local martial art. It began in the 14th century and only continued on to the rest of Japan in the first half of this century. For this reason it is not considered a traditional Japanese martial art.

The emphasis is on unarmed combat, as the name of the sport implies. Blows are

delivered with the fists or feet. For optimum performance, all movements require intense discipline of the mind. There are two methods of practising karate. The first is *kumite*, when two or more people spar together. The second is *kata*, when one person performs formal exercises.

Aikidō The roots of this solely defensive art can be traced to the Minamoto clan in the 10th century, but the modern form of *aikidō* was started in the 1920s by Ueshiba Morihei.

Aikidō draws on many different techniques, including jūdō, karate and kendō. Breathing and meditation form an integral part of training, as does the concentration on movement derived from classical Japanese dance and the awareness of *ki* (life force or will) flowing from the fingertips.

Jūdō This is probably the most well known martial art; it become a popular sport worldwide and regularly features in the Olympic Games.

The origins of this art are found in *jūjutsu*, a means of self defence favoured by the samurai, which was modernised into jūdō (the 'way of softness') by Kano Jigoro in 1882. The basic principles and subtle skills of the art lie in defeating an opponent simply by redirecting the opponent's strength against himself or herself.

RELIGION

In many respects, the term 'religion' can be misleading for Westerners when it is applied to either Japan or China. In the West and in Islam, religion is connected with the idea of an exclusive faith. Religions in Japan, for the most part, are not exclusive of each other. They tend to mingle and find expression in different facets of daily life, and their utility in different daily needs.

Shintō (the native 'religion' of Japan), Buddhism (a much travelled foreign import originating in India), Confucianism (a Chinese import that is less a religion than a code of ethics), and even Christianity all play a role in contemporary Japanese social life, and are defining in some way of the Japanese world view. If you are sceptical of the inclusion of Christianity, you need only attend a Japanese wedding to find certain Christian elements mingling happily with more traditional practices.

Shintō and Buddhism, the major religions in Japan, have coexisted for many centuries in relative harmony. A notable break in this amicable relationship occurred during the Meiji period, when nationalist fervour introduced 'State Shintō' as the state religion. Severe restraints were placed on Buddhism, which came under attack from nationalist zealots. The balance was restored with the abolition of State Shintō after the Allied occupation in 1945.

Shintō

Shintō is an indigenous religion that acquired its name, 'the way of the gods', to distinguish it from Buddhism, a later import. It seems to have grown out of an awe for manifestations of nature that included the sun, water, rock formations, trees and even sounds. All such manifestations were felt to have their god *(kami)*, a belief that led to a complex pantheon of gods and a rich mythology. In particularly sacred spots, shrines were erected. Important to Shintō is the concept of purification before entering such sacred domains.

Shintō is a religion without a founder and without a canon; indeed it is not a religion in the sense that you could convert to it. In a sense Shintō is an expression of the Japaneseness of the Japanese. It encompasses myths of the origin of Japan and the Japanese people, beliefs and practices in local communities and the highly structured rituals associated with the imperial family. Until 1945, Shintō belief dictated that the emperor was a kami, or divine being.

Japanese Myths

The chief sources for Japanese myth are the *Kojiki* (Records of Ancient Matters; 712) and the *Nihon Shoki* (Chronicle of Japan; 720). The myths contained in these works have much in common with those of neighbouring countries and the South-East Asian and Mongolian area.

The creation of Japan is ascribed to Izanagi-no-Mikoto and Izanami-no-Mikoto. Standing on the Floating Bridge of Heaven, they dipped the Heavenly Jewelled Spear into the ocean. Brine dripped from the spear and created the island of Onogoro-jima, where the two were married. Izanami gave birth to the islands of Japan and to its deities.

Izanami gave birth to 35 gods, but in giving birth to the fire deity she was burned and died. Izanagi ventured into the Land of the Dead (Yomi-no-Kuni). He found Izanami horribly transfigured by death, and in her shame she joined the Eighty Ugly Females to pursue him. He escaped only by blocking the entry to Yomi with a huge boulder, thus separating the lands of the living and the dead. On his return to the Land of the Living, Izanami purified himself in a stream. This act created more deities, the three most important being Amaterasu Ōmikami (the sun goddess, from whom the imperial family later claimed descent), Tsukuyomi-no-Mikoto (the moon god) and Susano-ō-no-Mikoto (the god of oceans).

According to the legend, Amaterasu ruled the High Plain of Heaven and Susano-ō was given charge of the oceans. Susano-ō missed his mother and stormed around causing general destruction for which he was exiled by his father. In a fit of pique, Susano-ō visited his sister and they had such a quarrel that Amaterasu rushed off to hide in a cave, plunging the world into darkness. All the gods assembled round the cave entrance to find a way to make Amaterasu return.

Finally, Ame-no-Uzume-no-Mikoto performed a ribald dance causing much laughter among the onlookers. Amaterasu, attracted by the commotion, peeped out of her cave and was quickly hauled out to restore light to the High Plain of Heaven. The site of these events is near Takachiho in Kyūshū. Susano-ō was deprived of his beard, toenails and fingernails and banished to earth, where he landed in Korea before heading to Izumo in Japan.

Okuninushi, a descendant of Susano-ō, took control of Japan, but passed it on to Ninigi, a grandson of Amaterasu. Myth merges into history with Ninigi's grandson, Jimmu, who became the first emperor of Japan. Amaterasu is credited with having supplied the emperor with the Three Treasures (mirror, sword and jewel) – symbols of the emperor's authority.

Shintō & Buddhism With the introduction of Buddhism in the 6th century, the Japanese formed a connection between the religions by considering Buddha as a kami (spirit god) from neighbouring China. In the 8th century the kami were included in Buddhist temples as protectors of the Buddhas. Assimilation progressed with the belief that kami, like human beings, were subject to the suffering of rebirth and similarly in need of Buddhist intercession to achieve liberation from this cycle. Buddhist temples were built close to Shintō shrines and Buddhist *sutras* (collections of dialogues and discourses) were recited for the kami.

Later, the kami were considered incarnations of Bodhisattvas (Buddhas who delay liberation to help others). Buddhist statues were included on Shintō altars or statues of kami were made to represent Buddhist priests.

State Shintō There had been something of a revival of interest in Shintō during the Edo period, particularly by neo-Confucian scholars interested in Japan's past. The work of some of these scholars in calling for a return to imperial rule with Shintō as a state religion helped to lay the groundwork for just this occurrence in the Meiji Restoration.

During the Meiji period, Shintō shrines were supported by the government, Shintō doctrines were taught in school and the religion became increasingly nationalistic. It was a relatively brief affair. After Japan's WW II defeat, the Allied forces dismantled the mechanisms of State Shintō and forced the emperor to refute his divine status, a principal tenet of Shintō.

Shintō Shrines The most famous Shintō shrines are the Meiji-jingū and Yasukuni-jinja in Tokyo, the Ise-jingū at Ise and the Izumo Taisha at Matsue. (See the Highlights section in the Facts for the Visitor chapter for more about the major shrines.)

Shrines differ in architectural styles but follow a defined pattern. At the entrance to the shrine is the *torii* (gateway) marking the boundary of the sacred precinct. *Shimenawa*, plaited ropes decorated with strips of white paper *(gohei)*, are strung across the top of the torii. They are also wrapped around sacred rocks or trees or above the actual shrine entrance. Flanking the main path are often pairs of stone lion-like creatures called *komainu*. One usually has its mouth open in a roar and the other has its mouth closed.

Further along the approach is an ablution basin *(chōzuya)* where visitors use the ladle *(hishaku)* to rinse both hands before pouring water into a cupped hand to rinse their mouths.

In front of the *haiden* (hall of worship) is an offering box *(saisen-bako)*, above which hangs a gong and a long rope. Visitors lob a coin – ¥5 or ¥50 coins have an auspicious hole – into the box, then sound the gong twice, make two deep bows, clap loudly twice, bow again twice (once deeply, once lightly) and then step back to the side. Unlike Buddhist temples, no entrance fee is charged for entering a Shintō shrine.

Amulets are popular purchases at the shrine. *Omamori*, special talismans, are purchased at shrines to ensure good luck or ward off evil – taxi-drivers often have a 'traffic-safety' one dangling from the rear-view mirror. Votive plaques *(ema)* made of wood with a picture on one side and a blank space on the other are also common. On the blank side visitors write a wish, for instance, success in exams, luck in finding a sweetheart or safe delivery of a healthy child. Dozens of these plaques can be seen attached to boards in the shrine precincts.

Fortunes *(omikuji)* are selected by drawing a bamboo stick at random from a box and picking out a fortune slip according to the number indicated on the stick. Luck is classified as *dai-kichi* (great good fortune); *kichi* (good fortune); *shō-kichi* (middling good fortune); and *kyō* (bad luck). If you like the fortune slip you've been given, you can take it home. If you've drawn bad luck, you can tie it to the branch of a tree in the shrine grounds – presumably some other force can then worry about it.

The *kannushi* (chief priest) of the shrine is responsible for religious rites and the administration of the shrine. The priests dress in blue and white; on special occasions they don more ornate clothes and wear an *eboshi* (a black cap with a protruding, folded tip). The *miko* (shrine maidens) dress in red and white. The ceremonial *kagura* dances performed by the miko can be traced back to shamanistic trances.

The main training centres for priests are Kokugakuin University in Tokyo and Kōgakukan University in Ise. Marriage is allowed and most of the posts are hereditary, mainly held by men.

Shintō Rites & Festivals These events are important components of Japanese life. For newborn children the first shrine visit occurs on the 30th or 100th day after birth. On 15 November, the Shichigosan rite is celebrated by taking children aged seven (shichi), five (go) and three (san) to the shrine to be blessed. Seijin-no-Hi, the day of adulthood,

is celebrated on 15 January by young people who have reached the age of 20.

Virtually all marriages are performed according to Shintō ritual by taking a vow before the kami. Funerals, however, are almost always Buddhist. Both religions coexist equally in traditional Japanese homes, where there are two altars: a Shintō *kamidana* (a shelf shrine) and a Buddhist *butsudan* (Buddha stand).

Shintō also plays a role in professional and daily life. A new car can be blessed for accident-free driving, a purification rite is often held for a building site or the shell of a new building, and completed buildings are similarly blessed. One of the most common purification rites is *oharai*, when the priest waves a wand to which are attached thin strips of paper.

Shintō *matsuri* (festivals) occur on an annual or occasional basis and are classed as grand, middle-size or minor. In divine processions, a ceremonial palanquin *(mikoshi)* is paraded on the shoulders of participants. Other rites include *misogi* (water purification), tug-of-war, archery, horse-racing, sumō (wrestling), gagaku (sacred music) and lion dances.

Although there are hundreds of Shintō festivals throughout the year, a selection of the most interesting or spectacular ones might include:

Onta Matsuri
    first Sunday in February at Asuka
Tagata Hōnen-sai
    15 March at Tagata-jinja Shrine
Hana-taue
    first Sunday in June at Chiyoda
Osore-zan Taisai
    20-24 July on Mt Osore-zan
Nachi-no Hi Matsuri
    14 July at Kumano Nachi Taisha
Oyama-sankei
    first day of the eighth lunar month at Hirosaki
Takachiho-no-Yo-Kagura
    late November to early February around Takachiho
On-matsuri
    16-18 December in Nara

Buddhism

Japanese Buddhism has adapted along individual lines with some decisive variances from other forms of the religion.

Origins of Buddhism The founder of Buddhism was Siddhartha Gautama, the son of King Suddhodana and Queen Mahamaya of the Sakya clan. He was born around 563 BC at Lumbini on the border of present-day Nepal and India.

In his 20s, Prince Siddhartha left his wife and newborn son to follow the path of an ascetic. Despite studying under several masters, he remained dissatisfied and spent another six years undergoing the most severe austerities. During this period he gave a graphic account of himself: 'Because of so little nourishment, all my bones became like some withered creepers with knotted joints; my buttocks like a buffalo's hoof; my backbone protruding like a string of balls...' Realising that this was not the right path for him, he gave up fasting and decided to follow his own path to enlightenment. He placed himself cross-legged under a Bodhi tree at Bodhgaya and went into deep meditation for 49 days. During the night of the full moon in May, at the age of 35, he became 'the enlightened' or 'awakened one' – the Buddha (Nyorai in Japanese).

Shortly afterwards, Buddha delivered his first sermon, 'Setting in Motion the Wheel of Truth', at Deer Park near Sarnath. Then, as the number of his followers grew, he founded a monastic community and codified the principles according to which the monks should live. The Buddha continued to preach and travel for 45 years until his death at the age of 80 in 483 BC. To his followers, Buddha was also known as Sakyamuni (the sage of the Sakya clan or 'Shaka' in Japanese). Buddhists believe that he is one of the many Buddhas who appeared in the past and that more will appear in the future.

Approximately 140 years after Buddha's death, the Buddhist community diverged into two schools: Hinayana (the Lesser Vehicle) and Mahayana (the Greater Vehicle). The essential difference between the two was that Hinayana supported those who strove for the salvation of the individual, whereas Mahayana supported those who strove for the salvation of all beings. Hinayana prospered in South India and later spread to Sri Lanka, Burma, Thailand, Cambodia, Indonesia and Malaysia. Mahayana spread to inner Asia, Mongolia, Siberia, Japan, China and Tibet.

The basis of Buddhism is that all suffering in life comes from the overindulgence of our desires. Suppression of our sensual desires will eventually lead to a state of nirvana where desire is extinct and we are free from its delusion.

Buddha, who was not a god and did not even claim to be the only enlightened one, felt that the way to nirvana was for our karma (central spirit) to follow the eight-fold path of right thinking, right behaviour and the like. For an over-affluent Western world that is beginning to doubt the potency of the materialist concept of life, Buddhism has obvious charms.

Development of Buddhism in Japan Buddhism was introduced to Japan via Korea in the 6th century. Shōtoku Taishi, acknowledged as the 'father of Japanese Buddhism', drew heavily on Chinese culture to form a centralised state and gave official recognition to Buddhism by constructing temples in and around the capital. Horyū-ji Temple, close to Nara, is the most celebrated temple in Japan from this period.

Nara Period The establishment of the first permanent capital at Heijō-kyō (present-day Nara) in 710 also marked the consolidation of Buddhism and Chinese culture in Japan.

In 741, Emperor Shōmu issued a decree for a network of state temples (Kokubun-ji) to be established in each province. The centrepiece of this network was Tōdai-ji Temple, with its gigantic Vairocana Buddha (Daibutsu).

Nara Buddhism revolved around six schools – Ritsu, Jōjitsu, Kusha, Sanron, Hossō and Kegon – which covered the whole range of Buddhist thought as received from

Zen Buddhism

Probably the most widely known aspect of Japanese Buddhism in the West today was introduced as a separate school from Sung China. Its origins can be traced to Daruma, an Indian priest whose teaching spread to China in the 5th century. Daruma stressed meditation and striving for enlightenment from within, rather than seeking 'outside' help.

Japanese New Year dolls portray Daruma as a fierce, squat, lustrous red figure who is legless – his legs were reputed to have withered away after endless years of meditation.

Although Zen emphasises the direct, intuitive approach to enlightenment rather than rational analysis, there are dozens of books available on the subject. Two favourites are *Zen & Japanese Culture* (Princeton University Press, 1971) by D T Suzuki and *Zen Flesh, Zen Bones* (Penguin Books, London, 1971) compiled by Paul Reps.

Two major schools of Zen were formed in Japan: Rinzai and Sōtō. Eisai (1141-1214), originally a Tendai monk, visited China twice before returning to set up bases for the Rinzai school in Kamakura and Kyoto. Rinzai retained eclectic links with preceding Japanese schools and retained some Esoteric Buddhism rituals in its teachings.

The main technique for enlightenment involved a dialogue between master and disciple which concentrated on *kōan* (topical riddles) usually culled from the experience of previous masters. The Rinzai school found support among influential samurai who were attracted to the spartan discipline. The meticulous attention to detail in all aspects of daily life found expression in components of Japanese culture such as Nō drama, flower arrangement *(ikebana)*, tea ceremony *(chanoyu)*, tea gardens *(tei-en)*, calligraphy *(shodō)* and martial arts *(budō)*.

Dōgen (1200-1253) introduced the Sōtō Zen school from China. The main technique of this school consisted of long sessions of *zazen* (sitting Zen) – practise itself was considered enlightenment.

Dōgen sought support for his school among provincial samurai and the common people. He settled first in Kyoto, but soon shifted his base to the rural setting of the Eihei-ji Temple (near Fukui) which is now the thriving headquarters and training centre of the Sōtō school. Sōtō has a larger membership than Rinzai and branches have flourished abroad, notably in the USA. ■

17th Century Wood-block Print

China. Three of these schools have continued to this day: the Kegon school, based at the Tōdai-ji Temple; the Hossō school, based at the Kōfuku-ji Temple and Yakushi-ji Temple; and the Ritsu school, based at the Tōshōdai-ji Temple.

Heian Period In 794, the capital was moved from Nara to Heian-kyō (present-day Kyoto). During the Heian period, political power drifted away from centralised government into the hands of aristocrats and their clans who became a major source of Buddhist support.

The new schools, which introduced Mikkyō (Esoteric Buddhism) from China, were founded by separate leaders on sacred mountains away from the orthodox pressures of the Nara schools.

The Tendai school (derived from a Chinese school on Mt Tian-tai in China) was founded by Saichō (762-822), also known as Dengyō Daishi, who established a base at the Enryaku-ji Temple on Mt Hiei-zan, near Kyoto.

Saichō travelled to Mt Tian-tai in China, where he studied meditation and the Lotus Sutra. On his return, he expanded his studies to include Zen meditation and Tantric ritual. The Tendai school was only officially recognised a few days after his death, but the Enryaku-ji Temple developed into one of Japan's key Buddhist centres and was the source of all the important schools (Pure Land, Zen and Nichiren) in the following Kamakura period.

The Shingon school (derived from the Chinese term for mantra) was established by Kūkai (714-835), often referred to as Kōbō Daishi, at the Kongōbu-ji Temple on Mt Kōya-san and the Tō-ji Temple in Kyoto.

Kūkai trained for government service but decided at the age of 18 to switch his studies from Confucianism and Taoism to Buddhism. He travelled as part of a mission to Chang-an (present-day Xian) in China, where he immersed himself in Esoteric Buddhism. On his return, he made a broad impact on cultural life, not only spreading and sponsoring the study of Mikkyō, but also compiling the first Chinese-Japanese dictionary and the *hiragana* syllabary which made it much easier for Japanese to put their language into writing.

During this period, assimilation with Shintō continued. Many shrine temples (*jingū-ji*) were built for Buddhist rituals in the grounds of Shintō shrines. Theories were propounded which held the Shintō kami to be manifestations of Buddhas or Bodhisattvas. The collapse of law and order during these times inspired a general feeling of pessimism in society and encouraged belief in the Mappō or End of the Law theory, which predicted an age of darkness with a decline in Buddhist religion. This set the stage for subsequent Buddhist schools to introduce the notion of Buddhist saviour figures such as Amida.

Kamakura Period In this period, marked by savage clan warfare and the transfer of the capital to Kamakura, three schools emerged from Tendai tradition.

The Jōdo (Pure Land) school, founded by Hōnen (1133-1212), shunned scholasticism in favour of the Nembutsu, a simple prayer that required the believer to recite Namu Amida Butsu or 'Hail Amida Buddha' as a path to salvation. This 'no-frills' approach – easy to practise, easy to understand – was popular with the common folk.

Shinran (1173-1262), a disciple of Hōnen, took a more radical step with his master's teaching and broke away to form the Jōdo Shin (True Pure Land) school. The core belief of this school considered that Amida had *already* saved everyone and hence to recite the Nembutsu was an expression of gratitude, not a petition for salvation.

The Nichiren School bears the name of its founder, Nichiren (1222-82), a fiery character who spurned traditional teachings to embrace the Lotus Sutra as the 'right' teaching. Followers learned to recite Namu Myōhō Rengekyō or 'Hail the Miraculous Law of the Lotus Sutra'. Nichiren's strident demands for religious reform of government caused antagonism all round and he was frequently booted into exile.

The Nichiren school increased its influence in later centuries; the famous Hokke-ikki uprising in the 15th century was led by Nichiren adherents. Many of the new religious movements in present-day Japan – Sōka Gakkai for example – can be linked to Nichiren.

Later Developments During the Tokugawa period (1600-1867), Buddhism was consolidated as a state institution. When the shogunate banned Christianity, a parallel regulation rigidly required every Japanese to become a certified member of the local temple.

During the Meiji period, Shintō was given priority and separated from Buddhism, which suffered a backlash of resentment. Today, Buddhism prospers in Japan both in the form of traditional schools and in a variety of new movements.

Buddhist Gods There are dozens of gods in the Japanese Buddhist pantheon. Images vary from temple to temple, depending on the religious schools or period of construction, but three of the most common images are those of Shaka (Sanscrit: Sakyamuni), the Historical Buddha; Amida (Sanskrit: Amitabha), the Buddha of the Western Paradise and Miroku (Sanskrit: Maitreya), the Buddha of the Future. For the optimistic follower who is prepared to wait around a while, some sources schedule the appearance of Miroku in about 5670 million years.

Kannon (Sanskrit: Avalokitesvara) is the 'one who hears their cries' and is available in no less than 33 different versions, including the goddess of mercy, a female form popular with expectant mothers. When Christianity was banned, Japanese believers ingeniously kept faith with the Holy Virgin by creating a clone 'Maria Kannon'.

Jizō is often depicted as a monk with a staff in one hand and a jewel in the other. Pieces of clothing or red bibs draped around Jizō figures are an attempt to cover the souls of dead children. According to legend, this patron of travellers, children and expectant mothers helps the souls of dead children perform their task of building walls of pebbles on the banks of Sai-no-kawara, the river of the underworld. Believers place stones on or around Jizō statues as additional help.

Recently, there have been public murmurings about the maintenance of Jizō statues and the emotional blackmail involved when mothers of aborted babies receive demands from temples for donations.

Buddhist Temples Temples vary widely in their construction, depending on the type of school and the historical era of construction. A selection of the finest Buddhist temples would include many in and around Kyoto, Nara and Kōya-san as well as the Eihei-ji Temple (near Fukui) in Chūbu; the Chūson-ji Temple (Hiraizumi) in Tōhoku; Zenkō-ji Temple in Nagano; and, close to Tokyo, the temple complexes of Nikkō and Kamakura. (See the Highlights section in the Facts for the Visitor chapter for a list of major temples.)

An admission fee, ranging between ¥200 and ¥500, is usually charged at the entrance to these very important temples. An additional fee is sometimes necessary to visit the museum of temple treasures, the temple gardens or for a cup of tea complete with ceremony. Talismans and fortunes (see the Shintō section) are often on sale near the entrance or in one of the halls. An attractive souvenir available for about ¥1000 at many temples is the *shuenshu*, a cloth-covered, pocket-sized booklet with a concertina of folding pages. Railway stations, tourist attractions and temples provide ink pads and stamps for visitors to print souvenir logos in their booklet. For a small fee, you can ask a temple monk to give an artistic touch to your booklet by adding calligraphy.

The entrance is usually marked by a gate, often of gigantic proportions and sometimes flanked by Niō, muscle-bound god kings from Hindu tradition, who are stripped for action as guardians. The central image, in the main hall, has offerings of incense sticks, or food or flowers placed before it. Visitors stand in front of the image, press their palms together and pray.

In the temple surroundings, there are often cemeteries – at Kōya-san there is a centuries-old cemetery that stretches for many hectares.

Common Signs in Temples	Kanji Script
entrance	入口
exit	出口
follow the route	順路
garden	庭／苑
gate	門
hall	堂
no admittance	立入り禁止
pagoda	塔
palace	宮殿
pavilion	宮／パビリオン
pavilion	亭／あずまや
pond	池
shrine	神社／神宮
teahouse	茶室
temple	寺院
toilet	手洗い
tower	塔

Shugendō

This somewhat offbeat Buddhist school incorporates ancient Shamanistic rites, Shintō beliefs and ascetic Buddhist traditions. The founder was En-no-Gyōja, to whom legendary powers of exorcism and magic are ascribed. He is credited with the enlightenment of kami (spirit gods), converting them to *gongen* (manifestations of Buddhas). Practitioners of Shugendō, called *yamabushi* (mountain priests), train both body and spirit with arduous exercises in the mountains.

Until the Meiji era, many of Japan's mountains were the domain of yamabushi who proved popular with the locals for their skills in sorcery and exorcism. During the Meiji era, Shintō was elevated to a state religion and Shugendō was barred as being culturally debased. Today, yamabushi are more common on tourist brochures than in the flesh, but Shugendō survives on mountains such as Dewa Sanzan and Omine-san.

Confucianism

Although Confucianism is essentially a code of ethics, it has exerted a strong enough influence to become part of Japanese religion. Confucianism entered Japan via Korea in the 5th century. To regulate social behaviour, Confucius took the family unit as his starting point and stressed the importance of the five human relationships: master and subject, father and son, elder brother and younger brother, husband and wife, friend and friend.

The strict observance of this social 'pecking order', radiating from individual families to encompass the whole of society, has evolved over centuries to become a core concept in Japanese life. The influence of Confucianism can be seen in such disparate examples as the absolute loyalty demanded in Bushidō (the code of the samurai), the extreme allegiance to the emperor in WW II, the low status of women and the hierarchical ties in modern Japanese companies.

Folklore & Gods

Japan has a curious medley of folk gods. Common ones include the following:

Shichifuku-jin are the seven gods of luck – a happy band of well-wishers plucked from Indian, Chinese and Japanese sources. Their images are popular at New Year, when they are often depicted as a group on a treasure ship *(takarabune)*.

Ebisu is the patron of seafarers and a symbol for prosperity in business. He carries a fishing rod with a large red, sea bream dangling on the line and can be recognised by his beaming, bearded face.

Bishamon is the god of war. He wears a helmet, a suit of armour and brandishes a spear. As a protector of Buddhism, he can be seen carrying a pagoda.

Daikoku, the god of wealth, has a bag full of treasures slung over his left shoulder and a lucky mallet in his right hand.

Benzaiten is the goddess of art, skilled in eloquence, music, literature and wisdom. She holds a Japanese mandolin (biwa) and is often escorted by a sea snake.

Fukurokuju looks after wealth and longevity. He has a bald, dome-shaped head, and a dumpy body and wears long, flowing robes.

Jurojin also covers longevity. He sports a distinguished white beard and holds a cane to which is attached a scroll listing the life span of all living beings.

Hotei, the god of happiness, is instantly recognisable (in Japan and elsewhere in Asia) by his large paunch and Cheshire-cat grin. Originally a Chinese beggar priest, he is the only god in this group whose antecedents can be traced to a human being. His bulging bag provides for the needy and is never empty.

A variety of fabulous creatures inhabit Japanese folklore and crop up regularly in shops, festivals and shrines:

Tanuki is often translated as 'badger', but bears a closer resemblance to a North American raccoon. Like the fox, the tanuki is thought of as a mischievous creature and is credited with supernatural powers, but is more a figure of fun than the fox. Statues usually depict the tanuki in an upright position with straw headgear and clasping a bottle of sake.

Kitsune is a fox, but for the Japanese it also has strong connections with the supernatural and is worshipped in Japan at over 30,000 Inari shrines as the messenger of the harvest god. The Fushimi

Inari Taisha Shrine near Kyoto is the largest of its kind and is crammed with fox statues.

Maneki-neko, the Beckoning Cat, is a very common sight outside shops or restaurants. The raised left paw attracts customers and their money.

Tengu are mountain goblins with a capricious nature, sometimes abducting children, sometimes returning those who were missing. Their unmistakable feature is a long nose, like a proboscis.

Kappa are amphibious creatures about the size of a 12 or 13 year old boy and have webbed hands and feet. They have a reputation for mischief, such as dragging horses into rivers or stealing cucumbers. The source of their power is a depression on top of their heads which must always contain water. A crafty method to outwit a kappa is to bow to it. When the kappa – Japanese to the core – bows back, it empties the water from its head and loses its power. The alternatives are not pleasant. Kappa are said to enjoy ripping out their victim's liver through the anus!

Christianity

Portuguese missionaries introduced Christianity to Japan in the 16th century. In 1549, Francis Xavier landed at Kagoshima, on Kyūshū. At first, the feudal lords (daimyō) seemed eager to convert together with their subjects. However, the motivation was probably less a question of faith and more an interest in gaining trade advantages.

The initial tolerance shown by Oda Nobunaga was soon reversed by his successor, Toyotomi Hideyoshi, who considered the Jesuits a colonial threat. The religion was banned in 1587 and 26 Christians were crucified in Nagasaki 10 years later. After expelling the remaining missionaries in 1614, Japan clammed up to the outside world for several centuries. During this time a small number of Christians kept their faith active as a type of 'back-room Buddhism'. Christian missions were allowed back at an early stage during the Meiji era to build churches and found hospitals and schools, many of which still exist.

Despite these efforts, Christianity has not met with wide acceptance among the Japanese who tend to feel more at home with Shintō and Buddhism. The number of Christians in Japan is a very small portion of the population – possibly one million.

New Religions

A variety of new religions has taken root in Japan. They cover a wide range of beliefs from founder cults to faith healing. Easily the largest of these new religions is Sōka Gakkai (Creative Education Society). Founded in the '30s, it follows Nichiren's teachings and numbers over 20 million followers. (The Clean Government Party (Komeito) was founded in 1964 as a political offshoot of Sōka Gakkai, but now tends to play down the association. It is the second-largest opposition party and, as its name implies, takes a dim view of corruption.)

LANGUAGE

It is something of a cliché that Japanese spend years studying English at school and often at university or college without even being able to string a coherent English sentence together at the end of it all. This is at least partly due to the language-teaching techniques employed in Japanese classrooms, but part of the problem can also be attributed to translation difficulties. Structurally, Japanese and English are so different that word-for-word translations will often produce almost incomprehensible sentences.

To English speakers, Japanese language patterns often seem to be back to front and lacking in essential information. For example, where an English speaker would say 'I'm going to the shop' a Japanese speaker would say 'shop to going', omitting the subject pronoun (I) altogether and putting the verb at the end of the sentence. To make matters worse, many moods which are indicated at the beginning of a sentence in English occur at the end of a sentence in Japanese, as in the Japanese sentence 'Japan to going if' – 'if you're going to Japan'.

Fortunately for visitors to Japan, it's not all bad news. Unlike other languages in the region (Chinese, Vietnamese and Thai among others), Japanese is not tonal and the pronunciation system is fairly easy to master. In fact, with a little effort, getting together a repertoire of travellers' phrases ('Would you like a jellybaby?' etc) should be no trouble –

the only problem will be understanding what people say back to you.

The biggest problem for visitors to Japan who have never studied Japanese is the writing system. Japanese has one of the most complex writing systems in the world, using three different scripts (four if you include the increasingly used Roman script *romaji*). The most difficult of the three, for foreigners and Japanese alike, is *kanji*, the ideographic script developed by the Chinese. Unfortunately for the Japanese, while this script works perfectly well for the Chinese language, the Japanese language does not fare so well. There is a kind of imperfect fit between the Japanese spoken language and kanji that results in a large number of variant readings (pronunciations) for any given character.

Even worse, because of the differences between Chinese grammar and Japanese grammar, the Japanese were forced to supplement kanji with an alphabet of syllables, or a syllabary, known as *hiragana*. Finally, Japanese has a special script (another syllabary) that is used largely for representing foreign-loan words such as *terebi* (TV) and *femunisuto* (feminist); this script is known as *katakana*.

The romaji used in this book attempts to follow the Hepburn system of romanisation with macrons being used to indicate long vowels. Most place names will use a combination of romaji and English – the romaji suffix will in most cases be separated from the proper name by a hyphen and followed by its English translation. For example: Tōdai-ji Temple (*ji* is the romaji word for temple); Shimabara-hantō Peninsula (*hantō* means peninsula) and Ise-jingū Shrine (*jingū* means shrine). These suffixes, however, will not be hyphenated when they are not followed by a direct English translation: for example, Suizenji Garden (the 'ji' for temple will not be hyphenated) and Oshima-kōen Park (the *shima* for island will not be hyphenated).

If you're thinking of tackling the Japanese writing system before you go or while you're in Japan, your best bet would be to start with hiragana or katakana. The reasoning behind this is that there are around 2000 kanji in everyday use and it takes at least a year of pretty solid work before any real progress is made in learning them. Hiragana and katakana, on the other hand, only have 48 characters each and can be learned within a week. You can practise your katakana on

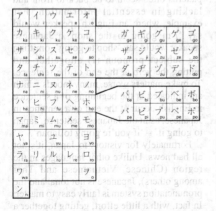

Katakana

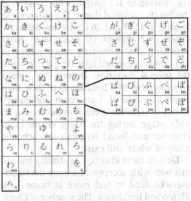

Hiragana

restaurant menus, where such things as *kōhii* (coffee) and *keiki* (cake) are frequently found, and practise your hiragana on train journeys as station names are indicated in hiragana.

If all this seems a bit daunting, don't be put off. The Japanese are a very courteous people and will reward your attempts to make yourself understood in their language with liberal dollops of praise. Remember that the Japanese response to praise is a humble deprecation, not a big smile and a 'thank you'. The expression *sono koto wa arimasen* ('not at all') is an appropriate response when someone flatters you.

The following selection of Japanese phrases will see you through some of the more common situations experienced by travellers to Japan. For a more comprehensive guide to making yourself understood in Japan, try Lonely Planet's *Japanese Phrasebook*.

Pronunciation

a   as the 'a' in 'father'
e   as the 'e' in 'get'
i   as the 'i' in 'macaroni'
o   as the 'o' in 'lot'
u   as the 'u' in 'flu'

Vowels appearing in this book with a macron over them (*ā, ē, ō, ū*) are pronounced in the same way as standard vowels except that the sound is held twice as long. This is a vital difference as anyone who has confused *komon* (advisor) with *kōmon* (anus) can tell you.

Consonants are generally pronounced as in English, with the following exceptions:

f   this sound is produced by pursing the lips and blowing lightly
g   as the 'g' in 'goal' at the start of a word; and nasalised as the 'ng' in 'sing' in the middle of a word
r   more like an 'l' than an 'r'

Greetings & Civilities

The all-purpose title *san* is used after a name as an honorific and is the equivalent of Mr, Miss, Mrs and Ms.

Good morning.
  ohayō gozaimasu
  お早うございます。

Good afternoon.
  konnichiwa
  こんにちは。

Good evening.
  kombanwa
  こんばんは。

How are you?
  o-genki desuka?
  お元気ですか？

Fine. (appropriate response)
  ē, okagesamade
  ええ、おかげさまで。

Goodbye.
  sayōnara
  さようなら。

See you later.
  de wa, mata
  では、また。

Excuse me.
  sumimasen
  すみません。

I'm sorry.
  gomen nasai/sumimasen
  ごめんなさい／すみません。

I am disturbing you. (when entering a room)
  o-jama shimasu/shitsurei shimasu
  おじゃまします／失礼します。

Thank you.
  arigatō gozaimasu
  ありがとうございます。

No, thank you.
iie, kekkō desu
いいえ、結構です。

Thanks for taking care of me. (when leaving)
o-sewa ni narimashita
おせわになりました。

Please. (when offering something)
dōzo
どうぞ。

Please. (when asking for something)
onegai shimasu
お願いします。

OK.
daijōbu (desu)/ōke
大丈夫（です）／オーケ

Yes.
hai
はい。

No.
iie
いいえ。

No. (for indicating disagreement)
chigaimasu
ちがいます。

No. (for indicating disagreement
– less emphatic)
chotto chigaimasu
ちょっとちがいます。

Small Talk

I don't understand.
wakarimasen
わかりません。

Please say it again more slowly.
mō ichidō, yukkuri itte kudasai
もう一度、ゆっくり言って下さい。

What is this called?
kore wa nan-to iimasuka?
これは、何といいますか？

My name is...
watakushi no namae wa...desu
私の名前は......です。

What's your name?
o-namae wa, nan desuka?
お名前は、なんですか？

Where are you from?
o-kuni wa dochira desuka?
お国はどちらですか？

It's up to you. (when asked to make a choice)
omakase shimasu
おまかせします。

Is it OK to take a photo?
shashin o totte mo ii desuka?
写真を取ってもいいですか？

Nationality

Australia
ōsutoraria
オーストラリア

Canada
kanada
カナダ

Denmark
denmāku
デンマーク

Germany
doitsu
ドイツ

France
furansu
フランス

Holland
oranda
オランダ

Italy
itaria
イタリア

Japan
nihon
日本

New Zealand
nyūjīrando
ニュージーランド

Sweden
suēden
スエーデン

Switzerland
suisu
スイス

United Kingdom (England)
igirisu
イギリス

USA
amerika
アメリカ

Accommodation

Where is...?
...wa, doko desuka?
...... は、どこですか？

Do you have any vacancies?
aita heya wa arimasuka?
空いた部屋はありますか？

a single room
shinguru rūmu/hitori heya
シングルルーム

a double room
daburu rūmu
ダブルルーム

room with a bath
basu tsuki no heya
バス付きの部屋

I don't have a reservation.
yoyaku wa shite imasen
予約はしていません。

Getting Around

How much is the fare to...?
...made, ikura desuka?
..... まで、いくらですか？

Does this (train, bus, etc) go to...?
kore wa...e ikimasuka?
これは..... へ行きますか？

Is the next station...?
tsugi no eki wa...desuka?
次の駅は...... ですか？

Please tell me when we get to...
...ni tsuitara oshiete kudasai
...... に着いたら教えてください。

Where is the ...exit?
...deguchi wa doko desuka?
...... 出口はどこですか？

east/west/north/south
higashi/nishi/kita/minami
東／西／北／南

Do you have an English subway map?
eigo no chikatetsu no chizu ga arimasuka?
英語の地下鉄の地図がありますか？

Where is this address please?
kono jūsho wa doko desuka?
この住所はどこですか？

Excuse me, but can you help me please?
sumimasen ga, oshiete kudasai?
すみませんが、教えて下さい。

Emergencies

Help me!
tasukete!
助けて！

Watch out!
ki o tsukete!
気をつけて！

Thief!
dorobō!
どろぼう！

Call the police!
keisatsu o yonde kudasai!
警察を呼んで下さい！

Call a doctor!
isha o yonde kudasai!
医者を呼んで下さい！

Food

Do you have an English menu?
eigo no menyū wa arimasuka?
英語のメニューはありますか？

I'm a vegetarian.
watashi wa saishoku-shugi desu
私は菜食主義です。

Do you have any vegetarian meals?
saishoku-shugiryōri wa arimasuka?
菜食主義の料理はありますか？

What do you recommend?
o-susume wa nan desuka?
お勧めはなんですか？

Please bring the bill.
o-kanjō onegai shimasu
お勘定お願いします。

Shopping

How much is this?
kore wa ikura desuka?
これは、いくらですか？

It's too expensive.
taka-sugimasu
高すぎます。

I'll take this one.
kore o itadakimasu
これを頂きます。

I'm just looking.
miru dake desu
見るだけです。

Health

How do you feel?
kibun wa ikaga desuka?
気分はいかがですか？

I don't feel well.
kibun ga warui desu
気分が悪いです。

It hurts here.
koko ga itai desu
ここが痛いです。

I have asthma.
watashi wa zensoku desu
私は喘息です。

I have diarrhoea.
geri o shite imasu
下痢をしています。

I have a toothache.
ha ga itamimasu
歯が痛みます。

I'm allergic to antibiotics/penicillin.
kōsei busshitsu/penishirin ni arerugii desu
抗生物質／ペニシリンにアレルギーです。

Numbers

0	*zero/rē*	０
1	*ichi*	一
2	*ni*	二
3	*san*	三
4	*yon/shi*	四
5	*go*	五
6	*roku*	六
7	*nana/shichi*	七
8	*hachi*	八
9	*kyū/ku*	九
10	*jū*	十
11	*jūichi*	十一
12	*jūni*	十二
20	*nijū*	二十
21	*nijūichi*	二十一
30	*sanjū*	三十
100	*hyaku*	百
200	*nihyaku*	二百
1000	*sen*	千
5000	*gosen*	五千
10,000	*ichiman*	一万
20,000	*niman*	二万
100,000	*jūman*	十万
1,000,000	*hyakuman*	百万

Facts for the Visitor

VISAS & EMBASSIES

Tourist and business visitors of many nationalities are not required to obtain a visa if staying in Japan less than 90 days. Visits involving employment or other remunerated activity require an appropriate visa.

Stays of up to six months are permitted for citizens of Austria, Germany, Ireland, Mexico, Switzerland and the UK. Stays of up to three months are permitted for citizens of Argentina, Belgium, Canada, Denmark, Finland, France, Iceland, Israel, Italy, Malaysia, Netherlands, New Zealand, Norway, Singapore, Spain, Sweden, the USA and a number of other countries.

Visitors from Australia and South Africa are among those nationals requiring a visa. This is usually issued free, but passport photographs are required and a return or onward ticket must be shown. Visas are valid for 90 days.

Japanese Embassies

Visas for Japan are available through Japanese embassies and consulates, including the following:

Australia
112 Empire Circuit, Yarralumla, Canberra, ACT 2600 (☎(06) 733-244); there are also consulates in Brisbane (☎ (07) 221-5188), Melbourne (☎ (03) 867-3244), Perth (☎ (09) 321-3455) and Sydney (☎ (02) 231-3455).

Canada
255 Sussex Drive, Ottawa, Ontario K1N 9E6 (☎ 236-8541); there are also consulates in Edmonton (☎ 422-3752), Montreal (☎ 866-3429), Toronto (☎ 363-7038), Vancouver (☎ 684-5868) and Winnipeg (☎ 943-5554).

France
7 Ave Hoche, 75008-Paris (☎ 147-66-02-22)

Germany
Bundeskanzlerplatz, Bonn-Center HI-701, D-5300 Bonn 1 (☎ (0228) 5001)

Hong Kong
25th Floor, Bank of America Tower, 12 Harcourt Rd, Central (☎ 5221184-8)

Ireland
22 Ailesbury Rd, Dublin 4 (☎ 69-40-33)

Israel
Asia House, 4 Weizman St, 64 239 Tel-Aviv (☎ 03-257-292)

New Zealand
7th Floor, Norwich Insurance House, 3-11 Hunter St, Wellington 1 (☎ 731-540); there is also a consulate in Auckland (☎ 34-106)

Singapore
16 Nassim Rd, Singapore 1025 (☎ 235-8855)

Thailand
1674 New Petchburi Rd, Bangkok 10310 (☎ 252-6151)

UK
43-46 Grosvenor St, London W1X OBA (☎ (071) 493-6030)

USA
2520 Massachusetts Ave, NW Washington DC 20008-2869 (☎ 939-6800); there are also consulates in Anchorage (☎ 279-8428), Atlanta (☎ 892-2700), Boston (☎ 973-9772), Chicago (☎ 280-0400), Honolulu (☎ 536-2226), Houston (☎ 652-2977), Kansas City (☎ 471-0111), Los Angeles (☎ 624-8305), New Orleans (☎ 529-2101), New York (371-8222), Portland (☎ 221-1811) and San Francisco (☎ 777-3533)

Foreign Embassies in Japan

See the Tokyo chapter for a list of foreign embassies.

Visa Extensions

It has become difficult to extend visas. With the exception of nationals of the few countries whose reciprocal visa exemptions allow for stays of six months, 90 days is the limit for most visitors. Those who do apply should obtain two copies of an Application for Extension of Stay (available at Immigration Bureaus), a letter stating the reasons for the extension (along with any supporting documentation you may have) and your passport. There is a processing fee of ¥4000. Many long-term visitors to Japan get around the extension problem by briefly leaving the country, usually going to Hong Kong, South Korea or Taiwan; however, the immigration officials can be very difficult when they return.

Working Holiday Visas

Australians, Canadians and New Zealanders between the ages of 18 and 25 (the age limit can be pushed up to 30) can apply for a working holiday visa. This visa allows a six month stay and two six-month extensions. The visa's aim is to enable young people to travel extensively during their stay and for this reason employment is supposed to be part time or temporary, although in practice, many people work full time.

A working holiday visa is much easier to obtain than a proper visa and is popular with Japanese employers as it can save them a great deal of inconvenience. Applicants must have the equivalent of A$2000 of funds and an onward ticket from Japan, or A$3000 in funds without the ticket.

Working Visas

The ever-increasing number of foreigners clamouring for a role in the Asian economic miracle has prompted much stricter visa requirements for Japan. Immigration laws introduced in June 1990 designate legal employment categories for foreigners and specify standards of experience and qualifications. Working visas must be organised outside Japan.

Arriving in Japan and looking for a job is quite a tough proposition these days, though people still do it. It is necessary for your prospective employer to obtain a Certificate of Eligibility. Without it you are not able to work legally. It takes 90 days to issue, and you will be required to apply for a work visa with the certificate at an embassy or consulate overseas, not in Japan itself.

Alien Registration Card

Anyone, and this includes tourists, who stays for more than 90 days is required to obtain an Alien Registration Card. This card can be obtained at the municipal office of the city, town or ward in which you're living but moving to another area requires that you re-register within 14 days.

You must carry your Alien Registration Card at all times as the police can stop you and ask to see the card. If you don't have the card, you will be taken back to the station and will have to wait there until someone fetches it for you.

CUSTOMS

Customs allowances include the usual tobacco products, three 760 ml bottles of alcoholic beverages, 57 grams of perfume and gifts and souvenirs up to a value of ¥200,000 or its equivalent. Liquor is not cheap in Japan, so it's worth bringing some for personal consumption or as a gift; there is no possibility of reselling it for profit. The penalties for importing drugs are very severe.

Customs officers also confiscate literature, such as men's magazines, which shows pubic hair. Depictions of just about every kind of sexual liaison and contortion are readily available at newsagents in Japan, but all pubic hair is carefully erased.

There are no limits on the import of foreign or Japanese currency. The export of foreign currency is also unlimited but a ¥5 million limit exists for Japanese currency.

MONEY
Currency

The currency in Japan is the *yen* (¥) and banknotes and coins are easily identifiable. There are ¥1, ¥5, ¥10, ¥50, ¥100 and ¥500 coins; ¥1000, ¥5000 and ¥10,000 banknotes. The ¥1 coin is an aluminium lightweight, the ¥5 and ¥50 coins have a hole in the middle.

Exchange Rates

Exchange rates in mid-94 included the following:

A$1	=	¥77.30
C$1	=	¥77.20
DM1	=	¥63
HK$1	=	¥13.60
NZ$1	=	¥62.50
S$1	=	¥68.45
UK£1	=	¥158.30
US$1	=	¥105.10

The Japanese are used to a very low crime rate and often carry wads of cash for the almost sacred ritual of cash payment. Unfortunately, this habit also extends to trips abroad and greatly endears the Japanese tourist to the worldwide fraternity of muggers and rip-off artists. Foreign travellers in Japan can safely copy the cash habit, but should still take the usual precautions.

Changing Money

You can change cash or travellers' cheques at an 'Authorised Foreign Exchange Bank' (signs are always displayed in English) or at some of the large hotels and stores. These are easy to find in cities, but much less common elsewhere. The safest and most practical way to carry your money is in travellers' cheques, preferably in US dollars, although other major currencies are acceptable. Exchanging Korean or Taiwanese currency in Japan is a fruitless task, so avoid bringing any if you're arriving from those countries.

Banking Hours

Banks are open Monday to Friday from 9 am to 3 pm and closed on Saturday, Sunday and national holidays. Japan may be a hi-tech place, but to change money you have to show your passport, fill in forms and wait until your number is called which can take anything up to half an hour. If you're caught cashless outside regular banking hours, try a large department store or major hotel.

Automatic telling machines (ATM) are now widespread throughout Japan, but are closed on Sunday. Commercial districts often have ATMs operating on weekends and late at night; some of these also provide international access.

Money Transfers

If you are having money sent to a bank in Japan, make sure you know *exactly* where the funds are going: the bank, branch and location. Telex or telegraphic transfers are much faster, though more expensive, than mail transfers. A credit card cash advance (see below) is a worthwhile alternative, American Express transfers require a trusty friend back home.

Bank & Post Office Accounts

Banking operations have been cautiously modernised over the last few years in Japan – good news for the customers who have had to put up with a creaky system. Surprisingly, for a hi-tech country like Japan, the present cosy arrangement between the banks discourages competition and encourages inefficiency and expensive bank charges for simple things like paying a bill. Interest rates on deposits – in most cases very low at present – are to be linked to market rates and raised to appropriate levels. At least Japanese banks turn on their ATMs at weekends nowadays.

If you open a savings account at one of the major banks, you'll receive a savings book and a cash card which will allow you to draw cash at any branch of the bank or from a cash-dispensing machine. An easy option is to open a post office savings account *(yūbin chokin)* at the main post office in one of the major cities; this will allow you to withdraw funds from any post office. You should be able to get things started by using the following Japanese phrase: *Yūbin chokin no kōza o tsukutte kudasai* (I would like to open a post office savings account).

The central post office in Tokyo took 10 minutes to open a post office savings account for me – I was even offered a choice of designs for my passbook and given two packs of tissues!

Robert Strauss

Credit Cards

The use of credit cards is becoming more widespread in Japan, but outside major cities, cash still reigns supreme. American Express, Visa, MasterCard and Diners Club are the most widely accepted international cards. The main offices are:

American Express
    Ogikubo Head Office, 4-30-16 Ogikubo, Suginami-ku, Tokyo (☎ 3220-6010; 0120-376-100 toll free 24 hours)
Diners Club
    Senshu Building, 1-13-7 Shibuya, Shibuya-ku, Tokyo (☎ 3499-1311; 3797-7311 emergency; 3499-1181 after hours)
MasterCard
    Union Credit Co, 1-10-7 Kaji-chō, Chiyoda-ku,

Tokyo (☎ 3254-6751); in an emergency dial
0051 and ask for a collect call to 1-314-275-6690
Visa
Sumitomo Credit Co, Taihei Building, 5-2-10
Shimbashi, Minato-ku, Tokyo (☎ 3459-4800;
3459-4700 emergency)

Costs

Japan has been made even more expensive
by the all-powerful yen. It's probably the
most expensive country in the world to travel
in at the moment, but there are ways of
keeping the outlays to an almost bearable
level. A cup of coffee can indeed cost you
¥600 (US$6) or more in an expensive place
but it is equally possible to drop into one of
the many chain coffee shops and pay ¥190.
If you want coffee, rather than a break in a
coffee shop, it will cost just ¥110 from one
of the ubiquitous vending machines.

Similar comparisons could be made in the
food or accommodation areas, but transport
doesn't offer much latitude for savings – it's
expensive whichever way you look at it.

A skeleton daily budget, assuming you
stay at the cheapest places (¥2200 per night
in a hostel), eat modestly (¥1500) and spend
¥1500 on short-distance travel would work
out to ¥5000 (US$50). Add at least ¥1000 for
extras like snacks, drinks, admission fees
and entertainment. More expensive accommodation costs around ¥4200 to ¥5500 for a
minshuku (Japanese-style B&B), cheap
ryokan or business hotel.

Food costs can be kept within reasonable
limits by taking set meals. A fixed 'morning
service' breakfast (*māningu sābisu* or *setto*)
is available in most coffee shops for around
¥350. At lunch time there are set meals
(*teishoku*) for about ¥650. Cheap noodle
places, often found at stations or in department stores, charge around ¥300 for a filling
bowl of noodles. For an evening meal,
there's the option of a set course again or a
single order – ¥600 to ¥700 should cover
this. Average prices at youth hostels are ¥450
for a Japanese breakfast and ¥700 for dinner.

Transport is a major expense, although
there are ways to limit the damage. The Japan
Rail Pass is well worth the money if you

intend to travel widely in a short space of
time. Overnight buses are cheaper than the
train, and enable you to save on accommodation. Hitching is not only easy, it also puts
you in touch with a cross section of Japanese
society. If you want to avoid emptying your
wallet at an alarming rate, you should only
use taxis as a last resort. Most cities in Japan
have fast, efficient public transport, so you
rarely need taxis anyway.

Foreigners approaching the zero budget in
the urban wilderness can keep hunger at bay
by cruising for free food samples in department stores; but at the other extreme, high
rollers will have no problems off-loading
their cash. Japan specialises in establishments catering to the ostentatious flattery of
business accounts – the higher the bill, the
greater the prestige of the guests.

Tipping

The total absence of tipping does reduce
costs a little; nobody expects a tip so it's best
to keep it that way. However, if you feel your
maid at a top-flight ryokan has given service
surpassing that of a fairy godmother, you can
leave her a small present, perhaps a souvenir
from your home country. If you give cash,
the polite way is to place it in an envelope.

Bargaining

Prices in Japan are fixed, though in some of
the bargain electronic shopping areas, such
as Akihabara in Tokyo, a certain amount of
bargaining is usually required to get the best
possible price. Generally, shops will only
come down 10% to 15% from the original
price. Don't push too hard, asking politely
for a discount is enough in Japan – the sales
clerk will tell you if one is available. In the
big department stores, as in the West, the
marked price is as low as you're going to get.

Consumer Taxes

Unfortunately, Japan does have a 3% consumer tax, introduced in 1989 and extremely
unpopular with the Japanese public. If you
eat at expensive restaurants and stay at 1st
class accommodation you will encounter a
service charge – a disguised form of tipping

– which varies from 10% to 15%. A local tax of 3% is added for restaurant bills exceeding ¥5000 or for hotel bills exceeding ¥10,000. This means it is sometimes cheaper to ask for separate bills. At onsen (hot-spring) resorts, a separate onsen tax applies. This is usually 3% and applies at cheap accommodation, even youth hostels.

WHEN TO GO

The Japanese make a lot of fuss about the fact that Japan has four distinct seasons; indeed many young Japanese are genuinely surprised to hear that other parts of the world are also subject to seasonal change. For the Japanese, each of the seasons has its pleasures (though spring with its clear skies and cherry blossoms is probably the most celebrated), but for the visitor, the best times to visit are the more climatically stable seasons of spring and autumn.

Spring can be a magnificent season to visit Japan. The only drawback is that the cherry blossom season is a holiday period for the Japanese, and many of the more popular travel destinations tend to be flooded with Japanese tourists who head out of the cities in droves. Still, if you're not on too tight a budget, finding accommodation even at this time of the year won't be impossible.

Synchronising your trip with the cherry blossom season can be tricky, however. For one, the blossoms are notoriously fickle, blooming any time from early April to late April. Moreover, when the blossoms do come, their moment of glory is brief, lasting generally a mere week. Still, if you're going to be travelling in Japan during April, chances are you'll come across cherry blossoms somewhere, as they creep slowly across Japan beginning in the south and making their way northwards (their progress is followed obsessively on all the TV channels).

While a great deal is made of the cherry blossoms, spring remains a good time to be travelling in Japan whether you see them or not: temperatures are pleasant, rainfall is low and there is a high proportion of clear days.

Autumn (September to November) may lack the attraction of the cherry blossoms,

but it is an equally good time to travel, with pleasant temperatures and the beautiful landscapes provided by russet shades of the forests and the carpets of red leaves on the ground. This is most certainly the time to visit historical centres such as Kamakura or Kyoto – the temples and shrines set against the backdrop of autumn leaves make a magnificent scene.

The extremes of the Japanese climate make travelling in either summer or winter less pleasant than at other times. The Japan Sea side of Honshū and Hokkaidō receive huge winter snowfalls and, from December to February, very cold temperatures prevail. On the other hand, summer (June to August) can be uncomfortably humid. Still, there are advantages that need to be considered. One thing to bear in mind is that both seasons are less popular with the Japanese and all the major travel destinations (with the exception of ski resorts in winter) will be less crowded than they would be in autumn or spring. Winter can be especially attractive, with temples and shrines blanketed in snow. However, traditional Japanese buildings are rarely heated so it can be miserably cold. In Hokkaidō, where temperatures really plummet over the winter months, there is the attraction of colourful festivals and the famous Sapporo ice sculptures where a small city is carved from ice.

All things considered, the ideal trip to Japan would see you in Hokkaidō and Northern Honshū during the height of summer, in southern Honshū, Kyūshū and Shikoku from late summer to early autumn and in Central Honshū during autumn. Peak holiday seasons, particularly the late April to early May 'Golden Week', can also cause travel problems. See the Holidays & Festivals section for details.

WHAT TO BRING

For the serious traveller, the number one rule in Japan is much the same as anywhere else – travel light. There's nothing so useful as more space in your bag. The advantages of travelling light are even more important for rail travellers, as trains usually have little space for storing bags.

Clothing will depend very much on where and when you are in Japan and what you are doing. Japan extends a long way from north to south. The north of Hokkaidō can be under deep snow at the same time as the Okinawa Islands are basking in tropical sunshine. Japan also varies considerably in altitude; so, even at the height of summer, you'll need good, cold-weather gear if you're intent on climbing Mt Fuji. Generally, however, Japan's climate is somewhat similar to that of continental USA; while it can get very cold and icy in winter, high summer is definitely T-shirt weather and much of the year is pleasantly mild.

There is a distinct wet season between June and July, but rain seems to be possible at almost any time of year and an umbrella is well worth having. Almost every shop and hotel in Japan seems to have an umbrella stand outside, often with a neat locking arrangement so umbrellas can be stowed safely.

Unless you're in Japan on business, you are unlikely to meet situations where 'coat and tie' standards are enforced; casual clothing is all you'll need. Also, laundrettes are reasonably common, so you can usually count on recirculating your wardrobe fairly regularly. Some hotels, hostels and other accommodation have laundry facilities for their guests' use. If you do need more clothes, only extra-large gaijin may have trouble finding big enough sizes; others should have no problems.

The same rule, but underlined, applies to shoes. If your feet are big, make sure your shoes will outlast your stay in Japan. Choose them carefully – you want shoes which are not only comfortable for walking but which are also easy to slip on and off for the frequent indoor occasions where they must be abandoned. Remember that slippers are almost always provided for indoor and bathroom use, so you don't need to bring anything other than your outdoor shoes. Bring a towel – even in an expensive ryokan, a towel is not necessarily provided or it may

be of a size Westerners will consider more like a washcloth. Most hotels and ryokan will supply a *yukata*, that all-purpose Japanese 'dressing gown', but not always and it's such a vital piece of apparel that you should buy yourself one as soon as possible. They make a fine souvenir of Japan.

TOURIST OFFICES

The Japan National Tourist Organisation (JNTO) produces a great deal of literature, which is available both from its overseas and TIC offices (see below). Publications include *Your Guide to Japan*, a handy booklet giving information on places of interest, calendar events and travel data; the *Tourist Map of Japan* and *Your Travelling Companion Japan – with tips for budget travel*, which has money-saving tips on travel, accommodation and places to eat. Most publications are available in English and, in some cases, other European and Asian languages. Separate brochures are available on a number of important tourist destinations.

Local Tourist Offices

JNTO operates three local Tourist Information Centres (TIC):

Tokyo
    Kotani Building, 6-6, Yuraku-chō 1-chōme, Chiyoda-ku, Tokyo 100 ; open from 9 am to 5 pm weekdays and from 9 am to noon on Saturday closed on Sunday and national holidays (☎ 03-3502-1461)
Tokyo International Airport (Narita)
    Passenger Terminal 2, PO Box 2204, Narita Airport, Chiba 282 open from 9 am to 8 pm every day of the year (☎ 0476-34-6251)
Kyoto
    1st Floor, Kyoto Tower Building, Higashi-Shiokoji-chō, Shimogyo-ku, Kyoto 600 open from 9 am to 5 pm weekdays and from 9 am to noon on Saturday; closed on Sunday and national holidays (☎ 075-371-5649)

TIC offices have counters for making some hotel or ryokan reservations, but cannot make transport bookings; they can, however, direct you to agencies which can, such as the Japan Travel Bureau (JTB) or the Nippon Travel Agency (NTA). 'Teletourist' is a round-the-clock taped information service on current events in town operated by the TIC's Tokyo (☎ 3503-2911) and Kyoto (☎ 361-2911) offices. JNTO also operates Goodwill Guides, a volunteer programme with over 30,000 members who wear a blue and white badge with a dove and globe logo.

Japan Travel-Phone JNTO operates a nationwide toll-free phone service available from 9 am to 5 pm, seven days a week. The main aim is to provide assistance for visitors unable to get to the TIC offices in Tokyo or Kyoto. To contact an English-speaking travel expert, call ☎ 0120-22-2800 for information on eastern Japan; ☎ 0120-44-4800 for western Japan. You can also use this service to help with language problems when you're stuck in a hopeless linguistic muddle. It's said that foreigners with Japanese dates, but minimal language skills, have even used the service to smooth the amorous path of acquaintance!

❶Tourist Information System JNTO has recently set up a network of 75 information offices with English speaking staff. They are scattered across the country from Naha to Sapporo, and information on them is provided in the relevant areas in this book. For listings of their addresses, telephone numbers and opening hours, pick up a copy of JNTO's *Tourist Information Centers & ❶ Tourist Information System* pamphlet.

Other Information Offices Away from Tokyo or Kyoto there are information offices *(annai-jo)* in almost all the major railway stations but the further you venture into outlying regions, the less chance you have of finding English-speaking staff. If you want a licensed, professional tourist guide try TIC, a large travel agency such as JTB, or phone the Japan Guide Association in Tokyo on ☎ 3213-2706.

For any information on Japan Railways (JR) including schedules, fares, fastest routings, lost baggage and discounts on railway services, hotels and rent-a-cars call the JR East-Infoline in Tokyo on ☎ 3423-0111. The service is available from 10 am to 6 pm, Monday to Friday, but not on holidays.

Overseas Reps

JNTO has a number of overseas offices including the following:

Australia
  Level 33, The Chifley Tower, 2 Chifley Square, Sydney, NSW 2000 (☎ (02) 232-4522)
Canada
  165 University Ave, Toronto, Ontario M5H 3B8 (☎ (416) 366-7140)
France
  4-8 rue Sainte-Anne, 75001 Paris (☎ (01) 42-96-20-29)
Germany
  Kaiserstrasse 11, 6000 Frankfurt am Main 1 (☎ (069) 20353)
Hong Kong
  Suite 3606, Two Exchange Square, 8 Connaught Place, Central (☎ 525 5295)
South Korea
  10 Da-Dong, Chung-Ku, Seoul (☎ (02) 752-7968)
Switzerland
  13 rue de Berne, 1201 Geneva (☎ (022) 731-81-40)
Thailand
  Wall Street Tower Building, 33/61, Suriwong Rd, Bangkok 10500 (☎ (02) 233-5108)
UK
  167 Regent St, London W1 (☎ (071) 734-9638)
USA
  Chicago: 401 North Michigan Ave, IL 60611 (☎ (312) 222-0874)
  Dallas: 2121 San Jacinto St, Suite 980, LB-53, TX 75201 (☎ (214) 754-1820)
  Los Angeles: 624 South Grand Ave, Suite 2640, CA 90017 (☎ (213) 623-1952)
  New York: Rockefeller Plaza, 630 Fifth Ave, NY 10111 (☎ (212) 757-5640)
  San Francisco: 360 Post St, Suite 401, CA 94108 (☎ (415) 989-7140)

BUSINESS HOURS & HOLIDAYS

Shops are typically open seven days a week from around 10 am to 8 pm. Department stores close slightly earlier, usually 6.30 or 7 pm, and also close one weekday each week. If a city has several major department stores, opening hours will probably be organised so that Mitsukoshi closes on Monday, Daimaru closes on Tuesday, and so on. Large companies usually work a 9 am to 5 pm five-day week, some also operate on Saturday mornings. (See the Money section for banking hours and the Post & Telecommunications section for post office hours.)

Calendar & Holidays

In 1873, the Japanese switched from the lunar calendar to the Gregorian calendar used in the West. They still follow the animal zodiac of the lunar calendar but indulge in an earlier celebration for the arrival of the lunar New Year on 1 January.

Years are counted in Japan according to two systems: Western and Imperial. The Western system sets the date from the birth of Christ. The Imperial system calculates the years from the accession of the emperor. The reign of each emperor is assigned a special name. The reign of the previous emperor, Hirohito (1926-89), is known as the Shōwa (Enlightened Peace) era. Thus 1988 was Shōwa 63. The present emperor, Akihito, reigns in the Heisei era, so 1989 was Heisei 1 and 1990, Heisei 2.

When a public holiday falls on a Sunday, the following Monday is taken as a holiday. You can expect a total sell-out for travel and lodging during the New Year (29 December to 6 January), Golden Week (27 April to 6 May) and mid-August.

National holidays include the following:

Ganjitsu
(New Year's Day) 1 January
Seijin-no-hi
(Adult's Day) 15 January
Kenkoku Kinen-no-bi
(National Foundation Day) 11 February
Shunbun-no-hi
(Spring Equinox) 21 March (approximately)
Midori-no-hi
(Green Day) 29 April
Kenpo Kinen-bi
(Constitution Day) 3 May
Kodomo-no-hi
(Children's Day) 5 May
Keiro-no-hi
(Respect-for-the-Aged Day) 15 September
Shubun-no-hi
(Autumn Equinox) 23 September (approximately)
Taiiku-no-hi
(Sports Day) 10 October

Bunka-no-hi
(Culture Day) 3 November
Kinro Kansha-no-hi
(Labour Thanksgiving Day) 23 November
Tennō Tanjōbi
(Emperor's Birthday) 23 December

CULTURAL EVENTS

Japan has hundreds of national and local festivals throughout the year. The biggest and most famous can attract thousands of spectators, but the smaller local ones can also be a lot of fun.

National Festivals

Shōgatsu (New Year)
1-3 January. New Year celebrations include much eating and drinking, visits to shrines or temples and the paying of respects to relatives and business associates.

Seijin-no-hi (Adult's Day)
15 January. Ceremonies are held for boys and girls who have reached the age of majority (20). To celebrate the end of winter and drive out evil spirits, the Japanese indulge in *setsubun* or bean throwing while chanting '*fuku wa uchi oni wa soto*' (in with good fortune, out with the devils).

Hina Matsuri (Doll Festival)
3 March. During this festival old dolls are displayed and young girls are presented with special dolls *(hina)* which represent ancient figures from the imperial court.

Knickers Giving Day
14 March. This is a slightly bizarre recent addition to the collection of festivals in Japan. The idea is that men should reciprocate the gift of chocolates on 14 February, St Valentine's Day, with a gift of panties for their lady!

Hanami (Blossom Viewing)
February – April. The Japanese delight in the brief blossom-viewing seasons. The usual sequence is plum in February, peach in March and cherry in late March or early April.

O Higan (Equinoctial Week)
March and September. At this time, family graves are visited and temples hold memorial services for the dead.

Golden Week
29 April-5 May. Golden Week is so called because it takes in Green Day (29 April), Constitution Day (3 May) and Children's Day (5 May). This is definitely not a time to be on the move since transport and lodging in popular holiday areas can be booked solid.

Kodomo-no-hi (Children's Day)
5 May. This is a holiday dedicated to children,

especially boys. Families fly paper streamers of carp *(koi)*, which symbolise male strength.

Tanabata Matsuri (Star Festival)

7 July. The two stars Vega and Altair meet in the Milky Way on this night. According to a myth (originally Chinese), a princess and a peasant shepherd were forbidden to meet, but this was the only time in the year when the two star-crossed lovers could organise a tryst. Children copy out poems on streamers and love poems are written on banners that are hung out on display. An especially ornate version of this festival is celebrated from 6 to 8 August in Sendai.

O Bon (Festival of the Dead)

13-16 July and August. According to Buddhist tradition, this is a time when ancestors return to earth. Lanterns are lit and floated on rivers, lakes or the sea to signify the return of the departed to the underworld. Since most Japanese try to return to their native village at this time of year, this is one of the most crowded times of year to travel or look for accommodation.

Shichi-Go-San (Seven-Five-Three Festival)

15 November. Traditionally, this is a festival in honour of girls who are aged three and seven and boys who are five. Children are dressed in their finest clothes and taken to shrines or temples where prayers are offered for good fortune.

Local Festivals

Japan has plenty of local *matsuri* (festivals) that take place throughout the year. Kyoto, Nara and Tokyo are especially famous for local festivals, but elsewhere too there are special *matsuri* which often involve the display of *mikoshi* (portable shrines). The religion section includes details of major Shintō *matsuri*.

Festival details are also provided throughout this book under relevant sections for individual cities or regions. The TIC in Tokyo and Kyoto provide up-to-date listings of festivals and should have a useful JNTO leaflet entitled *Annual Events in Japan*. If you do base a visit around festivals, remember that accommodation can be swamped by visitors from all over the country, so book well in advance.

POST & TELECOMMUNICATIONS

The symbol for post offices is a white and red T with a bar across the top. Red mailboxes are for ordinary mail, blue ones for special delivery. The Japanese postal system is reliable and efficient and, for regular postcards and airmail letters, not markedly more expensive than other advanced countries.

Addresses

In Japan, finding a place from its address can be a near impossibility, even for the Japanese. The problem is twofold – firstly, the address is given by an area rather than a street and secondly, the numbers are not necessarily consecutive. Prior to the mid-50s numbers were assigned by date of construction! During the occupation after WW II, an attempt was made to bring some 'logic' to Japanese addresses and many streets were assigned names, but the Japanese reverted to their own system as soon as the Americans left.

To find an address, the usual process is to ask directions – even taxi drivers often have to do this. The numerous local police boxes are there, in part, to give directions. Businesses often include a small map in their advertisements or on their business cards to show their location.

Starting from the largest area and working down to an individual address, first comes the *ken* (prefecture) as in Okayama-ken or Akita-ken. Four areas in Japan do not follow this rule – Tokyo-to, Kyoto-fu, Osaka-fu (those cities and the areas around them) and the island of Hokkaidō. After the prefecture comes the *shi* or city. Thus Okayama city in Okayama Prefecture is properly Okayama-shi, Okayama-ken. In country areas, there are also *gun*, which are like counties, and *mura* or 'villages'.

Large cities are then subdivided first into *ku* (wards), then into *chō* or *machi* and then into *chōme*, an area of just a few blocks. The chōme is the smallest division, so an address like 4-4 3-chōme should locate the actual place you want. For the poor gaijin, the system often seems to be changed back and forth without rhyme or reason and an address like 2-4-8 Nishi Meguro can also be written 4-8 Nishi Meguro 2-chōme. The building number is either a single numeric or a hyphenated double numeric. When there are three hyphenated numerics the first one is the chōme, so 1-2-3 is building 2-3 in 1-chōme.

You can buy maps which show every building in every chōme and there are often streetside signs indicating building locations, but they are very hard to interpret.

Postal Rates

The airmail rate for postcards is ¥70 to any overseas destination; aerograms cost ¥80. Letters weighing less than 10 grams are ¥80 to other countries within Asia, ¥100 to North America or Oceania (including Australia and New Zealand) and ¥120 to Europe, Africa and South America.

Sending Mail

Sending parcels overseas from Japan often works out 30% cheaper with Surface Airlift (SAL) and only takes a week longer.

District post offices (the main post office

in a ward or *ku*), are normally open from 8 am to 7 pm on weekdays, 8 am to 3 pm on Saturday and 9 am to 12.30 pm on Sunday and public holidays. Local post offices are open 9 am to 5 pm on weekdays and 9 am to 1 pm on Saturday. Main post offices in the larger cities may have some counters open 24 hours a day.

Mail can be sent to Japan, from Japan or within Japan when addressed in Western (romaji) script, but it should, of course, be written as clearly as possible.

Receiving Mail

Although any post office will hold mail for collection, the poste restante idea is not well known and can cause confusion in smaller places. It is probably better to have mail addressed to you at a larger central post office. Letters are usually only held for 30 days before being returned to sender. When inquiring about mail for collection ask for *kyoku dome yūbin*.

American Express will hold mail for their cardholders or users of American Express travellers' cheques. Normally, mail will be held for 30 days only unless marked 'Please hold for arrival'. American Express offices in Japan include the following:

Fukuoka
Nichido Fukuoka Daini Building, 1-3 Shimakawabata-chō, Hakata-ku, Fukuoka 812
Kyoto
L. Avenue Kawaramachi, 52 Daikoku-chō Sanjōsagaru Kawaramachi-dōri, Nagagyō-ku, Kyoto 604
Nagoya
Nagoya Hirokoji Building 1F, 2-3-1 Sakae, Naka-ku, Nagoya 460
Naha, Okinawa
Okinawa Tourist Service, 2-21-8 Maejima, Okinawa 900
Okinawa Tourist Service, 1-2-3 Matsuo, Okinawa 900
Osaka
Ushu Honmachi Building, 3-1-6, Honmachi, Chūō-ku, Osaka 541
Sapporo
Onose Building, 1F, 3-1 Nishi Kita Sanjō, Chūō-ku, Sapporo 060
Tokyo
American Express Tower, 4-30-16 Ogikubo, Suginami-ku, Tokyo 167-01
Shinjuku Gomeikan Building 1F, 3-3-9 Shinjuku, Shinjuku-ku, Tokyo 160
Toranomon Mitsui Building, 3-8-1 Kasumigaseki, Chiyoda-ku, Tokyo 100
Yūrakuchō Denki Building South 1F, 1-7-1 Yūrakuchō, Chiyoda-ku, Tokyo 100

Some embassies will hold mail for their nationals, check before you depart. Hotels and youth hostels are another possibility.

Telephone

The Japanese public telephone system is very well developed; there are a great many public phones and they work almost 100% of the time. It would be very unusual to see a vandalised phone in Japan. Local calls cost ¥10 for three minutes; long-distance or overseas calls require a handful of coins which are used up as the call progresses; any unused coins are returned.

Most payphones will also accept prepaid phonecards (terefon kādo). It's much easier to buy one of these than worry about having coins to hand; they are readily available from vending machines, telephone company card outlets and many shops in ¥500 and ¥1000 denominations. Phonecards are magnetically encoded, and after each call a small hole is punched to show how much value

remains. The phone also displays the remaining value of your card when you insert it. Since you get a small discount on calls made with a phonecard, card collecting is a popular activity. Larger denomination phonecards are no longer available due to the recent surge in availability of black-market phonecards (¥1000 can buy you around five or more used cards which have had their value restored). Using such phonecards is illegal.

Japanese telephone numbers consist of an area code plus a local code and the number. You do not dial the area code when making a call within that area.

International Calls International payphones are becoming much more common on the streets of Japan. An overseas call (paid or operator-assisted) can be made from phones with a gold sign which specifically notes that it handles international calls, from grey IDD phones and from credit card phones (blue with a chrome face).

If you're having problems finding an international phone, try the big hotels, the main railway station, the main shopping arcade or Nippon Telegraph & Telephone (NTT) offices. (You can also try offices of NTT's international counterpart, Kokusai Denshin Denwa (KDD).) Once you've found one, calls are charged by the unit (there's no three minute minimum) so, if you talk fast enough, you could get a call through for ¥100!

To place an international call through the operator, dial ☎ 0051 – international operators all seem to speak English. To make the call yourself, simply dial ☎ 001 (KDD), 0041 (ITJ) or 0061 (IDC) (rates between these three companies vary very little) then the international country code, the local code and the number. Another option is to dial 0039 for home country direct which takes you straight through to a local operator in the country dialled. You can then make a reverse-charge (collect) call or a credit card call with a telephone credit card valid in the destination country.

In some hotels or other tourist locations,

you may find a home country direct phone where you simply press the button labelled USA, UK, Canada, Australia, NZ or wherever to be put through to your operator. Dialling codes include:

Country	Direct Dial	Home Country Direct
Australia	☎ 001-61	☎ 0039-611
Canada	☎ 001-1	☎ 0039-161
Hong Kong	☎ 001-852	☎ 0039-852
Netherlands	☎ 001-31	☎ 0039-311
New Zealand	☎ 001-64	☎ 0039-641
Singapore	☎ 001-65	☎ 0039-651
Taiwan	☎ 001-886	☎ 0039-886
UK	☎ 001-44	☎ 0039-441
USA	☎ 001-1	☎ 0039-111*

*for mainland USA you can also dial ☎ 0039-121, for Hawaii you can also dial ☎ 0039-181

Fax, Telex & Telegraph

Japan may be an economic miracle but getting a fax out of the place can still be a real hassle. Most post offices do not offer a fax service, and large hotels generally do not allow you to use their facilities unless you are a guest. The Kokusai Denshin Denwa (KDD) international telegraph office (☎ 3275-4343), one block north of Ōtemachi subway station in Tokyo, has fax and telex facilities. The Shinjuku KDD (☎ 3347-5000) close to the south exit of Tokyo's Shinjuku station can also handle faxes. Faxes can be sent from 9 am to 6 pm Monday to Friday and to 5 pm on Saturday.

Budget travellers, particularly those staying at the Kimi Ryokan in Tokyo, can use the Kimi Information Centre, around the corner from the ryokan. You have to pay a registration fee of ¥2000, but after this you pay the fax charges individually. The centre will also receive faxes for you.

TIME

Despite Japan's east-west distance, the country is all on the same time, nine hours

ahead of Greenwich Mean Time (GMT). Thus, when it is noon in Japan, it is 3 am in London, 11 am in Hong Kong, 1 pm in Sydney, 3 pm in Auckland, 10 pm the previous day in New York, 7 pm the previous day in San Francisco and 5 pm the previous day in Honolulu. Daylight-saving time is not used in Japan. Times are all expressed on a 24 hour clock.

ELECTRICITY

The Japanese electric current is 100 V AC, an odd voltage found almost nowhere else in the world. Furthermore, Tokyo and eastern Japan are on 50 Hz, western Japan including Nagoya, Kyoto and Osaka is on 60 Hz. Most North American electrical items, designed to run on 117 V, will function reasonably well on Japanese current. The plugs are flat two pin, identical to US and Canadian plugs.

LAUNDRY

Some youth hostels and ryokan have washing facilities, but failing this the best option is to seek out a koin rōndori (coin laundry). In suburban Japan there is almost always one with easy walking distance. Costs range from ¥200 to ¥300 for a load of washing and ¥100 for every seven to 10 minutes of drying time. Those staying in business hotels or more up-market accommodation can use the hotel laundry service, though it will cost more than doing it yourself.

WEIGHTS & MEASURES

Japan uses the international metric system. One odd exception is the size of rooms, which is often given in tatami mat measurements known as jō. Tatami sizes vary regionally in Japan, which tends to complicate things. In Tokyo a tatami mat measures 1.76 by 0.88 metres, while in Kyoto a tatami mat measures 1.91 by 0.96 metres (see the Long-Term Accommodation section later in this chapter for more on tatamai mat measurement).

BOOKS & MAPS

There's no need to stock up on books, particularly books about Japan, before you leave home (although it would definitely be cheaper to do it this way). If you're passing through Tokyo there are bookshops with excellent selections of books on all aspects of Japanese culture. Outside Tokyo, the choice of foreign-language books is nowhere near as good, though many larger cities will have a branch of Kinokuniya and/or Maruzen with a foreign section. In the back blocks, however, you may be hard pressed to find anything in English other than the occasional newspaper and copy of *Time*.

Most of the following books should be available in Tokyo, often in paperback rather than in original hardbacks.

People & Society

Ruth Benedict's *The Chrysanthemum & the Sword* (available in paperback) is, in some ways, still regarded as the classic study of Japanese culture and attitudes. However, the fact that it was written in the USA during WW II, at a time when meeting the Japanese in Japan was clearly impossible, makes some of its conclusions a little questionable.

Japanese Culture (1973, now in paperback) by H Paul Varley is a slightly academic but nevertheless interesting account of the main currents in the development of Japan's culture. *Appreciations of Japanese Culture* (Kodansha, 1981) by Donald Keene is a readable, eclectic collection of essays by a renowned scholar of Japanese culture.

The Japanese Today (Belknap, 1988) by Edwin O Reischauer, is a recently revised standard textbook on Japanese society and a must for those planning to spend time in Japan. Ian Buruma's *A Japanese Mirror* (Penguin) provides an interesting examination of Japanese popular culture.

For a fascinating insight into the Japanese language and the position of women in Japanese society look for *Womansword – what Japanese words say about women* (Kodansha, 1987) by Kittredge Cherry. *Japan as it Is* (Gakken, 1985; updated in 1990) is a collection of one-page essays on a

whole range of matters relating to Japan, each one with its facing page in Japanese.

The two volumes of *Discover Japan – Words, Customs & Concepts* (Kodansha, 1987) were originally published as *A Hundred Things Japanese* and *A Hundred More Things Japanese* and consist of a series of short essays on things Japanese by a wide variety of writers.

Japanese Religion – A Survey by the Agency for Cultural Affairs (Kodansha, 1989) gives a good overall perspective of Japanese religions and their place in the lives of contemporary Japanese. (See the Religion section in the Facts about the Country chapter for more details.)

A few recent releases on Japan make for interesting reading while you are in the country. Jonathan Rauch's *Outnation – A Search for the Soul of Japan* (Littlebrown, 1992) is an intelligent and penetrating account of his six months in Japan. In her book *In the Realm of a Dying Emperor* (Vintage, 1993), Norma Field has written a beautiful account of a side of Japan that gets little attention internationally. It goes too far to say that this is a book about dissidence, but it deals primarily with three Japanese whose lives have been at odds with mainstream Japanese society and gives pause to thought for all those who see Japanese culture as monolithic and de-individualising. Pico Iyer's *The Lady and the Monk* is an unabashed romanticisation of Japan (mainly Kyoto) by a writer whose primary strength is as an essayist. It still makes for a great read, even if you might want to balance some of his reflections with the reality of modern Japan. Finally, a book that gets many recommendations is *Max Danger – the Adventures of an Ex-Pat in Tokyo* (Tuttle, 1981). The book has quite a following in Japan.

History

Inside Japan (Penguin, 1987) by Peter Tasker, is probably the best wide-ranging introduction to modern Japanese culture, society and the economy. Richard Storey's *A History of Modern Japan* (Penguin) is a concise and consistently interesting history

Manga – Japanese Comics

It's a well-known fact that in comparisons of mathematical ability, Japanese high school students regularly show up better than their peers in other advanced nations. What is not so well known is that Japanese students would also come out well ahead in their consumption of comic books. In fact, the Japanese are the world's number one consumers of comic books (manga).

Manga is a catch-all word covering cartoons, magazine and newspaper comic strips and the comic books which take up so much space in so many Japanese shops. A Japanese comic book is rarely a slim volume (weekly comics as thick as phone directories are not unusual) and there's a version to appeal to every market niche. The text will always be in Japanese but there's usually an English subtitle on the front cover announcing at whom it's aimed, whether it's a 'Lady's Comic', a 'Comic for Business Boys' or even an 'Exciting Comic for Men', (for 'exciting' read 'soft-core porn').

Japanese comic-strip artists (there are thousands of them to cater for the insatiable demand) are often as well known and wealthy as pop stars. There's no question that it's a big business: Shōnen Jump, the most popular comic, has weekly sales which top four million copies. It's also an inventive business. Japanese comic artists pioneered multi-panel movements, perspectives which brought the reader into the action, close-ups, curious angles and a host of movie-like techniques. Along with inventiveness came recognition in the form of annual awards, regular reviews and serious critiques.

The curious Westerner leafing through a manga may be somewhat surprised at the explicitness of the action. Japanese censors may black out the pubic hair in imported copies of Playboy, but it certainly all hangs out when it comes to comic books. Even the 'Lady's Comics' may give you a few surprises with their sexual activity. But manga also tackle very serious subjects: jitsuma manga ('practical comics') and benkyō manga ('study comics') actually set out to teach everything from high school subjects to international finance.

The ready acceptance of the dark side of so many manga would seem to indicate an avid interest in areas that are repressed in daily Japanese life. Of course (so the Japanese reasoning goes), it's only natural that adults should want to recapture something of their childhood by turning to comics after 11 hours in the office. And while we may level an accusing finger at the violence and sexual content of the manga, we also have to acknowledge that Japan is still probably the safest place in the world to walk the streets at night.

Those interested in Japanese comics can join the crowds leafing through recent issues in bookshops. Many smaller hotels, hostels and ryokan will have stacks of old issues for their guests' amusements. Japan Inc (University of California Press, Berkeley, 1988) by Shōtarō Ishinomori, is an English translation of a popular manga series on international finance and Japanese-US trade relations; it also contains an interesting introductory history of manga. ■

of modern Japan. *The Japanese Achievement* (Sidgwick & Jackson, 1990) by Hugh Cortazzi, provides a detailed yet highly readable survey of Japan's history and culture from earliest times to the present day.

Olive Statler's *Japanese Inn* traces the history of Japan through the comings and goings of visitors at an inn on the old Tōkaidō road. This engrossing book is available in paperback and makes excellent travel reading.

The Economic Superpower

As Japan elbows its way to the front of the industrial pack, the countries left behind have produced a flood of 'What was that?' and 'How did it happen?' style books. *The Enigma of Japanese Power* by Karel van Wolferen is an attack on the Japanese 'system' and a book for the finger pointers and accusers who reckon Japan got to the top by playing dirty. The bad news keeps on coming with books like *Japan – The Coming Collapse* (Orion, 1992) by Brian Reading.

Japan's most forceful recent reply was in *The Japan That Can Say No* by Akio Morita (chairman of Sony) and Shintaro Ishihara (former cabinet minister and politician). They argue that Japan is big enough to play a real role in world politics and need no longer be at the USA's beck and call, and that the USA is now dependent on Japan's superior technology.

Other views on the growth of Japan as an economic superpower are found in *Trading Places: How America Allowed Japan to Take the Lead* (Charles E Tuttle) by Clyde V Prestowitz Jr and *The New Masters – Can the West Match Japan?* (Hutchinson Business Books, 1990) by Phillip Oppenheim. Ezra Vogel saw it coming more than 10 years ago in *Japan as Number One: Lessons for America* (Harvard University Press, 1979). Of course, Japan has hardly reached the top before someone is foreshadowing its descent – Bill Emmott describes it in *The Sun Also Sets*.

Travel Guides

Edward Seidensticker's *Low City, High City* (1983) traces the history of Tokyo from 1867 to 1923 – the tumultuous years from the Edo period to the great earthquake. He followed that book with *Tokyo Rising: The City Since the Great Earthquake* (Knopf, New York, 1990) which traces Tokyo's history from the '20s, through the destruction of WW II and the period of explosive growth to today's super city status. Much regret is expressed for the loss of the city's traditional elements and their replacement with faceless modern architecture; there is also a great deal of interest in Tokyo's freestyle entertainment possibilities. A new addition to books on Tokyo is Paul Waley's *City of Stories* (Weatherhill, 1991). It makes for good reading, and is a good substitute to wading through the two volumes of Seidensticker's history of Tokyo.

If you're travelling along the San-yō coast of Western Honshū, or visiting Inland Sea islands between Honshū and Shikoku, you won't find a more enjoyable companion than Donald Richie's *The Inland Sea*. Originally published in 1971, it's now available in paperback and manages to be both amusing and educational.

Oliver Statler's *Japanese Inn* is an excellent introduction to the personalities of Japanese history; it was followed by *Japanese Pilgrimage* (available in paperback), the story of a walking tour of the Shikoku pilgrimage circuit. *The Roads to Sata* by Alan Booth (Penguin) is a wonderful account of a four month trip on foot from the tip of Hokkaidō to the southernmost point of Kyūshū. Alan, a long-time Japan resident and writer on things Japanese, died in early 1993. His book rates as one of the most intelligent reflections on Japan, with the author never giving way to the temptation (as so many foreign commentators do) to generalise about the Japanese.

Okubo Diary (Stanford University Press) by the British anthropologist Brian Moeran, is a memoir of his stay in a tiny Kyūshū village. *Unbeaten Tracks in Japan* (Virago Books, 1984) by Isabella Bird recounts the 'off the beaten track' travels of a doughty Victorian-era lady and includes an interesting account of the dying Ainu culture in Hokkaidō.

The Japan Travel Bureau (JTB) produces an illustrated book series with pocket-sized books covering various aspects of Japan including lifestyle, eating, festivals, the salaryman, Kyoto, Nikkō and other subjects in a bouncy, highly visual style.

Language Guides

Japanese Phrasebook (Lonely Planet, 1994) offers a convenient collection of survival words and phrases for your trip to Japan. Tae Moriyama's *The Practical Guide to Japanese Signs* (Kodansha, 1987) is a convenient introduction to some commonly encountered Japanese signs. It not only identifies them but explains how they came about and has been followed by a second volume.

The popularity of Japanese studies has spawned an incredible number of specialist publications. Some of them are quirky enough to make them worth browsing through or taking home as an off-beat souvenir, even if you have nothing but a casual acquaintance with the language. Just to give you an idea of the range available, you can choose from Charles de Wolf's *How to Sound Intelligent in Japanese – a vocabulary builder* (Kodansha, 1993) (sample sentence: 'As George Berkeley denied the existence of matter, one might say he was a kind of monastic spiritualist'); or, from the sublime to the ridiculous, Peter Constantine's *Japanese Street Slang* (Tengu Books, 1992) (sample sentence: 'I jerked off so much yesterday my dick is sore'). Have fun.

Bookshops

Most major Japanese cities will have a branch of Maruzen or Kinokuniya, both of which usually stock a good selection of English-language books and smaller selections of books in French, German and, occasionally, Spanish.

The best city to stock up on English-language books is Tokyo, but Osaka and Kyoto in Kansai, Sapporo in Hokkaidō, Hiroshima in Western Honshū and Fukuoka in Kyūshū also have bookshops with well-stocked foreign-language sections. See the appropriate city entries for more information.

Maps

The Japanese word for map is *chizu*. The JNTO's free *Tourist Map of Japan* is a reasonable 1:2,000,000 English-language map of the whole country which is quite adequate for general route planning. Lonely Planet's *Japan Travel Atlas* (in production as we go to press) is an excellent guide to the country in a convenient full-colour book format.

The *Japan Road Atlas* (Shobunsha, Tokyo, ¥2890) covers all of Japan at 1:250,000 except for Hokkaidō, which is covered at 1:600,000. Most towns are shown in kanji (Japanese script) as well as romaji (Roman script). However, mountains, passes, lakes, rivers and so on are only shown in romaji. Locating exactly where a small town or village is on the map is sometimes difficult and places are often left off. (Check the map of Iriomote-jima Island on page 14 of the atlas, for example – none of the island's half-dozen little towns appears on the map!) Despite these drawbacks, the atlas is the best mapping available for detailed exploration of the country, both by car and rail, as every railway station is marked. Another useful map which provides both Japanese and English place names is the *Bilingual Atlas of Japan* (Kodansha, 1992).

Japan Guide Maps (JGM) produce a series of English-language maps covering the whole country area by area; the map of Kyūshū, at 1:500,000, is typical. Although they're not bad, these maps are not as good as equivalent Japanese-language maps, which are often free. Check the Service & Parking Area (SAPA) maps which are available free at expressway service centres.

Giveaway town maps may also have enough romaji detail to make them useable for non-Japanese speakers, however, much of this mapping is often wildly exaggerated in scale and appearance. Stylised maps, where all roads are completely straight and all corners right angles, are very common.

MEDIA

The insatiable Japanese hunger for information has given rise to an information industry equal to any in the world. Tokyo has seven TV channels; cinemas do a roaring trade despite high admission charges; bookshops are overflowing with weekly magazines, newspapers and books; and a very efficient translation network allows the Japanese access to a wide range of foreign publications and films. Recently, satellite pay TV has also become popular.

The Japanese are world leaders in tabloid consumption. There are more than 160 local and national newspaper companies in Japan, some of the larger ones producing morning and evening editions of the same paper. A 1991 survey found that over 52 million newspapers are sold daily in Japan, 1.24 for every household. (What this must be doing for the world's forests doesn't bear thinking about.) Japan's most popular paper, the *Yomiuri Shimbun* has the largest daily circulation in the world, pulling in around 10 million readers daily.

Japan also produces a staggering range of weekly and monthly magazines. The enormous success of weekly tabloids such as *Focus* and *Friday*, with their uniquely lurid, gossip-column approach, has spawned racks of imitations.

The Japanese are also world leaders in the TV field; 99% of all households have at least one TV set and there are 111 TV stations in Japan. No other group, except perhaps the Americans, embraces contemporary advertising-jingle culture as thoroughly as the Japanese.

Newspapers & Magazines

In the major urban centres at least, you won't have any problem finding English-language newspapers and magazines. However, since English publications are produced in Tokyo, the further you get from the capital, the scarcer they become.

The *Japan Times*, with its good international news section and unbiased coverage of local Japanese news, is read by most newcomers looking for work because of its employment section – the Monday edition has the most extensive listings. The paper costs ¥160 and in Kyūshū and other far-flung parts of Japan will usually be a day old when you get it. The *Daily Yomiuri* rates alongside the *Japan Times* in its coverage of local and international news, and is particularly worth picking up on Friday, when it has an eight-page supplement, 'View From Europe', culled from the British *Independent* and on Saturday when a similar 'World Report' from the *Los Angeles Times* is included.

The *Mainichi Daily News* is another good English-language newspaper widely available in Tokyo and its environs. If you oversleep and miss the morning papers, the *Asahi Evening News* is not bad. All these newspapers can be picked up from newsstands in the major cities, particularly at railway stations, or at hotels that cater to foreign tourists and businesspeople.

Foreign magazines and newspapers are available in the major bookshops, though they tend to be three or four times more expensive than they would be in their country of origin. US magazines such as *Newsweek* and *Time* are popular and widely available despite a ¥700 (US$7) cover price. For the more specialist magazines, you'll need to visit the big bookshops in Tokyo, Osaka and Kyoto.

The Japanese also publish a number of magazines in English, mainly for their ever-growing English-speaking community. Most of these magazines are a kind of community service, providing what's-on information for theatres and cinemas, details about various cultural events as well as classifieds for anything from marriage partners to used cars. The Tokyo-based *Tokyo Journal* is the pick of the crowd with its comprehensive what's-on listings and informative, readable articles on local cultural and topical issues. Also based in Tokyo is the very similar *Tokyo Time Out*.

Kansai Time Out, produced in the Kansai region around Osaka, has excellent information about goings-on of interest to both foreign visitors and local residents. Like the *Tokyo Journal*, it also carries features on various aspects of life in Japan. In the Nagoya area, *Eyes* is a useful what's-on magazine.

If you're studying Japanese, *Nihongo Journal* and the *Hiragana Times* are monthly bilingual magazines for Japanese learners. The *Nihongo Journal* is particularly good, having an accompanying tape for pronunciation and listening comprehension practice and good listings of Japanese-language schools. Both magazines require that you have acquired the rudiments of Japanese and can at least read hiragana and a smattering of kanji.

Radio & TV
The common consensus is that Japanese radio is pretty dismal, mainly because it places far more emphasis on DJ jive than it does on music. Given the quality of Japanese pop music, this is probably just as well. For English-language broadcasts, the possibilities are pretty much limited to the appallingly banal US armed services' Far East Network (FEN).

Even the FM stations are fairly uninspiring although J-WAVE in Tokyo has increased the music content and cut the talk. Bring a good supply of tapes and a Walkman if music is essential to your sanity.

Like radio, most TV is inaccessible to the non-Japanese speaker and, even if you do speak the language, most programmes seem to be inane variety shows. It's worth watching a few hours as a window into the culture, but it won't take long to figure out what the programmes are all about.

TVs can be fitted with an adapter so that certain English-language programmes and movies can be received in either Japanese or English. The Japanese Broadcasting Corporation (NHK) even broadcasts a nightly bilingual news report. Unfortunately, Japanese TV news is not the most informative in the world, often running extended reports on the daring rescue of a cat from a tree while the Middle East teeters on the brink of another all-out war. This, combined with the sometimes rather slow and halting simultaneous interpretation by an unusually laconic

American, makes the evening news in English not quite the daily event it could be.

Finally, many Japanese hotel rooms will have a pay cable TV with video channels. It is unlikely that English-language movies will be available but the porn channel which is often available needs no translation.

FILM & PHOTOGRAPHY
The Japanese are a nation of photographers. No social occasion is complete without a few snaps and an exchange of the photos taken at the last get together. This, combined with the fact that the Japanese are major producers of camera equipment and film, means there is no problem obtaining photographic equipment or print film. Slide film is not as readily available and is best brought from home.

A 36 exposure Kodachrome 64 slide film costs about ¥850 without processing. The very popular disposable cameras are even sold from vending machines. They typically cost from ¥1000 to ¥2000; more expensive ones have a built-in flash.

Processing
Processing print film is fast and economical in Japan, although the standards are not always the best and prices vary (¥2000 for a 36 exposure film is typical). In the big cities it is usually possible to have Fuji or Sakura slide film processed within 24 hours (¥1000 for 36 exposures) and the results appear to be of a consistently high standard. Kodachrome slide film, however, can only be processed by the Imagica Kodak depot in Ginza, Tokyo but the processing is fast (24 hours) and the results are good. There is no problem honouring pre-paid Kodachrome film either. Away from Tokyo, send Kodachrome film to: Far East Laboratories Ltd, 2-14-1 Higashi Gotanda, Shinagawa-ku, Tokyo.

HEALTH
Travel health depends on your predeparture preparations, your day-to-day health care while travelling and how you handle any medical problem or emergency that does develop. However, looking after your health

in Japan should pose few problems since hygiene standards are high and medical facilities widely available, though expensive. The average life expectancy among the Japanese is now 80 years for women and 74 for men, a sure sign that they are doing something right.

Travel Health Guides

There are a number of useful books on travel health:

Staying Healthy in Asia, Africa & Latin America, Moon Publications. Probably the best all-round guide to carry, as it's compact but very detailed and well organised.

Travellers' Health, Dr Richard Dawood, Oxford University Press. Comprehensive, easy to read, authoritative and also highly recommended, although it's rather large to lug around.

Where There is No Doctor, David Werner, Hesperian Foundation. A very detailed guide intended for someone, like a Peace Corps worker, going to work in an undeveloped country, rather than for the average traveller.

Travel with Children, Maureen Wheeler, Lonely Planet Publications. Includes advice on travel health for younger children.

Predeparture Preparations

Health Insurance A travel insurance policy to cover theft, property loss and medical problems is a wise idea. With such a wide variety of policies available, it may be best to consult your travel agent for recommendations. The international student travel policies handled by STA Travel or other student travel organisations are usually good value. Some policies offer a choice between lower and higher medical expense options; choose the high-cost option for Japan. Check the small print:

*   Some policies specifically exclude 'dangerous activities' which can include scuba diving, motorcycling, even trekking. If such activities are on your agenda you don't want that sort of policy. A locally acquired motorcycle licence may not be valid under your policy.
*   You may prefer a policy which pays doctors or hospitals direct rather than you having to pay on

the spot and claim later. If you have to claim later make sure you keep all documentation. Some policies ask you to call back (reverse charges) to a centre in your home country where an immediate assessment of your problem is made.
*   Check if the policy covers ambulances or an emergency flight home. If you have to stretch out you will need two seats and somebody has to pay for them!

Medical Kit A small medical kit is a good thing to carry even though most items will usually be readily available in Japan. Your kit could include:

*   Aspirin or paracetamol – for pain or fever
*   Antihistamine (such as Benadryl) – useful as a decongestant for colds, allergies, to ease the itch from insect bites or stings or to help prevent motion sickness. Antihistamines may cause sedation and interact with alcohol so care should be taken when using them.
*   Kaolin preparation (Pepto-Bismol), Imodium or Lomotil – for stomach upsets
*   Rehydration mixture - for treatment of severe diarrhoea. This is particularly important if travelling with children, but is recommended for everyone.
*   Antiseptic such as Betadine, which comes as impregnated swabs or ointment, and an antibiotic powder or similar 'dry' spray - for cuts and grazes.
*   Calamine lotion – to ease irritation from bites or stings
*   Bandages and Band-aids – for minor injuries
*   Scissors, tweezers and a thermometer (mercury thermometers are prohibited by airlines)
*   Insect repellent, sunscreen (can be difficult to find in Japan), suntan lotion and chapstick
*   A couple of syringes, in case you need injections in a country with medical hygiene problems. Ask your doctor for a note explaining why they have been prescribed.

Health Preparations Make sure you're healthy before you start travelling. If you are embarking on a long trip make sure your teeth are OK; there are lots of places where a visit to the dentist would be the last thing you'd want to do. If you're short-sighted bring a spare pair of glasses and your prescription. If you require a particular medication take an adequate supply as it may not be available locally. Take the prescription or, better still, part of the packaging showing the generic rather than the brand name (which may not be available locally) as it will make getting replacements easier. It's a wise idea to have the prescription with you to show you legally use the medication – it's surprising how often over-the-counter drugs from one place are illegal without a prescription or even banned in another.

Immunisations No immunisations are required or necessary for Japan.

Basic Rules

Care in what you eat and drink is the most important health rule; stomach upsets are the most likely travel health problem (between 30% and 50% of travellers in a two-week stay experience this) but the majority of these upsets will be relatively minor. Don't become paranoid; trying the local food is part of the experience of travel after all.

Tap water is safe to drink all over Japan but drinking from mountain streams should be done with caution. On Rebuntō Island (Hokkaidō), travellers have been warned that the springs could be contaminated with fox faeces which contain tapeworm cysts. There have been reports of the schistosomiasis parasite still lurking in the countryside in rice paddies or stagnant water – avoid wading around barefoot in these places.

Food hygiene in Japan rarely causes complaints. Most of the raw food can be eaten without health worries although raw freshwater fish and raw wild boar meat should be avoided. The consumption of *fugu* (globefish) – for which you will need a fat wallet – is perhaps the one Japanese dish which can pose real dangers. (See the Food section for more details.)

Medical Problems & Treatment

Motion Sickness Eating lightly before and during a trip will reduce the chances of motion sickness. If you are prone to motion sickness, try to find a place that minimises disturbance – near the wing on aircraft, close to midships on boats or near the centre on buses. Fresh air usually helps, reading or cigarette smoke doesn't. Commercial anti-

motion-sickness preparations, which can cause drowsiness, have to be taken before the trip commences; when you're feeling sick it's too late. Ginger is a natural preventative and is available in capsule form.

Sexually Transmitted Diseases Sexual contact with an infected sexual partner spreads these diseases. While abstinence is the only 100% preventative, using condoms is also effective. Gonorrhoea and syphilis are the most common of these diseases; sores, blisters or rashes around the genitals, discharges or pain when urinating are common

---

Toilets

Western toilets are on the increase in Japan. On one trip aboard the bullet train, I was intrigued to see queues outside the Western toilet while the Japanese one remained vacant. A Dutch couple told me that back in the '70s, there were instructive diagrams on the correct use of Western toilets as part of a drive to dissuade toilet-goers from standing on the seat and aiming from on high.

It's quite common to see men urinating in public, typically in the evening in a bar district. In Shinjuku (Tokyo) I watched a tipsy, soberly suited salaryman slip behind a policeman and pee against the wall a couple of feet behind him. When the salaryman was finished, he turned round, thanked the policeman, exchanged bows and tottered into the railway station.

Japanese toilets are Asian style – level with, or in the floor. The correct position is to squat facing the hood, away from the door. This is the opposite to squat toilets in most other places in Asia. Make sure the contents of your pockets don't spill out. Toilet paper isn't always provided so carry tissues with you. Separate toilet slippers are often provided just inside the toilet door. These are for use in the toilet only, so remember to change out of them when you leave.

Mixed toilets also exist. Men and women often go through separately marked entrances, but land up in the same place. No-one feels worried, and privacy is provided by cubicles – women are supposed to simply ignore the backs turned to them at the urinals. The kanji script for 'toilet' is 手洗い, for 'men' 男 and for 'women' 女. ■

symptoms. Symptoms may be less marked or not observed at all in women. Syphilis symptoms eventually disappear completely but the disease continues and can cause severe problems in later years. The treatment of gonorrhoea and syphilis is by antibiotics.

There are numerous other sexually transmitted diseases, for most of which effective treatment is available. However, there is no cure for herpes and there is also currently no cure for AIDS.

HIV/AIDS HIV, the Human Immunodeficiency Virus, may develop into AIDS, Acquired Immune Deficiency Syndrome. HIV is a major problem in many countries. Any exposure to blood, blood products or bodily fluids may put the individual at risk. In many developing countries transmission is predominantly through heterosexual sexual activity. This is quite different from industrialised countries where transmission is mostly through contact between homosexual or bisexual males or contaminated needles in IV drug users. Apart from abstinence, the most effective preventative is always to practise safe sex using condoms. It is impossible to detect the HIV-positive status of an otherwise healthy-looking person without a blood test.

HIV/AIDS can also be spread through infected blood transfusions; most developing countries cannot afford to screen blood for transfusions. It can also be spread by dirty needles – vaccinations, acupuncture, tattooing and ear or nose piercing can potentially be as dangerous as intravenous drug use if the equipment is not clean. If you do need an injection, it may be a good idea to buy a new syringe from a pharmacy and ask the doctor to use it. You may also want to take a couple of syringes with you, in case of emergency.

Women's Health
Gynaecological Problems Poor diet, lowered resistance due to the use of antibiotics for stomach upsets and even contraceptive pills can lead to vaginal infections when travelling in hot climates. Keeping the genital area clean, and wearing skirts or

---

Traditional Japanese Medicine
As in so many other fields, China has exerted a strong influence over traditional Japanese medicine. Acupuncture (hari-kyū) is well known in the West as an oriental medical technique using hair-thin needles (gold, silver, or steel) inserted at key points (tsubo) of the body to restore the flow of ki (loosely translated as 'life energy'). Closely associated with acupuncture is okyū (moxibustion) which stimulates the key points of the body by burning small amounts of mogusa (a powdered herb) over the points.

Shiatsu (acupressure) is also related to acupuncture, but uses the application of finger pressure on the key points of the body. Kampo is based on Chinese herbalism with Japanese additions. Several hundred drugs derived from animal, mineral or plant sources are used in small doses, sometimes mixed with water. Many of these remedies have been concocted after centuries of experimentation and can prove helpful, although bats, dragonflies or lizards may be among the ingredients.

Onsen (mineral baths) are an old favourite with the Japanese. Legend recounts how samurai warriors, injured in battle, would find their way to a remote mineral bath where they were revived by the waters and recouped their energy to return to the fray. Nowadays, you find mineral baths all over Japan, each one reputed to be beneficial for particular ailments. ■

---

loose-fitting trousers and cotton underwear will help to prevent infections.

Yeast infections, characterised by a rash, itch and discharge, can be treated with a vinegar or even lemon-juice douche or with yoghurt. Nystatin suppositories are the usual medical prescription. Trichomonas is a more serious infection; symptoms are a discharge and a burning sensation when urinating. Male sexual partners must also be treated, and if a vinegar-water douche is not effective medical attention should be sought. Metronidazole (Flagyl) is the prescribed drug.

Pregnancy Most miscarriages occur during the first three months of pregnancy, so this is the most risky time to travel as far as your own health is concerned. Miscarriage is not uncommon, and can occasionally lead to severe bleeding. The last three months should also be spent within reasonable distance of good medical care. A baby born as early as 24 weeks stands a chance of survival, but only in a good modern hospital. Pregnant women should avoid all unnecessary medication, but vaccinations and malarial prophylactics should still be taken where possible. Additional care should be taken to prevent illness and particular attention should be paid to diet and nutrition. Alcohol and nicotine, for example, should be avoided.

Women travellers often find that their periods become irregular or even cease while they're on the road. Remember that a missed period in these circumstances doesn't necessarily indicate pregnancy. In most places, you can seek advice and have a urine test to determine whether you are pregnant or not.

Contraception

Although oral contraceptives are available from clinics specialising in medical care for foreigners, it is preferable to bring adequate supplies with you. Only in 1990 was the marketing of oral contraceptives officially authorised in Japan, and even now the low-dosage varieties widely available in the West

---

Condoms

Well, it's just something you can't do without these days, isn't it? If you arrive in Tokyo unprepared, look out for the Condomania stores in Roppongi (appropriately) and Harajuku. These places are always crowded so, if you're the shy type, making that embarassing purchase might be something of an ordeal – but then again why else would you be in there? Condomania stocks everything from Small Pecker ('protection for the little guy'), to Peter Meter ('the rubber that's also a ruler'), not to mention Lickety Sticks (in four flavours – caffeine-free also available) and Nose Condoms ('for the safe practice of brown nosing'). No sniggering please, this is serious business. ■

---

are hard to get hold of. Meanwhile the condom reigns supreme. Condoms are widely available in Japan, but generally only locally produced varieties, which tend to be small and made with very thin rubber – a dangerous combination when you consider the HIV-AIDS threat. It's a good idea to bring your own, or buy foreign made condoms at the American Pharmacy in Hibiya, Tokyo. There are also two branches of the condom shop, Condomania, in Tokyo's Roppongi and Harajuku. Both have a wide variety of condoms.

Medical Assistance

The TIC has lists of English-speaking hospitals and doctors in the large cities. Dental care is widely available at steep prices. If you need a medicine not readily available in Japanese pharmacies try the American Pharmacy (☎ 3271-4034) close to the Yuraku-chō TIC in Tokyo. A peculiarity of the Japanese medical system is that most drugs are supplied not by pharmacies but by doctors. Critics say that as a result, doctors are prone to over-prescribe and choose the most expensive drugs.

Emergencies Emergency services in Japan will usually only react fast if you speak Japanese. Try the Tokyo English Lifeline (TELL) (☎ 3403-7106) for emergency assistance in English. The Japan Helpline (☎ 0120-461-997) is an emergency number which operates 24 hours a day, seven days a week. Don't clog the line unless you really do have an emergency.

Counselling & Advice Adjusting to life in Japan can be tough but there are several places to turn for help. The TELL phone service provides confidential and anonymous help. If they don't have the right answers at hand, they can pass you on to someone who might. Tokyo Tapes (☎ 3262-0224) has a wide variety of tapes available to help you deal with problems.

WOMEN TRAVELLERS

Japan never gives you a chance to make up your mind up firmly about anything. Just when you've decided something works one way, something happens to convince you the opposite is true. This policy of opposites applies to women travellers as well.

The crime rate in all categories is very low in Japan so the risk of rape or assault is minimal. Women should take normal precautions of course, but can travel by subway at night or wander the streets of the entertainment districts (dodging the reeling salarymen) with little concern.

The major concern of women travellers in many countries – 'Will I be physically safe?' – is not a worry in Japan, though jam-packed rush-hour subways or buses can still bring out the worst in the Japanese male. When movement is impossible, roving hands are frequently at work and women often put up with this interference because, in Japan, it would simply be impolite or unseemly to make a fuss! Actually a loud complaint might have little effect in any case, since the usual Japanese reaction would be to look in the opposite direction and pretend this distasteful occurrence was not happening in their carriage. One woman visitor has suggested that it is not a Western woman's duty to reinforce Japanese mores and, if possible, the offending hand should be grabbed, held up and the whereabouts of its owner inquired about (or better still, it should be bitten!).

There are some aspects of Japanese life which are not anti-female but certainly strike women as peculiar on first encounter. Public toilets, for example, are often not sex segregated although there may be doors labelled male and female. It can be a real shock to a Western woman when she enters the door marked 'women' and finds a row of urinals with men lined up at them! It's an equal shock to the unprepared Western male when he steps back from a urinal and finds women all around him.

Comic books (*manga*) and other mass media often portray women in wildly exploitative situations. Many of the manga themes would raise howls of protest from women's groups in the West but men openly read these comics in trains and other public places.

Women in Japan are, however, very much second class citizens. Pay levels for women relative to those for men are lower than any other advanced nation. In most companies, women are considered temporary workers, filling in a few years between school and marriage. They are referred to as OLs, office ladies, and it is considered highly unlikely that they will rise above the most menial ranks. The steady path to the top is strictly reserved for the salarymen. Many women work in occupations where they are purely decorative – they may be the smiling, bowing greeters at department store entrances or the coffee servers in big companies.

Many manual jobs, which in the West would have a small but visible percentage of female workers, are strictly banned to women in Japan. Many manufacturing companies, for example, bar women from working on the assembly lines; one wonders if there is a female taxi or bus driver anywhere in Japan?

Yet, some of this is changing. Japan has been suffering a severe shortage of workers, particularly for those menial tasks the Japanese are simply no longer willing to undertake, and a blind eye is being turned to illegal immigration. In this situation, Japanese companies are being forced to relax male-only hiring policies.

The yuppie syndrome has also hit Japan in a big way and is changing the typical pattern where a woman works for only a few years and then devotes herself to raising a family. Furthermore, younger women are often the most affluent of Japanese consumers and much more attention is being paid to them by advertisers – young women do not have to squander a large part of their income on nightly circuits of the bars and entertainment districts the way an aspiring salaryman has to.

Finally, some observers feel that the very basis of women's deference to men is withering. For the past generation, the father figures to whom young children are taught to defer have simply not been there, they've been away winning the economic wars every day and consolidating the victory in the bars every night. A whole generation of women has grown up with that important, and superior, male figure hardly in sight.

DANGERS & ANNOYANCES
Theft
The low incidence of theft and crime in general in Japan is frequently commented on, though of course, theft does exist and its rarity is no reason for carelessness. Airports and the crowded Tokyo rail network are reputed to be among the haunts of pickpockets and other sneak thieves, so take extra care in these places. It's probable the stolen goods are on their way overseas before the owner even realises their disappearance.

Lost and found services really do seem to work so, if you leave something behind on a train or other transport, it's always worth inquiring if it has been turned in.

Earthquakes
Japan is a very earthquake-prone country although most will only show up on instrumentation. If you experience a strong earthquake, head for a doorway or supporting pillar. Small rooms, like a bathroom or cupboard, are often stronger than large rooms but even a table or desk can provide some protection from falling debris. Of course, it is better to be outside than inside, but keep away from buildings because of the danger of falling glass or other debris.

Fire
Although modern hotels are subject to high safety standards, traditional Japanese buildings with their wooden construction and tightly packed surroundings can be real fire traps. Fortunately, most old buildings are small places where you are unlikely to be trapped on the 40th floor but it's wise to check fire exits and escapes. Onsen (hot-spring/spa) centres, where buildings are often traditional in design with floors covered in grass tatami mats and where much

---

The Yakuza
The Yakuza, perhaps because they are often referred to as the 'Japanese Mafia', are much misunderstood by foreign visitors to Japan. Enjoying deep penetration into Japanese society, powerful right-wing political support, operating as vast syndicates with interests in everything from real estate to hospitals (plus, of course, obvious contenders such as prostitution, drugs and gambling), the Yakuza is a highly organised and widely tolerated component of Japan's hierarchical society.

Naturally the Yakuza occupy (at least nominally) a lowly position in this hierarchy, but the yakuza themselves compensate for this with a bravado that looks to historical antecedents. Many yakuza see themselves as custodians of the flickering flames of honour and chivalry, traditional values that are all but extinguished in contemporary Japanese society. Japan's ultra-nationalist right – which also looks for a return to 'traditional values' – enjoys Yakuza support, and the black propaganda vans you will encounter cruising urban Japan are often driven by Yakuza.

There are thought to be close to 90,000 Yakuza members in Japan and Yakuza earnings are probably over US$10 billion annually. The largest group is the Yamaguchi-gumi, based in Kōbe. It claims over 20,000 'employees' and pulls in about a fifth of total Yakuza annual earnings.

How do you pick a yakuza? Short-cropped permed hair is à la mode amongst the lower orders. Those with money often drive a US *yakuzamobile* (nobody else fancies US cars very much). Yakuza will also affect an arrogant swagger *(iburi)* and a gruff manner of speech *(aragoto)*. A bodyful of tattoos is *de rigueur* (cherry blossoms signify the brief but cheerful life of an ardent criminal), but don't forget to look out for that telling detail: failure in one's obligations to the group is punished by the amputation of a little finger at the first joint. Repeated convictions move to the next joint and so on until, presumably, there are no fingers left – a sign of the honourable but bumbling custodian of Japan's samurai past. ■

drunken revelry takes place, can pose particular dangers.

Beaches & Swimming

Few public beaches have lifeguards and summer weekends bring many drowning accidents. Watch for undertows or other dangers. Severe sunburn is possible in Japan, just as in more obviously 'hot' places. However, as yet, the Japanese seem unaware of the dangers of overexposure. Bring a good sunblock lotion if you will be outdoors for long hours in the summer.

Noise

In Japanese cities the noise assault on the auditory senses can be overwhelming, so it's no wonder so many pedestrians are plugged in to Walkmans. Pedestrian crossings are serenaded by electronic playtime music, loudspeaker systems broadcast muzak or advertisements, bus passengers are bombarded with running commentaries in Mickey Mouse tones and accommodation may include TVs turned up full volume in dining rooms or lounges. Earplugs can help.

Size

Even medium-sized foreigners need to mind their head in Japanese dwellings, though, in some homes, padded bags attached to the top of door frames appear to acknowledge the problem. The Western frame may find it hard to fit into some seats and those with long legs will often find themselves wedged tight. Toilets in cramped accommodation necessitate contortions and careful aim. Sitting cross-legged takes a little practice to avoid the embarrassment of standing up only to find your legs so numb that you promptly topple over.

Some physiotherapists maintain that Asian people, many of whom spend a lifetime stretching their knee joints in the cross-legged position, suffer much less from knee problems than Westerners.

Wildlife

Japan is hardly a high danger region when it comes to wildlife, although in Okinawa Pre-

fecture much fuss is made about the 'deadly *habu*' snake. To avoid an unhappy encounter with a deadly habu don't go traipsing barefoot through the undergrowth. Snake bites do not cause instantaneous death and antivenenes are available. Keep the victim calm and still, wrap the bitten limb tightly, as you would for a sprained ankle, and then attach a splint to immobilise it. Then seek medical help, if possible with the dead snake for identification. Don't attempt to catch the snake if there is any remote possibility of being bitten again. Tourniquets and sucking out the poison are now comprehensively discredited. On the mainland islands the *mamushi* is also poisonous.

There are still bears in remote areas of Hokkaidō and they can be fiercely protective of their cubs. Foxes, also found in Hokkaidō, can carry diseases and should be avoided. Japan also has wasps, mosquitoes and other biting or stinging insects but not in extraordinary numbers or of unusual danger. Jellyfish and other marine dangers also exist and local advice should be heeded before entering the water.

Smoking

One dangerous habit you're almost certain to indulge in while visiting Japan is passive smoking. Japan looks like being the last advanced nation to face up to the dangers of smoking – cigarettes are readily available and, at ¥220 to ¥240 for a pack from a vending machine, they're also cheap. Although the anti-smoking lobby is growing and there are now more nonsmoking seats on aircraft and more nonsmoking carriages on trains, Japan is still a long way behind California or Singapore.

WORK

The high value of the yen makes Japan a very attractive place for a working holiday. That said, it should be remembered that the Japanese economy is no longer booming and the job market for foreigners has shrunk considerably. English teaching in particular has been hard hit by the current recession, with many schools closing down and private classes harder to come by. The entertainment industry, a source of hostessing work, is also suffering as many companies cut back on their employees' entertainment expense accounts.

The largest number of foreign workers in Japan these days are from less developed countries. They are taking on work in fields the Japanese themselves no longer have a taste for. Building sites and restaurants are just two areas that have become increasingly dominated by (often illegal) foreign workers. Most users of this book are more likely to be doing work the Japanese *can't* do – English teaching and foreign modelling for example.

Finding casual work is certainly still possible, particularly if you look neat and tidy. (Appearances are *very* important in Japan, suit and tie for the men please, businesslike dresses for the women.) But you will need to be determined and you should have a sizeable sum of money to carry you through the lean period while you are looking for work and possibly to get you out of the country in the event you don't find any (it happens). Many foreigners who have set up in Japan over the last few years maintain that a figure of around US$5000 and upwards is necessary to make a go of it in Japan. People do it with less, but they are taking the risk of ending up penniless and homeless before they find a job.

Once upon a time, blonde hair and blue eyes were all that was needed for an English-teaching job but nowadays, real qualifications are essential. Be wary of anyone who is prepared to employ you without qualifications – there are some very exploitative deals, especially in Tokyo.

English Teaching

Teaching has, for many years, been the easiest work for native-English-speaking foreigners to find. This is definitely no longer the case. Unless you have the basic minimum of a university degree, it would be foolish to roll up in Japan in the hope that a teaching job will come your way. Even very qualified teachers have been finding it diffi-

cult to find jobs in the current economic climate. Many prospective teachers, watching their savings dwindle as they search for that elusive position, recommend trying to line up a job before arriving in Japan. Big schools, like Nova for example, now have recruitment programmes in the USA and the UK – US and British English being the two preferred accents for teaching.

Australians, New Zealanders and Canadians, who have the advantage of being able to come to Japan on a working holiday visa (see Visas), are in a slightly better position. Schools are generally more willing to take on unqualified teachers if they don't have to bother with the voluminous paperwork involved in sponsoring a teacher for a work visa. Nevertheless, Australian and New Zealand (to a lesser extent Canadian) accents are considered less desirable than US and British accents and this can be an impediment to getting a job in one of the better schools. Many working holiday visa recipients find themselves working for small, unreliable outfits that are badly managed and generally unrewarding to work for (both financially and in terms of job satisfaction).

Suitably qualified teachers who want to work in Japan should seriously consider contacting the Japan Association of Language Teachers (JALT) at Shamboru Dai 2 Kawasaki 305, 1-3-17 Kaizuka, Kawasaki-ku, Kawasaki-shi, Kanagawa-ken 210 (☎ 044-245-9753; fax 044-245-9754). It's a useful forum for getting the low down on the teaching situation in Japan and sometimes finding work. Membership is ¥7000 yearly, which includes an 80 page monthly newsletter and a twice-yearly journal.

Private Schools Over the last couple of years many of Japan's private schools have been going under, and in those that remain formal qualifications will be essential. The Monday edition of the *Japan Times* is the best place to look for teaching jobs, although word of mouth is also useful and some larger schools simply rely on direct inquiries from would-be teachers.

Tokyo is the easiest place to find teaching

jobs, as even schools on other islands advertise or recruit in Tokyo. Heading straight to another of Japan's major population centres (say Osaka, Fukuoka, Hiroshima or Sapporo), where there are smaller numbers of competing gaijin, is also a good bet.

Check the fine print carefully once you have an offer. Find out how many hours you will teach, whether class preparation time is included and whether you get sick leave and paid holidays. Find out how and when you will be paid and if the school will obtain your visa. It's worth checking with other foreign staff to find how they are treated. Check also whether your school is prepared to serve as a guarantor in the event that you rent an apartment.

Government Schools The JET programme provides 2000 teaching assistant positions for foreign teachers. The job operates on a yearly contract and will have to be organised in your home country. The programme gets very good reports from many of the teachers involved with it.

Teachers employed by the JET programme are known as Assistant English Teachers (AETs). Although you will have to apply in your home country in order to work as an AET with JET, it's worth bearing in mind that many local governments in Japan are also employing AETs for their schools. Such work can be obtained in Japan without having to go home.

International Schools Big cities like Tokyo and Yokohama with large foreign populations have a number of international schools for the children of foreign residents. Work is available for experienced, Western-trained teachers in all disciplines and the schools will usually organise your visa.

Rewriting
Since the general standard of translation in Japan ranges from bad to comical, transforming 'Japlish' into English has become a big industry. Technical documents and manuals pose particular problems and, ideally, visitors hoping to work as translators

should also have the appropriate technical knowledge. Rewriting work is harder to come by than teaching but try the *Japan Times*. Office jobs usually pay ¥2000 to ¥3000 per hour.

Hostessing
Hostessing evolved from the geisha culture in which highly trained and cultivated women entertained powerful men with their repartee and artistic accomplishments. Geisha establishments are very expensive but most company expense accounts will stretch to the odd night at a hostess club where the women will pour drinks for the salarymen, listen to their troubles and generally provide an amiable atmosphere. Although hostessing has been described as 'psychological prostitution', there is no pressure to grant sexual favours; it's more a matter of slipping on the mask, making light conversation and giggling at the crude innuendos and general role playing.

Since working visas are not issued for hostessing, it's a mildly illegal activity to which the authorities seem to turn a blind eye. An introduction is usually required, but at any gaijin house there will usually be women working in this field. Rates for western women working as hostesses typically range from ¥2000 to ¥3000 per hour (plus even more in tips), with bonuses for bringing customers to the club. This only requires meeting the customer downstairs and escorting him through the door; most hostesses soon foster a small circle of admirers. An ability to speak Japanese is an asset in this kind of work, but is not essential – many Japanese salarymen want to practice their English with a hostess.

Modelling
Modelling jobs for foreigners are increasingly dominated by professional models so any hope of getting into the field will require a proper portfolio of photographs. Nonprofessionals are more likely to pick up casual work as extras in advertising or film and, once again, news of possible work circulates mainly by word of mouth.

Working the Streets

In big cities, particularly Tokyo, you'll see Westerners busking, or peddling everything from Nepalese jewellery to moving toy pandas. Although peddling is somewhat illegal, apologising and moving on is usually enough to defuse any unwanted police attention. The Yakuza (Japanese Mafia) may also show an interest since they often control the lively entertainment districts and will want a fee from any outsider who appears on their turf.

Buskers seem to work best as a team, while solo street selling can be tough work unless you know how to sell (the Japanese certainly have the money to spend). The street selling business is controlled by Israelis, so you need to be an Israeli yourself or have an introduction from one if you want to get in on the act. It's said that Israelis are intercepted at Narita Airport by others with connections in the street-selling game.

STUDYING IN JAPAN

The Japanese obsession for acquiring new skills and developing personal interests has resulted in schools and courses for almost every aspect of Japanese culture. The Tokyo Tourist Information Centre (TIC) has a wealth of information material available. Applicants for cultural visas should note that attendance at 20 class hours per week are required. Those wishing to work while studying need to apply for permission to do so.

Japanese Language

Studying Japanese has become so popular that schools cannot keep up with demand and there are long waiting lists of foreign students. This has also led to many fly-by-night operations springing up. These tend to have poor facilities and teachers with limited training and experience (like us with English, most Japanese are deluded into thinking that being a native speaker automatically qualifies them for teaching the language). The TIC leaflet *Japanese & Japanese Studies* lists government-accredited schools that belong to the Association of International Education. The association can

also be contacted directly (☎ 3485-6827). Also available at the TIC is *The Guide to Japanese Career & Vocational Schools*. It has an extensive list of vocational and language schools, as well as details of the Monbusho Japanese Government Scholarship. *Nihongo Journal* is an excellent monthly language magazine for students of Japanese, and advertises Japanese language schools.

Costs at private Japanese-language schools vary enormously depending on the school's status and facilities. There is usually an application fee of ¥5000 to ¥30,000, an administration charge of ¥50,000 to ¥100,000 and annual tuition fees of ¥350,000 to ¥600,000. Add accommodation and food, and it is easy to see that studying is not a viable option for most people unless they also have an opportunity to work.

Martial Arts

Aikidō, jūdō, karate and kendō can be studied in Japan as well as less popular fields such as *kyūdō* (Japanese archery) and sumō. Relevant addresses include:

All-Japan Jūdō Federation, c/o Kodokan, 1-16-30 Kasuga, Bukyō-ku, Tokyo (☎ 3818-4199)

Amateur Archery Federation of Japan, Kishi Memorial Hall, 4th Floor, 1-1-1 Jinan, Shibuya-ku, Tokyo (☎ 3481-2387)

International Aikidō Federation, 17-18 Wakamatsuchō, Shinjuku-ku, Tokyo (☎ 3203-9236)

Japan Kendō Federation, c/o Nippon Budokan, 2-3 Kitanomaru-kōen, Chiyoda-ku, Tokyo (☎ 3211-5804/5)

Nihon Sumō Kyokai, c/o Kokugikan Sumō Hall, 1-3-28 Yokoami, Sumida-ku, Tokyo (☎ 3623-5111)

World Union of Karate-dō Organisation, 4th Floor, Sempaku Shinkokai Building, 1-15-16 Toranomon, Minato-ku, Tokyo (☎ 3503-6640)

HIGHLIGHTS

Visitors to Japan have few preconceptions of any highlight they definitely do not want to miss – there is no Taj Mahal, Statue of Liberty, Sydney Opera House or Eiffel Tower in Japan. Nevertheless there are many interesting things to see and areas of interest worth pursuing.

Castles

Although the Meiji Restoration was bad news for Japan's castles, the preceding Tokugawa Shogunate had not been good for their preservation either. The 'one kingdom, one castle' rule had resulted in many surplus castles being destroyed or dismantled. During the centuries of peace under the Tokugawas, castles were simply redundant; when they caught fire there was often no hurry to reconstruct them. Then, in 1873, the sixth year of the Meiji era, the government ordered the destruction of 144 of these feudal symbols and only 39 remained.

World War II further reduced Japan's castles and today only 12 original castle donjons remain. The '60s saw an enormous spate of castle reconstructions, but these were all rebuilt like Hollywood movie sets, very authentic looking from a distance but constructed from very 'unfeudal' concrete and steel.

Perhaps the greatest original castle is Himeji-jō, the huge and impressive 'White Egret' Castle. It's an easy day trip from Kyoto. The contrasting black Matsumoto-jō

is also well preserved and in very original condition. Hirosaki-jō Castle has some interesting surroundings including a samurai quarter. Conveniently near Kyoto are the pretty lakeside Hikone-jō and the small Inuyama-jō Castle.

Although Matsuyama-jō Castle was rebuilt only a few years before the Edo era ground to a halt, it has a spectacular setting overlooking the town and the appearance of a complete and battle-ready fortress. Shikoku's other original castles at Kōchi, Uwajima and Marugame are smaller, less impressive affairs. Maruoka-jō has the oldest surviving castle donjon in Japan, though otherwise, it's not of great interest.

Matsue-jō Castle has a fine setting and some interesting nearby streets. Bitchu-Matsuyama Castle at Takahashi represents an earlier era, hidden away on a high hilltop rather than standing proudly at the centre of its town. Kumamoto-jō Castle is a modern reconstruction, but its design is very interesting; the museum has informative displays about castle construction. Edo Castle was once the largest castle in the world; today its

Osaka Castle

huge moats and walls surround the Tokyo Imperial Palace.

Gardens

Japan is famed for its beautiful gardens and whether they are the larger Edo 'stroll gardens' or the small contemplative Zen gardens the emphasis is always on exquisite attention to detail. The Japanese love to rate things and the 'big three' in the garden category are the Kairaku-en (Mito), the Kenroku-en (Kanazawa) and the Kōraku-en (Okayama). Not all visitors are likely to agree with the official listings; Mito, for example, gets the nod principally because it has lots of lawn.

Kyoto has almost too many gardens to mention, including gardens that virtually define the rock garden and the Zen dry-landscape garden concepts. Among the best smaller Zen gardens outside Kyoto are the beautiful Kōmyō-ji at Dazaifu, the Jōei-ji in Yamaguchi and the Raikyū-ji at Takahashi.

Other large gardens include the Ritsurin-kōen in Takamatsu, the Suizenji-kōen with its miniature Mt Fuji in Kumamoto and the Iso-teien in Kagoshima with a real smoking volcano as borrowed scenery. Hikone has the very beautiful Genkyū-en Garden and also one of Japan's few surviving original castles. Close to Tokyo, the Sankei-en Park in Yokohama is also very fine.

Historical Japan

Feudal castles are not the only symbols of 'old Japan' which have disappeared over the years. The destruction of WW II, the Japanese penchant for knocking down the old and putting up the new, plus the often flimsy and inflammable construction of so many old Japanese buildings have combined to leave few reminders of an earlier Japan. Apart from temples, shrines and castles there are, however, some intriguing reminders of the country's history.

Hakodate, in Hokkaidō, is a fascinating old port town with some very interesting Meiji period Western-style buildings. Similar buildings can be seen in the port towns of Nagasaki and Kōbe. Hakone, near

Tokyo, was a post town on the Tōkaidō Highway and preserves a short stretch of that historic road. Tsumago and Magome also maintain their old post town atmosphere.

Takayama, north of Nagoya, has many fine old buildings and a farmhouse village (Hida Folk Village) consisting of more than a dozen houses of the *gasshō-zukuri* or 'hands in prayer' architectural style. The houses were all dismantled and reconstructed as a village after a huge dam was built in the region. Similar farmhouse villages can be found at Kawasaki and Takamatsu. Kanazawa, which escaped bombing during WW II, is another town with many reminders of an earlier era.

Kurashiki is famed for its canal district and old warehouses, many of which have been converted into museums. A little further along the San-yō coast is Tomo-no-Ura, an interesting small port you can explore by bicycle. On the opposite San-in coast, the town of Hagi exemplifies the kind of contradiction so typical of Japan. While the town is famous for its role in the ending of the Edo era and the beginning of the Meiji Restoration, it is equally famous for its finely preserved Edo period buildings. Uchiko in Shikoku has a single old street where wealthy wax merchants once lived.

Nagasaki's atomic destruction distracts from its earlier history as a gateway between Japan and the outside world. During the centuries of seclusion under the Tokugawa Shogunate, Nagasaki was virtually the only peephole to the outside world and is still a remarkably cosmopolitan city today. The small town of Chiran, near Kagoshima in southern Kyūshū, has an old street of well-preserved samurai buildings and a more modern historic reminder in the form of a kamikaze museum.

Shrines

Japan's dual religions means there are two sets of indigenous religious structures – Shintō shrines and Buddhist temples. The shrines are known as *jinja, jingū* or *gū* and the arched torii is an indicator that you are entering a shrine rather than a temple.

The three great shrine centres are Ise, Nikkō and Izumo Taisha. Ise has the imperial shrine to Amaterasu, the mythical ancestor of the Japanese imperial line. Nikkō has the shrine to Ieyasu Tokugawa, founder of the Tokugawa Shogunate. Izumo Taisha has the largest and, it is claimed, oldest shrine hall in Japan. Kyoto is, of course, particularly well endowed with impressive shrines.

Other important or interesting shrines include the very popular Meiji-jingū Shrine in Tokyo, the Itsukushima-jinja with its much photographed floating torii on Miyajima Island and the hilltop Kotohira-gū Shrine in Shikoku. Kyūshū has two particularly interesting shrines. The Tenman-gū Shrine at Dazaifu near Fukuoka is dedicated to the legendary Sugawara-no-Michizane, who was exiled there from Kyoto. Just outside Takachiho the Ama-no-Iwato-jinja has the very cave where the sun goddess Amaterasu once hid.

In Northern Honshū, you can see shrines frequented by worshippers of Shugendō in the spectacular surroundings of the sacred mountains of Dewa Sanzan, near Tsuruoka.

Temples
Distinguishing a Buddhist temple from a Shintō shrine is simply a matter of examining the entrance. While shrines are entered through an arched torii, a temple *(dera* or *ji)* is entered through a gateway, usually flanked by guardian figures. The most important temples in Japan are concentrated in Kyoto and Nara and the surrounding Kansai region.

Important Kyoto temples include the Daitoku-ji, with its gardens; the ancient Kiyomizu-dera with its superb hillside site; the 13th century Sanjūsangen-dō and the Tō-ji, founded by Kōbō Daishi. Nara has the fine Tōshōdai-ji and the Tōdai-ji, with its Great Buddha. Also in the Kansai region is Kōbō Daishi's mountaintop Kōya-san, the wonderful Hōryū-ji and the Byōdō-in in Uji, one of the most famous buildings in Japan.

Close to Tokyo, Kamakura offers some of the best temple tramping in Japan; Kōtoku-in Temple has the best known giant Buddha statue in Japan. Although the 88 temples in

Kōbō Daishi's circuit of Shikoku have no great significance individually; taken together, however, they make up the most important pilgrimage route in Japan. The Kōsan-ji, at nearby Setoda in the Inland Sea, is a Disneyland of temples – all modern reproductions of important temples crammed together in one location. Onomichi, on the Honshū coast near Setoda, has an interesting temple walk.

Scenery & Natural Attractions
Expressways, railways, factories, skyscrapers and a teeming population would scarcely seem to leave room for natural attractions. Yet, despite the population density, Japan is a mountainous country with many areas of great natural beauty.

Just as the Japanese rate the three best gardens, they also rate the three best views. These are the 'floating' torii of Miya-jima Island (see the Shrines section), the long sandspit of Amanohashidate and the bay of Matsushima, with its pine-covered islands. The misty, island-dotted waters of the Inland Sea would also have to be one of the most beautiful sights.

Some of the most spectacular mountain scenery in Japan is found in Nagano-ken (Kamikōchi and Hakuba) and northern Gifu-ken (Takayama and the Shōkawa Valley region).

Mt Fuji, the much climbed symbol of Japan, can actually seem like Shinjuku Station at rush hour when you get close up, but from a distance it's as beautiful as it has ever been. Mt Bandai-san and its lakes in the Tōhoku region offer more superb scenery.

Hokkaidō, the second-largest but least densely populated island, offers wonderful mountain scenery around Lake Mashu-ko in the Daisetsuzan National Park and around Tōya-ko and Shikotsu-ko lakes in the west. The Shiretoko-hantō and Shakotan-hantō peninsulas have fine coastal scenery.

If you can possibly squeeze in an extra few days on Hokkaidō, the islands of Rishiri-tō and Rebun-tō in the north offer superb hiking.

Kyūshū has some wonderful volcanic

scenery, particularly in the immense caldera of Mt Aso, the bleak, volcano-studded Kirishima National Park, and rumbling Sakurajima near Kagoshima. At the extreme western end of the country, Iriomote-jima Island has dense jungle and good scuba diving.

Modern Japan

Ancient temples and shrines, feudal castles and Zen gardens are all very well but Japan is also the land of *pachinko* pinball parlours, love hotels, robot-operated production lines and multi-storey buildings filled with nothing but bars. It's also the first (and, thank God, still the only) place to have suffered atomic destruction. The atomic bomb museums at Hiroshima and Nagasaki are something no visitor to Japan should avoid.

Hiroshima is also a good place to see the modern Japanese industrial machine in peak form. It's easy to arrange a factory visit at many centres in Japan, but the huge Mazda car factory in Hiroshima is certainly worth a visit. After work, the Japanese salarymen head for the huge entertainment districts, where the neon burns bright and the bill at the end of the evening would bankrupt the average Third World country. Even if you don't venture inside a single bar, these colourful areas are fascinating to wander around. Interesting ones include Tokyo's up-market Roppongi area and, in the Shinjuku district, the decidedly raunchier Kabuki-chō area. Shinjuku in Tokyo is also 'modern Japan' at its most modern; with two million people passing through its railway station everyday, Shinjuku is probably the busiest place in the world.

Osaka's Namba district is another good example of a busy entertainment district, while Nakasu Island in Fukuoka is said to have a higher concentration of bars than anywhere else in Japan – hence the world?

If you travel north in search of bars and nightlife, then you should head for the Kokubun-chō district in Sendai and the Susukino district in Sapporo, Hokkaidō.

The Japanese passion for hot springs (*onsen*) is well documented and, in many

places, is a very tasteful and ritualistic activity. In others, it is most definitely not. The spa town of Beppu in Kyūshū is the Las Vegas of onsen towns with bright lights and bad taste in full swing.

Love hotels are another side of Japan and it's surprising that an enterprising publisher hasn't yet produced a coffee-table book on love hotel architecture. In some places there are major enclaves of love hotels, the Dōgenzaka area of Tokyo's Shibuya district is a good example.

ACCOMMODATION

Japan offers a wide variety of accommodation, Japanese-style and Western-style establishments catering to all budgets from shoestring travellers to the ultra-rich.

Compared to the rest of Asia, Japanese budget places make a sizeable dent in the pocket. The average cost at a youth hostel is around ¥2200, although there are slight seasonal variations. By staying at the cheapest places, you will conserve funds, but you will also cut yourself off from an essential part of the Japan experience – trying out different types of accommodation. You will considerably add to your enjoyment if you manage to vary your accommodation routine to include at least one night at a traditional ryokan (Japanese-style inn), *shukubō* (temple lodging) and minshuku (Japanese B&B).

Cheap places to stay are often further out of town, which can mean an expensive taxi ride if you arrive late. If you get really stuck in the late hours, the nearest *kōban* (police box) should be able to point you in the right direction for a place to stay. Business hotels are often conveniently close to the station, but you're generally looking at an absolute minimum of ¥5000 in one of these. Capsule hotels or love hotels are useful late-night alternatives.

Reservations

Generally, it is quite feasible to look for a room when you arrive in a new town, though reservations are best made a few days in advance. During peak holiday seasons, you should book as far ahead as possible, particularly if you have a special choice. Out of season, calling a day in advance is usually sufficient.

The information office (annai-jo) at a main railway station can usually help with reservations, and is often open until about 6.30 pm or later. Even if you are travelling by car, the railway station is a good first stop in town for information, reservations and even cheap car parking. The Japanese run their accommodation according to an established rhythm which favours checkouts at around 10 am and check-ins between 5 and 7 pm; unannounced latecomers disturb their pattern.

Making phone reservations in English is usually possible in most cities. Providing you speak clearly and simply, there will usually be someone around who can get the gist of what you want. However, once you head into the outlying areas, making telephone reservations in Japanese can be a major hassle for both sides. In practice, a combination of phrasebook consultation, memorised scraps of Japanese and your telephone partner's morsels of English usually get results. One way to avoid this linguistic jousting is to ask a passing Japanese for help or to ask the desk staff of your last place of accommodation to phone your reservation through.

Information on accommodation listings is provided in this section's accommodation categories. JNTO offices abroad and TIC offices in Tokyo and Kyoto also stock some of these publications as well as their own lists. JNTO publishes *Reasonable Accommodations in Japan*, a useful leaflet with details of 200 hotels, ryokan and business hotels in 50 major cities in Japan. Other useful publications include *Directory of Welcome Inns*, a very extensive listing, and *Japanese Inn Group*, which has a number of ryokan throughout Japan that are used to dealing with foreigners.

Gaijin Houses   外人ハウス
This is the cheapest category of accommodation, especially for long-term stays, but you should be prepared for basic dorms or shared tatami rooms and probably a communal kitchen. Prices for the cheapest houses start around ¥1600 per night. Some places offer reductions for stays longer than a month.

Most of the gaijin houses are in Tokyo and Kyoto. You can find advertisements or listings of these places in publications such as *Tokyo Journal*, *Kansai Time Out* or *Kyoto Visitor's Guide*. TIC offices no longer provide information on gaijin houses, after they were told by authorities that most of them are illegal.

Youth Hostels   ユースホステル
For anyone wanting to keep to a low budget, youth hostels are the best option and it is quite feasible to plan an entire itinerary using them. By far the best source of information on hostels is the (Japan) *Youth Hostel Handbook* available for ¥580 from the Japan Youth Hostel Association (JYHA) (☎ 3269-5831), Hoken Kaikan, 1-2 Sadohara-chō, Ichigaya, Shinjuku-ku, Tokyo 162.

Branch offices in Tokyo which stock the handbook and can supply information are in the 2nd level basement of Sogo department store, Yuraku chō (two minutes on foot from TIC); the 4th floor of the Keiō department store, Shinjuku; and the 7th floor of the Seibu department store, Ikebukuro. Many hostels throughout Japan also sell the handbook.

The *Youth Hostel Map of Japan* (approximately ¥225) is a map with one-line entries for each hostel on the reverse. JNTO publishes *Youth Hostels in Japan*, a concise English listing of youth hostels.

The JYHA handbook is mostly in Japanese, though there is some English at the front in the symbol key and on the locator map keys. The hostels on each map are identified by name (in kanji) and a page number. Each hostel is accompanied by a mini-map, photo, address in Japanese, fax and phone details, a row of symbols, access instructions in Japanese, open dates, bed numbers and prices for bed and meals.

By looking at the photos and the symbols it is quite easy to single out hostels which might be interesting. The reversed swastika symbol means that the hostel is a temple. Pay careful attention to the closing and opening dates: many hostels – particularly those in rural areas – close over New Year or shut down in the winter. For the musically inclined, the handbook even has a page with the words and music for the 'Youth Hostel Song'.

The *Youth Hostel Map of Japan* has hostel addresses in English, but it can still be a struggle trying to work out a romaji version of the address. The *IYHF Handbook* has a ridiculously skimpy set of entries for Japan and is not worth considering for a Japan trip.

Youth Hostel Categories There are various categories of youth hostel in Japan: JYHA hostels, privately run and government-subsidised hostels, ryokan hostels and hostels run by youth organisations, shrines and temples. In general, the atmosphere is more relaxed at privately run hostels, ryokan and religious establishments; the other hostels can sometimes feel as if they are being run as military camps.

Membership & Regulations You can stay at over 70 municipal hostels without a youth hostel membership card. Elsewhere, you will need a JYHA membership card or one from an affiliate of the International Youth Hostel Federation (IYHF) otherwise you must pay an extra charge. It is much simpler if you become a member in your own country, as JYHA registration requires that members have lived in Japan for a year, have an Alien Registration Card and pay a ¥2000 joining fee.

Nonmembers must pay an additional ¥600 per night for a 'welcome stamp'. Six welcome stamps plus a photograph entitles you to a IYHF International Guest Card valid worldwide for the rest of the year. If you purchase all six stamps at once the price is reduced to ¥2800, a saving of ¥800.

Youth hostel membership has a minimum age limit of four years but no maximum age – you will meet plenty of Japanese wrinklies and often a few foreign ones approaching their 70s as well.

Hostel charges currently average ¥2200 per night; some also add the 3% consumption tax *(shōhizei)*. Private rooms are available in some hostels at ¥3500 per night upwards. Average prices for meals are ¥450 for breakfast and ¥750 for dinner. Although official regulations state that you can only stay at one hostel for three consecutive nights, this probably depends on the season.

Almost all hostels require you to use a regulation sleeping sheet which you can rent for ¥100 if you do not have your own. As a friendly gesture, some hostels have introduced a special reduction – sometimes as much as ¥500 per night – for foreign hostellers.

Hostellers are expected to check in between 3 and 8 pm. Checkout is usually required before 10 am and dormitories are closed between 10 am and 3 pm. Bath time is usually between 5 and 9 pm, dinner time is between 6 and 7.30 pm, breakfast time is between 7 and 8 am.

Hostel Food The food at hostels varies widely: some places provide stodgy and unimaginative fare while others pull out all the stops to offer excellent value. At consecutive hostels in Hokkaidō, you may be served a luscious Jenghis Khan hotpot one night, sukiyaki the next and sashimi the following night – all accompanied by copious complimentary beer.

The hostel breakfast is usually Japanese style, for which it takes a little time to acquire a taste. Many travellers skip *natto* (fermented soybeans), *Nōre* (seaweed) and raw egg and head off in search of a *māningu* set breakfast of coffee, toast and a boiled egg from a nearby coffee shop. It can even work out cheaper doing it this way. Many hostels now allow alcohol on the premises. Some require you to help with the washing-up, others prefer to keep you out of the kitchen.

Reservations Advance reservations are essential for the New Year holiday weeks, March, the late April/early May Golden Week, and July and August. You should state the arrival date and time, number of nights, number and sex of the people for whom beds are to be reserved and the meals required. When corresponding from abroad *always* include two International Reply Coupons.

In Japan, computer bookings can be made in Tokyo and Osaka and increasing numbers of youth hostels are plugging into the system. Many hostels also have fax numbers. For confirmation, return postage-paid postcards are available from post offices or to make things even simpler, use the pre-printed cards available from JYHA headquarters in Tokyo.

Telephone bookings are fine if you can muster enough Japanese. One way to simplify things is to ask a Japanese, perhaps a fellow hosteller or a member of the youth hostel staff, to make the booking for you.

Out of season you can probably get away with booking a day or so in advance. Hostels *definitely* prefer you to phone, even if it's from across the street, rather than simply rolling up without warning. If you arrive without warning, you shouldn't expect any meals.

The one time I turned up on a youth hostel's doorstep unannounced, I received a very sour reception and a long lecture in Japanese about phoning ahead – even though I later discovered that I was the only person staying in a completely empty hostel!

Robert Strauss

Advantages & Disadvantages Youth hostels are comfortable, inexpensive by Japanese standards, and usually good sources of information when used as a base for touring. They are also a good way to meet Japanese travellers and other foreigners. By carefully studying the JYHA handbook, you can select interesting places and weed out possible duds. Many hostels have superb sites: some are farms, remote temples, outstanding private homes or elegant inns.

Some hostels, however, have very early closing hours, often 9 pm, and a routine strongly reminiscent of school or perhaps even prison. In the high season you are likely to encounter waves of school children or throngs of students. Some hostels organise meetings in the evening with games, songs and dances, which any resident gaijin may find difficult to decline. The novelty of these can wear thin. If you are reliant on public transport, access to some youth hostels is complicated and time-consuming.

Shukubō　宿坊
Staying in a shukubō or temple lodging is one way to experience another facet of traditional Japan. Sometimes you are allocated a simple room in the temple precincts and left to your own devices. You may also be allowed to participate in prayers, services or

---

The Japanese Bath

The Japanese bath is another ritual which has to be learnt at an early stage and, like so many other things in Japan, is initially confusing but quickly becomes second nature. The all-important rule for using a Japanese bath is that you wash *outside* the bath and use the bath itself purely for soaking. Getting into a bath unwashed, or equally dreadful, without rinsing all the soap off your body, would be a major error.

Bathing is done in the evening, before dinner; a pre-breakfast bath is thought of as distinctly strange. In a traditional inn there's no possibility of missing bath time, you will be clearly told when it's time to head for *o-furo* (the bath) lest you not be washed in time for dinner! In a traditional inn or a public bath, the bathing facilities will either be communal (but sex segregated) or there will be smaller family bathing facilities for families or couples.

Take off your *yukata* or clothes in the ante-room to the bath and place them in the baskets provided. The bathroom has taps, plastic tubs (wooden ones in very traditional places) and stools along the wall. Draw up a stool to a set of taps and fill the tub from the taps or use the tub to scoop some water out of the bath itself. Sit on the stool and soap yourself. Rinse thoroughly so there's no soap or shampoo left on you, then you are ready to climb into the bath. Soak as long as you can stand the heat, then leave the bath, rinse yourself off again, dry off and don your yukata. ■

zazen meditation. At many temples the meals are vegetarian *(shōjin ryōri).*

The TICs in Tokyo and Kyoto both produce leaflets on temple lodgings in their regions. Kōya-san, a renowned religious centre, includes over 50 shukubō and is one of the best places in Japan to try this type of accommodation.

Over 70 youth hostels are temples or shrines – look for the reverse swastika symbol in the JYHA handbook. The suffix -ji or -in also provides a clue that the hostel is a temple. A few which proved interesting (the number in brackets refers to the JYHA handbook) include: Takayama (4101), Takaoka (3207), Otoyu (7404) and Yoshino (5508).

Toho & Mitsubachi
トーホー・ミツバチ・ライダーハウス
The Toho network is a diverse collection of places which have banded loosely together offering a more flexible alternative to youth hostels at a reasonable price. Most of the 70 places are in Hokkaidō, although there are a few in northern and central Japan. The emphasis seems to be on informal hospitality, outdoor pursuits, and accommodation with original architecture such as log cabins. Some members of Toho function as rider houses *(mitsubachi)* which offer reasonable accommodation to those touring on motorcycles. The main drawback (or attraction for some travellers) of these places is that most of them are difficult to reach. English is rarely spoken.

Prices average ¥3000 per person per night, without meals, or ¥4200 with two meals. A list of Network members is available, in Japanese only, for ¥150 plus postage. The list is published by Mr Shinpei Koshika (☎ 011-271-2668), Sukkarakan, South 3 West 8, Chūō-ku, Sapporo 060, Hokkaidō. You will need to know some Japanese to make the most of this list. An English version of this booklet is reportedly being produced.

Cycling Terminals
サイクリングターミナル
Cycling terminals *(saikuringu tāminaru)* provide low-priced accommodation of the bunk-bed or tatami-mat variety and are usually found in scenic areas suited to cycling. If you don't have your own bike, you can rent one at the terminal.

At around ¥2500 per person per night or ¥4000 including two meals, terminal prices compare favourably with those of a youth hostel. For more information contact the Japan Bicycle Promotion Institute (☎ 03-3583-5444), Nihon Jitensha Kaikan Building, 1-9-3 Akasaka, Minato-ku, Tokyo.

Camping Grounds & Mountain Huts
キャンプ場・山小屋
Camping is one of the cheapest forms of accommodation, but official camping grounds are often only open during the Japanese 'camping season' (July to August), when you can expect an avalanche of students. Facilities range from bare essentials to de luxe. JNTO publishes *Camping in Japan*, a limited selection of camping grounds with details of prices and facilities.

In some restricted areas and national parks, camping wild is forbidden, but elsewhere, foreigners have reported consistent success. Even if there is no officially designated camping ground, campers are often directed to the nearest large patch of grass. Provided you set up camp late in the afternoon and leave early, nobody seems to mind, though it would be common courtesy to ask permission first (assuming you can find the person responsible). Public toilets, usually spotless, and water taps are very common, even in remote parts of Japan.

The best areas for camping are Hokkaidō, the Japan Alps, Tōhoku and Okinawa.

Mountain huts are common in many of the hiking and climbing areas. Unoccupied huts provide a free roof over your head. Other huts, in the Japan Alps for example, are run privately and offer bed and board (two meals) at around ¥5000 per person.

Kokuminshukusha　国民宿舎
Kokuminshukusha (people's lodges) are government institutions offering affordable accommodation in scenic areas. Prices average ¥5500 to ¥6000 per person per night including two meals.

Kokumin Kyūka Mura 国民休暇村

National vacation villages or *kokumin kyūka mura* are also government sponsored and many offer camping or sports facilities in national parks. Prices are similar to those of the people's lodges.

Kaikan 会館

Kaikan (literally 'meeting hall') is hotel-style accommodation sponsored by government or public organisations. Non-members are often accepted. A typical price per person per night is around ¥5500, including two meals.

Minshuku 民宿

A minshuku is usually a family-run private lodging, rather like a B&B in Europe or the USA. Minshuku can be found throughout Japan and offer one way to peep into daily Japanese life. The average price per person per night with two meals is around ¥5500. You are expected to lay out and put away your bedding and bring your own towel.

JNTO publishes a booklet, *Minshukus in Japan*, which lists details of about 300 minshuku. The Japan Minshuku Association (☎ 03-3371-8120), New Pearl Building, Room 201, 2-10-8 Hyakunin-chō, Shinjuku, Tokyo, has a leaflet in English describing the minshuku concept and providing advice on staying at one; a list of minshuku is also available. The Japan Minshuku Center (☎ 03-3216-6556), Tokyo Kotsu Kaikan Building, 21 Yuraku-chō, Chiyoda-ku, Tokyo 100 can help with computer bookings; a similar office operates in Kyoto. Some of the places listed in the Japanese Inn Group's handy little booklet (see the following Ryokan section) are really minshuku rather than ryokan. The line between the two accommodation categories can be fuzzy.

Ryokan 旅館

For a taste of traditional Japanese life, a stay at a ryokan is mandatory (see Staying at a Ryokan). Ryokan range from ultra-exclusive establishments (priced accordingly and available only to guests bearing a personal recommendation) to reasonably priced places with a homey atmosphere, and there are corresponding fluctuations in what you get for your money. Prices start around ¥4200 (per person, per night) for a 'no-frills' ryokan without meals. For a classier ryokan, expect prices to start at ¥8000. The really exclusive establishments – Kyoto is a prime centre for these – will charge ¥25,000 and often much more, if you book way in advance and they like the look of your face.

Ryokan owners prefer to charge on a room and board (breakfast and dinner) per person basis. If, like many foreigners, you find yourself a bit overpowered by the fulsome and unusual offerings of a Japanese breakfast, it should be possible to have dinner only, but in many ryokan, opting out of both meals is unacceptable. The bill is reduced by about 10% if you decline breakfast.

A 10% to 20% service charge is added to your bill. If the total charge for accommodation, food, drink and other services per person per night is ¥10,000 or less, a 3% tax applies – a bill over ¥10,000 attracts 6% tax. Tipping is not expected.

Ryokan Guides & Addresses The Japanese Inn Group (☎ 075-351-6748), c/o Hiraiwa Ryokan, 314 Hayao-chō, Kaminoguchi-agaru, Ninomiyacho-dōri, Shimogyo-ku, Kyoto 600, publishes an excellent listing of inexpensive ryokan, used to foreign guests, with full details on access, prices, facilities and mini-maps for each establishment. Prices start at ¥4200 for a single room without meals.

JNTO publishes the *Japan Ryokan Guide*, a listing of government-registered members of the Japan Ryokan Association (JRA). Prices start around ¥8000 and rise to astronomical heights. JRA produces a trilingual pamphlet called *Enjoy Japanese Home-Life at Ryokan* which uses cartoons and copious text to explain the intricacies of a ryokan stay.

Pensions ペンション

Pensions are usually run by young couples offering Western-style accommodation based on the European pension concept and many offer sports and leisure facilities. They

Staying at a Ryokan

On arrival at the ryokan, you leave your shoes at the entrance steps, don a pair of slippers, and are shown by a maid to your room which has a *tatami* (reed mat) floor. Slippers are taken off before entering tatami rooms. Instead of using numbers, rooms are named after auspicious flowers, plants or trees.

The interior of the room will contain an alcove *(tokonoma)*, probably decorated with a flower display or a calligraphy scroll. One side of the room will contain a cupboard with sliding doors for the bedding; the other side will have sliding screens covered with rice paper and perhaps open onto a veranda with a garden view.

The room maid then serves tea with a sweet on a low table surrounded by cushions *(zabuton)* in the centre of the room. At the same time you are asked to sign the register. A tray is provided with a towel, cotton robe *(yukata)* and belt *(obi)* which you put on before taking your bath. Remember to wear the left side over the right – the reverse order is used for dressing the dead. In colder weather, there will also be an outer jacket *(tanzen)*. Your clothes can be put away in a closet or left on a hanger.

Dressed in your yukata, you will be shown to the bath *(o-furo)*. At some ryokan, there are rooms with private baths, but the communal ones are often designed with 'natural' pools or a window looking out into a garden. Bathing is communal, but sexes are segregated. Make sure you can differentiate between the bathroom signs for men 男 and women 女 – although ryokan used to catering for foreigners will often have signs in English. Many inns will have family bathrooms for couples or families.

Dressed in your yukata after your bath, you return to your room where the maid will have laid out dinner – in some ryokan, dinner is provided in a separate room but you still wear your yukata for dining. Dinner usually includes standard dishes such as miso soup, pickles *(tsukemono)*, vegetables in vinegar *(sunomono)*, hors d'oeuvres *(zensai)*, fish – either grilled or raw (sashimi), and perhaps tempura and a stew. There will also be bowls for rice, dips and sauces. Depending on the price, meals at a ryokan can become flamboyant displays of local cuisine or refined arrangements of *kaiseki* (a cuisine which obeys strict rules of form and etiquette for every detail of the meal and setting).

After dinner, while you are pottering around or out for a stroll admiring the garden, the maid will clear the dishes and prepare your bedding. A mattress is placed on the tatami floor and a quilt put on top. In colder weather, you can also add a blanket *(mōfu)*.

In the morning, the maid will knock to make sure you are awake and then come in to put away the bedding before serving breakfast – sometimes this is served in a separate room. Breakfast usually consists of pickles, dried seaweed *(nori)*, raw egg, dried fish, miso soup and rice. It can take a while for foreign stomachs to accept this novel fare early in the morning.

The Japanese tendency is to make the procedure at a ryokan seem rather rarefied for foreign comprehension and some ryokan are wary of accepting foreign guests. However, once you've grasped the basics, it really isn't that hard to fit in. ■

are common in rural areas. Pensions seem to specialise in quaint names like Pension Fruit Juice, Pension Pheasant or Pension Morning Salada and often have decidedly quaint

---

Shoes & Slippers

Knowing which shoes to wear in a Japanese inn can initially be very confusing, but is a good thing to learn early on. Seeing *gaijin* take off their shoes as they arrive reassures the inn-keeper that they know what they're doing and will not make some truly awful faux pas like using soap in the bath.

When you enter a traditional inn there will be a *genkan*, a step up from street level, where you remove your shoes and put on slippers. There will usually be a series of pigeonholes where your shoes are stored and a large basket of assorted size slippers for you to select from. In the evening, the slippers will be lined up along the step, waiting for returning guests and new arrivals. In the morning, the process is reversed and guests' shoes will be lined up on the street side of the step. The sight of large numbers of waiting slippers is a good clue that an otherwise unidentified (in English at least) building is actually an inn of some type.

Wearing the slippers, you can now proceed to your room but must remove them again at the door, or on a small standing area just inside your room. You now go barefoot or in socks on the tatami matting which covers the floor. Further complications await if you head for the toilet, as there'll be another pair of slippers just inside the door for use only in that room. Toilet slippers are usually some garish colour, making it immediately obvious that you have committed a grave misdeed if you forget to change back to the regular slippers afterwards!

Shoes outside, slippers inside, bare or socked feet in your room and toilet slippers in the toilet still does not encompass all the possibilities. Some inns will provide wooden sandals or the traditional *geta* sandals at the front door so you can make short trips out of the inn without having to use your own shoes. In *onsen* (spa towns) or other holiday centres many guests will, after their evening bath, wander the town wearing their *yukata* (cotton robes) but shoes simply do not look right with a yukata; geta are far more appropriate. If there's a garden to wander in, yet another pair of sandals for that area may be awaiting you. ∎

---

décor as well, sometimes like a romantic Japanese dream of a European country cottage.

Prices average ¥6000 per person per night or ¥8500 including two meals. Food is often excellent, typically a French dinner and an American breakfast. JNTO publishes *Pensions in Japan*, a selection of pensions all over Japan.

Capsule Hotels カプセルホテル

In the '70s, the Japanese architect Kurokawa Kisho, came up with the idea of modifying a shipping container to hold a bed, bath and all 'mod cons'. A site was found for his construction which can still be seen in Tokyo's Ginza area.

Capsule hotels *(capseru hoteru)* have reduced the original concept to a capsule measuring two metres by one metre by one metre – about the size of a coffin. Inside is a bed, a TV, reading light, radio and alarm clock. Personal belongings are kept in a locker room.

This type of hotel is common in the major cities and often caters to travellers who have partied too hard to make it home or have missed the last train. There are a few for women only, but the majority are only for men. Some capsule hotels have the added attraction of a sauna.

An average price is ¥3800 per night or ¥1400 for a three hour stay. You could try one as a novelty, but it's not an experience recommended to those who easily become claustrophobic.

Business Hotels ビジネスホテル

These are economical and practical places geared to the single traveller, usually lesser-ranking business types who want somewhere close to the station. Rooms are clean, Western style, just big enough for you to turn around in and include a miniature bath/WC unit. A standard fitting for the overstressed businessman is a coin-operated TV with a porno channel. Vending machines replace room service.

Cheap single rooms can sometimes be found for ¥4500, though the average rate is

A Night in Capsuleland

My one experience of a capsule hotel was at Capsuleland in Fukuoka and, like much else in Japan, it was initially a little bewildering. Shoes were left at the entrance, just like in a traditional Japanese inn, but there the similarity ended. There was no space to take anything (apart from myself) into the capsule – a locker room was available for clothes and personal effects and, at the entrance, larger secondary lockers for bigger bags.

In the locker was a pair of pyjamas, emblazoned with the hotel's logo. Most of the other inmates seemed to wear their pyjamas all the time both in the hotel and outside in the neighbouring streets. (When I returned to the hotel later in the evening I realised I was getting close when, still a block or two away, I began to see men in blue and yellow short pyjamas!)

The hotel had a coffee bar, restaurant, TV lounge, sauna, massage room, toilets, washing facilities and a large communal bath. The capsules didn't lock (all my valuables were supposedly in the locker), and there was just a screen to pull down at the entrance. The capsule was exactly the length and width of the mattress but, also squeezed in, was a small shelf, a light, controls for a radio, alarm and the air-con and, mounted in the 'ceiling' of the capsule, a TV set complete with the obligatory porno channel. The capsules were stacked two high but were surprisingly quiet and, since the lighting was all artificial and there was no way of telling day from night, I slept way past my normal waking time.

Tony Wheeler

around ¥6000; some business hotels also have twin rooms. Cheaper business hotels usually do not have a service charge, though places costing ¥7000 or more often add a 10% charge.

The Japan Business Hotel Association at 43 Kanda-Higashi, Matsusita-chō, Chiyoda-ku, Tokyo, publishes the *Business Hotel Guide*, a handy pamphlet which lists business hotels throughout Japan along with phone numbers, prices, addresses and access details. Ask for a copy at JNTO or TIC. The Japanese version is useful if you need to give directions to a taxi driver – match up the phone numbers in the Japanese and English

versions. Popular business hotel chains include Green Hotel found near so many railway stations, Sun Route, Washington, Tōkyū Inns and Hokke Club. The Hokke Club hotels are unusual in their conveniently early check-in and late checkout times. Most Japanese hotels kick you out by 10 or 11 am and won't let you check in until 3 or 4 pm.

Hotels ホテル
De luxe and 1st class hotels offering the usual array of frills and comforts have sprung up in most of Japan's major cities and are comparable to the best in the USA and Europe. Singles start around ¥7500 and rise

to a cool ¥20,000 or way beyond if you fancy a suite. The Japan Hotel Association has 389 government-registered members, all neatly listed in an informative JNTO leaflet, *Hotels in Japan*.

Some of the leading hotel chains, such as ANA Hotels, Holiday Inns, The New Otani Hotels, Prince Hotels and Tōkyū Hotels have overseas offices. Bookings can also be made through the overseas offices of major Japanese travel agencies such as Japan Travel Bureau (JTB), Kintetsu International, Tokyu Tourist Corporation, Nippon Travel Agency (NTA) and Japan Air Lines (JAL). Most of these agencies also have schemes for discount hotel coupons such as JTB's 'Sunrise Super Saver', NTA's 'NTA Hotel Pass' or JAL's 'Room & Rail'.

Expect to pay 10% or more as a service charge plus a 3% consumer tax; add another 3% local tax if the bill exceeds ¥10,000. Asking for separate bills for meals can sometimes reduce the tax paid.

Love Hotels   ラブホテル

Love hotels are one of the wild cards in Japanese accommodation. Their primary function is to serve as a short-time base for couples to enjoy some privacy. Customers are not necessarily singles in search of sex; the hotels are also used by married couples who often lack space at home for relaxing together.

To find one on the street, just look for flamboyant facades with rococo architecture, turrets, battlements and imitation statuary. The design of the hotels emphasises discretion: entrances and exits are kept separate; keys are provided through a small opening without contact between desk clerk and guest; photos of the rooms are displayed to make the choice easy for the customer. There's often a discreetly curtained parking area so your car cannot be seen once inside.

The rooms can fulfil most fantasies with themes ranging from harem extravaganza to sci-fi. Further choices can include vibrating beds, wall-to-wall mirrors, bondage equipment and video recorders to recall the experience (don't forget to take the video cassette with you when you leave).

Charges on an hourly basis are at a peak during the day and early evening. Love hotels are of more interest to foreign visitors after 10 pm, when it's possible to stay the night for about ¥5000 per room (rather than per person), but you should check out early enough in the morning to avoid a return to peak-hour rates. Outside love hotels there will usually be a sign in Japanese (occasionally in English) announcing the rates for a 'rest' (usually two hours) or a 'stay' (overnight).

Long-Term Accommodation

If you're intending to stay longer in Japan, a job offer which appears lucrative at first sight may seem markedly less so when you work out your rent and other living costs. Ideally, you can avoid many hassles by negotiating decent accommodation as part of your work contract.

If at all possible, get a Japanese to help you with your search and negotiations since Japanese landlords are notoriously wary of foreign tenants and often prefer to do business with a local go-between. If you are on good terms with a Japanese friend, this person may offer to act as a *hoshō-nin* (guarantor). This represents considerable commitment and the guarantor's *hanko* (seal) is usually required on your rental contract.

A pitfall which is often overlooked is that you may have to lay out four, possibly as much as seven months' rent *in advance*. For starters, there's one to two months' rent payable as *reikin* (key money). This is nonrefundable and a form of extortion to line the wallets of landlords. Then there's a *shikikin* (damage deposit) of one to three months' rent. This is refundable at a later date as long as both sides agree there's no damage. Avoid later squabbles over shikikin by making duplicate inventories, signed by both parties, before you move in. The *fudōsan-ya* (estate agent) will of course want *tesūryō* – one month's rent as a non-refundable handling fee. Finally, you have to pay *maekin* which is one month's rent in advance and is also non-refundable.

These high up-front costs are cogent reasons why foreigners looking for long-term employment in Japan should arrive with a sizeable financial float. This will allow more time to choose a decent job and avoid the scenario – assuming your stay was mostly motivated by financial gain – of leaving Japan with very little to show for your stay and an embittered feeling about the place.

Standard contracts often run for two years and some *ōya-san* (landowners) may require the additional payment of maintenance fees and fire insurance. When *kōshin* (renewal) comes up, you should expect a raise in your *yachin* (monthly rent). When you decide to move on, make absolutely sure you give notice *at least* one month in advance. Otherwise you will be landed with payment of an extra month's rent.

What to Look For It's usually best for budget travellers to find their feet in a gaijin house before putting out feelers for other accommodation. Inner city rentals are obviously high, as are those for chic suburban areas. Commuting costs often reduce the apparent gain of lower rental costs outside town and you may not like your nightlife being curtailed by transport timetables.

At the top end of the housing market are *manshon* which are modern concrete condominiums or rental apartments. At the lower end are *danchi*, functional concrete blocks of public flats, which are sought after by those with moderate or low incomes.

Japanese are often amazed at the spaciousness of Western housing since the average Japanese family in the city makes do with much less space in their apartment. If you want a house or apartment similar to urban sizes in the West, you can expect to pay several million yen a month.

In major cities like Tokyo and Kyoto, gaijin houses are the cheapest options for long-term stays, but you should be prepared for basic dorms or shared tatami rooms and a communal kitchen. Prices for the cheapest houses start around ¥1600 per night. If you negotiate for a monthly price, you may be able to reduce the rent to ¥30,000 per month.

Once you move up a bracket to your own room with separate facilities (kitchen, bathroom) in an apartment with easy access to the city centre, you can expect monthly rental to start around ¥55,000. If you share facilities in this type of set-up with one other flat mate, the monthly rental is about ¥10,000 cheaper.

Where to Look There are several methods to hunt for housing – it depends what you want and how long you intend to stay.

Asking other foreigners at work or play in schools, clubs, bars, gaijin houses, etc is one way of locating long-term accommodation. If you strike it really lucky, you may find somebody leaving the country or moving on who is willing to dump their job contacts, housing and effects in one friendly package.

Notice boards are another good source and are often found at tourist information offices, international clubs, conversation clubs, etc. Even if there's nothing on the board, ask someone in charge for a few tips.

Regional and city magazines aimed at foreigners often have classified ads offering or seeking accommodation. For Tokyo, you should look at *Tokyo Journal* or *Weekender*; for the Kansai area (Osaka, Kōbe, Kyoto, Nara) you should peruse *Kansai Time Out*; and further afield in Ishikawa Prefecture (Kanazawa for example) you could buy *Suimairu-Ishikawa* which is a monthly magazine devoted to house rental. There are plenty of other magazines all over Japan with suitable ads. TIC or the local tourist office should know which publications are best, particularly if you decide to live somewhere more remote like Hokkaidō or Okinawa.

Newspapers also have classified ads for rentals. The Friday edition of the *Japan Times* is a good example. If you want to get an idea of long-term accommodation costs before travelling to Japan, pick up a copy of this edition. JNTO offices and Japanese embassies usually have back copies lying around.

Common abbreviations in rental ads

include K – kitchen, D – dining room, L – living room, UB – unit bath (combined bath and toilet). An ad specifying 3LDK, for example, means three bedrooms and one living room combined with dining kitchen. The size of rooms is usually given in standard tatami mat measurements, known as *jō*. There are several tatami sizes, but as a general rule of thumb, one tatami mat equals one jō which is 1.8 metres by 0.9 metres (1.62 sq metres). A room decribed as being 4.5 jō, for example, is 7.29 sq metres: a medium-sized room by Japanese standards but poky by Western standards.

Using a fudōsan-ya (estate agent) is the most expensive option and really only feasible if you intend to stay a long time and need to determine exactly the type and location of your housing. English-language magazines such as *Tokyo Journal* and *Kansai Time Out* carry ads from estate agents specialising in accommodation for foreigners.

Additional Costs Before you sign your contract, ask the landlord for precise details about gas, electricity and water. Check if a telephone is already installed since installation of a new telephone is a costly business. You can expect to pay around ¥75,000 but you've then purchased the right to have a phone line anywhere in Japan. This right is negotiable, either privately or through private agencies which deal in phone rights. If you move and want to take your phone line with you, the charge for transferral is around ¥13,000.

Japan is introducing schemes for recycling garbage: in some cities residents are asked to separate it into *moeru-gomi* (burnable), *moenai-gomi* (non-burnable), and *shigen-gomi* (recyclable). If you hear a noisy truck grinding through your area with a loudspeaker announcing 'chirigami kōkan', your area will have a system to save used newspapers and magazines. In return for your used newspapers and magazines, you will be given rolls of toilet paper and garbage liners.

FOOD

With its obvious influence on nouvelle cuisine, Japanese food has been receiving more and more attention from food connoisseurs in the West over recent years. Japanese restaurants are becoming increasingly common in Western cities, and consequently more Westerners are coming to Japan with some idea of what to expect.

It is unlikely, however, that Japanese restaurants outside Japan could possibly prepare the visitor for the sheer diversity of cuisine inside Japan. For one, there is an enormous range of regional cuisines, some of which are variations on Japanese standards and others unique to the localities in which they're found. The Japanese are also adept at modifying foreign dishes and making them their own; the pizza you order at the little 'Italian' place on the corner in Tokyo will probably be unlike any pizza you've had before.

This diversity in Japanese cuisine is increasing as Japanese eating habits, like everything else in Japan, continue to change in response to foreign influences. A Japanese today is just as likely to breakfast on toast or cereal as on the traditional breakfast of pickles and watery rice. A Japanese lunch might be anything from pasta, to Chinese noodles, to a British pub meal. Many young Japanese claim they can't eat rice and say that they'd rather have McDonald's for dinner than sushi.

The Western influence on Japanese eating habits began just before the turn of the century. From the 7th century through to this time the Japanese were not eaters of red meat, restricting their diet, in accordance with Japanese Buddhist precepts, to rice, fish and vegetables. The change came with the Meiji Restoration, when meat-eating was embraced, along with a vast range of other barbaric practices, as part of the national policy of strengthening Japan. The reasoning was, that if the Japanese were to become as strong as the barbarians apparently poised to overrun their country, they would have to adopt, among other things, the barbarians' carnivorous ways.

Today, in the big cities, almost any cuisine that takes your fancy is available. Outside these centres, the only non-Japanese food you're likely to come across is the occasional Chinese restaurant or a McDonald's, Kentucky Fried Chicken or Shakey's Pizza. Fast food has taken off in a big way across Japan, but to be honest it's not such a great bargain. Usually the Chinese noodle shops will give you a healthier and cheaper meal than the fast-food outlets.

If you're on a real budget, many of the coffee shops do very good set breakfasts, known as *māningu sābisu* (morning service) from around ¥350. They generally include two pieces of incredibly thick toast, a dollop of jam and butter, a hard-boiled egg, a small salad and a cup of coffee. For lunch, a noodle or *soba* shop will fill you up for around ¥450. For dinner, you may have to push your budget up to around ¥700 to ¥800 for a decent meal to include both meat and vegetables.

The bakeries which are found everywhere in Japan (there's almost always one in larger railway stations) are another good place for an economical breakfast or a cheap snack at any time of day. They often have tables and chairs or a bar so you can have a cup of coffee or cold drink with your baked goods.

Even within this fairly basic price range, there will usually be an enormous selection of restaurants and cuisines to choose from. Because of the long hours they work, many Japanese are forced to eat most of their meals outside. Consequently, railway stations, business districts and shopping areas will usually have a large number of fast and reasonably priced restaurants.

Unlike Japanese restaurants in the West, Japanese restaurants in Japan tend to specialise in a particular kind of dish or cuisine. The following sections describe some of the restaurants and dishes you are likely to encounter in Japan.

Okonomiyaki   お好み焼き

This is an inexpensive Japanese cuisine, somewhat like a pancake or omelette with anything that's lying around in the kitchen thrown in. The dish is usually prepared by the diner on a hotplate on the table. Typical ingredients include vegetables, pork, beef and prawns.

Rāmen   ラーメン

This is a Chinese cuisine that has been taken over by the Japanese and made their own. These restaurants are generally the cheapest places to fill yourself up in Japan. Rāmen dishes are big bowls of noodles in a chicken stock with vegetables and or meat and are priced from around ¥400 upwards.

chāshūmen   チャーシューメン
   rāmen with roasted pork
gomokumen   五目メン
   rāmen with a combination of five ingredients (meat, egg and vegetables)
gyōza   餃子
   Chinese fried meat and vegetable dumpling
miso rāmen   みそラーメン
   rāmen with miso

Soba   そば

This is a traditional Tokyo noodle dish, made with buckwheat noodles. The noodles come in a hot or cold fish-stock soup with various other ingredients.

kake soba   かけそば
   soba with slices of spring onion
tempura soba   天ぷらそば
   soba with tempura – prawns and vegetable
kamo-namban   かもなんばんそば
   soba with spring onion and chicken
kitsune soba   きつねそば
   soba with thinly sliced tōfu
tsukimi soba   月見そば
   soba with a raw egg on top (literally 'moon viewing')

Udon   うどん

This Osaka dish is similar to soba, except that the noodles are white and thicker.

kake-udon   かけうどん
   udon with spring onions
kamo-namban   かもなんばんうどん
   udon with chicken and spring onions

nabeyaki-udon なべやきうどん
  udon with tempura

Sukiyaki & Shabu-Shabu
すき焼き・しゃぶしゃぶ
Restaurants usually specialise in both these dishes. Sukiyaki is generally cooked on the table in front of the diner. It is prepared by cooking thinly sliced beef, vegetables and tōfu in a slightly sweetened soya sauce broth. The difference between sukiyaki and shabu-shabu is in the broth that is used. Shabu-shabu is made with a stock-based broth.

Sushi

Sushi & Sashimi 寿司・刺身
These are probably the most famous of Japanese dishes. The difference between them is that sashimi is thin slivers of raw fish served with soy sauce and *wasabi* (hot horseradish), while for sushi, the raw fish is set atop a small pillow of lightly vinegared rice.

amaebi 甘海老
  sweet prawn (raw)
awabi あわび
  abalone
ebi 海老
  prawn or shrimp
hamachi はまち
  yellowtail
ika いか
  squid
ikura いくら
  salmon roe
kappa maki かっぱ巻
  cucumber in *norimaki* (seaweed roll)

maguro まぐろ
  tuna
tai 鯛
  sea bream
tamago たまご
  sweetened egg
toro とろ
  fatty tuna
uni うに
  sea urchin roe

Tempura 天ぷら
This dish has controversial origins, some maintaining that it is a Portuguese import. Tempura is what fish & chips might have been – fluffy, non-greasy batter and delicate, melt-in-your mouth portions of fish, prawns and vegetables.

Yakitori 焼き鳥
Various parts of the chicken, skewered on a stick and cooked over a charcoal fire. Yakitori is great drinking food and the restaurants will serve beer and sake with the food. Some common yakitori dishes:

kawa かわ
  chicken skin
negima ねぎま
  chicken and spring onion
piiman ピーマン
  green capsicum
rebā レバー
  liver
sei-niku せいにく
  dark chicken meat
sasami ささみ
  chicken breast
tsukune つくね
  chicken meat balls

Robatayaki/Izakaya ろばた焼き／居酒屋
Robatayaki or izakaya restaurants are celebrated as the noisiest in the world. Enter and you will be hailed by a chorus of welcoming *irasshaimases*, as if you were some long-lost relative. Orders are made by shouting. The food, a variety of things including seafood, tōfu and vegetables, is cooked over a grill. Again, this is a drinking cuisine. Both

sashimi and yakitori are popular robatayaki dishes – others include:

agedashi-dōfu 揚げとうふ
  deep fried tōfu in a fish-stock soup
jagabatā じゃがバター
  potatoes grilled with butter
niku-jaga 肉じゃが
  cooked meat and potato
shio-yaki 塩焼き
  a whole fish grilled with salt
tōmorokoshi とうもろこし
  corn on the cob
yaki-onigiri 焼きおにぎり
  broiled rice balls

When Japan was getting me down, a robatayaki was always my favourite choice of a place to eat. The noisy bonhomie may simply be part of the background décor but it certainly made me feel better. The food was familiar and recognisable, and ordering was never any problem at all as everything was either out on view and you could simply point or the menu was illustrated.

Tony Wheeler

Nabemono 鍋物
This winter cuisine consists of a stew cooked in a heavy earthenware pot. Like sukiyaki, it is a dish cooked on the table in front of the diner.

Unagi うなぎ
This is Japanese for 'eel'. Cooked Japanese style, over hot coals and brushed with soy sauce and sweet sake, this is a popular and delicious dish.

Kaiseki 懐石料理
The origins of kaiseki are in the tea ceremony, where a number of light and aesthetically prepared morsels would accompany the proceedings. True kaiseki is *very* expensive – the diner is paying for the whole experience, the traditional setting and so on.

Etiquette
When it comes to eating in Japan, there are quite a number of implicit rules, but they're fairly easy to remember. If you're worried

Fugu ふぐ
Only the Japanese could make a culinary speciality out of a dish which could kill you. The fugu, pufferfish or globefish, puffs itself up into an almost spherical shape to deter its enemies. Its delicate flesh is highly esteemed and traditionally served in carefully arranged fans of thinly sliced segments. Eat the wrong part of the humble pufferfish, however, and you drop dead. It's said a slight numbness of the lips indicates you were close to the most exciting meal of your life, but fugu fish chefs are carefully licensed, and losing customers is not encouraged. Every year there are a few deaths from pufferfish poisoning but they're usually from home-prepared fish.

Fugu can only be eaten for a few months each year and the very best fugu restaurants, places which specialise in nothing else, close down for the rest of the year. It's said that the fugu chef who loses a customer is honour bound to take his own life. ■

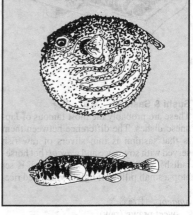

about putting your foot in it, relax – the Japanese almost expect foreigners to make fools of themselves in formal situations and are unlikely to be offended as long as you follow the standards of politeness of your own country.

Among the more important eating 'rules' are those regarding chopsticks. Sticking them upright in your rice is considered very bad form, that's how rice is offered to the dead! So is passing food from your chopsticks to someone else's – another Buddhist death rite involves passing the bones of the cremated deceased among members of the family using chopsticks.

When eating with other people, the general practice is to preface actually digging into the food with the expression *itadakimasu*, literally 'I will receive'. Similarly, at the end of the meal someone will probably say *gochisōsama deshita*, a respectful way of saying that the meal was good and satisfying. When it comes to drinking, remember that you're expected to keep the drinks of your fellow drinkers topped up. Don't fill your own glass: wait for someone to do this for you.

In Japan, there is a definite etiquette to bill-paying. If someone invites you to eat or drink with them, they will be paying. Even among groups eating together it is unusual for bills to be split. Generally, at the end of the meal, something of a struggle will ensue to see who gets the privilege of paying the bill. If this happens, it is polite to at least make an effort to pay the bill – it is extremely unlikely that your Japanese 'hosts' will acquiesce. Exceptions to this rule are likely among young Japanese such as students.

When eating Japanese food, it's worth considering that a great deal of effort has gone into its preparation; don't pour soya sauce over it and mix it up with your chopsticks. The accompanying sauces are for dipping food into. Finally, don't forget to slurp your noodles: the Japanese claim that it enhances the flavour.

Chopsticks Nowadays, more and more Westerners are getting used to the idea of chopsticks, which is just as well because you're going to have a hard time in Japan if you don't learn how to use them. The Japanese, for the most part, remain convinced that foreigners are unable to use *hashi*, as chopsticks are known in Japan, and dextrous wielding of this wooden 'cutlery' will invariably prompt admiring exclamations of *Jōzu nē!* ('So skilful!') from nearby diners.

Japanese chopsticks are longer than their Chinese equivalents and are pointed. Almost every restaurant uses disposable wooden chopsticks, although, at last, there seems to be a move away from the use of these due to ecological considerations. If you feel strongly about this, travel with your own chopsticks.

Ordering Ordering at a Japanese restaurant is made easier by the fact that many restaurants display plastic replicas of their dishes in the front window. Rather than point randomly at an indecipherable menu, you can drag one of the serving staff outside and point to the dish in the window. Another alternative is to ask what's recommended: *o-susume wa nan desuka?*

Eating on the Cheap
Like anywhere else, the cheapest way to fill yourself up in Japan is to cook for yourself. Unfortunately, however, apart from some youth hostels, there are not many places where you can do this.

Non-vegetarians will be pleased to hear that meat is not always as horrendously expensive in Japan as outsiders are led to believe. If you are cooking your own food and can abstain from *biifu* (beef), buying meat needn't leave you particularly out of pocket. One of the best options is to go to the meat section of one of the department store food halls and ask for *ramu* (lamb). Lamb is not a very popular meat with the Japanese and consequently is very cheap. The other cheap option is pork *(buta-niku)*. As most meat is either stir-fried or cooked in broths it's most likely to come chopped or very thinly sliced.

Yasaiya (vegetable shops) can be found on almost every street corner of the more suburban areas. Prices are generally quite reasonable.

For the real shoestring traveller, another popular eating alternative is the bakery. The Japanese don't seem to like eating their crusts – sandwiches and slices of bread are served with these horrid, chewy appurtenances neatly trimmed off. This means that if you ask for *pan no mimi* at the bakery you can buy yourself a whole bag of crusts for next to nothing. If you get fed up with your diet of crusts, you can always spend a pleasant afternoon at the park feeding the ducks.

Cheapest of all is to eat for free. Every supermarket and department store food floor seems to be continuously offering sample titbits and a judicious circuit will often provide some interesting free snacks!

DRINKS
Nonalcoholic Drinks
Most of the drinks you're used to at home, or at least varieties of them anyway, will be available in Japan. One convenient aspect of pounding city footpaths, especially in warm weather, is the ubiquitous drink-dispensing machine. These have everything from hot coffee to that favourite soft drink, Pocari Sweat.

Coffee Coffee drinkers will find travelling in Japan difficult at times. Although there will be a coffee shop on every second street corner, in most instances the coffee they serve up is bitter and expensive – from ¥350 to ¥450 a cup. True, many of the machines dispensing drinks will provide the caffeine addict with a quick fix – but have you ever tried drinking hot coffee from a can? For one, how do you hold it? Two, how do you stop your lips getting stuck to the hot metal surface every time you take an anguished sip? Fortunately, a few chains of cheap coffee shops have opened up in the bigger cities. The most popular of these is Doutor; coffee here (five or six varieties) sells for ¥190. The fast-food chains, Mister Donut for

example, are also a good place for a cheap cup of coffee.

Tea & Other Drinks Of course, as everyone knows, the Japanese are tea drinkers. Unlike the tea Westerners drink, Japanese tea is green and does not contain caffeine. As a visit to the tea section of any Japanese department store will show, Japanese tea comes in a variety of forms: among these green leaf, ground green leaf and green leaf with bits of rice in it. During the summer many Japanese drink *mugicha*, a cold barley water drink.

Alcohol
Japanese culture features a serious interest in drinking and, unlike most other Asian countries, drinking is a popular pastime for both sexes. It is routinely taken to excess, presumably as a release from the straitjacket of proper conduct at work. Office workers are expected to join their group boozing sessions to promote bonding inside the group.

By 11 pm in most major Japanese cities, it can seem that everyone on the streets is in various stages of inebriation. Fortunately, the Japanese are fairly good-natured drunks and it's extremely rare to see any trouble – though it does happen, especially in the hot summer months. A recent survey estimated that around 12% of the male population gets drunk every day, while nearly 70% get drunk once a week. Drunkenness is readily tolerated as an excuse for bad behaviour, but for those foolish enough to drink and drive, the police enforce very strict penalties.

Hangovers
In Japan, just as in the West, hangovers *(futsukayoi)* have their popular remedies. Salted plums *(umeboshi)* in green tea *(sencha)* are one tip for the morning after. Tea made from boiled cloves is also used. Another herbal cure, recommended in rural Tōhoku, requires a handful of *senburi* (a herb) to be steeped for three hours in a cup of hot water – the resulting brew is revoltingly bitter. Less punishing options are a bowl of *rāmen* noodles, rice soup *(ochazuke)* or persimmons *(kaki)*.

Finally, if herbal cures don't help, you can always try evoking sympathy from the Japanese by cradling your head in your hands and moaning *Kino o nomisugimashita* ('Yesterday, I drank too much')!

Robert Strauss

Beer Introduced at the end of the last century, beer is now the favourite tipple of the Japanese. The quality is generally excellent and the most popular type is a light lager. The major brewers are Asahi, Suntory, Sapporo and Kirin. Beer is dispensed everywhere, from vending machines to beer halls and even in temple lodgings.

A standard can of beer from a vending machine is about ¥220; elsewhere the price of your beer starts around ¥500 and climbs upwards depending on the establishment. Draught beer *(nama biiru)* is widely available and imported beers are common.

Sake Rice wine is a Japanese staple which has been brewed for centuries. Once restricted to imperial brewers, it was later produced at temples and shrines across the country. In recent years, consumption of beer has overtaken that of sake, but it's still a standard item in homes, in restaurants and in drinking dens. Large casks of sake are often seen piled up as offerings outside a shrine or temple and it plays a part in most celebrations or festivals. Although sake doesn't have quite the cultural significance that wine does in the West, it is still taken very seriously by many Japanese.

It takes about 20 days to ferment the brew from water, rice and malted rice. Ageing is not considered important for sake and most is drunk soon after processing.

There are cloudy, white and unrefined types of sake, but the commonest form is the clear one. The three grades of sake in descending order are *tokkyū* (premium), *ikkyū* (first grade) and *nikyū* (second grade). The latter is the routine choice. There is a further division of these grades into *karakuchi* (dry) and *amakuchi* (sweet). Apart from national brewing giants, there are thousands of provincial brewers producing local brew *(jizake)*.

Sake is usually served *atsukan* (warm) but may be served *hiyazake* (cold) or *reishū* as a summer drink with ice. A different way to sample it cold, is in *masu* (little wooden boxes, traditionally used as measures) with a pinch of salt on the corner of the box. When served warm, sake enters the bloodstream extra fast – so don't underestimate its average alcohol content of 17%, which is slightly stronger than wine.

A variety of containers (ceramic pots, glass jars and bottles) are used, but bars and restaurants favour the slim, clay flask *tokkuri*, holding 180 ml, which usually costs around ¥250 and provides several servings in miniature cups *(sakazuki)*. The flask and cups are sold in decorative sets which make inexpensive gifts. And remember, custom dictates that you never eat rice at the same time as you drink sake.

Shōchū For those looking for a quick and cheap escape route from the world of sorrows, *shōchū* is the answer. It's a distilled spirit (averaging 30% alcohol content) which has been resurrected from its previous low-class esteem – it was used as disinfectant in the Edo period – to the status of a trendy drink. You can drink it as *oyuwari* (with hot water) or as a highball *chūhai* (with soda and lemon). A bottle (720 ml) sells for about ¥600 which makes it a relatively cheap option compared to other spirits.

Wine, Imported Drinks & Whisky Japanese wines are available from areas such as Yamanashi Prefecture, Nagano Prefecture, Hokkaidō and Tōhoku. Standard wines are often blended with imports from South America or Eastern Europe. The major producers are Suntory, Mann's and Mercian. Prices are expensive – expect to pay at least ¥1000 for a bottle of something drinkable.

Imported wines are often stocked by large liquor stores or department stores in the cities. Bargains are sometimes available at around ¥600, but most of the imports cost considerably more.

Prices for imported spirits such as brandy or cognac have been elevated to absurd levels by market gouging and customer pretentiousness. If you want imported spirits for your own consumption or as gifts, the simplest thing is to make full use of your duty-free allowance when entering Japan.

Whisky is available in most drinking

establishments and is usually drunk *mizu-wari* (with water) or *onzarokku* (on ice). Local brands, such as Suntory or Nikka, are sensibly priced and most measure up to foreign standards. The price of imported whisky reflects exploitation of the snob appeal of foreign labels. Expensive foreign labels are popular as gifts, since the greater the cost of the gift, the higher the esteem in which the recipient is held.

Drinking Customs The usual form when drinking in company is to fill your companion's glass and allow your own glass to be filled by your companion. Raise your glass slightly while it is being filled. Once everyone's glass has been filled, the usual starting signal is a chorus of *kampai!* which means 'cheers!'. Constant topping up means you can be faced with a bottomless glass – just put your hand over the glass if you've had enough.

The Japanese make a habit of paying the bill for their foreign friends, particularly if they wish to make an impression or the acquaintance is slight. The custom of *warikan* (each person paying his own share) is common in a group where everyone knows each other well.

Drinking Places What you pay for your drink depends on where you drink, what you drink and who (a hostess) helps you drink it. Appearances can be misleading: swanky establishments imply high prices, but it is also quite possible for an outwardly drab-looking place to cater to an exclusive clientele who pay the requisite fortune. Avoid the painful shock of an unexpectedly hefty bill by asking about prices and cover charges *before* sitting down.

Izikaya and *yakitori-ya* are establishments with reasonable prices for standard drinks (beer, shōchū or whisky) and food in a casual atmosphere resembling that of a pub. *Aka-chōchin*, which display a 'red lantern' outside the premises, are similar pubs for the working man – down-to-earth in price and décor.

In the summer, many department stores open up beer gardens on the roof. They are a popular spot to cool off with an inexpensive beer. Beer halls are affordable and popular places to swill your beer in the German tradition. The bars which are found in their hundreds jammed into tiny rooms on floor after floor of large buildings are often used by customers as a type of club – if you drop in without introduction from a regular, the reception may be cool.

In many bars you may find yourself paying for *otsumami* (charms), which are minute snacks often served without being requested. To encourage regular patronage, bars also operate the 'keep bottle' system – you buy a bottle and keep it at the bar to consume whenever you visit. Apart from the initial cost of the bottle, you will also have to pay an 'ice charge' when you have a drink from your bottle.

Hostess bars are invariably expensive, often exorbitant. They cater mainly to those entertaining on business accounts. Hostesses pamper customers with compliments or bend a sympathetic ear to their problems. The best way to visit is in the company of a Japanese friend who knows the routine – and may pick up the tab.

Japan, of course, is also the origin of the now ubiquitous karaoke bar. If you've never sung in a karaoke bar, it's worth trying at least once, though after that, the experience might seem a bit empty. Customers sing to the accompaniment of taped music and, as the evening wears on, voices get progressively more ragged. Sobbingly mournful *enka* (folk ballads) are the norm, though foreigners might find tapes of *My Way* or *Let it Be* to exercise their vocal chords.

ENTERTAINMENT

Japan has a reputation as a country brimming with entertainment establishments that present their clients with bills that would go a long way to financing Operation Desert Storm. Such bars exist. They are generally a modern manifestation of Japan's traditional geisha culture. It's unlikely that you will inadvertently wander into any such places, and in most cases if you don't look like you can foot the bill at the end of the night you'll be politely turned away at the door.

Expensive hostess bars are not the whole picture, however. Most large Japanese cities have numerous bars with affordable prices that attract an interesting mixture of local foreigners and residents. These are often the best places to meet Japanese – it only takes a couple of drinks for most Japanese to let their guard down and drop their customary distancing politeness.

Japan is also the best place in Asia to catch up with movies and live music. The only drawback is the expense involved. Cinema tickets, for example, range from ¥1800 to ¥2000, which probably makes Japan the most expensive place in the world to catch a movie. Live music prices are also high, ranging from around ¥1500 for a local act to ¥6000 and upwards for international stars. Unless you are in Japan for a long stint (or Richard Clayderman is playing), you can probably skip the international acts; but it is worth trying to catch a couple of Japanese bands while you are in the country – they can be surprisingly good.

Cinemas

If you are willing to fork out a fistful of yen for your movie-going pleasure, Japan's major cities (in particular Tokyo) offer the opportunity to catch up with everything from the latest Hollywood blockbusters to rare art-house releases. In Tokyo, the best place to get the detail is on what's playing where is *Tokyo Journal*. Screening times are indicated, and the magazine also includes useful maps for finding the cinemas – very important. *Kansai Time Out* has info on movie screenings for the Kansai area (Osaka, Kyoto and Kōbe) and in the Nagoya area *Eyes* does the same thing.

Japanese cinemas screen foreign movies with their original soundtracks and subtitled in Japanese. Standards at cinemas have also been steadily improving over recent years. Old practices like only partially dimming the lights during the screening and letting the next batch of patrons into the cinema before the previous screening is over are gradually disappearing.

Discos

Before you think about heading off to a disco, bear in mind that you are going to be hit for a ¥4000 to ¥5000 cover charge. This will usually include two or three drinks, but it still makes for an expensive night of dancing. In the big cities like Tokyo, Osaka, Kyoto, Fukuoka and Sapporo there are usually a few bars around with no cover charge that have dancing on Friday and Saturday nights. Details on a few particularly interesting discos, where the décor and patrons make the expense worthwhile for those who can afford it have been included in this book. Check the Tokyo chapter in particular.

Live Houses & Bars

Live houses and bars are the cheapest nightlife option for travellers and foreign residents in Japan. It's well worth making a point of at least calling into one 'gaijin bar' while you are in Japan. It will probably be your best opportunity to meet young Japanese in an informal setting, and will probably change your opinion of modern Japanese society.

Very few of the gaijin bars recommended in this book have entry charges, and where they do they are usually the price of a drink ticket just to ensure that you do spend some money while you are there. Drink prices generally average out at ¥500 for a beer to ¥700 for spirits.

Live houses are venues for local bands and are often worth checking out. Performances tend to start and finish early (say 7.30 to 10 pm). Keep an eye on magazines like *Tokyo Journal* and *Kansai Time Out*. Occasionally interesting international acts play at small clubs in Japan: the Neville Brothers, for example, put in the occasional appearance at *Taku Taku*, a famous Kyoto blues establishment.

THINGS TO BUY

The Japanese are obsessive shoppers, and

consequently everything from tiny speciality shops to some of the world's largest and most luxurious department stores give visitors ample opportunity to empty their pockets before going home. True, some items are overpriced, but many things, including electronic gear like cameras and video cameras, are much cheaper than you might expect. The current high value of the yen means that you are unlikely to come up with prices for such things that are competitive with prices in Hong Kong and Singapore, however.

As well as all the electronic gadgetry available in Japan, there are a wide range of traditional crafts to choose from, though for good stuff you're really going to be spending big money. It pays to shop around if you have anything particular on mind. The big department stores, which often have the best selections of Japanese gift items, can vary enormously in their prices from one store to another. In some shops, you are paying for extras such as the high level of service (a feature of all Japanese shops anyway), loca-

tion and interior décor, all of which are very important to the well-heeled Japanese but lesser considerations to the traveller looking for a bargain.

Tax-Free Shopping

Shopping for tax-free goods in Japan may not necessarily give you the bargains you might expect. Although tax-free shops enable foreigners to get an exemption of the 10% to 30% sales tax levied on most items, these still may not always be the cheapest places to shop. Other bulk-buying shops are often a better deal. The best advice is to shop around and compare prices before making a purchase.

Photographic Equipment

Tokyo is an excellent hunting ground for photographic equipment. Almost all the big-name brands in camera equipment are Japanese, and for these locally produced items, prices can be very competitive. The prices for accessories, such as motor drives and flash units, can even be competitive with Singapore and Hong Kong. In addition, shopping in Japan presents the shopper with none of the rip-off risks that abound in other Asian discount capitals.

As always, be prepared to shop around. Tokyo's Shinjuku area (see the Tokyo chapter) is the best place for buying camera equipment, although Ginza too has a good selection of camera shops. If you're short of time, however, I'd suggest heading straight to Shinjuku's Yodobashi Camera, which is virtually a department store devoted to cameras, camera accessories and darkroom equipment. The range is enormous and prices generally compare well with elsewhere in Tokyo.

One possibility that few visitors consider is buying second-hand camera equipment. Both Shinjuku and Ginza have a fair number of second-hand shops where camera and lens quality is usually very good and prices are around half what you would pay for new equipment. Buying second-hand is a particularly good option if you are only in the market for lenses, which are much more easily tested in the shop.

Electronic Equipment & Hi-Fi
Some bargains can be picked up, but there are a few things to take note of before you rush into any purchases. The main problem is that much of the electrical gadgetry on sale in Japan is designed for Japan's curious power supply (100 V at 50 or 60 Hz) and will usually require a transformer for use overseas. Other problems include the incompatibility of Japanese TVs, video recorders and FM radios with foreign models. The safest bet is to go for export models – the prices may be slightly higher, but in the long run you'll save the expense of converting the equipment to suit the conditions in your own country. Two places to look for export models are the International Arcade in Ginza and the big LAOX store in Akihabara, Tokyo.

For battery-operated items such as Walkmans and Diskmans, scout around the hundreds of electrical shops in Akihabara. A little bargaining (don't get too carried away – this is not Bombay) will generally bring the price down around 10% or so.

Computers
The computer market, both hardware and software, is one area in which the Japanese are lagging behind. Although Japanese manufacturers have grabbed a large part of the market for laptop computers, you're still better off looking in Hong Kong or Singapore for these and other computer goods.

Music & Instruments
From CDs to electric guitars, musical equipment can be a lot cheaper in Japan than elsewhere. At branches of Tower Records and HMV Records (Tokyo, Yokohama, Osaka and Kyoto) imported US CDs range between ¥1900 and ¥2200. Japanese CDs average around ¥2300, although you can occasionally come across real bargains. Wave, located in Tokyo's Roppongi, Shibuya and Ikebukuro districts, has excel-

lent selections of both Japanese and Western music in CD, LP and tape format.

The Japanese are great music lovers and, consequently, there are plenty of musical equipment shops in all the major cities. Bargains can usually be had on Japanese-made instruments, while foreign-made ones will generally be more expensive than they are in other parts of the world. For example, a Japanese-assembled Fender guitar will be about half the price of the same US-assembled model. For musical equipment, it is usually possible to negotiate lower prices than those marked.

Pearls
The Japanese firm Mikimoto developed the technique of producing cultured pearls by artificially introducing an irritant into the pearl oyster. Pearls and pearl jewellery are still a favourite purchase for a visitor to Japan but it would be wise to check prices in your own country before buying. Size, quality and colour will all have a bearing on the price. Toba, in the Ise area (Kansai region) is a centre for the production of cultured pearls.

Cars, Motorcycles & Bicycles
Information on purchasing these vehicles can be found in the Getting Around chapter.

Clothes
Japanese-made clothes and shoes are excellent quality and needn't cost the earth. In up-market and fashionable districts, most of the clothes shops are exclusive boutiques with exclusive prices. In less fashionable areas, there are countless retail outlets for an industry providing economical, mass-produced versions of designer clothes. In such shops, it is possible to pick up a suit for around ¥12,000 – perfect if you're a newly arrived English-language teacher with a backpack full of travel-soiled jeans and T-shirts.

Toys
Japanese toys are surprisingly disappointing, even dull; if you're on a business trip to Japan don't promise your children you'll

bring them back some unimaginable technological wonder. Despite the numerous
Japanese toy shops, the displays are unimaginative and the toys even more so. They're
curiously uninvolving toys; a high percentage of them seem to be of the 'turn it on, sit
back and watch it perform' type.

As in the West, there are many TV spin-off
marketing ploys in Japan, but they're likely
to be for TV programmes which have had no
impact at all outside Japan, and hence have
little interest to non-Japanese children.
Teenage Mutant Ninja Turtles had not made
an appearance in Japan long after they had
swept the English-speaking children's
world.

Japanese Arts & Crafts
As well as all the hi-tech knick-knacks produced by the Japanese, it is also possible to
go home loaded down with Japanese traditional arts & crafts. Anything from carp
banners to kimono can make good souvenirs
for the converted Japanophile.

Ningyō *Ningyō* (Japanese dolls) are
intended for display, not for playing with.
Often quite exquisite, with coiffured hair and
dressed in kimono, they make excellent souvenirs or gifts. Also available are the
gogatsu-ningyō, dolls dressed in samurai
suits used as gifts on Boy's Day. The most
famous dolls are made in Kyoto and are
known as *kyō-ningyō*.

Ningyō can be bought in tourist shops,
department stores and special doll shops. In
Tokyo (see the Tokyo chapter) Asakusabashi's Edo-dōri is well known for its many
doll shops.

Kasa *Kasa* (Japanese umbrellas) are another
classic souvenir item. They come in two
forms: *higasa*, which are made of paper,
cotton or silk and serve as a sunshade; and
bangasa, which are made of oiled paper and
keep the rain off. Again, department stores
and tourist shops are your best bet for finding
kasa.

Koinobori *Koinobori* are the carp banners

that you see flying from poles in Japan. The
carp is much revered for its tenacity and
perseverance, but you might like the banners
for their simple elegance. They're available
from Shibuya's Oriental Bazaar in Tokyo
and are occasionally sold in tourist shops.

Katana *Katana* (Japanese swords) make a
fantastic souvenir – it's just that good ones
are going to cost more than all your other
travel expenses put together! The reason for
their expense is both the mystique attached
to them as the symbols of samurai power and
the great care that went into making them.
Sword shops that sell the real thing will also
stock *tsuba*, sword guards, and complete sets
of samurai armour. Department stores, on the
other hand, stock realistic (to the untrained
eye at least) imitations at affordable prices.

Shikki *Shikki* (lacquerware) is another Japanese craft that has been mastered to a
superlative degree. The lacquer-making
process, involving as many as 15 layers of
lacquer, is used to create objects as diverse
as dishes and furniture. As you might expect,
examples of good lacquerware cannot be had
for a song, but smaller items can be bought
at affordable prices from department stores.
Popular, easily transportable items include
bowls, trays and small boxes.

Washi *Washi* (Japanese paper) has been
famous for more than 1000 years as the finest
hand-made paper in the world. Special shops
stock sheets of washi and products made
from it, such as notebooks, wallets and so on.
As they're generally inexpensive and light,
washi products make excellent gifts and souvenirs. Again, you'll find them in the big
department stores. Tokyo's Ginza also has a
large washi shop in the same building as the
Contax Gallery (see the Central Tokyo map
in the Tokyo chapter).

Stoneware & Porcelain The difference
between stoneware and porcelain is in the
firing process. Stoneware is fired at temperatures of between 600°C and 900°C and is
frequently admired for its earthiness and

imperfections. Porcelain, on the other hand, is fired at much higher temperatures (1300°C to 1400°C) and is transformed into a glass-like substance in the process. Imperfections in porcelain are considered just that – imperfections – and are discarded.

Numerous pottery villages still exist in various parts of Japan. Many of them feature pottery museums and working kilns which can be visited. Of course, it is also possible to buy examples of stoneware and porcelain. Not too far from Tokyo is Mashiko (see the

Around Tokyo section); in Western Honshū is Imbe, near Okayama, famed for its *bizen-yaki* pottery; in the Kansai region is Tamba Sasayama, with its Tamba pottery; in Kyūshū, the home of Japanese pottery, Koishiwara, Karatsu, Imari and Arita are all sources of different pottery styles.

Ukiyo-e Ukiyo-e wood-block prints (literally 'pictures from the floating world'), originally were not an art form. Wood-block printing originated in the 18th century as one of Japan's earliest manifestations of mass culture and, as such, was used in advertising and posters. The name derives from a Buddhist term indicating the transient world of daily pleasures, ukiyo-e uniquely depicting such things as street scenes, actors and courtesans.

Today, tourist shops in Japan stock modern reproductions of the work of famous ukiyo-e masters such as Hokusai whose scenes of Mt Fuji are favourites. It is also possible to come across originals by lesser-known artists at prices ranging from ¥5000 to ¥40,000. Try the Oriental Bazaar in Shibuya, Tokyo if you're looking for reasonably priced originals. In Ginza, Tokyo, there are a couple of galleries that stock contemporary wood-block prints – many of them deal with very modern themes and are strikingly innovative.

Kimono & Yukata Kimono are seldom worn by Japanese women nowadays. Indeed, most young Japanese women would have no idea how to dress themselves in a kimono. Still, they are worn occasionally, mostly on ceremonial occasions such as a school graduation or wedding day.

For most non-Japanese, the cost of a kimono is prohibitively expensive. For a 'bottom of the range' kimono, prices start at around ¥60,000 and soar to ¥1 million or more. The best option for those interested in owning their own kimono is to look for an antique silk kimono in places like Shibuya's Oriental Bazaar in Tokyo. Alternatively, if you're in Japan during March or September, these are the months that the Daimaru store has sales of its rental kimono. Be warned, however: these sales are also popular with local Japanese.

For those not in the kimono league, another option might be to look for a yukata (the cotton bathrobes worn in ryokan). These have a distinctively Japanese look and are not only affordable (from around ¥3500 up) but also highly useable.

Getting There & Away

Flying into Tokyo is only one of a diverse range of ways of getting to Japan and only a tiny part of the whole story. For a start there are many other airports in Japan, some of which make better entry points than Tokyo's inconvenient Narita International Airport. It's also possible to arrive in Japan by sea from a number of nearby countries, particularly South Korea. Japan can also serve as the starting or finishing point for the popular Trans-Siberian Express trip across Russia.

AIR

There are flights to Japan from all over the world, usually to Tokyo but also to a number of other Japanese airports. Although Tokyo may seem the obvious arrival and departure point in Japan, for many visitors this may not be the case. If, for example, you were travelling from Tokyo to western Japan then out to Hong Kong or Australia, it could be much more convenient to fly out of, say, Fukuoka rather than backtrack all the way to Tokyo.

Arriving in Japan

Airports There are international airports on the main island of Honshū (Nagoya, Niigata, Osaka and Tokyo), Kyūshū (Fukuoka, Kagoshima, Kumamoto and Nagasaki), Okinawa (Naha) and Hokkaidō (Sapporo).

Tokyo Despite having more international flights than any other airport in Japan, Tokyo is far from the best place to make your first landfall. For a start, Narita International Airport is 60 km from central Tokyo and a rush-hour traffic jam can mean a two hour drive to the city. Even the airport bus services take 1½ hours at the best of times.

Train services are faster, particularly since the JR Narita and private Keisei lines were extended all the way to the airport terminal. (Until the lines were completed in March 1991, visitors had to take a bus the short distance between the terminal and the Narita railway station.)

Unless you've got direct access to a major bank's central vault, don't even consider taking a taxi between the airport and central Tokyo. (See the Getting Around section of the Tokyo chapter for more details on airport transport.)

Air Travel Glossary

Apex Apex, or 'advance purchase excursion' is a discounted ticket which must be paid for in advance. There are penalties if you wish to change it.

Baggage Allowance This will be written on your ticket: usually one 20 kg item to go in the hold, plus one item of hand luggage.

Bucket Shop An unbonded travel agency specialising in discounted airline tickets.

Bumped Just because you have a confirmed seat doesn't mean you're going to get on the plane – see Overbooking.

Cancellation Penalties If you have to cancel or change an Apex ticket there are often heavy penalties involved, insurance can sometimes be taken out against these penalties. Some airlines impose penalties on regular tickets as well, particularly against 'no show' passengers.

Check In Airlines ask you to check in a certain time ahead of the flight departure (usually 1½ hours on international flights). If you fail to check in on time and the flight is overbooked the airline can cancel your booking and give your seat to somebody else.

Confirmation Having a ticket written out with the flight and date you want doesn't mean you have a seat until the agent has checked with the airline that your status is 'OK' or confirmed. Meanwhile you could just be 'on request'.

Discounted Tickets There are two types of discounted fares – officially discounted (see

Promotional Fares) and unofficially discounted. The lowest prices often impose drawbacks like flying with unpopular airlines, inconvenient schedules, or unpleasant routes and connections. A discounted ticket can save you other things than money – you may be able to pay Apex prices without the associated Apex advance booking and other requirements. Discounted tickets only exist where there is fierce competition.

Full Fares Airlines traditionally offer first class (coded F), business class (coded J) and economy class (coded Y) tickets. These days there are so many promotional and discounted fares available from the regular economy class that few passengers pay full economy fare.

Lost Tickets If you lose your airline ticket an airline will usually treat it like a travellers' cheque and, after enquiries, issue you with another one. Legally, however, an airline is entitled to treat it like cash and if you lose it then it's gone forever. Take good care of your tickets.

No Shows No shows are passengers who fail to show up for their flight, sometimes due to unexpected delays or disasters, sometimes due to simply forgetting, sometimes because they made more than one booking and didn't bother to cancel the one they didn't want. Full-fare passengers who fail to turn up are sometimes entitled to travel on a later flight. The rest of us are penalised (see Cancellation Penalties).

On Request An unconfirmed booking for a flight, see Confirmation.

Open Jaws A return ticket where you fly out to one place but return from another. If available this can save you backtracking to your arrival point.

Overbooking Airlines hate to fly empty seats and since every flight has some passengers who fail to show up (see No Shows) airlines often book more passengers than they have seats. Usually the excess passengers balance those who fail to show up but occasionally somebody gets bumped. If this happens guess who it is most likely to be? The passengers who check in late.

Promotional Fares Officially discounted fares like Apex fares which are available from travel agents or direct from the airline.

Reconfirmation At least 72 hours prior to departure time of an onward or return flight you must contact the airline and 'reconfirm' that you intend to be on the flight. If you don't do this the airline can delete your name from the passenger list and you could lose your seat. You don't have to reconfirm the first flight on your itinerary or if your stopover is less than 72 hours. It doesn't hurt to reconfirm more than once.

Restrictions Discounted tickets often have various restrictions on them – advance purchase is the most usual one (see Apex). Others are restrictions on the minimum and maximum period you must be away, such as a minimum of 14 days or a maximum of one year. See Cancellation Penalties.

Standby A discounted ticket where you only fly if there is a seat free at the last moment. Standby fares are usually only available on domestic routes.

Tickets Out An entry requirement for many countries is that you have an onward or return ticket, in other words, a ticket out of the country. If you're not sure what you intend to do next, the easiest solution is to buy the cheapest onward ticket to a neighbouring country or a ticket from a reliable airline which can later be refunded if you do not use it.

Transferred Tickets Airline tickets cannot be transferred from one person to another. Travellers sometimes try to sell the return half of their ticket, but officials can ask you to prove that you are the person named on the ticket. This is unlikely to happen on domestic flights, on an international flight tickets may be compared with passports.

Travel Agencies Travel agencies vary widely and you should ensure you use one that suits your needs. Some simply handle tours while full-service agencies handle everything from tours and tickets to car rental and hotel bookings. A good one will do all these things and can save you a lot of money but if all you want is a ticket at the lowest possible price, then you really need an agency specialising in discounted tickets. A discounted ticket agency, however, may not be useful for other things, like hotel bookings.

Travel Periods Some officially discounted fares, Apex fares in particular, vary with the time of year. There is often a low (off-peak) season and a high (peak) season. Sometimes there's an intermediate or shoulder season as well. At peak times, when everyone wants to fly, not only will the officially discounted fares be higher but so will unofficially discounted fares or there may simply be no discounted tickets available. Usually the fare depends on your outward flight – if you depart in the high season and return in the low season, you pay the high-season fare. ■

Airport transport isn't the end of the Tokyo horror story. Narita is not a particularly user-friendly airport and immigration formalities can be extremely slow and tedious. When you finally do reach Tokyo, the city itself is big, expensive and may seem overwhelmingly confusing. All in all, if you can plan your arrival elsewhere in Japan, then do so.

There is one exception to this tale of woe. When Narita International Airport opened, China Airlines (along with most domestic airlines flights) stayed at the convenient old Haneda Airport. This was because Air China (mainland China) did not want to fly to the same airport as China Airlines (Taiwan). Consequently, visitors preferring to make Tokyo their entry point can avoid the hassles of Narita International Airport by flying China Airlines to Haneda Airport instead.

Osaka Osaka, Japan's third-largest city, has many international flights. Its airport is conveniently close to the town and there are direct bus services between the airport and nearby Kyoto, Japan's number one tourist destination. International connections include Canada, the USA and many countries in Europe, Asia and Australasia.

Kansai International Airport Due to open in early 1994, the Kansai International Airport will be the first Japanese airport to function 24 hours a day and will serve the key Kansai cities of Kyoto, Osaka and Kōbe. At the time of writing, transport details with these cities (and others, including Tokyo) had not been finalised. But, given the hype the new airport has been getting in Japan, one

would expect transport from the airport to be frequent and efficient.

Nagoya Nagoya may have few attractions in its own right, but the town is conveniently located between Tokyo and Osaka and the airport is reasonably close. From Nagoya, flights connect with Australia, Canada, Guam, Hong Kong, Indonesia, the Philippines, Singapore, South Korea, Taiwan, Thailand and the USA.

Fukuoka Fukuoka, at the northern end of Kyūshū, is the major arrival point for Western Japan. The airport, conveniently located near the city, has flight connections with Australia, North America and a number of Asian destinations.

Naha Okinawa Island, south-west of the main islands of Japan, is a convenient arrival or departure point for Hong Kong and Taiwan. There are also connections with Guam and the USA.

Niigata Niigata, north of Tokyo, is connected with Seoul in South Korea and with Khabarovsk in Russia. From Khabarovsk, the Trans-Siberian Express and Aeroflot operate to Moscow. A *shinkansen* (bullet train) line connects Niigata with Tokyo.

Other Airports On the island of Kyūshū, Kagoshima Airport has flights to Hong Kong, Kumamoto Airport has flights to South Korea, and Nagasaki has flights to Shanghai and Seoul.

On Hokkaidō, Sapporo Airport has connections with South Korea.

Kansai International Airport
Everybody is very tight-lipped about transport details from the new airport to Kansai destinations. The only thing for certain is that there will be ultra-fast rail connections with Osaka, Kyoto and Nara and a high-speed ferry connection with Kōbe. No prices are available yet. Rail and car connections with the airport will be via a five-km bridge (the airport is on an artificial island) and times for rail connections are as follows: Osaka – 30 minutes to Namba; 50 minutes to Umede; Kyoto 85 minutes; Nara 75 minutes; Kōbe 30 minutes (by ferry). ■

A	B	C
D	E	F
G	H	I

Food & Drink
A: Drying fish (TW)
B: Drying octopus (TW)
C: Fishmongers (CT)
D: Sake Barrels (RI)
E: Animal bread (CT)
F: Drying fish (TW)
G: Plastic food display (CT)
H: Sembei cracker shop (CT)
I: Melons (CT)

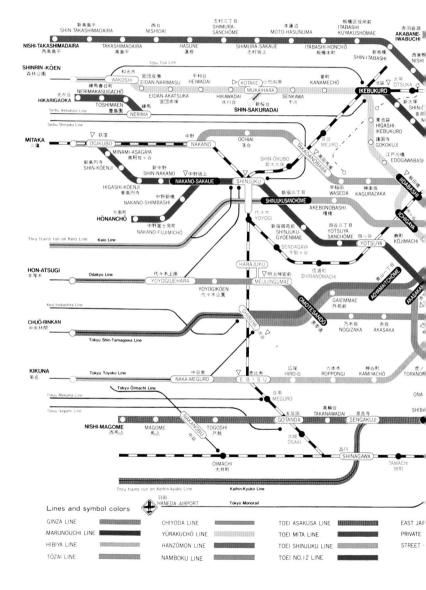

SHIN-TAKASHIMADAIRA 新高島平　NISHIDAI 西台　SHIMURA-SANCHŌME 志村三丁目　MOTO-HASUNUMA 本蓮沼　ITABASHI KUYAKUSHOMAE 板橋区役所前　AKABANE-IWABUCHI 赤羽岩淵

NISHI-TAKASHIMADAIRA 西高島平　TAKASHIMADAIRA 高島平　HASUNE 蓮根　SHIMURA-SAKAUE 志村坂上　ITABASHI-HONCHŌ 板橋本町　SHIN-ITABASHI 新板橋　NISHI 西巣鴨

Tōbu Tōjō Line

SHINRIN-KŌEN 森林公園

WAKOSHI 和光市　EIDAN-NARIMASU 営団成増　HEIWADAI 平和台　KOTAKE-MUKAIHARA 小竹向原　KANAMECHŌ 要町　IKEBUKURO 池袋　ŌTSUKA 大塚

HIKARIGAOKA 光が丘　NERIMAKASUGACHŌ 練馬春日町　EIDAN-AKATSUKA 営団赤塚　HIKAWADAI 氷川台　SHIN-SAKURADAI 新桜台　SENKAWA 千川

TOSHIMAEN 豊島園　NERIMA 練馬

Seibu Ikebukuro Line

Seibu Shinjuku Line

HIGASHI-IKEBUKURO 東池袋　GOKOKUJI 護国寺　EDOGAWABASHI 江戸川橋

MITAKA 三鷹　OGIKUBO 荻窪　NAKANO 中野　OCHIAI 落合　SHIN-ŌKUBO 新大久保　TAKADANOBABA 高田馬場　MEJIRO 目白　IIDABASHI 飯田橋

MINAMI-ASAGAYA 南阿佐ヶ谷　SHIN-NAKANO 新中野　WASEDA 早稲田　KAGURAZAKA 神楽坂

SHIN-KŌENJI 新高円寺　NAKANO-SAKAUE 中野坂上　SHINJUKU 新宿　ICHIGAYA 市ヶ谷

HIGASHI-KŌENJI 東高円寺　NAKANO-SHIMBASHI 中野新橋　SHINJUKUSANCHŌME 新宿三丁目　AKEBONOBASHI 曙橋　KŌJIMACHI 麹町

HŌNANCHŌ 方南町　NAKANO-FUJIMICHŌ 中野富士見町　YOYOGI 代々木　SHINJUKU-GYOENMAE 新宿御苑前　YOTSUYA-SANCHŌME 四谷三丁目　YOTSUYA 四ツ谷

Thru trains run on Keiō Line　Keiō Line　SENDAGAYA 千駄ヶ谷

HON-ATSUGI 本厚木　Odakyū Line　YOYOGIUEHARA 代々木上原　HARAJUKU 原宿　MEIJIJINGUMAE 明治神宮前　SHINANOMACHI 信濃町　AOYAMA-ITCHŌME 青山一丁目　AKASAKA

YOYOGIKŌEN 代々木公園

Keiō-Inokashira Line

GAIEMMAE 外苑前　OMOTESANDŌ 表参道

CHŪŌ-RINKAN 中央林間　Tokyu Shin-Tamagawa Line　SHIBUYA 渋谷　NOGIZAKA 乃木坂　AKASAKA 赤坂

KIKUNA 菊名　Tokyu Tōyoko Line　NAKA-MEGURO 中目黒　EBISU 恵比寿　HIRO-O 広尾　ROPPONGI 六本木　KAMIYACHŌ 神谷町　TORANO...

Tokyu Mekama Line　Tokyu Ōimachi Line　MEGURO 目黒　ONA...

Tokyu Ikegami Line　TAKANAWADAI 高輪台　SENGAKUJI 泉岳寺　SHIBA...

NISHI-MAGOME 西馬込　MAGOME 馬込　NAKANOBU 中延　TOGOSHI 戸越　GOTANDA 五反田　ŌSAKI 大崎

ŌIMACHI 大井町　SHINAGAWA 品川　TAMACHI 田町

Thru run on Keihin-kyuko Line　Keihin-Kyūko Line

HANEDA-AIRPORT 羽田　Tokyo Monorail

Lines and symbol colors

GINZA LINE		CHIYODA LINE		TOEI ASAKUSA LINE		EAST JA...
MARUNOUCHI LINE		YŪRAKUCHŌ LINE		TOEI MITA LINE		PRIVATE...
HIBIYA LINE		HANZŌMON LINE		TOEI SHINJUKU LINE		STREET...
TŌZAI LINE		NAMBOKU LINE		TOEI NO.12 LINE		

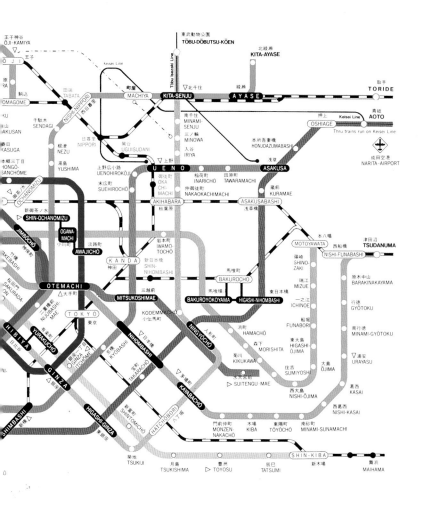

Types of stations

GINZA   Junctions of subway lines.

KANDA   Junctions of Subway, East Japan Railway and Private Railway lines.

▽   Stations with a Pass Office.

(C) Dec. 1991 TRTA

A: Sumō Tournament, Nagoya (RI)
B: Lanterns, Kasuga Taisha Shrine, Nara (RI)
C: Monk, Asakasa Shrine, Tokyo (RI)
D: Temple calling cards (CT)
E: Sumiyoshi-jinja Shrine, Osaka (RI)
F: Shuri Castle, Naha, Okinawa (CT)

To/From Europe

Most direct flights between Europe and Japan fly into Tokyo but some continue to Osaka. Flight times vary widely depending on the route taken. The most direct route is across Scandinavia and Russia. Since Russia became hard up for cash, there have been far more flights taking this route as the Russians have opened their airspace in return for hefty fees.

The fastest nonstop London-Tokyo flights on the Russian route take just under 12 hours. Flights that stop in Moscow take an extra 2½ hours. Finnair's Helsinki-Tokyo flight over the North Pole and the Bering Strait takes 13½ hours. Before the Russians opened their skies, the popular route was via Anchorage, Alaska. Some flights still operate that way and take about 17 hours, including the Anchorage stopover. Finally, there are the old trans-Asian routes across the Middle East and South Asia, which take anything from 18 to 30 hours depending on the number of stops en route.

Return economy air fares between London and Tokyo are around UK£1000 and are valid for 14 days to three months. A ticket valid for a year away costs about UK£1300. Although a wide variety of cheaper deals are available, generally, the lower the price, the less convenient the route. Expect to pay around UK£900 to UK£1000 for a one-year valid return ticket with a good airline via a fast route. For a less convenient trans-Asian route, count on UK£700 or lower and about half that for one-way tickets.

In London, STA Travel (☎ (071) 937-9962) at 74 Old Brompton Rd, London SW7 or 117 Euston Rd, London NW1; Trailfinders (☎ (071) 938-3366) at 46 Earls Court Rd and at 194 Kensington High St, London W8 7RG (☎ (071) 938-3444) and Travel Bug (☎ (061) 721-4000) all offer rock-bottom return flights to Tokyo and can also put together interesting Round-the-World routes incorporating Tokyo on the itinerary. The weekly 'what's on' magazine *Time Out* or the various giveaway papers are good places to look for travel bargains but take care with shonky bucket shops and prices that seem too low to believe. The really cheap fares will probably involve cash-strapped Eastern European or Middle Eastern airlines and may involve complicated transfers and long waits along the way.

The Far East Travel Centre (FETC) (☎ (071) 734-9318) at 3 Lower John St, London W1A 4XE, specialises in Korean Airline ticketing and can fly you from London Gatwick via Seoul to your choice of Nagasaki, Nagoya, Osaka, Sapporo and Tokyo. This is a good option for visitors who don't want to take the conventional Tokyo route.

The Japan Centre (☎ (071) 437-6445) 66-68 Brewer St, London W1R 3PJ, handles all sorts of ticket permutations. Its basement has a shop section (☎ (071) 439-8035) with books and assorted Japanese paraphernalia as well as a Japanese restaurant with reasonable prices. It's worth a visit for a taste of Japan.

An alternative route to Japan from Europe is to fly to Hong Kong and buy an onward ticket from one of Hong Kong's very competitive travel agencies. London-Hong Kong flights are much more competitively priced than London-Tokyo ones. If you have to go to Hong Kong en route to Tokyo, a London-Hong Kong-London ticket plus a Hong Kong-Tokyo-Hong Kong ticket can work out much cheaper than a London-Hong Kong-Tokyo-London ticket.

London remains one of the best places in Europe to purchase keenly priced airline tickets although Amsterdam is also very good.

To/From North America

West coast flights to Japan go straight across the Pacific and take about 10 hours. From the east coast, flights usually take the northern route over Alaska – the new nonstop flights take about 13 hours. The big time change on the trans-Pacific flights is a sure-fire recipe for jet lag and there's also a date change as you cross the International Date Line.

Seven-day advance purchase return fares are US$910 to US$1125 from the west coast (depending on the season) and US$1156 to

US$1370 from the east. Regular economy fares are much higher – US$874 to US$935 (one way) from the west coast, US$1195 to US$1279 from the east coast.

Better deals are available if you shop around. From the east coast, return fares as low as US$759 to US$879 and one-way fares of US$749 are possible. From the west coast fares can drop to US$559 and US$689 with Korean Airlines. There are also good deals available via Vancouver with Canadian Airlines International. From San Francisco or Los Angeles, fares to Tokyo range from US$629 to US$769 or to Nagoya from US$579 to US$779. Check the Sunday travel sections of papers like the *Los Angeles Times* or the *New York Times* for travel bargains. Council Travel and STA Travel are two good discount operations specialising in student fares and other cheap deals. They have offices all across North America.

Fares from Canada are similar to those from the USA. Canadian Airlines International, which operates out of Vancouver, often matches or beats the best fares available from the USA. Travel Cuts, the Canadian student travel organisation, offers one-way Vancouver-Tokyo flights from C$800 and returns from C$1000 or more depending on the season.

To/From Australasia

The cheapest fares between Australia and Japan are generally with Garuda; one-way/return fares start at around A$750/1100. Tickets are valid for four months, or for an additional A$100, for one year; both fares allow a stopover in Bali.

Japan Air Lines (JAL), All Nippon Airways (ANA) and Qantas all have direct flights between Australia and Japan. You can fly from most Australia state capitals to Tokyo, Osaka, Nagoya and Fukuoka. There's only a one hour time change between Australia and Japan and a direct Sydney-Tokyo flight takes about nine hours.

A return excursion Sydney-Tokyo fare is around A$1500, valid for four months. If you have a working holiday visa, the validity is extended to one year. STA Travel offices or

the numerous Flight Centres International are good places to look for discount ticket deals.

Air New Zealand and Japan Air Lines each fly Auckland-Tokyo three times weekly (about 11 hours flying time); return fares start around NZ$1399. Air Pacific flies Auckland-Tokyo twice weekly via Fiji (stops permitted) for about NZ$1569.

To/From Asia

Most Asian nations have air links with Japan. South Korea is particularly popular because it's used by many travellers as a place to take a short holiday from Japan when their visas are close to expiring. The immigration authorities treat travellers returning to Japan after a short break in South Korea with great suspicion. Hong Kong has traditionally been popular as a bargain basement for airline ticketing, but prices are no longer as cheap as they once were.

Many carriers fly Bangkok-Japan, and the competitive pressures mean frequent price changes. Typical fares include Bangkok-Tokyo on United Airlines (one-way/return 9900/11,900 Baht) and Bangkok-Taipei-Tokyo on China Airlines (8900/14,500 Baht).

South Korea Numerous flights link Seoul and Pusan with cities in Japan but the cheapest travel is by ferry. (See the following Sea section for information on sea-travel bargains between Korea and Japan.)

Hong Kong There are direct flights between Hong Kong and a number of cities in Japan, though the biggest choice and best deals will be to Tokyo. Agents like the Hong Kong Student Travel Bureau or Phoenix Travel can offer one-way tickets from around HK$2300 to HK$2900, and return tickets from HK$3000 to HK$5000, depending on the period of validity. Discounted tickets are generally only available on flights to Narita, Osaka and Nagoya, though DragonAir fly to Kagoshima at competitive rates (HK$3000 return).

Taiwan Agents handling discounted tickets advertise in the English-language *China Post*. There are flights from Taipei to Fukuoka, Naha, Osaka or Tokyo. If you are stopping off in Taiwan between Hong Kong and Japan, check on China Air tickets, which allow a stop-over in Taipei before continuing on to Tokyo's very convenient Haneda airport.

Flights also operate between Kaohsiung and Osaka or Tokyo.

China CAAC has several flights a week from Beijing to Tokyo and Osaka, via Shanghai. Japan Airlines (JAL) flies from Beijing and Shanghai to Tokyo, Osaka and Nagasaki. There are flights between Dalian and Fukuoka/Tokyo on All Nippon Airways.

Chinese visas obtained in Japan are outrageously expensive – US$80 to US$120 depending on which agent you use. You'll save money if you can obtain the visa elsewhere, but as Chinese tourist visas are only valid for one to three months from date of issue it's useless to obtain one too far in advance.

Other Asian Centres There are regular flights between Japan and other major centres like Manila, Bangkok, Kuala Lumpur, Singapore and Jakarta. Some of the cheapest deals between Europe and Japan will be via South Asia – Bangladesh Biman will fly you from London to Dhaka to Tokyo at about the lowest price going.

To/From Other Regions
There are also flights between Japan and South America, Africa and the Middle East.

Round-the-World & Circle Pacific Tickets
Round-the-World (RTW) fares are put together by two or more airlines and allow you to make a circuit of the world using their combined routes. A typical RTW ticket is valid for one year, allows unlimited stopovers along the way and costs about UK1400, A$3500 or US$2700. An example, including Tokyo in Japan, would be a British Airways/United Airways combination flying London, New York, Tokyo, Singapore, London. A South Pacific version might take you London, New York, Los Angeles, Tahiti, Sydney, Tokyo, London. There are many versions involving different combinations of airlines and different routes. Generally, routes which stay north of the equator are usually a little cheaper than routes that include countries like Australia or South America.

Circle Pacific fares are a similar idea and allow you to make a circuit of the Pacific. A typical combination includes Los Angeles, Tokyo, Bangkok, Sydney, Auckland, Honolulu, Los Angeles (US$2188). Sydney can generally be interchanged with most East coast Australian capitals or Cairns.

Enterprising travel agents put together their own RTW and Circle Pacific fares at much lower prices than the joint airline deals but, of course, the cheapest fares will involve unpopular airlines and less popular routes. It's possible to put together a RTW from London for as little as UK£700. Travel agents in London have also come up with another variation on these combination fares – the Circle Asia fare. A possible route would be London, Hong Kong, Tokyo, Manila, Singapore, Bangkok, London.

SEA

To/From South Korea
South Korea is the closest country to Japan and a very popular visa-renewal point. Many long-term visitors to Japan who are teaching English or who are engaged in some other kind of work, drop over to Korea when their permitted period of stay in Japan is about to expire, then come back to start a fresh stay. Expect to have your passport rigorously inspected.

Pusan-Shimonoseki This popular ferry service is the cheapest route between South Korea and Japan. Daily departures with the Kampur Ferry Service's vessels *Kampu* or *Pukwan* leave Pusan at 5 pm and arrive in Shimonoseki at 8.30 am the next morning. One-way fares start from about US$65 for students, continue up through US$85 for an open tatami-matted area and peak at between US$100 and US$150 for a cabin. There's a 10% discount on return fares and children under six travel free. Fares for children aged six to 12 are half price. (See the Shimonoseki section of the Western Honshū chapter for more details.)

Pusan-Osaka Services between Pusan and Osaka take nearly 24 hours and operate four times a week. One-way fares start at about US$80 for students in the larger cabins. Regular fares range from about US$100 for the multi-berth cabins or from US$125 per person for a two-berth cabin. Children under six travel free, children aged six to 12 qualify for half fare. The services are operated by a Korean and a Japanese ship. You cannot use Korean currency on the Japanese ship so, if you're leaving Korea on that boat, make sure you've disposed of all your *won* before boarding.

Pusan-Fukuoka There is both an ultra-fast hydrofoil service and a ferry service running between Pusan and Fukuoka. The Hydrofoil, which whizzes across in a few hours costs around US$120 one way, US$210 return. The service operates daily. Costs for the Camellia-line ferry service are US$85 one way, US$120 return.

To/From China
There is a regular boat service between Shanghai and Osaka/Kōbe. The ship departs once weekly, one week to Osaka and the next week to Kōbe, and takes two days. Off-season it's kind of empty but can be crowded during summer. The cost is US$130.

Another ship runs from Kōbe to Tanggu (near Tianjin). Departures from Kōbe are every Thursday at noon, arriving in Tanggu the next day. Economy/1st-class tickets cost US$247/333. The food on this boat gets poor reviews so bring a few emergency munchies. Tickets can be bought in Tianjin from the shipping office (☎ 312243) at 89 Munan Dao, Heping District. In Kōbe, the office is at the port (☎ 078-321-5791).

To/From Taiwan
A weekly ferry operates between Taiwan and Okinawa, sometimes via Ishigaki and Miyako in Okinawa Prefecture. The Taiwan port alternates between Keelung and Kaohsiung. Departure from Okinawa is on Thursday or Friday; departure from Taiwan is usally on Monday. The trip takes 16-19 hours. Fares from Okinawa range from ¥15,600 economy class to ¥24,300 1st class; fares are slightly cheaper from Taiwan than from Japan.

You can buy tickets from travel agents in your port of departure, but you can also buy them direct from the ferry company, Arimura Sangyo, which has an office in Naha (☎0988-64-0087) and Osaka (☎ 02-424 8151). In Taiwan you can buy tickets from Yeong An Maritime Company (☎ 02-771-5911) in Taipei, or in Kaohsiung (☎ 07-551-0281) and Keelung (☎ 02-424-8151).

To/From Other Places
For travellers intending to take the Trans-Siberian Railway to Moscow, there's a weekly ferry service between Yokohama and the Russian port of Nakhodka near Vladivostok.

TRANS-SIBERIAN RAILWAY
A little-used option of approaching or leaving Japan is via the Trans-Siberian railway. It won't be particularly attractive to those looking at getting out of Japan in a hurry – visas and bookings take time – but for those with time to spare and an interest in avoiding expensive flights, it might be an attractive option.

There are three Trans-Siberian railway routings: one is directly across Russia followed by a flight from either Vladivostok or Khabarovsk – an expensive routing. The cheaper options are the Chinese Trans-Mongolia and Russian Trans-Manchuria routings, which both end in China, from where there are ferry connections to Japan via Tianjin and Shanghai.

Information on ferry connections between Japan and China is included in the Sea section of this chapter. Air connections with Vladivostok and Khabarovsk are via Niigata in Northern Honshū. Discounted tickets are not available on these flights and they both cost ¥65,000 one way, ¥128,000 return – not cheap. Ferry connections between Nakhoda (near Vladivostok) and Yokohama have been suspended.

Those looking at travelling between China and Japan will be best off travelling by ferry. Air connections between the two countries remain very expensive – one of the cheapest options is Fukuoka-Shanghai (¥42,000 one-way, ¥87,600 return) with China Air.

For more information on using this route contact national tourist agencies such as the Japan National Tourist Organisation (JNTO), China International Travel Service (CITS), Intourist (Russia) or Ibusz (Hungary). In Japan the Tourist Information Centres (TIC) in Tokyo and Kyoto and the Japan-Soviet Tourist Bureau (JSTB) should have more information. The JSTB has offices in Tokyo (☎ 03-3432-6161) and Osaka (☎ 06-531-7416).

More detailed information is available in a number of publications – see Robert Strauss' *Trans-Siberian Handbook* (Compass Publications, 1993) in particular. Those making their way to Japan via China (or vice versa) should pick up a copy of *China – a travel survival kit* (Lonely Planet, 1994), which has invaluable information on travel in China as well as information on Trans-Siberian travel.

LEAVING JAPAN

The availability of discounted tickets in Japan has improved greatly over the last few years. The average Japanese travel agent still tends to charge its clients the earth, but in Japan's major cities there is an increasing number of agents that provide tickets for

price-conscious foreigners. Worthy of a special mention is STA Travel, who are computerised and can organise tickets efficiently (many Japanese agents are not and can't). For information on STA and other discount agents check with local gaijin-oriented info magazines. In Tokyo, the best place to look is *Tokyo Journal*. In the Kansai Region (Kyoto, Osaka and Kōbe) check with *Kansai Time Out*.

Departure Tax

It's very likely (in fact almost certain, given the costs of constructing it) that the new Kansai International Airport will require a departure tax, but at present the only airport with departure tax is Narita at Tokyo. Departure tax is ¥2000. Don't spend all your money getting to the airport!

WARNING

This chapter is particularly vulnerable to change – prices for international travel are volatile, routes are introduced and cancelled, schedules change, special deals come and go, and rules and visa requirements are amended. Airlines and governments seem to take a perverse pleasure in making price structures and regulations as complicated as possible. You should check directly with the airline or travel agent to make sure you understand how a fare (and ticket you may buy) works. In addition, the travel industry is highly competitive and there are many lurks and perks. The upshot of this is that you should get opinions, quotes and advice from as many airlines and travel agents as possible before you part with your hard-earned cash. The details given in this chapter should be regarded as pointers and are not a substitute for careful, up-to-date research.

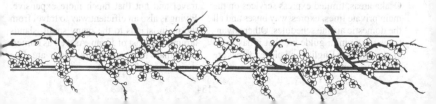

Getting Around

Japan has an enormous variety of travel possibilities and, like everything else in Japan, its transport network is extremely well organised. The Japanese are used to departures and arrivals timed to the minute and they plan trips with schedules that require split-second timing.

TIMETABLES

In many popular areas of Japan, transport schedules are so frequent that timetables hardly matter – does it really make any difference if the train departs at 10.30 or 10.40 am? If, however, you really want to know what goes where and when, then you need a *jikokuhyō* or 'book of timetables'.

These come in a variety of forms including a completely comprehensive monthly *ōki-jikokuhyō* which lists just about everything that moves and takes passengers in and around Japan. This can be useful if you're really exploring the back blocks of Japan and need to know about buses to remote villages or ferries between small islands. Most travellers find it's altogether too much of a good thing since it's the size and weight of a telephone directory and is completely in Japanese. Deciphering a 1000 page kanji timetable is not most people's idea of fun travel! In any case, the ōki-jikokuhyō is always available at stations (often tied to the ticket-office counter with a piece of string) and at most ryokan, youth hostels, minshuku and other accommodation.

An easier alternative is JTB's *Mini-Timetable* which costs ¥310 and is issued monthly. It's about the size of a pocket dictionary and lists JR shinkansen services, limited and ordinary expresses, intercity and express trains in the Tokyo, Nagoya and Osaka areas, limited express services on the main private lines, expressway buses and all the domestic airline schedules. Other advantages of the mini guide are that it has some explanations in English and places names are shown in romaji on maps and main timeta-

bles. You're still going to have to do some deciphering of kanji but even a short-stay visitor should find this no problem.

TRAVEL AGENCIES

Information and tickets can also be obtained from travel agencies of which there are a great number in Japan. Virtually every railway station of any size will have at least one travel agency in the station building to handle all sorts of bookings in addition to train services. The Japan Travel Bureau (JTB) is the big daddy of Japanese travel agencies.

DISCOUNT TICKETS

There are some agencies that deal in discounted tickets both for international and domestic travel. Typical savings on shinkansen tickets are around 20%, which is good news for long-term residents who are not eligible for Japan Rail Passes. Discount ticket agencies are found in the major cities and these agencies sometimes advertise in the English-language journals produced for long-term residents. (See the Tokyo chapter for details of discounters in that city.)

BAGGAGE FORWARDING

In Japan, it's important to travel light, particularly on trains. However, if you have too much baggage, there are highly efficient forwarding services which you can use to send your baggage ahead to a final destination.

AIR

Rail travel has such a pervasive image in Japan that it's easy to forget there's a dense network of air routes. In many cases, flying can be much faster than even shinkansen rail travel and not that much more expensive. Flying is also an efficient way to travel from the main islands to the many small islands around the coast of Japan. As well as numerous small local operators, there are five major domestic airlines.

Local Air Services

Japan Air Lines (JAL) is the major international carrier and also has a domestic network linking the major cities. All Nippon Airways (ANA) is the second largest international carrier and operates a more extensive domestic system. Japan Air Systems (JAS) only does a couple of overseas routes but flies to many destinations in Japan. Air Nippon Koku (ANK) and South-West Airlines (SWAL) are smaller domestic carriers. ANK links many smaller towns all over Japan while SWAL is particularly good for connections through Okinawa and the other South-West Islands.

The Domestic Airfares Chart shows some of the major connections and the one-way fares. There's a 10% discount on round-trip fares if the return flight is made within seven to 10 days. The airlines have some weird and wonderful discounts if you know what to ask for. JAL, for example, has a women's group discount available for groups of three or more women. Or a husband and wife discount if their combined age totals 88 or more!

If you're flying to or from Tokyo, note that most domestic airlines use the convenient Haneda Airport, while all international flights, except those with China Airlines, use Narita. If you're flying to Tokyo to make an international connection out of Narita it would be rather embarrassing to end up at Haneda – make sure you're on one of the less frequent domestic Narita flights or that you have plenty of time (around three hours) to make the transfer from Haneda to Narita.

TRAIN

As in India, rail is *the* way to travel in Japan but there are few other similarities. Japanese rail travel is usually fast, frequent, clean, comfortable and often very expensive. The services range from small local lines to the

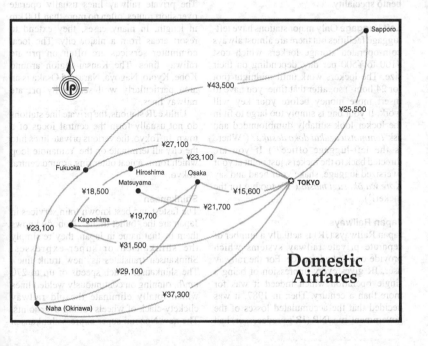

¥43,500

¥25,500

¥27,100

¥23,100

Fukuoka

Hiroshima

Osaka

TOKYO

Matsuyama

¥18,500

¥15,600

¥21,700

¥19,700

Kagoshima

¥23,100

¥31,500

Shinkansen

¥29,100

¥37,300

Naha (Okinawa)

Sapporo

Domestic Airfares

shinkansen super-expresses or 'bullet trains' which have become a symbol of modern Japan.

Railway Stations

Railway stations in Japan are usually very well equipped. The main station is often literally the 'town centre' and in many cases will be part of a large shopping centre with a wide variety of restaurants, bars, fast-food outlets and other facilities.

Meals The Japanese railway system is not renowned for its high-class cuisine, though you may find that the shinkansen dining cars turn out pretty good food. Anyway, you certainly won't starve, as apart from the dining cars, there are snacks, drinks, ice creams and meals sold from the aisles. A good bet is to come prepared with a *bentō* (boxed lunch). At almost every station there will be a shop selling bentō, typically for ¥1000 or less. Some towns and stations have a particular bentō speciality.

Left Luggage Only major stations have left-luggage facilities but there are almost always coin-operated storage lockers which cost ¥100 to ¥500 per day, depending on their size. The lockers work until midnight (not for 24 hours) so, after that time, you have to insert more money before your key will work. If your bag is simply too large to fit in the locker look suitably dumbfounded and ask *Tenimotsu azukai doko desuka?* ('Where is the left-luggage office?') If you are directed back to the lockers, just point at your oversized luggage, shake your head and say *Kore wa ōki sugi masu!* ('It's too big for the locker!').

Japan Railways

Japan Railways (JR) is actually a number of separate private railway systems which provide one linked service. For the railway user, JR gives every impression of being a single operation which indeed it was for more than a century. Then in 1987, it was decided that the accumulated losses of the government-run JNR (JR's predecessor) had

simply gone too far and the government privatised it. To most Japanese, JR is known as *kokutetsu* – *koku* means 'national', *tetsu* means 'line' or literally 'iron', short for 'iron road'.

The JR system covers the country from one end to the other and also provides local services around major cities like Tokyo and Osaka. There are over 20,000 km of railway line and over 20,000 services daily. In many cities, the JR central station forms the hub of the town centre, and is surrounded by hotels, restaurants, entertainment areas, bus services, car rental agencies, travel agencies, airline offices and the like. Shinkansen lines are totally separate from the regular railways and, in some places, the shinkansen stations are a fair distance from the regular JR station. JR also operate buses and ferries, and ticketing can combine more than one form of transport.

Private Railways

The private railway lines usually operate over short routes, often no more than 100 km in length. In many cases, they extend to resort areas from a major city. The local commuter services are often on private railway lines. The Kansai region around Kōbe, Kyoto, Nagoya, Nara and Osaka is an area particularly well served by private railway lines.

Unlike JR stations, the private line stations do not usually form the central focus of a town. In Tokyo, the various private lines into the city all terminate on the Yamanote loop which forms a neat outer ring around central Tokyo.

Shinkansen

The fastest and best known train services in Japan are the 'bullet trains'. Nobody knows them by that name in Japan, they're simply the shinkansen or super-expresses. Shinkansen translates as 'new trunk line'. The shinkansen reach speeds of up to 270 km/h, running on continuously welded lines which totally eliminate the old railway clickety-clack of wheels rolling over joints. The new Nozomi super express shinkansen recently came into use. They are still not as fast as the high-speed trains in France, but the Japanese service has established an incredible record for speed, reliability and safety. In more than 30 years of operation, there has never been a fatality.

The shinkansen service efficiency starts even before you board the train. Your ticket indicates your carriage and seat number, and platform signs indicate where you should stand for that carriage entrance. The train pulls in precisely to the scheduled minute and, sure enough, the carriage door you want is right beside where you're standing. Your departure from the train is equally well organised. As you approach the station, a recorded voice announces, in English and Japanese, that you will soon be arriving and should make your way to the door as the stop will be a short one.

On each shinkansen route, there are two types of services: a faster express service stopping at a limited number of stations and a slower service stopping at all shinkansen stations. There is no difference in fare. There are, however, regular and Green Car (1st class) carriages. If you want to avoid the Japanese cigarette passion, there are a limited number of non-smoking carriages *(kin-en-sha)*; request one when booking. Unreserved carriages will always be available, even on the shinkansen, but at peak holiday periods they can be very crowded and you may have to stand for the entire trip.

Shinkansen Routes There are three shinkansen routes, all starting from Tokyo. One runs via Nagoya, Kyoto, Osaka and Hiroshima to Shimonoseki at the western end of Honshū and on to Fukuoka/Hakata on the northern coast of Kyūshū. Another runs via Sendai to Morioka, almost at the north-eastern end of Honshū. The third line runs north from Tokyo to Niigata on the north coast of central Honshū.

Tokyo-Osaka-Hakata The Tōkaidō line runs from Tokyo to Osaka and continues to Fukuoka/Hakata as the San-yō line. Three types of trains run on this route – the Hikari

(Light), the Kodama (Echo) and the new Nozumi. The difference is a combination of speed and the number of stops – while the Hikari stops only at Nagoya and Kyoto on the Tokyo-Osaka run, the Kodama stops at all the shinkansen stations. The Nozumi also stops at Nagoya and Kyoto, but does the trip around 20 minutes quicker. From Tokyo to Kyoto, the Nozumi service takes around two hours 20 minutes, the Hikari two hours 40 minutes, and the Kodama four hours. All the way to Hakata from Tokyo takes five hours by Nozumi, six hours by Hikari.

Most westbound Hikari services continue beyond Osaka but stops vary from one departure to the next, so check your schedule carefully. There's a similar pattern eastbound from Hakata: some Hikari services terminate in Osaka, others continue on to Tokyo. Kodama services usually operate shorter segments along the Tokyo-Osaka-Hakata route. For example, Tokyo-Osaka, Osaka-Hakata, Osaka-Hiroshima, Hiroshima-Hakata, or the reverse.

Departures from Tokyo or Osaka are generally every 10 to 15 minutes from around 6 am to 11 pm, and all arrivals are before midnight. Services use the Tokyo central station. On a clear day, the Tokyo-Kyoto shinkansen run provides fine views of Mt Fuji – the shinkansen train passing by with Mt Fuji in the background being a favourite travel brochure picture.

Tokyo-Sendai-Morioka-Yamagata The Tōhoku line would have continued all the way to Sapporo on Hokkaidō if costs had not aborted that plan. There are three services: two of them – the Yamabiko, which is the express, and the Aoba, which is the local train – travel to Morioka or one of the main stops en route (Fukushima or Sendai); the third is the Tsubasa, which travels via Fukushima to Yamagata.

Depending on the stops, Yamabiko trains take as little as 1¾ hours to Sendai or 2½ to three hours 20 minutes to Morioka. Except for a few late evening services which terminate at Fukushima, the Aoba services all terminate in Sendai and take about 2½ hours.

Direct Tsubasa services from Tokyo to Yamagata are extremely rare, but some Yamabiko services (approximately once every 1½ hours) allow connections to Tsubasa trains at Fukushima. The entire trip from Tokyo to Yamagata takes around 2½ hours.

There are more than 50 departures from Tokyo's Tokyo and Ueno stations every day, roughly half going all the way to Morioka and the rest terminating at Sendai or Fukishima. The scenery on this route is not as impressive as on the Tokyo-Osaka-Hakata route.

Tokyo-Niigata The Jōetsu line is frequently held up as a prime example of Japanese political corruption. Niigata is not really of sufficient importance to require a shinkansen railway line so passenger usage has always been relatively low. To make matters worse, the route had to tunnel straight through the mountainous spine of Honshū, which made it a very expensive project. So why did it get built? Because Niigata was the home town of Prime Minister Kakuei Tanaka, whose political activities also included taking a couple of million US dollars in bribe money from Lockheed Aircraft !

There are about 40 departures a day from Tokyo's Ueno station, more than 30 going all the way to Niigata. The express services are known as Asahi (Sunrise), the slower ones as Toki (Crane). The Tokyo-Niigata trip takes from one hour 50 minutes to two hours 20 minutes.

Travellers on the Trans-Siberian Railway through Russia will arrive at Niigata if flying to Japan from Khabarovsk in Russia.

Other Train Services
While the shinkansen routes run most of the length of Honshū, a network of JR lines, supplemented by a scattering of shorter private lines, cover much of the rest of Japan. Although these services are efficient, they are nowhere near as fast as the shinkansen, and typically take about twice as long. (See

the following section on Classes for more information about non-shinkansen trains.)

Even slower than the regular trains, but enormously popular nevertheless, are JR's steam locomotive (SL) services. After retiring its last steam trains in 1975, JR has now revived several services as special holiday attractions. On the Yamaguchi line from Ogōri to Tsuwano in Western Honshū, there's a steam train service operating throughout the summer and autumn months. Other SL services operate on the Hōhi line from Kumamoto to Mt Aso in Kyūshū and on the private Oigawa line from Kanaya, near Shizuoka, about 200 km south-west of Tokyo, to Senzu. SL services are very popular, so make enquiries and reservations well ahead of time.

Classes
All JR trains, including the shinkansen, have regular and Green Car (1st class) carriages. The seating is slightly more spacious in 1st class, but most people will find the regular carriages quite OK.

The slowest trains stopping at all stations are called *futsū*. A step up from this is the 'ordinary express' or *kyūkō* which stops at only a limited number of stations. A variation on the kyūkō trains is the *kaisoku* or 'rapid' services. Finally, the fastest regular (non-shinkansen) trains are the *tokkyū* or 'limited express' services.

The longer the route, the more likely you are to find faster train services. Local futsū trains are mainly limited to routes of less than 100 km. In the back blocks of Japan these local trains are called *donko* and may well operate with older equipment than the mainline trains.

Reservations
Tickets can be bought at any JR station to any other JR station. Tickets for local services are usually dispensed from a vending machine but for longer distances you must go to a ticket window. For reservations, complicated tickets, Japan Rail Pass validations and the like, you will need a JR Travel Service Centre. These are found at Narita Airport and

at the main JR stations in Hakata, Hiroshima, Kyoto, Kumamoto, Nagoya, Niigata, Nishi-Kagoshima, Osaka, Sapporo, Sendai, Shimonoseki, Tokyo (Tokyo, Ueno, Ikebukuro, Shinjuku and Shibuya stations), and Yokohama. Large stations that don't have a Travel Service Centre will have a Green Window ticket counter – (Midori-no-Madoguchi or Guriin Uindō). Any major station should have these counters with their green band across the glass.

Major travel agencies in Japan also sell reserved-seat tickets and you can buy shinkansen tickets through JAL offices overseas if you will be flying JAL to Japan.

On futsū services, there are no reserved seats. On the faster kyūkō, tokkyū and shinkansen services you can choose to travel reserved or unreserved. However, if you travel unreserved, there's always the risk of not getting a seat and having to stand, possibly for the entire trip. This is a particular danger at weekends, peak travel seasons and on holidays. Reserved-seat tickets can be bought any time from a month in advance to the day of departure.

Validity & Stopovers Your ticket is valid for two days for a 100 to 200 km trip, with an extra day for each extra 200 km. During that time, you can make as many stopovers as you want so long as the ticket distance is more than 100 km. You cannot stop in Fukuoka, Hiroshima, Kitakyūshū, Kōbe, Kyoto, Nagoya, Osaka, Tokyo, Sapporo, Sendai or Yokohama if your ticket also starts or finishes in one of those cities. In other words, if you bought an Osaka-Kitakyūshū ticket you could not stop at Hiroshima but you could stop at other smaller stations along the way. Additional surcharges are on a per-trip basis, so that every time you break your journey, you must pay the relevant surcharge for the next sector. Therefore, if you're planning a multi-stop trip, you're better off getting a simple futsū ticket and paying express surcharges to the conductor as you go along.

Costs

Basic fares can easily be calculated from a straightforward distance/fare table in the JNTO *Railway Timetable*. Rural lines have a slightly higher fare structure than trunk lines. Shinkansen fares are simply the basic fare plus a super-express distance surcharge. Shinkansen tickets show the three figures – total, basic fare and shinkansen surcharge. (See the following Surcharges section.) Typical basic fares, though not including the new Nozomi super express, are:

Tokyo or Ueno	Distance (km)	Futsū	Shinkansen
Nagoya	366	¥5970	¥10,380
Kyoto	514	¥7830	¥12,970
Osaka	553	¥8340	¥13,480
Okayama	733	¥9990	¥16,050
Hiroshima	895	¥11,120	¥17,700
Shimonoseki	1089	¥12,570	¥20,690
Hakata	1177	¥13,180	¥21,300
Fukushima	273	¥4530	¥8330
Sendai	352	¥5670	¥10,190
Morioka	535	¥8030	¥15,370
Niigata	334	¥5360	¥9880

Surcharges Various surcharges are applied to the base level fares, starting with a ¥500 fee for a reserved seat. The shinkansen fares include this fee, so deduct ¥500 for the cost of travelling by shinkansen in an unreserved carriage. Some surcharges vary with the season – see Travel Seasons later in this section. Above the basic futsū fare, the surcharge for kyūkō (ordinary express) and tokkyū (limited express) services are:

Distance (Up to)	Kyūkō Surcharge	Tokkyū Surcharge
50 km	¥520	¥720
100 km	¥720	¥1130
150 km	¥930	¥1750
200 km	¥1030	¥2060
300 km	¥1240	¥2270
400 km	¥1240	¥2470
600 km	¥1240	¥2780
600 km +	¥1240	¥3090

The express surcharges (but not the shinkansen super-express surcharge) can be paid to the train conductor. There's an additional surcharge for Green Car (1st class) travel. Further surcharges apply for overnight sleepers and these vary with the berth type from ¥5150 for a regular three-tier bunk, ¥6180 to ¥10,300 for various types of two-tier bunks, and up to ¥13,100 to ¥16,850 for a standard or 'royal' compartment. Note that there are no sleepers on the shinkansen services as none of these run overnight. Japan Rail Pass users must still pay the sleeper surcharge. Sleeper services mainly operate on trains from Tokyo or Osaka to destinations in Western Honshū and Kyūshū.

The Nozomi super express has higher surcharges than other shinkansen and cannot be used with a Japan Rail Pass. As a guideline, the surcharge for Tokyo-Nagoya is ¥5160 as opposed to ¥4410 by other shinkansen; for Tokyo-Hakata ¥9920 as opposed to ¥8120 by other shinkansen.

Travel Seasons Some of the fare surcharges are different during the off-peak and peak seasons as opposed to the rest of the year. Off-peak dates are between 16 January and 28 February, all of June and September, and from 1 November to 20 December, except Friday, Saturday, Sunday, national holidays and the day before national holidays. Peak season dates are 28 April to 6 May (Golden Week), 21 July to 31 August, 25 December to 10 January and 21 March to 5 April. During these peak seasons, travelling is very difficult and trains are heavily booked. The rest of the year is 'normal season'! On shinkansen services, for example, you get a ¥200 discount during the off-peak season or pay a ¥200 surcharge during the peak season.

Discounts & Special Fares If you buy a return ticket for a trip which is more than 600 km each way, you qualify for a 20% discount on the return leg. You can also get coupons for discounted accommodation and tours combined with your rail travel. There's even a JR prepaid card which you can use for ticket vending machines to gain a 6% or 7% discount on the larger denomination cards.

There are a number of excursion tickets, known as *shūyū-ken* or *furii* (sounds like 'free') *kippu*. A *waido shūyū-ken* or 'wide

excursion ticket' takes you to your destination and back and gives you unlimited JR local travel in the destination area. There are waido shūyū-ken available to travel from Tokyo to Hokkaidō and then around Hokkaidō for up to 20 days. A Kyūshū or Shikoku waido shūyū-ken gets you to and from either island and gives you 20 days of travel around them. You can even go to Kyūshū one way by rail and one way by ferry.

Variations include a *mini shūyū-ken* (a shorter time span, smaller area waido shūyū-ken), a *rutō shūyū-ken* (a multi-stop ticket along a certain route) and an *ippan shūyū-ken* (a sort of do-it-yourself return ticket with certain stops). One interesting variation is a five day *seishun jūhachi kippu*, literally a 'Youth 18 Ticket'. The latter are strictly speaking aimed at Japanese university students and are only available during university vacation periods (2 February to 20 April, 20 July to 10 September, 10 December to 20 January).

Still, it seems that many foreign residents have successfully used these tickets, even if they look a few years the wrong side of 18. Basically, they allow you to buy five train tickets to anywhere in Japan for ¥11,300. The only catches are that you can only travel on local trains and each ticket must be used within 24 hours. However, even if you only use one to go to Kyoto and back from Tokyo (with a few side trips thrown in), you'll be saving money.

Japan Rail Pass
One of Japan's few travel bargains is the unlimited travel Japan Rail Pass. The pass lets you use any JR services for seven days for ¥27,800, 14 days for ¥44,200 or 21 days for ¥56,600. Green Car (1st class) passes are ¥37,000, ¥60,000 and ¥78,000 respectively. Children aged six to 11 get a 50% discount. The pass cannot be used for the new super express Nozomi shinkansen service, but is OK for everything else. The only additional surcharge levied on the Japan Rail Pass is for overnight sleepers. Since a reserved seat Tokyo-Kyoto shinkansen ticket costs ¥12,970, you only have to travel Tokyo-

Kyoto-Tokyo to make a seven day pass come close to paying off.

The pass can only be bought overseas and cannot be used by foreign residents in Japan. The clock starts to tick on the pass as soon as you validate it, which can be done at certain major railway stations or even at the JR counter at Narita Airport if you're intending to jump on a JR train immediately. Don't validate it if you're just going into Tokyo and intend to hang around the city for a few days. The pass is valid *only* on JR services, you will still have to pay for private railway services.

Schedules & Information

The most complete timetables can be found in the *jikokuhyō* (book of timetables) but JNTO produce a handy English-language *Railway Timetable* booklet which explains a great deal about the railway services in Japan and gives timetables for the shinkansen services, JR limited expresses and major private lines. If your visit to Japan is a short one and you will not be straying far from the major tourist destinations, this booklet may well be all you need.

The TIC offices at Narita Airport, Tokyo and Kyoto can also supply information on specific schedules. Major JR stations all have JR train information counters, however, you can only be certain of finding someone who speaks English at the really big foreign tourist points, like Tokyo station.

If you need to know anything about JR – time schedules, fares, fastest routings, lost baggage, discounts on rail travel, hotels and car rental – call the JR East-Infoline in Tokyo on ☎ 3423-0111. The service is available in English and operates from 10 am to 6 pm, Monday to Friday, but not on holidays.

BUS

In addition to its local city bus services, Japan also has a comprehensive network of long-distance buses. These 'highway buses' are nowhere near as fast as the shinkansen and heavy traffic can delay them even further, but the fares are comparable with those of the local train (futsū) without any

reservation or express surcharges. The trip between Tokyo and Sendai, for example, takes about two hours by shinkansen, four hours by limited express and nearly eight hours by bus. Tokyo-Kyoto is less than three hours by shinkansen and more than eight hours by bus.

Bus services have been growing in recent years, partly because of the gradual extension of the expressway network, partly because of the closing of uneconomical JR lines and partly because of escalating rail fares. Of course, there are also many places in Japan where railways do not run and bus travel is the only public transport option.

The main intercity bus services run on the expressways and usually stop at expressway bus stops where local transport is available to adjacent centres. The main expressway bus route runs between Tokyo, Nagoya, Kyoto and Osaka and stops are made at each city's main railway station. There are also overnight services and the comfortable reclining seats are better for a night's sleep than sitting up in an overnight train.

Bookings can be made through JTB offices or at the Green Window in large JR stations. The Japan Rail Pass is valid on some highway buses although, of course, the shinkansen would be far preferable! Note, however, that the storage racks on most buses are generally too small for backpacks. Other popular bus services include routes from Tokyo to Sendai, Yamagata and Hirosaki in Northern Honshū and to Niigata and areas around Mt Fuji in Central Honshū. There are extensive networks from Osaka and Hiroshima into areas of Western Honshū and around the smaller islands of Hokkaidō, Kyūshū and Shikoku.

Night Services

An option that is becoming increasingly popular among travellers is the network of night buses. They are relatively cheap, spacious (allowing room to stretch out and get some sleep) and save on a night's accommodation. They typically leave at around 10 or 11 pm and arrive the following morning at around 6 or 7 am.

Costs

Some typical prices out of Tokyo include:

Destination	Fare
Aomori	¥10,000
Sendai	¥7700
Niigata	¥5150
Nagoya	¥6300
Kyoto	¥8030
Osaka	¥8450
Hiroshima	¥11,840
Hakata	¥15,000

CAR

One of the common myths about travel in Japan is that it's virtually impossible for a gaijin to travel by car: the roads are narrow and congested making travel incredibly slow; getting lost forever is a constant fear since we cannot read the signs; the driving is suicidal; fuel is prohibitively expensive; parking is impossible and we're altogether better off sticking to the trains.

None of these myths is necessarily true. Of course, driving in Tokyo *is* a near impossibility but not many visitors rent cars to get around New York or London either. The roads are actually fairly well signposted in English so, on the major roads, getting lost is unlikely. The minor roads are more likely to test your navigational ability but as Japan is compact, you can never be lost for long. The driving is a long way from suicidal – polite and cautious is probably a better description. Fuel is expensive but no more so than most of Europe, in fact it's cheaper than many countries in Europe. As for parking, it is rarely free, but neither is it impossibly expensive.

All in all, driving in Japan is quite feasible, even for the mildly adventurous. In some areas of the country it can prove much more convenient than other forms of travel and, between a group of people (two adults and a couple of children for example), it can also prove quite economical. You will certainly see more of the country than all but the most energetic public transport users.

On the Road

Licence You'll need an International Driving Permit backed up by your own national licence. The international permit is issued by your national automobile association and costs around US$5. Make sure it's endorsed for cars and motorcycles if you're licensed for both.

Foreign licences and International Driving Permits are only valid in Japan for six months. If you are staying longer you will have to get a Japanese licence from the licence office *(shikenjo)*. You need your own licence, passport photos, Alien Registration Card or Certificate of Residence, the fee and there's also a simple eyesight test to pass.

Even when driving, the Japanese manage to convey respect towards others, sometimes with near disastrous results. I was being driven by a Japanese lady out in the rural parts of Wakayama Prefecture, when we met another car at a junction. My friend bowed regally, and waited. The other driver bowed equally regally, and waited. Suddenly, both drivers shot forwards at the same instant, then lurched to a violent halt.

This sequence continued: more bows, more lurching forwards until we were within a few feet of each other. Just as I was bracing myself for impact, my friend bowed even deeper and longer over the steering wheel. When she raised her head again, the other car had driven off. Highway code?

Robert Strauss

Fuel There's no shortage of petrol (gas) stations, the cost of petrol is about ¥150 to ¥160 per litre (about US$5.00 per US gallon) and the driveway service will bring a tear to the eye of any driver who resents the Western trend to self-service. In Japan, not only does your windscreen get washed but you may even find your floor mats being laundered and the whole staff coming out, at the trot, to usher you back into the traffic and bow respectfully as you depart.

Maps & Navigation Get a copy of the *Japan Road Atlas* (Shobunsha, Tokyo, 1990, ¥2890). It's all in romaji with sufficient names in kanji to make navigation possible even off the major roads. If you're really intent on making your way through the back blocks, a Japanese map will prove useful even if your knowledge of kanji is nil. When you really get lost, a signposted junction will offer some clues if you've got a good map to compare the symbols.

These days, there is a great deal of signposting in romaji so getting around is not a great feat. Road route numbers also help; for example, if you know you want to follow Route 9 until you get to Route 36 the frequent roadside numbers make navigation child's play. If you are attempting tricky navigation, use your maps imaginatively – watch out for the railway line, the rivers, the landmarks. They're all useful ways of locating yourself when you can't read the signs. Bring a compass, you'll often find it useful and, if you really get lost, Japan's compact size will always come to the rescue – 'If I head generally north I'm going to hit the main road or the coast in 20 km'.

If you're a member of an automobile association in your home country you're eligible for reciprocal rights at the Japan Automobile Federation (JAF). Its office is directly opposite the entrance to the Tokyo Tower at 3-5-8 Shiba-kōen, Minato-ku, Tokyo 105. The JAF has a variety of publications, including a useful *Rules of the Road* book and will make up strip maps for its members.

Road Rules

Driving in Japan is on the left – like most other countries in the region stretching from India, through South-East Asia and down through Australia and the Pacific. One of the minor curiosities about this is that when the Japanese buy imported cars they like them to be really different – eg, to have the steering wheel on the left side. This might have some sort of logic to it with German or US cars (they drive on the right) but none whatsoever with British cars (like the Japanese, the British drive on the left). Nevertheless, most Jaguars, Rolls-Royces and Minis sold in Japan will be left-hand drive. Apart from being on the wrong side of the road from the European or North American perspective, there are no real problems with driving in Japan. There are no unusual rules or interpretations of them and most signposts follow international conventions. The JAF has an English-language *Rules of the Road* book for ¥1860 (slightly discounted if you're a member of an overseas association). See the previous Maps & Navigation section for more about the JAF.

You see very little evidence of the police on Japanese roads, they're simply not there most of the time. I did see a taxi driver grabbed for running a red light in Kyoto once, but I never saw a speed trap and on most roads, there's very little opportunity to break the speed limit anyway. On the expressways, lots of cars exceed the speed limit and on one occasion I saw a police car cruising sedately along the inside lane at more-or-less the limit, while cars whizzed by at something above it. When speed traps *are* used, they will probably be on the one nice open stretch of road where the speed limit is way below the speed most people will be inclined to travel.

Tony Wheeler

Speed traps, however, are notorious in Hokkaidō and their presence is advertised in a strange manner: the incredibly rusty hulk of what was once a police car is simply mounted on a pedestal beside the road. Passing drivers nonchalantly activate their hi-tech radar detector defence systems and accelerate. Hokkaidō is definitely one of those places in Japan where you not only need to make use of a car, but you can also really enjoy yourself.

Robert Strauss

A blind eye may be turned to moderate speeding but for drinking and driving you get locked up and the key is thrown away. Don't do it.

Rental

There are a great many car rental companies in Japan and although you'll find many of them represented at Narita Airport, renting a car at Narita to drive into Tokyo is absolutely not a good idea. Heading off in the opposite direction towards Hokkaidō makes a lot more sense. Car rental offices cluster round railway stations and the best way to use rent-a-cars in Japan is to take a train for the long-distance part of your trip, then rent a car when you get to the area you want to explore. For example the northern (San-in) coast of Western Honshū is a good place to drive – but don't drive there from Tokyo, take the train to Kyoto and rent a car there.

Japanese car rental companies are set up for this type of operation and offer lots of short-term rates – such as for people who just want a car for half a day. However, they're not much good at one-way rentals; you're always going to get hit for a repositioning charge and if the car has to be brought back from another island, the cost can be very high indeed. Typical one-way charges within the island of Honshū are ¥6000 for 100 km and ¥2400 for each additional 50 km. It makes a lot of sense to make your trip a loop one and return the car to the original renting office. Some of the main Japanese car rental companies and their Tokyo phone numbers are:

Car Rental Company	Telephone
Budget	☎ 03-3263-6321
Nippon	☎ 03-3485-7196
Nissan	☎ 03-3587-4123
Toyota	☎ 03-3264-0100

Rental costs are generally a flat rate including unlimited km. Typical rental rates for a small car (a Toyota Starlet or Mazda 121 – one step up from the Japanese microcars) is ¥8000 to ¥9000 for the first day and ¥5500 to ¥7000 per day thereafter. Move up a bracket (a Mazda 323 or Toyota Corolla) and you're looking at ¥10,000 to ¥13,500 for the first day and ¥8000 to ¥9000 thereafter. On top of the rental charge there's a ¥1000 per day insurance cost. Of course, you can also rent luxury cars, sports cars, even imported cars, but why give yourself headaches you don't need? Something easy to park is probably the best thing to have in Japan.

It's also worth bearing in mind that rental costs go up during peak seasons: 28 April to 6 May, 20 July to 31 August and 28 December to 5 January. The increase can make quite a difference to costs. A car that costs ¥8800 a day usually will go up to ¥9700 during any of the peak seasons.

Communication can be a major problem when renting a car, although waving your driving licence and credit card and pointing at a picture of the type of car you want to rent usually makes it pretty clear what you want. Some of the offices will have a rent-a-car

phrasebook with questions you might need to ask in English and Japanese – 'The cassette deck has jammed and my favourite Dylan tape is stuck in it'. Nippon Rent-a-Car even has an 'English-speaking desk' (☎ 03-3485-7196) where you can ring for assistance in English.

Check over your car carefully – perhaps it's an expectation that cars will only be used locally, but rental cars in Japan don't seem to be checked as thoroughly as those in the West. Check all the tyres are in good order and that the jack and tool kit are all in place.

I once rented a car with a radio that didn't work until I'd succeeded in unjamming the cassette mechanism, and when I had a puncture, I discovered the spare was totally unuseable since some previous renter had hit a kerb hard enough to make it pretzel shaped.

Tony Wheeler

Apart from maps and a phrasebook, other essentials are a compass (see Maps & Navigation in the On the Road section later in this chapter) and your favourite cassette tapes. Non-Japanese speakers will find very little to listen to on Japanese radio and the cassettes will help pass time in traffic jams. A Japanese-language tape is a good idea if you're keen to learn some Japanese as you drive.

Your rented car will, incidentally, almost certainly be white. Like refrigerators and washing machines, cars in Japan seem to be looked upon as white goods – 80% or 90% of the cars on the road are white. A few hot shots have red sports cars, a few members of the avant-garde drive black or grey cars, but apart from that it's white-white-white.

Purchase

Since few foreign tourists drive themselves around Japan, the manufacturers have never promoted the overseas delivery options which are so popular with expensive European cars. Presumably, it could be done if you really wanted to. Long-term visitors or residents are more likely to be looking for a second-hand vehicle to use while in Japan and sell on departure. However, think carefully before making this decision. There are so many drawbacks to running a car in

Japan's crowded cities that the alternative of renting a car on the odd occasion when you really need one may be preferable.

Buying cars in Japan is subject to the same pitfalls as in most other places in the world – a Tokyo used car salesman would sell his grandma-san just like anywhere else – but the stringent safety inspections mean that you're unlikely to buy an unsafe vehicle. Once it's three years old, every car has to go through a *shaken* (inspection) every two years which is so severe that it quickly becomes cheaper to junk your car and buy another. The shaken costs about ¥100,000 and once the car reaches nine years of age it has to be inspected every year. This is the major reason you see so few old cars on the road in Japan. A car approaching an unpassable shaken drops in value very rapidly and, if you can find one, could make a good short-term purchase. The shaken system is currently being reexamined by the government and, by the time you have this book is in your hands, it should be worth enquiring into the latest situation.

Another obstacle to buying a car in Japan is that you must have an off-street parking place before you can complete the registration formalities. Exemption from this requirement is one reason why the little microcars are so popular in Japan. To qualify as a microcar, a vehicle must have an engine of less than 660 cc, be less than 140 cm wide and less than 330 cm long.

Language is likely to be the major handicap in buying a car, so it's very useful to have a Japanese speaker to help with the negotiations. Foreign residents often sell their cars through the various English-language papers.

Roads

When & Where to Drive If you're going to drive yourself in Japan, do it sensibly. There's absolutely no reason to drive in the big cities or to drive in the heavily built-up areas like the San-yō coast of Western Honshū. If you're simply going from town A to town B and then stopping for a while, you're much better off taking the train.

In the less urbanised areas, however, a car can be useful. The northern San-in coast of Western Honshū, for example, is a world apart from the congested southern coast and slow public transport makes a car much more feasible. Hokkaidō is another good area for a drive-yourself trip. There are many areas where a car can be useful for a short excursion into the surrounding countryside, such as the loop from Kagoshima in Kyūshū down to Chiran and Ibusuki on the Satsuma Peninsula or for a couple of days to make a circuit of (say) Okinawa Island. Car rental companies cater to this with short rental periods of a day or half day.

Expressways The expressway system will get you from one end of the country to another but it is not particularly extensive. Also, since all the expressways charge tolls, it is uniformly expensive – about ¥27 a km. Tokyo to Kyoto, for example, will cost about ¥9000 in tolls. This does have the benefit of keeping most people off the expressways so they are often delightfully uncrowded. The speed limit on expressways is 80 km/h but seems to be uniformly ignored. At a steady 100 km/h, you will still find as many cars overtaking you as you overtake, some of them going very fast indeed.

There are good rest stops and service centres at regular intervals. A prepaid highway card, available from tollbooths or at the service areas, saves you having to carry so much cash and gives you a 4% to 8% discount in the larger card denominations. Exits are usually fairly well signposted in romaji but make sure you know the name of your exit as it may not necessarily be the same as the city you're heading towards.

Other Roads On Japan's lesser roads, the speed limit is usually 50 km/h, and you can often drive for hours without ever getting up to that speed! The roads are narrow, traffic is usually heavy, opportunities to overtake are limited and no-overtaking restrictions often apply in the few areas where you could overtake safely. Sometimes you never seem to get out of built-up areas and the heavy traffic and frequent traffic lights can make covering 300 km in a long day's drive quite a feat. It's worth contemplating that just after WW II, only 1.5% of the roads in Japan were paved.

Generally, however, the traffic does keep moving, slow though that movement may be. The further you travel from the main highways, the more interesting the countryside becomes. Occasionally you'll come to stretches which are a wonderful surprise. Along a beautiful winding mountain road without a car in sight, it's easy to appreciate why the Japanese have come to make such nice sports cars.

Parking

Along with congestion and navigational difficulties, the impossibility of finding a parking space is the other major myth about driving in Japan. While there are few places you can park for free and roadside parking is virtually nonexistent, finding a place to park is usually not too difficult and the cost is rarely excessive.

Parking meters are rare and when they do exist are often a distinct technological step beyond what we have in the West. One type has an electronic 'eye' to detect if your car is still sitting there when your time is up. If so, a light on top of the meter then starts to flash to alert a passing meter inspector to come and issue the ticket! Even more sinister are the meters which lock your car in place. When your time's up a barrier rises up between the front and back wheels and you cannot move the car until you've paid the fine directly into the meter! Under normal circumstances, meters usually cost ¥100 for each half hour.

Off-street parking is usually in car parks – often very small ones with an attendant in a booth who records your licence plate number on arrival and charges you when you leave. Sometimes you have to leave the keys with the attendant. The charge might be ¥200 or ¥300 an hour but if you can read the small print, you may get a pleasant surprise or a nasty shock. Sometimes the first half hour or hour is free, particularly at railway station car parks. At some car parks the rate increases dramatically after, say, three hours to discourage long-term car parking. Unfor-

tunately, it takes a lot of Japanese small print to discover these regulations. Even in big city multistorey car parks, the charges are rarely as high as in equivalent car parks in, say, Australia or the USA.

Railway station car parks are usually a good bet, as they are conveniently central and reasonably priced. Watch for interesting car parking technology, particularly the rotating vertical conveyer belts where your car disappears into a sort of filing cabinet. Car parking spaces seem to be zealously guarded and many daytime car parks are chained up at night to prevent anyone getting a free space for the evening.

In one city I saw a series of meters which operated from 7 am to 7 pm. So they were free after 7 pm, right? No way, for no visible reason, after 7 pm it was 'no parking'!

Tony Wheeler

MOTORCYCLE

Japan is the home of the modern motorcycle and you certainly see a lot on the road. Once upon a time they were all small displacement machines but now there are plenty of larger motorcycles as well. During the holidays you will see many groups of touring motorcyclists and, as usual in Japan, they will all be superbly equipped with shiny new motorcycles, efficient carriers and panniers, expensive riding leathers and, when the inevitable rain comes down, excellent rainproof gear.

Buying or Renting a Motorcycle

If you enjoy motorcycles and you're staying long enough to make buying and selling a motorcycle worthwhile, then this can be a great way of getting around the country. A motorcycle provides the advantages of your own transport without the automotive drawback of finding a place to park. Nor do you suffer so badly from the congested traffic.

Although Japan is famed for its large-capacity road burners, these bikes are less popular in Japan for a number of reasons including outright restrictions on the sale of machines over 750 cc. The motorcycle

Foreign & Unusual Motorcycles

Just as expensive European cars have carved out a lucrative market in Japan, so have foreign motorcycles. The occasional Italian Ducati or Moto-Guzzi, German BMW or British Triumph can be seen among the throngs of Kawahondazukis, but the real foreign standout is the Harley-Davidson. Japanese motorcyclists have a real passion for 'hogs' and many HD riders even have their bikes kitted out like the California Highway Patrol and ride them in what looks like a US police uniform!

Old motorcycles also have a following, though you rarely see them on the road. There are Japanese magazines for vintage motorcycle enthusiasts and from the number of for-sale advertisements for old motorcycles, there must be many carefully restored machines hidden away – older Japanese ones as well as European and US collectors' items. Corin Motors in Ueno (see Buying or Renting a Motorcycle) have a small museum of old motorcycles and the Honda showroom, beside the Aoyama Itchōme subway station, displays some old Honda racing motorcycles including Mike Hailwood's beautiful six cylinder Honda of the mid-60s. ■

licence-testing procedure also varies with the size of machine and before you can get a licence for a 750 cc motorcycle, you must prove you can lift one up after it has fallen over! Not surprisingly, this cuts down on the number of potential big motorcycle riders.

The 400 cc machines are the most popular large motorcycles in Japan but, for general touring, a 250 cc machine is probably the best bet. Apart from being quite large enough for a compact country like Japan, machines up to 250 cc are also exempt from the expensive shaken (inspections).

Smaller machines are banned from expressways and are generally less suitable for long-distance touring but people have ridden them from one end of Japan to another on little 50 cc 'step-thrus'. An advantage of these is that you can ride them with just a driving licence, and don't need to get a motorcycle licence.

Buying a new machine from Japan's multitude of motorcycle dealers is no problem, though you will find a better choice of large capacity machines in the big cities. Used motorcycles are often not much cheaper than new ones and, unless you buy from another gaijin, you will face the usual language problems in finding and buying one. Because of the small demand for large motorcycles, their prices tend to drop more steeply than small ones, but on the other hand, the popularity of the 250 cc class means these machines hold their value better. As with

everything else in Japan, you rarely see a motorcycle more than a couple of years old.

There are numerous used motorcycle dealers around Ueno station in Tokyo, on the streets parallel to Shōwa-dōri and north of the Ueno subway station. Some of these larger dealers actually employ gaijin salespeople who speak Japanese and English. Corin Motors (☎ 03-3841-4112) is a collection of nearly 20 motorcycle shops along Korin-chō, a block from the Disneyland bus exit. They're open from 9 am to 7 pm, Monday to Saturday. As with used cars the English-language papers and magazines are a good place to look for a foreigner's motorcycle for sale.

Renting a motorcycle for long-distance touring is not as easy as renting a car, although small scooters are available in many places for local sightseeing.

On the Road

As with car driving, your overseas licence and International Driving Permit are all you need to ride a motorcycle in Japan. Crash helmets are compulsory and you should also ensure your riding gear is adequate to cope with the weather, particularly rain. For much of the year the climate is ideal for motorcycle touring but when it rains it really rains.

Touring equipment – bags, panniers, carrier racks, straps and the like – are all readily available from dealers. Remember to pack clothing in plastic bags to ensure it stays dry, even if you don't. An adequate supply of tools and a puncture repair outfit can prove invaluable.

Riding in Japan is no more dangerous than anywhere else in the world, which is to say it is not very safe and great care should be taken at all times. Japan has the full range of worldwide motorcycle hazards from single-minded taxi drivers to unexpected changes in road surface, heedless car-door openers to runaway dogs.

BICYCLE

If you're keen about long-distance bicycle touring, exploring Japan by bicycle is perfectly feasible. Although the slow average speed of traffic on Japanese roads is no problem for a bike rider, pedalling along in a constant stream of heavy traffic is no fun at all. Reportedly, the Japan Cycling Association warns cyclists not to ride more than 100 km per day because of the danger from car exhaust fumes. Japanese cyclists seem to have a higher tolerance of heavy traffic and doggedly follow routes down recommended major highways. Tunnels can be an unnerving experience at first.

The secret of enjoyable touring is to get off the busy main highways and onto the minor roads. This requires careful route planning, good maps and either some ability with kanji or the patience to decipher country road signs, where romaji is much less likely

to be used. Favourite touring areas for foreign cyclists include Kyūshū, Shikoku, the Japan Alps (if you like gradients!), the Noto-hantō Peninsula and definitely Hokkaidō. Valiant Japanese cyclists have been known to ride as far up Mt Fuji as the road permitted and then shouldered their steeds so that they could conquer the peak together.

There's no point in fighting your way out of big cities by bicycle. Put your bike on the train or bus and get out to the country before you start pedalling. To take a bicycle on a train you may be required to use a bicycle carrying bag: they're available from good bicycle shops.

The Maps & Navigation section for car travel earlier in this chapter also applies to bicycles but there is also a series of Bridgestone *saikuringu mapu* (cycling maps). They identify many places in romaji as well as kanji but, as yet, only cover part of the country in Central Honshū. The cycling maps show where bicycles can be rented, identify special bicycle tracks and accommodation which is popular with cyclists and even show steep road gradients.

The Japan Bicycle Promotion Institute (Nihon Jitensha Kaikon Biru) (☎ 03-3583-5444) is also known as the Bicycle Cultural Centre and is across from the US Embassy at 1-9-3 Akasaka, Minato-ku, Tokyo. The institute has a museum and is a useful source of information about the special inns for

---

Cycling in Japan

In 1899, the British adventurer John Foster Frazer, cycling across the country en route from Europe to the USA, declared Japan 'the wheelman's paradise'. Foster may not have had to contend with the traffic on Route 1 or the bewildering complexities of Tokyo urban expressways, but his original judgement remains sound. Japan is still a great country to explore on two wheels.

Unchanged since Foster's day are the topography and the climate, both important considerations for the would-be bicycle tourer. Japan's topographic wild card is its mountains. Even the coastal roads can have their hilly moments. (I cursed a former edition of this book atop a very large hill on the Niigata coastline for describing the area as 'ideal for cycling' – well, perhaps it was and my legs weren't.)

The Tōkaidō coastline, stretching from Tokyo south-westwards through Nagoya and past Osaka is mostly flat, but it is also polluted, congested and unrelievedly boring. Avoid Route 1 at all costs. On the other hand, the Japan Sea coastline, windswept, sometimes hilly but rarely congested, is a cyclist's delight. It provides the cyclist with good roads, abundant wildlife and some of the freshest seafood in Japan. Hokkaidō, Shikoku and Kyūshū offer more of the same on even quieter roads.

That said, my own favourite cycling territory is in the mountains of Central Honshū – hard work but rewarded by spectacular scenery, delicious hot springs in which to soothe aching bones and, best of all, a glimpse of rural Japan that few city dwellers get a chance to see,

Climatic conditions require some serious consideration, particularly for cyclists planning a lengthy tour of Japan. Winter is something of a mixed bag. November and December are often sunny though cold and can be good months for touring Japan's coastal regions. In January and February, however, snowfalls, rain and cold conditions make much of Japan – particularly the Japan Alps, Northern Honshū and Hokkaidō – unattractive to all but the most masochistic of cyclists. Summer, on the other hand, is swelteringly hot and humid, a good time to stick to the coast or the cooler latitudes of Hokkaidō.

The rainy season is best avoided for obvious reasons; and while it generally arrives in May and lingers for just a few weeks, it can't always be relied on to end on time, as I discovered on one sodden trip from Niigata to Kyoto. Typhoons blow up with immense ferocity in late summer and can play havoc with a tight itinerary. This leaves spring and autumn, the best seasons to be cycling in Japan: both are blessed with cool weather and minimal rainfall and see the Japanese countryside at its best.

The single biggest frustration for the cyclist in Japan is probably the lack of Romanised street names. This situation is improving gradually, but it can still be maddeningly difficult to find your way out of urban centres onto the road of your choice. (On one memorable occasion I managed a 90 minute circumnavigation of the Kanazawa ring road that brought me back to where I'd started.) A handy way of avoiding such confusion and the frustration of inner-city traffic is to put your bike on a train. To do this, a carry bag is required. Specialist carry bags, known in Japanese as *rinko bukuro* or *rinko baggu*, are available in bike shops, though I have made do with a blanket, two garbage bags and some sticky tape without any hassle. Strictly speaking, a ticket is required for your bike on the train (though it is rarely checked). Ask for a *temawarihin kippu*, a bargain at ¥260 and valid for any single journey. Ferries are also an opportunity to rest aching legs, and taking your bike aboard is no problem, though sometimes an extra charge will be required.

The best machine for touring Japan is a lightweight touring road machine or else a suitably equipped hybrid or cross bike. While mountain bikes are all the rage they are hardly required for Japan's well-paved roads. If you do bring a mountain bike, be sure to fit slimmer profile, preferably slick tyres, unless you're planning to spend all your time on mountain trails. Bikes with suspension forks require too much maintenance to consider as viable touring machines.

Perhaps the most important question for the cyclist looking at a holiday in Japan is costs. However you look at it, Japan is not cheap. Try to bring your own bike and accessories – even though Japan produces some of the world's best cycling equipment, prices will be cheaper at home. Camping is a good antidote to Japan's high accommodation costs, and many cyclists sustain themselves on a diet of instant noodles and sandwiches. Bear in mind, however, that after a long rainy day a comfortable inn with home cooking becomes a great temptation and it's easy to stray from a tight budget. Worst of all, if you're really pinching the pennies you'll never get into the bars, restaurants and hot springs where you can meet the Japanese at their most relaxed and welcoming. Even if you're planning to camp out and eat cheaply, it would be wise to budget US$30 per day.

Japan is a reasonably safe country to cycle in but, on a cautionary note, accidents happen more frequently than you might imagine. Comprehensive insurance is a must, as is a decent lightweight helmet. Also, despite Japan's reputation as a crime-free country, bicycles do get stolen, and of late professional gangs of bike thieves have been targeting big cities, especially around railway stations. I have lost no less than three expensive bikes over the last eight years. Bring a lock.

An essential purchase for those planning to tour Japan by bike is a copy of *Cycling Japan* (Kodansha, 1993), edited by Brian Harrell, long-term Japan resident and bike expert who also publishes the useful newsletter *Oizake* (Tailwind), another useful source of information (available for US$15 annually from B Harrell, 2-24-3 Tomigaya, Shibuya-ku, Tokyo, ☎ 03-3485-0471.

Cycling Japan is packed with information on everything from where to but a large-frame bike to insurance policies to the best *onsen* accommodation. The rest of the book suggests itineraries, from Hokkaidō to Kyūshū. For off-road aficionados the wilderness of the Oku-Shiga forest trail sounds particularly inviting, not least because it passes through the Shiojiri vineyards. Fill your drink bottle with a Honshū Muscator or a drop of Chardonnay?

John Ashburne

cyclists (cycling terminals or *saikuringu ter-minaru*), maps, routes and types of bicycles suitable for foreign dimensions.

Useful Japanese phrases for cyclists include *Kanazawa...yuki wa kono michi desuka?* ('Is this the route to...Kanazawa?') and *Chizu o kaite kudasai* ('Draw a map, please').

Purchase & Rental

If you already have some experience of bicycle touring you will, no doubt, have your own bicycle and should bring this with you. Most airlines these days will accommodate bikes, sometimes as part of your baggage allowance, sometimes free. Often, all you have to do is remove the pedals before handing it over.

If you want to buy a bicycle in Japan, it is possible but nowhere near as simple as you might think. A glance at the bicycle park besides any big railway station – or simply at the bicycle-clogged streets and sidewalks around the station – will reveal that lots of Japanese ride bikes. But very few of them are anything you would want to ride more than a few km. Despite all the high-tech Japanese bicycle equipment exported to the West, 10-speed touring bikes and modern mountain bikes are conspicuous by their absence in Japan. The vast majority of bicycles you see around the cities are utilitarian single-speed machines; cleaner and more modern versions of the heavy single-speed clunkers you find all over China or India.

This doesn't mean you can't find bicycles suitable for touring, it's just that you have to search them out. Even when you find an outlet handling multi-geared bikes, you should buy with care since they're likely to be built for the average-size Japanese rather than the average-size gaijin. If you're short to average it may not be a problem, but a tall gaijin is liable to have real trouble finding a big enough machine. Specialist dealers are one place to look, bicycle shops near US military bases are another but easiest of all is to bring your own bicycle with you.

A number of adventure travel companies operate bicycle tours in Japan. It is not easy to rent a touring bike for a long trip but, in a great many towns, you can rent bicycles to explore the town. Look for bicycle-rental outlets near the railway station; typical charges are around ¥200 per hour or ¥800 for a day. In many towns, a bicycle is absolutely the ideal way to get around. In the mountain town of Tsuwano in Western Honshū, for example, it seems like there are more bicycles available for rent than there can ever be visitors to rent them. Also in Western Honshū, between Okayama and Kurashiki, there's an excellent half-day cross country bicycle path and a one-way rental system.

Many youth hostels have bicycles to rent – there's a symbol identifying them in the (Japan) *Youth Hostel Handbook*. The cycling inns found in various locations around the country (see the Accommodation section in the Facts for the Visitor chapter) also rent bicycles.

Many foreigners who have just arrived in Japan, on seeing the piles of discarded bicycles that litter most Japanese cities, make the assumption that you can just pick one up and ride into the sunset. Theoretically, yes...but Japan doesn't really work that way. About the only thing that a Japanese policeman on beat is diligent about is checking bike registrations. If you get picked up with a bike that is not registered in your name, you'll be hauled down to the local kōban and have to wait while they trace the original owner and check the bike in question wasn't stolen. Next question: if you threw it away, would you like the gaijin that's riding it around to have it?

A friend of mine who had acquired a stolen bike was picked up and taken to the local police station. Within a couple of hours the boys in blue had established the bike had actually been thrown away and had the former owner on the phone. 'How do you feel about this foreigner who's riding it around hanging on to it?' they asked. The former owner thought about it for a while and then decided 'no', he'd prefer to have it dragged back to the rubbish dump to which it rightfully belonged.

HITCHING

Hitching is never entirely safe in any country in the world, and we don't recommend it.

Travellers who decide to hitch should understand that they are taking a small but potentially serious risk. However, many people do choose to hitch, and the advice that follows should help to make their journeys as fast and safe as possible.

Japan can be an excellent country for hitchhiking, though this may partly be because so few Japanese hitchhike and gaijin with their thumbs out are also a very rare sight. Nevertheless, there are many hitchhikers' tales of extraordinary kindness from motorists who have picked them up. There are equally numerous tales of motorists who think the hitchhiker has simply lost his or her way to the nearest railway station, and accordingly takes them there!

The rules for hitchhiking are similar to anywhere else in the world. Make it clear where you want to go – carry cardboard and a marker pen to write in kanji the name of your desired destination. Write it in romaji as well, as a car-driving gaijin may just be coming by. Look for a good place to hitch: it's no good starting from the middle of town, though unfortunately, in Japan, many towns only seem to end as they merge into the next one. Expressway entrance roads are probably your best bet. A woman should never hitch alone, even in Japan.

Truck drivers are particularly good bets for long-distance travel as they often head out on the expressways at night. If a driver is exiting before your intended destination, try and get dropped off at one of the expressway service centres. The Service Area Parking Area (SAPA) guide maps (☎ 03-3403-9111 in Tokyo) are excellent for hitchers. They're available free from expressway service areas and show full details of each interchange (IC) and rest stop – important orientation points if you have a limited knowledge of Japanese.

In Japan, as anywhere else in the world, it's a hitchhiker's duty to entertain. Although the language gap can make that difficult, get out your phrasebook and try and use at least *some* Japanese. Finally, be prepared to reciprocate kindnesses. You may find your driver will insist on buying you food or

---

Hitching in the Snow

Even in Japan, hitching ain't always plain sailing, as this traveller discovered when trying to hitch from Kamitono, near Hiroshima.

All the traffic going through the tollgates had come from the nearby ski fields to the west. We stood by the tollgate at the side of the road for five hours with our destination written in kanji. Intermittent bouts of sleet and sunshine had worn our patience thin so, in frustration, we climbed some embankments out of view of the tollgate attendant and clambered over a two metre fence lining the expressway.

It was a sorry sight – three unshaven foreigners hitching in the snow on a Japanese expressway. Sorrier still, however, when the highway patrol appeared and spotted us trying to hide our bulging packs from view. They drove past in disbelief, stopped, reversed, and stared at us. We were casually leaning against a rail. We nervously looked back at the policemen and, after what seemed like an eternity, my friend said 'konnichiwa'.

Although we knew we shouldn't have been hitching on the expressway we feigned ignorance and escaped with a warning. We were told to return to the tollgate if we wanted to hitch. I've hitched in several countries and have come to the conclusion that skiers will never stop to pick you up – skiers seem to be a different species from the rest of us.

Peter Moorhouse

---

drinks at a rest stop and it's nice if you can offer fruit, rice crackers or even cigarettes in return.

WALKING

There are many opportunities for hiking and mountain climbing in Japan but few visitors set out to get from place to place on foot. Alan Booth did, all the way from Hokkaidō to Kyūshū and wrote of the four month journey in *The Roads to Sata*.

It would be quite feasible to base an itinerary on walks, preferably out of season to avoid the day-trippers. JNTO publishes a *Combined Mini-Travel Series* with ideas on walks in Japan, including: *Walking Tour*

Courses in Tokyo (036); Walking Tour Courses in Nara (053); and Walking Tour Courses in Kyoto (052). Hiking in Japan by Paul Hunt (Kodansha, Tokyo & London, 1988) has excellent walking suggestions throughout the country.

The Oirase Valley walk, near Lake Towada-ko (Tōhoku) is very pleasant. In the Japan Alps region, Kamikōchi is one of several bases for walks; and Takayama has a pleasant extended walking trail for several hours round the temple district. In the Kiso Valley, there's a good walk between Magome and Tsumago.

In the Japan Alps and Hokkaidō, it's quite easy to break down hikes into smaller walks. On Rebun-tō Island, at the northern tip of Hokkaidō, there is plenty of scope to spend several days doing different walks in spectacular scenery; the same applies to the other Hokkaidō national parks, especially Daisetsuzan. Shikoku has some fine walks, particularly up Mt Ishizuchi-san. In Kyūshū there are some excellent walks through areas of volcanic activity, such as on the Ebino-kōgen Plateau near Mt Kirishima-yama.

BOAT

Japan is an island nation and there are a great many ferry services both between islands and between ports on the same island. Ferries can be an excellent way of getting from one place to another and seeing parts of Japan you might otherwise miss. Taking a ferry between Osaka (Honshū) and Beppu (Kyūshū), for example, is a good way of getting to Kyūshū and (if you choose the right departure time) seeing some of the Inland Sea on the way.

The routes vary widely from two-hour services between adjacent islands to 1½-day trips in what are really small ocean liners. The cheapest fares on the longer trips are in tatami-mat rooms where you simply unroll your futon on the floor and hope, if the ship is crowded, that your fellow passengers aren't too intent on knocking back the booze all night. In this basic class, fares will usually be lower than equivalent land travel but there

are also more expensive private cabins. Bicycles can always be brought along and most ferries also carry cars and motorcycles.

There are long-distance routes from Hokkaidō to Honshū and many services from Osaka and Tokyo to ports all over Japan, but the densest network of ferry routes connects Kyūshū, Shikoku and the southern (San-yō) coast of Western Honshū, across the waters of the Inland Sea. Apart from services connecting A to B, there are also many cruise ships operating in these waters. Ferries also connect the mainland islands with the many smaller islands off the coast and those dotted down to Okinawa and beyond to Taiwan.

Information on ferry routes, schedules and fares can be found in the comprehensive monthly *ōki-jikokuhyō* and on information sheets from TIC offices. Ask for a copy of the Japan Long Distance Ferry Association's excellent English-language brochure. Some ferry services and their lowest fares include:

From Hokkaidō to Honshū	Fare
Muroran to Oarai	¥9570
Otaru to Maizuru	¥6590
Otaru to Niigata	¥5150
Otaru to Tsuruga	¥6590
Tomakomai to Nagoya	¥15,450
Tomakomai to Oarai	¥9570
Tomakomai to Sendai	¥8850

From Tokyo	Fare
to Kōchi (Shikoku)	¥13,910
to Kokura (Kyūshū)	¥12,000
to Kushiro (Hokkaidō)	¥14,420
to Nachi-Katsuura (Honshū)	¥9060
to Naha (Okinawa)	¥19,670
to Tokushima (Shikoku)	¥8200
to Tomakomai (Hokkaidō)	¥11,840

From Osaka	Fare
to Beppu (Kyūshū)	¥6900
to Imabari (Shikoku)	¥4500
to Kagoshima (Kyūshū)	¥10,300
to Kōchi (Shikoku)	¥4530
to Matsuyama (Shikoku)	¥4430
to Naha (Okinawa)	¥15,450
to Shin-Moji (Kyūshū)	¥4840
to Takamatsu (Shikoku)	¥2780

From Honshū	Fare
Hiroshima to Beppu (Kyūshū)	¥3600
Kawasaki to Hyuga (Kyūshū)	¥17,720
Kōbe to Hyuga (Kyūshū)	¥7620
Kōbe to Kokura (Kyūshū)	¥4840
Kōbe to Matsuyama (Shikoku)	¥3500
Kōbe to Naha (Okinawa)	¥15,450
Kōbe to Oita (Kyūshū)	¥5050
Nagoya to Sendai (Honshū)	¥9580

From Kyūshū	Fare
Hakata to Naha (Okinawa)	¥12,970
Kagoshima to Naha (Okinawa)	¥11,840
Kokura to Matsuyama (Shikoku)	¥3500

LOCAL TRANSPORT

All the major cities offer a wide variety of public transport. In many cities you can get day passes for unlimited travel on bus, tram or subway systems. The pass is called a 'one day open ticket' or a *furii kippu*, though, of course, it's not free. If you're staying for an extended period in one city, commuter passes are available for regular travel.

Train & Subway

Several cities, in particular Osaka and Tokyo, have mass transit rail systems comprising a loop line around the city centre and radial lines into the central stations. In Tokyo, these *kokuden* trains are operated by 11 private railways which connect with the Yamanote loop. Kokuden services are also often directly connected with subway services. Subway systems operate in Fukuoka, Kōbe, Kyoto, Nagoya, Osaka, Sapporo, Sendai, Tokyo and Yokohama. They are usually the fastest and most convenient ways of getting around the city.

For subways and local trains you will probably have to buy your ticket from a machine. Usually they're relatively easy to understand even if you cannot read kanji since there will be a diagram explaining the routes and from this you can find what your fare should be. However, if you can't work the fare out, an easy solution is to simply buy a ticket for the lowest fare on the machine. When you finish your trip, go to the *ryōkin seisanjo* or fare adjustment office before you reach the exit gate and they will charge you the additional fare. JR train and subway sta-

tions not only have their names posted above the platform in kanji and romaji but also the names of the preceding and following stations.

Bus

Almost every Japanese city will have a bus service but it's usually the most difficult public transport system for gaijin to use. The destination names will almost inevitably be in kanji (the popular tourist town of Nikkō is a rare exception) and often, there are not even numbers to identify which bus you want. Buses are also subject to the usual traffic delays.

Fares are either paid to the driver on entering or as you leave the bus and usually operate on one of two systems. In Tokyo and some other cities, there's a flat fare irrespective of distance. In the other system, you take a ticket as you board which indicates the zone number at your starting point. When you get off, an electric sign at the front of the bus indicates the fare charged at that point for each starting zone number. You simply pay the driver the fare that matches your zone number. Drivers usually cannot change more than ¥1000 but there is often a change machine in the bus.

In almost any town of even remote tourist interest, there will be *teiki kankō* (tour buses), usually operating from the main railway station. The tour will be conducted entirely in Japanese and may well go to some locations of little interest. However, in places where the attractions are widespread or hard to reach by public transport, tours can be a good bet.

Tram

A number of cities have tram routes – particularly Nagasaki, Kumamoto and Kagoshima in Kyūshū, Kōchi and Matsuyama in Shikoku and Hakodate in Hokkaidō. These are excellent ways of getting around as they combine many of the advantages of bus travel (particularly the good views) with those of subways (it's easy to work out where you're going). Fares work on similar systems to bus travel and there are also unlimited-travel day tickets available.

Taxi

Taxis are convenient but expensive and are found in even quite small towns; the railway station is the best place to start looking. Drivers are often reluctant to stop and pick you up near a station taxi stand, so either wait at the correct spot for a taxi off the rank or walk a couple of streets away. Fares vary very little throughout the country – flagfall (posted on the nearside windows) is ¥600 for the first two km, after which it's ¥90 for each 347 metres (slightly farther outside Tokyo). There's also a time charge if the speed drops below 10 km/h. A red light means the taxi is available, a green light means there's an additional night time surcharge, a yellow light means the cab is on a call.

Don't whistle for a taxi, a straightforward wave should bring one politely to a halt. Don't open the door when it stops, the driver does that with a remote release. He (if there are women taxi drivers in Japan they are very rare) will also shut the door when you leave.

Drivers are normally as polite as anybody else in Japan but, like the majority of Japanese, are not linguists. If you can't tell him where you want to go, it's useful to have the name written down in Japanese. At hotel front desks there will usually be business cards complete with name and location, which are used for just this purpose. Note that business names, including hotels, are often quite different in Japanese and English.

Taxi drivers have just as much trouble finding Japanese addresses as anyone else. Just because you've gone round the block five times does not necessarily mean your driver is a country boy fresh in from the sticks. Asking directions and stopping at police boxes for help is standard practice.

Tipping is not a standard practice unless you've got a lot of bags or your destination has been particularly difficult to find. A 20% surcharge is added after 11 pm at night or for taxis summoned by radio. Like many other places in the world, taxis in Japan seem to dissolve and disappear when rained upon.

Late at night, particularly in the big cities, can be a difficult time to find taxis. Public transport stops relatively early but, as the salarymen reel out of the bars taxis, become increasingly difficult to find and also become mysteriously reluctant to pick up foreigners. The reason is quite simple: the drunken carousers will be heading home to some far distant suburb while the poor gaijin will probably be heading for a hotel just a few km away. At times of severe taxi shortage, the Japanese custom is to hold up fingers to indicate how many times the meter fare you are willing to pay.

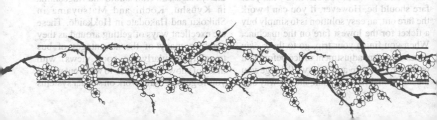

Tokyo is such a huge, sprawling city that you could spend a lifetime exploring it and still make new discoveries. Coming in on an airport limousine bus or by train, it often looks vaguely depressing: an unending sea of bleak concrete housing estates and office blocks traversed by overhead expressways crowded with trucks, buses and commuting Toyotas. But it doesn't take long to realise that, like all great cities, Tokyo is a bizarre conundrum, a riddle of contradictions that springs from the tension between the large-scale ugliness and the meticulous attention to detail that meets the attentive eye at every street corner; the tensions between the urgent rhythms of 20th century consumer culture and the quiet moments of stillness that are the legacy of other, older traditions.

While Tokyo sports some of the world's biggest and most lavish department stores, the average Tokyo suburb hasn't fallen prey to supermarket culture: the streets are lined with tiny specialist shops and restaurants, most of which stay open late into the night. Close to the soaring office blocks in the business districts and commercial centres are entertainment quarters; mazes of narrow alleys that blaze with neon lights by night and offer an intoxicating escape from the 12-hours-a-day working regimen that is the lot of Tokyo's surging crowds of office workers. In the shadow of the overhead expressways and the office blocks exist pockets of another Tokyo: an old wooden house, a kimono shop, a Japanese inn, an old lady in kimono and *geta* sweeping the pavement outside her home with a straw broom.

As might be expected of a city that has established itself as one of the economic powerhouses of the modern world, what confronts the visitor more than anything else is the sheer level of energy in Tokyo. Rush hour seems to begin with the first train of the day, sometime after 5 am, when drunken hordes of revellers from the night before start the two or three hour journey back to the so-called 'bedroom suburbs' in which they live.

On the busy train lines, even at 11 pm on a Monday evening there is standing room only. Crowds sweep you up, carry you in their wake, and a barrage of noise assaults you at every turn. Train drivers assume strange, masked voices to advise you of the stops. On escalators, female announcers who sound like chirping birds ask you to stand within the yellow lines. Shops blare out their personal anthems into the crowded streets, traffic lights and vending machines play digitised melodies, and politicians drive the streets in cars specially fitted with loud-speakers, thanking constituents for having voted for them in the recent elections.

In fact, some of the best sights Tokyo has to offer are often not the kind of things you can put in a guidebook. They jump out at you unexpectedly on a crowded street: the woman dressed in traditional kimono buying a hamburger at McDonald's; and the Buddhist monk with an alms bowl, standing serenely in the midst of jostling crowds of shoppers in Ginza. Tokyo is a living city. It is less a collection of sights than an experience.

HISTORY

Tokyo is something of a miracle; a city that has literally risen from the ashes (the result of US aerial bombing at the end of WW II) to become one of the world's leading economic centres.

Tokyo used to be known as Edo (Estuary), so named for its location at the mouth of the Sumida-gawa River. Edo first became historically significant in 1603, when Tokugawa Ieyasu established his shogunate (military government) there. From a sleepy backwater town, Edo grew into a city from which the Tokugawa clan governed the whole of Japan and which, by the late 18th century, had become the most populous city in the world. When the Tokugawa clan fell

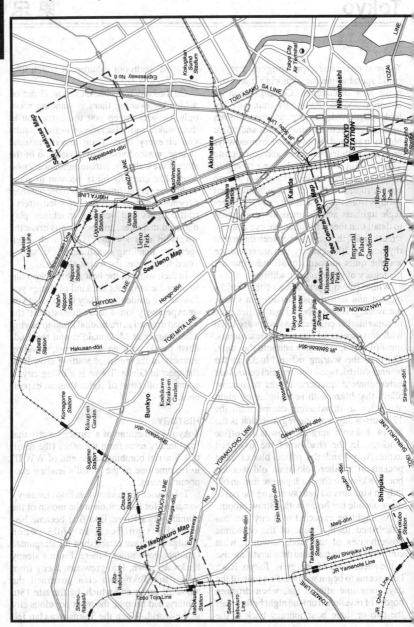

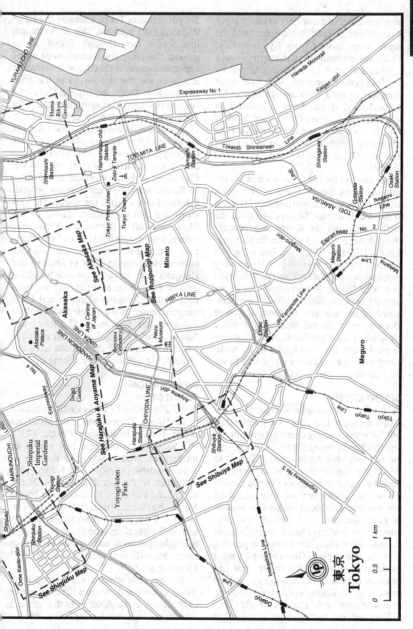

from power and the authority of the emperor was restored in 1868, the emperor and the capital were moved from Kyoto to Edo, which was renamed Tokyo (Eastern Capital).

After 250 years of isolation imposed by the Tokugawa Shogunate, Tokyo set about transforming itself into a modern metropolis. Remarkably, it has been successful in achieving this in spite of two major disasters that, in each case, practically levelled the whole city: the great earthquake and ensuing fires of 1923, and the US air raids of 1944 and 1945.

Not much of the old Japan is left in Tokyo; indeed, given the violence of the city's history – the periodic conflagrations (known to the locals as the 'flowers of Edo'), the earthquakes and the destruction brought about through war – it's a wonder that anything is left at all. What you find today is a uniquely Japanese version of a 21st century city: a weaving of the remnants of a shattered past with 'Blade Runneresque' cityscapes peopled by Orwellian legions of business-suited office workers. In short, if you're looking for traditional Japan you're better off heading for Kyoto or Kamakura, where recent history has been kinder to the traditional past. Tokyo is a place you visit to see the Japanese success story in action.

ORIENTATION

Tokyo is a vast conurbation spreading out across the Kantō Plain from Tokyo-wan Bay. But for visitors nearly everything of interest lies either on or within the JR Yamanote line, the rail loop that circles central Tokyo. In Edo times, Yamanote referred to 'Uptown'; the estates and residences of feudal barons, the military aristocracy and other members of the elite of Edo society in the hilly regions of Edo. Shitamachi, or 'Downtown', was home to the working classes, merchants and artisans. Even today the distinction persists, with the areas west of Ginza being the more modernised, housing the commercial and business centres of modern Tokyo, and the areas east of Ginza, centred in Asakusa, retaining more of the character of old Edo.

Essential for finding your way around Tokyo is a map of Tokyo's subway and Japan Railways (JR) network. The JR Yamanote line does a loop through Tokyo, above ground, that takes you through most of the important centres of the city, both Yamanote and, to a lesser extent, Shitamachi. It is actually possible to do the trip very cheaply, because buying a ticket to the next station for ¥120 doesn't stop you going in the less direct of the two possible directions and taking in the whole city on the way. Starting in Ueno, two stops to the south is Akihabara, the discount electronics capital of Tokyo. Continuing in the same direction, you come to Kanda, which is near Tokyo's second-hand bookshop district, Jimbō-chō. The next stops are Tokyo station, close to the Marunouchi office district, and Yūraku-chō station, a short walk from Ginza. From there, trains continue through to the teen-oriented, fashionable shopping areas of Shibuya and Harajuku. Another two stops on is Shinjuku, a massive shopping, entertainment and business district. Between Shinjuku and Ueno the train passes through Ikebukuro (really a down-market version of Shinjuku) and Nippori, one of the few areas left in Tokyo where you can find buildings that have survived Tokyo's 20th century calamities.

INFORMATION
Tourist Office

Practically on top of Hibiya subway station on the Hibiya, Chiyoda and TOEI Mita lines is the Tourist Information Centre, (TIC) (☎ 3502-1461), the single best source of information about Tokyo and the rest of Japan available in Tokyo. The Tokyo office is the best of the four TICs (two in Narita airport and one other in Kyoto) run by the Japan National Tourist Organisation (JNTO). It has an enormous range of information for travellers who know how to ask the right questions and, unlike the Kyoto centre, has no limit on the time you can spend harassing the staff.

The important thing to bear in mind at the TIC is that while there are a limited number of brochures available on racks that you can take for yourself, much more is available for those who ask for it. The pamphlet you need will very likely be tucked away in a dusty cabinet or a drawer somewhere and will remain there unless you can prompt one of the TIC staff members to find it for you. The centre also has information for those with specialised interests in Japan: anything from martial arts to the tea ceremony or Japanese paper making – all you have to do is ask.

One of the most useful things you can pick up at the centre is the *Tourist Map of Tokyo*. It includes a large map of Tokyo as well as smaller maps of Shinjuku, Ueno, Asakusa, central Tokyo, the transportation network and the Tokyo subway network.

The Tokyo TIC is at 1-6-6 Yūraku-chō, Tokyo 100, just beyond the expressway from the central Ginza area. To get there take the A2 exit of Hibiya subway station – the centre, distinguishable by a large red question mark and a sign reading 'Tourist Information Office', is directly opposite, on the other side of the road running towards Hibiya-kōen Park.

The centre is open Monday to Friday from 9 am to 5 pm and on Saturday from 9 am to noon. It is closed on Sunday and public holidays.

Money

Banks are open Monday to Friday from 9 am to 3 pm. Those that change travellers' cheques usually have a sign outside that reads 'Foreign Exchange'. The foreign-exchange counter is usually upstairs, and the exchange procedure can take up to 15 minutes. Money can be changed more quickly at many of the larger hotels.

Credit Cards Even in Tokyo, credit cards are used less frequently than they are in the West, though this situation is starting to change. Credit card facilities are available at major department stores, establishments that are used to doing business with foreigners and increasingly in restaurants.

American Express For reporting theft of your card or other problems, American Express has a 24 hour toll-free number:

☎ 0120-376-100. There are four American Express offices in Tokyo:

American Express Tower, 4-30-16 Ogikubo, Sug-
    inami-ku, Tokyo 167-01 (☎ 3220-6010)
Shinjuku Gomeikan Building, 1 Floor, 3-3-9
    Shinjuku, Shinjuku-ku, Tokyo 160 (☎ 3352-
    1555)
Toranomon Mitsui Building, 3-8-1 Kasumigaseki,
    Chiyoda-ku, Tokyo 100 (☎ 3508-2400)
Yūraku-chō Denki Building, South 1 Floor, 1-7-1
    Yūraku-chō, Chiyoda-ku, Tokyo 100 (☎ 3214-
    0068)

Other Cards Diner's Club (☎ 3499-1311; 3499-1181 after hours), JCB Card (☎ 3294-4649, 24 hours), MasterCard (☎ 3254-6751; in an emergency, dial 0051 and ask for a collect call to 1-314-275-6690) and Visa (☎ 3456-4800; 3459-4700 in an emergency) all have offices in Tokyo.

Post

Look for the red and white T with a bar across the top. Post boxes have two slots: the red-lettered slot is for Tokyo mail and the blue-lettered one is for mail going to other destinations. The Tokyo central post office (☎ 3284-9527) is next to Tokyo station in the Tokyo station plaza, Chiyoda-ku. Poste restante mail will be held there for 30 days. It should be addressed as follows:

Jane SMITH
Poste Restante
Central Post Office
Tokyo, JAPAN

International parcels and registered mail can be sent from the Tokyo international post office (☎ 3241-4891) next to Ōtemachi subway station.

Telephone

Tokyo public telephones are the same as those everywhere else in Japan. All except the pink phones take phonecards, and international phones are labelled in English. Tokyo also has an English-language directory assistance service (☎ 3201-1010) available Monday to Saturday from 10 am to 7 pm. Some of the discount travel agencies

(see the following Travel Agencies section)
also offer 5% to 10% discounts on other
items, such as phonecards.

Japan Travel-Phone This is a service
offered by JNTO for travellers having language or general travel problems anywhere
in Japan. While you are in Tokyo ring
☎ 3502-1461; in Kyoto ring ☎ 371-5649;
elsewhere, for information on eastern Japan
ring ☎ 0120-222-800, and for information
on western Japan ring ☎ 0120-444-800.
Your coin will be returned after you have
finished your call for the latter two numbers.
In Tokyo and Kyoto you will be charged for
a local call. The service is offered seven days
a week from 9 am to 5 pm.

Fax
The Kokusai Denshin Denwa (KDD) international telegraph office (☎ 3275-4343),
one block north of Ōtemachi subway station,
has fax and telex facilities. The Shinjuku
KDD (☎ 3347-5000) close to the south exit
of Shinjuku station can also handle faxes.
Faxes can be sent from 9 am to 6 pm Monday
to Friday and to 5 pm on Saturday.

Budget travellers, particularly those
staying at the Kimi Ryokan (see Places to
Stay), can use the Kimi Information Centre,
around the corner from the ryokan. You have
to pay a registration fee of ¥2000, but after
this you pay the fax charges individually.
The centre will also receive faxes for you.

Immigration Office
The Tokyo Regional Immigration Bureau is
best reached from Ōtemachi subway station
on the Chiyoda line. Take the C2 exit, cross
the street at the corner and turn left. Walk past
the Japan Development building; the
immigration bureau is the next building on
your right.

Foreign Embassies
Most countries have embassies in Tokyo,
though visas are generally expensive in
Japan.

Australia
2-1-14 Mita, Minato-ku (☎ 5232-4111)
Austria
1-1-20 Moto Azabu, Minato-ku (☎ 3451-8281)
Belgium
5-4 Niban-chō, Chiyoda-ku (☎ 3262-0191)
Canada
7-3-38 Akasaka, Minato-ku (☎ 3408-2101)
China
3-4-33 Moto Azabu, Minato-ku (☎ 3403-3380)
Denmark
29-6 Sarugaku-chō, Shibuya-ku (☎ 3496-3001)
France
4-11-44 Minami Azabu, Minato-ku (☎ 3473-0171)
Germany
4-5-10 Minami Azabu, Minato-ku (☎ 3473-0151)
India
2-2-11 Kudan Minami, Chiyoda-ku (☎ 3262-2391)
Indonesia
5-2-9 Higashi Gotanda, Shinagawa-ku (☎ 3441-4201)
Ireland
No 25 Kowa Building, 8-7 Sanban-chō,
Chiyoda-ku (☎ 3263-0695)
Israel
3 Niban-chō, Chiyoda-ku (☎ 3264-0911)
Italy
2-5-4 Mita, Minato-ku (☎ 3453-5291)
Laos
3-6-2 Minami Magome, Ota-ku (☎ 3778-1660)
Malaysia
2-1-11 Minami-Azabu, Minato-ku (☎ 3280-7601)
Myanmar (Burma)
4-8-26 Kita Shinagawa, Shinagawa-ku (☎ 3441-9291)
Nepal
7-14-9 Todoroki, Setagaya-ku (☎ 3705-5558)
New Zealand
20-40 Kamiyama-chō, Shibuya-ku (☎ 3467-2271)
Norway
5-12-2 Minami-Azabu, Minato-ku (☎ 3440-2611)
Philippines
11-24 Nanpeidai-chō, Shibuya-ku (☎ 3496-2731)
Russia
2-1-1 Azabudai, Minato-ku (☎ 3583-4224)
Singapore
5-12-3 Roppongi, Minato-ku (☎ 3586-9111)
South Korea
1-2-5 Minami-Azabu, Minato-ku (☎ 3452-7611)
Spain
1-3-29 Roppongi, Minato-ku (☎ 3583-8531)

Sri Lanka
1-14-1 Akasaka, Minato-ku (☎ 3585-7431)
Sweden
1-10-3 Roppongi, Minato-ku (☎ 5562-5020)
Switzerland
5-9-12 Minami Azabu, Minato-ku (☎ 3473-0121)
Taiwan (Association of East Asian Relations)
5-20-2, Shirogane-dai, Minato-ku, Tokyo (☎ 3280-7811)
Thailand
3-14-6 Kami Osaki, Shinagawa-ku (☎ 3441-7352)
UK
1 Ichiban-chō, Chiyoda-ku (☎ 3265-5511)
USA
1-10-5 Akasaka, Minato-ku (☎ 3224-5000)
Vietnam
50-11 Moto Yoyogi-chō, Shibuya-ku (☎ 3466-3311)

Cultural Centres

For the homesick, Tokyo has no shortage of Japanese and foreign-sponsored cultural institutes and libraries. The National Diet Library (☎ 3581-2331) is the largest library in Japan, with over 1.3 million books in Western languages. Books have to be requested on a special form. The library is close to Nagata-chō subway station on the Yūraku-chō and Hanzomon lines and is open Monday to Saturday from 9.30 am to 5 pm.

The library at the American Center (☎ 3436-0901) has books and magazines concerning the USA. It's close to Shibakōen subway station on the TOEI Mita line, and is open Monday to Friday from 10.30 am to 6.30 pm.

The British Council (☎ 3235-8031) has a library, and you can also inquire about other cultural activities. The office is close to Iidabashi subway station on the Yūraku-chō line. The library is open Monday to Friday from 10 am to 8 pm.

The Japan Foundation Library (☎ 3263-4504) is close to Kojimachi station on the Yūraku-chō line. It has some 30,000 English-language publications and is only open to foreigners. It has odd opening hours – basically 10 am to 5 pm, closed Sunday and Monday – so ring before you go out there to make sure that it isn't one of their scheduled days off.

For languages other than English, the Bibliotheque de la Maison Franco-Japonaise (☎ 3291-1144) is open from 10 am to noon, 1 pm to 6 pm, closed Saturday, and is close to Ochanomizu station on the JR Chūō line. The Goethe Institute Tokyo Bibliotek (☎ 3583-7280), with around 15,000 volumes, is open daily from noon to 6 pm (8 pm on Fridays) and closed on weekends. It is close to Aoyama Itchōme station on the Ginza line.

Finally, a nice place to get away from it all in Ginza is the World Magazine Gallery (☎ 3545-7227). The gallery has a huge selection of magazines from all over the world and a coffee shop on the same floor. It's in a big modern building behind the Kabuki-za Theatre in Ginza. It's open 11 am to 7 pm, closed on Sunday.

Clubs & Conversation Lounges

When millions of people compete for limited amounts of recreational space and facilities, membership of a club brings privileges denied to outsiders: the right to hit hundreds of small balls against a net on top of a building for example. Even studying at a language school, as any newly arrived 'English teacher' will soon discover, is not simply a matter of paying for the classes you attend. Students actually pay for a package that includes such things as the right to use the school's lounge for chatting with other students and the teachers. Not surprisingly, clubs have sprung up to give Japanese the opportunity to meet and talk to foreigners. Generally, activities centre around a lounge or a coffee shop, entry to which costs foreigners little or nothing – it is the Japanese who pay.

Mickey House (☎ 3209-9686) is an 'English bar' that offers free coffee and tea as well as reasonably priced beer and food. Entry is free for foreigners and it's a good place to meet young Japanese as well as long-term gaijin residents. It's a lively place with a fairly regular crowd, but it is definitely not a closed scene. This can be a good place to make contacts and pick up tips on living in Tokyo.

Mickey House is close to the JR Takadanobaba station on the Yamanote line. Facing towards Shinjuku station, take the exit on the left side of the station. Keeping the Big Box building to your right, walk straight up Waseda-dōri. Look for the Tōzai line subway station entrance on your left; Mickey House is on the 4th floor of the Yashiro building, several doors on. The bar is open Monday to Friday from 3 to 11 pm.

Another similar institution is the Corn Popper Club in Ebisu. It's developed into more of a singles club over recent years and even has a computer dating service. Despite this it has a warm, cosy kind of atmosphere, sells second-hand books and has games like chess, and Japanese games such as *shōgi* and *go*. To get there, walk straight ahead from the east exit (just follow the crowds heading for the Hibiya line to Roppongi) to the second traffic light and turn left. Corn Popper is about a 100 metres down on the left in the basement; there's an English sign outside.

Associations

On the club and association front there is something for everyone in Tokyo. The following is just a sprinkling of what's available. Those with more specialised interests should check with the TIC or the classified pages of the *Tokyo Journal*.

Buddhist English Academy has lectures every Friday at 7 pm for ¥500 in Shinjuku (☎ 3342-6605)

Corn Popper Club is very much an American affair, but if you're from the USA and into popcorn, coffee, tea, billiards and the occasional party, this could be just the club for you (☎ 3715-4473)

International Adventure Club monthly meeting at Tokyo British Club (☎ 3403-7595)

International Feminists of Japan meets twice monthly; ring Makiko (☎ 0423-97-5609)

International House of Japan is a prestigious association that runs academic seminars and is able to provide accommodation to its members at reasonable rates, although membership is expensive (¥200,000) and requires two nominations from members (☎ 3470-4611)

Japan Association of Translators meets third Saturday of every month (fax 3385-5180)

Japan Foundation has, among other things, library classes and free screenings of Japanese films

with English subtitles – a real rarity in Japan (☎ 3263-4503)

Will House International Club cultural exchange through sports, camps, music, seminars, etc (☎ 3380-8000)

Travel Agencies

The discount ticket situation out of Tokyo has improved somewhat in recent years, but it's still much better to arrive with a return ticket. Discounts are available if you shop around, but they're not as cheap as they are elsewhere in Asia and they tend to get booked out quickly. One of the best places to look is among the classified advertisements in the *Tokyo Journal*. Discounts are available on foreign and domestic air tickets, on JR tickets (particularly shinkansen), and on other items like phonecards.

Most of the discount travel agencies will have English-speaking staff, but service tends to be rushed and the bargains are generally only displayed in Japanese. An exception to this general rule is STA Travel, which has three offices in Tokyo, in Ikebukuro (☎ 5391-2922), Yotsuya (☎ 5269-0751) and Shibuya (☎ 5485-8380). Another long-standing agent worth trying is Across Traveller's Bureau, which has offices in Shinjuku (☎ 3374-8721) and Ikebukuro (☎ 5391-2871).

Bookshops

The English-language sections of several of the larger Tokyo bookshops would put entire bookshops in many English-speaking cities to shame.

The big bookshop area in Tokyo is Jimbō-chō, and although most of the bookshops cater only to those who read Japanese, there are a couple of foreign-language bookshops. The best among these is Kitazawa Shoten (☎ 3263-0011), which has an excellent academic selection on the ground floor and second-hand books on the 2nd floor, many of them hardback and not all that cheap. If you exit from Jimbō-chō subway station on Yasukuni-dōri and set off westwards in the direction of Ichigaya, Kitazawa is about 50 metres away on the left.

Kinokuniya (☎ 3354-0131) in Shinjuku (see the Shinjuku map) has a good selection of English-language fiction and general titles on the 6th floor, including an extensive selection of books and other aids for learning Japanese. There is also a limited selection of books in other European languages – mainly French and German. Kinokuniya is a good place to stock up on guidebooks if you are continuing to other parts of the world. It's closed on the third Wednesday of every month.

Maruzen (☎ 3272-7211) in Nihombashi near Ginza has a collection of books almost equal to Kinokuniya's and it is always a lot quieter. This is Japan's oldest Western bookshop, established in 1869. Take the Takashimaya department store exit at Nihombashi subway station and look for Maruzen on the other side of the road. It's closed on Sunday.

The 3rd floor of Jena (☎ 3571-2980) in Ginza doesn't have quite the range of some other foreign-language bookshops but it does have a good selection of fiction and art books and stocks a large number of newspapers and magazines. Take the Sukiyabashi Crossing exit of Ginza subway station and walk along Harumi-dōri towards the Kabuki-za Theatre. Jena is on the third block on your right. It's closed on public holidays.

Ikebukuro residents can check out Wise Owl on the east side of the station. The top floor has a good selection of English-language publications – the shop is particularly strong on Japanese culture and language.

Guide Books

There are plenty of books available on Tokyo, the history of the city and how to get around the 20th century metropolis that this city has become. For an interesting history of Tokyo from 1867 to 1923, look for Edward Seidensticker's *Low City, High City*. *Tokyo Rising: The City Since the Great Earthquake* (Tuttle, 1991), by the same author, continues the story to the present day. Paul Waley's *City of Stories* (Weatherhill, 1991) is another worthwhile book on Tokyo.

Probably the most fun book to come out on Tokyo is Don Morton and Naoko Tsunoi's *The Best of Tokyo* (Tuttle, 1989). The book has a comprehensive list of 'best ofs', from 'best garlic restaurant' and 'best traditional Japanese dolls' to 'best toilet'. It's a good companion with which to explore a more idiosyncratic side of the city. On a more practical note, look out for *Living for Less in Tokyo and Liking it!* (Kodansha, 1991). Compiled by the Japan Hotline team, it answers all the most commonly asked questions about Tokyo on everything from visas to discos. For a comprehensive pocket-sized guide to Tokyo, you can't go past Lonely Planet's *Tokyo city guide*.

The *City Source English Telephone Directory* is useful for long-term visitors. It has over 500 pages of telephone numbers and a wealth of useful practical information. The Nippon Telegraph & Telephone (NTT) English Information Service (☎ 3201-1010) will tell you the address of the nearest NTT office, where you can pick up a free copy.

Jean Pearce's *Footloose in Tokyo* (John Weatherhill, 1976) and *More Footloose in Tokyo* (John Weatherhill, 1984) are excellent guides to exploring Tokyo on foot. Even if you don't follow Pearce's routes, her introductions to some of Tokyo's most important areas make for interesting background reading. The first book contains most of the important areas in Tokyo.

Gary Walters' *Day Walks Near Tokyo* (Kodansha International, 1988) covers 25 countryside trails, most of which can be reached from central Tokyo in an hour.

Maps

A *Tourist Map of Tokyo* is available from the TIC (see the earlier Tourist Office section of this chapter). Excellent mapping is also available in *Tokyo – A Bilingual Atlas* (Kodansha, 1989).

Newspapers & Magazines

See the Media section in the Facts for the Visitor chapter for information about newspapers. Most of the jobs advertised in the Monday edition of the *Japan Times* are in

English. This is the best place to look for teaching and rewriting work.

Tokyo has a wealth of English-language magazines covering local events, entertainment and cultural listings. The pick of the pack is undoubtedly the *Tokyo Journal*; the Cityscope section alone is worth ¥600 a month for its comprehensive listings of movies, plays, concerts, art exhibitions and unclassifiable 'events'. The *Tokyo Journal*'s classified advertisements are particularly useful for those basing themselves in Tokyo for some time. Sections include housing, employment and education. There are also general advertisements for things like moving house on a budget and furniture rental. The *Tokyo Journal* is available in bookshops with English-language sections. The monthly *Tokyo Time Out* magazine is a more glossy rival to *Tokyo Journal* and has good features and an excellent classifieds section. It costs ¥500 and is available in the same places as its rival.

An excellent source of information about more tourist-oriented events is the *Tokyo City Guide*, a free, twice-monthly magazine (and not to be confused with Lonely Planet's *Tokyo city guide*). However, its listings are nowhere near as comprehensive as those in the *Tokyo Journal*, and it is pitched at well-heeled visitors. The magazine has some good features on places to visit in Tokyo, and the shopping and dining-out advertisements should give you some ideas on how to get rid of your money quickly. Along similar lines, though stronger on informative features, is *City Life News Tokyo*. Another one to look out for is *Tokyo Day and Night*, which is basically a monthly advertising broadsheet with area guides and good maps. All three of these can be picked up in the TIC, hotels and travel agencies.

If you're studying Japanese, all the articles in the *Hiragana Times* are in English and Japanese, and all the kanji include *furigana* (Japanese script used to give pronunciation for kanji) readings – great for improving your reading skills. The magazine has some good features on restaurants and events around Tokyo.

Medical Services

The TIC has a list of clinics and hospitals where English is spoken in Tokyo. For a clinic with foreign doctors, try the Tokyo Medical & Surgical Clinic (☎ 3436-3028) in Kamiya-chō on the Hibiya line. Appointments can be made from 9 am to 4.45 pm from Monday to Friday and to 1 pm on Saturday. The International Clinic (☎ 3583-7831) in Roppongi is another clinic with English-speaking staff. It is open from 9 am to 5 pm Monday to Friday and to noon on Saturday.

In the case of an emergency, the number for an ambulance is 119, but you will need to speak Japanese to make yourself understood. For information in English about your nearest medical treatment centre, ring the Tokyo Fire Department (☎ 3212-2323). For other emergency numbers (medical or otherwise) see the Emergencies section below.

American Pharmacy If you're having trouble finding what you want in Japanese pharmacies, try the American Pharmacy (☎ 3271-4034). It's just around the corner from the TIC, near Yūraku-chō station and Hibiya subway station, and is open Monday to Saturday from 9 am to 7 pm.

Emergencies

The police can be contacted by telephoning 110, and the fire brigade and ambulance by telephoning 119. Both these numbers will require Japanese-language skills. For English-language help in an emergency, ring Japan Helpline (☎ 0120-461-997), an emergency service which operates 24 hours a day, seven days a week – don't bother them unless it really is an emergency.

Earthquakes These are a risk throughout Japan, and the congested Tokyo region is no exception. The last big one was in 1923 and, while the question of whether the city is due for another biggie is subject to some academic debate, it is wise to err on the side of caution. There is no point in being paranoid, but it is worthwhile checking the emergency exits in your hotel and being aware of earthquake safety procedures (see the Earthquakes section in the Facts for the Visitor chapter). If an earthquake occurs, the Japanese Broadcasting Corporation (NHK) will broadcast information and instructions in English on all its TV and radio networks. Tune to channel 1 on your TV, or to NHK (639 kHz AM) or FEN (810 kHz AM) on your radio.

CENTRAL TOKYO　東京中心部
Imperial Palace　皇居

The Imperial Palace is the home of Japan's emperor and the imperial family, but there's very little to see. The palace itself is closed to the public for all but two days of the year: 2 January (New Year's Day) and 23 December (the emperor's birthday). Still, it is possible to wander around its outskirts and visit the gardens, where you can at least get a view of the palace with the Nijū-bashi Bridge in the foreground.

The present palace is a fairly recent construction, having been completed in 1968. Like much else in Tokyo, the original palace, built at the time of the Meiji Restoration, was a victim of the bombing in WW II. Before the construction of the Meiji Imperial Palace, the site was occupied by Edo-jō Castle, the seat of power of the Tokugawa Shogunate. In its time the castle was the largest in the world, though apart from the massive moat and walls, little remains to mark its former existence.

It is an easy walk from Tokyo station, or Hibiya or Nijūbashi-mae subway stations, to the Nijū-bashi Bridge. The walk involves crossing Babasaki Moat and the expansive (for Tokyo at least) Imperial Palace plaza. The vantage point, which is popular with photographers, gives you a picture-postcard view of the palace peeking over its fortifications, with the Nijū-bashi Bridge in the foreground.

Imperial Palace East Garden　皇居東御苑

This is the nicest spot in the immediate vicinity of the Imperial Palace. Enter through the Ōte-mon Gate, a 10 minute walk north of the Nijū-bashi Bridge. This was once the principal gate of Edo-jō Castle, while the garden is situated at what was once the centre of the old castle. Just inside the gate is a rest house where you can buy a map of the extensive garden for ¥150. Remarkably, there is no entry fee for the park, which is open daily except Monday and Fridays from 9 am to 4 pm (last entry at 3 pm).

Kitanomaru-kōen Park　北の丸公園

The park itself is fairly ordinary, but it is home to a few museums and the Budokan, if you're in the mood to pay homage to the venue at which so many live recordings have been produced over the years. The park is reached most easily from Kudanshita or Takebashi subway stations. Alternatively, if you're walking from the Imperial Palace East Garden, take the Kitahanebashi-mon Gate, turn left and look for Kitanomaru-kōen Park on your right.

Science Museum There's little in the way of English explanations but the museum does give out an excellent booklet in English when you buy your ticket. There are displays dealing with space development, nuclear energy and 'bikecology' ('Man and Bicycle', as the booklet helpfully explains). Entry is ¥515. The museum is open daily from 9.30 am to 4 pm. To get there, continue walking past the Budokan and the museum is on the left.

National Museum of Modern Art The emphasis here is on Japanese art from the Meiji period onwards. Admission is ¥400, and it is open from 10 am to 4.30 pm and closed on Monday.

Craft Museum Actually an annexe of the National Museum of Modern Art, this museum houses crafts such as ceramics, lacquerware and dolls. Admission is ¥400, and it is open from 10 am to 4.30 pm and closed on Monday. This museum and the National Museum of Modern Art are towards the back of the park, facing the Imperial East Garden.

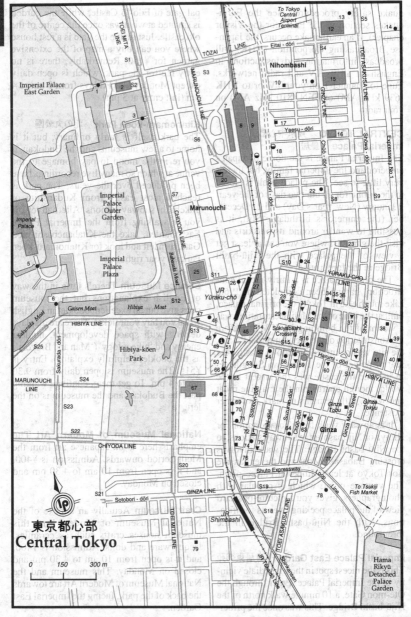

Imperial
Palace
East Garden

Nihombashi

Imperial
Palace

Imperial
Palace
Outer
Garden

Marunouchi

Imperial
Palace
Plaza

JR
Yūraku-chō

YŪRAKU-CHŌ
LINE

Gaisen Moat

Hibiya Moat

Sukiyabashi
Crossing

Hibiya-kōen
Park

Ginza
Tōkyū

Ginza
Tokyu

National Museum

Ginza

Shuto Expressway

JR
Shimbashi

東京都心部
Central Tokyo

0   150   300 m

Sotobori - dōri

To Tsukiji
Fish Market

Hama
Rikyū
Detached
Palace
Garden

PLACES TO STAY

2 Palace Hotel
パレス　ホテル
7 Tokyo Station Hotel
東京ステーションホテル
10 Yaesu Terminal Hotel
八重洲ターミナルホテル
17 Business Hotel Heimat
ビジネスホテル　ハイマート
23 Hotel Seiyo Ginza
ホテル西洋銀座
38 Hotel Ginza Dai-ei
ホテル銀座ダイエー
40 Hotel Atami-so
ホテル熱海荘
67 Imperial Hotel
帝国ホテル
73 Ginza Nikkō Hotel
銀座日航ホテル
76 Ginza International Hotel
銀座国際ホテル
77 Ginza Dai-Ichi Hotel
銀座第一ホテル
79 Sun Hotel Shimbashi
サンホテル新橋

PLACES TO EAT

31 Kawa Restaurant
かわレストラン
35 Kaiten-zushi Sushi
回転寿司
36 Volks Restaurant
フォルクス　レストラン
37 Tenya Restaurant
天屋レストラン
42 Nair's Indian Restaurant
ナイル　インド　レストラン
47 Saigon Restaurant
サイゴン
48 Dondo Restaurant
どんど
51 Yakitoris
焼き鳥屋
53 Ginza Palmy Building
銀座パーミイビル
55 New Torigin Restaurant
ニュー鳥ぎん
58 Munchen Beer Hall
ミュンヘン　ビアホール
60 Sapporo Maharaja Indian Restaurant
札幌マハラジャ
インドレストラン
62 Lion Beer Hall
ライオン　ビアホール
70 Sapporo Restaurant Indonesia
インドネシア
75 Kyubei Restaurant
久兵衛

OTHER

1 Ōte-mon Gate
大手門
3 Wadakura-mon Gate
和田倉門
4 Sakashita-mon Gate
坂下門
5 Nijū-bashi Bridge
二重橋
6 Sakurada-mon Gate
桜田門
8 JR Tokyo Station
ＪＲ東京駅
9 Daimaru Department Store
大丸百貨店
11 Maruzen Bookshop
丸善書店
12 Tōkyū Department Store
東急百貨店
13 Kite Museum
凧の博物館
14 Yamatane Museum of Art
山種美術館
15 Takashimaya Department Store
高島屋
16 Bridgestone Museum of Art
ブリヂストン美術館
18 Airport Limousine Bus Stop
空港リムジンバス
19 JR Highway Bus Terminal
バスターミナル
20 Central Post Office
中央郵便局
21 Yaesu Bookshop
八重洲書店
22 Meidi-ya International Bookshop
明治屋
24 American Express
アメリカンエクスプレス
25 Imperial Theatre & Idemitsu Art Museum
帝国劇場／出光美術館
26 Sogo Department Store
そごう百貨店
27 Kōtsū Building
交通会館
28 Printemps Department Store
プランタン
29 Kodak Imagica
コダック　イマジカ
30 Kirin City
キリン　シティ
32 Nikon Gallery
ニコン　ギャラリー

33 Matsuya Department Store
松屋百貨店
34 Ito-ya Stationery Shop
伊東屋
39 World Magazine Gallery
ワールド
マガジンギャラリー
41 Kabuki-za Theatre
歌舞伎座
43 Mitsukoshi Department Store
三越百貨店
44 Wakō Department Store
和光
45 Hankyū & Seibu Department Stores
阪急／西武百貨店
46 American Pharmacy
アメリカン
ファーマシー
49 TIC
50 Hibiya Chanter (Cinema District)
日比谷シャンテ
52 Hankyū Department Store
阪急百貨店
54 Sony Building
ソニービル
56 Yoseido Gallery
三笠会館
57 Jena Bookshop
イエナ洋書店
59 Mitsubishi Building
三菱ビル
61 Matsuzakaya Department Store
松坂屋
63 Toshiba Ginza Seven
東芝銀座セブン
64 Hakuhinkan Toy Park
博品館トイパーク
65 Riccar Art Museum
リッカー美術館
66 Nishiginza Electric Centre
西銀座電力センター
68 International Arcade
インターナショナル
アーケード
69 Taikō Festival Shop
タイコー
フェスティバル
71 Henry Africa
ヘンリー　アフリカ
72 Hachikan-jinja Shrine
八幡神社
74 Takumi Souvenirs
たくみ土産物店
78 Tokyo P/N (National Panasonic Showroom)
東京Ｐ／Ｎ
（ナショナル
パナソニック）

SUBWAY STATIONS

S1 Ōtemachi (Chiyoda Line)
大手町（千代田線）

S2 Ōtemachi (TOEI Mita Line)
大手町（都営三田線）

S3 Ōtemachi (Tōzai Line)
大手町（東西線）

S4 Nihombashi
日本橋

S5 Edobashi
江戸橋

S6 Tokyo-Ōtemachi
東京／大手町

S7 Nijūbashi-mae (Chiyoda Line)
二重橋前（千代田線）

S8 Kyobashi
京橋

S9 Takara-chō
宝町

S10 Ginza-Itchōme
銀座一丁目

S11 Yūraku-chō
有楽町

S12 Hibiya (TOEI Mita Line)
日比谷（都営三田線）

S13 Hibiya (Hibiya & Chiyoda Lines)
日比谷（日比谷線／千代田線）

S14 Ginza (Marunouchi Line)
銀座（丸の内線）

S15 Ginza (Hibiya Line)
銀座（日比谷線）

S16 Ginza (Ginza Line)
銀座（銀座線）

S17 Higashi-Ginza
東銀座

S18 Shimbashi (TOEI Asakusa Line)
新橋（都営浅草線）

S19 Shimbashi (Ginza Line)
新橋（銀座線）

S20 Uchisaiwai-cho
内幸町

S21 Toranomon
虎ノ門

S22 Kasumigaseki (Chiyoda Line)
霞ケ関（千代田線）

S23 Kasumigaseki (Hibiya Line)
霞ケ関（日比谷線）

S24 Kasumigaseki (Marunouchi Line)
霞ケ関（丸の内線）

S25 Sakuradamon
桜田門

Yasukuni-jinja Shrine　靖国神社

If you take the Tayasu-mon Gate exit (just past the Budokan) of Kitanomaru-kōen Park, across the road and to your left is the Yasukuni-jinja Shrine, literally 'Peaceful Country Shrine'. Given that the shrine is actually a memorial to Japan's war dead, the title is something of a misnomer.

In the years leading up to and during WW II, Yasukuni-jinja was the most important shrine for state Shintō in Tokyo. Not surprisingly, it's a subject of controversy today. Despite a Japanese constitutional commitment to a separation of religion and politics and a renunciation of militarism, in 1979 a group of class-A war criminals were enshrined here. Also, the shrine has become the object of yearly visits by leading Liberal Democratic Party (LDP) politicians on the anniversary of Japan's defeat in WW II (15 August). Whatever your personal feelings about honouring Japanese war dead, it's an interesting shrine to have a look at. In the vicinity of the shrine, you may see rather evil-looking black vans that broadcast right-wing propaganda from speakers mounted on their roofs.

Yūshūkan Museum Next to the Yasukuni-jinja Shrine is the Yūshūkan Museum, with treasures from the Yasukuni-jinja Shrine and other items commemorating Japanese war dead. There are limited English explanations, but there is an English pamphlet. Interesting exhibits include the long torpedo in the large exhibition hall which is actually a *kaiten*, or 'human torpedo', a submarine version of the kamikaze. There are displays of military uniforms, samurai armour and a 'panorama of the Divine Thunderbolt Corps in final attack mode at Okinawa'. Admission is ¥200, and the museum is open daily from 9 am to 5 pm.

Ginza　銀座

Ginza is the shopping area in Tokyo that *everyone* has heard of. Back in the 1870s, Ginza was one of the first areas to modernise, featuring a large number of novel – for Tokyoites of that time – Western-style brick buildings. Ginza was also home to Tokyo's first department stores and other Western emblems of modernity such as gas lamps.

Today, other shopping districts rival Ginza

in opulence, vitality and popularity, but Ginza retains a distinct snob value. Ginza is still the place to go and be seen emptying the contents of your wallet. If you are an impecunious traveller, on the other hand, this is still an interesting area to browse through, full of galleries and display rooms, most of which are free; and you can at least afford a cup of coffee at one of the discount coffee shops that are tucked away on the fringes of the Ginza area.

The best starting point for a look at Ginza is the Sukiyabashi Crossing, which is a 10 minute walk from the Imperial Palace. Alternatively, take the Sukiyabashi Crossing exit at Ginza subway station.

Showrooms Right on the Sukiyabashi Crossing is the Sony building (☎ 3573-2371), which has fascinating displays of Sony's many products. You're free to fiddle with many of the items. The high-definition TV display is particularly interesting, and there is a viewing room where you can watch the technology in action. Shows take place at regular intervals during the day.

On Chūō-dōri next to the Lion Beer Hall is Toshiba Ginza Seven (☎ 3571-5971), which displays Toshiba products. It has a large audiovisual display area, with collections of CDs and videos to test Toshiba products with. Tokyo P/N (☎ 5568-0461), the National Panasonic showroom, is down Shōwa-dōri and across the expressway. It has a reputation for its lively hi-tech displays.

Galleries Ginza is overflowing with galleries, many of them so small that they can be viewed in two or three minutes. Others feature work by unknown artists who have hired the exhibition space themselves. Wander around and visit any galleries that seem particularly interesting. They are scattered throughout Ginza but are concentrated in the area south of Harumi-dōri, between Ginza-dōri and Chūō-dōri.

If you have an interest in ukiyo-e woodblock prints, a few minutes south-west of the Sukiyabashi Crossing, next to the railway tracks, is the Riccar Art Museum (☎ 3571-

3254). Admission is ¥300; it's open from 11 am to 6 pm daily except Monday. Do not enter by the Riccar building's main door but through another entrance at the side. The gallery is on the 7th floor.

The Idemitsu Art Museum holds Japanese and Chinese art and is famous for its collection of work by the Zen monk Sengai. It's a five minute walk from either Hibiya or Yūraku-chō stations, on the 9th floor of the Kokusai building, next door to the Imperial Theatre. Admission is ¥550, and it is open from 10 am to 5 pm daily except Monday.

Probably the best of the photographic galleries in the area are the Nikon Gallery (☎ 3572-5756), the Contax Gallery (☎ 3572-1921) and the Canon Photo House Ginza (☎ 3573-7821). They're sponsored by the respective camera companies and have free, changing exhibits. The Nikon Gallery is on the 3rd floor of the Matsushima Gankyōten building, opposite the Matsuya department store on Chūō-dōri, and is open from Tuesday to Sunday from 10 am to 6 pm.

The Contax Gallery is on the 5th floor of the building next door to the Sanai building on Chūō-dōri; there is no English sign at ground level. Admission is free, and it is open from Tuesday to Sunday from 10.30 am to 7 pm. The Canon Photo House is on one of the side streets between Chūō-dōri and Shōwa-dōri and is open from 10 am to 6 pm daily except Sunday.

Kabuki-za Theatre Further east of Sukiyabashi Crossing, on Harumi-dōri, is the Kabuki-za Theatre (☎ 3541-3131). Even if you don't plan to attend a kabuki performance, it's worth wandering down and taking a look at the building. Performances usually take place twice daily and tickets range from ¥2000 to ¥14,000, depending on the seat. If you only want to see part of a performance you can ask about a restricted ticket for the 4th floor. For ¥600, plus a deposit of ¥1000, you can get an earphone guide that explains the kabuki performance in English as you watch it. However, the earphone guide is not available with restricted tickets. For phone bookings, ring

at least a day ahead; the theatre won't take
bookings for the same day.

Tsukiji Fish Market 築地魚市場
This is where all that sushi and sashimi turns
up after it has been fished out of the sea
(preferably as far away from the murky
waters surrounding Japan as possible). The
day begins very early, with the arrival of fish
and its wholesale auctioning. The wholesale
market is not open to the general public,
which is probably a blessing, given that
you'd have to be there before 5 am to see the
action. You are free to visit the outer market
and wander around the stalls that are set up
by wholesalers and intermediaries to sell
directly to restaurants, retail stores and other
buyers. It is a fun place to visit, and you don't
have to arrive *that* early: as long as you're
there sometime before 8 am there'll be something going on. Watch out for your shoes –
there's a lot of muck and water on the floor.

The done thing is to top off your visit with
a sushi breakfast in one of the nearby sushi
shops. There are plenty of places on the right
as you walk from the market back to Tsukiji
subway station. The market is closed on
Sunday and public holidays.

AKIHABARA 秋葉原
Akihabara is the discount electrical and electronics centre with countless shops ranging
from tiny specialist stores to electrical
department stores. You could go there with
no intention of buying anything and within
half an hour find half a dozen things that you
couldn't possibly live without.

The range of products is mind boggling,
but before you rush into making any purchases, remember that most Japanese
companies use the domestic market as a
testing ground. Many products end their
days there without ever making it onto overseas markets. This may pose difficulties if
you take something home and later need to
have a fault repaired. Also, the voltage for
which the product was made may not be the
same as that available in your home country.
Some larger stores (Laox is a reliable option)

have tax-free sections with export models for
sale.

Many of the prices can be quite competitive with those you are used to at home,
though it's unusual to find prices that match
those of dealers in Hong Kong or Singapore.
You should be able to knock another 10% off
the marked prices by bargaining, though this
is often not the case with the tax-free items
in the bigger stores. To find the shops, take
the Electric Town exit of Akihabara station.
You'll see the sign on the platform if you
come in on the JR Yamanote line.

UENO 上野
Ueno Hill was the site of a last-ditch defence
of the Tokugawa Shogunate by about 2000
Tokugawa loyalists in 1868. They were duly
dispatched by the imperial army and afterwards the new Meiji government decreed
that Ueno Hill would be transformed into
one of Tokyo's first parks.

Today, Ueno-kōen Park is Ueno's foremost attraction. The park has a number of
museums, galleries and a zoo that, by Asian
standards at least, is pretty good. The park is
also famous as Tokyo's most popular site for
hanami (cherry blossom viewing) when the
blossoms come out in early to mid-April.

Ueno is an interesting area to stroll
around. Opposite the station is the
Ameyoko-chō arcade (look for the large
romaji sign over the entrance), a market area
where you can buy anything from dried fish
to imitation Rolex watches. Only two stops
away on the Ginza subway line is
Kappabashi-dōri, the place to go if you want
to buy, as a souvenir, some of the plastic food
used for window displays.

Ueno-kōen Park 上野公園
Saigō Takamori Statue This slightly
unusual statue of a samurai walking his dog,
near the southern entrance to the park, is a
favourite meeting place. Saigō Takamori's
history is a little complicated. He started out
by helping the cause of the imperial forces
of the Meiji Restoration but, after frustrated
attempts to defeat them, ended his life by
committing seppuku. The turnabout in his

Shitamachi
Today there is little left of Shitamachi, and the only way to get some idea of the circumstances in which the lower classes of old Edo lived is by visiting somewhere like Ueno's Shitamachi Fūzoku Shiryōkan (History Museum). In its time, Edo was a city of wood, and the natural stained-wood frontages and dark tiled roofs gave the city an attractiveness that is little in evidence in modern Tokyo. Nevertheless, the common people lived in horribly crowded conditions, in flimsy wooden constructions often with earthen floors. Conflagrations regularly swept great swaths across the congested wooden buildings of the city. In a perverse attempt to make the best of misfortune, Edo dwellers almost seemed to take pride in the fires that periodically purged their city, calling them *Edo-no-hana*, or 'flowers of Edo'.

The flowers of Edo occurred with such frequency that it has been estimated that any Shitamachi structure could reckon on a life span of around 20 years, often less, before it would be destroyed by fire. Preventive measures included building houses that could be completely sealed: with the approach of a fire, the house would be sealed and left with candles burning inside, starving the interior of oxygen. Private fire brigades operated with standard bearers who would stake their territory close to a burning building and exact payment if they managed to save it.

Modern building techniques have eliminated most of 'Edo's flowers'; and you can still see the occasional wooden structure that has miraculously survived into the late 20th century.

Chris Taylor

loyalties occurred when the Meiji government withdrew the powers of the military class to which he belonged. See Kagoshima in the Kyūshū chapter for more about Saigō Takamori.

Tokyo National Museum The Tokyo National Museum is the one museum in Tokyo that it is worth going out of your way to visit. Not only is it Japan's largest museum, housing some 87,000 items, it also has the world's largest collection of Japanese art. Only a portion of the museum's huge

collection is displayed at any one time. The museum is open from 9 am to 4 pm daily except Monday; admission is ¥400.

The museum has four galleries, the most important of which is the Main Gallery. It's straight ahead as you enter, and houses a very impressive collection of Japanese art, from sculpture and swords to lacquerware and calligraphy. The Gallery of Eastern Antiquities, to the right of the ticket booth, has a collection of art and archaeological finds from all of Asia east of Egypt. The Hyōkeikan, to the left of the ticket booth, has a collection of Japanese archaeological finds. There is a room devoted to artefacts used by the Ainu people, the indigenous ethnic group of Japan who now live only in Hokkaidō.

Finally, there is the Gallery of Hōryūji Treasures, which is only open on Thursday, and then only 'weather permitting'. The exhibits (masks, scrolls, etc) are from the Hōryū-ji Temple in Nara. Because they are more than 1000 years old, the building often remains closed if it's raining or humid.

National Museum of Western Art The National Museum of Western Art has an impressive permanent collection and is also frequently host to special exhibits on loan from other museums of international repute. There is a special emphasis on the French impressionists, with originals by Rodin, including 'The Thinker', and paintings and sketches by, among others, Renoir and Monet. Admission is ¥400, and it is open daily from 9.30 am to 4.30 pm except Monday.

Tokyo Metropolitan Museum of Art The Metropolitan Museum of Art has a number of different galleries that run temporary displays of contemporary Japanese art. Galleries feature both Western-style art such as oil paintings and Japanese-style art such as sumi-e (ink brush) and ikebana (flower arranging). The admission charge varies according to the exhibition, but entry to the museum itself is free, and there are often interesting displays with no admission

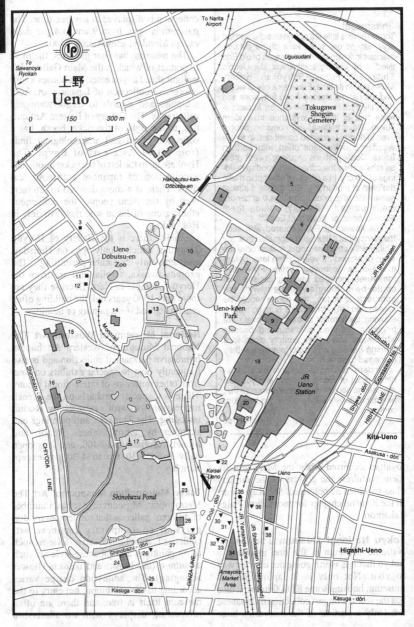

上野
Ueno

To
Sawanoya
Ryokan

To Narita
Airport

Uguisudani

Tokugawa
Shogun Cemetery

0   150   300 m

Kototoi - dōri

Hakubutsu-kan-
Dōbutsu-en

Keisei Line

Ueno
Dōbutsu-en
Zoo

Monorail

Ueno-kōen
Park

JR Shinkansen

JR
Ueno
Station

Kuromon - chō

Shōwa - dōri

Expressway No 1

HIBIYA LINE

Kita-Ueno

Shinobazu - dōri

CHIYODA
LINE

Shinobazu Pond

Keisei
Ueno

Asakusa - dōri

Ueno

Chūō - dōri

GINZA LINE

Shinobazu - dōri

JR Yamanote Line

JR Shinkansen (Underground)

Higashi-Ueno

Ameyoko
Market
Area

Kasuga - dōri

Kasuga - dōri

PLACES TO STAY

3 Ryokan Katsutarō
旅館勝太郎
11 Hotel Ohgasio
鴎外荘
12 Suigetsu Hotel
酔月ホテル
23 Kinuya Hotel
キヌヤ　ホテル
24 Hotel Parkside
ホテル　パークサイド
25 Hotel Pine Hill Ueno
ホテル　パインヒル上野
38 Ueno Capsule Kimeya
Hotel
上野カプセル　きめやホテル

PLACES TO EAT

26 Yoshibei Restaurant
芳兵衛
27 Izu-ei Restaurant
伊豆栄
29 McDonald's
マクドナルド
30 Kappazushi
Restaurant
かっぱ寿司
31 Maharaja
Restaurant
マハラジャ
32 Samrat Indian
Restaurant
サムラート　インドレストラン

33 Spaghetti House
スパゲティ　ハウス
36 Irohazushi Restaurant
いろは寿司

OTHER

1 Tokyo University of
Fine Arts
東京芸大
2 Kanei-ji Temple
寛永寺
4 Gallery of Hōryūji
Treasures
法隆寺宝物館
5 Tokyo National
Museum
国立博物館
6 Gallery of Eastern
Antiquities
東洋アンティーク　ギャラリー
7 Rinno-ji Temple
輪王寺
8 National Science
Museum
科学博物館
9 National Museum of
Western Art
西洋美術館
10 Tokyo Metropolitan
Museum of Art
東京都美術館
13 Five Storeyed Pagoda
五重塔

14 Tōshō-gū Shrine
東照宮
15 Ueno Zoo
上野動物園
16 Aquarium
水族館
17 Benzaiten Temple
弁財天
18 Kiyomizu Kannon-dō
Temple
清水観音堂
19 Tokyo Metropolitan
Festival Hall
東京文化会館
20 Japan Art Academy
芸術院会館
21 Ueno-no Mori Art
Museum
上野の森美術館
22 Saigō Takamori Statue
西郷隆盛像
28 Shitamachi History
Museum
下町風俗資料館
34 Ameyoko Centre
Building
アメ横センタービル
35 Ameyoko-chō Arcade
アメヤ横丁
37 Marui
Department Store
丸井百貨店

charge. It's open daily, except Monday, from 9 am to 5 pm.

National Science Museum The National Science Museum (Kokuritsu Kagaku Hakubutsukan) may be of more interest to the Japanese than to foreigners. As well as a wide range of general scientific displays, there are displays on the origin of the Japanese people, on Japanese technology and so on. Not all the exhibits are labelled in English, but an English pamphlet is available for ¥300. It is open from 9 am to 4 pm daily except Monday; admission is ¥400.

Shitamachi History Museum The Shitamachi History Museum is away from the other museums, at the south-eastern corner of Shinobazu Pond. It re-creates life in Edo's Shitamachi, the plebeian downtown

quarters of old Tokyo, through an exhibition of typical Shitamachi buildings. The buildings include a merchant's shop, a sweet shop, the home and business of a copper-boiler maker, and a tenement house. You can take off your shoes and look around inside. Upstairs, the museum has many utensils and items from the daily life of the average Shitamachi resident. You are free to pick many of them up and have a closer look. It is open from 9.30 am to 4 pm daily except Monday; admission is ¥200.

Ueno Zoo Established in 1882, Ueno zoo was the first of its kind in Japan. It's not really worth going out of your way to see, but if you do you are unlikely to come away feeling depressed (unlike many other Asian zoos). Among the Japanese the zoo is very popular for its pandas (not on view on

Fridays). Admission is ¥400, and it is open from 9.30 am to 4 pm.

Tōshō-gū Shrine Dating from 1651, this is a shrine, like its counterpart in Nikkō, to Tokugawa Ieyasu, who unified Japan. There is a ¥100 entrance fee to the shrine, which is open from 9 am to 5.30 pm except in winter, when it's open from 9 am to 4.30 pm.

Ameyoko-chō Arcade アメ横
This area, opposite Ueno station, was famous as a black-market district after the war and is still a lively shopping area, where many bargains can be found. Shopkeepers there are much less restrained than those in other shopping areas in Tokyo, calling to prospective customers in the crowded alleyways. This is a good area in which to wander and get something of the feeling of Shitamachi. Look for the big romaji sign opposite Ueno station.

AROUND UENO 上野周辺
Korin-chō 上野バイク街
See the Motorcycle section of the Getting Around chapter for information about the busy Korin-chō area, or Ueno Baiku-gai (Bike St), the motorcycle shopping centre in the shadow of Ueno station. There's an interesting motorcycle museum on the 3rd and 4th floor of the clothing shop of Corin Motors.

Kappabashi-dōri カッパ橋道具街
Just two stops from Ueno subway station on the Ginza line is Kappabashi-dōri. This is where you go if you're setting up a restaurant. You can get flags that advertise the food in your restaurant, personalised cushions, crockery and most importantly, all the plastic food you need. Whether you want a plate of spaghetti bolognese complete with an upright fork, a steak and chips, a lurid pizza or a bowl of rāmen, it's all there. Items aren't particularly cheap, but some of them are very convincing and could make unusual Japanese mementos.

Kappabashi-dōri is about five minutes

from any of the Tawaramachi subway station's exits.

ASAKUSA 浅草
Asakusa's most famous attraction is the Sensō-ji Temple, also known as the Asakusa Kannon Temple. Like Ueno, though, Asakusa is an interesting area just to look around. It has long been the very heart of Shitamachi. In Edo times, Asakusa was a halfway stop between the city and its most infamous pleasure district, Yoshiwara. In time, however, Asakusa developed into a pleasure quarter in its own right, eventually becoming the centre for that most loved of Edo entertainments, kabuki. In the very shadow of the Sensō-ji Temple a fairground spirit prevailed and a whole range of very secular entertainments were provided, from kabuki theatres to brothels.

When Japan ended its self-imposed isolation with the commencement of the Meiji Restoration, it was in Asakusa that the first cinemas opened, in Asakusa that the first music halls appeared and in Asakusa's Teikoku Gekijo Theatre (Imperial Theatre) that Western opera was first performed before Japanese audiences. It was also in Asakusa that another Western cultural export to the Japanese – the striptease – was introduced. A few clubs still operate in the area.

Unfortunately, Asakusa never quite recovered from the bombing at the end of WW II. Although the Sensō-ji Temple was rebuilt, other areas of Tokyo assumed Asakusa's role of the pleasure district. Asakusa may be one of the few areas of Tokyo to have retained something of the spirit of Shitamachi, but the bright lights have shifted elsewhere – notably to Shinjuku.

Sensō-ji Temple 浅草寺
Sensō-ji Temple enshrines a golden image of the Buddhist Kannon, goddess of mercy, which according to legend was miraculously fished out of the nearby Sumida-gawa River by two fishermen in 628. In time, a temple was built to house the image, which has remained on the spot ever since, through successive rebuildings of the temple.

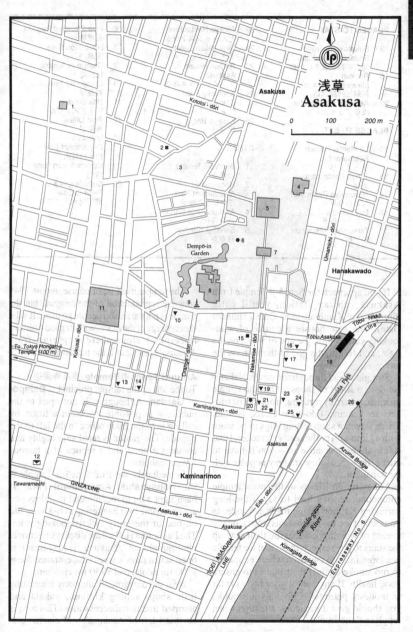

浅草
Asakusa

0   100   200 m

Asakusa

Kototoi - dōri

1

2

3

4

5

6

7

Dempō-in
Garden

Hanakawado

8

9

11

10

Tōbu Nikkō
Line

To Tokyo Hongan-ji
Temple (100 m)

15

16

17

Tōbu-Asakusa

18

Kokusai - dōri

Orange - dōri

Nakamise - dōri

Umamichi - dōri

13   14

19

23   24

20

21   22

25

Kaminarimon - dōri

Sumida Park

26

12

Asakusa

Azuma Bridge

Tawaramachi

GINZA LINE

Kaminarimon

Asakusa - dōri

Edo - dōri

Sumida-gawa River

Expressway No. 6

Asakusa

TOEI ASAKUSA LINE

Komagata Bridge

If you approach the Sensō-ji Temple from Asakusa subway station, you'll enter through the Kaminari-mon Gate (Thunder Gate). The gate houses a couple of wild-looking gods: Fūjin, the god of wind, on the right; and Raijin, the god of thunder, on the left.

Straight ahead through the gate is Nakamise-dōri, a street of shops within the temple precinct, where everything, from tourist trinkets to genuine Edo-style crafts, is sold. There's even a shop selling wigs to be worn with a kimono. Try the *sembei* (crackers) that a few shops specialise in – you'll have to queue, though, as they are very popular with the Japanese.

Nakamise-dōri leads to the main temple compound, but it's hard to say if the long surviving Kannon image really is inside, as you cannot see it – not that this stops a steady stream of worshippers making their way up the stairs to pay respect. In front of the temple is a large incense cauldron where people go to rub smoke against their bodies to ensure good health. If any part of your body (as far as modesty permits) is giving you trouble, you should give it particular attention when 'applying' the smoke.

The temple itself is, of course, a post-1945 concrete reproduction of the original, but the temple is not the reason people go there. It's the sheer energy of the place, with its gaudy, almost fairground atmosphere lingering from Asakusa's past, that is the real attraction.

Around Sensō-ji Temple 浅草寺周辺

To the left of the temple precinct is **Dempō-in Garden**. Although it is not open to the public, it is possible to obtain a ticket by calling in to the main office to the left of the pagoda. The garden is rated very highly and contains a pond and a replica of a famous Kyoto teahouse.

Immediately west of Sensō-ji Temple is the **Hanayashiki Amusement Park**. It hasn't got a lot to recommend it, unless you are overcome by a hankering to risk your life on one of the fairly rickety-looking rides. The Panorama Hall inside displays historical photographs of Asakusa. Hanayashiki is open seven days a week; the entrance fee is ¥500 for adults and ¥250 for children.

Near the playground are many interesting little shops selling kimono, yukata and assorted traditional accessories. This area is all that's left of Asakusa's old cinema district, but the only cinemas remaining seem to restrict their screenings almost exclusively to Japanese pornography – at least they all carry the familiar lurid posters depicting naked women trussed up, their meek eyes casting plaintive looks at the tattooed torturers standing over them.

Sumida-gawa River Cruise 'Cruise' might be considered too grand a term for the boat journey up the Sumida-gawa River. It may not be the most scenic river cruise you've ever experienced, but it's a good way of getting to or from Asakusa.

The cruise departs from next to Asakusa's Azuma Bridge and goes to Hamarikyū-teien Garden, Hinode Pier and Odaiba Seaside Park. Probably the best option is to buy a ticket to Hamarikyū-teien Garden for ¥720 (the ticket includes the ¥200 entry fee for the garden). After looking around the garden it is possible to walk into Ginza in about 10 to 15 minutes. Boats leave every 20 to 30 minutes from 9.40 am to 6.15 pm and cost ¥520 to Hamarikyū-teien Garden, ¥560 to Hinode Pier and ¥960 to Odaiba Seaside Park.

SHINJUKU 新宿

Shinjuku is a city in itself and is without doubt the most lively part of Tokyo. If you had only a day in Tokyo and wanted to see the modern Japanese phenomenon in action, Shinjuku would be the place to go. It's an incredible combination of high-class department stores, discount shopping arcades, flashing neon, government offices, stand-up drinking bars, hostess clubs and sleazy strip bars.

Shinjuku is a sprawling business, commercial and entertainment centre, and the action never seems to stop. It is calculated that up to two million people a day pass through Shinjuku station, making it one of the busiest stations in the world. And if the thought of two million jostling Japanese isn't daunting enough in itself, the station is also regarded by foreign residents and visitors alike as the most confusing in the world.

On the western side of the station is Tokyo's highest concentration of skyscrapers, several of which have fascinating hi-tech interiors. A recent addition to the skyline is the Tokyo Metropolitan Government Offices, which have to be seen to be believed. Despite this, it is the eastern side of the station that is far and away the most lively part of Shinjuku to visit.

From Shinjuku station's eastern exit, your first sight will be of the Studio Alta building, with its huge video screen showing advertisements and video clips all day and night. The sheltered area underneath the screen is Shinjuku's most popular meeting place, though like the Almond coffee shop in Roppongi, it has become so popular that finding the person you're meeting is something of an ordeal – gaijin at least stand out in the crowd.

To the right of the Studio Alta building, about 100 metres up Shinjuku-dōri and on your left, is the Kinokuniya bookshop (see the earlier Bookshops section in this chapter). The sheltered area here is also a popular meeting place. All around Kinokuniya there are shops selling discounted clothes and shoes. There are also some cheap second-hand camera shops on the backstreets. The area abounds in fast-food restaurants, cheap noodle shops, reasonably priced Western food, and some of the best Chinese food in Japan.

West Side 新宿西口

Shinjuku's west side does have a couple of attractions. If you're after camera equipment, it's home to Tokyo's largest camera stores: Yodobashi Camera and Sakuraya Camera. Yodobashi Camera has practically everything you could possibly want that relates to photography, including a huge stock of film, darkroom equipment, tripods, cameras, lenses and other accessories. Its prices are usually very reasonable. Yodobashi even has a limited selection of second-hand photographic equipment. The stores are behind the Keio department store.

Shinjuku NS Building If you're in the mood for a bit of eccentric hi-tech, the interior of

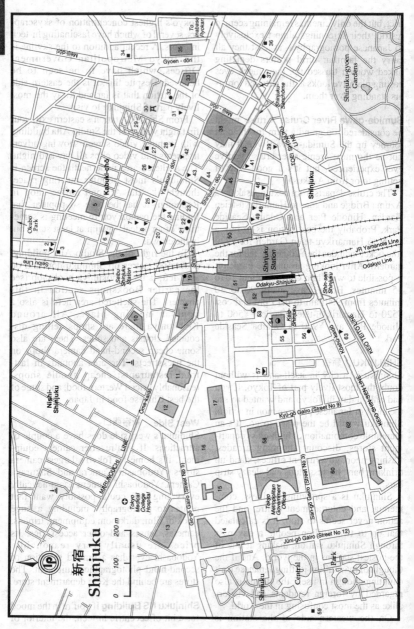

新宿 Shinjuku

PLACES TO STAY

3 Green Plaza Shinjuku
   (capsule hotel)
   グリーンプラザ新宿
9 Shinjuku Prince Hotel
   新宿プリンスホテル
10 Star Hotel Tokyo
   スターホテル東京
13 Tokyo Hilton
   International
   東京ヒルトンホテル
14 Century Hyatt Hotel
   センチュリーハイアット
   ホテル
27 Shinjuku-ku
   Capsule Hotel
   新宿区カプセルホテル
34 Hotel Sun Lite
   Shinjuka
   ホテル サンライト新宿
36 Winning Inn Shinjuku
   (capsule hotel)
   ウィニング イン新宿
47 Central Hotel
   セントラル ホテル
58 Keio Plaza Inter-
   Continental Hotel
   京王プラザインター
   コンチネンタル ホテル
59 Shinjuku
   New City Hotel
   新宿ニューシティ ホテル
61 Shinjuku
   Washington Hotel
   新宿ワシントンホテル
64 Shinjuku Park Hotel
   新宿パークホテル

PLACES TO EAT

1 Pekin Chinese
   Restaurant
   北京飯店
2 Tainan Taami Taiwanese
   Restaurant
   台南 台湾レストラン
4 Tokyo Kaisen Ichiba
   Chinese Restaurant
   東京海鮮市場
6 Kaiten-zushi Revolving
   Sushi Restaurant
   回転寿司
7 Ban Thai Restaurant
   バン・タイ レストラン
8 Yōrōnotaki Restaurant
   養老の滝

20 Ibuki Restaurant
   伊吹レストラン
24 Champer Thai
   Restaurant
   チャンバー タイ
25 Tōkaien Korean
   Restaurant
   東海苑 韓国レストラン
26 Yatai Mura (Kao Keng &
   Other Restaurants)
   屋台村
28 Hofbräuhaus Beer Hall
   ホーフブロイハウス
   ビアホール
31 Tokyo Dai Hanten
   Chinese Restaurant
   東京大飯店
39 Daikokuya Restaurant
   大黒屋
41 Tsunahachi Restaurant
   つな八
42 Irohanihoheto
   Restaurant
   いろはにほへと
43 El Borracho Mexican
   Restaurant
   エル ボラッチョ
   メキシカン
46 Tatsukichi Restaurant
   たつ吉
48 Kaiten-zushi Revolving
   Sushi Restaurant
   回転寿司
49 Suehiro Restaurant
   スエヒロ
63 Rose de Sahara
   Restaurant
   ローズ ド サハラ

OTHER

5 Koma Theatre
   コマ劇場
11 Kaisai Kaijo Building
   海上ビル
12 Shinjuku Nomura
   Building
   新宿野村ビル
15 Shinjuku Sumitomo
   Building
   新宿住友ビル
16 Shinjuku Mitsui Building
   新宿三井ビル
17 Shinjuku Centre
   Building
   新宿センタービル
18 Odakyu Department Store
   小田急デパート

19 Charlie's Not Here
   チャーリーズ
   ノット ヒア
21 Studio Alta Building
   スタジオ アルタ ビル
22 Konika Plaza
   コニカ プラザ
23 Kirin City
   キリン シティ
29 Golden Gai-jinja
   ゴールデン街
30 Hanazono-jinja Shrine
   花園神社
32 Milo's Garage
   ミロズ ガレージ
33 Marui Men's
   Department Store
   丸井紳士服デパート
35 Isetan Park City
   伊勢丹パークシティ
37 Rolling Stone
   ローリング ストーン
38 Isetan
   Department Store
   伊勢丹
40 Mitsukoshi
   Department Store
   新宿三越
44 Kinokuniya Bookshop
   紀伊国屋書店
45 Marui Department Store
   & Virgin Megastore
   丸井デパート
50 My City Department Store
   マイ シティ
51 Odakyū Department Store
   小田急百貨店
52 Keio Department Store
   京王百貨店
53 Airport Limousine
   Bus Stop
   空港リムジンバス
54 Highway Bus Terminal
   ハイウェイ バス
55 Yodobashi Camera
   淀橋カメラ
56 Sakuraya Camera
   カメラのサクラヤ
57 Post Office
   新宿郵便局
60 Shinjuku NS Building
   新宿ＮＳビル
62 KDD Building
   ＫＤＤビル

this building is hollow, featuring a 1600 sq metre atrium from which you can look up and see sunlight coming in through the glass roof. Overhead, at 110 metres, is a 'sky bridge'. The atrium itself features a 29 metre pendulum clock that is listed in the *Guinness*

Book of Records as the largest in the world. The 29th and 30th floors have a large number of restaurants, including a branch of the Spaghetti Factory. On the 5th floor, you can browse through the showrooms of the Japanese computer companies in the OA Centre.

Shinjuku Sumitomo Building The
Sumitomo building bills itself as 'a building that's actually a city', a concept that the Japanese seem to find particularly appealing (Sunshine City in Ikebukuro is another 'city' building.)

Like the Shinjuku NS building, the Sumitomo building has a hollow core. The ground floor and the basement feature a 'jewel palace' (a jewellery shopping mall) and a general shopping centre. There is a free observation platform on the 51st floor, which is a good deal when you consider the inflated prices being charged by Tokyo Tower and the Sunshine building for entry to their observatories.

Pentax Forum On the 1st floor of the Shinjuku Mitsui building is the Pentax Forum (☎ 3348-2941), a must for photography buffs. The exhibition space has changing exhibits by photographers sponsored by Pentax. Undoubtedly, the best part of the Pentax Forum, however, is the vast array of Pentax cameras, lenses and other optical equipment on display. It is completely hands-on – you can snap away with the cameras and use the huge 1000 mm lenses to look through the windows of the neighbouring buildings. Admission is free, and it's open daily from 10.30 am to 7 pm.

Metropolitan Government Offices Altogether there are three towering blocks, the centerpiece of which had a brief spell of glory as the tallest building in Japan – recently knocked off its pedestal by the Yokohama Landmark Tower. The buildings were designed by whizz-kid Kenzo Tange, and whatever your feelings about them you'll have to agree that they are something of a marvel. The aim was to produce a 'people-friendly' city hall, but the resulting

edifice, with its Ministry of Truth overtones, looks like it was hauled off the set of a high-budget production of Orwell's *1984*. Head up to the 45th floor of the No 1 building for one of the best free views of the Tokyo skyline.

East Side 新宿東口
Shinjuku's east side is an area to wander through and get lost in rather than an area in which to search out particular sights. There's plenty to see.

Kabuki-chō Tokyo's most notorious red-light district is the area next to the Seibu Shinjuku station, north of Yasukuni-dōri. To get there, head north from the eastern exit of Shinjuku station; Kabuki-chō starts on the other side of the first major intersection you come to. It's still a safe area to stroll around, but most of what goes on is pretty much off limits to foreigners. There are, however, several strip clubs in the area that are frequented by foreigners (at least one of them occasionally advertises in the tourist hand-out magazines), though you can figure on spending around ¥5000 if you wander into one of these places. Further explorations of Kabuki-chō's seedy offerings will require a Japanese escort or exceptional Japanese-language skills.

This is one of the more imaginative red-light areas in the world, with 'soaplands' (massage parlours), love hotels, no-pants coffee shops (it's the waitresses who doff their undies, not the customers), peep shows, so-called pink cabarets ('pink' is the Japanese equivalent of 'blue' in English), porno video booths and strip shows that involve audience participation. As you walk through streets lined with neon signs and crowded with drunken salarymen, high-pitched female voices wail out invitations to their establishments through distorting sound systems, and Japanese punks earn a few extra yen passing out advertisements for telephone clubs, where young Japanese men pay an hourly fee for a room, a telephone and a list of girls' telephone numbers: if the two like the sound of each other, they can make a date to meet.

Kabuki-chō is not wall-to-wall sex; there are also some very straight entertainment options, including cinemas and some of the best restaurants in Tokyo.

Hanazono-jinja Shrine Nestled away in the shadow of Kabuki-chō is this quiet, unassuming little shrine. It only takes around five minutes to poke around all it has to offer, but it's a nice place to sit down and take a break from the urban madness of Shinjuku. The shrine is particularly pleasant when it's lit up in the evening.

Shinjuku-gyoen Park This park is one of Tokyo's best escapes, with a Japanese garden, a French garden, a hothouse containing tropical plants and, near the hothouse, a pond containing giant carp. Admission is ¥200, and it's open Tuesday to Sunday from 9 am to 4.30 pm.

IKEBUKURO 池袋

Ikebukuro has been treated to something of a facelift over the last couple of years. It still lacks the exuberance of Shinjuku or the classiness of Harajuku, but there's quite a bit to see one way or another. It's home to the world's largest department stores (Seibu and Tōbu), one of the tallest buildings in Asia (the Sunshine City building) the second-busiest station in Tokyo, the world's largest automobile showroom (Toyota Amlux) and the escalator experience of lifetime (Tokyo Metropolitan Art Space). Despite all the attractions, it's still difficult to shrug off the feeling that the whole area is slightly déclassé. It is almost like a Shinjuku waiting to happen, but for some reason the bright lights and the revellers never arrive.

There are sights on both sides of the station. The western side, until recently notable only for a sleazy red-light area and some discount clothes shops has seen a lot of development over the last couple of years.

East Side 池袋東口

Sunshine City Billed as a city in a building, this 'workers' paradise', as it's referred to in the promotional literature, is basically 60 floors of office space and shopping malls, with a few overpriced cultural and entertainment options thrown in. If you've got ¥620 to burn, you can take a lift (reportedly the fastest in the world) to the lookout on the 60th floor and gaze out on Tokyo's murky skyline.

Not in the Sunshine City building itself but in the Bunka Kaikan building of Sunshine City is the Ancient Orient Museum. Admission is ¥400. It's open daily from 10 am to 4.30 pm, except Monday, and is strictly for those with a special interest in ancient odds and ends such as coins and beads.

Also of interest to some might be the Sunshine Planetarium (¥800) and the Sunshine International Aquarium (¥1440).

Toyota Amlux Even if you are not an auto buff, this place has to be seen to be believed – Japanese eccentric hi-tech at its best. There are auto display areas, features on auto production and historical exhibitions, but best of all is the building itself, with its subteranean lighting and ambient sound effects. It is open from 11 am to 8 pm weekdays (except Monday) and from 10 am to 7 pm weekends; entry is free.

Department Stores Until a few years ago, the Ikebukuro branch of Seibu was allegedly the largest department store in the world. But in June 1992, Tōbu snatched the honour from under Seibu's nose by adding an extra nine stories to their store on the other side of the station. Both are worth checking out, but Seibu still seems the busiest, and feels like it's the biggest even if it isn't. You can easily spend an entire afternoon just wandering around the basement food floor of Seibu sampling the little titbits on offer. The 12th floor has an art museum and the top floor is restaurant city, with something like 50 restaurants, many of them offering great lunch specials. Across the road from the Seibu annexe is a Wave record shop. Seibu is open daily, except Thursday, from 10 am to 6 pm.

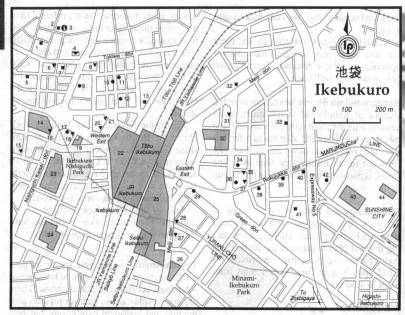

Sezon Museum of Art In the annexe of the Seibu department store is the Sezon Museum of Art, which has changing art exhibits, usually of a very high standard.

West Side 池袋西口

There's not really a lot to see on the west side, but anyone who hasn't been to Ikebukuro for a couple of years should check out the area between the Tokyo Metropolitan Art Space and the southern end of the station. The **Metropolitan Plaza** building is packed with classy boutiques, restaurants and a massive HMV Records (6th floor – great browsing). Just across the road is the **Spice 2** building, which does a repeat performance of the Metropolitan Plaza.

Tokyo Metropolitan Art Space Part of the 'Tokyo Renaissance' plan launched by the Department of Education, this huge cultural bunker was plonked down just where Tokyo needed it most – on the west side of

Ikebukuro. Designed to host performance art, the building has four halls. Those without a ticket for anything should treat themselves to the soaring escalator ride – it doesn't get much more exciting than this in Ikebukuro!

AROUND IKEBUKURO 池袋周辺
Rikugi-en Garden 六義園

Just three stops from Ikebukuro, near the JR Komagome station on the Yamanote line, is the Rikugi-en Garden, a very pleasant place for a walk, with landscaped views unfolding at every turn of the pathways that crisscross the grounds. The garden is rich in literary associations; its name is taken from the six principles of Japanese *waka* poetry (poems of 31 syllables), and the garden itself recreates in its landscaping famous scenes from Chinese and Japanese literature (good luck finding them). The garden was established in the late 17th century by Yanagisawa Yoshiyasu, and after falling into disuse, it

PLACES TO STAY	16	Cattleya Restaurant カトレア	19	Marui Sports 丸井スポーツ
1	Kimi Ryokan 貴美旅館	18	Pekintei Restaurant 北京亭	22	Tōbu Department Store 東武百貨店
2	Hotel Castel (love hotel) ホテル カステル	20	McDonald's マクドナルド	23	Tokyo Metropolitan Art Space 東京芸術劇場
5	Ikebukuro Plaza (capsule hotel) 池袋プラザ (カプセル ホテル)	21	Pizzeria Capri ピッツァリア カプリ	25	Seibu Department Store 西武百貨店
7	Hotel Star Plaza Ikebukuro ホテル・スタープラザ池袋	27	Taiyuzushi Restaurant 大雄寿司	26	Wave Record Shop ウェーブ レコードショップ
13	Hotel Sun City Ikebukuro ホテル・サンシティ池袋	28	Café Presto カフェ プレスト	29	Wise Owl Bookshop ワイズ オウル ブックショップ
24	Hotel Metropolitan ホテル・メトロポリタン	31	Saigon Restaurant サイゴン	30	Mitsukoshi Department Store 三越百貨店
32	Hotel Sun Route Ikebukuro ホテル・サンルート池袋	35	Komazushi Restaurant こま寿司	34	Pronto Coffee プロント コーヒー
33	Hotel Grand Business ホテル・グランド ビジネス	37	Shakey's Pizza シェーキーズ ピッツァ	36	Bic Camera ビック カメラ
41	Capsule Kimeya Hotel カプセル きめやホテル			38	Munchen Beer Hall ミュンヘン ビアホール
44	Prince Hotel プリンス ホテル	OTHER		39	Jack & Betty Club ジャック & ベティー
		3	Kimi Information Service 貴美インフォメーション	40	Tōkyū Hands Store 東急ハンズ
PLACES TO EAT	4	Post Office 郵便局	42	Toyota Amlux トヨタ アムラックス
6	Sushi Kazo Restaurant 寿司和	9	Cinema Rosa シネマ ローザ	43	Sunshine City Building サンシャイン シティ
8	Toneria Izakaya トネリヤ居酒屋	10	Winners' Bar ウィナーズ バー		
15	Capricciosa Restaurant カプリチョーサ	11	Doutor Coffee ドトール コーヒー		
		12	Reggae Bar Kingston レゲー バー キングストン		
		14	Marui Department Store 丸井百貨店		
		17	Horindo Bookshop 芳林堂書店		

was restored by the founder of the Mitsubishi group, Iwasaki Yataro. Admission is ¥200, and it is open Tuesday to Sunday from 9 am to 5 pm.

HARAJUKU & SHIBUYA 原宿・渋谷

Harajuku and Shibuya are the up-and-coming fashion centres of Tokyo. Harajuku is probably somewhat younger in its orientation than Shibuya, but it's difficult to pin the area down, as there are all kinds of surprises in the backstreets and in the basements of unlikely buildings. Harajuku has many shops catering to Tokyo teenagers on the lookout for fashion alternatives – second-hand, punk and '50s and '60s fashions to name a few possibilities. Shibuya, on the other hand, is like Ginza with a bit more

energy. The atmosphere there is vibrant but more mainstream than that in Harajuku. It's where young fashionable Japanese go to do some shopping and hang out.

Harajuku 原宿

You can go to Shibuya any time, but the day to visit Harajuku is Sunday, when Tokyo's subcultures put themselves on public display in the nearby Yoyogi-kōen Park, performing anything from avant-garde theatre to Sex Pistols-style punk. For some reason there aren't as many performers in the park as there used to be, but it's still worth a look.

The activity starts at 1 pm, when the road through the park is closed to traffic. Just five minutes from the park, on Takeshita-dōri, are the shops that serve as the source of the

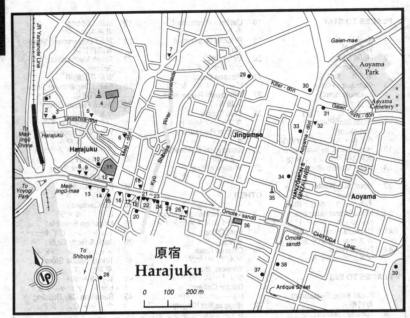

原宿
Harajuku

0   100   200 m

bizarre fashions you see in Harajuku. The streets can be like rush hour on the Yamanote line, but it is still worth exploring Takeshita-dōri and the surrounding area on a Sunday.

Late on Friday and Saturday nights, you can see another side of Japanese youth culture, when car enthusiasts parade up and down Kōen-dōri between NHK and Shibuya station.

Meiji-jingū Shrine The Meiji-jingū Shrine is without a doubt Tokyo's, if not Japan's, most splendid Shintō shrine. It is difficult to believe that it is so close to the crowds in Harajuku. Completed in 1920, the shrine was built in memory of Emperor Meiji and Empress Shōken, under whose rule Japan ended its long isolation from the outside world. Unfortunately, like much else in Tokyo, the shrine was destroyed in the bombing at the end of WW II. Rebuilding was completed in 1958.

The Meiji-jingū Shrine might be a recon-struction of the original, but unlike so many of Japan's postwar reconstructions, it has been rebuilt with all the features of a Shintō shrine preserved. The shrine itself was built with Japanese cypress, while the cypress for the huge torii gates came from Alishan in Taiwan.

Meijijingū-gyoen Park The English explanation on the entry ticket to the park points out that this park was originally part of the garden of a 'feudal load' and that the garden itself has 'spots in it'. Don't let this put you off, however: the park has some very peace-ful walks and is almost deserted on weekdays. It's particularly beautiful in June, when the irises are in bloom, but entry is a somewhat steep ¥400. The entrance is on the left before you reach the shrine; the garden is open daily from 9 am to 4.30 pm.

Meijijingū Treasure Museum As you approach the Meiji-jingū Shrine, there are so many signs indicating the way to the treasure museum that you tend to feel obligated to go there. In fact, the collection of items from the lives of the emperor and empress is pretty unexciting. It includes official garments, portraits and other imperial odds and ends. Admission is ¥200, and it is open daily from 9 am to 4.30 pm, except on the third Friday of each month.

Yoyogi-kōen Park The park has nothing in particular to recommend it, apart from the Sunday afternoon crowds of Japanese youth, rock bands, mime troupes and assorted alternatives to mainstream culture. There's no need to be coy about photography; everyone goes there to be seen, and being photographed is like achieving momentary star status.

Ota Memorial Art Museum The Ota Memorial Art Museum (Ota Kinen Bijutsukan) has an excellent collection of ukiyo-e woodblock prints and offers a good opportunity to see works by Japanese masters of the art, including Hiroshige. To get there, walk away from the JR Harajuku station down Omotesando (the big boulevard opposite the entrance to the Meiji-jingū Shrine) and take the first turn to your left. The museum is a few doors down and is open daily from 10.30 am to 5.30 pm, except from the 25th to the end of the month, when it is closed. Entry is very expensive at ¥800.

Shibuya 渋谷
Shibuya is one of the most trendy shopping areas in Tokyo, but its appeal is predominantly to the young – it's one of those areas in Tokyo notable for an absence of old people. It's not an area rich in sights, but there's plenty to see if you take the time to explore.

The best place to start is Shibuya station.

TOKYO

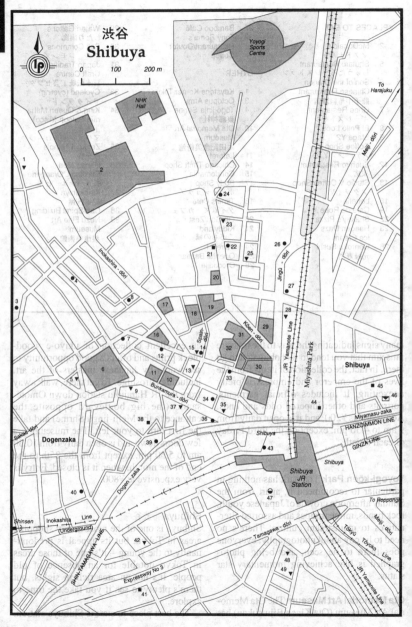

渋谷
Shibuya

PLACES TO STAY

21 Shibuya Tōbu Hotel
   渋谷東武ホテル
38 Hotel Ivy Flat
   ホテル
   アイビーフラット
41 Hotel Sun Route
   Shibuya
   ホテル
   サンルート渋谷
44 Shibuya Tōkyū Inn
   渋谷東急イン
45 Shibuya Business
   Hotel
   渋谷ビジネスホテル

PLACES TO EAT

1 Sunda Restaurant
   サンダレストラン
5 Chef's Gallery
   Chinese Restaurant
   シェフギャリー
   中華料理店
9 Bougainvillea
   Restaurant
   ブーゲンビリアレストラン
13 Samrat Indian
   Restaurant
   シャムタイレストラン
15 Victoria Station
   Restaurant
   ビクトリア駅レストラン
23 Siam Thai Restaurant
   シャムタイレストラン
25 Jūnikagetsu
   Restaurant Building
   １２ヵ月レストランビル
28 Suehiro Restaurant
   末広

35 Only Malaysia
   Restaurant
37 Warung I Balinese
   Restaurant
42 Tainan Taami
   Chinese Restaurant
48 Ninnikuya Garlic
   Restaurant
   ニンニクヤガーリック料理店
49 Kantipur Nepalese
   Restaurant

OTHER

2 NHK Broadcasting
   Centre & Tenji Plaza
   ＮＨＫ放送センター展示広場
3 Kanze Nō-gakudō
   Theatre
   観世能楽堂
4 Tsutsuma Factory
   つつま工場
6 Tōkyū Department
   Store
   東急百貨店
7 The Cave/Bistro de
   Hanna
8 Tower Records
   タワーレコード
10 One-Oh-Nine Building
   １０９ビル
11 One-Oh-Nine '30s
   Store
12 Club Quattro
   クラブ　クワトロ
14 Octopus Army
16 The Beam
   ザ　ビーム
17 Tōkyū Hands
   東急ハンズ
18 Parco Part III
   パルコ　パートⅢ

19 Parco Part I
   パルコ　パートⅠ
20 Parco Part II
22 Tobacco & Salt
   Museum
   たばこと塩の博物館
24 Eggman
   エッグマン
26 Tepco Electric Energy
   Museum
27 Bic Camera
   ビックカメラ
29 Marui Department
   Store
   丸井百貨店
30 Seibu Department
   Store
   西武百貨店
31 Seibu Seed
   西武シード
32 Loft Department
   Store/Wave
   Record Shop
   ロフト百貨店
   ウェーブレコード店
33 Hub Bar
34 Shot Bar
36 109 Building
   １０９　ビル
39 Aspen Glow
40 Dr Jeekhan's
43 Hachikō Statue
   ハチコー像
46 Shibuya Post Office
   渋谷郵便局
47 South Exit Bus Station
   南出口バス停

Take the Hachikō exit to see the bronze **statue of Hachikō**, Tokyo's most famous dog. The statue is a popular meeting place, although as with other Tokyo meeting places, its popularity sometimes makes it less than an ideal spot to meet someone. The story goes that Hachikō waited for his master every day at the railway station for 10 years, unable to come to terms with the fact that his master had died one day at work and wouldn't be coming home again...ever. It's a touching tale, and the dog was much admired throughout Japan for its uncompromising

loyalty, a quality that still plays a big part in Japanese social life.

Opposite Hachikō, roads radiate in a number of directions. If you take the largest of the roads, cross at the first set of traffic lights and bear left at the first, you come to the enormous Seibu department store complex. On the second small street on your left is the Wave record shop and Loft, also run by Seibu. Loft is like a youth-oriented department store – lots of junk and interesting oddments.

Further up the road from Seibu are the

Parco I, II and III department stores (three branches), touted by some as the ultimate in shopping splendour and convenience in Tokyo. The upper floors of all the stores provide some great lunch specials.

Next is Tōkyū Hands, a wonderful store full of do-it-yourself and hobby equipment, hardware, toys and bizarre oddments.

If you continue away from Parco and turn right at the end of the road, on your left is Tower Records, another great record shop and the place to pick up imported US CDs.

Near Parco III, look for **Spain-dōri**, a narrow little lane that has nothing particularly Spanish about but is always chock-a-block with teenies on a shopping spree. Features worth looking out for are Octopus Army, a youth-oriented clothing bazaar at the bottom end of the lane and the Chinese shop selling silk hats with tassles and other incredibly kitsch items about halfway up.

Love Hotel Hill Take the main road to the left of the Hachikō plaza, and at the top of the hill, on the side streets that run off the main road, is a concentration of love hotels catering to all tastes. The buildings alone are interesting, as they represent a broad range of architectural pastiches, from miniature gothic castles to Middle-Eastern temples. It's OK to wander in and take a look. Just inside the entrance there should be a screen with illuminated pictures of the various rooms available. You select a room by pressing the button underneath a room's picture and proceeding to the cashier. This is not an area for cheap love hotels, however. Prices for an all-night stay start at around ¥7000.

New additions to the area include Dr Jeekhan's (*jikan* means 'time' in Japanese), the ultimate in video-game parlours. You even get to dress up in a spacesuit and shoot aliens with a laser gun. Payment is by way of debit cards (¥6000 to ¥10,000). Just down the road is Comic Wonderland, another of those buildings that have to be seen to be believed – the exterior is one huge comic illustration. Inside is an animation 'simulation theatre'. Finally, between these two

places on the other side of the road, is the On Air Theatre, which has a streetside café – a great place to sit and watch couples furtively hunting for a hotel room.

Tobacco & Salt Museum The Tobacco & Salt Museum is another in Japan's long list of quirky museums. There are diagrams and exhibits explaining the history of tobacco use and production (salt gets the same treatment) and a display of cigarette packets from around the world.

There's not much in the way of English explanations, but you get a useful English pamphlet when you pay your ¥100 admission fee. There's a cheap coffee shop on the ground floor. The museum is open daily, except Monday, from 10 am to 6 pm.

Tepco Electric Energy Museum The Tepco Electric Energy Museum is the building in Jingū-dōri with the bulbous silver roof, but it's of no real interest. There are no English explanations. Admission is free, and it's open from 10.30 am to 6.30 pm, but is closed on Wednesday.

Gotō Planetarium Directly to the east of Shibuya station in the Tokyū Bunkakan, this planetarium will probably have little to offer most travellers because it is all in Japanese. All the same, the heavens projected onto the 20 metre dome are pretty amazing. It's open from 11.10 am to 6 pm (closed on Monday) and entry is ¥700.

AKASAKA 赤坂

East of Shibuya and Harajuku and north of Roppongi is exclusive Akasaka, with expensive restaurants and clubs and a thriving cultural scene. Near the Akasaka-Mitsuke subway station is the **Suntory Art Museum**, on the 11th floor of the Suntory building. It has a collection of over 2000 traditional artefacts, including lacquerware and pottery. It's open daily, except Monday, from 10 am to 5 pm (to 7 pm on Friday).

Hie-jinja Shrine 日枝神社
While it's not one of Tokyo's major sights, if

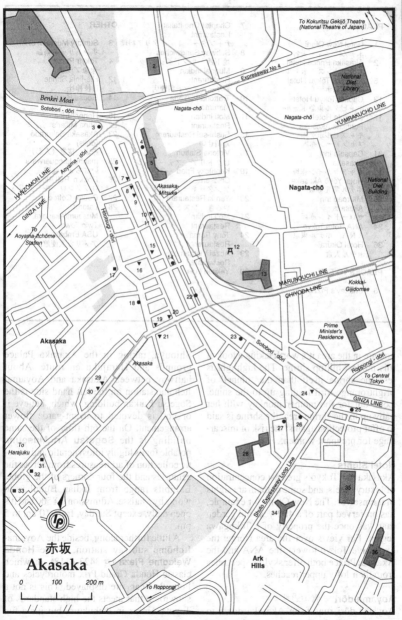

To Kokuritsu Gekijō Theatre
(National Theatre of Japan)

Expressway No 4

National
Diet
Library

YUMRAKUCHO LINE

Benkei Moat
Sotobori - dōri

Nagata-chō

Nagata-chō

HANZOMON LINE

Aoyama - dōri

Akasaka-
Mitsuke

Nagata-chō

National
Diet
Building

GINZA LINE

Hitotsugi - dōri

To
Aoyama-itchōme
Station

MARUNOUCHI LINE

Kokkai-
Gijidōmae

CHIYODA LINE

Akasaka

Prime
Minister's
Residence

Akasaka

Sotobori - dōri

Roppongi - dōri

To Central
Tokyo

GINZA LINE

To
Harajuku

Shuto Expressway Loop Line

Ark
Hills

赤坂
Akasaka

To Roppongi

0   100   200 m

PLACES TO STAY

1 Hotel New Otani
   ホテル ニュー大谷
2 Akasaka Prince Hotel
   赤坂プリンス ホテル
5 Akasaka Tōkyū Hotel
   赤坂東急ホテル
13 Capitol Tōkyū Hotel
   キャピタル東急ホテル
17 Capsule Hotel
   Fontaine Akasaka
   キャプセルホテル
   フォンテーン赤坂
31 Capsule Inn
   Akasaka
   キャプセルイン赤坂
32 Hotel Yōkō Akasaka
   ホテル陽光赤坂
33 Marroad Inn
   Akasaka
   マロードイン赤坂
34 ANA Hotel Tokyo
   ＡＮＡ ホテル東京
36 Hotel Ōkura
   ホテル大倉

PLACES TO EAT

6 Shakey's Pizza

7 Chapter One Italian
   Restaurant
   チャプター 1 イタリア料理
8 Subway Sandwiches
   地下鉄 サンドイッチ
9 Mughal Indian
   Restaurant
   ヌガールインド料理店
10 Trattoria/Pizzeria
   Marumo
11 Moti Indian
   Restaurant
15 Sushi-sei Restaurant
   寿司せい
16 Victoria Station
   ビクトリア ステーション
19 Kentucky Fried
   Chicken
   ケンタッキーフライドチキン
20 Yaruki Restaurant
   やるき レストラン
21 Moti Indian
   Restaurant
24 Tony Roma's
   Restaurant
29 Aozai Vietnamese
   Restaurant
30 Yakitori Luis

OTHER

3 Suntory Museum of Art
   サントリー美術館
4 Tōkyū Plaza
   東急プラザ
12 Hie-jinja Shrine
   日枝神社
14 Goose Bar
   グース バー
18 Henry Africa
22 Anna Miller's
23 Akasaka Sakuradō
   (dolls)
   赤坂 桜堂 (人形)
25 Inachu Lacquerware
   いなちゅう漆器
26 Rock n' Roll Alba
   ロックンロール アルバ
27 Doutor Coffee
28 Laforet
   Museum/Akasaka
   Twin Tower
35 USA Embassy
   アメリカ大使館

you are in the area it's worth taking a look at this modest hilltop shrine. The highlight is less the shrine itself than the 'tunnel' of bright orange torii leading up to the shine. Look out for the mother monkey with her baby up in the shrine area; the shrine is said to offer protection against the risk of miscarriage for pregnant women.

Hotel Sights

Akasaka has Tokyo's greatest concentration of luxury hotels, and some of them are sights in themselves. The New Otani, for example, has preserved part of a 400-year-old garden that was once the property of a Tokugawa regent. For views over the area (forget the expensive Tokyo tower), the ANA and the Akasaka Prince both offer skyline spectacles from their lofty upper reaches.

Aoyama-dōri 青山通り

Aoyama-dōri runs from Akasaka down to Shibuya, taking in the Akasaka Palace grounds and Harajuku en route. About halfway between Akasaka and Aoyama-Itchōme station on the left-hand side is the Sogetsu Kaikan building, which, believe it or not, is devoted to avant-garde flower arrangement. On the 6th floor of the same building is the **Sogetsu Art Museum**, notable for its highly idiosyncratic and eclectic collection of art treasures from across the centuries and the four corners of the globe. Exhibits range from Indian Buddhas to works by Matisse. Admission is ¥500 and it's open daily, except Sunday, from 10 am to 5 pm.

A little further along, beside the Aoyama-Itchōme subway station, is the **Honda Welcome Plaza** (☎ 3423-4118), in which classic Honda Grand Prix motorcycles and Formula I cars are displayed. This is not a showroom that meets the high standards of Toyota Amlux in Ikebukuro, but it's a fun place all the same – check out the projection room with its 'sonic floor', where you get the sensation of being in a motor race. It's open daily from 9.30 am to 6.30 pm, and from 10 am to 6 pm on weekends and public holidays; entry is free.

ROPPONGI 六本木

Playground of the rich, the beautiful and hordes of lecherous off-duty English teachers, Roppongi comes to life at nightfall. There's no reason to go there by day, but by night it's the glittering disco capital of Tokyo. Actually, the way you feel about the whole Roppongi scene is going to depend a lot on how you feel about discos and the kind of crowds they attract. See the Places to Eat and Entertainment sections for more information on Roppongi. There are, however, some attractions in the vicinity of Roppongi that can be visited before nightfall and the onset of disco fever.

Tokyo Tower 東京タワー

This Eiffel Tower lookalike is really more impressive from a distance; up close the 330 metre tower is the familiar tourist rip-off. The Grand Observation Platform (¥750) is only 150 metres high; if you want to peer through the smog at Tokyo's uninspiring skyline from 250 metres up, it will cost you a further ¥520 to get to the Special Observation Platform. The tower also features an overpriced aquarium (¥800), a wax museum (¥750), the Holographic Mystery Zone (¥300) and showrooms.

The tower is a fair trudge from Roppongi: take the Hibiya subway line one stop to Kamiya-chō station. The observation platforms are open daily from 9 am to 6 pm. They close at 8 pm from 16 March to 15 November, except in August, when they are open until 9 pm.

Zōjō-ji Temple 増上寺

Behind the Tokyo Tower is this former family temple of the Tokugawas. It has had a calamitous history, even by Tokyo's standards, having been rebuilt three times in recent history, most recently in 1974. It's still

a pleasant place to visit if you're in the vicinity of the tower. The main gates date from 1605 and are included among the nation's 'Important Cultural Properties'. On the grounds there is a large collection of statues of Jizō, the patron saint of travellers and the souls of departed children.

OTHER ATTRACTIONS
Parks & Gardens

Although the Japanese purport to be ardent lovers of nature and see this as one of the qualities that distinguishes them from other races, Tokyo, like many other Japanese cities, is not particularly green and has a shortage of park space. If you've been hitting the bitumen and haven't seen a tree for days, try the following parks.

Hibiya-kōen Park This park is not one of Tokyo's best but it is close to Ginza and makes a reasonably quiet retreat from the boutiques and department stores.

Koishikawa Kōraku-en Garden Next to the Kōraku-en amusement park and baseball stadium, this has to be one of the best and least-visited (by foreigners at least) gardens in Tokyo. Established in the mid-17th century, it incorporates elements of Chinese and Japanese landscaping. Admission is ¥200, and it is open Tuesday to Sunday from 9 am to 4.30 pm.

Hamarikyū-teien Garden Often referred to in English as the Detached Palace Garden, a visit can be combined either with a visit to Ginza or, via the Sumida-gawa River Cruise, with a visit to Asakusa (see the Asakusa section of this chapter). The garden has walks, ponds and teahouses. Admission is ¥200, and it is open Tuesday to Sunday from 9 am to 4.30 pm.

Museums & Galleries

There's an enormous number of museums and galleries in Tokyo. In many cases their exhibits are small and specialised and the admission charges prohibitively expensive for travellers with a limited budget and a

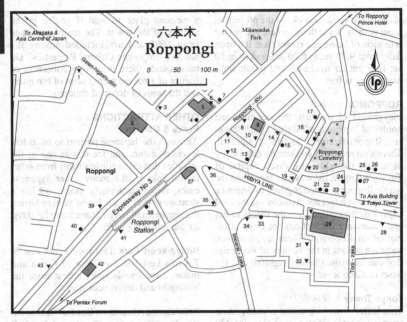

六本木
Roppongi

0   50   100 m

tight schedule. For an up-to-date and more complete listing, get hold of the TIC's *Museums & Art Galleries* pamphlet.

Nezu Art Museum This well-known collection of Japanese art includes paintings, calligraphy and sculpture, and there are also Chinese and Korean art exhibits, and teahouses where tea ceremonies are performed. From Omote-sando subway station, walk down Omote-sando away from Harajuku. Turn right at the end of the road and look for the museum on the left. Admission is ¥550, and it is open daily from 9.30 am to 4.30 pm, but is closed on Monday.

Bridgestone Art Museum Contemporary art by Japanese and European artists is displayed in this museum, five minutes from Tokyo, Nihombashi and Edobashi stations. Admission is ¥550, and it is open from 10 am to 5.30 pm, except Monday.

Sumō Museum The Kokugikan Sumō Stadium, where the museum is located, is a hop, skip and a jump from Ryōgoku station on the Sobu line. Admission is free, and it is open Monday to Friday from 9.30 am to 4.30 pm.

Japanese Sword Museum For corporate warriors with a hankering for Japan's samurai past, the Sword Museum has a collection of over 6000 swords. Entry is ¥550, and it is open daily from 9 am to 4 pm, except Monday. The nearest station is Sangubashi station on the Odakyū line.

Lookouts

The expensive lookouts in the Tokyo Tower and the Sunshine building are covered in the previous Roppongi and Ikebukuro sections. For free lookouts, check the Shinjuku West Side section for information on the Tokyo Metropolitan Government Offices, and the Akasaka section for Hotel view points. Less

PLACES TO EAT		35	Tsunahachi Restaurant	13	Motown House
			綱八	15	Lexington Queen
1	Capricciosa Italian	36	Sicilia Italian		Disco
	Restaurant		Restaurant	16	Maggie's Revenge
	カプリチョーサ	37	シシリア	17	Gaijin Zone
3	Shojikiya Restaurant	37	Almond Coffee Shop		外人ゾーン
	正直屋		アーモンドコーヒー店	18	Charleston Bar
6	Hub Pub	39	Raja Indian Restaurant		チャールストン バー
8	Tainan Taami Taiwan-	41	Moti Indian Restaurant	21	Jack & Betty Club
	ese Restaurant	43	Bengawan Solo		ジャック アンド
11	Pronto Coffee Shop		Indonesian		ベティ クラブ
	プロント		Restaurant	22	Pips Disco
12	Tsubohachi		ブンガワンソロ	24	Gas Panic
	Restaurant		インドネシア	25	Déjà Vu Bar
	つぼ八		料理店	26	Bogey's Bar
14	Seryna Restaurant			27	Henry Africa Bar
19	Shunsai Restaurant		**OTHER**	29	Roy Building
	しゅんさい				ロイ ビル
20	Kushisuke Restaurant	2	Hotel Ibis	33	Kento's Oldies but
	くしすけ		ホテルアイビス		Goodies
23	Bikkuri Sushi	4	Victoria Station	38	Serendip Bookshop
	びっくり寿司		ビクトリア ステーション	40	Meidi-ya International
28	Haagen Dazs	5	Haiyū-za Building		Supermarket
	Ice Cream		俳優座		明治屋国際
30	Mr Donut	7	Suntory Shot Bar		スーパーマーケット
	ミスタードーナッツ		サントリー ショット バー	42	Wave Building
31	Hard Rock Café	9	Square Building		ウエイブ ビル
	ハードロック カフェ		(Birdland & Java		
32	Spago's Californian		Jive Nightclubs)		
	Restaurant		スクエアビル		
34	Roman-tei Restaurant	10	Gas Panic		

well known and also free is the view from the 36th floor of the Kasumigaseki building in Kasumigaseki. Even a look through a telescope there is free.

Amusement Parks

Tokyo Disneyland Only the Japanese signs reveal that you're a long way from Orange County – Tokyo Disneyland is a near-perfect replica of the Anaheim, California, original. A few rides may be in slightly different locations, but basically you turn left from the entrance to the African Jungle, head straight on to Fantasyland or turn right to Tomorrowland.

Its opening hours vary seasonally from 8.30 am to 10 pm in summer to 10 am to 6 pm in winter, but phone ☎ 0473-54-0001 to be sure. It's open daily, except for

about a dozen days a year (most of them in January) when it is closed all day. A variety of tickets are available, including an all-inclusive 'passport' which gives you unlimited access to all the rides for ¥4800 (children aged 12 to 17, ¥4400; those aged 4 to 11, ¥3300). As at the original Disneyland, there are often long queues at popular rides (30 minutes to one hour is normal). Crowds are usually lighter in the mornings and heavier on weekends and holidays.

To get to Tokyo Disneyland, take the Tōzai subway line to Urayasu station. Follow the 'direct bus to Disneyland 340 m' sign out of the station. A shop-lined laneway leads to the Disneyland bus station. A ticket on this bus costs ¥200. Alternatively, take the Yūraku-chō subway line to Shin-kiba station and the JR Keiyo line to Mahihama station, which is right in front of Disneyland's main gate. A variety of shuttle buses also run from Tokyo (¥600), Ueno (¥600) and Yokohama (¥1000) stations, from Narita (¥2000) and Haneda (¥700) airports and from the various nearby Disneyland hotels.

Tokyo Disneyland also has a ticket office (☎ 3201-3511) on the 1st floor of the north wing of the Denki building next to JR Yūraku-chō station. It's open daily from 10 am to 6.30 pm, except on Sunday and national holidays.

Kōraku-en Amusement Park Next to Kōraku-en subway station on the Marunouchi subway line is an amusement park that gets good reports from some travellers. It's nowhere near as big or glossy as Disneyland, but that's what makes it good for many people. The 'Ultra Twister' roller coaster ride is the most popular ride. The park is open Tuesday to Sunday from 10 am to 7 pm and entry is ¥1100 for adults, ¥650 for children (rides not included).

ORGANISED TOURS

Guided tours of Tokyo are a very expensive way of seeing places that you could see more cheaply on your own. If you simply *must* join a tour, first stop should be the TIC, which has comprehensive listings of what's available.

Probably the widest range of tours is available from JTB's Sunrise Tours (☎ 3276-7777). Both morning and afternoon tours are available, as well as tours for those with more specialised interests; industrial tours (¥10,560) and village life and crafts tours (¥11,170) are examples. The Hato Bus Company (☎ 3435-6081) has an all-day Panoramic tour (¥9300) that takes in all the major sights of Tokyo.

Night tours are a popular alternative to the standard run of sights. Possibilities include a kabuki night tour that includes a meal and a geisha show (¥13,420) and the nudge-nudge, wink-wink 'adults only' Fascinating Night tour (¥11,310), which includes a kushiage dinner, geisha show and topless review.

FESTIVALS

Tokyo has many festivals worth seeing if you're in town at the right time of year, including the following:

Ganjitsu (New Year's Day)
1 January. This is the one day in the year (well, the night before is, anyway) that the trains run all night. It is customary for Japanese to visit Buddhist and Shintō shrines to pray for luck in the coming year. For a look at the action, head to Meiji-jingū Shrine, Sensō-ji Temple or the Yasukuni-jinja Shrine. The day after New Year's Day is one of the two occasions each year when the Imperial Palace is open to the public and the imperial couple display themselves before adoring crowds. Enter the inner gardens by the Nijū-bashi Bridge between 9 am and 3.30 pm.

Dezome-shiki
6 January. Firemen dressed in Edo-period costumes put on a parade involving acrobatic stunts on top of bamboo ladders. The parade takes place on Chūō-dōri in Harumi from 10 am onwards.

Seijin-no-hi (Adult's Day)
15 January. Those who turn 20 get a national holiday for reaching the age when they are legally able to drink and smoke. A traditional display of archery is held at Meiji-jingū Shrine.

Setsubun
3 or 4 February. Throughout Japan, beans are scattered from the inside of a building outwards, which is the direction it is hoped the 'devils' will take, and from the outside inwards, which is the direction that good luck is meant to take. In Tokyo, ceremonies are held at Zōjō-ji Temple, Kanda-jinja Shrine and Sensō-ji Temple. Sensō-ji Temple offers the added attraction of a classical dance.

Hari-kuyō
Early February. Check with the TIC for the dates of this typically quirky Japanese festival held for pins and needles that have been broken in the preceding year. At Sensō-ji Temple, women lay their pins and needles to rest by 'burying' them in tōfu and radishes.

Hina Matsuri (Doll Festival)
3 March. Throughout Japan, girls display miniature imperial figures on shelves covered with red cloth. From about mid-February onwards, a doll fair is held in Asakusabashi – check with the TIC for exact details.

Kinryū-no-Mai
18 March. A golden dragon dance is held at Sensō-ji Temple to celebrate the discovery of the

golden image of Kannon that now rests there. Two or three dances are performed during the day.

Hanami (Blossom Viewing)

Early to mid-April. This is one festival you can't help hearing about if you happen to be in Japan when the blossoms come out. Interest in the progress of the sakura (cherry blossoms) verges on a national obsession, with panoramic views of famous cherry blossom viewing parks and close ups of the blooms themselves taking up as much TV viewing time as major sports do in other parts of the world. In Tokyo, *the* place to go for hanami is Ueno-kōen Park. Other famous spots around Tokyo include Yasukuni-jinja Shrine and Koishikawa Kōraku-en Garden.

Hana Matsuri (Buddha's Birthday)

8 April. Celebrations are held at Buddhist temples all over Japan. In Tokyo, celebrations take place at Sensō-ji Temple and Zōjō-ji Temple, among others.

Ueno Tōshō-gū Taisai

17 April. Ceremonies, traditional music and dance are held at Ueno's Tōshō-gū Shrine in memory of Tokugawa Ieyasu.

Kanda Matsuri

Mid-May. This festival is held on odd-numbered years on the Saturday and Sunday closest to 15 May and is a traditional Edo festival that celebrates a Tokugawa battle victory. A whole range of activities take place at Kanda-jinja Shrine.

Sanja Matsuri

May. On the 3rd Friday, Saturday and Sunday of May, at Sensō-ji Temple in Asakusa, up to 100 mikoshi carried by participants dressed in traditional clothes are paraded through the area in the vicinity of the temple.

Sannō-sai

10 to 16 June. Street stalls, traditional music and dancing, and processions of mikoshi are all part of this Edo Festival, held at Sannō Hie-jinja Shrine, near Akasaka-Mitsuke subway station.

O Bon

13 to 15 July. This festival takes place at a time when, according to Buddhist belief, the dead briefly revisit the earth. Dances are held and lanterns lighted in their memory. In Tokyo *bon odori* dances are held in different locations around town.

Sumida-gawa Hanabi Taikai

Last Saturday of July. The biggest fireworks display of its kind in Tokyo is held on the Sumida-gawa River in Asakusa.

Tsukudajima Sumiyoshi-jinja Matsuri

Sunday closest to 7 July. There are several three-day festivals that take place in Tokyo every three years. In this one, activities centre around the Sumiyoshi-jinja Shrine, with dragon dances and mikoshi parades among other things. The next

festival will take place in 1992. The Sumiyoshi-jinja Shrine is across the Sumida-gawa River (via the Tsukuda-ōhashi Bridge) from Tsukiji subway station on the Hibiya line.

Fukagawa Hachiman Matsuri

15 August. In this, another tri-annual, three day Edo festival, foolhardy mikoshi-bearers charge through eight km of frenzied crowds who dash water on them. The action takes place at Tomioka Hachiman-gū Shrine, next to Monzen-Naka-chō subway station on the Tōzai line.

Ningyō-kuyō

25 September. Childless couples make offerings of dolls to Kannon in the hope that she will bless them with children. More interesting for spectators is the ceremonial burning by priests of all the dolls that remain from previous years. It takes place at Kiyomizu-dō Temple in Ueno Park from 2 pm to 3.30 pm.

Furusato Tokyo Matsuri (Metropolitan Citizen's Day)

First Saturday and Sunday in October. A wide range of activities are held at different locations around town. In particular, check out Asakusa's Sensō-ji Temple and Ueno-kōen Park.

Oeshiki

12 October. This festival is held in commemoration of Nichiren (1222 to 1282), founder of the Nichiren sect of Buddhism. On the night of the 12th, people bearing large lanterns and paper flower arrangements make their way to Hommon-ji Temple. The nearest station is Ikegami station on the Tōkyū Ikegami line.

Kanda Furuihon Ichi

27 October to 3 November. A huge sale of second-hand books is held in the Jimbō-chō area. There are 30% reductions on books. Go to the Jimbō-chō intersection and start your explorations there (see the Bookshops section of this chapter).

Meiji Reidaisai

30 October to 3 November. A series of events is held at Meiji-jingū Shrine in commemoration of the Meiji emperor's birthday. Particularly interesting to watch are displays of horseback archery in traditional clothes. Other events include classical music and dance.

Shichi-go-san (Seven-Five-Three Festival)

15 November. As the title implies, this is for children aged seven, five and three. The children (boys aged five and girls aged three and seven) make a colourful sight, as they are dressed in traditional clothes and taken to different shrines around town, notably Meiji-jingū Shrine, Yasukuni-jinja Shrine and Sannō Hie-jinja Shrine.

Gishi-sai

14 December. The day's events commemorate the deaths of the 47 rōnin (masterless samurai) who committed seppuku after avenging the death

of their master. The activities involve a parade of warriors to Sengaku-ji Temple – the rōnin's burial place – and a memorial service from 7.30 pm onwards. The temple is directly west of Sengaku-ji subway station on the TOEI Asakusa line.

PLACES TO STAY

Tokyo is probably one of the most expensive cities in the world when it comes to finding somewhere to sleep. Central Tokyo would be an ideal place to be based but the only possibilities in that part of town are five-star hotels or very expensive business hotels – you won't get value for money even if you find something you can afford. If your budget doesn't reach five-star levels you can find cheaper accommodation with easy access to central Tokyo by staying somewhere on the Yamanote line.

Around the Yamanote line, business and entertainment districts like Shinjuku or Ikebukuro will have capsule hotels from around ¥3500 per night or business hotel singles from ¥5000 to ¥6000 per night. For the same price, a couple could even find a room in a down-market love hotel from 10 or 11 pm – for an extra couple of thousand you could get a fantasy theme room.

The cheapest short-term accommodation will be in a youth hostel, from around ¥2000 per person. Another alternative is a gaijin house, a form of accommodation restricted to Tokyo, Kyoto and Osaka. Until fairly recently these were limited to long-term residents, but increasingly it is possible to find gaijin houses that are willing to accept weekly or in some cases even nightly payment. In Tokyo, gaijin houses are scattered all over the city, almost always outside the Yamanote line and often a good 30 to 40 minutes away from central Tokyo. Given the considerable expense involved in staying in Tokyo, for many visitors gaijin houses are the only real accommodation option.

For a taste of traditional Japan, Tokyo also has a number of ryokan. As elsewhere in Japan, they tend to be divided into those that are reasonably priced and accustomed to foreigners and those that cost the earth and turn

foreigners away if they do not have an introduction. Ueno and Asakusa – older areas with their own tourist attractions as well as direct subway connections with central Tokyo – have a number of ryokan that are used to dealing with foreign guests. Other ryokan are scattered around town and can even be found in bustling commercial centres like Shinjuku. Prices can often be very reasonable – from around ¥4500 per person.

Other traditional accommodation options, such as minshuku, are more rustic and are not available in Tokyo. There are, however, some shukubō (temple lodgings) available out of town for those who want to offset the frantic rhythms of the big city with the calming influence of a Buddhist temple. Staying in a temple requires a high degree of sensitivity to the rules and etiquette that prevail, and many temple lodgings refuse to accept foreigners on the grounds of bad experiences in the past.

Places to Stay – bottom end

The accommodation situation in Tokyo is not what it is in other cities around Asia. If you're happy spending from ¥5000 to ¥6000 or more a night for a single room, there's no shortage of accommodation but things are definitely harder if you are travelling on a budget.

The problem for shoestring travellers is that Japan has for many years been *the* place in Asia to make a few bucks before hitting the road again. Most people fly into Tokyo and stay there until they have enough money to leave. For some years this large long-term foreign population has put a squeeze on budget accommodation. By late '93, however, the bad dollar-yen exchange rate and the downward slide of the Japanese economy had combined to slow down the influx of gaijin coming in search of work and it was getting easier to find cheaper places again. How long things will stay this way is anyone's guess, but for the time being, while it's still a good idea to book ahead, arriving in Tokyo without a booking is not the end of the world. There should be a number of budget places around with vacancies.

Youth Hostels The cheapest short-term accommodation options in Tokyo are the youth hostels in Iidabashi and Yoyogi. The only problem is the usual youth hostel regulations – you have to be out of the building between 10 am and 3 pm (10 am and 5 pm at Yoyogi) and you have to be home by 10 pm – a real drawback in a city like Tokyo. Finally, there's a three night limit to your stay and the hostels can often be booked right out during peak holiday periods.

If you can handle these drawbacks, the common consensus is that the *Yoyogi Youth Hostel* is the better of two evils (the Yoyogi branch gets its fair share of bad reports). The Iidabashi branch might be a showcase for Japan's youth hostels (it's on the 18th floor of a towering office block, giving you great views of Tokyo), but the staff and the general atmosphere are much more businesslike and officious.

The *Tokyo International Youth Hostel* (Iidabashi; ☎ 3235-1107) doesn't require that you be a member but does ask that you book ahead and provide some identification (a passport will do) when you arrive. To get there, exit from Iidabashi station (either JR or subway) and look for the tallest building in sight (it's long, thin and glass fronted). There is a basic charge of ¥2650 per person per night, and a sleeping sheet costs ¥150 for three nights. The Narita Airport TIC has a step-by-step instruction sheet on how to get to the hostel from the airport most cheaply.

The *Yoyogi Youth Hostel* (☎ 3467-9163) requires that you be a youth hostel member and charges ¥2100. There are no meals available, but there are cooking facilities. To get there, take the Odakyū line to Sangubashi station and walk towards the Meiji-jingū Shrine gardens. The hostel is enclosed in a fenced compound – not a former prison camp but the National Olympics Memorial Youth Centre – in building No 14. Staff may let you exceed the three night limit if it is not crowded.

Ryokan The *Kimi Ryokan* (☎ 3971-3766) deserves a special mention in any listing of Tokyo's budget accommodation. The Kimi is in Ikebukuro, which isn't a bad location from which to see Tokyo: 10 minutes from Shinjuku; 20 minutes from Ginza. The rooms are cheap by Tokyo standards, nicely designed in Japanese style (tatami mats and futons) and the place is friendly, clean and relaxed about the hours you keep – just remember to take your room key with you if you're going to be out after 11.30 pm.

The Kimi lounge area is a good meeting place, with an excellent notice board; the Kimi bulletin board has metamorphosed into the nearby Kimi Information Centre. If you're planning to stay at the Kimi, phone and book a few weeks ahead, as there's nearly always a waiting list. Alternatively, arrive early in the morning and wait for someone to leave.

The Kimi is over on the west side of the station and fairly easy to find if you follow the Ikebukuro map. Prices range from ¥3500 (there are only a couple of these and they're rarely free) to ¥4300 for singles, from ¥7000 to ¥8000 for doubles and from ¥7500 for twins.

The *Asia Centre of Japan* (☎ 3402-6111), near Aoyama-Itchōme subway station on the Ginza line, is a popular option in the upper-budget category. This is another place that attracts many long-term stayers, and even though it's a lot bigger than the Kimi, it's still often fully booked. The station is under the easily recognisable Aoyama Twin Tower building on Aoyama-dōri. Walk past the building towards Akasaka-Mitsuke, turn right (towards Roppongi) and the Asia Centre is a short walk up the third street on the left. Rooms have pay TV, and singles cost from ¥4900, twins/doubles from ¥6400. Rooms with bathrooms are significantly more expensive.

An easy place to get to from Narita Airport is the *Suzuki Ryokan* (☎ 3821-4944) in Nippori. Some of the rooms there have private bathrooms and all have TV. Take the Keisei line from Narita and get off at Nippori station, the last stop before Ueno station.

Walking in the direction of Ueno, go to the end of the station and turn right. After you've crossed the tracks straight ahead, there's a flight of stairs that takes you up to a road. The Suzuki Ryokan is a few doors down on the right – look for the English sign. Rooms cost ¥4200 per person, or ¥5000 with private bathrooms.

Close to the JR Gotanda station on the Yamanote line is the *Ryokan Sansui-sō* (☎ 3441-7475). This is not the greatest of locations, but it's only a few stops from Shibuya, the nearest main railway terminus. Take the exit furthest away from Shibuya and exit on the left-hand side. Turn right, take the first right after the big Tōkyū department store and then the first left. Turn left and then right, walk past the bowling centre and look for the sign on the right directing you down the side street to the ryokan. Prices for singles/doubles without bath are ¥4700/ 8000, with bath ¥5000/8400; triples without bath cost ¥11,000.

In Ueno, which is a good place to be based for sightseeing, even if it is a bit of a trek from the bright lights, there are several budget ryokan. The *Sawanoya Ryokan* (☎ 3822-2251) is within walking distance of Nezu subway station on the Chiyoda line (see the Ueno map). If you're coming from Narita International Airport, it would probably be easier and just as cheap if there are more than one of you to catch a taxi from Ueno station. Singles cost ¥4300 to ¥4600; doubles cost ¥8000 without bath and ¥8600 with; triples cost ¥10,800 without bath and 12,300 with.

A bit closer to Ueno station is *Ryokan Katsutaro* (☎ 3821-9808). If you follow the road that runs alongside Shinobazu Pond for about 10 minutes, you'll see the ryokan on the right. Singles/doubles/triples cost ¥4200/7800/10,500 without bath; doubles/ triples with bath cost ¥8400/12,600. On the left, before you get to Ryokan Katsutaro, is the larger *Suigetsu Hotel* (☎ 3822-9611), which has a laundrette and rooms with private bathrooms. You can also change money there. Singles/doubles cost ¥6500/ 11,400; triples cost ¥14,400. This is one

hotel where you really pay through the nose for a Japanese-style room with your own bath – ¥17,820 for a single! Western-style singles/doubles with bath cost ¥7300/12,300.

One stop away from Ueno on the JR Yamanote line (Uguisudani station) is the *Sakura Ryokan* (☎ 3876-8118). Take the southern exit and turn left. Pass the Iriya subway station exits on the left – the Sakura Ryokan is on the right-hand side of the second street on your left. If you're exiting from Iriya subway station on the Hibiya line, take the No 1 exit and turn left. Singles/ doubles without bath cost ¥5000/9000; triples cost from ¥12,000 to ¥13,500. There are also Western-style rooms available with bath from ¥6000 for a single.

Three stops away from Ueno on the Ginza line is Asakusa, which also has a few reasonably priced ryokan. *Ryokan Mikawaya Bekkan* (☎ 3843-2345) is just around the corner from the Sensō-ji Temple in an interesting area. It's on a side street off the shop-lined street leading into the temple. From the Kaminari-mon Gate, the street is a few streets up on the left – there's a toy shop and a shoe shop on the corner. The ryokan is on the left-hand side of the road. Singles/ doubles without bath cost ¥5700/10,400.

In Nishi Asakusa (near Tawaramachi subway station, which is one stop away on the Ginza line from Asakusa station) is the *Kikuya Ryokan* (☎ 3841-6404/4051). It's just off Kappabashi-dōri and prices are ¥4500/7800 for singles/doubles; triples cost ¥11,000. This place get good reports as a quiet and friendly place to stay.

There are several other budget alternatives worth checking out, although they are popular with long-term visitors and often full. In Ikebukuro, *House Ikebukuro* (☎ 3984-3399) has singles/doubles/triples for ¥4000/6000/7700. Near Kotake-Mukaihara subway station, a few stops out of Ikebukuro on the Yūraku-chō line, is the *Rikkō Kaikan Guest Room*, with singles/ doubles from ¥4000/8000.

The *YMCA Asia Youth Centre* (☎ 3233-0611) takes both men and women but is pretty expensive for what it offers. It's halfway between Suidobashi and Jimbō-chō subway stations. Rooms with bathroom cost ¥7000/13,000 for singles/doubles; triples cost ¥16,800. The *Tokyo YWCA Sadohara Hostel* (☎ 3268-4451), near the Ichigaya exit of Ichigaya subway station, accepts couples and is cheaper. Singles/doubles with toilet cost from ¥6180/14,420.

A place that verges on belonging to the gaijin house category is *Apple House* (☎ 0422-51-2277). The advantage of this place is that it is big and has three branches all close to each other. Rates can be paid on a night-by-night basis (which is not possible in most gaijin houses) and the guesthouse has good facilities (kitchen, laundry, fax, satellite TV, etc). Singles are ¥2800 to ¥3400 nightly, ¥18,000 to ¥20,000 per person weekly, ¥65,000 to ¥73,000 monthly; share twins are ¥2200 to ¥2800 nightly, ¥18,000 to ¥20,000 weekly, ¥36,000 to ¥39,000 monthly. Cheaper rates are available for four-bed dormitory style accommodation (¥2000 per person per night).

To get to Apple House take the Chūō line from Shinjuku station (platform No 10) to Higashi Koganei station and ring the guesthouse. Somebody will come to the station and meet you. However, ring to make sure they actually have a vacancy before you make your way all the way out there.

Capsule Hotels Capsule hotels are a strictly male domain and you find them wherever there are large numbers of salarymen, bars, hostess clubs and other drains for company expense accounts. Close to the western exit of Ikebukuro station is the *Ikebukuro Plaza* (☎ 3590-7770), which costs ¥3800 per night. An even cheaper option is the *Capsule Kimeya Hotel* (☎ 3971-8751), where capsules cost ¥3200. It's over on the east side of Ikebukuro, not far from Sunshine City.

Shinjuku is the kind of area you would expect to find capsule hotels thick on the ground – and they are. Right in the heart of Kabuki-chō, Shinjuku's infamous red-light district, is the *Shinjuku-ku Capsule Hotel*

(☎ 3232-1110). It's open from 5 pm to 10 am and costs ¥4100. See the Shinjuku map for a couple of other capsule hotels.

Gaijin Houses The influx of Westerners into Tokyo has dropped off somewhat and there seem to be more gaijin houses offering short-term (nightly or weekly) rates nowadays. The general shortage of cheap accommodation in Tokyo means that some of the more popular places still have have long waiting lists, but there is still the chance of turning up a bed on your first day. It's worth ringing around when you get into town if you're short of cash. Typically prices range from ¥40,000 to ¥70,000 a month for a bed in a shared room, with no deposits or key money required.

Of course you should be prepared for the worst, in which case you may have to book into a cheaper ryokan or a youth hostel until a cheaper room in a gaijin house becomes available. Watch out for rip-offs – there have been reports of travellers paying nearly ¥1000 a night for the privilege of sleeping in a car parked outside a gaijin house.

Gaijin house conditions often leave much to be desired. Rooms are usually very small and chances are you're going to be sharing one to keep expenses down. Facilities are often pretty limited – one shower and toilet for 40 people is a typical shock-horror story. This kind of thing is OK for a while, but if you're going to be based in Tokyo for an extended period, you'll probably want to start looking for something better.

If you ring a gaijin house, there is always someone who speaks English. Generally someone will be able to meet you at the station and take you to the house. Unless otherwise indicated, the prices given here are per person per month. Those looking for short-term accommodation should try the houses with daily and weekly rates first.

1A House: shared rooms ¥30,000 per month, ¥7000 per week, ¥1000 per night; 20 minutes from Shinjuku (☎ 0422-51-2277)

Abbey House: singles ¥42,000; eight minutes from Hibarigaoka station on the Seibu-Ikebukuro line (☎ 0424-23-4162)

Bilingual House: singles/twins from ¥55,000/66,000; five different locations on the Seibu-Shinjuku line (☎ 3200-7082)

Cosmopolitan House: singles/doubles ¥40,000/59,000; 20 minutes from Shinjuku (☎ 3926-4746)

Friendship House: shared rooms ¥9200 to ¥10,400 per week, singles ¥16,750 per week; five locations including Higashi-Kōenji (Marunouchi line) and Kichijōji (JR) (☎ 3327-3179)

Happy Birthday: shared rooms ¥30,000; four locations including Iidabashi (Yūraku-chō line) and Otsuka (Yamanote line) (☎ 5802-4461)

Japan House: shared rooms ¥42,000; Kamata station (Keihin-Tōhoku line) (☎ 3962-2495)

Liberty House: shared rooms weekly from ¥9000, monthly from ¥29,000; seven minutes from Ikebukuro and Shinjuku (☎ 5272-7238)

Maharaja Palace: (somewhat infamous gaijin house) shared rooms weekly from ¥9000, singles/doubles monthly ¥59,000/70,000; 15 minutes from Gotanda, 30 minutes from Shibuya (☎ 3728-7061/5499-3779)

Marui House: daily stays singles/doubles ¥2600/3800, cheaper monthly rates available; good location in Ikebukuro, close to Kimi Ryokan (☎ 3962-4979)

Mom's House: ¥55,000 to ¥60,000; houses well located in Hiroo and Harajuku among other places; (☎ 5568-0123 – ask for Tsuneo)

Tokyo English Centre: shared ¥2000 daily, ¥52,000 monthly; Fujimigaoka station (Keio-Inokashira line) (☎ 5370-8440)

Stone House: private ¥46,000; shared ¥30,000; close to Yagiri station on the Keisei line (☎ 0473-68-0802)

Tokyo English House: ¥2900 a day; ¥18,000 a week; ¥60,00 a month; shared rooms also available at cheaper rates; three minute walk from Horikiri Shōbu-en station on the Keisei line (☎ 3335-0572/3693-4300)

Yellow Fence: private ¥70,000; shared ¥45,000; three minutes from Kami-Igusa station on the Seibu Shinjuku line (☎ 3301-4963)

YTC House: shared ¥45,000; close to Sugamo station (Yamanote line) (☎ 3946-5266/3942-2887)

Places to Stay – middle

Hotels The middle price bracket in Tokyo principally comprises business hotels. There's very little to distinguish one from another, and their main attraction is usually convenience. Every district in Tokyo has numerous business hotels with singles/

doubles from about ¥6000/10,000. Generally, each room will have a built-in bathroom with shower, bath and toilet, a telephone, pay TV and other features like disposable toothbrushes and shaving equipment.

An interesting late-night alternative is a love hotel. There are plenty of these in any of Tokyo's entertainment districts but particularly in Shinjuku, Shibuya, Roppongi and Ikebukuro. All-night rooms range in price from about ¥7000 to ¥8000, but 'all night' doesn't start until 10 or 11 pm, when the regular hour-by-hour customers have run out of energy.

One of the major problems with accommodation in Tokyo is actually finding the place you've decided you want to stay at. Although the following is a very selective list of mid-range hotels, they do at least have English-speaking staff who'll give you instructions over the phone on how to get to the hotel from the nearest station. Wherever possible, locations are indicated on the relevant area maps in this chapter.

Central Tokyo Any hotels in this area tend to be expensive, simply because real-estate values are so high. Nevertheless, there are a few mid-range places.

Business Hotel Heimat: singles/doubles ¥7000/9000; across from the Marunouchi exit of JR Tokyo station (☎ 3273-9411)

Ginza Capitol Hotel: singles ¥8300; twins ¥13,800; two minutes from Tsukiji subway station (☎ 3543-8211)

Ginza International Hotel: singles/doubles ¥13,000/17,000; twins ¥19,000; two minutes from Shimbashi station (☎ 3574-1121)

Hotel Atami-sō: singles ¥9800; twins ¥19,000; two minutes from Higashi-Ginza subway station (☎ 3541-3621)

Hotel Ginza Dai-ei: singles ¥8750; doubles or twins ¥13,000; one minute from Higashi-Ginza subway station (☎ 3545-1111)

Sun Hotel Shimbashi: singles ¥7500; twins ¥12,600; three minutes from Shimbashi station (☎ 3591-3351)

Tokyo City Hotel: singles/doubles ¥8400/12,000; twins ¥12,500; two minutes from Mitsukoshi-mae station (☎ 3270-7671)

Tokyo Station Hotel: singles ¥13,000; twins ¥17,000; doubles ¥19,000; in the JR Tokyo station (☎ 3231-2511)

Yaesu Terminal Hotel: singles/doubles ¥9700/15,500; one minute from the JR Tokyo station (☎ 3281-3771)

Ueno & Asakusa

The cheaper ryokan in these areas are better value, but if they're all full, the business hotels there are generally cheaper than those in other areas around Tokyo.

Asakusa Plaza Hotel: singles/doubles ¥6700/10,500; next to Asakusa subway station (☎ 3862-7551)

Ikenohata Bunka Centre: singles ¥5655; twins ¥11,330; three minutes from Yushima subway station (☎ 3822-0151)

Kinuya Hotel: singles without bath ¥5300; with bath ¥6700; doubles ¥10,800; next to Keisei Ueno station (☎ 3833-1899)

Hotel Parkside: singles/doubles ¥9300/16,500; near Ueno's Shinobazu Pond (☎ 3836-5711)

Hotel Pine Hill Ueno singles ¥7500; doubles and twins ¥14,000; three minutes from Yushima or Okachimachi stations (☎ 3836-5111)

Shinjuku

Shinjuku is a good hunting ground for business hotels that cater to foreigners.

Business Hotel Shinjuku Inn: singles ¥7200; doubles or twins ¥11,000; five minutes north of Shinjuku Gyoen-mae subway station (☎ 3341-0131)

Hotel Sun Lite Shinjuku: singles from ¥7700 to ¥8500; twins from ¥12,000 to ¥14,000; doubles from ¥11,000 to ¥14,000; 10 minutes from the east exit of Shinjuku station (☎ 3356-0391)

Shinjuku New City Hotel: singles/doubles ¥9700/19,000; twins ¥15,300; 10 minutes from the west exit of Shinjuku station, behind Shinjuku Central Park (Shinjuku Chūō-kōen) (☎ 3375-6511)

Shinjuku Park Hotel: singles from ¥6800 to ¥7300; twins ¥11,800; seven minutes from Shinjuku station in the direction of Shinjuku-gyoen Park (☎ 3356-0241)

Shinjuku Washington Hotel: singles/doubles ¥10,000/16,500; 10 minutes from the west exit of Shinjuku station, just south of the NS building (☎ 3343-3111)

Star Hotel Tokyo: singles/doubles ¥11,500/17,300; three minutes from the west exit of Shinjuku station (☎ 3361-1111)

Tokyo Business Hotel: singles without bathroom ¥4800; twins ¥10,300; seven minutes north of Shinjuku Gyoen-mae subway station (☎ 3356-4605)

Ikebukuro

There are innumerable business and love hotels in the Ikebukuro area, as well as some of the most popular cheaper ryokan.

Dai-Ichi Inn Ikebukuro: singles/doubles from ¥8300/16,000; close to the east exit of Ikebukuro station (☎ 3986-1221)

Hotel Grand Business: singles ¥7700 to ¥8200; twins ¥12,800 to ¥13,400; five minutes from the east exit of Ikebukuro station (☎ 3984-5121)

Hotel Star Plaza Ikebukuro: singles from ¥6500 to ¥7000; doubles ¥10,000; five minutes from the west exit of Ikebukuro station (☎ 3590-0005)

Hotel Sun City Ikebukuro: singles from ¥6500 to ¥7000; doubles/twins from ¥9500 to ¥10,500; close to the west exit of Ikebukuro station (☎ 3986-1101)

Hotel Sun Route Ikebukuro: singles from ¥8500; doubles/twins from ¥14,000/15,000; five minutes north of the east exit of Ikebukuro station (☎ 3980-1911)

Shibuya

Shibuya is a trendy area and an expensive one to base yourself in. If you're looking for more inexpensive business hotels, Ueno, Ikebukuro and even Shinjuku represent much better value for money. The following hotels are all within easy striking distance of Shibuya station.

Hotel Ivy Flat: singles ¥10,500; twins ¥16,500; five minutes from the Hachikō exit of Shibuya station (☎ 3770-1122)

Hotel Sun Route Shibuya: singles ¥6500; doubles/twins ¥13,000/15,900; five minutes from Shibuya station on south side of the expressway (☎ 3464-6411)

Shanpia Hotel Aoyama: singles/doubles ¥11,470/18,120; five minutes from the Hachi-kō exit of Shibuya station (☎ 3407-2111)

Shibuya Business Hotel: singles/doubles ¥8270/11,100; two minutes from the station on the east side of the Yamanote line behind Shibuya post office (☎ 3409-9300)

Shibuya Tōkyū Inn: singles from ¥12,200 to ¥13,200; doubles/twins ¥17,000/17,600; one minute from the east exit of Shibuya station (☎ 3498-0109)

Shibuya Tōbu Hotel: singles from ¥11,600; doubles/twins from ¥16,200/19,800; five minutes from Shibuya station, up past the Parco department stores (☎ 3476-0111)

Roppongi & Akasaka

These are good areas to be based in if you want access to central Tokyo and a lively nightlife (it's possible to walk down to Roppongi from Akasaka). Like Shibuya, Akasaka and Roppongi are not areas in which you are going to find any accommodation bargains.

Hotel Ibis: singles/doubles ¥13,000/20,000; two minutes from Roppongi subway station (☎ 3403-4411)

Hotel Yōkō Akasaka: singles/doubles ¥9500/13,000; three minutes from Akasaka subway station (☎ 3586-4050)

Marroad Inn Akasaka: singles/doubles ¥9600/12,000; five minutes from Akasaka subway station (☎ 3585-7611)

Shanpia Hotel Akasaka: singles ¥9990; twins ¥16,890; four minutes from Akasaka subway station (☎ 3586-0811)

Toshi Centre Hotel: singles ¥7500; twins ¥12,000; seven minutes from Akasaka-Mitsuke subway station (☎ 3265-8211)

Places to Stay – top end

Although Tokyo is one of the world's most expensive cities, its top-end hotels are no more expensive than similar hotels anywhere else, and you get Japan's legendary high standard of service.

Top-end hotels are naturally found mostly in central Tokyo. Given that all such hotels have very high standards, location should be a prime factor in deciding where you stay. The Imperial Palace and Ginza areas have a certain snob appeal, but the Akasaka area, which combines a good central location with nearby entertainment options, would be an equally good choice. The west side of Shinjuku station has a concentration of top-notch hotels, and is a good area in which to see Tokyo at its liveliest.

The hotels that lead the pack in Tokyo are reportedly the *Hotel Seiyo Ginza*, which also happens to be the most expensive, the *Akasaka Prince*, the *New Otani* and the *Hotel Ōkura*. The *Imperial Hotel* in Central Tokyo is probably the best known hotel in the city. The following prices are for the least expensive rooms available in each hotel.

Akasaka Prince Hotel: singles ¥24,000; doubles/twins ¥36,000/32,000; next to Nagata-chō subway station (☎ 3234-1111)

Akasaka Tōkyū Hotel: singles ¥21,000; doubles/twins ¥31,000/29,000; next to Nagata-chō or Akasaka-Mitsuke subway stations (☎ 3580-2311)

ANA Hotel Tokyo: singles ¥23,000; doubles/twins ¥31,000; near Akasaka subway station (☎ 3505-1111)

Asakusa View Hotel: singles ¥15,000; doubles/twins ¥21,000/28,000; 10 minutes from Asakusa subway station (☎ 3847-1111)

Capitol Tōkyū Hotel: singles ¥25,000; doubles/twins ¥35,500; near Nagata-chō subway station (☎ 3581-4511)

Century Hyatt Tokyo: singles ¥30,000; doubles/twins ¥34,000; west exit of Shinjuku station (☎ 3349-0111)

Dai-Ichi Hotel Tokyo: doubles/twins ¥30,000/34,000; close to Shimbashi station (☎ 3501-4411)

Ginza Dai-Ichi Hotel: singles ¥18,000; doubles/twins ¥29,000/25,000; near Higashi-Ginza and Shimbashi stations (☎ 3542-5311)

Ginza Nikkō Hotel: singles ¥16,800; doubles/twins ¥22,800/26,800; close to Shimbashi station (☎ 3571-4911)

Ginza Tōbu Tokyo Renaissance Hotel: singles ¥17,000; doubles/twins ¥31,000; close to Higashi-Ginza subway station (☎ 3546-0111)

Ginza Tōkyū Hotel: singles ¥17,500; doubles/twins ¥29,800; near Higashi-Ginza station (☎ 3541-2411)

Hotel Metropolitan: singles ¥16,000; doubles/twins ¥21,000; near the west exit of Ikebukuro station (☎ 3980-1111)

Hotel Ōkura: singles ¥28,500; doubles/twins ¥37,000/40,000; near Kamiya-chō subway station (☎ 3582-0111)

Hotel New Otani: singles ¥25,500; doubles/twins ¥33,500/32,500; near Nagata-chō subway station (☎ 3265-1111)

Hotel Seiyo Ginza: singles ¥45,000; twins ¥62,000; 10 minutes from Higashi-Ginza subway station (☎ 3535-1111)

Imperial Hotel: singles ¥30,500; doubles/twins ¥35,500; near Hibiya-kōen Park) (☎ 3504-1111)

Keio Plaza Inter-Continental Hotel: singles ¥15,000; doubles/twins ¥27,000; near west exit of Shinjuku station (☎ 3344-0111)

Le Pacific Meridien Tokyo: singles ¥21,000; doubles/twins ¥25,000; close to Shinagawa station (☎ 3445-6711)

Palace Hotel: singles ¥22,000; doubles/twins ¥32,000/28,000; near Tokyo station and Ōtemachi subway station (☎ 3211-5211)

Roppongi Prince Hotel: singles ¥19,500; doubles/twins ¥24,500/23,000; close to Roppongi subway station.

Takanawa Prince Hotel: singles ¥20,000; doubles/twins ¥25,000/24,000; near Shinagawa station (☎ 3447-1111)

Tokyo Hilton International: singles ¥27,000; doubles/twins ¥34,000; near Shinjuku station (☎ 3344-5111)

PLACES TO EAT

One of the best things about Tokyo is the food. It's possible to get *anything* in Tokyo. Scanning the food section of the *Tokyo Journal*, 124 restaurants are reviewed, and the entries begin with *Piga Piga* (an African restaurant with live African music) and end with *Miyun* (My Dung; a restaurant run by a 'Saigonese woman serving Vietnamese dishes with a French flair').

Of course, Tokyo isn't all trendy ethnic cuisine at chalked-up prices. The city harbours a multitude of dining spots, ranging from exclusive Japanese and foreign restaurants to inexpensive places where you slurp your noodles standing at the counter. Plastic food displays in the window tell you how much your meal is going to cost before you go inside. Even in the lowliest of establishments, you will get a hot towel and a glass of water when you sit down.

It's not really necessary to look for restaurants in Tokyo. They are just there, everywhere you look. Railway stations are the haunt of Chinese noodle rāmen shops and obentō (boxed meals) stands. In the upper floors of department stores there are often *resutoran-gai*, or 'restaurant streets' with Japanese, Chinese and Italian restaurants offering special lunch-time prices. Big commercial districts like the east side of Shinjuku just brim with restaurants – everything from revolving sushi to pizza. Often the problem is not finding a place to eat but deciding *which* one.

Despite the high cost of everything else in Tokyo, meals are one thing that need not be that expensive. For the best cheap eats, try to be a bit adventurous: avoid the Western-style fast-food barns and experiment with the Japanese and Chinese restaurants that are popular with local office workers for lunch and after work. You can usually get a large bowl of noodles for between ¥350 and ¥450 in most rāmen shops. Other budget options that are popular with the Japanese are the

curry rice shops and the revolving sushi shops where three sushi pieces on a plate will set you back between ¥100 and ¥150.

During the day, the best eating areas are the big shopping districts like Shibuya, Shinjuku, Harajuku and Ginza. Shinjuku could well take the prize as Tokyo's best daytime gourmet experience, with rows of restaurants in the big department stores and, at street level, an endless selection of reasonably priced restaurants and the best affordable Chinese food in Tokyo. Shinjuku is the busiest commuter junction in Tokyo, and there are a vast number of restaurants around the station and in the frenetic entertainment area. There are also many restaurants underground, along the 1½ km of shopping streets which run from around the station.

At night, Shinjuku is again in the running with the best Chinese food in Tokyo at affordable prices, plus a fantastic selection of Japanese, Korean and various 'ethnic' (Thai, Turkish, Mexican, etc) restaurants. Places in central Tokyo, on the other hand, are really too expensive for evening meals although you can find cheap yakitori bars near the Yūraku-chō station area and *Nair's* Indian restaurant is reasonable. The Ueno and Ikebukuro areas, where many travellers stay, abound in small Japanese and Chinese noodle bars, though Ikebukuro has an increasing number of up-market alternatives, including French, Italian and Vietnamese restaurants. Anyone with some money to spend should remember that Roppongi is not just a night-club area – it has some of the best eating out in Tokyo.

For a serious restaurant crawl get Rick Kennedy's *Good Tokyo Restaurants*. Many of the places recommended are too expensive for travellers on a budget, but if you're planning a longer stay the book is definitely a worthwhile investment. The *Tokyo Journal* runs a regular restaurant guide, and is the best source for more off-beat dining alternatives.

The following cuisine guide first describes restaurants serving Japanese food by area. Places serving international cuisine are listed by area in the Other Cuisines section and are then described more fully under separate cuisine sections.

Japanese

Of course, besides all the international places, there are more Japanese restaurants in Tokyo than you could poke a piece of sushi at. Mostly they specialise – you'll be hard pressed to come up with a 'Japanese restaurant', the kind you find at home that serves sushi, tempura *and* sukiyaki. Affordable options include raucous izakaya/robotayaki restaurants, simple neighbourhood okonomiyaki and yakitori bars, revolving sushi restaurants and department store tempura restaurants. At the other extreme, Tokyo abounds in exclusive restaurants with very high prices; you may not even get in without an introduction. Some individual recommendations follow in the area descriptions.

Central Tokyo & Ginza If you are even remotely on a budget, Ginza is for the most part best avoided as a place to eat out in the evening. During the day, though, it's a different story. There are some very economical lunch-time teishoku deals to be had in the department stores. As in other parts of Tokyo, it's on the upper floors of the department stores that you'll find the restaurant areas. *Restaurant City* on the 8th floor of the Matsuya department store has a wide variety of restaurants with not too outrageous prices. It's conveniently close to the centre of Ginza on Ginza-dōri and is open until 9 pm daily (closed on Thursday). The store itself closes at 6 pm but the restaurant floor has its own elevator.

Another floor of restaurants can be found in the 2nd basement level of the Matsuzakaya department store, also on Ginza-dōri but just the other side of Harumdōri. Another place worth checking out is the Ginza Palmy building. The basement floors are chock-a-block with Japanese restaurants that are very popular with office workers

Seeking out affordable Japanese food in Ginza after hours is not a completely lost cause. A good starting place is the Yūraku-

chō station area close to the TIC. Here you'll find some long-running, inexpensive yakitori bars, although this area is being rapidly gentrified and the old yakitori places are being replaced by up-market restaurants. Even if you don't eat here, it's a tremendously atmospheric area to take a stroll through – all those red-faced businessmen munching on skewered chicken and knocking back beers. A similarly rowdy spot is the *Sapporo Lion Beer Hall* (☎ 3571-2590), just down the road from the Matsuzakaya department store. It's as good an introduction to Japanese beer culture as any, and the extensive menu includes everything from Japanese snacks to German sausages – food and beers will set you back from ¥2000 to ¥2500. It's open from 11.30 am to 10.15 pm daily.

Just south of Harum-dōri is *New Torigin*, hidden away down a very narrow back alley but there is a signpost in English and the restaurant is quite easy to find. There's a menu in English, and this authentic, very popular little place does excellent food including yakitori at ¥120 to ¥200 per stick and the steamed rice dish known as Kamameshi at ¥700. A complete meal with a beer costs about ¥1500.

If you wander around Ginza, you'll undoubtedly stumble across other reasonably priced Japanese restaurants. Places to look out for include the revolving sushi restaurant *Kaiten-zushi*, north of Harumi-dōri. It's easy to miss as it's on the 2nd floor – look out for a men's clothing store at ground level. Just down the road from here is a branch of *Tenya*, the tendon (tempura and rice) chain that has rice and tempura dishes from ¥490. *Dondo*, just a couple of doors up from the TIC has good udon from ¥750.

Ueno & Asakusa In the older areas – Shitamachi or 'low' city of pre-Meiji Tokyo – there are fewer foreign restaurants and more traditional Japanese food. Just south of Ueno station, and a good area to browse in and grab a bite to eat is Ameyoko market. All the restaurants have plastic food displays, so you should have an idea of what you are getting and how much you are going to pay for it. Look out for *Irohazushi*, an inexpensive sushi restaurant. It's on the left, just after you enter the market area. *Kappazushi*, a little further up on one of the side streets is a similar kind of restaurant, also with affordable sushi.

Ueno is also home to some very traditional up-market Japanese restaurants. One place that isn't *that* expensive, but on the down side isn't particularly accommodating to foreigners who don't speak Japanese, is *Izu-ei*. The restaurant specialises in *unagi*, or eel, and has an incredible interior – bamboo umbrellas, plants and soft lighting. A meal here will cost from ¥1200 up, though you will probably be looking at around ¥2500 when you are finished. There are a few other traditional restaurants along Shinobazu-dōri, and it's worth wandering along the street and peering in at the interiors.

A final tip on Ueno is to try the station itself. Most Tokyo JR railway stations have a number of places to eat, but Ueno station is one of the best. Just get lost in the network of tunnels in the station (easy to do) and look out for the shops with monster-size bowls of rāmen. Other places serve generic Japanese cuisine – everything from sashimi to udon.

In Asakusa, the area between Sensō-ji Temple and Kaminarimon-dōri is the best place to seek out Japanese food. On Kaminarimon-dōri itself *Tenya*, a tiny mod-con tendon shop, has tempura and rice dishes from ¥490 – a bargain. A bit further up the road towards Asakusa subway station, *Naowariya* is a classy soba shop, with dishes ranging from ¥1100. To the right of the entrance to Sensō-ji Temple is *Tonkya*, a small, family-run tonkatsu establishment (closed Thursday), where you can eat well from ¥700. To the left is a branch of *Yoshinoya*, a chain that can be found all over Tokyo, specialising in very inexpensive gyūdon (beef and rice).

There are a number of Japanese restaurants in the lane running parallel to and to the east of Nakamise-dōri, the colourful acade that leads into the precincts of Sensō-ji

Temple. One place to look out for is the *Ramen House Asakusa*, recommended for its playful subversion of standard rāmen cuisine – try a 'sausage rāmen' or a 'beef patty rāmen', you won't get a chance to do so anywhere else. Prices range from ¥800. On the subject of rāmen, the cheapest rāmen in Asakusa (possibly in all of Tokyo) can be had at *La Mentei* – ¥280 for a bowl.

On the same street as the Ramen House Asakusa is *Tatsumiya* (☎ 3842-7373), an old Edo-period restaurant full of interesting bric-a-brac that specialises in *nabe ryōri* ('stew', or literally 'pot cuisine') during the winter months. Prices for this speciality average ¥2500. At midday, bentō are available for ¥850. Evening courses that allow you to sample a wide range of goodies will cost ¥4200. Tatsumiya is closed on Monday.

Finally, close to Asakusa subway station is *Kamiya* (☎ 3841-5400), claimed to be the oldest bar in Japan. There's a beer hall on the ground floor where you order and pay for beer and food as you enter. Upstairs, both Western and Japanese food are served. Kamiya is renowned for a cocktail of its own invention called denki buran – the *buran* stands for brandy – and it comes in two varieties: 60 proof and 80 proof. The Kamiya is closed on Tuesday.

Ikebukuro Ikebukuro is not the kind of area you go to looking for Japanese food but, if you are in the area, there are a number of places worth checking out. First on anyone's itinerary should be the 'restaurant cities' in Seibu, Tōbu and Marui department stores – great lunch-time specials and hundreds of places to choose from. Other than the department stores, the busy shopping area over on the east side of Ikebukuro is the place to look for somewhere to eat. There are a couple of revolving sushi places, *Taiyuzushi* and *Komazushi* that are both very popular. Also worth checking out is the *Jack & Betty Club*. It's not a place for Japanese food, so much as Japanese interpretations of Western favourites like steak and pizza, all at very low prices.

Shinjuku Shinjuku is the busiest and most energetic commuter junction in Tokyo, and there are a vast number of restaurants around the station and in the east-side entertainment area. Many of the Japanese restaurants in Shinjuku are livelier and rowdier than those in, say, Asakusa. The large numbers of businessmen and young people here make Shinjuku a good place to eat out at night and sample some of the places that specialise in beer and snacks – after all enough snacks soon become a meal.

The east side of the station is the best place to seek out something to eat. Over behind Mitsukoshi department store is a long-time favourite for tempura: *Tsunahachi* (☎ 3352-1012). It's a little expensive (sets around ¥2000) and you'll probably have to queue to get fed, but it's worth both the wait and the money. Not far away is the lively *Daikokuya* (☎ 3352-2671), a popular student hang-out. It has all-you-can-eat deals (yaki-niku ¥1700, shabu-shabu and sukiyaki ¥2300, add ¥1000 and it's all you can drink too). Daikokuya is in a basement location.

In a similar vein to Daikokuya is *Irohanihoheto* (what a mouthful) (☎ 3359-1682). This is a big izakaya that is popular with students. It's on Yasukuni-dōri on the 6th floor of the Piccadilly movie house. Another high-decibel boozing and eating experience can be had in the Shinjuku branch of the popular robotayaki chain *Yōrōnotaki*. Cheap beer, great food listed on an illustrated menu, and the restaurant can be found in the basement on Yasukuni-dōri on the fringes of Kabuki-chō.

At the end of the day, however, the best advice for Shinjuku is just to strike off and see what you come up with. Look out for one of the numerous *kaiten-zushi*, or 'revolving sushi' restaurants or take an escalator to the top floors of one of the department stores. The back lanes of Kabuki-chō are also packed with Japanese restaurants (among other things).

Harajuku & Shibuya Trendy shopping districts, pizzerias, ethnic bars and coffee shops are thicker on the ground than Japanese cuisine in Harajuku and Shibuya. Affordable restaurants in Harajuku include *Genroku* (☎ 3498-3968) on Omote-sandō. It's a revolving sushi shop in a league of its own, with sushi from ¥130 a plate. On the corner of Omote-sandō and Meiji-dōri is *Suehiro* (☎ 3401-4101), a branch of the popular chain that specialises in beef dishes, including shabu-shabu and sukiyaki. It's a classy kind of place that will probably be a bit too expensive for most visitors.

Walk a little further down Omote-sandō and look out for *Gojinhasero*, a great basement noodle shop next door to the Body Shop. This is one place where it's worth spending a bit extra for your noodles. Prices range from ¥700 and the servings are enormous.

Surprisingly, another part of Harajuku worth checking out is Takeshita-dōri. There are a few Japanese restaurants on this trendy stretch of road. *Shūtarō* (☎ 3402-7366) is a tonkatsu and katsudon specialist and most dishes are around the ¥1000 mark.

Shibuya is department-store city, and there are some great lunch-time deals for Japanese food in any of the innumerable *depāto*s that litter the area. Places to start are the 7th floor of Parco 1 or the 8th floor of the One-Oh-Nine building. Another alternative, though a bit more up-market, is *Jūnikagetsu* (meaning '12 months' for all you Japanese students) Restaurant building.

The alternative to department stores and restaurant buildings in Shibuya can be found in the maze of side streets north of Bunkamura-dōri. There shouldn't be any problem in digging up a revolving sushi shop or a beer and snacks place.

Akasaka & Roppongi The Akasaka/Roppongi area is a gourmet paradise, but in most cases, prices will be out of the reach of visitors on a budget. Still, it pays to hunt around a bit. Even in Roppongi there are small yakitori bars and noodle shops that are no more expensive than elsewhere in Tokyo.

In Akasaka, take a stroll in the streets running off and parallel to Sotobori-dōri. All the best deals in this area are in Western food, however. Many of the Japanese restaurants are fairly exclusive or have reputations that make them expensive to eat in. Examples include *Tenichi*, where set-course tempura in opulent surroundings starts at ¥6500, or *Sushi-sei*, a branch of the famous sushi chain.

Exeptions to the rule can be found in places like *Yaruki*, a boisterous izakaya with affordable prices over by Akasaka subway station. (It has an illustrated menu for easy ordering.) Also not far from the subway station is *Yakitori Luis* (☎ 3585-4197), a very popular yakitori place where prices start at ¥200 per snack.

In Roppongi, a special mention is in order for *Bikkuri Sushi*, a long-standing, late-night revolving sushi that gets a lot of patronage from those who frequent gaijin hang-outs like Déja Vu or Gas Panic (it's almost next door to the latter), like to eat good sushi and watch people. Another place to look out for is *Tsubohachi*, a small yakitori bar where a little English is spoken and which stays open until 5 am.

up-market Japanese cuisine is well represented in Roppongi, with places like *Sushi-sei* (☎ 3401-0578), a branch of the famous sushi chain, and *Seryna* (☎ 3403-6211), perhaps Roppongi's best known Japanese restaurant. The latter has an extensive menu that gives you a chance to sample items from across the spectrum of Japanese cuisine – but be prepared for an expensive evening out.

Other Cuisines

Tokyo is a fabulous city to dine out on non-Japanese cuisines. Italian, French, Indian and a host of obscure ethnic restaurants combine to make Tokyo the gourmet capital of Asia. The drawback of course is that the current poor exchange rate and high prices also make Tokyo the most expensive city in Asia for eating out. That said, many of the restaurants recommended here do such good business that they are able to keep their prices down, and even if you are on a strict budget it's worth splashing out at least once on a good Balinese or Ethiopian meal for

between ¥1500 and ¥2000. Other interesting restaurants have cross-ethnic cuisines or embrace a theme like 'garlic'.

Central Tokyo & Ginza Ginza has an excellent range of international cuisine, but bear in mind that most of it is very pricey. The following list includes a few more reasonably priced options:

French – *Maxim de Paris*
German – *Lorelei, Munchen Beer Hall, Volks*
Indian – *Maharaja, Nair's*
Indonesian – *Restaurant Indonesia*
Vietnamese – *Saigon*

Ueno & Asakusa If you're determined to avoid Japanese food there are plenty of fast-food specialists, but fewer foreign restaurants in the Ueno and Asakusa areas. *Samrat* and *Maharaja* in Ueno serve good Indian food.

Ikebukuro Not quite the backwater it used to be, Ikebukuro has some good French, Italian and even Vietnamese food.

Chinese – *Pekintei*
French – *Chez Kibeau*
German – *Munchen*
Italian – *Café Presto, Cattleya, Pizzeria Capri, Capricciosa*
Vietnamese – *Saigon*

Shinjuku As well as a wide variety of Japanese restaurants and fast-food centres there are also some superb places for foreign food in Shinjuku; the Kabuki-chō area to the east of the station has countless restaurants of all types.

African – *Rose de Sahara*
Cambodian – *Angkor Wat* (in Yoyogi)
Chinese – *Pekin, Tainan Taami Tokyo Kaisen Ichiba, Tokyo Dai Hanten*
German – *Hofbräuhaus Beer Hall*
Korean – *Tōkaien*
Mexican – *El Borracho*
Thai – *Ban Thai, Champer, Kao Keng*

Harajuku & Aoyama These are trendy areas and most of the international restaurants are out of the price range of the average traveller.

TOKYO

There are some good coffee shops to sit around in, however, and watch the fashionable world pass by.

Cafés – *Stage 2, Studio V, Time's Café, Café de Rope, Bamboo Café*
Chinese – *Son of the Dragon*
French – *L'Orangerie*

Shibuya Shibuya has numerous fast-food restaurants and places serving a wide variety of international cuisines. Places to try here include:

Balinese – *Warung I*
Chinese – *Tainan Taami, Chef's Gallery*
Indian – *Maharaja, Samrat*
International – *Sunda, Ninnikuya*
Malaysian – *Only Malaysia*
Nepalese – *Kantipur*
Thai – *Siam Thai*

Akasaka Aksaka is really one of the best places to eat out in Tokyo. Most of the restaurants are clustered together in a compact enclave between Sotobori-dōri and Hitotsugi-dōri.

American – *Subway Sandwiches, Tony Roma's, Victoria Station*
Indian – *Moti* (two branches), *Mughal, Taj*
Italian – *Chapter One, Pizzaria/Trattoria Marumo*
Vietnamese – *Aozai*

Roppongi *Hard Rock Cafe* (see Entertainment) is a Tokyo institution and just behind it is *Spago's*, an up-market Californian restaurant. Next door to the Hard Rock is *Tony Roma's*, where you can pay a lot of money for ribs. Burgers and other beef dishes plus a good salad bar can be found at the *Victoria Station* chain. The Roppongi branch is in the Haiyū-za building, on the other side of Roppongi Crossing from Almond.

Some other less expensive international possibilities include:

Chinese – *Buryōmon, Tainan Taami*
French – *Shunsai*
Indian – *Moti, Samrat*
Indonesian – *Bengawan Solo*
Italian – *Capricciosa, Sicilia*
Thai – *Sabai*

Fast Food
Most of the budget-priced Japanese and Chinese restaurants serve their food just as quickly and often more cheaply than the fast-food chains, but if you simply can't do without a Big Mac or a Shakey's pizza, Tokyo won't deprive you of the pleasure: these places can be found all over the city.

It seems that almost all the major fast-food chains in the world are trying to muscle in on the lucrative Japanese market. *Shakey's Pizza, Kentucky Fried Chicken* and *McDonald's* seem to have a branch next to every railway station in Tokyo. Others, such as *El Polo Loco* and *Pizza Hut*, also have a shop here and there. In another interesting move, the McDonald's phenomenon has spawned some Japanese variations on the same theme: *Mos Burger, Lotteria* and *Love Burger*, to name a few. Also worth seeking out are the Japanese food chains like *Yoshinoya* (with gyūdon – beef and rice – dishes) and *Tenya* (with tendon – tempura and rice – dishes).

The fast-food places are particularly popular with teenagers, so eating in them may mean being squeezed onto a table with a contingent of giggling school uniforms. Some of the chains offer pretty good lunchtime specials – ¥650 for all the Shakey's pizza you can eat is an example.

The budget-priced coffee shop, of which there is an ever-increasing number, is another good fast-food option. The major chain is *Doutor* (look for the big yellow and brown signs). Doutor sells coffee for ¥190 and German hotdogs for ¥190. You can put together a good lunch, including a ¥150 piece of cake, for around ¥550 – not bad in Tokyo. *Pronto* is another chain that specialises in inexpensive coffee, and in the evenings they become shot bars with beers from ¥330. The *Mister Donut* places are good for an economical donut, orange juice and coffee breakfast.

African
Prices are not exactly cheap at *Rose of Sahara* (☎ 3379-6427) in Shinjuku, but this restaurant occupies a unique niche in the

Tokyo restaurant scene and is worth a visit on a special occasion. Courses start from ¥3500. The adventurous might like to try the guinea fowl in orange sauce.

American

Tokyo has a few places that devote themselves to bringing out the best in a much overlooked and even maligned cuisine. *Victoria Station*, applauded by long-time residents as having the only decent salad bars in town, is a chain with branches in Roppongi, Akasaka and Shibuya. *Tony Roma's* is an expensive charcoal ribs specialist, and generally more popular with Japanese than with foreigners. It has branches in Akasaka and Roppongi. *Subway*, the sandwich specialist now has an increasing number of shops around Tokyo, and even has a branch in Ginza. Other branches can be found in Akasaka and Shibuya.

Over in Shimokitazawa, a trendy student area on the Odakyū line out from Shinjuku, is *Big Ben Rock'n'Roll Diner* (☎ 3411-6565). It serves nachos, fajitas and 'rock'n'roll burgers', all at around ¥1500; beers are ¥600. Take the south exit of Shimokitazawa station, walk straight ahead and look for Big Ben on the left.

British

British-style pubs are a popular import and Tokyo has no shortage of them. *1066* (☎ 3719-9059) in Naka-Meguro has hearty English food (roast lunch on Sunday) and British beer on tap. There is also live folk music regularly – the entrance fee includes a banquet. On a smaller scale, *The Hub* (☎ 3478-0414), in Roppongi, is another British pub.

Cambodian

There's not much else to do in Yoyogi by night (one stop from the JR Shinjuku station on the Yamanote line), but it's worth a special trip to visit *Angkor Wat* (☎ 3370-3019). This place has been around for some time, and despite a move to more spacious (but less atmospheric) quarters, the food is as good as ever. The staff are friendly and speak Japanese, Mandarin, Khmer and some English, so

there should be someone who can help you with the Japanese menu.

The food has much in common with Thai cuisine, including spicy salads and great coconut-based curries. To get to Angkor Wat, take the Yamanote line to the JR Yoyogi station. Walk in the opposite direction to Shinjuku station to the end of the platform, exit the station on the left-hand side, cross the road, walk straight ahead and after about 100 metres look for Angkor Wat in a lane on your right.

Chinese

Tokyo is really the only place in Japan where you can get good, authentic Chinese food. Even in Yokohama's Chinatown, most of the food has been tampered with according to Japanese tastes. The main reason that Tokyo is an exception to a rule that extends throughout Japan is the large number of Chinese who have come to the city over the last 10 years. Cities like Nagasaki, Kōbe and Yokohama tend to have long-settled Chinese communities who cater mainly to Japanese diners.

Some of the most authentic Chinese food you're likely to come across (there's no sweet and sour pork here) outside China or Taiwan is at the Taiwanese restaurant *Tainan Taami*. There are branches in Roppongi (☎ 3408-2111), Suidobashi (☎ 3263-4530), Shinjuku (☎ 3232-8839) and Shibuya (☎ 3464-7544), but the pick of the bunch is the Shinjuku branch, located in the nether regions of Kabuki-chō.

The menu is complete with photographs of the dishes to make ordering easy. Most of the dishes are small serves ranging in price from ¥300 to ¥600 – try as much as possible, and whatever you do, don't order rice. If you want rice, the restaurant is famous for its *zongzi* – sticky rice, pork and other oddments wrapped in a lotus leaf and steamed. All of the Tainan Taami restaurants feature long queues, and generally you get to order while you are in line.

Just two doors down from Tainan Taami is *Pekin* (☎ 3208-8252), a very down-to-earth Chinese noodle shop that is always crowded with Chinese. The décor may leave a lot to be desired and the staff may be surly, but you can get a good bowl of noodles there for around ¥550. Unfortunately, there's no English sign so look for the glass front window through which you can see the chefs at work.

On the same road in the other direction, away from the Seibu Shinjuku station, is a unique Chinese restaurant known as the *Tokyo Kaisen Ichiba* (☎ 35273-8301), literally the 'Seafood Market'. You can't miss the building, a girder and glass construction with a fish market downstairs. Upstairs you get to eat the fish. This place has slightly up-market prices but simply picking the cheapest things on the menu at random (around ¥1200 per serve) will provide some delicious surprises. This place even has an English menu these days. Go there late, when the Kabuki-chō workers knock off, for some great people watching.

For yum cha or dim sum, one of the few possibilities in Tokyo is at the multi-storey (12 floors) *Tokyo Dai Hanten* (☎ 3202-0121) in Shinjuku. Most of the food is overpriced and not particularly special, but the yum cha service is not bad, if a bit more expensive than in other parts of the world. This is one of the few places in Tokyo where correct yum cha form is observed by having the food brought around on trolleys.

Other good Chinese restaurants around Tokyo include Ikebukuro's *Pekintei*. It's between the Marui department store and the west exit of Ikebukuro station. In Harajuku, close to the lower end of Takashita-dōri, is *Son of the Dragon*, or *Ryūnoko* as it used to be known before it caught on with the gaijin set; it's a small and unpretentious Sichuanese restaurant. It has an English sign outside these days. Finally, for Chinese nouvelle cuisine, Shibuya's *Chef's Gallery* (☎ 3476-0899) is an up-market but cosy little place cluttered with *objets d'art*. The chefs are from Hong Kong, Shanghai and Beijing, and courses start at ¥6000.

French

French restaurants in Tokyo are generally not very affordable, but *Pas A Pas* (☎ 3357-7888) is a tiny, informal place that resembles a living room more than a restaurant; it has a great atmosphere and great food. You can order any combination of starter, main course and dessert for ¥3500. To get there, take the Marunouchi line to Yotsuya-Sanchōme subway station, take the Yotsuya-Sanchōme exit, turn right, walk past the Marusho bookshop, cross the road and take the second street on the left. *Pas A Pas* is a few doors down on the left on the 2nd floor.

Another affordable French restaurant is Ikebukuro's *Chez Kibeau* (☎ 3987-6666), a home-style place run by Kibo (get it?), owner of the Kimi Ryokan. Anyone staying at the Kimi can pick up a map from reception for getting there. Main courses range from around ¥1500. In the Roppongi area, *Shunsai* (☎ 3405-4501) is surprisingly economical (¥2500 to ¥3000 per head) and has a great atmosphere.

Naturally, Tokyo also has its fair share of expensive French restaurants. *Maxim de Paris* (☎ 3572-3621), in Ginza's Sony building, receives a special mention in this category. By all accounts a dead ringer for the original in Paris, this dining experience is going to set you back around ¥6000 at lunch time and a cool ¥20,000 in the evenings. Harajuku's Hanae Mori building (5th floor) is home to another acclaimed French restaurant: the word on the streets is that *L'Orangerie* (☎ 3407-7461) has Tokyo's best Sunday brunch buffet (11.30 am to 3.30 pm). Be warned though, at ¥3965 it won't be the cheapest brunch of your life.

Garlic

In case the heading had you worried, there's no country called Garlic (otherwise we'd have a travel survival kit for it). No, garlic restaurants are one of those uniquely quirky Tokyo institutions. There are a few of them about these days. The idea is that anything goes as long as you can ladle heaps of garlic into it (keep a distance from friends the next day). If you see one, don't even think about walking past – go in.

A favourite with many is *Ninnikuya*

(☎ 3476-5887), a small basement den on the wrong side of the station in Shibuya – great smells and an English menu. Ebisu's *Ninniku Dokoro* (☎ 3403-3667) is probably the longest-running garlic restaurant in Tokyo. It's only about a 10 minute walk from Ebisu station, but it's not that easy to find. Give them a ring from the station for instructions.

Indian

Ginza has a couple of good Indian restaurants. *Maharaja* (☎ 3572-7196), which has branches all over Tokyo, is a bit pricey in the evening, but it has good lunch-time specials from ¥900 and an excellent tandoori mixed grill for ¥1250. The Ginza branch is opposite the Mitsukoshi department store, about 50 metres down Harumi-dōri towards the Kabuki-za Theatre. Maharaja is in the basement – look for the plastic sample dishes in a glass cabinet at floor level. The Shibuya branch is on the 8th floor of the 109 building.

If you continue towards the Kabuki-za Theatre along Harumi-dōri and turn left at the first major intersection, not far up on your left is *Nair's*, a Tokyo institution. It's almost impossible to get in for lunch, but dinner is also good value. The curries are very reasonably priced and made to Nair's unique recipe. It's closed on Thursday. There's also a branch in the Restaurant City floor of Ikebukuro's Seibu.

Moti has two branches in Roppongi (☎ 3479-1939) and two more in Akasaka (☎ 3582-3620, 3584-6640). It also qualifies as something of a Tokyo institution in that it was an early pioneer of Indian food in the city. Queues for a table are the order of the day in any of the Motis, but the food and atmosphere make the wait worthwhile. You can expect to pay about ¥2500 per head.

Another Indian restaurant with several branches is *Samrat*. If you're sightseeing in the Ueno area, Samrat (☎ 3568-3226) has a good lunch-time special of chicken, mutton or vegetable curry with rice and naan for ¥850. Other branches are in Shibuya (☎ 3496-9410) and Roppongi (☎ 3478-5877). Main courses average ¥1500.

Taj (☎ 3352-1111) has branches on the 7th floor of Isetan Park City in Shinjuku and another branch in Akasaka (☎ 3586-6606) – prices are higher than at Samrat or Moti. Also in Akasaka is *Mughal* (☎ 3582-9940), with main courses from ¥1500.

Indonesian

Bengawan Solo (☎ 3403-3031) in Roppongi is deservedly the most popular of Tokyo's Indonesian restaurants. The atmosphere is great, and the food is delicious and not particularly expensive. You can find Bengawan Solo across the road from the Wave building.

Warung I (☎ 3464-9795) in Shibuya is a popular Balinese restaurant. The restaurant itself is not at ground level, but at least the English sign is. Look for the sign announcing 'Black & Brown' – Warung is in the building next door.

A final Indonesian suggestion is Ginza's *Restaurant Indonesia*, a friendly place with reasonable prices. It's beneath the railway tracks south of Yūraku-chō station.

Italian

Tokyo abounds in Italian restaurants. The top floor of almost every department store has one, and every shopping district has a myriad of places serving up spaghetti and pizza. Of course, not all such places serve up authentic Italian fare, but it's surprising how good many of them are. As an example, anyone in the Ikebukuro area should try *Cattleya* in the basement of the Marui department store on the west side. It has decent pasta in large or small portions at prices that begin at around ¥650. Also on Ikebukuro's west side is *Pizzeria Capri* with a wide range of pizzas and a newly opened branch of *Capricciosa*. *Café Presto*, over on the east side of Ikebukuro, has meals upstairs. Downstairs has been overrun by a rowdy gaijin set.

Akasaka and Roppongi are trendy areas in which you'd expect to find some good Italian cuisine. In Akasaka, *Chapter One* (☎ 3583-6643) is expensive by night, but has good lunch specials for around ¥1000. A particularly good and inexpensive place with real Italians on the staff is *Pizzeria/Trattoria Marumo* (☎ 3585-5371). It has very good pasta and pizzas, with main courses under ¥1000 and affordable drinks. In Roppongi, a long-time favourite is *Sicilia* (☎ 3405-4653). Look for the queue snaking out on to the street. You can figure on spending around ¥2500 per head there.

Finally, for many Tokyo residents addicted to the occasional pasta binge, the *Capricciosa* chain is the final say on Italian food. The attraction is reasonable prices combined with mammoth servings. If there are three of you, two dishes at about ¥1300 will be more than enough. There are two branches in Roppongi, and others scattered around Tokyo, including Shimokitazawa (☎ 3487-0461) (a lively student area) and Shibuya (☎ 3407-9482).

Korean

Korean restaurants are very popular in Japan, and Tokyo is full of them. Most neighbourhoods have a couple of Korean barbecue restaurants – good places to have a few beers and sizzle bits of meat with some friends. The biggest Korean restaurant in Tokyo is *Tōkaien* (☎ 3200-2924), a nine-floor monster on Yasukuni-dōri in Shinjuku. The staff are generally accommodating to bewildered gaijin. Japanese, Mandarin, Korean, and even a little English, are spoken here. Reckon on about ¥1500 per head on any of the first four floors. The upper floors have banquets and are more exclusive.

Malaysian

This is easy. *Only Malaysia* (☎ 3496-1177), so it claims, derives its name from the rather astounding fact that it *is* the only Malaysian restaurant in town. It's easy to miss the sign at ground level, so look carefully. Prices are affordable and the food is delicious.

Mexican

There are actually quite a number of Mexican restaurants around these days, but old Tokyo hands will have a soft spot for a Shinjuku establishment that has been around for years: *El Borracho* (☎ 3354-7046). The place looks like it has been around for a while – note the graffiti scrawled over every available nook and cranny of the walls. Figure on around ¥2500 per head in this very popular restaurant.

Thai

Thai restaurants were always at the cutting edge of Tokyo's ethnic cuisine explosion and, even though they've well and truly established themselves now, they continue to grow in popularity. Shinjuku, in particular Kabuki-chō, has emerged as one of the best places to seek out good Thai food, largely as a result of the large numbers of Thai 'workers' labouring in Tokyo's premiere red-light area these days. For the average traveller looking at holding down expenses, it's better to save your money for Thailand. Thai food is expensive in Tokyo. For those earning money in Tokyo, it's a different matter. There's some great Thai food out there.

One of the pioneers of Thai cuisine in Tokyo is the *Ban Thai* (☎ 3207-0068) in Shinjuku. The food is excellent, but as usual you're going to have to wait for it – the queues can be very long. The menu has pictures to help you order, and there's a very good banquet, although it's rather expensive at ¥3500 per person. The restaurant lies in the heart of Shinjuku's Kabuki-chō red-light area, on the 3rd floor of the Dai-Ichi Metro building.

Cheaper than Ban Thai is *Champer* (☎ 3226-5921) over on Yasukuni-dōri. This basement restaurant manages to recreate the atmosphere of a Thai street-stall area. The staff are all Thai and the food is good and cheap. Check out the lunch-time specials ranging from ¥780 to ¥980. Finally, if you are in Kabuki-chō by night, take a stroll over to what has become the *yatai-mura* (the street stall village), a small enclave of Thai, Filipino and Chinese stalls catering to the area's foreign workers. Yatai Mura has a good Thai stall *(Kao Keng)* where the menu is *only* in Thai, but whose friendly staff have enough English to help you out.

The *Siam Thai Restaurant* (☎ 3770-0550) in Shibuya is not a particularly big place, but it's nicely laid out, with rough-hewn wooden tables and chairs. The food's comparable with that of Ban Thai and the meals are a bit less expensive. There's a good lunch-time set menu for ¥750. To get there, walk straight ahead from the pedestrian crossing at the Hachikō exit of Shibuya station, turn left at the second major intersection and look for the Siam on your right about 100 metres before you reach the Pizza Hut.

Turkish

Babaros in Akasaka combines a bar and Turkish food. It has main courses from ¥1800 and is good place for a get together with friends.

Vegetarian

Eating out in Japan can be a hassle for strict vegetarians. Most people working in Japanese restaurants won't really understand the concept of vegetarianism – simply taking the meat out of a dish that has been cooked in a meat stock is the standard response to customers who profess to be noncarnivorous. There are some vegetarian restaurants springing up around town, however, and there are always Indian restaurants that are used to catering for vegetarians. The TIC has a list of Tokyo's natural food restaurants that includes some vegetarian possibilities.

Vietnamese

Vietnamese cuisine is a fairly recent and increasingly popular entry into the Tokyo dining scene. Even Ikebukuro has a Vietnamese restaurant these days. *Saigon* (☎ 3989-0255), over on the east side of Ikebukuro station, attracts a good number of foreign diners, is inexpensive and not that difficult to find (there's an English sign).

Other Vietnamese restaurants around town include another *Saigon* (☎ 3271-3833) in Ginza. Prices are around ¥2000 per head for an evening meal (there are cheaper lunch-time sets available) and it can be found close to the TIC, in the same building as the American Pharmacy. *Aozai* (☎ 3583-0234) is a Vietnamese restaurant in Akasaka that has built up quite a following. Evening courses start at ¥3500.

ENTERTAINMENT

Tokyo comes into its own by night. Among the memories that linger longest will be the bright lights, neon kanji, huge video screens and the backstreet red lanterns strung up over the entrances to hole-in-the-wall drinking spots. The only drawback to a night on the town in Tokyo (and you should have at least *one*) is that entry prices and drink prices tend to mount up very quickly. There's really no way of doing nightlife centres like Roppongi on a shoestring. Areas like Shinjuku can be cheaper, but even there clubs often have a nominal entry fee, and a bottle of beer may cost, say, ¥800.

As well as all the nightlife attractions you'd expect to find in any big city, Tokyo offers the more traditional Japanese entertainment options.

Kabuki

The best place to see kabuki in Tokyo is the *Kabuki-za Theatre* (☎ 3541-3131) in Ginza. Performances and times vary from month to month, so you'll need to check with the TIC or with the theatre directly for programme information. Earphone guides providing 'comments and explanations' in English are available for ¥600 for those who find themselves becoming disoriented and confused during the performance. Prices for tickets vary from ¥2000 to ¥14,000, depending on how keen you are to see the stage. One distraction you may encounter is a large group of school children on a school outing – the excitement of the proceedings gives rise to a lot of chatting and giggling.

Kabuki performances can be quite a marathon, lasting from 4½ to five hours. If you're not up to it, you can get tickets for the 4th floor for less than ¥1000 and watch only part of the show but earphone guides are not available in these seats. Fourth floor tickets can be bought on the day of the performance. There are generally two performances daily, starting at around 11 am and 4 pm.

Japan's national theatre, *Kokuritsu Gekijō Theatre* (☎ 3265-7411), also has kabuki performances, with seat prices ranging from ¥1200 to ¥7200. Again, earphone guides are available. Check with the TIC or the theatre for performance times.

Nō

Nō performances are held at various locations around Tokyo. Tickets will cost between ¥3000 and ¥10,000, and it's best to get them at the theatre itself. Check with the TIC or the appropriate theatre for times.

The *Kanze Nō-gakudō Theatre* (☎ 3469-6241) is a 10 to 15 minute walk from Shibuya station. From the Hachikō exit, turn right at the 109 building and follow the road straight ahead past the Tōkyū department store. The theatre is on the right, a couple of minutes down the third street on the left after Tōkyū.

The *Ginza Nō-gakudō* (☎ 3571-0197) (Ginza Nō Stage) is about a 10 minute walk from Ginza subway station. Turn right into Sotobori-dōri at the Sukiyabashi Crossing and look for the theatre on the left.

The *Kokuritsu Nō-gakudō* (☎ 3423-1331) (National Nō Theatre) is in Sendagaya. Exit Sendagaya station in the direction of Shinjuku on the left and follow the road which hugs the railway tracks; the theatre is on the left.

Bunraku

Osaka is the home of bunraku, but performances do take place in Tokyo several times a year at the *Kokuritsu Gekijō Theatre* (☎ 3265-7411). Check with the TIC or the theatre for information.

Sumō

Sumō may not be in the same league, culturally speaking, as the preceding entries, but there are definite connections: sumō is actually a highly ritualised event that is as much a spectacle as it is a sport. The actual jostling in the ring can be over very quickly, and great importance is attached to the pomp that precedes and follows the action.

Sumō tournaments at Tokyo's *Ryōgoku Kokugikan Stadium* (☎ 3866-8700) in Ryōgoku take place in January, May and September and last 15 days. The best seats are all bought up by those with the right connections, but balcony seats are usually available from ¥6000 and bench seats at the back for about ¥1000. If you don't mind standing, you can get in for around ¥500. Tickets can be bought up to a month prior to the tournament, or simply turn up on the day.

The stadium is adjacent to Ryōgoku station on the northern side of the railway tracks.

Tea Ceremonies

A few hotels in Tokyo hold tea ceremonies which you can observe and occasionally participate in for a fee of about ¥1000. The *Hotel New Otani* (☎ 3265-1111) has ceremonies on its 7th floor on Thursday, Friday and Saturday from 11 am to noon and 1 to 4 pm. Ring them before you go to make sure the show hasn't been booked out. The *Hotel Okura* (☎ 3582-0111) and the *Imperial Hotel* (☎ 3504-1111) also hold daily tea ceremonies.

Music

There's a lot of live music in Tokyo, ranging from big international acts to lesser known performers from the West who end up playing in clubs and other small venues. And, of course, there are many local bands. On any night there are hundreds of performances around town. The best place for information on both mainstream and alternative live music and events is the *Tokyo Journal*.

Live Houses A number of live houses have reasonable entry charges and drink prices, and provide good opportunities to hear interesting live music.

For anyone new to Tokyo, a good area to check out is Shibuya. In Shibuya there is a number of venues, ranging from the mainstream to the alternative. *Club Quattro* (☎ 3477-8750) has something happening almost every night of the week, and is the sort of place that you can catch on-the-rise or alternative Western acts, as well as some of the more adventurous home-grown stuff. Close by, *The Cave* sometimes has live acts, but is mostly gloom with strobes and dancing – good, sweaty fun. For local acts and a very young local crowd Shibuya has *Eggman* (☎ 3496-1461) and *La Mama* (☎ 3464-0801).

A place that should be high on any list of live houses in Tokyo is *Club Z* (☎ 3336-5841). This place is fairly roomy by Tokyo standards and usually has something interesting happening on Saturday nights. The club is next to Kōenji station on the Chūō line. Facing in the direction of Shinjuku, exit on the left side of the station and make a sharp right. Follow the road beside the railway tracks for about 50 metres and then cross the road. Club Z is opposite the railway tracks, next to Nippon Rent-a-Car, in the basement.

Also in Kōenji, not far from Club Z, is *Inaoiza* (☎ 3336-4480), a hole-in-the-wall place with a small stage for live music. It's a kind of Bohemian musician's hangout and often, if no-one is booked to perform, there will just be an impromptu jam session. Live music has to stop at 10.30 pm because of the neighbours, but the action continues with lots of local English teachers, hostesses and out-of-the-ordinary Japanese dropping in after work for a few drinks. Inaoiza also has good food – ask for their menu – and a great, friendly atmosphere. The only problem is finding it. Your best bet is to ask someone at Club Z, or wander around Kōenji until you find someone who knows it – we're not giving anything else away.

In Harajuku, *Crocodile* (☎ 3499-5205) has something happening seven nights a week. To get there from the JR Harajuku station, walk down Omote-sando and turn right at Meiji-dōri. Cross the road and continue straight ahead, passing an overhead walkway. Crocodile is on your left, in the basement of the New Sekiguchi building.

Another good live house is *Rock Mother* (☎ 3460-1479) in Shimokitazawa. The whole area is worth a look: it's a kind of down-market Harajuku or a youth-oriented Shinjuku with lots of cheap places to eat and drink – very popular with students. To get to Rock Mother, take the Odakyū line to Shimokitazawa station and exit via the southern exit (Minami-guchi). After you leave the station, turn left, then right, then left again. Follow the road around to the right and look for the club on your left.

In Roppongi there are a number of places that specialise in live 'oldies-but-goodies'. The bands are often surprisingly good at what they do – producing perfect imitations of '50s rock'n'roll or of the Beatles – and Japanese audiences often turn out in their bobby socks. The *Cavern Club* (☎ 3405-5207) is where a Japanese Beatles look-a-like band (it helps if you squint, or knock a few Kirins back very quickly) performs nightly. There's a live music charge of ¥1300. *Lollipop* (☎ 3478-0028) and *Kento's* (☎ 3401-5755) both feature '50s standards and have a ¥1300 live music charge – good wholesome fun for all the family.

Citta in Kawasaki is where many lesser-known overseas rock acts end up playing. For information on the upcoming schedule of events here, check the *Tokyo Journal*.

Jazz Jazz is very big in Tokyo, although some places seem to take it rather too seriously. Quiet, solemn audiences hanging on the musicians' every note: that's the Japanese for you – a serious lot when it comes to enjoying themselves. Still, if you're interested in jazz, there are a lot of places to try, and all the big names who are visiting Tokyo will have listings in the *Tokyo Journal*.

In Roppongi, the *Pit Inn* (☎ 3585-1063) is a long-running jazz venue. Walking away from Roppongi subway station, turn right at Almond, cross over the road and look for the Pit Inn on your left, about 100 metres down the road. Another Roppongi jazz club is *Birdland* (☎ 3478-3456), in the basement of the Square building, the hub of much of the disco activity in Roppongi. Admission is around ¥3000. Cross the intersection at Almond, continue walking away from Roppongi subway station, take the second right turn and you'll bump into the Square building. Look for all the beautiful people lounging around outside waiting to see where the happening spot is that night.

Harajuku is another area with a couple of well-known jazz spots. Right across from the station is *Keystone Korner Tokyo* (☎ 5232-1980), a venue that hosts some great acts, but unfortunately forces you to pay through the nose for the privilege of seeing them – ¥8000 is an average entry fee. *Blue Note Tokyo*

(☎ 3407-5781) is another expensive, classy venue.

Other Nightlife

There's so much happening that it's difficult to make recommendations. Most people seem to find their own favourite watering holes wherever they happen to be, but some areas have high concentrations of pubs, clubs and discos that are popular with both foreigners and Japanese. At bars that have gained some notoriety as the hang-outs of wild and crazy gaijin, there will also be a number of Japanese who come along for the thrill.

Ikebukuro *One Lucky* (☎ 3985-0069) is a favourite among foreign residents and guests of the nearby Kimi Ryokan. 'One Rucky', as it's affectionately called by its Japanese patrons, is a one-man show where the master-san prepares all the food (a delicious set-menu dinner for ¥700), pours the drinks (a beer is ¥500) and, most importantly, takes a photograph of everyone who visits. There's a bookcase of photo albums containing the master's social shots, dated so that you can refer back and see how drunk you looked on your last visit.

From the Kimi Ryokan, turn left, left again and then right. Follow this road and, when it forks at a small bakery, bear left. The last intersection of this road before the main road is a paved pedestrian path. Turn left here and look out for the small neon sign advertising One Lucky around 100 metres down on the left. One Lucky is closed on Monday.

On the way to One Lucky, you will pass *Rum Bullion*, or the Reggae Bar, previously a popular late night foreigner's hang-out, but recently out of favour. It's a pleasant little place, but the ¥500 admission charge is ill-considered and only serves to keep people away. The *Reggae Bar Kingston*, also on the west side, behind the Rosa Cinema, has a ¥2000 cover charge with a few drinks thrown and has become a fairly popular place with both gaijin and Japanese. It's about the only dance venue frequented by foreigners in Ikebukuro. Also worth checking out is the

Winner's Bar. The DJ has everything and encourages requests. What's more, if you eat something you get a chance to be a winner – we're not giving any more away.

Finally, over on the east side of Ikebukuro, you might want to check out *Café Presto*. Be warned, this place gets rough sometimes and it's dubious how much longer the owners are going to put up with the large numbers of gaijin who hang out here and get very rowdy.

Shinjuku Shinjuku's nightlife opportunities are underrated by many of Tokyo's residents. There's actually plenty there, but you have to know where to look for it. Just wandering under the bright lights of Kabuki-chō and ducking into one of the revolving sushi shops or one of the yakitori bars for a bite to eat is a good prelude to a night out.

For a few drinks and some yakitori and karaoke in decidedly odd surroundings, try *Yamagoya*. Feel free to indulge in a spot of karaoke, but don't worry – no-one's going to drag you on stage. You enter Yamagoya by a narrow flight of stairs and end up in what seems like the hull of an old wooden ship. Huge wooden beams, every inch of them carved with names and graffiti, crisscross overhead, and wooden stairs continue down two more levels. The bottom level is the gloomiest and most dungeon-like – watch your head. Look for the wooden sign with kanji hung outside the entrance.

Just around the corner from Yamagoya is the *Rolling Stone* (☎ 3354-7347). Something of a Tokyo institution, it's not for the faint-hearted, but it is an interesting alternative to the Roppongi scene. It's fairly quiet on weeknights, but gets packed into on Friday or Saturday nights. There's a ¥200 cover charge and beers cost ¥800 per bottle. A few doors down from the Stone is *Reggae Splash Touch House*, a small live venue with some jamming late at night – they may not let you in if they don't like the look of you. Down on the other side of Yasukuni-dōri, actually inside the entrance to Hanazono-jinja Shrine (what a great place for a club), is *Milo's Garage* (☎ 3207-6953), a dance club with

different 'happenings' every night of the week. Entry ranges from ¥1500 to ¥2000, but this usually includes a couple of drinks. It's a good place to go with a group of friends for a dance as it rarely gets crowded and hasn't really been discovered by the gaijin set.

Harajuku Harajuku is one of those rare areas in Tokyo that are more active by day than by night. *Oh God* (☎ 3406-3206) is popular with foreign residents; in fact some people rave about it. It has a bar, pool tables, movie screenings every night and the food gets very good reports. Walk down Omote-sando and take the first lane on the right after Meiji-dōri. Oh God is in the basement of the building at the end of the lane. Almost next door is *Zest* (☎ 3499-0976) another popular pub-cum-restaurant.

In a different league altogether is the trendy *Cay* (☎ 3498-5790), a venue that combines Thai food and live music – very expensive, with meal and music charge coming in at between ¥7000 and ¥10,000.

Roppongi Roppongi is still worth checking out, but many of the long-running institutions that used to be good for a few beers are on a downward slide. The only way to escape the sleaze nowadays is to go up-market and pay a ¥4000 cover charge for one of the discos. If you can afford to do this (and cover charges always include a few drink tokens), it's possible to have a good night in the area.

The main point of orientation is the Roppongi Crossing, with the Almond Coffee Shop – a favourite meeting spot – on the corner. Follow the road under the metropolitan expressway in the opposite direction to the Wave building, take the second turn to the right and on the first corner on the right is the Square building, which has eight floors of discos. They all charge ¥3500 to ¥4500 (¥500 less for women) entry with a couple of drink tokens thrown in. A long-running favourite is *Java Jive* (☎ 3478-0087), where a reggae band alternates with recorded music throughout the night. Currently hippest of the Square group is *Buzzzz* (☎ 3470-6391), an enormous place with a giant TV monitor and the occasional big metallic fly (get it?) dangling from the ceiling.

Across from the Square building is another disco building with *Lollipop* and *Cipango*, the latter described by *Tokyo Journal* as 'Saturday night fever in Mexico'. Close by, in a basement location, is the *Lexington Queen* (☎ 3401-1661), a disco with a reputation as a haunt of the beautiful set, though standards seem to have taken a dip in recent years.

For serious drinking without the distraction of all those sweaty bodies hopping around, popular options are places like *Henry Africa* (☎ 3405-9868), *Déjà Vu* (☎ 3403-8777) and *Motown*. Henry Africa and Motown are frequented mostly by the business set and beers are ¥800. Déjà Vu offers beers for ¥500 and has a younger crowd; during the summer, drinkers spill out of the open-fronted entrance into the street. Close by Déjà Vu is *Gas Panic*, a place that's worth a look and then best avoided – the occasional knifing doesn't seem to do anything to lessen its popularity. Gas Panic has even opened up a second branch over by the Square building – Saturday nights there are definitely Tokyo at its worst. Quieter and somehow a little more civilised (despite the name) is *Gaijin Zone*, a bar with dancing and cheap beer.

A tour of late-night hang-outs can be completed with a visit to the *Charleston* (☎ 3402-0372), lauded as Tokyo's 'best sleaze pick-up bar' in the book *The Best of Tokyo*. Actually it lost its legendary status in the pick-up/sleaze stakes to the nearby Déjà Vu and Gas Panic some years ago, but it's still worth a look late on a Saturday night.

Couples who would like to take a look at Roppongi by night and then have a quiet drink somewhere, might want to check out *Bogey's Bar* (☎ 3478-1997), a bar modelled on Rick's Bar in the film Casablanca – it's a cool, laid-back kind of place with unobtrusive live piano. It's on the 4th floor of the building next to Déjà Vu. *Maggie's Revenge* (☎ 3479-1096) is a small folk club operated by an Australian woman. It has been running

for years, has a warm, convivial atmosphere and is good for a quiet drink.

Finally, Tokyo has its own *Hard Rock Cafe* (☎ 3408-7018), with a ready supply of hamburgers, rock music and expensive cocktails. You can't miss the King Kong figure clambering up its exterior, near Roppongi Crossing, in a lane beside the Roy building. The queues for this place have got ridiculous on Friday and Saturday nights, and unless you've never been to a Hard Rock Cafe, it's dubious whether the wait is worth it.

Bay Area Over the last few years the bay area, also known as Shibaura, around Hamamatsu-chō station on the JR Yamanote line has developed a happening scene in the form of warehouse dance clubs. The big ones are *Gold* (☎ 3453-3545), *Juliana's* (☎ 5484-4000) and *O'Bar 2218* (☎ 3453-1300). Gold is an enormous place with a capacity for 2000 sweaty bodies. When it's good it's very very good, but it does have the occasional off night too. It has a cover of ¥3000 with one drink. Juliana's has a certain reputation as the OL (office lady) dance capital of Tokyo and costs ¥4000 during the week and ¥5000 on Friday and Saturday nights. It's taken off as *the* place for *ike-ike gyaru*, which can be translated as 'go-go girls'. Tokyo being what it is, the girls seem to be there for the 'glamour' of being a go-go queen.

Both Gold and Juliana's are closer to Tamachi station than Hamamatsu-chō. For Juliana's, take the east exit (left-hand side with your back to Hamamatsu-chō), walk straight ahead and take the first left. Juliana's is around 500 metres up on the left. To find Gold, instead of turning left for Juliana's continue straight ahead from the station, cross over a canal and take the third left. From here you'll cross two more canals – Gold is just down the road on the left after the second canal.

Cinemas
Foreign movies are screened with their original soundtracks and Japanese subtitles. There is usually a fairly good selection of alternative movies playing around town.

Tokyo cinemas have been steadily improving over the years, and nowadays there are some top-class cinemas around – without a doubt the best in Asia. Essential is *Tokyo Journal*'s Film Maps section. Without it, it is very difficult to find the cinema you are looking for. Ticket prices are fairly expensive at around ¥1800, but if you can plan ahead (even by a few hours) there are ticket agencies around town selling tickets at discounted prices – generally at a saving of ¥500. Outlets include: the basement of the Tokyo Kōtsū Kaikan building in Ginza; the 5th floor of Shinjuku's Studio Alta building; the 2nd floor of Shibuya's 109 building; and the 1st floor of Laforet in Harajuku. You can find these on the district maps in this chapter.

THINGS TO BUY

An ever-strengthening yen has all but banished shopping bargains from the streets of Tokyo. Even in cut-price Akihabara, electronics capital of Tokyo, you should look carefully at whether prices are indeed cheaper than you'd be paying at home – chances are they won't be. It's still worth checking, however.

For general souvenir items, most of the big department stores in Tokyo have good selections of things like Japanese dolls, ceramics, lacquerware, fans, etc. Department stores offer convenience, but it's worth bearing in mind that goods are often overpriced. You're likely to find less glamorous but possibly more interesting souvenirs in Tokyo's flea markets, where you can buy Japanese antiques and all kinds of curiosities from daily life.

There are a number of flea markets worth visiting. The following is a list of some of the bigger ones:

Tōgō-jinja Shrine – 4 am to 4 pm on the first and fourth Sunday of each month; Harajuku station – turn left and take the next right after Takeshita-dōri

Nogi-jinja Shrine – dawn to dusk on the second Sunday of each month; from Nogi-zaka subway station on the Chiyoda line – the shrine is on the other side of Gaien-higashi-dōri

Hanazono-jinja Shrine – 7 am to 5 pm second and third Sunday of every month; close to Isetan department store on the east side of Shinjuku station

Roppongi – 8 am to 8 pm fourth Thursday and Friday of every month; in front of the Roy building, close to Roppongi subway station;

Iidabashi Antique Market – 6 am to 6 pm first Saturday of every month; Central Plaza, Ramura building close to Iidabashi JR and subway stations

Sunshine City Ikebukuro – 8 am to 10 pm third Saturday and Sunday of every month; Alpa shopping arcade

Vending Machines
There are no prizes for guessing that Japan has a larger number of vending machines per capita than any other country in the world. You cannot walk for five minutes without bumping into one. A major reason must be that in crime-free Japan they go unmolested. In most civilised countries, plonking a beer vending machine down on a suburban street corner would be unthinkable.

There are presently thought to be around 4.5 million vending machines in Japan, and demand is still growing. A recent local cartoon showed a company official exhorting employees to work harder to meet the growing need for vending machines; in the next frame the answer is unveiled – a huge vending-machine vending machine.

You can buy almost anything from vending machines. Soft drinks, coffee and cigarettes are the most common vending machine products, but beer vending machines are also reasonably common. Other less common machines sell goods ranging from rice and vegetables to neckties and computer software. Condom vending machines can sometimes be found outside pharmacies, and pornography (magazines and videos) can be found in some areas.

Probably the most controversial vending machine venture in recent years has been for the sale of used panties. Ostensibly once owned and worn by female high-school students, the panties come in vacuum-sealed packs of three (with a photo of the erstwhile owner) and are targeted at the average fetishistic man about town. The cost? Around ¥3000 to ¥5000, making them the perfect, reasonably priced Japanese souvenir for the folks at home.

Chris Taylor

Folkcrafts & Antiques

Not far from Ikebukuro station's eastern exit, on the 1st floor of the Satomi building (☎ 3980-8228), there are more than 30 antique dealers. They are open Friday to Wednesday from 10 am to 7 pm.

One of the best places to look for antiques and interesting souvenirs is in the basement of the Hanae Mori building (☎ 3406-1021) in Harajuku. There are more than 30 antique shops there. Not far from the Hanae Mori building, the Oriental Bazaar (☎ 3400-3933) is open every day except Thursday and is an interesting place to rummage through. It has a wide range of good souvenirs – fans, folding screens, pottery, etc – some at very affordable prices.

The Tokyo Antique Fair takes place three times a year and brings together more than 200 antique dealers. The schedule for this event changes annually, but for information on the schedule you can ring Mr Iwasaki (☎ 3950-0871) – he speaks English.

Japanese Dolls

Edo-dōri, next to Asakusabashi station, is the place to go if you're interested in Japanese dolls. Both sides of the road have large numbers of shops specialising in traditional Japanese dolls as well as their contemporary counterparts. *Kawaii ne*!

Photographic Equipment

Check the Shinjuku section for information on the big camera stores there. Many places deal in second-hand photographic equipment; foreign-made large-format equipment is usually ridiculously expensive, but Japanese equipment can often be bought at very good prices. One of the best places to look, surprisingly, is in Ginza. If you walk along Harumi-dōri, there's a place opposite the Sony building on the Sukiyabashi Crossing. On the same side as the Sony building, towards the Kabuki-za Theatre, there are a couple more places. They're all on ground level and the windows are full of cameras and lenses. The other area to seek out second-hand camera equipment is the east side of Shinjuku.

Clothes

Areas like Ginza aren't ideal for clothes shopping: the high prices take all the fun out of buying things! Generally, the big department stores, with the exception of their sale floors and big annual sales, are also expensive. The best places for clothes are the smaller discount shops that abound in areas such as Shinjuku, Harajuku and Ikebukuro.

Reasonably priced clothing stores are scattered all over the east side of Shinjuku – there are quite a few around the Kinokuniya bookshop. In Harajuku, Omote-sando and Takeshita-dōri make good hunting grounds, although it's likely to be pretty much youth oriented. In Ikebukuro, around the western exit of the station, there is a large number of discount fashion shops.

The prohibitively high prices asked for new kimono and other traditional Japanese clothing items make second-hand shops the best option. The Oriental Bazaar and the basement of the Hanae Mori building in Harajuku are good places to look. (See the preceding Folkcrafts & Antiques section for more information.) If you've got money to burn and are set on getting a new kimono or similar item, check the big department stores like Isetan and Seibu. In March and September, there are big sales of rental kimono at Daimaru.

Kids' Stuff

Japanese are particularly creative when it comes to finding things to keep their kids occupied, and Tokyo has some great toy shops. Even if you don't have any children of your own, some of the shops make for fun browsing. Places to take a look at are Loft in Shibuya and Kiddyland in Harajuku. The latter has five floors of stuff that your kids would probably be better off not knowing about. The biggest toy shop in Japan (the world?) is in Ginza. Hakuhinkan Toy Park even has a child-oriented theatre and restaurants on its upper floors. You can probably leave your kids in one of these places and take a permament vacation – they won't notice...really!

GETTING THERE & AWAY

Air

With the exception of China Airlines, all international airlines touch down at Narita Airport rather than at the more conveniently located Haneda Airport. Narita Airport has had a controversial history, its construction having met with considerable opposition from farmers it displaced, and from student radicals. Even today, it is very security conscious which can slow down progress in and out of the airport.

Arrival Immigration and customs procedures are usually straightforward, although they can be very time consuming for non-Japanese. One thing worth bearing in mind is that backpackers coming in from anywhere remotely third-worldish (the Philippines, Thailand, etc) should be careful that they have *nothing* of an incriminating nature with them – Japanese customs officials these days are very thorough. You can change money in the customs hall after having cleared customs or in the arrival hall. The rates will be the same as those offered in town.

Narita has two terminals: No 1 and No 2. This doesn't complicate things too much as both have railway stations that are connected to JR and Keisei lines. The one you arrive at will depend on the airline you are flying with. Both terminals have clear English signposting for limousine bus and train services and, as long as you don't get intimidated by the hi-tech sterility of the place, there's no need to get flustered.

Airline Offices Following is a list of the major airline offices in Tokyo.

Aeroflot
No 2 Matsuda Building, 3-4-8 Toranomon, Minato-ku (☎ 3434-9671)

Air China (formerly CAAC)
AO1 Building, 3-2-7 Akasaka, Minato-ku (☎ 3505-2021)

Air France
(☎ 3475-1511)

Air India
Hibiya Park Building, 1-8-1 Yūraku-chō, Chiyoda-ku (☎ 3214-1981)

Air Lanka
Dowa Building, 7-2-22 Ginza, Chūō-ku (☎ 3573-4261)

Air New Zealand
Shin Kokusai Building, 3-4-1 Marunouchi, Chiyoda-ku (☎ 3287-1641)

Alitalia
Tokyo Club Building, 3-2-6 Kasumigaseki, Chiyoda-ku (☎ 3580-2181)

All Nippon Airways (ANA)
Kasumigaseki Building, 3-2-5 Kasumigaseki, Chiyoda-ku (☎ 3272-1212, international; ☎ 3552-6311, domestic)

American Airlines
201 Kokusai Building, 3-1-1 Marunouchi, Chiyoda-ku (☎ 3214-2111)

Asiana Airways (☎ 3472-6600)

Bangladesh Biman
Kasumigaseki Building, 3-2-5 Kasumigaseki, Chiyoda-ku (☎ 3593-1252)

British Airways
Sanshin Building, 1-4-1 Yūraku-chō, Chiyoda-ku (☎ 3593-8811)

Canadian Airlines International
Hibiya Park Building, 1-8-1 Yūraku-chō, Chiyoda-ku (☎ 3281-7426)

Cathay Pacific
Toho Twin Tower Building, 1-5-2 Yūraku-chō, Chiyoda-ku (☎ 3504-1531)

China Airlines
Matsuoka Building, 5-22-10 Shimbashi, Minato-ku (☎ 3436-1661)

Continental Airlines
Suite 517, Sanno Grand Building, 2-14-2 Nagata-chō, Chiyoda-ku (☎ 3592-1631)

Delta Airlines
Kokusai Building, 3-1-1 Marunouchi, Chiyoda-ku (☎ 5275-7000)

Dragon Air (☎ 3589-5315)

Finnair
NK Building, 2-14-2 Kojimachi, Chūō-ku (☎ 3222-6801)

Garuda Indonesian Airways
Kasumigaseki Building, 3-2-5 Kasumigaseki, Chiyoda-ku (☎ 3593-1181)

Japan Airlines (JAL)
Tokyo Building, 2-7-3 Marunouchi, Chiyoda-ku (☎ 5489-1111, international; ☎ 3456-2111 domestic)

Japan Air System (JAS)
No 18 Mori Building, 2-3-13 Toranomon, Minato-ku (☎ 3438-1155)

Japan Asia Airways (☎ 3455-7511)

KLM
Yūraku-chō Denki Building, 1-7-1 Yūraku-chō, Chiyoda-ku (☎ 3216-0771)

Korean Air
Shin Kokusai Building, 3-4-1 Marunouchi, Chiyoda-ku (☎ 3211-3311)

Lufthansa
    3-2-6 Kasumigaseki, Chiyoda-ku (☎ 3580-2111)
Malaysian Airlines (MAS)
    3rd Floor, No 29 Mori Building, 4-2 Shimbashi,
    Minato-ku (☎ 3503-5961)
Northwest Orient Airlines
    5-12-12 Toranomon, Minato-ku (☎ 3533-6000)
Philippine Airlines
    Sanno Grand Building, 2-14-2 Nagata-chō,
    Chiyoda-ku (☎ 3593-2421)
Qantas
    Tokyo Shoko Kaigisho Building, 3-2-2
    Marunouchi, Chiyoda-ku (☎ 3593-7000)
Sabena Belgian World Airlines
    Building 2-2-19 Akasaka, Minato-ku (☎ 3585-
    6151)
Scandinavian Airlines (SAS)
    Toho Twin Tower Building, 1-5-2 Yūraku-chō,
    Chiyoda-ku (☎ 3503-8101)
Singapore Airlines
    Yūraku-chō Building 709, 1-10-1 Yūraku-chō,
    Chiyoda-ku (☎ 3213-3431)
Swissair
    Hibiya Park Building, 1-8-1 Yūraku-chō,
    Chiyoda-ku (☎ 3212-1016)
Thai Airways International
    Asahi Seimei Hibiya Building, 1-5-1 Yūraku-
    chō, Chiyoda-ku (☎ 3503-3311)
United Airlines
    Kokusai Building, 3-1-1 Marunouchi, Chiyoda-
    ku (☎ 3817-4411)
Virgin Atlantic Airways
    3-13 Yotsuya, Shinjuku-ku (☎ 5269-2680)

Train

Arriving in Tokyo by train is a simple affair.
Most of the major train lines terminate at
either Tokyo or Ueno stations, both of which
are on the JR Yamanote line. As a general
rule of thumb, trains for the north and north-
east start at either Ueno or Tokyo station and
southbound trains start at Tokyo station. For
day trips to areas such as Kamakura, Nikkō,
Hakone and Yokohama, the most convenient
means of transport is usually one of the
private lines. With the exception of the Tōbu
Nikkō line, which starts in Asakusa, all of
them start from somewhere on the Yamanote
line.

Shinkansen There are three shinkansen
lines that connect Tokyo with the rest of
Japan: the Tōkaidō line passes through
Central Honshū, changing name along the
way to the San-yō line before terminating at

Hakata in Northern Kyūshū; the Tōhoku line
runs north-east via Utsunomiya and Sendai
as far as Morioka; and the Jōetsu line runs
north to Niigata. Of these lines, the one most
likely to be used by visitors to Japan is the
Tōkaidō line, as it passes through Kyoto and
Osaka in the Kansai region. All three
shinkansen lines start at Tokyo station,
though the Tōhoku and Jōetsu lines make a
stop at Ueno station.

Other JR Lines As well as the Tōkaidō
shinkansen line there is a Tōkaidō line ser-
vicing the same areas but stopping at all the
stations that the shinkansen zips through
without so much as a toot of its horn. Trains
start at Tokyo station and pass through
Shimbashi and Shinagawa stations on their
way out of town. There are express services
to Yokohama and the Izu-hantō Peninsula,
via Atami, and from there trains continue to
Nagoya, Kyoto and Osaka.

If you are keeping expenses down and
travelling long distance on the Tōkaidō line,
there are some late-night services that do the
Tokyo to Osaka run, arriving early the next
morning. One of them will have sleepers
available.

Travelling in the same direction as the
initial stages of the Tōkaidō line, the
Yokosuka line offers a much cheaper service
to Yokohama and Kamakura. Like the
Tōkaidō line, the Yokosuka line starts at
Tokyo station and passes through Shimbashi
and Shinagawa stations on its way out of
Tokyo.

Northbound trains start in Ueno. The
Takasaki line goes to Kumagaya and
Takasaki, with onward connections from
Takasaki to Niigata. The Tōhoku line
follows the Takasaki line as far north as
Omiya, from where it heads to the far north
of Honshū via Sendai and Aomori. Getting
to Sendai without paying any express surcharges will involve changes at Utsunomiya
and Fukushima. Overnight services also
operate for those intent on saving the
expense of a night's accommodation.

Private Lines The private lines generally

service Tokyo's sprawling suburbia and very few of them go to any areas that visitors to Japan would care to visit. Still, where private lines do pass through tourist areas, they are usually a cheaper option than the JR lines. Particularly good bargains are the Tōkyū Toyoko line, running between Shibuya station and Yokohama; the Odakyū line, running from Shinjuku to Odawara and the Hakone region; the Tōbu Nikkō line, running from Asakusa to Nikkō; and the Seibu Shinjuku line from Ikebukuro to Kawagoe.

Bus

There are buses plying the expressways between Tokyo and various other parts of Japan. Generally they are little or no cheaper than the trains but are sometimes a good alternative for long-distance trips to areas serviced by expressways. The buses will often run direct, so that you can relax instead of watching for your stop as you would have to do on an ordinary train service.

There are a number of express buses running between Tokyo, Kyoto and Osaka. Overnight buses leave at 10 pm from Tokyo station and arrive at Kyoto and Osaka between 6 and 7 am the following morning. They cost from ¥8000 to ¥8500. The buses are a JR service and can be booked at one of the Green Windows in a JR station. Direct buses also run from Tokyo station to Nara and Kōbe. And from Shinjuku station there are buses running to the Fuji and Hakone regions, including, for Mt Fuji climbers, direct services to the fifth stations, from where you have to walk.

Ferry

A ferry journey can be a great way to get from Tokyo to other parts of the country. Fares are not too expensive (by Japanese standards anyway) and there is the advantage that you save the expense of a night or two's accommodation.

From Tokyo, there are long-distance ferry services to Kushiro (☎ 5400-6080) and Tomakomai (☎ 3578-1127) in Hokkaidō (2nd class ¥14,420 and ¥11,840 respec-

tively); to Kōchi (☎ 3578-1127) (2nd class ¥13,910) and Tokushima (☎ 3567-0971) (2nd class ¥8200) in Shikoku; to Kokura (☎ 3567-0971) in Northern Kyūshū (2nd class ¥12,000); and to Naha (☎ 3273-8911 or 3281-1831) on Okinawa (¥19,670).

Departures may not always be frequent (usually once every two or three days for long-distance services) and ferries are sometimes fully booked well in advance, so it pays to make inquiries early. The numbers given above for ferry companies will require some Japanese-language skills or the assistance of a Japanese speaker. If you have problems, contact the TIC at Narita or in Tokyo.

GETTING AROUND

Tokyo has an excellent public transport system. There are very few worthwhile spots around town that aren't conveniently close to a subway or JR station. When the rail network lets you down, there are generally bus services, though these are harder to use if you can't read kanji.

Most residents of and visitors to Tokyo find themselves using the railway system far more than any other means of transport. In fact, the only real drawback with the Tokyo railway network is that it shuts down somewhere between midnight and 1 am and doesn't start up again until 5 or 6 am. Subway trains have a habit of stopping halfway along their route when closing time arrives. People who get stranded face the prospect of an expensive taxi ride home or of waiting the rest of the night for the first morning train.

Undoubtedly, the most useful line in Tokyo is the JR Yamanote line, which does a loop around the city, taking in most of the important areas. You can do the whole circuit in an hour for the ¥120 minimum fare – a great introduction to the city. Another useful above-ground JR route is the Chūō line, which cuts across the centre of town between Shinjuku and Akihabara.

Apart from the JR Yamanote and Chūō lines, there are 10 subway lines, of which seven are TRTA lines and three are TOEI lines. This is not particularly important to remember, as the subway services are essentially the same, have good connections from one to the other and allow for ticket transfer between the two systems.

Avoiding Tokyo's rush hour is a good idea, but unfortunately almost impossible. Things tend to quieten down between 10 am and 4 pm, when travelling around Tokyo can actually be quite pleasant, but before 9.30 am and from about 4.30 pm onwards there are likely to be cheek-to-jowl crowds on all the major train lines. The best advice for coping with the late evening crowds is probably to be as drunk as everyone else.

To/From Narita Airport

Narita International Airport is used by almost all the international airlines but only by a small number of domestic operators. The airport is 66 km from central Tokyo, which means that getting into town is going to take from 50 minutes to 1½ hours, depending on your mode of transport.

All things considered, rail is the best mode of transport between Narita and Tokyo. For one, you are not going to get snarled up in the traffic and, two, if you don't mind taking a bit longer getting into town (80 minutes by rapid as opposed to 50 minutes by express), the train can be cheaper (depending on how you do it).

Those departing from Narita should remember that there is a ¥2000 departure tax.

Train There are three rail services between Narita airport and Tokyo: the private Keisei line and the JR Narita Express (N'EX) and Airport Narita services. From the airport, unless you plan to based in Ueno or Asakusa, the N'EX service is probably the most convenient as it runs directly into Tokyo, Shinjuku and (less frequently) Ikebukuro stations. Those heading out to the airport should bear in mind that it is important to note which terminal (No 1 or No 2) to alight at. The N'EX platforms in Tokyo, Shinjuku and Ikebukuro stations will have a list of the airline companies that operate from each of the terminals. Check to see which terminal

the airline you are flying with is based in and get off at the appropriate terminal.

The N'EX services are fast, extremely comfortable and include services like drink dispensing machines and telephones, but they don't come all that cheap. If you don't mind standing, tickets are ¥500 cheaper. To Tokyo station takes 53 minutes and costs ¥2890; to Shinjuku station takes 80 minutes and costs ¥3050; to Ikebukuro station takes 90 minutes and costs ¥3050; and to Yokohama station takes 90 minutes and costs ¥4100. JR also has Airport Narita rapid trains that take 90 minutes and costs ¥1260 to Tokyo central, ¥1850 to Yokohama, and don't stop at Shinjuku or Ikebukuro. The latter service is also less frequent, running only once an hour between 7 am and 10 pm. N'EX services run approximately half hourly between the same hours, but Ikebukuro services are very infrequent and in most cases you will be better off heading to Shinjuku and taking the Yamanote line from there.

One other point worth bearing in mind is that N'EX services only have reserved seats – you can buy them at the ticket window in the JR station from a computerised vending machine with a video screen on the N'EX platforms. Airport Narita train tickets can be bought at the ticket vending machines at the airport railway station.

On the private Keisei line, there are three trains running between Narita Airport and Ueno stations: the Skyliner, which runs nonstop and takes one hour (¥1740) and the limited express (tokkyū) service, which takes 70 minutes (¥940). You can buy tickets at the Keisei ticket office in the northern wing of the arrival lounge at Narita Airport or at the station. Ueno is the final destination of the train and is connected to the rest of Tokyo by the JR Yamanote line and the Hibiya and Ginza subway lines.

Going to the airport from Ueno, the Keisei station is right next to the JR Ueno station. You can buy advance tickets for the Skyliner service at the ticket counter, while limited express and express tickets are available from the ticket dispensing machines. From

People

A: Sanja Festival, Sensō-ji Temple (CT)
B: Japanese hippy (CT)
C: Geisha (CT)

D: School children (CT)
E: Gion Matsuri Festival (RI)
F: Shintō priest (MM)

A	B	C
D	E	F
G	H	I

Architecture

A: Screened entrance (CT)
B: Yasukuni-jinja Shrine, Tokyo (CT)
C: Hida Folk Village (CT)
D: Shin-kyō Bridge, Nikkō (CT)

E: Tokyo tower (CT)
F: Kintai-kyō Bridge, Iwakuni (TW
G: Genbaku Dōmu, Hiroshima (JW
H: Nishi Hongan-ji Temple, Kyoto
I: Interior (CT)

the JR station on the Yamanote line, take the southern exit (you should come out under the railway bridge, more or less opposite the Ameyoko market area) and turn right. The station is about 50 metres away on your right.

Limousine Bus Ticket offices, marked with the sign 'limousine', can be found in both wings of the arrival building. The limousine buses are just ordinary buses and take 1½ to two hours (depending on the traffic) to travel between Narita Airport and a number of major hotels around Tokyo. Check departure times before buying your ticket, as services are not all that frequent. The fare to hotels in eastern Tokyo is ¥2800, while to Ikebukuro, Akasaka, Ginza, Shiba, Shinagawa, Shinjuku or Haneda Airport it is ¥2900. There is also a bus service straight to Yokohama, which costs ¥3300. The trip to Yokohama City Air Terminal (YCAT) takes at least two hours.

TCAT From 6.15 am to 8.50 pm limousine buses also run every 15 minutes to Narita from the Tokyo City Air Terminal (TCAT) and cost ¥2700. The TCAT is next to Suitengu-mae subway station on the Hanzōmon line in Nihombashi. There is also a frequent shuttle bus service between the TCAT and Tokyo station, costing ¥200 and departing from the Yaesu side at Tokyo station (look for the signs). If you are leaving Tokyo, you can check in your luggage at the TCAT before taking the bus out to the airport. Some travellers swear by this service.

To/From Haneda Airport
Most domestic flights and China Airlines (Taiwan) flights use the convenient Haneda Airport.

Getting from Haneda Airport to Tokyo is a simple matter of taking the monorail to Hamamatsu-chō station on the JR Yamanote line. The trip takes just under 20 minutes; trains leave every 10 minutes and cost ¥270. Taxis to places around central Tokyo will cost around ¥6000. There's a regular bus service between Haneda and the YCAT that

takes around 30 minutes. Limousine buses also connect Haneda with TCAT (¥900), Ikebukuro and Shinjuku (¥1100).

There is a direct bus service between Haneda and Narita (¥2900) which can take up to two hours, depending on the traffic. The alternative is to take the monorail in to Tokyo, and then connect with one of the Narita services running from various stations on the Yamanote line (see the preceding Train section).

Train
The Tokyo train system can be a bit daunting at first, but you soon get the hang of it. All the subway lines are colour coded, so even if you can't read a thing you soon learn that the Ginza line is orange. For all local journeys, tickets are sold by vending machines called *jidō kippu uriba*. Above the vending machines will be a rail map with fares indicated next to the station names. Unfortunately, the names are almost always in kanji only. Probably the best way around this problem is to put your money in the machine and push the lowest fare button (usually ¥120). This will get you on the train and when you get to your destination you can correct the fare at the fare adjustment office. You can get your money back before you press the ticket button by pressing the button marked *torikeshi*.

If you get tired of fumbling for change every time you buy a ticket, the JR system offers the option of 'orange cards'. The cards are available in denominations of ¥1000, ¥3000 and ¥5000. Fares are automatically deducted from the cards when you use them in the orange-card vending machines.

For long-term residents, passes called *teiki-ken* are available between two stops over a fixed period of time, but you really have to use the ticket at least once a day for it to pay off. The incentive for buying one is as much for the saving in time spent queuing for tickets as for any pecuniary advantage.

Also available are the so-called *furii kippu*, tickets for a day's unlimited travel on either the subway system or the JR system, within the bounds of the Yamanote line.

These tickets are not 'free' at all, and given that you generally need to use both systems, you won't get your money's worth.

Bus

Many Tokyo residents and visitors spend a considerable amount of time in the city without ever using the bus network. This is partly because the train services are so good and partly because the buses are much more difficult to use. In addition, buses are at the mercy of Tokyo's sluggish traffic flow. Services also tend to finish fairly early in the evening, making buses a pretty poor alternative all round.

When using the buses, it's useful to have the name of your destination written in Japanese so that you can either show the driver or match up the kanji yourself with that on the route map. Fares are paid as you enter the bus.

Taxi

Taxis are so expensive that you should only use them when there is no alternative. Rates start at ¥600, which gives you two km (after 11 pm 1.5 km), after which the metre starts to click an additional ¥90 for every 340

metres; you also click up ¥90 for every two minutes you sit idly gazing at the scenery in a typical Tokyo traffic jam.

If you have to get a taxi late on a Friday or Saturday night and are able to find one, be prepared for delays and higher prices. At these difficult times, gaijin may find themselves shunned like lepers because taxi drivers assume their ride is likely to be a short one, whereas the drunken salaryman holding up two fingers (to indicate his willingness to pay twice the meter fare) is probably bound for a distant suburb.

Tram

Tokyo's only remaining tram (streetcar) service (the Toden Arakawa line) runs from opposite Ōtsuka station on the JR Yamanote line. It passes the Sunshine City building in Ikebukuro, heads on to Zoshigaya and then terminates in Waseda, not far from Waseda University. The line is perhaps worth using for a visit to Zoshigaya, an old residential area under threat from Tokyo's rapacious property developers. There are a number of small temples in the area, as well as Zoshigaya cemetary, the final resting place of Lafcadio Hearn and Natsume Sōseki.

Around Tokyo   東京の附近

Tokyo itself may be a tangle of expressways and railway lines, a congested sprawl of high-rises, department stores and housing estates, but an hour or so by rail is all you need to reach some of Japan's most famous sights. Apart from the Ogasawara Islands, all the attractions in this chapter can be visited as day trips from Tokyo, although in several cases it would be worth staying away overnight.

Foremost among the attractions around Tokyo are Kamakura and Nikkō. If you have limited time and are interested primarily in Japan's important historical sites, these are the places you should visit, along with Kyoto and Nara. More in the line of a pleasant outing, it's also worth visiting Hakone or the Mt Fuji region, where the fortunate are occasionally blessed with magnificent views of Mt Fuji.

Most of the other sights around Tokyo are less interesting for short-term visitors, despite heavy promotion by the Tourist Information Centre (TIC). For long-term residents, areas like the Izu-hantō Peninsula and the Boso-hantō Peninsula are pleasant retreats from Tokyo, but cater largely to the needs of Japanese tourists and to many foreign visitors may seem like a never-ending succession of entry fees, roped walkways and orderly queues.

This chapter begins with places to the far west of Tokyo and moves clockwise, finishing with the Izu Seven Islands to the east and the Ogasawara Islands further south.

Izu-hantō Peninsula 伊豆半島

The Izu-hantō Peninsula, west of Tokyo, is noted for its abundant hot springs, but unless you have a particular interest in hot-spring resorts – an extremely popular holiday option for the Japanese – there's nothing to take short-term visitors here except for some very pleasant scenery. There are no particularly outstanding destinations on the peninsula, and travel costs to and around the area tend to mount up very quickly.

Although it's possible to get around the peninsula in one long and hurried day, it's better to stay overnight at a halfway point, such as Shimoda. The ideal accommodation of course is going to be a hot-spring (onsen) hotel – the hot-spring water is piped into segregated bathing areas in the hotel – but realistically this is going to be out of the price range of many travellers. Fortunately, many minshuku and ryokan around the peninsula also have onsen bathing areas and can provide a futon at more affordable rates.

A suggested itinerary for circuiting the peninsula is to start at Atami – a hot-spring resort town whose name means 'hot sea' – and travel down the east coast to Shimoda; from there you can cut across to Dogashima on the west coast and travel up to Mishima or Numazu, where there are railway stations with direct access to Tokyo. There are frequent and reliable bus services between all the main towns on the peninsula, and some of the towns are also serviced by ferries.

ATAMI   熱海

Atami probably has more appeal to Japanese couples looking for a naughty hot-spring weekend than it has to Westerners for its sightseeing potential. Its easy access from Tokyo by shinkansen and its fame as a hot-spring resort make it an expensive place to spend the night. Head down to Itō or Shimoda if it's cheaper accommodation and less tourist development that you are looking for.

There is an information counter (☎ 0557-81-6002) at Atami railway station, where they can help you with finding accommodation; there should be an English speaker on hand.

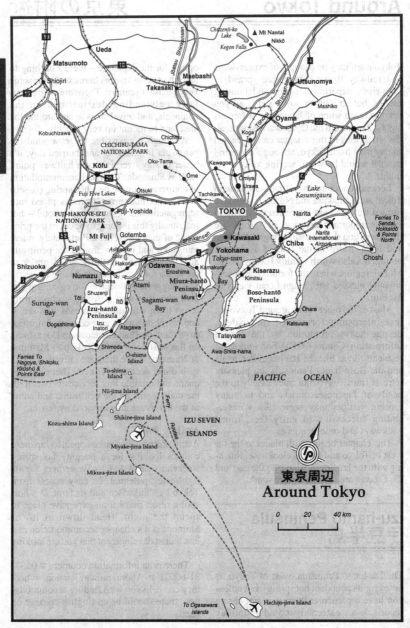

東京周辺
Around Tokyo

0   20   40 km

MOA Art Museum ＭＯＡ美術館

Atami's prime attraction is the MOA Art Museum. The museum, housed in the world headquarters of the Church of World Messianity, has a collection of Japanese and Chinese art that includes a few 'national treasures' and a good number of 'important cultural properties'. The museum is open from 9.30 am to 4.30 pm and closed on Thursday. Admission is a very hefty ¥1500. The museum is about 10 minutes by bus from Atami station – take the bus from the No 4 bus stand outside the station to the last stop (*MOA bijitsukan* – ¥140).

Izusan-jinja Shrine 伊豆山神社

About 10 minutes to the north of Atami station by bus, this is not an important shrine but it's situated in tranquil and expansive grounds. There is also a local history museum (¥150, 9 am to 3.30 pm, closed Monday). Take a bus from No 4 bus stand and get off at Izusan-jinja-mae (¥170).

Places to Stay & Eat

Atami is a very expensive place to spend the night. Most of the hotels quote rates that include two meals and, with the exception of the occassional minshuku, they all have hot-spring water piped in for bathing. Most places are about a km south of Atami station in the beachfront area. In this area you can find the *Atami Kinjō-kan* (☎ 0557-81-6261), which has rates ranging from ¥26,000 to ¥40,000 per person including two meals.

One exception to Atami's sky-high rates is the *Grand View Atami* (☎ 0557-85-0051), which has rooms with two meals from ¥8000. It's very close to the station. From the harbour side of the station turn right, follow the road, bearing left and look out for it on the left. Most of the other affordable accommodation is further afield. South of Atami, close to Izutaka and Ajiro stations are the *Taka Minshuku* (☎ 0557-85-2222) and the *Ajiro Minshuku)* (☎ 0557-68-0136), where rates are ¥7500 to ¥10,000 per person with two meals.

Getting There & Away

An ordinary Tōkaidō line train from Tokyo station will get you to Atami in one hour 45 minutes for ¥1850. The shinkansen takes only 50 minutes but costs ¥4000. Ordinary trains leave Tokyo every 40 minutes during the day. It is also possible to approach Atami via Shinjuku by taking the Odakyū line to Odawara (¥1550, one hour 10 minutes), and then connecting with the Tōkaidō line, at which point the remaining 20 minutes to Atami will cost ¥390.

ITŌ 伊東

Itō is another hot-spring resort and is famous as the place where Anjin-san (William Adams), the hero of James Clavell's *Shogun*, built a ship for the Tokugawa Shogunate. Among the sights around the town are the gourd-shaped Lake Ippeki-ko , the Cycle Sports Centre and the Izu Cactus Garden (ask for *Izu Shaboten-kōen*; buses depart from the the No 10 bus stand outside Itō station), which is 35 minutes by bus from Izu station and costs a mere ¥1550 for admission.

The Lake Ippeki-ko , Ikeda Art Museum and Izu Cactus Garden can all be visited by taking a bus from No 10 stop outside Itō station. If you still have time after this, you could continue on to Atagawa by train and visit the Atagawa Banana & Crocodile Park, a theme park that seems eccentric even by Japanese standards.

Itō station has a tourist information counter (☎ 0557-37-3291) which can help with finding accommodation and so on.

Lake Ippeki-ko 一碧湖

The gourd-shaped (which means it's roughly circular) Ippeki-ko is around four km in circumference, and is a pleasant enough spot. There's boat hire on the lake – 30 minutes for ¥600. To get there, take a bus from either No 5 or 10 bus stops outside Itō station. The 25 minute journey costs ¥470. Lake Ippeki-ko can be combined easily with a visit to the Ikeda 20th Century Art Museum.

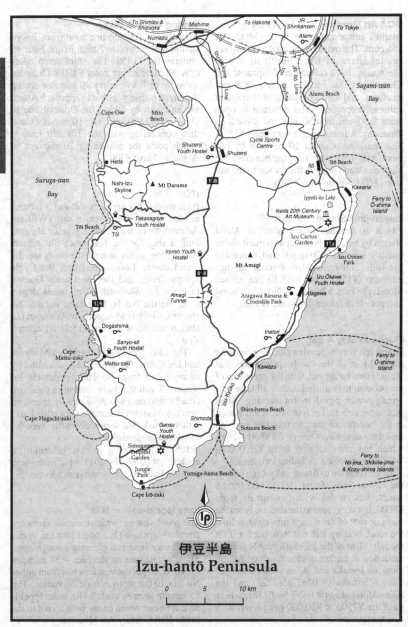

伊豆半島
Izu-hantō Peninsula

0   5   10 km

Ikeda 20th Century Art Museum
池田20世紀美術館

The Ikeda 20th Century Art Museum has a collection of paintings and sculptures by Matisse, Picasso, Dali and others. The museum is 25 minutes from Itō station and is open daily from 10 am to 4.30 pm. Admission is ¥800. To get there, take the same buses as for Lake Ippeki-ko and get off at Ikeda Bijitsukan. The trip costs ¥530.

Izu Ocean Park   伊豆海洋公園

The Izu Ocean Park (ask for *Izu Kaiyō-kōen*) has 12 natural swimming pools as well as opportunities for snorkelling and scuba diving. It's 45 minutes by bus from Itō. Admission is ¥1550 in July and August, the peak months, and ¥550 during the rest of the year.

Festivals

On the first Sunday of July, Itō holds the Tarai-nori Kyoso which involves paddling down the Matsukawa River in washtubs using rice scoops as oars although what this race is in aid of, no-one seems to know.

Places to Stay

The *Itō Youth Hostel* (☎ 0557-45-0224) costs ¥2280 depending on the season, but is 15 minutes out of town by bus and not that easy to find. Other accommodation options can be found in the numerous pensions that exist out of town. The Lake Ippeki-ko area is good for pensions: *Pension Itōsansō* (☎ 0557-36-4454) has rooms from ¥6900. Most of the other pensions range from ¥8800 per night. There is also a host of accommodation possibilities in the Izu Kōgen (plateau) area, which is easily accessible from Izu Kōgen station. If you don't mind spending ¥7000 to ¥8000 on a room, there will be plenty of places to choose from. The best advice would be to check with the Itō station information counter for vacancies.

Getting There & Away

Itō is about 25 minutes from Atami station on the JR Itō line. When you arrive at Atami station, a sign on the platform in romaji tells you when and from which platform the next train for Itō leaves. The JR limited express (tokkyū) 'Odoriko' service also runs from Tokyo station to Itō, taking one hour 50 minutes and costing ¥4000. Direct ordinary trains from Tokyo station are quite a bit cheaper at ¥2160 and take about two hours 10 minutes.

SHIMODA   下田

If you only have time for one town on the peninsula, make it Shimoda, the most pleasant of the hot-spring resorts. It's a peaceful place with a few historical sites as well as the usual touristy stuff.

Shimoda is famous as the residence of the American Townsend Harris, the first Western diplomat to live in Japan. The Treaty of Kanagawa, which resulted from Commodore Perry's visit, ended Japan's centuries of self-imposed isolation by opening the ports of Shimoda and Hakodate to US ships and establishing a consulate in Shimoda in 1856.

Ryōsen-ji & Chōraku-ji Temples
了仙寺・長楽寺

About a 25 minute walk from Shimoda station is Ryōsen-ji Temple, famous as the site of another treaty, supplementary to the Treaty of Kanagawa, signed by Commodore Perry and representatives of the Tokugawa Shogunate. Today the temple is less interesting than its next-door neighbour, Chōraku-ji Temple, which has a **sex museum** featuring a collection of erotic knick-knacks – pickled turnips with suggestive shapes and stones with vagina-like orifices in them. This odd museum is open from 8.30 am to 5 pm daily and admission is ¥500.

The museum also has a series of pictures depicting the tragic life of the courtesan Okichi-san. The story goes that Okichi-san was forced to give up the man she loved in order to attend to the needs of the barbarian Harris, and was thereafter stigmatised by her relationship with him, a situation that drove her to drink and culminated in her suicide. The pictures seem to suggest that the traditional Japanese way of life had been compromised in the confrontation with the West, and Okichi-san is regarded as a kind of sacrifice to internationalism, a symbol of

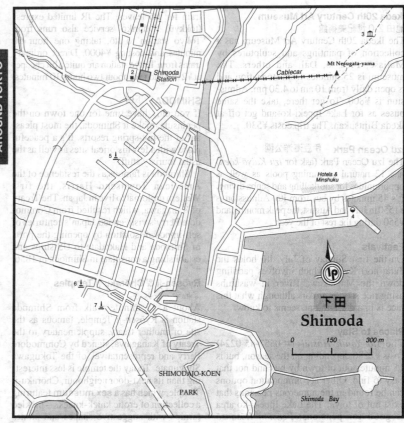

1 Kokuminshukusha New Shimoda
   国民宿舎ニュー下田
2 Station Hotel Shimoda
   ステーションホテル下田
3 Photography Museum
   写真とカメラの記念館
4 Bay Cruises
   遊覧船
5 Hōfuku-ji Temple
   宝福寺
6 Ryōsen-ji Temple
   了仙寺
7 Chōraku-ji Temple
   長楽寺

the defilement of Japanese culture by contact with things foreign.

Hōfuku-ji Temple 宝福寺
On the way to Ryōsen-ji Temple is Hōfuku-ji Temple, which has a museum that memorialises the life of Okichi-san and includes scenes from the various movie adaptations of her life.

Mt Nesugata-yama 寝姿山
Cablecars lurch their way up Mt Nesugata-yama every 10 minutes, parking at the top of what is less a mountain than a hill. The park

has a photography museum, a small temple, good views of Shimoda and Shimoda Bay and a reasonably priced restaurant. A return cablecar trip, including admission to the park, costs ¥1100. It's impossible to miss the 'mountain', as it's directly in front of the Shimoda station square. The park is open from 9 am to 5.30 pm.

Bay Cruises
From the Shimoda harbour area, there are numerous bay cruises. Most popular with the Japanese is a 'Black Ship' cruise, which departs every 40 minutes (approximately) from 9.40 am to 3.30 pm and costs ¥800 for a 20 minute spin around the bay. Three boats a day (9.40 and 11.20 am and 1.25 pm) leave on a Cape Irō-zaki course. You can leave the boat at Irō-zaki and travel onwards by bus or stay on the boat to return to Shimoda. One-way tickets to Irō-zaki cost ¥1335 and the trip takes 40 minutes.

Festivals
From 16 to 18 May, the Kuro-fune Matsuri (Black Ship Festival) is held in Shimoda. It commemorates the first landing of Commodore Perry with parades and fireworks displays.

Places to Stay & Eat
As in the other peninsula resort towns, there is a wealth of accommodation in Shimoda, most of it overpriced. The *Gensu Youth Hostel* (☎ 0558-62-0035) is 25 minutes by bus from the town (from No 2 bus stand outside Shimoda station) and has beds for ¥2400. The hostel is opposite a bus stop and a post office. Even further from town is the *Amagi Harris Court Youth Hostel* (☎ 0558-35-7253), which is around five km inland from Kawazu station, between Itō and Shimoda. It has beds for ¥2400. You can get there from Kawazu station by boarding a Shuzenji-bound bus, and getting off at the first stop after the Yukano Onsen. There are hiking trails and waterfalls in this area.

Staff at the information counter (☎ 0558-22-1351) across the square from the station will book accommodation. If you want a cheap room, ask for a minshuku or kokuminshukusha (people's lodge); you should be able to get a room for ¥4500 to ¥6000, without meals. If you want to find something yourself and you don't mind going up-market, the best hunting ground is the area that fronts onto Shimoda Bay. The left-hand side of the road is crowded with hotels, ryokan and minshuku for more than a km. Be warned, though, many of these places are very expensive, even though they offer the attraction of a hot-spring bath.

There is reasonably inexpensive business hotel accommodation in the *Station Hotel Shimoda* (☎ 0558-22-8885), right next to the station. Singles/twins cost ¥5500/11,000. Also not far from the station and affordable is the *Kokuminshukusha New Shimoda* (☎ 0558-23-0222), a really pleasant place that costs ¥6500 per person with two meals.

Getting There & Away
Shimoda is as far as you can go by train on the Izu-hantō Peninsula; the limited express from Tokyo station takes two hours 45 minutes and costs ¥5850. Alternatively, take an Izu Kyūkō line train from Itō station for ¥1340; the trip takes about an hour. There are a few express services each day from Atami station, but the express surcharges makes them expensive.

Bus platform No 5 in front of the station is for buses going to Dogashima, while platform No 7 is for those bound for Shuzenji.

SHIMOGAMO HOT SPRING　下加茂温泉
The Shimogamo area is another place to loll around in hot water, but as it's off the railway line it's a bit less developed than other onsen areas around the peninsula. Buses run to the area from in front of Shimoda station. There's plenty of accommodation along the Aono-gawa River, including the *Minshuku Fukuya* (☎ 0558-62-1003), a pleasant place with rates from ¥6500 to ¥7000 per person with two meals. Not far from here is the Yumiga-hama Beach, an excellent beach by Japanese standards.

CAPE IRŌ-ZAKI 石廊崎

Cape Irō-zaki, the southernmost point of the peninsula, is noted for its cliffs and lighthouse. It also has a jungle park, a tropical garden and some fairly good beaches; if that sounds appealing, you can get to the cape by bus or boat (see the Bay Cruises entry of the Shimoda section) from Shimoda. Buses from Shimoda to the Irō-zaki lighthouse take around 55 minutes and cost ¥840.

DOGASHIMA 堂ヶ島

From Shimoda, it's a very scenic bus journey to Dogashima, on the other side of the peninsula. There are no breathtaking views, but the hilly countryside and narrow road that winds its way past fields and small rural townships make for an interesting trip. Along the way is **Cape Matsu-zaki**, recommended for its traditional-style Japanese houses and quiet sandy beach.

The main attractions at Dogashima – a touristy but pleasant place to wander around – are the unusual **rock formations** that line the seashore. The frequent boat trips available include a visit to the town's famous shoreline cave which has a hole in the roof that lets in light. A 20 minute trip costs ¥850, while two hour tours cost ¥1850. Paths from the right of the jetty follow the cliffs to the hole in the cave roof.

Places to Stay

The nearby town of Matsu-zaki has the *Sanyo-sō Youth Hostel* (☎ 0558-42-0408), where beds cost ¥2400. The hostel is a good couple of km to the east of town, but you can catch a Shimoda-bound bus and get off at the yūsu-hosteru-mae bus stop.

Getting There & Away

Buses to Dogashima from platform No 5 in front of Shimoda station take about an hour and cost ¥1200.

To do a complete circuit of the peninsula, there are a number of bus stops in Dogashima on the road opposite the jetty. The fare to Shuzenji from stop No 2 is ¥1920. A more interesting and not that much more expensive alternative is to catch a ferry to Numazu,

which is connected with Tokyo by the Tōkaidō line. Boats also go to Tōi, where the Takasagoya Youth Hostel is near the harbour. From Tōi, it is possible to continue to Heda and Shuzenji by bus or take another boat to Numazu.

HEDA 戸田

Further up the west coast of Dogashima is the small town of Heda, which has a pleasant beach and fewer tourists. To get to Heda from Dogashima, you may have to change buses at Tōi or take the boat from Dogashima and change to a bus at Tōi. Tōkai buses run between Shuzenji and Heda, taking around one hour and costing ¥1040.

For accommodation, there is the *Takasagoya Youth Hostel* (☎ 0558-98-0200) in the nearby town of Tōi, and beds here are ¥2300. The hostel is close to the harbour. To get to it, walk alongside the river until you reach the second bridge. Turn left at the bridge away from the river, cross over the main road and look for the youth hostel on your right after the next intersection.

SHUZENJI 修善寺

Shuzenji is just another hot-spring resort with overpriced accommodation, but there is a rail connection with the Tōkaidō line in this town, which serves, along with Mishima and Atami, as one of the three rail entry points to the peninsula.

There's not much in the way of sights in Shuzenji, but if you do stop over the **Shuzen-ji Temple** is around 2½ km southwest of railway station and is worth a look. It dates back to 807 AD, and was rebuilt in 1489. Take a Tōkai or Izu-Hakone bus from stand Nos 1 or 2 outside Shuzenji station. The 10 minute ride costs ¥190. Ask for Shuzenji Onsen. This area is also where you'll find ryokan accommodation, shops, restaurants and the **Shigetsu-den Hall**, another minor sight.

The *Shuzenji Youth Hostel* (☎ 0558-83-0146) is around 1½ km north-east of this area. Take the road to the right before Shuzen-ji Temple (coming from Shuzenji station) and keep bearing to the right. The road forks around a km up the road; take the right fork and look out for the hostel, a big white building off on its own on the left.

MISHIMA 三島

Mishima is another of the Tōkaidō line entry points to the Izu-hantō Peninsula. The **Rakuju-en Garden** is a short walk from the station, while **Garden** is a short walk from the station, while **Mishima-taisha Shrine**, around one km to the south-east of the station, is a five minute bus journey away.

Festivals

Mishima-taisha Shrine is the venue for an annual festival involving horseback archery and parades of floats from 15 to 17 August.

Getting There & Away

A Tōkaidō line shinkansen from Tokyo takes one hour five minutes to get to Mishima and costs ¥4310. Ordinary trains take twice as long and cost ¥2160. From Mishima station, it's half an hour on the private Izu Hakone line to Shuzenji.

It's only 10 minutes by train from Mishima to Numazu, from where it is possible to continue into the peninsula by boat or by bus (see the Dogashima section of this chapter for details).

Ōkitsu 興津

In the days when feudal lords were required to make regular visits to Edo (Tokyo today), Ōkitsu was the 17th stop on the old Tōkaidō Highway between Kyoto and Edo. Many visitors to Japan will already be familiar with the town's **famous inn**, a survivor from the feudal era, as it plays the key role in Oliver Statler's popular book *Japanese Inn*. The **Seiken-ji Temple** with its attractive garden is about a km west of the station.

Ōkitsu can be easily reached via the Tōkaidō line from Numazu or from Mishima.

SHIMIZU & SHIZUOKA 清水・静岡

A little further west, and also on the Tōkaidō line, are the towns of Shimizu and Shizuoka. Tokugawa Ieyasu 'retired' to Shizuoka and the **Kunōzan Tōshō-gū Shrine** in Shimizu

has a number of his possessions in its treasure house. Only moats and ramparts mark the site of **Shizuoka Castle**, destroyed during WW II, but the town also boasts the interesting prehistoric site of **Toro Iseki** which dates from the Yayoi period (see the History section in the Facts about the Country chapter). The site museum displays the artefacts excavated here and there are reconstructions of Yayoi dwellings. The site is about 2½ km south-east of the JR station.

Hakone 箱根

If the weather cooperates and Mt Fuji is clearly visible, the Hakone region can make a wonderful day trip out of Tokyo. You can enjoy cablecar rides, visit an open-air museum, poke around smelly volcanic hot-water springs and cruise Lake Ashino-ko . The weather, however, is crucial, for without Mt Fuji hovering in the background, much of what Hakone has to offer is likely to diminish in interest. Visibility permitting, a one day circuit of the region offers some of the best opportunities for a glimpse of Japan's most famous mountain.

An interesting loop through the region takes you from Tokyo by train and toy train to Gōra; then by funicular and cablecar up Mt Soun-zan and down to Lake Ashino-ko; by boat around the lake to Moto-Hakone where you can walk a short stretch of the Edo era Tōkaidō Highway; and from there by bus back to Odawara, where you catch the train to Tokyo. (If you're feeling energetic, you can spend 3½ hours walking the old highway back to Hakone-Yumoto, which is on the Tokyo line.)

ODAWARA 小田原

Odawara is billed in the tourist literature as an 'old castle town', which it is; the only problem is that the castle, like many of Japan's castles, is an uninspiring reconstruction of the original. That said, the castle is worth visiting during the cherry blossom season, as there are some 1000 sakura trees

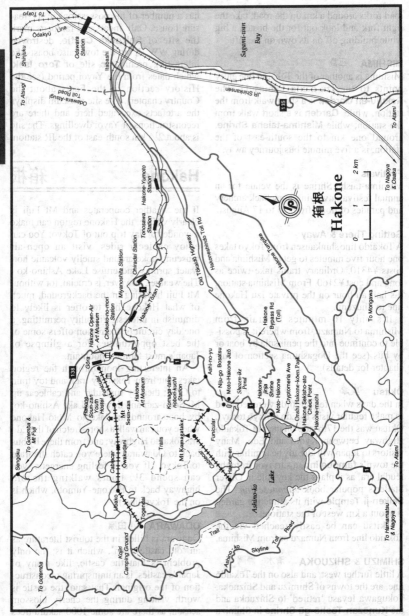

箱根
Hakone

planted on the grounds. The castle and surrounding park area is a 10 minute walk south-east of Odawara station and admission is ¥250. It's open from 9 am to 4.30 daily. There is very little else of interest in the town, which is principally a transit point for Hakone.

HAKONE OPEN-AIR ART MUSEUM
彫刻の森美術館

Between Odawara and Gōra on the Hakone-Tōzan line is the Chōkoku-no-mori Bijutsukan, or the Hakone Open-Air Art Museum as it's usually referred to in English. The museum is next to Chōkoku-no-mori station, a little before Gōra station, the final stop on the line. The museum itself features sculptures by Western artists such as Rodin and Moore in a 30 sq km park. There are also a couple of indoor exhibits, including a Picasso collection.

Admission is a hefty ¥1500, and the Hakone 'free pass' (see the following Getting Around section for details) is *not* accepted, though it will earn you a discount. The museum is open from 9 am to 5 pm between March and October; during the rest of the year it closes at 4 pm.

GŌRA 強羅

Gōra is the terminus of the Hakone-Tōzan line and the starting point for the funicular and cablecar trip to Togendai on Lake Ashino-ko . The town also has a couple of its own attractions, which may be of minor interest to travellers. If you are in this area between 11.30 and 2.30, check out the Gyōza Centre, a famous dumpling shop with nine kinds of gyōza or dumplings – ¥500 is enough to fill you up.

Gōra-kōen Park 強羅公園

Just a short walk beside the funicular tracks up Mt Soun-zan is Gōra-kōen Park. For ¥820 you can enjoy the French Rock Garden, along with a collection of 'seasonal flowers, alpine plants and tropical plants'. The park is open from 9 am to 9 pm from 21 July to 21 August; during the rest of the year, it closes at 5 pm.

Hakone Art Museum 箱根美術館

Further up the hill, 10 minutes from Gōra station, is the Hakone Bijutsukan, which has a moss garden and a collection of ceramics from Japan and other Asian nations. It is open from 9.00 am to 4.30 pm, closed Thursday and admission is ¥800. While the moss garden is very pleasant, unless you have a special interest in ceramics, it is probably overpriced.

MT SOUN-ZAN & ŌWAKUDANI
早雲山・大涌谷

Almost everyone going to Gōra will continue to the top of Mt Soun-zan on the funicular. If you don't have a Hakone 'Free Pass' (see the following Getting Around section), you'll need to buy a ticket at the booth to the right of the platform exit. You could walk to the top but it's a steep climb and the funicular does it in a mere 10 minutes for only ¥290.

Mt Soun-zan is the starting point for what the Japanese refer to as a 'ropeway', a 30 minute, four km cablecar ride to Togendai by Lake Ashino-ko. On the way, the gondolas pass through Ōwakudani, giving you a chance to get out and have a look at the volcanic hot springs; the gondolas pass by every 52 seconds. If the weather is fine, there are great views of Mt Fuji, both from the gondolas and from Ōwakudani. The journey from Gōra to Togendai costs ¥1180 one way, ¥2080 return; keep the ticket if you pause at Owakudani.

The volcanic activity at Ōwakudani includes clouds of steam, bubbling mud and mysterious smells but hopefully no walls of rapidly advancing molten lava. The black, boiled eggs on sale here are cooked in the boiling mud, which it is believed results in certain medicinal properties being imparted. Buy a couple if you feel in need of a volcanic pick-me-up. Next to the cablecar stop, there's a building with restaurants, shops selling tourist junk and a reasonably priced stand-up noodle bar. If you want to sit down, the restaurant has a good lunch selection (the katsudon is not bad, at ¥850) with a view of Mt Fuji thrown in (weather permitting).

The Ōwakudani Natural Science Museum

AROUND TOKYO

has displays relating to the geography and natural history of Hakone. It's open daily from 9 am to 4.30 pm, and admission is ¥400.

LAKE ASHINO-KO   芦ノ湖

Lake Ashino-ko is touted as the primary attraction of the Hakone region, and although it's generally nothing to get excited about, the lake does a Cinderella transformation when the majestic form of Mt Fuji appears over the surrounding hills, its snow-clad slopes glimmering on the water. More often than not, though, the venerable mount is hidden behind a dirty grey bank of clouds. If so, you have the consolation of a ferry trip across the lake and a postcard of the view.

At Kojiri, Moto-Hakone and Hakone, you can hire rowing boats (¥500 to ¥600 per half hour) or pedal boats (¥1500 per half hour). The truly indolent can take chauffeur-driven motor boats for a ¥6000 jaunt around the lake. See the following Getting Around section for more details about lake transport.

MT KOMAGA-TAKE   駒ヶ岳

Mt Komaga-take is a good place from which to get a view of the lake and Mt Fuji. From Togendai, boats run to Hakone-en, from where a cablecar (¥610 one way, ¥1030 return) goes to the top. You can leave the mountain by the same route or by a five minute funicular descent (¥360 one way, ¥620 return) to Komaga-take-nobori-kuchi. Buses run from there to Hakone-Yumoto (¥740) and to Odawara (¥910).

Rock Carvings   元箱根石仏群

Not that far from Mt Komaga-take-nobori-kuchi are a group of Buddhas and other figures carved in relief on rocks that lay between Mt Komaga-take and Mt Kami Futago. They date from the Kamakura era (1192 to 1333) and still look very good despite the battering from the elements they must have received in the intervening centuries. On one side of the road is the Niju-go Bosatsu, a rock carved with numerous Buddha figures. Across the road, the Moto-Hakone Jizō carving, patron saint of

travellers and souls of departed children, is the largest of a number of rock carvings.

To get there from the funicular, turn right and follow the road down until you reach a T-junction. Turn left here and then left again; the carvings are around 400 metres up the road from this point.

MOTO-HAKONE   元箱根

Moto-Hakone is a pleasant spot with a few places where you can eat or get an overpriced cup of coffee. There are a couple of interesting sights within easy walking distance of the jetty.

Hakone-jinja Shrine   箱根神社

It's impossible to miss Hakone-jinja Shrine, with its red torii rising from the lake itself. Walk around the lake towards the torii; huge cedars line the path to the shrine, which is in a wooded grove. The well-maintained shrine is nothing special, but the general effect is quite atmospheric. There is a treasure hall on the grounds. It is open from 9.30 am to 4 pm and costs ¥300.

Cryptomeria Ave   旧街道杉並木

Cryptomeria Ave or 'Sugi-namiki' is a two km path between Moto-Hakone and Hakone-machi lined with cryptomeria trees planted more than 360 years ago. The path runs behind the lakeside road used by the buses and other traffic.

Old Tōkaidō Highway   旧東海道石畳

Up the hill from the lakeside Moto-Hakone bus stop is the old Tōkaidō Highway, the road that once linked the ancient capital Kyoto with Edo, today the modern capital, Tokyo. It is possible to take a 3½ hour walk along the old road to Hakone-Yumoto station, passing the Amazake-jaya Teahouse, the Old Tōkaidō Road Museum and Soun-ji Temple along the way.

HAKONE-MACHI   箱根町

Hakone-machi is further around the lake beyond Moto-Hakone. Known in Japanese as Hakone Sekisho-ato, the Hakone Check Point was operated by the Tokugawa Shogunate from 1619 to 1869 as a means of controlling the flow of anything unwanted in and out of Edo from people and arms to ideas. The present-day check point is a recent reproduction of the original. Further back towards Moto-Hakone is the **Hakone History Museum** (Hakone Sekisho Shiryōkan), which has some samurai artefacts. It's open daily from 9 am to 4.30 pm, and admission is ¥200.

FESTIVALS

The Ashino-ko Kosui Matsuri, held on 31 July at Hakone-jinja Shrine in Moto-Hakone, features fireworks displays over Lake Ashino-ko . On 16 August, in the Hakone Daimonji-yaki Festival, torches are lit on Mt Myojoga-take so that they form the shape of the Chinese character for 'big' or 'great'. The Hakone Daimyō Gyoretsu on 3 November is a re-enactment of a feudal lord's procession by 400 costumed locals.

PLACES TO STAY

Hakone's local popularity is reflected in the high price of most accommodation in the area. The *Hakone Soun-zan Youth Hostel* (☎ 0460-2-3827) costs the standard ¥2300. To get there, you need to take the funicular from Gōra to Soun-zan, turn right, then left and then look out for the hostel around 100 metres up on your left. Look out for the wooden sign with Japanese writing and the YHA triangle outside the hotel. One problem with this place is that it has no cooking facilities, no meals and nowhere to eat in the near vicinity – bring some instant noodles along.

Most of the other accommodation in the Hakone region is clustered around the area's many onsens: Yumoto Onsen (Yumoto Hakone); Gōra Onsen; Miyanoshita Onsen (two stops before Gōra); Sengokuhara Onsen (north of Lake Ashino-ko); and Ashinoko Onsen (close to Moto-Hakone). There is also accommodation in Odawara, but the atmosphere in this area is more urban than in Hakone.

Naturally, Hakone being a famous sight-seeing so close to Tokyo, there is a lot of *very* expensive accommodation in the area. A famous case in point is the *Fujiya Hotel* (☎ 0460-2-2211), one of Japan's earliest Western-style hotels, where room rates start at ¥41,000. The hotel is around 250 metres west of Miyanoshita station on the Hakone-Tōzan line. Fortunately, for those who don't want to stay in a youth hostel and who are still intent on overnighting in Hakone, there are some reasonable alternatives, mainly in the form of pensions, ryokan and minshuku.

Between the Fujiya Hotel and Miyanoshita station is the *Pension Yamaguchi* (☎ 0460-2-3158), where rates with two meals are ¥9200. The pension is a quaint white building, and it only has a total of five rooms. To get to it, turn left out of Miyanoshita station (presuming you're facing the direction of Gōra) walk up to the main road. About 90 metres up the main road is a smaller road on the right that doubles back parallel to the main one. Walk down it for about 100 metres and look for the pension on the left.

Over in the Sounzan area, not far from the youth hostel is another pension with similar rates: *Hakone-no-Yama* (☎ 0460-2-1882). From the Sounzan cablecar turn right (opposite direction to the youth hostel), and follow the road round, taking the first left. Take the second left, and the pension is at the end of this lane (it has an English sign).

The Japanese Inn Group has a couple of guesthouses in Hakone, and like most of the Inn Group's guesthouses they are not that easy to find. The *Fuji Hakone Guest House* (☎ 0460-4-6577) is over in the Sengokuhara area, north of Lake Ashino-ko, and has singles from ¥5000 to ¥6000 and twins from ¥10,000 to ¥12,000. It's a 45 minute bus journey from stop No 4 at Odawara to the Senkyoro-mae bus stop. The guesthouse is close to the Porsche Museum and a swimming pool; there's also a sign advertising its location, but you'll probably end up having to ring them up anyway.

The other Inn Group Hotel, *Moto Hakone Guesthouse* (☎ 0460-3-7880), is in a better location over in Moto-Hakone, and has rates of ¥5000 per person. To get there, walk away from the lake starting at the bus stop closest to the harbour; the guesthouse is up a road to the right just before the next bus stop (Ashino-ko-mae).

GETTING THERE & AWAY

There are basically three ways of getting to the Hakone region: by the Odakyū express bus service from the Shinjuku bus terminal on the western side of Shinjuku station; by JR from Tokyo station; and by the private Odakyū line from Shinjuku station.

Train

JR trains run on the Tōkaidō line between Tokyo station and Odawara. Ordinary trains take 1½ hours, cost ¥1420 and run every 15 minutes or so. Limited express trains take one hour 10 minutes and the express surcharge is ¥1430. Shinkansen do the journey in 42 minutes, cost ¥3570 and leave Tokyo station every 20 minutes.

Trains also service Odawara from Shinjuku station on the private Odakyū line. Quickest and most comfortable is the Romance Car, which takes one hour 25 minutes, costs ¥1780 and leaves every half hour. There's also an express service, taking one hour 35 minutes, which at ¥990 is by far the cheapest way of reaching Odawara.

At Odawara, it is possible to change to the Hakone-Tōzan line, which takes you to Gōra. Alternatively, if you are already on the Odakyū line, you can continue on to Hakone-Yumoto and change to the Hakone-Tōzan line there simply by walking across the platform. The latter is the most sensible course of action.

For those coming from or continuing on to the Kansai region, Kodama shinkansen run between Odawara and Shin-Osaka station. The journey takes three hours 20 minutes, costs ¥11,380 (you can use your Japan Rail Pass) and runs every 20 minutes.

Bus

The Odakyū express bus service has the advantage of running directly into the Hakone region, to Lake Ashino-ko and to

Hakone-machi for ¥1830. The disadvantage is that the bus trip is much less interesting than the combination of Romance Car, toy train (Hakone-Tōzan line), funicular, cablecar (ropeway) and ferry. Buses run from the west exit of Shinjuku station 11 times daily and take around two hours.

GETTING AROUND

Train

The Odakyū line offers a Hakone furii pasu (Hakone free pass), which costs ¥4850 in Shinjuku or ¥3500 in Odawara (which is the place to buy it if you are travelling on a JR Rail Pass) and allows you to use any mode of transport within the Hakone region for four days. The fare between Shinjuku and Hakone-Yumoto is also included in the pass, although you will have to pay a ¥620 surcharge if you want to take the Romance Car. This is a good deal for a Hakone circuit, as the pass will save you at least ¥1000 even on a one-day visit to the region.

You can get to Gōra from Odawara or Hakone-Yumoto stations on the Hakone-Tōzan line (literally the 'Hakone climb mountain line'). The ride itself is very enjoyable, involving several switchbacks in a small train that heaves and puffs against the steep gradient. The journey takes around an hour from Odawara (¥520) or 40 minutes from Hakone-Yumoto (¥340).

Bus

The Hakone-Tōzan bus company and Izu Hakone bus company service the Hakone area, and between them they manage to link up most of the sights. If you finish up in Hakone-machi, Hakone-Tōzan buses run between here and Odawara for ¥1000.

Ferry

Ferry services crisscross Lake Ashino-ko, running between Togendai, Hakone-machi and Moto-Hakone for ¥950 every 30 minutes or so. The new 'Pirate Ship' has to be seen to be believed – tourist kitsch at its worst, but fun all the same.

Mt Fuji Area 富士

Curiously, in a country where people have had such an impact on the landscape, Japan's most familiar symbol is a natural one. The perfectly symmetrical cone of Mt Fuji is the most instantly recognisable symbol of the country; combine it with a shinkansen hurtling past and you have the essential picture-postcard Japan cliché. Apart from the mountain itself, the Mt Fuji area also has a series of attractive lakes around its northern side.

MT FUJI 富士山

Japan's highest mountain stands 3776 metres high, and when it's capped with snow in winter, it's a picture-postcard perfect volcanic cone. Fuji-san, as it's known in Japanese (*san* is the Chinese reading of the ideograph for 'mountain'), last blew its top in 1707, when streets in Tokyo were covered in volcanic ash. On an exceptionally clear day, you can see Mt Fuji from Tokyo, 100 km away, but for much of the year you'd be pushed to see it from 100 metres away. Despite those wonderful postcard views, Mt Fuji is a notoriously reclusive mountain, often hidden by cloud. The views are usually best in winter and early spring, when a snow cap adds to the spectacle.

Information

Climbing Mt Fuji and *Mt Fuji & Fuji Five Lakes* brochures are available from the TIC and provide exhaustive detail on transport to the mountain and how to climb it, complete with climbing schedules worked out to the minute. There is a tourist information office in front of the Kawaguchi-ko station.

Mt Fuji Views

You can get a classic view of Mt Fuji from the shinkansen as it passes the city of Fuji. There are also good views from the Hakone area and from the Nagao Pass on the road from Hakone to Gotemba. The road that encircles the mountain offers good views, particularly near Yamanaka-ko and Sai-ko lakes.

Climbing Mt Fuji

Officially the climbing season on Fuji is July and August, and the Japanese, who love to do things 'right', pack in during those busy months. The climbing may be just as good either side of the official season but transport services to and from the mountain are less frequent then and many of the mountain huts are closed. You can actually climb Mt Fuji at any time of year, but a mid-winter ascent is strictly for experienced mountaineers.

Although everybody – from small children to grandparents – makes the ascent in season, this is a real mountain and not to be trifled with. It's just high enough for altitude sickness symptoms to be experienced, and as on any mountain, the weather on Mt Fuji can be viciously changeable. On the summit it can quickly go from clear but cold to cloudy, wet, windy, freezing cold and not just miserable but downright dangerous. Don't climb Mt Fuji without adequate clothing for cold and wet weather: even on a good day at the height of summer, the temperature on top is likely to be close to freezing.

The mountain is divided into 10 'stations' from base to summit but these days most climbers start from one of the four fifth stations, which you can reach by road. From the end of the road, it takes about 4½ hours to climb the mountain and about 2½ hours to descend. Once you're on the top, it takes about an hour to make a circuit of the crater. The Mt Fuji Weather Station on the southwestern edge of the crater is on the actual summit of the mountain.

You want to reach the top at dawn – both to see the *goraiko* (sunrise) and because early morning is the time when the mountain is least likely to be shrouded in cloud. Sometimes it takes an hour or two to burn the morning mist off, however. To time your arrival for dawn you can either start up in the afternoon, stay overnight in a mountain hut and continue early in the morning, or climb the whole way at night. You do not want to

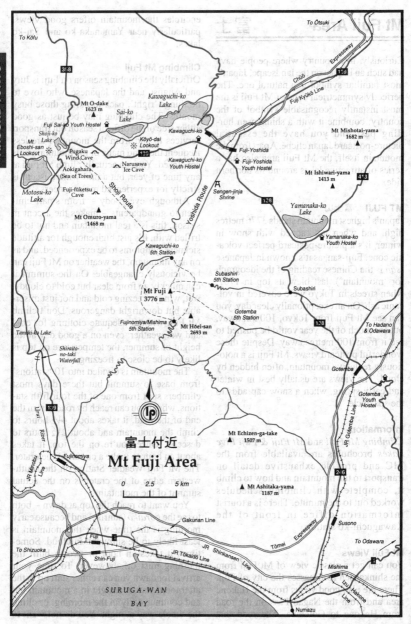

富士付近
Mt Fuji Area

0   2.5   5 km

Climbing Mt Fuji

I'd started out on a hot August night; at 10 pm the temperature had been around 27°C (80°F) but by 4 am it was below freezing and the wind was whistling past at what felt like hurricane speed. With a surprising number of other *gaijin* and a huge number of Japanese, I'd reached the top of Mt Fuji.

Climbing Fuji-san is definitely not heroic: in the two month 'season' as many as 180,000 people get to the top – 3000-odd every night. Nor is it that much fun – it's a bit of a dusty slog and when you get to the top it's so cold and windy that your main thought is about heading down again. But, with Fuji, the climb and the views aren't really what you do it for. To Japanese Fuji climbers, it's something of a pilgrimage; to gaijin, it's another opportunity to grapple with something uniquely Japanese.

Like many other climbers, I made my Fuji climb overnight. Although seeing the sunrise from mountaintops is a 'must do' in many places, on Fuji it is almost imperative that you arrive at dawn, as this is the one time of day when you have a good (but not guaranteed) chance of a clear view: most of the time, the notoriously shy mountain is discreetly covered by a mantle of cloud.

So at 9.30 pm I got off the bus at the Kawaguchi-ko Fifth Station, which is where the road ends and you have to start walking. I'd bought some supplies (a litre of 'Pocari Sweat' and a packet of biscuits) at a Seven-11 in the town of Kawaguchi-ko, and wearing a shirt and a coat, I was all set. The night was clear but dark, and I was glad I'd got some new batteries for my torch before I'd left Tokyo.

My experience of climbing holy mountains is that you always get to the top too early: you work up a real sweat on the climb, and then you freeze waiting for dawn. So I hung around for a while before starting out. Surprisingly, about half my fellow passengers on the bus had been gaijin, most of them a group of Americans planning on converting the Japanese to Mormonism!

By the time I reached a marker at 2390 metres I'd already stopped to unzip the lining from my coat, but on the rest of the climb to the top I put on more and more clothes.

Despite the daily hordes climbing the mountain, I still managed to lose the path occasionally, but by 11 pm I was past 2700 metres and thinking it was time to slow down even more if I wanted to avoid arriving too early. By midnight I was approaching 3000 metres – virtually halfway – and at this rate I was going to be at the top by 2.30 am, just about in line with the four hours 35 minutes it was supposed to take, according to the tourist office leaflet! In Japan, even mountain climbing is scheduled to the minute.

It was also getting much cooler. First I added a T-shirt under my shirt, then a hat on my head, then gloves. Next I zipped the jacket lining back in place, and finally, I added a sweater to the ensemble. Although I'd started on my own, some of the other faces I met at rest stops were becoming familiar by this point, and I'd fallen in with two Canadians and a Frenchman.

Huts are scattered up the mountainside, but their proprietors have been fairly cavalier about matching huts with stations: some stations have a number of huts, while others have none. The proprietors are very jealous of their facilities, and prominent signs in English as well as Japanese announce that even if it is pouring with rain, you can stay outside if you aren't willing to fork over the overnight fee. Fortunately, at 1.30 am we were virtually swept into one hut, probably in anticipation of the numerous bowls of *rāmen* (noodles) we would order. We hung out in this comfortable 3400 metre hideaway until after 3 am, when we calculated a final hour and a bit of a push would get us to the top just before the 4.30 am sunrise.

We made it, and looking back from the top, we suddenly saw hordes of climbers heading up towards us. It was no great surprise to find a souvenir shop (there is absolutely no place in Japan that tourists might get to where a souvenir shop is not already waiting for them). The sun took an interminable time to rise, but eventually it poked its head through the clouds, after which most climbers headed straight back down. I spent an hour walking around the crater rim but I wasn't sorry to wave Fuji-san goodbye. The Japanese say you're wise to climb Fuji, but a fool to climb it twice. I've no intention of being a fool.

Tony Wheeler

arrive on the top too long before dawn, as it's likely to be very cold and windy, and if you've worked up a sweat during the climb, you'll be very uncomfortable.

Although nearly all climbers start from the fifth stations, it is possible to climb all the way up from a lower level. These low-level trails are now mainly used as short hiking routes around the base of the mountain, but gluttons for punishment could climb all the way on the Yoshida Route from Fuji-Yoshida or on the Shoji Route from near Lake Shoji-ko. There are alternative sand trails on the Kawaguchi-ko (Yoshida), Subashiri and Gotemba routes which you can descend very rapidly by running and *sunabashiri* (sliding), pausing from time to time to get the sand out of your shoes.

Fifth Stations There are four 'fifth stations' around Fuji, and it's quite feasible to climb from one and descend to another. On the northern side of Fuji is the Kawaguchi-ko Fifth Station, at 2305 metres, which is reached from the town of Kawaguchi-ko. This station is particularly popular with climbers starting from Tokyo. The Yoshida route, which starts much lower down, close to the town of Fuji-Yoshida, is the same as the Kawaguchi-ko route for much of the way.

The Subashiri Fifth Station is at 1980 metres, and the route from there meets the Kawaguchi-ko one just after the eighth station. The Gotemba Fifth Station is reached from the town of Gotemba and, at 1440 metres, is much lower than the other fifth stations. From the Gotemba station it takes seven to eight hours to reach the top, as opposed to the 4½ to five hours it takes on the other routes. The Fujinomiya or Mishima Fifth Station, at 2380 metres, is convenient for climbers coming from Nagoya, Kyoto, Osaka and western Japan. It meets the Gotemba route right at the top.

Equipment Make sure you have plenty of clothing suitable for cold and wet weather, including a hat and gloves. Bring drinking water and some snack food. If you're going to climb at night, bring a torch (flashlight). Even at night it would be difficult to get seriously lost, as the trails are very clear, but it's easy to put a foot wrong in the dark.

Mountain Huts There are 'lodges' dotted up the mountainside but they're expensive – ¥4000 for a mattress on the floor squeezed between countless other climbers – and you

don't get much opportunity to sleep anyway, as you have to be up well before dawn to start the final slog to the top. No matter how miserable the night might be, don't plan to shelter or rest in the huts without paying. The huts also prepare simple meals for their guests and for passing climbers. Camping on the mountain is not permitted.

Getting There & Away
See the following Fuji Five Lakes and Gotemba sections for transport details to Kawaguchi-ko and Gotemba, the popular arrival points for Tokyo Fuji climbers. Travellers intending to head west from the Fuji area towards Nagoya, Osaka and Kyoto can take a bus from Kawaguchi-ko or Gotemba to Mishima on the shinkansen line.

Kawaguchi-ko Route From Kawaguchi-ko, there are bus services up to the fifth station from April to mid-November. The schedule varies considerably during that period. The trip takes 55 minutes and costs ¥1610. During the peak climbing season there are buses until quite late in the evening – ideal for climbers intending to make an overnight ascent. Taxis also operate from the railway station to the fifth station for around ¥7210 plus tolls – not much different from the bus fare when divided among four people.

There are also direct buses from the Shinjuku bus terminal to the Kawaguchi-ko Fifth Station. These take 2½ hours and cost ¥2160. This is by far the fastest and cheapest way of getting from Tokyo to the fifth station. If you take two trains and a bus, the same trip can cost nearly ¥6000.

Subashiri Route From Subashiri, buses take 55 minutes and cost ¥1040 to the Subashiri Fifth Station. They start from or finish at the Gotemba station.

Gotemba Route From Gotemba, buses to the Gotemba Fifth Station operate four to six times daily, but only during the climbing season. The 45 minute trip costs ¥950.

Fujinomiya or Mishima Route The southern route up the mountain is most popular with climbers from western Japan approaching the mountain by shinkansen. There are bus services from the Shin-Fuji (¥2380) and Mishima railway stations (¥2300) to the fifth station, taking just over two hours. The Shin-Fuji bus goes by the Fujinomiya station, taking 1½ hours and costing ¥2000.

FUJI FIVE LAKES 富士五湖

The five lakes arched around the northern side of Mt Fuji are major attractions for Tokyo day-trippers, offering water sports and some good views of Mt Fuji. Yamanaka-ko is the largest of the lakes, but it doesn't offer much in the way of attractions – unless you count an enormous swan-shaped hovercraft that does 30 minute circuits of the lake for ¥900.

On Lake Kawaguchi-ko there is a town of the same name which, like Gotemba, is a popular departure point for climbing Mt Fuji. North of the station, on the lower eastern edge of the lake is a cablecar (ropeway) up to a **Fuji viewing platform** at 1104 metres. It costs ¥340 one way, ¥620 return. Motor boat hire (¥7000 for 20 minutes!) and cruise boats leave from lower eastern end of the lake, directly north of the station. Other sights in Kawaguchi are a couple of small museums and an overpriced art museum (¥800).

At Fuji-Yoshida, around 1½ km south of the station, is **Sengen-jinja Shrine**, which dates from 1615 (although this area is thought to have been the site of a shrine as early as 788 AD) and is dedicated to the kami of the mountain. In the days when climbing Mt Fuji was more of a pilgrimage and less of a tourist event, a visit to this shrine was a necessary preliminary to the ascent. The entrance street to the shrine still has some Edo-era pilgrims' inns. Until the Meiji Restoration, women were only allowed to climb Fuji once every 60 years, as the mountain kami was female and would have been jealous of other women.

Fuji-Yoshida also has a futuristic theme park in **Fuji Highland**. It's a kilometre west of the station, but this place even has its own station *(hairando eki)*, so you could head over by train if you wanted to check it out. The park features a giant roller-coaster ride with double loops, caves and top speeds of 90 km/h. Another favourite is Zola, which the Japanese call a 'shooting coaster' – if you like hurtling through darkness while firing a laser gun at things this will be just your ticket. The park is open daily from 9 am to 5.30 pm, except Tuesday; entry is ¥1700.

The area around the smaller Lake Sai-ko is less developed than the areas around the larger lakes. There are good views of Mt Fuji from the western end of the lake and from the Kōyō-dai lookout near the main road. Close to the road are the **Narusawa Ice Cave** and the **Fugaku Wind Cave**, both formed by lava flows from a prehistoric eruption of Mt Fuji. There's a bus stop at both caves, or you can walk from one to the other in about 20 minutes. The **Fuji-fūketsu Cave**, further to the south, is often floored with ice.

The views of Mt Fuji from further west are not so impressive, but tiny **Lake Shoji-ko** is said to be the prettiest of the Fuji Five Lakes. Continue to Mt Eboshi-san, a one to 1½ hour climb from the road to a lookout over what the Japanese call the **Sea of Trees** to Mt Fuji. Next is Lake Motosu-ko, the deepest of the lakes, while further to the south is the wide and attractive drop of the **Shiraito-no-taki Waterfall**.

Organised Tours

In good weather, the Fuji area might be one of the few occasions in Japan that it is worth taking a tour bus. Two tour buses set off from Mishima station daily at 9.40 and 10.15 am. The first takes 8½ hours and visits Gotemba, Lake Yamanaka-ko, a Fuji fifth station, the Naruwasu ice cave, Shin-Fuji and then heads back to Mishima. It costs ¥6390. The second tour has a similar, though slightly shortened, agenda and costs ¥4940.

Places to Stay

There are three youth hostels in the Fuji area: the *Marimo (Yamanaka-ko)* (☎ 0555-62-4210), *Kawaguchi-ko* (☎ 0555-72-1431) and *Fuji*

Sai-ko (☎ 0555-82-2616). The first two cost ¥2500 a night, while the Sai-ko is ¥2300 or ¥2450, depending on the season. The Marimo is the trickiest to find as it's around 300 metres off the main road that circles the lake, somewhere on its south-west rim. The Kawaguchi-ko is about 500 metres south-east of Kawaguchi station. The Sai-ko is on the south-eastern end of the lake of the same name, on the road that circles the lake. It conveniently has its own bus stop *(yūsu hosteru mae)*, and buses from Kawaguchi station take around 35 minutes (ask for Saiko Minshuku). The *Fuji-Yoshida Youth Hostel* (☎ 0555-22-0533) in the town of the same name is ¥2100.

There are numerous hotels, ryokan, minshuku and pensions around the Fuji Five Lakes, particularly at Kawaguchi-ko. The tourist information office at the Kawaguchi-ko station can make reservations. The Japanese Inn Group is represented by the *Hotel Ashiwada* (☎ 0555-82-2321), at the western end of Lake Kawaguchi-ko. Rooms are ¥6500 per person or ¥7000 with attached bathrooms. The map included in the Japanese Inn Group for this particular hotel is so vague (upside down for a start) that the hotel doesn't deserve to be found by anyone.

Getting There & Away

Fuji-Yoshida and Kawaguchi-ko are the two main travel centres in the Fuji Five Lakes area. Buses operate directly to Kawaguchi-ko from the Shinjuku bus terminal in the Yasuda Seimei 2nd building, beside the main Shinjuku station in Tokyo. The trip takes one hour 45 minutes and there are departures up to 16 times daily at the height of the Fuji climbing season. The fare is ¥1520. Some buses continue to Yamanaka-ko and Motosu-ko lakes.

You can also get to the lakes by train, although it takes longer and costs more. JR Chūō line trains go from Shinjuku to Ōtsuki (one hour and ¥2890 by limited express; ¥1260 by local train or futsū). At Ōtsuki you cross the platform to the Fuji Kyūkō line local train which takes another hour at a cost of ¥1110 to Kawaguchi-ko. The train actu-

ally goes to Fuji-Yoshida first (¥990, 50 minutes), then reverses out for the final short distance to Kawaguchi-ko. On Sunday and holidays from March to November there is a direct local train from Shinjuku which takes two to 2½ hours and costs ¥2330.

From Fuji-Yoshida and Kawaguchi-ko, buses run north to Kōfu, from where you can continue north-west to Matsumoto.

Getting Around

There's a comprehensive bus network in the area, including regular buses from Fuji-Yoshida station that pass by the four smaller lakes and around the mountain to Fujinomiya on the south-western side. From Kawaguchi-ko, there are nine to 11 buses daily making the two hour trip to Mishima on the shinkansen line.

GOTEMBA 御殿場

Gotemba is an unexciting town – just an arrival point for Mt Fuji climbers. Views of the mountain from the Gotemba area are unexceptional until you get north near Lake Yamanaka-ko. It may not be the kind of sight that most travellers will be interested in, but not far from Gotemba is the **Fuji Safari Park**. If the idea of elephants, tigers and lions cavorting in the shadow of Fuji-san piques your curiosity, Fuji Kyūkō buses leave from Gotemba station for the park, take 40 minutes and cost ¥700. There are also buses from Mishima station for ¥980. The park is open daily from 9 am to 4.30 pm and entry is ¥2500.

Places to Stay

The *Gotemba Youth Hostel* (☎ 0550-82-3045) is ¥2300 a night. It's a good three km east of the railway station. If you catch a bus, you need to get off at the *tōzan kampu iriguchi* (the Tōzan camping ground entrance). Follow the road (in the direction of the mountains) and take the third right. The hostel is around 300 metres down on the left.

Getting There & Away

From Shinjuku station in Tokyo, the Odakyū

line runs four express services daily to Gotemba; they take one hour 36 minutes and cost ¥2420. There's one JR Tōkaidō line service daily direct from Tokyo station to Gotemba, which would be good for Japan Rail Pass holders. It takes 2½ hours and costs ¥1850.

Getting Around

Buses run 15 to 17 times daily between Gotemba and Kawaguchi-ko, from where services continue west via the lakes. Services from Kawaguchi-ko to Mishima, which is on the shinkansen line, operate via Gotemba.

North of Tokyo
東京の北部

North of Tokyo are the Saitama and Tochigi prefectures, which include numerous places of interest, such as the old town of Kawagoe, the Chichibu-Tama National Park and the temple and shrine centre of Nikkō, one of Japan's major tourist attractions.

KAWAGOE 川越

The principal attraction in Kawagoe (population 294,000) is a number of **clay-walled stores** (*kurazukuri*), many of them have been designated as 'national treasures'. The clay-walled buildings, built by wealthy merchants, are significant mainly for the fact that they are fireproof. Most of them were built after a disastrous fire swept the town in 1893, and several now operate as museums. The buildings are strung out along one street, and once you've walked up it, there's very little else to do.

Getting There & Away

The Seibu Shinjuku line from Tokyo's Seibu Shinjuku station operates to the conveniently located Hon-Kawagoe station. From the station, take the middle of the three roads that radiate out – most of the old buildings are along this road or on side streets off it. The Tōbu Tojo line also runs to Kawagoe but the

station is inconveniently situated a ¥1000-taxi-ride from the old part of town.

CHICHIBU-TAMA NATIONAL PARK
秩父多摩国立公園

Hikes in the Chichibu-Tama National Park are more likely to appeal to Tokyo residents than to short-term visitors to Japan. The park is divided into the Chichibu and the Oku-Tama regions – these are connected by a hiking trail that goes via Mt Mitsumine.

Chichibu Region 秩父

The Chichibu region has two walks and the famous **Chichibu-jinja Shrine**, which is near Chichibu and Seibu Chichibu stations. The shorter walk starts from Yokoze station, one stop before Seibu Chichibu station. You can walk the trail as a circuit via Mt Buko-san or turn off to the Urayama-guchi station via the **Hashidate Stalactite Cavern**.

From Urayama-guchi station it is possible to continue to Mitsumine-guchi station, the starting point for the longer walk which connects Chichibu with Oku-Tama. There is reasonably priced accommodation available on the trail at the *Mountain Hut Kumitori San-sō*. The trail goes past **Mitsumine-jinja Shrine**, about a 40 minute walk from the station. The shrine was founded some 2000 years ago and has long been favoured as a mountain retreat by members of the Tendai Buddhist sect. The walk takes about eight hours to Kamozawa, from where buses run to Oku-Tama station.

Nagatoro Near Nagatoro station there is a rock garden and the **Nagatoro Synthetic Museum**, which houses a collection of rocks and fossils. From mid-March to mid-November, boats leave from Oyahana-bashi Bridge, 700 metres from Kami-Nagatoro station, to shoot the **Arakawa River rapids**. The trip lasts 50 minutes and costs ¥2600.

Places to Stay *Chichibu Youth Hostel* (☎ 0494-55-0056) is about a 15 minute walk from Lake Chichibu-ko bus stop and costs ¥1840 or ¥1990 depending on the time of

秩父多摩国立公園
Chichibu-Tama National Park

Not to scale

PLACES TO STAY

1 Chichibu Nagatoro
   SL Hotel
   秩父長瀞SLホテル
2 Nishichu Ryokan
   西中旅館

3 Chikujukan Ryokan
   ちくじゅかん旅館
4 Chichibu Youth Hostel
   秩父ユースホステル
5 Mountain Hut
   Kumotori San-sō
   山小屋雲取山荘

6 People's Lodge
   Hatonosu-sō
   国民宿舎鳩ノ巣荘
7 Mitake Youth Hostel
   ユースホステル御嶽
8 Komadori San-sō
   駒鳥山荘

year. The *Chichibu Nagatoro SL Hotel* (☎ 0494-66-3011) is good value. It charges ¥4100 per person, including two meals, and is close to the Mt Hodo-san cablecar and to Nagatoro station.

Not far from Chichibu station is the *Nishichu Ryokan* (☎ 0494-22-1350), costing ¥3500 per person or ¥5000 with two meals. Down the road towards Chichibu station is the more expensive *Chikujukan Ryokan*

(☎ 0494-22-1230), which costs ¥12,500 per person with two meals.

Getting There & Away The cheapest and quickest way of getting to the Chichibu area is via the Seibu Ikebukuro line from Seibu Ikebukuro station. The limited express Red Arrow service goes direct to Seibu Chichibu station in 1½ hours for ¥1270. Alternatively, JR trains depart from Ueno station to Kumagaya station on the Takasaki line (one hour 10 minutes, ¥1090), where you will have to change to the Chichibu Tetsudō line to continue to Chichibu station (45 minutes, ¥760). All things considered, unless you are travelling on a JR rail pass, it would be cheaper to set off from Ikebukuro even if you are based in Ueno.

Oku-Tama Region 奥多摩
Like the Chichibu region, Oku-Tama has some splendid mountain scenery and a few good hiking trails.

Ōme Railway Park Steam locomotives are on display, and there is a memorial hall housing model trains in the railway museum, about a 15 minute walk from Ōme station. It is open from 9 am to 4.30 pm, but closed on Monday; admission is ¥100.

Mitake From Mitake station it is possible to walk via Mt Sogaku-yama and Mt Takamizu-yama back to Kori station. A shorter (one hour) walk to Sawai station takes in Mitake Gorge and the Gyokudo Art Museum.

Mt Mitake-san Buses run from Mitake station to the Mt Mitake-san cablecar terminus, from where a cablecar (¥500) takes you close to the summit. About 30 minutes on foot from the cablecar terminus on Mt Mitake-san is **Mitake-jinja Shrine**, said to date back some 1200 years.

Other Attractions Buses run from Oku-Tama station to the nearby artificial Lake Oku-Tama-ko. The **Nippara Stalactite**

Cavern is 40 minutes by bus from Oku-Tama station.

Places to Stay The *Mitake Youth Hostel* (☎ 0428-78-8501) is very close to the Mt Mitake-san cablecar terminus and charges ¥2300 per person. About a 15 minute walk from the cablecar terminus in the opposite direction from the youth hostel is the *Komadori San-sō* (☎ 0428-78-8472), which costs ¥5000 per person or ¥7500 with meals. The *People's Lodge Hatonosu-sō* (☎ 0428-85-2340) charges ¥3000 per person or ¥5100 with two meals, and is a short walk from Hatonosu station.

A good alternative if you're in the area for the hiking is the *Mountain Hut Kumitori San-sō* (☎ 0485-23-3311), with a per person charge of ¥4500 with meals – there are cheaper rates without them, but in this neck of the woods you will need to bring your own food or forage for berries. The hut is a few hours up the trail that connects the Chichibu and Oku-Tama regions.

Getting There & Away You can get to Oku-Tama by taking the JR Chūō line from Shinjuku station to Tachikawa station (¥430) and changing there to the JR Ōme line, which will take you on to Oku-Tama station (¥590). The first leg takes 40 minutes, the second 70 minutes.

NIKKŌ 日光
Nikkō is not only one of the most popular day trips from Tokyo, it is also one of Japan's major tourist attractions due to its splendid shrines and temples. Visitors must contend with the jostling crowds found at any of Japan's big-name attractions, but on weekdays they rarely reach the Yamanote-line proportions that you find in Kyoto. All things considered, it's worth trying to slot Nikkō into even the most whirlwind tour of Japan.

History
Nikkō's history as a sacred site stretches back to the middle of the 8th century, when a Buddhist priest established a hermitage there. For many years it was a famous train-

AROUND TOKYO

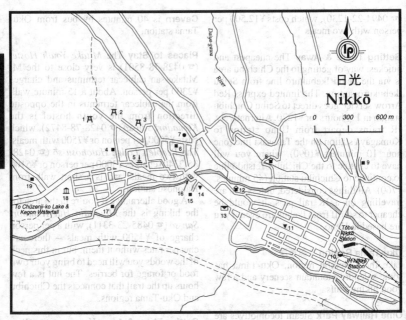

日光
Nikkō

0   300   600 m

To Chūzenji-ko Lake &
Kegon Waterfall

Daiya-gawa River

Tōbu
Nikkō
Station

JR Nikkō
Station

PLACES TO STAY

4   Nikkō Pension
    Green Age Inn
    日光ペンション
    グリーンエイジINN
6   Hotel Seikoen
    ホテル清晃苑
8   Nikkō Youth Hostel
    日光ユースホステル
9   Logette St Bois
    ロジェチサンボワ
12 Daiyagawa
    Youth Hostel
    日光大谷川ユースホステル
15 Nikkō Kanaya Hotel
    日光金谷ホテル
17 Turtle Inn Nikkō
    タートルイン日光

19 Nikkō Green Hotel
    日光グリーンホテル

PLACES TO EAT

11 Yōrō-no-taki
    Restaurant
    養老の滝
14 Yakitori Restaurant
    焼き鳥屋

OTHER

1   Taiyūin-byō Shrine
    家光大猷院廟
2   Futara-san-jinja Shrine
    二荒山神社

3   Tōshō-gū Shrine
    東照宮
5   Rinnō-ji Temple
    輪王寺
7   Nikkō Tōkan-sō
    Ryokan
    日光東観荘
10 Bus Terminal
    バスターミナル
13 Post Office
    郵便局
16 Shin-kyō Bridge
    神橋
18 Nikkō Museum
    日光博物館

ing centre for Buddhist monks. By the 17th century the area's significance had seriously declined. That is, until it was chosen as the site for the mausoleum of Tokugawa Ieyasu, the warlord who took control of all Japan and established the shogunate which ruled for 250 years until the Meiji Restoration ended the feudal era.

Tokugawa Ieyasu was laid to rest among Nikkō's towering cedars in 1617, but it was his grandson Tokugawa Iemitsu who commenced work in 1634 on the shrine that can be seen today. The original Tōshō-gū Shrine was completely rebuilt using a huge army of some 15,000 artisans from all over Japan.

The work on the shrine and mausoleum took two years to complete and the results continue to receive mixed reviews. In contrast with the minimalism, that is generally considered the essence of Japanese art, every available nook and cranny of Ieyasu's shrine and mausoleum is crowded with detail. Animals, mythical and otherwise, jostle for your attention from among the glimmering gold-leaf and red lacquerwork. The walls are decorated with intricate patterning, coloured relief carvings and paintings of, among other things, flowers, dancing girls, mythical beasts and Chinese sages. The overall effect is more Chinese than Japanese. Tōshō-gū Shrine, despite continuing accusations of vulgarity and that it goes against the grain of all that is quintessentially Japanese, remains a grand experience.

It is worth bearing in mind that what you see in Nikkō was constructed as a memorial to a warlord who devoted his life to conquering Japan. Tokugawa Ieyasu was a man of considerable determination and was not above sacrificing a few scruples in order to achieve his aims. He is attributed with having had his wife and eldest son executed because, at a certain point, it was politically expedient for him to do so in order to ingratiate himself with other feudal powers. More than anything else, the grandeur of Nikkō is intended to inspire awe; it is a display of wealth and power by a family that for nearly three centuries was the supreme arbiter of power in Japan.

Information & Orientation

First stop in Nikkō should be the Kyōdo Centre, with its excellent tourist information office (☎ 0288-53-3795), on the road up to Tōshō-gū Shrine. The office has a wealth of useful pamphlets and maps. There is another tourist information office in the Tōbu-Nikkō station.

It's a straight 30 minute walk uphill from the JR and Tōbu stations to the shrine area – fine if you're not lugging a heavy pack. The alternative is to take bus No 1, 2, 3 or 4 up to the Shin-kyō bus stop for ¥180.

Those interested in hiking in the Nikkō area should pick up a copy of *Nikko-Yumoto-Chuzenji Area Hiking Guide*. It costs ¥150, is available from some of the pensions in the area as well as at the information counters in Nikkō, and has maps and information on local flora and fauna.

Tickets Ticketing arrangements for the sights in Nikkō have become a bit more organised in recent years, though there's still room for confusion. Basically it works like this: Futara-san-jinja Shrine costs ¥200; Rinnō-ji Temple costs ¥710; and Tōshō-gū Shrine costs ¥1030. In the interests of saving a few yen, the best idea is to buy a 'two-shrines-one-temple' ticket *(nisha-ichiji-kōtsū-baikan-ken)* for ¥750. This covers all three of the above sights, with the one exception that it doesn't include entry to the Nemuri-Neko (sleeping cat) in Tōshō-gū Shrine, a sight that will set you back ¥430. Even if you do visit the Nemuri-Neko, though, you are still making a considerable saving than buying each of the tickets separately.

Shin-kyō Bridge 神橋

Taking the road from the Tōbu Nikkō line station to the Tōshō-gū Shrine area, the first point of interest is the Shin-kyō Bridge. The story goes that the monk, Shōdō Shōnin, who first established a hermitage in Nikkō in 782, was carried across the river at this point on the backs of two huge serpents. Today's bridge is a 1907 reconstruction of the mid-17th century original. It costs ¥300 to cross the bridge on foot.

Rinnō-ji Temple 輪王寺

The original temple on this site was founded 1200 years ago by Shōdō Shōnin, and it remains a temple of the Buddhist Tendai sect. The Sambutsu-dō (Three Buddha Hall) has huge gold-lacquered images, the most impressive of which is the *senjū* (1000 armed

Kannon). The central image is Amida Nyorai, flanked by *batō* (a horse-headed Kannon), whose special domain is the animal kingdom.

The Hōmutsu-den (Treasure Hall), also on the temple grounds, has a collection of treasures associated with the temple, but admission (¥250) is not included in the two-shrines-one-temple ticket.

Tōshō-gū Shrine　東照宮

A huge stone torii marks the entrance to Tōshō-gū Shrine, while to the left is a five storeyed pagoda, originally dating from 1650 but reconstructed in 1818. The building is remarkable for its lack of foundations: the interior is said to contain a long suspended pole that swings like a pendulum in order to restore equilibrium in the event of an earthquake.

The true entrance to the shrine is through the torii at the Omote-mon Gate, protected on either side by Deva kings. Through the entrance to the right and directly ahead are the **Sanjinko** (Three Sacred Storehouses). Look out for the upper storey of the last of the storehouses, on which you can see imaginative relief carvings of elephants by an artist who had never seen the real thing. To the left of the entrance is the **Shinkyūsha** (Sacred Stable), a suitably plain building housing a carved white horse. The stable's only adornment is an allegorical series of **relief carvings** depicting the life-cycle of the monkey. They include the famous 'hear no evil, see no evil, speak no evil' threesome who have become emblematic of Nikkō.

Just beyond the stable is a granite water font at which, in accordance with Shintō practice, worshippers cleanse themselves by washing their hands and rinsing their mouths. Next to the gate is a **sacred library** containing 7000 Buddhist scrolls and books; it is not open to the public.

Pass through another torii, climb another flight of stairs, and on the left and right are a drum tower and a belfry. To the left of the drum tower is the **Honji-dō Hall**, which has a huge ceiling painting of a dragon in flight known as the Roaring Dragon. There's a

queue to stand beneath the dragon and clap hands – do so and the dragon will respond with a perfunctory roar.

Next comes the **Yōmei-mon Gate**, which bustles with a teeming multitude of Chinese sages, children, dragons and other mythical creatures. Worrying that its perfection might arouse envy in the gods, the final supporting pillar on the left-hand side was placed upside down as a deliberate error.

Through the Yōmei-mon Gate and to the right is the Nemuri-neko (Sleeping Cat). The Sakashita-mon Gate here opens onto a path that climbs up through towering cedars to **Ieyasu's tomb**, a relatively simple affair. If you are using the two-shrines-one-temple ticket it will cost an extra ¥430 to see the cat and the tomb. To the left of the Yōmei-mon Gate is the **Jinyōsha**, a storage depot for Nikkō's mikoshi (portable shrines), which come into action during the May and October festivals. The **Honden** (Main Hall) and the **Haiden** (Hall of Worship) can also be seen in the enclosure.

Futara-san-jinja Shrine　二荒山神社

Shōdō Shōnin founded this shrine. It's dedicated to the mountain Nantai, to the mountain's consort Nyotai and to their mountainous progeny Tarō. It's a bit of a repeat perforance of the Tōshō-gū Shrine on a smaller scale, but worth a visit all the same.

Taiyūin-byō Shrine　大猷院廟

The Taiyūin-byō enshrines Ieyasu's grandson Iemitsu (1604-51) and is very much a smaller version of Tōshō-gū Shrine. The smaller size gives it a less extravagant air and it has been suggested that it is more aesthetically worthy than its larger neighbour – this is best left for the experts to quibble over. Many of the features to be seen in the Tōshō-gū are replicated on a smaller scale: the storehouses, drum tower and Chinese gate for example. The shrine also has a wonderful setting in a quiet grove of cryptomeria.

Lake Chūzenji-ko　中禅寺湖

On a quiet day it's a 50 minute bus trip up to Lake Chūzenji-ko along a winding road

東照宮

Tōshō-gū Shrine (Nikkō)

Not to Scale

Ieyasu's Tomb

Honden (Main Hall)

Haiden (Hall of Worship)

Jinyōsha

Yōmei-mon Gate

Honji-dō Hall (Roaring Dragon Ceiling)

Steps

Sakashitamon Gate

Nemuri-neko (Sleeping Cat)

Sanjinko (Three Sacred Storehouses)

Granite Water Font

Walking Paths

Shinnyūsha (Sacred Stable) (Three Monkeys)

Omote-mon Gate

Main Approach (Ōmotesar-dō)

Five Storeyed Pagoda

Car Park

complete with hairpin bends. There's some beautiful scenery, including the 97 metre **Kegon Waterfall** and the lake, but don't cut short a visit to the shrine area just so as to fit in a visit to the lake. The waterfall features an elevator (¥520 return) down to a platform where you can observe the full force of the plunging water. Also worth a visit is the third of the **Futara-san-jinja shrines**, complementing the ones in Tōshō-gū Shrine area and on Mt Nantai.

For good views of the lake and Kegon Waterfall, Akechidaira bus stop (the last stop but one) has a cablecar (ropeway) up to a

viewing platform for ¥600 return. From this point, it is a pleasant 1½ km walk up to the lake area. The lakeside **Chūzenji Onsen** has another cablecar heading up to the Chanokidaira viewing platform. The six minute ride costs ¥440.

As you might expect, Lake Chūzenji-ko has the usual flotilla of cruise boats all clamouring to part you from your yen. It's worth the money in many ways. The lake, which reaches a depth of 161 metres, is a deep blue in colour, and this along with the mountainous backdrop make for a pleasant cruise. An alternative to the cruises are the rowboats that are available for ¥1000 per hour.

Just by the cablecar is the hi-tech **Nikkō Nature Museum**. It has displays and films on the Nikkō region's flora and fauna, though none of it will be particularly accessible to those who don't understand Japanese. Entry is ¥800 and it's open from 9 am to 5 pm, closed the fourth Wednesday of every month.

Buses run from Tōbu Nikkō station to Chūzenji Onsen at 10 to 20 minute intervals from 6.20 am to 7.30 pm and cost ¥1050.

The wonderful little *Guide in Nikkō* points out that the Kegon Waterfall is 'greatly noted for committing suicide', and that nowadays 'more than one hundred people are coming here every year, intending to commit suicide'. The Kegon Waterfall can claim something of a historical pedigree as a destination for those set on doing away with themselves, as it was first used for this purpose by a Tokyo high school student 'who jumped down from the top for the first time' in 1893. It's actually not clear whether he committed suicide from being 'too much absorbed in philosophy', as the guidebook suggests, or whether he was suffering from a chronic complex about his height. His final words read: 'How long the time is! How spacious the heaven and earth! I am going to measure the greatness with my body, which is only five feet tall'.

Kinugawa Onsen & Nikkō Edo Village
鬼怒川温泉・日光江戸村

South-east of Nikkō on the Tōbu Kinugawa line are Kinugawa Onsen and the Nikkō Edo Village. Kinugawa itself is an onsen town with little of interest for the foreign visitor, but the Edo Village may be of interest to some travellers, especially those with children. It's an imaginative recreation of an Edo period village, with samurai quarters, a 'temple of hell', ninja displays and even a 'ninja maze' – visitors to the latter are given the opportunity to test their 'ninja skills' and are recommended to 'call out for help' if they can't get out. Mid '93 saw the opening of the 'Great Red Light Theatre', in which ninja skills are not needed for a good time.

The village is open daily from 9 am to 4 pm (3 pm from December to March) and entry is ¥2500. There are shuttle buses

running from Kinugawa Onsen station for ¥410 to the village.

Festivals

The Gohan Shiki on 2 April is a rice-harvesting festival held at Rinnō-ji Temple in which men (in days past, samurai lords) are forced to eat great quantities of rice in a tribute to the bounty supplied by the gods. Sacred dances are also performed by the priests as an accompaniment to the ceremonial pig-out.

On 16 and 17 April, the Yayoi Matsuri – a procession of portable shrines – is held at Futāra-san-jinja Shrine.

The Tōshō-gū Shrine Grand Festival on 17 and 18 May is Nikkō's most important annual festival. It features horseback archery and a 1000-strong costumed re-enactment of the delivery of Ieyasu's remains to Nikkō.

The Tōshō-gū Shrine Autumn Festival is held on 17 October and needs only the equestrian archery to be an autumnal repeat of the performance in May.

Places to Stay

Nikkō's importance as a tourist attraction makes it one of the few places in Japan, apart from Tokyo and Kyoto, where travellers on a budget actually get some choice as to where to stay. If you're willing to spend ¥1500 or so over the standard youth hostel rates, there are some very good accommodation options close to the central shrine and temple area.

Some travellers opt to stay up in the Lake Chūzenji-ko area, and come away very pleased with the experience. Room rates tend to be higher up around the lake, but it's a beautiful area to be situated in.

Youth Hostels The *Nikkō Daiyagawa Youth Hostel* (☎ 0288-54-1974) is the more popular of the town's two hostels. It costs ¥2300 per night and is behind the post office on a side street that runs parallel to the main street. A 10 minute walk away, on the other side of the Daiya-gawa River, is the *Nikkō Youth Hostel* (☎ 0288-54-1013), where beds are ¥2450 or ¥2650, depending on the time of year.

Pensions & Minshuku Nikkō's many pensions offer very reasonable rates and clean, comfortable surroundings. Per person costs are around ¥5000 but in many cases you can reduce expenses by sharing rooms with other travellers. Nikkō is very popular so book ahead. All of the following pensions have someone who can answer your questions in English.

One of the more popular pensions in Nikkō is the *Turtle Inn Nikkō* (☎ 0288-53-3168), with rooms from ¥3900 per person without bath and from ¥5500 with. Meals are also available at ¥1000 for breakfast and ¥2000 for dinner. It's by the river, beyond the shrine area. It's quite a walk from the stations, and you'd be better off taking a bus to the *sōgō-kaikan-mae* bus stop, backtracking from there around 50 metres to the fork in the road and following the river for around five minutes. Also popular is the *Logette St Bois* (☎ 0288-53-3399), which has both Western and Japanese-style singles/doubles starting at ¥5500/11,000 for rooms without baths. It's across the river, about a km north of the station.

Other pensions with similar rates include *Humpty Dumpty* (☎ 0288-53-4365). Very close to Humpty Dumpty are a couple of inexpensive minshuku: *Narusawa Lodge* (☎ 0288-54-1630) and *Ringo-no-Ie* (☎ 0288-53-0131); both have rates of ¥4500 per person or ¥6000 with two meals.

There's not a great deal in the way of affordable accommodation over by Lake Chūzenji-ko, but one place that might just squeeze into this category is the *Chūzenji Pension* (☎ 0288-55-0720). This delightful little pension charges from ¥8800 per person with two meals. To find it from the Nikkō-Chūzenji road, turn left at the lakeside, cross the bridge and look out for the pension on the left about 100 metres down the road. It's set back a little. If you hit the Sazanami coffeeshop, you've gone too far.

Hotels Not far from the Shin-kyō Bridge is the *Nikkō Kanaya Hotel* (☎ 0288-54-0001), an expensive hotel that combines classiness with a great location. Plan on spending around ¥20,000 per person (including two meals), and bear in mind that at least part of your bill includes the hotel's historical associations: it's been running since the 1870s. During peak holiday periods – Golden Week and the summer holidays for example – room prices soar to nearly double the normal rates. There are a few places over in the vicinity of the shrine that are less likely to burn a hole in your wallet. The *Nikkō Green Hotel* (☎ 0288-54-1756) has rooms from ¥6200 to ¥12,000, and meals are also available. The *Hotel Seikoen* (☎ 0288-53-5555) is a bit more expensive, with rates ranging from ¥13,000 with two meals.

Finally, two places that take full honours in the ambience category are the wonderfully named *Nikkō Pension Green Age Inn* (☎ 0288-53-3636), which looks like a Tudor mansion, and the *Nikkō Tōkan-sō* (☎ 0288-54-0611). Rates at the former start at ¥9000 with two meals, while at the Tōkan-sō the same deal will set you back ¥13,000.

Up in Chūzenji, the *Lakeside Hotel* (☎ 0288-55-0321) is a very classy place that gets good reports – and it would want to with the prices it charges. Prices start at around ¥12,000 per head; twins here range from ¥19,000 to ¥23,000. The *Sachi-no-Ko Hotel* (☎ 0288-55-0223) is a nifty little white structure, all post-modern angles, and it charges from ¥12,000 to ¥18,000 with two meals.

Places to Eat
Many travellers staying in Nikkō prefer to eat at their hostel or pension, but there are also a number of places on the main road between the stations and the shrine area. Across the road from the fire station is a branch of the robotayaki chain *Yōrō-no-Taki* – cheap beer and a good selection of snacks and meals. Further up, close to the Shin-kyō Bridge, is a great little yakitori bar – look for the entrance scrawled with English recommendations. It seems that countless travellers have been won over by the charm of the old lady who runs this place and the great food she prepares. There's an English menu, and meals start at an economical ¥300

– try the *yaki-udon*, a bargain at only ¥500. This place closes early – around 7 pm. In the shrine area itself there are a couple of shops selling tourist trinkets and quite reasonable food – they'll even provide an English menu if you look like you are having difficulties.

Next to the Tōbu Nikkō station is a tiny coffee and cheesecake shop, which is a good place to hang out while waiting for the next train.

For an up-market lunch or dinner, the restaurant at the *Nikkō Kanaya Hotel* is recommended both for its atmosphere and for its meals, which cost from ¥1500 to ¥3500.

Getting There & Away

The best way to visit Nikkō is via the Tōbu-Nikkō line from Asakusa station in Tokyo. The station, which is separate from Asakusa subway station, is in the basement of the Tōbu Department Store, but is well signposted and easy to find from the subway. Limited express trains cost ¥2530 and take one hour 45 minutes. These trains require a reservation (on a quiet day you'll probably be able to organise this before boarding the train) and run every 30 minutes or so from 7.30 to 10 am; after 10 am they run hourly. Rapid trains require no reservation, take 15 minutes longer than the limited express and cost ¥1270. They run once an hour from 6.20 am to 4.30 pm. Tickets for these are purchased with the automatic vending machine.

As usual, travelling by JR trains works out to be more time consuming, more expensive and only really of interest to those on a Japan Rail Pass. The quickest way to do it would be to take the shinkansen from Ueno to Utsunomiya (¥4510, 50 minutes) and change there for an ordinary train (no other options) for the 45 minute, ¥720 journey to Nikkō. The trains from Utsunomiya to Nikkō leave on average once every half hour. Not all Nikkō line trains run the full distance to Nikkō – you may have to get off at an intermediate station and wait for the next Nikkō-bound train.

A limited express service taking 1½ hours (¥3690) and an ordinary service taking one

hour 50 minutes (¥1850) also run between Ueno and Utsunomiya.

Nikkō-Kinugawa Free Pass These 'free passes', not 'free' at all, are becoming more and more popular. Unlike the Hakone pass, the Nikkō pass doesn't pay if you are only taking a one-day trip into the area. If you are going to spend a few days in the area, exploring Chūzenji and other nearby sights, it would probably be a worthwhile investment. The ticket costs ¥5490 and is available from Tōbu railways in Asakusa. It includes transport from Asakusa to Nikkō (but not the express surcharge) and all bus costs between Nikkō and Chūzenji, Yumoto Onsen, Kunigawa, Kirifuri Plateau and Lake Ikariko.

MASHIKO 益子

Mashiko is a centre for country-style pottery, with about 50 potters, some of whom you can see working at their kilns. The town achieved fame when the potter Hamada Shōji settled there and, from 1930, produced his Mashiko pottery. Today he is designated as a 'living national treasure' and has been joined in Mashiko by a legion of other potters. The noted English potter Bernard Leach also worked there for several years.

Mashiko's kilns are spread out over quite a wide area and getting to see them requires a lot of footwork. Pick up the *Tourist Map of Mashiko* from the tourist information counter at Utsunomiya station (see the following Getting There & Away section) or from TIC in Tokyo before you go. **Hamada House** and **Tsukamoto kiln** are recommended, but bear in mind that there are some 115 kilns in the area, and you could literally spend weeks seeking them out. Hamada House has both wood-fire kilns and modern automated contraptions, and visitors can play around with the machinery themselves.

Getting There & Away

It is possible to combine Mashiko with a visit to Nikkō if you set off from Tokyo very early and use the JR route. See the Nikkō Getting There & Away section for travel details to

Colourful Characters, Yoyogi-kōen Park, Tokyo (CT)

A	B	C
D	E	F
G	H	I

Statues & Sculptures
A: Daibatsu (MM)
B: Wooden Buddha image (CT)
C: Bronze statue detail (CT)
D: Statue with saxophone (TW)

E: Statue, Kumamoto (TW)
F: Modern sculpture (CT)
G: Ninna-ji Temple (TW)
H: Jizō (CT)
I: Meditating Buddha (CT)

Utsunomiya. From Utsunomiya, buses run regularly during the day to Mashiko, taking one hour and costing ¥1100 one way. Ask at tourist information counter outside Utsunomiya for instructions for getting to the bus stop and bus times. This office also has tourist maps of Mashiko.

East of Tokyo
東京の東部

East and south-east of Tokyo much of Chiba-ken is suburbs or market gardens. There are few compelling reasons to visit the area. However, a large majority of visitors to Japan will arrive or depart from Narita Airport, and if you have a few hours to kill at the airport, there are some points of interest in the town of Narita.

NARITA 成田
If you're not going to the airport, the only real reason to go to Narita is to visit **Narita-san Shinshō-ji Temple**. While the temple was founded some 1000 years ago, the main hall is a 1968 reconstruction. The temple itself remains an important centre of the Shingon sect of Buddhism and attracts as many as 10 million visitors a year. Taxis and buses run to the temple from the JR and Keisei Narita stations.

If you've got to kill time in the airport area, there's also the **Museum of Aeronautical Sciences** and the **Chiba Prefectural Botanical Garden**, both right beside the airport. There's a brochure *For Passengers Transiting at Narita* about the airport vicinity attractions, and tours are operated from the airport.

Festivals
The main festivals centred around Narita-san Shinshō-ji Temple are Setsubun, on 3 or 4 February, and the Year End Festival, on 25 December. Things get very hectic at the temple on both these occasions and a high tolerance level for crowds is a must.

Places to Stay
If you have to stay at Narita – perhaps because you are catching an early flight – there are several accommodation options in the vicinity, though none in the real budget category.

Not far from Narita-san Shinshō-ji Temple is the *Kirinoya Business Hotel* (☎ 0476-22-0724) with singles/doubles for ¥4630/8300. To get there, leave the temple by the front gate and turn left; the hotel is about five minutes down the road on the left.

Not much further from the temple is the *Business Hotel Teradai* (☎ 0476-23-0744), with singles from ¥4000 to ¥4500 and doubles from ¥7000 to ¥8000. To get there, continue walking straight ahead from the Kirinoya Ryokan and cross the bridge and an intersection; the hotel is on your right.

Being so close to the airport, Narita also has a representative selection of up-market hotels such as the *ANA* (☎ 0476-33-1311), the *Holiday Inn* (☎ 0476-32-1234), and the *Tokyū Inn* (☎ 0476-33-0109). All these places have rates of ¥20,000 and up.

Getting There & Away
From Narita Airport there are buses going into the city of Narita every 20 minutes or so from bus gate No 5. The trip takes 25 minutes and costs ¥370. The easiest way to get to Narita is via the Keisei line, which starts in Ueno. For information on using this service, see the Tokyo Getting There & Away section.

BOSO-HANTŌ PENINSULA 房総半島
The Boso-hantō Peninsula's attractions are almost certainly only for long-term residents, although the displays by **women divers** at Shira-hama and Onjuku beaches may be of interest to foreign visitors. The women dive to the sea bottom in search of edible goodies such as shellfish and seaweed.

The peninsula's main attraction is its beaches, most of which are easily accessible by train. The tourist literature promises a number of unusual activities at the beaches, including 'houseback rising', 'summering', 'sand bath' and 'dragnet fishing'.

Places to Stay

The Boso-hantō Peninsula is a very popular resort with the Japanese, so there are many minshuku and youth hostels. Youth hostels include the *Kujūkurihama Youth Hostel* (☎ 0475-33-2254) (¥2200) at Awa-Amatsu, the *Tateyama Youth Hostel* (☎ 0470-28-0073) (¥1530) at Cape Nojima-zaki and the *Hiranoya Youth Hostel* (☎ 0439-87-2030) (¥1900) at Kisarazu.

Getting There & Away

Train The Boso-hantō Peninsula can be reached on either the Sotobō line or the Uchibō line, both running from Tokyo station. From Tokyo to Ohara Beach costs ¥3050 and takes one hour 25 minutes via the Sotobō line. A cheaper option is to go to Goi on the Uchibō line, which costs ¥970 and takes one hour five minutes. Onward travel from this point will be expensive.

Ferry An unusual approach to the peninsula is to take a ferry from Kawasaki's Ukushima Port. One leaves every 45 minutes, taking 70 minutes to Kisarazu and costing ¥1030.

Getting Around

The transport network around the peninsula is very good. Most of the beaches are serviced by JR trains; there is also a private line that cuts across the peninsula from Goi to Ohara, as well as a good network of local buses.

South-West of Tokyo
東京の南西部

South-west of Tokyo are the cities of Kawasaki and Yokohama, which have virtually merged with the capital to create one immense urban corridor. Beyond this huge city is the fascinating old town of Kamakura and the Miura-hantō Peninsula.

KAWASAKI　川崎

Kawasaki (population one million) is a fairly uninteresting industrial city. However, it does have the colourful Horinouchi entertainment district, an interesting enclave of love hotels and the Nihon Minka-en Garden.

Nihon Minka-en Garden　日本民家園

The Nihon Minka-en Garden is an open-air museum with 22 traditional Japanese buildings collected from the surrounding country and reassembled on one sight to give visitors a glimpse of the way of life of an older Japan.

Most of the structures are farmhouses, although there are also a Shintō shrine and a kabuki stage. The oldest of the buildings dates back to 1688.

The garden is open Tuesday to Sunday from 9.30 am to 4 pm, except over New Year, when it is closed. Admission is ¥300. The garden is about a 10 minute walk from Mukōgaoka-yuen station on the Odakyū line.

Festivals

Kawasaki hosts the famous Jibeta Matsuri. Processions of costumed people carry wooden phalluses to celebrate the vanquishing of a sharp-toothed demon with an appetite for male sexual organs. The demon had taken up residence in a fair maiden and had already emasculated two bridegrooms before a local blacksmith came up with the ingenious idea of deflowering the maiden with an iron phallus. This scheme can't have been particularly appealing to the maiden but defeat of the demon gave rise to much celebration and an annual re-enactment of the forging of the metal phallus.

The festival takes place in the late afternoon of 15 April, commencing with a procession, followed by a re-enactment of the forging and rounded off with a banquet. The action takes place close to Kawasaki Taishi station.

Getting There & Away

Take the Odakyū line from Tokyo's Shinjuku station to Mukōgaoka-yuen station. From the southern exit, look for the start of the monorail and follow the line until it bears left, when you must bear right. The Nihon

Minka-en is up the hill and on the right-hand side, opposite a parking lot.

YOKOHAMA 横浜

The site of present-day Yokohama (population three million) was little more than mud flats 150 years ago, but with the end of Japan's long isolation from the outside world, the city was the closest port to Tokyo open to foreign traders. Since then Yokohama has grown to be the second largest city in Japan, sprawling outwards from its original small-town beginnings at the water's edge and forming a vast continuous conurbation with Tokyo.

For the most part, Yokohama is like a dull extension of Tokyo, lacking the bright lights, historical sites and vibrant, international-city atmosphere of the capital. Still, it remains a fairly popular get-away for Tokyoites mainly for its international restaurants (notably in the sizeable Chinatown area) and its laidback harbour atmosphere. Until recently, Yokohama's attractions could be summed up in the harbour, a lively Chinatown and the Sankei-en Garden. In the last few years, however, a massive development project in the Sakuragi-chō area has raised the 70 storeyed Landmark Tower (with the fastest lift in the world...like...*wow!*), a large amusement park (with the biggest ferris wheel in the world), a marine museum and various other attractions. Also worth a look is the elegant 860 metre Yokohama Bay Bridge, south of the Yamashita Park area

Information & Orientation

The Yokohama International Tourist Association (☎ 045-641-4759) and the Kanagawa Prefectural Tourist Association (☎ 045-681-0007) are both on the ground floor of the same building that houses the Silk Museum. Both offices have at least one staff member who speaks English and useful brochures, including the *Yokohama Paradise Tourist Map*, which is probably the most useful of the lot. It's also worth picking up a copy of *Sightseeing in Kanagawa – handbook for visitors*, a useful pocket-size book that covers all the sights in Kanagawa-ken

(notably Hakone, Kamakura and Yokohama). Some of the information in the latter booklet is inaccurate or out of date, but for the most part it can be relied on.

Arriving in Yokohama can be slightly confusing. Most of the sights are quite a way from Yokohama station, and it makes more sense to go to Sakuragi-chō or Kannai stations. From Sakuragi-chō station the Minato Mirai 21 development area, with the enormous Landmark Tower, are very close; it is then possible to take a boring 25 minute walk over to Yamashita Park. Kannai station is closer to Yamashita Park, the harbour area, Chinatown and a number of other sights such as the Silk Museum and the Foreigners' Cemetery.

Sankei-en Garden 三渓園

The Sankei-en Garden is not particularly old, having been established in 1906 by a Yokohama silk merchant, but it is beautifully landscaped and features a three storeyed pagoda that is 500 years old. The pagoda, along with an old villa and farmhouses, was moved to the garden and reconstructed there.

There are separate ¥300 admission charges to the outer and inner gardens. The inner one is a fine example of traditional Japanese garden landscaping. The garden is open daily from 9 am to 4.30 pm. The No 8 bus, from the road running parallel to the harbour behind the Marine Tower, operates with less than commendable frequency. If one does happen along, ask for the Sankei-en-mae bus stop. Alternatively, locals recommend taking the train to Negishi station and changing here for a city bus bound for Sakuragi-chō (Nos 54, 58, 99, 101 or 108). Get off at the Honmoku stop, and from here it's an easy five-minute walk to the south entrance of the park.

Minato Mirai 21 みなとみらい

This new development (the '21' stands for '21st century' – of course) just north of Sakuragi-chō station is another of those Japanese excursions into the metropolis-of-the-future theme. The whole thing won't be completed until the year 2000, but there's a

AROUND TOKYO

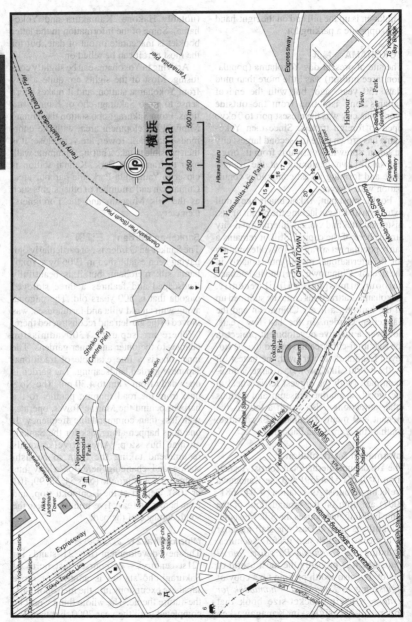

横浜

Yokohama

0   250   500 m

PLACES TO STAY

2 Yokohama Royal Parkhotel
   横浜ロイヤルパークホテル
4 Kanagawa Youth Hostel
   神奈川ユースホステル
14 Hotel Yokohama
   ザ ホテル横浜
15 Hotel New Grand
   ホテルニューグランド
16 Star Hotel Yokohama
   スターホテル横浜
19 Astor Hotel
   アスターホテル

PLACES TO EAT

8 Pizzeria Suginoki
   杉の木
10 San Marina Restaurant
   サンマリナ
11 Parkside Gourmet Plaza
   パークサイドグルメプラザ
12 Hachisch Restaurant

13 Hof Brau Restaurant

OTHER

1 Yokohama Museum of Art
   横浜美術館
3 Yokohama Maritime Museum
   日本丸メモリアルパーク
5 Iseyama Shrine
   伊勢山皇大神宮
6 Nogeyama Park & Zoo
   野毛山動物園
7 JTB

9 Silk Museum
   シルク博物館
17 Marine Tower
   マリンタワー
18 Doll Museum
   横浜人形の家
20 International Seamen's Hall
   横浜海員会館

using this service to get to the 70th floor viewing platform.

Other attractions near the Landmark Tower include the **Yokohama Maritime Museum** and *Nippon Maru* sailing ship, both open from 10 am to 5 pm and closed on Monday; ¥300 entry. The Yokohama Museum of Art is devoted to modern art and costs ¥500. It's open 10 am to 5 pm, closed on Thursday. **Yokohama Cosmo World**, the amusement park with the world's largest ferris wheel (it also functions as a clock, which probably makes it the world's largest clock as well) is free to enter, but rides range from ¥100 to ¥600. It's open from 1 to 9 pm and closed on Monday. Some visitors might also want to check out the Minato Mirai 21 **Yokohama Pavilion**, a five-part complex that is fairly dull for the most part, but has a miniature version of 21st century Yokohama called Yokohama Gulliver Land. The complex is open from 9 am to 5 pm and is free.

Yokohama Bay Bridge 横浜ベイブリッジ
Well, yes, it's just a bridge, but it is a particularly impressive one. There's actually a walkway on the bridge – Sky Walk – which leads you to a viewing area out over the bay. During the summer the Sky Walk is open from 9 am to 9 pm, while during winter (November to March), it's open from 9 am to 6 pm. Entry is ¥600.

Marine Tower マリンタワー
Viewing towers seem to be a popular feature of almost every major Japanese city. Basically the idea is to queue for 15 minutes, fork out a wad of cash (in this case ¥700), catch a crowded lift commanded by a chirping hostess in a silly hat to the top floor of a high tower (in this case 106 metres) and then peer through wafting smog at the sea on one side and an apparently infinite expanse of concrete on the other. The tower (don't be put off by my cynicism) is open from 10 am to 9 pm.

Chinatown 中華街
About a five to 10 minute walk from the Marine Tower and the harbour is Chinatown,

fair bit to be ogled at already. One of the highlights is the new **Landmark Tower** (tallest building in Japan), with its super fast lift. On an incidental note, the record for the world's fastest lift was previously held by the Sunshine 60 building in Ikebukuro. The Landmark Tower's lift hits a top speed of 45 km/h, which is nine km/h faster than its Ikebukuro rival. You can be sure that you will pay through the nose for the privilege of or *chukagai*, as it is known in Japanese. Even if you've seen plenty of Chinatowns before, the gaudy colours and lively street scenes in this area make a welcome change from the rest of Yokohama. Be warned: this place gets packed on the weekends.

Other Attractions

The **Silk Museum** takes you on a tour of the world of silk and silk production with characteristic Japanese thoroughness. Entry is ¥300 and it's open 9 am to 4.30 pm, closed on Monday. About five minutes from the Silk Museum is the harbourfront **Yamashita-kōen Park**. Moored in the harbour next to the park is the *Hikawa Maru*, a passenger liner that is open to the public. The boat is open from 9.30 am to 10 pm and has a beer garden in the summer months. Admission is ¥800.

Three companies operate harbour cruises from the pier next to the *Hikawa Maru*: Marine Rouge; Marine Shuttle; and Sea Shuttle. Of these the Sea Shuttle is the cheapest with quick runs around the harbour area for ¥500. The Marine Shuttle and Marine Rouge have longer 90 minute 'cruises' for ¥2000 and ¥2500 respectively. Close to the Marine Tower is the Yokohama Doll Museum, which has 1200 dolls from around the world. Admission is ¥300 and it is open from 10 am to 5 pm daily. Just beyond the expressway is the **Harbour View Park** and the nearby **Foreigner's Cemetery**, containing the graves of more than 4000 foreigners.

Places to Stay

The *Kanagawa Youth Hostel* (☎ 045-241-6503) costs ¥2300. From Sakuragi-chō station, exit on the opposite side to the harbour, turn right and follow the road alongside the railway tracks (look for the graffiti on the right). Cross the main road, turn left into the steep street with a bridge and a cobble-stoned section and the youth hostel is up the road on the right.

Most other accommodation in Yokohama is aimed at business travellers or Japanese tourists, and prices can be very high indeed. The *Yokohama International Seamen's Hall*

(☎ 045-681-2141) is a reasonably inexpensive place that is well located; singles/doubles cost ¥5300/11,100. Walk away from the harbour along the road beside the Marine Tower to the third intersection and turn right. Very close by is the *Astor Hotel* (☎ 045-651-0141), which also has reasonable rates. Singles/doubles are ¥6200/12,500. The hotel is recognisable by the big dragon painted onto the side of the building.

There are a number of hotels along the harbour front facing Yamashita-kōen Park, but all of them are very expensive. The *Hotel Yokohama* (☎ 045-662-1321) is an up-market option by the waterfront, with rates starting at ¥19,500. The *Hotel New Grand* (☎ 045-681-1841) has rates from ¥13,000. The *Star Hotel Yokohama* (☎ 045-651-3111) has singles/doubles ranging from ¥9500/15,000.

Places to Eat

Yokohama's chief gourmet attraction is its Chinatown, the only one within easy striking distance of Tokyo. Due to this there are lengthy queues for meals most days of the week, though the weekends naturally see the area at its crowded worst. The best bet is to take a stroll, check out the plastic food displays and weigh the goods against the length of the queue. Places with a good reputation include *Keika Hanten* (☎ 045-641-0051), *Kato Hanten* (☎ 045-641-0335), *Manchin Rō* (☎ 045-681-4004), *Kashō Rō* (☎ 045-681-6781) and, for dim sum (expensive), *Manchin Rō Tenshin Po* (045-651-4004), though this is just a sampling of the wide variety available.

Yokohama's reputation as a good place to eat does not rest on its Chinese food alone. In the area of the Silk Museum, a couple of good places for lunch are *San Marina*, an inexpensive Italian seafood place, and *Pizzaria Suginoki*, a place whose window-display plastic pizzas look as if they should have been changed back during the Meiji Restoration. Also close by is the uninspiring but reliable *Parkside Gourmet Plaza*, a basement huddle of restaurants and coffee shops.

Finally, behind the Yokahama Hotel, those

with some money to spend on a more up-market meal might want to check out *Hachisch* (☎ 045-664-0844), a cosy little French restaurant with a great name and prices from around ¥2000. Also close by is *Hof Brau* (☎ 045-662-1106), a restaurant that has been running for some 35 years and whose menu features a combination of Russian, Hungarian and Italian cuisines at very reasonable prices (without drinks ¥1000-1500 per head).

Getting There & Away
Train There are numerous trains from Tokyo, the cheapest being the Tōkyū Tōhoko line from Shibuya station to Sakuragi-chō station for ¥260. The trip takes 44 minutes by ordinary train and 35 minutes by limited express (same price). Trains also stop at Yokohama station on the way to Sakuragi-chō station.

The Keihin Tōhoku line from Tokyo station is a bit more convenient, going through to Kannai station, but at ¥610 it's considerably more expensive. To Yokohama station is ¥440. The Tōkaidō line from Tokyo or Shinagawa stations also runs to Yokohama station, taking around 30 minutes and costing ¥470.

It is convenient to continue on to Kamakura on the Yokosuka line from Yokohama station. The Tōkaidō shinkansen stops at Shin-Yokohama station, a fair way to the north-west of town, on its way into the Kansai region. If you enter or leave Yokohama this way, Shin-Yokohama station is connected with Yokohama, Sakuragi-chō and Kannai stations via the Yokohama line.

Ferry There are two international ferry services running between Yokohama and Shanghai. The Japan-China International Ferry (☎ 3294-3351) has once monthly sailings with prices ranging from ¥29,900 for tatami-style 2nd class to ¥56,600 for a private room. The Shanghai Ferry (☎ 5202-5781) has sailings approximately every three weeks and has prices ranging from ¥30,000 for a 2nd class B ticket.

Getting Around
To/From the Airport Buses run from Narita and Haneda airports to the Yokohama City Air Terminal (YCAT) (☎ 045-459-4800) by the eastern exit of Yokohama station. It's only 30 minutes to Haneda but it takes 2½ hours and costs ¥3200 to get to Narita.

KAMAKURA   鎌倉
Kamakura may not have as much to offer historically as Kyoto or Nara but a wealth of notable Buddhist temples and Shintō shrines make this one of Tokyo's most interesting day trips. The town has some relaxing walks and a peacefulness that is hard to come by in, say, Kyoto – tour-group city.

History
Kamakura may be a picturesque backwater today, but from 1192 to 1333 it was the Japanese capital. In the 10th century the power of the emperor was restricted to ceremonial and cultural affairs, and real power had for some time rested in the hands of the Fujiwara clan. As the power of the Fujiwaras declined, other clans began jostling for their bit of the action, until the Taira, led by Taira Kiyomori, and the Minamoto, led by Minamoto Yoshitomo, commenced an all-out struggle for supreme power. The struggle culminated in a battle in 1159 that completely routed the Minamoto forces.

Although many executions followed, by chance Yoshitomo's third son's life was spared and the boy was sent to spend his days in an Izu-hantō Peninsula temple. As soon as the boy, Minamoto Yoritomo, was old enough, he began to gather support for a counterattack on his clan's old rivals. In 1180 he set up his base at Kamakura, an area that shared the advantages of being far from the debilitating influences of Kyoto court life, close to other clans loyal to the Minamoto and naturally easy to defend, being enclosed by the sea on one side and densely wooded hills on the others.

A series of victories over the Taira led to Minamoto Yoritomo being appointed shōgun of Japan in 1192 and governing the country from Kamakura. The lack of an heir

AROUND TOKYO

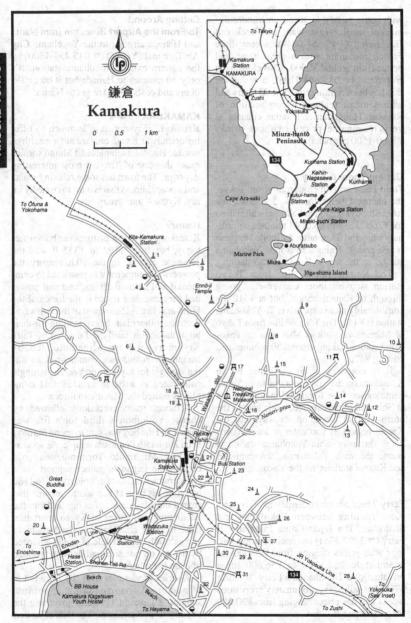

鎌倉

Kamakura

0   0.5   1 km

	TEMPLES & SHRINES			
1	Engaku-ji Temple 円覚寺	11	Kamakura-gū Shrine 鎌倉宮	22 Hongaku-ji Temple 本覚寺
2	Tōkei-ji Temple 東慶寺	12	Jomyo-ji Temple 浄明寺	23 Myohon-ji Temple 妙本寺
3	Meigetsu-in Temple 明月院	13	Hōkoku-ji Temple 報国寺	24 Anyo-in Temple 安養院
4	Jōchi-ji Temple 浄智寺	14	Sugimoto-dera Temple 杉本寺	25 Daiho-ji Temple 大宝寺
5	Zeniarai-benten Shrine 銭洗い弁天	15	Tomb of Minamoto Yoritomo 源頼朝の墓	26 Myoho-ji Temple 妙法寺
6	Kaizo-ji Temple 海蔵寺	16	Hokai-ji Temple 宝戒寺	27 Ankokuron-ji Temple 安国論寺
7	Kenchō-ji Temple 建長寺	17	Hachiman-gū Shrine 鶴岡八幡宮	28 Hossho-ji Temple 法性寺
8	Raigo-ji Temple 来迎寺	18	Eisho-ji Temple 英勝寺	29 Chosho-ji Temple 長勝寺
9	Kakuon-ji Temple 覚園寺	19	Jufuku-ji Temple 寿福寺	30 Myocho-ji Temple 妙長寺
10	Zuisen-ji Temple 瑞泉寺	20	Hase-dera Temple 長谷寺	31 Gosho-jinja Shrine 五所神社
		21	Daigyo-ji Temple 大巧寺	32 Kuhonu-ji Temple 九品寺

after Yoritomo's death, however, gave power to the Hōjos, the family of Yoritomo's wife.

The Hōjo clan ruled Japan from Kamakura for more than a century, until finally in 1333, weakened by the cost of maintaining defences against threats of attack from Kublai Khan in China, the Hōjo clan fell from power at the hands of the forces of Emperor Go-daigo. Though the restoration of imperial authority was somewhat illusory, real power reverting to another of Japan's clans, the capital nevertheless shifted back to Kyoto and Kamakura disappeared from the history books.

Orientation & Information

The sights in Kamakura are spread over a fairly wide area and, although most of them can be seen on foot, there are times when it is necessary to catch a bus. There's not much chance of getting lost, as the temples are well signposted in both English and Japanese. You can either start at Kamakura station and work your way around the area in a circle or start north of Kamakura at Kita-Kamakura station and visit the temples between there and Kamakura on foot. The latter route is

preferable, and the following itinerary moves south from Kita-Kamakura station.

The useful TIC booklet *Sightseeing in Kanagawa* covers Kamakura and other sights in the region. The Kamakura station information counter sells a great map which includes walking routes as well as opening hours and prices for the shrines and temples around Kamakura. If you arrive at Kita-Kamakura station, there are vendors as you exit the station selling very similar maps with points of interest marked in both English and Japanese.

Engaku-ji Temple 円覚寺

Engaku-ji Temple is on the left as you exit Kita-Kamakura station. It is one of the five main Rinzai Zen temples in Kamakura. Rinzai is distinguished from the other major school of Zen Buddhism in Japan, Sōtō, by its use among other things of riddles, stories concerning the lives of Zen masters and formal question-and-answer drills as aids to attaining enlightenment. Sōtō, on the other hand, relies more exclusively on meditation.

Engaku-ji Temple was founded in 1282, allegedly as a place where Zen monks might be able to pray for soldiers who had lost their lives defending Japan against the second of Kublai Khan's invasion attempts. Today the only real reminder of the temple's former magnificence and antiquity is the **San-mon Gate**, which is a 1780 reconstruction. At the top of the long flight of stairs through the gate is the **Engaku-ji bell**, cast in 1301 and the largest bell in Kamakura. The Main Hall inside the San-mon is quite a recent reconstruction, dating from the mid-60s.

The temple has a ¥200 entry fee and is open from 8 am to 5 pm from April to September and from 8 am to 4 pm during the rest of the year.

Tōkei-ji Temple 東慶寺

Tōkei-ji Temple, across the railway tracks from Engaku-ji Temple, is notable for its grounds as much as for the temple itself. On weekdays, when visitors are few, it can be a pleasantly relaxing place. Walk up to the cemetery and wander around.

Historically, the temple is famed as having served as a kind of women's refuge. Women could be officially recognised as divorced after three years as nuns in the temple grounds. Today no nuns live in the temple precincts; the grave of the last abbess can be found in the cemetery. The temple is open daily from 8.30 am to 5 pm and entry is ¥50.

Jōchi-ji Temple 浄智寺

A couple of minutes further on from Tōkei-ji Temple is Jōchi-ji Temple, another temple with pleasant grounds. Founded in 1283, this is considered one of Kamakura's five great Zen temples. It is open daily from 9 am to 4.30 pm, and admission is ¥100.

Kenchō-ji Temple 建長寺

Kenchō-ji Temple is about a 10 minute walk beyond Jōchi-ji Temple. It is on the left after you pass through a tunnel. This is not only Kamakura's most important Zen temple but something of a showcase generally. The grounds and the buildings are well maintained and still in use. The first of the main buildings you come to, the Buddha Hall, was moved to its present site and reassembled in

1647. The second building, the Hall of Law, is used for Zazen meditation. Further back is the Dragon King Hall, a Chinese-style building with a garden to its rear. The temple bell, the second largest in Kamakura, has been designated a 'national treasure'. The temple is open daily from 9 am to 4.30 pm and admission is ¥200.

Ennō-ji Temple 円応寺

Across the road from Kenchō-ji Temple is Ennō-ji Temple, distinguished primarily by its collection of statues depicting the judges of hell. The temple is open daily from 10 am to 4 pm.

Hachiman-gū Shrine 八幡宮

Further down the road, where it turns towards Kamakura station, is Hachiman-gū Shrine. The shrine was founded by Minamoto Yoriyoshi, of the same Minamoto clan that was later to rule Japan from Kamakura. There is some debate as to whether Hachiman, the deity to which the shrine is dedicated, has always been regarded as the god of war; his dedication may simply be a reflection of the fact that Hachiman is also the guardian deity of the Minamoto clan. Whatever the case, this Shintō shrine presents the visitor with a drastically different atmosphere to the repose of the Zen temples clustered around Kita-Kamakura station.

If you enter the shrine from the direction of Kita-Kamakura station, you are actually entering from the rear and not by the proper entrance gates. This is not a problem; after taking a look at the shrine, follow the stairs down to the square below the shrine. To the right is a gingko tree beneath which it is said that a famous political assassination was carried out in 1219, making the tree very old indeed.

At the foot of the stairs there is a dancing platform and the main avenue which runs to the entrance of the shrine. At the entrance on the left is an **arched bridge**, which in times past was designated for the passage of the shōgun and no-one else. The bridge is so steep that every crossing must have been quite a test of the shogunate's athletic prowess.

National Treasure Museum To the left of the dancing platform (assuming you're continuing to walk away from the shrine) is the Kokuhō-kan. This is one museum which is recommended, as it provides your only opportunity to see Kamakuran art, most of which is hidden away in the temples. The museum is open from 9 am to 4 pm, closed Monday, and admission is ¥150.

Kamakura Station Area   鎌倉駅周辺
It is possible to continue on to Kamakura station by exiting through the big torii gates at the entrance to Hachiman-gū Shrine and walking straight ahead down Wakamiya-dōri. The avenue has a green centre strip, complete with sakura trees and a pathway. Kamakura station is on the right-hand side, down the first main street you come to after the second torii gate, and is a good place to get some food before continuing.

Apart from Hachiman-gū Shrine, there are no sites of historic importance in the immediate vicinity of the station; most places require a short bus trip from one of the bus stops in front of the station.

Great Buddha   大仏
The Daibutsu (Great Buddha) was completed in 1252 and is Kamakura's most famous sight. Once housed in a huge hall, the statue today sits in the open, its home having been washed away by a tsunami in 1495. Cast in bronze and weighing close to 850 tonnes, the statue is 11.4 metres tall. Its construction is said to have been inspired by Yoritomo's visit to Nara (where there is another, even bigger Buddha statue) after the Minamoto clan's victory over the rival Taira clan. Even though Kamakura's Great Buddha doesn't quite match Nara's in stature, it is commonly agreed that it is artistically superior.

The Buddha itself is the Amida Buddha, worshipped by the followers of the Jodō and Shinshū sects of Japanese Buddhism. These

sects continue to attract followers, particularly from among ordinary people who find the monastic discipline and obscure rites of Zen inaccessible. The statue remains the figurehead of Japan's most popular Buddhist sects.

To get to the Great Buddha, take a bus from the Nos 2, 7 or 10 bus stops in front of Kamakura station and get off at the Daibutsu-mae bus stop. The Great Buddha can be seen daily from 7 am to 5.30 pm, and admission is ¥150.

Hase-dera Temple   長谷寺
If you walk back towards Kamakura station and turn right at the intersection where the bus goes left, this small street will take you to Hase-dera Temple, also known as Hase Kannon Temple. The pleasant grounds have a garden and an interesting collection of **statues of Jizō**, the patron saint of travellers and souls of departed children. Ranked like a small army of urchins, the statues are clothed to keep them warm by women who have lost children by abortion or miscarriage. The main point of interest in the grounds, however, is the Kannon statue.

Kannon, the goddess of mercy, is a Boddhisattva – a Buddha who has put off enlightenment in order to help others along the same path. This altruism has given Kannon a reputation for compassion and mercy, leading people to call on her for help in times of trouble. The nine metre wooden carved **jūichimen** (11 faced Kannon) here is believed to be very ancient, dating from the 8th century. The 11 faces are actually one major face and 10 minor faces, the latter representing 10 stages of enlightenment. However, in keeping with her reputation for mercy and compassion, it is also commonly believed that the 11 faces allow Kannon to cast an eye in every direction and maintain an unrelenting vigilance for those in need of her assistance.

From October to February, Hase-dera Temple is open from 7 am to 4.40 pm. During the rest of the year it closes at 5.40 pm. Admission is ¥200.

Buddhism in Kamakura
The Buddhism that established itself in Japan during the 6th century belonged to the Mahayana (Greater Vehicle) school. This school maintained that enlightenment, or release from the cycle of birth and death, was available not only to those special few with the ability to unswervingly follow Buddhist precepts (the eight-fold path) but to all sentient beings. This, it was claimed, had been disclosed by the Buddha (Gautama) himself in his last sermon, the *Lotus Sutra*.

It was not until some five centuries later, during the Kamakura period, that Buddhism spread to all of Japan. Initially the Kamakura period was marked by disillusionment with the institutions of Buddhism and the monastic orders, and a widespread belief that history had entered the Mappō (Later Age), a period of Buddhist decline, during which individuals would no longer be able to achieve enlightenment through their own efforts. This led to the flourishing of several alternatives to established Buddhist doctrine – notably Zen and the Pure Land school of Buddhism.

Adherents of the Pure Land school preached that in the Later Age salvation could only be achieved through devoting oneself to the transcendent Buddha Amida. Such, it was believed, was the infinite mercy of the Amida, that all who called on him sincerely would achieve salvation in the Pure Land after death. This denial of responsibility for one's own enlightenment was, in a sense, a 'soft option' and thus accounted for the sect's popularity among the lower orders of society who did not have the 'luxury' of devoting themselves to the rigours of pursuing personal enlightenment. This also contrasted with Zen, a Chinese import that strove to bring out the Buddhahood of the individual through meditative practice that sought out the empty centre of the self.

Zen, which literally means 'meditation', with its rigorous training and self-discipline, found considerable support among an ascendant warrior class and made a considerable contribution to the evolution of the samurai ethic. Doctrinal differences on the question of whether *satori* (enlightenment) could be attained suddenly or whether it was a gradual process accounted for Zen breaking into the Rinzai and Sōtō sects.

The contending schools of Pure Land and Zen, along with the views of charismatic leaders such as Nichiren, led to revitalisation of Buddhism within Japan during the Kamakura period. All the major Buddhist sects active in Japan today can trace their antecedents back to that period. ■

Other Shrines & Temples

If you're still in the mood for temple tramping, there are plenty more in and around Kamakura – somewhere in the vicinity of 70 temples and shrines.

From the Great Buddha it is best to return to Kamakura station by bus and take another bus out to the temples in the western part of town. These have the advantage of being even less popular with tourists than the temples in Kita-Kamakura; they may lack the grandeur of some of Kamakura's more famous temples, but they more than make up for this with their charm. There is also a delightfully restful village-like atmosphere in the town's outer fringes.

Egara Ten-jin Shrine This Shintō shrine would not be particularly noteworthy if it were not associated so closely with academic success. Students write their academic aspirations on *ema* (small wooden plaques), which are then hung to the right of the shrine.

In the grounds there's another ancient gingko tree said to be around 900 years old. Buses from stop No 6 in front of Kamakura station run out to Egara Ten-jin Shrine; get off at the Tenjin-mae bus stop.

Zuisen-ji Temple The grounds of this secluded Zen temple make for a pleasant stroll, and include Zen gardens laid out by the Musō Kokushi, the temple's founder. The temple is open daily from 9 am to 5 pm and has a ¥100 admission charge. It is possible to get there from Egara Ten-jin Shrine on foot in about 10 to 15 minutes; turn right where the bus turns left in front of the shrine, take the next left and keep following the road.

Sugimoto-dera Temple This interesting little temple, founded in 734 AD, is reputed to be the oldest in Kamakura. Ferocious temple guardians are poised on either side of the entrance, while the temple grounds and the thatch-roofed temple itself are littered with banners announcing *jūichimen Sugimoto Kannon* ('11 faced Kannon of Sugimoto') in Chinese characters. The temple houses three Kannon statues, though they are not in the same league as the famous statue at Hase-dera Temple.

The temple is open daily from 8.30 am to 4.30 pm and admission is ¥100. To get to the temple, take a bus from the No 5 stop in front of Kamakura station and get off at the Sugimoto Kannon bus stop.

Hōkoku-ji Temple Down the road (away from Kamakura station) from Sugimoto-dera Temple, on the right-hand side, is Hōkoku-ji Temple. This is a Rinzai Zen temple with quiet landscaped gardens where you can relax under a red parasol with a cup of Japanese tea. This is also one of the more active Zen temples in Kamakura, regularly holding Zazen classes for beginners. The temple is open from 9 am to 4.30 pm and entry is ¥100.

Festivals
Setsubun is the bean-throwing ceremony held throughout Japan on 3 or 4 February. The best celebrations in Kamakura are at Hachiman-gū Shrine.

The Kamakura Matsuri is a week of celebrations held from the second Sunday to the third Sunday in April. It includes a wide range of activities, most of which are centred around Hachiman-gū Shrine.

During the Bonbori Matsuri, held from 7 to 9 August, hundreds of lanterns are strung up around Hachiman-gū Shrine.

The Hachiman-gū Matsuri is held from 14 to 15 September. Festivities include a procession of mikoshi and, on the 16th, a display of horseback archery.

The Menkake-gyōretsu, on 18 September, is a masked procession held at Goryō-jinja Shrine.

Places to Stay
The *Kamakura Kagetsuen Youth Hostel* (☎ 0467-25-1238) has beds at ¥2500. You can walk to the hostel from Hase-dera

Temple by continuing to walk away from the Great Buddha along the road that runs in front of the temple. When you reach the T-junction, turn right and look for the hostel on the corner of the next road on the left. Hase station is also a five minute walk away in the direction of Hase-dera Temple.

Just around the corner from Kamakura station is the *Ryokan Ushio* (☎ 0467-22-7016), where rates start at ¥4500 per person. It's a little tricky to find. Take the busy shopping street that runs parallel to the train tracks next to the station (there's a torii gate at the entrance) and take the third left. About 20 metres down this road you should see a sign on the left pointing into an alley. The ryokan is at the bottom of the alley.

Further up this shopping street is the *City Pension Shangri La* (☎ 0467-25-6363), which has twins for ¥6000 and also has four person rooms available at economical rates. It's in a modern white building on the left side of the road as you walk up from the station.

Not far from the youth hostel is *BB House* (☎ 0467-25-5859), which provides accommodation for women only and costs ¥5000 per person, including breakfast. It's behind the Kamakura Hotel (you'll need to take one of the side streets next to the hotel to get to it).

Places to Eat
Around the square facing the station is a *Kentucky Fried Chicken* and a *Love Burger*, but for real food, head through the torii gate next to the Kentucky Fried into the 'Shopping Town' street that runs parallel with the train tracks. There is a large number of budget-to-medium priced places on both this street and Wakamiya-dōri, the main road that runs parallel to it.

On the Shopping Town street look out for the little curry place on the left just after you enter from the station square. Further up, close to the Ryokan Ushio, is *Niraku-sō*, a good Chinese restaurant.

Getting There & Away
Trains on the Yokosuka line that are blue

with a white stripe operate from Tokyo, Shimbashi and Shinagawa stations – take your pick. The trip takes about 55 minutes and fares are ¥930 from Tokyo and Shimbashi and ¥880 from Shinagawa. It is also possible to catch a train from Yokohama on the Yokosuka line. If you're planning to get off at Kita-Kamakura station, it is the stop after Ōfuna.

A cheaper but more complicated option begins with a one hour 15 minute ride on the Odakyū line from Shinjuku in Tokyo to Katase-Enoshima station for ¥530 by express. When you leave the station, cross the river and turn left. Enoshima station is a 10 minute walk away, and there you can catch the Enoden line to Kamakura for ¥220 (24 minutes). This is not a bad way to get to Kamakura if you were planning to take in Enoshima anyway.

It is possible to continue on to Enoshima, either via the Enoden line from Kamakura station or by bus from stop No 9 in front of Kamakura station.

Free Pass There is a bewildering selection of 'free passes' for sightseeing in Kamakura and Enoshima, and they all represent fairly good savings. The JR Kamakura-Enoshima Free Pass, allows for transport on the JR between Ōfuna and Kamakura, on the Shōnan monorail between Ōfuna and Enoshima and on the Enoden line between Fujisawa and Enoshima. From Tokyo station the pass costs ¥1890.

Odakyū offers a similar deal from Shinjuku station. The 'A ticket' is particularly good because it offers the added convenience of use of the buses within the Kamakura area. It costs ¥1980 from Shinjuku station.

Getting Around
The transport hub for the Kamakura area is Kamakura station. In front of the station are 10 bus stops serviced by the Enoden and Keihin and Kyūkō bus companies. There are no English signs for the bus destinations, but it is possible to ask at the station tourist information counter.

ENOSHIMA 江ノ島
Avoid this popular beach on weekends, when it's packed with day-trippers. At the end of the beach is a bridge to **Eno-shima Island**, where the Enoshima-jinja Shrine is reached by an 'outdoor escalator' that costs ¥250 – you *can* walk though. The shrine houses a *hadaka-benzaiten* – a nude statue of the Indian goddess of beauty. Other sights around the island include the **Enoshima Tropical Garden** (Enoshima Shokubutsu-en), which is open from 9 am to 5 pm daily and costs ¥200.

Getting There & Away
Buses and trains run frequently between Kamakura and Enoshima (see the Kamakura Getting There & Away section). The Tōkaidō line goes to Ōfuna station from Tokyo station, at a cost of ¥760. At Ōfuna, change to the Shōnan monorail to Shōnan Enoshima station for ¥290. Alternatively, trains run on the Odakyū line from Shinjuku station to Katase-Enoshima station. The 'Romance Car' takes one hour 10 minutes and costs ¥1030, while an express takes five minutes longer and costs ¥530.

MIURA-HANTŌ PENINSULA 三浦半島
Strictly for long-term residents suffering from boredom, the Miura-hantō Peninsula has beaches and the usual collection of overpriced, touristy marine parks, harbours and tropical gardens.

Aburatsubo Marine Park
油壺マリンパーク
This park has around 6000 fish in an aquarium that surrounds the viewer. It also offers 'synchronised swimming with girls and dolphins and laser light shows all put to music'. If this is your scene, start saving for the ¥1600 entry charge. The park is a 15 minute bus trip from Misaki-guchi station.

Joga-shima Island 城ヶ島
Excursion boats to nearby Joga-shima Island depart from the pier, which is a 10 minute walk from the Aburatsubo bus stop. The 35 minute trip costs ¥850. It's said that on a clear day you are able to see Mt Fuji from the boat

but you'd have to be *very* lucky. The island is actually connected to the mainland by a bridge, and buses go there from Misaki-guchi station.

Other Attractions
About five km north of Joga-shima Island, **Cape Ara-saki** has beaches with unusual rock formations. Take a bus from Misaki-guchi station to the Nagai bus stop and change for a bus to the Ara-saki bus stop. It takes about an hour to walk the **Mito-hama Beach Hiking Course** from Misaki-guchi station and back. The path takes you past a fishing village, beaches and a small shrine.

Getting There & Away
The cheapest and easiest way to the Miura-hantō Peninsula is to take the Keihin Kyūkō line from Tokyo station or Shinagawa station through to Misaki-guchi station, where buses go to different places around the peninsula. From Shinagawa the train takes one hour 20 minutes and costs ¥800.

An alternative point of entry to the peninsula is Yokosuka, which is serviced by the Yokosuka line (it passes through Kamakura) from Tokyo and Shinagawa stations. The fare is ¥1090.

Izu Seven Islands
伊豆諸島

The Izu Seven Islands are peaks of a submerged volcanic chain that projects out into the Pacific from the Izu-hantō Peninsula. There is still considerable volcanic activity: in November 1986 Mt Mihara-yama erupted and the residents of Ō-shima Island were evacuated to Tokyo.

Until recently the chain was considered more appropriate as a place of exile than of scenic beauty, but today it's a popular holiday destination for Tokyo residents. To escape the crowds, avoid the holiday periods and head for the remoter islands. See the earlier Around Tokyo map.

Ō-SHIMA ISLAND 大島
The main attraction of Ō-shima Island – at 91 sq km the largest of the group – is the active volcano **Mt Mihara-yama**. Buses run to the summit from Motomachi Port. **Oshima-kōen Park** has a natural zoo and a camping ground.

Information
The Izu Seven Islands Tourist Federation (☎ 03-3436-6955) in Tokyo has information on minshuku, and there is also the Ōshima Tourist Association (☎ 04992-2-2177), which offers help to travellers.

Places to Stay
The *Ō-shima-kōen Park* and *Umi-no-Furusatsu-mura* camping grounds are the cheapest places to stay, the latter having pre-pitched tents at ¥4000 for seven people. There are also lodges with beds for ¥2000 per person. The *Mihara Sansō Youth Hostel* (☎ 04992-2-2735) charges ¥2500 per bed, while the *Izu Oshima People's Lodge* (☎ 04992-2-1285) costs ¥7000 per person, including two meals.

Getting There & Away
Air There are three flights a day from Tokyo to Ō-shima Island with Air Nippon Koku (ANK). The 40 minute flight costs ¥6550 one way and ¥11,800 return.

Ferry Ferry services run once daily to Ō-shima Island from Tokyo's Takeshiba Pier (10 minutes from Hamamatsu-chō station) and from Atami and Itō. The trip from Tokyo takes seven hours and costs ¥3310 (2nd class). From Atami it takes two hours and costs ¥2380. There are also services from Itō and Shimoda, though these are less frequent. High-speed services taking about one hour are available from Atami (¥5350) and Itō (¥5030).

For information about departure times, contact Tōkai Kisen (☎ 03-3432-4555). The TIC also has up-to-date information on getting to Ō-shima Island.

TO-SHIMA ISLAND 利島

To-shima Island, 27 km south-west of Ō-shima Island, is the smallest of the Izu Seven Islands, with a circumference of only eight km. The island is mountainous, although its volcano is now dormant, and there are no swimming beaches. Much of the island is used for the cultivation of camellias, which makes it a picturesque place to visit between December and February, when the flowers are in bloom.

Places to Stay

The island has a few ryokan and minshuku – for information contact the Izu Seven Islands Tourist Federation (☎ 03-3436-6955).

Getting There & Away

Ferries leave from Tokyo's Takeshiba Pier. The trip takes around nine hours and fares start at ¥3680 in 2nd class. Boats also depart from Ō-shima Island and cost ¥620.

NII-JIMA ISLAND 新島

Nii-jima Island has an area of 23 sq km, and its beaches have made it so popular that there are now over 200 minshuku on the island. Even with this abundance of accommodation, it's a good idea to ring the Niijima Tourist Association (☎ 04992-5-0422) if you're visiting during a holiday period.

The 10 hour boat trip from Tokyo's Takebashi Pier costs ¥4450 in 2nd class. There are also boats from Ō-shima and To-shima.

SHIKINE-JIMA ISLAND 式根島

Six km south of Nii-jima Island is tiny Shikine-jima Island, with an area of only 3.8 sq km. The island has swimming beaches, hot springs and plenty of accommodation.

Ferries to Shikine-jima Island depart from Takeshiba Pier daily, take 10 hours and cost ¥4450 in 2nd class. From Nii-jima Island, boats cost ¥200.

KOZU-SHIMA ISLAND 神津島

This 18 sq km island is dominated by an extinct volcano, **Mt Tenjo**. The island also has good beaches, **Tokyo-ji Temple** and a

cemetery for former exiles, including 57 feudal warriors, from the days when the island served as a resort for Japanese unwanted by their compatriots on the mainland.

Places to Stay

There are around 180 minshuku on the island with costs of around ¥6000 with meals; bookings can be made through the Kozushima Tourist Association (☎ 04992-8-0011).

Getting There & Away

Ferries leave from Takeshiba Pier and cost ¥4710 in 2nd class. From Nii-jima boats cost ¥610.

MIYAKE-JIMA ISLAND 三宅島

Known as Bird Island due to the 200 species of birds that live there, the island is 180 km south of Tokyo and is the third largest of the Izu Seven Islands, with a circumference of 36 km. It has a volcano, which last erupted in 1962, some good beaches, a couple of small lakes and an onsen. You can either explore the island in a hired car or on a rented bicycle or make use of the local bus services.

Places to Stay

For reasonably priced minshuku, contact the Miyake-jima Tourist Association (☎ 04994-6-1144). There are camping grounds at Sagiga-hama, Okubo-hama and Miike-hama beaches; you'll need your own equipment, however.

Getting There & Away

By boat from Tokyo costs ¥4980 in 2nd class. There are also two flights a day with Air Nippon (☎ 03-3780-7777) for ¥8210 one way or ¥14,780 return.

MIKURA-JIMA ISLAND 御蔵島

Mikura-jima Island is only 20 km from Miyake-jima Island but is not of great interest. Accommodation is limited, camping is not allowed and transport connections are infrequent.

HACHIJO-JIMA ISLAND   八丈島

Hachijo-jima Island, 290 km south of Tokyo, is the southernmost and second largest of the Izu Seven Islands (68 sq km). It has a pleasant semi-tropical climate and is becoming increasing popular among young Japanese. Sights include the now dormant volcano, some good beaches, a botanical garden, **Tametomo-jinja Shrine** and **Sofuku-ji Temple**. Bicycles and cars can be rented.

There are some interesting local customs which are now maintained as tourist attractions, including a form of **bull-fighting** found throughout Asia in which two bulls try to push each other out of a ring. Bull fights are held daily at Jiyugaoka and admission is ¥800. The Runin Matsuri (Exile Festival) is held from 28 to 30 August, with a costumed procession, drum beating and folk dancing.

Places to Stay

For accommodation information, ring the local tourist association (☎ 04996-2-1377).

Getting There & Away

Ferries from Tokyo, via Miyake-jima Island, taking around 10½ hours, cost ¥6240 in 2nd class and depart daily during the summer season. Alternatively, there is a more frequent air service (six flights a day) between Haneda Airport and the island with Air Nippon (☎ 03-3780-7777). The flight takes one hour and costs ¥11,110 one way, ¥20,160 return.

Ogasawara Island
小笠原諸島

Although technically part of Tokyo-to, these islands are far to the south of the Izu Seven Islands. They have a climate similar to that of the Okinawa islands. Like those islands, they were occupied by US forces long after they had left the mainland islands.

The main group of islands include **Chichi-jima** ('Father Island'), **Haha-jima** ('Mother Island') and **Ani-jima** islands, on which you will find a number of minshuku and where **scuba diving** is popular. Further south are the Kazan (Volcano) Islands, which include **Iwo-jima** Island, one of the most famous battle sites of WW II. The island is still off limits to visitors because it contains live ammunition.

Boats to Chichi-jima Island leave approximately once weekly from Tokyo, take around 28½ hours and cost ¥22,140 for 2nd class tickets. For more information ring Ogasawara Kaiyun (☎ 03-3451-5171). Boats between Chichi-jima and Haha-jima take around two hours, leave daily and cost ¥3300 in 2nd class.

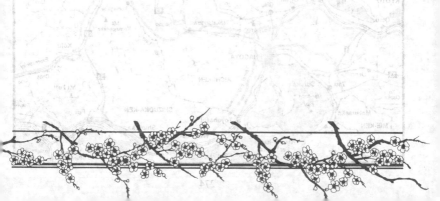

Central Honshū

本州の中央部

Central Japan, known in Japanese as *chūbu*, extends across the area sandwiched between Tokyo and Kyoto.

This chapter covers the prefectures at the heart of the Chūbu region: Aichi-ken, Gifu-ken, Nagano-ken, Toyama-ken, Ishikawa-ken and Fukui-ken. Niigata-ken and Sado-ga-shima Island have been included in the Northern Honshū chapter and Shizuoka-ken

and Yamanashi-ken are in the Around Tokyo chapter.

Chūbu divides into three geographical areas with marked differences in topography, climate and scenery. To the north, the coastal area along the Sea of Japan features rugged seascapes. The central area inland encompasses the spectacular mountain ranges and highlands of the Japan Alps, while the south-

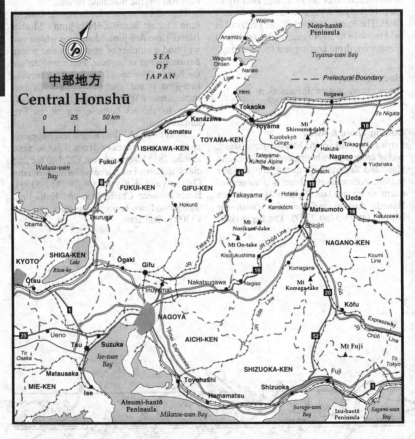

ern Pacific coast area is heavily industrialised, urbanised and densely populated.

Transport in the southern area is excellent, with Nagoya functioning as the major transport hub and southern gateway to the region. The mountainous inland area is served by the JR Takayama line and JR Chūō line, which run roughly parallel from north to south. The main transport hubs and gateways for this area are Takayama to the west and Matsumoto to the east. Another useful rail connection is provided by the JR Shin-etsu line which links Tokyo with Nagano. Transport in the northern area centres around the JR Hokuriku line, which follows the coast along the Sea of Japan, providing an efficient link between the main transport hubs of Kanazawa and Toyama.

Bear in mind that transport outside main cities in Chūbu, especially around the Japan Alps, is severely restricted between November and May. Access to ski resorts is an obvious exception.

The attractions of Chūbu lie in the central and northern areas, each of which can be skimmed in five days, but preferably give yourself two weeks for both.

The central area includes highlights such as well preserved traditional architecture (Takayama and the Kiso Valley), superb mountain scenery and hiking (most of Nagano-ken, especially Kamikōchi) and remote rural communities such as those in the Shōkawa Valley.

The northern area highlights include the cultural and artistic centre of Kanazawa, the unspoilt beauty of the Noto-hantō Peninsula and the Eihei-ji Temple in Fukui-ken.

Nagoya 名古屋

Nagoya (population 2,154,000) is Japan's fourth-largest city and centre of the Chūkyō industrial zone, Japan's third largest. Nagoya is mainly a commercial and industrial city with little to offer the traveller, though many people pass through on their way to other places. It's a convenient transport hub for

trips to Ise-jingū Shrine and the Kii Peninsula further south or, if you head north, for excursions to Gifu and Inuyama or longer trips into the Japan Alps.

Nagoya rose to power as a castle town during the feudal age. All three of Japan's great historical heroes, Oda Nobunaga, Toyotomi Hideyoshi and Tokugawa Ieyasu were born in the town or near by. Tokugawa Ieyasu built Nagoya-jō Castle for one of his sons in 1612. Not much of the past remains, however. During WW II, the city was flattened by US aerial bombing. Today, like many other Japanese urban centres, it's a prosperous, clean and well organised city that offers no compelling reasons to linger more than a couple of hours. The two major sights are Nagoya-jō Castle and Atsuta-jingū Shrine.

Orientation

The city was completely rebuilt after WW II on a grid system with expansive avenues and side streets connecting in straight lines. This makes it easy to find one's way around the central part of the city.

From the east exit of Nagoya station, Sakura-dōri runs directly eastwards to the TV tower, a useful landmark, on Hisaya-ōdōri. The area either side of Hisaya-ōdōri, south of the TV tower, is the Sakae entertainment district. Nagoya-jō Castle is north of the TV Tower.

Nagoya station is vast, a city in itself. The shinkansen platforms are on the west side of the station. The Meitetsu and Kintetsu lines are on the east side of the station, which is also handy for connections with the subway system, the Meitetsu bus centre and the city centre.

Information

There's an information stand inside Nagoya station – take the central exit and look out for it in the middle of the hall; however, it's not of great use to non-Japanese speaking travellers. If you need information on Nagoya or other areas in Central Honshū, a much better source is the Nagoya International Centre (☎ 052-581-5678, ext 24/25), which is on

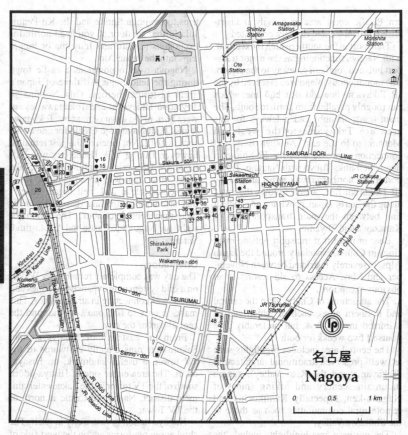

名古屋
Nagoya

0   0.5   1 km

the 3rd floor of the International Centre (Kokusai Centre) – a 10 minute walk east along Sakura-dōri. It's open daily from 9 am to 8.30 pm and is staffed by English-speaking Japanese.

The staff here seem to have almost as much material on hand as the TIC in Kyoto. *Live Map Nagoya* is a useful colour map of the city, with hotels and sights accurately sited. Other brochures you might want to pick up include JNTO's *Japan: Nagoya & Inuyama*, and another JNTO leaflet entitled *Nagoya & Vicinity*. These are available at the Tourist Information Centre (TIC) in Kyoto

or Tokyo and at JNTO offices abroad. There's also a library, TV newscasts from the USA and a bulletin board.

Useful local publications with restaurant, entertainment and festival listings include *Eyes* (¥250), *Nagoya Avenues* (¥250) and *The Alien* (¥200). All are published monthly, with *Eyes* and *Nagoya Avenues* aimed at the more mainstream market and *The Alien* aimed more at a younger, alternative set – lots of nightlife suggestions.

Post Office The main post office is a couple of minutes on foot, north of Nagoya station;

PLACES TO STAY		47	Nagoya Tōkyū Hotel 名古屋東急ホテル	OTHER	
7	Nagoya Green Hotel 名古屋グリーンホテル	48	Ryokan Meiryu 旅館名龍	1	Nagoya-jō Castle 名古屋城
10	Sun Hotel Nagoya サンホテル名古屋	49	Marutame Ryokan まるため旅館	2	Tokugawa Art Museum 徳川美術館
11	Nagoya Dai-Ichi Washington Hotel 名古屋第一ワシントンホテル		PLACES TO EAT	4	Aichi Arts Centre 愛知芸術文化センター
12	Nagoya Dai-Ni Washington Hotel 名古屋第二ワシントンホテル	3	Carina Pizza カリナピザ	5	Nagoya TV Tower テレビ塔
17	Kimiya Ryokan きみや旅館	8	Irohanihoheto Restaurant いろはにほへと	6	Tokyu Hands Department Store 東急ハンズ
18	Hotel Castle Plaza ホテルキャッスルプラザ	9	Fujiko Yakitori Grill 富士子焼き鳥グリル	15	Nagoya International Centre 国際センタービル
19	Fitness Hotel 330 Nagoya フィットネスホテル ３３０名古屋	13	Tsubahachi Restaurant つぼ八	23	Nagoya Central Post Office 中央郵便局
20	Nagoya Dai-Ichi Hotel 名古屋第一ホテル	14	Hassam Deel Deli ハッサムディールデリ	24	City Bus Terminal 市バスターミナル
21	Sun Plaza Hotel サンプラザホテル	16	Yoshinoya Restaurant 吉野屋	26	Nagoya Station 名古屋駅
22	Eki-Mae Mont Blanc Hotel 駅前モンブランホテル	35	Okonomiyaki-gai (restaurants) お好み焼き街	31	Meitetsu & Kintetsu Department Stores 名鉄デパート 近鉄デパート
25	Nagoya Terminal Hotel 名古屋ターミナルホテル	36	Kentucky Fried Chicken ケンタッキーフライドチキン	32	Across the Border (bar) アクロスザボーダー （バー）
27	Business Hotel Dai-Ni Kifune ビジネスホテル第２きふね	37	McDonald's マクドナルド	39	Marui Department Store 丸井デパート
28	Business Hotel 3-Star Nagoya ビジネスホテル ３スター名古屋	38	Mr Donut ミスタードーナッツ	40	Mitsukoshi Department Store 三越デパート
29	City Hotel Nagoya シティホテル名古屋	43	Asilo Pizzeria アシロピッツァリア	41	Sakae Bus Terminal 栄バスターミナル
30	Meitetsu Grand Hotel 名鉄グランドホテル	44	Tsubahachi Restaurant つぼ八	42	Matsuzakaya Department Store 松阪屋デパート
33	Nagoya Hilton 名古屋ヒルトン	45	Lian Hua Restaurant 蓮花		
34	Nagoya Kokusai Hotel 名古屋国際ホテル	46	Suien Restaurant & Underground Cafe (bar) 翠園アンダーグラウンド キャフェー		

it has a 24 hour window for express and registered mail.

Emergencies Nagoya International Centre (☎ 052-581-5678, ext 24/25) can provide advice needed for dealing with emergencies. There's a medical clinic (☎ 052-201-5311) in the same building.

Home Visits
Nagoya International Centre (☎ 052-581-

5678, ext 24/25) can put you in touch with Japanese families willing to invite you to their homes for a few hours for tea and a chat.

Planning Your Itinerary
There are just a couple of significant sights in Nagoya; they can be knocked off in half a day or ignored. Inuyama, Gifu and Seki are within easy reach by train. Ise-jingū Shrine and Takayama are both feasible as day trips if you make an early start.

Nagoya-jō Castle 名古屋城

Tokugawa Ieyasu built Nagoya-jō Castle on the site of an older castle in 1610-14 for his ninth son in. It was destroyed in WW II and replaced in 1959 with a ferroconcrete replica. Look out for the three-metre replicas of the famous *shachi*, a dolphin-like sea creature, that stand at either end of the roof.

The interior houses a museum with armour and family treasures which escaped the bombing. The castle also boasts an elevator to save you all the puff of climbing stairs. The Ninomaru Garden has a teahouse in an attractive setting in the castle grounds. Admission costs ¥400 and it's open from 9.30 am to 4.30 pm.

The castle is a five minute walk from Shiyakusho station on the Meijo subway line.

Tokugawa Art Museum 徳川美術館

The collection of the Tokugawa Art Museum includes prints, calligraphy, painted scrolls, lacquerware and ceramics which previously belonged to the Tokugawa family. A special exhibition is mounted in November, at which time you may feel you are getting your money's worth for the high admission charge. The museum is open from 10 am to 5 pm daily except on Monday; admission is ¥1000.

To reach the museum from the castle, take bus No 16 from Shiyakusho subway station and get off at the Shindeki stop.

Atsuta-jingū Shrine 熱田神宮

This shrine, one of the most important in Japan, dates from the 3rd century and is said to house the *kusanagi-no-tsurugi* (the sacred sword – literally the 'grass-cutting sword'), one of the three imperial regalia (the others being the curved jewels and the sacred mirror) of the imperial family. The sacred sword, like the other two imperial regalia, was according to mythology, handed down to the imperial family by the goddess Amaterasu Ōmikami.

From Shiyakusho subway station (close to the castle), take the Meijo line south to Jingū-nishi station (seven stops). To reach the

shrine from Nagoya station, take the Meitetsu Nagoya Honsen line to Jingū-mae (four stops) and then walk for five minutes. The shrine is open from 9 am to 4 pm, and closed the last Wednesday and Thursday of every month; entry is ¥300.

Nagoya Port Area 名古屋港周辺

The Nagoya port area has seen considerable development over the last few years. Attractions include the hi-tech **Nagoya Port Aquarium** (what is this Japanese fascination with aquariums?), the **Port Tower**, with good views of the harbour, the Maritime museum on the 3rd floor of the Port Tower and the **Fuji Antarctic Exploration Ship**. All of them can be visited with a combination ticket for ¥2000, provided you roll up before 1 pm. Take the Meijo subway line to Nagoya-kō (Nagoya Port) subway station. The attractions are signposted in English.

Higashiyama-kōen Park 東山公園

If you need a break from the concrete jungle and want to amble around some extensive greenery, this vast park contains a zoo, a botanical garden and an amusement centre. That said, don't even consider extending your stay in Nagoya just to see this place – it's not worth it.

The Owls of Mt Hōraiji-san

Tourist literature all over the world provides surprises and I was particularly impressed by an item in a glossy brochure about Aichi-ken. According to the brochure, there is something quite amazing in the remote north-eastern regions of the prefecture which border on Shizuoka-ken. Midway up Mt Hōraiji-san is Hōrai-ji Temple which is well known for owls which cry 'bupposo'. Since their calls resemble the Japanese sounds 'bup', 'po' and 'so' which mean 'Buddhism', 'ways' and 'priest' respectively, the birds are considered holy.

To an irreverent foreigner it might seem that the birds are suffering from a dose of hiccups or indigestion.

Robert Strauss

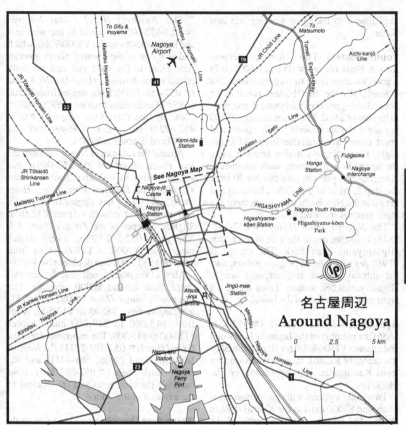

To Gifu &
Inuyama

Nagoya
Airport

To
Matsumoto

Aichi-kanjō
Line

JR Chūō Line

Tomei
Expressway

Meitetsu
Komaki
Line

Meitetsu Inuyama Line

41

19

JR Tōkaidō Honsen Line

22

Seto Line

Meitetsu

Hongo
Station

Fujigaoka

Nagoya
Interchange

Kami-iida
Station

JR Tōkaidō
Shinkansen
Line

Meitetsu Tushima Line

See Nagoya Map

Nagoya-jō
Castle

Nagoya
Station

HIGASHIYAMA LINE

Higashiyama-
kōen Station

Nagoya Youth Hostel

Higashiyama-kōen
Park

JR Kansai Honsen Line

Nagoya

Kintetsu

Atsuta-
jinja
Shrine

Jingū-mae
Station

Meitetsu

Nagoya Honsen

Line

名古屋周辺

Around Nagoya

0   2.5   5 km

Nagoyako
Station

23

Nagoya
Ferry Port

1

CENTRAL HONSHŪ

From Nagoya station, take the Higashiyama subway line and get off at Higashiyama-kōen station (16 minutes). It's open from 9.30 am to 4.30 pm, closed on Monday and entry is ¥400.

Festivals

The Atsuta Festival, held on 5 June at the Atsuta-jingū Shrine, features displays of martial arts and fireworks.

On the first Saturday and Sunday of June, the Tenno Matsuri Festival takes place in Deki-machi. Large *karakuri* (mechanical puppets) are paraded on floats in the precincts of the Susano-o-jinja Shrine.

Nagoya Matsuri Festival, held in mid-October, is the big event of the year. Displays include costume parades, processions of floats with karakuri, folk dancing, music and a parade of decorated cars.

Places to Stay

Accommodation in Nagoya is clustered largely around the station and the Sakae commercial and entertainment district. Nagoya's excellent subway system means that basing yourself in the station area is no impediment to taking an evening trip into Sakae.

Youth Hostels The *Aichi-ken Seinen-Kaikan Youth Hostel* (☎ 052-221-6001) is in a good location close to Nagoya station. As a result, it's the first budget place to be booked out – reserve in advance if you want to be sure of a bed. The hostel charges ¥2500 per night. Japanese-style family rooms and guest rooms are available from ¥4100 per night. From Nagoya station (eastern exit), the hostel is a 20 minute walk south-east. Alternatively, you can take bus No 20 from the stop in front of the Toyota building and get off at the Nayabashi stop. From there, it's three minutes south on foot.

The *Nagoya Youth Hostel* (☎ 052-781-9845) is further out to the east of town near Higashiyama-kōen Park. The charge is ¥1980 per night. From Nagoya station, take the subway on the Higashiyama line to Higashiyamakōen station. From there, it's eight minutes on foot to the hostel.

Ryokan The *Ryokan Meiryu* (☎ 052-331-8686) is a member of the Japanese Inn Group and charges ¥4500/8000 for singles/doubles. It's centrally located, three minutes on foot from Kamimaezu subway station on the Meijo line.

Two other options with per-person costs of around ¥4000 exist in the *Kimiya Ryokan* (☎ 052-551-0498), which is north of the Nagoya International Centre building, and the *Marutame Ryokan* (☎ 052-231-7130), which is close to Higashi Betsuin subway station on the Meijo line. English is spoken at the Kimiya, but not at the Marutame – they may not want to take you at the latter if you don't speak Japanese.

Hotels Most of the hotels are around the station and Sakae areas.

Station Area Most of the business hotels in the station area are fairly pricey, and the cheaper ones tend to be located around the west exit rather than the more convenient east exit.

The *Business Hotel 3-Star Nagoya* (☎ 052-452-0033) is close to the west exit and has singles/twins for ¥5000/7500, which makes it one of the cheaper places around. Also close to the west exit and similarly priced is the *Business Hotel Dai-Ni Kifune* (☎ 052-452-7535). It has singles from ¥5200 to ¥5400 and twins/doubles at ¥8200/8000. Close by, the *City Hotel Nagoya* (☎ 052-452-6223) has singles at ¥5400, twins at ¥8500 and doubles at ¥8800.

Around the east exit of Nagoya station, the *Sun Plaza Hotel* (☎ 052-563-0691) has singles from ¥6400 and doubles from ¥12,400. The *Eki-Mae Mont Blanc Hotel* (☎ 052-541-1121) has singles from ¥7600, and twins and doubles from ¥12,000. Slightly cheaper is the *Fitness Hotel 330 Nagoya* (☎ 052-562-0330), where singles range from ¥7000 to ¥7500, twins from ¥11,000 to ¥13,000 and doubles cost ¥9500.

Most of the other hotels near the east exit range from around ¥8000 upwards. The *Nagoya Terminal Hotel* (☎ 052-561-3751) has singles from ¥8500 to ¥10,500, twins from ¥15,000 to ¥17,000 and doubles ¥13,000 to ¥15,000. The enormous *Meitetsu Grand Hotel* (☎ 052-582-2211), the *Nagoya Dai-Ichi Hotel* (☎ 052-581-4411) and the *Hotel Castle Plaza* (☎ 052-582-2121) offer basically the same rates and are all close to the east exit of the station.

Sakae Area The Sakae area is a more lively part of town to be based in terms of eating out and nightlife. One of the cheapest options around is the *Nagoya Dai-Ichi Washington Hotel* (☎ 052-951-2111), which has a limited number of hole-in-the-wall singles for ¥4600; larger singles are ¥7200, while twins range from ¥9300. Close by, the *Nagoya Dai Ni Washington Hotel* (☎ 052-962-7111) has singles from ¥5800, and twins and doubles from ¥11,600. Just across the road, the *Sun Hotel Nagoya* (☎ 052-971-2781) has singles at ¥6000 and twins at ¥9700. Also in the same area is the *Nagoya Green Hotel* (☎ 052-951-9801), where singles range from ¥6400 to ¥6800, and twins and doubles from ¥10,000.

The Sakae area also has a number of very up-market hotels. Probably the best is the *Nagoya Tōkyū Hotel* (☎ 052-251-2411), which has singles at ¥14,500, twins at ¥24,000 and doubles at ¥21,000. The *Nagoya Kokusai Hotel* (☎ 052-961-3111) is another up-market possibility, with singles from ¥9500 to ¥15,000, and twins and doubles from ¥19,000. Not far from Sakae, close to Fushimi subway station, the *Nagoya Hilton* (☎ 052-212-1111) is all you would expect of the Hilton chain and has singles from ¥16,000, and twins and doubles from ¥24,000.

Places to Eat

Probably the most famous of Nagoya's regional specialities is *kishimen*, another of those variations of noodles in stock soup (there's a bewildering variety of them throughout Japan). There's no real need to seek kishimen out though – it's nothing to write home about. Nagoya has a good range of traditional Japanese dining options, as well as some very good Chinese and International dining.

Those just passing through Nagoya (changing trains perhaps) should take the central exit for the main part of the station and look out for the basement *Gourmet One* dining arcade. There are a number of Japanese-style restaurants down here, as well *Sarosa*, a dining hall with a selection of Singapore-style hawker stands selling everything from rāmen to curry rice at good prices. Fast-food aficionados will find little in the station area, and a fix will require a 20 minute hike or subway trip into the Sakae area, where you will find reminders of home in *McDonald's, Kentucky Fried Chicken, Mr Donut* and their ilk. There is a branch of *Yoshinoya*, the excellent Japanese beef and rice chain (open 24 hours) across from the east exit of Nagoya station.

For lively izakaya-style Japanese eating and drinking, look out for one of the several branches of the *Tsubohachi* chain. Along similar lines is *Irohanihoheto*, another beer and yakitori (among other things) chain that has made its reputation on quality food and

reasonable prices – figure on ¥2000 per head with drinks. The basement of the Sakaemachi building has *Okonomiyaki-gai*, a 'street' of cheap okonomiyaki restaurants that are popular with students and other young people. One other place to look out for, close to Sakae subway station, is *Fujiko*, a corner stall doing a brisk business in yakitori – take-away only, but cheap and tasty.

For good Taiwanese food (an excellent and little-known cuisine), try *Lian Hua* on the west side of Sakae subway station. It has an illustrated menu and a good selection of authentic Taiwanese street-stall snacks. An evening meal would come to ¥2000 to ¥2500 per head with a drink. Just around the corner is *Suien*, another authentic Chinese restaurant (this time Shanghainese) with a limited illustrated menu (some of the best stuff is in Japanese and Chinese only). It's a cheap place to eat and has draught beer available.

For good Italian pizza and pasta, check out *Carina Pizza*, north of the TV tower. A bit more conveniently located is *Asilo*, another popular and slightly trendy Italian restaurant. Main courses in both places range from around ¥700 to ¥800. Finally, not far from the station (just across the road from the Nagoya International Centre building) is *Hassam Deel*, a great little deli with sandwiches and other snacks – it's popular with foreign residents.

Entertainment

Nagoya, while a big city, isn't as exciting as Tokyo or Osaka. But it does have a bit of a nightlife scene and a few bars that attract an interesting mix of gaijin and Japanese. Probably the hippest places in town (dark and loud – not necessarily the best place to meet people) are the *Underground* and the *Underground Cafe*, which are on the 3rd and 4th floors of the same building, respectively. The Underground is basically a dance space with good soul sounds and a cover charge of ¥1000 to ¥2000 on some nights of the week, while the Underground Cafe is more of a drinking spot – both get packed on Friday and Saturday nights.

More straight drinking options are available in *Westridge*, which is over in Fushimi, and *Across the Border*, probably the most popular gaijin hang-out, not far from the Nagoya Hilton. The night to be at Westridge is Monday, when there's live music and all beers cost only ¥300 (check with one of the monthly magazines – see the Information section – to confirm that this is still the case). The place gets incredibly crowded.

Things to Buy
Nagoya and the surrounding area are known for various arts & crafts such as *arimatsu-narumi shibori* (elegant tie-dying), cloisonné (enamelling on silver and copper), ceramics and seki blades (swords, knives, scissors, etc). Nagoya International Centre can provide details on tours of specific factories or museums as well as shopping.

The major shopping centres are in Sakae and around Nagoya station. The Radio Centre Ameyoko building in Sakae is crammed from top to bottom with shops selling camera gear, hi-fi equipment and electrical goods. For souvenir items (handmade paper, pottery, tie-dyed fabric, etc) you can browse in Sakae in the giant department stores such as Matsuzakaya, Marui and Mitsukoshi, or try Meitetsu, an equally vast department store, next to the station.

Getting There & Away
Air Nagoya is served with domestic flights by All Nippon Airways (ANA), Japan Airlines (JAL) and Japan Air Systems (JAS) for cities such as Tokyo (Narita), Sapporo, Sendai, Fukuoka and Naha. As the bus takes 45 minutes from Nagoya's Komaki Airport to the city centre, the shinkansen from Tokyo is much quicker.

An increasing number of international flights are using Nagoya's Komaki Airport, which does not suffer from the chronic congestion of Tokyo's Narita Airport. This is definitely an option to be considered since direct flights are now available to Nagoya from Hong Kong, Seoul, Manila, Singapore, Vancouver and Sydney.

Train The JR shinkansen is the fastest rail service to Nagoya. The journey on the Hikari shinkansen takes one hour and 52 minutes from Tokyo (¥10,380), one hour and 2 minutes from Osaka (¥6060) and 50 minutes from Kyoto (¥5340).

Ise-shima National Park is connected with Nagoya on the Kintetsu line, which runs via Ise-shi station and Toba to Kashikojima. Nagoya to Ise takes one hour and 20 minutes (¥2280). If you want to use JR, it will take at least two hours (¥2890); take the JR Kisei line to Taki and then change for Ise.

Nara is connected with Nagoya on the Kintetsu line. Nagoya to Nara takes two hours and 16 minutes.

For the Japan Alps and related sidetrips, you can take the JR Chūō line to Nagano via Matsumoto. To reach Takayama from Nagoya, you should take the Meitetsu Inuyama line to Inuyama (Unuma station) and then change to the JR Takayama line.

Inuyama is connected with Nagoya station on the Meitetsu Inuyama line. The trip takes about 30 minutes.

Gifu is connected with Nagoya station on the JR Tōkaidō Honsen line. The trip takes about 30 minutes.

Bus A JR bus operates between Tokyo and Osaka with stops in Nagoya and Kyoto. The approximate times and prices for Nagoya are as follows: Tokyo – six hours, ¥4500; from Kyoto – 2¾ hours, ¥2000; Osaka – 3½ hours, ¥2400. The Nagoya International Centre will have up-to-date details.

Ferry The Taiheiyo Ferry (☎ 03-661-7007) runs between Nagoya and Tomakomai (Hokkaidō) via Sendai. Ferries depart from Nagoya-futō Pier which is 40 minutes by bus from the Meitetsu bus centre or you can take the Meijo subway south to its terminus at Nagoya-ko station.

The passenger fare from Nagoya to Sendai is ¥9580 and the trip takes 21 hours. There are evening departures every second day. The fare from Nagoya to Tomakomai is ¥15,450 and the full trip takes about 40 hours.

Hitching To hitch east from Nagoya to Tokyo, or west to Kyoto or Osaka, your best bet is the Nagoya Interchange on the Tomei Expressway. Take the subway on the Higashiyama line from Nagoya station to Hongo station (13 stops) – one stop before the terminus at Fujigaoka. The interchange is a short walk east of the station.

Getting Around

To/From the Airport Express bus services run between the airport and the Meitetsu bus centre (3rd floor, stop No 5). The trip takes 45 minutes and the one-way fare is ¥640. Taxis take about 35 minutes and cost about ¥3000.

Bus There is an extensive bus system but the subway is easier to handle for those with a limited grasp of Japanese. The main bus centre is the Meitetsu bus terminal which is on the 3rd floor of the Meitetsu department store on the south side of Nagoya station.

Subway Nagoya has an excellent subway system with four lines, all clearly signposted in English and Japanese. The most useful lines for visitors are probably the Meijo line, Higashiyama line and the new Sakura-dōri line. The last two run via Nagoya station. Fares range from ¥180 to ¥300 on all lines. Both the *Live Map Nagoya* and the JNTO brochure *Japan: Nagoya & Inuyama* have subway maps. If you intend to do a lot of travel by bus and subway, you can save money with a one-day pass (¥820), which is available at subway stations.

Taxi There is no shortage of taxis around the station and in Sakae, but the subway system should meet your needs unless you stay out until the wee hours.

Southern Gifu-ken
岐阜県の南部

The Gifu Prefecture consists almost entirely of mountains, with the exception of the plain

around the city of Gifu, the prefectural capital. In the south of the prefecture the two cities of interest to travellers are Gifu and Inuyama which are famed for *ukai* (cormorant fishing) and easily visited as sidetrips from Nagoya.

SEKI 関

Seki (population 68,000) is renowned as an ancient centre for swordsmiths. It still produces a few swords, but there isn't much growth in the sword market so the emphasis of production has been switched to cutlery and razor blades (Seki produces 90% of Japan's razor blades).

Swordsmithing demonstrations are given on the first Sunday of each month (five times daily), on 2 January, and during the second weekend in October. The best source of information on swordsmithing displays is the Seki Tourism Association (☎ 0575-22-3131). There are several minshuku and ryokan around Seki and some visitors combine a stay with an evening dinner on a boat while watching ukai.

From Gifu (Noisshiki station), the train runs on the Meitetsu Minomachi line to Seki in 50 minutes. There are also buses from Gifu to Seki which take about half an hour.

GIFU 岐阜

Gifu (population 410,000) was strongly hit by a colossal earthquake in 1891 and later given a thorough drubbing in WW II. The city is overlooked by Mt Kinka-zan, which is topped by a postwar reconstruction of Gifu-jō Castle. A cablecar runs from Gifu-kōen Park to the top of the mountain.

Gifu is not wildly attractive from an architectural viewpoint and most tourists go there for ukai and for handicrafts.

There's a tourist information office (☎ 0582-63-7291) at the JR station which provides maps and leaflets. The Meitetsu and JR stations are close to each other in the southern part of the city.

Cormorant Fishing 鵜飼い

The ukai (cormorant fishing) season in Gifu lasts from 11 May to October. Boats depart

Southern Gifu-ken

岐阜県南部

FUKUI-KEN

NAGANO-KEN

GIFU-KEN

AICHI-KEN

Zenshō-ji Temple

Gero

Gujō Hachiman

Mino

Seki

Mino Ota

Yaotsu

Mitake

Inuyama

Meiji-mura Village

Ōgata-jinja Shrine

Tagata-jinja-mae Station

Tajimi

Seto

Komaki

Kasugai

Ichinomiya

Ōgaki

Gifu

Nagaragawa Line

JR Takayama Line

Meitetsu Minomachi Line

Noisshiki Station

Meitetsu Komaki Line

Gakuden Station

Tagata-jinja Shrine

Meitetsu Line

JR Tōkaidō Line

Shinkansen

Tōkaidō-San...

Tōmei Expressway

Chūō Expressway

JR Chūō Line

To Nagoya

Prefectural Boundary

0   10   20 km

---

every evening, except after heavy rainfall, or on the night of a full moon. For details on ukai see the Western Kyoto section in the Kansai Region chapter.

Tickets are sold by hotels or, after 6 pm, at the booking office (☎ 0582-62-0104 for advance reservations) just below the Nagara-bashi Bridge. Tickets cost ¥2900.

The fishing takes place around Nagara-bashi Bridge, a short tram ride from Gifu JR and Meitetsu stations. If you don't want to join the partying on the boats, you can get a good view of the action by walking along the shingle to the east of the bridge.

Gifu-kōen Park 岐阜公園

Gifu-kōen park has a history museum (open from 9 am to 4.30 pm; closed Monday; admission ¥300) and an entomological museum (open daily from 9 am to 5 pm; admission ¥300). You can also take a cablecar up to the summit of Mt Kinka-zan (8 am to 6 pm; ¥980 return) and check out Gifu-jō Castle, a small but picturesque modern reconstruction of the original.

Shōhō-ji Temple 勝法寺

The main attraction of this orange and white temple is the papier-mâché Daibutsu (Great

Buddha) which is nearly 14 metres tall and was created from a tonne of paper sutras (prayers). Completed in 1747, the Buddha took 38 years to make. The temple is a short walk south-west of Gifu-kōen Park.

Arts & Crafts

Gifu is famous for its *kasa* (oiled paper parasols) and *chōchin* paper lanterns, which are stocked in all the souvenir shops.

If you want to see a shop that not only sells but also makes kasa, you should visit Sakaida Honten (☎ 0582-71-6958). It's a 12 minute walk south-east of JR Gifu station.

Ozeki Shōten (☎ 0582-63-0111) is a lantern factory. Take the tram from Gifu station and get off at the Daigaku-byō-in stop which is at the junction of the road leading to the tunnel. From there, it's a short walk east down the main road to the factory. A guided tour takes visitors through the processes of frame building, pasting and painting. Lanterns are also on sale here.

Both Sakaida and Ozeki are closed on Sunday.

Places to Stay

Gifu has plenty of ryokan and hotels, although ryokan tend to be fairly expensive. The information office at the station can provide further accommodation details.

Youth Hostel *Gifu Youth Hostel* (☎ 0582-63-6631) is perched close to the cablecar station on top of Mt Kinka-zan. If the cablecar is not operating, the hostel has to be reached via a circuitous ramble up the mountain. The recompense for getting lost is the low ¥1650 it costs for a bed for the night.

If the cablecar is not operating, or you simply prefer to walk, take the tram from Gifu station (15 minutes) and get off at the Yana-ga-se stop. Then walk east down the main road and turn left at the second crossroads. A short distance down this street, there's a path to your right which leads up the mountain to the hostel (about a 20 minute walk).

Alternatively, take the tram from Gifu station (20 minutes) and get off at the Daigaku Byō-in stop. Walk east down the main road towards the tunnel and just before the entrance, take the path to the right which leads uphill to the hostel, a walk which also takes about 20 minutes.

Hotels There are quite a number of business hotels in the station area. The *Grand Palais Hotel* (☎ 0582-65-4111) is directly opposite JR Gifu station and has singles/twins from ¥5500/11,000. On the next street north is the *New Gifu Hotel Plaza* (☎ 0582-63-0011), a standard business hotel with singles at ¥6000, and twins and doubles at ¥10,000. The nearby *Hotel Sunroute* (☎ 0582-66-8111) is more expensive, with singles from ¥7200, and twins and doubles from ¥13,900.

There are also a number of cheaper business hotels north of the Kin-machi tram stop. The *Business Hotel Asahi* (☎ 0582-66-1919) has singles at ¥4500 and twins at ¥8000. Just around the corner, the *Gifu Kaikan* (☎ 0582-63-7111) has 16 rooms ranging in price from ¥3700 to ¥5200, though it's often full.

Getting There & Away

From Nagoya station take the Meitetsu Honsen (main) line (30 minutes, ¥440) to Gifu. If you are going to watch ukai, you should then take the tram to Nagarabashi.

Gifu is also served by the JR Takayama line and the JR Tōkaidō line.

INUYAMA 犬山

The highlights of Inuyama (population 69,000) are its castle and activities such as ukai and river running. The riverside setting of the castle is quite attractive, but it's stretching the imagination a bit to claim that it's the 'Japanese Rhein', as claimed in some tourist brochures. Many of the sights have been moulded or hyped into tourist attractions which are of specific appeal to Japanese. For foreigners, probably the most interesting items are the castle, the teahouse, ukai and shooting the Kiso-gawa River rapids.

The Meiji-mura Village Museum should appeal to those interested in Western archi-

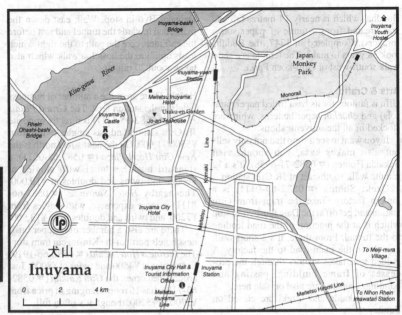

犬山
Inuyama

tecture; it requires at least half a day if you want to give it thorough attention.

Orientation & Information

The castle and the ukai area are within easy walking distance of Inuyama-yuen station, which is one stop north of Inuyama station. Inuyama City Hall's international section (☎ 0568-61-1800, ext 233) is open on weekdays from 9 am to 5 pm and from 9 am to noon on Saturday. The city hall is a couple of minutes on foot south-west of JR Inuyama station. Explanatory leaflets and maps are available and staff can help you find accommodation. There is another tourist information office at Inuyama-jō Castle.

Inuyama-jō Castle   犬山城

Dating from 1440, this is Japan's oldest castle and is preserved in its original state – a relative rarity in Japan. From the top storey of the castle, there's a fine view across the Kiso-gawa River.

The castle is a 15 minute walk west of Inuyama-yuen station. It's open daily from 9 am to 4.30 pm and entry is ¥300.

Uraku-en Garden & Jo-an Teahouse
有楽苑・如庵

Uraku-en Garden is 300 metres east of Inuyama-jō Castle in a corner of the grounds of the Meitetsu Inuyama Hotel.

The centre of attention in the garden is the Jo-an Teahouse which is rated as one of the finest in Japan. It was constructed in 1618 in Kyoto by Oda Urakusai, a younger brother of Oda Nobunaga. Urakusai was a renowned tea master who founded his own tea ceremony school.

Admission to the teahouse costs ¥800. It's open from 9 am to 5 pm but closes an hour earlier between December and February.

Cormorant Fishing   鵜飼い

Ukai takes place close to Inuyama-yuen station at Inuyama Bridge; the boat dock and booking office is just east of the bridge.

Tickets cost ¥2800 during July and August; ¥300 less during June and September. Book your ticket in Inuyama in the morning or call ahead and reserve tickets at the dock office (☎ 0568-61-0057) if your Japanese is up to it.

The boats go fishing every night from 1 June to 30 September except after heavy rainfall or on the night of a full moon. For details on ukai see the Western Kyoto section of the Kansai Region chapter.

Kiso-gawa River Trip 木曽川下り
Flat-bottomed, wooden boats shoot the rapids on a 13 km section of the Kiso-gawa River. The trip takes about an hour and entails little risk although you might get dampened by spray. If you want a slightly faster and noisier ride, you can take a motorised boat; for a quieter ride, choose a boat without a motor.

From Nagoya station take the Meitetsu line via Inuyama along the Meitetsu Hiromi line to Nihon Rhein Imawatari station. From there it's a five minute bus ride to the boat dock. The fare for the boat trip is ¥3400. Call Nihon Rhein Kankō (☎ 0574-28-2727) for more details.

Japan Monkey Park 日本モンキーパーク
Unless you are interested in the commercial exploitation of monkeys, you can skip this. Apart from the Japan Monkey Research Centre, a zoo and a botanical garden, there's also a collection of handicrafts related to monkeys.

Admission to the park costs ¥1100. It's open from 9.30 am to 5 pm daily but closes an hour earlier from early December to mid-February. A monorail zips you from Inuyama-yuen station to the park in four minutes.

The Little World Museum of the World
リトルワールド
This is a bizarre exhibition of modes of living in Africa, Asia, Europe and America. Compared with the cost of a Round-the-World airline ticket, the admission to this place seems cheap.

The museum is open daily from 9.30 am

to 6 pm but closes at 4.30 pm from 16 September to 15 March; admission costs ¥1200. To get there, take a bus from Inuyama station (25 minutes, ¥420) or take a bus from the Meitetsu bus station in Nagoya, a trip that can take up to two hours and costs ¥1180.

Festivals
On the Saturday and Sunday closest to 7 and 8 April, the Inuyama Matsuri takes place at the Haritsuna-jinja Shrine. This festival dates back to 1650 and features a parade of 13 three-tiered floats decked out with lanterns. Mechanical puppets perform to music on top of the floats.

Places to Stay
If you intend to stay in Inuyama, perhaps as an extension of an ukai jaunt, you should check with the information office in the Nagoya International Centre (see the earlier Nagoya section) or the Inuyama City Hall information office.

The cheapest option in Inuyama, and one of the cheapest in Japan, is *Inuyama Youth Hostel* (☎ 0568-61-1111), which is a 20 minute walk east of Inuyama-yuen station. The charge for a bed for the night is a bargain at ¥1170. The hostel is closed from 28 December to 3 January.

Around 200 metres north-west of the station is the *Inuyama City Hotel* (☎ 0568-61-1600), which has singles at ¥6500, twins at ¥11,000 and doubles at ¥10,000. Further north again, close to the Kiso-gawa River, is the expensive *Meitetsu Inuyama Hotel* (☎ 0568-61-1600), where singles/doubles will set you back ¥12,000/17,000.

Getting There & Away
Inuyama is connected with Nagoya station via the Meitetsu Inuyama line. The ordinary express takes 35 minutes and costs ¥520.

AROUND INUYAMA 犬山周辺
Meiji-mura Village Museum 明治村
In Meiji-mura, 20 minutes by bus from Inuyama, you can see more than 60 Meiji-era buildings brought together from all over

Japan. The clash of architectural styles on display, both Western and Japanese, provides a sense of the play of contradictions in the Meiji period, as Japan sought to transform itself into a unified modern nation and an international power. The aerial bombing of Japan late in WW II, natural disasters and unbridled modernisation have left few buildings of this era standing; this open-air museum provides one of the few opportunities to see what's left.

Notable buildings include a section of Frank Lloyd Wright's original Imperial Hotel, the mansion of the Japanese statesman Saigō Tsugumichi, the summer house of Lafcadio Hearn, a hall for martial arts, a bath house, a brewery, a kabuki theatre, a prison, two churches and dozens more spread over 100 hectares.

Even if you chug around on the village locomotive or tram, you'll still need at least half a day to enjoy the place at an easy pace.

The village is open from 10 am to 5 pm daily but closes an hour earlier between November and February. Admission costs ¥1240.

A bus departs every 15 minutes from Inuyama station for the 20 minute (¥410) trip to Meiji-mura. You can also take a one hour bus ride from Meitetsu bus station in Nagoya direct to Meiji-mura. Buses leave twice an hour. The round-trip fare, including admission to Meiji-mura, is ¥3000.

Oagata-jinja Shrine   大県神社
This shrine is dedicated to Izanami, the female Shintō deity, and draws women devotees who are seeking marriage or the birth of children. The precincts of the shrine contain rocks and other items resembling female genitalia.

Oagata-jinja is a 15 minute walk east of Haguro station, to the east of Meiji-mura, on the Meitetsu Komaki line.

The Hime-no-Miya Grand Festival takes place on the first two Sunday in March at Oagata-jinja Shrine. The local populace pray for good harvests and prosperity by parading through the streets bearing a portable shrine with replicas of female genitals.

Tagata-jinja Shrine   田県神社
This shrine is dedicated to Izanagi, the Shintō deity who is the male counterpart of Izanami. The main hall of the shrine has a side building containing a collection of phalluses of all dimensions, left as offerings by grateful worshippers.

Tagata-jinja is at Tagata-jinja-mae station, one stop further south from Haguro station, on the Meitetsu Komaki line.

The festival of Tagata Hōnen Sai takes place on 15 March at the Tagata-jinja Shrine. Replicas of male genitals are carted around in this male counterpart of the Hime-no-Miya Festival.

Tajimi   多治見
Tajimi (population 94,000) has a long history as a porcelain-producing centre and is famed for its Mino ware. There are thought to be more than a thousand potteries in the area, and it remains one of the largest porcelain-producing centres in Japan.

Close to Tajimi station (just over a km walk to the east) is the **Prefectural Porcelain Museum**, a small place that's open 9 am to 4.30 pm (closed Monday) and has an admission charge of ¥200. There's another porcelain museum just north of Tokishi station, the next stop on the Chūō line north of Tajimi.

Tajimi is not far to the east of Meiji-mura, but unless you have your own transport it is most easily reached from Nagoya on the JR Chūō line (32 minutes, ¥640).

GERO   下呂
Gero is favoured by Japanese tourists for its spas, but there is little appeal in its sprawl of concrete buildings. The waters of the spas are reputedly beneficial for the complexion.

Apart from its numerous spas, including several communal open-air ones, Gero boasts its own 'hot-spring temple' – **Onsenji Temple** – overlooking the town. Some travellers rave about the Takehara Bunraku performances held at **Gero Gasshō open-air museum**. The puppets are operated by one man and performances are held daily

Gardens
A: Leaf with dripping water (CT)
B: Garden scene (CT)
C: Miniature Zen garden (CT)
D: Chinoike Jigoku, Beppu (TW)
E: The Path of Philosophy, Kyoto (CT)
F: Kenroku-en Garden, Kanazawa (CT)

A	B	C
D	E	F
G	H	I

Advertising, Japanese style
A: Sports shop advertising (CT)
B: Rooster phone box (TW)
C: Fugu phone box (TW)
D: King kong (TW)

E: Tree-trunk toilet (TW)
F: Karate-chopped building (TW)
G: Kamikaze building (TW)
H: Emerging Mini (TW)
I: Pocari Sweat Vending Machine (CT)

(except Wednesday and Thursday) at 10 am and 3 pm. Other minor attractions include the Mine-ichigo Relics Park and Zenshō-ji Temple which is next to the station of the same name, one stop north of Gero.

To get there, take a Takayama line train from Gifu station or from Nagoya.

GUJŌ HACHIMAN 郡上八幡
The main claim to fame of this town is its Gujō Odori Folk Dance Festival, held from the first 10 days of July through to the first 10 days in September, when the townsfolk continue nearly four centuries of tradition and let their hair down for some frenzied dancing. During the four main days of the festival (from 13 August to 16 August) the dancing goes on through the night.

From Gifu, take a train to Mino Ota, then change to the Nagaragawa Railway for the 70 minute trip to Gujō Hachiman.

Northern Gifu-ken
岐阜県の北部

The major attractions of the mountainous Gifu Prefecture lie to the north in the Hida district, which is part of the Japan Alps. Takayama, the administrative centre of Hida, retains much of its original architecture and small-scale charm. From Takayama, you can make sidetrips to the spectacular mountain regions around Kamikōchi to the east (where there are numerous hot-spring resorts and excellent scope for short walks or long hikes) or you can visit the Shōkawa Valley for a look at rural life and architecture in remote farming villages to the west. If you go east from Takayama you can cross the Japan Alps to Matsumoto and Nagano, and if you head west, you can continue to Kanazawa.

Access to the remoter parts of Hida is restricted by severe weather conditions

CENTRAL HONSHŪ

岐阜県北部
Northern Gifu-ken

0   7.5   15 km

Prefectural Boundary

which often last from November to mid-May. Check first with Japan Travel-Phone, (☎ 0120-444800, toll free) or the Takayama tourist office if you plan to visit during the winter.

More details about the Japan Alps region can be found in the Nagano-ken section of this chapter.

TAKAYAMA 高山

Takayama (population 65,000) lies in the ancient Hida district tucked away between the mountains of the Japan Alps, and should be a high priority on any visit to Central

Honshū and the Japan Alps. Give yourself two days to enjoy the place and add a few more if you use it as a base to visit the mountains.

Takayama, with its traditional inns, shops and sake breweries, is a rarity; a Japanese city (admittedly a small one) that has managed to retain something of its traditional charm. Basically, it's a small, intimate place, easily tackled on foot or by bicycle, and a good town to take a break from the more urgent rhythms of larger urban centres.

Historically, the inhabitants of Takayama have long been known for their woodwork-

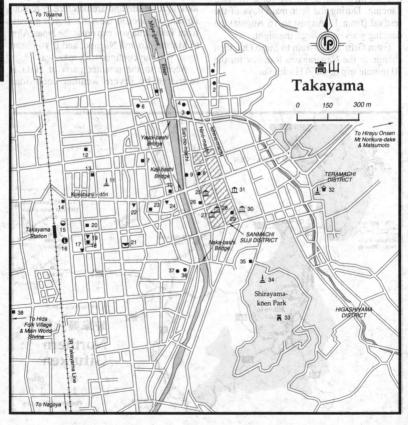

高山
Takayama

0   150   300 m

ing skills, and Hida carpenters were in demand to construct imperial palaces and temples in the Kyoto and Nara regions. The tradition continues to this day with the production of furniture and wood carvings.

Takayama entered history proper from the late 16th century, when it was established as the castle town of the Kanamori family. The present layout of the town dates from this period.

The Takayama Festival, held in April and October, is rated as one of the three great festivals in Japan and attracts over half a million spectators. If you go to the festival and want to stay in Takayama, then book your accommodation well in advance.

Orientation

All the main sights, except Hida Folk

Village, are in the centre of town, a short walk from the station. The streets are arranged in a grid pattern, similar to Kyoto or Nara, and this makes it easy to get around town. From the centre, you can continue east for 10 minutes along Kokubunji-dōri, which is the main street, until you reach Teramachi (Temple District) and Shiroyama-kōen Park in the Higashiyama (Eastern Mountain) district.

Hida Folk Village is a 10 minute bus ride west of the station.

Information

The Hida tourist information office (☎ 0577-32-5328), directly in front of JR Takayama station, is an excellent source of information on Takayama. There's even a video machine if you want a preview of the sights. The

PLACES TO STAY	PLACES TO EAT	11	Hida Kokubun-ji Temple 飛騨国分寺
5 Sumiyoshi Ryokan 寿美吉旅館	17 Hole in the Wall Restaurant 壁の穴	15	Takayama Bus Station 高山バスターミナル
7 Ryokan Kinkikan 旅館きんきかん	19 Nama-Soba Restaurant なまそばレストラン	16	Tourist Information Office 観光案内所
10 Hotel Alpha One ホテルアルファワン	22 Suzuya Restaurant すずやレストラン	21	Takayama Post Office 高山郵便局
12 Hida Hotel Plaza 飛騨ホテルプラザ	24 Nomeya Utaeya Restaurant 飲めや歌えやレストラン	25	Fujii Folkcraft Museum 藤井美術民芸館
13 Takayama Central Hotel 高山セントラルホテル		27	Hida Archaeology Museum 飛騨民族考古館
14 New Alps Hotel ニューアルプスホテル	**OTHER**	28	Hirata Folk Art Museum 平田記念館
18 Oshuku Matsuyama (minshuku) お宿松山 (民宿)	1 Festival Floats Exhibition Hall 高山屋台会館	29	Gallery of Traditional Japanese Toys 郷土玩具館
20 Daimaru Ryokan 大丸旅館	2 Lion Mask Exhibition Hall 獅子会館	30	Takayama Local History Museum 高山市郷土館
23 Ryokan Seiryu 旅館清龍	3 Kusakabe Heritage House 日下部民芸館	31	Wild Bird Museum 老田野鳥館
26 Ryokan Gōto 旅館河渡	4 Yoshijima-ke House 吉島家住宅	33	Takayama-jō Castle 高山城
32 Hida Takayama Tenshō-ji Youth Hostel 飛騨高山天照寺ユースホステル	6 Lacquerware Exhibition Hall 春慶会館	34	Shrōen-ji Temple 照蓮寺
35 Chatelet Inn Takayama シャトーレイン高山	8 Hachiga Folk Art Gallery 八賀民俗美術館	36	Jinya-mae Market 陣屋前朝市
38 Takayama Green Hotel 高山グリーンホテル	9 Miyagawa Market 宮川朝市	37	Takayama-jinya 高山陣屋

office is open from 8.30 am to 6.30 pm between 1 April and 31 October. During the rest of the year it closes at 5 pm.

Useful publications are *Japan: Hida Takayama* and *Takayama & Vicinity*, both published by JNTO. Those interested in the Takayama festivals should ask for a pale green booklet called *Background of Takayama Festival*, which has full details. Encyclopaedic coverage of Takayama is provided in *Information for Foreign Residents & Visitors*, which has over 50 pages of facts, figures and information.

If you want to arrange a home visit, a home stay, or would like to arrange for a volunteer interpreter for non-Japanese languages (or even sign language) call the International Affairs Office (☎ 0577-32-3333, ext 212).

Planning Your Itinerary

Takayama makes a good base for trips into the mountains (Kamikōchi, Hirayu Onsen, Shin-Hotaka cablecar or Norikura), or to the Shōkawa Valley with its traditional farmhouses.

Sights include more than a dozen museums, galleries, collections and exhibitions. Subject matter ranges from wild birds, toys and lion masks to folkcraft and archaeology. A small sampling is provided in this section, but check with the information office if you have a special interest.

The Hida Takayama Tenshō-ji Youth Hostel (☎ 0577-32-6345) can provide details of a nearby Zen temple run by a priest who speaks a little English and is willing to help genuinely interested people.

Walking Tour

From the station, you can complete a circular walking tour of the main sights in an hour. A walking tour of the Higashiyama district which passes through Teramachi and Shiroyama-kōen Park is also highly recommended. This walk takes about two hours and is particularly enjoyable in the early morning or late afternoon. The tourist information office in front of the station has a small, green booklet entitled *Temples &*

Shrines in Higashiyama Preserved Area which gives details of many of the temples.

Although Hida Folk Village is itself an enjoyable place to walk around, the approach to the village from the station offers only a dreary, urban stroll – the bus ride zips you through this in 10 minutes.

Takayama-jinya 高山陣屋

Originally built in 1615 as the administrative centre for the Kanamori clan, Takayama-jinya (Historical Government House) is worth visiting to see how the authorities governed at that time. The present buildings are reconstructions dating from 1816.

Apart from government offices, a rice granary and a garden, there's a torture chamber with explanatory detail. For foreigners who have the misfortune to tour this place during school holidays, a variation on this theme can be provided by dozens of raucous schoolkids mouthing 'gaijin'.

Admission costs ¥310 and it's open from 8.45 am to 5 pm, April to October, and closes half an hour earlier during the rest of the year.

Sanmachi Suji 三町筋

This is the centre of the old town, and consists of three streets (Ichi-no-machi, Ni-no-machi and San-no-machi) lined with traditional shops, breweries, restaurants, museums and private homes. The sake breweries are easily recognised by the round basket of cedar fronds hanging above the entrance. The best plan is to stroll around without trying to see everything and thus avoid risking an overdose of museums.

Hida Archaeology Museum The Hida Archaeology Museum displays craft items and archaeological objects in a traditional house. The house was constructed with secret passages and windows in case the owners needed to make a quick exit. Admission costs ¥300 and it's open from 8 am to 5 pm.

Fujii Folkcraft Museum This museum is close to the archaeology museum and displays folkcraft from Japan, China and Korea.

It's in an old merchant's house. Admission costs ¥300 and opening hours are from 9 am to 5 pm.

Hirata Folk Art Museum The Hirata Folk Art Museum is a merchant's house dating from the turn of the century. The displays include items from everyday Japanese life. Admission costs ¥200 and it's open from 9 am to 5 pm.

Gallery of Traditional Japanese Toys This gallery has an exhibition of some 2000 dolls and folk toys from the 17th century to the present day. The gallery is open from 8.30 am to 5 pm and entry costs ¥200.

Takayama Local History Museum This museum is devoted to the crafts and traditions of the region. Pride of place is allotted to rustic images carved by Enshū, a wood-carving priest who wandered around the region in the 17th century. Admission costs ¥300. It's open from 8.30 am to 5 pm, closed on Monday, with exception of the high-season summer months, when it's open daily.

Wild Bird Museum The Wild Bird Museum is devoted to the wild birds of the Japan Alps and surrounding areas. Admission costs ¥150 and it's open from 9 am to 5 pm daily except Wednesday.

Hachiga Folk Art Gallery This is a merchant house containing more folk arts and antiques, some of which depict Christian themes. Admission to the gallery costs ¥200 and it's open from 9 am to 5 pm but closed on Wednesday from December to March.

Kusakabe Heritage House　日下部民芸館
The Kusakabe Heritage House is a fine example of a wealthy merchant's home, with the living quarters in one section and warehouse in another. It is fitted out as it would have been if you'd walked in to talk business in the late 1890s. Admission costs ¥500. It's open from 9 am to 5 pm, but closes half an hour earlier from December to March.

Yoshijima-ke House　吉島家住宅
This house is on the same street as the Kusakabe Heritage House. Although Yoshijima-ke is also a merchant's house, it has more refined architectural details such as lattice windows which provide a lighter atmosphere. It is certainly worth a visit.

The house is open daily from 9 am to 4.30 pm, with the exception of the months from December to February, when it closes on Tuesday; admission costs ¥300.

Festival Floats Exhibition Hall　屋台会館
If you can't be in Takayama for the big festivals, you can still see four of the *yatai* (festival floats) which are displayed in this hall in seasonal rotation. The hall is adjacent to the grounds of the Sakurayama Hachiman-gū Shrine, where the autumn festival begins. Those yatai which are not on display are stored in tall *yatai-kura* (yatai storehouses) which can be seen in the town. For the technically minded – a collapsible top tier allows the yatai to pass through the doors.

The yatai, some of which date from the 17th century, are spectacular creations with flamboyant carvings, metalwork, and lacquerwork. The complex marionettes, manipulated by eight experts using 36 strings, are capable of amazing tricks and acrobatics. The marionettes on the Hotei Tai float perform astounding feats. Life-size figures standing next to the floats are dressed in the costumes worn in the festival parade.

Admission to the hall costs ¥460 and includes a glossy leaflet with information about the yatai. It's open from 9 am to 4.30 pm. At the ticket desk you will be offered a cassette recorder to guide you around the display or you may be assigned to a guide.

If you are near visiting tour groups, you can expect your ears to be blown off by flag-waving guides vying to drown each other's commentaries with bullhorns. There's a side room on the upper storey used for showing videos of the festival; it offers a convenient escape.

Lion Mask Exhibition Hall　獅子会館
Just below the Yatai Kaikan is the Lion Mask

Exhibition Hall, which has a display of over 800 lion masks and musical instruments connected with lion dances commonly performed at festivals in central and northern Japan. There are also frequent displays of ancient mechanical puppets – a good chance for a close-up view of these marvellous gadgets in action.

Admission costs ¥600 and this includes the mechanical puppet show (displays every 15 minutes). The hall is open from 8.30 am to 5 pm.

At the exit from the hall are souvenir shops and a machine that tells your fortune in English. Put ¥100 in the slot and a mechanical priestess toddles out from her shrine and drops your fortune into the tray below. If you want to continue feeling happy and secure in life, don't even open 'Written Oracle No 27: Excellent Luck'!

Written Oracle No 27: Excellent Luck
I was blessed with Written Oracle No 27: Excellent Luck. Here's a sample of how lucky I was: 'wish' – at first it appears to be realised very soon, but later it will be alright; 'missing thing' – it will be difficult to find, it will pass into another's hands; 'illness' – it will be a heavy illness, but take it easy; and 'travel' – it will do you less good, you will have much difficulty in finding your way to your home.

The last item was depressing news for someone writing about travel, but I hate to think what sort of fortune lies in store for those who get 'Poor Luck'. Still, the general prognosis was vaguely heartening: 'you'll have good luck in the near future, to get it you must be moderate in anything and abide your time without being tired'.

Robert Strauss

Hida Kokubun-ji Temple 飛驒国分寺
The original temple was built in the 8th century, but the oldest of the present buildings dates from the 16th century. The old ginkgo tree beside the three storeyed pagoda is impressively gnarled and in remarkably good shape considering it's believed to have stood there for 1200 years. Admission costs

¥200 and it's open from 9 am to 4 pm. The temple is a five minute walk from the station.

Teramachi & Shiroyama-kōen Park
寺町・城山公園
The best way to link these two areas in the Higashiyama district is to follow the walking trail. Teramachi has over a dozen temples (the youth hostel is in Tenshō-ji Temple) and several shrines which you can wander round at your leisure before continuing to the lush greenery of the park. Various trails lead through the park and up the mountainside to the ruins of Takayama-jō Castle. As you descend, you can take a look at Shōren-ji Temple, which was transferred to this site from the Shirakawa Valley when a dam was built there in 1960. Admission to the main hall costs ¥200.

From the temple it's a 10 minute walk back to the centre of town.

Hida Folk Village 飛驒民俗村
The Hida Minzoku-mura (Hida Folk Village) is a large open-air museum with dozens of traditional houses which once belonged to craftspeople and farmers in the Takayama region. The houses were dismantled at their original sites and rebuilt here. You should definitely include this museum in your visit to Takayama.

The admission charge (¥700) admits you to both the eastern and western sections of the village, which are connected part of the way by a pleasant walk through fields. Allow at least two hours if you want to explore the village on foot at a leisurely pace. On a fine day, there are good views across the town to the peaks of the Japan Alps. The village is open from 8.30 am to 5 pm.

Hida Minzokukan The eastern section of the village is centred around the Hida Minzokukan (Hida Folklore Museum) at the Minzokukan-mae bus stop. There are four buildings in the museum complex: Wakayama House, Nokubi House, Go-kura Storehouse (used for storage of rice as payment of taxes) and the Museum of Mountain Life.

Wakayama House is of interest for its precipitously slanted *gasshō-zukuri* roof, which is typical of the Hida area and used to prevent the accumulation of heavy snowfall. 'gasshō-zukuri' is a descriptive term that compares the roof style to 'hands folded in prayer'. The interior gives a good idea of a farmer's lifestyle in the 18th century. The 2nd and 3rd floors were used for rearing silkworms and have been filled with household implements of that era.

Nokubi House is a standard farmhouse – the interior is arranged around a central earthen floor and fireplace.

The Museum of Mountain Life is a random collection of mountaineering memorabilia: old skis, boots, stuffed roosters, swans and assorted feathered friends and pickled-looking fish.

To reach the western section of the Hida Folk Village, continue uphill from the Museum of Mountain Life along a pleasant path, which winds past fields until you rejoin the road. Keep walking uphill on the road until you reach the rows of souvenir shops and the ticket office for Hida-no-Sato Village which is on your left at the top of the hill.

Hida-no-Sato Village The western section of the village is centred round Hida-no-Sato Village at the Hida-no-Sato bus stop.

Hida-no-Sato stretches over 10 hectares and is divided into two parts: a village of 12 traditional old houses and a complex of five traditional buildings with artisans demonstrating folk arts & crafts. It takes about two hours, at a leisurely pace, to follow the circular route. The displays are well presented and offer an excellent chance to see what rural life was like in previous centuries.

Hida Folk Village is only a 20 minute walk from Takayama station, but the route through the urban sprawl is not enjoyable. Either hire a bicycle in town, or take the Hida Minzoku-mura bus from the bus station which takes 10 minutes to reach Hida-no-Sato (the western section of the village) and then continues downhill for a couple of minutes to Minzokukan-mae (the eastern section).

Main World Shrine

If you have time, drop in to see the colossal, Orwellian structure of Sukyo Mahikari Suza (Main World Shrine), with its golden roof topped by a glacé cherry – visible from miles around. Whether you are attracted or repelled by the architecture or the spiritual message, it's still an intriguing place.

Sukyo Mahikari is the name given to a movement started in 1959 by Kotama Okada who emphasised a spiritual life centred around the basic principles of the universe. The founder's daughter, Oshienushisama, arranged completion of the Main World Shrine in 1984. The activities of this spiritual movement, which has over half a million followers all over the world, concentrate on purification and include healing through the laying on of hands. Several experimental farms have been established near by to produce vegetables and grains by organic methods. There are four major ceremonies held annually and smaller ceremonies are held every month.

From the massive bus station at the base of the building, you ascend to the visitors' hall and continue to a vast platform with fine views of the Japan Alps. A long flight of stone steps leads up to the main hall. As you go, notice the Quetzalcoatl Fountain and the Towers of Light, standing like obedient spaceships with reversed swastika motifs.

Inside the doors of the main hall is a reception desk where you are required to deposit any cameras or daypacks. The main hall has seating for at least 1000 people in front of a gigantic shrine which is traversed by a shimmering blue aquarium. At the rear of the hall is a giant pipe organ from Denmark. A courteous attendant will probably give you instructions in Japanese, helping you through the motions of praying, bowing and clapping.

When you leave, you will be offered a saucer of sake at the reception desk. Leaflets are available here with background information about this spiritual movement.

The shrine is a 20 minute walk north-west of Hida Folk Village or you can take a bus from Takayama bus station.

Markets

The *asa-ichi* (morning markets) take place every morning from 7 am to noon. The Jinya-mae market is a small one in front of Takayama-jinya (Historical Government House) and the Miyagawa market is larger, strung out along the east bank of the Miyagawa River, between Kaji-bashi Bridge and Yayoi-bashi Bridge. Those in need of an early morning coffee can stop at a stand-up stall halfway in the middle of this market for a bargain cup at ¥170. The markets aren't astounding, but provide a pleasant way to start the day with a stroll past gnarled farmers at their vegetable stands and stalls selling herbs and souvenirs.

Festivals

Takayama is famed all over Japan for two major festivals which attract over half a million visitors. Book your accommodation well in advance.

Sannō Matsuri Festival takes place on 14 and 15 April. The starting point for the festival parade is Hie-jinja Shrine. A dozen yatai (festival floats), decorated with carvings, dolls, colourful curtains and blinds, are drawn through the town. In the evening the floats are decked out with lanterns and the procession is accompanied by sacred music. A famous feature of the floats is the marionettes, which perform amazing antics.

Hachiman Matsuri Festival, which takes place on 9 and 10 October, is a slightly smaller version of Sannō Matsuri.

Places to Stay

If you are going to stay in Takayama for the big festivals in April or October, you must book months in advance and expect to pay up to 20% more than you would at any other time. Alternatively, you could stay elsewhere in the region and commute to Takayama for the festival.

The information office outside Takayama station can help with reservations either in Takayama or elsewhere in the region. It has a list of places to suit all budgets. There are dozens of ryokan and

minshuku; prices for the cheapest ryokan start at ¥8000 per person, including two meals. The cheapest minshuku and kokuminshukusha charge ¥5000 per person, including two meals.

Youth Hostel *Hida Takayama Tenshō-ji Youth Hostel* (☎ 0577-32-6345) is a temple in the pleasant surroundings of Teramachi, but hostellers should be prepared to stick to a rigid routine. To get there from the station, it takes about 20 minutes to walk across town. A bed for the night costs ¥2100. You receive strict instructions on bath times and there are signs warning you that slippers must not be worn beyond a certain point. Punctually at 10 pm you are lulled to sleep by music and at 7 am you are awakened by the recorded twittering of birds.

Ryokan Most of Takayama's ryokan have rates of between ¥8000 to ¥15,000 per person including two meals, and in most cases you will need some Japanese in order to make the proprietors happy about taking you. Possibilities (there are seemingly millions of them) include the *Daimaru Ryokan* (☎ 0577-32-0630), which is close to the station and has rates from ¥9000. It's in a rather unryokan-looking white building – there's no English sign.

Just near the river is the *Sumiyoshi Ryokan* (☎ 0577-32-0228), a delightfully traditional-style place with rates from ¥8000. Straight ahead from the station and just over the river is the *Ryokan Gōto* (☎ 0577-33-0870), another traditional-style inn, with rates from ¥8500. The architecturally modern *Ryokan Seiryu* (☎ 0577-32-0448) is close to the town centre. Prices start at ¥10,000 per person including two meals.

If you want nothing but the finest classical ryokan and are willing to dig really deep into your bank account, then you should stay at *Ryokan Kinkikan* (☎ 0577-32-3131) in the centre of town. It has antique furnishings and an immaculate Japanese garden. Prices start around ¥16,000 per person.

Minshuku *Hachibei* (☎ 0577-33-0573) is a pleasantly faded, rambling place close to Hida-no-Sato Village. Take a bus to the Hida-no-Sato bus stop; from there it's an eight minute walk to the north. Prices start at ¥7000 per person and include two meals.

Close to the station is *Oshuku Matsuyama* (☎ 0577-32-1608). It's not in a particularly charming building and has rates of ¥7000 with two meals.

Kokuminshukusha Close to Hida Folk Village is *Kokuminshukusha Hida* (☎ 0577-32-2400). It's about 10 minutes on foot south-east of Hida Minzokukan. Prices start at ¥7000 per person and include two meals. This place is popular with Japanese tourists so advance reservations are recommended.

Business Hotels The *New Alps Hotel* (☎ 0577-32-2888) is just a minute's walk from the station. Singles/doubles start at ¥4500/9000, and this is very good value. Over by the river, the *Hotel Alpha One* (☎ 0577-32-2211; the Greek word for *alpha* and the numeral '1' are on the sign outside) is another reasonably inexpensive place, with singles from ¥5100 and twins/doubles at ¥10,400/9300. Around a 10 minute walk from the station is the *Takayama Central Hotel* (☎ 0577-35-1881), where singles are ¥5500 and twins range from ¥10,000.

More up-market possibilities include the *Hida Hotel Plaza* (☎ 0577-33-4600), with singles/twins from ¥8000/18,000, the *Takayama Green Hotel* (☎ 0577-33-5500), with twins/doubles from ¥15,000/18,000, and the *Chatelet Inn Takayama* (☎ 0577-34-0700), which has rates from ¥9000 to ¥30,000.

Places to Eat
Takayama is known for several culinary treats. These include *Hida-soba* (buckwheat noodles with broth and vegetables), *hoba-miso* (vegetables cooked with miso) and *sansai* (mountain greens). You might also want to try *midarashi-dango* (skewers of

grilled rice balls seasoned with soy sauce) or *shio-sembei* (salty rice crackers). Close to Takayama station (see the map) is a *Nama-Soba*, a soba restaurant where you can try Hida-soba. The restaurant also serves tempura and katsudon sets from around ¥800.

Bunched around the old part of town are eight sake breweries with pedigrees dating back to the Edo period. Formerly, the production processes for this *jizake* (local sake) were closed to visitors, but the breweries have recently started to arrange tours and tastings from early January to the end of February only. The information office at the station can arrange for prospective foreign imbibers to join these tours.

Central Takayama There are numerous restaurants and teahouses in the Sanmachi Suji area, which serve the constant flow of tourists but these have slightly elevated prices.

Suzuya (☎ 0577-32-2484) is a well-known restaurant with rustic décor in the centre of town, but is on the other side of the river from Sanmachi Suji. It serves all the local specialities and its teishoku lunches are good value – prices start from around ¥1000. Opening hours are from 11 am to 8 pm, but it's closed on Tuesday. To help you order, there's also an English menu.

Nomeya Utaeya is part of an izakaya chain, has a great atmosphere, reasonable food and drink prices and an illustrated menu for easy ordering. There's no English sign but you can look out for the red lanterns on the last alley before the bridge off the main shopping street leading from the station. For reasonable Italian fare, *Hole in the Wall* has pasta dishes from around ¥650. It's very close to the station.

For a complete change, you could try *Tom's Bellgins Bell* (☎ 0577-33-6507), a couple of blocks west of Yayoi-bashi Bridge. Its amiable Swiss owner, Tom Steinmann, fulfils all those cravings for things like rösti or fondue. Pizzas are a speciality and prices start around ¥1200.

Teramachi Area The Tenshō-ji Youth Hostel supplies a small map which shows cheap eateries in the area. The *Daikokuya* is an unpretentious noodle shop run by a lady who cooks standard buckwheat noodle dishes. The sansai soba is delicious and comes in various versions which cost about ¥700. If you walk down the steps from the hostel and turn left along the road, you come to a junction about 30 metres later. Take the road downhill to the right and you'll see the Daikokuya on your left, next to the river.

Hida Folk Village Area Clustered around the entrance to the folk village are a number of souvenir shops that also offer basic soba dishes. The food is nothing special and, as is often the case in souvenir shops/restaurants, tends to be a little pricey.

Things to Buy

Takayama is renowned for several crafts. *Ichii ittobori* (wood carvings) are fashioned from yew and can be seen as intricate components of the yatai floats or as figurines for sale as souvenirs. The craft of Shunkei lacquerware was introduced from Kyoto several centuries ago and is used to produce boxes, trays and flower containers. Pottery is produced in three styles ranging from the rustic Yamada-yaki to the decorative ceramics of Shibukusa-yaki. If your house feels empty, local makers of traditional furniture can help you fill it.

The Sanmachi Suji area has many shops selling handicraft items or you can browse in handicraft shops along the section of Kokubun-ji dōri between the river and the station.

If lacquerware is a specific interest, you should visit the Lacquerware Exhibition Hall, which is north-east of the station, a couple of blocks before Yayoi-bashi Bridge. More than 1000 lacquerware items are on display with an exhibit showing production techniques. The hall is open from 8.30 am to 5 pm; admission costs ¥300.

Hida Folk Village is full of shops selling souvenirs, but you might like to browse in the Gokura antiques shop. A venerable old lady presides over a dusty selection of antiques and bric-a-brac with price tags that look like telephone numbers.

Getting There & Away

Train Takayama is connected with Nagoya on the JR Takayama line. The fastest limited express (tokkyū) takes two hours and 16 minutes.

Express trains run from Osaka and Kyoto to Gifu or Nagoya and continue on the JR Takayama line to Takayama. The trip takes about five hours from Osaka and half an hour less from Kyoto. If you are travelling on a rail pass, the best course of action would be to take a shinkansen to Nagoya and change there to the Takayama line. Limited express trains from Nagoya to Takayama are not particularly frequent.

Toyama is connected with Takayama on the JR Takayama line. The fastest express from Toyama takes around 1½ hours whereas the local train (futsū) rambles to Takayama in just under three hours.

A bus/train combination runs from Takayama via Kamikōchi to Matsumoto. You take a bus from Takayama to Kamikōchi then change to another bus for Shin-Shimashima station on the Matsumoto Dentetsu line and continue by rail to Matsumoto.

Bus Staff from several tourist offices in the Japan Alps go to great lengths to warn travellers that many roads in this region close in the winter. This means that bus schedules usually only start from early May and finish in late October. For exact opening or closing dates either phone Japan Travel-Phone (☎ 0120-444800 toll free) or the tourist offices.

A bus service connects Takayama with Hirayu Onsen (one hour) and takes another hour to reach Kamikōchi. Direct buses run from Takayama via Hirayu Onsen to Shin-Hotaka Onsen and the nearby cablecar (ropeway).

Another bus route runs on the spectacular Norikura Skyline Road connecting Norikura with Takayama in 1¾ hours.

Details for the bus/train connection between Takayama and Matsumoto via Hirayu Onsen are given in the preceding section on rail connections.

The bus service between Kanazawa and Nagoya runs via Takayama and Shirakawa-gō, but only operates mid-summer.

Hitching Providing you are equipped for mountain conditions, hitching is quite feasible in the Japan Alps between May and late September.

I had several good hitches between Shirakawa-gō and Takayama and from Kamikōchi down to Matsumoto. On one occasion I was picked up by a petrol tanker and soon discovered that the only form of communication between myself and the driver was via his mania for foreign sports cars. We swapped names of sports cars in a type of monosyllabic, verbal ping-pong. When I mentioned I'd once driven an Austin Healey 3000 the driver almost went off the road in delirium.

Robert Strauss

Getting Around

With the exception of Hida Folk Village, the sights in Takayama can be easily covered on foot. You can amble from the station across to Higashiyama on the other side of town in 25 minutes.

Bus The bus station is on your left as you exit the station. There is a circular bus route around the town, and bus passes are available for one day (¥890) or two days (¥1350).

Although the main sights in town are best seen on foot or by bicycle, the walk to Hida Folk Village is tedious and unattractive. It's preferable to use the half-hourly bus service which takes 10 minutes and costs ¥200.

Bicycle There are several bicycle rental places near the station and in town. Rates are high at ¥250 for the first hour, ¥200 for each additional hour and ¥1250 for the day. The youth hostel charges ¥100 per hour or ¥700

for the day and is probably the best deal available.

Rickshaw For those who want a change from the shinkansen, there are several tourist rickshaws available for hire at prices which approach those of the shinkansen. A two hour ride costs ¥5000 per person and a half day ride costs ¥10,000 per person.

Ask at the tourist office if you want to arrange a ride or you can negotiate direct with the rickshaw-pullers who are usually found posing for photos in the streets of Sanmachi Suji.

SHŌKAWA VALLEY REGION 荘川

This is one of the most interesting regions in Japan and highly recommended as a day trip from Takayama or as a stopover en route between Takayama and Kanazawa.

Although much of what you see here has been specially preserved for, and supported by tourism, it still presents a view of rural Japan far removed from the usual images of Japan as a giant urban sprawl punctuated by oases of tranquil temples and Zen gardens. If you want to avoid large contingents of tourists, bear in mind that the peak seasons for this region are May, August and October.

In the 12th century, the remoteness and inaccessibility of the area is claimed to have attracted a few stragglers from the Taira clan who sought hideaways here and on Kyūshū after their clan was virtually wiped out by the Genji clan in a brutal battle at Shimonoseki in 1185.

In the present century, construction of the gigantic Miboro Dam in the '60s submerged many of the villages and the attention this attracted to the region also drew tourists interested in the unusual architecture of the remaining villages and their remote mountain surroundings.

There are many villages and hamlets spread around the Shōkawa Valley region, but Shirakawa-gō and Gokayama are two districts with dozens of specially preserved houses and are the two concentrations of villages most commonly visited by travellers.

CENTRAL HONSHŪ

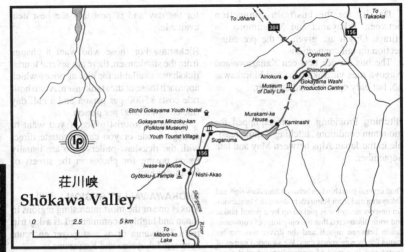

To Jōhana
To Takaoka
Ogimachi
Shimonashi
Ainokura
Gokayama Washi
Production Centre
Museum
of Daily Life
Murakami-ke
House
Kaminashi
Etchō Gokayama Youth Hostel
Gokayama Minzoku-kan
(Folklore Museum)
Youth Tourist Village
Suganuma
荘川峡
Shōkawa Valley
Iwase-ke House
Gyōtoku-ji Temple
Nishi-Akao
0 2.5 5 km
To
Miboro-ko
Lake
Shō-gawa River

SHIRAKAWA-GŌ DISTRICT & OGIMACHI 白川郷・荻町

The Shirakawa-gō district consists of several clusters of houses in villages stretching for several km. Ogimachi, the central cluster, is the most convenient place for bus connections, tourist information and orientation. When arriving by bus, ask to get off at the Gasshō-shuraku bus stop.

Information

The tourist information office (☎ 05769-6-1751/1013) is next to the Gasshō-shuraku bus stop in the centre of Ogimachi. It's open from 9 am to 5 pm. The office has a Japanese map of the whole region including a detailed map of Ogimachi itself. An English leaflet is also available.

Tenbōdai Lookout 展望台

To get your bearings on the village, climb up to the Tenbōdai lookout; from here, you'll obtain the view seen on most tourist brochures. From the Gasshō-shuraku bus stop, walk north down the main road for about 10 minutes and on your right you will see a wooded hill beside the road with a side street leading around the foot of the hill.

You can either follow the side street to the top of the hill or, after walking about 10 metres down the side street, take the steep path on your right which gets you to the top in about 15 minutes.

Shirakawa-gō Gasshō-no-Sato Village 白川郷合掌の里

This well-presented collection of over a dozen gasshō-zukuri buildings were largely collected from the surrounding region and reconstructed for display as an open-air museum. Several of the houses are used for demonstrating regional crafts such as woodwork, straw handicrafts, ceramics and painting in Chinese ink – most of these items are on sale either from the artisans or at the ticket office.

You can wander away from the houses for a pleasant stroll through the trees further up the mountain. If you don't take a picnic, you can stop at the rest house near the exit which is run by a chatty lady who offers tea, biscuits and home-made *mochi* (rice cakes) toasted over the *irori* (open hearth).

Admission costs ¥500. The village is open from 8.30 am to 5 pm between April and November, from 8 am to 6 pm during August and from 9 am to 4 pm between December

Gasshō-zukuri Architecture

The most striking feature of the villages are houses built in the *gasshō-zukuri* style. The poorest peasants had ramshackle hovels, but the leading families crammed several generations into massive buildings with up to four storeys.

The ground floor was used for communal living in open rooms and – not surprisingly, considering the bitter winters – the focal point was the *irori* (open hearth). The smoke from the fire drifted up into the upper storeys which were used for storage and, from the 18th century onwards, for the cultivation of silkworms which provided extra income. The acutely slanted thatched roof repelled heavy snowfall and its shape was considered to resemble 'hands in prayer' (gasshō-zukuri). ∎

and January. To reach the entrance, you have to walk west from the main road, cross a suspension bridge over the river, and continue through a dimly lit tunnel dripping with moisture.

Myōzen-ji Temple   明善寺
This temple, in the centre of Ogimachi, is combined with a museum displaying the traditional paraphernalia of daily life.

Admission costs ¥200 and it's open from 7.30 am to 5 pm. There are shorter opening hours during the winter.

Doburoku Matsuri Exhibition Hall
どぶろく祭展示館
This exhibition hall (Doburoku Matsuri-no-Yakata) is very close to Shirakawa Hachiman-jinja Shrine. The hall contains displays and a video show devoted to the Doburoku Matsuri Festival, an event clearly not lacking in liquid refreshment (*doburoku* is a type of unrefined sake), which is held in mid-October at the shrine.

Admission costs ¥310 and it's open from 8.30 am to 4.30 pm (9 am to 4 pm during winter).

Museum of Daily Life   民俗館
If you walk for about 15 minutes from the centre of Ogimachi back along the road

towards Takayama, you'll reach the Museum of Daily Life, which is on your right, just beyond the second bridge. On display are agricultural tools, rural crafts, equipment for the cultivation of silkworms and various household items from the past. Admission costs ¥200 and the museum is open from 8 am to 5 pm.

Places to Stay
Some of the gasshō-zukuri buildings function as minshuku and are a popular accommodation option in this region. If you don't speak Japanese, it would be a good idea to enlist the support of the tourist information office in introducing you to one. Per-person costs are generally ¥6000 including two meals. A couple of rustic possibilities include *Kandaya* (☎ 05769-6-1072), *Yosobē* (☎ 05769-6-1172) and *Furusato* (☎ 05769-6-1033).

Ryokan prices start at ¥8000 per person including two meals; minshuku prices, for the same deal, start at ¥6500. *Juemon*

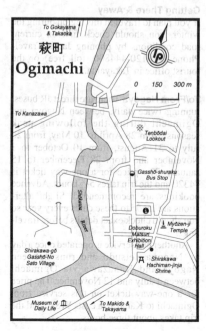

(☎ 05769-6-1053) is one minshuku which has received consistently favourable comments from foreign visitors.

If you want the cheapest option in the area, you'll have to travel to *Etchū Gokayama Youth Hostel* (☎ 0763-67-3331), which is a gasshō-zukuri house in a more remote location (about two km on foot from the bus stop on the main road) and close to Gokayama. See the following Gokayama Places to Stay section for more information on costs and finding the hostel.

Places to Eat

Breakfast and dinner are usually included in the price of your ryokan or minshuku. The main street in Ogimachi has several restaurants, including the atmospheric *Shiraogi*. The latter has dishes from around ¥800, but for a real treat try the *shiraogi-teishoku*, which at ¥2200 gives you a good sampling of the local cuisine.

Getting There & Away

If you plan to travel in this region during the winter, you should check first on current road conditions by phoning Japan Travel-Phone (☎ 0120-444800, toll free) or the tourist office in Takayama.

To/From Nagoya There are direct JR buses, running twice daily, between Nagoya and Ogimachi during the following peak seasons: from 28 April to 10 May, from 20 July to 31 August, from 10 October to 3 November and from 28 December to 15 January. The price for a one-way ticket is ¥4320 and the trip takes 5½ hours. Advance bookings are recommended. Slight alterations are made to these dates every year so you should check exact details before travelling.

Another bus service is operated once a day by Nagoya Tetsudō and runs between Nagoya and Kanazawa via Ogimachi between 1 July and 12 November. The price for a one-way ticket on this service from Ogimachi to Kanazawa costs ¥1880 and the trip takes about three hours.

To/From Takayama There are four daily bus connections with Ogimachi, made in two stages. The first stage is a bus service operated by Nohi bus company between Takayama and Makido (¥1800, one hour).

The second stage is a connecting bus service operated by JR between Makido and Ogimachi. The trip takes about an hour and a one-way ticket costs ¥1200 – unless, of course, you have a Japan Rail Pass.

To/From Kanazawa If you are not able to use the Nagoya Tetsudō bus described earlier, there are other options. One is to take the train from Kanazawa on the JR line to Takaoka, then from Takaoka station, take a bus to Ogimachi via Gokayama (two hours).

Another option is to take the train on the Jōhana line from Takaoka to Jōhana. From Jōhana there's a bus service to Ogimachi.

Getting Around

Ogimachi is easily covered on foot. If you want to visit Gokayama, you will have to wait for infrequent buses or hitch.

GOKAYAMA DISTRICT 五箇山

Gokayama is just inside the boundaries of Toyama-ken, a short distance north of Ogimachi. Prior to the Edo period, the feudal lords of Kanazawa used the isolated location of Gokayama as a centre for the secretive production of gunpowder. Many of the houses open to the public in this region have displays of equipment for making gunpowder. The construction of a road to Gokayama and the provision of electricity didn't occur until 1925.

In the Gokayama area, gasshō-zukuri houses are scattered in small groups along the valley. The following is a brief description of the sights as you travel north from Shirakawa-gō district and Ogimachi. There are bus stops at each group of houses.

Nishi-Akao 西赤尾

Nishi-Akao is about 20 minutes by bus from Ogimachi. The two attractions here are **Gyōtoku-ji Temple** and **Iwase-ke House** which was once the local centre for the production of gunpowder.

Suganuma 菅沼

Suganuma is four km beyond Nishi-Akao and lies just below the main road. The **Folklore Museum** consists of two houses: one displays items from traditional life; and across the path, the other is devoted to exhibits which explain the traditional techniques for gunpowder production. The combined admission charge is ¥300 and it's open from 9 am to 5 pm between May and November. For ¥1000 you can buy cassettes of the local music – a haunting combination of twanging stringed instruments and mournful wailing.

Close by is an attractive goup of gasshō-zukuri houses that are worth strolling around. From Nishi-Akao, take a Takaoka-bound bus for the 10 minute (¥220) ride to Suganuma.

Just to the south is a **Youth Tourist Village**. If you cross the bridge over the river and take the road to the right, you'll eventually puff your way uphill to the youth hostel (see Places to Stay).

Kaminashi 上梨

Kaminashi is on the main road, four km beyond Suganuma. **Murakami-ke House** dates from 1578 and has now become an interesting museum well maintained by the proud and enthusiastic owner who conducts visitors on a tour of the exhibits then sits them down around the irori and sings local folksongs. He provides a musical accompaniment for the songs using two curious musical instruments: a string of wooden blocks flicked expertly to produce a prolonged rattling sound and two bamboo sticks which are deftly twirled together to produce a rhythmic 'clack' sound. The owner also sells *suiboku* (water and black ink) paintings which he dashes off at great speed. Admission costs ¥300, and the house is open daily from 8.30 am to 5 pm. A detailed leaflet is provided in English.

Also close by and worth a look is **Hakusan-gū Shrine**. The main hall dates

from 1502 and has been designated an Important Cultural Property.

Takaoka-bound buses from Nishi-Akao take around 15 minutes to reach Kaminashi and cost ¥390.

Shimonashi & Ainokura 下梨・相倉

Shimonashi is on the main road, four km beyond Kaminashi. Just beyond the bus stop, there's a road on your left leading up a steep hill towards Ainokura. About 100 metres up this road, you reach **Gokayama Washi Production Centre** on your left. The production of washi (Japanese paper) has been a speciality of the region for several centuries and you can see the production process here. If you pay ¥450, you can even have a go at it yourself and keep your work of art. If you want to buy some of the elegant paper products, you can do so in the small shop. The centre is open daily from 8.30 am to 5 pm from April to November.

From here it takes another 25 minutes on foot, winding up the hill to reach the side street leading off to the left to Ainokura, an impressive village of gasshō-zukuri houses with fine views across the valley. The **Ainokura Museum of Daily Life** is in the village, is open from 8.30 am to 5 pm, closed on Tuesday and charges ¥200 admission.

If you are here when the tour buses are absent, or if you stay here in one of the minshuku, it should be possible to appreciate the slow, measured pace of village life. Frogs croak in flooded fields, farmers tramp through the mud and women in headscarves fan out across the fields to attack weeds and chat.

Places to Stay

Several gasshō-zukuri houses in the Gokayama area function as minshuku. Expect to pay around ¥6000 per person for a bed and two meals. The youth hostel near Suganuma offers the most inexpensive way to stay in accommodation of this kind.

The tourist information offices in Takayama and Ogimachi can help with reservations and there is an information office in the centre of Ainokura. Advance reservations are highly recommended particularly during the peak seasons of May, August and October.

Etchū Gokayama Youth Hostel (☎ 07636-7-3331) is a fine old gasshō-zukuri farmhouse and a great place to stay; it's only a few km off the main road.

A bed for the night costs ¥1900. For ¥700 you get a fine dinner which includes grilled trout, pickles, sansai (mountain greens), a huge slab of tōfu, tempura vegetables and rice. The owner and his family sit around a large irori as the smoke from the fire curls up through the rafters.

The hostel is not easy to find. The closest bus stop is at Suganuma which is only 12 minutes by bus from Kaminashi bus stop or 25 minutes by bus from Ogimachi. A sign in the Suganuma bus shelter warns hostellers arriving during the snowy season not to attempt the walk to the hostel before phoning from a nearby house to make sure the road is not blocked.

From the Suganuma bus stop on the main road, walk down the side street through the cluster of houses by the river and cross the large bridge. At the other end of the bridge, turn right and wind your way for several km uphill until you come to the hostel which is in a small cluster of houses perched on the mountainside. The total distance is about two km from the bus stop to the hostel.

In Suganuma itself, you could also try *Yohachi* (☎ 0763-67-3205), a rambling minshuku close to the river.

In Ainokura, you have a choice of several minshuku; check with the *minshuku annai-sō* (minshuku information office) which can help with reservations.

In Kaminashi, the *Kokuminshukusha Gokayama-sō* (☎ 0763-66-2316) costs of ¥5700 per person including two meals. The building is a bit of an architectural monstrosity, so if it's charm you're after, it might be worth looking elsewhere.

Getting There & Away

Gokayama is about 20 minutes from Ogimachi by infrequent bus . Hitching is a good way to avoid long waits for buses.

Gokayama is also served by the buses running between Kanazawa and Nagoya via Ogimachi, but only from July to November. For details, refer to the Ogimachi Getting There & Away section under . Remember that many roads in this region are closed during the winter.

HIRAYU ONSEN   平湯温泉

This is a hot-spring resort in the Japan Alps and of primary interest to visitors as a hub for bus transport in the region. The information office opposite the bus station has leaflets and information on hot-spring ryokan and nature trails in the area. If you have time, perhaps while waiting for a bus connection, the trail to **Hirayu-ōtaki Falls** is quite enjoyable – allow 1½ hours in total for the hike. Ask for the *Hirayu-ōtaki Kōsu Chizu*, which is a decent map with some details in English and includes directions to the nearby camping ground.

Getting There & Away

There are frequent bus connections between Hirayu Onsen and Kamikōchi, but *only* from late April to late October. The trip takes 65 minutes (¥1400) and runs via Nakanoyu. The section on Kamikōchi has more details regarding combined bus/rail connections with Matsumoto.

Buses to Norikura, Kamikōchi and Shin-Hotaka Onsen all run via Hirayu Onsen. Consequently, there are frequent bus connections between Takayama and Hirayu Onsen (¥1080, one hour).

There are bus services approximately three times a day between Norikura and Hirayu Onsen. The trip takes 45 minutes. The Norikura Skyline Road is *only* open from 15 May to 31 October. There are frequent bus connections between Hirayu Onsen and Shin-Hotaka Onsen (¥770, 35 minutes). If you want to continue to Toyama, there are bus connections twice daily (four hours).

SHIN-HOTAKA ONSEN   新穂高温泉

This is a hot-spring resort with the added attraction of the Shin-Hotaka cablecar, reportedly the longest of its kind in Asia, which whisks you up close to the peak of **Mt Nishi Hotaka-dake** (2908 metres) for a superb mountain panorama. The cablecar consists of two sections and a combined ticket costs ¥1240 one way and an extra ¥300 if you take your backpack.

If you are fit, properly equipped and give yourself ample time, there are a variety of hiking options from Nishi Hotaka-guchi (the top cablecar station). One option which takes a bit less than three hours, would be to hike over to **Kamikōchi**.

Getting There & Away
There are frequent bus connections with Hirayu Onsen (¥770, 35 minutes) and Takayama (¥1850, 95 minutes). From Shin-Hotaka Onsen to Toyama there are buses twice daily (3½ hours).

FURUKAWA 古川
Furukawa, on the route between Takayama and Toyama, was originally a castle town. It's quite a pleasant place to visit, particularly if you like strolling around areas with white storehouses, old residences and shops; the old streets are arranged in the traditional grid pattern. The main draw for Furukawa is the festival in April. If you want to attend, you should stay in Furukawa and reserve your accommodation well in advance.

One slightly confusing but important point is that the station for Furukawa is called Hida-Furukawa.

Information
Information can be obtained at the station, but you may find it easier to use the tourist information office in Takayama which can also provide maps and leaflets, and arrange reservations.

Festivals
The major annual festival is Furukawa Matsuri which is held on 19 and 20 April. The festival features squads of young men, who, dressed in loincloths (the event is also referred to as the Hadaka Matsuri or 'Naked Festival'), parade through town with a giant drum. There are also processions with large yatai (festival floats) similar to those used in the Takayama festivals.

Places to Stay
Hida Furukawa Youth Hostel (☎ 0577-75-2979) is about three km west of Furukawa station (40 minutes on foot), or 1.2 km (15 minute walk) west of Hida Hosō station (two stops to the north of Furukawa). Ask for Shinrin-kōen, which is a park next to the hostel. Only 22 beds are available. To avoid disappointment make an advance reservation. A dorm bed costs ¥2500 and bicycles are available for hire. The hostel is closed from 30 March to 10 April.

The *Ryokan Tanbo-no-Yu* (☎ 0577-73-2014) is a straightforward ryokan whih costs ¥7000 per person. No English is spoken, so if you don't speak any Japanese you'll need some help to make a reservation. To find the ryokan, turn right from the station, then take the third left, the first right and look out for the ryokan (a nondescript tan-coloured building with a sign outside) on the corner as the road turns to the right.

Things to Buy
Furukawa is famous for handmade candles. In the centre of town, you can visit Mishima-ya, a shop which has specialised in traditional candle-making techniques for over two centuries.

Getting There & Away
Hida-Furukawa station is three stops north of Takayama on the JR Takayama line. The trip takes 15 minutes. There are also hourly buses from Takayama station to Hida-Furukawa station (30 minutes).

Nagano-ken 長野県

Most of Nagano-ken consists of the northern, central and southern ranges of the Japan Alps – hence its claim to being the 'Roof of Japan'.

Nagano-ken is one of the most enjoyable

19(s) 20(s) 21(s) 22(Na) 23(Na)
24(Ma) 25(To) 26(To) 27(N) 28

長野県
Nagano-ken

0   15   30 km

––– Prefectural Boundary

RAILWAY STATIONS

1 Minami Otari	8 Ariake
2 Hakuba Oike	9 Toyoshina
3 Iimori	10 Shin-Shimashima
4 Inao	11 Komagane
5 Shinano-ōmachi	12 Nagiso
6 Naganohara	13 Ichida
7 Naka-Kuruizawa	14 Nakatsugawa

CENTRAL HONSHŪ

regions to visit in Japan, not only for the beauty of its mountainous terrain, but also for the traditional architecture and culture which linger in many parts of the prefecture and which have been spared the industrial zoning often seen elsewhere in Japan. Agriculture is still a major source of income for this prefecture, but the lack of pollution has also attracted growing numbers of companies from the electronics and precision industries.

Included in this prefecture are numerous national parks and quasi-national parks which attract large numbers of campers, hikers, mountaineers and hot-spring aficionados. Several hikes in this prefecture are covered in *Hiking in Japan* by Paul Hunt. Skiers can choose from dozens of resorts during the skiing season which lasts from late December to late March.

Getting Around

Travel in the prefecture relies mainly on the JR lines which run parallel to the Japan Alps from south to north and it is this axis which dictates the itinerary for most visitors. There are two scenic routes which traverse the Japan Alps: one runs from Matsumoto via Kamikōchi to Takayama (Gifu-ken) and the other runs from Shinano-ōmachi via the Kurobe Dam to Tateyama (Toyama-ken). When making travel plans for the mountains, bear in mind that many roads are closed and bus services are stopped due to heavy snowfall from mid-October to early May. If possible try and avoid major sights and trails during peak tourist seasons (early May, July and August) when they tend to become clogged with visitors.

JNTO publishes *Japan Nagano Prefecture*, a brochure which provides concise details and mapping.

KARUIZAWA 軽井沢

Karuizawa lies at the foot of Mt Asama-yama and lays claim to being Japan's trendiest summer resort or 'holidayland'. Originally a prosperous post town on the Nakasen-dō Highway linking Tokyo and Kyoto, it was 'discovered' by Archdeacon A C Shaw in

1896 and quickly became a favourite summer retreat for the foreign community.

Since then many affluent urbanites, both foreign and Japanese, have set up summer residences and turned the place into a booming centre for outdoor pursuits such as golf, tennis, horse riding and walking. Naturally, the pursuit of shopping has received due attention in the shape of a 'Ginza' street duplicating all the fashionable boutiques, restaurants, shops and crowds which no city-dweller can do without. In comparison with the other attractions of Nagano-ken, this place gets a low rating.

Orientation & Information

Karuizawa extends over a large area. Kyū-Karuizawa (Old Karuizawa) is the core part and is close to Karuizawa station. Naka-Karuizawa (Central Karuizawa) is several km further east.

There are tourist information offices at JR Karuizawa station (☎ 0267-42-2491), Naka-Karuizawa station (☎ 0267-45-6050), and on Karuizawa Ginza (☎ 0267-42-5538). Office hours are from 9 am to 5 pm or for longer during peak season.

The JNTO brochure, *Karuizawa Heights*, has concise details and maps. The tourist offices can help with queries about day trips, hiking trails, transport and accommodation.

Mt Asama-yama 浅間山

Climbing is currently prohibited on Mt Asama-yama (2560 metres) for good reason: it is known to have erupted at least 50 times and has been active over the last few years.

For a close look, you can visit **Onioshi-dashi Rocks**, a region of lava beds on the northern base of the mountain, where there are two gardens with lookout platforms. The **Onioshidashi Rock Garden** is open from 8 am to 6 pm from May to September and to 5 pm for the rest of the year; entry is ¥200. The Asama Garden is open from 8.30 am to 5.30 pm and entry is ¥500. The gardens are next door to each other.

There are buses from Karuizawa and Naka-Karuizawa stations to the lookouts (55 minutes). Get off at the Onioshidashi-en stop.

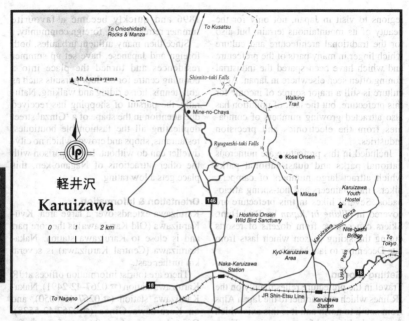

Usui Pass & Lookout 碓氷峠・見晴台

In Kyū-Karuizawa, a walking trail (allow 80 minutes) leads from Nite-bashi Bridge at the end of Karuizawa Ginza to this pass and a lookout with fine views of the surrounding mountains.

Hoshino Onsen Wild Bird Sanctuary 星野温泉野鳥の森

If you are interested in birds, you could stroll for a couple of hours along the bird-watching route. For dedicated 'twitchers' there are two observation huts.

Take a five minute bus ride from Naka-Karuizawa station to Nishiku-iriguchi. From there it's a 10 minute walk to the sanctuary.

Mine-no-Chaya to Mikasa Hike 信濃路自然歩道

If you have four or five hours to spare, this is a pleasant forest amble along a 10 km trail.

Take the bus from Naka-Karuizawa

station to Mine-no-Chaya (25 minutes). From there a trail leads to **Shiraito-taki Falls**, continues to **Ryugaeshi-taki Falls** and then leads via Kose Onsen to Mikasa. The JNTO brochure *Karuizawa Heights* has a map which shows the trail.

Places to Stay

As can be expected for a fancy summer resort, Karuizawa has no shortage of accommodation, ranging from luxury hotels, ryokan, minshuku and pensions to youth hostels and camping grounds. The tourist information office has lists to help with reservations. If you fancy a taste of the high life, you can even arrange to rent a villa.

The nearest youth hostel is in Komoro, six stops west of Karuizawa on the JR Shin-etsu Honsen line. The *Komoro Youth Hostel* (☎ 0267-23-5732) has beds at ¥2500. Considering the hostel is a good six km from Komoro station, it's not particularly convenient base for seeing Karuizawa. You might spend the day in Karuizawa and head over to Komoro in the evening, however.

Finding somewhere affordable to spend the night in Karuizawa is no mean feat. Even the pensions, the standard lower-end resort accommodation in Japan, are expensive. One of the cheaper pensions is *Pension Rosanta* (☎ 0267-42-3667) in Kyū-Karuizawa. It's a pleasant enough place and has per-person costs of ¥8500 to ¥9000 with two meals. It's around 300 metres walk directly north of the station and off a side street to the left.

Over in Naka-Karuizawa, the *Pension Memorizu* ('Memories') (☎ 0267-46-2505) is an atmospheric little place with costs ranging from ¥8500 to ¥13,000 per person with two meals. Look out for it on the right about 500 metres north from Naka-Karuizawa station.

Getting There & Away
Karuizawa is on the JR Shin-etsu Honsen line and can be reached in two hours (¥4720) from Ueno station in Tokyo. The rail connection with Nagano on the same line takes two hours if you do it by an ordinary service, 50 minutes by limited express.

Getting Around
Bus For both local and regional destinations, there is an extensive network of bus services radiating from both Karuizawa and Naka-Karuizawa stations.

Bicycle This is a pleasant way to get around the town. There are bicycle shops in front of Karuizawa station, Naka-Karuizawa station and in the centre of Kyū-Karuizawa. Rental rates start around ¥500 per hour or ¥1400 for four hours.

BESSHO ONSEN   別所温泉
This town was established around the hot springs during the Heian period. It flourished as an administrative centre during the Kamakura period and this cultural influence encouraged the construction of several temples, notably **Anraku-ji Temple** which is renowned for its octagonal pagoda, **Chūzen-**ji Temple and **Zenzan-ji Temple**. Anraku-ji Temple is 10 minutes on foot from Bessho Onsen station. If you have a couple of hours to spare for a five km rural hike, you can continue east to visit the temples of Chūzen-ji and Zenzan-ji.

If you want an inexpensive place to stay in Bessho Onsen, the *Ueda Mahoroba Youth Hostel* (☎ 0268-38-5229) is eight minutes on foot from the station. Nightly costs are ¥2500.

To reach Bessho Onsen, take the JR Shin-etsu Honsen line to Ueda then change to the Ueda Railway for the 30 minute ride to Bessho Onsen.

NAGANO   長野
Nagano (population 347,000), capital of the prefecture, has been around since the Kamakura period (1185-1333), when it was a temple town centred around Zenkō-ji Temple. Today Zenkō-ji Temple is still Nagano's main attraction, drawing in more than four million visitors every year. Nagano is also an important transport hub, providing access to the superb recreational facilities in the surrounding region.

Nagano shouldn't be a high priority, but it's worth staying overnight here and visiting Zenkō-ji.

Information & Orientation
JR Nagano station is at an angle to Chūō-dōri, the main road running north to Zenkō-ji Temple, and there is a slightly confusing warren of streets running out from the station and connecting with Chūō-dōri at various points. Once you've navigated these though, the rest is fairly straightforward. Chūō-dōri runs directly north, and is the main shopping area. It takes around 20 minutes on foot following Chūō-dōri to reach Zenkō-ji Temple.

There's an information office to the left after the central exit of JR Nagano station, though last time we called in no English was spoken. JNTO publishes *Japan Nagano Prefecture*, a brochure on both Nagano-ken and the city.

PLACES TO STAY

2 Zenkō-ji Kyōjo-in
   Youth Hostel
   善光寺教授院
   ユースホステル
4 Hotel Nagano
   Kokusai Kaikan
   ホテル長野国際会館
8 Nagano Washington
   Hotel
   長野ワシントン
   ホテル
9 Hotel Nagano Avenue
   ホテルナガノ
   アベニュー
11 Hotel New Nagano
   ホテルニューナガノ
13 Nagano Dai-Ichi Hotel
   長野第一ホテル
17 Nagano Royal Hotel
   長野ロイヤルホテル
18 Hotel Ikemon
   ホテル池門

PLACES TO EAT

3 Otaya Soba Restaurant
   太田屋そば

6 Thirty's Pizza
   サーティーズ ピザ
10 Kentucky Fried Chicken
   ケンタッキー
   フライドチキン
12 McDonald's
   マクドナルド
16 Kinryū Honten
   Chinese Restaurant
   金龍本店
19 Yōrōnotaki Restaurant
   養老の滝
20 Tsubohachi Restaurant
   つぼ八

OTHER

1 Zenkō-ji Temple
   善光寺
5 Central Post Office
   中央郵便局
7 Daiei Department Store
   ダイエーデパート
14 Midori Department Store
   みどりデパート
15 Nagano Railway Station
   長野駅
21 Bus Terminal
   バスターミナル

長野

Nagano

0   150   300 m

Zenkō-ji Temple 善光寺

The Zenkō-ji Temple is believed to have been founded in the 7th century, and was the home of the Ikkō Sanzon, allegedly the first Buddhist image to arrive in Japan (in 552). There have been subsequently several different stories concerning the image, which was, at times, either the subject of disputes, lost, rediscovered and finally, installed again.

Although the temple buildings have frequently been destroyed by fire, donations for reconstruction have always been provided by believers throughout Japan. The immense popularity of this temple stems from its liberal acceptance of believers, including women, from all Buddhist sects. The temple is affiliated with both the Tendai and Jōdo sects, and there are some 60 other Zenkō-ji temples scattered throughout Japan.

The approach to the temple passes from the Dai-mon Gate up a flight of steps to the Niō-mon Gate and then continues past shops selling religious paraphernalia to the immense San-mon Gate. Straight ahead lies the Kondō (Main Hall), a reconstruction dating from 707 and a National Treasure.

Once you've entered the inner sanctum of the Kondō, you'll see ticket machines on your right. Buy a ticket (¥300), take off your shoes (and place them in the bag provided), then proceed through the ticket collector's entrance. As you continue to the back of the hall, you'll see a large image of Buddha on your left. At the back of the hall, you descend a flight of steps into complete darkness – the absence of light is intentional and mandatory. Keep groping your way along the right-hand side of the tunnel until you feel something heavy, moveable and metallic – the key to salvation! Continue to fumble your way along the tunnel until you see light again.

Although the temple is usually thronged with lines of pilgrims passing through the tunnel, I was completely on my own during my 10 minute fumble for the key to salvation and found the experience quite eerie. There is a strong feeling of religious power in the temple – a feeling that was reinforced when I revisited the illuminated temple precincts later in the evening.
Robert Strauss

The temple is about 1½ km from JR Nagano station, at the northern end of Chūō-dōri. It's not a particularly interesting walk so, instead, you can take a 10 minute bus ride to Dai-mon Gate (¥190), or go by taxi (¥700) if you like. Another option is to take the Nagano Dentetsu line from the station and get off at the third stop – Zenkōji-shita station. From there it's a 10 minute walk westward to the temple.

Festivals

The Gokaichō Festival is held at Zenkō-ji Temple once every seven years from 10 April to 20 May. Millions of pilgrims attend this extravaganza, when a sacred image of Buddha, given to the emperor by a Korean king in 552, is put on display – the next is in 1999.

Places to Stay

Youth Hostel The *Zenkō-ji Kyōju-in Youth Hostel* (☎ 0262-32-2768) is a temple in a side street a couple of minutes on foot, east of Zenkō-ji Temple. Matronly guidance from the manager ensures an amicable, but strict regime. Keep things amicable by making an advance reservation. A bed for the night is ¥2500.

Shukubō Shukubō (temple lodgings) are available around Zenkō-ji Temple (☎ 0262-34-3591). Either call direct and make reservations in Japanese, or ask the tourist office to help.

Hotels The station area has a number of standard business hotels. The *Nagano Dai-Ichi Hotel* (☎ 0262-28-1211) is just to the east of the station and has singles from ¥5500 to ¥6200, twins at ¥11,000 and doubles at ¥10,000. Also close to the station is the *Hotel New Nagano* (☎ 0262-27-7200), where single rooms are ¥6000, twins range from ¥11,500 to ¥13,000 and doubles (there are only two of them) are ¥11,500. Almost directly opposite the station, the *Hotel Ikemon* (☎ 0262-27-2122) is another mid-range business hotel. It has singles at ¥6000, twins at ¥10,000 and very reasonably priced (by Japanese standards) doubles at ¥8000.

Slightly more up-market options exist in the *Nagano Washington Hotel* (☎ 0262-28-5111), about a 10 minute walk north of the station and with singles/twins from ¥6500/13,100, the *Nagano Royal Hotel* (☎ 0262-28-2222), with singles from ¥7500 to ¥8500, and doubles and twins from ¥13,000, and the *Hotel Nagano Avenue* (☎ 0262-23-1123), where singles/twins range from ¥7500/13,500.

Places to Eat

Midori, a department store immediately on your right as you exit the station, has a cluster of inexpensive restaurants on the 5th floor, a good place for a quick bite to eat if you're just passing through. Also close to the station are a number of the standard fast-food places: *McDonald's*, *Kentucky Fried Chicken* and *Mr Donut*.

If you are in Nagano overnight, the izakaya chains *Yōrōnotaki* and *Tsubohachi* have a few branches in town (check the map). There is a branch of each close to the station. Both have illustrated menus for easy ordering. Also close to the station is the *Kinryū Hanten*, a standard Chinese restaurant with just-affordable noodle dishes. For something out of the ordinary, try their *zajan-men* noodles (¥820), a northern Chinese speciality that is a little like spaghetti bolognese. Next door to the Kinryū Hanten is a restaurant specialising in pseudo-Italian fare – check the plastic food outside and decide for yourself whether you want to risk it. For not-bad pizzas, head up Chūō-dōri to *Thirty's Pizza*. It's basically a take-a-way/delivery service place, but you can also sit down inside and eat.

On the local speciality front, Nagano is famed for its soba, and there are many restaurants around Zenkō-ji Temple which serve the stuff up.

If you walk downhill from Dai-mon Gate along the left-hand side of Chūō-dōri, after about 300 metres you'll see a shop window with a mill grinding flour. This is *Ōtaya*, a restaurant which specialises in homemade

soba. Prices for a soba teishoku (set meal) start at around ¥750.

Getting There & Away

Trains from Ueno station in Tokyo via the JR Shin-etsu Honsen line take three hours and cost ¥3810, plus a ¥2770 limited express surcharge. The JR Shinonoi line connects Nagano with Matsumoto in 55 minutes. To Nagoya it takes three hours and costs ¥4420 plus a ¥2770 limited express surcharge.

Getting Around

Nagano is small enough to comfortably navigate on foot; see the earlier Zenkō-ji Temple section for information about getting around Nagano.

TOGAKUSHI   戸隠

Togakushi lies north-west of Nagano and is a popular destination for hikers, particularly in late spring and during autumn. In the winter, skiers favour the slopes around Mt Menō-yama and Mt Kurohime-yama. The one hour hike to **Togakushi-Okusha Sanctuary** includes a pleasant section along a tree-lined approach.

Access to Togakushi is via the small town of **Chōsha**, where a ski slope is located. For an inexpensive place to stay, there's *Togakushi Kōgen Yokokura Youth Hostel* (☎ 0262-54-2030) which is a couple of minutes from Chōsha bus stop and next to the ski slope. A bed for the night costs ¥2500.

There are frequent buses from Nagano station to Togakushi Kyampu-jō (¥1400) and to Chōsha (¥1300), both of which take about an hour for the trip and run via the scenic **Togakushi Birdline Highway**.

OBUSE   小布施

If you are interested in ukiyo-e, then you should make the short trip to Obuse, north-east of Nagano, and visit the **Hokusai-kan Museum**. This museum displays a collection of ukiyo-e works by the great master of this art form, Hokusai. The display consists of 30 paintings and two festival floats. Admission costs ¥500 and it's open from 9 am to 5 pm from April to October. During the rest of the year the opening hours are from 9.30 am to 4.30 pm. Souvenir sets of ukiyo-e postcards are on sale at the ticket counter.

To reach Obuse, take the Nagano Dentetsu line from Nagano (¥600, 20 minutes). The museum is eight minutes on foot from the station. Exit the station building and walk straight ahead, crossing a small intersection, until you reach the main road. Turn right here and continue down the main road past two sets of traffic lights. About 50 metres after the second set of lights, take the side street to your left which leads to the museum.

YUDANAKA 湯田中
This town is famous for its hot springs, particularly those known as **Jigokudani Onsen** (Hell Valley Hot Springs), which attract monkeys keen to escape the winter chill by with a hot soak.

Uotoshi Ryokan (☎ 0269-33-1215), a member of the Japanese Inn Group, charges ¥3900 to ¥4900 per person per night. The ryokan owner may offer to demonstrate *kyūdō* (Japanese archery) on request. You can either arrange to be picked up at the station or walk from there to the ryokan (seven minutes).

From Nagano, take the Nagano Dentetsu line for the 40 minute (¥1100) ride to Yudanaka.

KUSATSU 草津
From Yudanaka, there's a scenic route (closed in winter) across Shiga Heights to Kusatsu, one of Japan's most renowned hot-spring resorts, just inside the borders of Gumma-ken.

If you want to stay and sample the waters, there are dozens of ryokan. The *Kusatsu Kōgen Youth Hostel* (☎ 0279-88-3895) is about 25 minutes on foot from the centre of town, which is itself clustered round the Yuba hot-spring area. The youth hostel has bicycles for rent. To stay overnight costs ¥2500. It also operates as a ski school.

From Kusatsu, it takes 25 minutes by bus to Naganohara railway station which is on the Agatsuma line.

HAKUBA 白馬
The town of Hakuba, north-west of Nagano, is used as a staging point for access to outdoor activities in the nearby mountains. Skiing in the winter and hiking or mountaineering in the summer attract large numbers of visitors. The hiking trails tend to be less clogged during September and October. Even in mid-summer you should be properly prepared for hiking over snow-covered terrain. For information in English about Hakuba and the surrounding region, contact the tourist information office in Matsumoto.

Mt Shirouma-dake 白馬岳
The ascent of this mountain is a popular hike, but you should be properly prepared. There are several mountain huts which provide meals and basic accommodation along the trails.

From Hakuba station there are buses which take 40 minutes to reach Sarakura-sō (Sarakura Mountain Hut) which is the trailhead. From here, you can head west to climb the peak in about six hours; note that there are two huts on this route. If you don't feel like climbing the peak, you can follow the trail for about 1¾ hours as far as the Daisekkei (Snowy Gorge).

You could also take the trail south-west of Sarakura-sō and do the three hour climb to **Yari Onsen**. There's an open-air hot spring here with a mountain panorama and another mountain hut, in case you feel compelled to stay.

Tsugaike Natural Park 栂池自然公園
Tsugaike Natural Park (Tsugaike Shizen-en) lies below Mt Norikura-dake in an alpine marshland. A three hour hiking trail takes in most of the park which is renowned for its alpine flora.

From Hakuba Oike station it takes an hour by bus to reach the park. Between June and late October there's also a bus from Hakuba station which takes about 1½ hours.

Happō-one Ski Resort 八方尾根スキー場
This is a busy ski resort in the winter and a popular hiking area in the summer. From

Hakuba station, a five minute bus ride takes you to Happō; from there it's an eight minute walk to the cablecar base station. From the top station of the cablecar you can use two more chair lifts, and then hike along a trail for an hour or so to Happō-ike Pond on a ridge below Mt Karamatsu-dake. From this pond you can follow a trail leading to Mt Maru-yama (one hour), continue for 1½ hours to the Karamatsu-dake San-sō (mountain hut) and then climb to the peak of **Mt Karamatsu-dake** (2696 metres) in about 30 minutes.

Nishina Three Lakes   仁科三湖
While travelling south from Hakuba, there are three lakes (Nishina San-ko), which provide scope for short walks. Lake Nakazuna-ko and Lake Aoki-ko are close to Yanaba station and Lake Kizaki-ko is next to Inao station.

Salt Road   塩の道
In the past, Hakuba lay on the route of the Shio-no-Michi (Salt Road) which was used to carry salt on oxen from the Japan Sea to Matsumoto. Parts of this road still exist and there's a popular three hour hike along one section which starts at **Otari Folklore Museum** (Otari Kyodokan) – three minutes on foot from Minami Otari station – and continues via **Chikuni Suwa Shrine** before finishing at Matsuzawa-guchi. From there, it's a 15 minute bus ride to Hakuba Oike station which is two stops north of Hakuba station.

If you are thirsting for more background on salt, you could take the train further down the line to Shinano-ōmachi station and visit the Salt Museum (Shio-no-Michi Hakubutsukan).

Places to Stay
Hajimeno Ippo (☎ 0261-75-3527) is a minshuku which is a member of the Toho network. You'll probably need to know some Japanese and it's small, so advance reservations are a necessity. For a bed and two meals, prices vary between ¥4700 and ¥5200 according to the season (¥500 more expen-

sive in the winter). The minshuku is 12 minutes on foot from Iimori station (one stop south of Hakuba) and is usually closed in June and November.

Lavenue Sakae (☎ 0261-72-2212) is a minshuku close to Hakuba – seven minutes by bus from Hakuba station. Prices start at ¥6000 per person and include two meals.

Getting There & Away
Train Hakuba is on the JR Ōito line. From Matsumoto the trip takes about 1½ hours. From Shinano-ōmachi station allow 35 minutes.

If you continue north, the Ōito line eventually connects with the JR Hokuriku Honsen line at Itoigawa, which offers the options of heading north-east towards Niigata or south-west to Toyama and Kanazawa.

ŌMACHI   大町
The city of Ōmachi has several stations, but the one to use is called Shinano-ōmachi, which has tourist information facilities. The main reason for visiting Ōmachi is to start or finish the **Tateyama-Kurobe Alpine Route**, which is an expensive but impressive jaunt by various means of transport across the peaks between Nagano-ken and Toyama-ken. If you have time to kill in Ōmachi while waiting for connections, the **Salt Museum** (Shio-no-Michi Hakubutsukan) is just five minutes on foot from the station. It's open daily (closed Wednesday from November to April) from 8.30 am to 4.30 pm and entry is ¥400.

Places to Stay
An inexpensive place to stay is the *Kizaki-ko Youth Hostel* (☎ 0261-22-1820), which is 15 minutes on foot from Shinanosazaki station (just south of Lake Kizaki-ko) two stops north of Shinano-ōmachi station. A bed for the night costs ¥2500. From the station, walk north in the direction of the lake; at the bottom of the lake, turn left and look for the hostel on the right. Close to the hostel, clustered around the southern end of the lake, are numerous hotels, pensions and minshuku.

Poppo Minshuku (☎ 0261-23-1700) is a member of the Toho network. You'll probably need to know some Japanese since it's small, so advance reservations are a necessity. Prices start at ¥4300 for a bed and two meals. The minshuku is close to Ōmachi ski area, several km east of Inao station, and definitely not easy to find. The minshuku management recommends taking a bus from Shinano-ōmachi station to the Ōmachi ski area (15 minutes). It's closed during June.

Getting There & Away
Local trains on the JR Ōito line connect Ōmachi with Matsumoto in one hour. For connections with Hakuba on the same line allow 35 minutes. The main approach or departure is, of course, via the Tateyama-Kurobe Alpine Route – see the Toyama-ken section of this chapter for more details.

HOTAKA 穂高
Hotaka is a small town with a couple of interesting sights, but it's especially popular with hikers and mountaineers, who use it as a base to head into the mountains. Both the station and bicycle rental place (to your right as you exit on the east side of the station) have basic maps of the town. You can either walk around the area or rent a bicycle at ¥200 per hour. If you're staying at the youth hostel, you can also rent a bicycle there.

Rokuzan Art Museum 碌山美術館
The Rokuzan Art Museum (Rokuzan Bijutsukan) is 10 minutes on foot from the station and worth a visit. On display are sculptures by Rokuzan Ogiwara, a master sculptor whom the Japanese have claimed as the 'Rodin of the Orient'. Admission costs ¥500 and it's open from 9 am to 5 pm between April and October but closes an hour earlier during the rest of the year. It is closed on Monday.

Horseradish Farms わさび農場
Even if you're not a great fan of *wasabi* (horseradish), a visit to the Dai-ō Wasabi Farm is a good excuse to cycle or walk through fields crisscrossed with canals. The farm is the largest of its kind in Japan, and is a couple of kilometres directly east of Hotaka station. Notice the *dōsojin* (roadside guardians) carved on stones which usually depict a contented couple. The basic map provided at the station or at the adjacent bicycle rental office is sufficient for orientation.

Nakabusa Onsen 中房温泉
These remote hot springs are reached by bus (70 minutes) from Ariake station, one stop north of Hotaka. From here, there are several trails for extended mountain hikes.

Mt Jonen-dake 常念岳
From Toyoshina station, two stops south of Hotaka, it takes 10 minutes by taxi to reach Kitakaidō which is the start of a trail for experienced hikers to climb Mt Jonen-dake (2857 metres) – the ascent takes about eight hours. There are numerous options for mountain hikes extending over several days in the region, but you must be properly prepared.

Places to Stay
Azumino Youth Hostel (☎ 0263-82-4265) is four km west of Hotaka station (a one hour walk). A bed for the night costs ¥2500, and bicycles are available for hire. The hostel is closed from 17 January to 7 February.

Not far from Hotaka station are numerous pensions and ryokan. The *Hotaka Pension* (☎ 0263-82-4411) is just to the north of the station and has per-person costs from ¥5500 with two meals. The *Shioya Ryokan* (☎ 0263-82-2012) is just to the east of the station and has per-person costs of ¥5800 to ¥7000 with two meals.

MATSUMOTO 松本
Matsumoto (population 200,000) is worth a visit for its superb castle, and is a convenient base for exploration of the Japan Alps.

The city has been around at least since the eighth century, and was the castle town of the

CENTRAL HONSHŪ

松本

Matsumoto

0   100   200 m

Isemachi - dōri

Honmachi - dōri

Ekimae - dōri

Matsumoto Station

PLACES TO STAY

3 Nishiya Ryokan
　にしや旅館
4 Hotel Ote
　ホテル大手
5 Hotel New Station
　ホテルニュー
　ステーション
7 Hotel Iidiya
　ホテル飯田屋
14 Matsumoto Tourist Hotel
　松本観光ホテル
15 Matsumoto Tōkyū Inn
　松本東急イン

PLACES TO EAT

6 Yohayara Restaurant
　よはやら
8 Sushi Snack Restaurant
　寿司スナック
9 Yoronotaki
　養老の滝
10 McDonald's
　マクドナルド
11 Mr Donut
　ミスタードーナッツ

OTHER

1 Matsumoto-jō Castle
　松本城
2 Japan Folklore Museum
　日本民俗資料館
12 Central Post Office
　中央郵便局
13 Suzuki Educational Hall
　才能教育会館

Ogasawara clan during the 14th and 15th centuries. It continued to prosper and grow in size during the Edo period (1600-1868), and today is an unhurried medium-sized city that's worth an overnight stay, though not much longer.

One curious thing I've noticed at Matsumoto station is the musical delight of the station announcer who intones the name of the station like a muezzin calling from a mosque – 'Matsumoootooo'. The musical infatuation extends from the station to the city centre where every street seems to be lined with loudspeakers piping music at the pedestrians.

Robert Strauss

Information

Matsumoto city tourist information office (☎ 0263-32-2814) is on your right at the bottom of the steps leading from Matsumoto station's eastern exit. The English-speaking staff can provide maps and leaflets, help with accommodation and give plenty of other travel information. The office is open daily from 9.30 am to 6 pm; 9 am to 5.30 pm during the winter.

JNTO publishes two colour brochures: *Japan Matsumoto* which has good maps and *Japan Matsumoto & the Japan Alps* which provides wider regional coverage; and a concise leaflet entitled *Matsumoto &*

Kamikōchi. Despite its English title, the *Tourist Map of Matsumoto* is only useful for orientation if you read Japanese.

The main attraction of Matsumoto is the castle which is just 15 minutes on foot from the station.

Matsumoto-jō Castle 松本城

Even if you only spend a couple of hours in Matsumoto, make sure you see this splendid castle.

The main attraction in the castle grounds is the original three turreted castle donjon, built circa 1595, in contrasting black and white. Steep steps and ladders lead you up through six storeys. On the lower floors there are displays of guns, bombs and gadgets to storm castles – complete with technicolour graphics which are useful for those who can't read the Japanese descriptions. At the top, there's a fine view of the mountains. The structure includes slits and slots for archery and firearms, slatted boards to provide basic ventilation (or a means to bombard attackers) and a Tsukimi Yagura or 'Moon-Viewing Pavilion' which was used as a dainty retreat for those lighter moments when the castle was not under attack.

The castle is flood-lit at night and the park adjoining the castle moat is open to the public who stroll around here in the evenings. Opening hours are from 8.30 am to 4.30 pm daily but it is closed from 29 December to 3 January.

Admission to the castle costs ¥500 and is valid also for the Japan Folklore Museum. The castle is 15 minutes on foot from the station; if you take a bus, the stop for the castle is Shiyakusho-mae.

Japan Folklore Museum 日本民俗資料館

To the right of the entrance to the castle grounds is the Nihon Minzoku Shiryōkan (Japan Folklore Museum) which has exhibits on several floors relating to the archaeology, history and folklore of Matsumoto and the surrounding region. One floor is devoted to flora and fauna, including ducks, owls, beetles and extremely anaemic-looking bottled fish. Another floor displays the superb Honda collection of clocks and watches from the East and the West. There are some fascinating timepieces, including a Rolls-Royce clock, a banjo clock and an elephant clock.

Admission to the museum is included in the price of the castle admission ticket (¥500). Opening hours for the museum are the same as those for the castle.

Japan Ukiyo-e Museum 日本浮世絵博物館

Tourist brochures delicately refer to the 'ultra-modern' architecture of the Nihon Ukiyo-e Hakubutsukan (Japan Ukiyo-e Museum) though some have described it as 'an ugly metallic box'. Anyway, this shouldn't deter you from entering for a look at the Sakai collection of Japanese woodblock prints inside. If you have an interest in ukiyo-e, this museum should be on your list. Several generations of the Sakai family collected over 100,000 prints, paintings, screens and old books – the largest private collection of its kind in the world.

The displays are small in number, approximately 100 prints at a time, and frequently changed. This small-scale method of display allows the visitor to sustain interest without being swamped by large numbers of exhibits. English labelling is minimal, but an explanatory leaflet in English is provided, and there's a slide show upstairs which has an English commentary. Ukiyo-e postcards are also on sale. Admission is ¥700 and opening hours are from 10 am to 5 pm daily, except Monday.

Access to the museum is a real pain unless you take the eight minute taxi ride (¥1000) from the station.

A more complicated route is to go from Matsumoto station on the Matsumoto Dentetsu line and get off at the fourth stop, Ōniwa (¥170). Turn left out of the tiny station office and walk about 50 metres up the street to a main road. Bear left again, and continue for about 300 metres, passing under an overpass, and then turn right at the road mirror. Carry on down this street to the traffic lights then continue straight across for another 100 metres. The Japan Ukiyo-e Museum is on your left, just beyond the **Japan Judicature Museum**. (The latter is only really worth a visit (¥500 admission) if you like judicial documents and police weapons and uniforms from the Edo and Meiji periods.) The walk from Oniwa station to the Japan Ukiyo-e Museum takes about 20 minutes.

Matsumoto Folkcraft Museum
松本民芸館

The Matsumoto Folkcraft Museum (Matsumoto Mingeikan) has a collection of Japanese folk art with a few items from other parts of Asia and the rest of the world. Admission costs ¥200. It's open from 9 am to 5 pm, closed on Monday. The museum is 15 minutes (¥280) by bus from Matsumoto. Take a bus in the direction of Utsukushigahara and get off at the Shimo-Kanai Mingeikan-guchi bus stop.

Utsukushigahara-kōgen Plateau
美ケ原高原

From April to mid-November, this alpine plateau is a popular excursion from Matsumoto. Buses stop at Sanjiro Bokujo (Sanjiro Ranch) and there are pleasant walks and the opportunity to see cows in pasture (a source of Japanese fascination) and **Utsukushigahara-kōgen Bijutsukan** (an open-air museum) which charges ¥1400 for admission. It has a bizarre series of 120 sculptures, including 'Venus of Milo in the Castle of Venus' and 'Affection Plaza', but to be honest there are likely to be few travellers who would find the exhibits worthy of the hefty admission charge. There is also a two day hiking trail to **Kirigamine**.

Matsumoto Dentetsu buses run up to the plateau from the Matsumoto bus terminal in around one hour 20 minutes and cost ¥1400 or ¥1850 depending on the routing they take.

Alps-kōen Park アルプス公園

For those interested in speed thrills, this park includes the 'Alps Dream Coaster', a 600 metre dry-sleigh run. Each ride costs ¥300. There's an exhibition hall with displays on the flora and fauna of the Japan Alps and the

history of Japanese mountaineering. There's also a small zoo. The park is 20 minutes by bus from Matsumoto. It's open daily from 9 am to 5 pm but is closed on Monday.

Suzuki Education Hall 鈴木才能教育会館

Those interested in the Suzuki method of teaching musical skills to children may want to watch lessons or listen to concerts. The hall (Suzuki Sainō Kyōiku Kaikan) is in the centre of the city, about 15 minutes on foot from the station. The tourist information office can help with arrangements.

Festivals

During the Heso Matsuri (Navel Festival), held from 6 to 7 June, revellers demonstrate that Matsumoto is the navel of Japan by prancing through the streets wearing costumes that appropriately reveal their navels.

During August, the Takigi Nō Festival features Nō theatre, by torch light, which is performed outdoors on a stage in the park below the castle. For those interested in phallic festivals, the Dōsojin Festival is held in honour of dōsojin (roadside guardians) on 23 September at Utsukushigahara Onsen. On 3 and 4 October, Asama Onsen celebrates the Asama Hi-Matsuri, a fire festival with torchlit parades which are accompanied by drumming. At the beginning of November, Matsumoto celebrates the Oshiro Matsuri (Matsumoto Castle Festival) which is a cultural jamboree including costume parades, puppet displays and flower shows.

The tourist information office has precise dates and more information.

Places to Stay

The tourist information office at the station has lists of accommodation and can help with reservations. If your main objective is to use Matsumoto as a staging point to visit the Japan Alps, there's no real reason to stay in the town itself unless you get stranded here late in the day. Even if you do, there are several rural places within easy reach of the station.

Youth Hostels *Asama Onsen Youth Hostel*

(☎ 0263-46-1335) is a bit distant, regimented and drab, and it charges the standard youth hostel rate of ¥2500. It closes at 9 pm and lights go out punctually at 10 pm. The hostel is closed from 28 December to 3 January.

To reach Asama Onsen by bus from the Matsumoto bus terminal, there are two options: either take bus No 6 to Shita-Asama or bus No 7 to Dai-Ichi Koko-mae. The bus ride takes 20 minutes, and the hostel is then five minutes on foot. The bus ride provides the latest in technology with a video screen at the front of the bus which shows pictures of the next stop (useful at night!) interspersed with bizarre advertising for brooms and weddings.

Utsukushigahara Sanjiro Youth Hostel (☎ 0263-31-2021) is on an alpine plateau, nearly an hour's bus ride from Matsumoto. A bed for the night is ¥2300. It's closed from December to April. Take the bus bound for Utsukushigahara Bijitsukan and get off after 50 minutes at the Sanjiro bus stop. The hostel is two minutes on foot from there.

Ryokan The *Enjyoh Bekkan* (☎ 0263-33-7233) is a member of the Japanese Inn Group. Prices at this ryokan start at ¥4800/9000 for singles/doubles – excluding meals. The hot-spring facilities are available day and night. A Western-style breakfast is available for ¥800. From Matsumoto, take the 20 minute bus ride to Utsukushigahara Onsen and get off at the terminal. From there it's 300 metres to the ryokan.

For a very reasonably priced ryokan close to the station, the best bet is *Nishiya* (☎ 0263-33-4332). Some English is spoken here and per-person costs are ¥3600 without meals.

Hotels One of the cheapest business hotels around is the *Matsumoto Tourist Hotel* (☎ 0263-33-9000). It's about a 10 minute walk from the station and has a limited number of singles at ¥4700. More up-market rooms are also available at ¥7500/11,000 for singles/doubles. The *Hotel Iidaya* (☎ 0263-32-0027) is just across from the station and has singles from ¥5000 to ¥6700, and twins

and doubles from ¥10,000 to ¥12,000. Just across the road from the Iidiya is the *Hotel New Station* (☎ 0263-35-3850), which has singles from ¥6300 to ¥6800, twins from ¥10,600 to ¥13,400 and doubles at ¥10,600. Another reasonably priced option is the *Hotel Ōte* (☎ 0263-36-0516), which is just over the river, about a five minute walk from the station, and has singles/twins at ¥5000/9000.

More expensive hotels include the *Hotel Buena Vista* (☎ 0263-37-0111), with singles from ¥9000 to ¥10,000 and twins ¥15,000 to ¥21,000, and the *Matsumoto Tōkyū Inn* (☎ 0263-36-0109), where singles/twins/doubles are ¥8600/14,800/14,800. Both are close to the station.

Places to Eat

Matsumoto is renowned for its *shinshū-soba*, a variation on the soba theme which is eaten either hot or cold (*zaru-soba*) with wasabi and soy sauce. The local *okashi* are sponge cakes filled with bean paste. Other specialities more peculiar to the region include raw horsemeat, bee larvae, pond snails and *zazamushi* (crickets). The latter are unlikely to be of interest to all but the most adventurous of travellers, but if you want to try the soba, *Yohayara*, close to the station, is a good little soba shop with plastic food outside – drag the staff out and point.

If you're just passing through and you want a midday meal, there are a number of fast-food places close to the station, including *Kentucky Fried Chicken*, *McDonald's Mr Donut* (look out for the popular little rāmen shop next door) and even *Shakey's Pizza*. On the 2nd floor of the station there is an arcade with various restaurants offering inexpensive set meals. Alternatively, the basement of the bus terminal also has various cheap eateries. Almost next door to the station is *Sushi Snack* (yes, there's an English sign), a popular revolving sushi restaurant with plates from ¥120 to ¥200.

For evening meals, the best places to eat are the izakaya clustered around the station area. A good standby for non-Japanese speakers is the branch of the *Yōrōnotaki* chain – cheap beer, good food prices and an illustrated menu. Look out for the red and black illuminated sign.

Things to Buy
Some of the more interesting purchases available in Matsumoto are the *tanabata ningyō* (dolls used in the Tanabata Festival) and *temari*, which are the embroidered balls of silk that you see in all the souvenir shops – don't ask what use they might be put to.

Getting There & Away
Air JAS operates flights twice a day between Osaka and Matsumoto. There's a bus service connecting Matsumoto Airport with the city centre in 25 minutes.

Train & Bus From Tokyo (Shinjuku station), there are Azusa limited express services which reach Matsumoto in 2 hours 39 minutes and cost ¥3810 with a ¥2770 limited express surcharge. The fastest services on the JR Chūō Honsen line from Nagoya take 2½ hours. From Osaka, the fastest trip takes 3½ hours and requires a change of trains at Nagoya. The JR Shinonoi line connects Matsumoto with Nagano in 55 minutes. The trip from Matsumoto to Hakuba on the JR Ōito line takes about 1½ hours.

Both train and bus travel have to be combined for the connection between Matsumoto and Kamikōchi. From Matsumoto, take the Matsumoto Dentetsu line to Shin-Shimashima station – don't confuse this with the station called Shimojima. The trip takes 30 minutes and the fare is ¥670. From Shin-Shimashima station take the bus via Nakanoyu to Kamikōchi (¥2000, 75 minutes), though this service does not operate from mid-October through to April. From Kamikōchi you can continue by bus via Hirayu Onsen to Takayama.

There are regular buses from Tokyo (3¼ hours), Osaka (5½ hours) and Nagoya (3½ hours).

Getting Around
The castle and the city centre are easily covered on foot. Matsumoto bus terminal is diagonally across the main street to the right

as you leave the east exit of the station. The terminal is part of a large department store and this means you have to negotiate your way down to the basement before choosing your exit door, climbing the steps, and finding the bus stop back at ground level.

SHIRAHONE ONSEN　白骨温泉
This is a classic hot-spring resort which has retained some traditional inns with open-air, hot-spring baths in a mountain setting. Since it is close to Shin-Shimashima station, it could be visited as part of a trip to Kamikōchi; those with time to kill might like to test for themselves the truth of the saying that bathing here for three days ensures three years without a cold. Shirahone Onsen is also popular with hikers as a base for trails around **Norikura-kōgen Plateau**.

For a place to stay, you could try *Ōishi-kan Youth Hostel* (☎ 0263-93-2011), which is part of a ryokan, just a couple of minutes on foot from the bus terminal. A bed for the night is ¥2500.

From Matsumoto, travel by rail on the Matsumoto Dentetsu line to Shin-Shimashima station, then take a Matsumoto Dentetsu bus (one hour, ¥1350) to Shirahone Onsen. Bus connections are infrequent, so check carefully. Buses to Norikura-kōgen summit and to Norikura-kōgen Kyūka-mura (vacation village) also pass through Shirahone Onsen.

KAMIKŌCHI　上高地
Kamikōchi lies in the centre of the northern Japan Alps and has some of the most spectacular scenery in Japan. In the late 19th century, foreigners 'discovered' this mountainous region and coined the term 'Japan Alps'. A British missionary, Reverend Walter Weston, toiled from peak to peak and sparked Japanese interest in mountaineering as a sport. He is now honoured with his own annual festival and Kamikōchi has become a base for strollers, hikers, and climbers. Remember, Kamikōchi is *closed* from November to May.

Despite the thousands of visitors, Kamikōchi has so far resisted the temptation

Nature
A: Shin-kyō, The Sacred Bridge, Nikkō (RI)
B: Woodland scene, around Nara (CT)
C: Pinai Falls, Iriomote Island (TW)
D: Falls at Akame, Mie (AT)

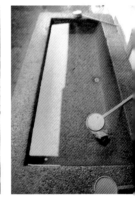

A: Traditional attire (CT)
B: Itsukushima-jinja Shrine, Miyajima (CT)
C: Buddha peeking through hole, Byōdō-in, Uji, Kyoto (MM)
D: Shrine purification area (CT)
E: Temple offerings (CT)
F: Kanji (lit. 'Three Rivers') (CT)

to go commercial. The best advice is probably to get there quick before the locals change their minds.

Orientation

On a fine day, the final stages of the approach to Kamikōchi on the road from Nakanoyu provide a superb mountain panorama: Taishō-ike Pond on your left, and a series of high peaks ranged in the background. From here, the road continues a short distance to the bus terminal which is the furthest point to which tourist traffic is officially allowed in this valley. A short distance on foot beyond

the bus terminal, the Azusa-gawa River is spanned by Kappa-bashi Bridge – at peak season, you probably only need to follow the sound of clicking shutters to find this photogenic subject. From this bridge, you can choose to follow a variety of trails.

Information

Tourist Office At the bus terminal, there is an information office (☎ 0263-95-2405) which is open from late April to mid-November only. It's geared mostly to booking accommodation, but also has leaflets and maps. It's preferable to make prior use of the

CENTRAL HONSHŪ

tourist information offices in Takayama or Matsumoto which have English-speaking staff.

Books & Maps JNTO publishes a leaflet entitled *Matsumoto & Kamikochi (MG-042)* which has brief details and a map for Kamikōchi. The tourist offices also have several large maps (covering Kamikōchi, Shirahone Onsen and Norikura-kōgen Plateau) which show mountain trails, average hiking times, mountain huts and lists of tourist facilities. However, they are all in Japanese. *Hiking in Japan* by Paul Hunt covers some trails in the area.

Emergencies Strollers are unlikely to suffer mishap, but those heading off on long hikes or climbs should be properly prepared.

There are medical facilities at the bus terminal and a helicopter is called in for heavy duty search & rescue operations. The mountain huts should be able to pass on messages via telephone or radio links. Some also have basic medical facilities.

Accidents can happen, but in many cases they occur through poor judgement of weather conditions, inadequate clothing and miscalculation of physical fitness. When I was in Kamikōchi, the season had hardly started before a rapid change of weather stranded a climber traversing an ice-bound ridge below Mt Yariga-take. When the weather cleared, a helicopter search revealed he'd dropped over the edge.

Robert Strauss

Planning Your Itinerary

If you want to avoid immense crowds, don't plan to visit between late July and late August, or during the first three weeks in October. Between June and mid-July, there's a rainy season which makes outdoor pursuits depressingly soggy.

It's perfectly feasible to visit Kamikōchi from Matsumoto or Takayama in a day, but you'll miss out on the pleasures of staying in the mountains and the opportunity to take early morning or late evening walks before the crowds appear.

Day Walks If you want to do level walking for short distances, without any climbing, then you should stick to the river valley. A typical three hour walk (round trip) of this kind would proceed east from Kappa-bashi Bridge along the right-hand side of the river to Myōjin-bashi Bridge (45 minutes) and then continue to Tokusawa (45 minutes) before returning. For variety, you could cross to the other side of the river at Myōjin-bashi Bridge.

West of Kappa-bashi Bridge, you can amble along the right-hand side of the river to Weston Monument (15 minutes) or keep to the left-hand side of the river and walk to Taishō-ike Pond (20 minutes). A bridge across the river between Weston Monument and Taishō-ike Pond provides variation for the walk.

Hiking There are dozens of long-distance options for hikers and climbers, varying in duration from a couple of days to a week. *Hiking in Japan* by Paul Hunt provides some ideas. The large Japanese maps of the area show routes and average hiking times between huts, major peaks and landmarks – but you've got to be able to read Japanese or get someone reliable to help decipher the maps. Favourite trails and climbs (which can mean human traffic jams on trails during peak seasons!) include Mt Yariga-take (3180 metres) and Mt Hotaka-dake (3190 metres) – also known as Mt Okuhotaka-dake. Other more distant popular destinations include Nakabusa Onsen and Murodō, which is on the Tateyama-Kurobe Alpine Route.

If you want to hike between Kamikōchi and Shin-Hotaka Onsen (see Shin-Hotaku under the Gifu-ken section of this chapter), there's a steep trail which crosses the ridge below Mt Nishi Hotaka-dake (2909 metres) at Nishi Hotaka San-sō (Nishi Hotaka Mountain Cottage) and continues to Nishi Hotaka Guchi, the top station of the cablecar for Shin-Hotaka Onsen. The hike takes nearly four hours (because of a steep ascent). Softies might prefer to save an hour of sweat and do the hike in the opposite direction.

Festivals

On the first weekend in June, the climbing season opens with the Weston Festival, which honours Walter Weston, the British missionary and alpinist.

Places to Stay

Accommodation is relatively expensive, advance reservations are essential during the peak season and the whole place shuts down from November to May. You'd be well advised to make reservations before arriving in Kamikōchi; the tourist information offices at Takayama and Matsumoto are convenient since they have English-speaking staff.

There is a handful of hotels, mostly around Kappa-bashi Bridge, which is a short walk from the bus terminal. *Gosenjaku Lodge* (☎ 0263-95-2221) provides a bed and two meals from ¥10,000. For a bed only, the price should be ¥6500. Just down the road a little, the rustic *Kamikōchi Nishiitoya San-sō* (☎ 0263-95-2206) is more expensive, with per-person costs with two meals coming in at ¥13,000. You might try negotiating for only a bed, but they may not be keen on the idea.

Dotted along the trails and around the mountains are dozens of mountain cottages or mountain huts *(san-sō* or *yama-goya)* which provide two meals and a bed for an average cost of around ¥6500. Given the usually lower standards of the food and lodging in such mountain accommodation, these prices are expensive. However, the proprietors have to contend with a short season and difficult access and most hikers are prepared to pay the premium for somewhere out of the cold.

Camping grounds are available at the Kamikōchi Konashidaira Kampu-jō, which is next to the visitor's centre about 10 minutes walk beyond Kappa-bashi Bridge, and at the Tokusawa Kampu-jō, which is about three km north-east of Kappa-bashi Bridge. Costs for tent hire tend to be rather high (¥3000 for a six person tent at Tokusawa).

The closest youth hostels are at Shirahone Onsen and on Norikura-kōgen Plateau, both within easy reach of Kamikōchi.

Places to Eat

Most visitors either take their meals as part of their accommodation package or bring their own. Several of the hotels around Kappa-bashi Bridge have restaurants. The bus terminal has vending machines and limited facilities for buying food.

Getting There & Away

Bus services for Kamikōchi cease from mid-November to late April and the exact dates can vary. If you plan to travel at the beginning or end of this period, check first with a tourist office or call Japan Travel-Phone (☎ 0120-222800, toll free).

The connection between Kamikōchi and Matsumoto involves travel by train and bus. For more details, see the Matsumoto Getting There & Away section in this chapter.

Between Takayama and Kamikōchi there are frequent bus connections but *only* from April to October. The bus runs via Nakanoyu and you have to change to another bus at Hirayu Onsen. From Takayama to Hirayu Onsen takes around an hour and costs ¥1360, and from Hirayu Onsen to Kamikōchi is around another hour of travel and costs ¥1400.

Between Norikura and Kamikōchi there are buses running via Hirayu Onsen approximately three times a day (two hours). The Norikura Skyline Road is *only* open from 15 May to 31 October. The whole trip takes around two hours and costs ¥2800.

There is also a relatively infrequent bus service between Kamikōchi and Shirahone Onsen. It takes one hour 15 minutes and costs ¥2000.

Getting Around

Once you've arrived in Kamikōchi, you're restricted to getting around on foot.

The road between Nakanoyu and Kamikōchi is closed to private cars between late April and early May, between late July and late August, from early October for about three weeks and on Sunday and public holidays between late April and early November. Parking charges are also high.

This policy leaves a few inches of space between the bumpers of the buses and taxis. It also gives an idea of the incredible numbers of visitors crammed into these peak visiting times and, conversely, the likelihood of lesser numbers of visitors and more tranquillity on the main trails at other times.

NORIKURA-KŌGEN PLATEAU & NORIKURA ONSEN
乗鞍高原・乗鞍温泉
This alpine plateau below Mt Norikura-dake (3026 metres) is popular with hikers and famous for the Norikura Skyline Road (closed from November to May), a scenic bus route which leads to the Tatami-daira bus stop at the foot of the mountain. From there, a trail leads to the peak in about 1½ hours. Norikura Onsen is a hot-spring resort on the plateau and a base for skiing and hiking which is open all year round.

Places to Stay
There is a choice of accommodation including ryokan, pensions and mountain huts. An inexpensive place to stay near the ski lifts is *Norikura Kōgen Youth Hostel* (☎ 0263-93-2748). It has nightly rates of ¥2500. On the way to the youth hostel, you might want to look out for the *Ryokan Mitake-sō* (☎ 0263-93-2016), an unassuming white building with a wooden annexe that has rates of ¥8000 to ¥10,000 per person with two meals. Close by is the *Pension Chimunii* (☎ 0263-93-2902), which has per-person costs of ¥7500 including two meals. It's a small place, so it would be wise to book ahead.

Getting There & Away
The bus between Norikura and Takayama operates along the Norikura Skyline Road between May and October and usually runs via Hirayu Onsen. The ride takes about 1½ hours.

From July to mid-October, there's a bus between Norikura and Shin-Shimashima station. The trip takes about an hour and costs ¥1250.

There are infrequent buses between Norikura and Shirahone Onsen and Kamikōchi.

KISO VALLEY REGION 木曽川
A visit to this region is highly recommended if you want to see several small towns with architecture carefully preserved from the Edo period. As a bonus, there's the opportunity to combine your visit to Magome and Tsumago with an easy walk. JNTO publishes a leaflet entitled *Kiso Valley*, which has details and maps for the region.

The thickly forested Kiso Valley lies in the south-west of Nagano-ken and is surrounded by the Japan Alps. It was traversed by the Nakasen-dō Highway, an old post road which connected Edo (present day Tokyo) with Kyoto and provided business for the post towns en route. With the introduction of new roads and commercial centres to the north, and the later construction of the Chūō railway line, the region was effectively bypassed and the once prosperous towns went into decline. During the '60s, there was a move to preserve the original architecture of the post towns and tourism has become a major source of income.

Magome was the birthplace of a famous Japanese literary figure, Shimazaki Tōson (1872-1943). His masterpiece, *Ie* (published in English in 1976 and entitled *The Family*), records the decline of two provincial families in the Kiso region.

On 23 November, the Fuzoku Emaki Parade is held along the old post road in Tsumago and features a procession by the townsfolk who dress in costume from the Edo period.

THE MAGOME TO TSUMAGO WALK
馬籠から妻籠への路
Magome 馬籠
Magome is a small post town with rows of traditional houses and post inns (and souvenir shops, of course) lining a steep street. The tourist information office (☎ 0264-59-2336) is a short way up, on the right-hand side of the street. The office is open from 8.30 am to 5 pm and dispenses tourist literature as well

as reserving accommodation. Close by is a museum devoted to the life and times of Shimazaki Tōson.

To walk from Magome to Tsumago, continue toiling up the street until the houses eventually give way to a forest path which winds down to the road leading up a steep hill to Magome-kōge Pass. This initial walk from Magome to the pass takes about 45 minutes and is not particularly appealing because you spend most of your time on the road. You can cut out this first section by taking the bus between Magome and Tsumago and getting off after about 12 minutes at the pass.

There's a small shop-cum-teahouse at the top of the pass where the trail leaves the road and takes you down to the right along a pleasant route through the forest. From the teahouse to Tsumago takes just under two hours – allow time to stop at waterfalls or ponder the Latin names thoughtfully labelled on plants beside the trail.

Tsumago 妻籠

Tsumago is so geared to tourism and well preserved, it feels like an open-air museum. Designated by the government as a protected area for the preservation of traditional buildings, no modern developments such as TV aerials or telephone poles are allowed to mar the scene. The tourist information office (☎ 0264-57-3123), open from 8.30 am to 5 pm, is halfway down the main street. Tourist literature on Tsumago and maps are available and the staff are happy to make reservations for accommodation.

Just down the street from the tourist information office, you can pop into the post office which sells an interesting assortment of commemorative stamps and postcards depicting life on the old post road.

About 50 metres beyond the post office, on the same side of the street, is the **Okuya Kyōdokan Folk Museum**, which is part of a magnificent house built like a castle. During the Edo period, felling of trees in the Kiso region was strictly controlled. In 1877, following the relaxation of these controls,

the owner decided to rebuild using *hinoki* (cypress trees).

If you continue from this house up the main street, the bus terminal can be reached by taking any of the side streets on your left.

Baggage Forwarding

As a special service for walkers on the trail between Magome and Tsumago, the tourist offices in both villages offer a baggage-forwarding service. For a nominal fee of ¥500 per piece of luggage, you can have your gear forwarded. The deadline for the morning delivery is 9 am and for the afternoon delivery, it's 1 pm. The service operates daily from 20 July to 31 August but is restricted to Saturday, Sunday and national holidays between 1 April and 19 July and throughout September and November.

Places to Stay & Eat

Both tourist information offices specialise in helping visitors find accommodation – telephone inquiries can only be dealt with in Japanese. There are many ryokan and minshuku. Prices for a room and two meals at a ryokan start around ¥9000 while minshuku prices for a similar deal start around ¥6500. *Minshuku Daikichi* (☎ 0264-57-2595) is a friendly place just four minutes on foot from the bus terminal. It has per-person rates of ¥6700.

Magome and Tsumago have several restaurants on their main streets. The local specialities include *gohei-mochi* (a rice dumpling on a stick coated with nut sauce) and sansai (mountain greens), which can be ordered as a set meal (sansai teishoku) for about ¥800.

Getting There & Away

The main railway stations on the JR Chūō line which provide access to Magome and Tsumago are Nakatsugawa station and Nagiso station respectively. Some services do not stop at these stations, which are about 12 minutes apart by limited express – check the timetable. By limited express, the trip between Nagoya and Nakatsugawa takes 55 minutes (¥2980); between Nakatsugawa and

Matsumoto it takes 85 minutes. Direct buses also operate between Nagoya and Magome and the trip takes just under two hours.

Buses leave hourly from outside Nakatsugawa station for Magome (30 minutes, ¥500). There's also an infrequent bus service between Magome and Tsumago (30 minutes, ¥580). If you decide to start your walk from the Magome-kōge Pass, take this bus and get off at the bus stop at the top of the pass.

From Tsumago, either walk to Nagiso station (1½ hours) or take the bus (nine minutes).

KISO-FUKUSHIMA & MT ONTAKE
木曽福島・御岳山

Kiso-Fukushima was an important barrier gate and checkpoint on the old post road. From the station, it takes about 20 minutes on foot to reach several old residences, museums and temples.

Mt Ontake (3063 metres) is an active volcano – entry to the crater area is prohibited. For centuries the mountain has been considered sacred and an important destination for pilgrims.

There are several trails to the summit. One popular trailhead is at Nakanoyu, 80 minutes by bus from Kiso-Fukushima station. From the trailhead, it takes about 3½ hours to hike to the summit. Another trailhead is at Tanohara, 1¾ hours by bus from Kiso-Fukushima station; from here the hike to the summit takes about three hours.

An inexpensive place to stay is *Kiso Ryōjōan Youth Hostel* (☎ 0264-23-7716) which is a short bus ride from Kiso-Fukushima station. Take the 25 minute bus ride to Ohara bus terminal – the hostel is three minutes on foot from there and provides a useful base for hiking or sightseeing in the area.

Kiso-Fukushima is on the JR Chūō line and limited expresses run to Nagoya in 1½ hours or to Matsumoto in 40 minutes.

NARAI 奈良井

Narai is another town on the old post road with a high proportion of traditional build-ings from the Edo period. It seems less exposed to large-scale tourism than Magome and Tsumago.

Orientation & Information

Narai's main street extends for about one km and lies to your left as you exit the railway station.

The station office is run by local senior citizens who go out of their way to load you down with Japanese brochures.

Things to See

About a five minute walk down the main street, and beneath a blue 'Shiseido' shop sign, is an interesting automat. Put ¥100 in the slot and you receive a neatly packaged old Japanese coin, or opt for a foreign one if you prefer.

At intervals along the street there are five old wells which were used by thirsty travellers during the Edo period. The sake brewery is easily recognised by its basket of fronds hanging from the roof above the entrance. Continuing down the street, there are side streets on the right-hand side which lead to tranquil temples.

Many of the houses lining the main street originally functioned as inns during the heyday of the old post road; most have been turned into museums though some still operate as ryokan. Nakamura-tei House was once a shop specialising in lacquer and is now a museum run by a friendly proprietor. Admission costs ¥150.

At the end of the main street, you pass a temple on your left, and just beyond is the Narai Minzoku Shiryōkan (Local History Museum) with a cart propped up against the wall. The energetic custodian does her best to guide you round the exhibits with a rapid-fire Japanese commentary and skilful mime to bridge the linguistic gap. On the upper floor, there's a delightful assortment of old implements and paraphernalia such as ice skates attached to geta (clogs), travelling lanterns, money boxes, local combs and bowls for tooth blacking powder, a collaps-ible candlestick, a large display of festival banners and dolls, straw snow shoes and a belt made out of leather with a design curiously similar to a bicycle chain. On the ground floor, there are antique household gadgets such as a kettle stand, a mochi (rice cake) pestle, a rice winnower and a staircase with drawers integrated into the steps. Admission costs ¥150.

If you feel like following the old post road, continue uphill for four km (about 1¾ hours) to **Torii-kōge Pass**. From there, it's another four km (1¾ hours) to the station at **Yabuhara**.

Getting There & Away
Narai is on the Chūo line, about 45 minutes by local train from Matsumoto.

TENRYU-KYŌ GORGE & MT KOMAGA-TAKE
天竜峡・駒ケ岳
Both Tenryū-kyō Gorge and Mt Komaga-take lie east of the Kiso Valley and are easily reached via the JR Iida line which runs roughly parallel to the Chūo line.

The main sightseeing approach for Tenryū-kyō Gorge is a 1½ hour boat trip down the Tenryū River and through the gorge. Boats leave from the dock close to Ichida station.

Mt Komaga-take (2956 metres) is a popular hiking destination. From Komagane station, a 55 minute bus ride takes you up to the base station of the cablecar at Shirabitaira. The eight minute cablecar ride whisks you up to Senjōjiki. From there, the hike to the peak takes about 2½ hours.

There are numerous pensions, minshuku and ryokan around the town, and several mountain huts along the trails. If you stay at *Komagane Youth Hostel* (☎ 0265-83-3856), you need to take a 15 minute bus ride from the station, then walk for 12 minutes.

Toyama-ken 富山県

The main attractions of this prefecture are two alpine routes across the northern Japan Alps and the mountain villages in the

Gokayama region, to the south of the prefecture on the border with Gifu-ken. Toyama serves as a transport hub for trips into the northern Japan Alps and Takaoka is a convenient staging post for a visit to Noto-hantō Peninsula or to Gokayama.

TOYAMA 富山
Toyama (population 321,000) is a heavily industrialised city with few attractions for the tourist. But it does provide a convenient access point for a visit to the northern Japan Alps.

Information
The information office in Toyama station has maps and leaflets.

Places to Stay
If you have to stay in Toyama, there are plenty of business hotels just a few minutes on foot from the station. The *Toyama Station Hotel* (0764-32-4311) is 100 metres down the street to your right as you exit the station (the hotel is on the left). Prices for singles/twins start at ¥6300/13,200. Almost next door is the *Toyama Business Hotel* (☎ 0764-32-8090), which has singles from ¥4600 to ¥5000 and a few twins at ¥8000.

The big *Dai-Ichi Inn* (☎ 0764-42-6611) next to the station has singles from ¥6500, twins from ¥14,000 and doubles at ¥13,000. The *Hotel Alpha One Eki-Mae* (☎ 0764-33-6000) has over 270 singles at ¥5200 to ¥5500, and a smaller number of twins from ¥10,000. It's just opposite the station.

Toyama Youth Hostel (☎ 0764-37-9010) lies way out to the north-east of the city, 45 minutes by bus from the station (bus terminal Nos 7 and 8). Rates vary from ¥2200 to ¥2350 depending on the season.

Getting There & Away
Air Daily flights operate between Toyama and Tokyo.

Train The JR Takayama line links Toyama with Takayama in about 1¾ hours. The Toyama Tateyama line links Toyama with Tateyama, which is the starting (or finishing) point for those travelling the Tateyama-

Kurobe Alpine Route. The Toyama Chihō Tetsudō line links Toyama with Unazuki Onsen, which is the starting point for a trip up the Kurobe-kyō Gorge.

The JR Hokuriku line runs west via Takaoka (15 minutes) to Kanazawa (40 minutes), Kyoto (3½ hours) and Osaka (four hours). The same line runs north-east via Naoetsu (75 minutes) to the ferry terminal for Sado-ga-shima Island and Niigata (three hours) to Aomori at the very tip of Northern Honshū.

TATEYAMA-KUROBE ALPINE ROUTE
立山黒部アルペンルート
Information
Be warned that this route is closed from late November to early May. For the precise dates, which vary each year, check with a tourist office or call Japan Travel-Phone (☎ 0120-222800, toll free). The season for heavy crowds of visitors lasts between

August and late October and reservations are advised for travel in these months.

JNTO publishes a leaflet entitled *Tateyama, Kurobe & Toyama* with details for the route which is divided into nine sections, using various modes of transport, between Toyama and Shinano-ōmachi. The best place to take a break, if only to escape the Mickey Mouse commentaries and enjoy the tremendous scenery, is Murodō. Transport buffs will want to do the lot, but some visitors find a trip from Toyama as far as Murodō is sufficient – and skip the expense of the rest. The following route description runs from Toyama to Shinano-ōmachi, but travel in either direction is possible.

The Route
From Toyama station, take the chug-a-lug Toyama Tateyama line for the 60 minute ride (¥1010) through rural scenery to Tateyama (at an altitude of 454 metres). Very close to Tateyama station is *Sugita Youth Hostel*

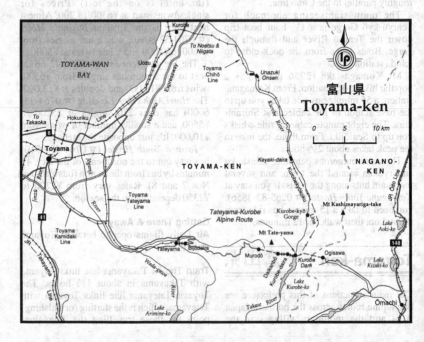

(☎ 0764-82-1754), a convenient place to stay if you are making an early start or a late finish on the route. A bed for the night is ¥2400.

From Tateyama, take the seven minute ride (¥620) in the cablecar to **Bijodaira**. From here, it's a 55 minute ride (¥1630) by bus via the alpine plateau of Midagahara to **Murodō** (altitude 2450 metres). You can break the trip at Midagahara and do the 15 minute walk to see **Tateyama caldera** – the largest non-active crater in Japan. The upper part of the plateau is often covered with deep snow until late into the summer – the road is kept clear by piling up the snow to form a virtual tunnel.

At Murodō, the natural beauty of the surroundings has been requited by a monstrous bus terminal to service the annual flood of visitors. From here, there are various options for short hikes. To the north, just 10 minutes away on foot is **Mikuriga-ike Pond** and 20 minutes further on is **Jigokudani** (Hell Valley Hot Springs). To the east, you can hike for about two hours – including a very steep final section – to the peak of **Mt O-yama** (2992 metres) for an astounding panorama. For the keen long-distance hiker, who has several days or even a week to spare, there are fine routes south to Kamikōchi or north to Keyaki-daira in the Kurobe-kyō Gorge.

Continuing on the route from Murodō, there's a 10 minute bus ride to Daikanbō via a tunnel dug through Mt Tate-yama. The ticket for this claustrophobic experience costs the hefty sum of ¥2060.

At **Daikanbō** you can pause to admire the view before taking the cablecar for the seven minute ride (¥1240) to Kurobe-daira, where another cablecar whisks you down in five minutes (¥820) to Kurobeko beside the vast **Kurobe Dam**. For the technically minded, this is the largest formed dome arch dam in Japan (492 metres long and 186 metres high).

At the dam, you can descend to the water for a cruise or climb up to a lookout point before taking the trolley bus from Kurobe Dam to **Ogisawa** (16 minutes, ¥1240). From there, a 40 minute bus ride (¥1250) takes you down to Shinano-ōmachi station – at an altitude of 712 metres.

For the technically minded, the trip from Toyama to Shinano-ōmachi covers 88.7 km and requires just over ¥10,000 in transport expenses for an adult.

KUROBE-KYŌ GORGE & UNAZUKI ONSEN
黒部峡・宇奈月温泉

From Unazuki Onsen, there's a tramcar line which provides a superbly scenic alpine run past hot-spring lodges and continues up the Kurobe-kyō Gorge to Keyaki-daira. Here you can hike to an observation point for a panorama of the northern Japan Alps. Keyaki-daira is also linked with Hakuba and Murodō by trails which are suitable for seasoned hikers, properly prepared and with several days to spare.

Getting There & Away
Take the train on the Toyama Chihō Tetsudō line from the separate terminus (next to Toyama station) to Unazuki Onsen. The trip from Toyama takes 1½ hours and the fare is ¥1550. If you're arriving on the JR Hokuriku line from the north, change to the Toyama Chihō Tetsudō line either at Kurobe (the stations are separate) or at Uozu (the stations are together).

When you arrive at the railway station at Unazuki Onsen, you then have to walk for five minutes to the station for the Kurobe Kyōkoku Tetsudō (tramcar line). The tramcar line only operates from early May to late November and open carriages are used on most runs. The fare from Unazaki Onsen to Keyaki-daira is ¥1300 and the trip takes 1½ hours. A surcharge is payable for travel on the daily run with enclosed carriages.

GOKAYAMA 五箇山
This remote region, famous for its gasshō-zukuri architecture, lies next to the southern border of Toyama-ken with Gifu-ken. Details for Gokayama are given in the section on Shōkawa Valley in Gifu-ken.

Getting There & Away

To visit Gokayama, you can either take a bus from Takaoka station (one hour and 50 minutes to Suganuma, ¥1600) or you can take a Jōhana line train from Toyama to Jōhana (50 minutes) and continue from there by bus (one hour to Suganuma). Several buses run further, linking Gokayama with Ogimachi and Shirakawa-gō. From Ogimachi you can take buses to Takayama.

TAKAOKA 高岡

Takaoka (population 175,000) is known for its **Daibutsu** (Great Buddha) statue and the local skill in producing bells. It's a useful staging post for heading north-west to Noto-hantō Peninsula or south-east to Gokayama and Takayama. There's an information office at the JR Takaoka station and the bus station is on your right as you exit the station.

The Daibutsu is about five minutes walk north of the station. Take the right fork of the road outside the station, and then the third left. Don't expect it to be overwhelming – it's by no means in the same league as its rivals in Kamakura and Nara. Entry is free.

Just 10 minutes on foot from the station is **Zuiryū-ji Temple** (☎ 0766-22-0179), which is also youth hostel. A bed for the night is ¥2400. Take the south exit from the station and walk straight ahead for 500 metres to the second intersection, then turn right and continue for 300 metres to the temple.

Getting There & Away

The JR Hokuriku line runs south-west via Kanazawa (25 minutes) and Kyoto (3¼ hours) to Osaka. The same line runs east to Toyama (15 minutes) and continues to Aomori at the very tip of northern Honshū.

Ishikawa-ken 石川県

KANAZAWA 金沢

During the 15th century, Kanazawa (population 442,000) came under the control of an autonomous Buddhist government, but this was ousted in 1583 by Maeda Toshiie, head of the powerful Maeda clan, which continued to rule for another three centuries. The wealth acquired from rice production allowed the Maeda to patronise cultural and artistic pursuits – Kanazawa is still one of the key cultural centres in Japan.

During WW II, the absence of military targets in Kanazawa spared the city from destruction and preserved several historical and cultural sites. As the capital of Ishikawa-ken, Kanazawa has its fair share of functional urban architecture. However, it has retained some attractive features from the old city, including the famous Kenroku-en Garden.

The main sights can be seen in a day or so and sidetrips to the Noto-hantō Peninsula and Eihei-ji Temple in Fukui-ken are highly recommended.

Orientation

Kanazawa is a surprisingly sprawling city, and the central city area is a 15 minute bus ride to the south-east of JR Kanazawa station. Fortunately the city has an excellent bus service, making it easy to get to the main sightseeing districts, which can then be covered on foot. The Katamachi district is the commercial and business hub of Kanazawa. From there it's a short walk east to Kenroku-en Garden and its surrounding attractions. The samurai houses in the Nagamachi district are a short walk west from Kohrinbo 109 shopping plaza, a useful orientation point in the centre of Katamachi. Just south of Katamachi, across the river, is the temple district of Teramachi, another interesting area to explore.

On the eastern side of Kanazawa, the hills rising behind the Higashiyama district are popular for walks and views across the city.

Information

Ignore the small information office indicated with a '?' sign next door to the ticket turnstiles inside JR Kanazawa station and head over to the JR ticket sales office in the station. At the back of the office is the excellent Kanazawa tourist information office

(☎ 0762-32-6200). The office has English-speaking staff and is open daily from 10 am to 6 pm.

An essential port of call for anyone planning an extended stay in Kanazawa is the International Culture Exchange Centre (☎ 0762-23-9575) in the Shakyo building close to Kenroku-en Park. The 4th floor of the centre has an English library and a useful noticeboard – sayonara sales, jobs, apartments and so on. The centre also offers particularly good deals on Japanese language tuition – ¥4000 per month with two 90 minute classes per week. Private classes are also available at ¥2000 per hour.

The Society to Introduce Kanazawa to the World (☎ 0762-22-7332) specialises in organising home visits, Goodwill Guides, language courses and home stays – if you give advance notice. Visitors with specific cultural interests can arrange to visit workshops, craft centres and theatres through the society.

Another organisation for long-termers is the Ishikawa Foundation for International Exchange (☎ 0762-62-5931), which organises

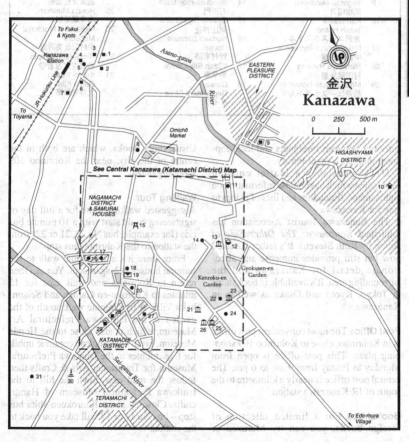

CENTRAL HONSHŪ

PLACES TO STAY		OTHER			
1	Kanazawa Central Hotel 金沢セントラルホテル	5	Hokutetsu Kankō Bus Company 北鉄観光バスターミナル	19	Post Office 郵便局
2	Kanazawa Station Hotel 金沢ステーションホテル	8	Meitetsu Marukoshi Department Store 名鉄丸越スカイプラザ	20	Kōrimbō 109 Shopping Plaza こうりんぼう１０９ ショッピングプラザ
3	New Central Inn Kanazawa ニューセントラルイン金沢	11	Terajima Samurai House 寺島応養邸	21	Ishikawa Prefectural Art Museum 石川県立美術館
4	Holiday Inn Kanazawa ホリデーイン金沢	12	Kenroku-en-shita Bus Stop 兼六園下バス停	22	Seison-kaku Villa 成巽閣
6	Garden Hotel Kanazawa ガーデンホテル金沢	13	Ishikawa Prefectural Museum of Handicrafts 石川県観光物産館	23	Ishikawa Prefectural Museum for Traditional Arts & Crafts 石川県立伝統産業工芸館
7	Kannazawa ANA Hotel 金沢全日空ホテル	14	Ishikawa-mon Gate 石川門	24	Nōgaku Bunka Kaikan 能楽文化会館
9	Yōgetsu Minshuku 民宿陽月	15	Oyama-jinja Shrine 尾山神社	25	Honda Museum 本多蔵品館
10	Kanazawa Youth Hostel 金沢ユースホステル	16	Nomura Samurai House 野村家跡	26	Nakamura Memorial Museum 中村記念美術館
27	Nakamuraya Ryokan 中村屋旅館	17	Yūzen Silk Centre 彩筆庵	30	Ninja-dera Temple 妙立寺／忍者寺
28	Murataya Ryokan 村田屋旅館	18	Daiwa Department Store ダイワ	31	Kutani Kosen Gama Kiln 九谷光仙窯
29	Matsui Youth Hostel 松井ユースホステル				

activities between foreigners and local Japanese and has a small library.

JNTO publishes a leaflet entitled *Kanazawa* which has concise information on sights, maps, timetables and lists of places to stay for Kanazawa.

The Kanazawa Tourist Association has published *Kanazawa: The Other Side of Japan* by Ruth Stevens. It's rather outdated now but still provides immense and affectionate detail for Kanazawa and the surrounding area. It's available in bookshops in Tokyo, Kyoto and Osaka as well as in Kanazawa.

Post Office The most convenient post office is in Kohrinbo, close to Kohrinbo 109 shopping plaza. This post office is open from Monday to Friday from 9 am to 6 pm. The central post office is nearly a kilometre to the south of JR Kanazawa station.

Bookshops For a limited selection of foreign books, you can try Maruzen or Utsunomiya Books, which are both in the centre of the city, near the Kohrinbo 109 shopping plaza.

Walking Tour
A suggested walking route for a full day of sightseeing could start with a 10 minute bus ride (for example, bus No 20, 21 or 22) from the station to the Kohrinbo bus stop.

From there it's a 10 minute walk to the samurai houses in Nagamachi. You can then return to Kohrinbo and walk east for 15 minutes to Kenroku-en Garden and Seison-kaku Villa. A five minute walk south of the garden is the Ishikawa Prefectural Art Museum, which is also close to the Honda Museum. From here you can continue uphill for five minutes to the Ishikawa Prefectural Museum for Traditional Arts & Crafts then follow the road east down the hill to the Ishikawa Prefectural Museum of Handicrafts. Close by is the Kenrokuen-shita bus stop – bus No 11 or 12 will take you back to the station.

Nagamachi Samurai Houses
長町武家屋敷跡

The Nagamachi district, once inhabited by samurai, has retained a few of its winding streets and tile-roofed mud walls. Nomura Samurai House, though partly transplanted from outside Kanazawa, is worth a visit for its decorative garden. Admission costs ¥400 and it's open from 8.30 am to 5 pm.

Close by is **Yūzen Silk Centre** (Saihitsuan), where you can see the silk-dyeing process. Admission costs ¥500 and includes an English leaflet, tea and a sweet. It's open from 9 am to noon and from 1 to 4.30 pm but is closed on Thursday.

Oyama-jinja Shrine   尾山神社

This shrine is not worth a special trip, but have a look if you are in the centre of the city and have time to spare. The shrine was dedicated to Maeda Toshiie in 1599. In the Meiji period, a couple of Dutchmen helped to design the three storeyed gate with a stained-glass window on the top storey.

Kenroku-en Garden   兼六園

Usually billed as the star attraction of Kanazawa, Kenroku-en Garden is also ranked by Japanese as one of their three top gardens – the other two are Kairaku-en in Mito and Kōraku-en in Okayama.

The name of the garden *(kenroku* translates as 'combined six') refers to a renowned Chinese garden from the Sung dynasty which required six attributes for perfection: seclusion, spaciousness, artificiality, antiquity, abundant water and broad views. In its original form, Kenroku-en formed the outer garden of Kanazawa Castle, but from the 17th century onwards it was enlarged until it reached completion in the early 19th century. The garden was opened to the public in 1871.

Using the explanatory leaflet and map which are provided at the entrance booth, you can spend a couple of hours wandering around the grounds (100.74 hectares!) admiring the paths, bridges, trees (5000), shrubs (3500), waterfalls and stone lanterns. Each season brings with it some special botanical attraction: winter, for example, sees the use of *yuki-tsuri*, intricate

umbrella-like structures which protect the trees from snow damage. The exits are clearly marked on the map.

Kenroku-en is certainly attractive, but its fame has attracted enormous crowds which, by sheer weight of numbers, make severe inroads into the intimacy and enjoyment of the place as a garden. To escape the rush hours, try and visit early in the morning or late in the afternoon.

Admission costs ¥300 and it's open daily from 6.30 am to 6 pm. From 16 October to 15 March opening hours are from 8 am to 4.30 pm.

Seison-kaku Villa   成巽閣

This retirement villa, on the south-eastern edge of Kenroku-en Garden, was built in 1863 by a Maeda lord for his mother. A visit to this stylish residence with its elegant chambers and furnishings is recommended. Admission costs ¥500 and includes a detailed explanatory leaflet in English. It's open daily from 8.30 am to 4.30 pm, and is closed on Wednesday.

Ishikawa Prefectural Art Museum
石川県立博物館

This museum specialises in antique exhibits of traditional arts with special emphasis on Kutani ceramics, Japanese painting, and Yūzen fabrics and costumes. The English caption for one art exhibit: 'Awake from a Dream by Honking' sounds like advice for a drowsy motorist. The exhibits are rotated throughout the year. Admission costs ¥350, but more is charged for special exhibitions. It's open from 9.30 am to 5 pm.

Nakamura Memorial Museum
中村記念美術館

The Nakamura Memorial Museum is reached via a narrow flight of steps below the Ishikawa Prefectural Art Museum. The museum displays the collection of a wealthy sake brewer, Nakamura Eishun. Exhibits are changed throughout the year, but usually include tea-ceremony utensils, calligraphy and traditional crafts. Admission costs ¥300 and includes green tea and a Japanese titbit. It's open from 9 am to 4.30 pm daily except Tuesday.

Honda Museum   藩老本多蔵品館

Members of the Honda family were chief retainers to the Maeda clan and this museum exhibits the family collection of armour, household utensils, and works of art. One cogent reason to visit this museum is the detailed, descriptive catalogue in English; the bullet-proof coat and the family vase are particularly interesting.

Admission costs ¥500. It's open from 9 am to 5 pm but is closed on Thursday between November and February. A sprightly, elderly guide sometimes conducts free tours in English.

Nō Theatre   能楽文化会館

Regular Nō performances are held at the Nō Theatre at 12.30 pm on the first Sunday of each month, on the second Sunday in April and on 15 January. It is also possible to attend rehearsals free of charge. Enquire at the Kanazawa station information counter for more information.

Museum for Traditional Arts & Crafts
伝統産業工芸館

This museum is an interesting shop window for the crafts of the region, ranging from ceramics, lacquerware and woodcarving to metalwork and the extraordinary precision

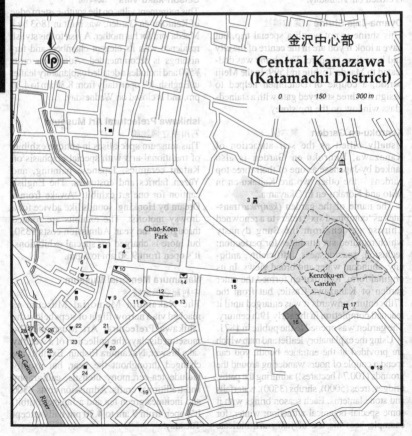

金沢中心部

Central Kanazawa
(Katamachi District)

0   150   300 m

of gold leaf techniques. Nothing is on sale, but prices are indicated for individual exhibits. For your own Buddhist altar, you'll need to shell out nearly three million yen but by contrast, the lacquered phone is a snip at ¥88,000. Of course, for the person with everything, there's always the gold-plated phone. Anglers will be entranced by the fly-tying exhibit where the heads of artificial flies get the gold leaf treatment.

Admission costs ¥250 and a detailed leaflet is provided in English. It's open daily from 9 am to 5 pm but closed every Thursday from December to March and every third Thursday between April and November.

Gyokusen-en Garden　玉泉園
If you want to visit a delightful garden with more intimacy and less crowds than Kenroku-en, Gyokusen-en is definitely recommended. The garden dates from the Edo period and consists of several gardens rising on two levels up a steep slope. You can take tea here for an additional ¥400.

Admission costs ¥400 and includes a very detailed leaflet in English. The garden is open from 9 am to 4 pm but is closed in the winter.

Ishikawa Prefectural Museum of Handicraft　石川県立観光物産館
This museum is a commercially oriented establishment with only the third floor functioning as a museum, which is, in fact, called the Hall of Traditional Arts & Crafts. Here you can observe demonstrations of the processes for making Japanese cakes, lacquerware, gold leaf, pottery and Yūzen silk. It's worth a visit as a change from gawking at static exhibits in a museum. Admission to the hall costs ¥200 and includes an English leaflet about the handicrafts. It's open from 9 am to 6 pm but opens an hour later between 21 November and 20 March. It's also closed on Thursday.

Ishikawa-mon Gate　石川門
This elegant gate with its lead tiles (useful if ammunition ran short) is all that's left of Kanazawa Castle, which burnt down so many times that the locals obviously got sick of rebuilding the thing.

CENTRAL HONSHŪ

PLACES TO STAY		13	K's Diner	4	Daiwa
			ケイズダイナー		Department Store
1	Kanazawa New	19	Hot House Restaurant		ダイワ
	Grand Hotel		ホットハウスレストラン	6	Cinema St
	金沢ニューグランドホテル	20	Kopkunka Thai		シネマ街
5	Kanazawa Tōkyū Hotel		Restaurant	7	Chipstix Bar
	金沢東急ホテル		コプクンカータイ料理		チプスティックスバー
8	Katamichi Shā Hotel	22	Tsubohachi	11	Sapporo Lion
	片町シャーホテル		Restaurant		Beer Hall
15	Kanazawa		つぼ八		サッポロライオンビヤホール
	Dai-Ichi Hotel	25	Irohanihoheto	12	Utsunomiya Books
	金沢第一ホテル		Restaurant		宇都宮書店
21	Marutaya Ryokan		いろはにほへと	14	Post Office
	村田屋旅館	28	Legian Indonesian		郵便局
24	Kanazawa		Restaurant	16	Ishikawa Prefectural
	Washington Hotel		レジアンインドネシア料理		Art Museum
	金沢ワシントンホテル				石川県立美術館
26	Kanazawa	**OTHER**		17	Kanazawa-jinja Shrine
	Prince Hotel				金沢神社
	金沢プリンスホテル	2	Ishikawa Prefectural	18	Shakyo Building
			Museum of		シャキョービル
PLACES TO EAT			Handicrafts	23	Katamichi Intersection
			石川県観光物産館		片町交差点
9	McDonald's	3	Kanazawa-jō	27	Pole Pole Bar
	マクドナルド		Castle Ruins		ポールポールバー
10	Mr Donut		金沢城跡		
	ミスタードーナッツ				

Terajima Samurai House 寺島応養邸
This is the residence of a middle-class retainer of the Maeda clan and was built in 1770. There's a peaceful garden and tea is available for ¥400 in the tea-ceremony room. Admission costs ¥300 and includes a detailed pamphlet in English. It's open from 9 am to 5 pm but is closed on Thursday.

Eastern Pleasure District ひがし茶屋街
If you follow the main road north from Terajima Samurai House and cross the Asano-gawa River, you reach the Eastern Pleasure District, which was established early in the last century as a centre for geisha to entertain wealthy patrons. There are several streets still preserved with the slatted, wooden facades of the geisha houses.

A former geisha house which is open to the public is Shima. Admission (including the enclosed garden) costs ¥300. It's open from 8.30 am to 4.30 pm but is closed on Monday. Yōgetsu is another former geisha house in this district which now functions as a minshuku – see the following Places to Stay section.

Teramachi District 寺町
Teramachi stretches beside the Sai-gawa River, just south of the city centre. This old neighbourhood was established as a first line of defence, and still contains dozens of temples and narrow backstreets: a good place for a peaceful stroll. **Ninja-dera Temple**, also known as Myōryū-ji Temple, is about five minutes on foot from the river. Completed in 1643, this temple resembles a labyrinthine fortress with dozens of stairways, corridors, secret chambers, concealed tunnels and trick doors – the Maeda lords did not want to be caught napping. The popular name of Ninja-dera refers to the temple's connection with *ninjutsu* (the art of stealth) and the *ninja* (practitioners of the art). Although the gadgetry is mildly interesting, mandatory reservation and a tour (conducted in Japanese) can make the visit unduly time-consuming.

Admission costs ¥500 and is by reservation (☎ 0762-41-2877) only. It's open from 9 am to 4.30 pm but closes half an hour earlier between December and February. The entrance ticket enjoins visitors to 'Refrain from amoking in the precincts'. For more information on the activities of the elusive ninja see the Iga-Ueno section of the Kansai chapter.

Those interested in the production of Kutani ceramics might like to visit the nearby **Kutani Kosen Gama Kiln** which is open to the public. There is no charge for admission and it's open daily from 8.30 am to noon and from 1 to 5 pm. The kiln is in an area of the city that was once known as the Western Pleasure District, a precinct which had similar functions to its counterpart in the eastern part of the city.

Edo-mura Village 江戸村
This is an open-air museum of transposed buildings dating from the Edo period – it's a long way from Kanazawa and you should allow at least half a day for your visit.

There are 20 buildings on display, including an inn, farmhouses, a samurai mansion and a pawnshop. One of the farmhouses has a tiny room above the entrance which housed the servants and at night the stairs were removed to stop them doing a flit.

Minibuses shuttle between Edo-mura Village and Danpūen which is a similar but smaller open-air museum concentrating on crafts.

Admission to the village costs a hefty ¥1100 and the ticket includes free transport to and from Danpūen. An explanatory English leaflet and map are provided. The village is open daily from 8 am to 6 pm between April and October but closes an hour earlier between November and March.

To reach Edo-mura Village, take bus No 12 (¥520, 45 minutes) from Kanazawa station. The bus goes via Yuwaku Onsen and climbs uphill for a few more minutes before dropping you off at the palatial Hakuunrō Hotel. Walk for about 10 minutes up the hill in front of the hotel and then climb the steps on the left to reach the entrance office for Edo-mura. The minibus for Danpūen leaves from this office every 20 minutes.

Markets

Omichō market lies on the main bus route between the station and the Kohrinbo area in the centre of the city. The most convenient bus stop for the market is Musashi-ga-tsuji. Omichō market is a warren of several hundred shops many of which specialise in seafood. Take a break from sightseeing and just wander around here to watch market life.

Festivals

Some of the major festivals celebrated here are:

Kagatobi Dezomeshiki
  6 January. Scantily clad firemen brave the cold, imbibe sake, and demonstrate ancient firefighting skills on ladders.

Dekumawashi (Puppet Theatre Festival)
  10 to 16 February. Displays of Jōruri, a traditional form of puppet theatre, are held in the evening at the village of Oguchi.

Asano-gawa Enyūkai
  Early April. Performances of traditional Japanese dance and music are held on the banks of the Asonagawa River.

Hyakumangoku Matsuri
  13 to 15 June. This is the main annual festival in Kanazawa and the highlight is a huge parade of townsfolk dressed in costumes from the 16th century. Other events include Takigi Nō (torchlit performances of Nō drama), Torō Nagashi (lanterns floated down the river at dusk) and a special tea ceremony at Kenroku-en Garden.

Bon Odori (Folk Dancing Festival)
  Mid-August. Folk dancing festivals are held in several places including the Futamata area, and the village of Hatta where the festival is called Sakata Odori.

Places to Stay

The tourist information office in the station can help with reservations for accommodation. Those with money to spend on a business hotel, should bear in mind that the station area is not particularly convenient for sightseeing in Kanazawa.

Station Area The station area has the usual abundance of business hotel accommodation. Directly in front of the station is the *Garden Hotel Kanazawa* (☎ 0762-63-3333), which has singles from ¥5800 to ¥6300, twins from ¥12,000 to ¥18,000 and doubles from ¥9500. Close by is the *Kanazawa Station Hotel* (☎ 0762-23-2600), where singles range from ¥6000 to ¥8000, twins from ¥12,000 to ¥18,000, and doubles from ¥11,500 to ¥15,000. The *New Central Inn Kanazawa* (☎ 0762-21-7800) and the *Kanazawa Central Hotel* (☎ 0762-63-5311) are opposite each other and both have rates of around ¥6200 for singles and ¥11,000 for twins.

Some up-market options near the station are: the *Holiday Inn Kanazawa* (☎ 0762-23-1111) has singles from ¥9500 to ¥10,500, twins from ¥15,000 to ¥20,000, and doubles from ¥15,000 to ¥18,000. Opposite the station is the flashy *Kanazawa ANA Hotel* (☎ 0762-24-6111), with singles from ¥11,000, twins from ¥20,000 and doubles from ¥19,000.

Central Kanazawa *Matsui Youth Hostel* (☎ 0762-21-0275) is small and relaxed, but closes at 10 pm. Nightly costs are ¥2400. Note that the hostel is closed from 31 December to 2 January.

From the station, take a bus from terminal No 7, 8 or 9 for the 14 minute ride to the city and get off at the Katamachi bus stop. Walk a few metres back up the street to a large intersection. Turn right here then take the second side street on your right. The hostel is halfway down this street. *Murataya Ryokan* (☎ 0762-63-0455) is a member of the Japanese Inn Group. The helpful manager is used to dealing with foreigners' queries on things to see and do in Kanazawa. Prices for singles/doubles start at ¥4200/8000; triples cost from ¥10,500. Western breakfast costs ¥400. To find this ryokan, follow the directions for Matsui Youth Hostel. Having turned right at the large intersection, take the first side street on your left and continue about 20 metres until you see the ryokan sign on your left.

On the business hotel front, most of the central Kanazawa accommodation is fairly expensive. Not far from the Katamichi intersection, the *Kanazawa Prince Hotel* (☎ 0762-23-2131) is a decent mid-range place with singles from ¥6000 to ¥7000, and twins and doubles from ¥11,600. Just north of the intersection, the *Katamichi Shā Hotel* (☎ 0762-23-3636) is a small, functional place with 22 singles at ¥5200. Also close to the intersection is the *Kanazawa Washington Hotel* (☎ 0762-24-0111), where singles range from ¥7000 to ¥9000, twins from ¥15,000 and doubles from ¥13,000.

One of the cheaper places around is the *Kanazawa Dai-Ichi Hotel* (☎ 0762-22-2011), which is just east of the Kohrinbo 109 building close to Kenroku-en Garden. Singles here range from ¥4800 to ¥5500, while twins range from ¥9000 to ¥10,000. The *Kanazawa Tōkyū Hotel* (☎ 0762-31-2411), next door to the Kohrinbo 109 building, is much more up-market, with rates from ¥11,000/18,000/20,000 for singles/twins/doubles. Around 300 metres to the north of here, the *Kanazawa New Grand Hotel* (☎ 0762-33-1311) has similar rates and standards.

Higashiyama District *Yōgetsu Minshuku* (☎ 0762-52-0497) is a geisha house dating from the previous century. Prices start around ¥6200 per person including two meals. The minshuku is close to Enkō-ji Temple, about 20 minutes on foot from the station; or 10 minutes by bus.

Kanazawa Youth Hostel (☎ 0762-52-3414) is way up in the hills to the east of the city and commands a superb position. Unfortunately, this also means that access to the hostel is mighty inconvenient, unless you have your own transport – bus services are infrequent.

A dorm bed costs ¥2500, but gaijin hostellers are given a ¥200 discount. Private rooms are a good deal at ¥3500 per person. The doors close at 10 pm and loudspeakers marshal the slumbering troops for breakfast in the morning. During peak season, the hostel takes members only. Bicycle rental is available. If you hear early morning whoops and shrieks, they are probably issuing from the zoo in 'Kiddyland' – an amusement park/aquarium opposite the hostel.

To reach the hostel from the station, take bus No 90 for Utatsuyama-kōen Park and get off after about 25 minutes at the Suizokukan-mae bus stop, which is virtually opposite the hostel.

Places to Eat

The station area is not particularly exciting on the dining front. The area around the Kitamachi intersection in central Kanazawa offers much more variety. For quality set lunches (from around ¥800), the 4th floor of Kohrinbo 109 shopping plaza has a variety of inexpensive places to eat. Similar restaurants are found on the upper floors of Daiwa department store, diagonally opposite Kohrinbo 109 plaza, and in Meitetsu Marukoshi department store, which is on the major intersection next to Omichō market. Connoisseurs consider the sushi restaurants in this market to serve the freshest and best sushi in town.

For evening meals, the izakaya chains *Tsubohachi* and *Irohanihoheto* both have several branches in Kanazawa. Check the Central Kanazawa map for their locations close to the Kitamachi intersection. Both have affordable prices and illustrated menus. *Sapporo Lion*, also close by, is a good (if a little pricey) place to knock back a beer and have some Japanese pub food – pizza, German sausages and so on.

Legian is a popular Indonesian restaurant down by the river. It looks a little down-at-heel, but the food is good and authentic. The Patio building on the first parallel street to the east of Katamichi-dōri has an excellent Thai restaurant, *Kopkunka*. It's not particularly cheap (Thai restaurants never are in Japan), and you should figure on around ¥2500 per head with drinks. Also on the ethnic front, the best Indian food is at *Hot House*. They have lunch specials from around ¥850; figure on ¥1500 to ¥2000 per head for evening meals.

Entertainment

Kanazawa is not a huge city and weeknights tend to be fairly quiet, but Friday and Saturday nights can be quite lively. There are a number of bars around town that see a good mix of gaijin (there are a lot of foreign students in Kanazawa) and local Japanese, and these are good places to meet people.

K's Diner is a popular gaijin hangout even though the décor is a little soulless. It's a good place for an early evening drink. Just around the corner from the Kohrinbo 109 plaza is *Chipstix*, a tiny bar that, at the time of writing, had been appropriated by the gaijin set. On Friday and Saturday nights the crowds spill out on the street. Upstairs is a karaoke room.

Late night drinkers gravitate to *Pole Pole*, one of those legendary bars that every self-respecting Japanese city has to have at least one of. It's grungy and dark, the floor is littered with peanut shells, and the music (reggae) is loud. The truly adventurous might want to order the house cocktail speciality: 'elephant wank'...or then again, maybe not. It's a little difficult to find the first time. It's in the same building as the Indonesian restaurant Legian – walk to Legian along the river and then walk through the building to find Pole Pole.

Things to Buy
Kanazawa is a centre for traditional crafts such as *kaga yūzen* (silk dyeing), *kutani-yaki* (colourful ceramics), *kaga maki-e* (lacquerware with raised lacquer design work), woodcarving using *kiri* (paulownia) and *kinpaku* (gold leaf) – a tiny gold leaf in your tea is meant to be good for rheumatism.

For a quick view or purchase of these crafts, you can visit Kankō Bussankan (Ishikawa Prefectural Museum of Handicrafts). The tourist information office can set up visits to workshops or direct you to museums of specific interest such as the one close to the station which specialises in the production of gold leaf.

Getting There & Away
Air Kanazawa Airport (Komatsu Kūkō) has air connections with Tokyo, Sendai, Fukuoka and Sapporo. There's also an international connection with Seoul (Korea).

Train Kanazawa is linked to south-western destinations by the JR Hokuriku line: Fukui

(55 minutes), Kyoto (2½ hours, ¥6580) and Osaka (3 hours, ¥7300). The same line runs north-east to Takaoka (45 minutes), Toyama (one hour), Naoetsu (2¼ hours) and Niigata (3¾ hours). To travel to Takayama (2½ hours), you need to change to the JR Takayama line at Toyama. The quickest way to travel between Tokyo and Kanazawa is by taking the Jōetsu shinkansen from Tokyo station to Nagaoka (one hour 40 minutes), and then travelling onwards by limited express to Kanazawa (three hours). The whole trip costs ¥13,210. There are two daily departures of the limited express Hakusan service from Ueno to Kanazawa. The journey takes just over six hours and costs ¥10,490.

The JR Nanao line connects Kanazawa with Wajima (Noto-hantō Peninsula) in 2¼ hours.

Bus There are regular bus services between Kanazawa and Tokyo (Ikebukuro, 7½ hours, ¥7700), Kyoto (four hours, ¥3990) and Nagoya (four hours, ¥3990). The Meitetsu bus service between Kanazawa and Nagoya operates from July to early November via Gokayama and Shirakawa-gō.

Getting Around
To/From the Airport A bus service connects Kanazawa Airport (Komatsu Kūkō) with Kanazawa station in 55 minutes (¥1000).

Bus The bus network is extensive and fares start at ¥170. From the station, bus Nos 10 and 11 will take you to the Kenroku-en-shita bus stop, a useful point if you just want to visit the main sights around Kenroku-en Garden. To ride from the station to the centre of the city, you can choose from several buses, including bus Nos 20, 21 and 30, and get off at the Kohrinbo bus stop.

The office of the Hokutetsu Kankō bus company outside the station sells *kaisūken* (discount tickets) and *teikiken* (discount commuter passes) if you want to travel frequently by bus for a day or more.

Bicycle Rental is available (¥1000 for the

day or ¥600 for four hours) at the station, but the hills and the urban traffic snarls aren't particularly inviting. The Kanazawa Youth Hostel also has bicycles for rent (cheaper prices), but it's quite a puff returning up the hill. The tourist information office in Kohrinbo 109 has details of bicycle rental places in the city centre.

Noto-hantō Peninsula
能登半島

For an enjoyable combination of rugged seascapes, traditional rural life and a light diet of cultural sights, this peninsula is highly recommended. Noto-hantō Peninsula is easily accessible from Kanazawa, Takaoka or Toyama. The wild, unsheltered western side of the peninsula contrasts with the calm and indented coastline of the eastern side.

Information

Kanazawa tourist information office (☎ 0762-22-1500) in JR Kanazawa station can help reserve accommodation and deal with most other queries regarding the Noto-hantō Peninsula.

The Society to Introduce Kanazawa to the World (☎ 0762-22-7332) publishes *Noto Peninsula, A Visitors' Guide*.

JNTO's leaflet entitled *Noto Peninsula* has concise information on sights, maps, timetables and lists of places to stay for the Noto-hantō Peninsula.

There are also information offices at Wajima station and Nanao station; Nanao also has its own Society to Introduce Nanao to the World (☎ 0767-53-1111) which arranges home visits.

Planning Your Itinerary

It's not really possible to do justice to the peninsula with a day trip in which you tick off all the sights in hurried procession; this leaves little time to savour the pace of rural life.

A better idea might be to spend perhaps two nights and three days gradually working your way around the coastline, which has plenty of youth hostels and minshuku.

Arts & Crafts

You won't have to look too far on your travels around the peninsula before seeing shops groaning with the main regional craft – lacquerware. A large proportion of the townsfolk in Wajima are engaged in producing Wajima-nuri, lacquerware renowned for its durability and rich colours.

Festivals

The Noto-hantō Peninsula has dozens of festivals throughout the year. Seihaku-sai Festival, held in Nanao from 13 to 15 May, includes a spectacular procession of festival floats. Gojinjō Daikō Nabune Festival, held in Wajima between 31 July and 1 August, features wild drumming performed by drummers wearing demon masks and seaweed headgear. Ishizaki Hoto Festival, held in Nanao in early August, is famed for its parade of tall lantern poles.

Full details for annual festivals and events are available from the tourist information offices in Kanazawa, Wajima or Nanao.

Accommodation

The peninsula is well provided with minshuku and youth hostels. Reservations are advisable during peak season and can be made through the Kanazawa, Wajima or Nanao tourist information offices.

Getting There & Away

Train The JR Nanao line runs from Kanazawa via Anamizu (where a change of trains is usually necessary) to Wajima in 2¼ hours. At Anamizu, the private Noto Tetsudō line branches off to Takojima on the tip of the peninsula.

Bus The Okunoto express bus service runs direct between Kanazawa and Maura via Wajima and Sosogi. The trip between Kanazawa and Wajima takes two hours and the ticket costs ¥2000 one way. A similar

能登半島

Noto-hantō Peninsula

0   5   10 km

service connects Kanazawa with Maura, takes two hours 45 minutes and cost ¥2300.

For information and reservations, call or visit the Hokuriku Tetsudō bus company (☎ 0762-37-5115) – the office is next to Kanazawa station.

Getting Around

Train The railway lines on the peninsula are not really useful for getting around. If you are using trains, Anamizu, even though it lacks sightseeing attractions, could serve as a provisional staging point to start or finish your tour.

Bus Local buses are infrequent and it's sometimes worth the added expense to use one of the scheduled tour buses (described later in this section) for short hops to reach more remote places.

Useful local bus lines include: Wajima to Monzen, Monzen to Anamizu and Wajima to Ushitsu via Sosogi and Kami Tokikuni. Local bus timetables are available at tourist information offices.

Tour Buses There are regular sightseeing buses which follow a variety of routes around the peninsula. Depending on the itinerary, the ticket price includes transport, a Japanese-speaking guide, admission fees for sights and lunch. In terms of transport, these buses are very convenient, the lunch is no great shakes and any pauses in the rapid-fire commentary from the guide are filled with recorded sounds ranging from jungle noises to songs and breaking waves. Ear plugs are advised.

There are many permutations, but most of the itineraries use Kanazawa or Wajima as a starting or finishing point. Some tours operate throughout the year, others only operate between March and November.

For example, by placing two itineraries back to back, you could construct your own two day tour with an overnight in Wajima (make your own reservation for accommodation). On the first day you could take the bus tour which goes from Kanazawa via Chiri-hama Beach, Myōjō-ji Temple, and Ganmon to Wajima. The bus leaves Kanazawa station at 9.10 am and arrives at Wajima station at 3.25 pm and the ticket costs ¥5050. The next day you could take the bus tour (¥5350) which goes from Wajima station (9.20 am) via Kami Tokikuni and Cape Rokkō-zaki to Tsukumo-wan Bay (4.10 pm). From there, you can return by train to Kanazawa.

The advantage of these tours is that you get to see all the major sights including those which are in more remote places. It's also worth noting that you can hop on or off the buses en route: a good way to shorten your exposure to the 'package'. A distinct disadvantage, apart from the cost and haste, is that you may well find the 'guided tourist missile' approach extremely wearing on the nerves.

Bicycle The peninsula should appeal to cyclists as its coastal terrain is flat, and inland there's only an occasional gradient. The camping grounds and youth hostels are spread out at convenient intervals. The tourist information offices (Kanazawa, Wajima, Nanao) have a very good map (in Japanese) entitled *Noto Hantō Rōdo Matsupu* which covers the area on a scale of 1:160,000.

KITA-KE HOUSE   喜多家

This residence of the Kita, a wealthy family which once administered over 100 villages in the region, is on the coast, about 30 minutes by bus north of Kanazawa. Kita-ke is built in local farmhouse style, and inside there are displays of weapons, ceramics, farming tools, folk art and documents. There is also a fine garden.

Admission costs ¥700 and includes a detailed leaflet in English. It's open from 8.30 am to 5 pm. To get there by train, take the JR Nanao line to Menden station then walk for 20 minutes.

CHIRI-HAMA BEACH   千里浜

This long beach has become an attraction for motorists, and at times it resembles a sandy motorway with droves of buses, motorcycles and cars roaring past the breakers. Without the motorised invasion the beach would be attractive, but the circus leaves behind the usual detritus of plastic, fast-food wrappings and dead sea birds.

An ugly tourist office sells souvenirs and medicines such as dried snake and what looked like small turtles. Outside, there's the pungent smell of fried squid and a stone plaque where chic bikers and their metal steeds queue up for a standard photo against the beach backdrop.

If you're still keen on visiting the beach, you can get to it on foot from Hakui station. It's around 20 minutes walk to the west of the station.

KETA-TAISHA SHRINE 気多大社

This shrine, set in a wooded grove close to the sea, is believed to have been founded in the eighth century, but the architectural style of the present building dates from the 17th century. The shrine is open from 8.30 am to 4.30 pm and is 10 minutes by bus from Hakui station. Get off at the Ichinomiya bus stop (¥210). Admission costs ¥100.

MYŌJŌ-JI TEMPLE 妙成寺

Myōjō-ji was founded in 1294 by Nichijō, a disciple of Nichiren, as the main temple of the Myōjō-ji school of Nichiren Buddhism. The temple complex is composed of several buildings including the strikingly elegant five storeyed pagoda (gojū-no-tō) which has just undergone extensive renovation. The grounds are relatively quiet – just one loudspeaker grinding out its message – and the structures have a pleasantly unembellished, weather-beaten feel.

Admission costs ¥350 and includes an excellent English leaflet with map. It's open from 8 am to 5 pm. To reach the temple from Hakui station, take the bus for 15 minutes and then walk for 15 minutes.

From the temple, it takes about 25 minutes on foot to reach **Shibagaki-hama Beach** with its small fishing community.

NOTO-KONGŌ COAST 能登金剛海岸

The stretch of rocky shoreline known as Noto-kongō extends for about 16 km between Fukūra and Sekinohana and includes a variety of rock formations such as Gammon, which resembles a large gate. Buses from Hakui station to Noto-kongō take just under an hour. There are pleasant sea views as the road winds along the coast passing fishing villages with their protective concrete breakwaters.

Ryūgo-ji Youth Hostel (☎ 0767-42-0401) is part of **Ryūgo-ji Temple** and you may, on request, be allowed to take part in a Zen meditation session. To reach the hostel, take a 20 minute bus ride from Togi in the direction of Monzen. Get off at the Sakami Ryūgoji-mae bus stop, then follow the road across the bridge to the hostel (about seven minutes). Nightly costs are ¥2400, but check to make sure that the temple is still running the hostel – at the time of writing there were reports that it might close.

Close to Monzen, there's the famous **Sōji-ji Temple** which was established in 1321 as the head temple of the Sōtō school of Zen. After a fire severely damaged the buildings in 1898, the temple was restored, but it now functions as a branch temple; the main temple has been transferred to Yokohama. Admission costs ¥300 and it's open daily from 8 am to 5 pm. To reach the temple from Anamizu station, take a 40 minute bus ride to the Sōji-ji-mae bus stop.

Notominazuki Youth Hostel (☎ 0768-46-2022) is at Minazuki, which is 35 minutes by bus from Monzen. There's a coastal hiking trail (about 2½ hours) between Minazuki and Kami-ōzawa. Nightly costs are ¥2400, and the hostel is closed from 29 December to 7 January.

WAJIMA 輪島

Wajima is a small town, but it has long been renowned as a centre for the production of lacquerware and has now become a major centre for tourism.

The tourist information office at Wajima station provides English leaflets, maps and timetable information and the staff will help you book accommodation.

Wajima Lacquerware Hall 輪島漆器会館

This hall is in the centre of town next to the Sim-bashi Bridge. The 2nd floor has demonstrations of lacquerware production techniques. The finished products are displayed in the museum section, and purchases can be made in the shop downstairs. Admission to the hall costs ¥200 and includes a shopping bag, a leaflet and a pair of chopsticks. The hall is open daily from 9 am to 5.15 pm.

Market　朝市
The morning market *(asa-ichi)* takes place daily between 8 am and noon – except on the 10th and 25th of each month. Despite its touristy trappings, the market might appeal for its array of chuckling old crones dangling seaweed, fish or ridiculous tourist tat in front of shoppers and drawing attention to their wares with a cheery *Dō deska?* ('How about it?'). Take your pick from tiny whitefish, large-finned fat fish, dried squid or comic toys resembling beetles, crabs or fish complete with tails, pincers or legs that wiggle.

To find the market, walk north along the river from the Wajima Lacquerware Hall and turn right just before Iroha-bashi Bridge.

Kiriko Kaikan　キリコ会館
This is a hall housing the huge lacquered floats used in the regional festivals. Admission costs ¥350. It's open from 8 am to 5 pm. From the station, the hall is 20 minutes on foot or you can take the six minute bus ride from the station and get off at the Tsukada bus stop.

Hegura-jima Island　舳倉島
Those interested in a day trip to an island can take the ferry to Hegura-jima Island which boasts a lighthouse, several shrines and no traffic. Birdwatchers flock to the island in spring and autumn. The main industries which support the islanders are fishing and tourism. If you want to extend your island isolation by staying overnight there are plenty of minshuku. Reservations can be made in Japanese by calling ☎ 0768-22-4961.

From early April to late October, the ferry departs Wajima at 8.30 am and reaches the island at 10.20 am. The return ferry leaves at 2.30 pm. During the winter, weather conditions can cause cancellation of the trip and the return ferry departs at 1 pm. A return ticket costs ¥3000.

Places to Stay
The tourist information office at Wajima station can help you find accommodation. Wajima has dozens of minshuku with prices starting at around ¥5500 per person and these include two meals (copious and delicious seafood). *Wajima Chōraku-ji Youth Hostel* (☎ 0768-22-0663) is 15 minutes on foot from the station on the other side of the Shim-bashi Bridge from the Wajima Lacquerware Hall. Nightly rates are ¥2400, and the hostel is closed from 31 December to 4 January and from 31 March to 4 April.

Getting There & Away
Wajima is a major transport hub for the peninsula. The bus station is opposite the railway station – for transport details see the Getting Around section at the beginning of the Noto-hantō Peninsula section.

SENMAIDA　千枚田
Senmaida (literally '1000 rice paddies') is an attractive terraced slope and, in fact, there are more than 2000 small paddies. It's about 30 minutes by bus north-east of Wajima (¥430). The appropriate bus stop is Shirayone.

SOSOGI　曽々木
The village of Sosogi, about 10 minutes by bus from Senmaida, has a couple of attractions. After the Taira were defeated in 1185, one of the few survivors, Tokitada Taira, was exiled to this region. The Tokikuni family, which claims descent from this survivor, eventually divided into two parts and established separate family residences here.

Shimo Tokikuni-ke (Lower Tokikuni Residence), built in 1590, is a smaller version of its counterpart, but it has an attractive garden. Admission costs ¥300 and includes an English leaflet. The residence is open from 8 am to 6 pm.

Kami Tokikuni-ke (Upper Tokikuni Residence), with its impressive thatched roof and elegant interior, was constructed early in the 19th century. Admission costs ¥310 and includes an English leaflet. It's open from 8 am to 5 pm. From Wajima station, the bus ride to Kami Tokikuni-ke takes about 40 minutes.

Close to the turn-off for Sosogi is *Sosogi Kajiyama Youth Hostel* (☎ 0768-32-1145) – seven minutes on foot from the Sosogi-guchi bus stop. The hostel is a convenient base for walking along the nearby coastal hiking trail. A bed for the night is ¥2500.

CAPE ROKKŌ-ZAKI 禄剛崎

The road east from Sosogi passes Cape Rokkō-zaki and winds round the tip of the peninsula to the less dramatic scenery of its eastern coast. At the cape, you can amble up to Noroshi Lighthouse where a nearby signpost marks the distances to Vladivostok, Shanghai and Tokyo. A coastal hiking trail runs west along the cape.

There is an infrequent local bus service which takes about an hour between Sosogi and the cape.

KIHEI-DON 喜兵衛どん

Farming implements and household utensils which belonged to wealthy farmers during the Edo period are displayed in this mildly interesting museum, which is about 45 minutes by bus from **Cape Rokkō-zaki**. Admission costs ¥400. It's open from 8 am to 6 pm. The museum is a 10 minute walk from Suzu-Iida station.

TSUKUMO-WAN BAY 九十九湾

Tsukumo-wan Bay, heavily indented and dotted with islands, is mildly scenic, but it's not really worth spending ¥610 on the boat tour despite the boat's glass bottom. From the bay, it's five minutes on foot to Noto-Ogi station and rail connections via Ushitsu to Kanazawa. If you want an inexpensive place to stay right next to the water, *Tsukumo-Wan Youth Hostel* (☎ 0768-74-0150) is only 15 minutes on foot from the station. A bed for the night is ¥2400.

USHITSU 宇出津

The limited attractions of Ushitsu are around Toshimayama-kōen Park which has good views out to sea. Close to the park is *Okunoto Youth Hostel* (☎ 0768-62-0436), where bicycle rental is available. Take the five minute bus ride in the direction of Ogi and get off at the Kōen-shita bus stop. The hostel is seven minutes on foot from the bus stop. The hostel's rates range from ¥2450 to ¥2750 depending on the time of year.

Fukui-ken 福井県

FUKUI 福井

Fukui (population 252,000) is yet another prefectural capital with nothing to see. It was given quite a drubbing in 1945 during the Allied bombing, and what was left largely succumbed to a massive earthquake in 1948. It was totally rebuilt, and is now known as a major textile centre. There's no real reason to linger here, but Fukui is useful as a staging point to visit sights in the prefecture. Between 19 and 21 May, Fukui celebrates the Mikuni Festival with a parade of giant warrior dolls.

If you need to stay in Fukui, there's the rather drab *Fujin Seinen Kaikan Youth Hostel* (☎ 0776-22-5625), around 500 metres north-west of the station next to Chūō-kōen Park, where a bed for the night is ¥2500. The *Hotel Akebono Bekkan* (☎ 0776-22-0506) is a member of the Japanese Inn Group and has singles/doubles at ¥4400/8360. From the station, walk straight ahead and take the second street on the left that crosses over the river. Close to the east exit of Fukui station (the main exit is the west exit) is the *City Hotel Fukui* (☎ 0776-23-5300), where singles range from ¥5500 to ¥6500, twins range from ¥11,000 and doubles are ¥9500.

Fukui lies on the JR Hokuriku Honsen line: 55 minutes east is Kanazawa and 40 minutes south-west is a major railway junction at Tsuruga which provides convenient access to Nagoya, Kyoto and Osaka.

EIHEI-JI TEMPLE 永平寺

Founded in 1244 by Dōgen, Eihei-ji Temple is now one of the two head temples of the Sōtō sect of Zen Buddhism and is ranked among the most influential centres of Zen in the world.

The temple is geared to huge numbers of visitors who come either as sightseers or for Zen training. Admission tickets can be bought from automats outside the temple, and plastic covers for shoes and umbrellas are doled out as you pass through the hall in the modern administration centre. Foreigners are equipped with a detailed English leaflet (including a list of rules for visitors) and groups are then led into a hall for an introductory talk in Japanese before being unleashed onto the circuit of the complex.

The complex has about 70 buildings, but the standard circuit usually concentrates on the seven major buildings: *tosu* (toilet), San-mon Gate, *yokushitsu* (bath), *daikuin* (kitchen), Butsuden (Buddha Hall), Hattō (Dharma Hall) and the Sō-dō (Priests' Hall).

Foreigners can apply for training in Zen and accommodation is also provided. If you apply in person, you should do so at least two weeks in advance – be prepared for a

To O-jima Island
To Otaru (Hokkaidō)
305
Tōjinbō
Mikuni-minato Station
Keifuku Mikuni Awara Line
Fukui
Sabae
Takefu
417
305
Mikata Five Lakes
Wakasa-wan Bay
Sotomo
Obama Station
Keifuku Dentetsu Eihei-ji Line
Higashi-Furuichi
Eihei-ji Station
8
Keifuku Honsen Line
Echizen Honsen Line
Katsuyama
Heisen-ji Temple
Eihei-ji Temple
158
Ōno
157
417
Kuzuryū-kyō Gorge
Kuzuryū Station
Etsumi Hokusen Line
FUKUI-KEN
Hokuriku Expressway
JR Hokuriku Line
Tsuruga
27
To Kyoto
Mikata Station
161
Lake Biwako-ko
303
Higashi-Obama Station

福井県
Fukui-ken

0   10   20 km

⎯ ⎯ ⎯ Prefectural Boundary

rigorous routine. By mail, applications must be made one month in advance, should include reply postage (from outside Japan, enclose international reply coupons) and should contain the following information: name, address, phone number, age, sex and preferred training dates. Apply to Kokusaibu Eihei-ji (International Department), Eihei-ji-chō, Yoshida-gun, Fukui-ken, 910-12.

Note, however, that the temple does not admit *sanrosha* (trainees) on the following dates: 1, 2, 3, 7, 26 January; 1 to 8, 15 February; 13, 21 to 29 April; 6, 17 May; 15 June; 2 July; 9 August; 13, 21 to 29 September; 5 October; 6, 17 November and 1 to 10, 22 December, plus on other days when special services are held.

Fees are ¥7000 for each overnight stay and two meals are provided.

Normal daily admission costs ¥400. The temple is open from 5 am to 5 pm; however, note that the temple is frequently closed for periods varying from a week to 10 days – before you visit, check with a tourist information office or use Japan Travel-Phone (☎ 0120-222800).

Places to Stay

A convenient youth hostel is *Eihei-ji Monzen Yamaguchi-sō* (☎ 0776-63-3123), which is five minutes on foot from Eihei-ji station. A bed for the night is ¥2500.

Getting There & Away

From Fukui, take the Keifuku Dentetsu Eihei-ji line to Eihei-ji station (¥710, 35 minutes). If you don't catch a direct train, you'll need to change trains at Higashi-Furuichi.

The temple is about 10 minutes from Eihei-ji station. Turn right as you exit the station and plod uphill past the souvenir shops.

ECHIZEN ŌNO DISTRICT 越前大野

The town of **Ōno** is known for its castle (a very recent reconstruction) and the morning market held on Shichiken-dōri between 21 March and 31 December. Further east from Ōno is the scenic **Kuzuryū-kyō Gorge**. From Fukui, the Etsumi Hokusen line provides convenient rail access to Ōno and the gorge.

About 10 km north of Ōno is the town of Katsuyama and the nearby **Heisen-ji Temple** with its moss garden in an attractive forest setting. Trains on the Echizen Honsen line link Katsuyama with Fukui in just under an hour.

TŌJINBŌ 東尋坊

About 25 km north-east of Fukui, are the towering rock columns and cliffs at Tōjinbō, which is a popular tourist destination. Visitors can take a 30 minute boat trip to view the rock formations or travel further up the coast to **O-jima Island**, a small island with a shrine and joined to the mainland by a bridge.

The Keifuku Mikuni Awara line connects Fukui with Mikuni-minato station. From there, it's a few minutes by bus to Tōjinbō.

TSURUGA 敦賀

The city of Tsuruga, south of Fukui and just north of Lake Biwa-ko, is a thriving port and major rail junction. The Shin Nihonkai ferry company operates four sailings a week between Tsuruga and Otaru (Hokkaidō). The trip takes 30 hours and passenger fares are good value at ¥6400 (2nd class, one way). Tsuruga-kō Port is 20 minutes by bus from Tsuruga station. If you don't mind walking, it's around two km to the north of Tsuruga station.

The Wakasa-wan Bay region, south-west of Tsuruga, has fine seascapes and coastal scenery. Close to Mikata station are the **Mikatago-ko** (Mikata Five Lakes). See the Wakasa-wan Bay section in the Western Honshū chapter for details.

The region described as Kansai in this chapter is also known as Kinki. While the term 'Kinki' is actually a more distinct geographical division, encompassing the prefectures of Shiga, Mie, Nara, Kyoto, Wakayama, Ōsaka, Kōbe and Hyōgo, the area is more frequently referred to colloquially as Kansai, a term which means 'west of the barrier'. This 'barrier' is an allusion to the historical barrier stations or checkpoints that separated Kansai from Kantō, the area 'east of the barrier'. The barriers were located in different places through Japanese history, but finally ended up in Hakone during the rule of the Tokugawa Shogunate from Edo (contemporary Tokyo) in Kantō.

Kansai's major drawcards are of course Kyoto and Nara, but the cities of Osaka and Kōbe are also vibrant and increasingly cosmopolitan urban centres. More and more foreigners are settling in the area, and *kansai-ben*, the local dialect, is gaining attention from foreign students of Japanese. Anyone interested in Kansai-ben should pick up a copy of Peter Tse's *Kansai Japanese* (Tuttle 1993), a lively introduction to the dialect. Kansai is also set to become the first port of call for many foreigners visiting Japan with the opening of the Kansai International Airport in mid-1994. Built on an artificial island in Osaka-wan Bay, it will be Japan's first 24 hour airport.

Kyoto, with its hundreds of temples and gardens, was the imperial capital between 794 and 1868, and is now a magnet for domestic and international tourism. It continues to function as the major cultural centre of Japan, but business and industry are closing in on the traditional architecture.

Nara predates Kyoto as an imperial capital and has an impressive array of temples, burial mounds and relics from early times.

Osaka and Kōbe are major centres in a sprawling industrial belt and are, for the most part, of limited interest to travellers, but even so not without their attractions. Osaka, along with Tokyo, is one of the best places to sample the Japanese hi-tech phenomenon, while Kōbe, along with Yokohama and Nagasaki, has a reputation as one of Japan's more cosmopolitan cities, especially in the dining-out department. Himeji, just east of Kōbe, has what is probably the best of Japan's many feudal castles.

In Mie-ken the main attractions are Ise-jingū, one of Japan's most important Shintō shrines, and the seascapes around the Shima-hantō Peninsula. In Wakayama-ken, the temple complex of Mt Kōya-san is a major centre of Japanese Buddhism, and offers temple accommodation, a welcome retreat for travellers exhausted by urban cityscapes.

Kyoto 京都

If there are two cities in Japan that *have* to be included on anyone's Japan itinerary, they are Tokyo and Kyoto (population 1.4 million). Some of what you've seen in Tokyo, you'll see again in Kyoto – the glare of neon by night, the large scale urban ugliness. But more than any other city in Japan, if you care to seek it out, Kyoto offers what all Westerners long for of Japan: raked pebble gardens, the sensuous contours of a temple roof, the tripping step of a latter-day geisha in pursuit of a taxi.

Despite this, first impressions are likely to be something of an anticlimax. The beauty of Kyoto doesn't force itself upon the visitor. You have to seek it out. Kyoto is a city that, like the other cities of Japan, has its eyes far more firmly on the future than on the past. But, happily, it is still a city where the past lingers on: more than 2000 temples and shrines; a trio of palaces; dozens of gardens and museums. Months or even years could be spent exploring Kyoto to turn up still new surprises.

The city's one major drawback is that its

fame attracts huge numbers of visitors (nearly 40 million annually), particularly during holidays and festivals. The spring and autumn periods, when Kyoto is at its most beautiful, are also very busy. An early start to the day can help, but sooner or later you are going to collide with the inevitable crowds of tour groups. The best advice if this annoys you is not to spend all your time on the major attractions. Often just a short walk from the big-name sights are lesser attractions that are near deserted because they don't figure on the standard tour group itinerary.

HISTORY

The Kyoto basin was first settled in the 7th century, and by 794 it had become Heian-kyō, the capital of Japan. Like Nara, a previous capital, the city was laid out in a grid pattern modelled on the Chinese Tang dynasty capital, Chang'an (contemporary Xi'an). Although the city was to serve as home to the Japanese imperial family from 794 to 1868 (when the Meiji Restoration brought the imperial family to the new capital Tokyo), the city was not always the focus of Japanese political power. During the Kamakura period (1185-1333), Kamakura

SEA OF JAPAN

Prefectural Boundary

0   30   60 km

関西地方
Kansai Region

KANSAI REGION

served as the national capital, and during the Edo period (1600-1867) the Tokugawa Shogunate ruled Japan from Edo – now Tokyo.

The problem was that from the 9th century the imperial family was increasingly isolated from the mechanics of political power and the country was largely ruled by military families, or shogunates. While Kyoto remained capital in name and was the cultural focus of the nation, imperial power was for the most part symbolic and the business of running state affairs was often carried out elsewhere.

Just as imperial fortunes have waxed and waned, the fortunes of the city itself have fluctuated dramatically. In the Ōnin War (1466-67) that marked the close of the Muromachi period, the Imperial Palace and most of the city was destroyed. Much of what can be seen in Kyoto today dates from the Edo period (1600-1867). Although political power resided in Edo, Kyoto was rebuilt and flourished as a cultural, religious and economic centre. Fortunately, Kyoto was spared the aerial bombing that razed other Japanese urban centres to the ground in the closing months of WW II.

Today, even though it has seen a rapid process of industrialisation, Kyoto remains an important cultural and educational centre. It has some 20% of Japan's National Treasures and 15% of Japan's Important Cultural Properties. There are 24 museums and 37 universities and colleges scattered throughout the city. And even if the city centre looks remarkably like the centre of a dozen other large Japanese cities, a little exploration will turn up countless reminders of Kyoto's long history.

ORIENTATION

Kyoto is a fairly easy city to navigate. JR Kyoto station is in the south of the city, and from there Karasuma-dōri runs north past Higashi Hongan-ji Temple, the commercial centre of town and the Imperial Palace. The commercial and nightlife centres are between Shi-jō-dōri and San-jō-dōri (to the south and north respectively) and between Kawaramachi-dōri and Karasuma-dōri (to

the east and west respectively). Although some of Kyoto's major sights are in the city centre, most of Kyoto's best sightseeing is on the outskirts of the city in the eastern and western parts of town. These areas are most conveniently reached by bus.

Kyoto has retained a grid system based on the classical Chinese concept. This system of numbered streets running east to west and avenues running north to south makes it relatively easy to move around with the help of a map from the Tourist Information Centre (TIC). Addresses are indicated with the name of the closest intersection and their location north *(agaru)* or south *(sagaru)* (literally 'up' or 'down' respectively) of that intersection.

Efficient bus services crisscross the city. There's a simplified bus map on the reverse of the TIC Kyoto map. The quickest way to shift between the north and south of the city is to take the subway. The TIC has a leaflet, *Walking Tour Courses in Kyoto*, which gives detailed walking maps for major sightseeing areas (Higashiyama, Arashiyama, northwestern Kyoto and Ōhara) in and around Kyoto.

INFORMATION
Tourist Office

The best source of information on Kyoto and the Kansai region is the TIC (☎ 075-371-5649); it's four minutes by foot north of Kyoto station. Opening hours are from 9 am to 5 pm on weekdays and from 9 am to noon on Saturday, closed on Sunday and holidays.

The staff here have maps, literature and an amazing amount of information on Kyoto at their capable fingertips. The TIC also functions as a tourist information office for the whole of Japan. To cope fairly with the daily flood of visitors, it deals with inquiries by numbers and imposes a time limit. Full details of the whole spectrum of accommodation are available and, unlike the Tokyo TIC, the Kyoto TIC will make reservations for you.

Volunteer Guides can also be arranged through the TIC if you allow the staff a day's notice.

Reservations are necessary to visit Kyoto Imperial Palace, the Imperial Villa and Saihō-ji Temple. Separate details for each are provided later, but the TIC can inform you about the procedures. Reservations for the Katsura-in Imperial Villa and the Shūgaku-in Imperial Villa have to be organised at the relevant offices, and cannot be organised by the TIC.

Post

Kyoto's central post office is conveniently close to JR Kyoto station (take the Karasuma exit, on the western side of the station). It's open from 9 am to 7 pm on weekdays, 9 am to 5 pm on Saturday and from 9 am to noon on Sunday and holidays.

Telephone

The Japan Travel-Phone (☎ 075-371-5649) is a service providing travel-related information and language assistance in English. Calls cost ¥10 for every three minutes and the service is available seven days a week, from 9 am to 5 pm. The Kyoto number can be particularly useful if you arrive between those hours on a day when the TIC is closed.

Books & Maps

For books on Kyoto you should visit the Maruzen bookshop (☎ 075-241-2161). At the time of writing the bookshop was about to open in newly refurbished premises. Opening hours are from 10 am to 7 pm but on Sunday and national holidays the shop closes half an hour earlier.

Kyoto: A Contemplative Guide (Tuttle, Tokyo, 1989 reprint) by Gouverneur Mosher treats a few sights in fond detail to give a taste of the amazing variety of exploration possible in Kyoto. The transport information is long out of date, but it's the sort of book well worth reading before, during or after your stay.

Must-See in Kyoto (JTB, Tokyo, 1988) is a pocket-sized book with copious illustrations and text about Kyoto. It has a bouncy style, is easy to read and covers all sorts of interesting sightseeing details.

Old Kyoto: A Guide to Traditional Shops, Restaurants & Inns (Kodansha, Tokyo, 1989 reprint) by Diane Durston helps with exploration in the backstreets of Kyoto.

For those anticipating a longer stay, the YWCA publishes *The Resident's Guide to Kyoto* (¥980). An updated edition may now be available from the YWCA Thrift Shop, Muromachi-dōri, Demizu-agaru, Kamikyo-ku, Kyoto 602. More up to date is *Easy Living in Kyoto* (Kyoto City International Foundation, 1992).

Tourist Map of Kyoto, Nara fulfills most mapping needs and includes a simplified map of the subway and bus systems. *Japan – Kyoto, Nara* provides a quick overview of sights. *Walking Tour Courses in Kyoto* details ways to see the sights in Kyoto on foot. Also available is a *City Bus & Subway* map – it's very detailed and names are supplied in kanji.

Newspapers & Magazines

Many of the magazines for foreigners that once provided information on Kyoto have gone out of business. At the time of writing, the TIC in cooperation with the municipal government was producing a monthly magazine called *Monthly Information Kyoto*. It was expected to close if and when the defunct *Kyoto Visitor's Guide* was resurrected. Whatever the case, one of these publications, with listings of festivals, performances and events, should be available at the TIC.

Probably the best source of information on Kyoto and the rest of the Kansai area is *Kansai Time Out*, a monthly English-language 'what's on' magazine (¥300). Apart from all the lively articles, it has a large section of small ads for employment, travel agencies, clubs, lonely hearts, etc. It's all in there: from the 'Kinki Macintosh Users Group' (it's OK, they're into computers) to Japan Animal Welfare Society (JAWS).

Those with a literary bent might want to look out for *Raw Conscience*, a local magazine with stories, poetry and articles written by local foreign residents.

KANSAI REGION

KANSAI REGION

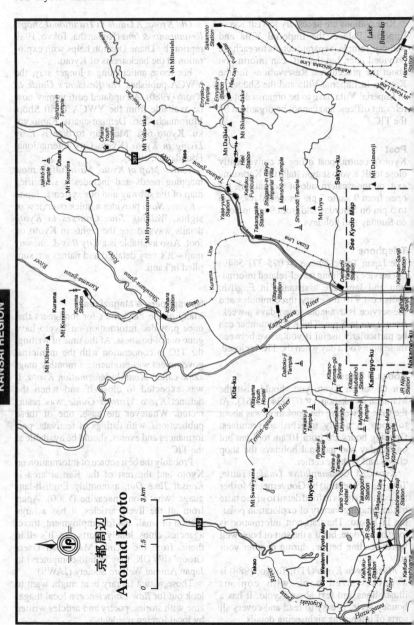

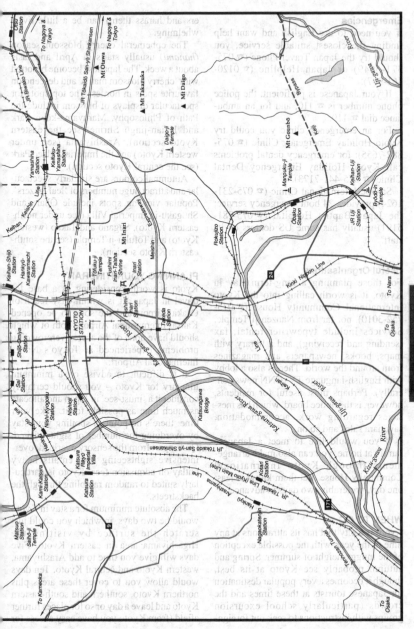

Emergencies

If you need to use English and want help finding the closest suitable service, you should try the Japan Travel-Phone (☎ 075-371-5649) or Japan Helpline (☎ 0120-461-997).

If your Japanese is proficient, the police phone number is ☎ 110, and for an ambulance dial ☎ 119.

For an emergency clinic you could try Kyoto Holiday Emergency Clinic (☎ 075-882-7655); for emergency dental problems call Kyoto Holiday Emergency Dental Clinic (☎ 075-441-7173).

Sakabe International Clinic (☎ 075-231-1624) provides 24 hour emergency service; the Japan Baptist Hospital (☎ 075-781-5191) usually has some US doctors on its staff.

Useful Organisations

For those planning a long-term stay in Kyoto, it is worth calling into the Kyoto International Community House (☎ 075-752-3010), not far from Nanzen-ji Temple. Services include typewriter rental, fax (sending and receiving), and a library with maps, books, newspapers and magazines from around the world. There's also a lobby with English-language TV (CNN news generally). Perhaps most useful for residents, however, is the notice board, which has messages regarding work, accommodation, sayonara sales and so on.

If you would like to meet a Japanese family at home, you can also make arrangements through Kyoto International Community House. Let them know at least one day, preferably two days in advance.

WHEN TO GO

Kyoto is a city that has its attractions at any time of the year, with the possible exception of the muggy height of summer. Spring and autumn probably see Kyoto at its best, though it becomes a very popular destination for Japanese tourists at these times and the crowds (particularly school excursion groups with instructions to seek out foreign-ers and harass them) can be a little overwhelming.

The ephemeral cherry blossom season *(hanami)* usually starts in April and lasts about a week. The Japanese become besotted with 'cherry blossom mania' and descend on favourite spots in hordes. The top spots for spectacular displays of blossom include the Path of Philosophy, Maruyama-kōen Park and Heian-jingū Shrine (see the eastern Kyoto section), Arashiyama (see under western Kyoto) and the Imperial Palace Park (see the central Kyoto section).

Autumnal colours are similarly spectacular and attract huge numbers of 'leaf-gazers'. Popular viewing spots include Ōhara and Shūgaku-in Imperial Villa (see under northeastern Kyoto), Sagano and Takao (western Kyoto) and Tōfuku-ji Temple (see the southeastern Kyoto section).

PLANNING YOUR ITINERARY

Kyoto is worth considering as a base for travel in Japan. It is within easy reach of Osaka Airport and the soon to be opened Kansai International Airport, both of which should have none of the acute overcrowding problems experienced at Tokyo's Narita International Airport.

It is difficult to advise on a minimum itinerary for Kyoto – you should certainly consider it a 'must-see' in Japan and allocate as much time as possible for it. Take your time: there's no point in spoiling your stay by overdoing the number of sights visited. Quite apart from the sensory overload, over-intensive sightseeing also entails heavy outlay on admission fees. Kyoto is particularly suited to random rambling through the backstreets.

The absolute minimum for a stay in Kyoto would be two days, in which you could just scratch the surface by visiting the Higashiyama area in eastern Kyoto. Five days will give you time to add Arashiyama, western Kyoto and central Kyoto. Ten days would allow you to cover these areas plus northern Kyoto, southern and south-eastern Kyoto and leave a day or so for places further afield (from Kyoto you have easy access for day trips to Nara, Yoshino, Lake Biwa-ko, Ise, Himeji and Osaka) or for in-depth exploration of museums, shops and cultural pursuits.

Kyoto is also an excellent place to indulge specific cultural interests, whether they be the arts, Buddhism or folkcrafts. The best place to find information on such activities is the TIC, which is used to dealing with both ordinary and extraordinary requests. For example, details are available on Zen temples which accept foreigners, specialist museums, Japanese gardens and villas, Japanese culinary arts and natural-food outlets, traditional crafts (silks, basketry, ceramics, pottery, temple paraphernalia, paper making, etc), Japanese drama, chanoyu (tea ceremony) and ikebana (flower arranging).

CENTRAL KYOTO 京都中心部

Central Kyoto looks much like any other Japanese city, but there are a few major sights in the area, such as the imperial palace, Nijō-jō Castle and several museums.

The area around Kyoto station (just below the city centre) is a fairly dull part of town; the main sights are Nishi Hongan-ji Temple and Tō-ji Temple. For further information, be sure to use the TIC, which is a couple of minutes on foot north of the station.

Kyoto Imperial Palace 京都御所

The original Kyoto Imperial Palace was built in 794 and was replaced numerous times after destruction through fires. The present building, on a different site and smaller than the original, was constructed in 1855. Enthronement of a new emperor and other state ceremonies are still held there.

The tour guide explains details while you are led for about 30 minutes past the Shishin-den Hall, Ko Gosho (Small Palace), Tsune Gosho (Regular Palace) and the Oike-niwa (Pond Garden).

Foreigners are privileged to be given preferential access – Japanese visitors have to wait months for permission – but the imperial palace does not rate highly in comparison with other attractions in Kyoto.

Reservation & Admission This is organised by the Imperial Household Agency (Kunaichō) (☎ 075-211-1215), which is a short walk from Imadegawa subway station. You will have to fill out an application form and show your passport; children should be accompanied by adults over 20 years of age. Permission to tour the imperial palace is usually granted the same day. Guided tours in English are given at 10 am and 2 pm; you should arrive no later than 20 minutes beforehand at the Seisho-mon Gate. Admission is free.

The agency's office is open weekdays from 8.45 am to noon and from 1 to 4 pm but note that on the first and third Saturday of the month it's open from 8.45 am to noon. There are no afternoon tours on the first and third Saturday, no tours on the second and fourth Saturday, Sunday, national holidays, during the New Year holiday (25 December to 5 January) or from 14 to 17 May.

This office is also the place to make advance reservations to see the Sentō Gosho Palace, and the Katsura-in and Shūgaku-in imperial villas. If you want to arrange reservations from abroad or from outside of Kyoto, the application forms are available from JNTO offices, the TIC or direct from the Imperial Household Agency – remember to include return postage or international reply coupons.

To reach the imperial palace, take the subway to Imadegawa or a bus to the Karasuma-Imadegawa stop.

Sentō Gosho Palace 仙洞御所

This is close to the Kyoto Imperial Palace. Visitors must obtain advance permission from the Imperial Household Agency and be over 20 years old. Tours (in Japanese) start at 11 am and 1.30 pm. The gardens, which were laid out in 1630 by Kobori Enshū, are the main attraction.

Nijō-jō Castle 二条城

This castle was built in 1603 as the official Kyoto residence of the first Tokugawa shōgun, Ieyasu. The ostentatious style of construction was intended as a demonstra-

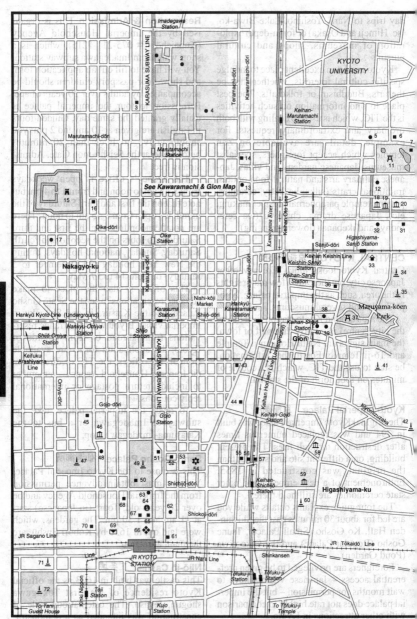

KANSAI REGION

KYOTO UNIVERSITY

KARASUMA SUBWAY LINE

Imadegawa Station

Kawaramachi-dōri

Teramachi-dōri

Keihan-Marutamachi Station

Marutamachi-dōri

Marutamachi Station

See Kawaramachi & Gion Map

Kamogawa River

Keihan-Ōto Line

Higashiyama-Sanjō Station

Sanjō-dōri

Keihan Keishin Line

Keishin-Sanjō Station

Keihan-Sanjō Station

Maruyama-kōen Park

Ōike-dōri

Ōike Station

Nakagyo-ku

Karasuma-dōri

Kawaramachi-dōri

Nishi-kōji Market

Hankyū Kawaramachi Station

Karasuma Station

Shijō-dōri

Hankyū Kyoto Line (Underground)

Shijō Station

Keihan-Shijō Station

Gion

Shijō-Ōmiya Station

Shijō Station

Keifuku Arashiyama Line

Kyōmizuzaka

Ōmiya-dōri

KARASUMA SUBWAY LINE

Keihan Hōnan Line (Underground)

Gojō-dōri

Gojō Station

Keihan-Gojō Station

Shichijō-dōri

Higashiyama-ku

Keihan-Shichijō Station

Shiokoji-dōri

JR Sagano Line

JR KYOTO STATION

JR Tōkaidō Line

JR Nara Line

Shinkansen

Line

Ōfuku-ji Station

Tōfuku-ji Station

Kinki Nippon

Tōji Station

To Tani Guest House

Kujō Station

To Tōfuku-ji Temple

京都
Kyoto

0   400   800 m

▲ Mt Kazan

tion of Ieyasu's prestige and to signal the demise of the emperor's power. To safeguard against treachery, Ieyasu had the interior fitted with 'nightingale' floors (intruders were detected by the squeaking boards) and concealed chambers where bodyguards could keep watch.

After passing through the grand Kara-mon Gate, you enter Ninomaru Palace which is divided into five buildings with numerous chambers. Access to the buildings depended on rank – only those of highest rank were permitted into the inner buildings. The Ohiroma Yon-no-Ma (Fourth Chamber) has spectacular screen paintings. Don't miss the excellent Ninomaru Palace Garden, designed by the tea master and landscape architect Kobori Enshū.

The neighbouring Honmaru Palace dates from the middle of last century and is only open for special viewing in the autumn.

Admission for Ninomaru Palace and garden is ¥500; it's open daily from 8.45 am until last admission at 4 pm (gates close at 5 pm). It's closed from 26 December to 4 January. A detailed fact sheet in English is provided. The Ninomaru Palace is so inundated with visitors that you have to choose your exit according to the numbered location of your shoes!

To reach the palace, take bus No 9, 12, 50, 52, 61 or 67 to the Nijō-jō-mae stop. Alternatively you can take the subway to Oike and then walk for 12 minutes.

Nijō-jinya 二条陣屋

Nijō-jinya (☎ 841-0972) was built in the 17th century as the home of a wealthy merchant and eventually functioned as an inn. It was fitted with a variety of contrivances to guard against fire and intruders. The house contains trap ladders, trap doors, concealed chambers for bodyguards and special screens to deter attackers.

Tours are conducted in Japanese four times daily (10 and 11 am and 2 and 3 pm), cost ¥700 and are only possible with advance reservation. If you speak Japanese, reservations can be made by phone (☎ 075-841-0972), or alternatively check with the

PLACES TO STAY

3 YWCA
6 YWCA
7 Three Sisters Inn
   洛東荘
14 Uno House
   宇野ハウス
16 International Hotel
   Kyoto
   京都国際ホテル
29 Yachiyo Ryokan
   八千代旅館
30 Miyako Hotel
   都ホテル
31 Kyoto Travellers Inn
   京都トラベラーズイン
33 Higashiyama Youth
   Hostel
   東山ユースホステル
36 Iwanami Ryokan
   岩波旅館
43 Ryokan Hinomoto
   旅館ひのもと
44 Hotel Rich II
   ホテルリッチ II
45 Kyoto Tōkyū Hotel
   京都東急ホテル
50 Pension Station Kyoto
   ペンション ステーション
   京都
51 Matsubaya Ryokan
   松葉屋旅館
52 Ryokan Kyōka
   旅館京花
53 Ryokan Murakamiya
   旅館村上家
55 Yuhara Ryokan
   ゆはら旅館
56 Ryokan Hiraiwa
   平岩旅館
57 Riverside Takase &
   Annexe Kyōka
   リバーサイド高瀬
   アネクス京花
61 Kyoto Century Hotel
   京都センチュリーホテル
65 Kyoto Tower Hotel
   京都タワーホテル
67 Hokke Club Kyoto/
   Kyoto New Hankyū
   Hotel
   法華クラブ京都／
   京都ニュー阪急ホテル
68 Kyoto Dai-San Hotel
   京都第3ホテル
70 Kyoto Grand Hotel
   京都グランドホテル

PLACES TO EAT

11 Time Paradox Eatery
   タイムパラドクス
21 Okutan Restaurant
   奥丹

OTHER

1 Imperial Household
   Agency
   宮内庁
2 Imperial Palace
   京都御所
4 Sentō Gosho
   Palace
   仙洞御所
5 Kyoto Handicraft
   Centre
   京都ハンディクラフト
   センター
8 Ginkaku-ji Temple
   銀閣寺
9 Hōnen-in Temple
   法然院
10 Anraku-ji Temple
   安楽寺
12 Kyoto Kaikan Hall
   京都会館
13 Ippō-dō Teashop
   一保堂
15 Nijō-jō Castle
   二条城
17 Nijō-jinya
   二条陣屋
18 Museum of
   Traditional Industry
   伝統産業会館
19 National Museum of
   Modern Art
   国立近代美術館
20 Kyoto Municipal
   Museum of Art
   市立美術館
22 Nomura Museum
   野村美術館
23 Eikan-dō Temple
   永観堂
24 Chōshō-in Temple
   聴松院
25 Nanzen-ji Temple
   南善寺
26 Nanzen-in Temple
   南善院
27 Tenju-an Temple
   天授庵
28 Konchi-in Temple
   金地院
32 Kanze Kaikan Nō
   Theatre
   観世会館能楽堂

34 Shōren-in Temple
   青蓮院
35 Chion-in Temple
   知恩院
37 Yasaka-jinja Shrine
   八坂神社
38 Kyoto Craft Centre
   京都クラフトセンター
39 Gion Corner
   祇園コーナー
40 Gion Kōbu Kaburenjō
   Theatre
   祇園歌舞練場
41 Kōdai-ji Temple
   高台寺
42 Kiyomizu-dera
   Temple
   清水寺
46 Costume Museum
   風俗博物館
47 Nishi Hongan-ji
   Temple
   西本願寺
48 Kungyoku-dō
   薫玉堂
49 Higashi Hongan-ji
   Temple
   東本願寺
54 Kikokutei Shōsei-en
   Garden
   渉成園
58 Kawai Kanjirō
   Memorial Hall
   河井寛次郎記念館
59 Kyoto National
   Museum
   京都国立博物館
60 Sanjūsangen-dō
   Temple
   三十三間堂
62 Kyoto Minshuku
   Reservation Centre
   民宿予約センター
63 Kintetsu
   Department Store
   近鉄デパート
64 TIC
66 Porta Shopping
   Centre
   ポルタショッピング
   センター
69 Post Office
   中央郵便局
71 Kanchi-in Temple
   観智院
72 Tō-ji Temple
   東寺

TIC. The house is a 10 minute walk south of Nijō-jō Castle.

Pontochō 先斗町
Pontochō is a traditional centre for night entertainment in a narrow street running between the river and Kawaramachi-dōri. It's a pleasant place for a stroll in the summer if you want to observe Japanese nightlife. Many of the restaurants and teahouses which have verandas over the river tend to prefer Japanese customers. The geisha houses usually control admittance of foreigners with a policy of introductions from Japanese only and astronomical charges. Many of the bars also function along similar lines, like a club. Don't bother with bars that use touts outside to entice you inside for fleecing.

KYOTO STATION AREA
京都駅周辺
Nishi Hongan-ji Temple 西本願寺
In 1591, Hideyoshi Toyotomi built this temple, known as Hongan-ji Temple, as a new headquarters for the Jōdo Shin-shū (True Pure Land) school of Buddhism, which had accumulated immense power. Later, Tokugawa Ieyasu saw this power as a threat and sought to weaken it by encouraging a breakaway faction of this school to found Higashi Hongan-ji (higashi means 'east') in 1602. The original Hongan-ji Temple then became known as Nishi Hongan-ji Temple (nishi means 'west'). It now functions as the headquarters of the Hongan-ji branch of the Jōdo Shin-shū school, with over 10,000 temples and 12 million followers worldwide.

The temple contains five buildings, featuring some of the finest examples of architecture and artistic achievement from the Azuchi-Momoyama period (1568-1600). The Daisho-in Hall has sumptuous paintings, carvings and metal ornamentation. A small garden and two Nō stages are connected with the hall. The dazzling Kara-mon Gate has intricate ornamental carvings. Both the Daisho-in Hall and the Kara-mon were transported here from Fushimi-jō Castle. Reservations (preferably several days in advance) for tours should be made either at the temple office (☎ 075-371-5181) or through the TIC. The tours (in Japanese) cover some but not all of the buildings and are conducted from Monday to Friday at 10 and 11 am and then 1.30 and 2.30 pm. On Saturday the tours are at 10 and 11 am. The temple is a 12 minute walk north-west of JR Kyoto station.

Higashi Hongan-ji Temple 東本願寺
When Tokugawa Ieyasu engineered the rift in the Jōdo Shin-shū school, he founded this temple as a competitor to Nishi Hongan-ji Temple. Rebuilt in 1895 after a fire, it is certainly monumental in its proportions, but less impressive artistically than its counterpart. A curious item on display is a length of rope, made from hair donated by female believers, which was used to haul the timber for the reconstruction. The temple is now the headquarters of the Ōtani branch of the Jōdo Shin-shū school.

Admission is free and the temple is open from 9 am to 4 pm. It's a five minute walk north of Kyoto station.

Kikokutei Garden 渉成園
Kikokutei Shōsei-en Garden is just east of Higashi Hongan-ji Temple and dates back to 1657. The landscaped garden arranged around a lake is gently falling into disrepair – a pleasant spot for a quiet stroll. Ask at the Nishi Hongan-ji Temple office for a free entry ticket.

Costume Museum 風俗博物館
This museum displays traditional costumes from early times to the Meiji era. It's on the 5th floor of the Izutsu building, opposite the north-eastern corner of Nishi Hongan-ji Temple. The museum is open from 9 am to 5 pm daily except Sunday; admission costs ¥400.

Tō-ji Temple 東寺
This temple was established in 794 by imperial decree to protect the city. In 818, the emperor handed over the temple to Kūkai, the founder of the Shingon school of Bud-

KANSAI REGION

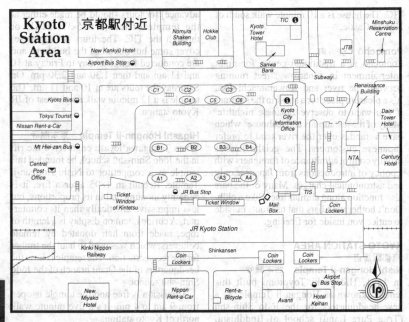

Kyoto Station Area 京都駅付近

dhism. Many of the temple buildings were destroyed by fire or fighting during the 15th century; most of those that remain today date from the 17th century.

The Lecture Hall (Kōdō) contains 21 images representing a Mikkyō (Esoteric Buddhism) mandala. The Main Hall (Kondō) contains statues depicting the Yakushi (Healing Buddha) trinity. In the southern part of the garden stands the five storeyed pagoda which, despite having burnt down five times, was doggedly rebuilt in 1643 and is now the highest (57 metres) pagoda in Japan.

Kōbō-san market fair is held here on the 21st of each month. Those held in December and January are particularly lively.

Admission to the temple costs ¥500 and there is an extra charge for entry to special exhibitions. An explanatory leaflet in English is provided. It's open from 9 am to 4 pm. The temple is a 15 minute walk southwest of Kyoto station.

Kanchi-in Temple

The Kanchi-in Temple, just outside the north gate of Tō-ji Temple, has a striking combination of gardens, good interior design, statues and a tearoom on a small, intimate scale.

Admission is ¥400 and it's open from 9 am to 5 pm. For an extra ¥500, you can take part in a tea ceremony inside an elegant tearoom.

EASTERN KYOTO 京都の東部

The eastern part of Kyoto, notably the Higashiyama (Eastern Mountains) district, merits top priority for a visit to its fine temples, peaceful walks and traditional night entertainment in Gion.

The following descriptions of places to see in eastern Kyoto begin with sights in the southern section; the sights in the northern section begin with the National Museum of Modern Art.

Allow at least a full day to cover the sights

in the southern section, and another full day for the northern section. JNTO publishes a leaflet, *Walking Tour Courses in Kyoto*, which covers the whole of eastern Kyoto.

Sanjūsangen-dō Temple 三十三間堂
The original temple was built in 1164 at the request of the retired Emperor Go-shirakawa. After it burnt to the ground in 1249, a faithful copy was constructed in 1266.

The temple's name refers to the 33 (*sanjūsan*) 'bays' between the pillars of this long, narrow building which houses 1001 statues of the Thousand-Armed Kannon (the Buddhist goddess of mercy). The largest Kannon is flanked on either side by 500 smaller Kannon images, neatly lined up in rows.

There are an awful lot of arms, but if you are picky and think the 1000-armed statues don't have the required number, then you should remember to calculate according to the nifty Buddhist mathematical formula which holds that 40 arms are the equivalent of 1000 arms, because each saves 25 worlds. Visitors also seem keen to spot resemblances to friends or family members among the hundreds of images.

At the back of the hall are 28 guardian statues with a great variety of expressive poses. The gallery at the western side of the hall is famous for the annual Tōshi-ya Festival, held on 15 January, when archers shoot arrows the length of the hall. The ceremony dates back to the Edo period when an annual contest was held to see how many arrows could be shot from the southern end to the northern end in 24 hours. The all-time record was set in 1686, when an archer successfully landed over 8000 arrows at the northern end.

The temple is open from 8 am to 5 pm (16 March to 31 October) and 8 am to 4 pm (1 November to 15 March). Admission is ¥400 and an explanatory leaflet in English is supplied.

The temple is a 15 minute walk east of Kyoto station, or you can take bus No 206 or 208 and get off at the Sanjūsangen-dō-mae stop.

Kyoto National Museum 京都国立博物館
The Kyoto National Museum is housed in two buildings opposite Sanjūsangen-dō Temple. There are excellent displays of fine arts, historical artefacts and handicrafts. The fine arts collection is especially highly rated, holding some 230 items that have been classified as National Treasures or Important Cultural Properties.

Admission costs ¥400 but note that a separate charge is made for special exhibitions. It's open daily from 9 am to 4 pm and closed on Monday.

Kawai Kanjirō Memorial Hall
河井寛次郎記念館
This museum was once the home and workshop of one of Japan's most famous potters, Kawai Kanjirō. The house is built in rural style and contains examples of his work, his collection of folk art and ceramics and his kiln.

The museum is open daily from 10 am to 5 pm (closed Monday), from 10 to 20 August and from 24 December to 7 January. Admission costs ¥700. The hall is a 10 minute walk north of the Kyoto National Museum or you can take bus No 206 or 202 from Kyoto station and get off at the Umamachi stop.

Kiyōmizu-dera Temple 清水寺
This temple was first built in 798, but the present buildings are reconstructions dating from 1633. As an affiliate of the Hossō school of Buddhism, which originated in Nara, it has successfully survived the intrigues of local Kyoto schools of Buddhism through the centuries and is now one of the most famous landmarks of the city.

The temple management recently bought a large tract of land beneath the temple and thereby saved the famed hilltop view of the city from being obliterated by an ugly high-rise development.

The main hall has a huge veranda, supported on hundreds of pillars, which juts out over the hillside. Just below this hall is the Otawa waterfall where visitors drink or bathe in sacred waters which are believed to have therapeutic properties. Dotted around the precincts are other halls and shrines. At

KANSAI REGION

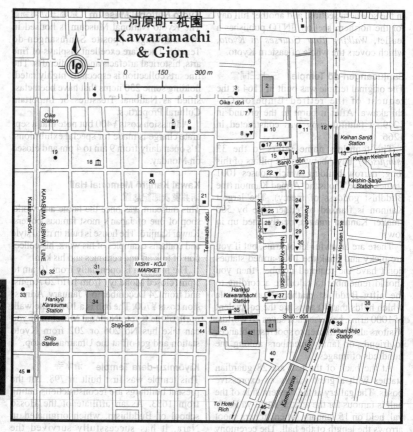

河原町・祇園
Kawaramachi & Gion

0   150   300 m

the Jishu Shrine, visitors try to ensure success in love by closing their eyes and walking about 18 metres between a pair of stones – if you miss the stone, your love won't be fulfilled!

The steep approach to the temple, known as 'Teapot Lane', is lined with shops selling Kyoto handicrafts, local snacks and souvenirs. Shopkeepers hand out samples of *yatsuhashi*, a type of dumpling filled with a sweet bean paste.

Admission to the temple costs ¥300 and it's open from 6 am to 6 pm. To get there from Kyoto station take bus No 207, 206 or 202

and get off at either the Kiyōmizu-michi or Gojō-zaka stops. Plod up the hill for 10 minutes to reach the temple.

Sannen-zaka & Ninnen-zaka Walk
三年坂・二年坂

One of the most enjoyable strolls around the backstreets and temples of Kyoto follows a winding route between Kiyōmizu-dera Temple and Maruyama-kōen Park. If you walk down from the entrance of Kiyōmizu-dera Temple along the right-hand road (Kiyōmizu-zaka) for about 200 metres, you'll see a small street on your right down

KANSAI REGION

a flight of steps. This is Sannen-zaka, a street lined with old wooden houses and shops selling local pottery, food and souvenirs. There are also pleasant teahouses with gardens – it's a good place to relax over a bowl of noodles.

Halfway down Sannen-zaka, the road bears sharp left. Follow it a short distance, then go right down a flight of steps into Ninnen-zaka, another street lined with historic houses, shops and teahouses. At the end of Ninnen-zaka, zig-zag left then right and continue north for five minutes to reach the entrance for Kōdai-ji Temple entrance.

Kōdai-ji Temple 高台寺

Kōdai-ji Temple was founded in 1605 by Kita-no-Mandokoro in memory of her late husband, Toyotomi Hideyoshi. The extensive grounds include gardens designed by the famed landscape architect, Kobori Enshū, and teahouses designed by the renowned master of the tea ceremony, Sen-no-Rikyū.

The temple was only recently opened to the public and is worth a look. It's open from 9 am to 5 pm and admission costs ¥500. An explanatory leaflet in English is provided.

Maruyama-kōen Park　円山公園

This park is a favourite spot for locals and visitors to escape the bustle of the nearby city centre and amble around the gardens, ponds, souvenir shops and restaurants. Peaceful paths meander through the trees up the hill.

Yasaka-jinja Shrine　八坂神社

This shrine is right next to Gion, west of Maruyama-kōen Park. This is a busy, colourful shrine which sponsors the Gion Matsuri Festival (for details, see the Festivals section later in this chapter).

Gion District　祇園

Gion is the famous entertainment and geisha district on the eastern bank of the Kamo-gawa River. Modern architecture, congested traffic and contemporary nightlife establishments have cut a swathe through its historical beauty, but there are still some places left for an enjoyable walk.

Hanami-kōji is a street running north to south which bisects Shijō-dōri. The southern section is lined with 17th century, traditional restaurants and teahouses many of which are exclusive establishments for geisha entertainment. If you wander around here in the late afternoon or early evening, you can often glimpse geisha or *maiko* (apprentice geisha) on their way to or from appointments.

At the bottom of this street you reach Gion Corner and the adjoining Gion Kōbu Kaburen-jō Theatre. For more detail on these two places, see the section on Entertainment later.

If you walk from Shijō-dōri along the northern section of Hanami-kōji, you will reach Shinmonzen-dōri running east to west at the fourth intersection. Wander in either direction along this street which is packed with old houses, art galleries and shops specialising in antiques – but don't expect flea-market prices here.

For more historic buildings in a beautiful waterside setting, wander down Shirakawa Minami-dōri which is roughly parallel with, and one block south of the western section of Shinmonzen-dōri.

Chion-in Temple　知恩院

Chion-in Temple was built in 1234 on the site where Hōnen had taught and eventually fasted to death. Today it is still the headquarters of the Jōdo school, which was founded by Hōnen, and a hive of religious activity.

The oldest of the present buildings date back to the 17th century. The two storeyed San-mon Gate at the main entrance is the largest in Japan and prepares the visitor for the massive scale of the temple. The immense main hall contains an image of Hōnen and is connected with the Dai Hōjō Hall by a 'nightingale' floor constructed to 'sing' (squeak) at every step.

The garden attached to the abbot's quarters is good for a quiet stroll.

The giant bell, cast in 1633 and weighing 74 tonnes, is the largest in Japan. The combined muscle-power of 17 monks is required to make the bell budge for the famous ceremony which rings in the new year.

The temple is open from 9 am to 4.30 pm (April to October) and from 9 am to 4 pm (November to March); admission costs ¥300. The temple is close to the north-eastern corner of Maruyama-kōen Park. From Kyoto station take bus No 18 or 206 and get off at the Chion-in-mae stop.

Shōren-in Temple　青蓮院

Shōren-in was originally the residence of the chief abbot of the Tendai school. The present building dates from 1895, but the main hall has sliding screens with paintings from the 16th and 17th centuries. The gardens are the most compelling reason to visit.

Admission to the temple costs ¥400, and it's open from 9 am to 5 pm. An explanatory leaflet in English is provided. The temple is a five minute walk north of the Chion-in Temple.

National Museum of Modern Art
国立近代美術館

This museum is renowned for its collection of contemporary Japanese ceramics and paintings. Exhibits are changed on a regular basis. Admission costs ¥400 and it's open from 10 am to 5 pm daily except Monday.

Kyoto Museum of Traditional Industry
伝統産業会館

If you want a break from temple gazing, you could pop in to the Kyoto Museum of Traditional Industry for exhibitions, demonstrations and sales of Kyoto handicrafts. For more details, refer to the Things to Buy section later in the chapter.

Heian-jingū Shrine　平安神宮

The Heian-jingū Shrine was built in 1895 to commemorate the 1100th anniversary of the founding of Kyoto. The buildings are gaudy replicas, reduced to a two-thirds scale, of the imperial palace of the Heian period.

The spacious garden, with its large pond and Chinese-inspired bridge, is also meant to represent the kind that was popular in the Heian period.

Two major events, Jidai Matsuri (22 October) and Takigi Nō (1 to 2 June), are held here. Jidai Matsuri is described later in the Festivals section, while details for Takigi Nō are under Dance & Theatre in the later Entertainment section.

Entry to the shrine precincts is free but admission to the garden costs ¥500. It's open from 8.30 am to 5.30 pm (15 March to 31 August) though closing time can be an hour earlier during the rest of the year.

Nanzen-ji Temple　南禅寺

The Nanzen-ji Temple began as a retirement villa for Emperor Kameyama, but was dedicated as a Zen temple on his death in 1291. Civil war in the 15th century destroyed most of the temple; the present buildings date from the 17th century. It operates now as headquarters for the Rinzai school of Zen.

At the entrance to the temple stands the massive San-mon Gate. Steps lead up to the 2nd storey which has a fine view over the city. Beyond the gate is the Hōjō Hall with impressive screens painted with a vivid depiction of tigers and a classic Zen garden called 'Leaping Tiger Garden'.

Admission to the temple costs ¥350 and it's open from 8.30 am to 5 pm. A brief explanatory leaflet in English is provided. The temple is a 10 minute walk south-east

from the Heian-jingū Shrine; from Kyoto station take bus No 5 and get off at the Eikan-dō-mae stop.

Dotted around the grounds of Nanzen-ji Temple are several subtemples which are often skipped by the crowds and consequently easier to enjoy.

Nanzen-in Temple This subtemple is on your left when leaving the Hōjō Hall – follow the path under the aqueduct. It has an attractive garden designed around a heart-shaped pond. Admission costs ¥350.

Tenju-an Temple This stands at the side of the San-mon Gate, a four minute walk west of Nanzen-in Temple. Constructed in 1337, the temple has a splendid garden. A detailed leaflet in English is provided. Admission costs ¥300.

Konchi-in Temple When leaving Tenju-an Temple, turn left and continue for 100 metres – Konchi-in Temple is down a small side street on the left. The stylish gardens fashioned by the master landscape designer Kobori Enshū are the main attraction. Admission costs ¥400. It's open from 8.30 am to 5 pm (March to November) but closes half an hour earlier during the rest of the year.

Nomura Museum　野村美術館

The Nomura Museum is a 10 minute walk north of Nanzen-ji Temple. Exhibits include scrolls, paintings, tea-ceremony implements and ceramics which were bequeathed by the wealthy business magnate Tokushiki Nomura. It's open from 10 am to 4 pm (closed on Monday), and admission is ¥600.

Eikan-dō Temple　永観堂

Eikan-dō Temple, also known as Zenrin-ji Temple, is made interesting by its varied architecture and its gardens and works of art. It was founded in 855 by the priest Shinshō, but the name was changed to Eikan-dō in the 11th century to honour the philanthropic priest Eikan.

The best approach is to follow the arrows and wander slowly along the covered walkways connecting the halls and gardens.

In the Amida-dō Hall, at the southern end of the complex, is the famous statue of Mikaeri Amida (Buddha Glancing Backwards).

There are various legends about this statue. One version maintains that Eikan was doing a dance in honour of Amida Buddha when the statue stepped down and joined in. When Eikan stopped in amazement, the Buddha looked over his shoulder and told him to keep on jiving.

On the right of this statue, there's an image of a bald priest with a superb expression of intense concentration.

From the Amida-dō Hall, head north to the end of the covered walkway. Change into the sandals provided, then climb the steep steps up the mountainside to the Taho-tō Pagoda where there's a fine view across the city.

The temple is open from 9 am to 4 pm and admission costs ¥400. An explanatory leaflet in English and a map are provided.

The Path of Philosophy 哲学の道

This walk, Tetsugaku-no-Michi, has long been a favourite with contemplative strollers who follow the traffic-free route beside a canal lined with cherry trees (and souvenir shops and vending machines) which come into spectacular bloom in April. It only takes 30 minutes to follow the walk, which starts after Eikan-dō Temple and leads to Ginkaku-ji Temple. During the day, be prepared for crowds of tourists; a night stroll will definitely be quieter. A map of the walk is part of *Walking Tour Courses in Kyoto*, a leaflet available from the TIC or JNTO.

Anraku-ji Temple

This is a temple of the Jōdo school and honours two monks, Anraku and Juren, who were involved in a juicy scandal.

In 1206, two ladies of the imperial court went to hear the two monks preach and felt so moved – nobody knows whether it was a call to love or a call to religion – that they became nuns. Emperor Go-Toba, feeling mighty piqued, summoned the monks to court to make them recant their faith. When the monks defied this offer of clemency, the emperor exiled their leader, Hōnen, and had the monks executed in 1207. On hearing the news, the two ladies, with the quaint names of Suzumushi (Bell Cricket) and Matsumushi (Pine Beetle), are reputed to have taken their lives.

The two monks and their ladies are buried in the temple grounds – the burial site is a still place to ponder the events of long ago.

The temple lies on the eastern side of the canal, a short walk south of Hōnen-ji Temple.

Hōnen-in Temple

This temple was founded in 1680 to honour Hōnen, the charismatic founder of the Jōdo school. This is a lovely, secluded temple with carefully raked gardens set back in the woods.

Entry is free. It's open from 7 am to 4 pm. The temple is a 12 minute walk from Ginkaku-ji Temple, on a side street just east off the Path of Philosophy. Cross the bridge over the canal and follow the road uphill.

Ginkaku-ji Temple 銀閣寺

Ginkaku-ji Temple is definitely worth seeing, but be warned that it is often swamped with busloads of visitors jamming the narrow pathways.

In 1482, Shogun Ashikaga Yoshimasa constructed a villa here which he used as a genteel retreat from the turmoil of civil war. Although its name translates as 'Silver Pavilion', the plan to completely cover the building in silver was never carried out. After Yoshimasa's death, it was converted to a temple.

The approach to the main gate runs between tall hedges before turning sharply into the extensive grounds. Walkways lead through the gardens which include meticulously raked cones of white sand (probably symbolic interpretations of a mountain and a lake), tall pines and a pond in front of the temple. A path also leads up the mountainside through the trees.

Admission costs ¥400 and it's open from 9 am to 5 pm. An explanatory leaflet in English is provided. From Kyoto station, take bus No 5 and get off at the Ginkaku-ji-mae stop.

NORTH-WESTERN KYOTO
京都の西北部

The north-western part of Kyoto is predominantly residential, but there are a number of superb temples with tranquil gardens in secluded precincts. For Zen fans, a visit to Daitoku-ji Temple and Ryōan-ji Temple is recommended. Kinkaku-ji Temple is another major attraction. The JNTO leaflet on walks also covers this area, but most of the walk is along unremarkable city streets.

Those who have the time and inclination to escape the tourist trail might consider a visit to the Takao district.

Daitoku-ji Temple 大徳寺

The precincts of this temple, which belongs to the Rinzai school of Zen, contain an extensive complex of 24 subtemples: two are mentioned below, but eight are open to the public. If you want an intensive look at Zen culture, this is the place to visit, but be prepared for temples which are thriving business enterprises and often choked with visitors.

My visit coincided with a ceremony marking the 400th anniversary of Sen-no-Rikyū's death. Dozens of smart geisha, some young, others a little long in the tooth, streamed through the grounds. The most incongruous foil to all this gentility were rows and rows of bright green, plastic porta-loos in precise lines on the path outside the subtemples. Zen and the art of porta-loo maintenance?

Robert Strauss

Daitoku-ji Temple is on the eastern side of the grounds. It was founded in 1319, burnt down in the next century, and rebuilt in the 16th century. The San-mon Gate contains an image of the famous tea master, Sen-no-Rikyū, on the 2nd storey.

According to some historical sources, Toyotomi Hideyoshi was so enraged when he discovered he had been demeaning himself by walking *under* Rikyū, that he forced the master to commit seppuku (ritual suicide) in 1591.

Daisen-in Subtemple
The famous Zen garden in this subtemple is worth a look –

that is, of course, if you can make any progress through the crowds. The jovial abbot posed for pictures, dashed off calligraphy souvenirs at lightning speed, held up his fingers in a 'V' for victory sign and completed the act with a regal bow and a rousing 'Danke schön' to each member of a German tour group. If you arrive at 9 am, you might miss the crowds.

Kōtō-in Subtemple
This subtemple is in the western part of the grounds. The gardens are superb.

Admission charges to the temples vary, but usually average ¥350. Those temples which accept visitors are usually open from 9 am to 5 pm. The temple bus stop is Daitoku-ji-mae. Convenient buses from Kyoto station are Nos 205 and 206.

Kinkaku-ji Temple 金閣寺

Kinkaku-ji Temple, the famed 'Golden Temple', is one of Japan's best known sights. The original building was constructed in 1397 as a retirement villa for Shōgun Ashikaga Yoshimitsu. His son converted it into a temple. In 1950, a young monk consummated his obsession with the temple by burning it to the ground. The monk's story was fictionalised in Mishima Yukio's *The Golden Pavilion*.

In 1955, a full reconstruction was completed which exactly followed the original design, but the gold-foil covering was extended to the lower floors. The temple may not be to everyone's taste – the tremendous crowds just about obscure the view anyway.

The temple is open from 9 am to 5.30 pm and admission costs ¥300. To get there from Kyoto station, take bus No 205 and get off at the Kinkaku-ji-michi stop; bus No 59 also stops close to the temple.

Ryōan-ji Temple 竜安寺

This temple belongs to the Rinzai school of Zen and was founded in 1450. The main attraction is the garden arranged in the *kare-sansui* ('dry landscape') style. An austere collection of 15 rocks, apparently adrift in a sea of sand, is enclosed by an earthen wall.

The designer, who remains unknown, provided no explanation.

This has encouraged others to use their imagination: oceans, islands, tigers – use your imagination. The viewing platform for the garden can become packed solid but the other parts of the temple grounds are also interesting and less of a target for the crowds. Here too, you are probably best advised to come as early in the day as possible.

Admission costs ¥350 and the temple is open from 8 am to 5 pm (8.30 am to 4.30 pm from December to March). Bus No 59 is convenient for this temple.

Ninna-ji Temple 仁和寺

Ninna-ji Temple was built in 842 and is the head temple of the Omura branch of the Shingon school of Buddhism. The present temple buildings, including a five storeyed pagoda, are from the 17th century. The extensive grounds are full of cherry trees. If you visit during the cherry blossom season, you may find the area full of drinkers, picnickers and tipsy ladies in flowing dresses dancing around in clouds of blossom.

The temple is open from 9 am to 5 pm and admission costs ¥350. Separate entrance fees are charged for the Kondō (Main Hall) and Reihōkan (Treasure House), which is only open for the first two weeks of October. To get there, take bus No 59 from Kyoto station and get off at the Omuro Ninna-ji stop which is opposite the entrance gate.

Myōshin-ji Temple 妙心寺

Myōshin-ji, a vast temple complex dating back to the 14th century, belongs to the Rinzai school of Zen. There are over 40 temples but only four are open to the public.

From the north gate, follow the broad, stone avenue flanked by rows of temples to the southern part of the complex. The ceiling of the Hattō (Lecture Hall) features the unnerving painting *Dragon Glaring in Eight Directions*. Admission costs ¥400 and it's open from 9.10 am to 3.40 pm.

Taizō-in Temple This temple is in the south-western corner of the grounds. The garden is

worth a visit. Admission costs ¥400 and it's open from 9 am to 5 pm.

The north gate of the Myōshin-ji Temple is an easy 10 minute walk from Ninna-ji Temple.

Kitano-Tenman-gū Shrine 北野天満宮

This shrine is of moderate interest, probably best visited for the market fair. The Tenjin-san market fair is held here on the 25th of each month. Those held in December and January are particularly colourful.

There's no charge for admission and it's open from 5.30 am to 6 pm. From Kyoto station, take bus No 50 and get off at the Kitano-Tenmangū-mae stop.

Kōryū-ji Temple 広隆寺

Kōryū-ji Temple was founded in 622 to honour Prince Shōtoku who was an enthusiastic promoter of Buddhism.

The Hattō (Lecture Hall), to the right of the main gate, houses a magnificent trio of 9th century statues: Buddha, flanked by manifestations of Kannon.

The Reihōkan (Treasure House) contains numerous fine Buddhist statues including the Naki Miroku (Crying Miroku) and the world renowned Miroku Bosatsu which is extraordinarily expressive. A national upset occurred in 1960 when an enraptured student clasped the statue and snapped off its little finger.

The temple is open from 9 am to 5 pm and admission costs ¥500. To get there from JR Kyoto station, first take a No 59 bus to the Omuro Ninna-ji stop and walk to the southern gate of Myōshin-ji Temple. From there you can take bus No 61, 62 or 63 to the Uzumasa-Kōryū-ji-mae stop.

Toei Uzumasa Eiga-Mura 東映太秦映画村

Toei Uzumasa Eiga-Mura (☎ 881-7716/ 1011) is a huge film set inside Toei's Uzumasa studios. This will probably only appeal to film buffs who enjoy wandering around historical reconstructions and town sets of the Edo and Meiji eras. Be prepared to share your tour with swarms of Japanese kids. If you fancy yourself as a film star, you can have your picture taken dressed in a kimono or other historical costume.

The studios are open to visitors from 9 am to 5 pm (16 March to 15 November), from 9.30 am to 4 pm during the rest of the year and are closed from 21 December to 1 January. Admission costs ¥1550 per person. From the southern gate of Myōshin-ji Temple take bus No 61, 62 or 63 and ask to get off at the Uzumasa Eigamura stop.

Takao District　高雄

This is a secluded district tucked far away in the north-western part of Kyoto. It is famed for autumn foliage and the temples of Jingo-ji, Saimyō-ji and Kōzan-ji.

To reach Jingo-ji Temple, take bus No 8 from Shijō-Omiya station – allow one hour for the ride. The other two temples are within easy walking distance.

There are two options for bus services to Takao: there is the hourly JR bus which takes about an hour to reach the Takao stop from Kyoto station; the other is the hourly Kyoto bus from Keihan-sanjō station which also takes one hour to Takao.

Hozu River Trip　保津川下り

Between 10 March and 30 November, there are seven trips (from 9 am to 3.30 pm) daily down the Hozu River. During the winter, the number of trips is reduced to three a day and the boats are heated. There are no boat trips from 29 December to 4 January.

The ride lasts two hours and covers 16 km between Kameoka and Arashiyama through occasional sections of choppy water – a scenic jaunt with minimal danger.

The price is ¥3700 per person. The boats depart from a dock which is eight minutes on foot from Kameoka station. Kameoka is accessible by rail from Kyoto on the JR Sagano (San-in) line. The Kyoto TIC provides an English leaflet and a photocopied timetable sheet for rail connections.

WESTERN KYOTO　京都の西部

Arashiyama and Sagano are two districts worth a visit in this area if you feel like strolling in pleasant natural surroundings

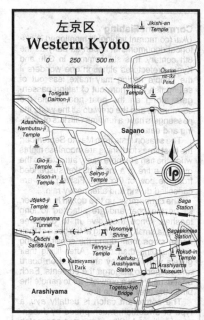

and visiting temples tucked into bamboo groves. The JNTO leaflet, *Walking Tour Courses in Kyoto*, has a rudimentary walking map for the Arashiyama area.

Bus Nos 71, 72 and 73 link Arashiyama with Kyoto station. Bus No 11 connects Keihan-sanjō station with Arashiyama. The most convenient rail connection is the 20 minute ride from Shijō-Omiya station on the Keifuku-Arashiyama line to Arashiyama station. There are several bicycle rental shops (¥600 for three hours, ¥1000 for the day) near the station, but it's more enjoyable to cover the relatively short distances between sights on foot.

Togetsu-kyō Bridge　渡月橋

Togetsu-kyō Bridge is the main landmark in Arashiyama, a couple of minutes on foot from the station. In July and August, this is a good vantage point to watch ukai (cormorant fishing) in the evening. If you want to get close to the action, you can pay ¥1300 to

Cormorant Fishing

Ukai (cormorant fishing) is mentioned in historical documents in Japan as early as the 8th century. It is still common in Gifu and Kyoto prefectures although one wonders if the people fishing may make less out of selling fish and more out of taking passengers along on the boat ride. While the cormorants and the crew do all the work, the passengers have a fun time with lots of drinking and eating.

The season lasts from May to September; the best times for fishing are moonless nights when the fish are more easily attracted to the glare of a fire in a metal basket suspended from the bow of the boat. Fishing trips are cancelled during and after heavy rain.

The cormorants, up to a dozen in number, sit on the boat and are attached to long leashes. Once they dive in to do some fishing, a small metal ring at the base of their necks stops them doing the sensible thing and guzzling their catch. After filling their gullets with fish, they are hauled on board and obliged to disgorge the contents. Each boat usually has a crew of four to handle the birds, the boat and the fire.

The cormorant catch is usually *ayu*, a type of sweetfish, much prized by Japanese foodies. A nifty cormorant can catch several dozen fish in a night. After completing their night's work, the cormorants are loaded into bamboo baskets in a strictly observed order of seniority – cormorants are very conscious of social ranking and will protest if this is not respected. Life expectancy for a cormorant ranges between 15 and 20 years, so they probably do have a point about seniority.

In Kyoto, the boat ride costs ¥1,200 (children half price). Advance bookings can be made through hotels or contact ☎ 010 8175 8611627. In Gifu, it costs more – about ¥2,600. ∎

join a passenger boat. The TIC can provide a leaflet and further details.

Tenryū-ji Temple 天竜寺

Tenryū-ji Temple is one of the major temples of the Rinzai school of Zen. It was built in 1339 on the former site of Emperor Go-Daigo's villa after a priest had dreamt of a dragon rising from the nearby river. The dream was interpreted as a sign that the emperor's spirit was uneasy and the temple was constructed as appeasement – hence the name *tenryū* (heavenly dragon). The present buildings date from 1900, but the main attraction is the 14th century Zen garden.

Admission costs ¥500 and it's open from 8.30 am to 5.30 pm (April to October) and has a 5 pm closing time during rest of the year.

Ōkōchi Sansō Villa 大河内山荘

This is the lavish home of Denjiro Ōkōchi, a famous actor in samurai films. The extensive gardens provide fine views over the city and are open to visitors. Admission costs a hefty ¥700 (including tea and a cake). The villa is a 10 minute walk through bamboo groves north of Tenryū-ji Temple.

Temples North of Ōkōchi Sansō Villa

If you continue north from Ōkōchi Sansō Villa, the narrow road soon passes stone steps on your left leading up to the pleasant grounds of Jōjakō-ji Temple. A further 10 minutes on foot brings you to Nison-in Temple, which is in an attractive setting up the wooded hillside.

If you have time for a detour, there are several small temples west of Nison-in Temple. Adashino Nembutsu-ji Temple is a rather bizarre temple where the abandoned bones of paupers and destitutes without next of kin were gathered. Thousands of stone images are crammed into the temple grounds. These thousands of abandoned souls are remembered each year with candles here in the Sentō Kuyō ceremony held on the evenings of 23 and 24 August.

Daikaku-ji Temple 大覚寺

Daikaku-ji Temple is 25 minutes walk northeast of Nison-in Temple. It was built in the 9th century as a palace for Emperor Saga who converted it into a temple. The present buildings date from the 16th century, but are still palatial in style with some impressive paintings. The large Osawa-no-Ike Pond was once used by the emperor for boating.

The temple is open from 9 am to 4.30 pm

and admission costs ¥500. Close to the temple entrance are separate terminals for Kyoto-shi (Kyoto City) buses (No 28 goes to Kyoto station) and Kyoto buses (No 71 goes to Kyoto station and No 61 to Keihan-sanjō station).

SOUTH-WESTERN KYOTO
京都の西南部

Katsura Rikyū Imperial Villa 桂離宮
This villa is considered to be one of the finest examples of Japanese architecture. It was built in 1624 for the emperor's brother, Prince Toshihito. Every conceivable detail of the villa, the teahouses, the large pond with islets and the surrounding garden has been given meticulous attention.

Tours (in Japanese) start at 10 am and 2 pm and last about 40 minutes. You should be there 20 minutes beforehand. An explanatory video is shown in the waiting room and a leaflet is provided in English.

An imperial villa tour can evolve into an interesting cultural experience with Japanese sticking close to the guide while the foreigners hang back. Both groups eagerly jostle for camera positions: the Japanese want everyone *in* the picture whereas the foreigners want everyone *out*. Meanwhile, the harassed security man brings up the rear, nervously twiddling his earphone, trying to shepherd all the straggling foreigners.

Admission is free, but you *must* make reservations through the Imperial Household Agency (see earlier details for the Kyoto Imperial Palace) and usually several weeks in advance. Visitors must be over 20 years of age.

To get to the villa from Kyoto station take bus No 33 and get off at the Katsura Rikyū-mae stop which is a five minute walk from the villa. The easiest access from the city centre is to take a Hankyū line train from Hankyū Kawaramachi station to Hankyū Katsura station which is a 15 minute walk from the villa.

Saihō-ji Temple 西芳寺
The main attraction at this temple is the heart-shaped garden, designed in 1339 by Musō Kokushi. The garden is famous for its luxuriant mossy growth – hence the temple's other name: 'Koke-dera' (Moss Temple). Visiting the temple is recommended only if you have time and patience to follow the reservation rules.

Reservations Reservations are the only way you can visit. This is to avoid the overwhelming crowds of visitors who used to swamp the place when reservations were not required.

Send a postcard at least one week before the date you require and include details of your name, number of visitors, address in Japan, occupation, age (you must be over 18) and desired date (choice of alternative dates preferred). The full address is Saihō-ji Temple, 56 Kamigaya-cho, Matsuo, Nishikyō-ku, Kyoto. Enclose a pre-stamped return postcard for a reply to your Japanese address. You might find it convenient to buy an *ōfuki-hagaki* (send and return postcard set) at a Japanese post office.

You should arrive at the time and on the date supplied by the temple office. After paying your ¥3000 'donation', you spend up to 90 minutes copying or chanting sutras or doing Zen meditation before finally being guided around the garden for 90 minutes.

Take bus No 73 from Kyoto station (45 minutes) or bus No 63 from Keihan-sanjō station (40 minutes).

SOUTH & SOUTH-EASTERN KYOTO
京都の南部・東南部
The district to the south of Kyoto is mostly devoted to industry (also famed for sake breweries), but Tōfuku-ji Temple and the foxy Fushimi-Inari Taisha Shrine are worth a visit.

To the south-east, Daigo-ji Temple is in rural surroundings and offers scope for a gentle hike to complement the architectural splendours. The city of Uji isn't exactly part of Kyoto, but it's easy to reach on a day trip, or as a convenient stop when travelling between Kyoto and Nara.

Tōfuku-ji Temple 東福寺
Founded in 1236 by the priest Enni, Tōfuku-

ji Temple now belongs to the Rinzai sect of Zen Buddhism. Since this temple was intended to compare with Tōdai-ji Temple and Kōfuku-ji Temple in Nara, it was given a name combining characters from the names of each of these temples.

Despite the destruction of many of the buildings by fire, this is still considered one of the five main Zen temples in Kyoto. The huge San-mon Gate is the oldest Zen main gate in Japan. The *tōsu* (lavatory) and *yokushitsu* (bathroom) date from the 14th century. The present temple complex includes 24 sub-temples; at one time there were 53.

The Hōjō (Abbot's Hall) was reconstructed in 1890. The gardens, laid out in 1938, are worth a visit. As you approach the northern gardens, you cross a stream over Tsūten-kyō (Bridge to Heaven), which is a pleasant leafy spot – the foliage is renowned for its autumn colour. The northern garden has stones and moss neatly arranged in a chequerboard pattern.

The nearby Reiun-in subtemple receives few visitors to its attractive garden.

Admission costs ¥300 for the main temple and admission charges for the subtemples are about the same. Opening hours are from 9 am to 4 pm. English leaflets are provided.

To reach Tōfuku-ji Temple by train, you can either take a JR train on the Nara line or a train from Keihan-sanjō station on the Keihan Honsen line. Get off at Tōfuku-ji station. Bus No 208 also runs from Kyoto station via Tōfuku-ji Temple. Get off at the Tōfuku-ji-mae stop.

Fushimi-Inari Taisha Shrine 伏見稲荷大社

This intriguing shrine was dedicated to the gods of rice and sake by the Hata family in the 8th century. As the role of agriculture diminished, deities were enrolled to ensure prosperity in business. Nowadays, the shrine is one of Japan's most popular, and is the head shrine for some 30,000 Inari shrines scattered the length and breadth of Japan.

The entire complex, consisting of five shrines, sprawls across the wooded slopes of Mt Inari. A pathway wanders four km up the

mountain and is lined with hundreds of red torii (arches). There are also dozens of stone foxes. The fox is considered the messenger of Inari, the god of cereals, and by extension the stone foxes, too, are often referred to as Inari. On an incidental note, the Japanese traditionally see the fox as a sacred, somewhat mysterious figure capable of 'possessing' humans – the favoured point of entry is under the fingernails. The key often seen in the fox's mouth is for the rice granary.

On 1 April, there is a festival at 11 am which features displays of flower arranging. On 8 April, there's a Sangyō-sai Festival with offerings and dances to ensure prosperity for national industry. During the first few days in January, thousands of festive believers pray at the shrine.

Local delicacies sold on the approach streets include barbecued sparrow and 'Inari-sushi' which is fried tōfu wrapped around sweetened sushi – commonly believed to be the favourite food of the fox.

To get to the shrine from JR Kyoto station, take a JR Nara line train to Inari station. From Keihan-sanjō station on the Keihan Honsen line (*honsen* means 'main'), get off at Fushimi-Inari station. There is no admission charge for the shrine.

Daigo-ji Temple 醍醐寺

Daigo-ji Temple was founded in 874 by the priest Shobo who gave it the name of Daigo (ultimate essence of milk). This refers to the five periods of Buddha's teaching which were often compared to the five forms of milk prepared in India – the highest form is called 'daigo' in Japanese.

The temple was expanded into a vast complex of buildings on two levels: Shimo Daigo (Lower Daigo) and Kami Daigo (Upper Daigo). During the 15th century, the buildings on the lower level were destroyed with the sole exception of the five storeyed pagoda. Built in 951, this pagoda still stands and is lovingly pointed out as the oldest of its kind in Japan and the oldest existing building in Kyoto.

In the late 16th century, Hideyoshi took a fancy to Daigo-ji Temple and ordered extensive rebuilding. It is now one of the main temples of the Shingon school of Buddhism. To explore Daigo-ji Temple thoroughly and leisurely, mixing hiking with temple viewing, you will need at least half a day.

Hōkō Hanami Gyōretsu Parade On the second Sunday in April, a parade called Hōkō Hanami Gyōretsu takes place in the temple precincts. This re-enacts in full period costume the cherry-blossom party which Hideyoshi held in 1598. As a result of this party, the temple's abbot was able to secure Hideyoshi's support for restoration of the dilapidated temple complex.

Sampō-in Temple This was founded as a subtemple in 1115, but received a total revamp under Hideyoshi's orders in 1598. It is now a fine example of the amazing opulence of that period. The Kanō paintings and the garden are special features.

The garden is jam-packed with about 800 stones – the Japanese mania for stones goes back a long way. The most famous stone here is Fujito-no-ishi which is linked with deception, death and a fabulous price that was spurned; it's even the subject of a Nō play, *Fujito*. Admission to Sampō-in Temple costs ¥500. It's open from 9 am to 5 pm (March to October) and closes one hour earlier during the rest of the year.

Hōju-in Treasure House This is close to the Sampō-in Temple, but is only open to the public from 1 April to 25 May and from 1 October to 25 November. Despite the massive admission fee of ¥700, it really should not be missed if you happen to be there at the right time. The display of sculptures, scrolls, screens, miniature shrines and calligraphy is superb.

Climb to Kami Daigo From Sampō-in Temple in Shimo Daigo (Lower Daigo), walk up the large avenue of cherry trees, through the Niō-mon Gate and past the pagoda. From there you can continue for a pleasant climb through Kami Daigo (Upper Daigo), browsing through temples and

shrines on the way. Allow 50 minutes to reach the top.

To get to the Daigo-ji Temple complex, take bus No 12 or bus 'Higashi' No 9 from central Kyoto to Rokujizo station (40 minutes). From there, it's an eight minute ride on the Toku (Special) No 12 bus to the Sampō-in-mae stop.

Mampuku-ji Temple 黄檗山万福寺
Mampuku-ji Temple was established as a Zen temple in 1661 by the Chinese priest Ingen. It is a rare example in Japan of a Zen temple built in the pure Chinese style of the Ming dynasty. The temple follows the Ōbaku school of Zen, which is linked to mainstream Rinzai Zen, but incorporates a wide range of Esoteric Buddhist practices.

Admission costs ¥400 and it's open from 9 am to 4.30 pm. The temple is a short walk from the two railway stations (JR Nara line and Keihan Uji line) at Ōbaku – about 30 minutes by rail from Kyoto.

Uji 宇治
Uji is a small city to the south of Kyoto. Its main claims to fame are the Byōdō-in Temple, tea cultivation and ukai (cormorant fishing). The stone bridge at Uji, the oldest of its kind in Japan, has been the scene of many bitter clashes in previous centuries – traffic jams seem to dominate nowadays.

Uji can be reached by rail in about 40 minutes from Kyoto on the Keihan-Uji line or JR Nara line.

Byōdō-in Temple This temple was converted from a Fujiwara villa into a Buddhist temple in 1052. The Phoenix Hall (Hōō-dō), more properly known as the Amida-dō, was built in 1053 and is the only original remaining building. The phoenix was a popular mythical bird in China and was revered by the Japanese as a protector of Buddha. The architecture of the building resembles the shape of the bird, and there are two bronze phoenixes perched opposite each other on the roof. The building was originally intended to represent Amida's heavenly palace in the Pure Land.

KANSAI REGION

Inside the hall is the famous statue of Amida and 52 Bosatsu (Bodhisattvas) dating from the 11th century and attributed to the priest-sculptor, Jōchō.

The temple, complete with its reflection in a pond, is a No 1 attraction in Japan and draws huge crowds. For a preview without the masses, take a look at the 10 yen coin. Admission costs ¥300 and it's open from 8.30 am to 5 pm (March to November) and from 9 am to 4 pm during the rest of the year. English leaflets are provided.

The nearby Hōmotsukan Treasure House contains the original temple bell and door paintings and the original phoenix roof adornments. Admission costs ¥300 and it is only open from 10 April to 31 May and from 15 September to 3 November. Opening hours are from 9 am to 4 pm. A brief leaflet is supplied in English.

The approach street to the temple complex is lined with souvenir shops many of which roast local tea outside. A small packet of the tea is popular as a souvenir or gift.

Between 17 June and 31 August, ukai trips are organised in the evening around 7 pm on the river near the temple. Prices start at ¥1500 per person. The TIC has a leaflet with up-to-date information on booking. More details about ukai are included in the Arashiyama section in Western Kyoto.

NORTHERN KYOTO　京都の北部

The area north of Kyoto provides scope for exploration of rural valleys and mountainous areas. Ōhara makes a pleasant day trip, perhaps twinned with an excursion to Mt Hiei-zan and the Enryaku-ji Temple or Shūgaku-in Rikyū Imperial Villa.

Shūgaku-in Rikyū Imperial Villa
修学院離宮

This villa, or 'detached palace', was begun in the 1650s by the abdicated emperor Go-Mizunoo, and work was continued after his death in 1680 by his daughter Akenomiya. Designed as an imperial retreat, the villa grounds are divided into three large garden areas on a hillside: lower, middle and upper. The gardens' reputation rests on their ponds,

pathways and impressive use of 'borrowed scenery' in the form of the surrounding hills; the view from the Rinun-tei Teahouse in the upper garden is particularly impressive.

Tours (in Japanese) start at 9 and 10 am; 1.30 and 3 pm (50 minutes). Get there early. An English leaflet is provided.

Admission is free, but you must make reservations through the Imperial Household Agency – usually several weeks in advance (see the earlier Kyoto Imperial Palace section for details).

From Kyoto station, take bus No 5 and get off at the Shūgaku-in Rikyū-michi stop. The trip takes about an hour. From the bus stop it's a 15 minute walk to the villa.

Shisendō & Manshū-in Temple
詩仙堂・曼殊院

Both these sights are in the vicinity of Shūgaku-in Rikyū Imperial Villa and both are less touristy than other major sights.

Shisendō (House of Poet-Hermits) was built in 1641 by Jōzan, a scholar of Chinese classics and a landscape architect, who wanted a place to retire at the end of his life. The garden provides relaxation – just the rhythmic 'thwack' of a bamboo *sōzu* (animal scarer) to interrupt your snooze.

Admission costs ¥400 and an English leaflet is provided; it's open from 9 am to 5 pm. The house is a five minute walk from the Ichijoji-sagarimatsu-mae bus stop on the No 5 route.

Manshū-in Temple was originally founded by Saichō on Mt Hiei-zan, but was relocated here at the beginning of the Edo period. The architecture, works of art and garden are impressive.

The temple is open from 9 am to 5 pm and admission costs ¥500; an English leaflet is provided. The temple is a 10 minute walk from Shūgaku-in Rikyū Imperial Villa.

Mt Hiei-zan & Enryaku-ji Temple
比叡山・延暦寺

A visit to Mt Hiei-zan and Enryaku-ji Temple is a good way to spend half a day hiking, poking around temples and enjoying the atmosphere of a key site in Japanese history.

Enryaku-ji Temple was founded in 788 by Saichō, the priest who established the Tenzai school of Buddhism. The Tenzai school did not receive imperial recognition until 1823, after Saichō's death. But from this time the temple continued to grow in power; at its height it possessed some 3000 temple buildings and an army of thousands of *sōhei*, or warrior monks. In 1581, Oda Nobunaga saw the temple's power as a threat to his aims to unify the nation. He destroyed most of the temple buildings along with the monks inside.

As it now stands, the temple area is divided into three sections: Tōdō, Saitō and Yokawa (of minimal interest). The Tōdō (Eastern Section) contains the Kompon Chū-dō (Primary Central Hall) which dates from 1642. Admission costs ¥400. It's open from 8.30 am to 4.30 pm (April to November) and from 9 am to 4 pm during the rest of the year. An English leaflet is provided. This part is heavily geared to group access with large expanses of asphalt for parking.

The Saitō (Western Section) contains the Shaka-dō Hall, dating from the Kamakura period. The Saitō, with its stone paths winding through forests of tall trees, temples shrouded in mist and the sound of distant gongs, is the most atmospheric part of the temple.

Getting There & Away

You can reach Mt Hiei-zan and Enryaku-ji Temple by either train or bus.

Train If you want to go via Lake Biwa-ko, you can take a train from Kyoto to one of two stations (Sakamoto or Eizan) close to the base of Mt Hiei-zan. The most convenient of these two is Sakamoto, which is near the base station of the cable railway which runs up Mt Hiei-zan to Enryaku-ji Temple.

To reach Sakamoto station, take the Keihan Kyozu line from Keihan-sanjō (in central Kyoto), then change to the Keihan Ishiyama line at Hama-ōtsu.

Eizan station is about 15 minutes walk east of Sakamoto, but it's worth mentioning for Japan Rail Pass holders because it's on the JR Kosei line. From Sakamoto station,

follow the road westwards (away from Lake Biwa-ko) to the Sakamoto cable railway station.

Although the views from the cable railway are excellent the rest of the train trip from Kyoto is unremarkable and tedious.

If you are starting from the north of Kyoto, you can also reach Yase-yuen by taking the train from Demachiyanagi station on the Eizan line.

Bus Bus Nos 17 and 18 run from Kyoto station to Ōhara in about 50 minutes. Get off before Ōhara at the Yase-yuenchi bus stop. From there it's a short walk to the cablecar station (departures every half hour) where you can ascend the mountain in two stages. A combined ticket (one way) for both sections costs ¥820. The lookout at the top cablecar station has fine views across Lake Biwa-ko, though skip it if the weather is dull; entry costs ¥300.

From Keihan-sanjō station in central Kyoto, you can take bus No 16 towards Ōhara and get off at the Yase-yuenchi bus stop.

From Kyoto station there are direct buses to Enryaku-ji Temple and Mt Hiei-zan at 9.50, 10.45 and 11.45 am and 1.50 pm (¥650, one hour 10 minutes). There are also direct buses from Keihan-sanjō station at 8.55, 9.35 and 11.06 am and 12.06, 1.05 and 3.05 pm (¥650, 52 minutes).

Ōhara 大原

Ōhara is in a drowsy rural area with some fine temples – the most famous are Sanzen-in Temple and Jakkō-in Temple. The Ōharame (Ōhara damsels), who once dressed in distinctive costume and toted loads of twigs on their heads are still promoted on postcards or dressed up to parade for photos.

From Kyoto station, bus Nos 17 and 18 run to Ōhara. The ride takes about 90 minutes. Allow half a day for a visit, possibly twinned with an excursion to Mt Hiei-zan and the Enryaku-ji Temple. JNTO includes a basic walking map for the area in its leaflet *Walking Tour Courses in Kyoto*.

Sanzen-in Temple To visit this temple, walk

out of the bus station up the road to the traffic lights. From there, take the small road to the right and turn left after the phone box. Then continue along a narrow path, lined with souvenir stalls, up the steep hill.

The oldest part of the temple is the main hall known as the 'Temple of Rebirth in Paradise', which was originally built in 985 by Eshin, a priest who retired from Mt Hieizan. The hall's ceiling is shaped like the hull of a ship, and the centrepiece of the hall is a set of statues – the Amitabha trinity.

The gardens are famous for their autumn colours. Part of the garden is jarringly modern compared with the venerable dignity of the classical section around the main buildings.

The temple is open from 8.30 am to 5.30 pm March to November and closes half an hour earlier during the rest of the year. Admission costs ¥500 and an English leaflet is provided.

Jakkō-in Convent This convent lies to the west of Ohara. Walk out of the bus station up the road to the traffic lights, then follow the small road to the left; the temple is at the top of a steep flight of stone steps.

The history of Jakkō-in Convent is exceedingly tragic – bring a supply of hankies. The actual founding date of the convent is subject to some debate (somewhere between the 6th and 11th centuries), but it acquired fame as the nunnery which harboured Kenrei Mon'in, a lady of the Taira clan. In 1185, the Taira were soundly defeated in a sea battle with the Minamoto clan. With the entire Taira clan slaughtered or drowned, Kenrei Mon'in threw herself into the waves with her son, the infant emperor; she was fished out – the only member of the clan to survive.

She was returned to Kyoto, where she became a nun living in a bare hut until it collapsed during an earthquake. Kenrei Mon'in was accepted into Jakkō-in Temple and stayed there, immersed in prayer and sorrowful memories, until her death 27 years later.

Jakkō-in is open from 9 am to 5 pm and admission costs ¥500.

ORGANISED TOURS

Some visitors on a tight schedule find it convenient to opt for a tour of the city. Travellers we spoke to who had done this felt that they had got to see a lot more of the sights than if they had tackled them on their own.

Two companies, Gray Line Kyoto Nara (☎ 075-691-0903) and JTB Sunrise Tours (☎ 075-341-1413), offer almost identical morning, afternoon and all-day tours. Morning and afternoon tours cost ¥5000, while all-day tours with a buffet lunch thrown in are ¥10,600. The same companies also offer Nara tours and Kyoto night tours that include tea ceremony, a 'Zen-style tempura supper' and traditional entertainment.

FESTIVALS

There are hundreds of festivals (matsuri) spread throughout the year. Listings can be found at the TIC or in *Kyoto Visitor's Guide*, *Monthly Guide Kyoto* and *Kyoto Monthly Guide*. The following are some of the major or most spectacular festivals. These attract hordes of spectators from out of town, sometimes twice as many as the resident population, so you need to book accommodation well in advance.

Aoi Matsuri (Hollyhock Festival)
15 May. This festival dates back to the 6th century and commemorates the successful prayers of the people for the gods to stop calamitous weather. Today, the procession involves imperial messengers in oxcarts and a retinue of 600 people dressed in traditional costume; hollyhock leaves are carried or used as decoration. The procession leaves around 10 am from the imperial palace and heads for Shimogamo-jinja Shrine where ceremonies take place. It sets out from here again at 2 pm and arrives at Kamigamo-jinja Shrine at 3.30 pm.

Gion Matsuri
16-17 July. Perhaps the most renowned of all Japanese festivals, this one reaches a climax on these days with a parade of over 30 floats depicting ancient themes, which are decked out in incredible finery.

Daimon-ji Gozan Okuribi
  16 August. This is a festival to bid farewell to the souls of ancestors. Enormous fires are lit on five mountains in the form of Chinese characters or other shapes. The fires are lit at 8 pm and it is best to watch from the banks of the Kamogawa River or pay for a rooftop view from a hotel.

Kurama-no-Himatsuri
  22 October. The origins of this festival are traced back to a rite using fires to guide the gods of the nether world on their tours around this world. Portable shrines are carried through the streets and accompanied by youths with flaming torches. The festival climaxes around 10 pm at Yuki-jinja Shrine in the village of Kurama which is 30 minutes by train from Kyoto station.

Jidai Matsuri (Festival of the Ages)
  22 October. This festival is of recent origin, dating back to 1895. More than 2000 people, dressed in costumes ranging from the 8th century to the 19th century, parade from the imperial palace to Heian-jingū Shrine.

PLACES TO STAY

Kyoto has a wide range of accommodation to suit all budgets. Choices range from the finest and most expensive ryokan in Japan to youth hostels or gaijin houses. Bear in mind that most of the cheaper places are further out of town. You can save time spent traversing the city if you organise your accommodation around the areas of interest to you. To help with planning, the following accommodation listings have been sorted according to location and price range. Gaijin houses usually offer reduced rates if you ask for weekly or monthly terms.

The TIC offers advice, accommodation lists and helps with reservations. Two useful TIC leaflets are *Reasonable Ryokan & Minshuku in Kyoto* and *Inexpensive Accommodations in Kyoto (Dormitory-Style)*.

Seven minutes walk from the TIC is the Kyoto Minshuku Reservation Centre (☎ 075-351-4547), On Building, 7th Floor, Shimogyo-ku. The centre provides computer reservations for minshuku not only in Kyoto, but all through Japan. Some English is spoken. Kyoto is a mega-attraction for tourists so try and book in advance, particularly during holiday seasons.

PLACES TO STAY – BOTTOM END
Central Kyoto
Uno House (☎ 075-231-7763) is a celebrated gaijin house that provides you with the dubious privilege of a real grungy accommodation experience. The attraction is the price and the absence of youth hostel regimentation. Dorm beds start at ¥1600, and private rooms range from ¥3600 to ¥5400.

Take bus No 205 or Toku 17 – make sure the kanji character for toku or 'special' (特) precedes the number – from Kyoto station (bus terminal A3) to the Kawaramachi-marutamachi-mae stop. The trip takes about 20 minutes.

Higher standards prevail at *Tani House Annexe* (☎ 075-211-5637), but it doesn't have dorm accommodation. It has doubles with bath and air-con for ¥6000 and triples for ¥7000. Take bus No 5 from Kyoto station (bus terminal A1) and get off at the Kawaramachi-sanjō-mae stop. The trip takes about 20 minutes.

One other place worth checking out is *Tōji An Guest House* (☎ 075-691-7017). It's around 10 minutes walk from Kyoto station, and has share accommodation at ¥2000. There's no curfew here, but it's often full with long-termers.

Eastern Kyoto
Higashiyama Youth Hostel (☎ 075-761-8135) is a spiffy hostel which makes an excellent base very close to the sights of Higashiyama. For a dorm bed and two meals, the charge is ¥3500. Private rooms are available for ¥5000 per person (including two meals). Bicycle rental costs ¥800 per day.

The old gripes about the regimentation of this hostel – one traveller referred to it as Stalag 13 in a welcome note to his friends – still apply. But if you're the kind of person who likes being in bed by 9.30 pm (tear the following Entertainment section of this chapter out of your book), this might be just your ticket. Meals are not a highlight, so you might prefer to skip them and find something more interesting in the town centre.

To get there, take bus No 5 from Kyoto

KANSAI REGION

station (terminal A1) to the Higashiyama-sanjō-mae stop (20 minutes).

ISE Dorm (☎ 075-771-0566) provides basic accommodation (42 rooms) at rates between ¥1500 and ¥3000 per day; monthly terms range between ¥31,000 and ¥60,000, and yearly terms are also possible. Facilities on offer include phone, fridge, air-con, shower and washing machine. This place has come in for quite a lot of criticism for its dirtiness and the rudeness of the management. Take a look at the place before you actually check in.

Take bus No 206 from Kyoto station (bus terminal A2) to the Kumano-jinja-mae stop. Allow 30 minutes for the ride.

North-Western Kyoto
Utano Youth Hostel (☎ 075-462-2288) is a friendly, well-organised hostel which makes a convenient base for covering the sights of north-western Kyoto.

Like the Higashiyama Youth Hostel, everything is ordered: 10 pm curfew, 10.30 pm lights-out and 6.30 am wakey-wakey. The men's bath is a large jacuzzi. There's an international phone just outside the front door. The buffet breakfast is good value for ¥400. If you want to skip the hostel supper, turn left along the main road to find several coffee shops offering cheap set meals (teishoku). Rates are ¥2500 without meals and ¥3700 with.

Ask at the hostel's front desk about postage stamps, one-day travel passes, '11 bus tickets for the price of 10', postcards and discount entry tickets (to Sanzen-in Temple, Manshu-in Temple and Movieland). There's also a meeting room with bilingual TV news, but for many travellers, fond memories are reserved for the heated toilet seats!

Take bus No 26 from Kyoto station (bus terminal C1) to the Yūsu Hosuteru-mae stop. The ride takes about 50 minutes.

Northern Kyoto
Aoi-Sō Inn (☎ 075-431-0788) has dorm beds for ¥1300, doubles for ¥5000 and triples for ¥7000. It's reported to be a quiet place with no evening curfew, and a coin laundry and kitchen are available. The inn is near the old imperial palace, a five minute walk west from subway Kuramaguchi Shin-mei (exit 2) between the Kuramaguchi Hospital buildings. Call first to check directions and vacancies.

Tani House (☎ 075-492-5489) is an old favourite for short-term and long-term visitors on a tight budget. There is a certain charm to this fine old house with its warren of rooms, jovial owners and quiet location next to Daitoku-ji Temple. Costs per night are ¥1500 for a space on the floor in a tatami room and ¥3600 to ¥4200 for a double private room. There's no curfew and free tea and coffee are provided. It can become crowded, so book ahead. Take the 45 minute ride on bus No 206 from Kyoto station (bus terminal B4) and get off at the Kenkun-jinja-mae stop.

Kitayama Youth Hostel (☎ 075-492-5345) charges ¥2400 for a dorm bed (without meals) or ¥3500 with two meals. Take bus No 6 from Kyoto station (bus terminal B4) to the Genkoan-mae stop (allow 35 minutes for the trip). Walk west past a school, turn right and continue up the hill to the hostel (five minutes on foot). This hostel would be an excellent base to visit the rural area of Takagamine which has some fine, secluded temples such as Kōetsu-ji Temple, Jōshō-ji Temple and Shōden-ji Temple.

Green Peace (☎ 075-791-9890) is a gaijin house that is really only an option if you are planning to stay three nights or longer – it no longer takes short-term visitors and doesn't quote nightly rates. Dorms cost ¥4500 for three nights, ¥9400 weekly and ¥26,000 monthly. Twin rooms cost ¥8200 for three nights, ¥17,000 weekly and ¥46,000 per month. Facilities include a kitchen, shower and even a friendship room.

To get there, take bus No 4 from Kyoto station (bus terminal A4) to the Nonogami-cho-mae stop. Allow 35 minutes for the ride.

Guest House Kyoto (☎ 075-491-0880) has single rooms at ¥2500 per day or ¥40,000 for one month. Twin rooms are ¥4000 per day or ¥50,000 for one month. Take bus No

205 from Kyoto station (bus terminal B3) to the Senbon-kitaoji-mae stop (50 minutes).

Takaya (☎ 075-431-5213) provides private rooms at ¥3000 per day or ¥50,000 for one month. Take the subway from Kyoto station to Imadegawa station (15 minutes).

Kyoto Ōhara Youth Hostel (☎ 075-744-2528) is a long way north out of town, but the rural surroundings are a bonus if you want to relax or dawdle around Ōhara's beautiful temples. A dorm bed costs ¥2300. From Kyoto station, you can take the subway to Kitaoji station and then take bus No 'north' 6 to Ohara (make sure the kanji for 'north' precedes the number or ask for *kita rokku*). Get off at the To-dera stop (near To-dera Temple). The TIC can give precise details for other train or bus routes to get you there.

West of Kyoto Station

Tani Guest House (☎ 075-681-7437, 075-671-2627) provides a dorm bed for ¥1900 and single/double rooms for ¥2200/4500. This is not connected with the management of the other Tani lodgings. To get there, take the JR line to Nishioji station (five minutes), then walk for 10 minutes.

PLACES TO STAY – MIDDLE
Central Kyoto & Station Area

Ryokan *Ryokan Hiraiwa* (☎ 075-351-6748), a member of the Japanese Inn Group, is used to receiving foreigners and offers basic tatami rooms. It is conveniently close to central and eastern Kyoto. Singles/doubles cost from ¥4000/8000 and facilities include bilingual TV, air-con and coin laundry. To get there from Kyoto station you can either walk (15 minutes) or take bus Nos 205, 42 or Toku (Special) 17 – make sure the kanji for toku precedes the number – from bus terminal A3. Get off at the third stop, Kawaramachi Shomen; from there it's a five minute walk.

Ryokan Kyōka (☎ 075-371-2709), a member of the Japanese Inn Group, has 10 spacious, Japanese-style rooms. Singles cost from ¥3600 to ¥4200 and doubles cost from ¥7200 to ¥8000. If you give advance notice,

a kaiseki dinner is available for between ¥3500 and ¥5000. It's about eight minutes on foot from Kyoto station, close to the Higashi Hongan-ji Temple.

Matsubaya Ryokan (☎ 075-351-4268) is a member of the Japanese Inn Group. Prices for singles/doubles are ¥4300/8600; triples cost ¥12,000. This ryokan is also close to Higashi Hongan-ji Temple.

Ryokan Murakamiya (☎ 075-371-1260), also a member of the Japanese Inn Group, is seven minutes on foot from Kyoto station. Prices for singles are ¥4000 and doubles range from ¥7600 to ¥8000; triples cost from ¥11,000 to ¥12,000.

Riverside Takase (☎ 075-351-7920) is a member of the Japanese Inn Group and has five Japanese-style rooms. The cost for singles/doubles starts at ¥3200/5400; triples cost from ¥8100. Take bus No 205 from Kyoto station (bus terminal A3) and get off at the third stop, Kawaramachi Shomen.

The recently built *Pension Station Kyoto* (☎ 075-882-6200) is a member of the Japanese Inn Group and a quiet place. Prices for singles/doubles are ¥4200/8400; triples cost ¥12,000. The pension is an eight minute walk from the station.

Yuhara Ryokan (☎ 075-371-9583) has a family atmosphere and a riverside location popular with foreigners. Prices for singles/doubles are ¥3800/7500. It's a 15 minute walk from Kyoto station.

Ryokan Hinomoto (☎ 075-351-4563) is a member of the Japanese Inn Group with a position right in the centre of the city's nightlife action. It's a small place that is a favourite with many frequent visitors to Kyoto. Singles cost from ¥3500 to ¥4500; doubles cost from ¥7000 to ¥8000; triples cost from ¥9900 to ¥10,500. Take bus No 17 or 205 from Kyoto station (bus terminal A3) and get off at the Kawaramachi-matsubara-mae stop.

Hotels In general, hotels work out slightly more expensive than staying in a ryokan and have far less character. Still, they are generally a lot more flexible about the hours you keep and are not without certain advantages.

KANSAI REGION

The following are some of the more reasonably priced business hotels in the central Kyoto region:

Hokke Club Kyoto (☎ 075-361-1251) – singles cost from ¥6400 to ¥7400; twins from ¥11,000; opposite JR Kyoto station

Hotel Rich (☎ 075-341-1131) – singles cost from ¥7700; twins from ¥12,400; doubles from ¥13,600; five minutes walk from Go-jō subway station

Karasuma Kyoto Hotel (☎ 075-371-0111) – singles cost from ¥8500; twins from ¥14,500; doubles from ¥18,000; next to Shi-jō subway station

Kyoto Central Inn (☎ 075-211-1666) – singles/twins cost from ¥6500/10,000; next to Kawaramachi station

Kyoto Dai-San Tower Hotel (☎ 075-343-3111) – singles cost from ¥6000 to ¥8000; twins from ¥10,000 and doubles from ¥13,500; five minutes walk from JR Kyoto station

Kyoto Dai-Ichi Hotel (☎ 075-661-8800) – singles/twins cost ¥6500/10,000; 10 minutes walk south-east of Kyoto station

Eastern Kyoto

Ryokan Mishima (Mishima Shrine) (☎ 075-551-0033) operates as part of a Shintō shrine and is a member of the Japanese Inn Group. Singles/doubles/triples cost ¥4000/7000/¥10,500. On request, you can fulfil your photographic fantasy by dressing up in Shintō robes. Take bus No 206 (east-bound) from Kyoto station (bus terminal A2) and get off at the Higashiyama-umamachi-mae stop.

Pension Higashiyama (☎ 075-882-1181) is a member of the Japanese Inn Group. It's a modern construction by the waterside and convenient for seeing the sights in Higashiyama. Prices for singles/doubles are ¥4200/8400; triples cost ¥12,000. For a break from Japanese breakfast, you could try the pension's American breakfast (¥800). Dinner is also available for ¥2000.

To get there, take bus No 206 from Kyoto station (bus terminal A2) for an 18 minute ride to the Chionin-mae stop.

Ryokan Ohto (☎ 075-541-7803) is a member of the Japanese Inn Group, has a riverside location and charges ¥3700 to ¥4500 for singles, ¥7400 for doubles and ¥11,000 for triples. You can get there via Nos

206 or 208 buses from Kyoto station (bus terminal A2) to Shichi-jō Ōhashi bus stop.

Not far from Kiyōmizu-dera Temple, the *Ryokan Sieki* (☎ 075-551-4911) is yet another member of the Japanese Inn Group and has singles from ¥3600 to ¥4500, doubles from ¥7500 to ¥8000 and triples from ¥11,000. It's 15 minutes from Kyoto station (bus terminal A2) by a No 206 bus; get off at Go-jō-zaka bus stop.

Three Sisters Inn (Rakutō-sō) (☎ 075-771-0225) is a popular ryokan, at ease with foreign guests. Per head costs are ¥9000. Take bus No 5 from Kyoto station and get off at the Dobutsu-en-mae stop – the inn is just to the north of Heian-jingū Shrine. *The Three Sisters Annexe* (☎ 075-761-6333), close by, is run by the same management, and has singles with/without bath for ¥6900/¥4900. Twins without bath are ¥9800.

Iwanami (☎ 075-561-7135) is a pleasant, old-fashioned ryokan with a faithful following of foreign guests. Book well in advance. Prices start at ¥8500 per person including breakfast.

Kyoto Traveller's Inn (☎ 075-771-0225) is a business hotel, very close to the Heian-jingū Shrine, offering both Western and Japanese-style rooms. Prices for singles/twins start at ¥5000/9000. There's no curfew and the Green Box restaurant on the 1st floor is open until 10 pm.

Northern Kyoto

Ryokan Rakucho (☎ 075-721-2174) is a member of the Japanese Inn Group. Prices for singles/doubles are ¥4500/7700; triples cost from ¥10,500 to ¥10,800.

The quickest way to get there is to take the subway from Kyoto station to Kitaoji station, walk east across the river and then turn north at the post office. To get there by bus, take bus No 205 from Kyoto station (bus terminal A3) and get off at the Furitsu-daigaku-mae stop.

Western Kyoto

Pension Arashiyama (☎ 075-881-2294) is a member of the Japanese Inn Group. Most of the rooms in this recently opened ryokan are

Western style. Singles/doubles are
¥4200/8400; triples cost ¥12,000. An American breakfast is available for ¥800.

To get there, take the 30 minute ride on
Kyoto bus Nos 71, 72 or 73 and get off at the
Arisugawa-mae stop.

PLACES TO STAY – TOP END
Central Kyoto
Ryokan Top-end ryokan accommodation in
Kyoto is, as you might expect, very expensive. Listed here are some of the ryokan that
occasionally have foreign guests.

Kinmata (☎ 075-221-1039) commenced
operations early in the last century and this
is reflected in the original décor, interior
gardens, antiques and *hinoki* (cypress) bathroom. Rooms cost from ¥25,000 to ¥35,000
per person, including two meals. Advance
reservation is essential. It's in the centre of
town, very close to the Nishiki-kōji market
– if you can afford to stay here, the cost of a
taxi will be a financial pinprick.

Hiiragiya (☎ 075-221-1136) is another
elegant ryokan favoured by celebrities from
East and West. Reservations are essential.
For a room and two meals, per-head costs
range from ¥30,000 to ¥80,000. Close by, the
Hiiragiya Annexe (☎ 075-231-0151) also
offers top-notch ryokan service and surroundings but at slightly more affordable
rates. Per-head costs range from ¥15,000 to
¥25,000 with two meals.

Tawaraya (☎ 075-211-5566) has been
operating for over three centuries and is
classed as one of the finest places to stay in
the world. Guests at this ryokan have
included the imperial family and royalty
from overseas. It is a classic in every sense.
Reservations are essential, preferably many
months ahead. Per head costs range from
¥33,000 to ¥75,000.

Hotels The up-market ryokan experience is
not for everyone, and there are a number of
high-class hotels in the central district.

Hotel Fujita Kyoto (☎ 075-222-1511) – singles cost
from ¥9800 to ¥17,000; twins from ¥14,500 to

¥31,000; doubles from ¥23,000 to ¥31,000; five
minutes walk from Marutomachi subway station
Holiday Inn Kyoto (☎ 075-721-3131) – economy
double for one/two persons costs ¥9000/13,000;
holiday doubles for one/two persons
¥10,000/14,000; free shuttle bus from south exit
of JR Kyoto station
International Hotel Kyoto (☎ 075-222-1111) –
singles cost from ¥9500 to ¥16,000; twins from
¥14,500 to ¥31,000; doubles from ¥23,000 to
¥27,000; 15 minutes by taxi from JR Kyoto
station
Kyoto Century Hotel (☎ 075-351-0111) – singles cost
from ¥9500 to ¥13,000; twins ¥19,000 to
¥22,000; doubles from ¥16,000 to ¥25,000; five
minutes walk from JR Kyoto station
Kyoto Grand Hotel (☎ 075-341-2311) – singles cost
from ¥12,000 to ¥17,000; twins/doubles from
¥18,000 to ¥26,000; 10 minutes walk from JR
Kyoto station
Kyoto New Hankyū Hotel (☎ 075-343-5300) – singles
cost from ¥10,000 to ¥12,000; twins from
¥17,000 to ¥27,000; doubles from ¥19,000 to
¥21,000; five minutes walk from JR Kyoto
station
Kyoto Tokyū Hotel (☎ 075-341-0111) – singles cost
from ¥12,000 to ¥13,000; twins from ¥14,500 to
¥40,000; doubles (only six) for ¥18,000; 15
minutes by taxi from JR Kyoto station

Eastern Kyoto
Yachiyo (☎ 075-771-4148) is an elegant
ryokan close to Nanzen-ji Temple. Prices per
person for a room and two meals range from
¥18,000 to ¥40,000.

Miyako Hotel (☎ 075-771-7111) is a
graceful, Western-style hotel perched up on
the hills and a classic choice for visiting
foreign dignitaries. The hotel surroundings
stretch over 6.4 hectares of wooded hillside
and landscaped gardens. For a change from
Western-style rooms, you could try the Japanese wing. Singles range from ¥15,000 to
¥19,000 and doubles range from ¥21,000 to
¥38,000.

OTHER ACCOMMODATION
Shukubō
Shukubō or temple lodgings are usually in
peaceful, attractive surroundings with
spartan tatami rooms, optional attendance at
early morning prayer sessions and an early
evening curfew. Guests use public baths near
the temples. There are quite a large number

of shukubō in Kyoto, but generally they are not interested in taking foreigners who cannot speak Japanese. The shukubō listed here have English speakers on hand. For more information and a list of the shukubō in Kyoto, check with the TIC.

Myōren-ji Temple (☎ 075-451-3527) charges ¥3500 with breakfast. Take bus No 9 from Kyoto station (bus terminal B1) to the Horikawa-Teranouchi-mae stop. *Hiden-in Temple* (☎ 075-561-8781) charges ¥4000 with breakfast. Take bus No 208 to the Sennyuji-michi-mae stop; another approach is to take the JR Nara line to Tōfuku-ji station.

Women-only Accommodation

In Japan's male-oriented society, this might be an interesting option for female travellers to explore. Generally, 'Ladies Hotels' feature rooms crammed with cuddly toys.

The *Kyoto Ladies Hotel* (☎ 075-561-3181) is near the southern end of Maruyama-kōen Park and has rooms from ¥4300 to ¥5900. Also in Higashiyama is *Uemura* (☎ 075-561-0377), a lady's ryokan close to Kōdai-ji Temple.

Rokuō-in Temple (☎ 861-1645) provides temple lodgings for women only – it's in western Kyoto, close to Rokuō-in station on the Keifuku Arashiyama line. Ask at the TIC for further information on these places and more ideas on the range of lodgings for women.

PLACES TO EAT

Kyoto is famed for *kyō-ryōri*, a local variation on *kaiseki* cuisine. Kaiseki features a wide range of Japanese dishes, and great attention is given to service. Sake accompanies the meal, and rice is served last. As you might expect, it's a very expensive experience. A modest kaiseki course might cost ¥6000 per person, a full spread ¥15,000, and then there are exclusive establishments where you can shell out ¥50,000 (if you are deemed fit to make a reservation). For lesser mortals with punier budgets, some restaurants do a kaiseki bentō (boxed lunch) at lunch time (11 am to 2 pm) at prices starting around ¥2000.

Another style of cooking for which Kyoto

is renowned is *shōjin ryōri*. This is a vegetarian cuisine (no meat, fish, eggs or dairy products are used), which was introduced from China along with Buddhism and is now available in special restaurants usually connected with temples. As it is a cuisine that has its origins in Buddhist asceticism, don't expect a hearty dig-in affair – great attention is given to presentation and dishes tend to be small tasters. Tōfu (bean curd) plays a prominent role in the menu and for a meal of this type, prices start at ¥2000.

The TIC and the Kyoto City Tourist Office have a *Kyoto Restaurant Guide* available free of charge. Another source of restaurant tips is the *IGS Kyoto Guide*, which is produced by the Kyoto Chamber of Commerce. It also includes information on shopping and hotels and is available at the TIC. *Old Kyoto: A Guide to Traditional Shops, Restaurants & Inns* would be a handy companion for extended exploration of Kyoto's culinary pleasures.

At the lower end of the food budget, there are plenty of fast-food eateries *(Shakey's Pizza, McDonald's, Kentucky Fried Chicken, Mr Donut*, etc) all over town.

Coffee shops and noodle restaurants are good for inexpensive meals or snacks. Good value is offered by the chain of *Doutor* coffee shops (big yellow and brown signs), which sell coffee for ¥190 and also have inexpensive snacks like cakes and hotdogs. Most of the major department stores have restaurants usually offering teishoku (set meals) which are good value at lunch time. Locals favour *Seven-Eight*, the 7th and 8th floors of Hankyū department store, which together form a large complex of inexpensive restaurants and are open until 10 pm. In the Porta shopping centre underneath Kyoto station there are also rows of restaurants with reasonable prices.

If you use the food section in the Facts for the Visitor chapter as a guide, you will soon develop your own skill at hunting for places to eat.

Japanese Cuisine

Central Kyoto Special mention is due to

Chikyuya, just around the corner from the Hankyū department store. This is a Kyoto institution, once the favoured haunt of Kyoto's alternative set and now doing a brisk business with a more mainstream clientele. Look for the queue outside. There's an Englshōgunnu (try the fried cheese) with an assortment of izakaya dishes. This is a place to get drunk and eat – cheap beer and sake – and watch out for the house speciality: the staff open the beer bottles with whatever happens to be on hand – chopsticks, ashtrays, lighters, big gaijin noses, whatever.

Taka Jyo (☎ 075-751-7090) is open daily from 11 am to 9.30 pm and serves noodles from ¥500 and a tempura bentō for ¥650. It's on Sanjō-dōri, about 100 metres east of Sanjō station. If you head west from this station along Sanjō-dōri, cross over the bridge and continue for about 150 metres, you'll find *Ukiya* (☎ 075-221-2978), a noodle restaurant on the right. Apart from inexpensive rice and noodle dishes (English menu), this place offers the free entertainment by way of daily noodle-making demonstrations between 2 and 4 pm. It's closed on Monday.

Gonbei (☎ 075-561-3350) is a well-known noodle restaurant in the heart of Gion, about 30 metres north of Shijō-dōri on Kiridoshi – look for the red lanterns outside. It is open until 11.30 pm but closed on Thursday.

The Pontochō area (a short walk north of Shijō-dōri) on the western bank of the Kamo-gawa River, there are clusters of exclusive riverside restaurants. *Yamatomi* (☎ 075-221-3268) is one of the cheaper places to sample a meal in this milieu. In the summer, there's a traditional dining platform outside, overlooking the river. The speciality of the house is *teppin-age*, a meal of vegetables, meat and seafood which you cook in a pot at your table. Set menus start at ¥2500. It's open from noon to midnight but is closed on Tuesday.

Eastern Kyoto In the Higashiyama area, tucked inside the north gate of Maruyama-kōen Park, there's a traditional restaurant

called *Hiranoya Honten* (☎ 075-561-1603) in restful surroundings. The speciality of the house is *imobō*, a meal made from a type of sweet potato and dried fish. Prices for a set meal start at ¥2000. It's open from 10.30 am to 8 pm.

If you walk north of Nanzen-ji Temple for a couple of minutes along the Path of Philosophy, you reach *Okutan* (☎ 075-771-8709), a restaurant inside the luxurious garden of Chōshō-in Temple. This is a popular place which has specialised in vegetarian temple food for hundreds of years. A course of 'yutōfu' (bean curd cooked in a pot) together with vegetable side dishes costs ¥3000. The restaurant is open from 10.30 am to 5.30 pm daily except Thursday.

About five minutes walk from Ginkaku-ji Temple, and virtually opposite the Ginkaku-ji-mae bus stop, is *Omen* (☎ 075-761-8926), a noodle shop named after the thick, white noodles *(omen)* it serves in a hot broth with vegetables. At ¥850, the noodles are reasonable value and the folksy décor is interesting – one drawback is that the place is often packed solid. It's open from 11 am to 11 pm daily except Thursday.

North-Western Kyoto You can combine a visit to Daitoku-ji Temple with a shōjin ryōri meal at *Izusen* (☎ 075-451-6665) inside the Daiji-in subtemple. It's open from 11 am to 5 pm and set meals start at ¥2500.

International Cuisine
Central Kyoto Central Kyoto, in particular the Kawaramachi area, is excellent for digging up reasonably priced alternatives to Japanese fare. To get an idea of what's available, the best starting place is Nishi-Kiyamachi-dōri (the one with a small canal running through the centre of it) and the lanes that run off it. There's a wide range of international and Japanese restaurants in this area, many with English menus.

One of the more interesting little restaurants actually on Kiyamachi-dōri is *Cous-Cous* (look for the English sign advertising African cuisine), a basement African restaurant with trendy décor and world music rhythms. Prices are reasonable (try the kuwa-kuwa – guinea fowl on a skewer – for ¥900) and the English-Japanese menu makes for easy ordering.

Not far from Cous-Cous is *Taj Mahal*, a branch of the successful Indian restaurant chain. Prices here are lower than in Tokyo branches, with huge vegetable thali sets ranging from ¥3000 and individual curries from ¥1000. Lunch time sets are also good value.

Also in the ethnic food line are a couple of pseudo-Balinese restaurants. *Bali Grill* is a small atmospheric little place on one of the alleys running off the southern end of Kiyamachi-dōri. It has dinner sets from ¥1800. *Curry Kingdom Balinesia* is further north on Kawamachi-dōri, and is slightly more expensive.

For inexpensive Italian food, top of anyone's list should be *Capricciosa*. This successful chain is renowned throughout Japan for its affordable and authentic pasta and pizza, delivered in enormous portions. Two portions here are easily enough to feed three people. Another place with an English menu and English-speaking staff is *Daniel's* (☎ 075-212-3268); during the day only pasta dishes are available, but by night the menu sports a wide variety of both pasta and pizza dishes. You can eat well here from around ¥1500. For more up-market Italian fare, check out *Pentola*, up on the northern end of Kiyamachi-dōri.

The *Ristorante Chiaro* (☎ 231-5547) does reasonable lunches from ¥850 (closed on Wednesday). It's opposite the Kyoto Royal Hotel on Kawaramachi-dōri (just north of the intersection with Sanjō-dōri). Near by is *Kerala* (☎ 251-0141), a restaurant serving regional Indian dishes; lunch prices start at ¥1500.

For Chinese food, *Gasshotei Gion* (☎ 531-2100) has prices starting at ¥800 and stays open until 3 am (closed on Sunday). It's on Tominagacho-dōri, one block north of Shijō-dōri.

Far East (☎ 252-2995) is a restaurant (open from 5 to 11 pm) and bar (open from 11 pm to 2 am), tucked down a side street off

the southern end of Kiyamachi-dōri. It's a popular meeting-point for locals and foreigners and prices start at ¥500 for all sorts of snacks, including Chinese food. There is a selection of international bottled beers at about ¥500 a bottle.

Eastern Kyoto A couple of minutes walk north of the Heian-jingū Shrine is *Time Paradox* (☎ 751-7531), a quirky eatery-cum-bar popular with university students and as a foreigners' den. The Western-style menu includes pizzas, omelettes, salads, soups, etc – prices start around ¥800. It's open from 5 pm to 1 am daily except Thursday.

Northern Kyoto *Knuckles Eatery* (☎ 441-5849) was started by an American to provide Western-style foods (knuckle sandwiches, bagels, cheesecake, etc). Even though management recently changed hands, it still remains a good place for authentic 'American cuisine'. It's on the southern side of Kitaoji-dōri at the Funaoka-kōen bus stop, two blocks east of Senbon-dōri. It's open from noon to 10 pm but closed on Monday.

The former owner of Knuckles now runs a 'California-style' restaurant known as *Fiasco* (☎ 075-415-0989). It looks set to develop into a popular spot, with an inventive menu, reasonable prices and live music performances on Saturday nights. Lunch time sets are ¥950 and are a good introduction to the restaurant. It's open 10 am to 11 pm, closed on Monday.

ENTERTAINMENT

Most of Kyoto's cultural entertainment is of an occasional nature, and you'll need to check with the TIC or a magazine like *Kansai Time Out* to find out whether anything interesting coincides with your visit. Regular cultural events are generally geared at the tourist market and tend to be expensive and, naturally, somewhat touristy.

While geisha entertainment is going to be well out of reach of all but the fabulously rich, Kyoto has a good variety of standard entertainment options: bars, clubs and discos, all of which are good places to meet young Japanese.

Traditional Dance & Theatre
Gion Corner (☎ 075-561-1119) presents shows every evening at 7.40 and 8.40 pm between 1 March and 29 November; it's closed on 16 August.

You should think carefully about whether tourist-oriented events of this kind are your scene before forking out the ¥2500 entry charge. While you get a chance to see snippets of the tea ceremony, Koto music, flower arrangement, gagaku (court music), kyōgen (ancient comic plays), Kyōmai (Kyoto-style dance) and bunraku (puppet play), you will be doing so with a couple of camera and video toting tour groups, and the presentation is a little on the tacky side. On top of this, 50 minutes of entertainment for ¥2500 is a little steep by anyone's standards. That said, if this is your only opportunity to dip into Japan's traditional entertainments and you have the cash, do it by all means – many people come away very pleased with the experience.

Dance The Miyako Odori (Cherry Blossom Dance) takes place four times a day throughout April at the Gion Kōbu Kaburen-jō Theatre, which adjoins Gion Corner. Maiko (apprentice geisha) dress elaborately to perform a sequence of traditional dances in praise of the seasons. The performances start in the afternoon at 12.30, 2, 3.30 and 4.50 pm. The cheapest ticket is ¥1650 (non-reserved on the tatami mat) and the ¥3800 ticket includes participation in a tea ceremony.

A similar series of dances, Kamogawa Odori, takes place from 1 to 24 May and from 15 October until 7 November at Pontochō Kaburen-jō Theatre (☎ 075-221-2025). Ticket prices start at ¥1650 (for a non-reserved seat on the 2nd floor).

Performances of *bugaku* (court music and dance) are often held in Kyoto shrines during festival periods. The TIC can provide information on performances.

Kabuki The Minami-za Theatre (☎ 075-561-0160) in Gion in central Kyoto is the oldest kabuki theatre in Japan. The major event of the year is the Kao-mise Festival (1 to 26 December) which features Japan's finest kabuki actors. Other performances take place infrequently and on an irregular basis. Those interested should check with the TIC. The most likely months for performances are May, June and September.

Nō For performances of Nō, the main theatres are Kanze Kaikan Nō Theatre (☎ 075-771-6114), Kongō Nō Stage (☎ 221-3049), and Kawamura Theatre (☎ 075-451-4513). Takigi-Nō is an especially picturesque form of Nō performed with lighting from blazing fires. In Kyoto, this takes place in the evenings of 1 and 2 June at Heian-jingū Shrine – tickets cost ¥2000 if you pay in advance (ask at the TIC for the location of ticket agencies) or pay ¥3000 at the entrance gate.

Musical Performances Musical performances featuring the koto, shamisen and shakuhachi are held in Kyoto on an irregular basis. The same is true of gagaku court music. Check with the TIC to see if any performances are scheduled to be held while you are in town.

Bars
Kyoto's more traditional nightlife is centred around Pontochō and Gion. Establishments with geisha entertainment are incredibly expensive – ¥100,000 for a night is quite normal – and usually require an introduction from a patron.

If you wander round Gion in the late afternoon or early evening, you can often catch sight of geisha or their apprentices (maiko) tripping off to an appointment. But for the average traveller, there will be little opportunity of falling through the backdoor into the world of geisha entertainment, and it's far more likely that you will end up knocking back a few beers or dancing in one of the bars or clubs that are frequented by mixed Japanese and gaijin crowds.

One of Kyoto's most popular gaijin hangouts is the *Pig & Whistle* (☎ 075-761-6022).

Like its counterparts in Osaka, it's an English-style pub with darts, pint glasses and (of course) fish & chips. Drunken giants should watch their heads on the rowing boat suspended from the ceiling. It's on the 2nd floor of the Shobi building, opposite Keihan-San-jō subway station.

Less British and more American in style is *Pub Africa*. It's not as good a place to meet people as the Pig & Whistle, mainly because the video screens showing movies tend to dominate everyone's attention, but it's still a good place for an early evening beer and something to eat. The menu is only in Japanese.

On the northern end of Kiyamachi-dōri, *Rub-a-Dub* is a funky little reggae bar with a shabby tropical look and good daiquiris. It's a good place for a quiet drink on weekdays, but on Friday and Saturday nights you'll have no choice but to bop along with the crowd.

A couple of other options exist in *Scoreboard* and *Backgammon*, two bars that are about as different as two bars could be. Scoreboard is a slick US-style 'sports bar', decorated with sporting paraphernalia and screening sporting events. Backgammon, on the other hand, is the kind of place where they hose out the drunks in the morning – loud metal sounds, an offbeat crowd, and look out for the upstairs dungeon connected to the action by an iron ladder. Enter at your own risk.

Another late night bar that's worth a recommendation is *Jam Rock House*. It's a little way south of the rest of the action on Kiyamachi-dōri (look for it on the left about 100 metres south of the Pink Tomato, which offers undisclosed sleazy services for Japanese salarymen). Jam Rock House has a great selection of records, and the young guy (Noaki) who runs the place is only too happy to take requests. The adventurous might want to try an 'Axl Rose' cocktail – 'for bad girls and boys only'.

On a final – and definitely not civilised – note, real late-nighters might want to check out *Step-Rampo*, a 10th floor bar with great views of Kyoto's nightlife area. The name means something like the 'faltering (literally 'chaotic') step', an appropriate name given that this place doesn't really get going until around 2 am, when it fills up with rejects from other Kyoto bars – one guy we met partied on here until 11 am one night.

Clubs
Yeah, you can dance the night away in the cultural heart of Japan and give the temples and shrines a miss the next day while you sleep off your hangover. One of the most popular places for this kind of thing is *Metro* (☎ 075-752-4765). It's part disco, part live house and even hosts the occasional art exhibition. Every night is a different theme (pick up a schedule in Rub-a-Dub), so it's a good idea to check ahead to make sure that it's not the once-a-month Diamond Night Transvestite Cabaret (or to make sure that it *is* the transvestite cabaret, whatever the case may be). Weekends usually feature an admission charge of ¥1500 to ¥2000 (with one drink), while Wednesday and Thursday are usually free. It's actually inside the No 2 exit of Keihan-Muratamachi subway station.

Teddy's has acquired something of a reputation as a gaijin dive, and things can get pretty rough here some nights, but (with the exception of Saturday night – ¥500) it doesn't have an entry charge and you can dance the night away for the price of a single beer (¥700) if you like – people do. In the same building are a couple of other gaijin hangouts you might like to take a look at: *Rag*, a popular live house, and *Cock-a-Hoop*, a very late night watering hole that serves as a magnet to Kyoto's alternative crowd in the early hours.

For straight disco action, *Maharahah* is part of the Tokyo (Aoyama) disco chain, and has become the focus of Kyoto's 'rave' nights. As John Ashburne from *Kansai Time Out* put it to us: 'it's part disco and part knocking-shop, full of poseurs and girls in impossibly short skirts dancing on tables with their nether regions at head height' – well, we wouldn't be seen dead in there...really...

THINGS TO BUY

Kyoto is brimming with tourist oriented shops. Even here in the cultural heart of Japan most of what's for sale is rubbish – ukiyoe T-shirts and cuddly toys. On the other hand, those in pursuit of a good souvenir to take home will have plenty of things to choose from – though it's worth shopping around a little for a good price.

The TIC provide shopping maps and can help you track down specialist shops. *Old Kyoto: A Guide to Traditional Shops, Restaurants & Inns* is useful for finding unusual traditional items sold (and often produced) by elegant shops with vintage character.

There are several crafts which are specific to Kyoto. *Kyō-ningyō* are display dolls, *kyō-shikki* is lacquerware with designs formed using gold or silver dust, *kyō-sensu* are ritual fans made from bamboo and Japanese paper, *kyō-yaki* are ceramics with elegant decorations, *zogan* is a damascene technique laying pure gold and silver onto figures engraved on brass, *nishijin-ori* is a special technique of silk textile weaving and *kyō-yūzen* is a form of silk-dyeing.

The main shopping haunts in the centre of town are around Kawaramachi-dōri, between Sanjō-dōri and Shijō-dōri. In the same area, Teramachi-dōri is lined with shopping arcades. In eastern Kyoto, the paved streets of Ninnen-zaka and Sannen-zaka (close to Kiyōmizu-dera Temple) are renowned for their crafts and antiques.

Kyoto's largest department stores (Hankyū, Takashimaya and Fujii Daimaru) are grouped on Shijō-dōri, close to Kawaramachi station. Kintetsu department store is one block north of the TIC.

If you want to do all your shopping under one roof, the following places offer a wide selection of Kyoto handicrafts. Kyoto Municipal Museum of Traditional Industry (☎ 075-761-3421), close to the Heian-jingū Shrine, holds exhibitions of Kyoto handicrafts and demonstrations of techniques. A selection of crafts is also on sale. Admission is free and it is open from 9 am to 4.30 pm but closed on Monday.

The Kyoto Craft Centre (☎ 075-561-9660) in Gion exhibits and sells handicrafts. It's open from 10 am to 6 pm daily except Wednesday.

The Kyoto Handicraft Centre (☎ 075-761-5080), just north of the Heian-jingū Shrine, is a huge cooperative which sells, demonstrates and exhibits crafts. It's open from 9.30 am to 6 pm.

If you are interested in seeing all the weird and wonderful foods required for cooking in Kyoto, wander through Nishiki-kōji market. It's in the centre of town, one block north of Shijō-dōri and just behind Daimaru department store.

Ippō-dō (☎ 075-211-4321) and Kungyoku-dō (☎ 075-371-0162) are two shops which are particularly appealing. Ippō-dō is an old-fashioned teashop selling all sorts of teas. Some English is spoken. It's on Teramachi-dōri, two blocks north of Kyoto City Hall and it's open from 9 am to 7 pm, closed on Sunday. Kungyoku-dō is a shop which has dealt in incense, herbs, spices and fine woods for four centuries. It's a haven for the olfactory senses, and is opposite the gate of the Nishi Hongan-ji Temple. It's open from 9 am to 7 pm but is closed on the first and third Sunday of each month.

For ideas about duty-free or discount items (cameras, hi-fi, watches, etc) you could try Ninomiya (☎ 075-361-7767). It's open daily from 10 am to 7 pm; closed on Wednesday.

Markets

On the third Saturday of each month, there is a flea market and general get-together of foreigners at the YWCA Thrift Shop, Muromachi-dōri, Demizu-agaru, Kamikyo-ku, Kyoto 602.

On the 21st of each month, there is a market fair, Kōbō-san, at Tōji Temple. On the 25th of each month, there's another market fair, Tenjin-san, at Kitano Tenman-gū Shrine. Arrive early and prepare to bargain.

GETTING THERE & AWAY

Air

Kyoto is served by Osaka Itami Airport – a major hub for domestic and international flights. The new Kansai International Airport was set to open in mid-1994 at the time of writing. There are frequent flights between Tokyo and Osaka – flight time is about 70 minutes but unless you are very lucky with airport connections you'd probably find it almost as quick and more convenient to take the shinkansen. The airport is an hour by bus from central Kyoto.

Train

Kyoto to Osaka If you are loaded with money, or have a Japan Rail Pass you can take the JR shinkansen line between Kyoto and Shin-Osaka – the trip takes only 16 minutes. To connect between Shin-Osaka and central Osaka, you can either take the JR Tōkaidō (San-yō) line to Osaka station or switch to the Mido-suji subway line for Osaka's Namba district.

The Japan Rail Pass is also valid on the JR Tōkaidō (San-yō) line which runs via Osaka. The trip between Kyoto and Osaka station takes 45 minutes and is ¥530 for a one-way ticket.

The Hankyū Kyoto line runs between Kyoto (Kawaramachi station) and Osaka (Umeda station – close to JR Osaka station). The fastest trip takes 47 minutes and is ¥330 for a one-way ticket.

The Keihan subway line in the east of Kyoto emerges from underground after Shijichō station and runs to Osaka's Yodoyabashi station, which is on the Mid-osuji subway line (convenient for connections with Shin-Osaka, Osaka and Namba). The fastest trip takes 40 minutes and costs ¥330 for a one-way ticket.

Kyoto to Nara Unless you have a Japan Rail Pass, the best option is the Kintetsu line linking Kyoto and Nara (Kintetsu Nara station) in 33 minutes by limited express (tokkyū) (¥900 one way). If you take a local or express train on this line, the ticket price drops to ¥500 for the 45 minute ride, but you will need to change at Yamato-Saidai-ji which is a five minute ride from Nara Kintetsu station.

The JR Nara line connects Kyoto with Nara JR station in one hour (¥740 one way).

Kyoto to Tokyo The JR shinkansen line is the fastest and most frequent rail link. The hikari super-express takes two hours and 40 minutes from Tokyo station and a one-way ticket including surcharges costs ¥12,970.

Unless you're travelling on a Japan Rail Pass or are in an extreme hurry, you'll probably be looking for a cheaper way to make the trip. Travelling by local trains takes around eight hours and involves at least two (often three or four) changes along the way. The fare is ¥7830, and you should call in to the TIC for details on the schedules and where changes are necessary for the particular time you are travelling.

Bus

JR buses run four times a day between Osaka and Tokyo via Kyoto and Nagoya. Passengers change buses at Nagoya. Travel time for the express buses between Kyoto and Nagoya is about 2½ hours (¥2200). The journey between Nagoya and Tokyo takes about 6¼ hours (¥5000). Other companies competing with JR on the same route include Meihan and Nikkyū. All buses run from the same point.

The overnight bus (JR Dream Bus) runs between Tokyo and Kyoto (departures in both directions). The trip takes about eight hours and there are usually two departures, at 10 and 11 pm. Tickets are ¥8030 plus a reservation fee. You should be able to grab some sleep in the reclining seats. If you find sleep a bit of a struggle, you can console yourself with the thought that you are saving on accommodation and will be arriving at the crack of dawn to make good use of the day. Buses run either to Yaesu bus terminal close to Tokyo station or to Shinjuku station.

Other JR bus possibilities include Kanazawa (¥3990), Tottori (¥3800), Hiroshima (¥5500), Nagasaki (¥11,100), Kumamoto (¥10,500), Fukuoka (¥9500), Kagoshima (¥12,600).

Hitching

For long-distance hitching, the best bet is to head for the Kyoto-Minami Interchange of the Meishin expressway which is about four km south of Kyoto station. Take the Toku No 19 bus (make sure the kanji for 'special' (toku) precedes the number) from Kyoto station and get off when you reach the Meishin expressway signs.

From here you can hitch east towards Tokyo or west to southern Japan.

GETTING AROUND
To/From the Airport

There are frequent airport limousine buses running between Osaka airport and Kyoto station. Buses also run between the airport and various hotels around town, but on a less regular basis. The journey should take around 55 minutes and the cost is ¥890.

The new Kansai International Airport will change this situation, but at the time of writing there were no details available on transport between the airport and Kyoto.

Bus

Kyoto has an intricate network of bus routes which provides an efficient way of getting around at moderate cost. Many of the bus routes used by foreign visitors have announcements in English. The core timetable for buses is between 7 am and 9 pm though a few run earlier or later.

The main bus terminals are Kyoto station, Keihan-San-jō station, and Karasuma-Shijō-station. On the northern side of Kyoto station is a major bus terminus with departure terminals clearly marked with a letter of the alphabet and a number.

The TIC has two bus maps: a simplified map on the reverse of the *Kyoto, Nara* brochure and a bus route map, studded with kanji, for advanced bus explorers.

Bus stops throughout the city usually display a map of bus stops in the vicinity on the top section. On the bottom section there's a timetable for the buses serving that stop.

Entry to the bus is usually through the back door and exit is via the front door. Inner city buses charge a flat fare (¥180) which you drop into a machine next to the driver. The machine gives change for ¥100 and ¥500 coins or ¥1000 notes, or you can ask the driver.

On buses serving the outer areas, you take a numbered ticket (*seiri-ken*) when entering. When you leave, an electronic board above the driver displays the fare corresponding to your ticket number.

To save time and money, you can buy a *kaisū-ken* (book of six tickets) for ¥1000 at bus centres or from the driver. There is also a deal offering 11 tickets for the price of 10.

There's a one-day pass (*ichinichi jōsha-ken*), which is valid for unlimited travel on city buses, private Kyoto buses and the subway. It costs ¥1050 and is available at bus centres and subway stations. A two-day pass (*futsuka jōshā-ken*), is also available and costs ¥2000. The passes can be picked up in subway stations and the City Information Office.

Bus No 59 is useful for travel between the sights of north-western Kyoto and Keihan-San-jō station. Bus No 5 connects Kyoto station with the sights of eastern Kyoto.

Three-digit numbers denote loop lines. Bus No 204 runs round the northern part of the city and Nos 205 and 206 circle the city via Kyoto station.

Subway

The quickest way to travel between the north and the south of the city is to take the subway, which operates from 5.30 am to 11.30 pm. There are eight stops, though the most useful ones are those in the centre of town. The minimum fare is ¥160.

Taxi

Kyoto is well-endowed with taxis. Fares start at ¥530 or ¥540, depending on the taxi, for the first two km.

MK Taxi (☎ 075-721-2237) provides a regular taxi service as well as tours with English-speaking drivers. For a group of up to four people, prices start at ¥12,620 for a three hour tour. Another company offering a

Bicycle

Renting a bicycle makes sense in peripheral areas of Kyoto such as Higashiyama, Arashiyama or northern Kyoto. Dense traffic in central Kyoto makes cycling unpleasant. Compared with bus travel, the savings on bicycle rental are minimal, but you can stop as you please. On the other hand, many of the peripheral areas are easily and enjoyably covered on foot.

Both the youth hostels at Higashiyama and Utano provide bicycle rental. In Higashiyama you could try Taki Rent-a-Bicycle on Kaminokuchi, east of Kawaramachi. Arashiyama station has several places for bicycle rental. Nippon Rent-a-Cycle is in front of the southern side of Kyoto station, close to the Hachijō west exit. Expect rental rates of around ¥1100 per day, but different rates apply depending on the kind of bicycle.

Lake Biwa-ko   琵琶湖

Lake Biwa-ko, Japan's largest freshwater lake, dominates Shiga Prefecture . The lake has a variety of attractions easily visited as day trips from Kyoto or as stop-offs when travelling to or from Tokyo. Ōtsu and Hikone are the major sightseeing centres. Mt Hiei-zan and Enryaku-ji Temple are covered under Northern Kyoto in the earlier Kyoto section of this chapter.

JNTO publishes a leaflet entitled *Lake Biwa, Ōtsu & Hikone*, which has useful mapping and concise information. The Kyoto TIC has more detailed information on transport, sights and events in this region.

If you want to stay overnight near the lake rather than staying in Kyoto, the main centres for accommodation are Omi-hachiman, Ōtsu and Hikone. There are youth hostels dotted around the lake, for example, at Ōmi-imazu (☎ 0740-25-3018), Ōmi-hachiman (☎ 0748-32-2938) and Ōtsu (☎ 0775-22-8009).

ŌTSU   大津

Ōtsu (population 260,000) developed from a 7th century imperial residence (the city was capital of Japan for a brief five years) into a lake port and major post station on the Tōkaidō highway between eastern and western Japan. It is now the capital of Shiga-ken. Ōtsu-e paintings are part of a folk tradition dating back to the Edo period, when the pictures were bought by pilgrims as souvenirs. They remain popular in this respect, though experts claim (they would, wouldn't they) that standards have slipped.

The information office (☎ 0755-22-3830) at the JR Ōtsu station is open from 8.45 am to 5 pm daily.

Mii-dera Temple   三井寺

Mii-dera Temple, formally known as Onjō-ji Temple, is a 10 minute walk from Hama-Ōtsu station. The temple, founded in the late 7th century, is the head branch of the Jimon branch of the Tendai school of Buddhism. It started its days as a branch of Enryaku-ji Temple on Mt Hiei-zan, but later the two fell into conflict, and Mii-dera was repeatedly razed by Enryaku-ji's warrior monks.

Admission costs ¥450. It's open from 8 am to 5 pm but closes half an hour earlier between November and March.

The Michigan   ミシガン

This reconstruction of a Mississippi paddle-wheel boat departs from Hama-Ōtsu Pier for trips on the lake. Fares start at ¥2400 (economy class) for 90 minute trips and there are special show-boat (Dixieland Jazz) and night-boat cruises with prices starting at ¥4600 (economy class). For reservations call the Biwa-ko Kisen Boat Company (☎ 0775-24-5000).

Festivals

The Ōtsu Matsuri Festival takes place on 9 and 10 October at Tenson-jinja Shrine which is close to JR Ōtsu station. Ornate floats are

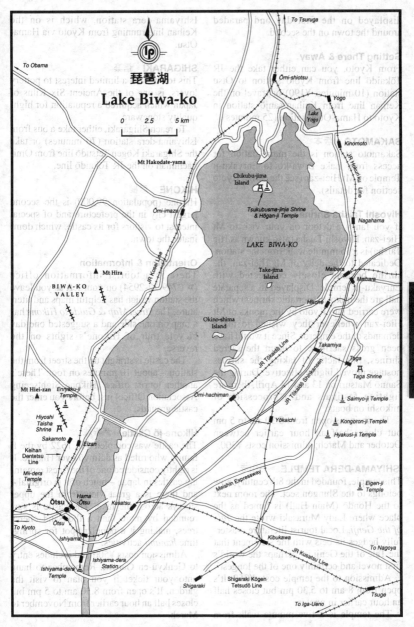

琵琶湖
Lake Biwa-ko

0   2.5   5 km

To Obama

To Tsuruga

Ōmi-shiotsu

Yogo

Lake
Yogo

Kinomoto

JR Hokuriku Line

Nagahama

Maibara

Chikubu-jima
Island

Tsukubusuma-jinja Shrine
& Hōgon-ji Temple

LAKE BIWA-KO

Take-jima
Island

Hikone

JR Tōkaidō Line

JR Kosei Line

Mt Hakodate-yama

Ōmi-imazu

BIWA-KO
VALLEY

Mt Hira

Okino-shima
Island

Takamiya

Taga

Taga Shrine

Saimyo-ji Temple

JR Tōkaidō Shinkansen

Ōmi-hachiman

Kongoron-ji Temple

Yōkaichi

Hyakusi-ji Temple

Mt Hiei-zan

Enryaku-ji
Temple

Hiyoshi
Taisha
Shrine

Sakamoto

Eizan

Keihan
Dentetsu
Line

Mii-dera
Temple

Eigen-ji
Temple

Ōtsu

Hama-
Ōtsu

Kusatsu

Meishin Expressway

To Kyoto

Ōtsu

Ishiyama

Kibukawa

JR Kusatsu Line

To Nagoya

Ishiyama-dera
Temple

Ishiyama-dera
Station

Shigaraki

Shigaraki Kōgen
Tetsudō Line

Tsuge

To Iga-Ueno

displayed on the first day and paraded around the town on the second.

Getting There & Away

From Kyoto, you can either take the JR Tōkaidō line from Kyoto station to Ōtsu station (10 minutes, ¥190) or travel on the Keihan line from Keihan-sanjō station in Kyoto to Hama-Ōtsu station (25 minutes).

SAKAMOTO 坂本

Sakamoto station is the main station for access from Lake Biwa-ko to Enryaku-ji Temple on Mt Hiei-zan (see the earlier Kyoto section for details).

Hiyoshi Taisha Shrine 日吉大社

If you fancy a detour on your visit to Mt Hiei-zan, Hiyoshi Taisha (also known as Hie Taisha) is a 15 minute walk from the station. Dedicated to the deity of Mt Hiei-zan, the shrine became closely connected with Enryaku-ji Temple. Displayed in a separate hall are the mikoshi (portable shrines) which were carried into Kyoto by the monks of Mt Hiei-zan whenever they wished to make demands of the emperor. Since it would have been gross sacrilege to harm the sacred shrines, this tactic of taking the shrines hostage proved highly effective. During the Sannō Matsuri on 13 and 14 April, there are fighting festivals and a procession of mikoshi on boats.

The shrine is open from 8.30 am to 5 pm but closes half an hour earlier between October and March; admission costs ¥300.

ISHIYAMA-DERA TEMPLE 石山寺

This temple, founded in the 8th century, now belongs to the Shingon sect. The room next to the Hondō (Main Hall) is famed as the place where Lady Murasaki wrote the *Tale of the Genji*. Local tourist literature masterfully hedges its bets with the statement that the Tale of the Genji is 'perhaps the world's first novel and certainly one of the longest'.

Admission to the temple costs ¥350. It's open from 8 am to 5.30 pm but closes half an hour earlier in winter.

The temple is a five minute walk from

Ishiyama-dera station, which is on the Keihan line running from Kyoto via Hama-Ōtsu.

SHIGARAKI 信楽

This town, with a limited interest to pottery lovers, is one of the Ancient Six Kilns of Japan which acquired a reputation for high-quality stoneware.

To reach Shigaraki, either take a bus from Ishiyama-dera station (70 minutes) or take the Shigaraki Kōgen Tetsudō line from Ōmi-hachiman on the JR Tōkaidō line.

HIKONE 彦根

Hikone (population 99,000) is the second largest city in the prefecture and of special interest to visitors for its castle, which dominates the town.

Orientation & Information

There is a tourist information office (☎ 0749-22-2954) on your left as you leave the station which has helpful maps and literature. The *Street Map & Guide to Hikone* has a map on one side and a suggested one-day bicycle tour of Hikone's sights on the reverse.

The castle is straight up the street from the station – about 10 minutes on foot. There's another tourist office (Hikone Sightseeing Association Office) just before you enter the castle grounds.

Hikone-jō Castle 彦根城

The castle was completed in 1622 by the Ii family who ruled as daimyō over Hikone. It is rightly considered one of the finest remaining castles in Japan – much of it is original – and there is a great view from the upper storeys across the lake. The castle is surrounded by more than a thousand cherry trees, making it a popular spot for springtime *hanami* activities.

Admission costs ¥500 and includes entry to Genkyū-en Garden. Remember to hang onto your ticket if you plan to visit the garden. It's open from 8.30 am to 5 pm but closes half an hour earlier from November to March.

Next to the main gate of the castle is Hikone-jō Castle Museum. Items on display came from the Ii family and include armour, Nō costumes, pottery and calligraphy. Admission costs ¥500 and it's open from 9 am to 4 pm.

Genkyū-en Garden below the castle is an attractive stroll garden. Buy yourself a bag of fish food for ¥20 at the gate and copy the other visitors who save the bloated carp the effort of movement by lobbing morsels straight into their blubbery lips. It's a tough life being an ornamental carp in Japan! Entry to this garden is included in the admission ticket for the castle.

Other Attractions

If you have more time in Hikone, you can follow the cycling route in the *Street Map & Guide to Hikone*. The route passes through the old town to the west of the castle, then south-west via Ichiba (Market Street) to Kawaramachi, where you can take a look at a candle-maker's shop (this is also the bar and nightlife district for Hikone) and then crosses to the other side of the Seri River.

From there, you can cross the town and visit a couple of Zen temples in the southeast. The most interesting of these is Ryōtan-ji Temple, which has a fine Zen garden. Admission to the temple costs ¥300 and it's open from 9 am to 5 pm but closes an hour earlier between December and February.

Cruises

There are four-times-daily departures from Hikone to Chikubu-jima Island (¥3240, return) – rather pricey given that it's only a 35 minute trip. There are also several daily departures to Take-jima Island (¥1700, 30 minutes).

Festivals

Hikone-jō Matsuri takes place at the castle on 3 November. Children dress up in the costume of feudal lords and parade around the area.

Getting There & Away

Hikone is only one hour (¥1090) from Kyoto on the JR Tōkaidō line. If you take the shinkansen, the best method is to ride from Kyoto to Maibara (25 minutes) and then backtrack from there on the JR Tōkaidō line to Hikone (10 minutes). Maibara is useful to travellers as a major rail junction for the JR Tōkaidō line, JR Hokuriku line and JR shinkansen line. From Osaka it takes 1½ hours (¥1850) via the Tōkaidō line to Hikone.

NAGAHAMA   長浜

Nagahama's main claim to fame is the Nagahama Hikiyama Matsuri held from 14 to 26 April. Costumed children perform Hikiyama kyōgen (comic drama) on top of a dozen festival floats which are decked out with elaborate ornamentation.

Nagahama is a 10 minute ride north of Maibara on the JR Hokuriku line. From Nagahama there are frequent boats making the 25 minute trip to Chikubu-jima Island.

CHIKUBU-JIMA ISLAND   竹生島

This tiny island is famed for its Tsukubusuma-jinja Shrine and the Hōgon-ji Temple which is one of those included on the Kansai Kannon temple pilgrimage.

The island is connected by boat with Hama-Ōtsu, Hikone, Nagahama and Ōmiimazu. Prices and departure times tend to vary so check them with the Kyoto TIC or the Hikone tourist information office.

Osaka   大阪

Osaka (population 2.6 million) is a difficult city to sum up. Second only to Tokyo in economic importance (third, after Yokohama, in population), Osaka suffers from even more of a lack of open spaces, greenery and historical sites than Japan's capital city.

There's no use pretending that it's an attraction for the average visiting foreigner, but for those who are not visiting Tokyo and who are basing themselves in, say, Kyoto, there's something to be said for at least making a day trip to Osaka and dipping into the modern Japanese urban experience. Despite its lack of major attractions, Osaka is a bustling, vibrant city with great dining, good nightlife and a mind-boggling selection of shopping areas.

HISTORY

Osaka was a trading port as far back as the 7th century, but it wasn't until the late 16th century that the city rose to prominence. It was at this time that Toyotomi Hideyoshi, having unified all of Japan, chose Osaka as the site for his castle. Merchants set up around the castle and the city quickly grew into a flourishing economic centre.

Even though the Toyotomi clan was defeated by the Tokugawas early in the 17th century, in a conflict that saw Osaka Castle razed to the ground, the Tokugawas rebuilt the castle and the city maintained its importance.

Today the Osaka region's economy is actually larger than that of entire developed countries like Canada and Australia. It has even been argued that, given the very real risks of another major earthquake levelling Tokyo, Osaka might one day take over from Tokyo as Japan's capital city. Whatever the future might hold for Osaka, its residents have a fierce pride in their city and tend to be a little contemptuous of all the attention that is received by Tokyo.

ORIENTATION

Umeda, in Kita-ku, the northern ward, and Shinsaibashi and Namba, in Minami-ku, the southern ward each have distinct features. Kita-ku is the business part of town with a scattering of high-rises and trendy department stores, while Minami-ku, with its bustling entertainment quarters, great restaurants and discount shopping, is a far more exciting part of town to look around if you just have a short stay in town.

Osaka station is in Umeda, but if you're coming from Tokyo by shinkansen you will arrive at Shin-Osaka station, which is to the north of Osaka station. Osaka station is two

stops, or about 10 minutes from Shin-Osaka by subway on the Mido-suji line. The same line continues to Minami-ku, probably the best area to be based in if you can afford the the hotel rates.

INFORMATION

The Osaka Tourist Association has offices at both Shin-Osaka (☎ 06-305-3311) and Osaka (☎ 06-345-2189) stations, though the main office is the one in Osaka station. Both are open from 8 am to 8 pm. Many travellers have problems finding the tourist office in Osaka station. It's in the south-east corner of the station complex, and to find it you should take the Midōsuji exit. Osaka airport also has an information counter (☎ 06-856-6781). All three offices can help with booking accommodation, but you will have to visit the office in person for this service.

Information available at the tourist offices include two excellent publications: *Osaka – information of Osaka city*, a fold out map with essential information on the reverse side, and the *Osaka Visitor's Guide*, a monthly magazine with maps, what's-on listings, as well as a restaurant and hotel guide.

Also available and worth picking up are *Meet Osaka*, a pocket-size reference guide and *Subway Lines in Osaka*, a fold-out rail guide to the Osaka region. A new addition to the above is *Streetalk*, an excellent publication with maps and information on restaurants and nightlife in both Osaka and Kōbe. Those planning on setting up house in Osaka should look out for *Kansai Flea Market*, a small monthly that has accommodation, employment and nightlife notices. It's also available from the information counters. Finally, see the Kyoto section for information on *Kansai Time Out*.

Post & Telecommunications

The main post office (☎ 06-347-8034) is between Osaka and Umeda stations. For telex and fax services try the major hotels or the international telegraph and telephone office (KDD) (☎ 06-343-2571) in Umeda's Shin-Hanshin building.

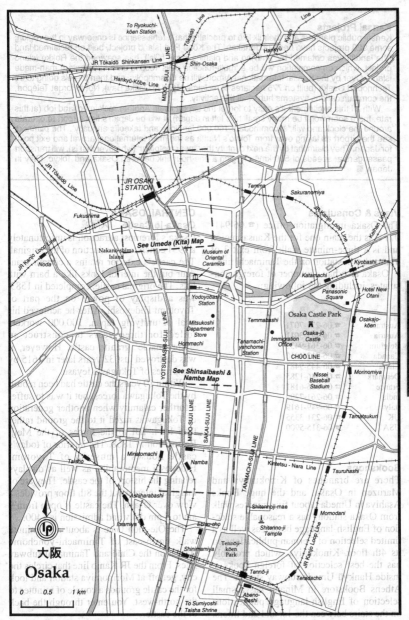

KANSAI REGION

To Ryokuchi-kōen Station

Tōkaidō Line

Kyoto Line

Hankyū

JR Tōkaidō Shinkansen Line

Shin-Osaka

MIDŌ - SUJI LINE

Hankyū-Kōbe Line

JR Tōkaidō Line

JR Kanjō Loop Line

JR OSAKI STATION

Temma

Sakuranomiya

JR Kanjō Loop Line

Keihan Line

Fukushima

See Umeda (Kita) Map

Nakanoshima Island

Museum of Oriental Ceramics

Kyobashi

Katamachi

Panasonic Square

Hotel New Otani

JR Kanjō Loop Line

Noda

Yodoyabashi Station

Mitsukoshi Department Store

Honmachi

Temmabashi

Tanamachi-yonchome Station

Osaka Castle Park

Immigration Office

Osaka-jō Castle

Osakajo-kōen

YOTSUBASHI SUJI LINE

CHŪŌ LINE

See Shinsaibashi & Namba Map

Nissei Baseball Stadium

Morinomiya

MIDŌ-SUJI LINE

SAKAI-SUJI LINE

TANIMACHI-SUJI LINE

Tamatsukun

Taishō

Minatomachi

Namba

Kintetsu - Nara Line

Tsuruhashi

Ashiharabashi

Shitennōji-mae

Momodani

Iとамiya

Ebisu-chō

Shitennō-ji Temple

大阪

Shinimamiya

Tennōji-kōen Park

JR Kanjō Loop Line

Osaka

Tennō-ji

Tennō-ji

Teradacho

0   0.5   1 km

Abeno-Bashi

To Sumiyoshi Taisha Shrine

Kansai Projects

Kansai public planners and their ilk like to proclaim that a renaissance is underway in the region; some 920 projects have been undertaken. The Kōbe Port Island project, built on reclaimed land (the landfill was obtained by 'shaving and planing small hills'), has spawned the Rokko Island project, which on completion will be a 'multi-function polis' resting on a 520 hectare man-made island. Over by the Kansai International Airport will be Cosmopolis, and then there's going to be Technoport Osaka (built on 775 hectares of reclaimed land in Osaka Bay). Not to forget Teleport, the communications systems hub of all this activity.

With all this excitement it's easy to forget the airport itself. Another reclaimed land job (at this rate, there soon won't be many small hills left in Japan), it will be Japan's first airport to operate around the clock and will 'accommodate 160,000 landings and takeoffs annually'. The planners see the airport as taking over from Tokyo's Narita as the main international arrival and exit point for Japan. They claim that by the next century the 'linear motorcar' (whatever that is), will transport passengers at speeds of 500 km/h, forging a one-hour link between Osaka and Tokyo. Only in Japan. ■

Visas & Consulates

The Osaka immigration office (☎ 06-941-0771) is the main one for the Kansai region and is a three-minute walk from exit 3 of Temmabashi station on the Tanimachi line.

Osaka also has a number of foreign consulates, including the following:

Australia	☎ 06-271-7071
Austria	☎ 06-241-3011
Belgium	☎ 06-361-9432
Canada	☎ 06-212-4910
China	☎ 06-445-9481
Denmark	☎ 06-346-1285
France	☎ 06-946-6181
India	☎ 06-261-7299
Italy	☎ 06-949-1619
UK	☎ 06-231-3355
USA	☎ 06-315-5900

Bookshops

There are branches of Kinokuniya and Maruzen in Osaka, and the huge Books Asahiya in Umeda (about five minutes walk from Osaka station) has a reasonable selection of English-language books, as well as a limited selection of German publications on its 4th floor. Kinokuniya, which probably has the best selection of foreign books is inside Hankyū Umeda subway station. The Athens Bookstore in Minami has a small selection of English-language publications on the stairs between the 1st and 2nd floors.

CENTRAL OSAKA

Osaka-jō Castle　大阪城

Osaka's foremost attraction is unfortunately a 1931 concrete reproduction of the original. The castle's exterior retains a certain grandeur but the interior looks like a barn with lifts. The original castle, completed in 1583, was a display of power on the part of Toyotomi Hideyoshi. After he achieved his goal of unifying Japan, 100,000 workers toiled for three years to construct an 'impregnable' granite castle. However, it was destroyed just 32 years later in 1615 by the armies of Tokugawa Ieyasu.

Within 10 years the castle had been rebuilt by the Tokugawa forces, but it was to suffer a further calamity when another generation of Tokugawas razed it to the ground rather than let it fall to the forces of the Meiji Restoration in 1868. The interior of today's castle houses a museum of Toyotomi Hideyoshi memorabilia as well as displays relating to the history of the castle. They are of marginal interest but the 8th floor provides a view over Osaka. The castle is open from 9 am to 5 pm daily and admission is ¥400.

The Ōte-mon Gate is about a 10 minute walk north-east of Tanimachi-yonchōme station on the Chūō and Tanimachi subway lines. From the JR Kanjo line that circles the city, get off at Morinomiya station and look for the castle grounds a couple of minutes to the north-west. You enter through the back of the castle.

Shitennō-ji Temple　四天王寺

Shitennō-ji Temple, founded in 593, has the distinction of being one of the oldest Buddhist temples in Japan, but none of today's buildings are originals.

Most are the usual concrete reproductions but an exception, and a feature that is quite unusual for a Buddhist temple, is the big stone torii (entrance gate). It dates back to 1294, making it the oldest of its kind in Japan. Apart from the torii, there is little of real historical significance, and the absence of greenery in the raked-gravel grounds makes for a rather desolate atmosphere.

The temple is open from 9 am to 5 pm daily and admission is ¥500. It's most easily reached from Shitennōji-mae station on the Tanimachi line. Take the southern exit, cross to the left side of the road and take the small road that goes off at an angle away from the subway station. The entrance to the temple is on the left.

Tennōji-kōen Park　天王寺公園

About a 10 minute walk from the temple with which it shares its name, this park can be combined with a visit to Shitennō-ji Temple, although its prime attraction, the Keitaku-en Garden, has rather irregular opening hours.

The park has a botanical garden, a zoo and a circular garden known as Keitaku-en. The latter is only open from 9 am to 4.30 pm on Tuesday, Thursday and Sunday. The park is a 10 minute walk from Tennō-ji station on the JR Kanjo line. To get there from the Shitennō-ji Temple, exit through the torii, turn left, then right, then left again into the main road and look for the park on your right.

Sumiyoshi Taisha Shrine　住吉大社

This shrine is dedicated to Shintō deities associated with the sea and sea travel, in commemoration of a safe passage to Korea by a 3rd century empress.

Having survived the bombing in WW II, the Sumiyoshi Taisha Shrine actually has a couple of buildings that date back to 1810. The shrine was founded in the early 3rd century and the buildings that can be seen today are faithful replicas of the originals. They offer a rare opportunity to see a Shintō shrine that predates the influence of Chinese Buddhist architectural styles.

The main buildings are roofed with a kind of thatch rather than the tiles on most later shrines. Other interesting features are a collection of more than 700 stone lanterns donated by seafarers and businesspeople, a stone stage for performances of bugaku and court dancing and the attractive Taiko-bashi Bridge, an arched bridge with park surroundings.

The shrine is next to both Sumiyoshi-taisha station on the Nankai line and Sumiyoshi-tori-mae station on the Hankai line.

KITA-KU　キタ

There's not a lot to do in Kita-ku and if you've passed through the area on your arrival that might be enough to get a feel for what the northern part of town is about.

Umeda Sky Building

Just to the north-west of Osaka station, the Umeda Sky building is a twin-tower complex with the two towers joined at the top. There are viewing platforms, restaurants, cinemas. Buildings like this are springing up all over Japan, and unless you are a real architectural buff, once is generally enough for most people.

Hankyū Grand Building

This 32 storeyed building next to Osaka station is renowned for its restaurants which occupy the 27th to 31st floors – not a bad place to check out the lunch-time specials, though its prestige rating nudges the prices up a little. There is a free lookout on the 32nd floor.

Umeda Chika Centre

This labyrinthine underground shopping

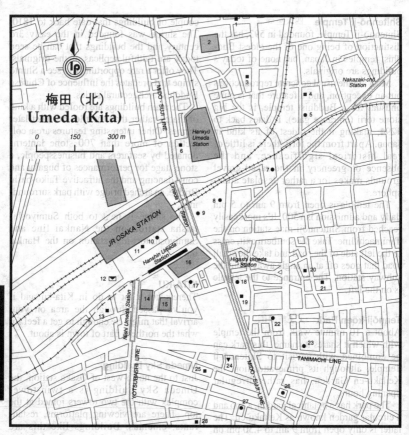

梅田（北）
Umeda (Kita)

0   150   300 m

complex can easily keep you occupied for a few hours with everything from cheap eats to antiques. The complex links Osaka station with Umeda station and can be entered from either.

Museum of Oriental Ceramics
With more than 1000 exhibits the museum is claimed to have one of the finest collections of Chinese and Korean ceramics in the world. Opening hours are from 9.30 am to 5 pm daily (closed on Monday) and admission is ¥400.

To get to the museum, go to Yodoyobashi

station on either the Mido-suji line or the Keihan line (different stations). Walk north to the river and cross to Nakano-shima Island. Turn right, pass the city hall on your left, bear left with the road and the museum is on the left.

Panasonic Square パナソニックスクエア
Billed as a 'Futuristic Electro-Fun Zone', Panasonic Square is a display forum for high-tech gadgetry developed by the Matsushita Electric Group of companies. It's very much hands-on and quite fun if you haven't already been to a similar place in

PLACES TO STAY			
1	Hotel Sunroute Umeda ホテルサンルート梅田	21	Hotel Kansai ホテル関西
2	Hotel Hankyū International ホテル阪急インターナショナル	25	Hotel New Central ホテルニューセントラル
3	Osaka Tōkyū Hotel 大阪東急ホテル	28	ANA Sheraton Hotel Osaka 大阪全日空ホテルシェラトン
4	Hotel Green Plaza Osaka ホテルグリーンプラザ大阪		
6	Hotel New Hankyū 新阪急ホテル		
11	Osaka Terminal Hotel 大阪ターミナルホテル		
13	Hotel Hanshin ホテル阪神		
14	Osaka Hilton 大阪ヒルトン		
15	Dai-ichi Hotel 大阪第一ホテル		
19	Umeda OS Hotel 梅田OSホテル		
20	Hokke Club Osaka 法華クラブ大阪店		

PLACES TO EAT		
24	Canopy Restaurant/Bar キャノピーレストラン	

OTHER		
5	Osaka Nō Theatre 大阪文楽劇場	
7	A'cross Travel アクロストラベル	
8	Hankyū Grand Building 阪急グランドビル	
9	Hankyū Department Store 阪急デパート	
10	Daimaru Department Store 大丸デパート	
12	Central Post Office 中央郵便局	
16	Hanshin Department Store 阪神デパート	
17	New Hankyū Building 新阪急ビル	
18	Books Asahiya 朝日屋書店	
22	Pig & Whistle Bar ピッグアンドウィッスル	
23	Umeda Gallery of Modern Art 梅田近代美術館	
26	American Consulate アメリカ領事館	
27	Bar Isn't It バーイズントイット	

KANSAI REGION

Japan. Highlights include Adventure Spaceship where multi-screen video projectors give you the illusion of approaching earth from outer space and a CD jukebox that you enter and request songs from by punching in a number.

Panasonic Square is open from 10 am to 6 pm daily except Wednesday and admission is ¥200. The easiest way to get there is to take the Keihan line to Kyōbashi station, take the southern exit, cross the river and turn right. Panasonic Square is on the 2nd floor of the Twin 21 Tower building.

MINAMI-KU ミナミ

This part of town south of Shinsaibashi subway station (on the Mido-suji line) is fun just to wander around but it really doesn't come into its own until night falls and the blaze of neon charges the atmosphere. North of Dōtomburi, between Midosuji-dōri and Sakaisuji-dōri, the narrow streets are crowded with hostess bars, discos and pubs. Expensive cars clog the streets, hostesses dressed in kimono and geta trot a few steps behind flushed businessmen, and young salarymen stagger around in drunken packs.

Amerika-Mura

Amerika-mura, or America village, is a compact enclave of trendy shops and restaurants (with a few discreet love hotels thrown in for good measure) that's worth a short stroll. Highlights include colourful graffiti, a massive Tower Records, the futuristic Wave complex, the ultra-kitsch Disney store (stock up on your Mickey Mice here) and the general ambience, courtesy of hordes of colourful Japanese teenies living out the myth of *Amerika*.

In the middle of Amerika-mura is a small 'park' (all concrete) area with benches. It's a good place to sit down for a while and watch the action.

Dōtomburi

You can start by exploring the wall-to-wall restaurants along the south bank of the Dōtomburi-gawa Canal, though don't restrict your gaze to ground level – almost every building has three or four floors of restaurants with prices ranging from reasonable to sky-high. South of Dōtomburi down to Namba station is a maze of colourful arcades with more restaurants, pachinko par-

KANSAI REGION

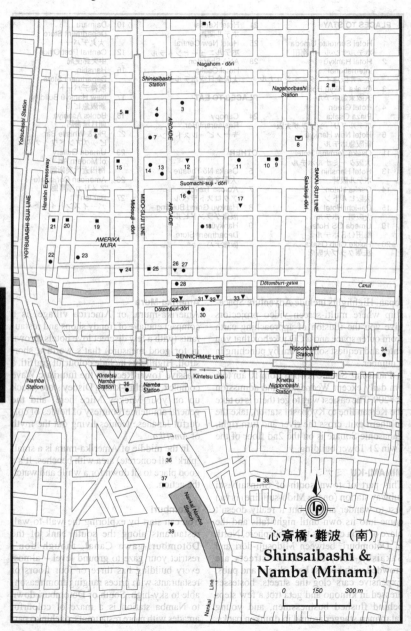

Nagahori - dōri

Shinsaibashi
Station

Nagahoribashi
Station

■ 1

■ 2

Yotsubashi Station

Hanshin Expressway

YOTSUBASHI-SUJI LINE

MIDŌSUJI-SUJI LINE

Midōsuji - dōri

SAKAI-SUJI LINE

Sakaisuji-dōri

ARCADE

ARCADE

● 5
● 4
● 3

● 7

● 15
● 14 ● 13
▼ 12
● 11
■ 10 ● 9
■

☑ 8

Suomachi-suji - dōri

● 16

▼ 17

AMERIKA
MURA

■ 21 ■ 20
■ 19

● 18

● 22
● 23

▼ 24
■ 25
26 ● 27

● 28

Dōtomburi-gawa

Canal

29 ▼
31 ▼ 32 ▼
33 ▼

● 30

Dōtomburi-dōri

SENNICHIMAE LINE

Nipponbashi
Station

● 34

Namba
Station

Kintetsu
Namba
Station

Namba
Station

Kintetsu Line

Kintetsu
Nipponbashi
Station

■ 35

● 36

● 37

■ 38

Nankai Namba Station

Nankai Line

● 39

心斎橋・難波（南）

**Shinsaibashi &
Namba (Minami)**

0   150   300 m

PLACES TO STAY	PLACES TO EAT	9	Murphy's Bar
			マーフィーズ
1	Hotel Do Sports	12	Capricciosa	11	Gimme Five Sports Bar
	Plaza		Restaurant		ギミーファイブ
	ホテルドゥスポーツプラザ		カプリチオサ	13	Athens Bookshop
2	Ark Hotel	17	Glenn's Bar & Grill		アテネ書房
	アークホテル大阪		グレンズ	14	Daimaru Department
5	Hotel Nikkō Osaka	24	Il Gemello Italian		Store Annex
	ホテル日航大阪		Restaurant		大丸アネックス
6	Hotel California		イルゲメロー	16	Pig & Whistle Bar
	ホテルカリフォルニア	26	Nanak Indian		ピッグアンドウィッスル
10	Asahi Plaza Hotel		Restaurant	18	Shanghai Bar
	East Shinsaibashi		ナナク		上海
	朝日プラザホテル心斎橋東	29	Moti Indian Restaurant	22	Cellar Bar
15	New Shinsaibashi		モーティ		セラー
	Hotel	31	Kani Doraku	23	Tower Records
	ニュー心斎橋ホテル		Restaurant		タワーレコード
19	Arrow Hotel		カニ道楽	27	Sam & Dave I (bar)
	アローホテル	32	Ebi Doraku Restaurant		サムアンドデイブ
20	Capsule Hotel		えび道楽	28	Kirin Plaza
	Asahi Plaza	33	Sawasdee Thai		キリンプラザ
	Shinsaibashi		Restaurant	30	Nakaza Theatre
	カプセルホテル		サワスディ		中座
	朝日プラザ心斎橋	39	Hard Rock Cafe	34	National
21	Asahi Plaza		ハードロックカフェ		Bunraku Theatre
	Hotel Amenity				国立文楽劇場
	Shinsaibashi	OTHER	35	Shin Kabukiza Theatre
	朝日プラザ				新歌舞伎座
25	Holiday Inn Nankai	3	Sam & Dave II (bar)	36	Takashimaya
	ホリデーイン南海大阪		サムアンドデイブ　II		Department Store
37	Nankai South Tower	4	Sogo		高島屋
	Hotel/Namba City		Department Store		
	南海サウスタワーホテル大阪		そごうデパート		
38	Business	7	Daimaru		
	Hotel Nissei		Department Store		
	ビジネスホテルニッセイ		大丸デパート		
		8	Minami		
			Post Office		
			ミナミ 郵便局		

lours, strip clubs, cinemas and who knows what else – take a camera.

National Bunraku Theatre

Although bunraku, or puppet theatre, did not originate in Osaka, the art form was popularised here. The most famous bunraku playwright, Chikametsu Monzaemon (1653-1724), wrote plays set in Osaka concerning the classes that traditionally had no place in Japanese art: merchants and the denizens of the pleasure quarters. Not surprisingly, bunraku found an appreciative audience among these people and a famous theatre was established to put on the plays of Chikametsu in Dōtomburi. Today's theatre is an attempt to revive the fortunes of bunraku.

Performances are only held at certain times of the year: check with the tourist information offices. Tickets normally start at around ¥3500 and English programme guides and earphones are available.

OTHER ATTRACTIONS
Osaka Aquarium – the Rim of Fire
大阪海遊館

In the Osaka bay area, this is one aquarium (and Japan has a glut of them) that is worth a visit. An escalator ride commences the trip, before you begin a slow, winding descent on foot through the 'Pacific Ring of Fire', taking a peek at marine life at eight different oceanic levels. The giant spider crabs in the Japan Ocean Deeps section look like something from another planet – very eery. Presentations have both Japanese and English captioning and have environment-friendly slant to them. The building itself is fascinating, with one reader writing in to suggest that with its two wings it looks like 'a large insect spreading its wings to fly' – this takes something an imaginative leap, but if you take a look you'll get the idea.

To get there, take the Chūō subway line to the last stop (Osaka-kō), and from here it's about a five minute walk to Tempō-zan Harbour Village (there's English signposting in the station), which is next to the aquarium. It's open daily from 10 am to 8 pm and entrance is ¥1950. Get there for opening time if you want to beat the crowds – on weekends and holidays long queues are the norm.

Expo Memorial Park   万国博記念公園
This park is the legacy of Expo '70, and houses a few interesting attractions such as the National Museum of Ethnology, Expo Land and a Japanese garden. To get there take the Mido-suji line to Senri Chūō station and change to bus Nos 114 or 115 to the park. Alternatively there is a monorail service from Senri-chūō that takes around five minutes and costs ¥200.

National Museum of Ethnology This
museum features everyday items from cultures around the world and makes extensive use of audio-visual equipment. Admission is ¥300 and it is open from 10 am to 5 pm but closed on Wednesday.

FESTIVALS
The major festivals held in Osaka include the following:

Sumiyoshi Taisha Odori
1 to 3 January. Children stage traditional dances every 30 minutes from 10 am to 3 pm at Sumiyoshi Taisha Shrine.
Toka Ebisu
9 to 11 January. Huge crowds of more than a million people flock to the Imamiya Ebisu Shrine to receive bamboo branches hung with auspicious tokens. The shrine is near Imamiya Ebisu station on the Nankai line.

Doya Doya
14 January. Billed as a 'huge naked festival', this event involves a competition between young men, clad in little more than headbands and imitation Rolex wrist watches, to obtain the 'amulet of the cow god'. This talisman is said to bring a good harvest to farmers. The festival takes place at 3 pm at Shitennō-ji Temple.
Shōryō-e
22 April. Shitennō-ji Temple holds night-time performances of bunraku.
Otaue Shinji
14 June. Women and girls dressed in traditional costumes commemorate the establishment of the imperial rice fields. The festival is held at the Sumiyoshi Taisha Shrine.
Tenjin Matsuri
24 to 25 July. Processions of portable shrines and people in traditional attire start at Temmangu Shrine and end up in the Okawa River (in boats). As night falls the festival is marked with a huge fireworks display.
Danjiri Matsuri
14 to 15 September. Reportedly Osaka's wildest festival, a kind of running of the bulls except with festival floats (*danjiri*), many weighing over 3000 kg. The danjiri are hauled through the streets by hundreds of people using ropes, and in all the excitement there have been a couple of deaths – take care. Check with the information office at Osaka station or the TIC in Kyoto, but generally the best place to see the action is west of Kishiwada station on the Nankai Honsen line (from Namba Nankai station).

PLACES TO STAY
The best place to stay when visiting Osaka is Kyoto. It's less than 20 minutes away by shinkansen, or around 40 minutes on the Keihan line, there's a far better choice of accommodation (particularly in the budget bracket) and it's a much nicer place. Business hotels in Osaka are concentrated in the central area and the cheaper places are inconveniently further out.

Youth Hostels
About 15 minutes from Kita-ku or 30 minutes from Minami-ku, is the *Osaka-fu Hattori Ryokuchi Youth Hostel* (☎ 06-862-0600), where beds are ¥1700. Take the Mido-suji line to Ryokuchi-kōen station and leave through the western exit. Enter the park and follow the path straight ahead past a fountain and around to the right alongside

the pond. You will find the youth hostel is a little further on the right.

Hotels – bottom end

The *Rinkai Hotel Dejimaten* (☎ 0722-41-3045), *Rinkai Hotel Kitamise* (☎ 0722-47-1111) and *Rinkai Hotel Ishizuten* (☎ 0722-44-0088) are close together and good for short or long-term stays; they should be cheaper by the month. Singles start from ¥2200 without bathroom at the Ishizuten and ¥2900 with bathroom at the Kitamise. Twins are also available at ¥2000 per head. Each of the hotels has cooking facilities and dining areas.

To get to the hotels, the best thing would be to call into one of the Osaka information counters and pick up a map. The hotels are a fair way out of town near Minato station on the Nankai line, which runs out of Namba station – take an express from platform 5 or 6 at Namba station, change to a Nankai line local train at Sakai and get off at the next stop, Minato station.

The *Ebisu-sō Ryokan* (☎ 06-643-4861) is a bit more expensive but more convenient and has singles/doubles from ¥4200/7400. The rooms are small, but have a TV, heater and fan. The ryokan is a 10 minute walk from the No 4 exit of Namba station or from the No 1 exit of Ebisu-chō station.

Hotels – middle

Minami Area The Minami area is probably the best place to be based; but, while it has a good selection of mid-range business hotels, it's also worth bearing in mind that Osaka is an important business centre, and there is often a squeeze on accommodation – particularly the smaller and less expensive places. It's wise to book ahead.

Worth a special mention is the wonderfully kitsch *Hotel California* (☎ 06-243-0333). The bar downstairs is a very Japanese interpretation of California style, complete with garish wooden marlin, parrots and vertical ducks hanging on the walls. The huge potted plants give the lounge the appropriate 'everglade' feel. The rooms are slightly larger than those in an average business hotel and prices start at ¥7500/12,000 for singles/doubles with bathroom. To get to the Hotel California, take the No 8 exit of Shinsaibashi station, turn right into the small street that runs off the main road next to the big Hotel Nikkō Osaka and the hotel is about 50 metres down on the left – you'll see the sign.

South-west of the Hotel California is the *Asahi Plaza Hotel Amenity Shinsaibashi* (☎ 06-212-5111), where singles/twins range from ¥6800/14,000. East of here is another Asahi hotel with mid-range rates: the *Asahi Plaza Hotel East Shinsaibashi* (☎ 06-241-1011) has singles/twins at ¥6500/12,500. In the Amerika-mura area of Shinsaibashi is the *Arrow Hotel* (☎ 06-211-8441), a modern hotel with singles at ¥7200, twins at ¥9200 and doubles at ¥8800.

Some other mid-range possibilities in Minami include:

Ark Hotel Osaka (☎ 06-252-5111) – singles cost from ¥7200; twins from ¥12,000; doubles at ¥11,500; next to Nagahoribashi subway station or 10 minutes walk east of Shinsaibashi subway station.

Business Hotel Namba Plaza (☎ 06-641-3000) – singles cost from ¥6400; twins from ¥10,000; five minutes walk east of Nankai Namba station.

Business Hotel Nissei (☎ 06-632-8111) – singles/twins cost ¥6300/11,000; next to Nankai Namba station.

New Shinsaibashi Hotel (☎ 06-251-3711) – singles/twins/doubles cost ¥8400/12,800/11,800; five minutes walk from Shinsaibashi subway station.

Osaka Station Area While this isn't the ideal place to be based, Osaka's efficient subway system means that you aren't far from the rest of town, and this area has the widest range of hotels to choose from.

Just north of Hankyū-Umeda station is the *Hotel Sunroute Umeda* (☎ 06-373-1111), where singles range from ¥7700, twins from ¥15,600 and doubles from ¥13,900. Not far to the south of here, the *Hotel Green Plaza Osaka* (☎ 06-374-1515) has singles from ¥6500, twins from ¥10,500 and doubles from ¥12,700. About five minutes south of Osaka station, near Books Asahiya, is the *Umeda OS Hotel* (☎ 06-312-1271). It has 208 single rooms from ¥7500 to ¥7900;

twins are also available from ¥10,500. About five minutes walk east of the OS is the *Hotel Kansai* (☎ 06-312-7971), a cheaper business hotel, where singles are ¥6200, twins ¥9200 and doubles ¥8200. Close by is the *Hokke Club Osaka* (☎ 06-313-3171), another cheaper option with the luxury of a noon checkout (as opposed to the usual 10 am); singles/twins are ¥5900/10,600.

Hotels – top end

Osaka is brimming with upper-end accommodation. The most expensive hotel in town, and presumably the best, is the *Hotel Hankyū International* (☎ 06-377-2100), just north of Hankyū-Umeda station. Singles here range from ¥27,000 to ¥33,000, twins from ¥42,000 to ¥46,000 and doubles from ¥40,000 to ¥42,000.

The following is a list of Osaka's major up-market hotels:

ANA-Sheraton Hotel (☎ 06-347-1112) – singles/doubles cost from ¥16,000/27,000; 10 minutes walk south of Osaka station.

Holiday Inn Nankai Osaka (☎ 06-213-8281) – singles/doubles cost from ¥11,500/18,000; five minutes north of Nankai Namba station.

Hotel Do Sports Plaza (☎ 06-245-3311) – singles cost from ¥10,800; twins from ¥18,500; doubles from ¥15,500; three minutes from Shinsaibashi subway station.

Hotel Hanshin (☎ 06-344-1661) – singles cost from ¥10,500; twins from ¥18,500; Japanese-style rooms also available from ¥19,000; three minutes south of JR Osaka station.

Hotel New Hankyū (☎ 06-372-5101) – singles cost from ¥11,500; twins from ¥19,000; next to Hankyū-Umeda station

Hotel New Otani Osaka (☎ 06-941-1111) – singles cost from ¥18,000; twins from ¥30,000; doubles from ¥31,000; next to Osaka-jō Kōen station on the JR loop line.

Hotel Nikkō Osaka (☎ 06-244-1111) – singles/doubles cost from ¥17,000/26,500; above Shinsaibashi subway station.

Nankai South Tower Hotel Osaka (☎ 06-641-1111) – singles cost from ¥17,000; twins and doubles from ¥28,000; above Nankai Namba station.

Osaka Dai-Ichi Hotel (☎ 06-341-4411) – singles cost from ¥10,500; twins from ¥20,000; doubles from ¥23,000; three minutes south of JR Osaka station.

Osaka Hilton Hotel (☎ 06-347-7111) – singles/ doubles cost from ¥25,000/30,500; next to JR Osaka station.

Osaka Tōkyū Hotel (☎ 06-373-2411) – singles cost from ¥12,000; twins from ¥22,000; doubles from ¥19,000; five minutes from JR Osaka station.

PLACES TO EAT
Kita

Once you get off the main thoroughfares, the backstreets of the Umeda area harbour a surprising variety of restaurants. If you just have a brief stop in Osaka (for lunch, for example), head over to the side streets east of Books Asahiya – rāmen shops, fast-food barns, sushi-ya, they're all well represented. South of this area is *Canopy*, an open-fronted (at least during the summer months) restaurant that stays open 24 hours a day daily. This is the place to pick up reasonably priced pizzas, burgers, fish & chips and anything else generically Western that you've been missing. When we were last in town they were selling beers at ¥300 – a bargain in Japan.

The *Food Park* in the Umeda Chika Centre has about 20 small restaurants with dishes ranging from noodles to sushi. Nothing is over ¥500 and ordering is made easy by the colour photographs of dishes displayed by each restaurant. On the 27th to 31st floors of the Hankyū Grand building there are plenty of restaurants and although they're a bit pricey there are a few good lunch-time specials.

Minami

The place to eat in Minami-ku is the restaurant-packed street of Dōtomburi. If you pick a place that is doing brisk business you are unlikely to be disappointed. Dōtomburi has a couple of famous Japanese restaurants whose extensive menus feature some very reasonably priced dishes. You can't miss *Kuidaore* (☎ 06-211-5300) as it has a mechanical clown posted outside its doors, attracting the attention of potential customers by beating a drum. The restaurant has eight floors serving almost every kind of Japanese food, and windows featuring a huge range of plastic replicas. Main-course meals cost from ¥1000.

Down the road, giving a little competition to the drum-pounding clown, is a restaurant that sports a huge mechanical crab helplessly waving its pincers around. The *Kani Doraku* (☎ 06-211-8975) *(kani* is Japanese for 'crab') specialises in crab dishes and they do all kinds of imaginative things to the unfortunate crustaceans. Most dishes are fairly expensive (over ¥3000) although there are a few exceptions.

Not to be outdone by the clown and the crab, Dōtomburi's prawn restaurant features – yes you guessed it – a big mechanical prawn. *Ebi Doraku* (☎ 06-211-1633) has all kinds of prawn dishes from around ¥1500.

Dōtomburi also has a wide range of international restaurants including *Sawasdee* (☎ 06-212-2301), a small Thai restaurant with friendly staff and great food. The restaurant is on the 2nd floor of the Shibata building, a short distance from Kani Doraku. Look for the English sign at ground level.

If you're in the mood for Indian food, the popular Tokyo restaurant *Moti* (☎ 06-211-6878) has a branch in Osaka. The restaurant is on the 3rd floor a few doors down Dōtomburi from its intersection with Midosuji-dōri. The food, prepared by Indian chefs, is not quite as good as in Tokyo but it's still pretty tasty; there are great curries from around ¥1000. Other Indian options around include *Nanak*, a popular chain with good curries and tandoori; the Osaka branch is just across from the Kirin Plaza down by Dōtomburi.

There are a host of other trendy international options in the Minami area. For Italian, check out the Shinsaibashi branch of the *Capricciosa* (☎ 06-243-6020) chain. Good prices and huge portions. The best Italian fare in town is served at *Il Gemello* (☎ 06-211-9542); homemade pasta at affordable prices.

If you're down by Dōtomburi, pop in and say 'Hi' to Glenn, a friendly Canadian-Japanese guy who runs *Glenn's Bar & Grill*; good beer prices and excellent lasagne and pizzas. It's open from 6 pm to 8 am (!) on Friday and Saturday, and late other nights of the week.

Finally, and also an entertainment option, Osaka now has its own branch of the *Hard Rock Cafe* (☎ 06-646-1470), with drinks and American style eats. It's south of Namba station down by the Namba City shopping complex.

ENTERTAINMENT
A big Japanese city with a large foreign community, such as Osaka, is bound to have a lively nightlife – and it does. The *Pig & Whistle* is probably the liveliest of Osaka's ex-pat bars, and does brisk business even on weekday nights. At the time of writing it was closing at midnight reportedly due to a late-night stabbing, but this doesn't seem to have done anything to keep the crowds at bay. It has a good mix of Japanese and resident gaijin.

Probably the second most popular place is *Sam & Dave II*, on the 4th floor of a building to the north of the Pig & Whistle. Sam & Dave II has more of a party atmosphere, with dancing, loud music and (importantly) *very* cheap beer. *Sam & Dave I* is south of here, close to Dōtomburi, and is a small basement place with good music. Two streets to the south of Sam & Dave II is a string of gaijin hang-outs that are worth popping into. *Gimme Five* touts itself as a 'sports bar' with continual sports coverage – you'll know if it's for you or not. Not far away, up on the 6th floor, is *Murphy's*, an Irish bar that seems to appeal largely to the business crowd. Also close by, *Reflex* is an up-market bar with live music and a sign that promises 'many pretty girls' – they weren't much in evidence on our last visit, but maybe they heard we were coming.

Other bars in Minami worth checking out are the hole-in-the-wall *Shanghai*, which is decorated with the complete Keith Richards guitar collection (in case you were wondering where all your guitars had got to, Keith). Over on the other side of Midōsuji-dōri in Amerika-mura (not far from Tower Records) is the *Cellar*, a lively little bar with live music most nights of the week and no cover charge.

There are also a few entertainment possibilities in Umeda. Reportedly the wildest of them is *Zombie Palace*, with its apocalyptic catch-cry 'kill a few brain cells and join dead' – we decided not to, having killed enough brain cells already in Japan. There's no cover charge, excepting nights with live entertainment. Umeda also has a branch of the *Pig & Whistle*. It's quieter than the Minami branch – a good place for a beer and a game of darts. Another place worth checking out is *Bar Isn't It*, just north of the ANA Sheraton Hotel.

GETTING THERE & AWAY

Air

As well as internal flights, Osaka is a major international air centre. Japan's first 24 hour airport (Kansai International Airport) is under construction offshore from Osaka on an artificial island, connected to the mainland by a bridge. It's due to open in 1994 and will make Osaka a much more important international arrival and departure point. The present airport is a much more convenient arrival port than its international counterpart in Tokyo (Narita Airport).

Train

Osaka is the centre of an extensive rail network that sprawls across the Kansai region. Kōbe is a mere 30 minutes away, even quicker by shinkansen, while Kyoto and Nara are each about 50 minutes from Osaka.

Shinkansen services operate between Tokyo station and Shin-Osaka station (just under three hours) via Kyoto, and from Shin-Osaka station on to Hakata in northern Kyūshū (about 3½ hours).

To get to Kyoto from Osaka, the quickest route, other than the shinkansen (just 16 minutes), is with the private Hankyū line, departing from Umeda station. The trip takes around 40 minutes by limited express. See the Kyoto Getting There & Away section for more information on possible other routings.

To get to Nara, your best bet is to take the JR Kansai line from Tennō-ji station and get off at Horyu-ji station. The trip takes around

30 minutes. The private Kintetsu line also operates between Namba station and Nara station, taking about 30 minutes.

It is possible to travel between Osaka and Kōya-san from Nankai Namba station via the private Nankai-Kōya line.

Ferry

Osaka has a twice-monthly international ferry service to Shanghai in China. The ferries leave from the Osaka Nankō International Ferry Terminal, which can be reached by taking the 'New Tram' service from Suminoe-kōen station to Nankoguchi station. The price for a 2nd-class tatami-stye berth is ¥23,000. For further information about Shanghai-bound ferries you can ring the Nitchū Kokusai Ferry company (☎ 078-392-1021), though don't expect any English to be spoken. A better source of information on sailing schedules and bookings would be the Kyoto TIC.

Ferries also depart from Nankō, Kanome-futō and Benten-futō piers for various destinations around Honshū, Kyūshū and Shikoku. For Beppu in Kyūshū (via Kōbe) the 2nd-class fare is ¥6900; for Miyazaki in Kyūshū the 2nd-class fare is ¥8230. Other possibilities in Kyūshū include Shinmoji in the north of the island near Shimonoseki and Shibushi in the south of the island. For Shikoku, possibilities include Kōchi (¥4530), Matsuyama (¥4900, 2nd class) Takamatsu (¥2800, 2nd class) and Tokushima.

GETTING AROUND

To/From the Airport

There are frequent limousine buses running between the airport and various parts of Osaka. Buses run to Shin-Osaka station every 15 minutes from 6.50 am to 8.15 pm and cost ¥340. The trip takes around 25 minutes. Buses run at about the same frequency to Osaka and Namba stations (¥440, half an hour).

There are also direct airport buses to and from Kyoto and Kōbe (see the Kyoto and Kōbe sections for details).

Train

Osaka has a good subway network and, like Tokyo, a JR loop line that circles the city area. In fact, there should be no need to use any other form of transport while you are in Osaka unless you stay out late and miss the last train. Subway and JR stations are clearly marked in English as well as hiragana and kanji so finding your way is relatively easy.

There are seven subway lines, but the one that most short-term visitors are likely to find most useful is the Mido-suji line, which runs north to south taking in the key areas of Shin-Osaka (shinkansen connection), Umeda (next to JR Osaka station) and Shinsaibashi/Namba, the main commercial and entertainment areas.

If you're going to be using the rail system a lot on any day, it might be worth considering a 'one-day free ticket'. For ¥800 you get unlimited travel on any subway, the so-called New Tram and the buses, but unfortunately you cannot use the JR line. You'd really need to be moving around all day to save any money but it might save the headaches of working out fares and where to buy tickets.

Bus

Osaka has a bus system though it is nowhere near as easy to use as the rail network. Japanese-language bus maps are available from the tourist offices.

Around Osaka
大阪周辺

SAKAI NINTOKU BURIAL MOUND
堺仁徳天皇陵

The history of Sakai's burial mound is a lot more interesting than its present reality. Today it merely looks like a mound. In its time, however, it is thought that some 800,000 workers laboured to fashion the final resting place of the 4th century Emperor Nintoku. To get to the mound, take the Hanwa line from Tennō-ji station in

Osaka to Mozu station, from where it is about a five minute walk.

KŌBE 神戸

Kōbe (population 1,477,000) is probably one of Japan's most attractive cities, and is a popular holiday destination for Japanese tourists. Despite this, there's not a lot to hold the average Western traveller, though the city would have to rate as one of the best in Japan to live.

Kōbe can be likened to Nagasaki on Kyūshū. Both cities are ports, have Chinese communities and in the late 19th century were settled by European traders. Both the Chinese and the European influences linger and can be found in the city's diverse restaurants and architectural styles.

All things considered, Kōbe shouldn't be a high priority on your schedule, but it's worth paying the place a visit as a day trip from Osaka or Kyoto. Accommodation in Kōbe is expensive even by Japanese standards.

Information & Orientation

The two main entry points into Kōbe are Sannomiya and Shin-Kōbe stations. Shin-Kōbe station is where the shinkansen pauses, and is in the north-west of town. A subway runs from here to the Sannomiya station, which has frequent rail connections with Osaka and Kyoto. It's also possible to walk between the two stations in around 15 minutes. Sannomiya (not Kōbe) station marks the city centre.

There are information counters in both Shin-Kōbe and Sannomiya stations, and English is spoken. At the very least, it's worth picking up a copy of the *Kōbe Guide Map*, which is regularly updated and has listings of restaurants and sights. Both counters are able to assist with accommodation bookings.

Bookshops There's a branch of Maruzen in Kōbe. Also, and something of a rarity in Japan, Wantage Books is a second-hand English bookshop. It's just down the road from Shin-Kōbe station.

Kitano-chō

Kitano-chō 北野町

Kitano-chō is where most of Kōbe's foreign architecture can be found. There are also a number of places of religious worship in the area: a Russian Orthodox church, a Moslem mosque, a synagogue and a Catholic church.

There is no real need to go out of your way to visit Kitano-chō. As in Nagasaki, Western-style homes are probably of limited appeal to Westerners who grew up surrounded by them. This area can also get very busy with Japanese tourists on the weekends. The other thing to consider is the way the entry fees

soon mount up. England house, for example, has an entry fee of ¥600, while the viewing platform at the highest point in Kitano is a hefty ¥800.

Persia House looks suitably middle eastern, and was the residence of the Persian (Iranian) consul in the 1930s. The building itself dates back to the 1890s and has a collection of folk arts and handicrafts from Iran. It's open from 9 am to 5 pm and entry is ¥300. Also worth taking a look at is Hunter House, a curious mixture of architectural styles. American House dates from 1929.

PLACES TO STAY

1 Shin-Kōbe
Oriental Hotel
新神戸オリエンタルホテル
4 Green Hill Hotel 2
グリーンヒルホテル第2
9 Green Hill Hotel 1
グリーンヒルホテル第1
10 Union Hotel
ユニオンホテル
20 Washington Hotel
ワシントンホテル
24 Business Hotel
Number One
ビジネスホテルナンバーワン
25 Sannomiya
Terminal Hotel
三宮ターミナルホテル
30 Kōbe Plaza Hotel
神戸プラザホテル

PLACES TO EAT

5 Gandhara
ガンダーラ
6 Wang Thai
ワンタイ
7 Chico 'N Charlies
チコアンドチャーリーズ
8 Moti
モーティ
11 Marrakech Restaurant
マラケシレストラン
12 Ju Ju Restaurant
樹樹レストラン
13 Abait Faim
Restaurant
アバイトフェイムレストラン
14 Nanyoshi Restaurant
なんよし
16 Acrophobia
(restaurant/bar)
アクロフォビア
17 Danny Boy Pub
ダニーボーイパブ
23 Häagen-Dazs
ハーゲンダッツ
27 Gaylord Indian
Restaurant
ゲイロードインド料理

OTHER

2 OPA Shopping Centre
ＯＰＡショッピングセンター
3 Wantage Books
ウォンテジ　ブックス
15 Garage Paradise Bar
ガレージパラダイス
18 Korea Consulate
大韓民国領事館
19 Rub-a-Dub-Dub
Reggae Bar
ラブァーダブダブ
21 Tokyu Hands
東急ハンズ
22 Bar Isn't It
バーイズントイット
26 Sogo
Department Store
そごうデパート
28 Daiei
Department Store
ダイエーデパート
29 Maruzen Bookstore
丸善
31 Hanshin Motomachi
Station
阪神元町駅

Kōbe Municipal Museum　神戸市立博物館

Kōbe Municipal Museum has a collection of so-called Namban (literally 'southern barbarian') art and occasional special exhibits. Namban art is a school of painting that developed under the influence of early Jesuit missionaries in Japan, many of whom taught Western painting techniques to Japanese students. Entry to the museum is ¥200 and it's open from 10 am to 4.30 pm, closed Monday.

Chinatown　南京町

Known as 'Nankinmachi' by locals, Kōbe's Chinatown is nothing to write home about if you've seen Chinatowns elsewhere. The restaurants all seem to offer the same Japanese/Chinese cuisine. Apart from eating and shopping in one of the little places selling kung fu shoes and silly silk hats decorated with tassels, there's little else to do. Chinatown is easy to find: it's a five minute walk south of Motomachi station.

Port Island　ポートアイランド

An artificial island, this is touted as one of Kōbe's premier tourist destinations. A monorail does a circuit of the island from Sannomiya station, and sights along the way (which you may or may not want to stop and have a look at) include a container terminal, the Kobe Municipal Youth Science Museum (¥600), the UCC Coffee Museum (¥210) and an international trade show hall.

Rokko Island　六甲アイランド

This new island development is reportedly the largest artificial island in the world, and is becoming increasingly popular as a base for Kōbe's foreign community. Probably the main attraction for visitors with a wad of yen to throw around on a good time, however, is the Aoia complex. It features an enormous water slide – the Super Whooper – in its Splash Garden area. The Super Whooper, which has some six km of water slides, is only open from July through September and has a ¥2900 entry charge (¥1500 after 3 pm). Also featured in the Aoia complex is Dynavox, a kind of bizarre hi-tech theme park, with virtual-reality games (Terabyss), a 'rocket coaster' in a huge kitchen with magic mice (whoever thought that one up?), a maze with a devil king (Daemon) and a hi-tech shooting gallery (Ga-zun). The Dynavox attractions each have individual entry charges – Terabyss ¥1500, Ga-zun ¥500 – but you can buy a ¥1500 or a ¥3500 book of ¥250 coupons.

Other Attractions

Featured prominently in all the tourist literature is 931 metre Mt Rokko-san. It's a pleasant trip by cablecar (¥560) to the top. To get there, take bus No 25 from Rokko station on the Hankyū line. Get off the bus at the Rokko cablecar station. You can continue onwards on the Arima cablecar (¥700). This is also a good area for some hiking. Some people take the cablecar up and then hike down. Further up from the cablecar terminus is the Herb Garden, which gets good reports from locals and visitors alike. Further up again are good views of Kōbe Harbour and Port Island.

Fifteen minutes north of Motomachi station is the Japanese-style Soraku-en Garden with a pond and some old buildings. The garden is a pleasant enough place for a stroll. It is open from 9 am to 5 pm (closed on Thursday) and admission is ¥150.

Cruises

From 1 March to 25 December, cruises depart daily from Kōbe's Naka pier. They usually last a couple of hours and cost ¥2750. Possibilities include the Akashi Bay cruise, a cruise around the new Kansai airport project and an evening Osaka Bay cruise. For more information ring Luminous Kankō (☎ 078-333-8414).

Places to Stay

Youth Hostels The *Kōbe Tarumi Youth Hostel* (☎ 078-707-2133) has beds for ¥2100, breakfast for ¥450 and dinner for ¥750, but it's a bit far out of town. Take a San'in line train from Kōbe station and get off after six stops at Tarumi station. The hostel is an eight minute walk to the east

along the road that parallels the south side of the railway tracks.

Hotels – middle Middle-range hotels in Kōbe are expensive even by Japanese standards. Unless you book ahead with one of the (marginally) cheaper places, you'll be hard-pressed to come up with anything under ¥7000 – and that's for a tiny single.

The Sannomiya station area has the greatest number of mid-range hotels. The *Green Hill Hotel 1* (☎ 078-222-1221) is about 10 minutes walk to the north (about equidistant between Shin-Kōbe and Sannomiya stations). It charges from ¥7000/12,000 for singles/twins. The *Green Hill Hotel 2* (☎ 078-222-0909) is further up the hill and down a side street. It has slightly bigger rooms at ¥8000/14,000.

About five minutes walk to the west of Sannomiya station, behind Motomachi station, is the *Kōbe Plaza Hotel* (☎ 078-332-1141), where singles range from ¥6800 to ¥8500 and twins range from ¥13,000 to ¥20,000. About five minutes walk south of Motomachi station is the *Kōbe Towerside Hotel* (☎ 078-351-2151), which is probably the cheapest place in town. Singles range from ¥4800 to ¥5600, and twins and doubles are ¥9500 – book ahead if you want one of the cheaper singles.

On the east side of Sannomiya station, the *Sunside Hotel* (☎ 078-232-3331) is slightly cheaper, with singles from ¥6200 to ¥6800, twins at ¥11,400 and doubles at ¥10,600. You might try squeezing into the small *Business Hotel Number One* (☎ 078-231-2525), a somewhat decrepit looking place with singles from ¥5800, twins from ¥13,000 and doubles from ¥12,000.

Right on top of Sannomiya station, the *Sannomiya Terminal Hotel* (☎ 078-291-0001) has comfortable rooms with all the usual features from ¥8500/16,600. Close by, the *Kōbe Tokkyū Inn* (☎ 078-291-0109) has singles from ¥8800, twins from ¥16,000 and doubles at ¥15,400. The *Washington Hotel* (☎ 078-331-6111) has slightly more expensive rates at ¥10,000/18,000.

Hotels – top-end Kōbe abounds in top-end accommodation. Close to Shin-Kōbe station is the *Shin-Kōbe Oriental Hotel* (☎ 078-291-1121) in a great gleaming monster of a building. Singles range from ¥13,000 to ¥22,000; twins from ¥23,000 to ¥37,000; and doubles from ¥23,000 to ¥33,000.

Near the waterfront, about 10 minutes walk south from Motomachi station, the *Hotel Okura Kōbe* (☎ 078-333-0111) has rooms from ¥17,000/24,000 for singles/doubles. About 10 minutes walk to the south-west of here, the *Kōbe Harbourland New Otani* (☎ 078-360-1111) is part of the prestigious Otani chain, and has singles from ¥10,000 to ¥14,000, twins from ¥22,000 to ¥35,000 and doubles from ¥27,000 to ¥37,000.

The Sheraton chain is represented over on Rokko Island, where you can find the *Kōbe Bay Sheraton Hotel* (☎ 078-857-7000). Singles are ¥17,000, twins ¥27,000 and doubles ¥23,000.

Places to Eat

Kōbe is teeming with restaurants, and the best advice is to wander around the southern part of the Kitano-chō area and take a look at what's on offer. Kōbe's two main culinary attractions are Kōbe beef and its ethnic restaurants. There are also French and Italian restaurants in abundance. Lunch-time specials are probably the best bet for sampling Kōbe's culinary diversity; this is a tourist town, a fact that is reflected in dinner prices.

For an idea of what's available take a stroll up Kitano-zaka. Here you'll find *Abat Faim*, a good Italian restaurant with reasonable prices but unfortunately no English menu. A few doors up the road is *Cookhouse Un Deux Trois*, as you guessed, a French restaurant with courses from ¥3000. On the other side of the road look out for *Ju Ju* (it means 'tree tree'), a very up-market Chinese restaurant. A little further up the road is the Corner House, a building with an Italian restaurant in the basement; *Den*, a French restaurant on the 5th floor and *Chico 'n Charly's*, an affordable Spanish/Mexican place, on the 4th floor.

Other Kitano highlights, some of them long-running favourites, include *Wang Thai*, for Thai food, *Marrakech*, for superb, if pricey Moroccan food, and just around the corner from Marrakech, *Moti*, a member of the popular chain of Indian restaurants.

Not far from Kitano-chō, look out for *Nanyoshi*, an atmospheric Japanese restaurant, and *Danny Boy*, an English-style pub with good counter meals. Take note of *Jardin*, a picturesque café with some food available across the road from Danny Boy.

The Kitana-chō area is also a good place to look for restaurants serving Kōbe beef. There are signs in English advertising most of them, but you'll be looking at a minimum of ¥5000 for a main course in the cheapest of these places.

Entertainment

Kōbe has a relatively large foreign community and a number of bars that see mixed Japanese and foreign crowds. A fairly recent arrival on the scene is *Acrophobia*, a friendly place with good food, affordable drinks and American Indian theme décor. *Rub-a-Dub-Dub* is a roomy reggae bar with food and drinks that gets quite lively on Friday and Saturday nights.

Garage Paradise Bar is a little expensive (¥1000 cover), but it's an atmospheric, laid-back kind of place with live piano music, a good place for a couple to visit. *Bar Isn't It* is a 'sports bar' that, like its counterparts in Osaka and Kyoto, features continuous sports coverage.

Getting There & Away

Train Shin-Kōbe station is the shinkansen stop for trains to Kyoto, Osaka and Tokyo (three hours 13 minutes) or into Western Japan and onto Fukuoka (two hours 54 minutes) in Kyūshū. The Sannomiya station has both JR and some private lines. The JR Sanyō line heads into Western Honshū via the castle town of Himeji. JR trains also run to Kyoto (one hour 15 minutes) and Osaka (20 minutes) on a regular basis, though it's worth bearing in mind that the private Hankyū line does the same journey cheaper, if a little slower. The Hanshin line runs also to Osaka.

Ferry There are ferries from Kōbe to Shikoku, Kyūshū and Awaji-shima Island. There are two departure points for ferries: Naka Pier, next to the port tower, and Higashi-Kōbe Ferry Terminal. Basically, the former has ferries to Matsuyama and Imabari (Shikoku) and Ōita (Kyūshū), while the latter has ferries to Takamatsu (Shikoku). The lowest fares are: Takamatsu ¥2370, Imabari ¥3600, Matsuyama ¥4430 and Ōita ¥5870. For information regarding departure times call Japan Travel-Phone (☎ 0120-444-800) or inquire at the TIC in Tokyo or Kyoto.

Osaka-Shanghai ferries also stop in Kobe. For more information, see the Osaka Ferry section.

Getting Around
To/From the Airport It is possible to take a bus directly to or from Osaka International Airport. The buses leave the airport every 20 minutes and cost ¥720 for the 40 minute trip. They start and terminate at Kōbe's Sannomiya station.

Local Transport JR, Kankyū and Hanshin railway lines run east to west across Kōbe, providing access to most of Kōbe's sights. A subway line also connects Shin-Kōbe station with Sannomiya station (¥160). Buses are frequent and reliable, and because of the fairly low level of traffic, taxis are often a reasonable option in Kōbe.

HIMEJI　姫路
If you see no other castles in Japan you should at least make an effort to visit Himeji-jō Castle, unanimously acclaimed as the most splendid Japanese castle still standing. It is also known as Shirasagi, the 'White Egret', a title which derives from the castle's stately white form. The surrounding town itself has little to offer as a tourist attraction, but there are plenty of places to grab a meal on the way to the castle.

Himeji can be easily visited as a day trip from Kyoto. A couple of hours at the castle,

姫路
Himeji

plus the 10 to 15 minute walk from the station is all the time you need there. The only other attraction worth lingering for is Himeji's historical museum, which has some interesting exhibits on Japanese castles. Walk to the castle down one side of the main street and back on the other to see the statuary dotted along both sides.

Orientation & Information

There's a tourist information counter at the station. The castle is straight up the main road from the station, and clearly visible to the north if you're simply passing through Himeji. If you have luggage with you, there are coin lockers at the station.

Himeji-jō Castle   姫路城

Himeji-jō Castle is the most magnificent of the handful of Japanese castles which survive in their original (non-concrete) form. Although there have been fortifications in Himeji since 1333, today's castle was built in 1580 by Toyotomi Hideyoshi and enlarged some 30 years later by Ikeda Terumasa. Ikeda was awarded the castle by Tokugawa Ieyasu when the latter's forces defeated the Toyotomi armies. In the following centuries the castle was home to 48 successive lords.

The castle has a five storeyed main donjon and three smaller donjons, the entire structure being surrounded by moats and defensive walls punctuated with rectangular, circular and triangular openings for firing guns and shooting arrows at visiting tourists. The walls of the donjon also feature *ishiotoshi* or openings that allowed defenders to pour boiling water or oil on to anyone that made it past the defensive slits and was thinking of scaling the walls. All things considered, visitors are recommended to pay the ¥500 admission charge and enter the castle by legitimate means.

It takes about 1½ hours to follow the arrowed route around the castle. The castle is open from 9 am to 6 pm (last entry 5 pm) in summer and it closes an hour earlier in winter.

Hyōgo Prefectural Museum of History
県立歴史博物館

This well laid out museum has good displays on Himeji-jō Castle and other castles around Japan and, indeed, the whole world. If you're at the museum at 2 pm you can try on a suit of samurai armour or a kimono. In the event of competition for this singular honour, the museum staff resolve the conflict by the drawing of lots.

The museum is a five minute walk north of the castle. Admission is ¥200, and it's open from 10 am to 5 pm daily except Monday.

Shosha-zan Engyō-ji Temple
書写山円教寺

Around eight km north-east of Himeji station is this seldom visited (by Western travellers at least) temple complex on Mt Shosha-zan. It's a well known pilgrimage spot and has been around for some 1000 years. Eight of the temple buildings and seven Buddha images have been designated important cultural properties. But most of all, this is a good spot to escape the crowds.

To get there, take a No 6 bus from Himeji station (¥220). The trip takes around 25 minutes. Get off at Shosha, and connect there with a cablecar (¥300). Entry to the temple area is free, and the cablecar operates every 15 minutes between 8.30 am and 6 pm.

Tegarayama Chūō-kōen Park
手柄山中央公園

Whatever you do, don't go out of the way to see this amusement park, about 10 minutes walk to the south-west of Himeji station. But if you are spending a night in town and you've seen the castle, you might want to wander over – it's cheap at least (¥200). There's some Disneyland look-a-like baroque castle architecture and an aquarium (*not* another one). It's open daily from 9 am to 4.30 pm.

Festivals

The Mega-Kenka Festival, held on 14 and 15 October, involves a conflict between three *mikoshi* (portable shrines) which are battered against each other until one smashes. The festival is held about a five minute walk from Shirahamanomiya station (10 minutes from

Himeji station on the Sanyō-Dentetsu line); just follow the crowds.

Places to Stay

There *are* some places to stay in Himeji, but in general they are overpriced and have little to recommend them. Basing yourself elsewhere and visiting Himeji as a day trip would be a far better option. There is no longer a youth hostel convenient to Himeji.

In town, *Hotel Sun Route New Himeji* (☎ 0792-23-1111) has rooms with all the usual business-hotel features and costs from ¥6300/13,500 for singles/doubles. It's a two minute walk from the station on the right-hand side of Ōtemae-dōri. The *Hotel Himeji Plaza* (☎ 0792-81-9000) is also close to the station and has singles from ¥5900 to ¥6900 and twins from ¥11,000 to ¥12,500. One of the cheaper places around is the *Himeji Oriental Hotel* (☎ 0792-84-3773). It has singles/twins at ¥5500/9000, and is about 10 minutes walk to the north-east of the station. See the map for other Himeji hotels.

Getting There & Away

The quickest way to get to Himeji is by shinkansen. From Shin-Osaka station the trip takes around 40 minutes, from Okayama it takes 30 to 40 minutes. JR trains also run between Osaka, Kyoto, Kōbe and Himeji, and the private Hankyū line runs between Kōbe and Himeji.

Nara 奈良

Nara (population 349,000), on first appearance an unispiring sort of town, has a large number of cultural relics and is, second to Kyoto, the major tourist destination in the Kansai region. Try to choose a fine day for sightseeing – doing the sights in Nara requires a lot of walking, and it's no fun at all in bad weather.

HISTORY

Prior to the 8th century, it had been the custom among the rulers of Japan to relocate the capital with the rule of each new emperor – perhaps to avoid the pollution of death. In 710, this custom was changed when Nara (then known as Heijōkyō) was made the permanent capital under Empress Gemmyō. Permanent status, however, lasted a mere 75 years. Several decades later, after a few more moves, the capital was shifted to Kyoto, where it remained until 1868.

Although brief, the Nara period was extraordinarily vigorous in its absorption of influences from China, a process that layed the foundations of Japanese culture and civilisation. The adoption of Buddhism as a national religion made a lasting impact on government, arts, literature and architecture. With the exception of an assault on the area by the Taira clan in the 12th century, Nara was subsequently spared the periodic bouts of destruction wreaked upon Kyoto, and a number of magnificent buildings have survived.

ORIENTATION

Nara retains the grid pattern of streets laid out in Chinese style during the 8th century. This makes it easy to cover the city centre and the major attractions in adjoining Nara-kōen Park on foot.

INFORMATION

If you are heading for Nara from Kyoto, the TIC in Kyoto has extensive material. In Nara, the best source of information is the Nara City Tourist Centre (☎ 0742-22-3900), which is open from 9 am to 9 pm. It's a short walk from JR Nara and Kintetsu Nara stations. There's a plush lounge for relaxing, a display of handicrafts and helpful staff doling out stacks of maps and literature about transport, sights, accommodation, etc.

The TIC can also put you in touch with volunteer guides who speak English and other foreign languages – try to book ahead. There are three such services: Goodwill Guides (☎ 0742-22-3900), Student Guides (☎ 0742-26-4753) and YMCA Guides (☎ 0742-27-4858). These services are a pleasant way for a foreigner to meet the Japanese (often bright students keen to practise their foreign languages), but they are not business ventures so you should offer to cover the day's expenses for your guide.

There are also information offices at both of Nara's stations which stock maps and have staff who can answer basic questions. The JR Nara station's office (☎ 0742-22-9821) is open from 8 am to 6 pm; the Kintetsu Nara station information office (☎ 0742-24-4858) is open from 9 am to 5 pm.

JNTO publishes a walking guide to Nara, *Walking Tour Courses in Nara*, which has maps and information on sights. The green *Japan: Nara City* map and red *Tourist Map of Kyoto & Nara*, also published by JNTO are useful. The staff has comprehensive listings of places to stay and, time permitting, will help you with reservations (Nara receives thousands of tourists, but they're mostly day-trippers).

For a more academic look at Nara's sights, pick up a copy of *Historical Nara* by Herbert Plutschow (Japan Times, Tokyo, 1983).

PLANNING YOUR ITINERARY

If you're torn between Nara and Kyoto, it's probably safe to say that Kyoto is a more rewarding sightseeing destination. Nara is also small enough that it's quite possible to pack the most worthwhile sights into one full day. It's preferable, of course, if you can spend at least two days here, but this will depend on how much time you have for the Kansai region. Those with time to spare would best be served by allowing a day for Nara-kōen Park and another day for the sights in western and south-western Nara. A one-day visit would be best spent tramping around Nara-kōen Park; trying to fit in the more distant sights as well would probably be too exhausting.

Day Walks

Traipsing around dozens of temples in quick succession can be tiring for mind and body. If you've got a day or half a day to spare, a walk in the forested hills around Nara is definitely recommended.

Take some food and drink and give yourself an easy schedule to get pleasantly lost, meet local farmers who confidently put you back on the wrong track, and keep following your nose and the erratic mapping until you reach Nara. It is the complete antithesis of a guided tour, and the sort of disorganised Western fun that most Japanese find most puzzling.

The Nara City Tourist Centre can provide maps and transport details. The Takisaka-michi and the Yamanobe-no-michi are popular walks. The tourist centre probably won't have any English maps, but you can make do with the Japanese ones, which are more detailed anyway. Ask the staff to circle a few of the key points on the route and write down the names in romaji.

The Takisaka-michi is the old highway leading from the Yagyū area to Nara city. It is cobblestone for part of the way, but most of it meanders through forests passing the occasional stone Buddhas and shrines by the wayside. I took an early bus from boarding bay 4 opposite Kintetsu station to Enjō-ji Temple. The ride took 30 minutes and cost ¥520. Bus Nos 100, 101 and 102 all go via Enjō-ji Temple and take another 17 minutes (and an extra ¥230) to reach Yagyū which is another possible place to start if you want a longer walk down the Takisaka-michi.

From Enjō-ji Temple you head off the road and through the forest. Together with my trail companion, who was half-Japanese but equally stymied by the mapping, we soon strayed down a sidetrack and came to a dead end in a farmer's yard. The farmer was very helpful, but obviously a little thrown by the sight of foreigners stumbling into his backyard.

This probably accounted for his extreme care in accompanying us back to the trail and pointing us in the wrong direction. We later realised there had been a misunderstanding since he was presumably used to going *up* the trail to take the bus to market, and we wanted to go *down* the trail to Nara without transport.

After that, the trail was easy to follow. The official walking time from Enjō-ji to Nara is about three hours, but it took us about five hours including numerous breaks for lunch, tea, photos, etc.

About halfway down the trail, there's a delightful old teahouse and antique shop (worth a stop for tea, mochi cakes and a chat). Further on, you pass tea plantations complete with dozens of electric fans on poles to circulate the air around the plants. There are various shrines and stone Buddhas along the way. Tucked away on a side track, almost obscured by

KANSAI REGION

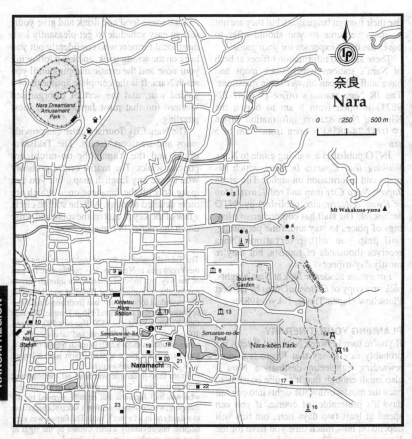

奈良
Nara

0   250   500 m

Mt Wakakusa-yama ▲

Nara Dreamland
Amusement
Park

Isui-en
Garden

Kintetsu
Nara
Station

JR
Nara
Station

Sarusawa-no-ike
Pond

Sarusawa-no-ike
Pond

Nara-kōen Park

Naramachi

trees, is the Sunset Buddha, so named because the last
rays of the sun light up its face.

The trail comes out near Shin-Yakushi-ji Temple.
Shortly before the temple I saw a vandalised vending
machine, a unique sight in Japan. If you are exhausted
by the time you reach the temple, the No 2 bus will
take you back to the city centre.

Robert Strauss

NARA-KŌEN PARK AREA　奈良公園周辺
The park was created from wasteland in
1880 and covers a large area. JNTO publishes a leaflet called *Walking Tour Courses
in Nara* which includes a map for this area.

Although walking time is estimated at two
hours, you'll need at least half a day to see a
selection of the sights and a full day to see
the lot.

The park is famous for its deer which
provide a cutesy backdrop for photos and are
fed by tourists who buy special packets of
biscuits for ¥100 from vendors (you'll get
strange looks from the Japanese if, as we saw
one misguided gaijin tourist doing, you eat
the biscuits yourself). Although they look
cute, these creatures, numbering over a thousand, have been spoilt rotten and can be a
nuisance.

PLACES TO STAY

1 Nara Youth Hostel 奈良ユースホステル
2 Seishōnen Kaikan Youth Hostel 青少年会館ユースホステル
9 Nara Green Hotel 奈良グリーンホテル
10 Nara Kokusai Hotel 奈良国際ホテル
17 Hote Nara ホテル奈良
18 Minshuku Yamaya 民宿山屋
19 Minshuku Sakigake ホテルサンルート奈良
20 Hotel Sunroute Nara 民宿さきがけ
21 Nara Hotel 旅館 松山
22 Ryokan Matsumae 奈良ホテル
23 Ryoka Seikan-sō せいかん荘

OTHER

3 Shōso-in Treasure Repository 正倉院
4 Nigatsu-dō Hall 二月堂
5 Sangatsu-dō Hall 三月堂
6 Daibutsu-den 大仏殿
7 Tōdai-ji Temple 東大寺
8 Neiraku Art Museum 寧楽美術館
11 Kōfuku-ji Temple 興福寺
12 Nara City Tourist Centre 奈良市観光案内所
13 Nara National Museum 奈良国立博物館
14 Kasuga Taisha Shrine 春日大社
15 Wakamiya-jinja Shrine 若宮神社
16 Shin-Yakushi-ji Temple 新薬師寺

Kōfuku-ji Temple

This temple was transferred here from Kyoto in 710 as the main temple for the Fujiwara family. Although the original temple complex had 175 buildings, fires and destruction through power struggles have left only a dozen still standing. There are two pagodas, a three storeyed one and a five storeyed one, dating from 1143 and 1426 respectively.

The National Treasure Hall (Kokuhōkan) contains a variety of statues and art objects salvaged from previous structures. A descriptive leaflet is provided in English.

Admission to the Kokuhōkan costs ¥500 and it's open from 9 am to 4.30 pm.

Nara National Museum

The Nara Koku-ritsu Hakubutsukan (Nara National Museum) is devoted to Buddhist art and is divided into two wings. The western gallery exhibits archaeological finds and the eastern gallery has displays of sculptures, paintings and calligraphy. The galleries are linked by an underground passage.

A special exhibition is held in May and the treasures of the Shōsō-in Hall, which is part of the Tōdai-ji Temple, are displayed here in November only. The exhibits include priceless items from the cultures along the Silk Road. If you are in Nara at these times, you should make a point of visiting the museum.

Admission to the museum costs ¥400 (special exhibitions excepted) and it's open from 9 am to 4.30 pm.

Neiraku Art Museum & Isui-en Garden

The art museum (Neiraku Bijutsukan) displays Chinese bronzes and Korean ceramics and bronzes. The garden, dating from the Meiji era, is beautifully laid out with abundant greenery and a fine view of Tōdai-ji Temple with the hills rising behind. It is recommended if you need a break.

Admission to the museum costs ¥520. The same ticket allows entry into the garden. It is open daily from 10 am to 4.30 pm in April, May, October and November, closed Wednesday during the rest of the year.

TŌDAI-JI TEMPLE

This temple is the star attraction in Nara. It is the largest wooden building in the world and houses the Great Buddha – one of the largest bronze images in the world. It also deserves a place in the record books for the largest concentration of tour groups, including hundreds of uniformed kids wearing yellow baseball caps being herded by dozens of guides with megaphones and banners.

KANSAI REGION

Emperor Shōmu ordered construction of the temple and casting of the Great Buddha (Daibutsu) during the 8th century. Fires, earthquakes and civil wars necessitated reconstruction in subsequent centuries. The present gigantic structure dates from the Edo period and is still only two-thirds the size of the original.

Daibutsu-den Hall

The Daibutsu-den (Hall of the Great Buddha) is not remarkably ancient, being a reconstruction dating from 1709.

The Daibutsu, however, was cast in 746 after a number of unsuccessful attempts. Over the centuries the statue took quite a beating from earthquakes and fires, losing its head a couple of times in the process. The present statue stands just over 16 metres high and consists of 437 tonnes of bronze and 130 kg of gold. Big isn't necessarily beautiful, but it's still impressive – even more so if you consider that it is only two-thirds the size of the original.

As you circuit the statue towards the back, you'll see a wooden column with a small hole at the base. Popular belief maintains that those who can squeeze through are ensured of enlightenment. (You'll probably see a lot of disappointed, firmly wedged adults reluctantly giving way to streams of nimble kids making quick work of enlightenment.)

Admission to the Daibutsu-den costs ¥400, and your ticket has a convenient list of the Daibutsu's vital statistics. Opening hours vary throughout the year. You might conceivably be able to reduce exposure to the hordes of visitors if you come very early or an hour before closing. Opening hours are as follows: November to February from 8 am to 4.30 pm; during March from 8 am to 5 pm; April to September from 7.30 am to 5.30 pm; during October from 7.30 am to 5 pm.

Shōsō-in

The Shōsō-in (Treasure Repository) is a short walk north of Daibutsu-den. If you discount the slight curve to the roof, the structure is reminiscent of a log blockhouse from North America. The building was used to house fabulous imperial treasures and its wooden construction allowed precise regulation of humidity through natural expansion and contraction. The treasures have been removed and are shown twice a year, in spring and autumn, at the Nara National Museum. The Shōsō-in building is open to the public at the same time.

Kaidan-in Hall

A short walk west of the entrance gate to the Daibutsu-den, you can visit this hall which was used for ordination ceremonies and is famous for its clay images of the Shi Tennō (Four Heavenly Guardians). The hall is open from 8 am to 4.30 pm and admission costs ¥400.

Nigatsu-dō & Sangatsu-dō Halls

If you walk east from the entrance to the Daibutsu-den, climb up a flight of stone steps, and continue to your left, you reach these two halls.

Nigatsu-dō Hall is famed for its Omizutori Festival (see the later section on Nara festivals for details) and a splendid view across Nara which makes the climb up the hill well worthwhile – particularly at dusk. The hall is open from 8 am to 5.30 pm and admission is free.

A short walk south of Nigatsu-dō is Sangatsu-dō Hall which is the oldest building in the Tōdai-ji Temple complex. This hall contains a small collection of fine statues from the Nara period. Admission costs ¥400 and it's open from 8 am to 5.30 pm.

Kasuga Taisha Shrine

This shrine was founded in the 8th century by the Fujiwara family and completely rebuilt every 20 years according to Shintō tradition, until the end of the 19th century. It lies at the foot of the hill in a pleasant wooded setting with herds of sacred deer waiting for hand-outs.

The approaches to the shrine are lined with hundreds of lanterns and there are many more hundreds in the shrine itself. The lantern festivals held twice a year at the shrine are a major attraction. For details about these and other festivals held at the nearby Wakamiya-jinja Shrine, see the later section on Nara festivals.

The Hōmotsu-den (Treasure Hall) is just north of the entrance torii for the shrine. The hall displays Shintō ceremonial regalia and equipment used in bugaku, Nō and gagaku performances. Admission costs ¥350 and it's open from 9 am to 4 pm.

TEMPLES SOUTH-WEST OF NARA

Shin-Yakushi-ji Temple   新薬師寺

This temple was founded by Empress Kōmyō in 747 in thanks for her husband's recovery from an eye disease. Most of the buildings were destroyed or have been reconstructed, but the present main hall dates from the 8th century. The hall contains sculptures of Yakushi Nyorai (Healing Buddha) and a set of 12 divine generals. Admission costs ¥500 and the temple is open from 8.30 am to 5.30 pm.

Hōryū-ji Temple   法隆寺

This temple was founded in 607 by Prince Shōtoku, considered by many the patron saint of Japanese Buddhism. It is renowned not only as the oldest temple in Japan, but also as a repository for some of the country's rarest treasures. Despite the usual fires and reconstructions in the history of the temple, several of the wooden buildings now remaining are believed to be the oldest of their kind in the world. The layout of the temple is divided into two parts: Sai-in (West Temple) and Tō-in (East Temple); it is the Sai-in precinct that lays claim to being Japan's oldest temple.

The entrance ticket costing ¥700 allows admission to the Sai-in Temple, Tō-in Temple and Great Treasure Hall. A detailed map is provided and a guidebook is available in English. The JNTO leaflet called *Walking Tour Courses in Nara* includes a basic map for the area around Hōryū-ji Temple. From 21 March to 19 November the temple is open from 8 am to 5.50 pm; for the rest of the year until 5.20 pm.

The main approach to the temple proceeds from the south along a tree-lined avenue and continues through the Nandai-mon Gate and Chū-mon Gate before entering the Sai-in precinct.

As you enter the Sai-in precinct, you see the Kondō (Main Hall) on your right, and a pagoda on your left. The Kondō houses several treasures, including the triad of the Buddha Sākyamuni with two attendant Bodhisattvas, the central image on the altar. The pagoda rises gracefully in five finely tapered storeys. The inside walls are lined with clay images depicting scenes from the life of Buddha. On the eastern side of the Sai-in Temple are the two concrete buildings of the Daihōzō-den (Great Treasure Hall), containing numerous treasures from Hōryū-ji Temple's long history. Renowned Buddhist artefacts in this hall include the Kudara Kannon and two miniature shrines: Tamamushi Shrine and the Shrine of Lady Tachibana.

If you leave this hall and continue east through the Tōdai-mon Gate you reach the Tō-in. The Yumedono (Hall of Dreams) in this temple is where Prince Shōtoku is believed to have meditated and been given help with problem sutras by a kindly, golden apparition.

At the rear of the Tō-in compound is the entrance to Chūgū-ji Nunnery, which is drab in appearance, but contains two famous art treasures: the serene statue of the Bodhisattva Miroku and a portion of the embroidered Tenjukoku (Land of Heavenly Longevity) mandala, which is believed to date from the 7th century and is the oldest remaining example of this art in Japan. Admission to this temple costs ¥300 and it's open from 9 am to 4.30 pm.

To get to the Hōryū-ji Temple, take the JR Kansai line from JR Nara station to Hōryū-ji station (15 minutes). A bus service shuttles the short distance between the station and Hōryū-ji Temple. On foot it takes about 25 minutes. There is also a direct bus service from Nara station to the temple; it takes around 40 minutes and costs ¥640.

Hōrin-ji Temple   法輪寺

Hōrin-ji Temple is about 10 minutes on foot

from Chūgū-ji Nunnery. In the Kondō (Main Hall) of the temple there are several images including a fine statue of Yakushi Nyorai (Healing Buddha) with a radiant smile. The pagoda was frazzled by lightning in 1944, but reconstructed in 1975. Admission costs ¥300 and an English leaflet is provided. It's open from 8 am to 5 pm daily but closes an hour earlier between December and February.

Hokki-ji Temple 法起寺

Hokki-ji Temple is a 10 minute walk from Hōrin-ji and instantly recognisable by its elegant three storeyed pagoda, which dates back to the 8th century. The temple has a cosy garden with a small pond. Admission costs ¥200. It's open from 8 am to 5 pm.

Jikō-in Temple 慈光院

Jikō-in Temple is about 25 minutes on foot from Hokki-ji. This Zen temple was founded in 1663 by Sekishu Katagiri who had studied at Daitoku-ji Temple in Kyoto and then devoted himself to Zen and the tea ceremony. Although the gardens and buildings are impressive, the ¥800 admission fee is a bit steep even with the free cup of matcha (powdered tea) thrown in. The view from the tearoom ranges over the garden to the encroaching urban sprawl. The temple is open from 8.30 am to 5 pm but closes at 5.30 pm in the summer.

To return to Nara by bus, you should turn left when leaving the temple and go down the hill a short distance to the main road. Turn left again and walk about 100 metres along the road until you cross a bridge over a river. The bus stop is just beyond the bridge. Buses to the nearby Kintetsu Kōriyama station are more frequent than those to Nara, but you can pick a train to Nara at the station.

Yakushi-ji Temple 薬師寺

Yakushi-ji was established by Emperor Temmu in 680. With the exception of the East Pagoda, the present buildings either date from the 13th century or are very recent reconstructions.

The main hall was rebuilt in 1976 and houses several images, including the famous Yakushi Triad (the Buddha Yakushi flanked by the Bodhisattvas of the sun and moon), dating from the 8th century.

The East Pagoda is a unique structure because it appears to have six storeys, but three of them are *mokoshi* (lean-to additions) which give a pleasing balance to its appearance. It is the only structure to have survived the ravages of time, and dates from 730.

Admission costs ¥500 and a leaflet in English is provided. It's open from 8.30 am to 5 pm.

To get to Yakushi-ji take a Kintetsu line train from Nara Kintetsu station to Saidai-ji, then change to the southbound Kintetsu Kashihara line and get off at the second stop – Nishinokyō station – which is very close to Yakushi-ji Temple.

Tōshōdai-ji Temple 唐招提寺

This temple was established in 759 by the Chinese priest Ganjin (Jian Zhen), who had been recruited by Emperor Shōmu to reform Buddhism in Japan. Ganjin didn't have much luck with his travel arrangements from China to Japan: five attempts were thwarted by shipwreck, storms and bureaucracy. Despite being blinded by eye disease, he finally made it on the sixth attempt and spread his teachings to Japan. The lacquer sculpture in the Miei-dō Hall is a moving tribute to Ganjin: blind and rock steady. It is shown only once a year on 6 June – the anniversary of Ganjin's death (6th day of the fifth month in the lunar calendar).

The Shin Hōzō (Treasure Hall) has some fine sculptures and images. Admission costs ¥100 and it's open during the same hours as the temple, but only from late March to late May, and from mid-September to early November.

Admission to the temple costs ¥300 and a detailed leaflet is provided in English, including a precise map of the extensive temple grounds. It's open from 8.30 am to 4.30 pm.

Tōshōdai-ji Temple is a 10 minute walk

from Yakushi-ji Temple; see the preceding section for transport details from Nara.

FESTIVALS

Nara has plenty of festivals throughout the year. The following is a brief list of the more interesting ones. More extensive information is readily available from Nara tourist offices or from the TIC in Kyoto.

Yamayaki (Grass Burning Festival)
15 January. To commemorate a feud many centuries ago between the monks of Tōdai-ji and Kōfuku-ji temples, Mt Wakakusa-yama is set alight at 6 pm with an accompanying display of fireworks. Arrive earlier to bag a good viewing position in Nara-kōen Park.

Mantōrō (Lantern Festival)
2-4 February. Held at Kasuga Taisha Shrine at 6 pm, this is a festival renowned for its illumination with 3000 stone and bronze lanterns; a bugaku dance also takes place in the Apple Garden.

Omizutori (Water-Drawing Ceremony)
1-14 March. The monks of Tōdai-ji Temple enter a special period of initiation during these days. On the evening of 12 March, they parade huge flaming torches around the balcony of Nigatsu-dō (on the temple precincts) and rain down embers on the spectators to purify them. The water-drawing ceremony is performed after midnight.

Kasuga Matsuri
13 March. This ancient spring festival features a sacred horse, classical dancing (Yamato-mai) and elaborate costume.

Takigi Nō
11-12 May. Open-air performances of Nō held after dark by the light of blazing torches at Kōfuku-ji Temple and Kasuga Taisha Shrine.

Mantōrō (Lantern Festival)
14-15 August. The same as the festival held in February.

Shika-no-Tsunokiri (Deer Antler Cutting)
Sunday & national holidays in October. Those pesky deer in Nara-kōen Park are pursued in a type of elegant rodeo into the Roku-en (deer enclosure) close to Kasuga Taisha Shrine. They are then wrestled to the ground and their antlers sawn off. Tourist brochures hint that this is to avoid personal harm, though it's not clear whether they mean the deer fighting each other, or the deer mugging the tourists.

On Matsuri
15 to 18 December. This festival, dating back to the Heian period, is held to ensure a bountiful harvest and to ward off disease. It takes place at Wakamiya-jinja Shrine (close to Kasuga Taisha

Shrine) and features a procession of people dressed in ancient costume, classical dances, wrestling and performances of Nō.

PLACES TO STAY

Although Nara is favoured as a day trip from Kyoto, accommodation can still be packed out for festivals, holidays and at weekends, so try and make reservations in advance if you plan to visit at these times. The Nara City Tourist Centre can help with reservations and has extensive lists of hotels, minshuku, pension, ryokan and shukubō.

Youth Hostels

The *Seishōnen Kaikan Youth Hostel* (☎ 0742-22-5540) is of a nondescript, concrete character, but cheap at ¥2060 per person per night, and the staff are helpful. It's a 30 minute uphill walk from the centre of town to the hostel. From JR Nara station you can take bus No 21 (in the direction of the Dreamland amusement park's south entrance) and get off at the Sahoyama-mae bus stop which is opposite the hostel. Buses run about twice an hour between 7 am and 9 pm.

The *Nara Youth Hostel* (☎ 0742-22-1334) is close to Kōno-ike Pond, which is a short walk from the other youth hostel. This is a ritzier hostel which *only* takes guests with a hostel membership card and charges ¥2500 per person per night. It tends to be booked out and is often swarming with schoolkids on excursions. From Nara Kintetsu station, take a bus in the direction of Dreamland, Kamo or Takanohara and get off at the Yakyūjō-mae stop, which is in front of a baseball stadium beside the hostel.

Ryokan & Minshuku

The *Ryokan Seikan-sō* (☎ 0742-22-2670) has wooden architecture and a pleasant garden. It's a 15 minute walk south of Kintetsu Nara station, close to Sarusawa-no-ike Pond. Prices for a Japanese-style room without bath start at ¥3800/7600 for singles/doubles.

The *Ryokan Hakuhoh* (☎ 0742-26-7891) is in the centre of town, just a five minute walk from JR Nara station. Prices for a Japanese-style room without bath are expensive at ¥5600/10,000 for singles/doubles.

The *Ryokan Matsumae* (☎ 0742-22-3686) is close to Nara-kōen Park, just south of Sarusawa-no-ike Pond. Prices for a Japanese-style room without bath start at ¥4500/8000 for singles/doubles.

There are also some minshuku in the city centre. *Sakigake* (☎ 0742-22-7252) is in an attractive, traditional style building and has rates of ¥5300 with two meals. Slightly cheaper is *Yamaya* (☎ 0742-24-0045), which costs ¥4200 per person, including breakfast. Don't expect English-speaking staff at either of these minshuku, though some English is spoken at each of the three ryokan listed above.

Shukubō
The Nara City Tourist Centre has a list of temples offering lodgings. *Shin-Yakushi-ji Temple* (☎ 0742-22-3736), which is in a quiet area near Nara-kōen Park, offers lodging and breakfast from ¥4000 per person per night.

Hotels
The city centre has a few business hotels. The *Nara Green Hotel* (☎ 0742-26-7815) is a small place with singles from ¥6400, twins from ¥12,000 and doubles at ¥11,000. It's close to the Kintetsu station. The *Nara Kokusai Hotel* (☎ 0742-26-6001) is close to JR Nara station and has a small number of singles at ¥7000; twin rooms here are expensive at ¥16,000. Close to the south-western corner of Nara-kōen Park, the *Hotel Sunroute Nara* (☎ 0742-22-5151) has singles from ¥7700 to ¥8700 and twins and doubles from ¥14,850 to ¥16,850.

Finally, not far from the Sunroute Hotel, the rambling *Hotel Nara* (0742-26-3300) is Nara's premiere hotel. It has singles at ¥11,000, twins from ¥18,500 to ¥21,000 and doubles from ¥20,000 to ¥21,000.

PLACES TO EAT
Nara is known for the full-course delights of kaiseki cuisine, which start at about ¥5000

for a basic version. This usually includes the local delicacy called *narazuke*, which consists of tart vegetables pickled in sake. If you've got the money to splurge on this kind of thing, *Yanagi-chaya* is an old teahouse where you can sample Nara kaiseki in garden surroundings. It's in Nara-kōen Park, just east of Kōfuku-ji Temple. Bentō (boxed lunches) start around ¥3500 and kaiseki set menus at around ¥6000.

There are plenty of inexpensive restaurants and fast-food places around both the stations. Opposite Kintetsu station are a couple of fast-food outfits, but the arcade and Marco Polo St, both of which run south from Kintetsu station, are probably the best hunting grounds for foreign and Japanese restaurants. Look out for *TacoDonald's* and *Parie de Rome* on the right side of Marco Polo St. Both have reasonably inexpensive lunch-time sets. Over on the arcade, there are a number of Japanese restaurants with good lunch-time deals. *Getsunitei* on the Kintetsu Nara station end of the arcade has mini-kaiseki lunches for ¥1500, which is about as cheap as kaiseki comes – a good opportunity to sample the local haute cuisine.

THINGS TO BUY
Nara has a long tradition for producing handicrafts such as *Nara-shikki* (lacquerware), *kogaku-men* (ancient masks), elaborate Nara round-fans, calligraphy materials and dolls made with the *itto-bori* (one chisel) carving technique. Tea utensils such as *akahada-yaki* ceramics and *chasen* (tea whisks) are also popular handicraft items. For a deer-related souvenir, you could buy *tsuno zaiku* (carved antlers) which are sawn off during the annual deer antler-cutting ceremony – though what you would want to do with them is anyone's guess.

A good place to look for handicrafts is the Naramachi area, a short walk south of Sarusawa-no-ike Pond in Nara-kōen Park.

GETTING THERE & AWAY
Air
Nara is served by Osaka Itami Airport and the new Kansai International Airport. You

will need to travel by bus to Osaka or Kyoto and then continue by rail to Nara – there is no direct connection with either airport.

Train

Nara to Kyoto Unless you have a Japan Rail Pass, the best option is the Kintetsu line (often indicated in English as the Kinki Nippon railway) linking Kyoto and Nara (Kintetsu Nara station) in 30 minutes by direct limited express (¥980 one way). Ordinary trains take 45 minutes and cost ¥540. The JR Nara line connects Kyoto with JR Nara station (¥680 one way, one hour).

Nara to Osaka The Kintetsu Nara line connects Osaka (Kintetsu Namba station) with Nara (Kintetsu Nara station) in half an hour by limited express (¥920). Express and local trains take about 40 minutes and cost ¥480.

The JR Kansai line links Osaka (Tennō-ji station) and Nara (JR Nara station) via Hōryu-ji (¥760, 50 minutes by express).

Bus

There is an overnight bus service between Tokyo and Nara which costs ¥8240 one way or ¥14,830 return. The bus leaves Nara at 10.30 pm and reaches Tokyo next day at 6.20 am. The bus from Tokyo leaves at 11 pm and arrives in Nara next day at 6.50 am. Check with the Nara City Tourist Office or the Tokyo TIC for further details.

GETTING AROUND
Bus

Nara has an excellent bus system geared to tourists and most of the buses have taped announcements in English. Outside Kintetsu station there's even a machine which gives advice in English for your destination. Just push the right destination button to find out your boarding terminal, bus number, ticket cost and departure time for the next bus.

Most of the area around Nara-kōen Park is covered by two circular bus routes. Bus No 1 runs counter-clockwise and bus No 2 runs clockwise. There's a ¥150 flat fare. You can easily see the main sights in the park on foot

and use the bus as an option if you are pushed for time or get tired of walking.

The most useful buses for western and south-western Nara (Tōshōdai-ji Temple, Yakushi-ji Temple and Hōryū-ji Temple) are Nos 52 and 97, which have taped announcements in English and link all three destinations with the Kintetsu and JR stations. Buses run about every 30 minutes between 8 am and 5 pm, but are much less frequent outside these times.

From Kintetsu station, allow about 20 minutes and a fare of ¥200 for the trip to Tōshōdai-ji Temple and Yakushi-ji Temple; add another 30 minutes and an extra ¥400 if you continue to Hōryū-ji Temple.

Taxi

Taxis are plentiful, but expensive. From JR station to either of the youth hostels costs about ¥800.

Bicycle

Nara is a convenient size for getting around on a bicycle. The Kintetsu Rent-a-Cycle Centre (☎ 0742-24-3528) is close to the Nara City Tourist Centre. From the centre, walk east down the main street to the first intersection, turn left into Konishi-dōri and walk about 70 metres until you see Supermarket Isokawa on your right. Opposite the supermarket is a small side street on your left – the bicycle rental centre is at the bottom of this street. Prices start at ¥720 for four hours or ¥1030 for the day. There's a discount for two day rental.

Around Nara

The southern part of Nara Prefecture was the birthplace of imperial rule and is rich in historical sights which are easily accessible as day trips from Nara or Kyoto – providing you make an early start.

The Tourist Division of Nara Prefectural Government publishes an excellent, detailed map called *Japan: Nara Prefecture*. The front page has a photo of two deer on a

KANSAI REGION

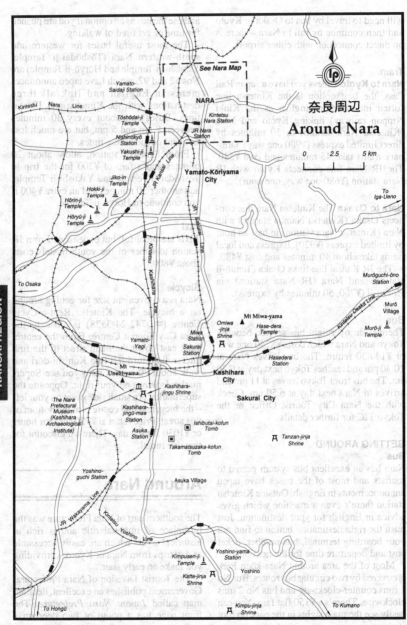

See Nara Map

NARA

奈良周辺
Around Nara

0   2.5   5 km

Kintetsu   Nara   Line

Yamato-
Saidaiji Station

Tōshōdai-ji
Temple

Nishinokyō
Station

Yakushi-ji
Temple

Jiko-in
Temple

Hokki-ji
Temple

Hōrin-ji
Temple

Hōryū-ji
Temple

Kintetsu
Nara Station

JR Nara
Station

**Yamato-Kōriyama
City**

To Osaka

To Iga-Ueno

Murōguchi-ōno
Station

Murō-ji
Temple

Murō
Village

Omiwa-
jinja
Shrine

Mt Miwa-yama

Hase-dera
Temple

Miwa
Station

Sakurai
Station

Hasedera
Station

**Kashihara
City**

Sakurai City

Yamato-
Yagi

Mt
Unebi-yama

The Nara
Prefectural
Museum
(Kashihara
Archaeological
Institute)

Kashihara-
jingu Shrine

Kashihara-
jingū-mae
Station

Asuka
Station

Tanzan-jinja
Shrine

Ishibutai-kofun
Tomb

Takamatsuzaka-kofun
Tomb

Asuka Village

Yoshino-
guchi Station

Kimpusen-ji
Temple

Katte-jinja
Shrine

Yoshino-yama
Station

Yoshino

Kimpu-jinja
Shrine

To Kumano

To Hongū

hillside. The Nara City Tourist Centre should have copies of this map, which gives an overall view of the prefecture and has insets providing precise locations for temples and other sights.

Sakurai and Yamato-Yagi are two cities which are easily reached by rail and are useful as transport hubs for visiting sights in the surrounding region. Travelling from Nara to Yamato-Yagi station you will need to go west to Yamato-Saidaiji first, then change to the southbound Kintetsu Kashihara line. The JR Sakurai line runs direct between Nara and Sakurai.

AROUND SAKURAI 桜井

There are a few interesting places to visit close to the town of Sakurai, which can be reached direct from Nara on the JR Sakurai line (30 minutes ¥310). To reach Sakurai via Yamato-Yagi (for example, from Kyoto or Osaka), take the Kintetsu Osaka line.

Ōmiwa-jinja Shrine 大神神社

This shrine is just north of Sakurai and can be reached by bus from Sakurai station. You can also walk to the shrine from Miwa station which is one stop north of Sakurai on the JR Sakurai line. Ōmiwa-jinja boasts the highest torii in Japan (32.2 metres), and is one of Japan's oldest Shintō shrines. Mt Miwa-yama is considered sacred because it is the abode of the shrine's kami (spirit gods), and there is a trail for pilgrims to hike up the wooded slopes.

Tanzan-jinja Shrine 談山神社

Tanzan-jinja lies south of Sakurai, and can be reached in about 25 minutes by bus (¥360) from Sakurai station. It is tucked away in the forests of Mt Tōnomine, famous for their autumn foliage colours. The central structure of the shrine is an attractive 13 storeyed pagoda. There's a hiking trail from the shrine leading down through the forests in less than two hours to Asuka (Ishibutai-kofun Tomb).

Hase-dera Temple 長谷寺

Two stops east of Sakurai on the Kintetsu Osaka line is Hasedera station which is a 20 minute walk from Hase-dera Temple. After a long climb up endless steps, you enter the main hall and are rewarded with a splendid view from the gallery, which juts out on stilts over the mountainside.

MURŌ-JI TEMPLE 室生寺

To visit Murō-ji Temple, you should return to Hasedera station and continue two stops further east down the Kintetsu Osaka line to Murōguchi-Ōno station. From there, it's a 15 minute ride by bus (¥340). The temple was founded in the 9th century and has strong connections with Esoteric Buddhism (the Shingon sect). Unlike other Shingon temples, women were never excluded from the precincts here. The five storeyed pagoda dates back from the 8th or 9th century and is the smallest in Japan. It's a peaceful, secluded place in thick forest and well worth a visit. It's open daily from 8 am to 4.30 pm and entry is ¥400.

IMAI-CHŌ

On the south-western edge of Yamato-Yagi, is the small town of Imai-chō , which – an extreme rarity for Japan – has preserved its houses virtually intact from the Edo period. To get there, take a train one stop south from Yamato-Yagi to Yagi-Nishiguchi. The town is a 10 minute walk south-west of the station.

KASHIHARA 橿原

Three stops south of Yamato-Yagi, on the Kintetsu Kashihara line, is Kashihara-jingū-mae station. There are a couple of interesting sights within easy walking distance, north-west of this station.

The Nara Prefectural Museum
奈良県立橿原考古博物館

This museum, which houses the Kashihara Archaeological Institute, is a must for archaeology buffs interested in the rich pickings from digs in the region. It's open from 9 am to 4.30 pm, closed on Monday, and entry is ¥300.

Kashihara-jingū Shrine 橿原神宮

This shrine at the foot of Mt Unebi-yama, dates back to 1889, when many of the buildings were moved here from the Kyoto Imperial Palace. The shrine is dedicated to Japan's mythical first emperor Jimmu, and an annual festival is held here on 11 February, the legendary date of Jimmu's enthronement. The vast, park-like grounds are pleasant for a stroll. The shrine is five minutes on foot from Kashihara-jingū-mae station.

ASUKA 飛鳥

One stop further south on the Kintetsu Kashihara line is Asuka station. You can rent bicycles here and head east to explore the area's temples, palace remains, tombs and strange stones. Alternatively, you can take a bus from Kashihara-jingū-mae station which makes stops within walking distance of many of the sights.

Two tombs worth seeing are Takamatsu-zuka-kofun and Ishibutai-kofun (*kofun* is 'tomb'). The former (excavated in 1972) cannot be entered, but has a museum (which is open from 9 am to 5 pm, closed Monday, entry ¥200) displaying a copy of the frescos. The Ishibutai-kofun can be entered, but has no frescos. Entry to the latter is from 9 am to 5 pm daily and tickets are ¥200.

The best museum in the area is Asuka Historical Museum, which has exhibits from regional digs. If you have time, take a look at Asuka-dera Temple, which dates from 596 and houses the oldest remaining image of Buddha in Japan – after more than 1300 years of venerable existence, you'll have to excuse its decidedly tatty appearance.

YOSHINO 吉野
History

In early times the remote mountainous regions around Yoshino were considered the mysterious abode of the kami (spirit gods) and later became a centre for Shugendō, a Buddhist school which incorporated ancient Shamanistic rites, Shintō beliefs and ascetic Buddhist traditions. The school has its origin in the banding together of Buddhist hermits who practised their faith deep in the mountains, though the legendary En-no-Gyōja, to whom powers of exorcism and magic are

ascribed, is frequently referred to as the founder of the school.

Yoshino came to historical prominence in the years following Emperor Go-Daigo's efforts to restore imperial rule from the Kamakura Shogunate. In 1333, Emperor Go-Daigo successfully toppled the Kamakura Shogunate with the help of disgruntled generals. The return to imperial rule, known as the Kemmu Restoration, only lasted three years. Go-Daigo failed to reward his supporters adequately and he was ousted in a revolt by one of his generals, Ashikaga Takauji, who set up a rival emperor.

Go-Daigo beat a hasty retreat to the remote safety of Yoshino where he set up a rival court. Rivalry between the two courts continued for 60 years, known as Nanbokuchō (Northern & Southern Courts period), until the Ashikaga made a promise (which was not kept) that the imperial lines would alternate.

Nowadays, Yoshino is Japan's top cherry blossom wonder. For a few weeks in spring, the blossoms from thousands of cherry trees form a floral carpet gradually ascending the mountainsides. It's definitely a sight worth seeing, but the narrow streets of Yoshino become jammed tight with thousands of visitors and you'll have to be content with a day trip unless you've booked accommodation long in advance. Early morning or late afternoon on a weekday is a good time to escape the crowds. Another severe impediment to enjoyment of the peaceful setting is an irritating loudspeaker system which relentlessly pursues you with a Mickey Mouse voice turned up at full pitch and volume to reverberate across the valley.

Orientation & Information

To walk from the top cablecar station to Kimpu-jinja, should take about 75 minutes at an easy pace. Allow a couple of extra hours to see the sights, or take a picnic for a lazy afternoon under the cherry trees and stay longer.

The village is often clogged with traffic inching its way through the narrow streets past souvenir shops and restaurants, many of which have dining areas on balconies overlooking the valley. Two local specialities are *kuzu* (arrowroot starch) and *washi* (handmade paper).

For information, you can try the tourist booth on your right as you exit the station, or ask at a similar booth which is in front of the top cablecar station. The official tourist information office is about 400 metres further up the street, on your right just after the Zao-dō Hall.

Things to See

As you walk up the main street, you pass through Kuro-mon Gate and should then veer slightly to the right up some stone steps to Ni-ō-mon Gate. This brings you to the massive, wooden structure of the Zaō-dō Hall, which is the main building of Kimpusen-ji Temple. For many centuries Kimpusen-ji has been one of the major centres for Shugendō. It's open from 8 am to 5 pm daily, and entry to the Zaō-dō Hall is ¥300.

About 500 metres further up the street you pass Katte-jinja Shrine on your right. The road forks uphill to the right, but keep to the left and follow the road until it twists up a hill to some shops. On your left, opposite the shops, there's a steep path leading up the mountain to Kimpu-jinja Shrine. Just past the shops, there's a bus stop (with infrequent buses to Kimpu-jinja) to your left on the Yoshino-ōmine driveway – good for motorised transport, but uninteresting as a walk.

There are plenty of streets or flights of steps leading off the main street to small temples and shrines. A short walk beyond the Kizō-in Temple Youth Hostel is the Chikurin-in Temple which provides expensive lodgings; you can pay to visit the garden only, with its ornamental pond and fine view across the valley.

Yoshimizu-jinja Shrine, on a side street opposite the tourist office, has a good platform for blossom viewing.

Mt Ōmine-san Pilgrimage Trail

From Kimpu-jinja Shrine in Yoshino, there's a Shugendō pilgrimage trail running all the way via the ranges of sacred Mt Ōmine-san to coastal Kumano. During the Heian period, the pilgrimage became immensely popular with pilgrims and yamabushi (Shugendō priests) trekking from as far as Kyoto and undergoing austere rites en route. Pilgrims who contravened the rules or lacked sufficient faith were given a gentle lesson by being hung over a precipice by their heels. Between May and September many pilgrims still hike this route.

Women were barred from the entire route until as recent as the 1960s. Today, there are still points at either end of the route beyond which women definitely may not pass; any who do try are met with fierce resistance.

Festivals

On 7 July, there's the bizarre Kaeru Tobi Festival, which commemorates the story of a man who insulted a yamabushi (literally 'mountain priest') of the Shugendō school and was turned into a frog. Don't be surprised if you see a man dressed as a frog parading around the village.

Places to Stay & Eat

The tourist information office in the centre of the village can organise accommodation or you can use the information booths outside Yoshino station or at the top cablecar station. Many of the temples offer lodgings, but you'll be looking at a minimum of ¥10,000 including meals. A slightly cheaper alternative is provided by several minshuku.

The cheapest option, at ¥1900 per person per night, is *Kizō-in Temple* (☎ 07463-2-3014), which doubles as the local youth hostel and provides an excellent opportunity to stay in a temple. Several of the hostel rooms look out across the valley.

Kizō-in Temple is easy to find. Just after Katte-jinja Shrine, the road divides. Take the right-hand fork up the steep hill for about 300 metres until you reach the imposing temple gate at the crest of the hill on your left.

On the same fork of the road, near the fork itself, is the *Kokuminshukusha Yoshino*

Sansō (☎ 07463-2-5051). It has a good reputation for its meals, and per-person costs with two meals included are from ¥5500.

The main street has dozens of restaurants and coffee shops. The former tend to close early after the day-trippers have left.

Getting There & Away

All rail connections to and from Yoshino run via Yoshino station. From the station you can reach the centre of Yoshino by simply walking uphill for 25 minutes or by taking a five minute cablecar ride (¥460 return).

From Kyoto you can take the train south on the Kintetsu Nara/Kashihara lines (they change halfway) to Kashihara-jingū-mae (50 minutes). At Kashihara-jingū-mae it's necessary to change to the Kintetsu Yoshino line for Yoshino station (40 minutes). You can do the whole trip in around one hour 15 minutes if you use limited express services and get good connections. The ticket price is ¥1060, with a ¥1020 limited express surcharge. It's possible to do the same trip from Nara by taking a train from Nara to Kashihara-jingū-mae station.

From Osaka (Abenobashi station close to Tennō-ji station) you can take the direct train on the Kintetsu Minami-Osaka line to Yoshino. Limited express services take one hour 12 minutes and tickets are ¥850, with a ¥720 limited express surcharge.

For rail connections to or from Wakayama Prefecture (for example, Mt Kōya-san), you can join the JR Wakayama line at Yoshino-guchi station.

IGA-UENO 伊賀上野

This rather drab town, an hour west of Nara by train, is dominated by a castle, which was once a base for ninja who were trained in martial and spiritual skills. The town also derives considerable literary and touristic clout from being the birthplace of Bashō, Japan's most celebrated haiku poet. In response to popular demands, the city elders have considerably installed a drop-in box for visitors' haiku poetry.

Ninjutsu

Those who have read *Shogun* by James Clavell, watched a few martial arts movies or taken an interest in the Teenage Mutant Ninja Turtles will know about this martial art. Although the Japanese claim it as their own, it's more probable that it was adapted in ancient times from the *Sonshi*, a Chinese tactical manual, used in Shugendō for training *yamabushi* (mountain priests).

Ninjutsu (the art of stealth) was perfected after the 13th century as a means for the practitioners *(ninja)* to serve their lords with mayhem such as assassination, stealthy thievery, sabotage and spying.

Two schools flourished during the 14th and 15th centuries: the Iga and Koga. Training took place in small family units. At one stage nearly 50 of these were active. Trainee ninja were taught the spiritual and physical skills of both overt and clandestine action along the lines of the Chinese theory of Yin and Yang. They developed tremendous agility in climbing, jumping and swimming, and could even sprint sideways or backwards.

To facilitate their spying and killing, they dressed in black for night operations and used a variety of gadgets. These included a collapsible bamboo stick for scaling walls, metal throwing stars *(shuriken)* and nasty little items called caltrops *(tennenbishi)* which had four spikes arranged to skewer the feet of pursuing enemies. ∎

Orientation & Information

The sights are contained in Ueno-kōen Park – the castle is visible from the station – which is a 12 minute walk from Ueno-shi station. Use the subway under the tracks, cross the road and continue uphill into the park.

There's an information office with maps and English leaflets just outside Ueno-shi station. If you have a large backpack which won't fit the lockers, you can pay ¥260 to deposit it at a luggage check beside the ticket window and save yourself the trouble of lugging your load around the park.

The area around Iga-Ueno is famous as a ceramics centre which produced classic items for the tea ceremony. There's a pottery museum, Iga Shigaraki Kotōkan, right next to Ueno-shi station.

Iga is also famous for producing virtually all of Japan's *kumihimo*, braided cords made from silk as adornments for swords and, in modern times, as classy kimono accessories.

Ninja Yashiki House　忍者屋敷

The house originally belonged to a village leader and was moved here from Takayama village in the Iga district.

Pink-suited *kunoichi* (ninja girls) go through a quick and wooden routine demonstrating how to slip through revolving doors. The group of visitors is then handed over to an old man who reveals a concealed cupboard and continues with perhaps the most impressive display when he deftly flips up a fake floorboard and retrieves a hidden sword in one rapid movement.

In the basement of the house is a museum with uniforms, martial implements and information in Japanese about ninjutsu (the art of ninja).

Admission costs ¥300 and it's open from 9 am to 5 pm but closed from 29 December to 1 January.

Ueno-jō Castle

This castle was built on the remains of a temple in 1608 by the lord of Iga and Ise, Todo Takatora. The present structure is a reconstruction from 1935. As you climb up steep stairs, there are exhibits of pottery, paintings, armour and ninja paraphernalia on each floor. It's worth a quick visit, particularly in the cherry blossom season and in combination with the Ninja House.

Admission to the castle costs ¥300. It's open from 9 am to 5 pm but closed from 29 December to 1 January.

Bashō Memorial Museum

The Bashō Ou Kinekan (Bashō Memorial Museum), is a brick and concrete building displaying some of Bashō's literary works. Unless you are a Bashō fan, you can safely skip this.

Those interested in curious literary trivia might like to know that Bashō is also the name for the Japanese banana tree and the poet was given his name after a disciple had planted one as a present at the gate of his retreat.

Admission costs ¥150 and it's open from 8.30 am to 5 pm daily except Monday, Thursday afternoons and days following a national holiday.

The Art of Swordsmithing

The first swords in Japan were made from polished stone but by the 6th century, bronze and iron were being used for long, straight swords. In later centuries the technology was refined to vary the hardness of the blade. The iron was folded and welded, often many thousands of times, to produce exceptional purity in the material and strength and beauty in the blade.

Each swordsmithing school had its own skills in tempering blades with specific mixtures of fire clay before polishing. The temper pattern on the edge of the blade progressed from simple designs to complex figures which distinguished one blade from another.

Early Japanese swords were made for stabbing: straight and usually single-edged. As mounted combat became more prevalent, warriors favoured a curved sword. Soldiers on foot found a short, heavy sword to be more effective.

In the Muromachi period, the most renowned samurai sword was the *katana* which had a long hilt for a fast draw and was wider and straighter than previous swords. The katana was often worn with a smaller, companion blade, the *wakizashi*, which was used for combat at close quarters or, if the game was up, for seppuku.

In the Edo period, swords and their mountings were covered with gold, silver or lacquer ornamentation. These works of art were displayed as paired sets of katana and wakizashi on special sword racks.

During the Meiji period, mass production of swords eroded their quality. After WW II, many swords were destroyed as part of a drive to stamp out militarism or carted away by souvenir-hunters. There has been a recent revival of interest in collecting Japanese swords; some swords have family histories stretching back many centuries and command huge prices. ■

KANSAI REGION

Festivals

Ninja Matsuri takes place on the first Sunday in April in the park.

Ueno Tenjin Matsuri takes place at Sugiwara-jinja Shrine between 23 and 25 October. Dating from the 16th century, the festival features a parade of mikoshi (portable shrines) on ornate floats which are accompanied by fearsomely attired demons.

Getting There & Away

Nara is one hour by express from Iga-Ueno on the JR Kansai line which also connects with Nagoya. The closest station for Ueno-kōen Park is Ueno-shi which lies between the stations of Iga-Kanbe to the south and Iga-Ueno to the north. It's a short trip to Ueno-shi (25 minutes from Iga-Kanbe; seven minutes from Iga-Ueno) but services are infrequent. You may prefer to take a taxi. Ise is 90 minutes by normal express train from Iga-Kanbe on the Kintetsu Osaka line.

Wakayama-ken
和歌山県

This remote and mountainous prefecture is on the south-western side of the Kii Peninsula. In the south, the Kumano region has several interesting Shintō shrines. In the north, the temple complex of Kōya-san is one of the major centres of Buddhism in Japan and merits a visit. The eastern parts consist of rocky coastlines and on the western side there are sandy beaches around Shirahama. Transport can be slow and infrequent, whether chugging along the coastline by rail or bussing through the remote, mountainous regions.

JNTO publishes a leaflet called *Shirahama & Wakayama Prefecture*, which gives concise details about sights and transport. The International Exchange Section (☎ 0734-32-4111) of Wakayama Prefectural Government publishes *Your Passport to Wakayama* which has detailed mapping and information.

There are some curious festivals in this prefecture. On 14 August, the town of Shimotsu celebrates the Grey Mullet Fishing Dance or you could wait until 10 October and choose between the Laughter Festival at Kawabe and the Crying Babies Sumō Festival in Shimotsu.

SHINGŪ 新宮

This town is nothing exceptional to look at, but functions as a useful transport hub for access to the three major Shintō shrines (Kumano Hayatama Taisha, Kumano Hongū Taisha and Nachi Taisha), known collectively as Kumano Sanzan. There's an information office at the station where you can get tourist information, pick up maps and check bus or train schedules.

If you are killing time between trains or buses, you could visit the gaudy Kumano Hayatama Taisha Shrine which is a 15 minute walk north-west of Shingū station. The shrine's Boat Race Festival takes place on 15 and 16 October. The nearby Shinpokan Museum houses treasures accumulated by the shrine.

Kamikura Shrine is famous for its Oto Matsuri Festival on 6 February when over a thousand men carrying torches ascend the slope to the shrine. The shrine is a 15 minute walk west of the station.

If you need a place to stay, you could try the *Shingū Hayatama Youth Hostel* (☎ 0735-22-2309) which is a 15 minute walk from the station, close to Kumano Hayatama Taisha Shrine. It's a relatively inexpensive youth hostel, with beds at ¥1900.

Getting There & Away

The JR Kisei line connects Shingū with Nagoya and Osaka. The fastest trip by limited express in either direction takes about four hours.

There are buses from Shingū to Shiko (45 minutes), which is the boat dock for trips through the Doro-kyō Gorge. Buses on this route continue via Hongū or the spa towns of Kawayu and Yunomine all the way through the Yoshino-Kumano National Park to Gōjō; some continue east to Nara or west to

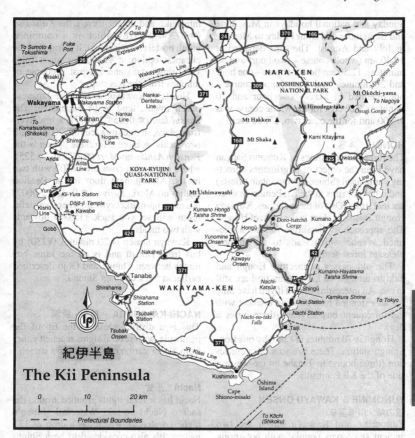

紀伊半島
The Kii Peninsula

0   10   20 km

--- Prefectural Boundaries

Hashimoto. The bus passes through spectacular scenery, but you need to allow over five hours for the journey from Shingū to Gōjō.

DORO-KYŌ GORGE 滝峡
Glass-roofed boats depart from the dock at Shiko for the dramatic two hour trip on the Kitayama-gawa River through what is generally considered to be Japan's most outstanding gorge. The fare is ¥3280 and boats operate at regular intervals from 8 am to 2.50 pm during the summer and from 9 am to 2.15 pm between November and February. Buses connect Shiko with Shingū and are

co-ordinated with boat times (¥960 one way, 42 minutes).

The glass-roofed boats ply the relatively tranquil lower end of the gorge as far as Doro-hatchō. If you want a less tranquil, wetter and more expensive ride you can shoot the rapids on rafts further upstream, but you will have to approach the gorge from the north and take a bus from Kumano station to Kitayama-mura. Check the latest details and timings with the TIC in Kyoto or Tokyo or make a toll-free call to the Japan Travel-Phone service. At the last check, rafts from Kitayama-mura operated on Saturday,

Sunday and national holidays in May, June and September and from Friday to Monday in July and August. The trips departed at 10.40 am (whole course – two hours and 50 minutes), 11.50 am (lower course – one hour and 20 minutes) and 1 pm (upper course – not operated in May – one hour and 20 minutes). The cost for the whole course was ¥8000 and for the other two, ¥5000 each.

HONGŪ 本宮
The three sacred shrines of Kumano Sanzan have been the object of pilgrimages attracting yamabushi (Shugendō mountain priests) and other pilgrims to the Kii Peninsula since ancient times. One of these shrines, Kumano Hongū Taisha, is close to the town of Hongū. The approach to the shrine follows a tree-lined avenue which leads to the shrine's pleasant forest setting.

The old passes connecting Hongū and Takijiri along a 40 km pilgrim trail are still in use. An interesting option if you have time for an extended hike and can connect with the infrequent bus services (three buses a day).

Hongū is 70 minutes (¥1380) by bus from Shingū station. There is also a bus connection (three hours) to Tanabe on the western side of the Kii Peninsula.

YUNOMINE & KAWAYU ONSEN
湯の峰・川湯温泉
Yunomine and Kawayu onsen are two ancient spa towns popular with hot-spring enthusiasts.

Yunomine consists of a narrow main street with the river and hot springs running down the middle. There are numerous hotels and minshuku on the wooded slopes either side of the street. Yunomine is on a bus route between Shingū and Gōjō, only 10 minutes from Hongū.

Kawayu Onsen is in a flatter, less attractive valley. The hot springs bubble out of the riverbed and there are numerous makeshift rotemburo (outdoor, hot-spring baths) dug out of the stones. However, these are not really worth a special visit – Yunomine is a better choice. Apart from a variety of

minshuku and hotels, there's the *Kajika-sō* (☎ 07354-2-0518) which is a combined youth hostel and minshuku. It's drab, but the cheapest option at ¥2300 per night (plus ¥100 onsen tax) and it's just a couple of minutes from the bus stop.

Hotels in Kawayu, as in other Japanese onsen towns, tend to be expensive. The *Sansui-kan* (☎ 07354-2-1011), a big riverfront place, charges upwards of ¥20,000 with two meals. A more affordable option is the *Pension Ashita-no-Mori* (☎ 07354-2-1525), where per-person costs are ¥8700 with two meals. Almost next door to the Pension Ashita-no-Mori, *Fujiya* (☎ 07354-2-0007) is a more up-market ryokan, where a tasteful room will set you back ¥15,000 upwards with two meals.

Kawayu Onsen is 20 minutes (¥280) by bus from Hongū and is on the same bus routes between Shingū and Gōjō described earlier in the section on Shingū.

NACHI-KATSUURA 那智・勝浦
This is a district, close to the tip of the peninsula, with several sights reached either from Nachi station or Kii-Katsuura station.

Nachi 那智
Nachi has several sights grouped around the sacred Nachi-no-taki Waterfall, Japan's highest waterfall, which has a drop of 133 metres. It's also considered to be a Shintō god. Nachi Taisha Shrine, one of the three great shrines of the Kii Peninsula, is adjacent to the waterfall as a natural homage to its kami. The Nachi-no-Hi Matsuri (Fire Festival) takes place here on 14 July. During this lively event portable shrines (mikoshi) are brought down from the mountain and met by groups bearing flaming torches.

Seiganto-ji Temple is next to the shrine. This temple is still popular with pilgrims as the starting point for the 33 Temple Pilgrimage.

The waterfall is about 10 minutes by bus from Nachi station, followed by a 20 minute walk.

Kii-Katsuura 紀伊勝浦

This resort town offers cruises around local islets and the renowned Bōki-dō Cave spa, which was popular with nobility in the Edo period. The catch is that the spa is inside one of Japan's largest hotels – the expensive Hotel Urashima. The cave spa is open to visitors from noon to 10 pm, and admission costs ¥2000. There's a cheaper (¥1000) open-air spa at Katsuura Gyoen ryokan which is open from 5 to 9 am, and from 3 pm to midnight.

The tourist office (☎ 07355-2-5311) is in front of the station.

Getting There & Away

A leisurely way of reaching the Kii Peninsula from Tokyo is the ferry between Tokyo Ferry Terminal (Ariake Pier in Toyocho) and Ukui Port close to Nachi. There's one sailing every second day (from ¥9060, 13 hours). There is a connecting bus (¥400, 20 minutes) between Nachi station and Ukui Port.

The same ferry runs between Ukui Port and Kōchi on Shikoku in about eight hours. Fares start at ¥5560 for this section of the trip or ¥13,910 for the whole trip between Tokyo and Kōchi.

TAIJI 太地

The earliest methods of whaling in Japan consisted simply of capturing whales that had become beached on the shore or trapped in bays. At the beginning of the 17th century, Taiji was one of the first communities to organise its whale hunting into a full-scale industry using hand harpooning and later resorting to net whaling. The rest of the story leading to the virtual extinction of many species of whale is well known and those who love whales will certainly be saddened by a visit to Taiji.

Things to See

The Whale Beach Park (Kujira Hama-kōen) is about five minutes by bus from Taiji station. Admission costs ¥1030 and it's open from 8.30 am to 5 pm. The entry ticket admits you to the Whale Museum, Whalers Museum, Marine Aquarium and Tropical Botanical Garden. It's a two km walk from Taiji station to Whale Beach Park. You can also approach the park from Katsuura station by bus (20 minutes, ¥440).

Places to Stay

The *Taiji Youth Hostel* (☎ 07355-9-2636) is three km from the station; 45 minutes on foot or nine minutes by bus. Get off at the Kōen-mae stop. Nightly costs at the hostel are ¥2000.

KUSHIMOTO 串本

This town is at the entrance to Cape Shiono-misaki, the southernmost point of Honshū. A short ferry ride connects with Kii Ō-shima Island (10 minutes, ¥170).

The cape is renowned for the Hashi-kui-iwa, a line of pillar-like rocks that have been imaginatively compared to a 'line of hooded monks' heading towards Kii Ō-shima Island. To take a look at the rocks, take a Shingū bound bus from Kushimoto station, and get off five minutes later at the Hashi-kui-iwa stop (¥130). For more local information contact the Kushimoto Tourist Association (☎ 07356-2-3171).

There are two youth hostels almost next to each other, on the tip of Cape Shiono-misaki. *Shiono-Misaki Youth Hostel* (☎ 07356-2-0570), with rates of ¥2200, is slightly cheaper than *Misaki Lodge Youth Hostel* (☎ 07356-2-1474), where nightly costs are ¥2300. Take a Shiono-misaki bound bus from Kushimoto station (20 minutes) and get off at the last stop – Sugu-mae.

Kushimoto is one hour from Shirahama by JR limited express, 3½ hours from Tennō-ji in Osaka, and two hours from Shingū by bus.

SHIRAHAMA 白浜

Shirahama is one of Japan's top, hot-spring resorts and comes complete with acres of swish hotels, golf courses, cabarets, an Adventure World and so forth. This probably makes it rather more interesting for Japanese than for most foreigners. The wonders of Shirahama are some distance from the station so you'll need to take a bus or rent a bicycle if you arrive by rail. The bus ride to the centre takes 17 minutes.

The Shirahama tourist information office (☎ 0739-42-2900) is in the station and open from 8.30 am to 5 pm. It's closed on Thursday. You could also try the Shirahama Tourist Association (☎ 0739-43-5511).

If you want to be independent, there's a bicycle rental place at the station – charges are ¥300 per hour or ¥1000 for the day.

Things to See & Do

Sakino-yu hot springs might appeal if you like the idea of taking a bath in the open air close to the sea. Take the bus from Shirahama station to Yuzaki bus stop (17 minutes), then walk for 10 minutes to the seaside segregated baths. Admission is free. Sakino-yu is open from 7 am to 7 pm in the summer and from 8 am to 5 pm in the winter but is closed on Wednesday. The springs are said to be good for all sorts of things ranging from constipation to the ailments of women.

Sandanheki Cliffs can be reached by bus (20 minutes) from the station. Get off at the Sandanheki-mae bus stop and admire all the souvenir stands before taking the elevator down to the Pirate's Cave at the foot of the cliffs. Various pirate items are displayed from the times when local pirates plundered passing shipping.

Close to these cliffs is Hama Blanca (Costa Branca) which promises the intriguing combination of laser lights, tropical theatre, a botanical garden and cabaret. Look out for the Jumbo Tomato Tree. Admission costs ¥1030 and it's open from 9 am to 5 pm.

Energy Land, close to Sakino-yu Hot Springs, has displays devoted to alternative energy sources. It's open 9 am to 4.30 pm, closed Wednesday and entry is ¥1200.

Just under a km to the south-west of Shirahama station is the Shirahama Adventure World. It has a safari park, aquarium and other attractions. It's not recommended, especially given the exhorbitant entry charge of ¥3000. It's open daily from 9 am to 5 pm.

At Tsubaki Onsen, two stops south of Shirahama on the JR line, there's the Tsubaki Monkey Park. The monkeys, some 250 of

them, are described as being 'popular with visitors' and 'humorous'. You'd *have* to be humorous if you wanted to live there, deal with all the crowds and stay sane.

Places to Stay

If you don't mind staying outside the town of Shirahama, the cheapest option is *Ohgigahama Youth Hostel* (☎ 0739-22-3433), which is close to some good beaches. The hotel is 10 minutes on foot from Kii-Tanabe station which is three stops (15 minutes) north of Shirahama station, or 30 minutes by bus from Shirahama station. From 1 July to 31 August the hostel charges ¥2000 per night, and ¥1800 thoughout the rest of the year.

In Shirahama itself, there are several kokuminshukusha and minshuku which charge around ¥5500 per person for accommodation and two meals. One place worth trying is the *Kokuminshukusha Hotel Shirahama* (☎ 0739-42-3039). It has per-person costs of ¥5400 per night with two meals, and is centrally located.

Getting There & Away

There are twice daily flights between Shirahama and Tokyo. The Kuroshio limited express on the JR Kisei line links Tennō-ji station in Osaka with Shirahama in two hours 15 minutes (¥3190 plus a limited express surcharge of ¥2150).

There is a bus service from Kii-Tanabe station which runs inland to Hongū via Yunomine and Kawayu in three hours. It follows the Nakaheji road which has been used by pilgrims for centuries.

GOBŌ 御坊

Gobō is famous for the nearby white, sandy beach of Enjuga-hama. Just beyond the western end of the beach, there's the Amerika-mura Village, so called because thousands of the locals emigrated from here to North America in the past and the place has now taken on the architectural style of their adopted homeland.

Close to Dōjōji station, one stop south of Gobō station, is Dōjō-ji Temple. The temple is home to a legend regarding a young woman who, when her love of a young monk was rejected, turned into a dragon and frazzled him to death. The story has been adapted by many Nō and Kabuki plays.

MINABE 南部

If you are passing through in early February, Minabe is famous for its 300,000 plum trees which blossom at this time.

YURA 由良

Close to Kii-Yura station is Kōkoku-ji Temple. The founder, Hotto Kokushi, is revered in culinary circles as the man believed to have introduced soy sauce to Japan from China. The town of Yuasa, just north of the temple, is famed for its homemade soy sauce. Avid foodies can see the sauce being produced and there's even a soy sauce museum.

ARIDA 有田

Cormorant fishing takes place on the Arida-gawa River from 1 June to 31 August. The standard method of cormorant fishing requires the use of a boat, but the people who fish on the Arida-gawa River wade in with a blazing torch in one hand and a cormorant on a leash in the other. If you join a group to see this style of fishing, it certainly won't come cheap. The going rate at present is ¥24,000 for a group of six.

Arida Orange Youth Hostel (☎ 0737-62-4536) is reached via Yuasa station. From the station take a bus (10 minutes) then walk for three minutes.

WAKAYAMA 和歌山

Wakayama (population 396,000) is the prefectural capital, a place of little interest to travellers beyond its function as a transport hub en route to other parts of the prefecture and beyond. The new Kansai International Airport is only 20 km to the north of Wakayama.

If you have time to kill in the city, it's only a 20 minute walk from Wakayama-shi station to Wakayama-jō Castle. The original castle was built in 1585 by Toyotomi

Hideyoshi and razed by bombing in WW II. The present structure is a passable postwar reconstruction.

Getting There & Away

Osaka is connected by rail with Wakayama via the Nankai Honsen line (70 minutes) and the JR Hanwa line (55 minutes). The Nankai line is serviced by Wakayama-shi (Wakayama city) station, which is about two km to the west of Wakayama station, where JR Hanwa line trains pull in. The two stations are connected by the JR Kisei line, which starts at Wakayama-shi station.

To visit Kōya-san from Wakayama you can go by rail on the JR Wakayama line to Hashimoto (¥780, one hour and 20 minutes) and then continue on the Nankai Dentetsu line express to Gokurakubashi station (¥320, 40 minutes).

From Wakayama Port, there's a ferry service to Komatsushima on Shikoku. From Fuke Port, just north of Wakayama, there are ferries to Sumoto (Awaji-shima Island) and Tokushima on Shikoku.

MT KŌYA-SAN & KŌYA-SAN 高野山

Mt Kōya-san is a raised tableland covered with thick forests and surrounded by eight peaks in the northern region of Wakayama Prefecture.

The major attraction on this tableland is the monastic complex, known as Kōya-san, which is the headquarters of the Shingon school of Esoteric Buddhism. It's one of the most rewarding places to visit in Japan, not just for the natural setting of the area, but also as an opportunity to stay in temples and get a glimpse of long-held traditions of Japanese religious life.

Over one million visitors come here annually so you should be prepared for congestion during peak holiday periods or festivals. Summer is a popular time to visit and escape from the lowland heat. You can miss large crowds by getting up really early for a stroll around the area before returning to take part in the morning religious service usually held around 6 am. Similarly, late-night strolls are most enjoyable for the peace and quiet. Apart from the obvious attractions of spring and autumn foliage, some hardy visitors like to wander round Kōya-san, mingling with skiers and pilgrims in the winter snow.

Although you could visit Kōya-san in a day, it's much better to reduce the travel stress and allow two days. This is one of the best places in Japan to treat yourself and splurge on a stay at a shukubō (temple lodging).

History

The founder of the Shingon school of Esoteric Buddhism, Kūkai (known after his death as Kōbō Daishi), established a religious community here in 816. Kōbō Daishi travelled as a young priest to China and returned after two years to found the school. He is one of Japan's most famous religious figures and is revered as a Boddhisattva, scholar, inventor of the Japanese kana syllabary and as a calligrapher. He is believed to be simply resting in his tomb, not dead but meditating, until the arrival of Miroku (Maitreya – Buddha of the Future).

Over the centuries, the temple complex grew in size and also attracted many followers of the Jōdo (Pure Land) school of Buddhism. During the 11th century, it became popular among the nobility and commoners to leave hair or ashes from deceased relatives close to Kōbō Daishi's tomb in handy proximity for his reawakening. This practice continues to be very popular today and accounts for the thousands of tombs around Okuno-in Temple.

In the 16th century, Oda Nobunaga asserted his power by massacring large numbers of monks at Kōya-san. The community subsequently suffered confiscation of lands and narrowly escaped invasion by Toyotomi Hideyoshi. At one stage, Kōya-san numbered over 1500 monasteries and many thousands of monks. The members of the community were divided into three groups: clergy (gakuryō), lay priests (gyōnin)) and followers of Pure Land Buddhism (hijiri).

In the 17th century, the Tokugawa Shogunate smashed the economic power of the lay priests who managed considerable estates in the region. Their temples were destroyed, their leaders banished and the followers of Pure Land Buddhism were bluntly pressed into the Shingon school. During the Edo period, the government favoured the practice of Shintō and confiscated the lands that supported Kōya-san's monastic community. Women were barred from entry to Kōya-san until 1872.

Today, Kōya-san is a thriving centre of Japanese Buddhism, with over 110 temples remaining and a population of 7000. As the headquarters of the Shingon school, it numbers over 10 million members and presides over nearly 4000 temples all over Japan.

Orientation & Information

At the top cablecar station there's a tourist information office which doles out information and makes reservations for temple lodgings.

The Kōya-san Tourist Association (☎ 0736-56-2616) has an office in the centre of town in front of the Senjuin-bashi-mae bus stop. Some English is spoken and a detailed brochure and maps are provided. Both tourist offices are open from 8.30 am to 5.30 pm in summer and from 9 am to 4.30 pm in winter. If enlightenment is imminent and you'd like to tell the folks abroad, there's an international phone booth beside the office.

The precincts of Kōya-san are divided into the Garan (Sacred Precinct) in the west and Okuno-in Temple with its vast cemetery in the east.

Okuno-in Temple　奥の院

Anybody worth their salt in Japan has had their remains or just a lock or two of hair interred here to ensure pole position when the Buddha of the Future and Kūkai return to the world.

The Tōrō-dō (Lantern Hall) houses hundreds of lamps including two believed to have been burning for over 900 years. Behind the hall you can see the closed doors of the Gobyō, Kūkai's mausoleum.

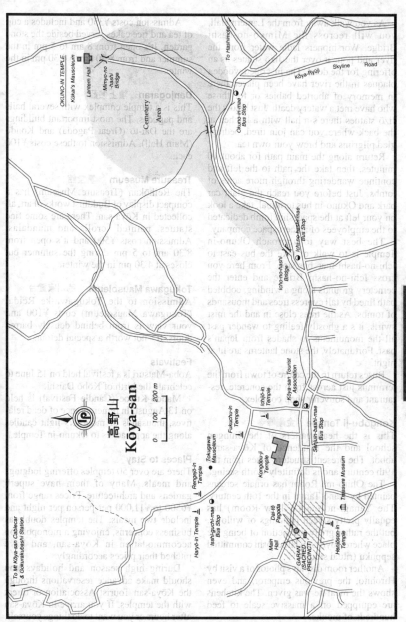

KANSAI REGION

As you walk away from the Lantern Hall, you will recross the Mimyo-no-hashi Bridge. Worshippers ladle water from the river and pour it over the Jizō statues as an offering for the dead. The inscribed wooden plaques in the river have been placed there in memory of aborted babies or for those who have met a watery death. Just below the Jizō statues there's a hall with a kitchen at the back where you can join tired, bedraggled pilgrims and brew your own tea.

Return along the main path for about 10 minutes, then take the path to the left and continue wandering through more acres of tombs. Just before you reach the giant car park and Okuno-in bus terminal, take a look on your left at the spaceship tomb dedicated to the employees of an aerospace company.

The best way to approach Okuno-in Temple is to walk or take the bus east to Ichi-no-hashi-mae bus stop. From here you cross Ichi-no-hashi Bridge and enter the cemetery grounds along a winding, cobbled path lined by tall cypress trees and thousands of tombs. As the trees close in and the mist swirls, it's a ghostly feeling to wander past all the monuments to shades from Japan's past. Fortunately, the stone lanterns are lit at night.

Buses return to the centre of town from the terminus just across from the concrete, restaurant and souvenir shop complex.

Kongōbu-ji Temple 金剛峰寺

This is the headquarters of the Shingon school and the residence of Kōya-san's abbot. The present structure dates from the 19th century and is definitely worth seeing.

The Ohiro-ma Room has ornate screens painted by Kanō Tanyu in the 16th century. The Yanagi-no-ma (Willow Room) has equally pretty screen paintings of willows, but the rather grisly distinction of being the place where Toyotomi Hideyoshi committed seppuku (ritual suicide).

Another room displays photos of a visit by Hirohito, the previous emperor, and even shows the meal he was given. The kitchens are equipped on a massive scale to feed hundreds of monks.

Admission costs ¥350 and includes a cup of tea and rice cakes served beside the stone garden. It's open from 8 am to 5 pm in the summer and from 8.30 am to 4.30 pm in the winter.

Danjogaran 壇上伽藍

This is a temple complex with several halls and pagodas. The most important buildings are the Dai-tō (Great Pagoda) and Kondō (Main Hall). Admission to these costs ¥100 each.

Treasure Museum 霊宝館

The Reihōkan (Treasure Museum) has a compact display of Buddhist works of art, all collected in Kōya-san. There are some fine statues, painted scrolls and mandalas. Admission costs ¥500 and it's open from 8.30 am to 5 pm during the summer but closes at 4.30 pm in the winter.

Tokugawa Mausoleum 徳川家霊台

Admission to the Tokugawa-ke Reidai (Tokugawa Mausoleum) costs ¥100 and your view is from behind densely barred doors. It's not worth a special detour.

Festivals

Aoba-Matsuri is a festival held on 15 June to celebrate the birth of Kōbō Daishi.

Mandō-Kuyoe (Candle Festival) is held on 13 August. In remembrance of dead relatives, thousands of mourners light candles along the approaches to Okuno-in Temple.

Places to Stay

There are over 50 temples offering lodgings and meals. Many of them have superb gardens and architecture. Prices range from ¥6500 to ¥11,000 per person per night and include two meals. The temples double as business concerns, enjoying a monopoly on accommodation in Kōya-san, and have pitched their prices accordingly.

During high season and holidays you should make advance reservations through the Kōya-san Tourist Association or direct with the temples. If you arrive in Kōya-san after hours or you want to do things yourself, the following shukubō all have English speaking staff and are at the lower to middle end of the price spectrum.

Henjōson-in Temple (☎ 0736-56-2434) was once a youth hostel, but is now one of the more expensive temple lodgings where English is spoken. A room for the night and two meals costs ¥8000. For this you get a pleasant room with a garden view, tatami furnishings, an excellent vegetarian dinner served in your room and the use of a terrific, wooden (smooth cedar) tub in the men's bathroom. There's even a temple bar and barmaid! The temple is close to the treasure museum and if you take the bus you should get off at Reihōkan-mae bus stop.

Haryō-in Temple (☎ 0736-56-2702) functions as a kokuminshukusha and is one of the cheapest temple accommodations around. It's a couple of minutes on foot from the Isshi-guchi-mae bus stop. A room for the night and two meals costs ¥5100.

Daien-in Temple (☎ 0736-56-2009) is another reasonably priced option. Per-person costs with two meals range from ¥6000 to ¥8000. *Seinan-in Temple* (☎ 0736-56-2421) has costs from ¥6600 to ¥9300; *Fukuchu-in Temple* (☎ 0736-56-2021) has costs ranging from ¥6600 to ¥18,400; and *Ichijō-in Temple* (☎ 0736-56-2214) has rates of ¥7000 to ¥10,000.

Places to Eat

The culinary speciality of Kōya-san is shōjin ryōri (vegetarian food) – no meat, fish, onions or garlic – which you can sample by ordering your evening meal at your temple lodgings. Two tasty tōfu specialities are *goma-tōfu* (sesame tōfu) and *kōya-tōfu* (local tōfu).

There are various coffee shops dotted around town for breakfast – a convenient one is at the main crossroads close to the tourist office.

Opposite Okuno-in-mae bus stop and the adjoining monstrosity of a car park, there's a large restaurant and souvenir shop. For lunch you could try the restaurant on the 2nd floor which serves a variety of dishes (choose from the window display and buy a ticket at the desk) including *sansai rāmen* (mountain vegetables with noodles) for ¥700. Mountain vegetable dishes are a local speciality available at restaurants all over town – tasty and nutritious.

Entertainment

Nightlife is restricted to walks in the graveyard, a couple of nondescript pubs and a pachinko parlour just across the road from the tourist office. Beer and sake are freely available in shops and in the temple lodgings – no religious quibbles about grain or rice.

Getting There & Away

All rail connections to and from Mt Kōya-san run via Gokurakubashi which is at the base of the mountain. A cablecar provides frequent connection between the base and the top of the mountain (five minutes). Buses run on two routes from the top cablecar station via the centre of town to Ichi-no-hashi Bridge and Okuno-in Temple. The fare to Okuno-in is ¥360.

From Osaka (Namba station) you can go direct by ordinary express on the Nankai Dentetsu line to Gokurakubashi station (one hour and 30 minutes). Most visitors buy a combined rail and cablecar ticket to Kōya-san for ¥1100. For the slightly faster, limited express service with reserved seats you pay a supplement almost equal to the ordinary express fare.

From Wakayama you can go by rail on the JR Wakayama line to Hashimoto (¥780, one hour and 20 minutes) and then continue on the Nankai Dentetsu express to Gokurakubashi station (¥320, 40 minutes).

If you are heading into the Kii Peninsula, you should take the train from Gokurakubashi to Hashimoto and then backtrack by rail to Gōjō (10 minutes). There are two buses a day between Gōjō and Shingū (¥3900, 5½ hours).

For rail connections to Yoshino, you must first travel from Mt Kōya-san (via Gokurakubashi) to Hashimoto and then continue on the JR Wakayama line to Yoshino-guchi station where you can change to the Yoshino

Kintetsu line for a short trip to Yoshino station.

Getting Around

Apart from Okuno-in Temple, which is 40 minutes on foot from the centre of town, all the other sights in the Garan area are conveniently reached from the centre on foot. As you walk, look out for the street drain covers; they have a temple motif!

Bicycles are available for hire at ¥350 per hour or ¥1050 for the day. The Kōya-san Tourist Association Office has more details.

There are three convenient bus services. One links the cablecar station with Ichi-no-hashi Bridge; another runs between the cablecar station and Okuno-in; and one more runs between the cablecar station and Daimon Gate. The stop opposite the tourist office in the centre of town is called Senjuin-bashi-mae. An all-day bus pass is available for ¥800.

Shima-hantō Peninsula
志摩半島

The Ise-Shima National Park on the Shima-hantō Peninsula has Japan's most sacred Shintō shrine and offers a variety of sea-scapes with narrow inlets and bays dotted with oyster rafts and seaweed poles. It's easily reached from Nagoya, Kyoto or Osaka and is worth a two day visit.

JNTO publishes *Ise-Shima*, a leaflet providing basic mapping and concise information for the area.

FESTIVALS

The Hatsumōde Festival celebrates the new year between 1 and 3 January. Millions of worshippers pack the area and accommodation is booked out for months in advance.

The Kagurai-sai Festival is celebrated on 5 and 6 April at Ise-jingū Grand Shrine. This is a good chance to see performances of kagura (sacred dance), bugaku (sacred dance and music), Nō and Shintō music.

Those in search of strange festivals might like to be around for the Hamajima Lobster Festival on 6 June when local folks prance around a giant paper lobster. Or else drop in on the Nakiri Waraji Festival which takes place in September (during the typhoon season). An enormous *waraji* (straw sandal) is floated out to sea to protect the locals. It's not surprising that this monstrous footwear is also claimed to scare off the sea monster.

PLACES TO STAY & EAT

Ise and Toba are prime tourist centres so there's plenty of accommodation, but it's probably preferable to stay in the quieter, more attractive places of the Ise-Shima area, such as Kashikojima or Futamigaura, which are within easy reach of Ise by train.

There are a couple of fast-food places – *Lotteria* and *Mr Donut* – next to Ise-shi station, which do budget breakfasts and lunches. Naturally, seafood is a speciality of the area and the dinners offered at youth hostels and ryokan are a good way to sample the local fare without busting your budget.

Youth Hostels

Youth Hostel Taikōji (☎ 05964-3-2283) is a temple hostel in Futamigaura. Take a four minute bus ride from the station, then walk for five minutes. The price is ¥1700 per night.

Ise-Shima Youth Hostel (☎ 05995-5-0226) is close to Anagawa station (two stops north of Kashikojima) – seven minutes on foot. You must be a member and the price is ¥2500 per night but a reduction may be given for foreign hostellers.

Ryokan

The *Hoshide Ryokan* (☎ 0596-28-2377) is a quaint, wooden ryokan with some nice traditional touches, seven minutes on foot from Ise-shi station. It's a member of the Japanese Inn Group and the friendly owners offer vegetarian or macrobiotic food. Singles/doubles cost ¥4000/7000. *Ishiyama-sō* (☎ 0599-52-1527) is a member of the Japan-

伊勢・志摩
Ise-shima Region

ese Inn Group on an island in Ago-wan Bay. The owner picks you up at Kashikojima Pier in his boat and spurts you back in a couple of minutes to the ryokan. Singles/ doubles cost ¥4500/9000. Some rooms have sliding doors less than a metre above the water. You can dip your toes in the water and watch the boats crisscrossing the bay. Dinner is good value at ¥1500 for a large spread of seafood.

Those who don't mind spending a little extra for the ryokan experience might want to try *Yamada-kan* (☎ 0596-28-2532), an atmospheric old ryokan about 500 metres south of Ise-shi station, close to Ise-jingū

Shrine. Per-person costs start at ¥9000 with two meals.

Hotels

Just to the east of Ise-shi station, the *Ise City Hotel* (☎ 0596-28-2111) is a standard business hotel, with singles from ¥6500 and twins from ¥13,000.

Shima Kankō Hotel (☎ 0599-43-1211) sits above Kashikojima, commanding a panoramic view across Ago Bay and its prices are commensurate with the view. Doubles start around ¥20,000 and Japanese-style rooms start a bit lower at ¥18,000. There are no single rooms. The hotel has Japanese and Western restaurants offering fine seafood and nouvelle cuisine respectively.

GETTING THERE & AWAY

Ise is well endowed with direct rail connections for Nagoya, Osaka and Kyoto. The most convenient direct routings are on private lines. Japan Rail Pass users will have to be prepared to make several time-consuming changes to reach their destination.

From Nagoya, the limited express on the Kintetsu line takes 80 minutes to Uji-Yamada station, one stop south of Ise, and takes another half hour to reach its terminus at Kashikojima. The fare is expensive (¥2280 one way to Ise-shi, ¥2970 to Kashikojima), but this is the quickest route. If you opt for JR services, your best bet is an express from Nagoya, which takes up to two hours and requires a change at Taki for the short ride to Ise-shi station.

From Osaka (Namba station), the limited express on the Kintetsu line takes about 1¾ hours to Uji-Yamada station and the one-way fare is ¥2570. There are also limited expresses on the same line, departing from Osaka (Uehon-machi station) and continuing via Ise-shi station to Toba in a total journey time of about two hours.

From Kyoto, the limited express takes two hours to Ise-shi station and continues for about an hour to reach its terminus at Kashikojima. The one-way fare from Kyoto to Ise-shi station costs ¥3010.

ISE-JINGŪ GRAND SHRINE   伊勢神宮

Dating back to the 3rd century, Ise-jingū Grand Shrine is the most venerated Shintō shrine in Japan. Shintō tradition has dictated for centuries that the shrine buildings (over 200 of them) are replaced every 20 years with exact imitations built on adjacent sites according to ancient techniques – no nails, only wooden dowels and interlocking joints. The present structures date from 1993 and were replaced at a cost exceeding ¥5 billion.

Although you cannot enter the buildings, it's possible to peek at their exterior architecture; interesting in that it represents classic

Japanese style before the arrival of Chinese influence in the 6th century. That said, some foreign visitors come away unenthusiastic about the experience. This is a place that is of immense historical and spiritual importance to Japan, but the actual shrine itself is unlikely to bowl you over visually.

There are two parts to the shrine – Gekū (Outer Shrine) and Naikū (Inner Shrine) – which are six km apart and linked by a frequent bus service. Over 100 other shrines are associated with the Grand Shrine.

No admission is charged and the shrines are open from sunrise to sunset. There are restrictions on photography and smoking.

Gekū   外宮

The Gekū (Outer Shrine) dates from the 5th century and enshrines the god of food, clothing and housing, Toyouke-no-Ōkami.

A stall at the entrance to the shrine provides a leaflet in English with a map. The main hall is approached along an avenue of tall trees and surrounded by closely fitted wooden fences which hide most of the buildings from sight. Only the emperor and imperial emissaries can enter.

From Ise-shi station, it's a 12 minute walk down the main street to the shrine entrance. Frequent buses leave from stop No 11 opposite the shrine entrance and run to Naikū (Inner Shrine) and Toba. A similar bus service operates to and from Uji-Yamada station.

Naikū   内宮

The Naikū (Inner Shrine) is thought to date from the 3rd century and enshrines the sun goddess, Amaterasu-Ōmikami, who is considered the ancestral goddess of the imperial family and the guardian deity of the Japanese nation. Since Naikū also houses the sacred mirror, one of the three imperial regalia (the other two are the curved jewels and the sacred sword) of the emperor, it is held in even higher reverence than Gekū.

Entrance to the shrine precincts is via Uji-bashi Bridge. One path leads to the left and passes Mitarashi, a place for pilgrims to purify themselves in the Isuzu-gawa River.

The obese carp here slither around with their slobbery lips permanently raised out of the water for yet more food. The path continues along a tree-lined avenue to the main hall. Photos are only allowed from the foot of the stone steps. Here too, you can only catch a glimpse of the interior; and wooden fences obstruct the surrounding view.

On your return to the bridge, take the path to your right and visit the sacred white horse which seems a little bored with its easy life: comfortable accommodation and plenty of fodder in return for a couple of monthly appearances at the shrine.

Buses run from Ise-shi station to the Naikū, take around 15 minutes and cost ¥360. Get off at Naikū-mae stop. From the shrine there are buses (¥1000, 45 minutes) to Toba which run along the Ise-Shima Skyline Road via Kongōshō-ji Temple on the top of Mt Asama-yama. If you have time, take a look around the temple, which is famous for its Moon Bridge, a footprint of Buddha – he seems to have left plenty around Asia – and eerie rows of memorial poles adorned with paraphernalia from the deceased. It makes a pleasant break from the bus trip with its obnoxious commentary including wailing songs, drumming and a quacking ditty extolling the virtues of the Kashikojima area to the south.

FUTAMIGAURA 二見浦

If you take the train from Ise towards Toba on the JR line, you might want to stop off at Futaminoura station (note the name difference) and take a detour of an hour or so out to Futamigaura. The big attractions are Futami Okitama-jinja shrine and the Meotoiwa (Wedded Rocks). These two rocks are considered to be male and female and have been joined in matrimony by sacred ropes (shimenawa) which are renewed each year in a special festival on 5 January.

The rocks are a 20 minute walk from the station. The small town is packed with places to stay, restaurants and souvenir shops.

TOBA 鳥羽

Unless you have a strong interest in pearls or enjoy a real tourist circus, you can safely give this place a miss. The information office at the station has a map in English. You can dump your packs here or in the lockers at the aquarium or at Mikimoto Pearl Island. Storage charges are about ¥200.

Buses run between Toba and Ise via Naikū and Gekū shrines. The JR line runs from Ise-shi station via Futamigaura to Toba and then on to Kashikojima.

There are ferry connections from Toba Port to Irako on the Atsumi Peninsula in Aichi Prefecture. The trip takes an hour and costs about ¥1030.

Mikimoto Pearl Island ミキモト真珠島
This is the place to go if you want to know more about pearls than you ever wanted to know. There are copious explanations in English – a relative rarity in Japan.

The establishment is a monument to Kokichi Michimoto who devoted his life to producing cultured pearls and, after irritating a lot of oysters with a variety of objects, finally succeeded in 1893.

The demonstration halls show all the oyster tricks from growing and seeding to selection, drilling and threading of the finished product. The demonstrators' English vocabulary is limited to their set piece. It must be a weirdly repetitive job, both threading pearls and reciting a text which has been learned by rote.

The Mikimoto Memorial Hall gives minute detail on Mikimoto's path through life and his pearls of wisdom. The Pearl Museum shows what you can do with pearls. The Liberty Bell pearl is one-third the size of the original and required over 12,000 pearls for its construction.

If you feel hungry, there's an expensive coffee shop selling sandwiches and cheesecake but no oysters.

There is a separate lounge and observation room for foreigners to watch the diving displays, which take place at 45 minute intervals. A nice thought in chilly or windy weather. From here you can watch a boat putter into view and drop off the ama (women divers) divers in their white outfits.

There are several thousand ama still operating in these coastal areas – but despite valiant efforts by regional tourist organisations to make you think they're after pearls, they are actually after shellfish or seaweed.

After the divers in the demonstration have retrieved their shells, they surface with a whistling sound to catch their breath again. There is a taped commentary in English which tells you all about the divers and their watery ways. Just ask if you'd like the attendant to put in a tape in another language.

Admission costs ¥850 and it's open from 8.30 am to 5 pm in the summer and from 9 am to 4 pm in the winter.

Toba Aquarium 鳥羽水族館

There seems little appeal in paying a large wad of yen to see this cutesy collection of sea creatures in cramped quarters. Those on view include sea otters, Baikal seals, one distinctly dead-looking eel lying on its back, a distressed dugong being chased by a diver, a sea-lion show and three common seals in a pathetically tiny cage with a large basin, about as big as a bathtub, as their sole source of water. There's now a new annexe to the Toba Aquarium, a hundred metres or so walk along the waterfront.

Admission to the aquarium and annexe is ¥2000, and it's open from 8 am to 5 pm from 21 March to 30 November; during the rest of the year it is open from 8.30 am to 4.30 pm.

Brazil Maru ぶらじる丸

This former passenger liner that carted passengers, mostly peasant emigrants, between Japan and South America has been converted into a floating entertainment and shopping centre. The restaurants specialise in exotic South American dishes.

AGO-WAN BAY & KASHIKOJIMA
英虞湾・賢島

Ago-wan Bay is a pleasant stretch of coastline, with sheltered inlets and small islands. Kashikojima is the terminus of the Kintetsu line, only 40 minutes from Ise, and a good base for exploration of Ago-wan Bay.

There's an information office at the station which has a map of the area in Japanese.

From the station, it's a three minute walk down to the pier. A ferry runs between Kashikojima and Goza. The 25 minute ride spins you past oyster rafts along the coast.

Goza is a sleepy fishing community where the main attractions are a fish market and elderly ama, dressed in wetsuits and white headcloths, waddling on and off boats in the harbour. There are bus connections between Goza and Ugata, which is close to Kashikojima, but the bus follows a new road which bypasses the previous scenic coastal road.

Shirahama camping ground is on a beach close to Goza.

SOUTH OF KASHIKOJIMA 賢島から南へ
If you want to continue down the Kii Peninsula, avoiding the tortuous road, the easiest way is to backtrack to Ise and then go by rail on the JR Kisei line.

The regions around Owase and Kumano offer good opportunities for hiking, but check locally for information on facilities and trails before you head into remote areas.

From Kumano, the railway crosses into Wakayama-ken and continues down to Shingū on its way round the Kii Peninsula.

Owase 尾鷲
The spectacular Ōsugi Gorge lies to the north of Owase, between Mt Hinodega-take and Mt Ōkōchi-yama. Owase has Japan's highest average rainfall at 4000 mm.

The *Business Hotel Phoenix* (☎ 05972-2-8111) and the *Business Hotel Mochizuki* (☎ 05972-2-0040) are both close to Owase station – five minutes on foot. Both have rates of around ¥4600/9000 for singles/doubles.

Kumano 熊野
Kumano can be used as a base to do the white-water raft trip from Kamikitayama-mura to Doro-hatchō via the Doro-kyō Gorge. The *Kumano Seinen-no-ie Youth Hostel* (☎ 05978-9-0800) is cheap at ¥1640 per night and is only an eight minute walk from the station. Note that it is closed from 29 December to 3 January.

Western Honshū is known in Japanese as Chūgoku, or literally the 'middle lands' (the same kanji, incidentally, that the Chinese use to refer to China). There are three main routes from the Kansai Region through the western end of Honshū to the island of Kyūshū. Most visitors choose the southern route through the San-yō region. This is a heavily industrialised and densely populated area with a number of important and interesting cities including Kurashiki and Hiroshima. The island-dotted waters of the Inland Sea, sandwiched between Honshū and Shikoku, are also reached from ports on the San-yō coast. As an additional reason for choosing this route, the Tokyo-Kyoto-Osaka-Hakata shinkansen rail route also runs along the San-yō coast.

The usual alternative to this route is the northern San-in coast. By Japanese standards, the north coast is comparatively uncrowded and rural. Although there are not as many large cities as on the southern route, the north coast route takes you to the historically interesting town of Hagi. Matsue, Izumo and Tsuwano are also interesting towns worth a stop. Despite the lower population density, travel along the San-in coast is likely to be slower, as the train services are less frequent and not so fast. Road travel, too, may be slower, as there are not the long stretches of expressway found along the southern coast. Still, as the traffic is lighter, the San-in coast is an excellent part of Japan to visit using your own transport.

Finally, there is the central route, a fast road route between Kyoto or Osaka and Shimonoseki at the western end of Honshū. The Chūgoku Expressway runs the full length of Western Honshū, more or less equidistant from the north and south coasts. Attractions along this route are comparatively limited and can usually be visited as side trips from the north or south coast routes. Some of these central excursions, particularly the one to the

mountain town of Takahashi, are well worth the trip.

GETTING THERE & AWAY
Although there are flights to a number of cities in the region and ferry connections between the major ports and surrounding islands, the shinkansen is the main means of getting to and through Western Honshū. Travelling from one end of the region to the other takes less than three hours by shinkansen.

Okayama-ken　　岡山県

Okayama Prefecture includes the twin towns of Okayama and Kurashiki along with numerous other interesting towns and tourist attractions. The Seto-ōhashi Bridge forms the main road and rail link from Honshū to Shikoku.

International Villas
In a brave attempt to attract foreign visitors to the less frequently visited areas of the country, the Okayama Prefectural Government has established six International Villas scattered around the prefecture. They're small and well equipped and rooms cost ¥3500/6000 for singles/doubles on the first night and ¥3000/5500 on subsequent nights (¥500 less per person for students). The villas have kitchen and cooking facilities, instructions in English on where to shop locally or where to find local restaurants, and even bicycles for visitors' use.

The villas are located in the mountain village of Fukiya; in Koshihata and Hattoji (where the villas are restored thatched-roof farm cottages); in Ushimado, overlooking the Inland Sea; in Kasaoka, also near the coast; and in Takebe, to the north of Okayama city. For more information contact the international exchange section of the pre-

Western Honshū
中国地方

fectural government office on ☎ 0862-24-2111, extension 2805. Members of the staff speak English and they can be faxed on 0862-23-3615.

OKAYAMA 岡山

Okayama (population 593,000) is so close to the smaller, but touristically more attractive, town of Kurashiki that it's very easy to stay in one town and day-trip to the other. Although Okayama is not as interesting as Kurashiki, there are a number of important places to visit including one of Japan's 'big three' gardens.

Orientation & Information

The town's main street, Momotarō-dōri, leads directly from the station to Okayama-jō Castle and Kōraku-en Garden. Tram lines run down the middle of the street.

JR Okayama station has a tourist information counter (☎ 0862-22-2912) and the staff are helpful. Okayama and Kurashiki publish

excellent information in English but not all of it may be available at the same time or in the same place. In particular, look for the *Okayama-Kurashiki – New Sites of Discovery* brochure. As well as the tourist information counter, Okayama station also has a 'Traverers Aid' section, but it rarely seems to be open.

The Kinokuniya (5th floor) and Maruzen (2nd floor) bookshops both have good English-language sections. Note the Zap!! Life Museum among the shops across from the station.

Kōraku-en Garden 後楽園

The Japanese penchant for rating and numbering things is apparent once again at this park, which is said to be one of the three finest in Japan. The other official members of the big three are the Kairaku-en Garden in Mito (Northern Honshū) and Kenroku-en Garden in Kanazawa (Central Honshū).

Constructed between 1687 and 1700,

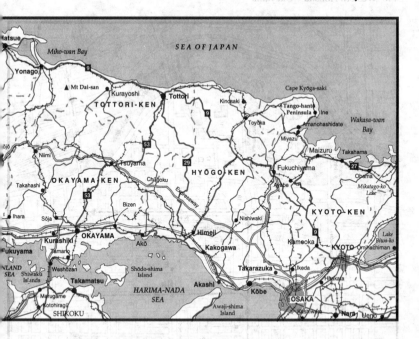

Kōraku-en is a stroll garden. (Kōraku-en means 'the garden for taking pleasure later', taken from the Chinese proverb that 'the lord must bear sorrow before the people and take pleasure after them'.) Part of its attraction in crowded Japan is the expanse of flat lawn but there are also attractive ponds, a hill in the centre, a curious tiny tea plantation and rice paddy and a neatly placed piece of 'borrowed scenery' in the shape of Okayama-jō Castle. Look for the Nō stage, the pretty little Ryuten building where poetry composing contests were once held, and the nearby Yatsu-hashi zigzag bridge.

Opening hours are from 7.30 am to 6 pm in summer and from 8 am to 5 pm in winter. Entry is ¥250 (see the 'combined entry' note in the Okayama-jō Castle section). An excellent English brochure describing the garden's attractions is available. You can rent rowing boats and swan-shaped paddle boats in the river channel between the garden and the castle.

From the station take the Higashi-yama

Momotarō – the Peach Boy

Okayama-ken and neighbouring Kagawa-ken on the island of Shikoku are linked with the legend of Momotarō, the tiny 'Peach Boy' who emerged from the stone of a peach and, backed up by a monkey, a pheasant and a dog, defeated a three-eyed, three-toed, people-eating demon. There are statues of Momotarō at JR Okayama station, and the main road of the town is named after him. Another statue of the boy stands at the end of the Kōraku-en Garden island in Okayama. Mega-shima Island, off Takamatsu in Shikoku, is said to be the site of the clash with the demon. Momotarō may actually have been a Yamato prince who was deified as Kibitsuhiko. His shrine, the Kibitsu-jinja, is visited on the Kibi Plain bicycle ride described in the Around Okayama section. ∎

WESTERN HONSHŪ

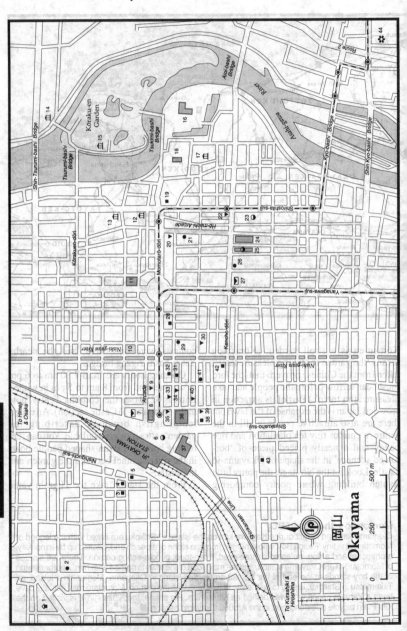

Okayama

岡山

To Himeji & Osaka

To Kurashiki & Hiroshima

JR OKAYAMA STATION

Kōraku-en Garden

Nishi-gawa River

Asahi-gawa River

Shin Tsurumi-bashi Bridge
Tsurumi-bashi Bridge
Tsukimi-bashi Bridge
Aoi-bashi Bridge
Kyō-bashi Bridge
Shin Kyō-bashi Bridge

Route 2

Kōrakuen-dōri
Momotarō-dōri
Hō-machi Arcade
Shiroshita-suji
Yanagawa-suji
Kenchō-dōri
Shiyakusho-suji
Nishiguchi-suji
Arcade

Shinkansen Line

0   250   500 m

tram to the Shiroshita stop (¥140) for the garden or castle. Alternatively take an Okaden bus from stand 9 at the station to the Kōrakuen-mae bus stop (¥150).

Okayama-jō Castle 岡山城

U-jō (Crow Castle) was built in 1597 and it is said that its striking black colour is a daimyō's jest at Himeji's pristine 'White Egret Castle'. Like so many other great castles in Japan, U-jō was destroyed in WW II; only the small Tsukima-yagura (Moon-Viewing Turret) survived the wartime destruction. It was rebuilt in 1966, a modern reinforced concrete construction like most of the postwar reconstructions. Nevertheless, there is an interesting display inside and much of it is labelled in English. At the

Ōte-mon Gate entrance at the south-western corner of the moat, note the interesting sign about the prestige derived from building castle walls with 'big' stones.

Entrance to the castle costs ¥250 but you can get combined tickets to the castle plus the Orient Museum for ¥350; the castle plus Kōraku-en Garden for ¥400; or the castle, the garden and the Hayashibara Museum for ¥550. The castle is open from 9 am to 5 pm daily. See the Kōraku-en Garden section for information on getting to the castle.

Museums

Close to the castle's back entrance, near the corner of the moat, the Hayashibara Museum of Art houses a private collection of Japanese and Chinese artefacts. It's open daily from 9 am to 4.30 pm and entry is ¥300. Beside the main entrance to the Kōraku-en Garden is the **Okayama Prefectural Museum** which has displays connected with local history. It's open from 9 am to 6 pm (closed on Monday) and entry is ¥150. Just north of the Kōraku-en Garden is the **Yumeji Art Museum**, displaying work by artist Yumeji Takehisa. It's open from 9 am to 5.30 pm (closed on Monday) and entry is ¥600.

Just north of the end of Momotarō-dōri, where the tram line turns south, is the excellent **Okayama Orient Museum**. The small collection of Middle Eastern art is beautifully displayed although the absence of any non-Japanese description can be very annoying: one is left wondering where these intriguing-looking places are. Entry is ¥200 and it's closed on Monday. Behind this museum is the **Okayama Prefectural Museum of Art**; entry is ¥300 and it is also closed on Monday.

Other Attractions
Only a block east of the station, the canal-like Nishi-gawa River, flanked by its gardens and sculptures, makes for a pleasant short stroll.

South-east of central Okayama is the Tōko-en Garden, which is easy to overlook in a town with one of the 'big three' gardens. It's worth trundling out on the tram to visit this small, attractive early 17th century garden just beyond the river. The garden is centred around a large pond. It actually predates the Kōraku-en Garden by 70 years. It's open daily from 9 am to 5 pm and entry is ¥300. Beyond the Tōko-en Garden is the **Sōgen-ji Temple**, which also has a noted garden. It's open from 6 am to 6 pm and entry is ¥100.

Festivals
The Saidai-ji Eyō (Naked Festival) takes place from midnight on the third Saturday in February at the Kannon-in Temple in the Saidai-ji area. A large crowd of near-naked men fight for two sacred wooden sticks *(shingi)* while water is poured over them!

Places to Stay
Youth Hostels *Okayama Seinen-kaikan Youth Hostel* (☎ 0862-52-0651) is west of the railway station and costs ¥2300.

Business Hotels One of the cheaper places around is the *Makibi Kaikan* (☎ 0862-32-0511), just south of the station. It's on the 5th floor of an educatational institute and only has 24 rooms, so it may be booked out. Singles/twins are ¥4780/8460. Another less expensive business hotel not far from the station is the *Hotel Maira* (☎ 0862-22-5601), which has singles/twins at ¥5500/11,000. The *Okayama Castle Hotel* (☎ 0862-34-5678) is east of the station and singles/doubles cost from ¥5700/9800. The *Okayama Terminal Hotel* (☎ 0862-33-3131) is beside the station and has singles at ¥6200 to ¥7500, doubles and twins from ¥16,000, plus a 10% service charge. At the top of Momotarō-dōri, opposite the station, is the expensive *New Okayama Hotel* (☎ 0862-23-8211); further down is the *Washington Hotel* (☎ 0862-31-9111).

In the quieter area west of the station, there are more hotels only a few minutes walk from the centre of things. The *Matsunoki Hotel* (☎ 0862-53-4111) is a pleasant, newish place where Japanese-style rooms with bathroom cost ¥7000/15,000 per night, room only, for singles/doubles. Breakfast costs ¥700, dinner ¥1500 and there's a cheaper annexe which has rooms without bathrooms. A few steps back towards the station is the *New Station Hotel* (☎ 0862-53-6655) which charges ¥4800/8500 for singles/doubles. There are a number of other cheaper small hotels in the same area as well as the more expensive *Dai Ichi Inn* (0862-53-5311), which has singles/twins from ¥5500/16,000.

Places to Eat
Okayama has a familiar collection of eating places in and around the railway station, including a *Mr Donut* and a *McDonald's* on Momotarō-dōri. The small street parallel to and immediately south of Momotarō-dōri has a varied collection of places to eat,

including the popular *Mura Ichiban Robatayaki* (fully illustrated menu) on the 2nd floor of the Communication building, the *Pizza & Salad St Moritz* and many others.

Curiously, Okayama is brimming with Italian restaurants, from relatively inexpensive pizzerias through to pricey ristorante. There are at least two branches of the *Pizza Patio* in town, one close to the station and one over by the Hō-machi arcade. Both of them have an excellent selection of pizzas and pasta dishes, with prices starting at around ¥650. On Kencho-dōri, between the Kinokuniya bookshop and the station, there are more Italian-style places, including the *Pizza House Skipper*, with its sign anouncing 'skipper skip dog' and *Cucina Italiano*, a more up-market option.

For Japanese food, it's worth heading over to the Hō-machi Arcade, where, among others, you'll find *Itcho*, a good sushi bar with affordable prices. Just down from here is another Italian place, *Ristorante Italiano*, and *Kirin City*, a very snazzy bar with good counter lunches.

Places for a drink and something to eat in the evenings include the *Lager Bar*, which has tacos and pizzas on its menu. Another interesting option is *Bierstube*, a German establishment with a quote from Goethe on its frontage. The *Jack & Jill Public House* might also be worth checking out.

In summer, there's a beer garden on the roof of the *New Okayama Hotel*, which is just in front of the station. Take the elevator to floor R; a fully illustrated menu of snacks to go with your beer is provided. In the arcade behind the hotel is the *Sushi Land – Marine Polis*, a revolving sushi restaurant.

Getting There & Away

All Nippon Airways (ANA) fly to Okayama from Tokyo several times daily; the airport is about 40 minutes from the city by bus. Okayama is on the main shinkansen line, unlike nearby Kurashiki. By shinkansen it only takes about an hour to get from Osaka to Okayama (¥5750). Himeji is about halfway between the two cities.

See the Kurashiki section for details on travelling between Okayama and Kurashiki. When travelling west, it's quicker to transfer from the shinkansen at Okayama than at Shin-Kurashiki. You also change trains at Okayama if you're heading to the island of Shikoku, across the Seto-ōhashi Bridge.

Buses run from in front of the station, from the Tenmaya bus station in the Tenmaya department store and from the nearby Uno bus station.

Getting Around

Getting around Okayama is a breeze since the Higashi-yama tram route will take you to all the main attractions. There are only two tram routes, both starting from directly in front of the station. With your back to the station, the Higashi-yama tram route is the one on the right, the easily recognised *yama* 山 is the second character on the front. Trams charge a standard ¥140 anywhere in town.

AROUND OKAYAMA　岡山周辺

There are a number of places of interest in the Okayama-Kurashiki area including the pottery centre of Bizen, the Inland Sea, the Seto-ōhashi Bridge lookout at Washūzan and, best of all, the enjoyable Kibi Plain bicycle route.

Kibi Plain Bicycle Route
吉備路サイクリングルート

An excellent way to spend half a day seeing a less visited part of Japan is to follow the Kibi Plain bicycle route. The route follows bicycle paths for most of its length and visits a number of temples, shrines and other sites. You can rent a bicycle (*renta saikaru*) at one JR station along the route and leave it at another.

Take a local JR Kibi line train from Okayama three stops to Bizen Ichinomiya (15 minutes, ¥200), ride 15 km to Sōja and from there take a JR Hakubi/San-yō line train back through Kurashiki to Okayama. It's easier travelling in that direction because the bicycle path is not so easy to pick up leaving Sōja, a fairly big town. Bicycles cost ¥300 for two hours, ¥200 for each additional

吉備自転車ルート
Kibi Plain Bicycle Route

1 Hōfuku-ji Temple 宝福寺	7 Kibitsu-jinja Shrine 吉備津神社	12 Bitchū Kokubun-ji Temple 備中国分寺
2 Sōja Shrine 総社宮	8 Koikui-jinja Shrine 鯉喰神社	13 Kōmorizuka Burial Mound こうもり塚古墳
3 Sesshu's Birthplace 雪舟誕生の地	9 Tsukuriyama Burial Mound 造山古墳	14 Sumotoriyama Burial Mound
4 Takamatsu-jō Castle Site 髙松城址	10 Bitchū Kokubun-niji Convent 備中国分尼寺跡	すもとり山古墳
5 Ikeda Zoo 池田動物園	11 Kibiji Archaeological Museum 吉備路郷　館	15 Anyo-ji Temple 安養寺
6 Kibitsuhiko-jinja Shrine 吉備津彦神社		

hour or ¥800 for a day. Officially they're available from 9 am, but you can actually start earlier.

From the JR Bizen Ichinomiya station turn right, then right again to cross the railway line and in just 300 metres you reach the Kibitsuhiko-jinja Shrine, which fronts a large pond. From here you soon pick up the bicycle path following a canal through the fields until it rejoins the road just before the Fudenkai Temple. Ignore this red herring, as it's not a temple of much interest: only 200 metres further is the **Kibitsu-jinja Shrine**, a large shrine with a commensurately large car

park. A wide flight of steps leads up to this attractive hilltop shrine. Have your fortune told (in English) for ¥100 by the serve-your-self oracle in the courtyard. The shrine, built in 1425, is unusual in having both the oratory and main sanctum topped by a single roof. The legendary peach boy, Momotarō, is connected with the shrine.

Pedalling on, you pass the uninteresting-looking Koikui-jinja Shrine, also connected with the legendary figure Kibitsuhiko, and you reach the huge 5th century **Tsukuri-yama-kofun Burial Mound**, rising like a rounded hill from the surrounding plain. You really need to be in a hot-air balloon or a helicopter to appreciate that it's really a 350 metre long keyhole-shaped mound, not a natural hill. Just north of here is the birthplace of Sesshū (1420-1506), the famous artist. He was once a novice monk at the **Hōfuku-ji Temple**, which is three km northwest of JR Sōja station.

Finally, there are the foundation stones of the **Bitchū Kokubun-niji Convent**, the nearby **Kibiji Archaeological Museum** (closed on Monday), the excavated **Kōmori-zuka Burial Mound** and the **Bitchū Kokobun-ji Temple** with its picturesque five storeyed pagoda. From here it's a few more kilometres into Sōja.

There are countless drink-vending machines along the way, and occasionally the bicycle path passes close enough to a main road to divert for food. If you start early you can arrive in Sōja in time for lunch, or buy a sandwich from the *Little Mermaid* bakery near the station and eat on the train on your way back. If this bicycle ride appeals to you, you can easily plot others on the network of tracks that cover the area. A walking path also runs very close to the bicycle route.

Takamatsu-jō Castle & Ashimori
高松城・足守

Places of interest on the Kibi Plain, but not on the bicycle route, include the site of Takamatsu-jō Castle where Hideyoshi defeated the Lord of Shimizu. Hideyoshi hastened the siege by flooding the castle and the remains of the great dykes can still be seen.

North-west of the Takamatsu Castle site is Ashimori, with its well-preserved samurai residence and the **Omizu-en Garden**, another stroll garden in the Enshū style. The castle is around 15 minutes on foot northeast of Bitchū Takamatsu station on the JR Kibi line but the samurai residence and the garden are some distance north of Ashimori station. The best way to get to Omizu-en is to take a bus to Ashimori-machi from outside Okayama station. The trip takes 40 minutes and costs ¥600.

Although there is little to be seen at the site of Takamatsu-jō Castle, the castle played a crucial part in the finale to the chaotic 'Country at War' century. In 1582, Hideyoshi besieged the castle on behalf of the ruthless Oda Nobunaga and agreed to allow the castle's defenders to surrender on condition that their commander, Lord Shimizu, committed suicide. On the very eve of this event, word came from Kyoto that Oda Nobunaga had been assassinated. Hideyoshi contrived to keep this news from the castle garrison and in the morning his unfortunate opponent killed himself. Hideyoshi then sprinted back to Kyoto and soon assumed command himself.

Imbe 伊部

East of Okayama, on the JR Akō line, is Imbe, the 700 year old pottery village renowned for its unglazed Bizen-yaki pottery. In Imbe, high-quality examples of this pottery, much prized by tea ceremony connoisseurs, are produced in wood-fired kilns and are very expensive. Clustered around the north side of Imbe station are the **Okayama Prefectural Bizen Ceramics Art Museum** (9.30 am to 4.30 pm, closed Monday, ¥500), the **Bizen Ceramic Crafts Museum** (9.30 am to 5.30 pm, closed Wednesday, free) and the **Bizen Ceramics Centre** (10 am to 4.30 pm, closed Monday, free), all of which display the pottery of the area.

North-east of Imbe is the **Shizutani Gakkō school** which was established in 1670. Picturesquely sited and encircled by a beautiful wall, it was one of the first schools established specifically for commoners. It's quite a way to the north of town, and locals recommend taking a taxi, which will set you back ¥2500 one-way. Try hitching if you're really keen.

Seto-ōhashi Bridge Area
児島・鷲羽山・瀬戸大橋

From the peninsula south of Kurashiki and Okayama, the Seto-ōhashi Bridge connects Honshū (Japan's biggest island) with Shikoku (its fourth-largest). The bridge (or more correctly bridges, since there are six of them stepping from island to island across the strait) was opened in 1988 and has considerably shortened travel time to Shikoku. The long span at the Honshū end is the world's longest double-level suspension bridge carrying both road and rail traffic.

The **Washū-zan Hill**, near the end of the peninsula, was long renowned as a lookout point over the Inland Sea. Now it looks out over the bridge as well. The best views are from the No 2 viewing platform at an elevation of 133 metres. Shitaden buses from Kurashiki run direct to the platform in one hour 20 minutes and cost ¥790.

If you are particularly interested in taking a look at the bridge, the best way to do so is via a boat tour around it from **Kojima**. During the summer months (from March to November), boats depart approximately hourly between 9 am to 4.30 am. Cruises last for around an hour and cost ¥1540. The cruise boats leave from just a couple of hundred metres to the south-east of Kojima station.

There's really nothing to linger for in Kojima. The **Seto-ōhashi Memorial Bridge Museum** is probably fascinating for bridge engineers, but for the average visitor the ¥500 admission charge is money better spent elsewhere. It's open from 9 am to 4.30 pm and closed Monday. Just to the north of the museum is the **Nozaki Residence**, the home of a late-Edo period salt merchant – nice but not worth the effort. Entry is ¥500 and the house is closed on Monday.

There are a number of hotels, pensions and ryokan in the Kojima/Washū-zan area, but particularly well located is the *Washūzan Youth Hostel* (☎ 0864-79-9280), which is at the foot of the hill, right at the end of the peninsula. It charges ¥2100, and buses run from in front of Kojima station. Ask for the *yūsu-hosuteru-mae basu-no-tei*. Those looking for up-market digs should ask at the Kojima station tourist information counter (☎ 0864-72-1289).

Buses run to Kojima from Kurashiki and Okayama and the JR Seto-ōhashi line from Okayama to Shikoku runs through Kojima station before crossing the bridge. Buses run from Kojima station to Washū-zan in 20 minutes (¥240), but are not all that frequent. There's also the Shimotsui Narrow Gauge Railway which runs from Kojima (near the

Seto-ōhashi Memorial Museum) at one end, via Washūzan station to Shimotsui station at the other. Shimotsui is an interesting little fishing port and ferries cross from here to Marugame on Shikoku.

KURASHIKI 倉敷

Kurashiki's claim to fame is a small quarter of picturesque buildings around a stretch of moat. There are a number of old black-tiled warehouses which have been converted into an eclectic collection of museums. Bridges arch over, willows dip into the river and the whole effect is quite delightful – it's hardly

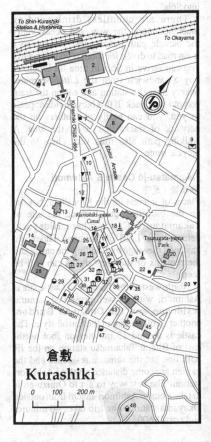

倉敷

Kurashiki

0   100   200 m

surprising that the town is a favourite with tourists. Kurashiki means 'warehouse village'.

In the feudal era, the warehouses were used to store rice brought by boat from the surrounding rich farmlands. As this phase of Kurashiki's history faded, the town's importance as a textile centre increased and the Kurabō Textile Company expanded. Ōhara Keisaburō, the owner of the company, gathered together a significant collection of European art and, in the 1920s, opened the

Ōhara Museum to display it. It was the first of a series of museums which have become the town's principal attraction and is still one of the finest.

Orientation & Information

As in so many other Japanese towns, the main street leads straight out from the railway station. It's about one km from the station to the old canal area. If you walk from the station, the typical urban Japanese scenery is enough to make you wonder

PLACES TO STAY		12	Rentenchi Italian Restaurant 煉天地	27	Ōhara Museum Annexe 大原美術館分館
3	Kurashiki Terminal Hotel 倉敷ターミナルホテル	16	Kiyū-tei Steakhouse 亀遊亭ステーキハウス	28	Kurashiki City Art Museum 市立美術館
4	Young Inn ヤングイン	23	Kanadean Restaurant カナディアンレストラン	29	Mizushima Washūzan Bus Stop 水島鷲羽山バス停
5	Ryokan Ohguma 旅館おおぐま	24	Kamoi Restaurant	31	Kurashiki Museum of Folkcraft 倉敷民芸館
7	Kurashiki Station Hotel 倉敷ステーションホテル	25	El Greco Café エルグレコ		
15	Kurashiki Kokusai Hotel 倉敷国際ホテル	35	Kama Izumi Restaurant かまいずみ	32	Kurashiki Ninagawa Museum 倉敷蜷川博物館
22	Kamoi Minshuku	**OTHER**		34	Kurashiki Archaeological Museum 倉敷考古館
30	Lady's Hotel レディスホテル	1	JR Kurashiki Station JR倉敷駅	37	Tourist Information/ Travellers' Rest Area 観光案内所
33	Tsurugata Inn & Restaurant 鶴形イン	2	Mitsukoshi Department Store 三越		
36	Ryokan Kurashiki 旅館くらしき	8	Tenmaya Department Store 天満屋	38	Japan Rural Toy Museum 日本郷土玩具館
39	El Paso Inn エルパソイン	9	Post Office 郵便局	41	Torajirō Kojima Museum & Orient Museum 児島虎次郎記念館
40	Kawakami Minshuku かわかみ民宿	13	Ōhashi House 大橋家		
43	Tokuchan Kan Minshuku 特産館民宿	14	Museum of Natural History 自然史博物館	42	Kurabō Memorial Hall 倉紡記念館
45	Kurashiki Ivy Square Hotel 倉敷アイビースクェア	17	Ōhara House 大原家	44	Ivy Square アイビースクェア
48	Kurashiki Youth Hostel 倉敷ユースホステル	18	Seigan-ji Temple 誓願寺	46	Ivy Academic Hall アイビー学館
PLACES TO EAT		19	Kanryū-ji Temple 観竜寺	47	Kojima Washūzan Bus Stop 小島鷲羽山バス停
6	McDonald's マクドナルド	20	Achi-jinja Shrine 阿智神社		
10	Domino Café ドミノ	21	Honei-ji Temple 本栄寺		
11	Etoile	26	Ōhara Museum of Art 大原美術館		

WESTERN HONSHŪ

whether you are in the right town. But when you turn into the canal area, everything changes; Ivy Square is just beyond the canal. A number of shops along the main street, Kurashiki Chūō-dōri, sell Bizen-yaki pottery.

The staff at the station's information counter (☎ 0864-26-8681) will make accommodation bookings, and there is also a helpful tourist information office near the bend in the canal. Most of the museums and galleries are closed on Monday and the number of visitors drops dramatically, so Monday is a good time to enjoy Kurashiki without the crowds (but also without the museums).

Around the Canal
The museums and galleries which are the town's major attraction are concentrated along the banks of the canal. At times, the canal area can seem like rush hour at Tokyo station, so, if you want to see how pleasant the area looks without throngs of tour groups, you should wander the canal banks early in the morning or on a Monday. It's not necessary to visit all (or indeed any) of the museums; some are definitely more interesting than others.

Ōhara Museum of Art This is undoubtedly Kurashiki's number one museum, housing the predominantly European art collection of the textile magnate Ōhara Keisaburō. Rodin, Matisse, Picasso, Pissarro, Monet, Cézanne, Renoir, El Greco, Toulouse-Lautrec, Gauguin, Degas and Munch are all represented here. The museum's neo-classical facade is Kurashiki's best known landmark, to which the constant procession of tour groups being photographed outside attests. Entry is ¥600; opening hours are from 9 am to 5 pm and it's closed on Monday.

Your ticket also takes you to the museum's folk art and Chinese art collections and to the contemporary art collection, housed in a new building behind the main one. You have to exit the old building and walk down the street to enter the new gallery where you will find works by Pollock, Rothko, de Kooning, Henry Moore and others.

Kurashiki Ninagawa Museum Between the Ōhara Museum and the tourist office is the interesting Kurashiki Ninagawa Museum which houses a collection of Greek, Etruscan and Roman antiquities, together with more modern European marbles and other items. Entry is ¥600 and it's open from 8.30 am to 5 pm daily.

Kurashiki Museum of Folkcraft The folkcraft museum's collection is mainly Japanese but also includes furniture and other items from many other countries. The collection is housed in an attractive complex of linked kura (warehouses). Entry is ¥500 and it's open from 9 am to 4.15 pm (December to February) or 5 pm (March to November). It's closed on Monday.

Japan Rural Toy Museum This interesting museum displays folkcraft toys from Japan and around the world. Japanese rural toys are also on sale. Entry is ¥310 and it's open from 8 am to 5 pm daily.

Kurashiki Archaeological Museum Directly across the canal from the tourist office, this museum is strictly for the archaeology buffs and those interested in bits of ancient pottery – it's very dry! There are finds from burial mounds from the Kibi Plain and an Inca room with some pre-Columbian pottery from Peru but even this isn't very interesting. Entry is ¥300 and it's open Tuesday to Sunday from 9 am to 4.30 pm.

Other Museums If you've not had your fill of museums there's also the Kurashiki City Museum of Natural History (¥100, open from 9 am to 5 pm, closed Monday) and the Kurashiki City Art Museum (¥200, same opening hours).

Ivy Square アイビースクエア
The Kurabō textile factories have moved on to more modern premises and their fine old Meiji-era red-brick factory buildings (dating

from 1889) now house a hotel, restaurants, shops and yet more museums. Ivy Square, with its ivy-covered walls and open-air café, is the centre of the complex.

The **Torajirō Kojima Museum** displays work by the local artist who helped Ohara establish his European collection, along with some fine pieces from the Middle East in the associated Orient Museum. The museums are open Tuesday to Sunday from 9 am to 5 pm and admission is ¥300.

The museum in the **Kurabō Memorial Hall** tells the story of Kurashiki's growth as a textile centre. It's open daily from 9 am to 5 pm and entry costs ¥100.

The curious **Ivy Academic Hall** (Ivy Gakkan) tries to trace the development of Western art through reproductions of notable paintings. The hall is open from 9 am to 5 pm daily and entry costs ¥100.

Ōhashi House　大橋家住宅

The Ōhashi family were retainers to the Toyotomi family, who were on the losing side of the upheavals leading to the establishment of the Tokugawa Shogunate. The Ōhashi family abandoned its samurai status and eventually ended up in Kurashiki, where they became wealthy merchants and built this house in 1796. In its heyday it would have been a fine example of an upwardly mobile merchant's residence but today it's very worn and shabby. Entry is ¥300 and it's open from Tuesday to Sunday from 9 am to 5 pm.

Shrines & Temples

The Achi-jinja Shrine tops Tsurugata-yama Park, overlooking the old area of town. The Honei-ji Temple, Kanryū-ji Temple and the Seigan-ji Temple are also found in the park.

Places to Stay

Kurashiki is a good town for staying in a traditional Japanese inn. Although there's a good selection of minshuku and ryokan, business hotels are not as well represented as in other towns.

Youth Hostels

Kurashiki Youth Hostel (☎ 0864-22-7355) is south of the canal area and costs ¥2500 per night. It's a long climb to its hilltop location, but the view is great and the staff are friendly. From the station you can take a bus to the shimin kaikan stop and then walk uphill to the hostel.

Minshuku & Ryokan

There are several good-value minshuku conveniently close to the canal. The *Tokuchan Kan* (☎ 0864-25-3056) is near Ivy Square and offers a room-only price as well as a room and two meals at ¥6000 per person, though prices go up in high season. Right by the canal near the toy museum the small *Kawakami Minshuku* (☎ 0864-24-1221) is slightly cheaper at ¥5150.

The *Kamoi Minshuku* (☎ 0864-22-4898) is easy to find (at the bottom of the steps to the Achi-jinja Shrine) and conveniently close to the canal area. Although this minshuku is new, it looks quite traditional: an atmosphere enhanced by the antiques throughout the building. The cost per person, including two good meals in this very pleasant minshuku, is ¥5500. The food should be good, as the Kamoi also has a popular restaurant by the canal.

There are also more expensive ryokan around the canal. The canal-side *Tsuragata Inn Kurashiki* (☎ 0864-24-1635) is operated by the Kokusai Hotel. The building dates from 1744 and nightly charges in this tasteful ryokan range from ¥17,000 to ¥36,000. The ryokan's restaurant also serves outsiders, mainly at lunch time, and there is a café.

Also by the canal, the *Ryokan Kurashiki* (☎ 0864-22-0730) is old, elegant and expensive, costing from ¥15,000 to ¥30,000 per person with two meals. Either of these ryokan would make a good introduction to staying at a fine traditional inn.

Most of the traditional ryokan and minshuku are around the canal area, an exception being the *Ryokan Ohguma* (☎ 0864-22-0250) which is near the station. It's to the right as you leave the station, down the small arcade which angles off the main road. It costs ¥7000 per person with two meals.

Hotels

Canal Area Part of the Ivy Square complex, the *Kurashiki Ivy Square Hotel* (☎ 0864-22-0011) has singles at ¥6500 or ¥9000 with bath. Doubles and twins range from ¥9000 to ¥10,500 without bath, ¥11,500 to ¥15,000 with bath. Rooms without a bath or shower have a toilet and sink only – there are large communal baths and showers. For all the prices at Ivy Square, add a 10% then 3% surcharge.

Backing on to the Ōhara Museum is the expensive *Kurashiki Kokusai Hotel* (☎ 0864-22-5141), with singles/doubles from ¥8800/13,200. There are also more expensive Japanese-style rooms in this popular and attractive hotel.

Also close to the canal is the stylish *El Paso Inn* (☎ 0864-21-8282). It only has a couple of singles, but doubles range from ¥9900 and twins from ¥11,000. A real oddity in the canal area is the *Lady's Hotel* (☎ 0864-22-1115); the sign announces this in English. It's a hotel aimed specifically at young OLs (office ladies), which seems to involve painting the rooms pink or a lurid shade of green and dotting stuffed toys around the place.

Station Area The JR-operated *Hotel Kurashiki* (☎ 0864-26-6111) is inside the station building and has singles from ¥7500 to ¥8500 and twins from ¥14,000. The *Kurashiki Terminal Hotel* (☎ 0864-26-1111) is immediately to the right as you come out of the station and the entrance is on the 9th floor. It's a typical business hotel with singles at ¥6000 to ¥7500, and twins or doubles from ¥12,000.

The *Young Inn* (☎ 0864-25-8585), behind the Terminal Hotel, has singles/doubles without bath for ¥3600/6500, quite a bargain. There are also slightly more expensive rooms with bathroom in this vaguely hostel-like hotel.

The *Kurashiki Station Hotel* (☎ 0864-25-2525) is a short distance along Kurashiki Chūō-dōri towards the canal. The entrance is

around the side of the building, with reception on the 5th floor. The rooms in this older but cheaper business hotel are minute and utterly straightforward; singles cost from ¥5000 to ¥5800, and doubles from ¥8300 to ¥12,000.

Places to Eat

If you plan to eat out in the canal area of Kurashiki, don't leave it too late. Many of the restaurants you may notice at lunch time will be closed by early evening. The hordes of day-trippers will have disappeared by then and many of the visitors actually staying in Kurashiki will be eating in their ryokan or minshuku.

El Greco (you can't miss its ivy-clad walls), right by the canal and close to the Ōhara Museum, is a fashionable place to stop for a snack. The menu, in English on one side, offers ice cream for ¥400, cake for ¥200 and a drink for about ¥400. It's closed on Monday.

Also beside the canal is the *Kamoi Restaurant*, run by the same people as the popular Kamoi Minshuku. Plastic meals are on display and the restaurant closes early in the evening as well as all day on Monday. At the northern end of the canal is *Kiyū-tei*, a steakhouse in an old traditional Japanese house. The fixed evening meal of soup, salad, steak, bread and coffee costs ¥2500.

Just back from the canal is *Kama Izumi*, a pleasant, modern restaurant with plastic meals in the window and a fully illustrated menu. You can get good tempura and noodles for ¥1400 and the restaurant stays open until at least 8 pm. There's a snack bar in Ivy Square and several restaurants in and near the square. A special treat, south-east of Tsuragata-yama Park, is *Kanadean*, a small place specialising in 'Asian' cuisine. It has milk tea and 15 kinds of spicy curries all at ¥500. It's open from 11 am to 9 pm. Look out for the blue lattice-work windows and the blue sign. There are also a number of places to eat along Kurashiki Chūō-dōri. *Domino*, labelled the 'Human's Café', is a neat little place, popular with young OLs, where you can get a good teishoku lunch for

¥400 to ¥600. A typical meal would be spaghetti, salad and a drink for ¥550. Not far away the *Rentenchi Italian Restaurant* has coffee at ¥300 and pasta dishes from ¥650. Next door, *Etoile* offers expensive French cuisine and a bilingual menu (Japanese and French).

The station has that old stand-by *McDonald's*, while close to the south exit is a branch of *Art Coffee*, with good coffee for ¥200.

Getting There & Away

Kurashiki, only 16 km from Okayama, is not on the shinkansen line. Travelling westwards, it's usually faster to disembark at Okayama and take a San-yō line local train to Kurashiki. These operate several times an hour; the trip takes just over 15 minutes and costs ¥470. If you're eastbound, get off at the Shin-Kurashiki station, two stops on the San-yō line from Kurashiki.

To get to Washūzan and Shikoku from Kurashiki, you can either travel by train to Okayama and change trains there for Washūzan or take a bus (from outside the station or from the canal area stops shown on the map) direct to Kojima or Washūzan.

Getting Around

Walk – it's only 15 minutes on foot from the station to the canal area, where everything is within a few minutes stroll.

TAKAHASHI　高梁

This small town, midway between Kurashiki and the central Chūgoku Expressway, gets few Western visitors even though it has a temple with a very beautiful Zen garden and is overlooked by an atmospheric, even spooky, old castle.

Orientation & Information

While the town is Takahashi, the railway station is Bitchū-Takahashi, which is a little confusing. The Raikyū-ji Temple is about a km to the north of the station, on the east side of the tracks, though to get there you'll need to walk north on the west side and then cross over. Bitchū-Matsuyama-jō Castle is about

five km north of the station, up a steep hillside. If you are not up to the walk, a taxi will run you up there for ¥900. The tourist information counter at the railway station has helpful staff and useful information in English. There are also bicycles for hire at the station for ¥200 per hour.

Raikyū-ji Temple　頼久寺

The classic Zen garden in this small temple is said to be the work of the master designer Kobori Enshū and dates from 1604. It contains all the traditional elements of this style of garden, including stones in the form of turtle and crane islands, a series of topiary hedges to represent waves on the sea and it even incorporates Mt Atago in the background as 'borrowed scenery'. Entry is ¥300 and it is open from 9 am to 5 pm daily.

Bitchū-Matsuyama-jō Castle　備中松山城

High above Takahashi stands the highest castle in Japan, a relic of an earlier period of castle construction when fortresses were designed to be hidden and inaccessible, unlike the later, larger constructions designed to protect the surrounding lands. The road winds up the hill to a car park, from where you have a steep climb to the castle itself. On a dark and overcast day you can almost feel the inspiration for a film like Kurosawa's *Throne of Blood*. Entry to the castle is ¥200 but this is no tourist castle – you'll probably have to rouse the caretaker from his hut and you may even have the place all to yourself.

The castle was originally established in 1240 and in the following centuries was enlarged until it finally covered the whole mountain top. The castle fell into disrepair after the Meiji Restoration, but the townspeople took over its maintenance from 1929 and it was finally completely restored in the 1950s.

Other Attractions

Takahashi has some picturesque old samurai streets with traditional walls and gates, mainly in the area around Raikyū-ji Temple. Around 500 metres to the north of Raikyū-ji

Temple is a fine **samurai residence**. It has rather irregular hours of opening, but if you are there between 9 am and 4 pm it should be open. Entry is ¥200. If you walk up to Raikyū-ji, you'll pass the **Local History Museum** (*kyōdo shiryō-kan*), a fine wooden Meiji structure dating from 1904. It has displays of items associated with area's mercantile and agricultural past, and is open daily from 10 am to 4 pm; entry ¥200. The Shōren-ji Temple, directly east of the station, has unique terraced stone walls. It's open from 9 am to 5 pm and is free.

Places to Stay
There are ryokan and minshuku in town, as well as the *Takehashi Youth Hostel* (☎ 0866-22-3149). It costs ¥2300 and is about a km north of the station, just south of Raikyū-ji Temple.

The best alternative to the youth hostel is the terrifically atmospheric *Minshuku Jōrin-ji* (☎ 0866-22-3443), which has rooms with breakfast for ¥3500. This temple-look-a-like is about 500 metres east of the station, just north of Shōren-ji Temple.

The *Business Hotel Takehashi* is just west of the station and has singles/twins at ¥4500/7600.

The *Takahashi-shi Cycling Terminal* (☎ 0866-22-0135) is a 20 minute bus trip from the JR station at the Wonderland amusement park. Accommodation at the terminal, including meals, is ¥4200. You can rent bicycles from the terminal for ¥400 for four hours, but think twice before setting out to ride up to the castle!

Getting There & Away
Although Takahashi is not on any of the regular tourist routes through Western Honshū, it would not take a great effort to include it in an itinerary. The town is about 50 km north of Okayama or 60 km from Fukuyama. It's on the JR Hakubi line so a stop could be made when travelling between Okayama on the south coast and Yonago (near Matsue) on the north coast. For those travelling by car on the Chūgoku Expressway, a visit would entail about 30 km extra,

leaving the expressway at Niimi and rejoining it at Hokubo, or vice versa.

FUKIYA 吹屋
The beautifully situated village of Fukiya, north-west of Takahashi, was once a rich copper mining centre and has many attractive buildings from the latter years of the Edo period and the first years after the Meiji Restoration. One of the prefecture's International Villas is in the village. To get to Fukiya, take a JR limited express (tokkyū) from Okayama to Bitchū-Takahashi station, from there it is about an hour by bus.

Hiroshima-ken 広島県

FUKUYAMA 福山
Fukuyama (population 365,000) is a modern industrial town of little interest to the tourist, but its convenient situation on the Osaka-Hakata shinkansen route makes it a good jumping-off point to the pretty fishing port of Tomo-no-Ura or to Onomichi, which in turn is a jumping-off point for Inland Sea cruises. If you do have a few hours to spend in Fukuyama, you can visit the art gallery and museum and the reconstructed castle.

Orientation & Information
Most of the places of interest as well as the hotels and restaurants are close to the station. Route 2 runs parallel to the railway line, about half a km south. There is a tourist information and accommodation booking counter (☎ 0849-22-2869) in the busy, modern railway station.

Fukuyama-jō Castle 福山城
Fukuyama jō Castle was built in 1619, torn down during the 'one realm, one castle' period, and reconstructed in 1966. It overlooks the railway station, which is only a couple of minutes walk away. As well as the imposing donjon of the castle itself, there are turrets, the fine Sujigane-Go-mon Gate and a bathhouse. The castle contains the usual collection of samurai armour and similar

福山
Fukuyama

0   125   250 m
Route 2

To Auto &
Clock Museum

To Kumashiki
& Okayama

To Hiroshima

JR FUKUYAMA
STATION

PLACES TO STAY

2 Fukuyama Grand Hotel
福山グランドホテル
6 Fukuyama Castle Hotel
福山キャッスルホテル
7 Fukuyama Kokusai Hotel/
Fukuyama Station Inn
福山国際ホテル／福山ステーションイン
8 Fukuyama Hotel
福山ホテル
9 Fukuyama New Kokusai Hotel
福山ニュー国際ホテル
10 New Castle Hotel
福山ニューキャッスルホテル
11 Fukuyama Tōbu Hotel
福山東武ホテル

PLACES TO EAT

12 Studebaker Restaurant
スチュードベーカー　レストラン
14 McDonald's
マクドナルド

OTHER

1 Gokoku Shrine
護国神社
3 Fukuyama Museum of Art
福山美術館
4 Hiroshima Prefectural History Museum
広島県立歴史博物館
5 Fukuyama-jō Castle
福山城
13 NTT
15 Tenmaya Department Store
天満屋
16 Main Post Office
中央郵便局

artefacts. The castle is open from 9 am to 4.30 pm, closed on Monday, and entry is ¥150. The castle may be nothing special inside but it looks wonderful at night.

Art Gallery & History Museum
美術館・歴史博物館
Immediately to the west of the castle hill are Fukuyama's Museum of Art (open from 9.30 am to 4.30 pm, closed Monday, entry ¥300) and the Hiroshima Prefectural History Museum (open from 9 am to 4.30 pm, closed Monday, entry ¥250).

Auto & Clock Museum　時計博物館
The Fukuyama Auto & Clock Museum, north of the town centre, charges an exorbitant ¥900 entry fee but the strange little collection makes an interesting change from the usual feudal artefacts. Anything old is a little strange in modern Japan so the 1950 Mazda motorcycle taxi looks particularly curious. The 1961 Datsun Fairlady sports car

would have been no competition at all for a British sports car of that period – 30 years on how things have changed! The museum also houses waxwork figures of US presidents Lincoln and Washington, James Dean, Elvis Presley, General MacArthur and a very dissolute looking Commodore Perry.

The information office's map identifies the museum as the 'Automobile Clock Museum', which conjures up wonderful visions of Japanese obsessiveness – 'This is the digital clock from a 1987 Toyota, and this is...'

Places to Stay
There are lots of business hotels close to the railway station. Two of the cheaper ones are

WESTERN HONSHŪ

the *Fukuyama Kokusai Hotel* (☎ 0849-24-2411) behind the station and the *Fukuyama New Kokusai Hotel* (☎ 0849-24-7000) in front. The New Kokusai only has single rooms at ¥5200, including service charges and tax. At the Fukuyama Kokusai there are a small number of singles and twins at ¥5000 and ¥9000 respectively. Next door to the Fukuyama Kokusai is the *Fukuyama Station Inn* (☎ 0849-25-3337). It's one of the cheapest places around, with singles from ¥4700 to ¥4900 and a small number of twins/doubles at ¥7800/7000.

Immediately in front of the station is the *Fukuyama Tōbu Hotel* (☎ 0849-25-3181) with singles from ¥6600 to ¥7700 and twins from ¥10,800 to ¥14,000. Near by is the *New Castle Hotel* (☎ 0849-22-2121), at the top of the Fukuyama hotel price range with rooms from ¥9000/18,000.

The *Fukuyama Castle Hotel* (☎ 0849-25-2111), directly behind the station, has singles at ¥6600 to ¥7700; twins from ¥10,800 to ¥14,200. The *Fukuyama Grand Hotel* (☎ 0849-21-5511) has singles from ¥7500 to ¥9000, twins from ¥14,000 to ¥18,000 and a few doubles at ¥15,000.

Places to Eat

The full complement of fast-food places can be found immediately south of the railway station. *Studebaker* is a Japanese-Italian restaurant curiously named after a US car manufacturer which went belly up in the early '60s. The menu features nine types of spaghetti, none of them bolognese or napolitana, but the food is good.

A good place to seek out a bite to eat is the 8th floor of the Tenmaya department store next to the station. It has several Japanese and Chinese eateries with good lunch-time sets. The alleys either side of *McDonald's* harbour a good number of rāmen shops that do a busy lunch-time trade with the salaryman set.

Getting There & Away

Fukuyama is on the main railway lines along the San-yō coast. If you are travelling between Fukuyama and Kurashiki, it's usually quicker to stick to the San-yō line all the way rather than travel from Fukuyama to Shin-Kurashiki station by shinkansen and transfer to the San-yō line there. There are frequent buses from the Fukuyama station area to Tomo-no-Ura. The trip takes around 30 minutes and costs ¥470.

TOMO-NO-URA 鞆の浦

The delightful fishing port of Tomo-no-Ura, with its numerous interesting temples and shrines, is just half an hour by bus south of Fukuyama. Although gaijin visitors are infrequent, an excellent English map and brochure is available and explanatory signs are dotted all around town. If you set aside a day to travel from Kurashiki to Hiroshima you can spend a pleasant morning exploring Tomo-no-Ura, get back to Fukuyama for lunch and visit Onomichi in the afternoon before continuing to Hiroshima.

Four km beyond Tomo-no-Ura is the Abuto Kannon Temple with superb Inland Sea views.

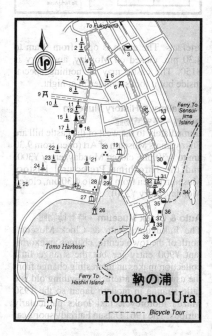

Bicycle Tour

Bicycles (*renta-saikaru*) are available at the ferry building and cost just ¥100 for two hours. The map shows an interesting circuit of the main attractions. Right across the road from the ferry landing is the **Muronoki Song Monument** with a sad poem composed by a Korean emissary whose wife had died en route to Tomo-no-Ura. Climb the headland to the ruins of **Taigashima Castle** where you will also find the **Enpuku-ji Temple** and a monument to the haiku poet Basho.

Cross the headland to the harbour and continue until you reach the steps leading to the Museum of History (¥150). It's open from 9 am to 4.30 pm. This interesting and well-presented museum features a great model of the sea bream fishing festival. Back on the road, have a look in the nautical equipment shop on the corner and then head down towards the harbour to the **Shichikyō-ochi Ruins**. This one-time sake shop isn't a ruin at all but played a small part in the Meiji Restoration when a fleeing anti-shogunate

group paused here long enough for one member of the group to compose a waka (31 syllable poem) extolling the virtues of the shop's sake.

Continue towards the **Iou-ji Temple** – although it's easier to park your bicycle at the bottom of the steep hill and walk up. From the temple, steep steps lead to a fine view over the town from the Taishiden Hill. Back on your bicycle, continue to the **Hōsen-ji Temple**, originally founded in 1358. The Tengai pine tree in the grounds spreads to cover 600 sq metres. Just beyond the temple, the **Sasayaki** (Whispering Bridge) commemorates an illicit romance which, according to a local tourist brochure, resulted in the lovers being 'drowned into the sea'. Beside the bridge is the **Yamanaka Shikanosuke Monument**, where, after a failed vendetta, the hapless Shikanosuke had had his 'head severed for inspection'.

The **Nunakuma-jinja Shrine** has a portable Nō stage used by Hideyoshi to enjoy performances during sieges. It has been des-

1	Ankoku-ji Temple 安国寺	15	Jokan-ji Temple 浄戒寺	29	Nautical Equipment Shop マリン店
2	Shōbō-ji Temple 正法寺	16	Sasayaki Bridge ささやき橋	30	Taichō-rō Guest House 対潮楼
3	Post Office 郵便局	17	Hosen-ji Temple 法宣寺	31	Josen-ji Temple 浄泉寺
4	Ji-tokuin Temple 慈徳院	18	Pine Tree 天蓋の松	32	Fukuzen-ji Temple 福禅寺
5	Zengyo-ji Temple 善行寺	19	Tomo-no-Ura Museum of History 鞆の浦歴史博物館	33	Muronoki Song Monument むろの木歌碑
6	Kogarasu-jinja Shrine 小烏神社	20	Tomo Castle Ruins 鞆城跡	34	Benten Island 弁天島
7	Hongan-ji Temple 本願寺	21	Ji-zōin Temple 地蔵院	35	Ferry Landing 渡船場
8	Daikan-ji Temple 大観寺	22	Nanzenbo-ji Temple 南禅坊寺	36	Taizan-kan Ryokan 対山館
9	Nunakuma-jinja Shrine 沼隈神社	23	Amida-ji Temple 阿弥陀寺	37	Basho Monument 芭蕉の句碑
10	Komatsudera-ji Temple 小松寺	24	Myoen-ji Temple 明円寺	38	Enpuku-ji Temple 円福寺
11	Kensyo-ji Temple 顕政寺	25	Iou-ji Temple 医王寺	39	Taigashima Castle Ruins 大雅島城跡
12	Myoren-ji Temple 妙蓮寺	26	Old Lighthouse 常夜灯	40	Yodohime-jinja Shrine よどひめ神社
13	Bus Terminal バスターミナル	27	Iroha-Maru Museum いろは丸展示館		
14	Yamanaka Shikanosuke Monument 山中鹿之助首塚	28	Shichikyō-ochi Ruins 七卿落遺跡		

ignated as an Important National Treasure. The shrine itself is picturesquely sited, with a gentle flight of stairs leading up to it. The **Ankoku-ji Temple** (entry ¥100) dates from 1270 and houses two wooden statues which are national treasures. It has a slightly tatty *kare-sansui* (waterless-stream garden) which was relaid in 1599.

From here you head back towards your starting point, pausing to take in 'eastern Japan's most scenic beauty' on the way. Whether it deserves the appellation or not you can can decide for yourself, but that is how it seemed to a visiting Korean dignitary in 1711. The **Taichō-rō Guest House**, built in 1690 for visitors from Korea, is in the Fukuzen-ji Temple compound and the cheerful priest will usher you in and let you sit to admire the view of Kōgō, Benten and Sensui islands.

Cruises

If you can rustle up five interested parties, you can putter around the bay and Sensui-jima Island in a small boat for ¥6000. Boats will also take you south to the Abuto Kannon, which is at the foot of the Numakuma-hantō Peninsula, a trip that will set a party of five back ¥9000. Ferries run on a regular basis to Sensui-jima Island from the harbour area. The five-minute trip costs ¥240 return. There are some quiet walking trails on the island and a couple of places to stay.

Festivals

The Tai-ami Sea Bream Fishing Festival takes place during the entire month of May.

Places to Stay

Rather than stay in Fukuyama, a night in Tomo-no-Ura, an altogether more picturesque location, would be a more pleasant experience. Right by the water, not far from the harbour is the *Taizan-kan* (☎ 0849-82-2111), though it's not cheap. Per person costs with two meals start at ¥15,000. Ask at the tourist information counter for information on the *Kokuminshukusha Kaihin Hotel* over on Sensui-jima Island. Costs here should be around ¥5000 per person with two meals.

Getting There & Away

It's only 14 km from Fukuyama to Tomo-no-Ura; a bus from stand No 2 outside JR Fukuyama station takes 30 minutes and costs ¥470.

ONOMICHI　尾道

Onomichi (population 97,000) is an undistinguished looking industrial town, hemmed in against the sea by a backdrop of hills. Along the base of this backdrop is a fascinating temple walk. It's well signposted in English, and English brochures are available at the station inquiry desk. The walk itself is pleasant although there is no way you would want to visit all of the 30-odd temples and shrines.

Temple Walk

You could easily spend the whole day following the temple walk; for a shorter version take a bus from outside the station and continue for three stops to the Nagaeguchi stop (¥110) near the cablecar station. From there, you can follow the walk all the way to the Jōdo-ji Temple, almost at the end of the route, then take a bus back to the station from the Jōdoji-shita bus stop.

The cablecar (¥270 one way) ascends to the top of Senkō-ji Hill where there is a museum and fine views over the town. As you ride the cablecar up, you can look down on the **Senkō-ji Temple**, then walk down to it along the Path of Literature where poets and authors have their works immortalised in stones beside the path. The temple, founded in 806, also has fine views over the town and sea. From the temple, you can continue downhill past the three storeyed **Tennei-ji Temple**. It was originally built with five storeys in 1388 but rebuilt with three in 1692.

The walk continues past the **Fukuzen-ji Temple**, originally dating from 1573, with its impressive gates carved with cranes and (look up) a dragon. The **Saikoku-ji Temple** is entered through the Niō-mon ('two kings') Gate, which is hung with gigantic two metre long straw sandals. From there, a steep flight

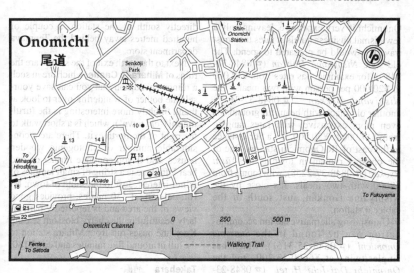

Onomichi

尾道

1	Saikoku-ji Temple 西国寺
2	Senkō-ji Hill Lookout & Museum 展望台
3	Jikan-ji Temple 慈観寺
4	Fukuzen-ji Temple 福善寺
5	Jyōsen-ji Temple 浄泉寺
6	Senkō-ji Temple 千光寺
7	Cablecar Station 長江口ケーブルカー駅
8	Rakutenjiguchi Bus Stop 楽天寺口バス停
9	Bōjiguchi Bus Stop 坊寺口バス停
10	Memorial Hall of Literature 文学記念碑
11	Tennei-ji Temple 天寧寺
12	Nagaeguchi Bus Stop 長江口バス停
13	Jikō-ji Temple 持光寺
14	Kōmyō-ji Temple 光明寺
15	Kibitsuhiko-jinja Shrine 吉備津彦神社
16	Jōdoji-shita Bus Stop 浄土寺下バス停
17	Jōdo-ji Temple 浄土寺
18	JR Onomichi Station JR尾道駅
19	Tsuchidōshita Bus Stop 土堂小下バス停
20	Watashibadōri Bus Stop 渡し場通りバス停
21	Bus Terminal バスターミナル
22	Onomichi Pier 尾道駅前桟橋
23	Nishiyama Honkan 西山本館
24	Yūshi Ryokan 友市旅館

of steps leads up to the temple, overlooked by a red three storeyed pagoda.

The **Jōdo-ji Temple** has an unusual two storeyed temple in its compound and a fine garden (entry ¥300) and teahouse moved here from Fushimi Castle. The temple houses a number of important art works including a painting damaged by the fire which destroyed the temple in 1325.

For anyone who hasn't seen enough tem-

ples for one day, between the station and the cablecar are Kōmyō-ji and Jikō-ji Temples, both of which are of lesser interest. The nearby Onomichi Cutural Hall *(Onomichi Bunka Kinen-kan)* is not geared to gaijin, but might be of interest to some. It's open daily from 9 am to 5.30 pm and admission is ¥200.

Places to Stay

A lot of the nicer accommodation in

Onomichi is very expensive, leaving only a few dismal business hotels at rates that most travellers would be prepared to spend. The old-style *Nishiyama Honkan* (☎ 0848-37-2480), for example, has rates from ¥12,000 to ¥20,000 per person with two meals. The *Nishiyama Bekkan* (☎ 0848-37-3145), another old place with beautiful grounds, is even more expensive, with rates ranging from ¥17,000 to ¥50,000. It's a fair distance to the east of JR Onomichi station. One of the cheaper ryokan in town is the *Yūshi Ryokan* (☎ 0848-37-2258), with rooms from ¥8000 with two meals. It's close by the Nishiyama Honkan, just south of the cablecar station.

Uninspiring alternatives to inn accommodation can be found in the *Sunroute Onomichi* (☎ 0848-25-3161), which has singles/twins at ¥6600/13,200, and the *Onomichi Dai-Ichi Hotel* (☎ 0848-23-4567), where rooms are ¥4950/15,000. Both of these hotels are just to the west of Onomichi station.

Getting There & Away

The Shin-Onomichi shinkansen station is three km north of the JR San-yō line station. Buses connect the two stations and also run straight to the cablecar station (¥160), but it's probably easier to reach Onomichi on the JR San-yō line and change to the shinkansen line either at Fukuyama (to the east) or Mihara (to the west). Hiroshima is one hour 30 minutes away on the San-yō line, and tickets cost ¥1420.

Ferries run from Onomichi to Setoda, the starting and finishing point for the popular Setoda-Hiroshima-Miyajima cruises. (See the Inland Sea section for details.) Ferries also operate from Onomichi to Imabari and Matsuyama, both on Shikoku.

ONOMICHI TO HIROSHIMA

尾道から広島へ

Mihara 三原

Mihara is on the San-yō shinkansen line and is a convenient departure or arrival point for Setoda on Ikuchi-jima, other islands of the Inland Sea and for Shikoku. The harbour is directly south of the station, a couple of hundred metres away behind the Tenmaya department store.

Next to the north exit of the station are the ruins of **Mihara-jō Castle**, which are in such a ruinous condition that you can save yourself the bother of wandering over to look at them. Slightly more interesting is the **furui-machi** ('old town'), which is a short walk to the right of the north exit. There are a considerable number of photogenic wooden houses, and if you continue further on and bear left, there is a string of small temples of minor interest. Just to the south of town, **Mt Hitsuei-zan**, at 330 metres, provides good views of the area and is reportedly particularly beautiful in the cherry blossom season. Kure line buses run from Mihara station to the hill in around five minutes and cost ¥180.

Takehara 竹原

Takehara is on the coastal JR San-yō line or can be reached by boat from Omi-shima Island. There is also a convenient bus service from Mihara that takes one hour and costs ¥940. Takehara was an important centre for salt production in the Edo period and still retains some interesting Edo-period houses. The old part of town is north of the station area. Follow the tree-lined avenue in front of the station, turn right into the main avenue about 200 metres up the road and follow it until you cross a river. A left turn here will take you up an attractive area with traditional-style homes, some of which are open to the public. **Shōren-ji Temple** is slightly north of this area and has an impressive 'bell gate', but little else to recommend it.

South of Takehara is **Ōkuno-jima Island**, which has the dubious distinction of harbouring the largest resort in central Honshū. It's all you would expect of a large Japanese resort, and boats run out to it from Takehara harbour (five minutes walk south of the station) in 30 minutes and cost ¥1640.

Kure 呉

The giant battleship *Yamato*, sunk off Nagasaki on a suicide mission to Okinawa during WW II, was just one of the many naval vessels built in Kure. The town, virtually a suburb of Hiroshima, is still an important shipbuilding centre and there is a naval museum on nearby Eta-jima Island – although it takes a long time to get there. The Nikyu-kyō Gorge is 15 km north-east of Kure.

NORTHERN HIROSHIMA-KEN
広島県の北部
Taishaku-kyō Gorge   帝釈峡
North of Onomichi, very close to the central Chūgoku Expressway, this 15 km limestone gorge could be a real chance to get off the beaten track. There are natural rock bridges, limestone caves and, for the Japanese, a major attraction in **Lake Shinryū-ko**, which has cruise boats.

Transport connections to the area are not as convenient as for most other attractions in this part of Japan, but this will be part of the fun for some. Probably the best means of transport is to take a bus direct from the Hiroshima bus centre. These buses take around two hours and cost ¥1750. Alternatively there are buses running to the area from both Bingo-Shōbara and Tōjō stations on the JR Geibi line. Tōjō station is closest (25 minutes by bus), but it is also a lot further from Hiroshima and not particularly convenient to anywhere else.

Sandan-kyō Gorge   三段峡
Sandan-kyō Gorge, about 70 km north west of Hiroshima, is another area that you could get lost in for a few days. The gorge itself isn't as interesting as the one at Taishaku, but this is not an area that is likely to be overrun by tourists.

Buses run from Hiroshima station and the Hiroshima bus centre to Sandan-kyō station at the southern end of the 16 km long gorge. The journey takes around two hours and costs ¥1240. Ordinary trains to JR Sandankyō station, the terminus of the Kabe line, 2½ hours and cost ¥1090. A walking trail leads through the gorge.

HIROSHIMA   広島
Although it's a busy, prosperous, not unattractive industrial city, visitors would have no real reason to leave the shinkansen in Hiroshima (population 1,085,000) were it not for that terrible instant on 6 August 1945 when the city became the world's first atomic bomb target. Hiroshima's Peace Memorial Park is a constant reminder of that tragic day and attracts a steady stream of visitors from all over the world.

The city's history dates back to 1589, when the feudal lord Mōri Terumoto named the city and established a castle there.

Orientation & Information
Hiroshima ('broad island') is a city built on a series of sandy islands on the delta of the Ōta-gawa River. JR Hiroshima station is east of the city centre and, although there are a number of hotels around the station, the central area, with its very lively entertainment district, is much more interesting. Peace Memorial Park and most of the atomic bomb reminders are at the northern end of an island immediately west of the city centre.

Hiroshima's main east-west avenue is Heiwa-dōri (Peace Blvd), but the busiest road (with the main tram lines from the station) is Aioi-dōri, which runs parallel to Heiwa-dōri. Just south of Aioi-dōri, and again parallel to it, is the busy Hon-dōri shopping arcade. A great deal of work was carried out in preparation for the 1994 Asian games to be held in Hiroshima, and by the time you have this book in your hands, the city should have its own underground rail system and monorail.

There is an information office in JR Hiroshima station where the staff can make accommodation bookings. For the benefit of those arriving by sea, Ujina, Hiroshima's port, also has an information counter. More comprehensive information can be obtained from the helpful tourist office in the Peace Memorial Park (☎ 082-247-6738); this office is open daily from 9.30 am to 6 pm from April to September and from 8.30 am to 5 pm the rest of the year. Hiroshima is a major industrial centre with a Mitsubishi heavy industries plant and the main Mazda

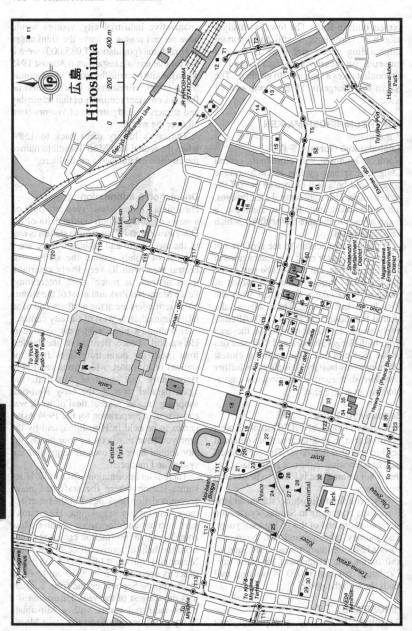

広島

Hiroshima

0   200   400 m

PLACES TO STAY

6 Hotel New Hiroden
ホテル ニューヒロデン
7 Hiroshima Ekimae
Green Hotel
広島駅前グリーンホテル
8 Hotel Sun Palace
9 Hotel Yamato
ホテルやまと
10 Hiroshima
Terminal Hotel
広島ターミナルホテル
12 Hiroshima
Station Hotel
広島ステーションホテル
13 Hiroshima Century
City Hotel
広島センチュリーシティホテル
14 Hiroshima City Hotel
広島シティホテル
15 Mikawa Ryokan
三河旅館
17 Hotel Silk Plaza
ホテルシルクプラザ
22 Hiroshima Green Hotel
広島グリーンホテル
30 Minshuku Ikedaya
民宿池田屋
34 ANA Hotel Hiroshima
広島全日空ホテル
35 Hokke Club Hotel
法華クラブ広島店
36 Hiroshima Tōkyū Inn
広島東急イン
39 Hiroshima
Kokusai Hotel
広島国際ホテル
51 Hiroshima
Central Hotel
広島セントラルホテル
52 Hiroshima
Union Hotel
ホテルユニオン広島
55 Sera Bekkan Ryokan
世羅別館

PLACES TO EAT

37 Andersen's Bakery &
Restaurant
アンデルセン
40 Spaghetteria
San Mario
サンマリオ
41 Rally's Steakhouse
ラリーズ
42 Yōrō-no-Taki
Restaurant
養老の滝
43 Suehiro Steak
Restaurant
スエヒロ

47 Tokugawa
Okonomayaki
Restaurant
お好み焼き徳川
48 Tonkatsu Tokugawa
とんかつ徳川
50 Kuimonoya &
Ottimo Restaurants
くいものや
53 Chikara Soba
Restaurant
ちから
54 Kumar Indian
Restaurant
くマー
56 Tokugawa
Okonomayaki
Restaurant
お好み焼き徳川

OTHER

1 Hiroshima-jō Castle
広島城
2 Science & Culture
Museum for
Children
こども文化科学館
3 Hiroshima Carp's
Baseball Stadium
広島市民球場
4 Hiroshima
Museum of Art
広島美術館
5 Prefectural
Art Museum
県立美術館
11 Pagoda of Peace
平和塔
16 World Peace
Memorial Cathedral
世界平和記念聖堂
18 Sogo Department
Store (Sogo Bus
Centre, Kinokuniya
Bookshop)
そごう
19 KDD (International
Telephone)
20 ANA
全日空
21 A-Bomb Dome
原爆ドーム
23 Atomic Bomb
Epicentre
爆心地
24 Children's Peace
Memorial
原爆の子の像
25 Korean A-Bomb
Memorial
韓国人原爆犠牲者慰霊碑

26 Tourist Information
Office
観光案内所
27 Peace Flame
平和の灯
28 Cenotaph
原爆慰霊碑
29 Laundrette
コインランドリー
31 Peace Memorial
Museum
平和記念資料館
32 Peace Memorial Hall
平和記念館
33 Former Bank
of Japan Building
旧日本銀行
38 Maruzen Bookshop
丸善
44 Fukuya
Department Store
福屋百貨店
45 Mac Bar
46 Tenmaya
Department Store
天満屋
49 Mitsukoshi
Department Store
三越
50 Harry's Bar
ハリーズ

TRAM STOPS

T1 Hiroshima ekimae
広島駅前
T2 Enkobashi
猿猴橋
T3 Matoba-chō
的場町
T4 Danbara Ohata-chō
段原大畑町
T5 Inarimachi
稲荷町
T6 Kanayama-chō
銀山町
T7 Ebisu-chō
胡町
T8 Hatchobori
八丁堀
T9 Tatemachi
立町
T10 Kamiya-chō
紙屋町
T11 Genbaku Dōmu-mae
(A-Bomb Dome)
原爆ドーム
T12 Honkawa-chō
本川町
T13 Tokaichimachi
十日市町
T14 Dobashi
土橋

WESTERN HONSHŪ

T15	Teramachi
	寺町
T16	Betsuin-mae
	別院前
T17	Jogakuin-mae
	女学院前
T18	Shukkeien-mae
	縮景園前
T19	Katei Saibansho-mae
	家庭裁判所前
T20	Hakushima Line Terminus
	白島
T21	Hon-dōri
	本通
T22	Fukuromachi
	袋町
T23	Chuden-mae
	中電前

(Matsuda in Japanese) car plant. Inquire at the tourist office about factory visits.

A good source of information, especially for those planning a lengthier stay in Hiroshima, is *Signpost*, a locally produced magazine with news on clubs, movies, restaurants and so on. Those planning on a long-term stay in Hiroshima might want to get hold of a copy of *Hiroshima Attention Please*, a comprehensive guide to the city. It's available at Maruzen bookshop.

The big department stores are Mitsukoshi (closed on Monday), Tenmaya (closed on Tuesday), Fukuya (closed on Wednesday) and Sogo (closed on Thursday).

Books English-language books can be found in the Kinokuniya bookshop on the 6th floor (through the men's department) or in the Sogo department store or in the Maruzen bookshop, near by in the shopping arcade and opposite Andersen's Restaurant. Maruzen's foreign-language books are on the 3rd floor.

John Hersey's *Hiroshima* (Penguin, 1946) is still the classic reporter's account of the bomb and its aftermath. In 1985 a new edition, available in paperback, followed up the original protagonists. Eleanor Coerr's children's book *Sadako & the Thousand Paper Cranes* tells the sad but inspiring story of a 12 year old girl's death from leukaemia, contracted due to exposure to the bomb's radiation.

The A-Bomb Dome 原爆ドーム

The symbol of the destruction visited upon Hiroshima is the A-Bomb Dome (Gembaku Dōmu) just across the river from Peace Memorial Park. The building was previously the Industrial Promotion Hall until the bomb exploded almost directly above it and effectively put a stop to any further promotional activities. Its propped-up ruins have been left as an eternal reminder of the tragedy, floodlit at night and fronted with piles of the colourful origami cranes which have become a symbol of Hiroshima's plea that nuclear weapons should never again be used. The actual epicentre of the explosion was just south of the A-Bomb Dome, and is marked by a small park.

The easiest way to get to the dome is to take a No 2, No 6 or Miyajima tram from the station and get off at the Genbaku Dōmu-mae stop, right beside the dome. I think it's better to get off the tram a few stops earlier and approach it by the shopping arcade parallel to Aioi-dōri. Walking down the busy arcade you pass bookshops, boutiques and a McDonald's restaurant: all the comfortable symbols of modern, prosperous Japan. Just before the river there's the Hiroshima Green Hotel then the arcade ends and you cross the road into a small park and *bang*, there you are, on the spot where the world ended for the people of Hiroshima.

Tony Wheeler

The A-Bomb Dome is the only blast survivor left in ruins, but some damaged buildings were repaired and still stand. On Rijō, just 380 metres south-east of the epicentre, the former Bank of Japan building looks rock solid; however, although the shell survived intact, the interior was totally destroyed and all 42 people in the bank at the time were killed. It was back in limited business two days later.

Peace Memorial Park 平和記念公園

From the A-Bomb Dome, cross the T-shaped Aioi-bashi Bridge to the Peace Memorial Park (Heiwa-kōen). It is thought that the

T-shape may have been the actual aiming point used by the bombardier. If so, his aim was acute. The park is dotted with memorials including the cenotaph which contains the names of all the known victims of the bomb and frames the A-Bomb Dome across the river. The flame burning beneath the arched cenotaph is not designed to be eternal – when the last nuclear weapon on earth has been destroyed it will be extinguished.

Near by is what for many is the most poignant memorial in the park – the Children's Peace Memorial inspired by leukemia victim Sadako. When she developed leukemia at 10 years of age she decided to fold 1000 paper cranes, the symbol of longevity and happiness in Japan, convinced that if she could achieve that target she would recover. She died having completed her 644th crane but children from her school folded another 356, with which she was buried. Her story inspired a nationwide bout of paper crane folding which continues to this day. Around the memorial are heaped not thousands but millions of cranes, regularly delivered by the boxload from schools all over Japan.

Just across the river from the park is a memorial to the bomb's Korean victims. Great numbers of Koreans were shipped from their homeland to work as slave labourers in Japanese factories during WW II, and more than one in 10 of those killed by the bomb was a Korean. The Korean memorial, erected long after the war (in 1970), carries a bitter reminder that no prayers were said for the Korean victims, and that despite the plethora of A-bomb monuments, not one had been erected in their memory.

A-Bomb Museum 平和記念資料館

Like its equivalent in Nagasaki, the A-bomb museum will win no awards for architectural inspiration, but its simple message is driven home with sledgehammer force. The exhibits tell the story of the bomb and the destruction it wrought on Hiroshima and its people. A model showing the town after the

The Hiroshima Bomb

Prior to the atomic bomb explosion, Hiroshima had not been bombed at all. This was a highly unusual situation, given that so many Japanese cities had been virtually flattened by repeated raids, and it is speculated that this was a deliberate policy in order to measure exactly how much damage the atomic bomb had done.

Dropped from the USAF B-29 *Enola Gay*, the bomb exploded at 8.15 am and approximately 75,000 people were killed almost immediately by the blast and subsequent fires. In comparison, all the bombing in WW II killed about 30,000 people in London and about another 30,000 in the rest of the UK. The Hiroshima death toll has probably now reached 200,000 as people continue to die from the radiation aftereffects. Even today, certain types of cancers still occur among Hiroshima's population in greater numbers than other comparable cities.

The first atomic explosion, the testing of a plutonium bomb, had taken place less than three weeks previously in the USA. The Hiroshima bomb used uranium, while the bomb dropped on Nagasaki three days later on 9 August used plutonium. On 2 September the Japanese surrendered. Ever since these events, there has been speculation as to whether it was necessary to drop the bomb, whether a demonstration of its capabilities could have prompted the Japanese surrender and whether a warning should have been given. Whether the Japanese would have resorted to using atomic weapons if they had invented them first has raised less speculation.

What is certain is that two bombs equivalent to a total of 38 kilotons of TNT brought Japan to its knees, despite a history of spectacular suicides which had shown that death was very often preferable to surrender. Also, the horrendous carnage at Okinawa had clearly shown that an invasion of the Japanese mainland was not going to be an easy task.

Today, nuclear weapons can have an explosive power equivalent to 50 megatons of TNT, over 1000 times greater than the Hiroshima and Nagasaki bombs combined. Given the devastating effects achieved by two relatively small nuclear bombs, why on earth do we still need thousands of much larger weapons just a button's push away?

Tony Wheeler

blast highlights the extent of the damage – seeing this, you might ponder what an insignificant little squib this bomb was, compared to the destructive potential of modern atomic weapons. The museum is open from 9 am to 6 pm (May to November), or 5 pm (December to April). Entry is ¥50.

Hiroshima-jō Castle   広島城
Also known as Ri-jō, or 'Carp Castle', Hiroshima-jō was originally constructed in 1589 but much of it was dismantled following the Meiji Restoration, leaving only the donjon, main gates and turrets. The remainder was totally destroyed by the bomb and rebuilt in modern ferro-concrete in 1958. There are some interesting displays including an informative and amusing video with some three-dimensional laser embellishments about the construction of the castle. It's open from 9 am to 4.30 pm (October to March) and closes an hour earlier between April and September; entry costs ¥300.

Shukkei-en Garden   縮景園
Modelled after Xihu (West Lake) in Hangzhou, China, the Shukkei-en Garden dates from 1620 but was badly damaged by the bomb. The garden's name literally means 'shrunk' or 'contracted view', and it attempts to recreat grand vistas in miniature. It may not be one of Japan's celebrated classic gardens, but it makes a pleasant stroll if you have time to spare. Entry is ¥200 and it's open from 9 am to 6 pm (5 pm from October to March).

Other Attractions
The **Hiroshima Museum of Art** (¥500, closed Monday) and the **Science & Culture Museum for Children** (free except for the planetarium) are both in Central Park just west of the castle. Hijiyama-kōen Park, directly south of JR Hiroshima station, is noted for its cherry blossoms in spring. The **Hiroshima City Museum of Contemporary Art** (¥300) is also in the park. To get to Hijiyama Park, take a No 5 tram from the station towards Ujina (Hiroshima's port) and get off at the Hijiyama-shita stop.

Fudō-in Temple, directly north of the station and about half a kilometre beyond the youth hostel, is one of the few old structures in Hiroshima which survived the bomb blast. **Mitaki-ji Temple** is north-west of the town centre.

Festivals
On 6 August paper lanterns are floated down the Ota-gawa River towards the sea in memory of the bomb blast.

Places to Stay
Hiroshima has places to stay for a range of budgets, both around JR Hiroshima staion and within walking distance of Peace Memorial Park.

Youth Hostels *Hiroshima Youth Hostel* (☎ 082-221-5343) is about two km north of the town centre; take a bus from platform 22 in front of the JR station or from platform 29 behind it. The hostel is very clearly marked; the nightly cost for members varies seasonally from ¥2090 to ¥2260.

Ryokan & Minshuku The *Mikawa Ryokan* (☎ 082-261-2719) is a short stroll from the JR Hiroshima station and has singles/doubles at ¥3500/6000, room only. Although the ryokan is convenient for train travellers, and staff are friendly, the rooms are very cramped and gloomy. In contrast, the *Minshuku Ikedaya* (☎ 082-231-3329) is modern, bright and cheerful. Singles/doubles are ¥4000/7000, room only. The helpful manager speaks good English and if your dirty washing is piling up, there's a laundrette on the corner of the road. The Ikedaya is on the other side of Peace Memorial Park in a quiet area but an easy walk via the park from the town centre. To get there, take tram No 6 or a Miyajima tram from the station and get off at the Dobashi stop.

There are a number of other budget places in the vicinity plus a compact enclave of colourful love hotels including one rejoicing in the name 'Hotel Adult'.

Hotels

The hotels around the station and central Hiroshima areas are:

Station Area The *Hiroshima Station Hotel* (☎ 082-262-3201) is right in the station building and costs from ¥7000/13,700 for singles/doubles. *Hotel Yamato* (☎ 082-263-6222) is slightly cheaper at ¥6000/12,300 and is close to the station, overlooking the river. Next to it is the *Hotel Sun Palace* (☎ 082-264-6111) which is cheaper again at ¥5500/10,000. Also near the station is the *Hiroshima Ekimae Green Hotel* (☎ 082-264-3939) with rooms at ¥5500/9600.

The expensive *Hiroshima Terminal Hotel* (☎ 082-262-1111), directly behind the station, has singles/doubles from ¥9700/16,000. Other typical business hotels around the station area include the *Hotel New Hiroden* (☎ 082-263-3456), with rooms from ¥7200, the *River Side Hotel* (☎ 082-227-1111), with rooms from ¥6400, the *Hiroshima Central Hotel* (☎ 082-243-2222), the *Hiroshima Union Hotel* (☎ 082-263-7878) and the *Hiroshima City Hotel* (☎ 082-263-5111).

Central Hiroshima The *Hiroshima Kokusai Hotel* (☎ 082-248-2323) is right in the city centre and has rooms from ¥7480/13,200 for singles/doubles. The *Hiroshima Green Hotel* (☎ 082-248-3939) is on the edge of the city centre and close to the riverside and Peace Memorial Park; it costs from ¥6000/10,500.

The *Hokke Club Hotel* (☎ 082-248-3371) has rooms which are small, even by cramped business hotel standards but the noon check-in/checkout is a good deal compared to the usual late check-in and early checkout of Japanese hotels. Singles/doubles cost from ¥6400/11,000.

Directly behind the Hokke Club, on Heiwa-dōri, is the expensive *ANA Hotel Hiroshima* (☎ 082-241-1111) with singles from ¥10,780, twins and doubles from ¥23,000. It's probably the city's best hotel and during the summer there's a rooftop beer garden. Across Heiwa-dōri from the ANA Hotel the *Hiroshima Tōkyū Inn* (☎ 082-244-

0109) is part of the popular chain and has rooms from ¥7590/12,320.

Hiroshima does have traditional Japanese ryokan but they're in modern, anonymous buildings. The *Sera Bekkan* (☎ 082-248-2251) is central and costs from ¥13,750 per person including two meals. All rooms have bathrooms.

Places to Eat

Hiroshima is noted for its seafood, particularly oysters. The familiar assortment of fast-food outlets including *Shakey's Pizza*, *McDonald's* and *Mr Donut* can be found in the Hon-dōri shopping arcade. *Andersen's* on Hon-dōri is a popular restaurant complex with an excellent bakery section – a good place for an economical breakfast, watching the world pass by from the tables in the front window. There are a variety of other restaurant sections in the Andersen's complex.

The *Kumar Indian Restaurant* (☎ 082-248-6502), only a couple of blocks south of Hon-dōri, has excellent curries, tandoori and the like. Lunch-time teishokus for between ¥800 and ¥1100 apply only on weekdays. Main courses are typically ¥1100, and the menu is in English. The other Indian restaurant to look out for the in the arcade area is *Tandoor* (☎ 082-247-5622), which also has good lunch time specials.

Also in the 'ethnic' department is *Kuimonoya* (☎ 082-541-1052), with hybrid Asian cuisine prepared by a Thai chef. It has a great dinner course for ¥2800, and the restaurant can be found on the 2nd floor of the Apple 2 building, which also houses Harry's Bar (see the Entertainment section). The 5th floor of the same building also has the excellent Italian restaurant *Ottimo* (☎ 082-541-1053), though this place is a bit pricey – figure on spending around ¥3500 to ¥5000 per person for dinner. Just off Hon-dōri arcade there's a cheaper Italian restaurant, *Spaghetteria San Mario*, with top-class pasta dishes. The menu is a little confusing (even the English one), but it's worth persevering – you can eat well here for less than ¥1000. There's another branch of this restaurant on the second floor of the

Sogo annexe on the Peace Park end of Hon-dōri arcade.

Just north of the Hon-dōri arcade, near the Kokusai Hotel, *Yōrō-no-Taki* is an excellent, boistrous robatayaki with cheap draught beer. Across the road is *Rally's* steakhouse. This whole area is great for seeking out good Japanese restaurants, and probably the best advice is to wander around the arcades looking at the window displays of restaurants until you find one you like. Look out for *Chikara*, a very interesting soba shop with economical prices, and for *Tonkatsu Tokugawa*, a snazzy place with a good selection of breaded-pork dishes.

Back down on Aioi-dōri is a branch of the *Suehiro* steak restaurant chain, always a reliable, if slightly expensive, option. There are two *Tokugawa* okonomiyaki restaurants in the centre – one behind the Mitsukoshi department store and the other on the edge of the Shintenchi entertainment district. Okonomiyaki is a sort of cook-it-yourself omelette. Each table has a hotplate in the centre, you're provided with whatever ingredients you select and cook your omelette yourself. The plastic meal displays show you what ingredients you get.

Entertainment
Like any large Japanese city, Hiroshima has its fair share of boozing establishments – somewhere in the vicinity of 4000 in this case. Shintenchi and Nagarekawa are the entertainment districts and they make for an interesting evening stroll. If you want to avoid the hostess scene, look out for shot bars – there are a fair few of them about.

The foreign community in Hiroshima have a few bars that they hang out in, and these are good places to meet people. Probably the two most popular are *Mac* and *Harry's Bar*. Mac is a tiny place on the 4th floor of a building on the corner of Chūō-dōri and one of the streets running into the arcade area; there's an English sign at ground level. It has an astoundingly wide selection of CDs and LPs, and the guy who runs the place will regale you with 'pick a song...any song'. He's probably got it.

Harry's Bar is in the basement of the Apple 2 building, and is much more up-market in appearance than Mac. As the sign outside notifies prospective customers, it's '15% off drink prices for foreigners'; reverse discrimination, of course, but then a cheap beer is a cheap beer.

Other nightlife options in Hiroshima include a branch of *Kento's*, the live 'oldies but goodies' standby. The band performing here go under the name of Lucky Lips. *Ahiru Nagaya* is a restaurant bar that's open until 2 am on Friday and Saturday; cryptically, it announces to patrons 'Ahiru Nagaya means "Duck House" and we're not talking about the food!' – figure that one out. Anyone with an interest in the local live band scene can check out *Woody Street*, a club on Aioi-dōri that has a different live act every night of the week. Last time we were in town, acts included Mysterious Persons, The Sod, Guntlet Draw and – best of all – Trio the Pants.

Getting There & Away
Air There are frequent flights between Hiroshima and other parts of Japan. Flights to Tokyo (Haneda) take around one hour 20 minutes and cost ¥21,600 one-way, ¥39,060 return. Flights from Sapporo take two hours five minutes and cost ¥35,450 one way. Okinawa is one hour 40 minutes away and flights cost ¥26,600. Other flight possibilities include Kagoshima and Oita.

Train Hiroshima has long been an important railway junction, one of the factors which led to it being the prime atomic bomb target in WW II. Today it is an important stop on the Tokyo-Osaka-Hakata shinkansen route, with some services originating or terminating in Hiroshima. By shinkansen, it takes about 4½ to five hours to reach Hiroshima from Tokyo (¥11,120 plus a tokkyū charge of ¥6580), 1½ to two hours from Kyoto and slightly less from Hakata.

The JR San-yō line passes through Hiroshima and onwards down to Shimonoseki, hugging the coastline for much of the way. If you're travelling this way, the ordinary local services move along fairly quickly and are the best way to visit the nearby attractions of Miya-jima Island and Iwakuni.

Bus Long-distance buses run from the shinkansen exit of Hiroshima station, although there is also a bus terminal on the 3rd floor of Sogo department store. Buses between Hiroshima and Tokyo take around 12 hours and cost ¥11,840; they run from the JR bus terminal next to Tokyo station. Buses to and from Nagoya take around eight hours and ¥7700. There are also buses to and from Kyoto (¥5500), Fukuoka (¥4430) and Nagasaki (¥6500).

Sea Hiroshima is an important port with a variety of Inland Sea cruises as well as connections to other cities. The Hiroshima to Matsuyama ferry and hydrofoil services are a popular way of getting to or from Shikoku. (See the Matsuyama section in the Shikoku chapter for details.) Ferries also operate to Beppu on Kyūshū and to Imabari on Shikoku. For information on the Imabari service (in Japanese) ring Hiroshima-Imabari Kōsoku-sen (☎ 082-254-7555); tickets cost ¥4360. For information on the Beppu service, ring Hirobetsu Kisen (☎ 253-0909); economy-class tickets are ¥4000.

Getting Around
To/From the Airport Hiroshima's airport is conveniently close to the south-west of town and trams do the trip in around 30 minutes (¥200).

Bus Buses are more difficult to use than the trams as they are not numbered and place names are in kanji only, but the stands outside the station are clearly numbered. Take a bus from stand No 1 to the airport, No 2 to the port.

Tram Hiroshima has an easy-to-use tram (streetcar) service which will get you pretty well anywhere you want to go for a flat fare of ¥130 (¥90 on the short No 9 route). There is even a tram which runs all the way to the Miyajima Port for ¥250. The tram routes are shown on the Hiroshima map. Note that the tram colours have no connection with the routes – it's popularly rumoured that Hiroshima ended up with their rainbow variety of trams by buying up other cities' old trams as they closed down their tram services. If you have to change trams to get to your destination you should ask for a transfer ticket (*norikaeken*) as you leave the tram and pay an additional ¥50.

MIYA-JIMA ISLAND 宮島
Correctly known as Itsuku-shima, Miya-jima Island is easily reached from Hiroshima. The famous 'floating' torii of the Itsukushima-jinja Shrine is one of the most photographed tourist attractions in Japan and, with the island's Mt Misen as a backdrop, is classified as one of Japan's 'three best views'. The other two are the sandspit at Amanohashidate (northern coast of Western Honshū) and the islands of Matsushima-wan Bay (near Sendai, Northern Honshū). Apart from the shrine, the island has some other interesting temples, some good walks and remarkably tame deer which even wander the streets of the small town. Look out for the signs warning of the dangers of fraternising with the horned varieties.

Orientation & Information
There's an information counter in the ferry building. Turn right as you emerge from the building and follow the waterfront to get to the shrine and the centre of the island's small town. The shopping street, packed with souvenir outlets and restaurants, is a block back from the waterfront.

Itsukushima-jinja Shrine 厳島神社
The shrine, which gives the island its real name, dates from the 6th century and in its present form from 1168. Its pier-like construction is a result of the island's holy status. Commoners were not allowed to set foot on the island and had to approach the shrine by boat, entering through the floating torii out in the bay. Much of the time, however, the shrine and torii are surrounded not by water but by mud. The view of the torii immor-

talised in thousands of travel brochures requires a high tide.

The shrine is open from 6 am to sunset and entry is ¥200. On one side of the floating shrine is a floating Nō stage built by a Mōri lord. The orange torii, dating from 1875 in its present form, is often floodlit at night. A 'son et lumière' is sometimes performed from 8.30 to 9 pm, particularly in summer. You can hear it on headphones in English as well as Japanese for ¥300.

The treasure house, west of the shrine, is open from 8 am to 5 pm and entry is ¥250. The collection of painted sutra scrolls dating from the 12th century are not usually on display and the exhibits are not of great interest except, perhaps, to the scholarly.

Temples & Other Buildings

Topping the hill immediately east of the Itsukushima Shrine is the Senjō-kaku (Pavilion of 1000 Mats) built in 1587 by Hideyoshi. This huge and atmospheric hall (entry ¥50) is constructed with equally massive timber pillars and beams and the ceiling is hung with paintings. It looks out on a colourful five storeyed pagoda dating from 1407. The Senjō-kaku should have been painted to match but was left unfinished when Hideyoshi died.

Miyajima has numerous other temples including the Daigan-ji just west of the shrine, which is dedicated to the god of music and dates from 1201. The colourful and glossy Daisho-in Temple is just behind the town and can be visited on the way down Mt Misen. This is a temple with everything – statues, gates, pools, carp, you name it. The rituals performed at the main Itsukushima Shrine are also administered by the Daigan-ji. West of Itsukushima Shrine is the picturesque Taho-tō Pagoda.

Miyajima History & Folklore Museum 歴史民俗資料館

This interesting museum combines a 19th century merchant's home with exhibits concerning trade in the Edo period, a variety of displays connected with the island and a fine garden. The museum is open from 8.30 am to 5 pm and there's an excellent and informative brochure in English. Entry is ¥250.

Mt Misen & Other Walks 弥山

The ascent of 530 metre Mt Misen is the island's finest walk; the uphill part of the round trip can be avoided by taking the two stage cablecar for ¥800 one way, ¥1400 return. It leaves you about a 15 minute walk from the top. Around the cablecar station there are monkeys as well as deer. On the way to the top look for the giant pot said to have been used by Kōbō Daishi (774-835) and kept simmering ever since! It's in the

smaller building beside the main temple hall, also said to have been used by the founder of the Shingon sect.

There are superb views from the summit and a variety of routes leading back down. The descent takes a good hour and walking paths also lead to other high points on the island, or you can just follow the gentle stroll through Momiji-dani (Maple Valley) which leads to the cablecar station.

Other Attractions

There's an aquarium, a popular beach, a seaside park and, across from the ferry landing, a display of local crafts in the Hall of Industrial Traditions.

Festivals

Island festivals include fire-walking rites by the island's monks on 15 April and 15 November, a fireworks display on 14 August and the Kangensai Boat Festival on 16 June.

Places to Stay & Eat

There is no inexpensive accommodation on Miya-jima Island, although the *Miyajima-guchi Youth Hostel* (☎ 0829-56-1444) is near the ferry terminal and JR Miyajima-guchi station on the mainland. It has rates of ¥2300.

If you can afford to stay on the island, it's well worthwhile: you'll be able to enjoy the island in the evening, minus the day-trip hordes. The *Kokuminshukusha Miyajima Lodge* (☎ 0829-44-0430) is west of the shrine and has rooms with bathroom from ¥5500 per person including meals. At the large and pleasant *Iwasō Ryokan* (☎ 0829-44-2233) or at the *Miyajima Grand Hotel* (☎ 0829-44-2411) you can count on at least ¥18,000 per person with meals. There are a number of fairly expensive hotels and ryokan along the waterfront including the *Kamefuku Hotel* (☎ 0829-44-2111), the *Kinsuikan Hotel* (☎ 0829-44-2133) and the *Miyajima Royal Hotel* (☎ 0829-44-2191).

A more moderately priced alternative is the friendly and very pleasant *Pension Miyajima* (☎ 0829-44-0039) which is just back from the ferry landing. Rooms with bathroom cost ¥6500 per person or ¥9500 with meals included. The food is superb at ¥3000 for dinner, ¥1000 for breakfast. Although there are many restaurants and cafés on Miya-jima Island most of them cater to the day-trippers and close early in the evening.

Getting There & Away

The mainland ferry terminal for Miya-jima Island is near the Miyajima-guchi station on the JR San-yō line between Hiroshima and Iwakuni. Miyajima trams from Hiroshima terminate at the Hiroden-Miyajima stop by the ferry terminal. The tram (50 minutes, ¥250) takes longer than the train (25 minutes) but runs more frequently and can be boarded in central Hiroshima. On some trams you may have to transfer at the Hiroden-Hiroshima stop.

From the terminal, ferries shuttle across to Miya-jima Island in just 10 minutes for ¥170. One of the ferries is operated by JR so Japan Rail Pass holders should make sure they use this one. Ferry services also operate to Miya-jima Island direct from Hiroshima. High speed ferries (¥1250) do the trip there and back eight times daily and take just over 20 minutes from Hiroshima's Ujina Port. The SKK (Seto Naikaikisen) Inland Sea cruise on the *Akinada* starts and finishes at Miyajima; the Miyajima to Hiroshima leg costs ¥1480.

Getting Around

Bicycles can be rented from the ferry building or you can walk. A free bus operates from in front of the Iwasō Ryokan to the Mt Misen cablecar station.

Southern Yamaguchi-ken
山口県の南部

IWAKUNI　岩国

The five arched Kintai-kyō Bridge is Iwakuni's major attraction, although the town also has a US military base (an unattraction, perhaps?) and a number of points of interest in the Kikko-kōen Park.

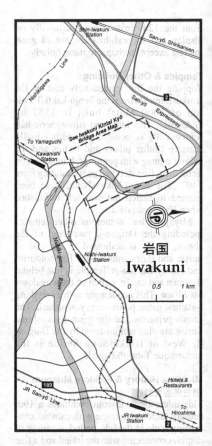

Orientation & Information

Iwakuni has three widely separated areas, which can, at first, be somewhat confusing for visitors. To the far west of the town centre is the Shin-Iwakuni shinkansen railway station, totally separate from the rest of town. In the central area is the old part of town with the bridge, the samurai quarter, the castle and all the other tourist attractions. To the east, in the modern part of town, is the JR Iwakuni station, as well as hotels, restaurants, bars and other conveniences. Tune your radio to 1575 AM for the US military radio station.

Kintai-kyō Bridge   錦帯橋

Also known as the 'Brocade Sash Bridge', the Kintai-kyō Bridge was built in 1673 and washed away by a flood in 1950. It was authentically rebuilt in 1953, albeit with some cunningly concealed steel reinforcements. The bridge is immediately recognisable by the five extremely steep arches. In the feudal era only samurai could use the bridge, which connected their side of the river with the rest of the town; commoners had to cross the river by boat. Today visitors have to pay a ¥210 toll to walk across and back. The ticket office at the entrance to the bridge also sells an all-inclusive ticket *(setto-ken)* for ¥820 that covers the bridge (¥210), the return cablecar (ropeway) trip (¥520) and Iwakuni-jō Castle (¥260), which is a saving of ¥170 if you plan to visit all three.

Samurai Quarter & Nishimura Museum
にしむら博物館

Some traces remain of the old samurai quarter by the bridge. The area is overlooked by Iwakuni-jō Castle and, beside the castle cablecar, is the Nishimura Museum with its extensive collection of samurai armour and equipment. It's said to be one of the best collections in Japan, but since only a small part of it is displayed at one time (and very little is labelled in English) it is unlikely to impress those already suffering from feudal-artefact overload. Entry is an expensive ¥500 and it's open from 8 am to 6 pm.

The old samurai quarter is now part of Kikko-kōen Park and includes some picturesque moats and remnants of the feudal buildings such as the Kagawa Nagaya-mon Gate, a fine old samurai gateway. Beside the moat, close to the cablecar station, is the Kinun-kaku Pavilion. Look for the swan houses in the moat. Also beside the cablecar car park is the Mekata House, a fine old samurai home. The Chokokan Library houses documents from the samurai period.

Iwakuni-jō Castle   岩国城

The original castle was built between 1603 and 1608 but stood for only seven years before the daimyō was forced to dismantle it and move down to the riverside. It was rebuilt in 1960 during Japan's great castle reconstruction movement; but modern Japanese castles were built for tourism, not warfare, so it now stands photogenically on the edge of the hillside, a short distance in front of its former hidden location. The well beside the path indicates where it was originally built.

You can get to the castle by cablecar or by the road (walking only) from beside the youth hostel. The cablecar costs ¥300 one way, or ¥520 return, but see the Kintai-kyō Bridge entry for the all-inclusive ticket.

Festivals

Traditional cormorant fishing (ukai) takes place at the Kintai-kyō Bridge every night from June to August except when rain makes the water muddy or on full-moon nights. Sightseeing boats operate on the Nishiki-gawa River during the fishing.

Places to Stay

Youth Hostels The *Iwakuni Youth Hostel* (☎ 0827-43-1092) is close to most of the attractions on the samurai side of the bridge. There are 106 beds and costs per night are ¥2300.

Ryokan If you were to stay in Iwakuni, the only real incentive to do so would be to stay in one of the traditional ryokan near the Kintai-kyō Bridge. One of the cheaper of these is the *Ryokan Yamane* (☎ 0827-41-0368), which has rooms from ¥8000 per person with two meals. Costs at the nearby *Shiratame Ryokan* (☎ 0827-41-0074) are slightly higher, with rooms at ¥10,000 to ¥16,000 per person with two meals.

Hotels The *Ogiya Station Hotel* at Shin-Iwakuni shinkansen station has rooms at ¥5000/10,000 but is a long way from anywhere. Around JR Iwakuni station, there's a choice of business hotels. The *Iwakuni Kinsui Hotel* (☎ 0827-22-2311) is right beside the station and has singles/twins at ¥7700/13,200. *City Hotel Andoh* (☎ 0827-22-0110) is only a couple of minutes walk from the station and has singles/doubles from ¥5500/9000. The *A-1 Hotel* (☎ 0827-

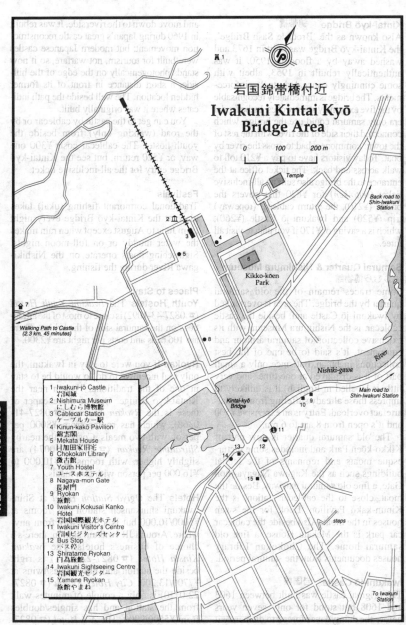

Top: Seto-ōhashi Bridge from Washū-zan Hill (TW)
Middle: Doga-shima Island from Izu-hantō Peninsula (CT)
Bottom: Floating torii, Miya-jima Island (JW)

Top: Fuji-san (CT)
Middle: Himeji from Himeji-jō Castle (JW)
Bottom: Ginza, Tokyo (CT)

21-2244) is not much further away and has clean, tidy, well-equipped rooms from ¥5000/8400 for singles/doubles.

Places to Eat

There are some small restaurants and cafés around the bridge and a wide variety of restaurants, bars and fast-food outlets around the station area including *Mos Burger*, *Lotteria* and the inevitable *Mr Donut*.

Getting There & Away

Iwakuni is only 44 km from Hiroshima, connected by shinkansen to the Shin-Iwakuni station (17 minutes, ¥1540), or regular JR San-yō line trains (44 minutes, ¥720) to the central JR Iwakuni station.

Getting Around

The Kintai-kyō Bridge is almost equidistant from the two main stations, about five km from either. Buses shuttle back and forth between Iwakuni station and the bridge (¥240) and Shin-Iwakuni station and the bridge (¥240).

YAMAGUCHI　山口

During the tumultuous Muromachi (Country at War) period from 1467 to 1573, Yamaguchi (population 129,000) prospered as an alternative capital to chaotic Kyoto. In 1550, the Jesuit missionary Francis Xavier paused for two months in Yamaguchi on his way to the imperial capital but quickly returned to the safety of this provincial centre when he was unable even to find the emperor in Kyoto! In the following centuries, Yamaguchi took turns with Hagi as the provincial capital and, like Hagi, Yamaguchi played an important part in the Meiji Restoration. Today it's a pleasantly peaceful town with a number of interesting attractions.

Orientation & Information

Ekimae-dōri is the main shopping street, running straight up from the station and crossing the main shopping arcade before it reaches Route 9. There's an information counter in the railway station.

Xavier Memorial Chapel
ザビエル記念聖堂

The Xavier Memorial Chapel overlooks the town centre from a hilltop in Marugame Park; this church was built in 1952 to commemorate the 400th anniversary of Francis Xavier's visit to the city. It was recently burnt out and at present only the walls remain standing, making it less of an attraction. No doubt, reconstruction will commence before too long.

Art Gallery & Museums

At the foot of the hill stands the Yamaguchi Prefectural Art Museum (open from 9 am to 4.30 pm, closed Monday, entry ¥180), where frequent special exhibitions are held. Just north is the Yamaguchi Prefectural Museum, which has the same opening hours and costs ¥120. The Yamaguchi History Museum is just off Route 9; it's open from 9 am to 5 pm (closed on Monday) and costs ¥100.

Kōzan-kōen Park & Rurikō-ji Pagoda
香山公園・瑠璃光寺五重塔

Further north again from the town centre is Kōzan-kōen Park, where the Rurikō-ji five storeyed pagoda, dating from 1404, is picturesquely sited beside a small lake. A small museum has photos and details of all 40 Japanese five storeyed pagodas, plus a map indicating where they're located. It's open daily from 9 am to 5 pm and entry is ¥200.

The Rurikō-ji Temple, with which the pagoda is associated, is also in the park and was moved here from a small village. The park's teahouse was also moved here – the Yamaguchi daimyō held secret talks in the house under the pretext of holding a tea ceremony. Next to the temple is a small museum of moderate interest; entry is ¥200. The park is also the site of Tōshun-ji Temple and the graves of the Mōri lords.

Jōei-ji Temple　常栄寺

The Jōei-ji Temple, three km north-east of the JR station, was originally built as a house and is notable for its beautiful Zen garden designed by the painter Sesshū. Visitors bring bentō (boxed lunches) and sit on the veranda to eat while admiring the garden.

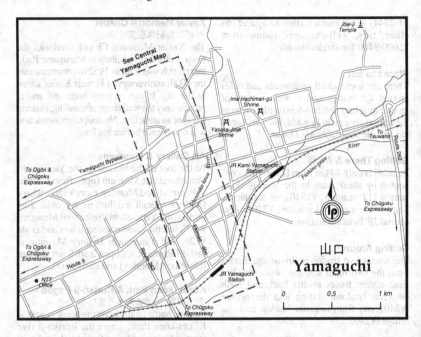

Entry to the garden is ¥300; it's open daily from 8 am to 5.30 pm.

Other Attractions

North of Route 9, the **Ichinosaka-kawa River** has a particularly pretty stretch, lined with cherry trees. Naturally they're at their best during the blossoming time in spring, but they're also lovely on summer evenings when large fireflies flit through the trees.

During the annual Gion Matsuri Festival in late July, the Sagi-mai Egret Dance is held in the **Yasaka-jinja Shrine**. The interesting **Ima Hachiman-gū Shrine** has a unique local architectural style that encompasses the gate, oratory and main hall under the same roof. The **Yamaguchi Dai-jingū Shrine** was a western branch of the great Ise-jingū Shrine near Nara in the Kansai District but is somewhat neglected today.

Places to Stay

Yamaguchi Youth Hostel (☎ 0839-28-0057)

is about four km from Miyano station (two stops east of Yamaguchi), and has 30 beds at ¥2300 per night. From Miyano station you can catch a bus to Miyano Onsen and get off at the last stop; the hostel is a few minutes walk to the north. You can rent bicycles there and a bicycle tour map is available.

The *Fukuya Ryokan* (☎ 0839-22-0531), just up Ekimae-dōri from the station, is popular, conveniently central and reasonably priced at ¥5500 per person with two meals.

There's the usual assortment of modern business hotels around the station area including the *Sun Route Kokusai Hotel Yamaguchi* (☎ 0839-23-3610), which has rooms from ¥6100/11,500 for singles/doubles. A short distance from the station down Ekimae-dōri the *Yamaguchi Kankō Hotel* (☎ 0839-22-0356) and the *Taiyō-dō Ryokan* (☎ 0839-22-0897) both have rooms with two meals included from between ¥6000 and ¥7000.

Yuda Onsen, a 10 minute bus trip from the

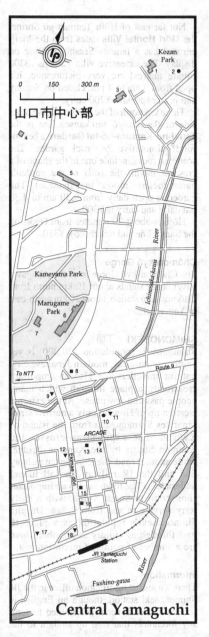

Central Yamaguchi

station, has a number of traditional ryokan including the expensive but historically interesting *Matsudaya Hotel* (☎ 0839-22-0125), which has rooms from ¥20,000 to ¥50,000 (!) per person with meals.

Places to Eat

The arcade off Ekimae-dōri has lots of restaurants, coffee bars and a *Lotteria* fast-food place in the arcade. Just a couple of doors down from the Fukuya Ryokan is *Yamabuki* (☎ 0839-22-1462), a pleasant old soba shop where you can eat well for ¥500. It's closed on the 1st and 15th of each month. Not far from the station, on the 2nd floor, is a pleasant little gallery restaurant, *Churamu*, with lunch-time spaghetti from ¥550.

There are a number of good places along Ekimae-dōri. *Mama No Ki*, close to the station is a pleasant *kissaten* (coffee shop) with a bargain-priced ¥330 morning setto (set-menu meal); notice how the regulars have their own cups and saucers (all different) pigeonholed behind the counter. Further up is *Jardin*, a good little bakery/patisserie, while at the top of the road, the *Green Park* restaurant is worth a try.

Getting There & Away
Yamaguchi is only 15 minutes by train (¥230) on the Yamaguchi line from the main shinkansen line station at Ogōri. JR buses run between Yamaguchi and Hagi, taking one hour 10 minutes and costing ¥1600.

Getting Around
Bicycles can be rented from the railway station and since the town's attractions are somewhat scattered (it's eight km just to the Jōei-ji Temple and back) and the traffic is not too chaotic, this is a good idea. The first two hours cost ¥310 or it's ¥820 for a day.

AROUND YAMAGUCHI 山口周辺
Ogōri 小郡
Ogōri, only 10 km south-west of Yamaguchi, is of no particular interest except as a place to change trains. It's at the junction of the San-yō Osaka-Hakata shinkansen line with the JR Yamaguchi line, which continues to Tsuwano and Masuda on the San-in coast.

Hōfu 防府
The **Hōfu Tenman-gū Shrine**, about a 10 minute walk north of Hōfu station, originally dates from 904 AD and is rated highly along with Dazaifu's (near Fukuoka on Kyūshū) Tenman-gū Shrine. It's open from 9 am to 4.30 pm daily and entry is ¥200. Close by is the **Suōkokubun-ji Temple**, a small and unimpressive structure that is said to date back originally to 741, though it has been rebuilt since then.

Not far east of Hōfu Tenman-gū Shrine, the **Mōri Hontei Villa** dates from the Meiji era and has a famous Sesshū painting on display. The extensive villa gardens (3300 square metres) are very picturesque. It's open from 9 am to 4 pm, closed on Sunday and is an expensive ¥700 entry.

Three km north of the station, on the other side of the San-yō shinkansen line is the **Tsuki-no-Katsura-no-tei Garden**, a beautiful if diminutive Zen rock garden. The scattered rocks include one in the shape of a crescent moon (the *tsuki* of the garden's name means 'moon' in Japanese). The garden is open daily from 9.30 am to 4.30 pm daily and entry is ¥300.

Hōfu is about 20 minutes from Ogōri on the Sanyō line and tickets cost ¥310.

Chōmon-kyō Gorge
The Chōmon-kyō Gorge is on the Abugawa River, and extends about 10 km north from Chōmon-kyō station, about 20 km north-east of Yamaguchi.

SHIMONOSEKI 下関
Shimonoseki (population 270,000) is yet another featureless, modern Japanese city, but for travellers it's also an important crossroads, a place through which many people pass and few pause. At the extreme western tip of Honshū only a narrow strait separates Shimonoseki from the island of Kyūshū. The expressway crosses the Kanmon Straits by the Kanmon Bridge, while another road, the shinkansen railway line and the JR railway line all tunnel underneath. The town is also an important connection to South Korea, with a daily ferry service to and from Pusan. Despite Shimonoseki's reputation as a place to pass through as rapidly as possible, there are a number of points of minor interest.

Information
There's a tourist information office in the JR Shimonoseki station, though no English is spoken and staff seem determined to send any foreigners that turn up straight to the

Pusan ferry terminal and out of Japan as quickly as possible. Beside the station is the large Sea Mall Shimonoseki shopping centre.

If you're arriving from Korea, note that the bank in the ferry terminal is only open from 9 to 9.30 am after the ferry arrival, but there are branches of the Bank of Tokyo and the Yamaguchi Bank near the station. Those arriving on a weekend should make sure they bring some Japanese yen with them. If you need a visa for Korea, the Korean consulate is about a km south of the station, beyond the ferry terminal.

Akama-jingū Shrine　赤間神宮

The bright red/orange Akama Shrine is dedicated to the child-emperor Antoku who died in 1185 in the naval battle of Dan-no-Ura. The battle took place in the Kanmon Straits which are overlooked by the shrine. In the Hōichi Hall stands a statue of 'Earless Hōichi', hero of a traditional ghost story retold by Lafcadio Hearn. The shrine is about three km east of the station, en route to Mt Hino-yama. Get off the bus at the Akamajingu-mae bus stop.

Mt Hino-yama　火の山

About five km north-east of JR Shimonoseki station there are superb views over the Kanmon Straits from the top of 268 metre Mt Hino-yama. The km-long Kanmon Bridge is right at your feet, ships shuttle back and forth through this narrow but important waterway and at night, the views of the city are wonderful. You can walk, drive or travel by cablecar to the top. The cablecar costs ¥200 one way, ¥400 return. Take a Ropeway-mae bus to the Mimosurogawa bus stop near the cablecar station or a Kokuminshukusha-mae bus right to the top – these depart hourly from stand No 3 at the station.

Sumiyoshi-jinja Shrine　住吉神社

The Sumiyoshi Shrine, dating from 1370, is north of Mt Hino-yama, near the Shin-Shimonoseki station. It's open from 9 am to 4 pm daily but closed from 8 to 15 December.

Aquarium　下関水族館

Shimonoseki's aquarium may or may not be the 'largest in the far east' as claimed in the aquarium's tourist brochure, but if it wasn't in Japan, it would just be another crummy Third World aquarium. There's a dolphin show and some of the fish, penguins and other sea creatures are crammed into tanks or enclosures far too small for them. An unfortunate giant leatherback turtle is squeezed into a small circular pool into which visitors toss coins; perhaps it can eventually buy its freedom.

On the hilltop overlooking the complex, a concrete 'whale' houses exhibitions showing all the reasons the Japanese give for slaughtering whales. The aquarium is south of the centre, just past the big Ferris wheel marking Marine Leisureland. In Japanese, aquarium is *suizokukan* and buses run from the station to the Suizokukan-mae bus stop. The aquarium is open from 9 am to 5 pm (6 pm in August) and entry is ¥500.

Chōfu　長府

If you have any time in Shimonoseki, a trip up to Chōfu would be the best way of utilising it. Chōfu is the old castle town area and, while little remains of the old coastal castle itself, there are old earth walls and samurai gates in Chōfu, along with a museum and some important temples and shrines. The **Kōzan-ji Temple** has a Zen-style hall dating from 1327 and the Chōfu Museum (9 am to 5 pm, closed Monday, ¥200) is also in the temple grounds. Other interesting temples and shrines include the Kakuon-ji Temple, the Iminomiya-jinja Shrine and the Nogi-jinja Shrine.

Buses run fairly frequently up Route 9 from Shimonoseki station to Chōfu. Two bus stops service the area: Matsubara to the south and Jōshita-machi to the north – the latter is the more convenient of the two.

Other Attractions

Across the road from the Grand Hotel in central Shimonoseki and by the Karato bus stop, is the Meiji-era former British consulate building of 1906. It's open from 10 am to

WESTERN HONSHŪ

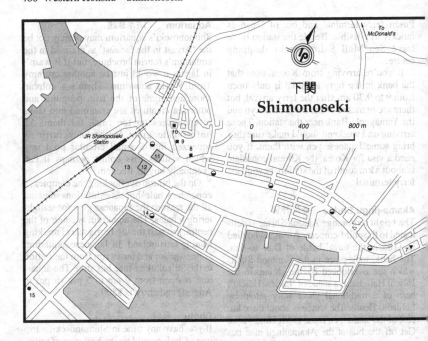

PLACES TO STAY

1 Hinoyama
   Youth Hostel
   下関火の山ユースホステル
2 Hotel San-yō
   山陽ホテル
4 Bizenya Ryokan
   備前屋旅館
6 Shimonoseki
   Grand Hotel
   下関グランドホテル
8 Shimonoseki
   Green Hotel
   下関グリーンホテル
9 Hotel Thirty Eight
   ホテル38下関

10 Shimonoseki
   Station Hotel
   下関ステーションホテル
12 Shimonoseki
   Tōkyū Hotel &
   Bank of Tokyo
   下関東急イン・東京銀行

PLACES TO EAT

7 Sunday's Sun
   & Jolly Pasta
   サンデイス・サン・
   ジョリーパスタ

OTHER

3 Akama-jingū Shrine
   赤間神宮

5 Former British
   Consulate
   旧英国領事館
11 Yamaguchi Bank
   山口銀行
12 Bank of Tokyo
   & Shimonoseki
   Tōkyū Hotel
   東京銀行・下関東急イン
13 Sea Mall
   Shopping Centre
   シーモール下関
14 Pusan Ferry Terminal
   下関港国際ターミナル
15 Korean Consulate
   大韓民国領事館

5 pm and closed on Monday. Just across Route 9 from here are two more Western-style buildings, though they'll be of little interest to most travellers. The Shimonoseki City Art Museum, opposite the aquarium, is of moderate interest and is open 9 am to 4.30 pm, closed Sunday; entry is ¥200.

Places to Stay
Youth Hostels The *Hinoyama Youth Hostel*

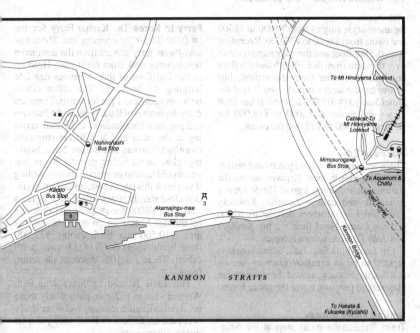

KANMON STRAITS

(☎ 0832-22-3753) is at the base of Mt Hino-yama, only 100 metres from the lower cablecar station. There are 52 beds at ¥1800 or ¥1950 depending on the time of year. Take a Hinoyama bus from the station; you can't miss the huge 'YH' sign on top of the building.

Ryokan & Minshuku Over in the Chōfu area is the *Chōfu Ryokan* (☎ 0832-45-0404), a rustic-looking little place with rooms, two meals included, for ¥6000. Further out of town still, in the Hino-yama area are several kokuminshukusha (people's lodges) also with costs of ¥6000 per person with two meals. They are clustered around the waterfront. Try the *Kaikan-sō* (☎ 0832-23-0108).

The *Bizenya Ryokan* (☎ 0832-22-6228) is part of the Japanese Inn Group. It's a basic place with rooms from ¥4000 to ¥5000 per person and is somewhat hidden away at the end of a narrow alley about two km from the centre of town. To get there, take a bus from JR Shimonoseki station (bus stop No 6) or Shin-Shimonoseki station (bus stop No 1) to the Nishinohashi bus stop. There are two petrol stations virtually side by side at this point.

Hotels A number of business hotels can be found close to the station including the *Hotel Thirty Eight* (☎ 0832-23-1138), only a couple of minutes walk away with singles from ¥4300 to ¥4800 and twins from ¥6400 to ¥8800. Close by is the *Shimonoseki Station Hotel* (☎ 0832-32-3511) with singles/doubles from ¥5000/8000.

Cross the road from the station and turn right to reach the *Shimonoseki Green Hotel* (☎ 0832-31-1007) with rooms at ¥5300/8100. Right next to the station is the *Shimonoseki Tōkyū Inn* (☎ 0832-23-0285) with singles at ¥6200 to ¥6900, twins at ¥11,200 to ¥12,000.

A couple of km from the JR station, the *Shimonoseki Grand Hotel* (☎ 0832-31-5000) has a wide variety of Western and

Japanese-style singles from ¥5000 to ¥8500 and twins from ¥8000 to ¥30,000. Reception is on the 8th floor and there are superb views over the strait from this 7th, 8th and 9th floor hotel. Even further from the station, just below the cablecar car park, you'll find the *Hotel San-yō* (☎ 0832-32-8666). It has great views and rooms at ¥6000 to ¥18,000 for singles, ¥10,000 to ¥13,000 for twins.

Places to Eat

There are lots of fast-food places and restaurants with plastic meal displays around the station area including a good *Vie de France* patisserie and café, a *Lotteria*, *Kentucky Fried Chicken* and others. Between the station and the Grand Hotel there's a big *Sunday's Sun/Jolly Pasta* restaurant complex.

For fugu (blowfish) fans, Shimonoseki is reputed to be an excellent place to dine on this deadly delicacy; around the station giant plastic fugu perch on top of the phone boxes.

Getting There & Away

Train Shinkansen trains stop at the Shin-Shimonoseki station, two stops from the JR Shimonoseki station in the town centre. There are frequent trains and buses between the two stations. By shinkansen, it's half an hour to Hakata, 40 to 80 minutes to Hiroshima and three to four hours to Osaka. The easiest way to cross over to Kyūshū is to take a train from the Shin-Shimonoseki station to Moji-ko and Kitakyūshū.

Car From Shimonoseki, the bridge and tunnel connect roads in Honshū with Kyūshū. Eastbound travellers can take Route 191 along the northern San-in coast, Route 2 along the southern San-yō coast or the Chūgoku Expressway through Central Honshū.

Ferry within Japan Ferries run regularly from early morning to late at night from the Karato area of Shimonoseki to Moji-ko on Kyūshū. From Kokura in Kitakyūshū there are ferries to Kōbe, Osaka and Tokyo on Honshū and to Matsuyama on Shikoku.

Ferry to Korea The Kampu Ferry Service (☎ 0832-24-3000) operates the Shimonoseki-Pusan ferry service from the terminal a few minutes walk from the station. Head up to the 2nd floor of this enormous desolate building for bookings. The office closes between noon and 1 pm for lunch. There are daily departures of the *Kampu* or the *Pukwan* at 5 pm from Shimonoseki and Pusan, arriving at the other end at 8.30 am (the next morning). You can board from 2 pm. Bookings close on the sailing day at 4.30 pm, but you would have to be snappy about boarding if you book this late as customs and immigration close shortly afterwards. One-way fares start from ¥6800 for students and continue up through ¥8500 for an open, tatami-mat area, ¥10,500 (six berth cabin), ¥12,000 (four berth cabin) and ¥14,000 (two berth cabin). There's a 10% discount on return fares.

This route is used by many long-term Western visitors to Japan, particularly those involved in English teaching and other shady occupations. Expect to have your passport rigorously inspected.

Hitching If you're hitching out of Shimonoseki, you'll need to get on the expressway. There's a complicated mass of junctions north of the youth hostel and Mt Hino-yama. Roads diverge in a variety of directions – to Kyūshu by the tunnel or bridge, to Hiroshima by the Chūgoku Expressway and to Yamaguchi by Routes 2 and 9.

The Inland Sea
瀬戸内海

The Inland Sea (Seto Naikai) has been described as the Aegean of Japan, and in many ways it does have the same appeal as that island-dotted stretch of sea. However the misty charm of the Seto Naikai is nothing like the sharper, angular look of the Greek islands.

The Inland Sea is bounded by the major islands of Honshū, Kyūshū and Shikoku. Four narrow channels connect the Inland Sea with the ocean. To the north the Kanmon Straits separate Honshū from Kyūshū and lead to the Sea of Japan; to the south, leading to the Pacific, the Hoya Straits separate Kyūshū from Shikoku; at the other end of Shikoku the Naruto Straits and Kitan Straits flow each side of Awaji Island, which almost connects Shikoku to Honshū.

For the visitor, the most interesting area of the Inland Sea is the island-crowded stretch from Hiroshima east to Takamatsu and Okayama. There are said to be more than 3000 islands, depending on what you define as an island! There are a number of ways of seeing the Inland Sea. One is to simply travel through it as there are numerous ferry services criss-crossing the sea or even running its full length, such as the service from Osaka on Honshū to Oita, near Beppu, on Kyūshū. Alternatively, but more expensively, there are Inland Sea cruises ranging from short day trips to longer overnight cruises. Also, you can visit single islands in the Inland Sea for a first-hand experience of a part of Japan which, though rapidly changing, is still quite different from the fast-moving metropolitan centres.

Information
Brochures, maps and general tourist information are readily available but Donald Richie's *The Inland Sea*, originally published in 1971 and now available in paperback, makes an excellent introduction to the region. Although much of the Inland Sea's slow moving and easy-going atmosphere has disappeared since his book was published, and indeed he emphasised its rapidly changing nature even at that time, it still provides some fascinating insights. Highpoints of the book include his encounter with a yakuza priest at the Oyamazumi Shrine on Omi-shima Island, his demolition job of the Kōsan-ji Temple at Setoda, the amusing search for a stone cat on Kitagi-shima and the wistful tale of the prostitutes of Kinoe on Osakikami-jima.

Cruises
Miyajima to Setoda The popular SKK (Seto Naikai-kisen) (☎ 082-321-5111) cruises between Miyajima and Setoda on Ikuchijima Island or on to Onomichi offer the easiest and most popular ways of seeing one of the finest stretches of the Inland Sea. *Popular* is the operative word; these cruises are all very touristy. The cruises offered by SKK are as follows:

Wan-uei-kurūzu A ('One-way cruise' A): depart Onomichi 11.20 am; Setoda 1.35 pm; Ōmi-shima Island 3.50 pm; Kure 5.05 pm; Hiroshima 5.30 pm; Miyajima 5.51 pm; ¥11,000 with lunch included
Wan-uei-kurūzu B ('One-way cruise' B): depart Miyajima 8.35 am; Hiroshima 9 am; Kure 9.35 am; Ōme-shima Island 10.35 am; Setoda 12.55 pm; Onomichi 2.55 pm; ¥11,000 with lunch included
Raundo-wan-dei-kurūzu ('Round one-day cruise'): depart Miyajima 8.35 am; Hiroshima 9 am; Kure 9.35 am; Ōmi-shima Island-Setoda-Kure 5.05 pm; Hiroshima 5.30 pm; Miyajima 5.50 pm; ¥12,000 with no lunch

Other Cruises There are shorter and longer cruises. The Japan Travel Bureau (JTB) and other tour operators have a variety of overnight cruises from Osaka. SKK have numerous other ships operating including day cruises from Hiroshima to Eta-jima, Miya-jima and Eno-shima islands.

ŌMI-SHIMA ISLAND   大三島
This hilly rather than mountainous island boasts the mountain god's **Ōyamatsumi-jinja Shrine**, which once commanded much respect from the Inland Sea's pirates. In actual fact, the pirates were more like a local navy than real pirates but, until Hideyoshi brought them to heel, they wielded real power in these parts. Along the way, an armour collection was built up in the shrine's treasure house, including more than half the armour in Japan: 80% of the armour and helmets designated as National Treasures are held here. Entry to the treasure house is ¥800 but despite the importance of the collection saturation soon sets in, and it's probably of more interest to those with a specific interest

in Japanese military accoutrements than to the average visitor.

In an adjacent building is a boat used by Emperor Hirohito in his marine science investigations, together with a somewhat tatty natural history exhibit. The shrine's history is actually one of the most ancient in Japan, ranking with the shrines at Ise and Izumo.

Miyaura Port is a 15 minute walk from the shrine. The *Omi-shima Suigun* restaurant is near the shrine.

Getting There & Away

The *Akinada* cruise from Hiroshima visits Omi-shima but you can also get there by ferry service from Onomichi, Mihara or Setoda on the neighbouring island of Ikuchi-jima, and also from Takehara, further west on the Honshū coast.

IKUCHI-JIMA ISLAND 生口島

At Setoda, the main town on the island, Ikuchi-jima is actually linked to neighbouring Takane-jima by a bridge. The town is noted for the **Kōsan-ji Temple**, a wonderful exercise in kitsch. Local steel-tube magnate Kanemoto Kōzō devoted a large slab of his considerable fortune from 1935 on to recreating numerous important temples and shrines all in this one spot and all in grateful homage to his mother. If you haven't got time to visit the originals, this is an interesting substitute.

Entry is ¥800 which includes the 1000 Buddhas Cave, the art museum and the treasure house. It costs another ¥200 to visit Kanemoto Kōzō's mother's quarters. The extraordinary 1000 Buddhas Cave includes an introductory 'hell', very Tiger Balm Garden-like with its tableaux of the damned being mangled, chopped, fried and generally hard done by. From there you follow winding tunnels and spiral stairs lined with 1000 Buddhas. One sour note at this temple is the poor Australian emu penned up in far too small an enclosure by the main entrance.

To get to the temple, turn right as you leave the boat landing then left up the shop-lined 600 metre long street. The **Setoda History**

& Folklore Museum is at the start of this street. Halfway up the same street you can turn left towards a temple on the hillside; around the back of this temple and much further up the hill is the **Kōjō-ji Temple**, dating from 1403, with a three storeyed pagoda and fine views over the island. You can also get there by turning left from the pier (towards the bridge) and heading straight up the hill.

Places to Stay

The *Setoda Youth Hostel* (☎ 08452-7-0244) costs ¥2200 and is a short walk from the dock. There's also the *Ikuchi-jima Tarumi Youth Hostel* (☎ 08452-7-3137) at ¥2300.

Getting There & Away

You can get to Ikuchi-jima Island by the regular cruise from Hiroshima or by ferries from Mihara or Onomichi on Honshū. Mihara has the widest range of services, some continuing on to Ōmi-shima Island and Imabari on Shikoku. It pays to shop around at the harbour area. Fares range from ¥290 to ¥1260, depending on the speed and luxury of the ferry. No matter how you want to travel, you shouldn't have to wait more than an hour.

INNO-SHIMA ISLAND 因島

Inno-shima Island is connected by bridge to Mukai-shima Island and on to Onomichi. The island has a pirate castle.

SHIWAKU ISLANDS 塩飽諸島

North of Marugame, on Shikoku are the scattered Shiwaku Islands, once the haunt of daring pirates and seafarers. Hon-jima is a larger island just west of the Seto-ōhashi Bridge with some fine old buildings and interesting sites.

SHŌDO-SHIMA ISLAND 小豆島

Shōdo-shima Island is easily reached from Honshū or Shikoku; it offers a number of interesting places to visit and makes an enjoyable short escape from big-city Japan. Although the second-largest island in the Inland Sea, Shōdo-shima is still small enough to explore quite easily. The island even has a miniature version of neighbouring Shikoku's 88 Temple Circuit, though since Shōdo-shima can't muster 88 temples, the itinerary is padded out with a number of other notable sites.

Orientation & Information

Tonoshō, at the western end of the island, is the usual arrival point from Takamatsu, Uno or Okayama and makes a good base from which to explore the island. Fukuda in the north-east and Sakate in the south-east are other busy ports. If you arrive on Shōdo Island from Takamatsu (the most popular jumping-off point) you'll find an information office just inside the ferry building.

Coastal Area

The island's olive-growing activities are commemorated at Olive Park on the south coast. Near by is the **Shōdo-shima Folk Museum** (¥300). The end of the peninsula to the south of Ikeda is marked by the **Jizōzaki Lighthouse** and offers fine views over the Inland Sea. Just north of Sakate is the turn-off to the small village of **Tanoura**, site of the village school in the book *Twenty Four Eyes* and the later film of the same name. There's a distinct feeling that this was Shōdo Island's sole brush with fame; the real school and its movie set version are both open for inspection (¥350 combined ticket). A statue of the teacher and her pupils (the movie version) also stands outside the Tonoshō ferry terminal.

South of Fukuda, on the eastern side of the island, huge rocks cut for Osaka-jō Castle now lie jumbled down a cliffside at **Iwagatani**. The rocks are classified as *zanseki* (rocks left over) or *zannen ishi* (rocks which were sorry not to be in time for shipment) and each bears the seal of the general responsible for their quarrying and dispatch. The north-eastern corner of the island is still one big quarry to this day. More unshipped castle rocks can be seen on the northern coast at **Omi**, along with the site of a shipyard used by Hideyoshi.

Central Mountains

The **Kanka-kei Cablecar** is the main attraction in the central mountains, making a spectacular trip up through the Kanka-kei Gorge in the shadow of Mt Hoshigajō-yama (¥600 one way, ¥1150 return). There's a walking track if you really want to walk one way. Around the eastern side of the mountain the island's tenuous connection with Greece (they both grow olives) is celebrated in the **Olive Sanctuary** where there's even a fake mini-Parthenon.

As you descend towards Tonoshō (rented scooters are allowed to travel down this road but not up it; perhaps it's too steep) you pass the Choshi-kei Gorge's **monkey mountain** (¥360) where wild monkeys come for a daily feed. Beside the car park is a restaurant offering *somen nagashi* noodles for ¥450. (A bowl of noodles are dropped into a sort of water racetrack which swirls around a circular channel in the middle of the table. You intercept them with your chopsticks as they come by!)

Near Tonoshō is the **Hosho-in Temple** with its huge and ancient juniper tree.

Festivals

The Shikoku-mura Village at Yashima, just outside Takamatsu on Shikoku, has a village kabuki theatre from Shōdo-shima. Farmers' kabuki performances are still held on the island: on 3 May at Tonoshō and on 10 October at Ikeda.

Places to Stay & Eat

Shōdo-shima Olive Youth Hostel (☎ 0879-82-6161) is on the south coast, just beyond Olive Park and the folk museum heading towards Kusakabe and Sakate. Nightly costs are ¥2500. The *Uchinomi-chō Cycling Terminal* (☎ 0879-82-1099) is in Sakate while in Ikeda there is the *Kokuminshukusha Shōdo-shima* (☎ 0879-75-1115).

Tonoshō has a variety of hotels, ryokan and minshuku, particularly along the road running straight back from the waterfront. The *Maruse Minshuku* (☎ 0879-62-2385), next to the post office is neat and tidy, costs

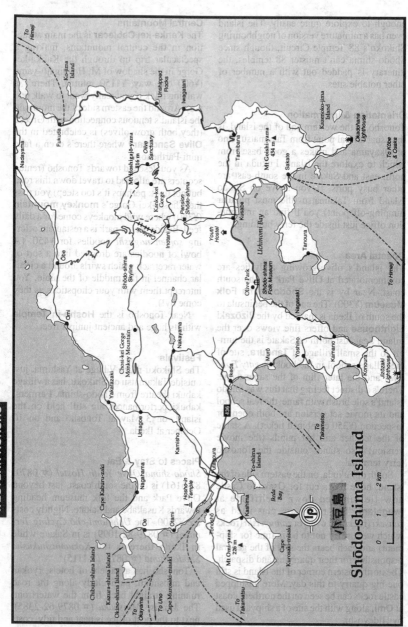

WESTERN HONSHŪ

小豆島

Shōdo-shima Island

0   1   2 km

¥4000 per person and has a restaurant downstairs.

North of the youth hostel, on the road to Inotani are a couple of pensions. *Pension Shōdoshima* (☎ 0879-82-0181) has per-person costs of ¥7000 with two meals.

Getting There & Away

There is a variety of ferry services from Honshū and Shikoku to various ports on the island. Popular jumping-off points include Uno on Honshū (trains go to Uno from Okayama) and Takamatsu on Shikoku. The regular Takamatsu to Tonoshō high-speed ferries take 35 minutes and cost ¥1000. Regular ferries take around an hour and cost ¥430.

Getting Around

There are plenty of bus services around the island and a host of bus tours (¥3000 to ¥5000) which seem to set off with every ferry arrival at Tonoshō. Alternatively, you can rent cars from a couple of agencies by the Tonoshō ferry terminal or motor scooters from Ryōbi Rent-a-Bike (☎ 0879-62-6578). The scooter agency operates out of a container near the ferry terminal; the daily hire cost is ¥2990 including fuel. The island is small enough to explore in a day if you start early, although a circuit of the coast and a mountain excursion will clock up well over 100 km.

AWAJI-SHIMA ISLAND　淡路島

Awaji-shima Island, the Inland Sea's largest island, forms the region's eastern boundary and almost connects Honshū with Shikoku. At the Shikoku end, the **Naruto-ōhashi Bridge** spans the Naruto Straits across the well-known **Naruto Whirlpools** to connect Shikoku with Awaji Island. (See the Around Tokushima section of the Shikoku chapter.) At the other end of the island, a tunnel is planned to connect the island with Honshū near Kōbe.

The island is densely populated, relatively flat and has some good beaches. It was the original home for the *ningyō jōruri* puppet theatre which preceded the development of

bunraku theatre. Short performances are given several times daily in the small puppet theatre in Fukura. The island has many minshuku.

Wakasa-wan Bay Area
若狭湾周辺

The area around Wakasa-wan Bay, the eastern end of the San-in coast, takes in parts of three prefectures: Fukui, Kyoto and Hyōgo-ken.

WAKASA-WAN BAY　若狭湾

At the eastern end of the bay, the **Mikatago-ko Lakes** (Mikata Five Lakes) are joined to the sea. **Obama** is a port town with the ruins of Obama-jō Castle and a number of interesting old temples including the Myōtsū-ji, the Mantoku-ji and the Jingū-ji. Tour buses operate from the JR Obama station and there are also boat trips around the picturesque Sotomo coastline with its inlets, arches and caves, just north of Obama. The town has a variety of accommodation including the *Obama Youth Hostel* (☎ 0770-52-2158). Continuing around the bay, more interesting coastal scenery can be reached by boat trips from Wakasa-Takahama. From Maizuru there are regular ferry services to Otaru in Hokkaidō. Ferries also run to Otaru from Tsuruga, at the other end of Wakasa-wan Bay (see the Fukui-ken section of the Central Honshū chapter).

AMANOHASHIDATE　天橋立

Amanohashidate (Bridge to Heaven) is rated as one of Japan's 'three great views', along with Miya-jima Island (near Hiroshima) and the islands of Matsushima-wan Bay (near Sendai). The 'bridge' is really a 'pier', a tree-covered sandspit 3½ km long with just a couple of narrow channels preventing it from cutting off the top of Miyazu-wan Bay as a separate lake.

The town of Amanohashidate consists of two separate parts, one at each end of the spit.

At the southern end there are a number of hotels, ryokan, restaurants, a popular temple and the JR Amanohashidate station. At the other end, a funicular railway (¥260 one way) and a chair lift run up the hillside to the Kasamutsu-kōen Park vantage point from where the view is reputed to be most pleasing. From here, incidentally, you're supposed to view the sandspit by turning your back to it, bending over and observing it framed between your legs! There's another hilltop viewpoint at the southern end of the spit.

A bridge and swing bridge cross the two channels at the southern end of the spit and cycling along the spit is a popular activity.

Places to Stay

There's an information counter at the railway station. The *Amanohashidate Youth Hostel* (☎ 07722-7-0121) is at Ichinomiya, close to the funicular to the lookout point. To get there take a Tankai bus from the JR Amanohashidate station and get off at the Jinja-mae bus stop, from where it's a 10 minute walk. The nightly cost is ¥2150 or ¥2350 depending on the season. The *Amanohashidate Kankōkaikan Youth Hostel* (☎ 07722-7-0046) is also near the park. It has the same rates as the Amanohashidate Youth Hostel

There are a number of ryokan and hotels, generally fairly expensive, near the station at the other end of the 'bridge'. The *Toriko Ryokan* (☎ 07722-2-0010) costs ¥11,000 per person including two meals. The *Shoehino Ryokan* is similarly priced. Other places include the *Hotel Taikyo* and the *Hotel Monju-sō*.

Getting There & Away

The coastal JR Miyazu line connects Obama with Amanohashidate and on to Toyooka where you change to the JR San-in line for Tottori. It takes about three hours by limited express from Kyoto, half an hour longer by tour bus.

Getting Around

You can cross the 'bridge to heaven' on foot, bicycle or on a motorcycle of less than 125 cc capacity. Bicycles can be hired at a number of places for ¥400 for two hours or ¥1600 a day. Tour boats also operate across Miyazu Bay.

TANGO-HANTŌ PENINSULA 丹後半島

Travelling westward, Amanohashidate marks the start of the Tango-hantō Peninsula, jutting north into the Sea of Japan. A coast road runs around the peninsula passing a number of small scenic fishing ports. The village of **Ine**, on a perfect little bay, is particularly interesting, with houses built out right over the water and boats drawn in under them as if in a carport. There's a large commercial fishing operation just beyond the village.

At the end of the peninsula, a large car park and restaurant marks the start of the one hour round-trip walk to the **Cape Kyōgasaki Lighthouse**. There are some pleasant coastal views but the lighthouse itself is nothing special.

KINOSAKI 城崎

The road around the Tango-hantō Peninsula rejoins the main coast before the city of Toyōka, which is linked to Kyoto by the JR San-in line. Toyōka itself is not worth more than a quick look from the train window, but the small onsen town of Kinosaki, two stops on, is a laid back place worth a stop. The **Gokuraku-ji Temple** has a good miniature rock landscape garden, and the **Gembu-dō Caves** are one stop south on the San-in line.

If you do stop in Kinosaki, take a stroll north from the station until you hit the stream that runs through the town. If you follow this for a couple of hundred metres away from the Maruyama River, you should be able to find Gokuraku-ji Temple on the left, around 100 metres south of the stream.

The Gembu-dō Caves are not a major event, but they might make a pleasant excursion. From the east exit of Gembudō station, it's necessary to take a five-minute ride (¥190) across across the Maruyama River to Gembudō-kōen Park. The caves are a couple of hundred metres south of the ferry drop off point.

Amanohashidate to Toyōka takes about 1½ hours on the JR Miyazu line. There you will have to change to the San-in line to go to Kinosaki or Gembu-dō Caves. Trains run to Kinosaki from Kyoto in around two hours 40 minutes.

TOTTORI 鳥取

Tottori (population 142,000) is a large, busy town some distance back from the coast. The main coast road passes through Tottori's northern fringe in a blizzard of car dealers, pachinko parlours and fast-food outlets. The town's main attraction is its famous sand dunes.There's a helpful tourist information booth (☎ 0857-22-8111) inside the station.

The Dunes 砂丘

Used as the location for Teshigahara Hiroshi's classic 1964 film *Woman in the Dunes*, the Tottori sand dunes are on the coast a couple of km from the city. There's a viewing point on a hillside overlooking the dunes along with a huge car park and the usual assortment of tourist amenities. The dunes stretch for over 10 km along the coast and, at some points, can be a couple of km wide. The section where the dunes are highest is popular with parachutists who stand at the edge of the dune, fill their chutes with the incoming seabreezes and leap off the dune top to sail down towards the sea.

1	Prefectural Museum 県立博物館
2	Tottori-jō Castle Ruins 鳥取城跡
3	Jinpu-kaku Villa & Museum 仁風閣
4	Kannon-in Garden 観音院
5	Washington Hotel ワシントンホテル
6	Hotel Taihei ホテル太平
7	Folkcraft Museum 民芸美術館
8	Tottori Hotel Green Morris 鳥取ホテルグリーンモリス

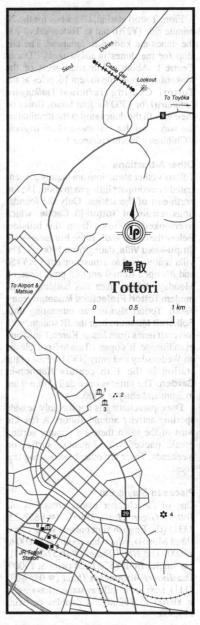

WESTERN HONSHŪ

From Tottori station, take a bus for the 20 minute ride (¥270) out to Tottori-sakyū , as the dunes are known in Japanese. The bus stop for the dunes is *sakyū-sentā* ('Dunes Centre'). About a km south-west of the lookout it is possible to rent bicycles at the Tottori Cycling Terminal *(saikinguru tāminaru)* for ¥300 for four hours. Buses on their way to the dunes stop at the terminal on the way – ask for *kodomo-no-kuni iriguchi* ('Children's World entrance').

Other Attractions

Tottori's other attractions are mainly concentrated in a compact little group about 1½ km north-east of the station. Only the foundations remain of **Tottori-jō Castle**, which overlooked the town from the hillside. Below the castle walls is the European-style **Jinpū-kaku Villa**, dating from 1906-07. The villa is now used as a museum; entry is ¥150 and it's open from 9 am to 5 pm, closed on Monday. Across from this building is the modern **Tottori Prefectural Museum** (entry ¥800). Tottori also has an interesting little **Folkcraft Museum** near the JR station, with folkcraft items from Japan, Korea, China and even Europe. It's open 10 am to 5 pm, closed on Wednesday and entry is ¥310. East of the station is the 17th century **Kannon-in Garden**. The latter is open daily from 9 am to 5 pm and entry is ¥500.

Dune-parachuting is not the only seaside sporting activity around Tottori. A few km west of the town there's a popular surfing break, packed with Japanese surfies on weekends. There are other breaks along this coast.

Places to Stay & Eat

One of the cheaper places around is the *Tottori Green Hotel Morris* (☎ 0857-22-2331) (the English sign outside simply says Hotel Morris), which has rooms at ¥4800 to ¥8800. The *Hotel Taihei* (☎ 0857-29-1111) has singles from ¥5200 and twins at ¥9000. The *Tottori Washington Hotel* (☎ 0857-27-8111), next to the railway station, has singles at ¥6700 to ¥7200 and doubles or twins ¥13,500.

There are plenty of restaurants (with the usual plastic food displays) around the station including *Mr Donut* and a big selection of fast-food operators along Route 9, the main road through town.

Getting There & Away

The coastal JR San-in line runs through Tottori and it takes about 1½ hours from Toyōka. The JR Inbi line connects with Tsuyama and on to Okayama, nearly three hours away on the south coast.

Tottori has an airport and ANA has flights from Osaka and Tokyo.

TOTTORI TO MATSUE   鳥取から松江へ

Mt Dai-sen   大山

Although not one of Japan's highest mountains, 1729 metre Mt Dai-sen looks very impressive because it rises straight from sea level – its summit only about 10 km from the coast. The popular climb up the volcano cone is a six to seven hour round trip from the ancient Daisen-ji Temple. Bring plenty of water and take care on the final narrow ridge to the summit. From the summit there are fine views over the coast and, in perfect conditions, all the way to the Oki Islands. Buses run to near the temple from Yonago and take about 50 minutes. The mountain snags the north-west monsoon winds in the winter, bringing deep snow and difficult conditions for winter climbers.

Yonago   米子

Yonago is an important railway junction connecting the north and south coasts and, as such, is a place to pass through rather than visit. From Yonaga Airport, there are flights to and from Osaka and Tokyo and on to the Oki Islands.

Shimane-ken   島根県

MATSUE   松江

Matsue (population 143,000) straddles the Ōhashi-gawa River, which connects Lake Shinji-ko to Lake Nakanoumi-ko and then the sea. A compact area in the north of the town includes almost all of Matsue's important sites: an original castle, a fine example of a samurai residence, the former home of writer Lafcadio Hearn and a delightful teahouse and garden.

Information

The tourist information office (☎ 0852-27-2598) at the JR station (on the left as you leave the station, just past Mr Donut) has a surprising amount of information in English and the staff are helpful. It's open daily from 9.30 am to 5.30 pm.

Matsue-jō Castle 松江城

Matsue's castle is not huge or imposing but it is original, dating from 1611. Modern Japan has so many rebuilt castles, externally authentic-looking but internally totally modern, that it can almost be a shock to step inside one where the construction is real wood, not modern concrete. Entry is ¥310 and it's open from 8.30 am to 5 pm.

The regional museum (Matsue Kyodokan) is within the castle precincts. The road alongside the moat on the north-eastern side of the castle is known as the Shiomi Nawate, at one time a narrow lane through the old samurai quarter. The high tile-topped walls still remain from that era and there are a number of places of interest. A No 1 or 2 bus from outside the JR station will get you to the castle.

Lafcadio Hearn Residence 小泉八雲旧宅

At the northern end of the Shiomi Nawate is the Lafcadio Hearn Memorial Museum and next to it is his former home. Hearn was a British writer (although he was born in Greece in 1850, educated in France and the UK and lived in the USA from 1869) who came to Japan in 1890 and was to remain there for the rest of his life. His first book on Japan, *Glimpses of Unfamiliar Japan*, is a classic, providing an insight into the country at that time. The Japanese have a great interest in the outsider's view of their country so Hearn's pretty little house is an important attraction, despite the fact that he only lived

in Matsue for just over a year. Hearn's adopted Japanese name is Koizumi Yakumo. While you're admiring the garden you can read his essay *In a Japanese Garden*, describing how it looked a century ago. Entry to the house is ¥190 and it's open daily from 9 am to 4.30 pm.

Lafcadio Hearn Memorial Museum 小泉八雲記念館

Next to the writer's home is his museum (the Koizumi Yakumo Memorial Museum) with displays about his life, his writing and his residence in Matsue. Entry is ¥205 and the museum is open from 8.30 am to 5 pm. The museum has an English brochure and map showing various points of interest around the town mentioned in his writings.

Tanabe Art Museum 田部美術館

This museum principally displays family items from the many generations of the region's Tanabe clan, particularly tea bowls and other tea ceremony paraphernalia. Opening hours are 9 am to 5 pm, closed Monday. Entry is ¥500.

Buke Yashiki Samurai Residence 武家屋敷

The Buke Yashiki is a well-preserved middle Edo period samurai residence built in 1730. There's a good English description leaflet of the various rooms and their uses in this large but somewhat spartan residence. This was not the home of a wealthy samurai! Entry is ¥205 and opening hours are from 8 am to 5 pm.

Meimei-an Teahouse 明々庵

A little further south is the turn-off to the Meimei-an Teahouse with its well-kept gardens and fine views to Matsue Castle. The teahouse was built in 1779 and was moved to its present site in 1966 (it had been moved once before in 1928). Look for the steep steps up from the road to the thatched-roof building. Entry is ¥200 and it's open from 9 am to 5 pm. You can sample some tea for ¥500.

Other Attractions

The **Kanden-an Teahouse** is about 20

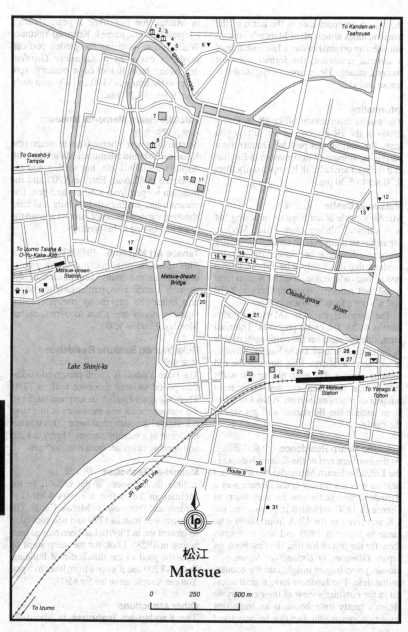

To Kanden-an
Teahouse

To Gesshō-ji
Temple

To Izumo Taisha &
O-Yu-Kake Jizo

Matsue-onsen
Station

Shiomi Nawate

Matsue-ōhashi
Bridge

Ōhashi-gawa   River

Lake Shinji-ko

JR San-in Line

JR Matsue
Station

To Yonago &
Tottori

Route 9

To Izumo

松江
Matsue

0   250   500 m

PLACES TO STAY	PLACES TO EAT		
15 Washington Hotel ワシントンホテル	4 Yakumo-an Restaurant 八雲庵	3	Tanabe Art Museum 田部美術館
17 Suimeiso Hotel 水明荘		5	Buke Yashiki Samurai Residence 武家屋敷
18 Ichihata Hotel ホテル一畑	6 Meimei-an Teahouse 明々庵	7	Matsue-jō Castle 松江城
19 Youth Hostel ユースホステル	12 McDonald's マクドナルド	8	Cultural Museum 松江郷土館
20 Young Inn Matsue ヤングイン松江	13 Kentucky Fried Chicken ケンタッキーフライドチキン	9	Prefecture Hall 県庁
21 Daiei Business Hotel ダイエー ビジネスホテル	14 Benkei Robatayaki 弁慶	10	Handicraft Centre 物産観光館
23 Business Ishida Hotel ビジネス石田ホテル	16 Kawa-kyo Restaurant	11	Ichihata Department Store 一畑デパート
25 Green Hotel Matsue グリーンホテル松江	26 Mr Donut ミスタードーナッツ	22	Yayoi Department Store やよいデパート
27 Matsue Tōkyū Inn 松江東急イン	OTHER	24	JTB JTB（交通公社）
28 Matsue Urban Hotel 松江アーバンホテル	1 Lafcadio Hearn Memorial Museum 小泉八雲記念館	29	Post Office 松江中央郵便局
30 Business Hotel Lake Inn ホテルレークイン	2 Lafcadio Hearn's Old House 小泉八雲旧居	31	Laundrette コインランドリー

minutes drive north-east of the centre. It dates from 1792 and is one of the finest teahouses in Japan. It's open from 9.30 am to 4 pm, closed Thursday.

About a km west of the castle is the **Gesshō-ji Temple**, which was converted from an ordinary temple to a family temple for Matsue's Matsudaira clan in 1664 but dismantled during the Meiji Restoration. The graves of nine generations of the clan remain and family effects are displayed in the treasure house.

Matsue has its own onsen (hot-spring) area, just north of the lake near Matsue-onsen station on the Ichihata-Dentetsu line. There are a number of hotels and ryokan in the area and a popular 'hell', a very hot spring known as the **O-Yu-Kake Jizō**. The sunset views over **Lake Shinji-ko** are very fine and best appreciated from the Matsue-ōhashi Bridge. The **Matsue Folk Art Centre**, across from the Ichihata Hotel in the onsen area by the lake, displays regional crafts. The **Matsue Prefectural Product & Craft Centre** is another regional craft centre, just south of the castle in the town centre.

Places to Stay

Youth Hostels *Matsue Youth Hostel* (☎ 0852-36-8620) is about five km from the centre of town in Kososhimachi, on the northern side of the lake at the first station you come to along the Ichihata line from Matsue-onsen station. There are 50 beds at ¥2500 a night. The hostel is closed from 1 to 20 November.

Budget Accommodation The *Pension Tobita* (☎ 0852-36-6933) in Hamasada-machi is in the same direction as the youth hostel and has Japanese and Western-style rooms at ¥5500 per person with breakfast only, ¥7000.

As usual, there are a lot of business hotels around the station including the unbusinesslike *Business Ishida* (no English sign) (☎ 0852-21-5931) in Teramachi, a simple Japanese-style hotel with tatami-mat rooms and shared bathrooms at ¥3600 per person. It's good value and conveniently close to the station: just continue walking past the tourist information office through the bicycle and car parks and it's right beside

WESTERN HONSHŪ

the elevated railway lines, just past the first road you cross.

Other possibilities, all with public bathrooms, include the *Daiei Business Hotel* (☎ 0852-24-1515) down by the river with rooms from ¥3700 and the *Business Hotel Lake Inn* (0852-21-2424), behind the station on the corner of Route 9, with singles/twins at ¥4200/7300. Not far from the Daiei Business Hotel down by the river is the *Young Inn Matsue* (☎ ☎ 0852-22-2000). It's a small place with an English sign and a limited number of twins from ¥3090 to ¥5500.

Hotels More expensive hotels include the *Matsue Tōkyū Inn* (☎ 0852-27-0109) just across the road from the station. This popular chain hotel has singles from ¥6800 to ¥8000, doubles and twins at ¥13,600 to ¥16,000. Also in front of the station, the *Green Hotel Matsue* (☎ 0852-27-3000) has singles from ¥5300 to ¥6000 and twins from ¥9600 to ¥11,600. The *Matsue Urban Hotel* is a cheaper place behind the Tōkyū Inn with singles from ¥4400.

The *Matsue Washington Hotel* (☎ 0852-22-4111) is across the river from the JR station but still convenient to the town centre. Singles are ¥6900 to ¥8100, twins ¥13,300.

Places to Eat

If you're wandering the Shiomi Nawate, the old samurai street in the shadow of the castle, pause for lunch at the *Yakumo-an Restaurant*, next to the samurai house. It's a delightfully genteel noodle house with a pond full of very healthy-looking carp. Noodle dishes range from ¥500 to ¥750 for Niku udon or Niku soba. Warigo-style noodles cost ¥550; they're a local speciality, a dish of buckwheat noodles over which you pour broth.

Matsue's *kyodo ryōri* or regional cuisine includes 'seven exotic dishes from Lake Shinji'. They are:

Suzuki or *hosho yaki* – steam baked,
   paper-wrapped bass
Shirauo – whitebait tempura or sashimi

Amasagi – sweet tempura or teriyaki
Shijimi – tiny shellfish in miso soup
Moroge ebi – steamed shrimp
Koi – baked carp
Unagi – broiled freshwater eel

Kawa-kyo, near the Washington Hotel north of the river, offers these seven local specialities on an English menu with prices from ¥250 (shijimi) to ¥1500 (hosho yaki).

There are a number of *Benkei* yakitori (grilled-food restaurants) around town: there's a particularly good one with an illustrated menu near the Washington Hotel in Higashihonmachi. The tourist office at the station can give you a list of good local restaurants including numerous Izumo soba (regional noodle dish) specialists.

Restaurants with plastic meal replicas and the usual fast-food places can be found in the station area. There's a *Mr Donut* in the station and a *Dom Dom* burger place in the nearby Yayoi department store where there's also an excellent basement supermarket.

Getting There & Away

Matsue is on the JR San-in line which runs along the north coast. It takes a little over 2½ hours to travel via Yonago to Kurashiki on the south coast. See the Izumo section which follows for information on the two railway lines running west from Matsue. Matsue is also a jumping-off point for the Oki Islands (see the Oki Islands section of this chapter for details).

Yonago is the airport for Matsue. There are ANA flights to Tokyo and JAS flights to the Oki Islands.

Getting Around

Airport buses run between Matsue-onsen station and the airport, taking about 40 minutes. Tour buses leave from stand No 8 in front of JR Matsue station. Other bus routes include Matsue-onsen (No 1), Kaga (No 4), Izumo (No 6) and Yonago (No 7). You pick up a ticket on entering the bus and the relevant fare for your starting point is displayed as you leave.

Matsue is a good place to explore by

bicycle: these can be hired at the Matsue and Matsue-onsen stations for ¥500 for two hours or ¥1000 per day.

AROUND MATSUE & IZUMO
松江・出雲周辺

There are a number of places of interest in the vicinity of Matsue and neighbouring Izumo.

Lake Shinji-ko　宍道湖

Sunset over the Yomega-shima islet in Lake Shinji-ko is a photographer's favourite and the lake also provides the region's seven favourite local delicacies (see Matsue's Places to Eat section). At the western end of the lake, the garden in the Gakuen-ji Temple in Hirata is noted for its autumn colours.

At the south-western corner of the lake, the town of Shinji has the *Yakumo Honjin* (☎ 0852-66-0136), one of the finest ryokan in Japan. Parts of the inn are 250 years old but if you stay here (from ¥15,000 per night)

ask for the old wing or you'll end up in the modern air-conditioned one. Casual visitors can have a look around for ¥300.

Shimane-hantō Peninsula　島根半島

North of Matsue, the coastline of the Shimane-hantō Peninsula has some spectacular scenery, particularly around Kaga, where Kaga-no-Kukedo is a cave you can enter by boat.

Fudoki-no-Oka & Shrines　風土記の丘

Five km south of Matsue, around the village of Yakumo-mura, there are interesting shrines and important archaeological finds. Fudoki Hill is a 1st century AD archaeological site with finds displayed in the Fudoki-no-Oka Shiryōkan (Archaeological Museum) which is open from 9 am to 5 pm, closed Monday. Near by is the **Okadayama Tumuli**, an ancient burial mound. Haniwa pottery figures were found here, similar to those of Miyazaki on Kyūshū.

West of Fudoki-no-Oka is the ancient

Kamosu-jinja Shrine, dedicated to Izanami, the mother of the Japanese archipelago. The shrine's Honden (Main Hall) dates from 1346. A little further west is the **Yaegaki-jinja Shrine** which is dedicated to the gods of marriage and commemorates a princess's rescue from an eight-headed serpent. The events are illustrated in fine 12th century wall paintings and the shrine sells erotic amulets to ensure fruitful marriages! There's a pretty little wood with shrines and ponds close by.

Fudoki-no-Oka is best visited on the way back from Bessho if you're going there. Get off at the Fudoki-no-Oka Iriguchi bus stop, walk to the archaeological centre and on to the two shrines then take another bus to Matsue from the Yaegaki-danchi Iriguchi bus stop, north of the Yaegaki-jinja Shrine.

Bessho 別所
About 15 minutes south of Fudoki-no-Oka is Bessho, which features the **Abe Eishiro Museum**, dedicated to the craftsman credited with revitalising the making of paper by hand. The museum is open from 9 am to 4.30 pm and you can also visit paper-making workshops in the village. A bus from stand No 3 at the JR Matsue station will get you to Bessho; it stops at Fudoki-no-Oka on the way back.

Yasugi 安来
East of Matsue on the Lake Nakanoumi-ko is Yasugi. The **Kiyomizu Temple** has a beautiful three storeyed pagoda and an important 11-faced statue of Kannon, the goddess of mercy. The **Adachi Art Museum** in Yasugi has a beautiful garden.

Tachikue-kyō Gorge 立久恵峡
Immediately south of Izumo is this km long, steep-sided gorge. It takes 30 minutes by rail to the gorge station from Izumo.

Mt Sanbe-san 三瓶山
Mt Sanbe is inland from Ōda and reaches 1126 metres; its four separate peaks are known as the Father, the Mother, the Child and the Grandchild. It's part of the Daisen-

Oki National Park and a popular skiing centre during the winter. Buses leave for Ōda from Izumo.

It takes about an hour to climb Mt Sanbe from Sanbe Onsen. Buses regularly make the 20 km run from Oda to Sanbe Onsen. Lake Ukinunonoike is near the hot springs.

If you follow the Go-gawa River south-west from Mt Sanbe, the Dangyo-kei Gorge is six km south of Inbara and there's a four km walking track along the ravine.

IZUMO 出雲
Only 33 km west of Matsue the small town of Izumo Taisha, just north of Izumo itself, has one major attraction: the great Izumo Taisha Shrine.

Orientation & Information
The Izumo Taisha Shrine is actually several km north-west of the central area of Izumo. There's no real reason to visit central Izumo since the shrine area, more or less one main street running straight up to the shrine, has two railway stations and a variety of (generally expensive) accommodation and restaurants. There's a tourist information office on the main street near the shrine entrance.

Izumo Taisha Shrine 出雲大社
Although this is the oldest Shintō shrine in Japan and is second in importance only to the shrines of Ise, the actual buildings are not that old. The main shrine dates from 1744, the other important buildings only from 1874. Nevertheless, the wooded grounds are pleasant to wander through and the shrine itself enjoys the 'borrowed scenery' of the Yakumo Hill as a backdrop. Okuninushi, to whom the shrine is dedicated, is kami (spirit god) of, among other things, marriage. So visitors to the shrine summon the deity by clapping four times rather than the normal two – twice for themselves and twice for their partner or partners to be.

The Haiden (Hall of Worship) is the first building inside the entrance torii and huge *shimenawa* (twisted straw ropes) hang over the entry. The main building is the largest shrine in Japan but the Honden (Main Hall) cannot be entered. The shrine compound is flanked by *jūku-sha*, long shelters where Japan's eight million kami (Shintō spirit gods) stay when they make their annual visit to Izumo.

On the south-eastern side of the compound is the Shinko-den (Treasure House) (open from 8 am to 4.30 pm) which has a collection of shrine paraphernalia. Behind the main shrine building in the north-western corner is the former Shōkokan (Treasure Hall) with a large collection of images of Okuninushi in the form of Daikoku, a cheerful chubby character standing on two or three rice bales with a sack over his shoulder and a mallet in his hand. Usually his equally happy son Ebisu stands beside him with a fish tucked under his arm.

Cape Hino-misaki 日御埼

It's less than 10 km from the Izumo Taisha Shrine to Cape Hino-misaki where you'll find a picturesque lighthouse, some fine views and an ancient shrine. On the way, you pass the pleasant **Inasano-hama Beach**, a good swimming beach just two km from Izumo Taisha station on the private Ichihata line. Buses run regularly from the station out to the cape, via the beach, taking just over half an hour to get to the cape.

The **Hinomisaki-jinja Shrine** is near the cape bus terminus. From the cablecar park, coastal paths lead north and south offering fine views, particularly from the top of the lighthouse (open from 8.30 am to 4 pm, entry ¥100). Beyond the cape is **Owashihama** and then Uryū, two picturesque little fishing villages where you can stay in minshuku.

Festivals

The lunar calendar month corresponding to October is known throughout Japan as Kami-nazuki (Month without Gods). In Izumo, however, it is known as Kami-arizuki (Month with Gods) for this is the month when all the Shintō gods congregate for an annual get-together at the Izumo Shrine. An important festival takes place here from 11

1 Former Treasury House
   彰古館
2 Izumo Taisha
   Shrine Hall
   本殿
3 Onatory
   拝殿
4 Treasure House
   宝物殿
5 Ichibata Bus Terminal
   一畑バス停留所
6 Inabaya Ryokan
   いなばや旅館
7 Takenoya Ryokan
   竹野屋旅館
8 Information Centre
   観光案内所
9 Satobara Ryokan
   藤原旅館
10 Hotel Matsuya
   ホテル松屋
11 Katō Ryokan
   加藤旅館
12 Ebisuya Youth Hostel
   えびすやユースホステル
13 Ichibata Izumo
   Taisha Station
   一畑出雲大社駅
14 Otorii Gate
   大鳥居
15 Izumo Ryokan
   出雲旅館

出雲大社
Izumo Taisha

0   250   500 m

Approximate Scale

to 17 October. The month of October is also a popular time for weddings at the shrine.

Places to Stay & Eat

There's no imperative reason to stay over-night in Izumo Taisha since it's easy to day-trip there from Matsue or simply pause there while travelling along the coast. If you do want to stop, there are a host of places along the main street of Izumo Taisha, which runs down from the shrine to the two railway stations.

The *Ebisuya Youth Hostel* (☎ 0853-53-2157) is just off the main street and costs ¥2400 or ¥2500 depending on the season. On the street near by is the *Katō Ryokan* (☎ 0853-53-2214) with Japanese-style rooms at ¥8000 per person including excellent meals. Other places along the main street include the *Hotel Matsuya* at ¥6200, the *Inabaya Ryokan* (☎ 0853-53-3180) with rooms including two meals from ¥10,000 to ¥20,000, the classy *Takenoya Ryokan* (☎ 0853-53-3131) at ¥13,000 to ¥25,000 and the *Satobara Ryokan* (☎ 0853-53-2009) at ¥10,000.

Izumo's soba (noodles) get high praise, particularly in the dish known as *warigo*, buckwheat noodles over which you pour a broth. There are a number of noodle shops along the main street.

Getting There & Away

Izumo Taisha has two railway stations, the JR one at the end of the street leading down from the shrine and the private Ichihata line station about halfway up the street. The Ichihata line starts from Matsue-onsen station in Matsue and runs on the northern side of Lake Shinji-ko to Izumo Taisha station. The JR line runs from JR Matsue station to JR Izumo station, where you transfer to an Izumo Taisha train. The private-line service also requires a change of train, at Kawato, but is more frequent (more than 20 services a day) and also takes you closer to the shrine. The private-line trip takes less than an hour and passes by rows of trees grown as windbreaks.

Izumo has an airport with JAS flights to and from Tokyo.

OKI ISLANDS　隠岐諸島

Directly north of Matsue, the Oki Islands with their spectacular scenery and steep cliffs are strictly for those who want to get away from it all. At one time, they were used to exile political prisoners and daimyō (on one occasion the emperor himself) who came out on the losing side of political squabbles. The islands consist of the larger Dōgo Island and the three smaller Dōzen Islands plus associated smaller islands. The seven km long cliffs of the Oki Kuniga coast of Nishino-shima Island, at times falling 250 metres sheer into the sea, are particularly noteworthy. The Kokobun-ji Temple on Dōgo Island dates from the 8th century. Bull-fights are an attraction during the summer months on Dōgo Island.

Places to Stay

On Dōgo Island the *Okino-shima Youth Hostel* (☎ 08512-7-4321) costs ¥2050 or ¥2300 per night depending on the season. On Chiburi-jima Island the *Chibu Youth Hostel* (☎ 08514-8-2355) costs ¥2300 a night as does the *Takuhi Youth Hostel* (☎ 08514-6-0860). The islands also have numerous minshuku and other accommodation.

Getting There & Away

There are ferry services to the Oki Islands from Shichirui or Sakaiminato. From Matsue, it's an hour by bus to Shichirui then 2½ hours by ferry. JAS flights operate to the islands from Yonago, Izumo and Osaka.

MASUDA　益田

Masuda is a modern industrial town with two temples, the Mampuku-ji and the Iko-ji. Both have notable gardens said to have been designed by the famed painter Sesshū, whose tomb is also in the vicinity. The temples are both about 10 minutes by bus from the JR station.

Masuda is the junction for the JR Yamaguchi line, which runs between Ogōri, Yamaguchi, Tsuwano and Masuda, and the

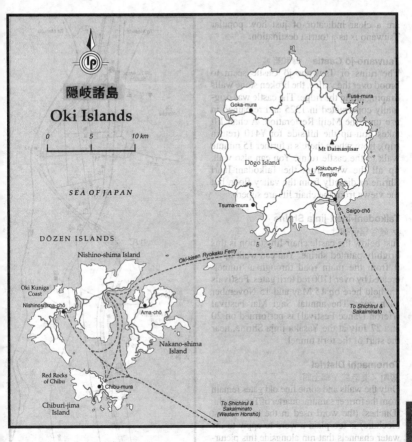

隠岐諸島
Oki Islands

0   5   10 km

SEA OF JAPAN

DŌZEN ISLANDS

Nishino-shima Island

Oki Kuniga
Coast
Nishinoshima-chō

Ama-chō

Nakano-shima
Island

Red Rocks
of Chibu

Chibu-mura

Chiburi-jima
Island

Oki-kisen Ryokaku Ferry

To Shichirui &
Sakaiminato
(Western Honshū)

Goka-mura

Dōgo Island

Mt Daimanjisan

*Kokubun-ji
Temple*

Tsuma-mura

Fuse-mura

Saigo-chō

To Shichirui &
Sakaiminato

JR San-in line, which runs from Shimonoseki, through Hagi and Masuda before continuing along the coast. Masuda is about 30 minutes from Tsuwano, one hour from Higashi-Hagi and two hours and 10 minutes from Izumo.

TSUWANO 津和野

Inland from Masuda is Tsuwano, a pleasant and relaxing mountain town with a fine castle, some interesting old buildings and a wonderful collection of carp swimming in the roadside water channels. The town is noted as a place to get to by the superb old steam-train service from Ogōri and as a place to get around by bicycle, of which there are quite a phenomenal number for rent.

Orientation & Information

Tsuwano is a long, narrow town wedged into a north-south valley. The steep sides of the valley rise on either side of the town. The Tsuwano-kawa River, JR Yamaguchi line and main road all run down the middle of the valley. The staff at the tourist information office by the railway station are very helpful. The number of souvenir shops around town are a clear indicator of just how popular Tsuwano is as a tourist destination.

Tsuwano-jō Castle   津和野城

The ruins of Tsuwano-jō Castle seem to brood over the valley, the broken stone walls draping along the ridge. The castle was originally constructed in 1325 and remained in use until the Meiji Restoration. A chair lift takes you up the hillside for ¥410 (return trip), from where there's a further 15 minute walk to the castle ruins. You can also walk up all the way from the Taikodani-Inari Shrine or directly from the valley floor, but the views from the chair lift are superb.

Taikodani-Inari-jinja Shrine
太鼓谷稲荷神社

Just below the castle chair-lift station is this brightly painted shrine. You can walk up to it from the main road through a 'tunnel' created by over 1100 red torii gates. Festivals are held here on 15 May and 15 November each year. The annual Sagi Mai Festival (Heron Dance Festival) is performed on 20 and 27 July at the Yasaka-jinja Shrine, near the start of the torii tunnel.

Tonomachi District
殿町・養老館・郷土館

Only the walls and some fine old gates remain from the former samurai quarter of Tonomachi. 'Ditches' (the word used in the local tourist brochure) is too plain a word to apply to the water channels that run alongside this picturesque road: the crystal-clear water in the channels is home to numerous large and healthy carp. It's said that these goldfish were bred to provide a potential source of food should the town ever be besieged. The feared attack never came and the fish have thrived.

At the northern end of the street is the **Catholic church**, a reminder that Nagasaki Christians were once exiled here. At the other end of Tonomachi, just north of the river, is the **Yorokan**. This was a school for young samurai in the late Edo period, a relatively innovative idea at that time. The building now houses an interesting small local museum with all sorts of farming and

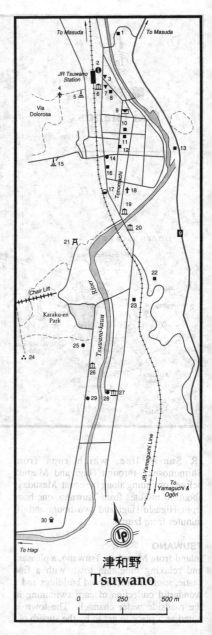

	PLACES TO STAY		**PLACES TO EAT**	18	Catholic Church
					津和野カトリック教会
1	Hotel Sun Route	3	HinokumaRestaurant	19	Yorokan Museum
	ホテルサンルート		日熊		養老館
8	Hoshi Ryokan	7	Shokyoto Restaurant	20	Kyōdokan Museum
	ほし旅館		小京都		津和野町立郷土館
10	Hiroshimaya			21	Taikodani-Inari Shrine
	Minshuku		**OTHER**		太鼓谷稲荷神社
	広島屋宿			24	Tsuwano-jō Castle
11	Meigetsu Ryokan	2	Tourist Information		Ruins
	名月		Office		津和野城跡
12	Minshuku Mitsuwa		観光案内所	25	Dento Kogeisha Paper
	民宿みつわ	4	Chapel of St Mary		Making Centre
13	Tsuwano Grand Hotel		マリア聖堂		津和野伝統工芸館
	津和野グランドホテル	5	Komyo-ji Temple	26	Jingasa Museum
16	Tsuwano Kankō Hotel		光明寺		津和野陣笠民芸館
	Shinjuku	6	Tsuwano Industry	27	Washi Kaikan Museum
	津和野観光ホテル新宿		Museum		和紙会館
22	Kokuminshukusha		産業資料館	28	Mori Ogai House
	Aonesansō	9	Post Office		森鷗外旧居
	国民宿舎青根山荘		郵便局	29	Nishi Amane House
23	Wakasagi-no-Yado	14	NTT		西周旧居
	Minshuku	15	Yomei-ji Zen		
	民宿わかさぎの宿		Temple		
30	Tsuwano		永明寺		
	Youth Hostel	17	Bus Station		
	津和野ユースホステル		バスターミナル		

cooking equipment. It's open from 8.30 am to 5.30 pm daily and entry is ¥200.

Across the river is the **Kyōdokan**, now a small local history museum with some displays concerning the Christian exiles. Hours are from 8.30 am to 5 pm and entry is ¥350, but it's not of great interest.

Chapel of St Mary マリア聖堂

The tiny Maria-Seido Chapel dates from 1948 when a German priest built it as a memorial to the exiled Catholics who died in the final period of Christian persecution before the anti-Christian laws were repealed in 1872. Tsuwano's own **Via Dolorosa** leads along the side of the valley from the chapel with markers for the stations of the cross. At the end of this winding pathway through the forest, a road leads down by the **Yomei-ji Zen Temple** which dates from 1420. The tomb of Mori Ogai (see Other Attractions section) is at the temple.

Other Attractions

The former homes of Mori Ogai, a highly

regarded novelist, and Nishi Amane, who played an important part in the Meiji Restoration Government, are in the south of the town. Near by is the **Sekishukan**, also known as the Washi Kaikan, a museum relating to washi (handmade paper) where you can watch the process of paper making. Entry is free.

The **Dento Kogeisha** centre also has paper-making displays. Across the road from it is the **Jingasa** with a museum of old items and costumes used in the annual Heron Dance Festival. The **Tsuwano Industry Museum** is right by the station and displays local crafts including paper making and sake brewing. It's open daily. South of the town is the **Washibara Hachiman-gū Shrine**, about four km from the station. Archery contests on horseback are held here on 2 April.

Festivals

The Sagi Mai (Heron Dance) Festival is a major annual festival held in July. Lighted lanterns are floated down the river in August.

Places to Stay

The information counter at the railway station will help with bookings at the town's many minshuku and ryokan.

Youth Hostels The *Tsuwano Youth Hostel* (☎ 08567-2-0373) has 28 beds at ¥2300 or 2400 per night depending on the season and is a couple of km south of the station.

Minshuku & Ryokan The *Wakasagi-no-Yado Minshuku* (☎ 08567-2-1146) is not in the town centre but it's a pleasant, friendly and frequently recommended place at ¥6000 per person with two meals. Other similarly priced minshuku and ryokan include the *Hoshi Ryokan* (☎ 08567-2-0136) with costs of ¥5500, *Hiroshimaya Minshuku* (☎ 08567-2-0204), also ¥5500, and *Minshuku Mitsuwa* (☎ 08567-2-0265). All are centrally located (see the map) and include two meals. The *Meigetsu Ryokan* (☎ 08567-2-0685) is a traditional and more expensive ryokan with costs from ¥8000 to ¥18,000. This is a place where you may get to try Tsuwano's famine food – carp!

Across the river and away from the centre is the government-run *Kokuminshukusha Aonesansō* (☎ 08567-2-0436) costing ¥5500 including two meals.

Hotels Hotels include the *Sun Route* (☎ 08567-2-3232), a bland modern hotel overlooking the town from the eastern slope of the valley with singles from ¥6800 to ¥9800 and twins from ¥10,600 to ¥24,600. *Tsuwano Kankō Hotel Shinjuku* is right in the centre of town while the *Tsuwano Grand Hotel* (08567-2-0888) is also on the eastern valley side, by Route 9; rates here are expensive at around ¥12,000 per person with two meals.

Places to Eat

If you're not eating at a minshuku or ryokan there are restaurants and cafés around town, some specialising in the local sansai (mountain vegetable) dishes. For a simple lunch-time meal there are a couple of places around the station. *Shokyoto* has curries, katsudon and coffee. *Hinokuma* has slightly more up-market Japanese cooking, but it's still affordable.

Getting There & Away

The JR Yamaguchi line runs from Ogōri on the south coast through Yamaguchi to Tsuwano and on to Masuda on the north coast. It takes about one hour 15 minutes by limited express from Ogōri to Tsuwano and about 30 minutes from Masuda to Tsuwano. A bus to Tsuwano from Hagi takes nearly two hours.

During the late April to early May Golden Week holiday, from 20 July to 31 August and on certain other Sunday and national holidays, a steam locomotive service operates between Ogōri and Tsuwano. It takes two hours each way and you should book well ahead.

Getting Around

Tsuwano is packed with bicycle rental places; at the height of the tourist season the town must be one enormous bicycle jam. Rental rates start from ¥400 for two hours, with a maximum of ¥800 for a day.

Northern Yamaguchi-ken 山口県の北部

Yamaguchi Prefecture, marking the western end of Honshū, straddles both the southern San-yō coast and the northern San-in coast. The northern stretch includes the historically important town of Hagi.

HAGI 萩

If there were a single reason for travelling along the northern coast of Western Honshū it would have to be Hagi (population 50,000), with its interesting combination of temples and shrines, a fascinating old samurai quarter, some picturesque castle ruins and fine coastal views. Hagi also has important historical connections with the events of the Meiji Restoration. It is ironical that the town's claim to fame is its role in propelling Japan directly from the feudal to the modern era while its attractions are principally its feudal past. Hagi is also noted for its fine pottery.

History

Hagi in Honshū and Kagoshima in Kyūshū were the two centres of unrest which played the major part in the events leading up to the Meiji Restoration. Japan's long period of isolation from the outside world under Tokugawan rule had, by the mid-19th century, created tensions approaching breaking point. The rigid stratification of society had resulted in an oppressed peasantry, while the progressive elements of the nobility realised Japan had slipped far behind the rapidly industrialising European nations and the USA. The arrival of Commodore Perry brought matters to a humiliating head as the 'barbarians' simply dictated their terms to the helpless Japanese.

Japan could not stand up against the West if it did not adopt Western technology, and this essential modernisation could not take place under the feudal shogunate. Restoring the emperor to power, even if only as a figurehead, was the route the progressive samurai chose and Yoshida Shōin of Hagi was one of the leaders in this movement. On the surface, he was also a complete failure. In 1854, in order to study the ways of the West first hand, he attempted to leave Japan on Perry's ship, only to be handed over to the authorities and imprisoned in Edo (Tokyo).

When he returned to Hagi he hatched a plot to kill a shogunate official, but talked about it so much that word leaked out to his enemies. He was arrested again and in 1859, at the age of 29, he was executed. Fortunately, while Shōin was a failure when it came to action he was a complete success when it came to inspiration and in 1865 his followers led a militia of peasants and samurai which overturned the Chōshū Government of Hagi. The Western powers supported the new blood in Hagi and Kagoshima and when the shogunate army

moved against the new government in Hagi, it was defeated. That the downfall of the shogunate had come at the hands of an army, not just of samurai but of peasants as well, was further proof of the changes taking place.

In late 1867, the forces of Kagoshima and Hagi routed the shogunate, the emperor was restored to nominal power and in early 1868, the capital was shifted from Kyoto to Tokyo, as Edo soon became known. To this day, Hagi remains an important site for visitors interested in the history of modern Japan and Yoshida Shōin 'lives on' at the Shōin-jinja Shrine.

Orientation & Information

Hagi consists of three parts: western and central Hagi are effectively an island created by the Hashimoto-gawa and Matsumoto-gawa rivers, while eastern Hagi (with the major JR station, Higashi-Hagi) lies on the eastern bank of the Matsumoto-gawa River.

The main road through central Hagi starts from JR Hagi station and runs north, past the bus station in the centre of town. There's a wide variety of shops along Tamachi arcade, close to the bus station. West of this central area is the old samurai quarter of Jokamachi, with its picturesque streets and interesting old buildings. More interesting old buildings can be found in Horiuchi to the north-west and Teremachi to the north-east of Jokamachi.

Hagi's tourist information office is a little difficult to find. On the main road through town, just south of the bus station, is a Ringer Hut, an outlet of the Japanese fast-noodle chain which looks a bit like a New England church building. Across the road from it is a bank-type building and the tourist office is in the back of that building. There's also an information counter at Higashi-Hagi station.

Hagi Pottery & Kilns   萩焼窯

Connoisseurs of Japanese pottery rank Hagi-yaki, the pottery of Hagi, second only to Kyoto's raku-yaki. As in other pottery centres in Japan, the craft came from Korea when Korean potters were brought back after

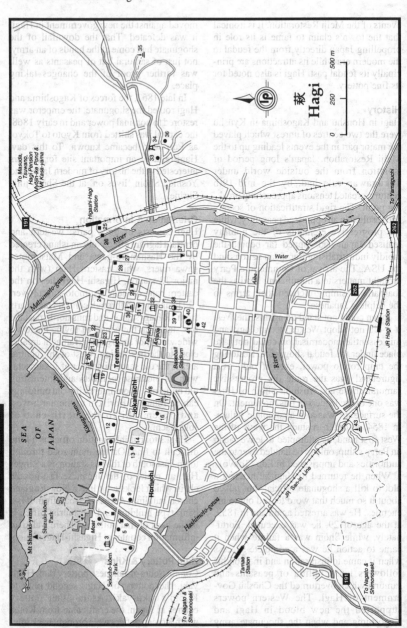

萩
Hagi

0   250   500 m

SEA
OF
JAPAN

PLACES TO STAY		40	Hagi-ko Restaurant はぎこレストラン	16	Takasugi Shinsaku House 高杉晋作旧宅
6	Youth Hostel 萩指月ユースホステル	42	Ringer Hut リーンガーハット	17	Ensei-ji Temple 円政寺
7	Shogetsu Kiln/ Kokuminshukusha Jōen 国民宿舎城苑		**OTHER**	18	Kido Takayoshi House 木戸孝允旧宅
10	Shizuki-sō Ryokan 指月荘	1	Hagi-jō Castle Ruins 萩城趾	19	Kumaya Art Museum 熊谷美術館
24	Hagi Grand Hotel 萩グランドホテル	2	Hagi-jō Kiln 萩城窯	20	Baizo-in Temple 梅蔵院
25	Hagi Royal Hotel	3	Hagi-yaki Museum 萩焼陶芸会館	21	Kyotoku-ji Temple 享徳寺
26	Riverside Hotel 萩リバーサイドホテル小川	4	Christian Cemetery キリシタン墓地	22	Hōfuku-ji Temple 保福寺
27	Hotel Orange ホテルオレンジ	5	Mori House 萩焼陶芸敷長屋	23	Kaicho-ji Temple 海潮寺
28	Hagi Travel Inn 萩トラベルイン	8	Tomb of Tenjuin 毛利天樹院墓所	30	Jonen-ji Temple 常念寺
29	Nakamura Ryokan 中村旅館	9	Fukuhara Gate 福原門	32	Ishii Chawan Museum 石井茶碗美術館
	PLACES TO EAT	11	Sufu House 旧周布家長屋門	33	Shōkasonjuku School 松下村塾
31	Restaurant & Tea Room Shizuki シズキ	12	Masuda House 益田家矢倉長屋	34	Shōin-jinja Shrine 萩陰神社
37	Akasi Restaurant 明石レストラン	13	Shizuki Kiln 指月窯	35	Tōkō-ji Temple 高光寺
39	Restaurant & Tea Room Kōdai レストラン高大	14	Sosuien Park そすい園	36	Itō Hirobumi House 伊藤博文旧宅
		15	Kikuya House	38	Bus Station 防長バス萩センター
				41	Tourist Office 観光案内所
				43	Daishō-in Temple 大照院

Hideyoshi's unsuccessful invasion in the late 1500s. There are a number of shops and kilns where you can see the pottery being made and browse through the finished products. Hagi-yaki is noted for its fine glazes and delicate pastel colours. The small notch in the base of each piece is also a reminder of the pottery's long history. In the feudal era only samurai were permitted to use the pottery, but by cutting a tiny notch in some pieces, the potters 'spoilt' their work and this pottery could then be used by the common folk.

The Shizuki Kiln in Horiuchi has particularly fine pieces. The western end of Hagi has several interesting pottery kilns near Shizuki-kōen Park. Hagi-yaki pottery can also be inspected in the Hagi-yaki Togei Kaikan Museum near the park; there's a big souvenir area downstairs.

Castle Ruins & Shizuki-kōen Park
萩城址・指月公園

There's not much of the old Hagi-jō Castle to see, apart from the typically imposing outer walls and its surrounding moat. The castle was built in 1604 but dismantled in 1874 during the Meiji Restoration; since Hagi played a leading part in the end of the feudal era and the downfall of the shogunate, it was appropriate that the town also led the way in the removal of feudal symbols.

Now the grounds are a pleasant park with the Shizukiyama-jinja Shrine, Hananoe Teahouse and other buildings. From the castle ruins you can climb the hillside to the 143 metre peak of Mt Shizuki-yama. The castle is open daily from 8 am to 5.30 pm and entry is ¥200; the entry ticket also covers the Mori House. Also in the park is the small Hagi Shiryōkan Museum, open daily from 9 am to 5pm with an entry fee of ¥300.

WESTERN HONSHŪ

Sekichō-kōen Park 石彫公園

About five minutes walk to the west of Suzuki-kōen is this new park with its collection of sculptural works from around the world (the park's name means 'sculpture park'). It's open daily and entry is free for the moment, though one wonders how long it will be before a price tag is put on passing through the entrance.

Mori House 毛利家

South of the park is Mori House, a row (terrace) house where samurai soldiers were once barracked. It's open daily and the same ticket covers entry to the castle ruins. There's an interesting Christian cemetery to the south of the samurai house.

Jokamachi, Horiuchi & Teremachi
春若町・堀内・寺町

Between the modern town centre and the moat that separates western Hagi from central Hagi is the old samurai residential area with many streets lined by whitewashed walls. This area is fascinating to wander around and there are a number of interesting houses and temples, particularly in the area known as Jokamachi. Teremachi is noted particularly for its many fine old temples.

Kikuya House The Kikuya family were merchants rather than samurai but their wealth and special connections allowed them to build a house well above their station. The house dates from 1604 and has a fine gate, attractive gardens and there are numerous examples of construction details and materials which would normally have been forbidden to the merchant class. Entry to the house is ¥370 and it is open from 9 am to 5 pm.

Other Houses Near by is Kido Takayoshi House (open from 9 am to 5 pm) and Takasugi Shinsaku House, which is still a private residence. Takasugi was a student of Shōin Yoshida and played a key role in the events leading up to the Meiji Restoration. Interesting houses in the Horiuchi area include the Masuda and Sufu houses.

Kumaya Art Museum The art museum in Jokamachi has a small and not terribly exciting collection including tea bowls, screens and other items in a series of small warehouses dating from 1768. The Kumaya family handled the trading and commercial operations of Hagi's ruling Mori family. Opening hours are from 9 am to 5 pm. Entry is an expensive ¥500.

Other Buildings The Horiuchi and Teremachi areas are dotted with temples and shrines: if you wander around the area you will pass by many of them. The **Fukuhara Gate** is one of the finest of the samurai gates in Horiuchi. Near by is the **Tomb of Tenjuin**, dedicated to Terumoto Mori, the founder of the Mori dynasty. There are numerous old temples in the Teremachi area including the two storeyed Kaicho-ji Temple, the Hōfuku-ji with its Jizō statues (the Buddha for travellers and the souls of departed children), the Jonen-ji Temple with its gate carvings and the Baizo-in Temple with its Buddha statues. The large Kyotoku-ji Temple has a fine garden.

Tea-bowl enthusiasts may find the **Ishii Chawan Museum** in the central Tamachi shopping arcade interesting. The museum is upstairs in the building at the far eastern end at the end of the arcade. It's closed on Tuesday and for much of December and January.

Tōkō-ji Temple 東光寺

East of the river stands this pretty temple with the tombs of five Mori lords. The odd-numbered lords (apart from number one) were buried here; the even-numbered ones at the Daisho-in Temple. The stone walkways on the hillside behind the temple are flanked by almost 500 stone lanterns erected by the lord's servants. It's open daily from 8.30 am to 5 pm and entry is ¥100.

Shōin-jinja Shrine 松蔭神社

West of the Toko-ji Temple is this Meiji era shrine to Shōin Yoshida, an important force in the Meiji Restoration. Events from his life are illustrated in the nearby **Shōin Yoshida**

Shrines & Temples

A: Saikoku-ji Temple (TW)
B: Meiji-jingū Shrine (CT)
C: Buddhist temple (CT)
D: Shimenawa (plaited ropes) (TW)
E: Hanging rope (MM)
F: Temple gate (TW)
G: Shrine maidens, Tōshō-gū Shrine (CT)
H: Shimenawa at shrine entrance (CT)

A	B
C	D
E	F

A: Pipers, Sanja Festival, Sensō-ji Temple, Asakusa, Tokyo (CT)
B: Sanja Festival, Sensō-ji Temple, Asakusa, Tokyo (CT)
C: Boy resting against float, Gion Matsuri Festival, Kyoto (RI)
D: Child at the Gion Matsuri Festival, Kyoto (RI)
E: Taking a break during the Gion Matsuri Festival, Kyoto (RI)
F: Sensō-ji Temple, Asakusa, Tokyo (CT)

Rekishikan (Shōin Yoshida History Hall) which is open from 9 am to 5 pm daily. Just south of the shrine is the **Itō Hirobumi House**, the early home of the four-term prime minister who was a follower of Shōin Yoshida and later drafted the Meiji Constitution. There are a number of other places connected with Shōin Yoshida in the vicinity including his tomb near the Toko-ji Temple and his school (the Shōkasonjuku) in the shrine grounds.

Daishō-in Temple 大照院
South of the centre, near the JR Hagi station, this funerary temple was the resting place for the first two Mori generations and after that, all even-numbered generations of the Mori lords. Like the better known and more visited Tōkō-ji Temple, it has pathways lined by stone lanterns erected by the Mori lord's faithful retainers. The original Mori lord's grave is accompanied by the graves of seven of his principal retainers, all of whom committed seppuku (ritual suicide) after their lord died. An eighth grave is that of a retainer to one of the retainers who also joined in the festivities. The shogunate quickly banned similar excessive displays of samurai loyalty. The temple is open daily from 8 am to 5pm and entry is ¥100.

Myōjin-ike Pond & Mt Kasa-yama
明神池・笠山
A couple of km east of the town, the Myōjin-ike Pond is actually connected to the sea and shelters a variety of saltwater fish. The road beside this small lagoon continues to the top of Mt Kasa-yama, a small extinct volcano cone from where there are fine views along the coast. Buses running from Hagi to Mt Kasa-yama take around 15 minutes and cost ¥240.

Other Attractions
At the south-eastern end of the Hagi 'island', carp can be seen swimming in the roadside **Aiba water channel**. East of the town and close to the main road to Masuda, is the **Hagi Hansharo**, an old reverberating furnace dating from 1858 which was used to make gun and ship parts.

Places to Stay
Hagi Youth Hostel (☎ 0838-22-0733) is south of the castle at the western end of the town, has 120 beds at ¥2300 per night and has rental bicycles. The hostel is closed from 16 January to 9 February. Tamae is the nearest JR station.

There are ryokan and minshuku in town with affordable prices. East of Shizuki-kōen park, a big modern place on the riverside, is *Shizuki-sō* (☎ 0838-22-7580), with rooms for ¥3600. Closer to the park again is *Kokuminshukusha Jō-en* (☎ 0838-22-3939) with rooms from ¥6000 including two meals. Over the river from Higashi-Hagi station is the *Nakamura Ryokan* (☎ 0838-22-0303), with per person costs from ¥8000 to ¥10,000 with two meals.

Pension Hagi (☎ 0838-28-0071) is a pleasant, modern pension 10 km east of town in the fishing port of Nagato-Ohi (pronounced *oy*). The pension is just back from the main road and costs ¥4700 per person including breakfast. JR Nagato-Ohi station is two stops from Higashi-Hagi and the pension's owner, Eukio Yamazaki, who learnt his excellent English in Papua New Guinea, will meet you at the station.

The *Hagi Royal Hotel* (☎ 0838-25-9595) is right by the Higashi-Hagi station and has rooms at ¥8800/17,000. Cheaper hotels in the same area include the *Riverside Hotel* (☎ 0838-22-1195), with rooms at ¥7000/15,000 and the *Hagi Travel Inn* (☎ 0838-25-2640), just across the river from the Higashi-Hagi station, with rooms at ¥5000/10,000. Just across the road from the Travel Inn is the *Hotel Orange* (☎ 0838-25-5880) with singles at ¥4000 and twins at ¥7000.

Places to Eat
There are numerous restaurants in the central area around the bus station, including a couple of nice cake and pastry places – *Kobeya* and *Gateaux Koube*. Just south-west of the station is *Hagi-ko*, a cheerful and bright place with lots of plastic meals to help you make your selection – spaghetti, noodles and other dishes cost ¥320 to ¥500 and a beer is ¥500.

A couple of places worth looking out for, both in the east of town, are *Restaurant & Tea Room Shizuki* and *Restaurant & Tea Room Kōdai*. The former, in a Tudor fronted building has French cuisine, and although a lot of it is pretty expensive, there are some good set lunches and dinners. The latter is well known for its Hagi cuisine and has a pricey (¥2000) but excellent *speshiaru rānchi* ('special lunch'). There are also less costly items on the menu.

Akasi is east of the centre, on the main through route, and is a better restaurant with good teishoku meals. There are some fast-food specialists including one of the *Ringer Hut* noodle restaurants (except here it's called *Pao*) across from the building with the tourist office.

Getting There & Away

The JR San-in line runs along the north coast through Tottori, Matsue, Masuda and Hagi to Shimonoseki. The faster expresses take four hours to or from Matsue.

JR buses to Hagi take 1½ hours from Ogōri, south of Hagi on the Tokyo-Osaka-Hakata shinkansen line. The buses go via Akiyoshi-dai, take one hour 10 minutes and cost ¥1900; there are also buses from Yamaguchi. Buses also operate between Tsuwano and Hagi, taking a little under two hours.

Getting Around

Hagi is a good place to explore on a bicycle and there are plenty of bicycle rental places including one at the youth hostel and several around the castle and JR Higashi-Hagi station. Bocho Bus Company tour buses operate from the Bocho bus station.

HAGI TO SHIMONOSEKi   萩から下関へ

There's some good coastal scenery, small fishing villages and interesting countryside along the coast road between Hagi and Shimonoseki, at the western extremity of Honshū.

Ōmi-shima Island, with its scenic, rocky coast, is immediately north of **Nagato** (population 28,000) and connected to the mainland by a bridge. The island is part of the Kita Nagato Coastal Park which extends eastwards beyond Hagi.

AKIYOSHI-DAI   秋芳洞

The rolling Akiyoshi-dai tablelands are about halfway between Yamaguchi on the southern San-yō coast and Hagi on the northern San-in coast. The green fields are dotted with curious rock spires and beneath this picturesque plateau are hundreds of limestone caverns, the largest of which, Akiyoshi-dō Cave, is open to the public.

The Akiyoshi-dō Cave is of interest principally for its size; the stalagmites and stalactites are not particularly noteworthy. In all, the cave extends about 10 km, a river flows through it and a pathway runs through the cave for about a km. At the mid-point of the cave walk you can take an elevator up to the surface where there is a lookout over the surrounding country. There are entrances to the cave at both ends of the pathway as well

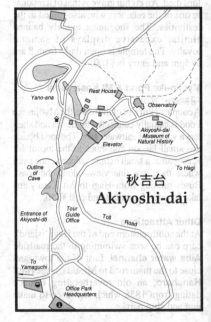

秋吉台
Akiyoshi-dai

as at the elevator, and buses run between the two ends if you do not want to retrace your steps. The cave is open from 8.30 am to 4.30 pm daily; entry is ¥1030.

The **Akiyoshi-dai Museum of Natural History** has exhibits concerning the cave and the surrounding area.

Places to Stay

The *Akiyoshi-dai Youth Hostel* (☎ 0837-62-0341) is close to the cave entrance and has 120 beds at ¥2300. There is also the *Rest House* and a variety of accommodation

around the cave area including the *Kokusai Kankō Hotel Shuhokan* (☎ 0837-62-0311) and the *Wakatakesanso Kokuminshukusha* (☎ 0837-62-0126). The latter is a fairly good option, with per-person costs of ¥5400 with meals.

Getting There & Away

It takes a little over an hour by bus from Yamaguchi or Hagi to the cave. Buses also run to the cave from Ogōri, Shimonoseki and other centres.

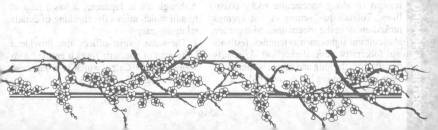

The northern part of Honshū, known in Japanese as Tōhoku, includes Fukushima, Miyagi, Iwate, Aomori, Akita and Yamagata prefectures. This chapter begins with a few sights north of Tokyo which are just beyond the day trips covered in the Around Tokyo chapter, then moves north along the east side of Tōhoku, continues round the northern tip, and descends the west side to include Niigata-ken and Sado-ga-shima Island.

The region is mostly mountainous and was originally inhabited by a people known in previous centuries as Ezo. The Ezo are believed to have been related to the Ainu, who now only remain on Hokkaidō. Although the Ezo were conquered and pushed back during the Kamakura period, it wasn't until the 17th century that the area came under complete government control.

During the Meiji era, the region suffered from years of neglect. This trend was only reversed after WW II, with a drive for development based heavily on industrial growth. Despite this, the region retains a strong reliance on agriculture and many Japanese still consider it as a place in the back of beyond – an economic laggard compared to the rest of Japan.

For those who want to see traditional rural life and enjoy vast areas of unspoilt natural scenery, the relative 'backwardness' of this region provides a strong incentive to visit.

The major cities, few in number, generally merit no more than a cursory stop before heading off into the back country, which offers hikes in volcanic and mountainous regions or along spectacular rocky coastlines. Tōhoku has scores of hot springs tucked away in the mountains and there are also cultural sights such as temples, festivals and folkcrafts. Several excellent ski resorts benefit from the long and severe winters with their accompanying heavy snowfalls.

INFORMATION

Since Tōhoku is less travelled by foreigners and sources of information are less common outside major cities, you may well find your queries answered more easily by phoning Japan Travel-Phone, toll free on ☎ 0120-22-2800 between 9 am and 5 pm.

Exploring Tōhoku (Weatherhill, 1982) by Jan Brown is a guide to the region which provides solid and very detailed background information including useful indices with place names in kanji.

For some literary refreshment en route you could dip into *The Narrow Road to the Deep North & Other Travel Sketches* (Penguin, 1970), which contains classic haiku penned by Bashō (1644-94), perhaps the most famous Japanese poet, on his travels in Tōhoku and elsewhere. To bring yourself up to date, you could also read *The Narrow Road to the Deep North: Journey into Lost Japan* (Jonathan Cape, 1990) by Lesley Downer. This is a well-written account of a walk which retraced one of Bashō's trips through the central and southern parts of Tōhoku.

The Japan National Tourist Organisation (JNTO) publishes a glossy brochure entitled *Tōhoku* that includes a map and brief details for sights, festivals and transport in Northern Honshū. JNTO also publishes leaflets for separate parts of Tōhoku and these are mentioned in the appropriate places in this chapter.

Tourist information offices in the northern prefectures of Tōhoku (Iwate, Aomori and Akita) can provide a very useful timetable entitled *Kita Tōhoku Kankō Jikokuhyō*. Although it's in Japanese, it has a map in romaji which makes the checking of details relatively easy.

The same tourist offices also provide a large map of northern Tōhoku entitled *Kita Tōhoku Kankō Chizu*, which is in Japanese and on a scale of 1:500,000.

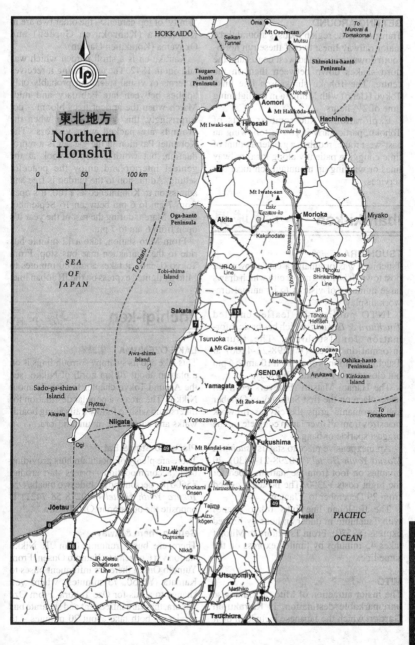

GETTING AROUND

Transport in the region focuses around three major railway lines: two of these run north-south down the east and west coasts and the third snakes down between them in the centre. The Tōhoku shinkansen line links Tokyo (Ueno) with Morioka in the lightning time of 2½ hours.

Exploration of the remoter parts of Tōhoku, particularly if you're following an east-west route, requires a greater amount of time chugging patiently along local railway lines or winding up mountains on local bus services.

Ibaraki-ken　　茨城県

TSUCHIURA　土浦

Tsuchiura was originally a castle town and post town. It is now a major city which draws large numbers of visitors to its annual firework display.

JNTO publishes a leaflet entitled *Tsuchiura & Tsukuba*, which has basic information for Tsuchiura. The tourist information office (☎ 0298-21-4166) at Tsuchiura station is open from 10 am to 6 pm but closed every second Thursday.

The Hanabi Matsuri (Firework Festival) takes place on the first Saturday in October and pyromania grips the city as firework maestros from all over Japan compete for the biggest sparkle or bang.

An inexpensive place to stay is *Tsuchiura Masuo Youth Hostel* (☎ 0298-21-4430), 20 minutes on foot from the station; a bed for the night costs ¥2300. The hostel is closed from 29 December to 3 January.

The JR Jōban line links Tokyo (Ueno) with Tsuchiura in under an hour by limited express (¥2520). From Tsuchiura to Mito, it takes 45 minutes by limited express on the same line.

MITO　水戸

The major attraction of Mito, an otherwise unremarkable destination, is **Kairaku-en Garden** which the Japanese include in their 'trinity' of top gardens – the other two are in Kanazawa (Kenroku-en Garden) and Okayama (Koraku-en Garden).

Kairaku-en is a stroll garden which was laid out in 1842. The top ranking it receives in terms of visual splendour probably only applies between late February and mid-March when the apricot trees bloom – not surprisingly, this is also a time when the grounds are packed with visitors. The Kobuntei Pavilion in the garden is a reproduction, but worth a stop to look at the genteel interior and enjoy the peaceful setting. Admission to the garden is free and admission to Kobuntei costs ¥160. It's open from 7 am to 6 pm between 16 September and 31 March; during the rest of the year it's open from 6 am to 7 pm.

From Mito station, take a 12 minute bus ride to the Kairakuen-mae bus stop. From Tokyo (Ueno), it takes about 80 minutes to Mito by limited express on the JR Jōban line.

Tochigi-ken　　栃木県

LAKE OZENUMA　尾瀬沼

This lake and its swampy surroundings is on a plateau about 70 km north of Nikkō (see the Around Tokyo chapter for details about Nikkō). The area is a popular destination for hikers who wish to follow trails along boardwalks and admire the mountain flora.

Places to Stay & Eat

There are plenty of mountain huts providing basic accommodation – prices start around ¥5500 per person and include two meals. *Oze Tokura Youth Hostel* (☎ 0278-58-7421) is opposite the bus stop in Oze Tokura.

Getting There & Away

There are buses running from JR Nikkō station via Chūzenji to Yumoto Onsen. From Yumoto Onsen there are infrequent buses to Kamata (¥1250, 75 minutes) where you change to a bus for Oze Tokura. From Oze Tokura, there are infrequent and separate bus services – both take about 20 minutes – to

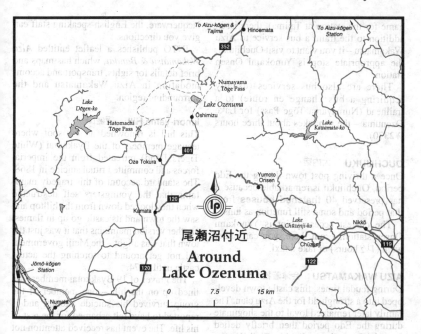

尾瀬沼付近

Around Lake Ozenuma

the two major trailheads (Hatomachi Tōge Pass and Oshimizu).

See the section on Numata (Gumma-ken) for transport between Numata and the trailheads for Lake Ozenuma.

If you're heading down from Fukushima-ken, the lake can be reached by taking a bus from Aizu-kōgen station (Aizu line) to Numayama Tōge Pass (¥2050, two hours) where trails lead to the lake.

bus ride from Jōmō-kōgen station on the JR Jōetsu shinkansen line.

If you want to visit Lake Ozenuma, with its surrounding network of hiking trails (often slippery and boggy), there are buses running from Numata station via Kamata to Oze Tokura (about 95 minutes, ¥1900). From Oze Tokura, there are infrequent and separate bus services – both take about 20 minutes – to the two major trailheads (Hatomachi Tōge Pass and Oshimizu).

Gumma-ken 群馬県

NUMATA 沼田
Numata is a convenient staging point for transport if you're travelling across from Nikkō with a sidetrip to Lake Ozenuma and then continuing to Kusatsu and across to Nagano-ken. Numata is on the JR Jōetsu line. It can also be reached with a 30 minute

Fukushima-ken 福島県

TAJIMA 田島
Tajima was formerly a post town on the Nikkō Kaidō Highway. You can stop here to visit the **Oku-Aizu Folk Museum** (Oku-Aizu Minzoku Shiryōkan) which exhibits crafts and household utensils.

From Aizu-Tajima station (the correct

name for the station at Tajima), there is, in addition to the train, a bus service to Aizu Wakamatsu – if you want to visit Ouchijuku, the appropriate stop is Yunokami Onsen station.

There are also bus services (usually requiring a bus change en route) to a trailhead (Numayama Tōge Pass) for Lake Ozenuma – the trip takes about three hours (¥2370).

OUCHIJUKU   大内宿
Once a thriving post town during the Edo period, Ouchijuku is remarkable because it has preserved 40 **thatched houses** from that period and some still function as inns.

The closest access point is Yunokami Onsen station. From there, you can either walk (1½ hours) or take a taxi.

AIZU WAKAMATSU   会津若松
During feudal times, this castle town developed into a stronghold for the Aizu clan. The family later remained loyal to the shogunate during the Edo period then briefly defied imperial forces in the Boshin Civil War (at the start of the Meiji era). The resistance was swiftly crushed and the town went up in flames – the heroic 'last stand of the samurai', complete with mass suicides by young warriors, has found its way into the annals of Japanese history and attracts many Japanese visitors to Aizu Wakamatsu.

Two bus lines conveniently circle from Aizu Wakamatsu station around the main sights – one clockwise and the other anticlockwise. Bicycle rental is also available at the station.

Information
The Aizu Wakamatsu tourist information office (☎ 0242-32-0688) is in the View Plaza of JR Aizu Wakamatsu station. Large, detailed maps of the area in English are available – excellent for orientation. The office is open from 9.30 am to 5.30 pm, 10 am to 5 pm on Sunday. If you want to visit nearby sake museums and breweries (tastings available!) or a hall exhibiting local

lacquerware, the English-speaking staff can give you directions.

JNTO publishes a leaflet entitled *Aizu Wakamatsu & Bandai*, which has maps and brief details for sights, transport and accommodation in Aizu Wakamatsu and the surrounding region.

Iimori-yama Hill   飯盛山
This hill is renowned as the spot where teenage members of the Byakkotai (White Tigers Band) retreated from the imperial forces and committed ritual suicide in 1868. The standard account of this tragedy maintains that the youngsters self destructed when they looked down from the hilltop and saw the town and its castle go up in flames; another version maintains that it was just the town that was alight – the Meiji government did not get around to torching the actual castle until 1874.

The graves of 19 Byakkotai members are lined up on the hill – one member of the group survived his suicide attempt and is reported to have felt ashamed for the rest of his life. The event has received attention not only from Japanese admirers of loyalty, but also from foreigners with similar sentiments. Close to the graves are two monuments: one from a German military attaché and another from Italian fascists.

One tourist brochure saw a link between the tragedy of the Byakkotai in 1868 and the opening of the first transcontinental railroad across the USA one year later; puzzling indeed.

Apart from a museum housing Byakkotai memorabilia, there's also the **Sazae-dō Hall**, a hexagonal building dating from the 18th century, which has an intricate set of stairs arranged as a double spiral. Admission to the hall costs ¥200 and it's open from 8 am to sunset.

The hill is a 15 minute bus ride from the railway station and can be climbed on foot – or use the hillside elevator.

Oyaku-en Garden   御薬園
This is a splendid garden complete with tea arbour, large central pond (and huge carp)

and a section devoted to the cultivation of medicinal herbs which was encouraged by former Aizu lords.

In the souvenir shop you can sample herbal tea, and packets of daimyō herbal brew are on sale.

Admission costs ¥300 and it is open from 8 am to 5 pm (April to October) and 8.30 am to 4.30 pm (November to March). The garden is a 15 minute bus ride from the station – get off at the Oyaku-en Iriguchi bus stop.

Samurai House 会津武家屋敷

Aizu Buke-yashiki is an interesting, large-scale reconstruction of the lifestyle of opulent samurai in the Edo period. An English leaflet and map are provided for you to guide yourself around dozens of rooms, which range from the kitchen to the principal residence. Don't miss the rice mill, where 16 grinding stones driven by water power are capable of producing 900 kg of rice in a day.

The toilet has a special sandbox for medical advisers to inspect their lord's daily deeds!

One irritation is the mass of souvenir shops scattered around the grounds which are geared to huge numbers of visitors. The house is open from 8.30 am to 5.30 pm (April to October) and 9 am to 4.30 pm (November to March). Admission costs a whopping ¥800. To reach the residence, take a 15 minute bus ride from the station and get off at the Buke-yashiki-mae bus stop.

Tsuruga-jō Castle 鶴ヶ城

The present castle is a reconstruction from 1965 and contains a historical museum. Admission costs ¥310 and it's open from 8.30 am to 5 pm.

Festivals

Aizu Aki Matsuri Festival, held from 22 to 24 September, features a large parade with participants dressed as daimyō and their

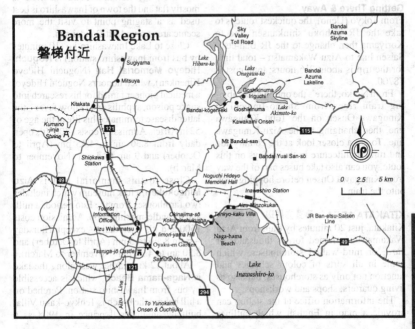

retainers, and there are performances of folk dances.

Places to Stay
For ryokan and minshuku accommodation, the tourist information office has lists of accommodation and can help with reservations. The *Aizu-no-Sato Youth Hostel* (☎ 0241-27-2054) is a 10 minute walk from Shiokawa station, which is 10 km from Aizu Wakamatsu and a little closer to Kitakata. Rates are fairly cheap at ¥1700 to ¥1900 depending on the time of year. Bicycle rental is available at the hostel.

Just south of Aizu Wakamatsu station is the *Green Hotel Aizu* (☎ 0242-24-5181), a serviceable business hotel with singles from ¥5500. The *Hotel Osakaya* (☎ 0242-22-5305) is way down the bottom of Ōmachi-dōri (it runs south from Aizu Wakamatsu station), and closer to Namukamachi station. It has singles from ¥6500 and twins from ¥12,000.

Getting There & Away
From Tokyo (Ueno), the quickest route is to take the JR Tōhoku shinkansen line to Koriyama then change to the JR Ban-etsu-Saisen line to Aizu Wakamatsu – total time for the trip is about 2½ hours; total cost is ¥8700.

From Nikkō, there's the option of combining train rides from Shimo-Imaichi to Kinugawa Onsen on the Tōbu Kinugawa line, then changing to the Aizu-Kinugawa line. To get a closer look at the countryside and rural architecture in the valleys on this route, you can also take buses part of the way from Kinugawa Onsen before hopping back onto the train.

KITAKATA AREA　喜多方周辺
Kitakata, just 20 minutes by train from Aizu Wakamatsu, is famed for its thousands of *kura*, or mud-walled storehouses, which come in all sorts of colour schemes and function not only as storehouses, but also as living quarters, shops and workshops.

The information office at the station can provide a map in English which outlines walking routes – allow three hours at an easy pace. Bicycle rental is also available near the station (¥250 per hour) and a horse-drawn tourist carriage (a sort of double-decker 'kuramobile') does the rounds in two hours (¥1200) – Japanese commentary only.

Brick-built, Western-style kura can be seen at **Mitsuya**, nine km north of Kitakata (15 minutes by bus from Kitakata station) on Route 121. The tiny community of **Sugiyama**, six km further north from Mitsuya, is almost solid with kura.

Six km west of Kitakata (25 minutes by bus from Kitakata station) is the **Kumano-jinja Shrine**, renowned for its Nagatoko Hall which was built over 900 years ago and has neither walls nor doors – more than 40 massive columns support the roof.

LAKE INAWASHIRO-KO　猪苗代湖
This is a large lake – the fourth-largest in Japan – and is popular with the Japanese as a place to take ferry rides and go camping. However, the terrain around the lake is mostly flat and the town of Inawashiro is best used as a staging point to visit the more scenic area around Mt Bandai-san.

Close to Lake Inawashiro-ko (10 minutes by bus from Inawashiro station) is **Noguchi Hideyo Memorial Hall** (Noguchi Hideyo Kinenkan), which honours Noguchi Hideyo, a medical pioneer famed for his research into snake poison, syphilis and yellow fever – the latter disease terminated his life at the age of 52 in Africa. Admission costs ¥400. It's open daily from 8.30 am to 4.45 pm (April to October) and 9 am to 4 pm (November to March).

Close to this memorial hall is **Aizu Minzokukan**, a folk museum which includes two farmhouses from the Edo period, a mill, and a candle-making shop. Admission costs ¥500 and it's open daily – except Thursday – from 8 am to 5 pm (April to October) and 8.30 am to 4.30 pm (November to March).

About 12 km further west along the lake is **Naga-hama Beach**, which is accessible by bus from Inawashiro station. Perched on a hill behind the beach is Tenkyo-kaku Villa, built by an imperial prince in 1908 as a summer residence. It has fine views across the lake. Cruises of the lake start and finish at Naga-hama Beach and cost ¥820 for 30 minutes.

Places to Stay & Eat

Next door to Tenkyo-kaku Villa (and sharing its view) is *Okinajima-sō Kokuminshukusha* (☎ 0242-65-2811), a comfortable place to stay. Prices start around ¥5450 per person and include two meals.

MT BANDAI-SAN & BANDAI-KŌGEN PLATEAU

磐梯山・磐梯高原

Mt Bandai-san erupted on 15 July 1888 and in the course of the eruption destroyed dozens of villages and their inhabitants. At the same time it completely rearranged the landscape to create a plateau and dam local rivers which then formed numerous lakes and ponds. Now designated as a national park, the whole area offers spectacular scenery with ample scope for walks or long hikes.

The most popular walk – sometimes jammed with hikers from end to end – takes about an hour and follows a trail between a series of lakes known as **Goshikinuma** (Five Coloured Lakes). The trailheads for the Goshikinuma walk are at Goshikinuma Iriguchi and at Bandai-kōgen-eki – the main transport hub – on the edge of Lake Hibara-ko. As can be expected of a main transport hub, Bandai-kōgen-eki is geared to the tourist circus – souvenir shops, restaurants and a vast asphalt expanse to accommodate the tour buses. The pleasure boat rides can safely be skipped, but there are various walking trails along the eastern side of the lake. Near by are several other lakes, including Lake Onagawa-ko and Lake Akimoto-ko, which also offer scope for walks along their shores.

Ura Bandai Youth Hostel is very close to Goshikinuma Iriguchi and makes a convenient base for extended hikes. The hostel has maps in Japanese which outline routes and approximate times for hikes in the areas.

The most popular hiking destination is Mt Bandai-san, which can be climbed in a day – start as early as possible and allow up to nine hours. A popular route for this hike starts from Kawakami Onsen (about 10 minutes by bus from the youth hostel) and climbs up to Mt Bandai-san, looping around the rim of the crater before descending to Bandai-kōgen-eki bus stop.

Places to Stay & Eat

There are numerous kokuminshukusha, pensions, minshuku and hotels in the area. There's a tourist information office at Idemitsu, between Goshikinuma Iriguchi and Bandai-kōgen-eki, but if you need help with booking accommodation (and you don't speak Japanese) it's probably easier to use the tourist office in Aizu Wakamatsu, which has English-speaking staff. Japanese speakers might try ringing the Bandai Inawashiro Minshuku Association (☎ 0242-62-3412). If you tell them where you are, they will be able to tell you the nearest minshuku with vacancies and make a reservation for you.

The *Ura Bandai Youth Hostel* (☎ 0241-32-2811) seems a little the worse for wear, but it's in a quiet spot next to one of the trailheads for the Goshikinuma walk. It's also a good base for longer mountain hikes. The hostel manager can provide maps and basic information for hikes in the area. Bicycle rental is also available – much cheaper than the rental at Lake Hibara-ko. Note that this hostel is closed from 1 December to 31 March. A bed for the night is ¥2300.

Take the bus bound for Bandai-kōgen from Inawashiro station and get off 30 minutes later at the Goshikinuma Iriguchi bus stop. The hostel is seven minutes on foot from the bus stop.

Other accommodation is scattered far and wide across the region. The *Ura-Bandai Kokumin Kyūka-mura* (☎ 0241-32-2421) has per-person costs of ¥3500 to ¥4500 without meals, but meals are available (¥2500 for dinner). Just to the south of it is the *Kyūka-mura Camping Ground*. Close by, expensive, Japanese-style accommodation is available at the *Hotel Shirokumo-sō* (☎ 0241-32-2311), where per-person costs range from ¥14,000 to ¥18,000 with two meals. Buses run direct from Inawashiro station to the Kyūka-mura, which is close to the camping ground and to the Hotel Shirokumo-sō.

Getting There & Away

There are buses from Aizu Wakamatsu station and Inawashiro station to the trailheads for the Goshikinuma walk. Buses from Aizu Wakamatsu to Lake Hibara-ko take 1½ hours (¥1560) and from Inawashiro to Bandai Kōgen-eki 25 minutes (¥810).

Between Bandai-kōgen-eki and Fukushima there is a bus service along two scenic toll roads – Bandai Azuma Lakeline and Bandai Azuma Skyline. The trip provides great views of the mountains and is highly recommended if you are a fan of volcanic panoramas.

The bus makes a scheduled stop (30 minutes) at Jōdodaira, a superb viewpoint, where you can climb to the top of Mt Azumakofuji (1705 metres) in 10 minutes and, if you still feel energetic, scramble down to the bottom of the crater. Across the road is Mt Issaikyō-yama, which belches steam in dramatic contrast to its passive neighbour – a steepish climb of 45 minutes is needed to reach the top with its sweeping views.

The bus fare between Fukushima and Bandai-kōgen-eki is ¥2700; the trip takes about three hours. This service only operates between late April and late October.

Between Bandai-kōgen-eki and Yonezawa there is another bus service along the scenic Sky Valley toll road. The trip takes two hours and the fare is ¥1700. This service only operates between late April and late October.

Miyagi-ken　宮城県

SENDAI　仙台

Sendai (population 918,000) is a fairly dull provincial Japanese city, even by dull provincial Japanese city standards. Still, there are a few sights around town, and the city's

clean, broad boulevards make for pleasant enough strolling – it's good at least for an overnight stay.

If you've been hiking the long road to the deep north, Sendai has some good restaurants and a couple of nightlife options (don't get too excited). Those coming from the bright lights of Tokyo, on the other hand, are probably better off skipping the place – spend the night in nearby Matsushima at least.

The dominant figure in Sendai's history is Date Masamune (1567-1636), who earned the nickname Dokuganryū ('one-eyed dragon') after he caught smallpox as a child and went blind in his right eye. Date adopted Sendai as his base and, in a combination of military might and administrative skills, became one of the most powerful feudal lords in Japan. An accomplished artist and scholar, Date also raised Sendai to the cultural centre of the Tōhoku region.

Unfortunately, there's not much evidence of high culture these days. During WW II, Sendai was demolished by Allied bombing, and the city was later rebuilt with streets and avenues laid out in a grid pattern. City planning has included liberal sprinklings of tree-lined boulevards, and Jūzenji-dōri in particular has a reputation among Japanese as being a romantic destination for an evening stroll.

Orientation

Sendai station is within easy walking distance of the city centre, and the grid layout of the streets makes orientation relatively simple. From the station, the broad sweep of Aoba-dōri, lined with many of the major department stores, banks and hotels, leads west to Aoba-yama Hill. The main shopping areas are along the mall-like Ichibanchō-dōri and Chūō-dōri – confusingly, the latter is known as Clis Road. Kokubunchō-dōri, west of Higashi Ichibanchō-dōri, is the largest entertainment district in Tōhoku, with thousands of bars and eateries.

Information

Sendai tourist information office (☎ 022-222-4069), on the 2nd floor of JR Sendai

宮城県
Miyagi-ken

0   30   60 km

--- --- --- Prefectural Boundary

PACIFIC OCEAN

station, may or may not have English-speaking staff on duty – don't count on it. Last time we were in town, the counter was posted with a couple of old dodderers who looked like they'd have trouble fielding questions in Japanese, let alone English. The Sendai English Hotline (☎ 022-224-1919) should be a more reliable source of travel information and advice.

The JR Travel Service Centre in the station deals with the exchange of Japan Rail Pass vouchers.

Aoba-jō Castle   青葉城跡

Aoba-jō Castle was built on Aoba-yama Hill in 1602 by Date Masamune. Its partial destruction during the Meiji era was completed by bombing in 1945. The castle ruins – a restored turret and that's about it – lie inside Aobayama-kōen Park where you can pause for a look at Gokoku-jinja Shrine or walk south to Yagiyama-bashi Bridge, which leads to a zoo. Admission costs ¥400. It's open from 9 am to 4.15 pm. From Sendai station, take bus No 9 for the 20 minute (¥220) ride to the Aoba-jōshi Uzumi-mon bus stop.

Sendai Municipal Museum   仙台市博物館

Just north of the castle ruins, the museum is of moderate interest and houses a collection of items associated with Sendai's history. It's open from 9 am to 4.45 pm, closed on Monday, and entrance is ¥400. It's an easy walk from the castle ruins.

Zuihō-den Hall   瑞鳳殿

This is the mausoleum of Date Masamune originally built in 1637, but later destroyed by bombing in WW II. The present building is an exact replica – faithful to the ornate and sumptuous style of the Momoyama period. The hall is open from 9 am to 4 pm daily and admission costs ¥515. From Sendai station, take either bus Nos 11 or 12 for the 15 minute (¥180) ride to the Otamaya-bashi stop.

Osaki Hachiman-jinja Shrine
大崎八幡神社

The original shrine building dates from the 12th century and was moved from outside Sendai to its present site by Date Masamune in 1607. The main building is a luxurious, black-lacquered edifice with eye-catching carved designs. Entrance is free and it closes at sunset. From Sendai station, take bus Nos

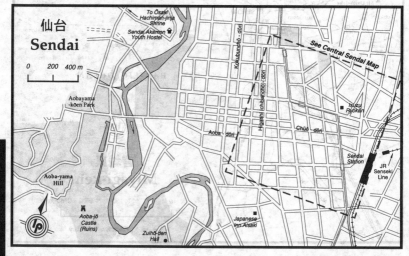

仙台
Sendai

0   200 400 m

To Osaki
Hachiman-jinja
Shrine
Sendai-Akamon
Youth Hostel

See Central Sendai Map

Aobayama-kōen Park

Kokubuncho-dōri

Higashi Ichibancho-dōri

Aoba - dōri

Chūō - dōri

Isuzu Ryokan

Aoba-yama Hill

Sendai Station

JR Senseki Line

Aoba-jō Castle (Ruins)

Zuihō-den Hall

Japanese Inn Aisaki

NORTHERN HONSHŪ

10 or 15 for the 20 minute (¥200) ride to the Hachiman-jinja-mae stop.

Festivals

The Tanabata Matsuri (Star Festival), held from 6 to 8 August, is the big annual event in Sendai. Several million visitors ensure that accommodation is booked solid at this time.

According to a myth (originally Chinese), a princess and a peasant shepherd were forbidden to meet, but 7 July – the time when the two stars Vega and Altair meet in the Milky Way – was the only time in the year when the two star-crossed lovers could sneak a tryst. Sendai seems to have stretched the dates a bit, but celebrates in grand style by decorating the main streets, holding parades and rounding off the events with a fireworks finale.

If you're in Sendai on the evening of 14 January, Osaki Hachiman-jinja is host to one of those parades where Japanese men brave sub-zero weather conditions to hop around almost naked in a show of collective madness. The festival is known as the Donto Matsuri.

Places to Stay

Youth Hostels *Sendai Dōchu-an Youth Hostel* (☎ 022-247-0511), just south of Sendai in an old farmhouse, has a high reputation for hospitality to foreigners – it's twinned with a youth hostel in Meiringen, Switzerland. Bicycle rental is available and there may still be a discount on the price of accommodation offered to foreign hostellers. Nightly rates are ¥2500.

From Sendai station, take the subway to Tomizawa station then walk for eight minutes to the hostel. Alternatively, you can walk to the hostel in 18 minutes from Nagamachi station which is one stop south of Sendai station. If you get lost, the hostel manager can give you directions over the phone.

Sendai Onnai Youth Hostel (☎ 022-234-3922) is north of Sendai station. Take bus No 24 bound for Shihei-chō (the stop is in front of the Sendai Hotel, opposite the station) and get off after about 15 minutes at the Tōhokukai Byō-in Shigakubu-mae stop. The hostel is two minutes walk away. A bed for the night is ¥2300 and bicycle rental is available at reasonable rates.

Sendai Akamon Youth Hostel (☎ 022-264-1405) is north-west of Sendai station – about 15 minutes by bus No 16 to the Nakanosebashi bus stop and then five minutes on foot. A bed for the night is ¥2300, and the hostel is closed from 28 December to 3 January.

Ryokan *Japanese Inn Aisaki* (☎ 022-264-0700), a member of the Japanese Inn Group, is behind the post office, a 15 minute walk from Sendai station. It's a friendly place with meals available. Prices for singles/doubles start at ¥4300 per person.

Hotels Sendai has no shortage of business hotels – the city centre is packed with them. One of the cheaper ones around is the *Sendai Pacific Hotel* (☎ 022-263-6611), just to the north of the station. It has singles at ¥5800 and doubles from ¥7500. Also not far from the station and not too expensive is the small *Business Hotel Yamato* (☎ 022-267-8990). It has singles/twins/doubles at ¥6000/10,000/9000. On the intersection of Chūō-dōri and Higashi Ichiban-dōri, a very central location, is the *Tokyo Dai-Ichi Hotel Sendai* (☎ 022-262-1355), with rooms from ¥6400 for singles and from ¥13,000 for twins.

There are many centrally located upmarket alternatives to these cheaper business hotels. Right next to the station, the *Hotel Metropolitan Sendai* (☎ 022-268-2525) has singles from ¥10,000 and doubles from ¥20,000. Equally classy and around 10 minutes' walk from the station is the *Sendai Kokusai Hotel* (☎ 022-268-1112). It has singles from ¥10,000 and doubles from ¥17,500. In case you were wondering, the most expensive hotel in town is the *Sendai Hotel* (☎ 022-225-5171), which has singles from ¥12,000. It's right next to the station.

Places to Eat

There are a multitude of dining options in the central city area. The fast-food barns are well

仙台中心部

Central Sendai

0   125   250 m

Hirose - dōri

Hirose-dōri
Subway
Station

Kōtōdai-kōen
Subway
Station

Kōdanchō - dōri

Higashi

Chūō
dōri

Ichiban - dōri

Aoba
dōri

dōri

Sendai
Subway
Station

JR Tōhoku Shinkansen

NORTHERN HONSHŪ

represented, with branches of *McDonald's*, *Lotteria*, *Kentucky Fried Chicken* and *Mos Burger*, to name a few. There's at least one branch of *Doutor's*, the successful Tokyo discount coffee chain, and also a branch of the equally successful *Italian Tomato* chain – it's on Chūō-dōri. The Japanese gyūdon (beef on rice) chain *Yoshinoya* has a branch up on Hirose-dōri – good economical fare. Ice-cream fans should look out for the branch of *Häagen Daazs*.

For some slightly more up-market Japanese cooking, check out *Santake*, a pleasant place with good tempura and udon dishes

from ¥650 to ¥1500. There's plenty to choose from at the lower end of the menu. Not far away is *Genroku-Zushi*, an excellent revolving sushi shop (the head of this chain is in Harajuku, Tokyo). Plates start at ¥120. For high quality rāmen in all-mod-con surroundings, head over to *Dondon Rāmen*. Prices here start at ¥600 and don't go above ¥800 for huge bowls of noodles.

A popular place with local residents is *Thaiway Corner*, a basement Thai kitchen run by a Japanese guy and his Thai wife. This is authentic Thai cuisine at affordable prices. It's opposite the NHK building just north of

PLACES TO STAY		PLACES TO EAT			
4	Hotel Hokke Club Sendai ホテル法華クラブ仙台	1	Kentucky Fried Chicken	11	Salotto Italian Restaurant イルサロット
13	Hotel Century Sendai ホテルセンチュリー仙台	2	La Terrasse Restaurant ラ テラス	12	Italian Tomato Restaurant イタリアントマト
18	Sendai Pacific Hotel 仙台パシフィックホテル	3	Häagen Daazs Restaurant	16	McDonald's マクドナルド
19	Sendai Hotel 仙台ホテル	5	Santake Restaurant さん竹	**OTHER**	
21	Hotel Metropolitan Sendai ホテルメトロポリタン仙台	6	Genroku-Zushi Restaurant	14	Red Shoes Bar
23	Business Hotel Yamato ビジネスホテルヤマト	7	元禄寿司 Yoshinoya Restaurant	15	Daiei Department Store ダイエー
25	Sendai Tōkyū Hotel 仙台東急ホテル	8	吉の屋 Doutor Coffee/Dondon Rāmen Restaurant	17 20	Village Vanguard Bar JR Sendai Station J R 仙台駅
26	Sendai Kokusai Hotel 仙台国際ホテル	9	どんどんラーメン Mr Donut ミスタードーナツ	22	Seiyō Department Store 仙台セイヨー
27	Hotel Sun Route Sendai ホテルサンルート仙台	10	McDonald's マクドナルド	24	Eastern Orthodox Church ハリストス正教会

the city centre. For Italian food, *Salotto*, another basement restaurant, is worth checking out. The English menu has pasta dishes from ¥800, and the restaurant often has good deals on wine (¥1000 for all you could drink in 90 minutes when we were in town last).

Finally, some of the department stores around town have restaurant floors with good lunch-time specials. For a starter you might try the 8th floor of Mitsukoshi or the 8th floor of Daiei department stores.

Entertainment

Sendai just wouldn't be a Japanese city if it didn't have its own famous nightlife area. In this case it's clustered around the northern end of Kokubunchō-dōri. It makes for an interesting evening stroll, but there probably isn't much that the average traveller could afford there. Interesting places that we stumbled across include *Sherlock Holmes*, *Baron Potato*, *Popeye the Hōrensō* (*hōrensō* means spinach), *Madame Lee Phone 63-5575* (yes, it's a bar), *Fancy Pub Spunky Sugar* and, the one place that probably sums the area up most

succinctly, *Member's Bar Rip Off* (sign us up, *please!*).

For a couple of affordable beers in a place that is frequented by other local gaijins, the best option is probably *Village Vanguard*, at the station end of Chūō-dōri. It's a bit of a dull jazz bar, with live acts occasionally perfoming on the weekends (there'll be a cover charge for this), but the reverse-discrimination foreigner discounts on the draught beer (¥300 for a draught Heineken!) make this a very affordable place to knock a few cold ones back. Another, trendier option is *Red Shoes*, which is just off Chūō-dōri, further west of the station. There are fewer foreigners here (the beer's more expensive), but the funky converted basement feel of the place provides the luxury of imagining that you aren't in Sendai. In Kokubun-chō, one bar that occasionally gets foreign customers and isn't a member's rip-off affair is *Simon's* – look out for it if you take a stroll through the area.

Getting There & Away

Air From Sendai Airport there are flights to

Osaka, Sapporo Airport (New Chitose Airport), Nagoya, Fukuoka, Komatsu (Kanazawa) and Okinawa. To get to and from Tokyo, the shinkansen is so fast, it's not really sensible to take a plane.

Train The JR Tōhoku shinkansen line takes two hours seven minutes by the Yamabiko service or two hours 34 minutes by the Aoba service between Tokyo (Ueno) and Sendai (¥10,390). Trains run around once every 20 minutes. The Tōhoku shinkansen line also connects Fukushima with Sendai in 26 minutes and continues north to Morioka in 50 minutes.

The JR Senzan line connects Sendai with Yamagata in one hour. The JR Senseki line links Sendai with Matsushima in 40 minutes.

Bus The Tōhoku Kyūkō (express night bus) runs between Tokyo (Tokyo station) and Sendai (¥5450 one way, 7¾ hours) and reservations are necessary.

Ferry Sendai is a major port with daily ferries operating to Tomakomai (Hokkaidō). The trip takes just under 17 hours and the fare is ¥8850. There are also ferries operating every second day to Nagoya (¥9580, 21 hours). Japanese speakers can make reservations on ☎ 022-263-9877 or in Tokyo on ☎ 03-3564-4161.

To get to Sendai-futō Pier from Sendai station, take the JR Senseki line to Tagajō station and then a 10 minute taxi ride.

Getting Around
To/From the Airport Sendai Airport is a 40 minute bus ride (¥780) south of Sendai.

Bus Sendai has a huge – and initially confusing – network of bus services. Most of the sights can be reached by bus direct from Sendai station. The tourist information office provides a bilingual leaflet with relevant bus numbers, bus destinations and the names of the appropriate bus stops. If you want to save time or avoid complicated bus routes while crossing between the sights, short hops by taxi are inexpensive.

Subway The present subway system runs from Izumi Chūō in the north to Tomizawa in the south. Pricing is according to sections, from ¥180 to ¥260, but few short-term visitors are likely to need to use it as it's not really useful for sightseeing. An extension of the subway is planned to run from east to west.

AKIU ONSEN　秋保温泉
This hot-spring resort, 50 minutes by bus west of Sendai, is a good base for sidetrips further into the mountains to see **Akiu-ōtaki Falls** and, further still, **Futakuchi Gorge** with its rock columns known as Banji-iwa. There are hiking trails along the river valley and there's a trail leading from Futakuchi Onsen to the summit of **Mt Daitō-dake** (about a three hour walk). Buses leave from the No 8 bus stop outside Sendai station and cost ¥740.

SAKUNAMI ONSEN　作並温泉
This is another hot-spring resort, west of Sendai, which can be reached from Sendai by bus (one hour) or by train on the JR Senzan line (40 minutes). Sakunami is renowned for its open-air hot springs and the production of kokeshi dolls. Take a bus from the No 10 bus stand next to Sendai station. The fare is ¥990. On the face of it, taking a train is quicker and cheaper (¥560), but Sakunami station is a fair trudge from the action.

MATSUSHIMA　松島
Matsushima and the islands in Matsushima-wan Bay are meant to constitute one of the *Nihon sankei*, or 'three great sights' of Japan – the other two are the floating torii of Miyajima Island and the sandspit at Amanohashidate. Besides the islands, there's also a lot of unprepossessing industrial scenery. Bashō (yes, Bashō was here too!) was reportedly so entranced by the surroundings in the 17th century that, according to a local brochure, his flow of words was reduced to: 'Matsushima, Ah! Matsushima! Matsushima!'.

It's certainly a picturesque place which

merits a half-day visit, but there are also impressive and less-touristed seascapes further east which are worth visiting.

Orientation & Information

Just to confuse things, there's a Matsushima station on the Tōhoku line, but the station that's more convenient to the sights and the harbour is Matsushima-Kaigen, which is on the Senseki line. From Matsushima-Kaigen station, it's only around 500 metres to the harbour, and sights are all within easy walking distance.

Matsushima Tourism Association (☎ 022-354-2618) is next to the dock and has a few brochures – English is not spoken.

Zuigan-ji Temple   瑞巌寺

Founded in 828, the present buildings of Zuigan-ji were constructed in 1606 by Date Masamune to serve as a family temple. This is one of Tōhoku's finest Zen temples and well worth a visit to see the painted screens and interior carvings of the main hall and the Seiryūden (Treasure Hall), which contains works of art associated with the Date family.

Admission costs ¥500 and includes an English leaflet. The temple is open from 8 am to 5 pm from April to mid-September, though for the rest of the year opening hours vary almost month by month; the core opening hours are from 8 am to 3.30 pm. The temple is five minutes on foot from the dock and is approached along an avenue lined with tall cedars.

Godai-dō Hall   五大堂

This is a small wooden temple reached by two bridges, just a couple of minutes on foot to your right as you get off the boat. The interior of the hall is only opened every 33 years – so you'll probably have to be content with the weatherbeaten exterior and the view out to sea.

Kanran-tei Pavilion   観瀾亭

This pavilion is about five minutes on foot from the dock; bear left after leaving the boat. Kanran-tei is claimed to have been presented to the Date family by Toyotomi

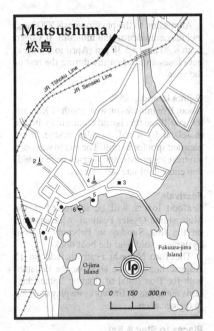

1 Matsushima Station (Tōhoku Line)
   松島駅（東北本線）
2 Zuigan-ji Temple
   瑞巌寺
3 Matsushima Century Hotel
   松島センチュリーホテル
4 Godai-dō Hall
   五大堂
5 Matsushima Kankō Hotel
   松島観光ホテル
6 Matsushima Cruise Boats
   松島遊覧船
7 Kanran-tei Pavilion
   観瀾亭
8 Aquarium
   マリンピア松島水族館
9 Matsushima-Kaigen Station
   (Senseki Line)
   松島海岸駅（仙石線）

Hideyoshi in the late 16th century and served as a genteel venue for tea ceremonies and moon-viewing. The garden includes a small museum housing a collection of relics from the Date family.

Admission to the pavilion costs ¥200 and includes entrance to the museum. It's open from 8.30 am to 5.30 pm (April to October) but closes an hour earlier during the rest of the year.

O-jima Island 雄島

About five minutes on foot, south of Kanran-tei, you'll see this island connected with the mainland by a red, wooden bridge. It's a pleasant spot for a stroll. The island was once a retreat for priests, and women were forbidden entry until late last century.

Festivals

Seafood lovers will be interested in the Matsushima Oyster Festival, which is held on the first Sunday in February – fresh oysters are sold near the boat dock.

The Tōrō Nagashi Festival, held on 15 August, honours the souls of the departed with the Bon ritual of floating lighted lanterns out to sea. A fireworks display adds zip to the occasion.

Places to Stay & Eat

Most of the accommodation in Matsushima itself is very pricey. The cheapest option around is the *Matsushima Youth Hostel* (☎ 0225-88-2220), at Oku-Matsushima to the east of Matsushima Bay, near Nobiru station. A bed for the night is ¥2500 and bicycle rental is available. The hostel is closed from 5 July to 12 July.

There are a couple of other options close to Nobiru station. The *Pension Marine Ship* (☎ 0225-88-3622) (you can't miss it, as it has 'Marine Ship' plastered across its unusual front section) has per-person costs from ¥8000 with two meals. It's around 600 metres south-east of the station, by the seafront. Very close to the station (walk seawards and turn right) is the *Minshuku Boyo-sō* (☎ 0225-88-2159), with per-person costs from ¥6000.

In Matsushima itself, the sky is the limit. If you want to splash out, one of the best choices is probably the *Ryokan Matsushima-jō* (☎ 0223-54-2883), which is a ryokan that looks like a castle – not a very authentic one

admittedly. Costs here range from ¥10,000 to ¥15,000 per person with two meals. Another odd-looking hotel (it looks vaguely Tibetan) is the *Matsushima Kankō Hotel* (☎ 0223-54-2121), which has rooms ranging from ¥8000 to ¥30,000.

Getting There & Away

Train The easy way to get to Matsushima is by train from Sendai. Trains run on the Senseki line, take around 40 minutes and cost ¥390. There are only around two services an hour (some of the trains on the Senseki line terminate before they reach Matsushima) to Matsushima, though there are three as far as Shiogama. This is important because travelling by train to Shiogama and then travelling onwards by boat to Matsushima is the most popular way of reaching the latter, taking in one of Japan's most self-celebrated strips of coastline on the way. The train fare to Shiogama is ¥310.

Ferry Shiogama itself is not particularly noteworthy, though it's a thriving fishing port and has a celebrated festival every 5 August, with a parade of colourful boats decked out with streamers and banners. The cruises to Matsushima are what is important for most visitors. The harbour is around 10 minutes on foot from Hon-Shiogama station – turn right at the station exit.

Cruises between Shiogama and Matsushima-Kaigan usually take about 50 minutes and operate from 8 am to 4 pm. There are hourly departures between April and November – less frequent departures during the rest of the year – and the one-way fare costs ¥1400. The loudspeakers on the boat are cunningly placed so that there is no escape from the full-blast Japanese commentary. Leaping overboard is about the only way of escaping this racket.

Apart from the standard boats, there are also more expensive ones shaped like peacocks or dragons. All the boats loop around the islands of Matsushima-wan Bay between Shiogama and Matsushima-Kaigan.

OKU-MATSUSHIMA　奥松島
On the eastern curve of Matsushima-wan Bay, Oku-Matsushima is less touristed and offers scope for exploration by bicycle or on foot along several hiking trails.

To reach Oku-Matsushima, take the JR Senseki line east from Matsushima-Kaigan to Nobiru station (two stops). From Nobiru station, it's a 10 minute bus ride to Otakamori village where a 20 minute climb up the hill provides a fine panorama of the bay.

Matsushima Youth Hostel is about 20 minutes on foot from Nobiru station. Bicycle rental is available and the manager can provide directions for the hiking trails.

Oshika-hantō Peninsula
牡鹿半島

AYUKAWA　鮎川

Ayukawa, at the base of peninsula, was once a major whaling centre and is now reliant on other types of fishing and tourism. The tourist information office, close to the dock for boats to Kinkazan Island, has helpful staff – only Japanese spoken – who will sit you down with a cup of coffee and arrange accommodation if you miss the last ferry to Kinkazan Island.

Just beside the tourist information office is **Oshika Whale Land**. Considering the sensitivity of most Western travellers to the plight of whales (steel yourself for pickled whale foetuses, diabolical harpoons, gruesome pictures of old whaling methods in open boats and giant diagrams where whales are compared in size to a bus or a shinkansen train), there are probably going to be few people prepared to fork out the ¥1000 admission charge. It's considered one of the peninsula's major sights by Japanese tourists.

Festivals
On 4 August, Ayukawa celebrates a whale festival with a parade of fishing boats and a fireworks display. Whales have been refusing to participate.

Places to Stay
An excellent place to stay is *Cobalt-sō Kokuminshukusha* (☎ 0225-45-2281). This modern people's lodge is in a superb position on a forested hilltop opposite Kinkazan Island. The lodge's minibus operates a 15 minute shuttle service to and from Ayukawa. For ¥6000 you get two meals and a well-maintained room. A variety of seafood is included in the evening meal. Close by is the much less attractive and more expensive *Hotel New Sakai* (☎ 0225-45-2515). It has rooms from ¥12,000 with two meals.

Getting There & Away
The gateway to this beautiful, secluded peninsula is **Ishinomaki**, about 30 minutes from Matsushima-kaigan by limited express on the JR Senseki line. It can also be reached via the Ishinomaki line from Ichinoseki on the Tōhoku line.

From Ishinomaki station there are buses (¥1430, 90 minutes) to Ayukawa at the base of the peninsula – you may be able to get a ¥100 discount by asking for a shūyū-ken or block of tickets. There is also a boat connection between Ishinomaki and Ayukawa which leaves Ayukawa at 8.00 am; a return ferry leaves Ishinomaki at 9.50 am (¥1850, two hours).

The bus ride down the peninsula is particularly enjoyable as the bus repeatedly climbs across forested hills before dropping down into bays and inlets where tiny fishing villages are surrounded by mounds of seashells and the ocean is full of rafts and poles for oyster and seaweed cultivation.

KINKAZAN ISLAND　金華山
For those in search of peace and quiet, an overnight stay on Kinkazan Island is highly recommended. The island features a pyramid-shaped mountain (445 metres), an impressive and drowsy shrine, a handful of houses around the boat dock, no cars, droves of deer and monkeys and mostly untended trails.

The island is considered one of the three holiest places in Tōhoku – women were banned until late last century – and you should respect the ban on smoking. On the first and second Sunday in October, there's a deer-horn cutting ceremony to stop the deer from causing injury to each other during the mating season.

From the boat dock, it's a steep 20 minute walk up the road to **Koganeyama-jinja Shrine**, which has several attractive buildings in its forested precincts. Below the shrine are grassy expanses where crows delight in hitchhiking on the back of deer which know a trick or two when it comes to cadging titbits from visitors. At ground level, the deers' droppings provide busy times for large numbers of irridescent dung beetles.

A steep trail leads from the shrine up the thickly forested slopes, via several wayside shrines, to the summit in about 50 minutes. From the shrine at the summit, there are magnificent views out to sea and across to the peninsula. On the eastern shore of the island is **Senjōjiki** or '1000 Tatami Mats Rock', a large formation of white, level rock.

A map of the island on green paper is provided by the shrine or the tourist information office in Ayukawa. It has neither contour lines nor scale and its only use is to demonstrate that there *are* trails and to provide the kanji for various places on the island (this may be useful when you come across one of the weatherbeaten trail markers).

I spent a full eight hours tramping around without meeting another person; the only sounds were crows cawing, frogs burping and boats hooting in the far distance. Deer danced across the bracken into the undergrowth and a huge male monkey suddenly barred my path with a belligerent baring of teeth and as a final comment proffered a close-up display of his ugly pink bum before retreating behind a rock.

Before setting off for an extended hike, stock up on food and drink either at the dock or at the shrine shop. Apart from the route up to the summit shrine, the trails are mostly untended and you should be cautious with some of the wooden walkways along the summit which are collapsing into rotten pulp. If you do get lost, head downhill towards the sea – there's a dirt road around all but the northern part of the island.

Robert Strauss

Places to Stay & Eat

Koganeyama-jinja Shrine (☎ 022-545-2264), 15 minutes on foot up the steep hill from the dock, has spartan rooms set aside for hostellers and basic meals are served. You can supplement the meals with food purchased from the shop outside the shrine – careful, the deer can mug the unwary! If you get up before 6 am you may be allowed to attend morning prayers. Most Japanese visitors seem to be day-trippers – this means the island is virtually deserted in the early morning and late afternoon.

The shrine also has a lodge for pilgrims which provides classier accommodation and food. Near the dock are a couple of unexciting minshuku.

Getting There & Away

Ferries depart Ayukawa hourly between 8 am and 3.30 pm. The return ferry departs hourly between 9 am and 5 pm. The trip takes 25 minutes one way and costs ¥880.

A variation in routing is provided by the ferry – a high-speed catamaran – between Kinkazan Island and Onagawa, which is the eastern gateway to the peninsula. There are four daily departures in both directions; the first ferry leaves between 9 and 10 am and the last leaves between 2 and 3 pm (¥1600 one way, ¥3020 return; half an hour).

ONAGAWA 女川

This fishing town serves as a gateway for the Oshika-hantō Peninsula. Having enjoyed the pristine scenery of the peninsula, you might like to know that the authorities have plonked an atomic power plant on the eastern coast, close to Natsuhama Beach. If you are interested, this plant has an Atomic Power Plant Superintending Centre which 'facilitates a proper understanding of atomic power generation' with the help of models and pictures. In Onagawa itself, there's the **Atomic Power PR Centre** which is described as an 'atomic museum' – this PR operation cost the regional power company ¥800 million. Now it is understandable why the scenic highway down the peninsula is called 'Oshika Cobalt Line'.

Onagawa is the terminus for the JR Ishinomaki line, 30 minutes from Ishinomaki where you can either catch a train south-west towards Sendai or west towards Furukawa (a change of train may be necessary, en route, at Kogota).

If you arrive at Onagawa Pier from Kinkazan Island, turn right as you leave the pier, continue for 200 metres, then turn left and proceed straight ahead for about 100 metres to the station.

KESENNUMA   気仙沼

North of Onagawa there is a road winding along the rugged coastline past the eroded rock formations of **Cape Kamiwari-zaki** (there's a camping ground near by) up to Kesennuma and the Karukawa-hantō Peninsula.

At the tip of Karukawa-hantō Peninsula, one hour by bus from Kesennuma, is **Cape O-saki**, which has a camping ground, a kokuminshukusha, the small Osaki-jinja Shrine, a tourist information office and the **Tsunami Museum** (Tsunami Hakubutsukan) – the latter demonstrates the horrifying effects of the *tsunami* or tidal wave with simulated earthquakes, films and scary wind effects.

Places to Stay

Karakuwa Youth Hostel (☎ 02263-2-2490) is on the peninsula and can be reached by bus or boat from Kesennuma in about an hour. Special guest rooms and bicycle rental are also available. Dorm beds cost ¥2500.

Getting There & Away

Kesennuma serves as a base to visit the peninsula and Ō-shima Island, which is 30 minutes by boat (¥250) from Kesennuma Port. The port, 10 minutes by bus from Kesennuma station, is also worth a morning visit to witness the busy fish market – Kesennuma is the largest fishing town in the prefecture.

Kesennuma is connected with Ichinoseki (Iwate-ken) by train on the JR Ōfunato line in about 1¾ hours. It's also possible to get there from Ishinomaki by travelling to Maeyachi on the Ishinomaki line and then changing there to the Kesennuma line to Kesennuma. Be prepared for long waits.

NARUKO ONSEN   鳴子温泉

This is a major hot-spring resort in the north-western corner of Miyagi-ken. The entrance to **Narugo-kyō Gorge** can be reached by a five-minute taxi drive (¥570) from Naruko station in the direction of Nakayama-daira. It's around three km away, so walking it shouldn't be a great strain (follow Route 44 west from the station). From the entrance there is a 50 minute walk along the river valley to Nakayama-daira. From Naruko station, there is a bus service which heads north for 30 minutes to reach more hot springs at **Onikōbe Onsen** which is also a popular ski resort in winter.

Naruko Onsen is one hour by train from Furukawa on the JR Rikū-tōsen line.

Iwate-ken   岩手県

HIRAIZUMI   平泉

Of the few cultural sights in Tōhoku, Hiraizumi is one that should not be missed.

From 1089 to 1189, three generations of the Fujiwara family created a political and cultural centre in Hiraizumi which was claimed to approach the grandeur and sophistication of Kyoto. This short century of fame and prosperity was brought to an end when the last Fujiwara leader, Fujiwara Yasuhira, displayed such greed and treachery that he incurred the distrust of Minamoto Yoritomo who ordered the annihilation of the Fujiwara clan and the destruction of Hiraizumi.

Only a couple of the original temple buildings now remain as the rest have been restored or added over the centuries.

Orientation & Information

Hiraizumi is now a small town and orientation is straightforward. The tourist information office is on your right as you exit Hiraizumi station; no English is spoken.

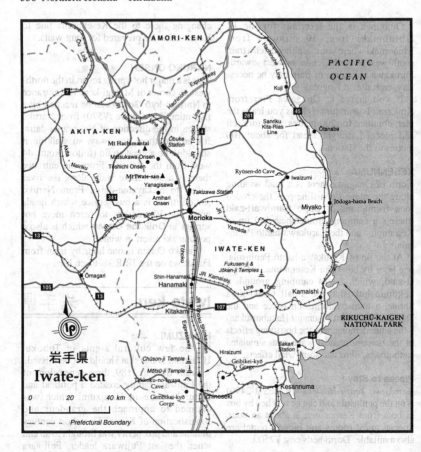

AMORI-KEN

AKITA-KEN

Mt Hachimantai ▲
Matsukawa Onsen
Tōshichi Onsen
Mt Iwate-san ▲
Yanagisawa
Amihari Onsen

Ōbuke Station

Akita Nairiku Line

JR Tazawako Line

JR Tōhoku Line

Morioka

Takizawa Station

Yamada Line

IWATE-KEN

Fukusen-ji &
Jōken-ji Temples

JR Kamaishi Line

**岩手県
Iwate-ken**

Shin-Hanamaki

Hanamaki

Tōhoku Shinkansen
JR Tōhoku Shinkansen

Kitakami

107

Tōno

Kamaishi

Chūson-ji Temple
Mōtsū-ji Temple
Takkoku-no-Iwaya
Cave
Gembikei-kyō
Gorge

Hiraizumi
Geibikei-kyō
Gorge

Sakari
Station

Ichinoseki

Kesannuma

45

**RIKUCHŪ-KAIGEN
NATIONAL PARK**

**PACIFIC
OCEAN**

Hachinohe Line

Hachinohe Expressway

Kuji

Sanriku
Kita-Rias
Line

281

Ōtanabe

Ryūsen-dō Cave

Iwaizumi

Miyako

Jōdoga-hama Beach

7

4

105

13

341

Omagari

Tōhoku Expressway

Prefectural Boundary

0   20   40 km

(lp)

JNTO publishes a leaflet entitled *Sendai, Matsushima & Hiraizumi*, which has a schematic map of Hiraizumi and brief details for sights, access and accommodation.

Gouverneur Mosher, who has written a sensitive guide to Kyoto (see the Kyoto section of the Kansai chapter), also wrote about Hiraizumi in a book entitled *Japan Caught Passing*, but it appears that this is out of print.

Chūson-ji Temple   中尊寺

Chūson-ji Temple was originally established in 850, but it was the first lord of the Fujiwara clan who decided in the early 12th century

to expand the site into a complex with over 40 temples and hundreds of residences for priests. A massive fire in 1337 destroyed most of the complex – even so, what you can see now is still most impressive.

The steep approach to the temple follows a long, tree-lined avenue past the Hondō (Main Hall) to an enclosed area with the splendid Konjiki-dō (Golden Hall) and several less interesting buildings.

Golden Hall   Built in 1124, the Konjiki-dō is small but packed with gold ornamentation, black lacquerwork and inlaid mother-of-pearl. The centrepiece of the hall is a statue of Amida with attendants. Beneath the three side altars are the mummified remains of three generations of the Fujiwara family. The fourth and last lord of the family, Fujiwara Yasuhira, was beheaded at the order of Minamoto Yoritomo, who further required the severed head to be sent to Kyoto for inspection before returning it for interment next to the coffin of Yasuhira's father. During the '60s, the protective shelter for the hall was renewed and the interior decoration was given a complete restoration.

Admission costs ¥500 – the ticket is also valid for admission to Kyōzō Sutra Treasury and Sankōzō Treasury. It is open daily from 8.30 am to 5 pm but closes 30 minutes earlier from November to March.

Kyōzō Sutra Treasury Built in 1108, this is the oldest structure in the temple complex. The original collection of over 5000 sutras was damaged by fire and the remains of the collection have been transferred to the Sankōzō Treasury.

Sankōzō Treasury This building houses temple treasures including the coffins and funeral finery of the Fujiwara clan, scrolls, swords of the Fujiwara clan and images transferred from halls and temples which no longer exist.

Mōtsū-ji Temple 毛越寺

Originally established in 850, this temple once rivalled Chūson-ji in size and fame. All that remains now are foundation stones and the attractive Jōdo (Paradise) Garden which gives a good impression of the luxurious, sophisticated lifestyle in the Heian period – as you wander around the pond, you can imagine nobles lazing around in boats, sipping sake and composing verses. The temple and gardens attract large numbers of visitors for Jōgyōdō Hatsukayasai, a performance of ancient dances, on 20 January; and for the Iris Festival, which is held from late June to mid-July when the irises bloom.

Admission to the gardens costs ¥500 and they are open from 8 am to 5 pm. Those

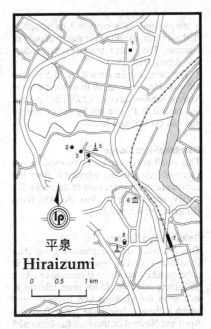

平泉
Hiraizumi

0   0.5   1 km

1	Kokuminshukusha Sun Hotel Koromogawa-sō 国民宿舎サンホテル衣川荘
2	Kyōzō Sutra Treasury 経蔵
3	Golden Hall 金色堂
4	Sankōzō Treasury 讃こう蔵
5	Chūson-ji Temple 中尊寺
6	Hiraizumi Folklore Museum 平泉郷土館
7	JR Hiraizumi Station JR平泉駅
8	Mōtsū-ji Youth Hostel 毛越寺ユースホステル
9	Mōtsū-ji Temple 毛越寺

staying at the youth hostel in the grounds do not have to pay for admission.

Takkoku-no-Iwaya Cave 達谷窟

A few km south-west of Mōtsū-ji Temple is

a temple built in a cave and dedicated to Bishamonten, the Buddhist guardian deity of warriors. The present structure is a reproduction dating from 1961.

The cave is open from 8 am to 5 pm but closes half an hour earlier from November to March. Admission costs ¥200. The cave can be reached in 10 minutes by bus or taxi; or you can cycle if you like.

Gembikei-kyō Gorge 巖美渓

This small gorge can easily be explored on foot and you can see where the river has carved elaborate shapes out of the rocks. It's easily accessible by bus or taxi from Hiraizumi or Ichinoseki.

Geibikei-kyō Gorge 猊鼻渓

This is a much more impressive gorge than Gembikei-kyō. The best way to reach it is either to take a taxi from Hiraizumi or take a 45 minute bus ride (¥570) from Ichinoseki station to the Geibikei-kyō Iriguchi stop, which is the entrance to the gorge. Between April and November, there are flat-bottomed boats with singing boatmen ferrying their passengers up and down the river between the sheer cliffs of the gorge. The trip takes 1½ hours and costs ¥1030. Boats depart hourly between 8.30 am and 4 pm.

Festivals

The Spring Fujiwara Festival, held from 1 to 5 May, features a costume procession, folk dances and performances of Nō. A similar Autumn Fujiwara Festival takes place from 1 to 3 November.

Places to Stay & Eat

Mōtsū-ji Youth Hostel (☎ 0191-46-2331) is part of Mōtsū-ji Temple and a pleasantly peaceful place to stay – guests at the hostel are not charged admission to the gardens. The temple is eight minutes on foot from Hiraizumi station.

North of the station is the *Kokuminshukusha Sun Hotel Koromogawa-sō* (☎ 0197-52-3311), where per-person costs with two meals range from ¥6700 to ¥7100.

Getting There & Away

To reach Hiraizumi from Sendai, take a JR Tōhoku shinkansen to Ichinoseki (35 minutes) then the bus which goes via Hiraizumi station to Chūson-ji Temple (¥320, 26 minutes). You can also take a JR Tōhoku Honsen line train from Sendai to Hiraizumi station, but a change of trains is usually necessary at Ichinoseki and the trip takes about two hours.

From Morioka to Ichinoseki on the JR Tōhoku shinkansen line takes 43 minutes. Trains between Ichinoseki and Morioka on the JR Tōhoku Honsen line are less frequent and take about 1¾ hours.

Getting Around

Frequent buses run from Ichinoseki station via Hiraizumi station to Chūson-ji Temple; the 20 minute walk from Hiraizumi station to Chūson-ji Temple is not particularly appealing. From the station, Mōtsū-ji Temple is an easy 10 minute walk. Bicycle rental is available outside the station at ¥500 for two hours and ¥200 for every additional hour thereafter.

KITAKAMI 北上

Kitakami is renowned for its Michinoku Kyodo Geino Matsuri Festival. This is held from 7 to 9 August and features folk-art performances not only from the Kitakami region, but also from many other parts of Tōhoku.

TŌNO 遠野

Tōno excited attention at the beginning of this century when a collection of regional folk tales were compiled by Kunio Yanagida and published under the title *Tōno Monogatari*. During the '70s, this work was translated into English by Robert Morse under the title *The Legends of Tōno* – it should still be available in specialist foreign-language bookshops like Kinokuniya or Maruzen in Tokyo. The tales cover a racy collection of topics from supernatural beings and weird occurrences to the strange ways of the rustic folk in traditional Japan.

The present city of Tōno was formed out

of a merger of eight villages in the '50s and is not uniformly interesting – just a few sights scattered around the more appealing rural fringes. The region still has some examples of the local style of farmhouse, known as *magariya*, where farmfolk and their prized horses lived under one roof – but in different sections.

Information

The tourist information office in Morioka has details about Tōno. The Tōno tourist information office (☎ 0198-62-3030) is outside JR Tōno station. The staff can provide an English brochure entitled *Come & See Traditional Japan in Tōno*, which has full details of transport, accommodation and sights. It also includes an accurate map for cycling routes on a scale of 1:70,000. Bicycle rental is available at this office and also at the youth hostel.

Once you've picked up your brochure and decided on your mode of transport, you might want to see the first two sights in the centre of town and then head for the more appealing sights on the rural fringes – such as the **Water Mill** (Suisha), which still functions, about 10 km north-east of Tōno station.

Tōno Municipal Museum 遠野市立博物館

The 3rd and 4th floors of the building house the museum. There are exhibits of folklore and traditional life and a variety of audiovisual and visual presentations of the legends of Tōno using slides, films, models and 'georamas'. The museum is about 500 metres south of the station.

Admission costs ¥300; a combined ticket for the nearby Tōno Folk Village is discounted to ¥500. The museum is open daily from 9 am to 5 pm. The museum is closed on the last day of every month between April and November, from 21 to 30 September and on Monday between November and March.

Tōno Folk Village 遠野昔話村

This 'village' consists of a restored ryokan, an exhibition hall for folk art and items connected with the local legends. There are a couple of souvenir shops selling local crafts.

Admission to the village costs ¥300; a combined ticket for the nearby Tōno Municipal Museum is discounted to ¥500. Opening hours are the same as for the Tōno Municipal

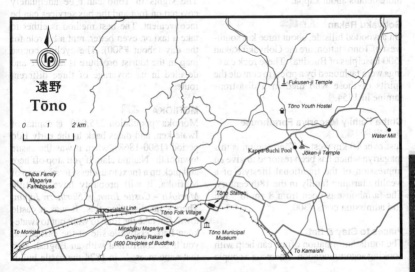

遠野 Tōno

0   1   2 km

Chiba Family
Magariya
Farmhouse

To Morioka

JR Kamaishi Line

Minshuku Magariya
Gohyaku Rakan
(500 Disciples of Buddha)

Tōno Folk Village

Tōno Station

Tōno Municipal
Museum

To Kamaishi

Fukusen-ji Temple

Tōno Youth Hostel

Water Mill

Kappa-Buchi Pool   Jōken-ji Temple

Museum. The village is a couple of minutes on foot from the museum.

Fukusen-ji Temple 福泉寺
This temple lies north-east of Tōno station, about 30 minutes by bicycle. Founded as recently as 1912, its major claim to fame is the wooden Fukusen-ji Kannon statue – 17 metres in height – which is claimed to be the tallest of its type in Japan. Admission costs ¥300.

Jōken-ji Temple & Kappa-Buchi Pool
常堅寺・カッパ淵
Jōken-ji Temple is about one km south of Fukusen-ji. Outside the temple is a distinctive lion statue; inside the temple is a famous image which some believe will cure their illness if they rub the part on its body which corresponds to the part where their own body ailment is.

Behind the temple is a stream and the Kappa-Buchi Pool. Kappa are considered to be mischievous, mythical creatures but legend has it that the kappa in this pool once put out a fire in the temple. The lion statue was erected as a gesture of thanks to honour the kappa. See the Folklore & Gods section in the Facts about the Country chapter for more details about kappa.

Gohyaku Rakan 五百羅漢
On a wooded hillside, about three km south-west of Tōno station, are the Gohyaku Rakan (500 Disciples of Buddha). These rock carvings were fashioned by a priest to console the spirits of those who died in a disastrous famine in 1754.

Chiba Family Magariya Farmhouse
千葉家曲り家農家
Just over 10 km west of Tōno station is this magariya which has been restored to give an impression of the traditional lifestyle of a wealthy farming family in the 18th century. The farmhouse is open from 8 am to 5 pm and admission costs ¥300.

Places to Stay & Eat
The tourist information office can help with booking accommodation – there are a couple of hotels and ryokan and at least a dozen minshuku.

Minshuku Magariya (☎ 0198-62-4564), about two km south-west of the station, is a popular place where you can stay inside a traditional farmhouse. Prices start around ¥8000 per person and include two meals.

Tōno Youth Hostel (☎ 0198-62-8736) provides a base for cycling or walking around the area. From Tōno station, take a bus bound for Iwate-Yamaguchi and get off at the Nitagai stop (about 12 minutes). From there it's 10 minutes on foot to the hostel. Bicycle rental is available at ¥500 for the day. A bed for the night is ¥2500.

Getting There & Away
Train On the JR Kamaishi line, it takes an hour to get from Tōno to Hanamaki (which is on the JR Tōhoku line) and an hour to Shin-Hanamaki (which is on the Tōhoku shinkansen line).

Bus There are buses departing four times a day from Kitakami to Kamaishi via Tōno. The trip to Tōno takes 70 minutes.

Getting Around
The sights in Tōno can't be adequately covered on foot and the bus services can be inconvenient. The best method is either to take a taxi or, even better, rent a bicycle for the day (about ¥500). The cycling course map in the tourist brochure is accurate and detailed in its coverage of three different routes.

MORIOKA 盛岡
Morioka (population 235,000) is capital of Iwate-ken, and dates back to the early Edo period (1600-1868), when it was the castle town of the Nambu clan. If you stop off here and pick up a (next to useless) tourist map of Morioka, it will probably have the title *Morioka – Castle Town of Northern Japan*. There's no disputing this. It was a castle town. But take the time to walk out to Iwate-kōen Park, erstwhile site of the castle, and you'll be confronted with an English sign that announces: '...in 1874 the castle build-

ings were sold and torn down'. So much for the castle town of northern Japan, and so much for Morioka.

This is one town in which there's almost nothing to see or do, and is probably best left off a busy itinerary. About all that can be said for it is that, at the terminus of the JR Tōhoku shinkansen line, it makes for a useful staging post for visiting the northern part of Tōhoku, and there are plenty of accommodation options around the city.

Information & Orientation

The Kita Tōhoku Tourist Information counter (☎ 0196-25-2090) is inside the Train Square coffee shop at the south exit of Morioka station on the 2nd floor. There should be at least one English-speaking staff on hand, and there is a good supply of information material. It's open from 8.30 am to 7.30 pm.

The city centre is east of the station, on the other side of the Kitakami-gawa River. Ō-dōri, which heads from this point through Iwate-kōen Park, is the main shopping street. From the station, it only takes around an hour to stroll around town and get a feel for what the place is about – don't expect any surprises.

Iwate-kōen Park   岩手公園

This park, in the centre of town, is really only of interest as a useful point for orientation. It was where Morioka-jō Castle once stood. Today there's nothing left but the moss-clad walls. Also on the grounds is a gravel playground for the kids, a small garden area and the Sakurayama-jinja Shrine – definitely not worth a special mention as far as shrines go.

Morioka Hashimoto Art Museum
盛岡橋本美術館

If you're really pressed for something to do, you might want to take a 30 minute bus journey out to this art museum. It's perched halfway up the slope of Mt Iwate-yama and combines various architectural styles including a magariya (traditional farmhouse). Hashimoto Yaoji (1903-79), a local artist, built the museum according to his own fancy,

rather than using blueprints from an architect. Some of his own sculptures and paintings are on display among the many other exhibits of folk arts & crafts; his taste as a collector included both Western and Japanese works of art. The museum is open from 10 am to 5 pm and admission costs ¥700.

From Morioka station, take an Iwate Kōtsū bus No 12 for the 30 minute ride to the museum (¥240).

Festivals

The Chagu-Chagu Umakko festival, held on 15 June, features a parade of brightly decorated horses through Morioka to Hachiman-gū Shrine.

Places to Stay

Youth Hostels *Morioka Youth Hostel* (☎ 0196-62-2220) is large and a bit bland, but the manager is helpful. A bed for the night is ¥2500. From Morioka station, take a bus from terminal No 11 – not all buses are suitable so check first – and get off after 15 minutes at the Takamatsu-no-ike-guchi stop. It's a three minute walk from here to the hostel.

Ryokan The *Ryokan Kumagai* (☎ 0196-51-3020), a member of the Japanese Inn Group, is in a great little building, even if the husband-and-wife team that run it seem to be asleep with the TV on all day. Singles/doubles start at ¥4500/8000; triples cost from ¥10,000.

Hotels Morioka has no shortage of business hotels. Affordable options close to the station include the *Morioka City Hotel* (☎ 0196-25-2611), which has singles from ¥6500 and doubles from ¥7800, and the *Morioka New City Hotel*, with singles/doubles at ¥5800/7800.

The *Hotel Rich* (☎ 0196-25-2611) is right next to the Kaiun-hashi Bridge just a couple of minutes from the station. Singles range from ¥6500 and doubles from ¥13,000. Next door to the station is the *Hotel Metropolitan Morioka* (☎ 0196-25-1211), an up-market business hotel with singles from ¥7000 to ¥8000 and twins from ¥15,000 to ¥20,000.

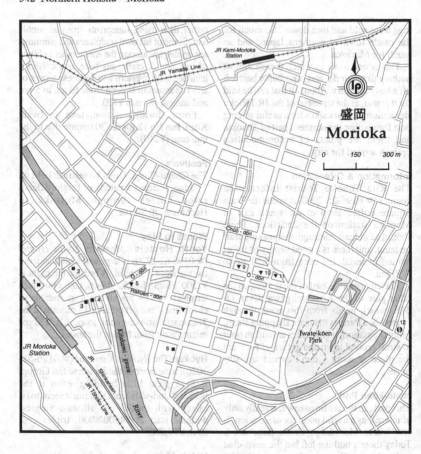

盛岡
Morioka

0   150   300 m

JR Kami-Morioka
Station

JR Yamada Line

Chūō - dōri

O - dōri

O - dōri

Rakuen - dōri

Kitakami-gawa River

Iwate-kōen
Park

JR Morioka
Station

JR Shinkansen

JR Tōhoku Line

PLACES TO STAY

1 Hotel Metropolitan
   Morioka
   ホテルメトロポリタン盛岡
2 Morioka
   New City Hotel
   盛岡ニューシティホテル
3 Morioka
   City Hotel
   盛岡シティホテル
4 Hotel Rich
   ホテルリッチ盛岡
6 Ryokan Kumagai
   熊谷旅館

8 Hotel Royal Morioka
   ホテルロイヤル盛岡

PLACES TO EAT

5 Chinese Restaurant
   中国飯店
7 Gyūdon Restaurant
   牛丼の米沢家
9 Kentucky
   Fried Chicken
   ケンタッキーフライドチキン
10 Mr Donut
   ミスタードーナッツ

11 Genroku-Zushi
   Restaurant
   元禄寿司

OTHER

12 Iwate Bank
   岩手銀行

Places to Eat

If you elect to spend a night or just a lunch time in Morioka, be warned, it's not the kind of place where places to eat just leap out at you. Fast-food freaks should head up to Ō-dōri, where they'll find *Kentucky Fried Chicken*, *McDonald's*, *Mr Donut* and other friends from home. Ō-dōri (and the side streets running off it) is the best place to look for other, more palatable cuisine. There's a good gyūdon (beef with rice) place along here and another close to the Ryokan Kumagai. Also on Ō-dōri is a branch of the excellent revolving sushi chain *Genroku Zushi* – plates cost from ¥120. There are a number of robatayaki and yakitori on the side streets off Ō-dōri, but unless you read Japanese menus they won't be much use to you. Near the Kitakami-gawa River end of Ō-dōri is a reasonable Chinese restaurant. It even has an English sign, and is called *Chinese Restaurant* – imaginative.

Things to Buy

The region around Morioka is famous for the production of Nambu Tetsubin (Nambu Ironware), which includes items such as tea kettles, flower pots and wind chimes. These ironware items make popular souvenirs and are on sale at many shops in the station and in the city centre.

Getting There & Away

From Morioka to Tokyo (Ueno) on the JR Tōhoku shinkansen line, the fastest trains take a mere 2¾ hours. If you are heading further north to Aomori by train, you should change to the JR Tōhoku line for the 2½ hour trip.

Lake Tazawa-ko, just west of Morioka, is reached via the JR Tazawa-ko line. To visit the Hachimantai area, north-west of Morioka, take the JR Hanawa line to either Obuke station or Hachimantai station, then continue by bus. To reach Miyako, on the eastern coast of Tōhoku, take the JR Yamada line.

Getting Around

Buses leave from the station and from the bus terminal, close to Iwate-kōen Park.

MT IWATE-SAN　岩手山

The volcanic peak of Mt Iwate-san is a dominating landmark, north-west of Morioka, and a popular destination for hikers. From Morioka station, you can take a bus north-west to **Amihari Onsen** (¥1240, 65 minutes), which is the start of one of the main trails to the summit. Another popular approach is to take the train north on the JR Tōhoku line to Takizawa station then change to a bus for Yanagisawa where you can join the steep trail to the summit.

MIYAKO　宮古

Miyako is a small city in the centre of the Rikuchū-kaigan National Park, which extends 180 km along the eastern coastline of Tōhoku from Kesennuma in the south to Kuji in the north. This huge coastal park does have some interesting rock formations and seascapes, but it really isn't necessary to devote too much time to them – the boat tours may seem like a good idea, but are often marred by an incessant, full-blast commentary hammering out of loudspeakers.

Information

Miyako tourist information office (☎ 0193-62-3574) is on your right as you exit the station. The staff speak a little English and can provide maps and train timetable details.

Jōdoga-hama Beach　浄土ヶ浜

This is a very attractive beach with white sand, dividing rock formations and a series of walking trails through the forests of pine trees on the steep slopes leading down to the beach.

From the concrete souvenir centre opposite the bus stop, a path leads down to the dock for excursion boats. A 40 minute boat trip (¥1000) to a few rock formations should be enough to introduce you to the loudspeakers and gluttonous seagulls. These seagulls seem to be such a source of amazement to sightseers that local souvenir shops now sell rubber versions of them.

You can skip the boat excursion and escape some of the crowds by leaving the tarmac road beyond the bus stop and climbing up trails into the hills where there are good views across the beach.

There are frequent buses to the beach from Miyako station (¥150, 15 minutes).

A daily excursion boat links Jōdoga-hama Beach with **Ōtanabe**. It stops at a couple of fishing ports and passes several rock formations en route. The trip (¥2900) takes nearly three hours, and is not an outstanding outing.

Places to Stay

Suehiro-kan Youth Hostel (☎ 0193-62-1555) is just three minutes on foot from Miyako station. Walk straight out of the station exit and continue 30 metres to the intersection with the main street, turn right and walk about 20 metres to the hostel, which is on the right-hand side of the street – there's a youth hostel sign next to the door. A bed for the night is ¥2500.

Getting There & Away

Train Morioka is linked with Miyako on the JR Yamada line (2¼ hours), which continues south from Miyako down the coast for another 75 minutes to Kamaishi.

The JR Kita-Rias line runs north from Miyako along the coastline to Kuji in about 1¾ hours – the scenery is mostly obscured by tunnels.

Bus Between Morioka station and Miyako station, there's a fast bus service with hourly departures for the 2¼ hour trip (¥1850). There are several bus services linking Miyako with Kamaishi via the southern coastline of Rikuchū-kaigan National Park.

RYŪSEN-DŌ CAVE 龍泉洞

Close to Iwaizumi (north-west of Miyako), is Ryūsen-dō Cave, one of the three largest stalactite caves in Japan. It contains a huge underground lake (said to be the clearest in the world) which is 120 metres deep.

From Iwaizumi station, it's a 10 minute bus trip to the cave. There are bus services from Morioka station direct to the cave and also buses from Miyako to the cave.

Aomori-ken   青森県

HACHINOHE 八戸

Travellers to Hokkaidō can take the ferry from Hachinohe-kō Port to either Tomakomai or Muroran.

The ferry for Tomakomai leaves three times daily at 8.45 am, 1 and 10 pm. The trip takes about nine hours and the cheapest passenger fare is ¥3900.

The ferry for Muroran departs twice daily at 5.45 am and 5.30 pm. The trip takes about eight hours and the cheapest passenger fare is ¥3900.

To reach the port, take a bus from Hon-Hachinohe station.

MISAWA 三沢

Misawa has a huge contingent of foreigners employed at **Misawa Air Force Base**, which is run by US and Japanese military authorities. Avid plane spotters may want to join a tour of the base to see the latest hardware such as F-16 and P-3 Orion combat planes. The tours take place every Friday afternoon and last 2½ hours. Prior permission is required from base officials – check first with the Sightseeing Section of the Misawa City Office (☎ 0176-53-5111).

Aviation pilgrims will probably also want to trek to **Sabishiro Beach**, just north of the air base, where the US flyers Pangborn and Herndon took off in 1931 and successfully coaxed their doughty monoplane, *Miss Veedol*, through the first nonstop trans-Pacific crossing. The flight took just over 41 hours and the pilots were able to claim the US$25,000 prize offered by the Japanese newspaper, *Asahi Shimbun*. The memories may be a bit faded by now, but an annual 'Miss Veedol' festival is still held there in September.

NOHEJI 野辺地

Noheji is a staging post for travel to the Shimokita-hantō Peninsula and also provides the option of a ferry connection to Hokkaidō.

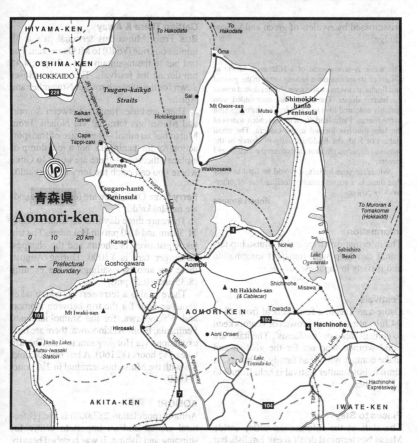

青森県
Aomori-ken

0   10   20 km

HIYAMA-KEN
OSHIMA-KEN
HOKKAIDŌ

Tsugaro-kaikyō Straits

Seikan Tunnel

Cape Tappi-zaki

Miumaya

Tsugaro-hantō Peninsula

Kanagi

Goshogawara

Mt Iwaki-san

Hirosaki

Jūniko Lakes
Mutsu-Iwasaki Station

AKITA-KEN

To Hakodate

To Hakodate

Ōma

Sai

Hotokegaura

Mt Osore-zan

Mutsu

Shimokita-hantō Peninsula

Wakinosawa

Noheji

Lake Ogawarako

Sabishiro Beach

Shichnohe

Misawa

Mt Hakkōda-san (& Cablecar)

AOMORI-KEN

Aomori

Aoni Onsen

Towada

Lake Towada-ko

Hachinohe

Hachinohe Expressway

IWATE-KEN

To Muroran & Tomakomai (Hokkaidō)

Prefectural Boundary

From Noheji station, there are buses (¥1180, 95 minutes) to Mutsu bus terminal which is the best access point for Mt Osore-zan. It might be quicker to do this section by train. From Noheji take the Ōminato line to Shimokita (one hour) and then change to the Kita-Kōtsu line for the six minute journey to Tanabu station (the next stop after Shimokita), which is the station for Mutsu.

There are three daily sailings from Noheji-kō Port to Hakodate (Hokkaidō), departing at 0.35 am, 12.30 pm and 5 pm. The trip takes 4¾ hours and the passenger fare is ¥1400.

MT OSORE-ZAN 恐山

This volcano has been held in awe as a mysterious, sacred place for many centuries – probably long before the founding of the **Entsū-ji Temple** on its slopes in the 9th century. Even the name, Osore, means fear or dread.

As you approach Osore-zan by road, the stench of sulphuric gas intensifies. Rhododendrons are the only plants that can hack it in this environment. After paying ¥300 admission, you can walk through the temple grounds, past the bathhouses and crunch your way along the trails of volcanic rock crisscrossed by rivulets of green and yellow sludge.

The scene is reminiscent of a Hitchcock movie as clouds of steam rise from hissing vents in the ground and flocks of ravens swarm over shrines dotted across the barren slopes. The shrines are surrounded with garishly coloured toys and children's whirligigs spin in the breeze. Paths lead down to the leaden waters of the lake that has formed in the caldera. The small statues of Jizō, the Buddhist deity in charge of the spirits of departed children, are covered with bibs and sweets.

Whatever your beliefs, it would be hard to deny that there is a strong, sinister feeling here of other-worldly power.

Robert Strauss

Information
The information office inside Mutsu bus terminal can help with transport information and leaflets in Japanese.

Festivals
Osore-zan Taisai, a festival held from 20 to 24 July, attracts huge crowds of visitors keen to consult *itako* or 'mediums'. The itako are blind women who act for the visitors and make contact with dead family members. A similar, but smaller festival is held from 9 to 11 October.

Places to Stay
The staff at the information office inside Mutsu bus terminal don't speak English, but they will do their best to help you book accommodation. There are plenty of minshuku in the drab confines of Mutsu and there are more expensive hotels and ryokan at Yagen Onsen, a scenic hot-spring resort in the mountains, about 80 minutes by bus from Mutsu.

Of the two youth hostels on the peninsula – both in remote locations – you might find that the most useful one is *Wakinosawa Youth Hostel* (☎ 0175-44-2341). This hostel is well-placed for an excursion along Hotokegaura, the spectacular western coast of the peninsula, and for the ferry connection to Aomori.

Getting There & Away
Bus From Mutsu bus terminal, it's a 35 minute bus ride (¥640) to Mt Osore-zan. The last bus to the mountain is at 3.20 pm, 4.45 pm during the festivals. The service closes down for the winter between November and April.

There are buses running between Aomori and Mutsu bus terminal via Noheji. From Mutsu bus terminal – the centre of transport action for the peninsula, but a real dump of a place otherwise – there are buses to Ōma, where you can catch the ferry to Hokkaidō.

Ferry From Ōma, there are ferries to Hakodate on Hokkaidō.

There are three daytime departures (6.30, 11.30 am and 4.10 pm) to Hakodate. The trip takes just over 1½ hours and the cheapest passenger fare is ¥1000. During August, there are also two sailings in the evening (8.35 and 10.20 pm).

There is also a ferry service which takes about an hour for the trip between Aomori and Wakinosawa, for the Shimokita-hantō Peninsula. From Wakinosawa, there are boat excursions via Hotokegaura to Sai. The trip takes 1½ hours (¥2160). A bus service links Sai with the Mutsu bus terminal in 2¼ hours (¥1960).

AOMORI 青森
Aomori (population 287,000) is the prefectural capital and an important centre for shipping and fishing. It was bombed heavily during WW II and has since been completely rebuilt – as a result, it's of limited appeal to the passing tourist.

Prior to the opening of the Seikan Tunnel linking Honshū and Hokkaidō, Aomori did booming business with its ferry services to Hokkaidō. Although this no longer applies, Aomori still serves as a useful transport hub for visits to Lake Towada-ko, the scenic region around Mt Hakkōda-san, the Shimokita-hantō and Tsugaru-hantō peninsulas.

Information
There's a tourist information office, where

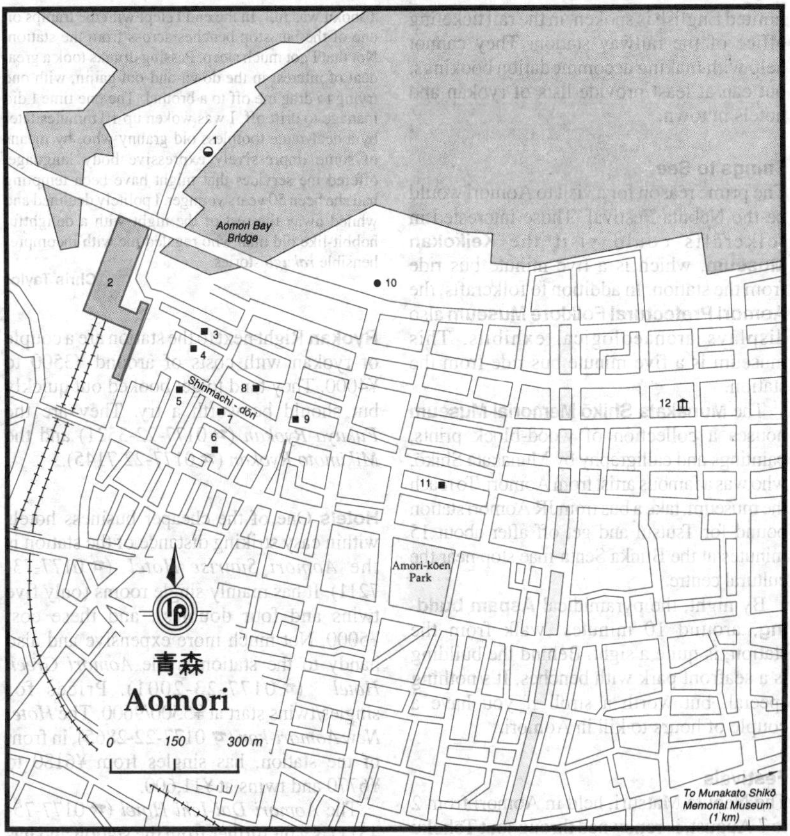

青森

Aomori

Aomori Bay Bridge

Shinmachi-dōri

Amori-kōen Park

0   150   300 m

To Munakata Shikō
Memorial Museum
(1 km)

PLACES TO STAY

3 Fukuya &
   Mikimoto Ryokan
   福屋／御木本旅館
4 Aomori Grand Hotel
   青森グランドホテル
5 Hotel New
   Aomori-kan
   ホテルニュー青森館
6 Aomori Kokusai
   Hotel
   青森国際ホテル

7 Aomori Sunrise Hotel
   青森サンライズホテル
8 Hotel Sunroute
   ホテルサンルート青森
9 Aomori Green Hotel
   青森グリーンホテル
11 Aomori Dai-Ichi Hotel
   青森第一ホテル

OTHER

1 Ferry Terminal
   青森港旅客船ターミナル

2 JR Aomori Station
   J R 青森駅
10 Aspam Building
   アスパムビル
12 Aomori Prefectural
   Museum
   青森県立郷土館

NORTHERN HONSHŪ

limited English is spoken, in the rail ticketing office of the railway station. They cannot help with making accommodation bookings, but can at least provide lists of ryokan and hotels in town.

Things to See

The prime reason for a visit to Aomori would be the Nebuta Festival. Those interested in folkcrafts could visit the **Keikokan Museum**, which is a five minute bus ride from the station. In addition to folkcrafts, the **Aomori Prefectural Folklore Museum** also displays archaeological exhibits. This museum is a five minute bus ride from the station.

The **Munakata Shikō Memorial Museum** houses a collection of wood-block prints, paintings and calligraphy by Munakata Shikō, who was a famous artist from Aomori. To reach the museum, take a bus from JR Aomori station bound for Tsutsui and get off after about 15 minutes at the Bunka Senta-mae stop near the cultural centre.

By night, the pyramidical **Aspam building**, around 10 minutes' walk from the station, is quite a sight. Behind the building is a seafront park with benches. It's nothing special, but worth a stroll if you have a couple of hours to kill in Aomori.

Festivals

The Nebuta Matsuri, held in Aomori from 2 to 7 August, is renowned throughout Tōhoku and Japan for its parades of colossal illuminated floats accompanied by thousands of dancers.

Places to Stay

Aomori is a popular place to break one's journey between Tokyo and Hokkaidō, and consequently in the peak seasons it's not that uncommon for *all* the accommodation in town to be booked out. Book ahead to be sure.

I arrived in Aomori at around 7.30 pm from Hakodate and started ringing around the ryokan...and then the hotels. An hour and a half later I was ringing Hirosaki, then Morioka. Nothing. It seemed as if every hotel in Tōhoku was full. In the end I slept with the tramps on one of the bus stop benches across from the station. Not that I got much sleep. Passing drunks took a great deal of interest in the down-and-out gaijin, with one trying to drag me off to a brothel. The one time I did manage to drift off, I was woken up 10 minutes later by a deaf-mute toothless old granny who, by means of some impressively expressive body language, offered me services that might have been tempting had she been 50 years younger. I politely declined and whiled away the rest of the night with a delightful hobbit-like old man who regaled me with incomprehensible *rakugo* stories.

Chris Taylor

Ryokan Right next to the station are a couple of ryokan with costs of around ¥3500 to ¥4000. They tend to get booked out quickly but should be worth a try. They are the *Fukuya Ryokan* (☎ 0177-22-3521) and the *Mikimoto Ryokan* (☎ 0177-22-7145).

Hotels One of the cheaper business hotels within easy striking distance of the station is the *Aomori Sunrise Hotel* (☎ 0177-73-7211). It has mainly single rooms (only five twins and four doubles), and these cost ¥5000. Not much more expensive and also handy to the station is the *Aomori Green Hotel* (☎ 0177-23-2001). Prices for singles/twins start at ¥5500/9600. The *Hotel New Aomori-kan* (☎ 0177-22-2865), in front of the station, has singles from ¥6180 to ¥6770 and twins at ¥11,600.

The *Aomori Dai-Ichi Hotel* (☎ 0177-75-4311) is a bit further from the station and has singles from ¥5500 to ¥6300 and twins from ¥10,800 to ¥11,800. More up-market options exist in the *Aomori Kokusai Hotel* (☎ 0177-22-4321), where singles/twins cost from ¥7000/13,000, and the *Hotel Sunroute* (☎ 0177-75-2321), where singles/twins cost from ¥6800/14,200.

Places to Eat

Shinmachi-dōri, the main shopping street, runs east from the station and has a couple of fast-food places – a *Mr Donut* and a *Kentucky Fried Chicken*. Other than that, the area around the station has a number of yakitori bars, though nothing outstanding.

Getting There & Away

Air JAS operates frequent flights to Tokyo, Osaka and Sapporo. From Aomori station, it's a 35 minute bus ride to Aomori Airport, just south of the city.

Train Aomori is connected with Hokkaidō by the JR Tsugaru Kaikyō line which runs via the Seikan Tunnel beneath the Tsugaru Straits to Hakodate in 2½ hours.

The JR Tōhoku Honsen line links Aomori with Morioka in just over two hours by limited express. From Morioka, you can zip back to Tokyo in 2½ hours on the shinkansen.

The JR Ōu line runs from Aomori, via Hirosaki, to Akita then continues down to Yamagata and Fukushima. From Akita, the JR Uetsu Honsen line runs down to Niigata.

Bus JR operates a frequent bus service between mid-April and mid-November from Aomori to Lake Towada-ko (¥2470, three hours). One hour out of Aomori, the bus reaches Hakkōda cablecar (ropeway), then continues through a string of hot-spring hamlets to the lake.

For a visit to Mt Osore-zan (Shimokita-hantō Peninsula), you can take a direct bus from Aomori via Noheji to the Mutsu bus terminal in 2¾ hours.

Ferry For a ferry connection to Shimokita-hantō Peninsula, you could take the one hour trip (¥2160) between Aomori and Wakinosawa.

MT HAKKODA-SAN   八甲田山

Just south of Aomori is a scenic region around Mt Hakkōda-san that is popular with hikers, hot-spring enthusiasts and skiers.

A bus service from Aomori reaches Hakkōda cablecar in 70 minutes then continues to Lake Towada-ko. The cablecar whisks you up to the summit of Mt Tamoyachi-yama in nine minutes (¥980 one way, ¥1650 return). From there you can follow a network of hiking trails. Some trails in this area are covered in *Hiking in Japan* by Paul Hunt.

To get there, take a JR bus from Aomori station bound for Lake Towada-ko and get off at the Hakkoda Ropeway-eki bus stop. The trip takes around an hour and costs ¥960.

TSUGARU-HANTŌ PENINSULA
津軽半島

The tip of this peninsula above Aomori can be visited by taking a 1¾ hour ride on the JR Tsugaru line from Aomori station to Miumaya. From there, a bus service (¥630, 45 minutes) follows the road around the coastline to **Cape Tappi-zaki**, which has superb views across the Tsugaru Straits. Just a couple of km east of this cape is the spot where the Seikan Tunnel wends its way underground, leaving the mainland and heading under the sea to Hokkaido.

HIROSAKI   弘前

Founded in the 17th century, the castle town of Hirosaki (population 174,000) developed into one of the leading cultural centres in Tōhoku. With the exception of its dreary modern centre – which can be avoided – it has retained much of its original architecture, including a large portion of its castle area, temple districts and even a few buildings from the Meiji era. Hirosaki is recommended for its pleasing atmosphere and a collection of sights that can be covered in one day at an easy walking pace.

Orientation & Information

The main station is JR Hirosaki station. All bus connections for destinations outside Hirosaki are made at Hirosaki bus terminal, a concrete monster of a building just a few minutes up the street from the JR station. Hirosaki is compact in size and easily covered on foot. To give yourself a quick start – and avoid the drab town centre – take a bus or a taxi from the station for a 15 minute ride to Neputa-mura, where you can start your circuit of the castle and the other sights. The information office at the station can provide an English brochure with a very sketchy map of the town.

Neputa-mura Museum   ねぶた村

This museum is set up as a type of 'village'

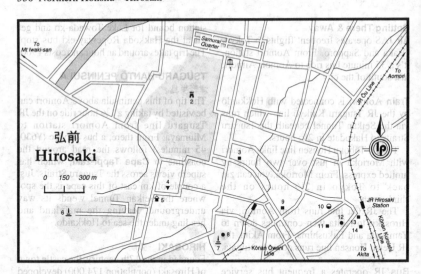

PLACES TO STAY

3   Hirosaki Grand Hotel
    弘前グランドホテル
5   Hirosaki Youth Hostel
    弘前ユースホステル
9   Hotel Hokke
    Club Hirosaki
    ホテル法華クラブ弘前
11 Hirosaki Dai-Ichi
    Hotel
    弘前第一ホテル
13 City Hirosaki Hotel
    シティ弘前ホテル

14 Business Hotel
    Shinjuku
    ビジネスホテル新宿

PLACES TO EAT

4   Yazo-u Sushiya
    Restaurant
    やぞう寿司屋

OTHER

1   Neputa-mura
    Museum
    津軽藩ねぷた村

2   Hirosaki-jō Castle
    弘前城
6   Chōshō-ji Temple
    長勝寺
7   Saishō-in Temple
    最勝院
8   Gojū-no-tō Pagoda
    塔
10 Hirosaki
    Bus Terminal
    弘前バスターミナル
12 Yamauta Live House
    やまうたライブハウス

(mura) which allows visitors to follow a circuit through several sections devoted to different topics. There is a fine display of floats used in the Neputa Festival and a man dutifully pops out every 10 minutes to give a drumming demonstration.

After passing through the garden with its pond full of greedy carp, you enter a crafts section where you can watch the production of pots, kokeshi and kites – or even have a go at making them yourself. On the 2nd floor is a room filled with a mind-boggling variety of figurines. There is also a souvenir shop where you can buy the professional product to compare with your own creation. (See the later section on Things to Buy.)

The museum is open from 9 am to 5 pm (April to mid-November) but closes an hour earlier during the rest of the year. Admission costs ¥500.

Samurai Quarter 津軽藩武家屋敷
Just north of the Neputa-mura Museum, you can walk around the residential district once

reserved for samurai. The traditional layout of the district now contains mostly modern buildings, but a couple of samurai houses have been restored and opened to the public.

Hirosaki-jō Castle   弘前城

Construction of the castle was completed in 1611, but the main donjon burnt down in 1627 after being struck by lightning. It was rebuilt in 1810 and this attractive structure has survived – a relative rarity today, when most of Japan's remaining castle structures are replicas. The castle grounds have been turned into a splendid park that attracts huge crowds for *hanami* (flower viewing) celebrations during the April cherry blossom season. There are over 5000 sakura trees in the park.

Saishō-in Temple   最勝院

About a 15 minute walk south of the castle, this temple is worth a visit to see the Gojū-no-tō Pagoda, a splendid five storeyed example constructed in 1667.

Chōshō-ji Temple   長勝寺

About 20 minutes on foot, west of the pagoda, you come to an avenue – flanked by temples on either side – which leads to Chōshō-ji Temple. After passing through the impressive temple gate, you can continue past a large, 14th century bell to the main hall which dates from the 17th century. Keeping to the left of the hall, you can follow a path through the trees to several timeworn shrines.

This peaceful temple district is a pleasant place to walk in the early morning or late afternoon.

Festivals

From 1 to 7 August, Hirosaki celebrates Neputa Matsuri, a festival famous throughout Japan for its beautifully painted floats which are illuminated from within. These are paraded in the evenings on different routes through the town to the accompaniment of flutes and drums. Like its more rowdy counterpart held in Aomori, this festival attracts thousands of visitors – book accommodation

well in advance if you plan to visit at this time.

Places to Stay

The *Hirosaki Youth Hostel* (☎ 0172-33-7066) is in a good location for the sights, but it's a bit drab. From Hirosaki station, take a bus from bus stop No 3 and get off after about 15 minutes at the Daigaku-byōin stop. Walk straight up the street for five minutes and the hostel is on your left down an alley. Nightly costs are ¥2500.

There are few business hotels in the station area, although this is not a particularly good part of town to be based in. The *City Hirosaki Hotel* (☎ 0172-37-0109) is right in front of the station and has singles from ¥7300 to ¥8000 and twins from ¥13,500 to ¥15,500. The *Business Hotel Shinjuku* (☎ 0172-32-8484) is a smaller, cheaper hotel just to the rear of the City Hirosaki. It has 19 singles at ¥6000 and just three doubles at ¥10,000. Also close by is the *Hirosaki Dai-Ichi Hotel* (☎ 0172-36-7861), where singles range from ¥5800 and twins from ¥10,000.

The *Hirosaki Grand Hotel* (☎ 0172-32-1515) is more centrally located and has singles from ¥5500 to ¥6000 and twins from ¥10,000 to ¥12,000. The *Hotel Hokke Club Hirosaki* (☎ 0172-34-3811) is also in the town centre, 10 minutes on foot from the station, and slightly more expensive at ¥6900 for singles and ¥10,000 to ¥13,000 for twins. It provides the rare luxury of a noon checkout, however.

Places to Eat

Close to the youth hostel is *Yazo-u Sushiya*, a sushi restaurant which does good teishoku (set-menu lunches) at prices starting from ¥1000. The boss and his wife are friendly – the fish is picked up fresh from the market every morning. Walk out of the youth hostel door and up the alley to the main street, then turn right and walk for about five minutes – the restaurant is on the other side of the road.

A good place to sample the local cuisine (mountain vegetables, river fish and so on) is *Kagi-no-Hana*. It has good teishoku from ¥1600.

Entertainment

If you want to combine food and entertainment then why not splurge on a visit to *Yamauta Live House*, a wooden-fronted building just five minutes on foot from the station. The place is run by a family which serves the drinks and food, then picks up musical instruments and launches into local music, known as *tsugaru-jamisen*.

The players lay down a fast rhythm using large plectrums on banjo-like instruments and are accompanied in a wailing, sometimes quavering voice by the well-proportioned lady of the house, encouraged by the audience shouting the Japanese equivalent of 'right on'! It's infectious music – the old lady sitting next to me was bouncing up and down like a steamhammer!

Robert Strauss

There is an extensive menu. If you order one of the teishoku and a couple of beers, you can expect to pay around ¥2500. The music starts around 8 pm.

Things to Buy

Neputa-mura has a shopping section where you can purchase kokeshi (wooden dolls), paper goldfish, tiny figurines, spinning tops that perform nifty stunts and *tako* (kites), a regional art form produced in bold designs and bright colours at prices from around ¥550. Hirosaki is famed for its apples and you can buy cans of unadulterated apple juice here at ¥110 each.

Hirosaki is also known for its exceptionally hard Tsuruga Nuri lacquerware, *kogin* embroidery and wickerwork using *akebi* (vine).

Getting There & Away

Train Hirosaki is connected with Aomori on the JR Ōu line (35 minutes by limited express). On the same line, trains south from Hirosaki to Akita take about 2½ hours by limited express.

Bus Between mid-April and early November, there are up to six buses from Hirosaki bus terminal to Lake Towada-ko (¥2200).

Morioka is linked with Hirosaki by a JR bus service which takes 2¼ hours (¥2880).

From mid-April to late October, there are buses from the Hirosaki bus terminal to Mt Iwaki-san.

AONI ONSEN   青荷温泉

The bus from Hirosaki to Lake Towada-ko climbs through the mountains and passes a series of remote hot-spring hamlets. One is Aoni Onsen (☎ 0172-52-3243), a rustic group of ryokan that prefer oil lamps to electricity and serve wholesome mountain food. To get there you'll have to get off the bus at Aoni Onsen Iriguchi then walk about an hour up the track. Advance reservations are necessary and you should expect to pay around ¥7000 per person with two meals.

The bus makes a short stop at **Taki-no-zawa**, a scenic lookout across the lake, before descending to Nenokuchi beside the lake.

MT IWAKI-SAN   岩木山

Soaring above Hirosaki is the sacred volcano of Iwaki-san, which is a popular climb for both pilgrims and hikers.

From mid-April to late October, there are buses from the Hirosaki bus terminal to Mt Iwaki-san. The trip takes 80 minutes to Hachigōme at the foot of the cablecar below the summit. After a seven minute ride (¥350) on the cablecar, it then takes another 45 minutes to climb to the summit (1625 metres). This route is the shortest and easiest – the youth hostel in Hirosaki has maps showing other climbing routes and times.

An autumn festival known as Oyama-sankei is celebrated on the mountain, usually in September. A colourful procession of local farmers wends its way from **Iwakisan-jinja Shrine** to the summit to complete ancient harvest thanksgiving rites.

KANAGI   金木

North of Hirosaki is Kanagi, a town which attracts thousands of Japanese literary types to the residence of the Tsushima family. Tsushima Shūji (1909-48) was one of Japan's famous writers, better known by his pen name of Dazai Osamu. Dazai's life was short and emotionally turbulent. He made four suicide attempts, on two occasions with women; one with a Ginza barmaid he barely knew and the other with his geisha mistress. At the age of 39 and struggling with tuberculosis, his fifth suicide attempt was successful. He threw himself into a river with his mistress of the time, a writer-cum-hairdresser. She died too.

Dazai is remembered most for his short fiction and essays. Several of his books have been translated into English, the best known titles being *The Setting Sun (Shayō)* and *No Longer Human (Ningen Shikkattu)*.

The Tsushima family residence, known as **Shayōkan** (after the novel mentioned above), has been preserved as a ryokan where guests can stay amidst bizarre furnishings from the Meiji era and ponder the short life span of this cult figure. The residence is a 10 minute walk from Kanagi station.

To reach Kanagi, take the train from either Aomori or Hirosaki to Goshogawara station. From there, it's a 30 minute ride by bus or train (Tsugaru Dentetsu line).

JŪSANKO LAKES 十三湖

If you are passing from Aomori towards Akita down the west coast of Tōhoku, you might like to make a short detour to spend a few hours hiking around this collection of lakes scattered inside a forest park and nod respectfully to the nearby **Nihon Canyon** – not the grandest in terms of size.

From Mutsu-Iwasaki station on the JR Gonō line, buses run five times daily and take about 10 minutes to reach the trailheads for the lakes. This service is stopped between early November and late April.

Akita-ken 秋田県

LAKE TOWADA-KO 十和田湖

This is a large crater lake with impressive scenery. It is rated by Japanese as the top tourist spot in Tōhoku which means you can expect lots of company! The main town on the lake is Yasumiya which is nothing special, just a staging post and centre for boat

trips around the lake. Unfortunately, however, the loudspeaker babble and hazy conditions may spoil the trip for you.

Nenoguchi, a small tourist outpost on the eastern shore of the lake, marks the entrance to the **Oirase Valley**. The 3½ hour hike up this valley to Ishigedo (refreshment centre and bus stop) is the most enjoyable thing to do around the lake. You can, of course, do the hike in the opposite direction. The path winds through thick deciduous forest following the Oirase-kawa River, with its mossy boulders, plunging waterfalls and tumbling tracts of white water. Early morning might be the best time to do the hike, particularly if you go during the peak viewing season in autumn.

The other main tourist spot on the lake, **Yasumiya**, is an accommodation centre and has numerous boat tours of the lake, most of limited interest to foreign visitors. There are four different courses available. Most take an hour and cost ¥1130.

There are frequent buses from mid-April to early November which link the valley with Aomori and Hirosaki. You can take a boat or a bus between Yasumiya and Nenoguchi.

Places to Stay

Hakubutsukan Youth Hostel (0176-75-2002) is tucked away *inside* the Grand Hotel, a few metres from the pier at Yasumiya.

I spent a frustrating quarter of an hour trying to find the hostel, as each time I asked, I was pointed in the direction of the Grand Hotel. Finally it dawned on me that the Grand Hotel has a quota of rooms reserved for hostellers – you just front up at the reception desk and receive the keys to a comfortable room for the price of a bunk bed elsewhere.

The dinner was plentiful, included a cook-your-own stew and was enlivened by a large group of handicapped kids firing food missiles and devoting themselves to disobedience with great gusto – a rare sight. Later that evening, the kids pinched my slippers outside the bathroom, and then screamed around the corridors until midnight when there was a one hour pause for sleep, followed by more bedlam until 5 am when they all started preparing for breakfast! At 8 am, the entire staff of the hotel lined up outside with banners and flags to wave goodbye to their young guests – I also joined the line to wave a cherished goodbye to treasured memories of a sleepless night.
Robert Strauss

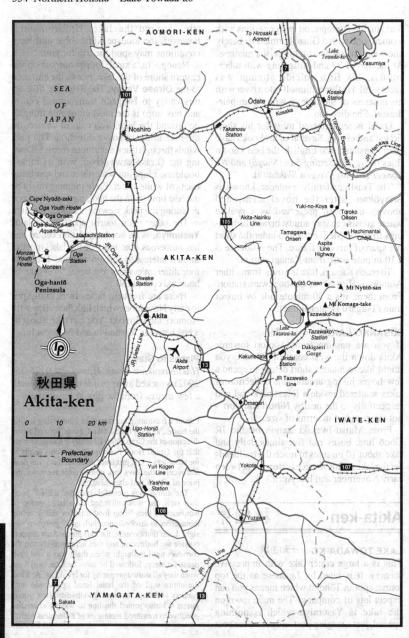

The *Oirase Youth Hostel* (☎ 0176-74-2031) is at Yakeyama, just north of Ishigedo. It charges ¥2500 per person.

There's nothing much to do in Yasumiya. You can walk along the lake shore past the Donald Duck boats, to a beach with a statue officially entitled 'Maidens by the Lake'; though, in the early morning mist or befuddled by a sleepless night, you might think you've run into two pudgy ladies playing 'pat-a-cake'! Some of the smart hotels have restaurants and terrace cafés. One menu offered 'smorked salmon' and 'crub meet salad'.

There are at least four camping grounds around the edge of the lake. The *Nenoguchi Camp Ground* (☎ 0176-75-2503) can take up to 800 campers and is just to the north of the start of the Oirase Valley walk.

The popularity of this area with Japanese tourists means that most of the non-youth hostel or camping accommodation alternatives are very pricey. If you've got the money to burn, a couple of possibilities include the *Towadako Grand Hotel Shinkan* (☎ 0176-75-1111), where per-person costs range from ¥14,000 to ¥20,000 with two meals, and the *Towada Hotel* (☎ 0176-75-2211), where the same deal costs ¥15,000.

Getting There & Away

There are two bus centres in Yasumiya: one for JR buses and one for other services. Both are a couple of minutes on foot from the pier.

Between mid-April and early November, there are up to six buses from Hirosaki bus terminal to Lake Towada-ko – more details are provided in the earlier Hirosaki Getting There & Away section.

Between mid-April and mid-November, JR operates a frequent bus service from Aomori to Lake Towada-ko (¥2470, three hours) – more details are provided in the Getting There & Away section for Aomori.

There are also direct buses from Ōdate (¥1570, two hours) and Morioka (2¼ hours, ¥2380).

If you want to visit the region around Mt Hachimantai, there are buses from Lake Towada-ko to Hachimantai Chōjō bus stop, the main point of access to the summit. This service only operates three times a day from May to late October; the trip takes about 2¾ hours and the ticket costs ¥2260 – a reserved seat costs ¥210 extra. From Hachimantai you can continue east to Morioka by bus or take the bus south to Lake Tazawa-ko.

HACHIMANTAI   八幡平

Further south from Lake Towada-ko, is the mountain plateau region of Hachimantai, which is popular with hikers, skiers and onsen enthusiasts.

The Aspite Line Highway, open from late April to November, runs east to west across the plateau. Transport connections revolve around Hachimantai Chōjō, the main access point and car park for the summit. Although the views are nice, the walks around the ponds on the summit only take an hour or so

Lake Towada-ko 十和田湖

To Aomori

Oirase Youth Hostel

Yakeyama

To Hirosaki

Ishigedo

Nenoguchi Camping Ground

OIRASE VALLEY

Taki-no-zawa

Lake Towada-ko

Nenoguchi

▲ Mt Kura-yama

0 2.5 5 km

Yasumiya

Hakubusukan Youth Hostel & Grand Hotel

To Towada Minami & Hachimantai

To Morioka

and are rather tame. Longer hikes are possible over a couple of days, for example, from nearby **Tōshichi Onsen** to Mt Iwate-san.

West of the summit, the road winds along the Aspite Line Highway past a number of hot-spring resorts before joining Route 341, which leads south to Lake Tazawa-ko and north towards Lake Towada-ko.

Places to Stay & Eat

Yuki-no-Koya (☎ 0186-31-2118) is a member of the Toho network and functions as an alternative youth hostel and mountain lodge – it has been highly recommended by some travellers. Prices start at ¥4300 per person including two excellent meals.

The lodge is on a major bus route, one km from the bus stop at Toroko Onsen which is on Route 341, just north of the turn-off for the Aspite Line Highway to Hachimantai.

Kyoun-sō (☎ 0195-78-2256), a member of the Japanese Inn Group, is at Matsukawa Onsen which is 50 minutes by bus from Obuke station on the JR Hanawa line; or 1¾ hours by bus direct from Morioka JR station. Visitors can use the open-air hot spring. Prices for singles/doubles start at ¥4800/9200 and for triples, from ¥13,200.

Hachimantai Youth Hostel (☎ 0195-78-2031) is east of the summit, 23 minutes by bus to Hachimantai Kankō Hoteru-mae bus stop. If you're coming by bus from Obuke station, the ride to this stop takes about 50 minutes. A bed for the night is ¥2500.

Getting There & Away

From Morioka, there are buses which take about 2¼ hours (¥1230) to Hachimantai Chōjō bus stop – this service only operates between late April and October. Another option is to take the train on the JR Hanawa line from Morioka to Obuke or Hachimantai stations, then change to the bus service.

For bus connections with Lake Towada-ko, see the earlier Getting There & Away section for that lake.

A bus service connects Hachimantai via Tamagawa Onsen with Lake Tazawa-ko in about 2½ hours (¥2060).

TAMAGAWA ONSEN　玉川温泉

This hot-spring resort, 41 km north of Lake Tazawa-ko on Route 341, has a variety of hot springs, baths and treatments. A paved path leads up the ravine through the steam and bubbling vents to open-air baths. Serious soakers who'd like to organise a stay can check rates and availability with the resort office (☎ 0187-49-2352).

LAKE TAZAWA-KO AREA　田沢湖周辺

Tazawa-ko is the deepest lake in Japan and a popular place for Japanese tourists keen on watersports. The foreign traveller may find more enjoyment by using the lake as a staging point for hikes along the trails of Mt Komaga-take and perhaps combining these with a stay in one of the remote hot-spring ryokan scattered around Nyūtō Onsen.

Orientation & Information

The main centre of activity, on the east side of the lake, is known as Tazawako-han – from there it's a 15 minute bus ride south to Tazawako bus terminal, which is next to Tazawako station. A tourist information office stands to your left as you exit the station. You can get leaflets and the staff will help with accommodation bookings.

The bus station at Tazawako-han has an information office where you can sort out timetables and pick up a map of the area – though the map is more useful for its bilingual Japanese/English place names than for its accuracy. Even if they don't want to stay, prospective hikers may want to visit the youth hostel to request a look at the plastic folder with its detailed hiking maps.

Things to Do

The lake offers boat excursions, swimming beaches, row boats and a road around the lake shore which can be followed by bus, car or on a bicycle rented at Tazawako-han. If you're interested in hiking around **Mt Komaga-take** there are many options.

The easiest way to start would be to take

a bus from Lake Tazawa-ko for the 50 minute ride to Komagatake-Hachigōme (Komagatake Eighth Station). From there it takes about an hour to climb up to the summit area where you can choose trails circling several peaks. One trail leads across to **Nyūtō Onsen** where there is another trail climbing up to the peak of Mt Nyūtō-san. Make sure you are properly prepared – see the comment earlier about the map folder in the youth hostel. The bus service operates from June to October only – during July and August there are departures three times a day and during the rest of the year the service only operates on Saturday, Sunday and national holidays.

Hot-spring enthusiasts will want to try some of the places around Nyūtō Onsen which is 40 minutes by bus from Lake Tazawa-ko.

Places to Stay

The staff in the information office at Tazawako-han bus station don't speak much English, but will try to help with accommodation bookings.

Tazawako Youth Hostel (☎ 0187-43-1281) is about five minutes on foot from the bus station at Tazawako-han. If you're arriving by bus, ask to get off at the Kōen Iriguchi bus stop which is virtually opposite the hostel's front door. A bed for the night costs ¥2300, and bicycle rental is available. Close by, in the south of Tazawako-han, is the *Tazawa-ko Camping Ground*.

To really get away from it all, you can stay in one of the hot-spring ryokan around Nyūtō Onsen. There are at least half a dozen to choose from, but *Tsurunoyu Onsen Ryokan* (☎ 0187-46-2814) and *Kuroyu Onsen Ryokan* (☎ 0187-46-2214) are rustic, traditional places with thatched roofs and a variety of open-air baths. If you book basic accommodation only – some guests cook for themselves – you can expect to pay around ¥3000 per person. However, you'd be missing out on well-prepared meals which usually include succulent mountain greens and fresh fish. Prices for accommodation and two meals start around ¥7500. The ryokan close from early November until late April.

Getting There & Away

Train Morioka is connected with Tazawako station by limited express (40 minutes) on the JR Tazawako line. Kakunodate, a short distance south-west of Lake Tazawa-ko, is reached in 20 minutes by local train on the same line. Connections to Akita take about 1½ hours and usually require a change to the JR Ōu line at Omagari.

Bus A bus service connects Lake Tazawa-ko via Tamagawa Onsen with Hachimantai in about 2½ hours (¥2060). From Hachimantai you can then catch a bus north to Lake Towada-ko or east to Morioka. There are also direct buses running from Lake Tazawa-ko to Morioka in 1¾ hours.

From the bus station at Tazawako-han, there's a bus service for the 40 minute ride to Nyūtō Onsen. Ask the driver to let you off at the stop closest to your ryokan but then be prepared to walk a couple of km.

KAKUNODATE 角館

This small town with its well-preserved samurai district and avenues of cherry trees is well worth a visit. You can cover the main sights in a few hours or devote a lazy day to browsing around town. There are half a dozen samurai houses open to the public along a couple of the main streets north-west of Kakunodate station – 15 minutes on foot. The **cherry tree promenade** beside the river is a major tourist attraction when the trees bloom in April.

Just outside Kakunodate, about 25 minutes away by bus or train (Jindai station), is **Dakigaeri Gorge** with a pleasant four km nature trail.

Orientation & Information

JNTO publishes a leaflet entitled *Kakunodate & Lake Tazawa-ko, Akita & Oga Peninsula*, which has a map of Kakunodate and brief details of the sights.

The tourist information office (☎ 0187-54-2995) is on your right as you leave the

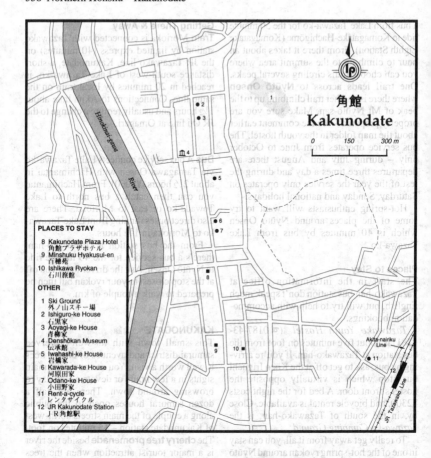

角館
Kakunodate

0   150   300 m

PLACES TO STAY
8 Kakunodate Plaza Hotel
   角館プラザホテル
9 Minshuku Hyakusui-en
   百穂苑
10 Ishikawa Ryokan
   石川旅館

OTHER
1 Ski Ground
   外ノ山スキー場
2 Ishiguro-ke House
   石黒家
3 Aoyagi-ke House
   青柳家
4 Denshōkan Museum
   伝承館
5 Iwahashi-ke House
   岩橋家
6 Kawarada-ke House
   河原田家
7 Odano-ke House
   小田野家
11 Rent-a-cycle
   レンタサイクル
12 JR Kakunodate Station
   J R角館駅

Akita-nairiku
Line

JR Tazawiko Line

station. The staff can help with reservations, lists of minshuku and provide a rough map which is good enough to keep one on the right track.

The town is small and easily covered on foot in three or four hours. Bicycle rental is available at the station.

Kawarada-ke House   河原田家

The interior of the house can be viewed from a path leading through the garden. Next door is the Samurai Shiryōkan, a cramped museum with an interesting assortment of martial equipment. Admission is ¥300 and it's open from 8.30 am to 4.30 pm.

Denshōkan Museum   伝承館

This museum houses exhibits of armour, calligraphy, ceramics and a large section devoted to the tools and products of the cherry-bark craft. In a room to the side is an artisan demonstrating the craft.

The museum is open daily from 9 am to 4.30 pm (April to October) and closes 30 minutes earlier and all day Thursday during the rest of the year. Admission costs ¥300.

Aoyagi-ke House 青柳家

Aoyagi-ke is really a large conglomeration of mini-museums, intriguing in their higgledy-piggledy presentation. One museum focuses on folk art, a treasure house exhibits heirlooms from the Aoyagi family and a 'new-fangled gadget' museum displays all the things that seemed so modern in the Meiji era. A flea market is crammed into the ground floor. In the middle of the grounds, a small restaurant sells decent soba for ¥500. It's curious watching the Japanese tourists ogling an old Bell & Howell cinécamera that was once such a novelty. The tide has long since turned and Japan now leads the world with innovative video equipment. Admission costs ¥500. It's open from 9 am to 5 pm.

Ishiguro-ke House 石黒家

This is a fine example of a samurai house with a sweeping thatched roof and meticulously laid out gardens. The friendly ladies at the admission desk lend foreign visitors a file with English information. The house is open from 9 am to 5 pm and admission costs ¥300.

Festivals

From 7 to 9 September, Kakunodate celebrates the Oyama Bayashi Festival where participants haul floats around and crash into each other.

Places to Stay & Eat

The tourist information office (☎ 0187-54-2995) at the station can help with reservations and provide a list of places to stay.

A long-time favourite with foreign visitors is *Minshuku Hyakusui-en* (☎ 0187-55-5715), which is an old house, 15 minutes on foot from the station. Excellent meals are served around an *irori* (open hearth). The owner believes that beer and sake should flow freely and guests are seated next to each other so there's less isolation and more chat. Prices start around ¥6000 per person without meals or from ¥8000 with two meals. A couple of rooms behind the irori have been turned into a musty, cobwebby museum; admission costs ¥200.

The *Ishikawa Ryokan* (☎ 0187-54-2030) is slightly closer to the station and has per-person costs of around ¥9000 with two meals. The only real business hotel in town is the *Kakunodate Plaza Hotel* (☎ 0187-54-2727), a drab kind of place with singles at ¥4500 and twins at ¥8500.

Things to Buy

Kakunodate is renowned for *kabazaiku*, a craft which uses cherry bark to cover household or decorative items. You can see the production process in the Denshōkan Museum and there are numerous shops selling the finished products. The canny merchants of Kakunodate have got just about everything covered with the bark – from cigarette lighters to geta (sandals) and even tissue boxes for the lady who has everything in her boudoir! The tea caddies are attractive and it's worth spending a bit more on the genuine article made entirely from wood, rather than buying the cheaper version which has an inner core made from tin.

Getting There & Away

Train Trains on the JR Tazawako line connect Kakunodate with Tazawako station (access to Lake Tazawa-ko) in about 20 minutes and continue to Morioka in about 45 minutes. A limited express between Morioka and Kakunodate takes around an hour and costs ¥2520. Ordinary services take just under two hours and cost ¥1090. Connections to Akita take about an hour by limited express (¥2190) and usually require a change to the JR Ōu line at Omagari.

Bus The bus station in Kakunodate is north of the railway station, about 10 minutes on foot. There are six buses daily to Akita – the trip takes 1½ hours (¥1220). From late July to late August, there is an infrequent bus service round Lake Tazawa-ko to Tazawako-han.

AKITA 秋田

Akita (population 302,000) is the prefectural

capital and a large commercial and industrial city. It has few sights of special interest to foreign travellers and is best used as a staging point for visits to Kakunodate, Lake Tazawako or the Oga-hantō Peninsula. The tourist information office at the station provides maps and details for transport and sightseeing.

If you have time to kill, it's just 10 minutes on foot from the station to **Senshū-kōen Park**, which was once the site of Kubota-jō Castle. The park provides the locals with greenery and contains the castle ruins. Also inside the park is **Hirano Masakichi Art Museum**, which houses both Western and Japanese works of art. Entry is ¥410, and it's open from 10 am to 5 pm, closed on Monday.

Festivals
From 4 to 7 August, Akita celebrates the Kantō Matsuri, which is one of the most famous festivals in Tōhoku. During the festival, there's a parade with over 160 men balancing giant poles, hung with illuminated lanterns, on their heads, chins, hips and shoulders. The poles can be 10 metres tall and weigh 60 kg.

Places to Stay
Kohama Ryokan (☎ 0188-32-5739), a member of the Japanese Inn Group, is five minutes on foot from Akita station. Prices for singles/doubles start at ¥4000/7600; triples start from ¥11,400.

Akita is also home to a dull selection of business hotels. For a relatively cheap overnighter close to the station, the *Hotel Hawaii Eki-mae* (☎ 0188-33-1111) has singles (over 300 of them) from ¥4000 to ¥5500, and twins from ¥5500 to ¥9000. You'll probably need to book ahead for the cheaper rooms. The *Akita Terminal Hotel* (☎ 0188-31-2222) is next door to the station, and has singles/twins at ¥7000/13,000.

Places to Eat
The local food specialities include two types of hotpot – *kiritampo* (made with rice cakes and chicken) and *shottsuru* (made from a local fish). Just 15 minutes' walk west of the station is Kawabata-dōri, the main street for eateries, which is packed with hundreds of pubs, restaurants and bars.

Getting There & Away
Air There are flights between Akita and Tokyo, Osaka, Nagoya and Sapporo. Akita's airport (Akita Kūkō) is south of the town, 50 minutes by bus (¥790) from JR Akita station.

Train Akita is linked with Morioka via the JR Tazawako line – two hours by limited express. This line is also useful to visit Kakunodate and Lake Tazawa-ko. The JR Uetsu line connects Akita with Niigata in four hours.

The JR Oga line links Akita with the Oga-hantō Peninsula in about an hour.

Bus A convenient bus service runs from Akita station via Kakunodate to Tazawako station.

1 Hirano Masakichi
   Art Museum
   平野政吉美術館
2 Hotel Hawaii Eki-mae
   ホテルハワイ駅前
3 Akita Terminal Hotel
   秋田ターミナルホテル
4 JR Akita Station
   JR秋田駅
5 Kohama Ryokan
   小浜旅館

秋田
Akita

0   200   400 m

Senshū-kōen
Park

OGA-HANTŌ PENINSULA 男鹿半島

This peninsula juts out for about 20 km and is worth visiting to see the contrasts in its rugged coastlines and grassy slopes. Most of the transport shuts down between November and late April as do the sights. Both local buses and sightseeing buses operate at other times during the year, but the commentary in Japanese can be intrusive.

The **Oga Aquarium** is the largest one in northern Japan and has a huge variety of fishy species on display. Admission costs ¥950 and it's open from 9 am to 4 pm. A 50 minute boat cruise (¥1650) operates along the spectacular coastline between the aquarium and Monzen.

At the northern tip of the peninsula, **Cape Nyūdō-zaki** has wide cliff-top lawns, fine seaviews and, to complete the picture, a striped lighthouse.

Festivals

A curious festival called Namahage is celebrated here on 31 December. The *namahage* are men dressed as fearsome demons complete with a straw cape over the body, a terrifying mask over the face and equipped with a wooden pail and knife. The demons roam around villages and visit houses where there are children and then admonish the youngsters against idleness. The house owners do their bit to welcome the demons and mollify the threats by giving the namahage rice cakes and sake.

This type of festival is common in northern Japan, but the one on this peninsula is particularly famous.

Places to Stay & Eat

Monzen Youth Hostel (☎ 0185-27-2823) is part of a temple and a useful base for exploring the peninsula. From Akita, take the train on the JR Oga line to Oga station, then change to a bus to reach the bus terminus at Monzen; from there it's a seven minute walk to the hostel. A bed for the night is ¥2300.

Oga Youth Hostel (☎ 0185-33-3125) is right next to the sea at Oga Onsen-gō, one of the gateways for visits to the peninsula. A bed for the night is ¥2500 and bicycle rental

is available. From Akita, take the train on the JR Oga line to Hadachi station; then take a 50 minute bus ride to Oga Onsen and get off at the Oga Grand Hoteru-mae stop – the hostel is 200 metres down the street, above the seashore. There is also a direct bus which takes 1¾ hours from Akita station to Oga Onsen.

Most of the other accommodation for the peninsula is also in the same area as Oga Youth Hostel at Oga Onsen-gō. You'll be unlikely to find any bargains, however. Rates are largely in the vicinity of those charged by the *Oga Grand Hotel* (☎ 0185-33-2151) just up the road from the youth hostel: ¥10,000 to ¥20,000 per person with two meals.

Getting There & Away

Trains on the JR Oga line connect Akita with the peninsula in about an hour (¥720). From here, a typical route would involve a bus to Monzen (35 minutes, ¥500), followed by an excursion boat to the Oga Aquarium. There are buses from the aquarium to Oga Onsen (15 minutes, ¥300), at which point you can take a bus back to Akita (two hours, ¥1000). There's nothing stopping you from doing the trip in reverse.

From Hadachi station, one stop before Oga station, there are buses to Oga Onsen, Cape Nyūdō-zaki and Oga Aquarium.

Yamagata-ken 山形県

JNTO publishes a brochure entitled *Yamagata Prefecture*, which gives details on sights and festivals and includes a useful map of the prefecture.

SAKATA 酒田

This large port city (population 100,000) has a couple of interesting sights and is a useful staging point for boat trips on the Mogami-gawa River or an island hop to Tobi-shima Island.

The **Homma Art Museum** is a couple of minutes on foot from the station. In the museum grounds is an impressive residence

AKITA-KEN

SEA
OF
JAPAN

Ou Line

Tobi-shima
Island

Sakata

Mogami-gawa
River

JR Rikuu
Saisen
Line

Zenpō-ji
Temple

Tsuruoka

Kiyokawa Station

Kusanagi Onsen

Mogami-kyō
Gorge

Furukuchi
Station

Shinjō

47

Sanze
Station

Dainichibō Temple

Mt Haguro-san

JR

Chūren-ji Temple

Hachigōme (Eighth Station)

Ōami

Mt Gas-san

Mt Yudono-san

112

48

YAMAGATA-KEN

Tendō

JR Sensan Line

Yamadera

NIIGATA-KEN

Mogami River

Yamagata

MIYAGI-
KEN

Yamagata
Expressway

Kaminoyama
Station

Kurosawa Onsen

Zaō Onsen

Mt Zaō-san

Zaō Bodaira

Imaizumi
Station

JR Shinkansen

Akayu
Station

山形県

Yamagata-ken

0   10   20 km

Yonezawa

121

Sky Valley Toll Road

JR Yonezawa

FUKUSHIMA-KEN

── ·· ── ·· ── Prefectural Boundary

of the Homma family and a delightful rock garden. Entry is ¥600, and the museum is open from 9 am to 4.30 pm, closed on Monday.

The **Domon Ken Memorial Museum** contains the photographs of the renowned Japanese photographer, Domon Ken. Domon Ken believed that photography should be involved with social issues, and his photographs often provide a sensitive insight into the underside of Japanese life in the postwar years. The museum is a 15 minute (¥280) bus ride to the south of town from Sakata station. Get off at the Domon Ken Kinenkan-mae stop. Entry to the museum is ¥410; it's open from 9 am to 4.30 pm, and closed on Monday.

From 15 to 17 February, the *Kuromori Kabuki* festival features performances of kabuki by farmers.

Places to Stay

There's business hotel accommodation in the station area at the *Hotel Alpha One Sakata* (☎ 0234-22-6111), which has singles at ¥4800 to ¥5700 and twins/doubles at ¥9800/9000. The *Sakata Tōkyū Inn* (☎ 0234-26-0109) is more expensive at ¥6300/11,000 for singles/doubles.

Getting There & Away

Sakata is on the JR Uetsu line: 1½ hours by limited express north to Akita or 2½ hours by limited express south to Niigata.

TOBI-SHIMA ISLAND   飛島

Ferries leave from Sakata-kō Port to Tobishima Island, a mere speck of a thing, some 2½ sq km in size. The main attractions are rugged cliffs, sea caves, black-tailed gulls and other feathered friends and, reportedly, excellent fishing. You can also organise boat trips out to smaller islands.

There are over a dozen ryokan and minshuku. The *Sawaguchi Ryokan* (☎ 0234-95-2246) also operates as the island's youth hostel – seven minutes on foot from the ferry pier. Rates vary from ¥2000 to ¥2200 depending on the time of year. Bicycle rental is available.

Ferries run daily from Sakata-kō Port to the island. The trip takes 1½ hours and the passenger fare is ¥2000.

MOGAMI-KYŌ GORGE   最上峡

Boat tours are operated through the Mogami-kyō Gorge on a section of the Mogami-gawa River between Sakata and Shinjō. It's harmless fun complete with a boatman singing a selection of the top 10 local folk hits – recent reports indicate that the boatmen have been extending their vocal prowess to include English. Let it be?

From Sakata, take the train to Furukuchi station on the JR Rikuu-saisen line – local trains take about an hour, though you'll probably have to change trains en route at Amarume. From Furukuchi station, it's eight minutes on foot to the boat dock. The boat trip takes an hour (¥1550) and you arrive at **Kusanagi Onsen** which is a 10 minute bus ride from Kiyokawa station on the JR Rikuu-saisen line. The main season is from April to November; winter boat trips can also be arranged.

TSURUOKA   鶴岡

Tsuruoka (population 99,000) was formerly a castle town and has now developed into a modern city with a couple of sights, but its primary interest is as the main access point for the nearby trio of sacred mountains, known collectively as Dewa Sanzan.

Information

The tourist information office doesn't appear to be geared to foreign visitors, but the staff speak a little English and are happy to dish out leaflets with maps in Japanese or to help with timetables and accommodation.

Chidō Museum   致道館

The Sakai family residence, with its collection of craft items and large garden, forms the nucleus of the intriguing Chidō Museum. The museum also includes two buildings from the Meiji era and a thatched-roof farmhouse. Entry is ¥510, and it's open from 9 am to 4.30 pm daily.

The museum is just west of Tsuruoka-kōen Park, a 10 minute bus ride from the station.

Zenpō-ji Temple 善宝寺

This temple, with its pagoda and large gateway, dates from the 10th century when it was dedicated to the Dragon King, guardian of the seas. The temple lies a few km west of Tsuruoka, about 30 minutes by bus from the station. Take a bus bound for Yunohama and get off at Zempōji bus stop (¥490).

Festivals

In early February, farmers perform in a festival of Kurokawa Nō performances at a special theatre in Kurokawa, which is just south of Tsuruoka. On 15 July, the Dewa Sanzan Hana Matsuri is held on the peak of Mt Haguro-san. Portable shrines are carried to the shrine at the top and flowers presented to visitors.

The Hassaku Festival takes place on Mt Haguro-san from 31 August to 1 September. Yamabushi (mountain priests) perform ancient rites for a bountiful harvest.

The Shōrei Festival, held on Mt Haguro-san on the night of 31 December, features parades of burning torches in an ancient rite to drive away affliction.

Places to Stay & Eat

There are dozens of shukubō at Tōge, a convenient base at the foot of Mt Haguro-san. The tourist information office at the station has lists and can help with reservations. Expect prices to start around ¥5500 per person including two meals – san-sai (mountain greens) and vegetarian temple food are a speciality. The bus terminal at Tōge also has an information office which can help with accommodation.

Tsuruoka Youth Hostel (☎ 0235-73-3205) is not in a convenient location. It's a 15 minute walk from Sanze station, which is three stops south-west of JR Tsuruoka station. A bed for the night is ¥2400, and the hostel is closed from 3 to 12 of June.

Business hotel accommodation around the station includes the Hotel Alpha One (☎ 0235-25-1212), a couple of minutes to

the south-west of the station, with singles from ¥4800 and twins/doubles at ¥9800; the Tsuruoka Washington Hotel (☎ 0235-25-0111), directly in front of the station, with singles/twins from ¥6000/10,000; and the Tokyo Dai-Ichi Hotel Tsuruoka (☎ 0235-24-7611), where singles range from ¥6200 to ¥7500 and twins from ¥11,500 to ¥15,000.

Getting There & Away

Train Tsuruoka is on the JR Uetsu line with connections north to Akita in 1¾ hours by limited express or connections south to Niigata in 2¼ hours by limited express.

Bus Between April and November there is a bus service between Tsuruoka and Yamagata (1¾ hours). Three of the daily departures go via the Yudonosan Hotel, which provides access to Mt Yudono-san. There is also a bus service between Tsuruoka and Sendai which takes 3¾ hours.

Buses to Mt Haguro-san leave from Tsuruoka station and take 35 minutes to reach Haguro bus terminal, in the village of Tōge, then continue for 15 minutes to the terminus at Haguro-sanchō. From July to October, there are a couple of buses which save the sweat of pilgrims by allowing them to travel from this terminus towards the peak of Mt Gas-san, as far as Hachigōme (Eighth Station) in 50 minutes (¥660).

Between June and late October there are infrequent buses direct to Sennin-Zawa on Mt Yudono-san. The trip takes 80 minutes (¥1390).

DEWA SANZAN 出羽三山

Dewa Sanzan (Three Mountains of Dewa), is the collective title for three sacred peaks – Mt Haguro-san, Mt Gas-san and Mt Yudono-san – that have been worshipped for centuries by yamabushi (mountain priests) and followers of the Shugendō sect. (See the Shugendō section under Religion in the Facts about the Country chapter.) During the pilgrimage seasons you can see many pilgrims (equipped with wooden staff, sandals and straw hat) and the occasional yamabushi (equipped with conch shell, check jacket and voluminous white pantaloons) stomping along mountain trails or sitting under icy waterfalls as part of the arduous exercises intended to train both body and spirit. You can also see plenty of older pilgrims happy to pay easy cash and avail themselves of the bus services and other labour-saving devices provided.

For details of access to the individual mountains, refer to Getting There & Away under Tsuruoka.

Mt Haguro-san　羽黒山

This mountain has several attractions and

easy access, thus ensuring a busy flow of visitors. From Tsuruoka station, there are buses to **Tōge**, a village consisting mainly of shukubō, at the base of the mountain. The orthodox approach to the shrine on the summit requires the pilgrim to climb hundreds of steps from here but the less tiring approach is to take the bus to the top. The climb is well worth the trouble and can be done at a very leisurely pace in about 50 minutes – take your time and enjoy the woods.

From the bus terminal at Tōge, walk straight ahead through an entrance gate and

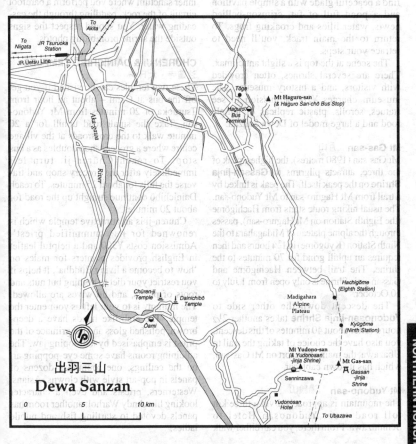

出羽三山
Dewa Sanzan

continue across a bridge into beautiful cryptomeria woods with trees forming a virtual canopy overhead. En route you pass a marvellous, weatherbeaten, five storeyed **pagoda** which dates from the 14th century. Then comes a long slog up hundreds of stone steps arranged in steep sections. Pause halfway at a teahouse for refreshment and a view across the hills to the sea.

As you continue up the steps, you come to a small water font on your right. You can make a pleasant excursion away from the main track by taking the path branching off to the right. At the end of the path you'll find a peaceful glade with a simple pavilion and a pond full of fat, crimson-bellied newts, water lilies and croaking frogs. To return to the main track, you'll need to retrace your steps.

The scene at the top is a slight anticlimax. There are several shrines, often crowded with visitors, and a history museum. The museum charges ¥200 admission to see statues, scrolls, plastic replicas of temple food and a large model of Dewa Sanzan.

Mt Gas-san 月山

Mt Gas-san (1980 metres), the highest peak of the three, attracts pilgrims to **Gassan-jinja Shrine** on the peak itself. The peak is linked by a trail from Mt Haguro-san to Mt Yudono-san. The usual hiking route starts from Hachigōme (the Eighth Station on Mt Haguro-san), passes through the alpine plateau of Midagahara to the Ninth Station (Kyūgōme) in 1¾ hours and then requires an uphill grind for 70 minutes to the shrine. The trail between Hachigōme and Gassan-jinja Shrine is only open from 1 July to 10 October.

The descent down the other side to **Yudonosan-jinja Shrine** takes another 2½ hours. After about 40 minutes of this descent, you also have the choice of taking the trail to Ubazawa, the main ski resort on Mt Gas-san, which has its own cablecar.

Mt Yudono-san 湯殿山

The mountain is approached via a three km toll road from Yudonosan Hotel to Senninzawa. From there, you can either walk uphill for another three km or pay ¥150 to take the convenient bus (a nice little earner for the shrine management) to the shrine approach. The shrine is then a 10 minute hike further up the mountain.

The sacred shrine on this mountain, **Yudonosan-jinja**, is not a building but a large orange rock continuously lapped by water from a hot spring. Admission costs ¥300 – another nice little earner! Take off your shoes and socks, pay the fee, receive your blessing with a type of feather duster, deposit your prayer slip into a nearby channel of water and then proceed into the inner sanctum where you perform a barefoot circuit of the rock, paddling through the cascading water. You should respect the signs outside the shrine prohibiting photos.

CHŪREN-JI & DAINICHIBŌ TEMPLES
注蓮寺・大日坊

These two temples can be visited if you get off the bus at Oami – about an hour from Tsuruoka or 20 minutes from Mt Yudonosan. Take the small road uphill for a 20 minute walk to the crossroads at the village centre where a grocery shop doubles as a bus stop. To reach Chūren-ji, turn left immediately after the grocery shop and traverse the hills for about 25 minutes. To reach Dainichibō continue straight up the road for about 20 minutes.

Chūren-ji is an attractive temple which is renowned for its 'mummified priest'. Admission costs ¥300 and a helpful leaflet in English provides pointers for males on 'how to become a living Buddha'. It helps if you restrict your diet to nothing but nuts and roots of plants, and no wives are allowed. The mummy is to your left as your enter the temple. The crab-like hands have a deep-brown, polished gloss and the grimace of the priest is emphasised by a drooping jaw. The adjoining rooms have some eye-popping art on the ceilings: one room has dozens of panels in pop-art style with clowns, Asians, Westerners, priests and even a character looking like Andy Warhol; another room has panels devoted to startling fish and nubile ladies!

Dainichibō also has its own mummified priest on display. There are infrequent buses to Tsuruoka from the bus stop at the grocery shop.

YAMAGATA 山形

Yamagata (population 249,000) is the prefectural capital and a thriving industrial city. For the foreign traveller, the city is not a sightseeing destination but a useful gateway to the sacred mountains of Dewa Sanzan, Yama-dera Temple and the skiing and hiking region around Zaō Onsen.

Information

The Yamagata tourist information office, in front of Yamagata station, has started an English Hot Line (☎ 0236-31-7865) for foreign travellers. The office is open from 10 am to 6 pm.

Festivals

The Hanagasa Festival, held in Yamagata from 6 to 8 August, is one of Tōhoku's major events. Large crowds of dancers wearing *hanagasa* (straw hats) cavort through the streets in the evenings.

Places to Stay

Yamagata Youth Hostel (☎ 0236-88-3201) is at Kurosawa Onsen, a 25 minute bus ride from Yamagata station. Rates vary seasonally from ¥2300 to ¥2400. It only has 20 beds so it would be wise to book ahead.

If you want to be based in town, there's a good selection of business hotels close to the station. Opposite the station is the *Hotel Yamagata* (☎ 0236-42-2111), which has singles from ¥4200 to ¥5200 and twins at ¥8800. Also close by is the *Green Hotel* (☎ 0236-22-2636), where singles range from ¥5000 to ¥5600 and twins come in at ¥9200; there are also three basic doubles available at ¥5800. The *Hotel Sakaiya* (☎ 0236-32-2311) has similar rates. Next door is the tiny *Business Hotel Akazawa* (☎ 0236-33-1616), which has singles at ¥4400 and doubles from ¥5400 to ¥8800.

Getting There & Away

Air There are flights from Yamagata to Tokyo and Osaka. Buses run from Yamagata to the airport (Yamagata Kūkō) in 40 minutes (¥620).

Train The JR Tōhoku shinkansen line was extended to Yamagata in 1992, making the travel time between Yamagata and Tokyo around 2½ hours. The cost is ¥5670 with a ¥5140 shinkansen surcharge.

The JR Senzan line runs from Yamagata via Yamadera to Sendai in about 70 minutes.

The JR Yonesaka line links Yamagata with Niigata in 3¼ hours by limited express and a change to the JR Uetsu line is usually necessary at Sakamachi.

Tsuruoka is connected with Yamagata via the JR Ōu line, JR Rikuu-saisen line and JR Uetsu line in about three hours – the direct connection is infrequent.

The JR Ōu line runs north from Yamagata along the centre of Tōhoku to Omagari (with

1 Yamagata Municipal Museum 山形市郷土館
2 Business Hotel Akazawa ビジネスホテルあかざわ
3 Hotel Sakaiya ホテルさかいや
4 Yamagata Tōkyū Inn 山形東急ホテル
5 Green Hotel グリーンホテル
6 Hotel Yamagata ホテル山形
7 JR Yamagata Station JR山形駅

山形 Yamagata

0   125   250 m

easy access to the region around Lake Tazawa-ko) in 2½ hours by limited express.

Bus For details of buses to Dewa Sanzan and Tsuruoka, see the section on Getting There & Away under Tsuruoka. There are frequent buses from Yamagata to Zaō Onsen (¥740, 45 minutes), more services to Yama-dera Temple and Sendai and night buses to Tokyo.

MT ZAŌ-SAN 蔵王山

The region around this mountain is very popular with skiers in the winter (the main skiing season is from December to April) and it is a pleasant hiking destination at other times of the year. The main ski resorts are centred around **Zaō Onsen** and **Zaō Bodaira**. There is an extensive network of ropeways and lifts, and night skiing is available until 9 pm.

The local scenic wonders, called *juhyō* or 'ice monsters', are conifers laden with ice and snow which look vaguely monstrous.

Information

Zaō Onsen tourist information office (☎ 0236-94-9328) can help with maps and advice on transport and accommodation.

Places to Stay & Eat

There are plenty of minshuku, pensions and ryokan, but advance reservations are essential if you visit during the peak season or at weekends. You might want to try one of the two minshuku at Zaō Onsen: *Lodge Chitoseya* (☎ 0236-94-9145) or *Yugiri-Sō* (☎ 0236-94-9253), which have prices starting around ¥6000 per person including two meals.

At Zaō Bodaira, you could try *Pension Alm* (☎ 0236-79-2256) or *Pension Ishii* (☎ 0236-79-2772), which have prices starting around ¥8000 per person including two meals.

Getting There & Away

There is a frequent bus service from Yamagata to Zaō Onsen (¥740, 45 minutes). Buses also run to Zaō Onsen from Kaminoyama station, just south of Yamagata.

To cope with demand during the winter – over a million visitors – there is a regular bus service direct from Tokyo.

YAMADERA 山寺

The main attraction is **Yama-dera Temple**, also known as Risshaku-ji Temple, which was founded here in 860 as a branch of the Enryaku-ji Temple near Kyoto. The temple buildings are laid out on wooded slopes. From the Konponchū-dō Hall, a few minutes on foot from the station, you continue past a treasure house and start a steep climb up hundreds of steps through the trees to the Niō-mon Gate. The trail continues a short distance uphill to the Okuno-in (Inner Sanctuary); trails lead off on either side to small shrines and lookout points. The temple is open from 8 am to 5 pm and admission is ¥200. Yamadera tourist information office (☎ 0236-95-2816) provides maps and help with finding accommodation.

Pension Yamadera (☎ 0236-95-2240) is just a one minute walk from the station.

Trains on the JR Senzan line link Yamagata with Yamadera station in 15 minutes and then take another hour to Sendai. There are also direct buses to Yamadera from Yamagata.

YONEZAWA 米沢

During the 17th century, the Uesugi clan built their castle in this town which later developed into a major centre for silk weaving. The town's production of rayon textiles has now eclipsed the previous role of silk.

The town is quiet and unpretentious – worth a brief stopover if you are passing through this part of the prefecture.

Things to See

A 10 minute bus ride from JR Yonezawa station, **Matsugasaki-kōen Park** contains the castle ruins and the Uesugi-jinja Shrine. The shrine's Keishō-den (Treasure House) displays armour and works of art belonging to many generations of the Uesugi family.

Just south of the shrine is the Uesugi Kinenkan (Uesugi Memorial Hall), which is a fine residence from the Meiji era with more relics from the Uesugi family.

The Uesugi-ke Byō Mausoleum is further west from the park, about 15 minutes on foot. A dozen generations of the Uesugi clan are entombed here in a gloomy row of individual mausoleums overshadowed by tall trees.

Places to Stay

There's not much in the way of budget accommodation in Yonezawa, and even most of the most business hotels are a fair trudge from the station. The *Hotel Otowaya* (☎ 0238-22-0124) is in front of the station and is an atmospheric vaguely castle-looking building. Singles range from ¥5800 and there are expensive twins available at ¥17,000. The *Yonezawa Station Hotel* (☎ 0238-21-4111) is a couple of minutes walk from the station, and has singles/twins at ¥4500/8000.

Getting There & Away

Train The JR Ōu line connects Yonezawa with Yamagata in 45 minutes and trains run east from Yonezawa on the same line to Fukushima in about an hour. The JR Yonesaka line links Yonezawa with Niigata via the JR Uetsu line.

Bus Between Yonezawa and Bandai-kōgen (Fukushima Prefecture) there is a bus service along the scenic Sky Valley toll road (¥1590, two hours). This service only operates between late April and late October.

Niigata-ken　新潟県

NIIGATA　新潟

Niigata (population 436,000), the capital of the prefecture, is an important industrial centre and functions as a major transport hub. The city itself has few sights and most foreign visitors use Niigata as a gateway for Sado-ga-shima Island or as a connection with Khabarovsk (Russia) as part of a trip on the Trans-Siberian Railway. See the Trans-Siberian Railway section in the Getting There & Away chapter for more details.

Information

The tourist information office (☎ 025-241-7914), on your left as you exit on the north side of Niigata station, has to win top marks for friendly service. There is usually an English-speaking staff member available to load you with city maps and leaflets and to assist with reservation of accommodation or transport queries – including queries relating to Sado-ga-shima Island.

JNTO publishes a glossy brochure entitled *Japan Niigata Prefecture* which has excellent maps and copious information on sights, transport and regional specialities. Also published by JNTO is a leaflet entitled *Niigata & Sado Island* which has specific information for these two destinations.

For literary companionship you might want to dip into *Yukiguni*, a novel written by the celebrated Japanese writer Kawabata Yasunari. It is available in an English translation under the title *Snow Country* and is the story of an affair between a geisha and a Tokyo dabbler, set in Echigo Yuzawa Onsen, on the southern border of Niigata Prefecture.

Things to See

Sights around town include **Hakusan-jinja Shrine**, where the local deity is worshipped as a god of marriage. The shrine grounds have a fine lotus pond. The **Prefectural Government Memorial Hall** is the only remaining Meiji-era prefectural hall in Japan and was modelled on the British Houses of Parliament, substituting the Shinano-gawa River for the Thames. The Nihon-kai Tower is a bit of a non-event and can be safely skipped.

Dotted around the outskirts of Niigata are several fine residences known as **Gono-no-Yakata** (Landlord Mansions) – highly recommended for those who like peering into noble pads and pottering around their gardens.

These can be visited on a bus tour, but you may prefer to skip the packaged approach which sometimes spoils the atmosphere. The

Sado-ga-shima Island

Ryōtsu

Aikawa

Ogi

To Sado-ga-shima Island

0   10   20 km

新潟県
Niigata-ken

0   15   30 km

Prefectural Boundary

To Hokkaidō

YAMAGATA -KEN

Awa-shima Island

JR Uetsu Line

JR Murakami Station

Iwafune-kō Port

Yonezaka Line

Sakamachi Station

Niigata Airport

Shimizu-en

Shibata

Ishishima-tel House

Itō-tei

Niigata

Suibara

Niitsu

Shibone

Yahiko Station

Sanjō

NIIGATA-KEN

Teradomari

Nagaoka

FUKUSHIMA -KEN

Kashiwazaki

Kawaguchi Station

Meide Station

To Sado-ga-shima Island

Tōkamachi

Jōetsu

Jōetsu Shinkansen

GUNMA -KEN

JR Hokuriku Line

Itoigawa

NAGANO-KEN

To Sado-ga-shima Island

NORTHERN HONSHŪ

tourist information office can provide full details and explain the best means of transport. You can see the lot in a full day, but it might be more rewarding to cover less at a slower pace.

Ito-tei House contains, in its attractive gardens, several farmhouses, individual tea arbours and an art collection displayed in a traditional warehouse (Northern Culture Museum).

Ichishima-tei House is an elegant mansion, built in 1897, with an extensive and relaxing garden. After your visit to this residence, you are close to **Shibata**, a small town which has another pleasant garden known as Shimizu-en.

Festivals

Kite-flyers may be interested in Shirone Takogassen, held in Shirone (about 15 km south of Niigata) for five days in early June. The festival features flying demonstrations of huge kites, kite battles and a kite market.

From 7 to 9 August, Niigata celebrates Niigata Matsuri Festival, the major annual bash with boat parades, thousands of folk dancers, a costume parade and a bumper fireworks display.

Places to Stay

The tourist information office can suggest accommodation to suit most budgets. There are plenty of business hotels around the station. The *Niigata Green Hotel* (☎ 025-246-0341) has singles from ¥4500; the *Hotel Kawai* (☎ 025-241-3391) has similar rates. The *Niigata Tōkyū Inn* (☎ 025-243-0109) has more up-market rooms at ¥7600/13,800 for singles/twins. The *Niigata Dai-Ichi Hotel* has similar standards but is a little cheaper at ¥5600/10,800.

Ryokan Furukawa-tei Honten (☎ 025-062-2013), a member of the Japanese Inn Group, is on the outskirts of Niigata in the town of Suibara. Prices for singles/doubles start at ¥4000/8000; triples cost from ¥12,000. The ryokan is 15 minutes on foot from Suibara station on the JR Uetsu line.

Getting There & Away

Air Niigata has flights to Khabarovsk (Russia) which connect with departures on the Trans-Siberian Railway. The Aeroflot office (☎ 025-244-5935) is a couple of minutes on foot from the station. Flights link Niigata with Ryōtsu on Sado-ga-shima Island in 25 minutes (¥7400). There are also flights to Tokyo, Osaka, Nagoya, Sendai and Sapporo.

Niigata Airport lies north-east of Niigata, 30 minutes by bus from Niigata station.

Train Niigata is connected with Tokyo (Ueno station) by the JR Jōetsu shinkansen line in between one hour 50 minutes and two hours 20 minutes depending on the service.

Travelling north, Niigata is linked via the JR Uetsu line with Tsuruoka (two hours) and Akita (four hours). Travelling south-west on the JR Hokuriku line, it takes four hours to Kanazawa, and direct trains also continue to Kyoto and Osaka. To travel from Niigata to Matsumoto requires a routing via Nagano which takes 3¾ hours.

Bus There are long-distance buses to Tokyo (¥5150, five hours) and a night bus to Kyoto (¥8750, 8¼ hours) and Osaka.

Ferry The Shin-Nihonkai Ferry from Niigata to Otaru (Hokkaidō) is excellent value at ¥5150 for a passenger ticket. The trip takes 18 hours and there are six sailings per week. The appropriate port is Niigata-kō which is 20 minutes by bus from Niigata station.

The ferry to Ryōtsu on Sado-ga-shima Island takes 2½ hours, the cheapest passenger fare is ¥1780 and there are between five and seven departures daily. The hydrofoil (also known as the 'jet foil') zips across in a mere hour, but costs a hefty ¥5460. There are at least five departures daily between April and early November and only two or three daily during the rest of the year.

The appropriate port is Sado Kisen terminal which is 10 minutes (¥160) by bus from the station.

AWA-SHIMA ISLAND　粟島

This is a small island, roughly 21 km in circumference, which has a couple of vil-

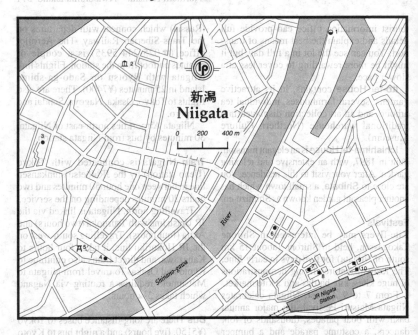

lages offering minshuku accommodation. There are also camping grounds for cyclists and hikers. It's a popular spot for fishing and you can also arrange boat trips.

The ferry departs from Iwafune-kō Port, close to Murakami station (JR Uetsu line), 60 km north-east of Niigata. The ferry trip takes 55 minutes and the cheapest ticket costs ¥1570. There are between three and 10 sailings daily, according to the season.

NAOETSU 直江津
The port town of Naoetsu, 111 km south-west of Niigata, provides ferry and hydrofoil services to Ogi, a small port in the south-west of Sado-ga-shima Island. Further details are provided in the following Sado-ga-shima Island section under Getting There & Away.

SADO-GA-SHIMA ISLAND 佐渡島
In medieval times, this was a place of exile for intellectuals who had lost favour with the government. Among those banished here

were the Emperor Juntoku and Nichiren, the founder of one of the most influential sects of Buddhism in Japan. When gold was discovered near Aikawa in 1601, there was a sudden influx of gold-diggers who were often vagrants shipped from the mainland as prisoners and made to work like slaves. Nowadays, the island relies on fishing, rice farming and tourism.

The two mountain ranges of this island in the south and north are connected by a flat, fertile plain. The best season to visit is between late April and early November – during the winter, the weather can be foul, much of the accommodation is closed and transport is reduced to a minimum.

It is possible to do a two day tour which hits all the sights, but the real attractions of the island are its unhurried pace of life and natural scenery. A minimum of three or four days would be preferable to visit the rocky coastlines and remote fishing villages, or to wander inland to the mountains and their temples.

Information

Sado tourist information office (☎ 0259-52-3163) provides pamphlets, books and advice for foreign visitors. It's open from 1 to 8 pm from Monday to Saturday but is closed on Sunday.

Niigata Kōtsū Information Centre (☎ 0259-27-5164) is in front of the pier at Ryōtsu. They have timetables for tour buses and local buses, but only minimal English is spoken.

The Sado Association publishes a glossy brochure entitled *Japan Sado Island* which has information on sights and transport, and an excellent map. JNTO publishes a leaflet entitled *Niigata & Sado Island*, which has specific information for these two destinations.

The Sado Kisen Ferry Company (☎ 025-245-1234) publishes an annual magazine in English which has excellent timetables, some sightseeing and transport information and a good map. These are available at the ferry terminal offices.

Ryōtsu　両津

This is the main town and tourist resort and a base to pick up information before travelling to more interesting places on the island. At Ryōtsu Ferry Terminal you can stop at the tourist information office for maps and timetables. The business and restaurant part of town is a 10 minute walk north of the terminal. Between April and November, there are daily performances of Ondeko and Okesa at 8.30 pm at the Ryōtsu Kaikan Hall which is in the same area. Admission costs ¥600, but a ¥100 discount is applied if the ticket is bought by guests at a ryokan in the town.

Sawata　佐和田

The town of Sawata, 16 km west of Ryōtsu, is on the main road between Ryōtsu and Aikawa. If you get off the bus at Shimonagaki, about one km east of the town, you can then walk for about 30 minutes up into the hills to **Myōshō-ji Temple**. This temple, set in dilapidated grounds, belongs to the Nichiren sect. From the shrine at the top of the steps, a pleasant path leads through the woods to rice paddies.

Aikawa　相川

From a tiny hamlet, Aikawa developed almost overnight into a boom town when gold was discovered near by in 1601. Gold mining continued to the end of the Edo period and the town once numbered 100,000 inhabitants. The mine was closed in 1867 – now the town's population has dwindled to a few thousand and the main source of income is tourism.

Aikawa is a major transport hub for bus services on the island. There are buses every thirty minutes between around 5 am and 8.30 pm to Ryōtsu (¥670, 55 minutes). The bus terminal is a ramshackle place. From Aikawa bus terminal, you can either walk for 40 minutes up a steep mountain or take a 10 minute ride by taxi or bus to **Sado Kinzan Gold Mine**. The mine finally ceased working in 1989 and one section has been turned into a museum where visitors descend into the chilly depths to see displays of mechanical puppets complete with sound effects to

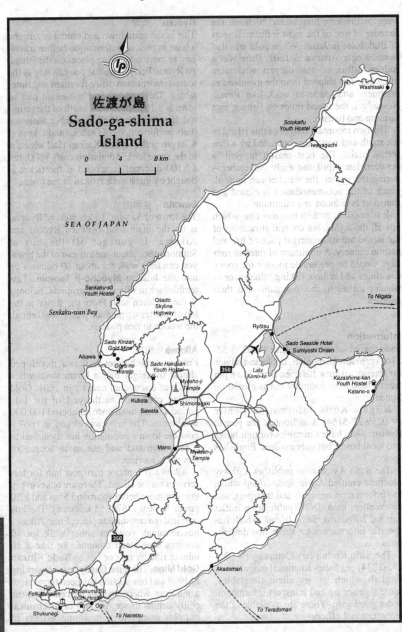

佐渡が島
Sado-ga-shima Island

0   4   8 km

SEA OF JAPAN

Senkaku-sō
Youth Hostel

Osado
Skyline
Highway

Senkaku-wan Bay

Sado Kinzan
Gold Mine

Aikawa

Dōyu no
Wareto

Sado Hakusan
Youth Hostel

Myōshō-ji
Temple

Kubota

Sawata

Shimonagashi

Washisaki

Sotokaifu
Youth Hostel

Iwayaguchi

To Niigata

Ryōtsu

Sado Seaside Hotel
Sumiyoshi Onsen

Lake
Kamo-ko

Kazashima-kan
Youth Hostel

Katano-o

Mano

Myōsen-ji
Temple

350

350

Akadomari

To Teradomari

Ogi
Folk Museam

Oki Sakuma Co
Youth Hostel

Shukunegi   Ogi

To Naoetsu

portray the tough existence led by miners in the past.

The museum annexe has models to explain the process of refining, trading and pressing the gold into coins. One showcase has miniature figures of miners shown splashing out their wages on wine and women. To reach the exit, you have to negotiate your way through an assault course of souvenir shops. Admission costs ¥600. It's open from 8 am to 6 pm. According to the ticket, groups of 300 or more are offered a substantial discount!

A short walk beyond the museum, further up the mountain, is Dōyu-no-Wareto (Sado Gold Mine), the original open-cast mine where you can still see the remains of the workings.

You can return on foot down the mountain road to Aikawa in about 30 minutes. On the way you pass several temples and the **Aikawa Folk Museum** (Kyōdo Hakubutsukan), which has more exhibits from the old mine. Admission costs ¥300 and it is open from 8.30 am to 5 pm.

Senkaku-wan Bay 尖閣湾

This bay, a 20 minute bus ride (¥270) north of Aikawa, is noted for its rock formations, which can be viewed on 40 minute boat excursions (¥650). There's a youth hostel near by – see the later Places to Stay section.

The scenery along the coast road further north is more interesting: fishing villages, racks of drying seaweed, sea mist and calm waters. You can make your own tour around the northern part of the island by taking the local bus (infrequent) from Aikawa to Iwayaguchi, then connecting with the local bus from Iwayaguchi to Ryōtsu. The full trip takes about 3½ hours and costs ¥1970. There's a youth hostel at Iwayaguchi – see Places to Stay.

My trip proceeded at the stately speed of maximum 20 km/h and was virtually a private tour – just the bus driver, myself and a little old lady from Niigata who karate-chopped the ticket machine, took swigs from a bottle in a paper bag and fast-talked the amiable

driver (a keen botanist) into stopping the bus at frequent intervals to point out plants of interest. After she got off the bus, the rest of the trip was like riding in a chauffeur-driven bus!

Robert Strauss

Mano 真野

Mano was the provincial capital and cultural centre of the island from early times until the 14th century. There are several temples in the vicinity of Mano. **Myōsen-ji Temple**, five km east of the town, lies in an attractive forest setting with a five storeyed pagoda. It was founded by Tamemori Endo, a samurai who became a follower of Nichiren.

There are local bus lines linking Mano with Ryōtsu (40 minutes), Sawata (15 minutes) and Ogi (one hour).

Akadomari 赤泊

This port provides an alternative ferry connection with Niigata. A local bus line links Akadomari with Ogi (35 minutes) and Sakata (70 minutes).

Ogi 小木

Ogi is a drowsy port which has been kept in business by the ferry connection with Naoetsu. The big tourist attraction, next to the ferry terminal, is a ride in a *taraibune* or 'tub boat' which is poled by a lady in traditional fisherwoman's costume – well, nobody wears it nowadays, it's just for the photos. The tub boats were once commonly used as a means to collect seaweed and shellfish but are no longer a common sight. A 15 minute spin in the tub costs ¥400 – you can fit in several passengers and the lady in charge may let you make a fool of yourself trying to steer.

On the hill overlooking the harbour there is a park with some fine views across the sea; the park is circled by an overgrown path.

Shukunegi 宿根木

This is a tiny fishing village with a drowsy temple, a few weather-beaten rows of wooden houses and a cove where a couple of old tubs moulder on the harbour. On the hill, just at the entrance to the village, you should definitely pop in to see the quirky **Ogi Folk Museum** (Ogi Minzoku Hakubutsukan) with its higgledy-piggledy (and dusty) collection of dolls, clocks, tools, ceramics, old TVs, radios, projectors and even thermos flasks! The hall at the back contains fishing paraphernalia, snapshots of countless generations of the village community – from babes in arms to aged pensioners – and a collection of postcards depicting the island belles of past decades as well as the island's sights – before the tourist boom. The museum is open from 8 am to 4 pm and admission costs ¥300.

There is an infrequent bus service running west from Ogi via Shukunegi to the museum, though since it's only four km, you could also walk or rent a bicycle in Ogi.

Festivals
The annual magazine published in English by the Sado Kisen Ferry Company has a detailed list and brief descriptions for many of the festivals on the island. There seem to be festivals happening almost every week although some seem engineered for tourists, rather than locals. The island is famed for its *okesa* (folk dances), *ondeko* (demon drum dances) and *tsuburosashi* (a phallic dance with two goddesses). The following are a brief selection.

Sado Geino Matsuri
   28 to 29 April. The festival is held in Mano with ondeko, folk songs and performances of tsuburosashi.
Kozan Festival
   25 to 27 July. The festival is celebrated in Aikawa with okesa, ondeko and fireworks.
Ogi Matsuri
   28 to 30 August. Celebrated in Ogi, this festival features lion dances, folk songs and tub-boat frolics.
Mano Matsuri
   15 to 16 October. This festival takes place in Mano and includes performances of local art forms and lion dances.

As a special favour to tourists, between April and November there are nightly performances of okesa and ondeko dances in Ryōtsu, Aikawa, Ogi and Sawata. The tourist information office in Sawata has exact details.

Places to Stay & Eat
The island is well supplied with minshuku, ryokan, kokuminshukusha, hotels and youth hostels. There are several camping grounds as well. You can get help with booking accommodation from the tourist information offices in the towns and villages described earlier as well as from the Sado Kisen Ferry Company offices at the ferry terminals. The following are a few suggestions in the budget and middle-range category.

Senkaku-sō Youth Hostel (☎ 0259-75-2011) is in the touristy area of Senkaku-wan Bay, close to Aikawa. If you like, you can upgrade your accommodation since this youth hostel is part of a ryokan. It's only open from April to the end of October. From Aikawa, take the Kaifu-sen bus line for the 20 minute ride north to the Himezu bus stop.

Sado Hakusan Youth Hostel (☎ 0259-52-4422) is only open from March to October. Take the bus from Ryōtsu bound for Aikawa, but get off after about 40 minutes at Kubota (about two km west of Sawata). Then it's a 25 minute walk up the side street virtually opposite the bus stop. If you phone the hostel, they'll fetch you at the bus stop. Guests can use a nearby hot spring.

Sotokaifu Youth Hostel (☎ 0259-78-2911) is in a tiny fishing hamlet in the middle of nowhere. Bicycles and scooters are available for rental so you might want to explore by this method of transport. To get there from Ryōtsu, take the Sotokaifu-sen bus line which runs via Washisaki, continues round the northern tip of the island and deposits you at the Iwaya-guchi bus stop – in front of the hostel door. This service operates two or three times a day (¥1070, 1¾ hours) – late April to late November only. A separate bus service continues down the coast to Aikawa in an hour.

Ogi Sakuma-sō Youth Hostel (☎ 0259-86-2565) is 20 minutes on foot from Ogi, in the far south of the island. It is only open between March and November. Guests can use a nearby hot spring.

Kazashima-kan Youth Hostel (☎ 0259-29-2003) is on the south-eastern side of the island. From Ryōtsu, take the Higashi Kaigan-sen bus line to Katano-o and get off after 45 minutes at the Yūsu-hosuteru-mae bus stop.

Sado Seaside Hotel (☎ 0259-27-7211) is at Sumiyoshi Onsen about two km (25 minutes on foot) from Ryōtsu Port. A free shuttle service is available to and from the port, and for the dance and music performances in Ryōtsu in the evening. The hotel has its own hot-spring bath which you can use any time. Seafood dinners are a speciality and good value with prices from ¥1800 to ¥2800. Per-person costs with meals are up around ¥10,000, but it is possible to get significantly cheaper rates if you do without the meals.

The island also has a large number of minshuku with per-person costs of around ¥5800 with meals. Reservations can be made at the Sado Kisen ship company in Niigata or at the Ryōtsu information counter.

Things to Buy
There are shops all over the island selling Mumyoi-yaki, pottery made from the clay rich in iron-oxides from the mines of Aikawa. Culinary souvenirs include Marudai miso and many of the things you may see hanging up to dry on the seashore – wakame seaweed and ika (dried cuttlefish). For the latter, the best advice is to keep chewing, you'll get there in the end.

Getting There & Away
Air Flights link Ryōtsu on Sado-ga-shima Island with Niigata in 25 minutes (¥7400).

Ferry The ferry from Ryōtsu on Sado-ga-shima Island to Niigata takes 2½ hours and the cheapest passenger fare is ¥1780; there are between five and seven departures daily. The hydrofoil (also known as the 'jet foil') zips across in a mere hour, but costs a hefty ¥5460. There are at least five departures daily between April and early November; just two or three during the rest of the year.

From Naoetsu (south-west of Niigata),

there are ferry and hydrofoil services to Ogi, a small port in the south-west of Sado-ga-shima Island. Between April and late November, there are four or more ferry departures daily; during the rest of the year the service is considerably reduced. The cheapest passenger fare is ¥1960 and the trip takes 2½ hours. The hydrofoil operates twice daily from April to late November and the ticket costs ¥5460. From Naoetsu station, it's a 10 minute bus ride (¥130) to the port.

From Teradomari (a short distance below Niigata), there is a ferry service to Akadomari, on the southern edge of Sado-ga-shima Island. The cheapest passenger ticket is ¥1220 and the trip takes two hours. Between April and late September, there are two or three departures daily; only one departure daily during the rest of the year.

Getting Around
Bus Local buses are fine on the main routes – between Ryōtsu and Aikawa, for example. However, services to other parts of the island are often restricted to two or three a day. If you plan to make extended use of local buses, a vital piece of paper is the Sado-ga-shima Basu Jikokuhyō, the island's bus timetable (in Japanese) which is available from bus terminals and tourist information offices. The timetable has a map showing the numbered bus routes for you to match up to the individual timetables.

Taxi A group of travellers could put together their idea of an itinerary, then approach the Sado Hired Car Service Association (☎ 0259-27-6962) in Ryōtsu. The *Sado Kisen* magazine has a list of sample itineraries ranging from ¥10,820 for a 2½ hour tour, to ¥40,690 for the 9½ hour blockbuster circuit.

Car This might make sense for a small group since it frees the visitor from the hectic schedules of tour buses and the infrequency of local buses. Sado Kisen Ferry Company in Ryōtsu provides car rental (☎ 0259-27-5195) at prices from ¥9790 for 24 hours. See the company's magazine for more details.

Bicycle This is quite feasible and an enjoyable way to potter off the beaten track. The tourist information offices can provide details for bicycle rental in Ryōtsu, Aikawa and Ogi. Sotokaifu Youth Hostel has bicycles and scooters available for hire.

Hitching This is not a very reliable method because most drivers are going short distances and traffic away from the main roads can be very limited. Time and patience are required.

Tours *Teiki kankō* (sightseeing buses) are available in neatly packaged itineraries –

ultra-convenient, sanitised, hectic and brassy. Tickets and departures are arranged at Sado Kisen offices or tourist information offices where you can pick up the appropriate *teiki kankō jikokuhyō* (sightseeing bus timetable). The one itinerary that merits a recommendation is the Skyline Course because it follows the spectacular Osado Skyline Highway from Ryōtsu to Aikawa – there is no local transport alternative for this particular highway. The trip takes about three hours and costs ¥3700. The 'Free Pass' costs ¥5150 and is valid for travel on all the regular sightseeing buses for two days.

Hokkaidō (population 5,644,000) is the northernmost and second largest of Japan's islands. Although it accounts for over one fifth of Japan's land area, only 5% of the Japanese population lives there. The real beauty of the place lies in the unpopulated wilderness regions where – in contrast to Honshū – there are no cultural monuments, but superb opportunities for outdoor activities such as hiking, camping, skiing, relaxing in hot springs and observing wildlife.

HISTORY & DEVELOPMENT
Until the Edo period, Hokkaidō, or Ezo as it was known prior to the Meiji Restoration, was a backwater in the currents of Japanese history. The island was largely left to its indigenous inhabitants, notably the Ainu, a people who are postulated by certain experts to be of Siberian origin, though such theories are still subject to debate.

In the 16th century, the Matsumae clan arrived from Honshū, establishing a foothold on the south-western tip of the island. The rest of Hokkaidō continued to be the domain of the Ainu, who lived a hunting and gathering existence.

The Meiji Restoration of 1868 saw a major policy shift in Japan's approach to its northernmost island. A colonial office was established to encourage settlers from other parts of Japan, and the new name Hokkaidō (literally the 'North Sea Road') was formally adopted. Foreign advisers were called in to help with the development of the island: Sapporo's grid-like layout was planned by a US architect, and US agricultural experts also introduced farm architecture which has endured as a characteristic of Hokkaidō's landscape.

Hokkaidō's sparsely populated landmass has made it an important agricultural base for Japan. The main crop is rice, but grain, vegetable and dairy farming are also crucial to the island's economy. The island is also an important base for forestry, pulp and paper industries, as well as fishing and mining.

One thing to look out for as you explore Hokkaidō is the increasing number of abandoned farmsteads. As farming proves less profitable, communities fracture and individuals move into the urban centres looking for work. Tourism has become a major source of income, particularly for remote communities that would otherwise find it hard to make a living from, for example, fishing or agriculture.

WHEN TO GO
Hokkaidō attracts hikers and campers between May and October – the peak months for tourism are June, July and August. While transport services are more frequent and extensive at this time of the year, it can also be difficult to escape the crowds and sometimes to find accommodation – a tent is a good idea. However, it's often possible to escape crowds and enjoy the last of the autumn weather from October to early November. After that, winter sets in for five months of heavy snowfalls and subzero temperatures. Skiers then form the bulk of the tourists, many of whom head for the ski resorts of Niseko or Furano, though some skip skiing to see Sapporo's Ice Festival in February. Whatever time of year you visit, don't underestimate the weather – take proper clothing to stay warm and dry.

PLANNING YOUR ITINERARY
Even if you only want to skim the surface of Hokkaidō, the absolute minimum would be a week. There is no pressing need to spend more than a day in Sapporo – to pick up information, organise transport, make bookings and change money – before heading for remoter parts. If you cut out a visit to Rishiri-Rebun-Sarobetsu National Park, you could visit the other four national parks at a comfortable pace in a fortnight. If you include this park, you'll need an extra week. It would

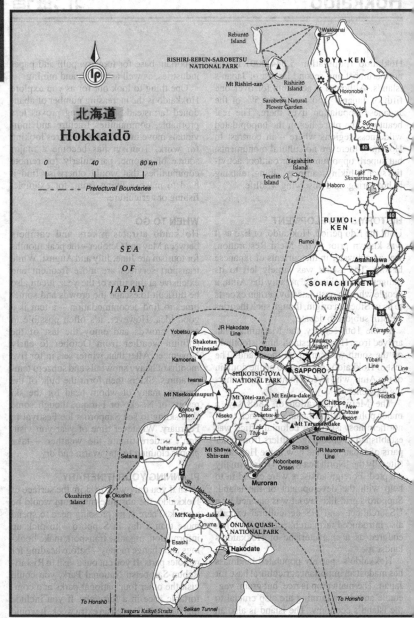

北海道

Hokkaidō

0 40 80 km

- - - - - Prefectural Boundaries

SEA

OF

JAPAN

Rebuntō
Island

RISHIRI-REBUN-SAROBETSU
NATIONAL PARK

Mt Rishiri-zan

Rishiritō
Island

Sarobetsu Natural
Flower Garden

Wakkanai

SOYA-KEN

Horonobe

Sōya

40
Line

Yagishiritō
Island

Teuritō
Island

Haboro

Lake
Shumarinai-ko

RUMOI-
KEN

Rumoi

Asahikawa

SORACHI-KEN

Takikawa

12

38
Line

JR
Furano
Line

Yobetsu

Shakotan
Peninsula

JR Hakodate
Line

Kamoenai

Otaru

Iwanai

Mt Nisekoannupuri

SHIKOTSU-TOYA
NATIONAL PARK

Kenbu
Onsen

Niseko

Mt Yōtei-zan

Oshamambe

Mt Shōwa
Shin-zan

Lake
Shikotsu-ko

SAPPORO

Mt Eniwa-dake

Okadama
Airport

New
Chitose
Airport

Lake
Tōya-ko

Mt Tarumaedake

Chitose

Yūbari
Line

Sekishō
Line

Line

Hidaka

Shiraoi

Noboribetsu
Onsen

Tomakomai

JR Muroran
Line

Setana

Muroran

Okushiritō
Island

Okushiri

JR
Hakodate
Line

Mt Komaga-dake

ONUMA QUASI-
NATIONAL PARK

Ōnuma

Esashi

JR
Esashi
Line

Hakodate

To Honshū

Tsugaru Kaikyō Straits

Selkan Tunnel

To Honshū

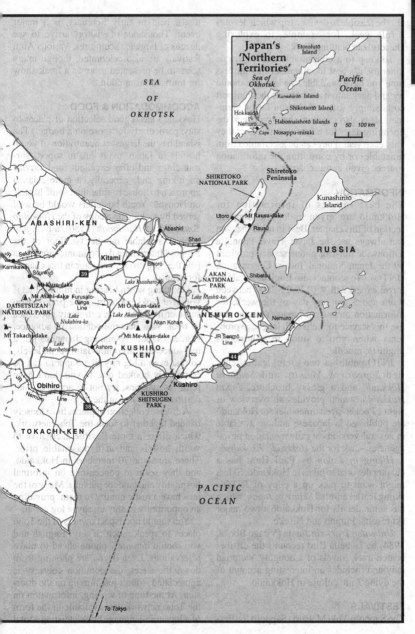

SEA

OF

OKHOTSK

Japan's
'Northern
Territories'

Etorofutō
Island

Sea of
Okhotsk

Pacific
Ocean

Kunashiritō Island

Shikotantō Island

Hokkaidō

Nemuro

Habomaishotō Islands

Cape Nosappu-misaki

0   50   100 km

SHIRETOKO
NATIONAL PARK

Shiretoko
Peninsula

Kunashiritō
Island

Utoro

Mt Rausu-dake

Rausu

Abashiri

ABASHIRI-KEN

Shari

RUSSIA

JR

Sekihoku Line

Kamikawa

Sōunkyō

Kitami

Bihoro

39

Mt Kuro-dake

Mt Asahi-dake

DAISETSUZAN
NATIONAL PARK

Lake Kussharo-ko

Furusato-
Ginga Line

Mt Ō-Akan-dake

Lake Akan-ko

Lake
Nukabira-ko

Mt Tokachi-dake

Lake
Shikaribetsu-ko

Akan Kohan

Mt Me-Akan-dake

AKAN
NATIONAL
PARK

Lake Mashū-ko

Shibetsu

Teshikaga

KUSHIRO-
KEN

NEMURO-KEN

Nemuro

JR Senmō
Line

44

Ashoro

Obihiro

Nemuro Line

38

TOKACHI-KEN

Kushiro

KUSHIRO
SHITSUGEN
PARK

PACIFIC
OCEAN

To Tokyo

also be feasible to devise a trip which devotes a full week, for example, to exploring Daisetsuzan National Park.

To keep to a comfortable and enjoyable itinerary, it's best to remember that the less time you have available, the less you should try and pack into it – otherwise the transport costs simply soar and the fun factor plummets. It is also essential that you check the operating dates for transport services as they vary each year. They can be ascertained from timetables or by consulting the information sources given in this chapter.

INFORMATION

The best sources of information for Hokkaidō are given under the Sapporo section of this chapter. Bear in mind that you can always use the Japan Travel-Phone, a nationwide toll-free phone service provided by the Japan National Tourist Organisation (JNTO). To contact an English-speaking travel expert call ☎ 0120-22-2800 between 9 am and 5 pm, any day of the week, for information on eastern Japan. You can also use this service for help with language problems when you're stuck in a hopeless linguistic muddle.

JNTO publishes two useful leaflets entitled *Sapporo & Vicinity* and *Southern Hokkaidō* and a glossy brochure, *Japan Hokkaidō*, which provides an overview of sights. Pocket-sized timetables for Hokkaidō are published in Japanese and are available in several versions at railway station newsagencies – ask for the *Hokkaidō Jikokuhyō*.

Hiking in Japan by Paul Hunt has a chapter devoted to hikes in Hokkaidō. Skiers might want to pick up a copy of JNTO's skiing leaflet entitled *Skiing in Japan*, which has some details for Hokkaidō's two major ski resorts: Furano and Niseko.

Unbeaten Tracks in Japan (Virago Books, 1984) by Isabella Bird recounts the off-the-beaten-track travels of a doughty Victorian lady and includes an interesting account of the dying Ainu culture in Hokkaidō.

FESTIVALS

The Sapporo Yuki Matsuri (Sapporo Ice Fes-

tival), held in early February, is a major event. Thousands of visitors arrive to see dozens of large ice sculptures. Various Ainu festivals are also celebrated, though many seem to be presented more as a freak show for tourist consumption.

ACCOMMODATION & FOOD

Hokkaidō has a good selection of places to stay, particularly for those on a budget. The island has the largest concentration of youth hostels in Japan, many are in superb surroundings and offer excellent food, advice on hiking and, generally, a more relaxed approach to house routine than some hostels on Honshū. Youth hostellers would be well served by picking up a copy of the *Hokkaidō Youth Hostel Handbook* (¥150), a bilingual booklet available on the 1st floor of the Sapporo International Communication Plaza (see the Sapporo section later in this chapter for details).

One thing worth bearing in mind is that if you visit Hokkaidō during the peak-season summer months it's an extremely good idea to book your accommodation in advance. Hordes of holiday-making Japanese put a real squeeze on accommodation at all levels, so that even a big city like Sapporo can be completely booked out. If you don't have prior reservations, try not to arrive at your destination too late in the day.

A diverse collection of places have loosely banded together to form the Toho network, which offers a more flexible alternative to youth hostels and at a reasonable price. There are some 70 members in Hokkaidō, and they seem to concentrate on informal hospitality and outdoor pursuits. Many of the inns have a rustic quality to them, providing an opportunity to stay in, say, a log cabin.

You should not expect owners of the Toho places to speak much (if any) English and you should *definitely* phone ahead to make reservations. Even if you are phoning from down the street, the common courtesy is appreciated – don't just turn up on the doorstep. At the time of writing, information on the Toho network was available in the form of a Japanese-language booklet listing a total

Japan's 'Northern Territories'

The collapse of the Soviet Union has no doubt been a boon for cartographers, suddenly presenting them with the lucrative task of redrawing the independent fragments of ex-Soviet territory. One Soviet possession they have not had to worry about, however, is a group of islands formerly belonging to Japan and occupied by the Soviet Union on 3 September 1945. The disputed islands are Kunashiri-tō, Etorofu-tō, Shikotan-tō and Habamaisho-tō, and their control gave the Soviet Union – and today, Russia – access to one of the richest fishing grounds in the world.

Arguably what the Russians need today – much more than fish – is Japanese investment. There's no doubt that conceding the islands to their former custodians would lead to a grateful flood of Japanese yen. Unfortunately, realities have been obscured by the issue of national pride and, no matter what the private feelings of Russian leaders are regarding the islands, the official line is one of no compromises. Boris Yeltsin has repeatedly cancelled trips to Tokyo, apparently because there is nothing to discuss. Japan refuses to pledge economic assistance until the islands are returned, and Russia vows that the islands will remain Russian.

In Japan, emotions run hottest in Hokkaidō, hardly surprising given that the nearest of the disputed islands is a mere four km off Cape Nosappu-misaki, just east of the town of Nemura. Hokkaidō is the scene of annual rallies and signature collecting drives. Neither is likely to cut any ice with Russia, where economic malaise is generating widespread nationalist fervour. ■

of 82 inns. Plans are afoot to produce an English version of the book, and it should be available by the time you have this book in your hands. See the Sapporo section for details on where to get the Toho network book.

Many of the youth hostels specialise in slap-up dinners which provide excellent value and include dishes such as 'Jingis Khan Hotpot' – a stew of lamb and vegetables cooked at the table.

GETTING THERE & AWAY

Air

There are numerous flights operated daily by Japan Airlines (JAL), All Nippon Airways (ANA) and Japan Air Systems (JAS) between Hokkaidō and the rest of Japan; a network of internal flights also makes it easier for those in a hurry to bridge the large distances on Hokkaidō.

Train

Two of the fastest rail connections from Tokyo are the Hokutōsei Express, which is a direct sleeper to Sapporo in 16 hours, and a combination of the shinkansen to Morioka followed by a limited express (tokkyū) via Aomori and Hakodate to Sapporo in 11 hours.

The trains cross from Honshū to Hokkaidō

via the Seikan Tunnel, the world's longest undersea tunnel, which is an eerie 53.85 km in length. Travellers who can't stand the idea of being underground, and under the sea, for so long can take a ferry from Aomori.

JR offers special round-trip deals to Hokkaidō which include a return ticket plus unlimited travel on JR buses and trains while you're there. For example, a 10 day pass of this kind commencing in Tokyo costs ¥23,000 – there are more permutations available. For details of these discount tickets check with travel agencies, JR Travel Service Centres (found in major JR stations – see the Tickets & Reservations section in the Getting Around chapter), or call the JR East-Infoline in Tokyo on ☎ 3423-0111. The JR East-Infoline service is available from 10 am to 6 pm, Monday to Friday, but not on holidays.

Ferry

If you have the time, the cheapest way to visit Hokkaidō is on one of the many long-distance ferries from Honshū – if you travel overnight, you also save on accommodation costs. The main ferry ports on Hokkaidō are Otaru, Hakodate, Muroran, Tomakomai and Kushiro. These are connected with major ports on Honshū such as Tokyo, Niigata, Nagoya, Sendai, Maizuru and Tsuruga.

From Northern Honshū (Tōhoku) there are short-hop ferry routes to several of the major ports on Hokkaidō.

GETTING AROUND

When planning a route around Hokkaidō, it's essential to remember the time (and expense) required because of the sheer size of the place. By way of illustration: the train journey from Hakodate in the extreme southwest to Wakkanai at the northernmost tip will take over nine hours by limited express; a flight from Sapporo to Wakkanai takes only 50 minutes but the round-trip ticket costs ¥24,220; the ferry from Otaru to the islands of Rishiri-tō and Rebun-tō, close to Wakkanai, takes 11 hours and costs ¥7720.

To/From the Airport

The main airport for Sapporo is New Chitose Airport, which is about 40 km south of the city. Sapporo has a subsidiary airport at Okadamo, which is about 20 km north of the city. Ask, if you're not certain, which airport is stated on your ticket.

Local Transport

Train The rail network on Hokkaidō has a couple of major lines with fast and frequent services while the remainder have slow or infrequent services. Many of the unprofitable lines have been phased out – several lines shown on old maps are no longer in operation – and more are due to be axed.

Bus Cities like Sapporo and Hakodate have excellent transport infrastructures, but buses to remoter regions tend to run infrequently or only during the peak tourist season. Some of the national parks have efficient bus services which do a circuit of the individual sights.

Car Rental If you can afford the extra expense, or can find passengers to share the costs, driving is highly recommended because this cuts out the problems with the slow or infrequent public transport. It also provides you with the mobility to reach remote areas at your own pace. Most of the

large cities have car rental agencies such as Nippon or Budget Rent-a-Car. Rates for smaller cars start around ¥7500 for 24 hours, but bear in mind the expressway tolls and fuel costs.

Bicycle This is a popular mode of transportation; many of the roads around the coastline have low gradients and there are plenty of cycling terminals and youth hostels which cater for cyclists.

Hitching The residents on Hokkaidō – and even tourists passing through – seem happy to oblige with a ride. In more remote regions, and especially during the off season for tourism, there may simply be a lack of traffic. If you ask around, it's sometimes possible to arrange a ride with other guests at youth hostels – the hostel manager usually knows who's going where.

Ferry The ferry from Otaru to the islands of Rebun-tō and Rishiri-tō, close to Wakkanai, is a slow but inexpensive way of reaching the northernmost part of Hokkaidō.

HAKODATE 函館

Hakodate (population 307,200) is a convenient gateway for Hokkaidō, and is a laid-back kind of place with something of a historical heritage. Sapporo is a much more happening city, but Hakodate has retained architectural influences from the last century. It was one of the first foreign trading ports to be opened up under the terms of the Kanagawa Treaty of 1854, and attracted foreign communities.

It's worth spending a day there to ride the trams (introduced in 1913), or stroll around the Motomachi district with its assortment of Western-style buildings. In fine weather the summit of Mt Hakodate-yama offers spectacular views across the city, day or night.

Orientation

Hakodate is not complicated when it comes to orientation. The western part of the city, within easy reach of Hakodate station by tram and bus, is the area with the bulk of the historical sights and is spread out below the slopes of Mt Hakodate-yama. Just east of the station is the sprawling city centre and a couple of km to the north-east are the mildly interesting remains of Goryōkaku fort.

Information

The Hakodate Tourist Information Office (☎ 0138-23-5440) is to the right as you exit the station. It's open from 9 am to 7 pm but closes at 5 pm in winter. The office has plenty of detailed maps and brochures in English, and can also help with finding accommodation.

JNTO publishes a leaflet entitled *Southern Hokkaidō*, which has a basic map and details on the sights, transport and accommodation in Hakodate.

Mt Hakodate-yama   函館山

The star attraction of Hakodate is the view from the summit of this mountain, preferably enjoyed on a clear night. A cablecar (the Japanese call these 'ropeways') whisks you up to the top in a few minutes and relieves you of ¥1130 for the return trip. Operating hours extend into the evening: from 9 am to 9 pm (1 February to 20 April), 9 am to 10 pm (21 April to 10 October), 10 am to 9 pm (11 October to 10 November) and 10 am to 8 pm (11 November to 31 January).

To reach the cablecar station from JR Hakodate station, take tram Nos 2, 3 or 5 and get off at the Jūjigai tram stop (about a six minute ride). The base station is then a seven minute walk uphill. Just to the right of the base station, take a look at the telephone booth shaped like a church!

If you feel fit, there's a mountain trail winding up the mountain, though it's closed from late November to late April. From Hakodate station, you can take a bus (20 minutes, ¥280) direct to the summit, but this service is suspended from late October until late April.

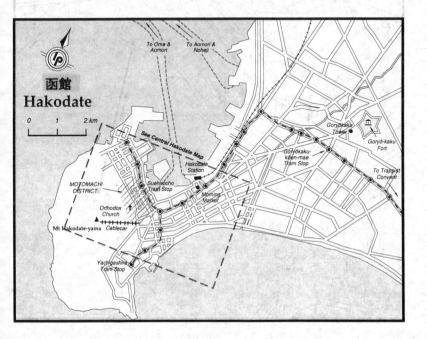

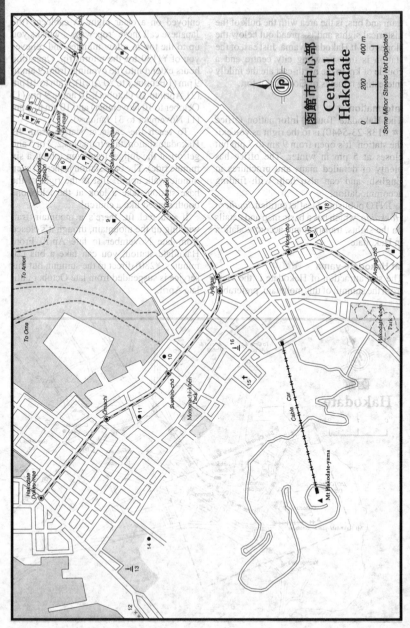

函館市中心部
Central Hakodate

0   200   400 m.

Some Minor Streets Not Depicted

Motomachi District 元町

This district, at the base of Mt Hakodate-yama, has retained several Western-style buildings from the turn of the century and is a pleasant place to stroll around.

The easiest building to recognise is the Eastern Orthodox Church, an attractive reconstruction dating from 1916 (the original was constructed in 1859). Entry is free, and from May to November the church is open from 10 am to 5 pm (4 pm the rest of the year); it's closed at lunch time, from noon to 1 pm. Other sights in Motomachi worth checking out include the Chinese Memorial Hall (a bit pricey at ¥500) and the Foreigner's Cemetery.

To reach Motomachi, take tram No 3 or 5 from Hakodate station to the Suehirocho tram stop, then walk uphill for about 10 minutes.

Goryōkaku Fort 五稜郭

Japan's first Western-style fort was built here in 1864 in the shape of a five pointed star. Five years later, forces loyal to the Tokugawa Shogunate held out for just seven days before surrendering to the attacking troops of the Meiji Restoration. All that's left now are the outer walls, and the grounds have been made into a park with the obligatory squads of cherry trees. Inside the grounds, keen historians or militarists can pay ¥100 admission to visit the Hakodate Museum, which displays the hardware used in the battle and the inevitable blood-stained uniforms.

The fort is a favourite destination for school outings, presumably with the aim of instilling pupils with an appreciation of self-sacrificing military valour – essential for a successful navigation of the Japanese education system.

Close to the park's entrance is the Goryōkaku Tower, which provides a bird's-eye view of the ruins and the surrounding area. The tower is open daily from 8 am to 8 pm from April to October, and from 9 am to 6 pm the rest of the year; admission is ¥520.

To reach the fort, take tram No 2, 3 or 5 for a 15 minute ride (¥180) to the Goryōkaku-kōen-mae tram stop. From there, it's a 10 minute walk to the fort.

Trappist Convent トラピスト修道院

This convent, founded in 1898, is on the outskirts of Hakodate, close to Yunokawa Onsen. Visitors come to see the architecture and gardens, but the real drawcard is the shop which sells delicious homemade biscuits, sweets and butter.

From Hakodate station, take bus No 19 for

the 35 minute ride to the Yunokawa-danchi-kitaguchi bus stop. From there, it's a 15 minute walk to the convent.

Yachigashira Spa 谷地頭温泉
This enormous spa, accommodating some 600 bathers, is not a major attraction, but is an inexpensive opportunity to take a look at Japanese onsen culture. Entry is just ¥300, and the spa can be reached by tram from Hakodate station. Get off at Yachigashira, the final stop. From 1 April to 31 October it's open from 6 am to 9.30 pm (from 7 am to 9.30 pm the rest of the year); it's closed on the 2nd and 4th Friday of every month and over New Year.

Markets
If you're an early bird, the asa-ichi (morning market) is open from 5 am to noon; closed on Sunday. It's a two minute walk from the west exit of Hakodate station.

Festivals
In mid-May, the festival of Hakodate Goryōkaku Matsuri features a parade with townsfolk dressed in the uniforms of the soldiers who took part in the Meiji Restoration battle of 1868.

Places to Stay
During the busy summer months, Hakodate is swamped with Japanese tourists heading northwards to other parts of Hokkaidō, and accommodation can be hard to find. If you don't have a reservation, it's a good idea to call into the tourist information office next to the station – the staff here will know which ryokan, minshukan or hotels, if any, have vacancies. They will also ring ahead and make same-day reservations for you.

Station Area *Minshuku Ryorō* (☎ 0138-26-7652) is a member of the Toho network. Prices start at ¥4500 per person including two meals, ¥3000 without any meals or an additional ¥500 if you only want breakfast.

To reach the minshuku – close to the morning market – take the west exit from the station then walk for six minutes keeping to

the left of the street until you come to the seventh side street. Go left down the side street and the minshuku is about 30 metres on your right.

Close to the Horai-chō tram stop is the *Minshuku Ryokan Nagashima* (☎ 0138-26-2101), a small ryokan with only 13 rooms. Per-person costs are ¥6500 with two meals. Five minutes walk east of the next tram stop (Aoyogi-chō) is the *Pension Aoyogi-kan* (☎ 0138-23-5736), which has four Japanese-style and five Western-style rooms at ¥6800 per person with two meals.

One of the cheapest hotels close to the station is the *Business Hotel New Ōte* (☎ 0138-23-4561). It has singles from ¥5000 to ¥5500 and twins from ¥9000 to ¥10,000. The *Miyagi Hotel* (☎ 0138-23-2204), to the north of the Ōte, is really only good for singles, which cost ¥5500. Close by is the *Hotel Dai-Ni Ocean* (☎ 0138-27-2700) with singles from ¥5500 to ¥6500, twins from ¥11,000 to ¥14,000 and doubles from ¥11,000 to ¥12,000. The *Aqua Garden Hotel* (☎ 0138-23-2200) has singles/twins at ¥5500/11,000 and the *Hakodate Plaza Hotel* (☎ 0138-22-0121) has singles/twins/doubles at ¥6500/11,000/10,000.

More up-market station area options include the *Hakodate Kokusai Hotel* (☎ 0138-23-5151), where singles range from ¥9000 to ¥18,000 and twins from ¥18,000 to ¥24,000. The *Hakodate Harbour View Hotel* (☎ 0138-22-0111) has singles at ¥8500 to ¥9000, twins from ¥19,000 to ¥24,000 and doubles from ¥22,000 to ¥24,000. The *Hotel Hakodate Royal* (☎ 0138-26-8181) has singles/twins from ¥8800/17,500.

Mt Hakodate-yama Area *Free Station* (☎ 0138-26-6817), a member of the Toho network, is in a quiet location below Mt Hakodate-yama. Per-person costs are ¥2500 without meals. Smoking is forbidden and male and female guests are segregated. Use of the nearby hot spring is included in the price. Special dishes can be ordered between July and September. From Hakodate station, take tram No 2 for the 15 minute ride south-west to the terminus at Yachigashira; Free Station is about 10 minutes walk away.

The recently opened *Hakodate Youth Guesthouse* (☎ 0138-26-7892) is close to Hakodate-kōen Park. It's slightly more expensive than the average youth hostel, and rooms are either doubles or triples; per-person costs are around ¥3500. At the time of writing, the hostel was only accepting parties of two or more, but it would be a good idea to check the current situation over the phone or with the tourist information office next to the station.

North of Hakodate If you want to stay out of Hakodate in some fine scenery, you could consider *Ikusandā Ōnuma Youth Hostel* (☎ 0138-67-3419) – see the section on Ōnuma.

Places to Eat
The station area doesn't offer a great deal in the way of restaurants, though there are a few rāmen shops and fast-food barns on the main street running out from the station. For something a little more up-market, try *Hisago Sushi* (☎ 0138-22-1506), a sushi restaurant that is popular with Japanese tourists. Sets range from ¥1000 to ¥2500.

There are a couple of restaurants up on the viewing platform of Mt Hakodate-yama, though they are more notable for their views than their food. At the foot of the mountain, in the Motomachi district, there are plenty of trendy eateries in converted Western-style buildings.

The main restaurant and entertainment area of Hakodate is north of the station in the vicinity of the Goryōkaku-kōen-mae tram stop (the first stop after the tram turns eastwards). This area is much more lively than the station area in the evenings, and there's a wider choice of dining options.

Getting There & Away
Air ANA and JAL connect Hakodate Airport with Haneda in Tokyo. There are seven flights daily and the one-way/return fare is ¥21,700/39,240.

Train Hakodate is connected with Aomori by the JR Tsugaru Kaikyō line, which runs via the Seikan Tunnel beneath the Tsugaru Kaikyō Straits to Hakodate in 2½ hours by limited express. The fare is ¥2880, plus ¥2150 limited express surcharge. Limited express sleeper services from Ueno in Tokyo (they continue on to Sapporo) take 14 hours 20 minutes. A combination of limited express and shinkansen (as far as Morioka) from Tokyo takes around seven to eight hours and costs ¥17,830 with express surcharges.

There is a limited express service available between Osaka and Hakodate. Like the Ueno-Sapporo service it is a sleeper train and takes 17 hours 30 minutes. Tickets cost ¥13,180 with a limited express surcharge of ¥3590.

Sapporo is linked with Hakodate in three hours and forty-five minutes by limited express via New Chitose Airport and Tomakomai. The fare is ¥4840 with a ¥2770 limited express surcharge.

Bus An overnight bus service links Hakodate with Sapporo (6½ hours, ¥4600). Buses leave from and arrive in Hakodate at the Hakodate Harbour View Hotel. In Sapporo they leave from the Ōtsu Shiei bus terminal.

Ferry Ferries link Hakodate with ports on Honshū such as Ōma (¥1000, 1¾ hours), Noheji (¥1400, 4¾ hours) and Aomori (¥1400, 3¾ hours).

Hakodate-kō Port is not convenient for access to the city centre. The taxi ride to the JR station costs ¥1140. The closest bus stop, Hokkudai-mae, is a seven minute walk from the ferry terminal; from there you can catch bus Nos 1 or 19 to the station. An expensive (¥6300) jetfoil service links Hakodate with Aomori in one hour 40 minutes, and this service leaves from the more convenient port to the south of JR Hakodate station.

Getting Around
To/From the Airport A bus service links Hakodate Airport with the city in around 20

minutes (¥290). Buses terminate in front of JR Hakodate station.

Bus & Tram One-day (¥900) and two-day (¥1500) open tickets, which entitle you to unlimited bus and tram travel, are available from the tourist information office or on buses or trams.

ŌNUMA　大沼

This small town, just north of Hakodate, is the gateway to **Ōnuma Quasi National Park**, which contains a trio of lakes beneath Mt Komaga-dake, the volcano that formed the lakes when it erupted. There are several camping grounds on the shores of the lakes as well as a network of hiking trails.

The main lakes, **Lake Ōnuma** and **Lake Onuma**, meaning 'big' lake and 'little' lake respectively, are really one big lake separated by a road and rail bridge. There are cruise boats that take in both lakes. Boats leave from the pier around 500 metres northwest of the station.

Places to Stay

Ikusandā Ōnuma Youth Hostel (☎ 0138-67-3419) is a 10 minute walk south of JR Ōnuma-kōen station. Walk out of the station and follow the road for a couple of hundred metres before taking the first right. The hostel is on the left-hand side shortly after you cross the railway tracks. Bicycles can be rented from the hostel and there are hot springs near by.

Takeda-sō (☎ 0138-67-2522) is a reasonably priced minshuku, three minutes on foot from Ōnuma-kōen station. Prices start at ¥6000 per person including two meals. To get there, take the first right turn out of the station and look out for it a couple of hundred metres down on the left.

Those who don't mind spending a little extra can try the *Pension Haine* (☎ 0138-67-3618), which is around five to 10 minutes walk from the station on the way to the hostel. Per-person costs are ¥8000 with two meals.

The nearest camping ground to the station is the *Ōmura Camping Ground*. It's only

about 600 metres from the station, a bit further on from the pier. Other camping grounds in the area are inconveniently located for those without their own transport.

Getting There & Away

Ōnuma-kōen station is about 40 minutes by local train (futsū) from Hakodate on the JR Hakodate line and tickets cost ¥470. There's also a bus service from Hakodate station to Ōnuma-kōen station (1¼ hours, ¥660).

ESASHI & OKUSHIRI-TŌ ISLAND
江差・奥尻島

Esashi is a major fishing town, 67 km west of Hakodate. The town is renowned for its annual festival, Ubagami Taisha Matsuri, which is held from 9 to 11 August and features a parade of more than a dozen ornate floats. Esashi can be reached from Hakodate by bus (2¼ hours, ¥1700) or by train in about three hours (infrequent service) on the JR Esashi line.

From Esashi, there is a ferry service to Okushiri-tō Island. The ferry departs twice daily and the trip takes 2¼ hours (¥2060). A bus service operates on the island, connecting the main town of Okushiri with several fishing villages, hot-spring resorts and the island's small airfield (there are flight connections to Hakodate). Another ferry service operates from Okushiri to **Setana**, which is further north from Esashi. Ferries depart once or twice daily and the trip takes 1¾ hours (¥1540). From Setana there is a bus service to Oshamambe (1¾ hours, ¥1150), which is on the JR Hakodate line.

In mid-1993 Okushiri-tō Island was devastated by a major earthquake that measured 8.1 on the Richter scale. The ensuing tsunami washed away many coastal homes and claimed some 400 lives. It will probably be some time before the island is ready for tourists, and it would be a good idea to ask at Sapporo tourist offices for details on the latest developments.

NISEKO　ニセコ

Niseko lies between Mt Yōtei-zan and Mt Nisekoannupuri and functions as a year-round resort: one of Hokkaidō's prime ski resorts during winter and a hiking base during summer and autumn. Numerous hot springs in the area are also popular.

Places to Stay & Eat
The Toho network has four inns in the Niseko area, but none of them are particularly easy to reach by public transport. *Nomad Yūbokumin* (☎ 0136-22-2281) is around seven km west of Kutchan station (two stops north of Niseko), and charges ¥4200 with two meals. *Niseko Ambishiasu (Ambitious)* (☎ 0136-44-3011) is five minutes by car from Niseko station, and if you speak enough Japanese to get the message across or can find someone to speak on your behalf, the owners will come and pick you up at the station; rates are ¥4000 with two meals. Japanese-speakers might try giving either *Hobo* (☎ 0136-46-3417) or *Pū House* (☎ 0136-44-1171) a ring for directions. They have rates of ¥4300 and ¥4000 respectively, with two meals.

Niseko Youth Hostel (☎ 0136-22-0553) is around 15 minutes walk from Kutchan station (two stops north of Niseko) and charges ¥2200. To get there, walk north of Kutchan station, turn left and follow the road for around 500 metres until it bears left. Look out for the hostel off to the right.

About a km north of the Tōzan-guchi bus stop is the *Pension Frypan* (☎ 0136-58-2932), which has rates of ¥7500 to ¥7800 with two meals.

Niseko also has a number of ultra-expensive resort-style hotels. The Prince hotel group is represented in the *Niseko Higashi-Yama Prince Hotel* (☎ 0136-44-1111). It's closer to Hirafu station than Niseko and charges princely sums for its rooms (¥18,000 upwards with meals).

Getting There & Away
Niseko is two hours 30 minutes from Sapporo on the Marine Liner rapid service via the JR Hakodate line; tickets cost ¥1850. There are also regular bus services connecting Niseko with Sapporo, New Chitose Airport and Otaru.

SHAKOTAN PENINSULA　積丹半島
This peninsula is renowned for its rugged coastline, steep cliffs and spectacular rock formations.

Places to Stay
Bikuni Youth Hostel (☎ 0135-44-2610) and *Shakotan Youth Hostel* (☎ 0135-46-5052) are convenient for the northern side of the peninsula, while *Shakotan Kamoi Youth Hostel* (☎ 0135-77-6136) is close to the terminus of the bus route on the southern side. They all have rates of around ¥2300.

Getting There & Away
On the northern side of the peninsula, a sightseeing bus runs from Otaru around the tip of the peninsula to Yobetsu in 2¼ hours (¥1300). On the southern side of the peninsula, a bus service runs from Iwanai to a lookout just beyond Kamoenai in about an hour (¥770).

OTARU　小樽
Otaru (population 162,200) is a major ferry port with services south to Honshū and north to the islands of Rishiri-tō and Rebun-tō. The town's importance as a port in the early development of Hokkaidō has left a small legacy of old Western-style buildings and an attractive canal area.

Information
The tourist information office (☎ 0134-29-1333), at the entrance to JR Otaru station, is open from 10 am to 6 pm daily, except on Saturday and Sunday, when the opening hours are from 9.30 am to 5.30 pm. A useful leaflet with maps and detailed information about Otaru in English is available there.

Things to See
Most of the attractions in town are east of Otaru station, close to the harbour, and consist of Western-style buildings dating back from early this century. While for most Western visitors they won't merit a special trip to Otaru, if you're in town most of the buildings are clumped together and worth a

1 Otaru Municipal Museum
  小樽市博物館
2 Otaru Green Hotel
  小樽グリーンホテル
3 New Green Hotel
  ニューグリーンホテル
4 Otaru Kokusai Hotel
  小樽国際ホテル
5 Business Hotel New Minato
  ビジネスホテルニュー港

小樽
Otaru

stroll. Rated highly are the Ex-Nippon Yusen Company building and the Mitsui Bank building.

The **Otaru Municipal Museum** is housed in an almost Chinese-looking building that, when it was first built in 1893, was a warehouse. It now houses a tastefully presented collection of items relating to local Otaru history. It's open from 9.30 am to 5 pm, closed Monday and entry is ¥100.

Perhaps the best of Otaru's attractions is the **Otaru Canal**, which runs east to west close to the harbour area. Beside the canal is a granite path with gas lamps – very romantic

at dusk. Sections of the canal are lined with photogenic old buildings.

Places to Stay
The tourist information office at the station can provide suggestions and help with booking accommodation.

The *Otaru Tengu-Yama Youth Hostel* (☎ 0134-34-1474) is close to the Tengu-Yama cablecar, a 10 minute bus ride from the station. On the business hotel front, one of the cheapest places around is the *Otaru Green Hotel* (☎ 0134-33-0333). It's just four minutes on foot from Otaru station, and prices for singles/doubles start at ¥3500/ 7000. Just across the road is the *New Green Hotel* (☎ 0134-33-6100). It has singles at ¥5000 and twins at ¥9400. Also close to the station is the *Business Hotel New Minato* (☎ 0134-32-3710), where singles range from ¥4200 to ¥5200 and twins from ¥5200 to ¥7600

Getting There & Away

Train Otaru is 50 minutes from Sapporo on the JR Hakodate line. Tickets are ¥560.

Bus A regular bus service runs directly between Otaru and Sapporo from in front of Sapporo station. It takes around 50 minutes and costs ¥500.

Ferry Long-distance ferries link Otaru with ports on Honshū such as Niigata (18 hours, ¥5000), Tsuruga (30 hours, ¥6400) and Maizuru (30 hours, ¥6400). There is also a service to the islands of Rishiri-tō and Rebun-tō off the northern tip of Hokkaidō. The overnight trip takes about 11 hours and the cheapest passenger ticket costs ¥7210.

Ferries for Niigata, Tsuruga and Maizuru leave from the Katsunai-futō Pier (ask for the *niigata feri noriba)*, while ferries for Rishiri-tō and Rebun-tō Islands run from the Hokkai Shōsen ferry terminal just to the north-west. Both piers are best reached from Minami-Otaru station. They are just under a km to the north of the station.

SAPPORO　札幌

Sapporo (population 1.6 million) is Hokkaidō's administrative hub, main population centre and a lively, prosperous city. The friendly locals and cosmopolitan flavour of the city, with its sweeping tree-lined boulevards, make it well worth a night or two. There may not be a wealth of 'sights', but there's plenty to do day and night. Like Hiroshima in western Honshū, Sapporo presents a good chance to take a peek at modern Japan without feeling squeezed by the pressing crowds that prevail in cities like Tokyo and Osaka.

Orientation

Sapporo is one of the only cities in Japan where it's almost possible to find places by their addresses. The reason is the precise grid pattern of the streets. The street names reflect this precision and, with the exception of the major Ō-dōri, are named according to compass points and numbers. Thus, if you know that a particular building is near the intersection of North 3 and West 3, you've narrowed it down to a manageable piece of turf.

From Sapporo station, West 3 makes a beeline straight through the administrative, commercial and entertainment areas of the city, crossing the huge Ō-dōri on the way. The area between the station and Ō-dōri is mainly administrative. This is where you'll find the airline companies, banks and so on. South of Ō-dōri is a shopping district, with large numbers of department stores and restaurants. Over South 4 is the Susukino entertainment area, which looks rather dull by day but comes to life at night. It's the largest entertainment area north of Tokyo, and besides the usual soaplands, peep shows, discos and shot bars there are some very good restaurants in the area.

Information

Sapporo is one of the best organised cities in Japan when it comes to dispensing English information to foreigners. While many Japanese tourist spots have simply given up trying to cater to the needs of foreign visitors, Sapporo has a number of information counters staffed by helpful English-speaking staff, and the municipal government also produces a wide range of English-language pamphlets and maps.

Most newcomers will arrive by train at Sapporo station. It's worth popping into the Lilac Paseo International Information Office (☎ 011-213-5062). It's open daily from 9 am to 5 pm, closed the second Wednesday of every month. The staff here have a wide range of maps and information on Sapporo and the rest of Hokkaidō – at the very least pick up a copy of the excellent *Sapporo Visitor's Handbook & Map*. Although the

Botanical Garden

JR Sapporo Station

Sapporo Station

Sapporo Station

NANBOKU LINE

Ōdori Station

Odori Station

Ōdori-kōen

Park

Nishi-Jūitchōme Station

TOZAI LINE

Tanuki - kōji Arcade

Susukino Station

Hosui Susukino Station

Nakajima-kōen Station

Toyohira-gawa River

札幌
Sapporo

0   200   400 m

Some Minor Streets Not Depicted

Nakajima- kōen
Park

PLACES TO STAY

2 Yugiri Ryokan
夕霧旅館
3 Sapporo House
Youth Hostel
札幌ハウスユースホステル
4 Sapporo Dai-Ni
Washington Hotel
札幌第2ワシントンホテル
5 Keiō Plaza Hotel
Sapporo
京王プラザホテル札幌
7 Nakamura Ryokan
中村旅館
9 Sapporo Dai-Ichi
Washington Hotel
札幌第1ワシントンホテル
13 Hotel New Otani
Sapporo
ホテルニューオータニ札幌
31 Prince Hotel
プリンスホテル
35 Susukino Green Hotel II
すすきのグリーンホテルII
36 Tōkyū Inn
東急イン
39 Susukino Green Hotel I
すすきのグリーンホテルI
43 Sapporo International
Inn Nada
札幌インターナショナルイン灘
46 Business Hotel Shintō
ビジネスホテル新東
47 Sapporo Central Hotel
札幌セントラルホテル
50 Susukino Green
Hotel III
すすきのグリーンホテルIII
51 Hotel Sunlight
ホテルサンライト
52 Quality Inn Sapporo
クオリティイン札幌
53 Sapporo Oriental Hotel
札幌オリエンタルホテル

PLACES TO EAT

20 Chart Italian Restaurant
チャート
イタリアンレストラン

21 Café Dior
カフェ ディオール
22 Cha-Cha-Cha
Italian Restaurant
チャチャチャ
イタリアンレストラン
26 Taj Mahal Indian
Restaurant
タジマハール
インド レストラン
30 Doutor Coffee
ドトール コーヒー
33 Kentucky Fried Chicken
ケンタッキー
フライドチキン
34 Sapporo Ichiban
Rāmen Restaurant
札幌一番ラーメン
38 Shakey's
Pizza/Mr Donut
シェーキーズピザ／
ミスタードーナッツ
40 Tsubohachi Restaurant
つぼ八
41 Rāmen Yokochō
Restaurant
ラーメン横丁
44 Delhi Palace Indian
Restaurant
デリー パレス
45 Tokei-dai Rāmen
Restaurant
時計台ラーメン

OTHER

1 Sapporo Central
Post Office
札幌中央郵便局
6 Batchelor Memorial
Museum
北方民族資料館
8 Immigration Office
札幌出入国管理局
10 SOGO
Department Store
そごうデパート
11 Tōkyū
Department Store
東急デパート

12 American Express
Office
アメリカンエクスプレス
14 Tokei-dai Clocktower
時計台
15 Sapporo International
Communication
Plaza
札幌国際コミュニケー
ションプラザ
16 Ōdori Post Office
大通り郵便局
17 Chūō Post Office
札幌中央郵便局
18 TV Tower
テレビ塔
19 Kinokuniya Books
紀伊國屋書店
23 Mitsukoshi
Department Store
三越
24 Maruzen Books
丸善
25 Parco
Department Store
パルコ
27 Daiei
Department Store
ダイエー
28 San-Ai
Department Store
三愛
29 Tower Records
タワーレコード
32 Blues Alley
ブルースアレー
37 York Matsuzakaya
Department Store
ヨーク松坂屋デパート
42 Susukino Nightlife
Information
すすきのガイドセンター
48 King Xhmu (disco)
キング シェムー
ディスコ
49 Al's Bar
アルス バー

staff are not authorised to book accommodation, they can make recommendations according to your budget. The office is in the north side of the station, and is easily missed because it's inside a coffee shop – look for the Lilac Paseo sign outside and the red Information sign inside.

Other offices around town include the Sapporo Tourist Association (☎ 011-211-

3341) and the Sapporo City Government's tourist section (☎ 011-211-2376); both have English-speaking staff.

Probably the most useful place, however, is the Sapporo International Communication Plaza (☎ 011-211-3678) on the 1st and 3rd floors of the MN building, just opposite the clocktower. The 1st floor office is devoted to the needs of tourists both in Sapporo and further afield around Hokkaidō. Large folders crammed with information on Hokkaidō are available, and well worth taking a look at if you're heading off to more remote parts of the island. The 3rd floor offers help for those planning a long-term stay in Sapporo. English-speaking staff can arrange home visits if you give advance notice.

There is a notice board with messages, teaching advertisements and invitations to 'Free Talk Parties'. There's also a selection of foreign newspapers and magazines to read in the comfort of the large lounge. It is also possible to organise youth hostel membership on the 1st floor.

If you plan to spend some time in Sapporo, pick up copies of *Monthly Hokkaidō* or *What's On in Sapporo* for listings of events.

Visas & Consulates Sapporo has a few consulates. The Consulate General of the United States (☎ 011-641-1115) is over in North 1 West 28. The Australian Consulate (☎ 011-242-4381) in North 1 West 3 on the 5th floor of the Daiwa Bank building. The Consulate General of the Republic of Korea (☎ 011-621-0288) is in North 3 West 21. The Consulate General of the Russian Federation (☎ 011-561-3171) is in South 14 West 12. Finally, the Consulate General of the People's Republic of China (☎ 011-563-5563) is in South 13 West 23.

Books Sapporo has branches of both Maruzen and Kinokuniya bookshops in the Chūō shopping district. Kinokuniya has a small selection of foreign books on its 2nd floor. The 3rd floor selection of foreign books in Maruzen, however, is much more extensive and is the best place to pick up reading material north of Tokyo.

The Sapporo Library has around 2300 English-language titles on its 2nd floor. It also has copies of English-language newspapers. It has slightly bewildering opening hours but is basically open from 9 am to 5 pm, except for Tuesday, when it's open from 1 pm to 5.15 pm, and on Monday when it's closed all day.

Botanical Garden 植物園
The Botanical Garden has more than 5000 varieties of Hokkaidō's flora on 14 hectares, and provides a relaxing spot for a stroll.

In the garden grounds is the Batchelor Memorial Museum, which houses the collection of Dr John Batchelor, an English missionary who took a keen interest in the culture of the Ainu and tribes from Siberia. Exhibits include handicrafts, tools, household utensils and old photos which document the demise of these cultures.

The garden is open daily from 9 am to 4 pm (29 April to 30 September) but closes half an hour earlier from October to early November and is closed on Monday. Admission is ¥400. Between 4 November and 28 April, only the greenhouse is open (10 am to 3 pm); admission is ¥150 and it is closed on Sunday.

Tokei-dai Clocktower 時計台
The Tokei-dai Clocktower was constructed in 1878 and has now become a cherished landmark for Sapporo residents and a useful orientation point for visitors. It's not particularly stunning, but you can enter the building and wander around a small museum of local history. If you're wondering why such an unimposing little structure should attract a constant stream of amateur photographers, it's because the clocktower is considered *the* symbol of Sapporo and no self-respecting Japanese would go home from a trip to the city without a picture of themselves posed in front of it.

Sapporo Beer Garden & Museum
サッポロビールビヤガーデン・博物館
The Sapporo Beer Garden and Museum are on the site of the original Sapporo Brewery. Dating back to 1876, it was the first brewery to be established in Japan. Tours of the museum are free, but reservations are required (☎ 011-731-4368). The tours, lasting about 80 minutes, are given throughout the year from 9 am to 3.40 pm.

The cavernous beer 'garden' (it's actually a hall) offers the opportunity for some serious drinking and pigging out – look out for the 'all you can eat and drink' offers, starting at around ¥3500. The standard dish is 'Ghengis-Khan Hotpot' – prices for other dishes on the menu start around ¥1000 and a mug of draught beer costs ¥450. The beer garden is open from 11.30 am to 9 pm, and reservations are recommended though not essential (☎ 011-742-1531).

From the north exit of the station, the brewery is a 15 minute walk east – or take the Higashi 63 bus and get off at the North 8 East 7 *(Kita-hachi higashi-nana)* bus stop. There are also special Beer Museum buses running from in front of the Gobankan Seibu department store close to JR Sapporo station.

TV Tower テレビ塔

This prominent landmark in Ōdōri-kōen Park provides good views of Sapporo from its 90 metre viewing platform. From May to September it's open from 9 am to 8.30 pm; through the rest of the year it's open from 9.30 am to 6.30 pm. Entry is ¥600.

Museums

The Hokkaidō Museum of Modern Art has a collection of modern art from overseas (mainly France) as well as works by local artists. Special exhibitions are also frequently held. The museum is open from 10 am to 5 pm and is closed on Monday; entry is ¥250.

The nearby Migishi Kotaro Museum of Modern Art is devoted to the works of the Sapporo artist of the same name (1903-34). It's probably only of interest to those with a special interest in the development of Japanese modern art. Its opening hours are the same as those of the Museum of Modern Art and entry is ¥250. Both museums are around five minutes walk north of Nishi-jūhatchōme subway station on the Tōzai line.

The Ainu Materials Display Room is in front of the Hokudai Botanical Garden and has a small display of items relating to Ainu history. It's open 9 am to 4.30 pm, closed on Monday, and entry is free.

An interesting off-beat museum is the Sapporo Salmon Museum. Salmon enthusiasts can pester one of the information offices about how to get there and when it's open.

Festivals

The Sapporo Yuki Matsuri (Sapporo Ice Festival), held in Odōri-kōen Park in early February, is probably Hokkaidō's major annual event. Since 1950 when the festival was first held, it has developed into a mass display of snow sculptures, many of which are very intricate buildings complete with internal illumination. If you plan to visit at this time, you should book accommodation well in advance or take a course in igloo construction.

Places to Stay

Youth Hostels Although there are three hostels in Sapporo, only one, Sapporo House, has convenient access – and it's hardly a place to rave about. The hostels are more of an option if you are stuck or don't mind the institutional atmosphere. *Sapporo House* (☎ 011-726-4235) is a seven minute walk from the station. Not a memorable place to stay – drab and prison-like. When leaving the station, take the south exit *(minami-guchi)*, turn right down the main street and keep walking until you reach the Keiō Hotel at the third intersection. Turn right here, continue under the bridge and the hostel is about 20 metres further ahead on your right. Beds are ¥2300.

Sapporo Miyagaoka Youth Hostel (☎ 011-611-9016) is close to Maruyama-kōen Park in the west of Sapporo, but it's only open from July to late September. *Sapporo Lions Youth Hostel* (☎ 011-611-4709) is further west, close to the Miyanomori Ski Jump. Transport from the station to both of these hostels is a bit complicated – a combination of subway, bus and walking – and neither is particularly appealing anyway.

Toho Network The *Sapporo International Inn Nada* (☎ 011-551-5882) is probably the most popular budget place to stay in Sapporo. It's close to the Susukino entertainment area and has no curfew, making it an ideal base for a late night foray into Hokkaidō's most happening nightclub district. Costs are ¥3500 per head, though this will probably mean sharing a room. Breakfast is available for ¥600 and there's a heating charge of ¥200 during winter. It's around a 10 minute walk west from Susukino subway station.

Even if you are staying elsewhere, those planning to do further travel around Hokkaidō should call in and pick up a copy of the Toho network book. An English version should be available (¥150) – at least plans were afoot to produce one at the time of writing.

Ryokan The most popular ryokan with foreigners is the *Yugiri Ryokan* (☎ 011-716-5482), which has per-head costs at around ¥3500 (depends on the room). The management don't speak English but seem to have reconciled themselves to the ways of visiting gaijin and try hard to please. It's a five minute walk north-west of the station, close to Hokkaidō University.

Nakamuraya Ryokan (☎ 011-241-2111) is a member of the Japanese Inn Group. Prices are relatively high at around ¥7000/13,000 for singles/doubles and ¥18,000 for triples, though discounts are sometimes available on polite request. The ryokan is a seven minute walk west of the station.

Hotels Despite the fact that Sapporo has close to a couple of hundred hotels, during summer *everything* gets booked out very quickly. It's wise to book ahead before arriving in Sapporo. If you are having problems finding somewhere with vacancies, give the Business Hotel Reservation Centre (☎ 011-221-0909) a ring, though you will need Japanese or the help of a Japanese speaker to get any sense out of them.

Station Area If you're going to be forking out the requisite cash for business hotel, you'd probably be better off down in the Susukino district, which is a much livelier part of town. Still, the station area is handy to many of the sights and isn't a dead loss as a place to base yourself.

Just a couple of minutes from the station, the *Sapporo Dai-Ichi Washington Hotel* (☎ 011-251-3211) has singles from ¥6190

and doubles at ¥17,600. It would be a good idea to book ahead for one of the cheaper singles. Singles at the nearby *Sapporo Dai-Ni Washington Hotel* (☎ 011-222-3311) are more expensive at ¥8910; doubles start at ¥16,500.

The station area also has some of Sapporo's top-class hotels. The opulent *Hotel New Otani Sapporo* (☎ 011-222-1111) has singles from ¥14,000 and doubles from ¥25,000. Similar high standards can be found at the *Keiō Plaza Hotel Sapporo* (☎ 011-271-0111), which has singles from ¥14,000 to ¥15,000 and doubles/twins at ¥25,000.

Susukino Area There are dozens upon dozens of hotels in the Susukino area, a fun part of town to be based in. One of the cheapest is the *Sapporo Central Hotel* (☎ 011-512-3121), a reasonably small hotel that tends to get booked out quickly. Singles are ¥5000, while doubles range from ¥7000 to ¥8000. Also reasonably priced is the *Sapporo Oriental Hotel* (☎ 011-521-5050), where singles/twins cost ¥6000/11,000. The *Quality Inn Sapporo* (☎ 011-512-5001) only has single rooms, and charges ¥6500 to ¥7500 per night.

There are three Green Hotels in the Susukino area. The cheapest is the *Susukino Green Hotel 3* (☎ 011-511-7211), which has singles/twins at ¥5500/13,000. The *Susukino Green Hotel 2* (☎ 011-511-9111) is considerably more expensive at ¥7700/14,200 for singles/twins. Singles at the *Susukino Green Hotel 1* (☎ 011-511-4111) start at ¥8000.

A couple of other places at the lower end of the price range include the *Business Hotel Shintō* (☎ 011-512-6611), which has singles/twins at ¥6000/10,000, and the *Hotel Sunlight* (☎ 011-562-3111), where singles/twins cost ¥6800/12,000.

Places to Eat
Sapporo is a big city and there's a lot to choose from in the dining category. As you'd expect, the fast-food huts are well represented, mainly in Susukino and the shopping district just to the north.

Hokkaidō is famous for its rāmen noodles,

and there are rāmen shops all over the city. Many of them have photographs of the dishes outside, which makes ordering slightly easier, but if you're having problems just ask for rāmen, the basic, no-frills (and cheapest) variety. A popular and tasty Sapporo variation is called *batā kōn rāmen*, or 'butter-corn noodles' – it's a lot better than it sounds. You can try this one at *Rāmen Yokochō*, one of the most popular rāmen places in Susukino or at *Tokei-dai Rāmen*. Another place to try Hokkaidō rāmen is *Sapporo Ichiban*, opposite the York Matsuzakaya department store.

Along with rāmen, there are some good and inexpensive revolving sushi shops in Susukino. *Kuru-Kuro Zushi* has an English sign outside, sushi plates from ¥130 and it is often packed out. *Kaiten Zushi* is a flashy place with the same deal. Sapporo has some good Indian cuisine in *Delhi Palace* in Susukino and *Taj Mahal* in the Chūō shopping district. The latter is part of a Japanese chain and, while the food is good, it's fairly expensive. The best deals are its lunch-time specials. Delhi Palace, on the other hand, has an Indian cook, authentic dishes and is inexpensive by Japanese standards – you can get a set dinner with a draught beer for around ¥2000.

There are quite a few Italian-style places around town, though we failed to stumble across anything particularly authentic. *Cha-Cha-Cha* and *Chart*, both in the Chūō shopping area, have slightly Japanised pasta dishes from around ¥800.

Finally, it's worth checking out the upper floors of some of the department stores for lunch-time specials. One of the best in town is the 8th floor of Parco. The restaurants are a little more expensive than usual, but if you don't mind spending ¥800 to ¥1000, there are some excellent lunches available. The Italian and Chinese restaurants are particularly good.

Entertainment

Susukino is wall-to-wall bars, karaoke parlours and kinky soaplands (Sapporo is the only city in Japan where soapland touts will

sometimes call out to passing single gaijin men). For just an idea of who and what is on offer, take a peek at the Susukino Nightlife Information Centre. All the information is in Japanese, but the advertising material on the walls needs no translation. That said, most of this kind of action is prohibitively expensive and of little interest anyway for visiting Westerners. This doesn't mean you should shun Susukino altogether though – there are loads of great places to eat and quite a few bars that are popular watering holes for local gaijin.

The best thing to do is to ask around for the latest 'in' spot. At the time of writing, one of the most popular bars in town was *Al's*. Look out for the English sign outside and head down into the basement. It has a ¥2500 cover charge on Saturday and ¥2000 the rest of the week. The cover charge will get you a handful of 'Al dollar bills' to buy some drinks with (four beers if you stick to a Japanese brew). It's popular with alternative locals and resident foreigners. Foreign DJs work the place on weekends; there's nowhere to dance, but people do anyway.

Blues Alley is a quiet place (perhaps a little boring by some people's standards), but it's a good place to meet people and sip a drink.

One place that has to be mentioned, even if it would probably break the average traveller's budget, is *King Xhmu* (everyone calls it 'King Mu's'), Sapporo's answer to *Juliana's* in Tokyo. This is an opulent disco if ever there was one. The only night of the week that sees a large number of foreigners is Thursday night, when anyone over 25 gets in free (you'll need ID no matter how old you look). Other days of the week it costs ¥3500 for women, ¥4000 for men, and ¥4000 for women, ¥4500 for men on Saturday. The entry charge buys you an electrically charged debit card with ¥2000 worth of drinks (beers are ¥500).

Even if you don't go to the disco (emphasis on techno beat), just wander down and take a look at the exterior. King Xhmu himself, massively carved in stone, presides wearily bemused over the neon of Susukino. The interior is no less fabulous – glowing demons with lasers for eyes leering over the dance floor.

Getting There & Away

Air Sapporo has flight connections with most of the major cities on Honshū and even Okinawa. There are dozens of flights daily from Tokyo – one-way/round-trip fares start at ¥23,850/43,100. The principal airlines offering services to Hokkaidō are JAS, ANA and JAL. Air Nippon Koku (ANK) also operates on internal routes for Hokkaidō. See the later Getting Around section for details on transport to/from the airport.

There are several international airlines with offices in Sapporo: Cathay Pacific (☎ 011-210-8473); Continental Airlines (☎ 011-221-4091); Korean Air (☎ 011-210 3311); Qantas Airways (☎ 011-242-4151). See the Getting There & Away chapter for details on international flights to and from Sapporo.

Train Two of the fastest rail connections from Tokyo include the Hokutōsei Express, a direct sleeper to Sapporo in 16 hours, and a combination of the shinkansen to Morioka followed by a limited express via Aomori and Hakodate to Sapporo in 11 hours. In the case of the former, if you are using a Japan Rail Pass, you will have to pay the sleeper supplement. It's also worth bearing in mind that this is a popular service and it only runs three times daily – book ahead. The cost is ¥13,180 with a ¥3590 limited express surcharge.

From Sapporo to Hakodate, it takes 3¾ hours by limited express via New Chitose Airport and Tomakomai.

The trip from Sapporo to Otaru on the JR Hakodate line takes 36 minutes. There are frequent trains running north-east on the JR Hakodate line to Asahikawa in 90 minutes (limited express). From Sapporo to Wakkanai, there's a sleeper service that leaves Sapporo around 10 pm and arrives in Wakkanai around 6 am, nicely timed to take the early ferry across to Rishiri-tō or Rebun-tō islands. If you're travelling on a Japan Rail Pass, you'll need to pay about ¥7400 in supplementary charges.

Bus Sapporo is linked with the rest of Hokkaidō by an extensive network of long-distance bus services such as those for Wakkanai (6¼ hours, ¥5850), Asahikawa (two hours, ¥1750), Kushiro (night bus – seven hours, ¥5700), Obihiro (4¾ hours, ¥3800), Kitami (4½ hours, ¥3400) and Hakodate (night bus – six hours, ¥4600). The night bus option is worth considering if you are backtracking, short on time or wish to save money on accommodation costs. However, it isn't exactly restful, and if you aren't backtracking you may lose out on some spectacular scenery.

Getting Around

To/From the Airport The main airport for Sapporo is New Chitose Airport, a 35 minute train ride (¥940) or 70 minute bus ride (¥750) south of the city. Sapporo has a subsidiary airport at Okadamo, which is a 35 minute bus ride (¥170) north of the city. If you're not certain which airport is stated on your ticket, ask.

Bus & Tram There are several bus terminals in Sapporo, but the main one is next to the station. City buses operate according to a system that is very common in Japan. Enter by the centre door and take a token as you do so. Exit by the front door, and calculate your fare by matching the number on your ticket with price indicated next to the same number on the board over the driver's seat.

There is a single tram line running from Ō-dori to Susukino. You probably won't need to use it, but if you do, there is a flat fare of ¥170.

Subway This is the most efficient way to get around Sapporo. There are three lines, the two most useful being the Nanboku line, which runs on a north-south axis and the Tozai line, which runs on an east-west axis. Fares start at ¥180, and special one-day passes are also available for ¥700; they are also valid for Sapporo's buses and trams.

ASAHIKAWA 旭川

Asahikawa (population 359,000) is an unimpressive urban sprawl and one of the largest cities on Hokkaidō. The city had its origins in the Meiji period as a farmer militia settlement and has since developed into a major industrial centre. For the traveller, its importance is largely as a transport hub: to the north, it's a long haul to Wakkanai; to the south, there are the attractions of Daisetsuzan National Park.

Information

There's an information counter in the station, though only Japanese is spoken. The staff here can help with finding accommodation, if the worst happens and you get stranded in Asahikawa.

Things to See

There's not a great deal to see in town, though there are some attractions that can be reached by bus. North of the station, **Tokiwa-kōen Park** has a Youth Science Museum and the Asahikawa Art Museum, but neither of these are likely to be of interest to many travellers.

More interesting is the **Yūkara Ori Folk-craft Museum**, with examples of dyed textiles from around the world and through the ages. It's open from 9 am to 5 pm daily from April to September and closed on Monday the rest of the year. To get there, take a bus No 56 or 67 from the stop in front of the station. The 15 minute trip costs ¥180.

The **Kawamura Kaneto Ainu Memorial Museum** is north-west of the city centre and is fairly touristy. It sometimes has Ainu dance displays. The museum is open from 9 am to 6 pm daily and entry is ¥300. Take a No 24 bus from in front of Asahikawa station for the 15 minute (¥150) trip to the Ainu Kinenkan-mae bus stop.

Places to Stay

Asahikawa Youth Hostel (☎ 0166-61-2751) is four km from the station. You can either take a 15 minute bus ride or hop in a taxi (¥1000). Buses bound for Kannondai-kōen

Park run from the central bus terminal across from the station; get off at the Yūsu-hosuteru-mae stop, a 15 minute ride from the station. Bicycle rental is available at the hostel and there are hot springs near by.

On the business hotel front, the *Asahikawa Station Hotel* (☎ 0166-23-9288), is a small hotel with singles from ¥3000 to ¥3500 and twins from ¥6000 to ¥6500. The rooms have no bathrooms. Along similar lines and around 10 minutes walk from the station is the *Hotel Sankei Kaikan* (☎ 0166-26-2288). This tiny place looks very unlike a hotel from the outside, but has 15 single rooms without bathroom from ¥3000 to ¥4000. About halfway between the station and Tokiwa-kōen Park, the *Orient Hotel* (☎ 0166-25-5111) has singles at ¥4800 and twins at ¥8400.

Going considerably up-market, the *Asahikawa Terminal Hotel* (☎ 0166-24-0111), right next to the station, has singles/twins at ¥6500/13,500. Not far away, the *Asahikawa Prince Hotel* (☎ 0166-22-5155) has singles from ¥5000 to ¥6800 and doubles from ¥10,800 to ¥16,200.

Getting There & Away

Train Asahikawa is linked with Sapporo in one hour 30 minutes by limited express on the JR Hakodate line. The price is ¥2160 with a ¥2250 limited express surcharge. The JR Furano line connects Asahikawa with Furano in an hour. The JR Sōya line runs north to Wakkanai – the trip takes just under four hours by limited express.

Bus Bus tickets can be bought from a booking office directly opposite the railway station. Buses themselves also leave and arrive in front of the station.

There are several bus services running from Asahikawa into Daisetsuzan National Park. One service runs twice daily (three times daily from mid-June to mid-October) to Tenninkyō Onsen via Asahidake Onsen (see the Asahidake Onsen section later for more details, including the youth hostel ticket refund). Another hourly bus service runs from Asahikawa via Kamikawa to Sōunkyō. The trip takes 1¾ hours and the ticket costs ¥1800.

A frequent bus service also operates between Sapporo and Asahikawa (two hours, ¥1750). Other bus services include Wakkanai (¥4300) and Obihiro (¥3090).

WAKKANAI   稚内

This windswept port on the northernmost fringe of Hokkaidō is visited by travellers heading for Rishiri-tō and Rebun-tō islands. Wakkanai station has an information counter where you can ask for timetables and maps. From the station, it's a 10 minute walk to the ferry terminal. Wakkanai has few sights. Unless your transport arrangements strand you there overnight, there's no compelling reason to stay.

Places to Stay
Youth Hostels *Wakkanai Youth Hostel* (☎ 0162-23-7162) is a 12 minute walk from the southern station for Wakkanai (in Japanese *minami wakkanai eki)*. It's open from 1 June to 31 October only. Bicycle rental is available. Beds cost ¥2500.

Wakkanai Moshiripa Youth Hostel (☎ 0162-24-0180) is a five minute walk from Wakkanai station and eight minutes on foot from the Wakkanai-kō Port. Bicycle rental is available. It's closed during November. Beds are ¥2500.

Hotels There isn't a lot in the way of hotels in this neck of the woods. Next to Wakkanai station is the *Wakkanai Sun Hotel* (☎ 0162-22-5311), which has singles at ¥7500 and twins from ¥12,000 to ¥20,000.

Most of the other hotels are down by Minami-Wakkanai station, the last stop before Wakkanai. Walk out of Minami-Wakkanai station and turn left to get to the *Hokkai Business Hotel* (☎ 0162-22-5630). It's a squat white structure with a couple of vending machines outside. Singles are ¥4500 and twins (there are only two of them) are ¥9000.

Getting There & Away
Air There are two ways to fly with ANK from Sapporo to Wakkanai – both take about an hour; the one-way/round-trip cost is ¥13,450/24,220. There is one daily flight from Sapporo's New Chitose Airport and two daily flights from Sapporo's Okadamo Airport. Make sure you know which airport you are going to be using.

Train From Sapporo to Wakkanai, there's a sleeper service that leaves Sapporo at around 10 pm and arrives in Wakkanai around 6 am, nicely timed to take the early ferry across to Rishiri-tō or Rebun-tō islands. If you're travelling on a Japan Rail Pass, you'll need to pay about ¥7400 in supplementary charges.

Other limited express services from Sapporo to Wakkanai take from 5½ hours to eight hours via the JR Hakodate and Sōya lines.

Bus A bus service runs from Sapporo via Asahikawa to Wakkanai in six hours and costs ¥5850.

Ferry Wakkanai is linked by ferries with Rishiri-tō and Rebun-tō islands. The ferry to Oshidomari on Rishiri-tō Island departs up to four times daily (between June and the end of August) and takes 90 minutes; the cheapest passenger ticket is ¥1850. From Oshidomari and Kutsugata (infrequent) there are ferry connections (¥720, 45 minutes) to Rebun-tō Island – these are linked to the arrivals/departures of the Wakkanai service.

There are direct ferries from Wakkanai to Kafuka on Rebun-tō Island up to three times daily (between June and the end of August); the ride takes 2¼ hours (¥2060). There is only one daily service directly from Wakkanai to Funadomari on Rebun-tō Island.

The port at Wakkanai is a 10 minute walk from the station – turn right as you exit the station.

Rishiri-Rebun-Sarobetsu National Park
利尻礼文サロベツ
国立公園

The Rishiri-Rebun-Sarobetsu National Park is made up of the two islands of Rishiri-tō and Rebun-tō, but also includes a 27 km strip of coast on the mainland of Hokkaidō known as the Sarobetsu Plain.

If you have the time, a visit to Rishiri-tō and Rebun-tō islands is a must. The best weather for hiking is during the tourist season which lasts from June to late September. You should plan on spending a minimum of four days if you want to visit both islands at an easy pace, including a hike or two.

RISHIRI-TŌ ISLAND　利尻島
This is an island dominated by the volcanic

peak of Mt Rishiri-zan which soars majestically out of the sea. A road circles the island and a bus service links the small fishing communities. The main activity for visitors is hiking on the various trails and lakes below the summit of the mountain. Providing you have warm clothes and proper footwear, the hike to the summit can be comfortably completed in a full day. Oshidomari and Kutsugata are the main ports for the island.

Information
Information booths at the ferry terminals of these two ports provide maps and information on transport, sights and hiking as well as making reservations for accommodation. The booths are opened for the arrival or departure of ferries.

Mt Rishiri-zan Hike　利尻山ハイク
There are three trails to the summit (1718 metres) but the most reliable ones lead from

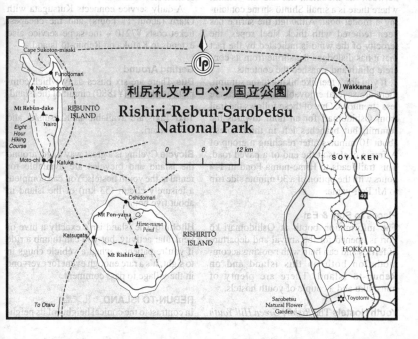

Oshidomari and Kutsugata. It doesn't make much difference which of these trails you take up, and which one you take down. Prepare properly for a mountain hike, aim for an early start and allow at least 10 hours for the ascent and descent. Advice and maps in Japanese (excellent hiking details with contour lines) are available from the information booths at the ports and from the youth hostels.

Just below the summit is Rishiridake-Sangoya, an unstaffed mountain hut, which perches on the edge of a precipice and provides the bare minimum for a roof over your head. Take your own food (purchase it from shops in the ports) and water. If you stay here, be warned that it's bloody cold at night and the wind contributes generously to the drop in temperatures. If you can't sleep, the night views are absolutely amazing and, providing the clarity holds, the views during the day extend as far as Sakhalin Island (Russia).

There is severe erosion on the sections between the mountain hut and the summit where there is a small Shintō shrine containing a model boat. Although the shrine has been tethered with thick steel ropes, the ferocity of the wind is indicated by the fact that it has dislodged the shrine from its concrete plinth and smashed the contents.

If you don't feel like hiking to the summit, there are several enjoyable hikes which are less strenuous. One of these follows the trail from Oshidomari for an hour towards the summit, but branches left in thick forest, about 10 minutes after reaching a group of A-frame chalets at the end of a paved road. This trail leads to Hime-numa Pond in 1¾ hours with the option of a 30 minute side trip to Mt Pon-yama.

Places to Stay & Eat
The information booth at Oshidomari-kō Port is opened for the arrival and departure of ferries and can help with booking accommodation both on this island and on Rebun-tō Island. There are plenty of minshuku and a couple of youth hostels.

Youth Hostels The *Rishiri Green Hill Youth*

Hostel (☎ 01638-2-2507) is a five minute bus ride or 25 minute walk from Oshidomari-kō Port. Bicycle and scooter rental is available. Beds are ¥2300.

Minshuku *Herasano-ya* (☎ 01638-2-2361) is a member of the Toho network and is three minutes on foot from Oshidomari-kō Port. Prices start at ¥7000 per person including two meals. It's closed from November until the end of April.

Getting There & Away
Air It's a 20 minute hop with ANK from Wakkanai and the round-trip ticket costs ¥10,580 – there are two flights daily during the peak summer season. The information office (☎ 01638-2-1770) at Rishiri Kūkō Airfield is open from 9 am to 5 pm.

Ferry For details of the service from Oshidomari via Kafuka (Rebun-tō Island) to Wakkanai, see the Getting There & Away section for Wakkanai.

A daily service connects Kutsugata with Otaru (about 11 hours) and the cheapest ticket costs ¥7210 – the same service also extends to Kafuka on Rebun-tō Island.

Getting Around
Bus There are six buses daily which complete a 1¾ hour (¥1880) circuit of the island.

Taxi Taxis are available in Kutsugata and Oshidomari.

Bicycle Cycling is a great way to get around the island and bicycles are available for rental at the youth hostels. You can complete a leisurely circuit (53 km) of the island in about five hours.

Hitching The island isn't exactly a hive of vehicular activity, but you can thumb a ride if you're patient – when a vehicle chugs in to sight, it's a rare enough event for everyone in the village to pass comment.

REBUN-TŌ ISLAND 礼文島
In contrast to the conical heights of its neigh-

bour, Rebun-tō is a low, sausage-shaped island which has one major road down the east coast. The main attractions of the island are the hiking trails which follow routes along the west coast past remote fishing communities. Between June and August, the island's alpine flowers – over 300 species – pull out all the stops for a floral extravaganza: a memorable experience.

Kafuka and Funadomari are the main communities and ports, at the southern and northern ends of the island, respectively.

Hiking on Rebun-tō Island

The classic hike down the entire length of the western coast is known as the *hachijikan haikingu Kōsu* (eight-hour hiking course). It's a marvellous hike across varied terrain: grassy cliff tops, fields of dwarf bamboo, forests of conifers, deserted, rocky beaches and remote harbours with clusters of fishing shacks and racks of seaweed. There doesn't seem to be much sense in following the example of many Japanese hikers who turn it into an endurance race – complete with certificate of survival! If you have the extra day, or simply want to pack less into the day, it would be more enjoyable to break the hike into two four-hour sections *(yonjikan haikingu Kōsu*, or four-hour hiking course) starting or finishing at Nishi-uedomari.

Information & Preparation

All the youth hostels and other places to stay on the island provide information on hiking, transport to trailheads and assign hikers to groups.

Although the eight-hour hike is not a death-defying feat, it has some tricky stretches, including steep slopes of loose scree and several km of boulder-hopping along beaches, which can become very nasty in the unpredictable weather of these northern regions. Much of the trail is several hours away from human habitation and, for the most part, those who slip off a cliff or twist an ankle will require rescue by boat. There's no need to be paranoid, but this is the reason why group hiking is encouraged. Beware of being marshalled into large groups because

things can then become too regimented. The best group size is four.

You'll need proper footwear, warm clothes and some form of rainwear. The hostels often provide packed lunches which hikers affectionately refer to as 'the Japanese Flag' – an aluminium container of rice with an *umeboshi* stuck in the centre. Take water or soft drinks with you. Do *not* drink the water from the streams. During the '30s, foxes were introduced from the Kurile Islands (Russia) and their faeces now contaminate the streams – it may be tapeworm gunk or something else.

Rebun Youth Hostel in Kafuka has an excellent guidebook in English entitled *Hiking Maps of Rebun*. The author details seven hikes and grades them according to difficulty and a really useful point is the inclusion of place names in kanji and romaji. The book is not for sale, but you can look through it and make notes, sketch maps and compile lists of place names.

Hiking Routes The eight-hour hike runs from Cape Sukoton-misaki on the northern tip, down to Moto-chi on the southern tip. The four-hour hike starts or finishes at Nishi-uedomari, a small fishing village midway down the trail. You can follow the trails in either direction – most people seem to hike from north to south – but make sure you have arranged transport and keep your timetable flexible to avoid spoiling things with the rush of a forced march.

Another popular hike is from Nairo, halfway down the east coast, to the top of Mt Rebun-dake. The peak is a tiddler at 490 metres, but it's a pleasant 3½ hour return hike.

Places to Stay & Eat

The information booth at the port can help find accommodation. There are many minshuku, a couple of hotels and a trio of youth hostels on the island.

Youth Hostels *Rebun Youth Hostel* (☎ 01638-6-1608) in Kafuka is a very friendly place, 13 minutes on foot from

Kafuka-kō Port. If you phone ahead, they'll pick you up at the port and when you leave, you may be given a lift back to the port. A bed costs ¥2300.

Momoiwa-sō Youth Hostel (☎ 01638-6-1421) is a 15 minute bus ride from Kafuka-kō Port. Take the bus bound for Moto-chi and get off at the Momoiwa Iriguchi stop; the hostel is about a seven minute walk from there, conveniently close to one of the trailheads for the eight hour hike. It's open from 1 June to 30 September only. Beds are ¥2300.

Rebun-tō Funadomari Youth Hostel (☎ 01638-7-2717) is a 20 minute walk from Funadomari-kō Port. It's open from 10 May to 15 October only. Beds are ¥2500.

Minshuku & Ryokan *Seikan-sō* (☎ 01638-7-2078) is a member of the Toho network, just a couple of minutes on foot from Funadomari-kō Port. If you speak some Japanese you can ring them up for a lift from the port. Prices start at ¥4500 per person including two meals. It's closed from October until the beginning of May.

Just south of the port area is the *Sakurai Ryokan* (☎ 01638-6-1030), a very modern looking ryokan with per-person costs from ¥8000 with two meals.

Getting There & Away
Air It's a 20 minute hop with ANK from Wakkanai and the round-trip ticket costs ¥12,080 – there are flights twice daily during the peak summer season. The information office (☎ 01638-7-2175) at Rebun Airfield is open from 9 am to 5 pm.

Ferry For details of the service from Kafuka providing connections to Oshidomari (Rishiri-tō Island) and to Wakkanai, see the Getting There & Away section for Wakkanai. There is one daily ferry between Funadomari and Wakkanai.

A daily service connects Kafuka via Kutsugata (Rishiri-tō Island) with Otaru in about 11 hours and the cheapest ticket costs ¥7720.

Getting Around
Most of the time you'll be getting around the island on foot. Youth hostels and other accommodation will usually help with your transport arrangements on arrival or departure. Taxis are available, but careful attention to the bus timetables should be enough to get you to the key points for hiking. A couple of the minshuku also have bicycles to rent.

Bus The main bus service follows the island's one major road from Kafuka in the south, to Cape Sukoton-misaki in the north. En route it passes Funadomari, the Kūkō-shita (airport) bus stop and Nishi-uedomari. Buses run on this route up to six times daily, but only four go to Cape Sukoton-misaki. Top marks must go to the solitary splendour of the cape's hi-tech toilet, where you can follow the needs of nature while listening to the recorded sounds of the waves outside! Another useful bus service runs five times daily from Kafuka to Moto-chi, a trailhead for the hike along the western coastline of the island. Pick up a copy of the island's bus timetable at the information office in Kafuka-kō Port.

Hitching Since there is only one major road, hitching is relatively simple. The only problem is that most of the traffic seems to consist of fisherfolk commuting, at most, one km from the beach to their home.

SAROBETSU NATURAL FLOWER GARDEN サロベツ原生花園
The Sarobetsu Gensai-kaen (Natural Flower Garden) is basically a tourist information office with a series of wooden walkways across swamps. It is the most well-known part of the Sarobetsu Plain, which lies a short distance south of Wakkanai, and is a vast swampy region famous for its flora. From June to late July, Japanese tourists come here for the vistas of flowers – mainly rhododendrons, irises and lilies.

During the flowering season, there are buses running from Toyotomi station to the garden in 14 minutes (¥380).

YAGISHIRI-TŌ & TEURI-TŌ ISLANDS
焼尻島・天売島

Yagishiri-tō and neighbouring Teuri-tō lie off the west coast of Hokkaidō and are popular with naturalists and ornithologists, who take boat trips out to the islands between June and August.

Excursion boats leave from Haboro and take 80 minutes (¥1300) to Yagishiri-tō before continuing for the 20 minute trip (¥600) to Teuri-tō Island. The service only operates between June and August.

A bus service connects Haboro with Horonobe, just south of the Sarobetsu Plain, and Rumoi, on the coast west of Asahikawa. Both Horonobe and Rumoi are also accessible by rail.

Daisetsuzan National Park
大雪山国立公園

This is Japan's largest national park (2309 sq km), consisting of several mountain groups, volcanoes, lakes and forests. It also includes Mt Asahi-dake, which at 2290 metres is Hokkaidō's highest peak. The park is spectacular hiking and skiing territory and the main centres of interest are Sōunkyō, Asahidake Onsen, Tenninkyō Onsen, Furano and Tokachidake Onsen. You can pick up maps and information (in English) about the park in Sapporo or try the tourist information offices locally. Only a couple of hikes on the more well-trodden trails have been mentioned here, but there are many more routes leading to more remote regions if you have several days or even a week to spare.

Those planning to take a look at the park should bear in mind that at least a few days are needed to get away from the park's tourist traps. It's dubious whether it's worth just heading up to Sōunkyō for an overnight trip. If you have limited time, Asahidake Onsen is a less touristy spot for a quick look at the park.

The main gateways to the park are

Asahikawa and Kamikawa in the north, Kitami in the east and Obihiro in the south. Bus services through the park are restricted to routes between Kitami and Kamikawa (continuing to Asahikawa) via Sōunkyō and a service between Asahikawa and Tenninkyō Onsen via Asahidake Onsen.

KAMIKAWA 上川
Kamikawa is a useful gateway to Sōunkyō in Daisetsuzan National Park, but it's definitely not an attraction in itself.

Places to Stay
Unless you're taking a very leisurely tour around Hokkaidō, there's no need (or reason) to stay in Kamikawa, which is a fairly dull kind of place. The *Yuwanto-Mura* (☎ 0165-82-2772), a member of the Toho network, is about four km from JR Kamikawa station. From the station, take the bus bound for Sōunkyō and get off after six minutes at the Rubeshibe-bashi stop; from there, it's about 20 minutes on foot. From the bus stop, backtrack a little, turn right, walk for 800 metres and turn right again; Yuwanto-Mura is 800 metres down the road on the right. Prices start at ¥4000 per person including two meals. Yuwanto-Mura is closed from 1 November to 20 December.

Getting There & Away
Local trains from Asahikawa take about 1¼ hours to Kamikawa on the JR Sekihoku line. Buses run from Kamikawa to Sōunkyō in 32 minutes (¥600).

ASAHIDAKE ONSEN 旭岳温泉
This unspoilt hot-spring resort consists of several houses surrounded by forest at the foot of Mt Asahi-dake (2290 metres) – the highest mountain on Hokkaidō. The nearby cablecar runs in two stages (12 minutes, ¥1300) to a point within easy hiking distance of the peak.

The base station of the cablecar has a restaurant and shop where you can buy *Daisetsuzan Attack* (¥1500), a very detailed map in Japanese. The youth hostel can provide advice on hiking and will loan you

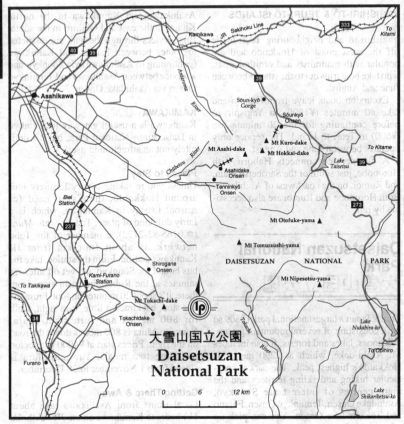

大雪山国立公園
Daisetsuzan National Park

a hiking map together with a compass and a jingle-bell. There are rotemburo (open-air, natural hot springs) at **Yudoku Onsen** and **Nakadake Onsen** along the trails over the peaks. Take warm clothing, appropriate footwear, and sufficient food and drink. During the peak hiking seasons, cablecars and lifts operate from as early as 6 am until as late as 7.30 pm.

There are dozens of hiking options in this region; the most popular hike follows trails from the Mt Asahi-dake cablecar via several peaks to **Sōunkyō** – allow about 6½ hours. From the top station of the Mt Asahi-dake

cablecar, it takes 1¾ hours to climb along a ridge overlooking steaming, volcanic vents to reach the peak of Mt Asahi-dake.

From there, you can continue via Mt Hokkai-dake (1½ hours) to **Mt Kurodake Ishimuro** (1½ hours) for a pause at the mountain hut and then continue via the peak of Mt Kuro-dake (30 minutes) to the top station of Sōunkyō chair lift (40 minutes). The lift takes 15 minutes to connect with a cablecar which whisks you down to Sōunkyō in seven minutes.

From Asahidake Onsen there's a trail through the forest to **Tenninkyō Onsen**, a small hot-spring resort with a scenic gorge and waterfall, which can be used as a base for extended hiking into the park.

Places to Stay & Eat

Daisetsuzan Shirakaba-sō (☎ 0166-97-2246) is an outstanding youth hostel at Asahidake Onsen. The evening meals are excellent and sometimes include fish caught from the mountain stream outside. There's an indoor hot-spring bath, an outdoor rotemburo where you can soak under the stars, a beautiful Canadian log cabin with a Japanese tatami-mat interior and the couple who run the place are well travelled and genuinely hospitable.

From the hostel – maps and advice are provided – you can hike up and over Mt Asahi-dake, or do more hiking towards Tenninkyō Onsen. Cross-country skiing is popular here in the winter too. Those coming in from Asahikawa by bus would be better off getting off at the kampu-jō-mae stop before Asahidake – the hostel is across the road. The hostel offers a refund for the bus ticket from Asahikawa for its guests. The charge for a bed is ¥2400.

Another accommodation option is the *Asahidake Park Hotel* (☎ 0166-97-2136), a delightfully eccentric little building that looks nothing like a hotel. Per-person costs with two meals range from ¥7500 to ¥8000. The similarly designed 'mountain lodge' *Ezo Matsu-sō* (☎ 0166-97-2321) is a little more up-market, with per-person costs (again with two meals) ranging from ¥9000 to ¥10,000. Another atmospheric place is the *Lodge Nutapu-Kaushipe* (☎ 0166-97-2150). Per-person costs with two meals are ¥6500. All three are close to each other below the cable-car station on the road to Asahikawa.

Getting There & Away

A bus service runs twice daily from Asahikawa to Tenninkyō Onsen via Asahidake Onsen; from mid-June to mid-October the service increases to three times daily. The last bus to Asahidake Onsen is at 3 pm; the last bus from Asahidake Onsen is at 5 pm. The trip takes 1½ hours and the

ticket costs ¥1180 – see the previous section for details of the youth hostel ticket refund.

SŌUNKYŌ　層雲峡温泉

Sōunkyō is the tourist hub of the park and consists of Sōunkyō Onsen, the hot-spring resort with an array of brutally ugly hotels, and Sōun-kyō Gorge itself – *kyō* means gorge in Japanese. For hikers, the gorge may seem a secondary attraction, rather tame compared to the role of Sōunkyō Onsen as a gateway for hikes into the interior of the park.

Information

The Kankō Centre next to the bus stop has a bus booking office and an accommodation booking office. The latter may be useful if you arrive at a busy time of year. No English is spoken, but the friendly staff do their best to help. Look out for the posters exhorting 'Open a Sōunkyō to the humans'.

Sōun-kyō Gorge　層雲峡

The gorge stretches for about eight km beyond Sōunkyō Onsen and is renowned for its waterfalls – Ryūsei-no-taki and Ginga-no-taki are the main ones – and for two sections of perpendicular columns of rock which give an enclosed feeling, hence their names: Ōbako (Big Box) and Kobako (Little Box).

Since the view from the road is restricted by tunnels, a separate cycling path has been constructed and local entrepreneurs derive a sizeable income from bicycle rental at ¥1200 per day – the local youth hostels probably offer the best deals for bicycle rental. You could also speed things up by taking a taxi to Obako (20 minute ride) and walking back in a couple of hours.

Hiking Routes

The combination of a cablecar (seven minutes, ¥750) and a chair lift (15 minutes, ¥220) provides fast access to Mt Kuro-dake for skiers and hikers. Discounts are given to youth hostellers and for return tickets.

The most popular hike is the one across to Mt Asahi-dake – see the section on Asahidake

Onsen for details. You can arrange to leave your baggage at either end and pick it up later after making the tedious loop back through Asahikawa by bus, or simply restrict your baggage to the minimum required for an overnight stay and return on foot by a different trail.

If you want to do simple day hikes from Sōunkyō Onsen and return there at the end of the day, you could climb from the chair lift station to the peak of Mt Kuro-dake in an hour and then descend in about 20 minutes to the mountain hut called Kurodake Ishimuro which provides basic accommodation and food during the peak hiking season. The return trip to this hut from Sōunkyō Onsen takes about four hours at a leisurely pace.

Places to Stay & Eat
Youth hostellers only have the option of the *Sōunkyō Youth Hostel* (☎ 0165-85-3418), about five to 10 minutes walk from the bus station in Sōunkyō. The hostel organises early morning hikes to Mt Kuro-dake during summer.

Apart from the youth hostel, there are dozens of other accommodation options. Most of the hotels are extremely expensive – one of the cheaper ones is the *Hotel Ginsen-kaku* (☎ 0165-85-3501), where room rates start at around ¥10,000.

A more homey and affordable option would be one of the many minshuku in the area. The *Kitakawa Minshuku* (☎ 0165-85-3515) costs ¥6000 per person with two meals. It has another branch (☎ 0165-85-3015) with the same rates. Also at the same price is the *Ginsen Minshuku* (☎ 0165-85-3503).

Sōunkyō is one of those Japanese tourist towns where everyone eats in their hotel or minshuku. Basic snacks (noodles and so on) are available during the day at both ends of the cablecar and above the Kankō Centre at *Milky House*.

Getting There & Away
Buses run from Sōunkyō to Kamikawa (32 minutes, ¥600). The bus service from

Sōunkyō to Kitami takes about two hours. The price is a hefty ¥2400, but you get to ride in a deluxe sightseeing bus with plush seats, chandeliers!, headphones, etc – a bizarre contrast with the wild scenery outside, especially if you've been out there hiking for a few days.

If you want to head south towards Obihiro, you'll have to use Route 273 which follows a scenic route via Lake Nukabira-ko, but which has *no* bus services – hitch or hire a car. From Obihiro, there's a bus (1¾ hours, ¥1600) to Lake Shikaribetsu-ko which is about 15 km from Lake Nukabira-ko. Incidentally, Obihiro will delight park-bench enthusiasts: it has the world's longest bench at 400 metres! Plenty of room for those who need to sit and think for a while.

FURANO 富良野
This is one of Japan's most famous ski resorts with over a dozen ski lifts and excellent facilities for powder skiing considered by some to be among the best in the world.

The JR Furano line links Asahikawa with Furano in 1¼ hours. There is also a railway line from Sapporo via Takikawa to Furano and trains take 2¼ hours. Buses also run directly from Sapporo to Furano in 2½ hours (¥1800).

Places to Stay
There are plenty of minshuku, ryokan, hotels and pensions – the information counter at Furano station can provide help with accommodation. For an inexpensive place to stay, you could try *Furano White Youth Hostel* (☎ 0167-23-4807), which is a 10 minute bus ride from Furano station. In winter take a bus bound for the *suki-jō* (skiing ground) and get off at the last stop – the youth hostel is 150 metres from the stop. In summer take a bus bound for Goryo and get off at the Kisen stop, which is around 200 metres from the hostel. Buses leave from Furano station. The hostel is closed from 11 to 27 April and from 5 November to 4 December. Rates are ¥2500.

TOKACHIDAKE & SHIROGANE ONSEN
十勝岳・白金温泉

A short distance north-east of Furano are the remote hot-spring villages of Tokachidake Onsen and Shirogane Onsen, which are bases for hiking and skiing. You can climb **Mt Tokachi-dake** in a day; some trails extend as far as Tenninkyō Onsen or Mt Asahi-dake, but these require between three and four days of hiking. An inexpensive place to stay at Shirogane Onsen is *Shirogane Center* (☎ 0166-94-3131), a youth hostel with rates at ¥2300. It's one minute on foot from the Shirogane Onsen bus stop.

From Kami Furano station on the JR Furano line, it's a 35 minute bus ride (¥490) to Tokachidake Onsen – up to three buses daily. From Biei station on the JR Furano line, it's a 30 minute bus ride (¥600) to Shirogane Onsen – up to four buses daily.

BIHORO 美幌
Bihoro lies east of Asahikawa, and north of Akan National Park. If you're not going to Shiretoko National Park, you can head south from here into Akan National Park.

From Bihoro, sightseeing buses follow a scenic route to the park, pausing after 50 minutes at **Bihoro Pass** which provides a superb view across Lake Kussharo-ko. The buses then continue around all the sights of the park for another 2¾ hours before reaching the terminus at Akan Kohan. It's best to use this expensive service in small doses – the incessant, babbling commentary and 'packaged' feel can be oppressive. The trip from Bihoro to Kawayu Onsen on the shore of Lake Kussharo-ko takes 65 minutes (¥2590).

Places to Stay
Bihoro Youth Hostel (☎ 0152-73-2560) is close to the town centre. From Bihoro station it's a six minute bus ride followed by a 10 minute walk. Take a bus bound for Tsubetsu or Ryoyo-jo and get off at the minami-san-chōme stop. The hostel is closed from 26 October to 24 November and from 16 to 19 May; rates are ¥2400.

ABASHIRI 網走
Abashiri (population 44,000) is of primary interest to travellers as a transport hub for access to Shari and the Shiretoko Peninsula. The town is primarily a harbour, though the harbour itself is closed from December to March each year due to ice floes. Abashiri is also the site of a maximum security prison – there's even a **Prison Museum** you can visit on Mt Tento-san, though entry is a little steep at ¥1030.

The tourist information office in Abashiri station has details about the few sights around Abashiri that can be reached by bus from the station. There's a lookout on **Mt Tento-san**, about four km from the station, which also features the **Museum of Ice Floes** (Okhotsk Ryū-hōkan) (¥500) and another museum, **Oroke Kinenkan**, which displays items from the culture of the Oroke, a nomadic tribe of Siberian origins, but now close to extinction.

Places to Stay & Eat
For reasonably priced accommodation close to the station, one of the best bets is the *Business Ryokan Miyuki* (☎ 0152-43-4425), a small place where per-person costs are ¥5500 with two meals. No English is spoken. To get there, turn right (east) out of the station and take the first turn right. Turn left after the park and look for the ryokan just after the first street on the right.

The *Minshuku Hokui Yonjū-Yondo* (☎ 0152-44-4325), a member of the Toho network, is a 30 minute walk from Abashiri station down Route 39 in the direction of Mt Tento-san or a five minute bus ride followed by a three minute walk. Prices start at ¥3800 per person including two meals. The hot springs can be used for an additional fee of ¥200.

Also in the same direction (turn left off Route 39 just before Abashiri-ko Lake) is *Amina-no-Sato* (☎ 0152-43-6806), another Toho network member, with per-person costs of ¥4500 with two meals. It's a long 45 minute walk from the station. Alternatively, take a Bihoro bound bus and get off at the entrance to Mt Tento-san (tento-san-Iriguchi). From there it's a five minute walk.

The nearest youth hostel is *Gensei-Kaen* (☎ 0152-46-2630), which is a 15-minute walk from Kitahama station – three stops east of Abashiri. The coastal strip close to the hostel is worth a visit between June and July when it is covered for many km with a blanket of flowers. The hostel charges ¥2500.

Getting There & Away

Abashiri is the terminus for the JR Sekihoku line which runs across the centre of Hokkaidō to Asahikawa – the fastest trains take about 3¾ hours.

It is also the terminus for the JR Senmō line which runs via Shari to Kushiro. From Abashiri to Shari takes 2¼ hours. It's hard to make good use of this line because trains are slow and infrequent. You might prefer to take the 65 minute bus ride (¥980) from Abashiri to Shari – there are up to four buses daily.

Shiretoko National Park
知床国立公園

This remote park (386 sq km) features a peninsula with a range of volcanic peaks leading out to the rugged cliffs around Cape Shiretoko-misaki. Two roads run along each side of the peninsula, but they peter out well before the tip which can be viewed as part of a long boat excursion from Utoro. Another road crosses the peninsula from Rausu to Utoro. Transport is restricted to infrequent buses and bicycle rental; hitching can prove quite successful. The main season for visitors is from mid-June to mid-September – most of the hikes are not recommended outside this season.

From Shari, the gateway to the peninsula, there is an efficient bus service to the large and rather bland resort of Utoro. However, as Iwaobetsu Youth Hostel is more convenient as a base for hiking, details about sights and hiking on the peninsula are concentrated in the Iwaobetsu section.

知床国立公園
Shiretoko National Park

SHARI 斜里

Shari functions as the gateway to Shiretoko-hantō Peninsula. A tourist information office at the station can provide timetables and leaflets in Japanese.

Places to Stay & Eat

The *Shari Youth Hostel* (☎ 01522-3-2220) is just five minutes walk from Shari station – take the east exit, turn left, left again, and look for the hostel on the left. Per-person costs are ¥2300. The hostel is closed from 1 November to 15 February.

Kaze-no-Ko (☎ 01522-3-1121) is a member of the Toho network. From Shari station, take the bus bound for Utoro and get off after 10 minutes (Nishi-nisen-basutei-mae stop). Prices start at ¥4000 per person including two meals.

Getting There & Away

The bus centre is to your left as you exit the station. There are up to eight buses daily from Shari to Utoro (¥1340), but only three or four continue to Iwaobetsu – the full trip from Shari to Iwaobetsu takes 70 minutes (¥1600). Buses to Rausu operate twice daily from July to mid-October.

UTORO　ウトロ

Although Utoro is the largest resort on the peninsula, the boat excursions are about the only things it has to offer. There's a tourist information office just behind the bus centre. The *Shiretoko Youth Hostel* (☎ 01522-4-2034) is a massive place ready to cater for large numbers. Take a bus from the Utoro bus terminal and get off at the Yūsu-hosuteru-mae stop. The hostel charges ¥2300. Bicycle rental is available.

Between May and early September, two boat excursions operate from Utoro: one runs once daily out to the soaring cliffs of Cape Shiretoko-misaki (¥6000, 3¾ hours); the other runs up to five times daily for a short cruise along the coastline as far as Kamuiwakka-no-taki Falls (¥2400, 90 minutes).

IWAOBETSU　岩尾別

Iwaobetsu is a hamlet, further up the coast from Utoro, and the *Shiretoko Iwaobetsu Youth Hostel* (☎ 01522-4-2311) deserves recommendation as a friendly and convenient base for exploring the peninsula. The hostel runs 'briefing' sessions every evening to outline hikes and trips available; organised outings are also arranged. Bicycle rental is available at ¥300 per day.

The hostel is closed from 25 October until 1 June. If you are fortunate enough to arrive when the hostel opens for the season, you can expect three consecutive nights of slap-up dinners and partying. Per-person costs are ¥2500.

To reach the hostel, either take a direct bus from Shari or Utoro for Shiretoko Goko (Shiretoko Five Lakes) (70 minutes, ¥1600 from Shari), and get off at Iwaobetsu. The hostel is only one minute from the Iwaobetsu bus stop. If you've missed the bus from Utoro, either hitch (it's only nine km) or phone the cheery and long-suffering hostel

manager, who has been known to fetch stranded foreigners.

A road almost opposite the youth hostel leads four km uphill to Iwaobetsu Onsen, which lies at the start of the trail up Mt Rausu-dake. The *Hotel Chi-no-Hate* (☎ 01522-4-2331) here is a bit frayed at the edges, and isn't particularly cheap (¥15,000 per person with two meals). Still, it's worth wandering up here for the rotemburo (open-air baths) just below the hotel's car park.

Shiretoko Peninsula Attractions

About 10 minutes by bus from Iwaobetsu Youth Hostel are the **Shiretoko Goko** (Shiretoko Five Lakes), where wooden walkways have been laid out for visitors to stroll around the lakes in an hour or so. You can pick up with the buses (there are five a day from Shari) in Shari, Utaro or Iwaobetsu.

Another 45 minutes by bus down the rough road towards the tip of the peninsula, you come to the **Shiretoko-ōhashi Bridge** just below the spectacular rotemburo which form part of **Kamuiwakka-no-taki Falls**. It takes about 20 minutes to climb up the rocky bed of the stream until you come to cascades of hot water emptying into a succession of pools. Bathers simply strip off and soak in the pools and enjoy the superb panorama across the ocean. A special sightseeing bus service operates to the lakes and the rotemburo once a day between mid-June and mid-September – passengers are given time to take a dip in the pools.

There are several hikes on the peninsula: Iwaobetsu Youth Hostel can provide more detailed advice on routes, trail conditions and the organisation of transport. Proper footwear and warm clothes are essential.

The hike to the top of **Mt Rausu-dake** starts from the hotel at Iwaobetsu Onsen. There's only one bus a day out to the hotel, so you'll probably have to walk for an hour up the road from Iwaobetsu Youth Hostel to reach the start of the trail – allow 4½ hours from there to reach the top (1660 metres) at a comfortable pace.

The hike to the summit of **Mt Iō-zan** (1562 metres) starts about 500 metres beyond

Shiretoko-ōhashi Bridge and requires about eight hours for the return trip.

The youth hostel owner also recommended another short hike from Shiretoko Pass – midway between Utoro and Rausu – to Lake Rausu-ko.

RAUSU 羅臼

This is an unimpressive fishing village, popular with Japanese for its *todo* (sea lion) meat.

Places to Stay

Rausu Youth Hostel (☎ 01538-7-2145) is reached by infrequent bus services either from Shibetsu to the south, or from Utoro to the west. It's a one minute walk from the Honmachi bus stop and nightly costs are ¥2300.

Akan National Park
阿寒国立公園

This large park (905 sq km) in eastern Hokkaidō contains several volcanic peaks, some large caldera lakes and extensive forests.

The main gateways on the fringe of the park are Bihoro in the north and Kushiro in the south. The major centres inside the park are the towns of Teshikaga, Kawayu Onsen and Akan Kohan. The main sights have been included with the descriptions of the last two towns as they provide the most convenient bases from which to see them.

The only efficient and speedy transport in the park is provided by sightseeing buses, which get you to the sights but also have the disadvantages of 'packaged' travel – see the comments in the Bihoro section. Bus services are most frequent between June and October. Kushiro would be a convenient choice to rent a car – ask at the tourist information office in Kushiro station. The JR Senmō line runs from Shari to Kushiro but trains are slow and infrequent. Hitching is a viable alternative.

KAWAYU ONSEN 川湯温泉

This hot-spring resort is a convenient base for visiting the nearby sights of Lake Kussharo-ko, Mt Iō-zan and Lake Mashū-ko.

About three km from Kawayu Onsen is **Lake Kussharo-ko**, the largest inland lake in Hokkaidō and a popular spot for swimming and camping. At **Sunayu Onsen** on the eastern shore, the hot springs warm the sand on the beach and at **Wakoto Onsen** on the southern shore, there are hot springs bubbling into open-air pools.

Mt Iō-zan, just outside Kawayu Onsen, is unmistakable for its steam and distinctive smell. A pleasant nature trail leads from the bus centre through dwarf pines to the mountain and takes 35 minutes. The scene is certainly impressive with hissing vents, billowing clouds of steam and bright yellow sulphur deposits. The egg business is big here; crates of them are boiled over the vents and sold at ¥350 for five – although the whole place provides an eggy whiff for free anyway.

Lake Mashū-ko is about 15 km south-east of Kawayu Onsen. Known to the Ainu as the 'Lake of the Devil', there is certainly an unusual atmosphere to this lake, which is surrounded by steep rock walls that reach a height of 300 metres. If you are fortunate enough to visit when the lake is not wreathed in mist, the clarity of the water and its intense blue colour is quite startling – its transparency depth of over 35 metres is said to be one of the deepest in the world. Visitors view the lake from three observation points which are equipped with souvenir stands and stalls selling sweet corn.

The observation points are best reached from Mashū station (two stops south of Kawayu Onsen station). Buses run from Teshikaga Onsen, about five minutes walk from the station, to the observation points. Observation points No 1 and 3 are closest. No 1 is a 35 minute bus journey (¥630), and No 2 takes 50 minutes (¥840).

Places to Stay & Eat

The *Mashū Youth Hostel* (☎ 01548-2-3098)

is the only youth hostel accommodation available in the area. From Mashū station take a bus bound for Bihoro or Kawayu and get off at the Yūsu-hosuteru-mae stop. If you arrive at Mashū station after 4 pm, ring the hostel for a lift with their minibus. Nightly rates are ¥2500. The hostel is closed from 1 December to 20 December. *Sanzoku-no-Ie* (☎ 01548-3-2725), a member of the Toho network, is a small minshuku about six minutes on foot from Kawayu Onsen station. Prices start at ¥4500 per person including two meals. It's open from May to late October.

Mashumaro (☎ 01548-2-2027), a member of the Toho network, is a five minute walk from JR Biruwa station – the stop between Kawayu Onsen and Teshikaga. Prices start at ¥4500 per person including two meals. It's closed during November and April.

Getting There & Away

The JR Senmō line links Kawayu station

with Shari in 55 minutes and with Kushiro in 1½ hours. Kawayu Onsen bus centre is a 10 minute bus ride from Kawayu station.

A sightseeing bus service operates from Kawayu Onsen via the main sights in the park to Akan Kohan (2½ hours, ¥3160).

TESHIKAGA　弟子屈

Teshikaga lies in the centre of the park and is a useful transport hub, but there's no pressing reason to stay here.

The sightseeing buses all pass through Teshikaga, which is 15 minutes south of Kawayu Onsen on the JR Senmō line (the relevant station is Mashū station, just to confuse things). Between Lake Akan-ko and Teshikaga is a particularly scenic stretch on Route 241, with an outstanding lookout at **Sokodai**, which overlooks Lake Penketō and Lake Panketō.

AKAN KOHAN　阿寒湖畔

This is a hot-spring resort on the edge of

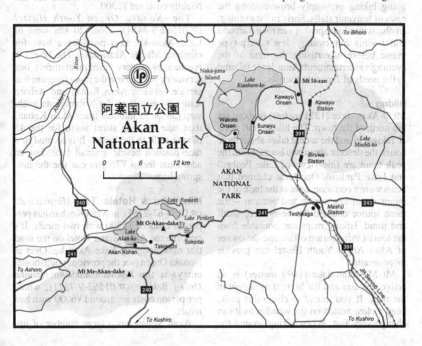

Lake Akan-ko. You can safely skip the boat trips (¥810) on the lake and the atrocious tourist facilities that purport to be part of an Ainu village, but we'd still recommend using this resort as a base for doing some interesting mountain hikes in the area.

On the eastern edge of the resort is a tourist information office where you can pick up information and hiking maps for the region – mostly in Japanese. The centre also has tanks where you can come face to face with *marimo*, a globe-shaped algae which is peculiar to the lake. These green fuzzballs can take 200 years to grow to the size of a baseball and have the ability to rise to the surface or sink to the bed of the lake, depending on the weather. They are interesting items, but severely overdone as a tourist attraction.

Behind the centre is a nature trail which leads through the woods to **Bokke** (a collection of spluttering mudholes beside the lake) and then returns to the town.

In town, you can stock up on food if you're going hiking or simply browse along the rows of souvenir stalls. Early in the evening, an obnoxious loudspeaker van roams around and booms out twangy Jew's harp-type music before advertising the time of the evening's entertainment: Ainu dance tailored to the needs of Japanese tourists.

Hiking

Mt O-Akan-dake (1371 metres) is about six km north of the town. The hiking trail starts at Takiguchi and the ascent takes about three hours, the descent about two hours. From the peak there are fine views of Lake Penketō and Lake Panketō. One local claimed that bears were a common sight at the base of the mountain in late spring and autumn – the same source claimed the bears were small and timid. Hiking maps are available from the tourist information office and the owner of Akan Angel Youth Hostel can provide more details.

Mt Me-Akan-dake (1499 metres) is an active volcano and the highest mountain in the park. If you intend to climb this peak, keep a close watch on the weather as it can change very fast. When hiking around the crater, watch out for the noxious effects of the sulphur fumes from the vents. There is a clear trail up the mountain which requires about 4½ hours for the ascent and 3½ hours for the descent if you return by the same trail. It's also possible to descend by a different trail on the west side of the mountain which joins the road leading to Nonaka Onsen Youth Hostel. Hiking maps are available from the tourist information office and the owner of Akan Angel Youth Hostel can provide more details.

Places to Stay & Eat

Youth Hostels The *Akan Angel Youth Hostel* (☎ 0154-67-2309) is a 12 minute walk from the bus terminal at Akan Kohan. If you phone ahead, the friendly owner may offer to fetch you and will give you a lift to the terminal when you leave. He can also provide advice on hiking in the area and often takes groups himself. Bicycle rental and a hot-spring bath (¥150 additional fee) are also available. Nightly costs are ¥2300.

The *Nonaka Onsen Youth Hostel* (☎ 01562-9-7454), about 20 km west of Lake Akan-ko, also provides a base for climbing Mt Me-Akan-dake. The hostel is reached by a very infrequent direct bus service or you can use the more frequent bus service between Akan Kohan and Ashoro station – get off at the Noboriyama-guchi stop (about 55 minutes from Akan Kohan) then take the side street south for the 45 minute walk to the hostel. It is located in a nice position beside a small lake. For an additional fee of ¥75 you can use the hot-spring bath.

Minshuku & Hotels The *Minshuku-dō* (☎ 0154-67-2755), in Akan Konhan has per-person costs of ¥5500 with two meals. It's opposite the Akan Grand Hotel on the road that runs alongside Lake Akan-ko. Over at Nonaka Onsen (see the previous youth hostel entry) is the *Kokuminshukusha Nonaka Onsen Bekkan* (☎ 01562-9-7321), where per-person costs are around ¥6000 with two meals.

Akan Kohan has a large number of up-market hotels with rates of over ¥10,000 per person with two meals. Possibilities include the *Akan Royal Hotel* (☎ 0154-67-2421), which has singles from ¥8000 and twins from ¥13,000 (including two meals), the *Akan Grand Hotel* (☎ 0154-67-2531) and the *Hotel Akanko-sō* (☎ 0154-67-2231), both of which are expensive.

Getting There & Away

Sightseeing buses run north-east from Akan Kohan to the main sights in the rest of the park as far as Kawayu Onsen. Other services connect with Ashoro and Obihiro (2¾ hours, ¥3500) to the south-west, Bihoro (1¼ hours, ¥1950) and Kitami to the north and Kushiro (2¼ hours, ¥2440) to the south.

KUSHIRO 釧路

Kushiro (population 205,000) is the industrial and economic centre of eastern Hokkaidō and one of the main gateways to Akan National Park.

If you have time to spare, you might want to visit the nearby **Kushiro Shitsugen** (Kushiro Marshlands Park), a swampy area famed for its flora and dwindling numbers of *tanchō-zuru* (red-crested white cranes).

Places to Stay & Eat

The *Kushiro Makiba Youth Hostel* (☎ 0154-23-0852) is a 15 minute walk from the station. Turn left out of the station and walk eastwards for 900 metres and take the first railroad crossing after the bridge. Follow this road for around 500 metres and look out for a small park on your left. The youth hostel is just after the park. Nightly costs are ¥2300, and bicycle and scooter rental are available.

Kushiro Youth Hostel (☎ 0154-41-1676) is a 15 minute bus ride from the station on a No 27 or No 30 bus (get off at the Yūsu Hosuteru-mae stop) and from there it's a two minute walk. The hostel is out by the Kushiro Marshlands Park, and is marginally cheaper than most Japanese youth hostels – ¥1800 to ¥2000 depending on the time of year. It's closed from 16 January to 25 January and from 16 to 19 May.

For other reasonably priced accommoda-

tion, the *Ryokan Kawatani* (☎ 0154-23-8221) is about 500 metres east of the station on the road that runs parallel to the train tracks – look out for the ryokan just before the bridge. It has per-person costs of ¥5500 with two meals.

Opposite the station is the *Kushiro Tōei Hotel* (☎ 0154-23-2121), a business hotel with singles/twins at ¥7000/12,000. The *Kushiro Tokkyū Inn* (☎ 0154-22-9200) is just to the east of the station and has similar rates. A cheaper business hotel is the *Kushiro Grand Hotel* (☎ 0154-25-1277), which is just behind the station and has singles from ¥5000 to ¥5900.

Getting There & Away

Air Flights connect Kushiro with Sapporo (40 minutes) and Tokyo (1¾ hours). Kushiro Airport is a 45 minute bus ride (¥800) from Kushiro station.

Train The JR Senmō line runs north through Akan National Park to Shari. The JR Nemuro line runs west to Sapporo (4¾ hours by limited express). The fare to Sapporo is ¥5670 with a ¥2970 limited express surcharge. Sapporo also has a night service to Kushiro that leaves at around 11 pm (check for the latest time), arriving at around 5.30 am in Kushiro.

Bus There are bus services from Kushiro to Akan Kohan (2¼ hours, ¥2440) and to Rausu (3½ hours, ¥2730) on the Shiretoko Peninsula. There's also a night bus to Sapporo (seven hours, ¥5700).

Ferry A regular ferry service connects Kushiro with Tokyo in 32 hours – the cheapest passenger fare is ¥14,000. Kushiro Nishi-kō Port (also known simply as the *ferii tāminaru*) is a 15 minute bus ride west of Kushiro station. Alternatively the ferry terminal is just over 500 metres south of Shin Fuji station, one stop west of Kushiro station.

CHITOSE 新千歳空港・千歳

New Chitose Airport, the main airport for Sapporo and Hokkaidō, is just a few minutes by bus from the actual city of Chitose, which is an expanding industrial centre.

The airport has its own station and bus centre so you can normally make your transport connections and speed your exit from Chitose. The information desk and car rentals counter are next to the exit on the 1st floor of the airport terminal. Ask at the information desk for a brochure called *Chitose*. It's in English and Japanese, and includes useful phone numbers, details of bus services and maps of the region. The bus centre is outside the exit.

Getting There & Away

Sapporo is a 35 minute train ride (¥900) by limited express on the JR Chitose line. There are convenient bus services to many destinations on Hokkaidō. Some useful ones include Sapporo (70 minutes, ¥750), Lake Shikotsu-ko (45 minutes), Lake Tōya-ko (2¼ hours), Noboribetsu Onsen (70 minutes) and Niseko (three hours).

TOMAKOMAI 苫小牧

This is a city renowned for its multitude of paper-making factories – it's Japan's leading paper manufacturing centre. This doesn't exactly recommend the place to the average foreign traveller, and Tomakomai's main point of interest is its port, which is the hub for ferry links with Honshū.

Places to Stay

Tomakomai is within easy reach of other more interesting destinations, so unless you have an early morning ferry or arrive late at night there shouldn't be any need to stay here. The nearest youth hostel is the *Utanai-ko Youth Hostel* (☎ 0144-58-2153), which is by the shore of Lake Utanai-ko, a popular spot for bird watching. This is one of Japan's cheaper youth hostels, with rates of ¥1450 from 1 May to 31 October and ¥1600 from 1 November to 30 April. From Tomakomai station it's a 30 minute bus ride in the direction of New Chitose Airport or Chitose. Take the Utanai-ko Yūsu Hosuteru-mae stop – from there it's a 10 minute walk in the direction of the lake.

Most of the business hotel accommodation around the station is fairly expensive. The *Tomakomai New Station Hotel* (☎ 0144-33-6121) in front of the station has singles at ¥7000 and twins at ¥13,500. On the street behind it, the *Tomakomai Green Hotel* (☎ 0144-32-1122) has singles at ¥6000 and twins at ¥11,500.

The *Business Hotel Okuni* (☎ 0144-34-6441) is cheaper but it's a couple of km to the east of the station and not particularly easy to find – a taxi might be the best bet. Prices for singles start at ¥4900.

Getting There & Away

Buses run between Shiraoi and Tomakomai in 35 minutes (¥300) and between Tomakomai and Lake Shikotsu-ko in 45 minutes (¥540). The JR Chitose line links Tomakomai with Sapporo in 44 minutes by limited express (¥1260 plus a limited express surcharge of ¥1630); Tomakomai to Hakodate takes three hours.

Ferry services link Tomakomai with Sendai (¥8850, 15 hours), Nagoya (¥15,450, 39½ hours), Tokyo (¥11,840, 31 hours) and Hachinohe (¥3900, 8½ hours). The Tomakomai ferry terminal is a 15 minute bus ride south-east of Tomakomai station.

SHIRAOI 白老

The big attraction in this small town is the reconstructed **Ainu village**, known as 'Poroto Kotan', and the **Ainu Minzoku Hakubutsukan**, which is an excellent museum of Ainu culture in a modern building inside the village. Shiraoi is only around 1½ hours from Sapporo by limited express, and is easily visited as a day trip.

This lacklustre and highly commercial village consists of a huge arcade of souvenir shops with about half a dozen model huts. For some reason, it has been thought necessary to keep the bears here in cages barely large enough for them to be able to move.

The museum, however, deserves a recommendation for its presentation and description (in English) of exhibits – definitely worth a visit. The museum guide (¥400), written in English and Japanese, is also an interesting read. Admission costs ¥515 and the museum is open from 8 am to 5.30 pm, April to October, and from 8.30 am to 4.30 pm, November to March. The village is a 10 minute walk from JR Shiraoi station – turn left when you walk out of the south side of the station. Most bus services drop passengers off at the Poroto Kotan bus stop opposite the approach road to the village.

Getting There & Away
Shiraoi is on the JR Muroran line, 25 minutes from Noboribetsu station and 30 minutes from Tomakomai. Buses run between Shiraoi and Tomakomai in 35 minutes (¥300).

Shikotsu-Tōya National Park
支笏洞爺国立公園

Shikotsu-Tōya National Park (983 sq km) is centred on Lake Shikotsu-ko, Lake Tōya-ko and Noboribetsu Onsen. The lakes have the added attractions of mountain hikes or close-up encounters with volcanoes, while Noboribetsu Onsen will appeal to hot-spring enthusiasts. Fast and easy access to the park from Sapporo or New Chitose Airport makes it a favourite with visitors who have only a short time to spend in Hokkaidō.

JNTO publishes a leaflet entitled *Southern Hokkaidō*, which provides a map of the park with information on sights, transport and accommodation.

LAKE SHIKOTSU-KO   支笏湖
Lake Shikotsu-ko is a caldera lake surrounded by several volcanoes. It's Japan's second deepest lake after Lake Tazawa-ko in Akita-ken. The main centre for transport and information is **Shikotsu Kohan**, which consists of a bus terminal, a tourist information office, a pier for boat excursions and assorted souvenir shops, restaurants and places to stay.

The information office (☎ 01232-5-2453),

close to the bus terminal, is open from 9.30 am to 4.30 pm and has maps and other information. From the boat pier, there are rather tame sightseeing cruises which stop off at a couple of places around the lake before returning to the pier (1½ hours, ¥1700). If you cross the bridge on your far left as you walk down to the lake shore, you can follow a nature trail around the forested slopes for an hour or so. The youth hostel provides bicycle rental (¥250 per hour or ¥800 per day) and this is a good way to follow the road around the edge of the lake as there is no bus service.

Hiking
The mountain hikes are perhaps the most interesting activities to do around the lake. The youth hostel or tourist information office can give more advice on access, routes and timings.

Mt Eniwa-dake (1320 metres) lies on the western side of the lake. The start of the trail is about 10 minutes on foot from Poropinai – the Eniwa-dake Yamaguchi bus stop is near by. It takes about 3½ hours to hike to the summit, where there is a fine panorama of the surrounding lakes and peaks. Don't bother with this hike if it rains – some of the steeper sections of the trail become dangerously slippery.

Mt Tarumae-zan (1038 metres) lies on the southern side of the lake and offers the rugged delights of wandering around the crater of an active volcano. The crater is an easy 40 minute hike from the seventh station, which can be reached from Shikotsu Kohan in three hours on foot – or in 20 minutes if you use the bus service that seems to run only on Sunday. From the crater, you can either return to the seventh station, or follow the trail north-west down the mountain for 2½ hours to Kokenodō-mon, a mossy gorge, which is 10 minutes from the car park at Shishamonai on the lake shore. From Shishamonai you'll have to walk or hitch the 15 km to Shikotsu Kohan.

Places to Stay & Eat
There are over a dozen minshuku, ryokan

and hotels on the edge of the lake; camping grounds are also available at Morappu, Poropinai and Bifue. The tourist information office can help with booking accommodation.

Shikotsu-ko Youth Hostel (☎ 0123-25-2311) is at Shikotsu Kohan, and just a couple of minutes from the bus terminal there. This is a well-organised and friendly hostel which has family rooms as well as the usual dormitory-style accommodation. Bicycle rental and a hot-spring bath (additional fee of ¥150) are also available. Overseas hostellers are eligible for a ¥500 discount. A 'briefing' session is held in the evenings to give advice on hiking in the area and the hostel may be able to help with organising transport to trailheads. Nightly rates are ¥2500. The hostel is closed from 1 to 10 December and from 16 to 19 May.

South of Shikotsu Kohan bus terminal around 500 metres (over the Chitose-gawa River) is the *Shikotsu Kohan Kokumin Kyūkamura* (☎ 0123-25-2341), a vacation village in wooded surroundings by the lake. Per-person costs range from ¥6000 to ¥7000 with two meals.

Getting There & Away

The bus service from Sapporo (Hokkaidō Chūō bus from in front of Sapporo station) to Lake Shikotsu-ko takes 80 minutes (¥1050); other bus services run from New Chitose Airport (47 minutes, ¥700) and Tomakomai (45 minutes, ¥540).

NOBORIBETSU ONSEN 登別温泉

This is perhaps the most popular hot-spring resort in Hokkaidō and offers at least 11 different types of hot-spring water to soothe ailments or simply invigorate. The resort is small and worth a visit if you are fascinated by hot springs.

The bus terminal is halfway up the main street. A couple of minutes further up the street there's a tourist office (☎ 0143-84-3311) on your left, where you can pick up a pink brochure in English about the resort, but very little English is spoken. The main sights are all accessible on foot from the main street.

Dai-Ichi Takimoto-kan 第一滝本館

The Dai-Ichi Takimoto-kan is a hotel, recently refurbished, with one of the largest bath complexes in Japan. Guests of the hotel are allowed to use the bath for free (it costs enough to stay there anyway), but visitors are admitted on payment of a large admission fee.

Plan to make the most of your ticket by spending half a day or longer wandering from floor to floor trying out all the mineral pools (very hot!), waterfalls, walking pools, cold pools (freezing!), jacuzzi, steam room, outdoor pool (with bar) and the swimming pool with its water slide. There are separate sections for men and women, but the swimming pool and water slide are mixed – swimwear is required. There are at least half a dozen different mineral pools each of which is considered beneficial for specific ailments such as rheumatism, blood pressure disorders and nervous problems. The bath has huge windows looking out over Jigokudani (Hell Valley).

Admission costs ¥2000 and you must enter between 9 am and 3 pm. Take a towel, and you'll need swimming gear if you want to use the water slide and swimming pool. The entrance to the bath section is at the top of the main street, just past the ramp leading to the hotel's lobby on the right.

Hell Valley 地獄谷

A five minute walk further up the hill from the Dai-Ichi Takimoto-kan, you reach the entrance to Hell Valley (Jigokudani), a valley of volcanic activity. A pathway leads up the valley close to steaming and sulphurous vents with streams of hot water bubbling out of vivid red, yellow and brown rocks. The scene is still quite imposing, but it has been suggested that in recent years the flow of the hot springs along the surface of the valley has been siphoned off for the town and hence reduced. Close to the entrance is a small shrine where visitors can sample hot mineral water – rather vinegary.

If you continue up the valley and bear left, you cross a road and come out on a point

支笏洞爺国立公園

Shikotsu-Tōya National Park

0   6   12 km

overlooking **Oyu-numa Pond** with its water bubbling violently and steam rising from the sickly coloured surface. If you have time to continue, the area is crisscrossed by a network of hiking trails.

Noboribetsu Marine Park Nixe
登別マリンパークニクス

Next to JR Noboribetsu station, this place is touted as a Scandinavian fantasy theme park. It has a castle, a high-tech aquarium and other attractions. Entry is ¥1900 and it's open from 9 am to 9 pm through summer, until 5 pm the rest of year.

Lake Kuttara-ko   倶多楽湖

About six km from Noboribetsu Onsen is this small caldera lake with exceptionally clear water which turns an intense blue on fine days. Buses run three times a day from Noboribetsu Onsen to the lake.

Mt Kuma-yama   熊山

About 50 metres uphill from the bus terminal, a road leads off to the right to the cablecar for Mt Kuma-yama (Bear Mountain). The cablecar ticket costs a whopping ¥2100 (return), and includes admission to the 'sights' on the mountain: a motley collection of Ainu huts, a bear museum and utterly repulsive concrete enclosures with over 130 depressed, bored, heavily scarred bears begging for food, fighting with each other or attempting to escape being sprayed by a hose.

Every hour or so, a bevy of elderly Ainu accompanied by a frisky bear cub do a weary performance of the Iomante Festival – once the most sacred Ainu festival. From the roof of the bear museum, there are fine views across to Lake Kuttara-ko and the surrounding mountains – probably the one good thing I could say about my visit to the mountain. As I returned on the ropeway, I still couldn't fathom why this subjugation and humiliation of human and beast was necessary.

Robert Strauss

Places to Stay & Eat
Youth Hostels *Kannon-ji Youth Hostel* (☎ 0143-84-2359) is part of a modern temple; you'll receive a friendly reception when you arrive and a ceremonial send-off with a gong when you depart. The food is excellent. From the bus terminal walk uphill for five minutes until you reach a junction next to a shrine; take the road to the left and walk for another three minutes until you see the temple (large insignia on the front wall) on your right. A hot-spring bath is available if you pay an extra ¥100. Nightly rates are ¥2500. At the time of writing this hostel was temporarily closed. It should be re-opened by the time this edition is available, but check just to be sure.

Akashiya-sō Youth Hostel (☎ 0143-84-2616) is a couple of minutes walk downhill from the bus terminal and on your left after the fire station. Nightly rates are ¥2500, and a hot-spring bath is available for an additional fee of ¥100. There are no meals available at the hostel.

Kanefuku Youth Hostel (☎ 0143-84-2565) is a 15 minute walk from the centre of Noboribetsu Onsen. It's on the left-hand side of the road if you're arriving on the bus from Noboribetsu station. Nightly rates are ¥2300.

Ryokan *Ryokan Hanaya* (☎ 0143-84-2521), a member of the Japanese Inn Group, is next to the Hanaya-mae bus stop, five minutes on

foot from the bus terminal. Singles/doubles cost ¥5000/8000 and triples ¥12,000.

On the left-hand side of the road before you reach the Kannon-ji Youth Hostel is the *Noboribetsu Tokiwa-sō* (☎ 0143-84-2041), a small place where per-person costs are ¥5900 with two meals.

Hotels Those wanting to stay in the *Dai-Ichi Takimoto-kan* (☎ 0143-84-2111) (see the above entry on the hotel's onsen facilities) are looking at spending ¥18,000 to ¥25,000 with two meals.

Getting There & Away
Between 1 June and late October, a bus service operates five times daily from Noboribetsu Onsen on a scenic route via Orofure Pass to Tōyako Onsen, on Lake Tōya-ko (¥850, 1¼ hours). The bus service from Sapporo to Noboribetsu Onsen takes one hour 40 minutes (¥1700) and runs via Tomakomai.

From Noboribetsu station on the JR Muroran line, it's a 13 minute bus ride to Noboribetsu Onsen.

LAKE TŌYA-KO　洞爺湖
Although Lake Tōya-ko is a large and attractive lake, most foreign visitors who come here concentrate on seeing the 'upstart' volcanoes near by. The centre of activity for the lake is **Tōyako Onsen**, a hot-spring resort on the south shore of the lake.

Mt Shōwa Shin-zan & Mt Usu-zan
昭和新山・有珠山
In 1943, after a series of earthquakes, Mt Shōwa Shin-zan was first formed as an upstart dimple in some vegetable fields and then continued to surge upwards for two more years to reach its present height (406 metres). It is still an awesome sight as it sits there, hissing and issuing steam and keeping the locals guessing about its next move.

At the base of the mountain is a large car park with tourist facilities. At the lower end of the car park is the **Masao Mimatsu Memorial Museum**. It's an intriguing museum which displays many items collected by the postmaster who actually owned the ground that turned into a volcano. For many years the old man kept possession of his land, but finally let it pass into the hands of the government.

Among all the photos and paintings, look out for the articles taken from English newspapers. Apparently, the Japanese government was keen to hush up the volcanic eruption which it thought might be misinterpreted and thereby hamper the progress of WW II. The postmaster was even requested to find a way to shield the volcanic glare or extinguish it so that the volcano couldn't be used by enemy aircrew for orientation! Admission to the museum costs ¥300 and it's open from 8 am to 5 pm.

At the top end of the car park is the cablecar for Mt Usu-zan, which operates from May to the end of September. The ride takes six minutes and the return ticket costs ¥1350. Those who stay at the Shōwa Shinzan Youth Hostel are eligible for a 10% discount.

Mt Usu-zan (729 metres) is a frisky volcano which has erupted frequently and was the force behind the creation of Mt Shōwa Shin-zan. The last eruption in 1977 destroyed the previous cablecar and rained down rocks and some 30 cm of volcanic ash onto Tōyako Onsen – you can see film clips of this eruption in the volcano museum in the resort. From the top station of the cablecar, there are superb views across the lake to the cone of Mt Yōtei-zan. A short trail leads up to a lookout where you can look into the desolate crater and keep an eye on the emission of smoke and fumes.

Getting There & Away The volcanoes are a 15 minute (¥290) bus ride south-east of Tōyako Onsen and about three km from Shōwa Shinzan Youth Hostel. From Tōyoko Onsen take a Tōnan bus to Shōwa Shinzan and get off at the last stop. Between May and late October buses run hourly between 9 am and 5 pm.

Tōyako Onsen Attractions

If you have time to spare after seeing the volcanoes, Tōyoko Onsen itself is not completely devoid of sights and things to do.

On the floor above the bus terminal is the **Volcano Science Museum**, which charges ¥400 for admission to displays explaining the origins and activities of volcanoes with special emphasis on Mt Usu-zan. Visitors can sit in a special room and experience the visual and aural fury of an eruption – the 16-woofer speakers will certainly clean your ears out! It's worth a visit and is open from 9 am to 5 pm.

Hot-spring enthusiasts could fork out ¥2000 (¥2500 on Sunday) and indulge in the bathing pleasures of the **Sun Palace Hotel** which is a 30 minute walk from the bus terminal and has facilities considered by some to be even more sophisticated than those of the Dai-Ichi Takimoto Honkan Hotel in Noboribetsu Onsen – see the earlier Noboribetsu Onsen section. The Sun Palace Onsen is open to visitors from 9 am to 4 pm.

Another diversion available is a boat trip out to **Naka-jima Island** in the middle of the lake. There's not a great deal out there, but it gives you a chance to see wild Ezo deer and perhaps visit the **Lake Tōya Forest Museum**. The latter is rather dull, with a couple of stuffed Ezo deer and slide shows featuring the changing of the seasons in the lake area. Boats out to the island take around 30 minutes and cost ¥980. During the summer, there are fireworks displays every evening. If you hire a bicycle, you can pedal around the lake in 2½ hours.

Places to Stay

Shōwa Shinzan Youth Hostel (☎ 0142-75-2283) is at the beginning of the steep road leading uphill to Mt Usu-zan and Mt Shōwa Shin-zan. To get there take an eight minute bus ride from Tōyako Onsen to the Noboriyama-guchi stop. The hostel is not particularly appealing, just a place to stay. Hostellers are eligible for a 10% discount on the Mt Usu-zan cablecar ticket. For an additional fee of ¥100 you can use the hot-spring bath. Bicycle and scooter rental is also available – a convenient way to pop into Tōyako Onsen for the evening fireworks display or to pedal around the lake. Nightly rates are ¥2300.

There are a few camping grounds around the lake. *Nakatōya Camping Ground* (☎ 0142-66-2121) is on the eastern edge of the lake and costs ¥300 per person. *Takinoue Camping Ground* (☎ 0142-66-2121) is around four km to the south also on the lakeside. Both offer tent rental during the summer months. *Green Stay Tōya-ko* (☎ 0142-75-3377) is open from April to October and is over on the west side of the lake.

Getting There & Away

The bus service between Tōyako Onsen and Noboribetsu Onsen is described under Getting There & Away in the Noboribetsu Onsen section earlier in this chapter. From Sapporo, unless you're on a Japan Rail Pass, probably the best way to reach Tōyako Onsen is by direct bus from in front of Sapporo station. Buses take 2¾ hours and cost ¥2550. There are also services from Muroran that take 1¾ hours and cost ¥1000.

Japan Rail Pass users should take an express service from Sapporo via the Chitose and Muroran lines. The trip takes one hour 50 minutes and costs ¥2880 with a ¥2560 limited express surcharge. Buses run from in front of Tōya station to Tōyoko Onsen in around 15 minutes and cost ¥280.

MURORAN 室蘭

Muroran (population 117,000) is a huge industrial hub, not worth a special visit unless you want to tour factories or use one of the city's handy ferry links with Honshū.

Places to Stay

Muroran Youth Hostel (☎ 0143-44-3357) is a 15 minute walk from Wanishi station. Foreign hostellers are eligible for a ¥500 discount. Bicycle rental is available. The hostel is closed from 16 to 25 January and from 16 to 19 May, and charges ¥2400.

Most of Muroran's business hotel accommodation is clustered around Muroran station and Higashi Muroran station. Next to Muroran station is the *Business Hotel Million* (☎ 0143-24-6511), which has singles from ¥3700. South of Muroran station (down Route 36) is the *Hotel Bayside* (☎ 0143-24-8090), which has singles at ¥4800 and twins at ¥8600. In front of Higashi Muroran station is the *Muroran Dai-Ichi Hotel* (☎ 0143-43-8881) with singles from ¥4100 to ¥5000, twins at ¥9000 and doubles at ¥8500. Next door, the *Muroran Palace Hotel* (☎ 0143-43-0888) has singles from ¥4300 to ¥4500 and doubles at ¥8500.

Getting There & Away

Train A direct limited express between Muroran and Hakodate on the JR Muroran line takes 2¼ hours; the loop north to Sapporo takes 1¾ hours.

Ferry Ferry services link Muroran with Hachinohe (¥3900, eight hours) and Aomori (¥3400, seven hours). Muroran-futō Pier is a three minute walk from Muroran station.

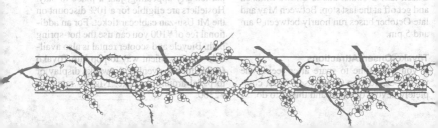

Shikoku 四国

In Japan's feudal past, the island of Shikoku (population 4,195,000) was divided into four (*shi*) regions (*koku*), which today have become four prefectures. Although Shikoku is Japan's fourth largest island, it's predominantly rural and very much off the tourist track. Apart from scenery, the Ritsurin-kōen Garden in Takamatsu and four castles (Kōchi, Marugame, Matsuyama and Uwajima) that managed to survive the Meiji Restoration and WW II, there are no overwhelming attractions. The construction of the Seto-ōhashi Bridge linking Shikoku with Honshū has made the island much more accessible. The island is set to become even more accessible with the construction of two more bridges: one to the east, from Naruto to Akashi (near Kōbe) via Awaji-shima Island; and the other to the west, island hopping from Imabari to Onomichi. The target completion date for both bridges is 1998.

THE 88 TEMPLE CIRCUIT

Japan's best known pilgrimage is Kōbō Daishi's 88 Temple Circuit of Shikoku. Kūkai (774-835), known as Kōbō Daishi after his death, is the most revered of Japan's saints. He founded the Shingon Buddhist sect in 807 after a visit to China. Shingon, often referred to as Esoteric Buddhism, is related to Tantric Buddhism, with its mystic rituals and multi-armed deities.

Kōbō Daishi was born in Shikoku, and it is said he personally selected the 88 temples which make up the circuit. Today, most pilgrims on the circuit travel by tour bus but some still walk – set aside six weeks and be prepared to walk over 1000 km if you want to join them. Some of the temples are only a few hundred metres apart and you can walk to five or six in a day. However, at the other extreme, it can be 100 km between temples. Oliver Statler's book *Japanese Pilgrimage* follows the temple circuit.

Individually, none of the temples is particularly interesting; it's the whole circuit that

counts. The pilgrims, known as *henro*, wear white robes *(hakui)*, carry a staff *(otsue)* and often top the ensemble with a straw hat *(kasa)*. Temple circuiters stamp their robes with the temples' red seals.

GETTING THERE & AWAY

Air services connect major cities in Shikoku with Tokyo, Osaka and other centres on Honshū. Numerous ferries ply the waters of the Inland Sea, linking Shikoku with the Inland Sea islands and with ports on the San-yō coast of Honshū. Takamatsu and Matsuyama are particularly busy Shikoku ports, though there are many others. The opening of the road and rail Seto-ōhashi Bridge in 1988 considerably simplified access to the island and there are frequent train services from Okayama to both Takamatsu and Matsuyama.

Kagawa-ken 香川県

TAKAMATSU 高松

Takamatsu (population 330,000) was founded during the rule of Toyotomi Hideyoshi (1537-98) as the castle town of the feudal lord of Kagawa. At that time, Takamatsu was known as Sanuki. The town was virtually destroyed in WW II but rapidly rebounded after the war. The completion of the Seto-ōhashi Bridge reinforced Takamatsu's importance as a major arrival point on Shikoku. Despite the new rail link, it remains an important port for Inland Sea ferry services, particularly to popular Shōdo-shima Island. The town has an important garden, the nearby Shikoku-mura Village Museum, and the very popular Kotohira-gū Shrine is an easy day trip.

One odd thing about Takamatsu is that it seems to have the highest concentration of urban cyclists in all of Japan. The occasional tinkling of a bell and the

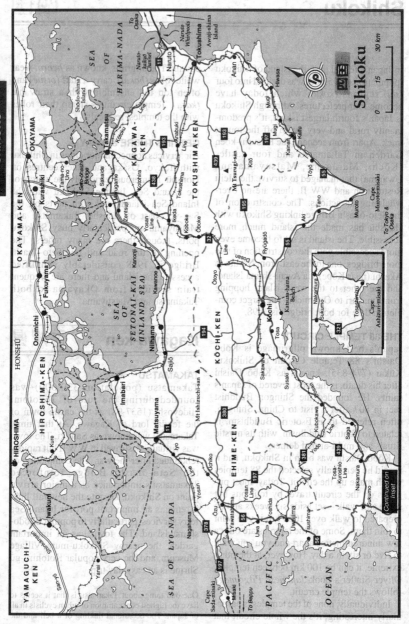

SHIKOKU

Shikoku

Continued on
Inset

tortured squeal of squeaky brakes behind you is commonplace on the footpaths of Japan. But in Takamatsu it's a step-by-step occurrence, so that you spend most of your strolling time keeping an eye on the oncoming traffic and an ear out for the ones at your rear. Take care, I almost got hit a few times.

Chris Taylor

Orientation & Information

There's an information counter in JR Takamatsu station (☎ 0878-51-2009), but don't expect any English to be spoken. All things considered, Takamatsu is a fairly straightforward kind of place, and you probably won't need their help. There's another information counter that can help with booking accommodation at the east entrance to Ritsurin-kōen Park, but this is a bit of a hike from the station and you'd probably be better off checking the accommodation around the station yourself before heading down there. The station is beside the ferry terminal buildings. Chūō-dōri, the main road in Takamatsu, leads out from the station, with the private Kotoden Chikkō station almost immediately on the left. A busy shopping arcade extends across Chūō-dōri and then runs parallel to it, passing through the entertainment district. The main shopping area is further south around the Kotoden Kawaramachi station area. Takamatsu is surprisingly sprawling, it's a long walk (two km) to the Ritsurin-kōen Garden from the station.

Ritsurin-kōen Garden　栗林公園

Although not one of Japan's 'big three' gardens, Ritsurin-kōen could easily be a contender for that list. The garden, which was first constructed in the mid-1600s, winds around a series of ponds with lookouts, tearooms, bridges and islands. The garden actually took more than a century to complete and was used as a villa garden for over 200 years prior to the Meiji Restoration. In one direction, Mt Shiun forms a backdrop to the garden but in the other direction, there is some much less impressive 'borrowed scenery' in the form of dull modern buildings.

In the garden, the Sanuki Folkcraft

Museum displays local crafts. The old Kikugetsu-tei Teahouse, also known as the Chrysanthemum Moon Pavilion, is a feudal-era teahouse. Entry to the garden is ¥310 and it's open from sunrise to sunset. There's an extra charge for the teahouse. You can get there by Kotoden or JR train, but the easiest way to get there is by a Kotoden bus (¥210) from platform No 2 at the JR station.

Takamatsu-jō Castle　高松城

There's very little left of Takamatsu Castle, which is just a stone's throw from the JR and Kotoden stations. The castle grounds, which now form the pleasant Tamamo Park, are only one-ninth their original size. When the castle was constructed in 1588, the moats on three sides were filled with sea water while the sea itself formed the fourth side of the castle. Entry is only ¥100, and it's open from 8.30 am to 6 pm, 9 am to 5 pm during January and February.

Yashima　屋島

The 292 metre high table-top plateau of Yashima stands five km from the centre of Takamatsu. Today, it's the site for the Yashima-ji Temple (No 84 on the temple circuit) and offers fine views over the surrounding countryside and the Inland Sea, but in the 12th century it was the site for titanic struggles between the Genji and Heike clans. The temple's treasure-house collection relates to the battle. Just behind the treasure house is the Pond of Blood, where the victorious warriors washed the blood from their swords, staining the water red.

A funicular railway runs up to the top of Yashima Hill from the left of the shrine at the bottom. The cost is ¥600 one way or ¥1200 return. At the top you can rent a bicycle (¥300 plus ¥1000 deposit) to pedal around the attractions – it's a long walk otherwise.

The two best ways of getting to Yashima are by Kotoden train or by Kotoden bus. From Kotoden Takamatsu Chikkō station it takes around 20 minutes (¥260) to Yashima station. From here you can take the cablecar to the top. Kotoden buses run directly to the top from in front of JR Takamatsu station, take around 30 minutes and cost ¥660.

Shikoku-mura Village 四国村
At the bottom of Yashima Hill is an excellent village museum with old buildings brought from all over Shikoku and neighbouring islands. There are explanations in English of the many buildings and their history. Highlights include a traditional suspension bridge (the vines are actually reinforced with steel cables but it certainly looks the part). There is only one authentic bridge left in Shikoku, across the Iyadani-kei Gorge, and villagers came from there to construct this replica. See the Iyadani-kei Gorge section later in this chapter.

Shōdo-shima Island is still famed for its traditional farmers' kabuki performances and the fine village kabuki stage came from that island. Other interesting buildings include a border guardhouse from the Tokugawa era, when travel was tightly restricted, and a bark steaming hut that was used in paper-making. There's also a water-powered rice hulling machine and a fine old stone storehouse. Entry is ¥500; the small museum in the village costs an extra ¥100 and you can safely skip it. The village is open from 8.30 am to 4.30 or 5 pm. See the Takamatsu Places to Eat section for information about the popular noodle restaurant just outside Shikoku-mura.

If you want to skip Yashima, you can visit Shikoku-mura directly; it's around seven minutes on foot north of Yashima station.

Other Attractions
Just offshore from Yashima is **Megi-jima Island**, also known as Oniga-shima or 'Demon Island'. It was here that Momotarō, the legendary 'Peach Boy', met and conquered the horrible demon. You can tour the caves where the demon was said to have hidden. See the Western Honshū chapter for the Momotarō story.

The caves are open from 8.30 am to 5 pm and entry is ¥500. Boats run to Megi-jima Island from the ferry area next to Takamatsu station, take 20 minutes and cost ¥260.

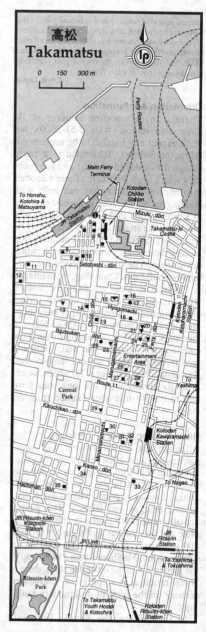

SHIKOKU

PLACES TO STAY		27	Takamatsu Washington Hotel 高松ワシントンホテル	29	Ristorante Verde Casa リストランテヴェルデカーサ
3	Station Hotel ステーションホテル	28	Royal Park Hotel ロイヤルパークホテル	30	McDonald's マクドナルド
4	Pearl Hotel パールホテル	31	Tokiwa Honkan 常盤本館	32	Mr Donut ミスタードーナッツ
6	Takamatsu Grand Hotel 高松グランドホテル	35	Keio Plaza Hotel 京王プラザホテル高松	34	Udon House Restaurant うどんハウス
8	New Getsukōen Hotel ニュー月光園ホテル		PLACES TO EAT		OTHER
9	Hotel New Frontier ホテルニューフロンティア	2	Mr Donut ミスタードーナッツ	1	Tourist Information Office 観光案内所
10	Takamatsu Terminal Hotel 高松ターミナルホテル	13	Tenkatsu Restaurant 天勝本店	5	ANA 全日空
11	Century Hotel	16	McDonald's マクドナルド	7	JAL 日航
12	Business Hotel Marukyu ビジネスホテル丸久	20	Kawa-Fuku Restaurant 川福本店	15	Post Office 高松郵便局
14	Takamatsu Tōkyū Inn 高松東急イン	21	Grill Yama グリル山	17	Mitsukoshi Department Store 三越
18	Hotel Kawaroku ホテル川六	23	Italian Tomato Restaurant イタリアントマト	22	Public Art Gallery 高松市美術館
19	Hotel Rich ホテルリッチ	24	Nanak Restaurant ナナックレストラン	33	NTT
26	Business Hotel Japan ビジネスホテルジャパン	25	Kamaizumi Restaurant かまいずみ		

Places to Stay

Youth Hostel The *Takamatsu Yashima-sansō Youth Hostel* (☎ 0878-41-2318) is just over five minutes walk north-east of Kotoden Yashima station. The hostel charges ¥2300 per night.

Hotels There are a number of budget business hotels a stone's throw from the station. The *Pearl Hotel* (☎ 0878-22-3382), is small, clean and quite acceptable with rooms from ¥5000 for singles and ¥9600 for doubles or twins. Also very close to the station is the *Station Hotel* (☎ 0878-21-6989) with singles from ¥6000 to ¥8500, and doubles or twins from ¥13,000.

Two of the cheapest places around are the *Business Hotel Japan* (☎ 0878-51-8689), south of the station in the shopping and entertainment district, and the *Business Hotel Marukyu* (☎ 0878-51-7305), which is south-west of Takamatsu station. Both are small and at the grotty end of the business

hotel spectrum, but offer singles/twins for ¥4000/7000.

A few minutes walk from the station, the *Takamatsu Terminal Hotel* (☎ 0878-22-3731) is a small, clean place with singles from ¥5200 and twins from ¥9500. Close by, the *Hotel New Frontier* (☎ 0878-51-1088) offers similar standards for ¥6000/10,000 for singles/twins.

The *Takamatsu Grand Hotel* (☎ 0878-51-5757), on top of the Kotoden Chikkō station, overlooks the Takamatsu Castle grounds and is conveniently situated only a few steps from the JR station. It's a little more up-market and singles/twins cost from ¥7000/ 12,500.

The *Takamatsu Tōkyū Inn* (☎ 0878-21-0109) is a popular chain hotel on Chūō-dōri, just beyond the arcade. Singles cost from ¥7700 to ¥14,000, doubles from ¥13,200 to ¥14,000. Much further down Chūō-dōri, almost at the Ritsurin-kōen Garden, is the *Keiō Plaza Hotel* (☎ 0878-34-5511) with singles from ¥7300 to ¥12,500 and twins from ¥13,500 to ¥22,000.

The *Royal Park Hotel* (☎ 0878-23-2222) has singles/doubles from ¥9000/16,000. A few steps away is the *Takamatsu Washington Hotel* (☎ 0878-22-7111). It has singles/twins from ¥7500/15,500.

Ryokan Takamatsu has a couple of expensive but centrally located ryokan. *Hotel Kawaroku* (☎ 0878-21-5666) is south of the shopping arcade, just off Chūō-dōri. Rooms cost from around ¥7000/12,000 for singles/doubles without meals and from around ¥15,000 per person with meals.

Near the Kotoden Kawaramachi station and close to the shopping arcade is the traditional *Tokiwa Honkan* (☎ 0878-61-5577), which costs from ¥15,000 to ¥20,000 per person including two meals.

Places to Eat
Every larger railway station in Shikoku seems to have an *Andersen's* bakery, also known as *Willie Winkie*. The one at JR Takamatsu station is good for an economical breakfast, though there's nowhere to sit down. Across the road is a *Mister Donut* and there are a number of other restaurants near by. The Kotoden Kawaramachi station is also a centre for a variety of cheap eats.

A bit of a hike from the station area, one of the cheapest places to slurp back some noodles in town is *Udon House* on Kankō-dōri. Look for the sign outside announcing 'all the rage'. It should be, with prices ranging from ¥300 for a hearty bowl of noodles.

The best selection of restaurants is found along the shopping arcade in the entertainment district. *Kawa-Fuku* is a pleasant restaurant offering good Sanuki noodles, tempura and other dishes from around ¥800 – try the *gyūdon* (beef with rice), which comes with a bowl of udon for ¥880. Just beyond Kawa-Fuku is the *Grill Yama*, which offers a variety of grilled meat dishes at up-market prices (from ¥1500). Look out for *Sushi Land Marin Polis* (yes, an English sign), across the road from Kawa-Fuku. This is a revolving sushi shop with reasonable prices.

The *Kamaizumi Restaurant*, a block east on Ferry-dōri, specialises in Sanuki noodles – you may see them being made in the window.

Just down the road from Kawa-Fuku and Grill Yama is a branch of the Indian restaurant chain *Nanak*. This place has lunch-time specials from ¥800 and evening specials from ¥2300. A curry and some naan in the evening will set you back around ¥1500. Further south of here is an up-market Italian restaurant, *Ristorante Verde Casa*, where you'll be looking at ¥1500 even for a lunch-time special – it's a fashionable, atmospheric little spot. More affordable Italian fare is available at a branch of the popular *Italian Tomato* restaurant chain on Bijutsukan-dōri.

Backtracking along the arcade across Chūō-dōri and continuing a few doors beyond the end of the arcade, you'll find *Tenkatsu*, a popular restaurant with a central bar around a large fish tank. (You know the fish is fresh, you see it die.)

If you're out at Yashima at lunch time, head for the restaurant with a water wheel, right beside the Shikoku-mura Village car park. For ¥350, you get a hearty bowl of Sanuki udon and a bowl of soup which you

---

Cruel Cuisine

Being cruel to your food is a Japanese tradition – you know the fish is fresh if it squeals when you eat it – and Takamatsu is certainly a centre for it. A prized dish here is *sugata-zukuri*: sea bream sliced seconds before it's placed in front of you. If you're quick with the chopsticks you can get the first mouthfuls down before it dies. I ate one night at Tenkatsu, where the bar encloses a large tank of fish and other sea life. When a customer ordered octopus, the unfortunate creature was scooped out of the tank and four tentacles were hacked off. Then, still living, but less than complete, the octopus was tossed back into the tank to crawl forlornly off to a corner.

Tony Wheeler

spice up with chopped spring onions and then dip the noodles in.

Getting There & Away

Air Japan Air Systems (JAS) has flights to and from Fukuoka and Tokyo; All Nippon Airways (ANA) has flights to and from Osaka and Tokyo.

Train The Seto-ōhashi Bridge has brought Takamatsu much closer to the main island of Honshū. From Tokyo, you can take the shinkansen to Okayama, change trains there and be in Takamatsu in five hours. The Okayama-Takamatsu section takes about an hour.

From Takamatsu, the JR Kotoku line runs south-east to Tokushima and the JR Yosan line runs west to Matsuyama. The Yosan line branches off at Tadotsu and becomes the Dosan line, turning south-west to Kotohira and Kōchi. The private Kotoden line also runs direct to Kotohira.

Bus Direct buses also operate between Tokyo and Takamatsu: the JR 'Hello Bridge' service costs ¥10,300 one way.

Ferry Takamatsu is an important ferry terminus with services to ports in the Inland Sea, and on Honshū, including Kōbe (4½ hours, ¥2370) and Osaka (5½ hours, ¥2370). Prior to the construction of the bridge, Uno, to the south of Okayama, was the main connection point to Takamatsu. It's still a quick way to make the Honshū-Shikoku trip since Uno-Okayama trains connect with the ferry departures. Takamatsu is also the easiest jumping-off point for visiting attractive Shōdo-shima Island. Takamatsu's ferry terminal buildings are right beside the JR Takamatsu station.

Getting Around

Takamatsu Airport is 16 km from the city and the bus, which departs from outside JR Takamatsu station, takes about half an hour.

Takamatsu has a local bus service but for most visitors, the major attractions, principally the Ritsurin-kōen Garden and Yashima,

can be easily reached on the JR Kotoku line or the more frequent Kotoden line service. The main Kotoden junction is Kawaramachi although the line ends at the Chikkō station, just across from the JR Takamatsu station.

Takamatsu seems to have an amazing number of cyclists, most of whom (sensibly) use the footpaths rather than the road. Inevitably, there seem to be many collisions; even late at night in the almost deserted arcades, Takamatsu's cyclists contrive to run into one another.

WEST OF TAKAMATSU　高松から西へ
Sakaide　坂出

Sakaide, a port city on the JR Yosan line, has nothing of interest for the traveller; it's at the southern end of the Seto-ōhashi Bridge.

Marugame　丸亀

On the JR Yosan line, just 25 minutes west of Takamatsu and close to the southern end of the Seto-ōhashi Bridge, there are some remains of the 1597 **Marugame-jō Castle** with its impressive stepped stone walls. The ruins are about a km south of the JR station. The Shiwaku Islands (see the Inland Sea section of the Western Honshū chapter) are reached from Marugame.

Tadotsu　多度津

At Tadotsu, the JR Dosan line to Kotohira and Kōchi branches off from the Yosan line. The **Toryo-kōen Park** has a magnificent display of cherry trees (sakura) during the blossom season.

Zentsū-ji Temple　善通寺

The Zentsū-ji Temple, No 75 on Kōbō Daishi's 88 Temple Circuit, is said to have been founded in 813 AD. This was Kōbō Daishi's birthplace so it has particular importance. The temple is one station north of Kotohira on the JR Dosan line.

Kanonji　観音寺

Kanonji (population 45,000) is noted for the **Zenigata**, the 350 metre diameter outline of a square-holed coin dating from the 1600s. The coin's outline and four kanji characters are formed by trenches which, it is said, were dug by the local population as a warning to their feudal lord not to waste the taxes they were forced to pay him. The huge coin is beside the sea, at the foot of Kotohiki Hill in Kotohiki Park, 1½ km north-west of Kanonji station. Also in the park is **Kanonji-jinme-in Temple** and the **Sekai-no-Koin-kan**, or World Coin Museum. The latter has coins through history from over 100 countries; it's open from 9 am to 5 pm daily except Monday, and entry is ¥300.

Kanonji can be reached by JR from Takamatsu in around 50 minutes. Those travelling between Takamatsu and Matsuyama could fit in a visit to both Kanonji and Kotohira provided they set off early enough. Buses run between Kotohira and Kanonji seven times daily between 7 am and 6 pm and cost ¥900.

KOTOHIRA 琴平

The Kompira-san Shrine at Kotohira is one of Shikoku's major attractions and for anyone in this part of Japan it shouldn't be missed, even if it is a little touristy. As you trudge up to the shrine, you might like to reflect how this is another of Japan's curiously misplaced shrines. On Omishima Island in the Inland Sea, the Oyamazumi-jinja Shrine is dedicated to the mountain god. Here, a mountain-top shrine is venerated by seafarers!

Orientation & Information

Kotohira is small enough to make orientation quite straightforward. The busy shopping arcade continues on until it reaches the shrine entranceway, lined with the inevitable souvenir shops. Those seeking to truly immerse themselves in the Japanese experience might want to use one of the latter, as seemingly every Japanese visitor does, to buy a walking stick for the walk up to the shrine.

In JR Kotohira station there is an information counter with friendly staff, though no English is spoken. They have lists of possible accommodation, though most of it is fairly expensive.

Kompira-san Shrine 金刀比羅宮

Kompira-san or, more correctly, Kotohira-gū, was originally a temple dedicated to the guardian of mariners but became a shrine after the Meiji Restoration. Its hilltop position gives superb views over the surrounding country and there are some interesting reminders of its maritime connections.

An enormous fuss is made about how strenuous the climb is to the top but, if you've got this far in Japan, you've probably seen a few long ascents to shrines already: this one isn't the most horrific to be found. If you really blanch at the thought of climbing all those steps (nearly 800 of them) you can be carried up in a palanquin – the carriers wait at the bottom. The countless tour guides are worse than the steps – bawling out over their megaphones, the noise totally spoils the tranquil atmosphere of the shrine.

The first notable landmark on the long climb is the Dai-mon Gate. Just to the right beyond the gate, the rather dull treasure house is open from 8 am to 6 pm in summer, 9 am to 5 pm in winter; entry is ¥200. A little further uphill is the reception hall known as the Shoin with the same ¥200 entry fee and similar opening hours to the treasure house. Built in 1659, it has some interesting screen paintings and a small garden.

Continuing the ascent, you eventually reach the large Asahino Yashiro also known as the Sunrise Hall. The hall, built in 1837 and dedicated to the sun goddess Amaterasu, is noted for its ornate woodcarving. From here, the short final ascent brings you to the Gohonsha (Main Hall) and the Ema-dō Pavilion, the latter crowded with suitably maritime offerings. Exhibits range from pictures of ships, both old and new, to models and even modern ship engines. The views from this level extend right down to the coast. Incurable climbers can continue another 600-odd steps up to the Inner Shrine.

Kanamaru-za Kabuki Playhouse 金丸座

Near the base of the steps is the Kyū Kompira Ōshibai, or Kanamaru-za, a fine old kabuki playhouse from the Edo period. It was built in 1835 and became a cinema before being

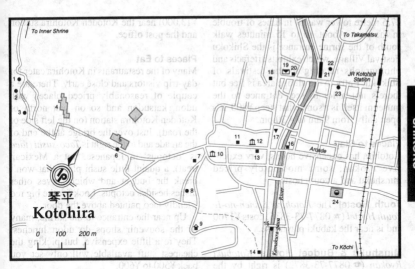

SHIKOKU

Kotohira

0   100   200 m

琴平

To Inner Shrine
To Takamatsu
To Kōchi
JR Kotohira Station
Arcade

PLACES TO STAY	PLACES TO EAT	8	Kanamaru-za Kabuki Playhouse
7 Kotohira Grand Hotel 琴平グランドホテル	17 Taco Sushi Restaurant たこ寿司		金丸座
9 Kotohira Seinen-no-Ie Youth Hostel 琴平青年の家ユースホステル	**OTHER**	10	Marine Museum 海の資料館
11 Shikishima-kan 敷島館	1 Kompira-san Main Hall 金刀比羅宮本殿	12	Sake Museum 酒資料館
13 Bizenva Ryokan 備前屋	2 Ema-dō Pavilion 絵馬堂	15	Saya-bashi Bridge 鞘橋
14 Kotohira Kadan Ryokan 琴平花壇旅館	3 Asahino Yashiro – Sunrise Hall 旭社	19	Post Office 琴平郵便局
16 Kotobuki Ryokan ことぶき旅館	4 Shoin Building 書院	21	Kotoden Kotohira Station 琴電琴平駅
18 Kotohira Royal Hotel 琴平ロイヤルホテル	5 Treasure House 宝物館	22	Fire Tower 高灯籠
20 Hotel Maruya まるやホテル	6 Dai-mon Gate 大門	23 24	KDD Bus Station バス停留所

restored to its current elegance in 1976. Inside, you can wander backstage and around the changing rooms, and admire the revolving stage. Entry is ¥300 and it's open from 9 am to 4 pm, closed Tuesday.

Other Attractions

At the bottom of the shrine steps there's a

Marine Museum (entry ¥300) with a variety of ship models and exhibits. There's also a Sake Museum along the shrine entranceway. At the southern end of the town, past the bus station and just before the Kotohira Kadan Ryokan, is the wooden **Saya-bashi covered bridge**. Note the curious **lantern tower** beside the Kotoden Kotohira station. The

27.6 metre tower was lit in times of trouble in the past. About 10 to 15 minutes walk south of the shrine entrance is the Shikoku Festival Village, which exhibits artefacts and photographs relating to the festivals of Shikoku. Entry to the village area is free but there's not a lot to see; entrance to the museum itself is a somewhat steep ¥800. It's open daily from 9 am to 4.30 pm.

Places to Stay

Kotohira has expensive hotels, very expensive ryokan, some moderately priced minshuku and a youth hostel.

Youth Hostel The *Kotohira Seinen-no-Ie Youth Hostel* (☎ 0877-73-3836) costs ¥1700 and is near the kabuki playhouse.

Minshuku & Budget Hotels *Kotobuki Ryokan* (☎ 0877-73-3872) is right by the riverside on the shopping arcade. It's conveniently situated, clean, comfortable and serves good food. The nightly cost per person with dinner and breakfast is ¥7000.

The *Hotel Maruya* (☎ 0877-75-2241), next to the post office, is similarly priced but nowhere near as friendly as the Kotobuki.

By Kotohira standards, the *Kompira Prince Hotel* (☎ 0877-73-3051) just creeps in the budget category with singles/doubles at ¥6490/9270. It's about 500 metres to the south-east of JR Kotohira station.

Ryokan & Expensive Hotels Kotohira has some expensive but very tasteful ryokan, particularly along the entranceway to the shrine steps. Costs per person, including dinner and breakfast, will probably be in the ¥13,000 to ¥20,000 range. The *Bizenya Ryokan* (☎ 0877-75-4131) and the *Shikishima-kan* (☎ 0877-75-5111) are both on the entranceway, while the *Kotohira Kadan Ryokan* (☎ 0877-75-3232) is just beyond the Saya-bashi Bridge.

Hotels include the *Kotohira Grand Hotel* (☎ 0877-75-3232) (¥18,000 with two meals) near the bottom of the steps up to the shrine and the grand and glossy *Kotohira Royal Hotel* (☎ 0877-75-1000) (singles from ¥13,000) near the Kotoden Kotohira station and the post office.

Places to Eat

Many of the restaurants in Kotohira cater for day-trip visitors and close early. There are a couple of reasonably priced places with udon, katsudon and so on just north of Kotoden Kotohira station (on the left side of the road). Just over the bridge at the end of the arcade and to the right is *Taco-sushi* (*taco* is 'octopus' in Japanese, not a Mexican treat), a quaint little sushi place that won't break the budget and which serves other dishes besides octopus. Look for the big red friendly taco painted above the door.

Up near the entrance to the shrine, many of the souvenir shops do udon lunches. They're a little expensive, but picking the cheapest stuff available will only set you back ¥500 to ¥600.

Getting There & Away

The JR Dosan line branches off the Yosan line at Tadotsu and continues through Kotohira and south to Kōchi. There is also a direct Takamatsu to Kotohira private Kotoden line. On either line, the journey takes around an hour from Takamatsu.

Tokushima-ken 徳島県

TOKUSHIMA 徳島

Tokushima (population 263,000), on Shikoku's east coast, is a pleasant enough modern city, but offers few attractions in its own right. Apart from the annual Awa Odori Festival, the only real reason for a visit is if you are in transit to somewhere else.

Orientation & Information

Orientation in Tokushima is very easy since it's neatly defined by two hills. One, with the castle ruins, rises up directly behind the station. From in front of the station, the main street, Shinmachibashi-dōri, heads south across the river to the cablecar station at the

SHIKOKU

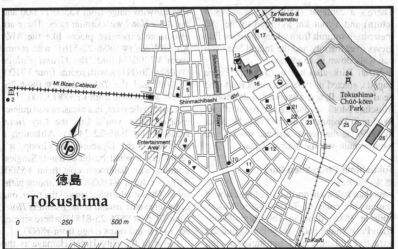

Mt Bizan Cablecar

徳島
Tokushima

0   250   500 m

PLACES TO STAY

5   Business Hotel
    New Tōyō
    ビジネスホテルニュー東洋
6   Washington Hotel
    ワシントンホテル
11 City Hotel Hamaya
    シティホテルはまや
12 Marston
    Green Hotel
    ホテルマーストングリーン
14 Tōkyū Inn
    東急イン
17 Grand Palace Hotel
    ホテルグランドパレス徳島
20 AWA Kankō Hotel
    阿波観光ホテル
21 Station Hotel
    ステーションホテル
22 Astoria Hotel
    アストリアホテル

23 Aivis Hotel
    エイヴィスホテル
26 Park Hotel
    パークホテル

PLACES TO EAT

8   Nisho-Moto
    Restaurant
    西元
9   Hashimoto Restaurant
    橋元
16 Mr Donut
    ミスタードーナッツ

OTHER

1   Wenceslão
    de Morães Museum
    モラエス記念館
2   Peace Pagoda
    平和塔

3   Cablecar Station
    眉山ケーブルカー駅
4   JAS
    日本エアシステム
7   Dancing Clock
    阿波おどり時計
10 Boat Rental
    貸しボート
13 Post Office
    徳島郵便局
15 Sogo
    Department Store
    そごう
18 JR Tokushima Station
    J R 徳島駅
19 Bus Station
    バスターミナル
24 Gokoku Shrine
    護国神社
25 Senshukaku-tien
    Garden
    徳島城表御殿庭園

base of Mt Bizan. The entertainment area and main shopping arcade is west of the river and south of the main street.

There's an information counter just inside the station and an international phone box by the counter. As elsewhere in Shikoku, an area that sees relatively few foreign visitors, don't

expect the staff to be geared up to the needs of gaijin backpackers.

Mt Bizan 眉山

A broad avenue with a central parade of palm trees runs south-west from the station to the foot of Mt Bizan, also known as Mt Otaki.

SHIKOKU

There's a cablecar (¥500 one way, ¥800 return) and a four km toll road to the 280 metre high summit from where there are fine views over the city and the Inland Sea. You can walk down in 15 minutes.

Bizan Park also has a 25 metre Peace Pagoda, erected in 1958 as a memorial to the dead of WW II, and a Wenceslão de Morães Museum. Morães, a Portuguese naval officer, lived in Tokushima from 1893 until his death in 1929. He married a Japanese woman and wrote a multi-volume study of Japan.

Tokushima-Chūō-kōen Park
徳島中央公園

Less than half a km north-east of the railway station, the ruins of Tokushima-jō Castle, built in 1586, stand in Tokushima-Chūō-kōen Park. In the park you will also find the attractively landscaped Senshukaku-teien Garden, which dates from the Momoyama period. Entry is free.

Other Attractions

Just south of the river, near the entertainment district, is the **dancing clock**, a curious contraption which pops up out of an otherwise undistinguished looking bus stop. You can rent rowboats on the Shinmachi-gawa River.

Festivals

The annual Awa Odori Festival from 15 to 18 August brings the citizens out into the streets in their traditional costumes and the dancing lasts almost all night. The town is also noted for its puppet theatres – performances are traditionally made by farmers before planting and after harvesting. You might catch a puppet performance at the beginning of June or in mid-August

Places to Stay

Hostel Tokushima Youth Hostel (☎ 0886-63-1505) is by the beach some distance out of town and costs ¥2500.

Hotels Hotels close to the railway station include the Station Hotel (☎ 0886-52-8181) with singles/doubles at ¥5300/10,200; the Astoria Hotel (☎ 0886-53-6151), where

singles/twins range from ¥5500/11,000 and the Aivis Hotel with similar rates. There are also more expensive places like the AWA Kankō Hotel (☎ 0886-22-5161) with rooms from ¥7200/14,000; the Grand Palace (☎ 0886-26-1111), with rooms from ¥9100/18,100; and the Tōkyū Inn (☎ 0886-26-0109) with rooms from ¥7900/13,700.

Close to the river, in a pleasant and quieter area of town, you'll find the City Hotel Hamaya (☎ 0886-22-3411). Although a member of the Japanese Inn Group, it's really just a small business hotel. Singles/doubles with bathroom cost from ¥5500/9100, or from ¥4500/8100 without bathroom. Over on the other side of the river, one of the cheapest around is the Business Hotel New Tōyō (☎ 0886-25-8181), where singles are ¥4700 and twins range from ¥8600.

Close to the City Hotel Hamaya is the glossy Marston Green Hotel (☎ 0886-54-1777), which really does have a green-tiled exterior. Singles/doubles start from ¥5900/10,500, and in summer, there's a beer garden on the 9th floor. Also near by are a number of other cheaper hotels, some fancy ryokan and a scattering of love hotels including one topped by a large sign announcing 'Soap'. (Soapland is a Japanese euphemism for sex and associated activities.) Across the river, on the edge of the entertainment district, is the Washington Hotel (☎ 0886-53-7111). Singles here range from ¥6700 to ¥8000, twins from ¥15,000 to ¥26,000 and doubles from ¥13,500 to ¥14,500.

Places to Eat

If you're just passing through Tokushima, you can pop down to the basement of Clement Plaza inside the station and raid the expansive delicatessen area for a wide range of cheap snacks. There's also a branch of Lotteria in the basement with cheap coffee – just ask for hotto kōhii.

Elsewhere around town, the dining possibilities don't just jump out and grab you. The entertainment area, just over the river, has a number of fast-food places like Mos Burger, Mr Donut and McDonald's, but for more interesting dining you're going to have to do some digging. One place that's worth checking out is an izakaya, *Nishi-Moto* (☎ 0886-52-5756). It's a lively place with reasonable prices and is open from 11.30 am to 11 pm, closed on Wednesday. Close by is *Hashimoto* (☎ 0886-22-8951), a popular soba place with prices from ¥500. It's also closed on Wednesday.

Getting There & Away
Air JAS connect Tokushima with Osaka and Tokyo.

Train & Bus Tokushima is less than 1½ hours from Takamatsu by limited express train (tokkyū). There are also railway lines westward to Ikeda on the JR Dosan line (which runs between Tadotsu and Kōchi) and south along the coastal Mugi line as far as Kaifu from where you will have to take a bus to continue to Kōchi.

Ferry Ferries connect Tokushima with Tokyo, Osaka and Kōbe on Honshū, with Kokura on Kyūshū, and with various smaller ports. It only takes two hours to Kōbe by hydrofoil.

Getting Around
It's easy to get around Tokushima on foot; from the railway station to the Mt Bizan cablecar station is only 700 metres. Bicycles can be rented from the underground bicycle park in front of the station.

AROUND TOKUSHIMA　徳島周辺
Naruto Whirlpools　鳴門の渦潮
At the change of tide, the water whisks through the narrow Naruto Channel with such velocity that ferocious whirlpools are created. Boats venture out into the channel, which separates Shikoku from nearby Awaji-shima Island, and travel under the modern Naruto-ōhashi Bridge to inspect the whirlpools close up. A brochure on the boat trips (¥1300) available at the JR Tokushima station information counter (ask for *naruto-no-uzu-ko*) gives details of tide times.

There's a fine view over the channel from **Naruto-kōen Park** at the Shikoku end of the

bridge and you can save the walk up to the top of the lookout by taking a long, ¥200 escalator ride. Getting to the bridge by public transport can be very time consuming although it's not a great distance. From Tokushima, take a train to JR Naruto station (¥310, 40 minutes) and an infrequent bus from there to the bridge (¥300, 20 minutes). It might be better to take a bus directly from Tokushima bus station. Ferries also run to the park from Awaji-shima Island.

Dochū Sand Pillars　土柱
About 35 km directly west of Tokushima is Dochū, where erosion has formed curious sand pillars standing about 15 metres high. It's reached via JR Anabuki station.

Mt Tsurugi-san　剣山
'Sword' peak (Mt Tsurugi-san) is actually gently rounded rather than sharp edged but, at 1955 metres, it is still the second highest mountain in Shikoku. A chair lift takes you to a point which is a 40 minute walk from the summit.

South of Tokushima　徳島の南部
The JR Mugi line runs south as far as Kaifu from where you can continue by bus to Cape Muroto-misaki and on to Kōchi. There are good views of offshore islands from Anan, while further south at Hiwasi, turtles come ashore to lay their eggs in the **Ohama-kōen Park** in late July and early August.

KOTOHIRA TO KŌCHI　琴平から高知へ
Although Kotohira is in Kagawa-ken and Kōchi is in Kōchi-ken, part of the distance between the two towns is in Tokushima-ken. The railway and road follow the Yoshino River Gorge much of the way, and the scenery is often spectacular.

Koboke & Ōboke　小歩危・大歩危
The eight km stretch of the Yoshino River between these two rock formations is particularly spectacular. Boat trips are made down the rapids to Koboke from a starting point near Ōboke (¥620). Both are stations on the Dosan line between Kotohira and Kōchi.

SHIKOKU

SHIKOKU

Iyadani-kei Gorge 祖谷渓

If you've seen the vine suspension bridge (steel reinforced) at the Shikoku-mura Village near Takamatsu, you might be interested in seeing the real thing; the **Kazura-bashi Bridge** which crosses the Iyadani-kei Gorge. From the Ōboke JR station, it's 12 km (¥860) to the bridge, but buses are infrequent and take an hour. Buses from Awa-Ikeda station (further to the north on the Dosan line) may be more frequent. They take around one hour 10 minutes and cost ¥1200.

At one time, many river gorges in the mountainous interior of Shikoku were crossed by similar bridges. However, the vines on the bridge have to be totally replaced every three years, and today the Kazura-bashi Bridge is the only one left. There's a miniature replica on the platform at Oboke station. There's a charge of ¥410 to cross the bridge, and it's open daily from sunrise to sunset.

Jōfuku-ji & Buraku-ji Temples 浄福寺・武楽寺

Further south towards Kōchi, and actually in Kōchi-ken, the Jōfuku-ji Temple has a *Youth Hostel* (☎ 0887-74-0301) where visitors sometimes make long stays. It has nightly costs of ¥2400. On the JR Toyonaga station platform, there's a sign in English directing people to the hostel. The next stop is Ōtaguchi, from where it's a 40 minute walk to the Buraku-ji Temple. The main hall there dates from 1151 AD.

Kōchi-ken 高知県

KŌCHI 高知

Kōchi (population 317,000) was the castle town of what used to be known as the Tosa Province, and the small but original castle still stands. Like Kagoshima in Kyūshū and Hagi in Western Honshū, the town can lay claim to having played an important role in the Meiji Restoration.

Orientation & Information

The main street in Kōchi, with a tram line down the centre, runs north-south, crossing the main shopping arcade and the other main street near Harimaya-bashi Bridge. The bridge (apart from some purely visual railings) has long gone but the citizens of Kōchi still recall a famous ditty about a bald monk buying a hair band at the bridge, presumably for a female friend. Apart from the castle, Kōchi's other attractions are all some distance from the town centre.

The information office at JR Kōchi station is just outside the station and to the left. There are excellent brochures in English, and there is usually a helpful staff member around who speaks good English.

Sakamoto Ryōma 坂本竜馬

Although it was the progressive samurai of Kagoshima and Hagi who played the major part in the dramatic events of the Meiji Restoration, the citizens of Kōchi claim it was their boy, Sakamoto Ryōma, who brought the two sides together. Unhappy with the

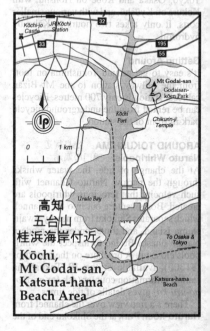

高知 五台山 桂浜海岸付近

Kōchi, Mt Godai-san, Katsura-hama Beach Area

rigid class structure institutionalised under Tokugawa rule, Sakamoto sought exile in Nagasaki, where he ran a trading company and helped build the powerful alliances that prompted the collapse of the shogunate. His assassination in Kyoto in 1867, when he was just 32 years old, cemented his romantic/tragic image and he appears, looking distinctly sour, on countless postcards and other tourist memorabilia in Kōchi. There's a notable statue of Sakamoto at Katsurahama Beach.

Dogs & Roosters

The Kōchi area is noted for its fighting dogs and long-tailed roosters. The mastiff-like dogs are ranked like sumō wrestlers and even wear similar aprons. You can see demonstration fights at Katsura-hama Beach, and buy toy fighting dogs from the souvenir shops. Breeders have persuaded the long-tailed rooster to produce tail feathers up to 10 metres long! You can see them at the Nagaodori Centre in the Oshino area of Nankoku City, out towards Kōchi Airport. The JR Gomen station, five stops west of Kōchi, is near by.

Kōchi-jō Castle　高知城

Kōchi's castle may not be one of the great castles of Japan but it is a real survivor, not a postwar concrete reconstruction. Although a construction on the site dates back to the 14th century, the present castle was built between 1601 and 1611, burnt down in 1727 and rebuilt in 1753. By this time, the peace of the Tokugawa period was well established and castles were scarcely necessary except as a symbol of a feudal lord's power. The Kōchi lord therefore rebuilt the castle with his living quarters (the Kaitokukan) on the ground floor, with doors opening into the garden. Kōchi-jō, therefore, is not a gloomy castle, as those which were strongly fortified against enemy attack tended to be.

At the bottom of the castle hill is the well-preserved Ōte-mon Gate. Inside the castle there is a small museum with exhibits relating to Sakamoto Ryōma, and from the castle there's a fine view over the town. The castle is open from 9 am to 5 pm and entry is ¥350. There's a very informative brochure on the castle available in English. The Kōchi History Museum is at the base of the hill but is not really worth the ¥250 entry fee.

Godaisan-kōen Park & Chikurin-ji Temple　五台山公園・竹林寺

The hilltop Chikurin-ji Temple and Kōchi's botanical garden are both in Godaisan-kōen Park, several km from the town centre. The temple is No 31 on the Shikoku temple circuit, and there's an attractive five storeyed pagoda at the top of the hill. The temple's treasure house has an interesting collection of old statues, some of them looking very Indian or Tantric, and is worth a look. The ¥200 entry fee also covers the temple garden, behind another building. On the other side of the car park is the Makino Botanical Garden and greenhouse, admission is ¥350.

To get to the park and temple take a bus, marked to the temple, from the Toden Seibu bus station which is next to the Seibu department store which is at the Harimaya-bashi junction. The journey takes about 20 minutes and the bus stops outside the temple steps. Buses run about once an hour until 5 pm and the fare is ¥300.

Katsura-hama Beach　桂浜

Only the Japanese could make a big deal out of a beach which is liberally dotted with large and permanent looking signs proclaiming 'No Swimming'. Nevertheless, Katsura-hama Beach is a popular 13 km excursion from Kōchi. Apart from the sand, there's a well-known statue of local hero Sakamoto Ryōma, an aquarium, a shell display and demonstration dog fights, which are held in the Tosa Tōken Centre.

Five minutes walk west of Katsura-hama Beach is the **Sakamoto Ryōma Memorial Museum**, which tells the local hero's life story in miniature dioramas. It's open daily from 9 am to 4.30 pm, and entry is ¥350.

Buses run from Kōchi bus station to Katsura-hama every 20 minutes; there's also a bus stop outside the Seibu department store, just beyond the Harimaya-bashi

SHIKOKU

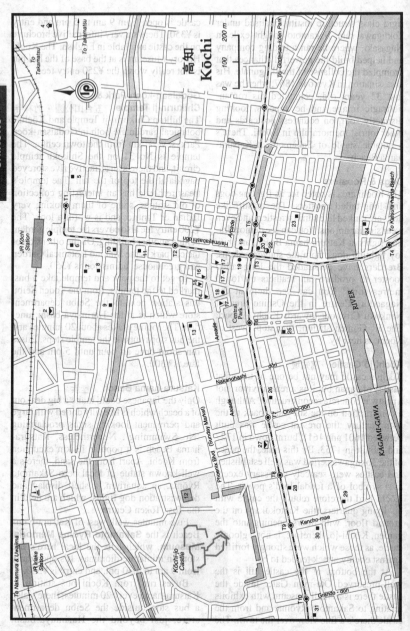

Kōchi

高知

0   100   200 m

To Takamatsu

To Takamatsu

To Takamatsu

To Godaisan-kōen Park

To Katsura-hama Beach

JR Kōchi Station

JR Irake Station

To Nakamura & Uwajima

Harimayabashi-dōri

Arcade

Arcade

Arcade

Central Park

Nakanohashi

Onashi-dōri

Phoenix Blvd (Sunday Market)

Kōchi-jō Castle

Kencho-mae

Grando-dōri

RIVER

KAGAMI-GAWA

-dōri

SHIKOKU

PLACES TO STAY		31	Orient Hotel Kōchi オリエントホテル高知	20	Seibu Department Store 西武デパート
4	Kōchi Ekimae Youth Hostel 高松駅前ユースホステル		PLACES TO EAT	21	Toden-Seibu Bus Station とでん西武 バスターミナル
5	Dai-Ichi Hotel 第一ホテル	14	Café Mousse カフェムース	22	Katsura-hama Bus Stop
6	Kōchi Hotel 高知ホテル	15	Murasaki Robatayaki むらさき炉端焼き		かつらはまバス停
7	Sun Route Hotel サンルートホテル	16	Okonomiyaki Yakisoba Hakobe お好み焼きやきそばはこべ	27	Post Office 郵便局
8	Business Hotel City Kōchi ビジネスホテルシティ高知	17	Tsukasa Restaurant (3 Branches) 料亭司		TRAM STOPS
9	Tosa Gyoen Ryokan 土佐御苑旅館			T1	Kōchi-eki 高知駅
10	Hotel Takasago ホテル高砂		OTHER	T2	Hasuike-machi はすいけまち
11	Kōchi Green Hotel 高知グリーンホテル	1	Anraku-ji Temple (No 30 on Circuit) 安楽寺	T3	Harimaya-bashi はりまやばし
13	Washington Hotel 高知ワシントンホテル	2	Main Post Office 高知中央郵便局	T4	Umenotsuji うめのつじ
23	Kōchi Business Hotel Honkan 高知ビジネスホテル本館	3	Bus Station (to Katsura-hama Beach & Matsuyama) バスターミナル（松山行き他）	T5	Toden-Seibu とでんせいぶまえ
24	Aki Hotel 民宿あき			T6	Horizume ほりずめ
25	Hotel Tosa ホテル土佐	12	Prefectural Museum - Kōchi History Museum 高知郷土文化会館	T7	Ohashi-dōri おおはしどうり
26	Kōchi Sunrise Hotel 高知サンライズホテル			T8	Kōchijō-mae 高知城前
28	Hotel New Hankyū 高知新阪急ホテル	18	Daimaru Department Store 大丸	T9	Kencho-mae 県庁前
29	Sansuien Ryokan 三翠園ホテル	19	Harimaya-bashi Bridge はりまや橋	T10	Grando-dōri グラルド通り
30	Kōchi Green Kaikan (hotel) 高知グリーン会館				

junction. The trip takes about 35 minutes and costs ¥580.

Market

If you're in Kōchi on Sunday, visit the popular and colourful street market along Phoenix Blvd, the road which leads to Kōchi-jō Castle. The market supplies everything from fruit, vegetables and goldfish to large stones for use in gardens.

Places to Stay

Youth Hostel *Kōchi Ekimae Youth Hostel* (☎ 0888-83-5086) is only a few minutes walk east of the railway station and costs ¥2400.

Budget Hotels For very basic business hotel accommodation, try the *Kōchi Business Hotel Honkan* (☎ 0888-83-0221). It has singles from ¥3500 to ¥3900 and twins from ¥7000 to ¥7600. Another place worth trying is the *Hotel Tosa* (☎ 0888-25-3332), where rooms start at ¥4500. It's not far from the Horizume tram stop. Further east, and just south of the Kencho-mae tram stop, the *Kōchi Green Kaikan* (☎ 0888-25-2701) is a small place with singles at ¥4500 and twins at ¥8400. Another cheapie is the *Business Hotel City Kōchi* (☎ 0888-72-2121), which has the advantage of being close to the station. It has singles from ¥4500 to ¥5000, twins at ¥9000 and doubles at ¥7800.

The *Kōchi Green Hotel* (☎ 0888-22-1800)

SHIKOKU

is also another straightforward, cheaper hotel that's not too far from the station. Singles are ¥6100, and twins and doubles range from ¥9800.

Expensive Hotels The *Washington Hotel* (☎ 0888-23-6111), on Phoenix Blvd, is conveniently central and close to the castle. Rooms cost from ¥8000/15,800 for singles/doubles.

The pleasant *Orient Hotel Kōchi* (☎ 0888-22-6565) is south of the castle and on the tram line. Rooms for one cost from ¥6700, for two from ¥11,000. The *Kōchi Sunrise Hotel* (☎ 0888-22-1281) charges from ¥6600/12,600 for singles/doubles. Not far from the station is the *Hotel Takasago* (☎ 0888-22-1288), a smaller hotel with slightly cheaper prices.

The large *Sansuien Hotel* (☎ 0888-22-0131), due south of the castle, includes some old buildings from the Kōchi daimyō's grounds. Costs per person with meals range from ¥14,000.

Places to Eat
Kōchi's best restaurants are clustered around the Daimaru department store near the Harimaya-bashi Bridge end of the shopping arcade. Here you'll find at least three branches of *Tsukasa*, a popular Japanese restaurant displaying plastic meals from tempura to sashimi, and offering fixed-price specials and friendly service.

On the 2nd and 3rd floors of a building just off the arcade, there's a branch of the *Murasaki Robatayaki*, easily recognisable by its thatched house motif. *Café Mousse* has snacks, cakes, ice cream and interesting desserts; look for the British Mini crashing out of the 2nd floor of the building around the corner. *Okonomiyaki Yakisoba Hakobe* offers the popular 'cook it yourself' omelette dish known as okonomiyaki. Sadists with a penchant for 'cruel cuisine' might want to check out *Shōseiko*, a Tosa-ryōri place that advertises its sashimi cuts as still living – look for the red lanterns outside, and figure on spending around ¥3000 per head.

Getting There & Away
Air ANA connects Kōchi with Osaka, Tokyo and Miyazaki in Kyūshū. Air Nippon Koku (ANK) also fly between Kōchi and Osaka while JAS fly to Fukuoka, Nagoya and Osaka.

Train Kōchi is on the JR Dosan line which runs from the north coast of Shikoku through Kotohira. It takes about 2½ hours by limited express from Takamatsu. From Kōchi, rail services continue westward to just beyond Kubokawa where the line splits south-west to Nakamura and north-west to Uwajima. From Uwajima, you can continue north to Matsuyama but this is a long and circuitous route.

Bus Travel between Kōchi and Matsuyama is faster by bus. These depart hourly from outside the bus station near the JR Kōchi station. If you want to travel right around the south coast, either west around Cape Ashizuri-misaki to Uwajima or east around Cape Muroto-misaki to Tokushima, you will have to travel by bus as the railway lines do not extend all the way.

Ferry Kōchi is connected by ferry to Osaka and Tokyo.

Getting Around
The tram service running north-south from the station intersects the east-west tram route at the Harimaya-bashi junction. Ask for a *norikaeken* (transfer ticket) if you have to transfer there. You can easily reach the castle on foot, though for the town's other attractions, you must take a bus.

AROUND KŌCHI 高知周辺
Apart from Katsura-hama Beach, there are a number of other interesting places easily reached from Kōchi.

Ryūga-dō Cave 竜河洞
This limestone cavern (one of the best three in Japan!) has typical stalactites and stalagmites plus traces of prehistoric habitation. A

bus bound for Odochi will get you to the cave in about an hour, entry is ¥850.

Aki　安芸

Further east is Aki, where Iwasaki Yatarō, founder of the giant Mitsubishi conglomerate, was born in 1834. His thatched-roof house is preserved, phone ☎ 0887-34-1111 if you want to see it. There are some old samurai streets around the castle remains.

Ino-chō Paper Museum
伊野町立紙の博物館

In Ino, just four stations west of Kōchi on the JR line, the Ino-chō Paper Museum demonstrates the traditional manufacturing techniques for Tosa paper making. The museum is open from 9 am to 5 pm daily except Monday; entry is ¥300.

CAPE MUROTO-MISAKI　室戸岬

Cape Muroto-misaki, south-east of Kōchi, has a lighthouse topping its wild cliffscape. The **Higashi-dera Temple** here is No 24 on the Shikoku temple circuit. Just north of Muroto is a chain of black-sand beaches known by local surfers as **'Little Hawaii'**. There's youth hostel accommodation on the cape at the *Hotumisaki-ji Youth Hostel* (☎ 0887-23-2488), where nightly costs are ¥2300.

You can reach the cape by bus from Kōchi and you can continue right round to Tokushima on the east coast. Tosa Dentetsu buses for Cape Muroto-misaki run from the Harimaya-bashi intersection, around 10 minutes on foot south of Kōchi station. The journey takes around two hours 20 minutes and costs ¥2650. For those continuing on to Tokushima, the JR Mugi line runs around the east coast from Tokushima as far as Kaifu.

CAPE ASHIZURI-MISAKI　足摺岬

South-west of Kōchi, Cape Ashizuri-misaki, like Cape Muroto-misaki, is a wild and scenic promontory ending with a lighthouse. As well as the coastal road, there's also a central **Skyline Rd**. Cape Ashizuri also has a temple (the Kongōfuku-ji, No 38 on the temple circuit), which, like the temple at Cape Muroto, also has its own youth hostel (☎ 0880-88-0038).

The usual point of access for the cape is **Nakamura**, from the station of which there are infrequent bus services to the tip of the cape for ¥1870. The cape's main attractions, including **Kongōfuku-ji Temple** and a wooded 'romance walk', are all within easy walking distance of the Ashizuri-misaki bus centre.

From Tosashimizu, at the northern end of the cape, ferries operate to Kōbe on Honshū. From Kōchi, there is a railway as far as Nakamura; travel from Nakamura around the cape and on to Uwajima is by bus.

NORTH-WEST TO UWAJIMA
宇和島方面へ

From Tosashimizu, the road continues around the southern coast of Shikoku to Uwajima in Ehime-ken. The scenery is particularly attractive through **Tatsukushi**, where there is a coral museum and a shell museum. Sightseeing boats and glass-bottom boats operate from the town.

Sukumo has a fine harbour and the *Sukumo Youth Hostel* (☎ 0880-64-0233). You can take boats out to remote Okinoshima Island from Sukumo.

Sukumo is less than an hour by bus from Nakamura by the direct road although much longer around the coast via the cape. On to Uwajima takes about two hours. From Sukumo, ferries make the three hour crossing several times daily to Saeki on Kyūshū.

Ehime-ken　愛媛県

MATSUYAMA　松山

Shikoku's largest city, Matsuyama, is a busy north coast town (population 443,000) and an important transport hub with frequent ferry links to Hiroshima. Matsuyama's major attractions are its castle, one of the finest survivors from the feudal era, and the Dōgo Onsen hot springs area with its magnificent old public bath.

Orientation & Information

The JR Matsuyama station is west of the

SHIKOKU

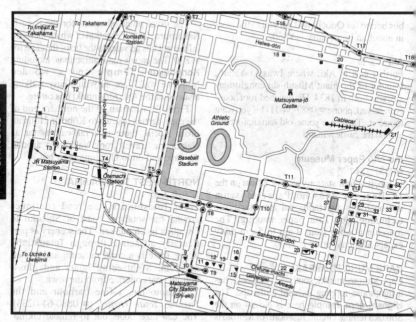

PLACES TO STAY

1   Hotel Sun Route
    Matsuyama
    ホテルサンルート松山
2   Terminal Hotel
    Matsuyama
    ターミナルホテル松山
4   Hotel New Kajiwara
    ホテルニューカジワラ
5   City Hotel American
    シティーホテルアメリカン
6   Central Hotel
    セントラルホテル
7   Hotel Nisshin
    ホテル日進
8   Tokyo Dai Ichi Hotel
    東京第一ホテル
17 Chateau-tel
    Matsuyama
    シャトーテル松山
18 Hotel Heiwa
    ホテル平和
19 Business Hotel Taihei
    ビジネスホテル泰平
20 Business Hotel
    New Kashima
    ビジネスホテルニューかしま

27 ANA Hotel
    Matsuyama
    全日空ホテル松山
28 Matsuyama Tokkyu Inn
    松山東急イン
33 Hotel Top Inn
    ホテルトップイン
34 Matsuyama
    International Hotel
    国際ホテル松山
39 Matsuyama
    Youth Hostel
    松山ユースホステル
41 Minshuku Miyoshi
    民宿みよし

PLACES TO EAT

3   Nakanoka
    中野家
9   Mister Donut
    ミスタードーナッツ
11 Munchen Beer Hall
    ミュンヘンビアホール
12 Atom Sushi Restaurant
    アトム寿司
15 Kirin City Pub
    キリンシティパブ

24 Restaurant Goshiki
    五志喜
25 Piccadilly Circus Bar
    ピカデリーサーカスバー
26 Spice House
    Restaurant
    スパイス王国
30 Murasaki Restaurant
    むらさき
31 Pound House
    Coffee Bar
    パウンドハウス
    コーヒーバー
32 Bar Icarus
    バーイカルス

OTHER

10 ANA & JAS
    全日空／日本エアシステム
11 New Grand Building
    ニューグランドビル
14 Shiki-do
    子規堂
16 Kinokuniya Bookshop
    紀伊国屋
21 Cablecar Station
    ケーブルカー駅

SHIKOKU

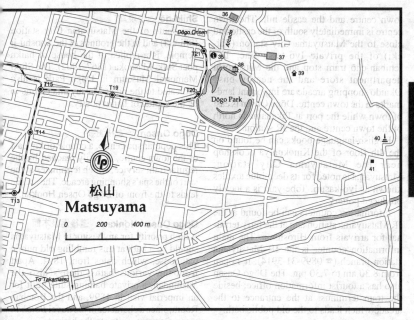

Matsuyama
松山

0   200   400 m

To Takamatsu

To Takamatsu

town centre and the castle hill. The town centre is immediately south of the castle and close to the Matsuyama City station (Shi-eki) of the private Iyo-tetsu line. The Ichiban-chō tram stop and the Mitsukoshi department store and the nearby busy Okaidō shopping arcade are important landmarks in the town centre. Dōgo Onsen is east of town while the port at Takahama is north of the town centre and the JR station.

English-language books can be found on the 4th floor of the Kinokuniya bookshop near the Matsuyama City station. Matsuyama is noted for its deep-blue textiles known as Iyo-kasuri. Tobe-yaki is a locally produced pottery.

Information counters can be found at the JR Matsuyama station and at the ferry terminal for arrivals from Hiroshima. The main information counter is the JR Matsuyama station branch (☎ 0899-31-3914); it's open from 8.30 am to 7.30 pm. The Dōgo Onsen also has a tourist information office: beside the tram terminus, at the entrance to the arcade which leads to the old public bath.

Matsuyama-jō Castle   松山城

Picturesquely sited atop a hill which virtually erupts in the middle of the town, Matsuyama-jō Castle is one of the finest original surviving castles. It only squeaks in with the 'original' label as it was restored just before the end of the Edo period. In the early years of the Meiji Restoration, rebuilding feudal symbols was definitely not a high priority.

The castle was built in 1602-03 with five storeys, but burnt down and was rebuilt in 1642 with three storeys. In 1784, it was struck by lightning and burnt down again, though, in those peaceful and slow-moving Edo years, it took until 1820 for a decision to be made to rebuild it and until 1854 for the reconstruction to be completed! It was completely restored between 1968 and 1986.

You don't even have to climb the steep hill up to the castle, a cablecar and/or chair lift will whisk you up there for ¥160 one way or ¥310 return. Entry to the castle costs ¥260.

Shiki-dō   子規堂

Just south of the Matsuyama City station (Shi-eki) and in the grounds of the Shoshu-ji Temple, is a replica of the house of haiku poet Shiki Masaoka (1867-1902). The Shiki Memorial Museum in Dōgo Park is also dedicated to the poet; Matsuyama claims to be the capital of haiku poetry.

Dōgo Onsen   道後温泉

This popular spa centre, a couple of km east of the town centre, is easily reached by the regular tram service, which terminates at the start of the spa's shopping arcade. The arcade leads to the front of Dōgo Onsen Honkan.

Dōgo Onsen Honkan   道後温泉本館

A high priority for any visitor to Matsuyama should be a bath at this rambling old public bathhouse, which dates from 1894. Apart from the various baths, there's also the Yūshinden, a private bathing suite built for an imperial visit in 1899, and the Botchan Room, since a character in the novel *Botchan* was a frequent visitor to the baths.

Dōgo Onsen Honkan is another place where the correct sequence of steps can be a little confusing. Pay your money outside – ¥250 for a basic bath; ¥620 for a bath followed by tea and a snack; ¥1200 for the private 'Bath of the Spirits' followed by the tea and snack – enter and leave your shoes in a locker. If you've paid ¥250, go to the 'Bath of the Gods' changing room. The changerooms are signposted in English so you won't wander into the wrong one and shock anybody, though if you're male, you may be slightly surprised to find matronly ladies looking after the male changing room. You'd be even more surprised if you took the wrong exit when heading for the bath in summer as only a cane blind separates the changing room from the street!

If you've paid ¥620 or ¥1200, first go upstairs to the balcony and get your yukata (dressing gown), then return to the appropriate changing room. You can leave valuables upstairs in the charge of the attendants who dispense the yukata, though it's hard to see why since there are lockers in the changing room.

After your bath, those destined for upstairs can don their yukata and retire to the veranda to sip tea and look down on onsen visitors clip-clopping by in yukata and geta.

Isaniwa-jinja Shrine 伊佐爾波神社

A few minutes walk from the Dōgo Onsen bathhouse, a long flight of steps leads up to the 1667 AD Hachiman Isaniwa-jinja Shrine.

Municipal Shiki Memorial Museum
子規記念博物館

In Dōgo Park, this museum is dedicated to the memory of local literary figure Shiki Masaoka.

Ishite-ji Temple 石手寺

It's quite a long walk (more than a km) east from the spa area to this temple, No 51 on the temple circuit. The temple dates from 1318, is noted for its fine Kamakura architecture, has a three storeyed pagoda and is overlooked by a Buddha figure high up on the hill. The name means 'stone hand', from a legend about a Matsuyama lord born with a stone in his hand.

At the entranceway to the temple is a 'pilgrim's supply shop'. If you're planning on making the pilgrimage around all 88 temples on the Shikoku circuit, the shop can supply maps, guidebooks, pilgrim's attire, hats, bells and staffs, in fact everything for the complete pilgrim. Matsuyama has seven other circuit temples.

Places to Stay

Matsuyama has three accommodation areas – around the JR station (business hotels); around the centre (business hotels and more expensive hotels); and at Dōgo Onsen (ryokan and Japanese-style hotels).

Youth Hostel *Matsuyama Youth Hostel* (☎ 0899-33-6366), near the Isaniwa Shrine in Dōgo Onsen, costs ¥2500 a night.

Hotels Some of the hotels in the following areas are:

Matsuyama Station Area The *Central Hotel* (☎ 0899-41-4358) is a cheaper business hotel with singles/twins from ¥4500/ 7000.

Other hotels within a stone's throw of the station include the *Hotel New Kajiwara* (☎ 0899-41-0402) with singles/twins from ¥5300/8400 and the *City Hotel American* (☎ 0899-33-6660), which is next door and has singles from ¥4500.

Slightly more expensive station area hotels include the *Hotel Sun Route Matsuyama* (☎ 0899-33-2811), where singles cost from ¥6600 and doubles or twins from ¥13,200. Next door to the station, the *Terminal Hotel Matsuyama* (☎ 0899-47-5388) has singles at ¥5500 and twins at ¥10,000. The featureless *Hotel Nisshin* (☎ 0899-46-3111) is a slightly longer walk from the station and has singles/doubles from ¥5500/9300.

Central Matsuyama The *Tokyo Dai Ichi Hotel* (☎ 0899-47-4411) is on the station side of the town centre and has singles from ¥6800, doubles or twins from ¥12,000. Rooms at the *Chateau-tel Matsuyama* (☎ 0899-46-2111) range from ¥6000 for singles and ¥11,000 for twins.

The expensive *ANA Hotel Matsuyama* (☎ 0899-33-5511) is near the Ichiban-chō tram stop and the Mitsukoshi department store which mark the town centre. Singles here range from ¥7100 to ¥19,000, twins from ¥15,000 to ¥30,000 and doubles from ¥12,000 to ¥19,500. Just across the road is the cheaper *Matsuyama Tokkyū Inn* (☎ 0899-41-0109), where singles range from ¥6800 to ¥12,000, twins from ¥14,000 to ¥20,000 and doubles are ¥14,000.

Immediately north of the castle hill is a quieter area, conveniently connected to the town centre by a tram line. One of the hotels in this area is the curiously old-fashioned *Business Hotel Taihei* (☎ 0899-43-3560), with rooms from ¥4500/8000; others are the *Hotel Heiwa* (☎ 0899-21-3515) and the *Business Hotel New Kashima* (☎ 0899-47-2100). The New Kashima is the cheaper of the latter two, with singles/twins from ¥4300/8000. Take a tram to Tetsubō-chō

SHIKOKU

tram stop and walk south to the main road to find them.

Dōgo Onsen Area For Japanese tourists, Dōgo Onsen, east of the town centre, is the big attraction and there are numerous Japanese-style hotels and ryokan in the area. Most of them are overpriced, but *Minshuku Miyoshi* (☎ 0899-77-2581), behind the petrol station near Ishite-ji Temple, is an exception at around ¥5000 per person. The *Funaya Ryokan* (☎ 0899-47-0278) is one of the best of the onsen ryokan but count on around ¥20,000 upwards per person, including meals.

Places to Eat

The long Ginten-gai and Okai-dō shopping arcade in central Matsuyama has *McDonald's, Kentucky Fried Chicken* and *Mister Donut*. There's another *Mister Donut* near the Matsuyama City station. There's good Japanese-style fast food just across from Matsushima station at *Nakanoka*, a 24 hour gyūdon specialist. The arcade leading from the Dōgo Onsen tram stop to the Dōgo Onsen Honkan bathhouse also has a number of restaurants with plastic meal replicas.

Next to the post office in the town centre, *Restaurant Goshiki* offers sōmen noodles and other dishes. Although there are plastic models in the window and an illustrated menu showing the multi-coloured noodles, this is another place where the artistically scrawled sign looks nothing like the printed kanji. Sōmen and tempura costs ¥850 and you can buy noodles in packets (one colour or mixed) to take home. The area around the Okaidō arcade is one of the best places to seek out a more interesting meal. One place worth checking out is the basement *Spice House*, a cosy Indian place with Indian chefs and reasonable prices – main courses from ¥1100. Also close by, look out for *Pound House*, a coffee bar with a delicious selection of cakes at ¥350.

For a cold beer and not bad pub food there are a couple of places near the Matsuyama City station. *Kirin City Pub*, looking pseudo-pubbish, is near the Kinokuniya bookshop.

Directly opposite the station is *Munchen*, a beer hall looking pseudo-German. Also in this area is the revolving sushi shop *Atom* (yes, there's an English sign). It's inexpensive and popular.

Finally, for straight drinking, *Piccadilly Circus* calls itself a 'British antique bar', and is decked out with all kinds of British paraphernalia. Drinks are expensive though. Cheaper and less pretentious is *Bar Icarus*, just down the road from the Pound Coffee shop. Apparently this is a popular place with the gaijin set on Sunday – you'll have to ask around if you want to find out where they hang out on other nights of the week. Finally, during summer, Matsuyama has a large number of rooftop beer gardens. Try the Sogo department store, the Matsuyama ANA Hotel or the Chateau Tel Hotel's *Terrace Garden*.

Getting There & Away

Air ANA connect Matsuyama with Osaka, Nagoya and Tokyo (both Narita International Airport and Haneda Airport). JAS have connections to Fukuoka, Miyazaki and Kagoshima, all in Kyūshū. JAL also flies to Tokyo while South-West Airlines (SWAL) have direct flights between Matsuyama and Naha in Okinawa.

Train & Bus The north coast JR Yosan line connects Matsuyama with Takamatsu and there are also services across the Seto-ōhashi Bridge to Honshū. Matsuyama to Okayama takes three hours 15 minutes. Another line runs south-west from Matsuyama to Uwajima and then east to Kōchi, though this is a rather circuitous route – it's faster to take a bus directly to Kōchi.

Ferry There are frequent ferry and hydrofoil connections with Hiroshima. Take the Iyotetsudō private railway line from Matsuyama City (Shi-eki) or Otemachi station right to the end of the line at Takahama (¥440 from Otemachi). From Takahama, a connecting bus whisks you the remaining distance to Matsuyama Kankō-kō Port. The hydrofoils zip across to Hiroshima in just over one hour for ¥4950 but there's not much to see en route – the view is much better from the regular ferries. Some services go via Kure, south-west of Hiroshima. The ferry takes from 2¾ to three hours depending on the port in Matsuyama and costs ¥3710 1st class and ¥1850 2nd class to Hiroshima from Matsuyama Kankō-kō.

Other ferries operate to and from Matsuyama and Beppu, Kokura and Oita on Kyūshū as well as Iwakuni, Kure, Mihara, Onomichi and Yanai in Honshū, but check which of the Matsuyama ports services operate from. From Matsuyama Kankō-kō, a hydrofoil zips across to Ocho (¥2660), Kinoe (¥3070), Omishima (¥3310), Setoda (¥4530) and Onomichi (¥4950).

Getting Around

Matsuyama has the private Iyo-tetsudō railway line and a tram service. The railway line is mainly useful for getting to and from the port for Hiroshima ferries.

The tram services cost a flat ¥150 anywhere in town. There's a loop line and major terminuses at Dōgo Onsen and outside the Matsuyama City station. The Ichiban-chō stop outside the Mitsukoshi department store and ANA Hotel is a good central stopping point. Tram numbers and routes are:

Tram No	Route
1 & 2	The Loop
3	Matsuyama City Station (Shi-eki)-Dōgo Onsen
5	JR Matsuyama Station-Dōgo Onsen
6	Kiya-chō-Dōgo Onsen

AROUND MATSUYAMA　松山周辺
Mt Ishizuchi-san　石鎚山

Mt Ishizuchi-san (1982 metres), the highest mountain in Shikoku (indeed in all western Japan), is easily reached from Matsuyama. It's also a holy mountain and many pilgrim climbers make the hike, particularly during the July-August climbing season. In winter it's snow-capped.

From Matsuyama, you can take a bus to Tsuchigoya, south-east of the mountain. Alternatively, you can take a bus from the JR

Iyo Saijō station on the Yosan line to the Nishi-no-kawa cablecar station on the northern side. This route passes through the scenic Omogo-kei Gorge, an attraction in its own right. Out of season, bus services to the mountain are infrequent. You can climb up one way and down the other or even make a complete circuit from Nishi-no-kawa to the summit, down to Tsuchigoya and then back to Nishi-no-kawa. Allow all day and an early start for the circuit.

The cablecar takes about five minutes straight up and down and costs ¥900 one way or ¥1700 return. The ride can be followed by an optional chair lift (¥200 one way, ¥350 return), which slightly shortens the walk to Jōju, where the Ishizuchi-jinja Shrine offers good views of the mountain. From Jōju, it's 3½ km to the top, first gently downhill through forest, then uphill through forest, across a more open area and finally a steep and rocky ascent. Although there's a path, and often steps, all the way to the top, the fun way to make the final ascent is up a series of *kusari*, heavy chains draped down the very steep rock faces. Clambering up these chains is the approved pilgrimage method. The actual summit, reached by climbing along a sharp ridge, is a little beyond the mountain hut on the top.

Imabari　今治

This industrial city is of no particular interest apart from its position beside the most island-crowded area of the Inland Sea. At this point, whirlpools rather like those at Naruto (see the Around Tokushima section earlier) form in the narrow channel separating Shikoku from Ō-shima Island.

There are numerous ferry services connecting Imabari with ports on Honshū including Hiroshima, Kōbe, Mihara, Nigata, Onomichi, Takehara and various ports on islands of the Inland Sea.

UCHIKO　内子

Half way between Matsuyama and Uwajima, and on the JR Yosan line, the small town of Uchiko has a street lined with old buildings dating from the last years of the

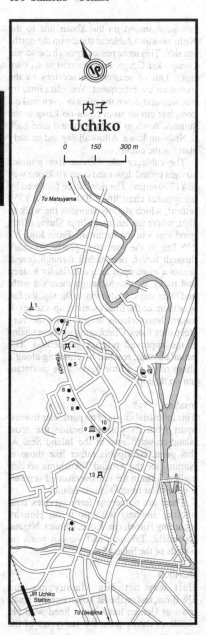

SHIKOKU

内子
Uchiko

0   150   300 m

To Matsuyama

Yōkaichi

To Uwajima

JR Uchiko
Station

1	Kōsho-ji Temple 高昌寺
2	Ōmori Rōsoku Candle Maker 大森和蝋燭店
3	Stone Lantern 常夜灯
4	Small Shrine 稲荷神社
5	Kami Hagi-tei House 上芳我邸
6	Small Craft Shop With Teahouse 茶室／民芸店
7	Hon Hagi-tei House 本芳我邸
8	Craft Shop 民芸店
9	Machi-ya Shiryōkan Museum 町家資料館
10	Amazake Chaya Teahouse あま酒茶屋
11	Sake Brewery 酒醸造所
12	Bus Station バス停留所
13	Hachiman Shrine 八幡神社
14	Uchiko-za Kabuki Theatre 内子座

Edo period and the early years following the Meiji Restoration. At that time, Uchiko was an important centre for the production of the vegetable wax known as *rō*, and some of the houses along Yōkaichi, the town's old street, belong to merchants who made their fortunes from producing rō.

Orientation & Information

Most of the places on Yōkaichi are closed on Monday, which makes it a bad day to visit. There's a map with *some* English outside the JR station but nothing else in Uchiko is labelled in English. Yōkaichi is an uneventful 20 minute walk to the north of Uchiko station.

Yōkaichi 八日市

Uchiko's picturesque old street, which extends for about a km, has a number of interesting old buildings along with souvenir shops, craft shops and teahouses. At the start of the street is an old sake brewery, across from which is the Amazake Chaya Teahouse (*amazake* is a sweet sake). A little further along the street is the Machi-ya Shiryōkan Museum and then the Hon Haga-tei House, a fine example of a wealthy merchant's private home. The Kami Haga-tei (entry ¥210) across the road is a wax merchant's house with a storehouse. At the end of the street the house of Omori Rōsoku is still engaged in traditional candle production, and you can see and buy these rō wax candles.

Uchiko-za Theatre　内子座

The Uchiko-za is an old kabuki theatre, originally built in 1915 and restored in the mid-80s. Entry is ¥210 and it's closed on Monday.

Getting There & Away

Uchiko can be reached by bus or train from Matsuyama and Uwajima. Ordinary train services from Matsuyama only take an hour. You need a couple of hours at least to explore Yōkaichi.

Getting Around

Yōkaichi is just over a km from the JR Uchiko station; if you're stopping off on the train and your time is limited, consider taking a taxi. The bus station is closer to Yōkaichi.

UCHIKO TO UWAJIMA　内子から宇和島へ

Only 10 km south-west of Uchiko, there are more interesting old houses and shops near the river in **Ōzu**, including the **Garyū-sansō** (closed Wednesday, entry ¥200), a wealthy trader's house built early this century. Traditional cormorant fishing (ukai) takes place in the river during summer. The *Ōzu Kyōdokan Youth Hostel* (☎ 0893-24-2258) has nightly rates of ¥2300. It's in the south-west of town, over the river next to the Ōzu-jō Castle ruins.

Twenty km south-west of Ōzu is **Yawatahama**, from where ferry services operate to Beppu (¥1740) and Usuki (¥1300) on Kyūshū – the crossing to either port takes about three hours. Yawatahama-kō Port is a 10 minute bus ride north of Yawatahama station.

Cape Sada-misaki extends 50 km towards Kyūshū, and from Misaki, near the end of the cape, ferries make the crossing to Saganoseki (near Oita and Beppu) in just over an hour (¥600) and to Beppu itself (¥1120).

UWAJIMA　宇和島

Uwajima (population 68,000) is a relatively quiet and peaceful place with a small but original castle, the shabby remnants of a fine garden, some pleasant temples and a notorious sex shrine. It makes an interesting pause between Kōchi and Matsuyama although an afternoon or a morning is long enough for a reasonable look around.

Orientation & Information

There is an information office in JR Uwajima station and another one across the road from the station. The staff in the latter are more likely to speak English, are very helpful and the office also rents bicycles, but it doesn't open until 9 am. Uwajima is a centre for cultured pearls: the tourist information office can tell you about shops dealing in them.

Uwajima-jō Castle　宇和島城

Uwajima-jō was never a great castle but it's an interesting 'little' three storeyed one and, dating from 1665, is an original, not a reconstruction. It once stood by the sea and although land reclamation has moved the sea well back, there are still good views over the town. Inside there are photos of its recent restoration and of other castles in Japan and overseas. Entry is free and it's open from 6 am to 5 pm, 9 am to 4 pm on Sunday and public holidays.

Taga-jinja Shrine & Sex Museum
多賀神社

Once upon a time, many Shintō shrines had a connection to fertility rites but this aspect was comprehensively purged when puritanism was imported from the West following the Meiji Restoration. Nevertheless, a handful of holdouts survived and Uwajima's Taga Shrine is certainly one of them: it's totally dedicated to sex. There's a tree trunk phallus and various other bits and pieces around the temple grounds, but the three

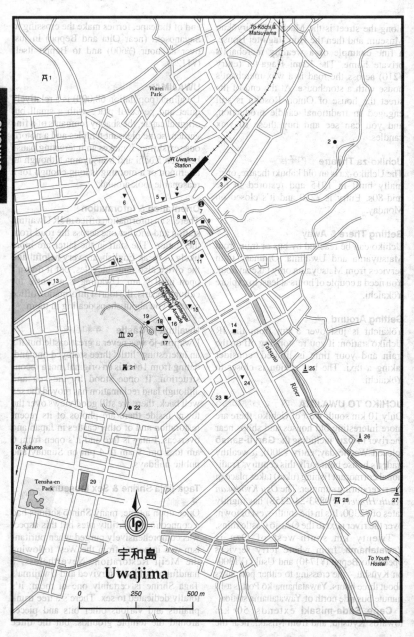

To Kōchi &
Matsuyama

Warei
Park

JR Uwajima
Station

Uwajima Gintengai Shopping Arcade

Tatsuno River

To Sukumo

Tensha-en
Park

To Youth
Hostel

宇和島
Uwajima

0   250   500 m

PLACES TO STAY		10	Hozumitei Restaurant ほずみ亭	19	Samurai Gate Koori Family 武家門
3	Terminal Hotel ターミナルホテル	13	Funahei Restaurant 舟平	20	Castle Museum 宇和島城資料館
8	Kokusai Hotel 国際ホテル	15	Pizza House Itariya	21	Donjon of Uwajima Castle 宇和島城
9	Grand Hotel グランドホテル	24	Gansui Restaurant 丸水	22	Naboritachi Gate のぼりたち門
12	Park Hotel パークホテル		OTHER	25	Seigō-ji Temple 西江寺
14	Dai-Ichi Hotel 第一ホテル	1	Taga-jinja Shrine 多賀神社	26	Ryugesan Tōkaku-ji Temple 東閣寺
16	Business Hotel Heiwa-sō ビジネスホテル平和荘	2	Municipal Bullfighting Ring 市営闘牛場	27	Kongōsan Dairyū-ji Temple 大竜寺
23	Kiya Ryokan 木屋旅館	7	Tourist Information Office 観光案内所	28	Uwatsuhiko-jinja Shrine 宇和津彦神社
	PLACES TO EAT	11	NTT	29	Municipal Date Museum 市立伊達博物館
4	Tomiya Restaurant とみや	17	Bus Centre バスセンター		
5	Kadoya Restaurant かどや	18	Post Office 宇和島郵便局		
6	Scratch Bakery Craft スクラッチベーカリークラフト				

storeyed sex museum is the temple's major attraction. Inside, it's packed floor to ceiling with everything from explicit Peruvian pottery to Greek vases, from the illustrated Kama Sutra to Tibetan Tantric sculptures, from South Pacific fertility gods to a show-case full of leather S&M gear, and from early Japanese shunga (pornographic prints) to their European Victorian equivalents, not to mention modern porno magazines. Saturation soon sets in; entry is ¥600.

Temples & Shrines

In the south-eastern part of town, a number of old temples and a shrine can be found by the canal. They include the Seigōzen-ji Temple, the Ryugesan Tōkaku-ji Temple, the Kongōsan Dairyū-ji Temple with its old tombs and the Uwatsuhiko-jinja Shrine.

Bullfights　市営闘牛場

Tōgyū is a sort of bovine sumō wrestling where one animal tries to shove the other out of the ring (actually, victory is achieved by forcing the other animal to its knees or forcing it to turn and flee from the ring).

Fights are held on occasionally at Uwajima's bullfight ring. You might be lucky enough to hook up with a Japanese tour group that has paid for a special performance, but otherwise fights are held on particular dates each year: 2 January; first Sunday of March and April; third Sunday of May; 24 July; 14 August; and the third Sunday of November.

Other Attractions

The **Tensha-en Gardens** are definitely not among Japan's classic gardens; they look distinctly worn and thin compared to the well-tended lushness of most Japanese gardens. They are open daily from 9 am to 4.30 pm and entry is ¥200.

is the **Municipal Date Museum** with a collection that includes a portrait of Toyotomi Hideyoshi and items connected with the Date lords. It's open from 9 am to 5 pm, closed Monday, and entry is ¥200.

Places to Stay

Youth Hostel The *Uwajima Youth Hostel* (☎ 0895-22-7177) is a long walk from the town centre: when you get to the temples

SHIKOKU

overlooking the town, it's another 650 metre walk, uphill. From the shrine, the hostel is a 1¼ km walk, but there are fine views back down to the town. The hostel charges ¥2500 per night.

Hotels & Ryokan The *Kiya Ryokan* (☎ 0895-22-0101) is a relaxed and friendly place with per-person costs from ¥5200 without meals, ¥9000 with. It's just south of the shopping arcade.

The *Grand Hotel* (☎ 0895-24-3911) is just south of the station and has singles from ¥4700 to ¥6000, twins from ¥9200 to ¥16,000 and a few doubles from ¥8200 to ¥10,000. The *Kokusai Hotel* (☎ 0895-25-0111), across the road from the Grand, is an expensive place with Japanese-style rooms pulling in per-person costs of ¥13,000 upwards with two meals. The *Dai Ichi Hotel* (☎ 0895-25-0001) is near the southern end of the arcade and is more affordable with singles/twins at ¥5200/9200.

One of the cheapest options in town is the *Business Hotel Heiwa-sō* (☎ 0895-22-7711), where singles are ¥3000. It's a small place, and definitely at the shabby end of the business hotel spectrum, but it's cheap. It's over by Uwajima-jō Castle opposite the post office.

Places to Eat

Remarkably, Uwajima is free of the usual US-style fast-food chains, having only an *Andersen's* bakery in the station and a burger place in the arcade. The arcade is principally inhabited by coffee bars, and the entertainment district, with many places to eat, sprawls on both sides.

Kadoya, one of the restaurants along the road by the station, is a friendly place with plastic replica meals in the window and some interesting dishes including the local speci-ality *tai-meshi*, sashimi in egg yolk and soy sauce mixed in with hot rice. It only stays open to 8 pm and is closed on Thursday. Kadoya is an expensive option, and *Tomiya*, a restaurant on the same stretch of road but closer to the station, is more affordable and has more variety – choose from the plastic display outside. Almost next door is *M House*, a pizza/coffee place that's worth a mention by virtue of the fact it's there.

South of the station in the arcade area, you're not going to be bowled over by the dining possibilities, but you might want to drop into *Pizza House Itariya*, a very unauthentic little pizzeria that throws in a few generic pasta dishes for good measure – prices range from around ¥650.

Finally, for a decent snack, on your way to the Sex Museum (or you might prefer a snack afterwards) look out for *Scratch Bakery Craft* (yes, English sign). It has pretty good pastries.

Getting There & Away

You can reach Uwajima by train from Matsuyama (via Uchiko and Uno), a one hour 40 minute trip by limited express. From Kōchi, it takes 3¾ to 4½ hours by limited express via Kubokawa, where you change trains. If you want to head further south and to Cape Ashizuri-misaki, you'll have to resort to buses as the railway line from Kōchi terminates at Nakamura.

Direct bus services operate to Honshū from Uwajima, and there is also a ferry connection to Beppu on Kyūshū which travels via Yawatahama.

Getting Around

Uwajima is a good place to explore by bicycle since it's quiet and the traffic is not too bad. The tourist office across from the station rents bicycles for ¥100 an hour.

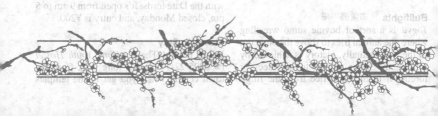

Kyūshū (population 14,500,000) is the third-largest and southernmost of the four major islands of Japan. Although somewhat isolated from the Japanese mainstream on Central Honshū, it has been an important entry point for foreign influence and culture. Kyūshū is the closest island to Korea and China, and it was from Kyūshū that the Yamato tribe extended their power to Honshū. Some of the earliest evidence of Japanese civilisation can be seen at the archaeological excavations around Miyazaki and at the many ancient stone carvings in the Usuki area. More recently Kyūshū was for many centuries the sole link to European civilisation. During the long period of isolation from the West, the Dutch settlement at Nagasaki in Kyūshū was Japan's only connection to the outside world.

For visitors, Nagasaki is one of Kyūshū's prime attractions, with its European-influenced history and its atomic tragedy. In the north, Fukuoka/Hakata is a major international arrival point and the terminus for the shinkansen line from Tokyo. In the centre of the island there is the massive volcanic caldera of Mt Aso, while more volcanic activity can be witnessed in the south at Sakurajima. Larger towns like Kagoshima and Kumamoto offer fine gardens and magnificent castles, while Beppu is one of Japan's major hot-spring centres. There are some good walking opportunities, particularly along the Kirishima volcano chain.

The climate is milder than other parts of Japan, and the people of Kyūshū are reputed to be hard drinkers and outstandingly friendly – a visit to a local bar may provide proof of both theories.

GETTING THERE & AWAY
Air
See the introductory Getting Around chapter for details of fares and routes. There are major airports at Beppu/Ōita, Fukuoka, Kagoshima, Kumamoto, Miyazaki and

Nagasaki. Fukuoka is the major international gateway for Kyūshū. There are also flights to islands off the coast of Kyūshū and to the islands south-west from Kagoshima down to Okinawa.

Train
The shinkansen line from Tokyo and Osaka crosses to Kyūshū from Shimonoseki and terminates in Fukuoka/Hakata. The major cities in Kyūshū are all connected by railway but not by high-speed shinkansen service.

Road and railway tunnels connect Shimonoseki at the western end of Honshū with Kitakyūshū on Kyūshū.

Ferry
There are numerous sea connections to Kyūshū; some of the more interesting ones are dealt with in more detail in the relevant sections of this chapter. Routes include:

Beppu or Ōita to Hiroshima, Kōbe, Matsuyama, Osaka, Takamatsu, Uwajima and Yawatahama
Fukuoka/Hakata to Okinawa
Hyuga to Kawasaki and Osaka
Kagoshima to Okinawa and Osaka
Kokura to Hitakatsu, Izumiotsu, Kōbe, Matsuyama, Osaka, Pusan, Tokushima and Tokyo
Kunisaki to Tokuyama
Saeki to Sukumo
Saganoseki to Misaki
Shibushi to Osaka
Takedazu to Tokuyama
Usuki to Yawatahama

In addition, local ferry services operate between Kyūshū and islands off the coast.

Fukuoka-ken   福岡県

The northern prefecture of Fukuoka will be the arrival point for most visitors to Kyūshū, whether they cross over from Shimonoseki or fly straight into Fukuoka city's international airport.

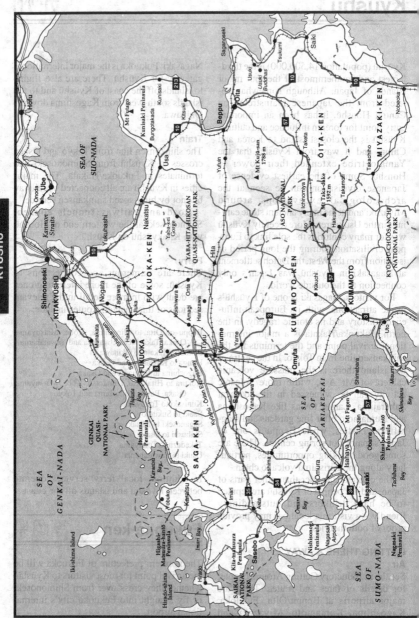

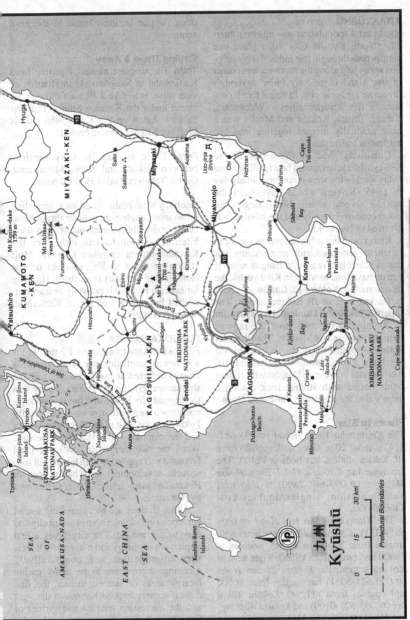

KYŪSHŪ

九州 Kyūshū

SEA OF AMAKUSA-NADA

EAST CHINA SEA

Tomioka

Shimo-jima Island

UNZEN-AMAKUSA NATIONAL PARK

Kami-jima Island

Hondo Island

Ushibuka

Nagashima Island

Koshiki-Retto Islands

Akune

Minamata

Hinagu

JR Kagoshima Line

Sendai

KAGOSHIMA-KEN

Okuchi

Ebino

Hitoyoshi

Yatsushiro

Yunomae

KUMAMOTO-KEN

Mt Kunim-dake 1739 m

Mt Ichifusa-yama 1722 m

Miya-zaki

Ebino-kōgen

Expressway

KIRISHIMA NATIONAL PARK

Mt Karakuni-dake 1700 m

Kirishima

Hayashida

Kobayashi

Saito

Saitobaru

MIYAZAKI-KEN

Miyazaki

Aoshima

Udo-jinja Shrine

Nichinan

Obi

Cape Toi-misaki

Kokubu

Expressway

Kirishima

Miyakonojo

10

Shibushi

Kushima

Shibushi Bay

KAGOSHIMA

Mt Sakurajima

Tarumizu

Kanoya

Ōsumi-hantō Peninsula

Nejime

Kiriko-wan Bay

Lake Ikeda-ko

Ibusuki

Tanakawa

Cape Sata-misaki

KIRISHIMA-YAKU NATIONAL PARK

Kaseda

Chiran

Fukiage-hama Beach

Satsuma-hantō Peninsula

Makurazaki

Bōnotsu

Hyuga

10

Sea of Yatsushiro-kai

SEA OF AMAKUSA-NADA

Prefectural Boundaries

九州 Kyūshū

0   15   30 km

KITAKYŪSHŪ 北九州

Kitakyūshū (population one million), literally 'North Kyūshū City', is a place you simply pass through; this industrial conurbation sprawling along the north-eastern corner of the island is unlikely to be anybody's favourite Japanese city. In actual fact it consists of five separate cities – Wakamatsu, Yahata, Tobata, Kokura and Moji – which have gradually merged together into one enormous traffic jam.

Curiously, one of the cities in the Kitakyūshū cluster would be a familiar name today worldwide were it not for a cloudy day in 1945. Kokura would have been the world's second atomic bomb target, but cloud obscured the city and the mission was diverted to Nagasaki.

Kitakyūshū has achieved pre-eminence in Japanese semiconductor manufacture but this is scarcely a reason to hang around. If you do have time to waste in Kitakyūshū, the reconstructed **Kokura-jō Castle** is about half a km west of JR Kokura station. The superb **Kitakyūshū Municipal Art Museum** is 20 minutes by road from the railway station; it's closed on Monday. The **Hiraodai Plateau**, south of Kokura, is reached via Ishihara and is somewhat similar to Akiyoshidai in Western Honshū with rolling fields dotted with strange rock outcrops; there's also the limestone **Senbutsu Cave**.

Places to Stay

The *Kitakyūshū Youth Hostel* (☎ 093-681-8142), about 20 minutes walk (uphill) from JR Yahata station, has beds at ¥2400. The Japanese Inn Group's *Hotel Town House Matsuya* (☎ 093-661-7890) is also near Yahata station; singles/doubles cost ¥4600/8000.

The *Kitakyūshū Dai Ichi Hotel* (☎ 093-551-7331) is a cheaper business hotel with singles from ¥5500 to ¥6200, doubles at ¥8000 and twins from ¥9500. Right next to Kokura station, the *Kokura Station Hotel* (☎ 093-521-5031) has singles from ¥6500 and doubles from ¥11,500. *Kokura Tōkyū Inn* (☎ 093-521-0109) and *Kokura Washington Hotel* (☎ 093-531-3111) are among the other popular business hotels in the town centre.

Getting There & Away

Train The simplest means of getting from Kitakyūshū to Shimonoseki in Honshū, or vice versa, is to take a JR train through the tunnel under the Kanmon Straits. The first railway station on the Kitakyūshū side is Moji but Kokura is more central.

Ferry There are regular ferry services between Kokura and Kōbe, Matsuyama, Osaka, Tokyo and other Honshū ports.

Hitching Kitakyūshū is one long, sprawling urban mess, unpleasant to drive through and nearly impossible to hitch out of. Travellers hitching to Honshū can either try the Kanmon tunnel entrance near JR Moji station or cross to Shimonoseki on the Honshū side and start from there. Hitching further into Kyūshū is probably best accomplished by getting well out of Kitakyūshū before you start.

FUKUOKA/HAKATA 福岡／博多

Fukuoka/Hakata (population 1.2 million) is a somewhat confusing city as the airport is always referred to as Fukuoka, and the shinkansen terminus as Hakata. Today it is the biggest city in Kyūshū but it was originally two separate towns – the lordly Fukuoka to the west of the Naka-gawa River and the common folks' Hakata to the east. When the two merged in 1889, the label Fukuoka was applied to both towns, but subsequent development has chiefly been in Hakata and many residents refer to the town by that name.

Although there are no compelling tourist attractions in Fukuoka it's a pleasant city and easy to get around. The city gives a real impression of energy and movement. It feels very cosmopolitan and, comparatively speaking, there seem to be many gaijin. Nearby areas of interest include the fine coastal scenery beyond Karatsu to the west and the interesting temples and shrines of Dazaifu, only a few km south.

Orientation

There are two important areas in central Fukuoka – Hakata and Tenjin. JR Hakata station is the transport terminus for the city and is surrounded by hotels and offices. The railway station is flanked by the Fukuoka Kōtsū bus centre on one side and the Hakata post office on the other.

West of Hakata is Tenjin, the business and shopping centre, which is focused along Watanabe-dōri. Underneath this busy street is Tenjin-chika-gai, a crowded underground shopping mall which extends for 400 metres. The Tenjin bus centre here is close to the terminus of the private Nishitetsu Omuta line. Slightly to the north, just off Shōwa-dōri, is the restaurant and entertainment district of Oyofuku-dōri.

Sandwiched between JR Hakata station and the shopping centre, on an island in the Naka-gawa River, is Nakasu, the businessman's entertainment centre of the city. It's a maze of restaurants, strip clubs, hostess bars, cinemas and department stores.

Information

Tourist Office The tourist information office (☎ 092-431-3003) in JR Hakata station is open from 9 am to 7 pm and has information and maps in English. The station is large and confusing at first but the office is more or less in the centre of the main floor.

Consulates For travellers going on to South Korea there's a Korean consulate (☎ 092-771-0461) west of Tenjin, very near the Akasaka subway station. There's also a British consulate (☎ 092-476-2525) and a US consulate (☎ 092-751-9331).

Books & Magazines *Rainbow* is a monthly English-language newsletter produced for Fukuoka-area gaijin and available from Fukuoka International Association Rainbow Plaza (☎ 092-733-2220), which is on the 8th floor of the IMS building in Tenjin. Rainbow also has videos on Japan, books, magazines and a noticeboard with events, accommodation and jobs. In the same building is the Magazine Centre on the 3rd floor, where you can browse free of charge through the latest English-language magazines. The 6th floor has a branch of Maruzen with a small collection of English books. The Kinokuniya bookshop on the 6th floor of the Tenjin Core building has an excellent selection of English-language books.

Shrines & Temples

The Shōfuku-ji Temple is a Zen temple originally founded in 1195 by Eisai, who introduced Zen doctrines to Japan and who is also credited with introducing tea. The temple was badly damaged during WW II and only occupies a quarter of its former area. It's within walking distance of JR Hakata station; don't confuse it with the Sōfuku-ji Temple, a little further away.

Also within walking distance of JR Hakata station is the Sumiyoshi-jinja Shrine, one of the oldest in Kyūshū; the main shrine was restored in 1623. The Kushida Shrine near the Hakata-gawa River opposite the south-eastern end of Nakasu Island is the starting point for the Hakata Yamagasa float race in July. The Hakozaki-gū Shrine has a stone anchor retrieved from the Mongol invasion attempt. To get there, take the Ni-go subway line to Hakozakimaya-mae.

Fukuoka-jō Castle　福岡城

Only the walls of Fukuoka-jō Castle remain in what is now Maizuru Park, but the castle's hilltop site provides fine views of the city. The Ōhori-kōen Park is adjacent to the castle grounds and has a traditional (though recently constructed) Japanese garden, Nihon-teien Garden, on its southern side. The garden has a ¥200 entry charge and is closed Monday. The Fukuoka City Art Museum is also in the park and is open from 9.30 am to 5.30 pm daily except Monday; admission is ¥200. You can get to the castle site by bus No 13 from Tenjin or by subway to Ōhori-kōen station.

Other Attractions

The red-brick building on Shōwa-dōri, close to west bank of the river, is of English design and dates from 1909. It used to house the

KYŪSHŪ

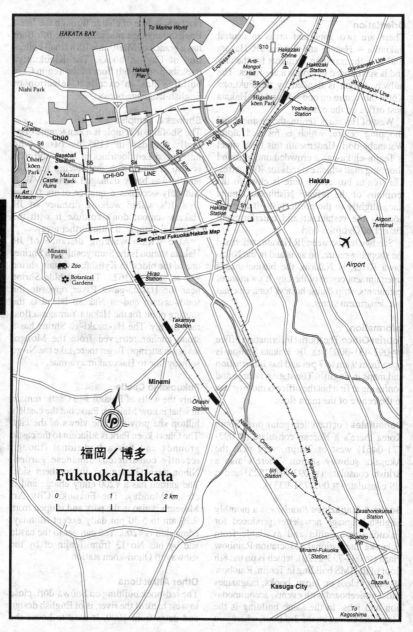

HAKATA BAY

To Marine World

Hakate Pier

Nishi Park

To Karatsu

Chūō

Baseball Stadium

Ōhori-kōen Park

Castle Ruins

Maizuru Park

Art Museum

Minami Park

Zoo

Botanical Gardens

Expressway

S10 Hakozaki Shrine

Anti-Mongol Hall

S9 Higashi-kōen Park

Hakozaki Station

Shinkansen Line

JR Sasaguri Line

Yoshikuta Station

S8

S7 NI-GO LINE

Naka River

S3

S2

S5 S4 ICHI-GO LINE

Hakata

JR Hakata Station

S1

Airport Terminal

Airport

See Central Fukuoka/Hakata Map

Hirao Station

Takamiya Station

Minami

Ōhashi Station

Nishitetsu Ōmuta Line

JR Kagoshima Line

IP

福岡／博多

Fukuoka/Hakata

0   1   2 km

Iijin Station

Zasshonokuma Station

Suehiro Inn

Minami-Fukuoka Station

To Dazaifu

Kasuga City

To Kagoshima

KYŪSHŪ

SUBWAY STATIONS

ICHI-GO LINE

S1 Hakata Station
博多駅
S2 Gion
祇園駅
S3 Nakasu-kawabata
なかすかわばた駅
S4 Tenjin
天神
S5 Akasaka
赤坂
S6 Ohori-kōen
大濠公園駅

NI-GO LINE

S3 Nakasu-Kawabata
なかすかわばた駅
S7 Gofuku-machi
ごふく町駅
S8 Chiyo-Kencho-guchi
ちよけんちょぐち駅
S9 Maidashi-Kyudabyōin-mae
まいだ至急病院前
S10 Hakozakimaya-mae
はこざきまやまえ駅

Fukuoka City Historical Museum, which is now in a new building west of the town centre.

Higashi-kōen Park is north-east of JR Hakata station, en route to the Hakozaki-gū Shrine. The **Genkō Historical Museum** (entry ¥300), also known as the Anti-Mongol Hall, displays items related to the abortive Mongolian invasions. To get there, take a JR train one stop from Hakata to Yoshizuka or take the subway towards Kaizuka and get off at the Maidashi-Kyudaibyoin-mae stop. Between Yoshizuka station and the museum is a large statue of Nichiren (1222-84) who predicted the invasion.

West of the city centre and clearly visible from many parts of town is the **Fukuoka Tower**. Like other Japanese towers elsewhere, you can take an elevator up to a viewing platform and take a look at the Fukuoka skyline. The tower is open from 9.30 am to 9 pm and entry is ¥800. Next to the tower is Momochi-kōen Park and beach. It's a popular spot for swimming. Get to this

area by the Ichi-go subway and get off at Fujisaki station.

Fukuoka's zoo and botanical gardens are south of Fukuoka-jō Castle in Minami Park. To get there, take bus No 56 (for Hibaru-eigyosho) or bus Nos 41 or 43 (for Dobutsu-en-yuki) from stop No 10 in the Tenjin bus centre. **Marine World Umi-no-Nakamichi** is a seaside amusement park and swimming pool reached by ferry across Hakata Bay from Hakata Pier.

Festivals

If you're in town on 3 January you can head out to Hakozaki-gū Shrine and see young men in loincloths chasing a wooden ball. The Hakata Yamagasa Festival, the city's major annual event, is held from 1 to 15 July; seven groups of men race through the city carrying huge floats which weigh about a tonne. The floats are displayed around the city from 1 to 14 July.

A major sumō tournament is held in Kyūshū in mid-November and, in early December, the Fukuoka Marathon, one of the world's most important marathon races, attracts world-class runners from many countries.

Places to Stay

Budget Accommodation Fukuoka itself has no youth hostel, but there is one in nearby Dazaifu, within easy commuting distance of the city (see the Dazaifu Places to Stay section). The information counter in JR Hakata station has a list of inexpensive hotel accommodation in Fukuoka and can make reservations.

If you've wanted to try a capsule hotel (for which you have to be male) then head for *Sauna Wellbe* (☎ 092-291-1009), which is north of Hakata and near the Nakasu Island entertainment district. A sign outside also announces 'Daiwa Club' in English. Your very own capsule costs ¥3700 for the night and there's a large bath, sauna, massage room, restaurant, bar, TV room and other amenities. Just around the corner is the *Capsule Inn Hakata* (☎ 092-281-2244).

KYŪSHŪ

KYŪSHŪ

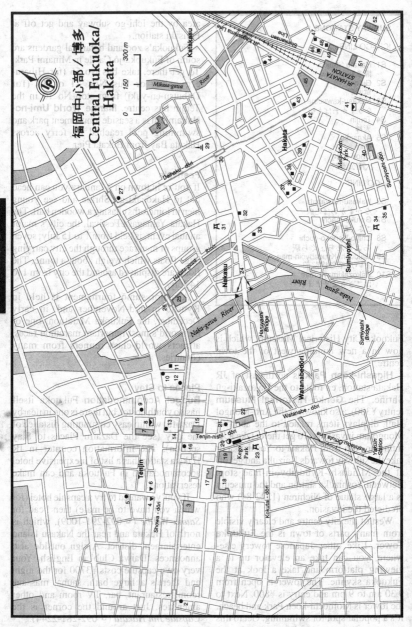

福岡中心部／博多
Central Fukuoka/
Hakata

0   150   300 m

PLACES TO STAY		6	Taiwan Yatai Restaurant 台湾屋台	20	Tenjin Bus Centre 天神バスセンター
3	Nishitetsu Grand Hotel 西鉄グランドホテル	24	Food Stalls 屋台	21	IMS Building I M Sビル
11	Hakata Tokyu Hotel 博多東急ホテル			22	Daimaru Department Store 大丸
32	Capsule Inn Hakata カプセルイン博多		OTHER	23	Kego-jinja Shrine 警固神社
33	Sauna Wellbe	1	Akasaka Subway Station 赤坂地下鉄駅	25	Tamaya Department Store 玉屋
35	Hokke Club Hakata 法華クラブ博多	2	Korean Consulate 韓国領事館	26	Nakasu-Kawabata Subway Station 中洲川端地下鉄駅
36	Chisan Hotel Hakata チサンホテル博多	5	Umie Bar ウミエ	27	JAL
37	Mitsui Urban Hotel 三井アーバンホテル	7	Matsuya Ladies 松屋レーディス	28	Shōfuku-ji Temple 聖福寺
38	Business Hotel Royal ビジネスホテルロイヤル	8	Main Post Office 中央郵便局	29	Tocho-ji Temple とちょう寺
39	Hakata Business Hotel 博多ビジネスホテル	9	Bollox (bar/dance space)	30	Gion Subway Station 祇園町地下鉄駅
40	ANA Hotel Hakata 日空ホテル博多	10	Former Historical Museum 元祖長浜屋	31	Kushida Shrine 櫛田神社
46	Green Hotel 2 グリーンホテル2	12	Thai International Airways 泰国航空		Sumiyoshi-jinja Shrine 住吉神社
47	Green Hotel 1 グリーンホテル1	13	ANA	41	Hakata Post Office 博多郵便局
48	Sun Life Hotel 1 サンライフホテル1	14	Tenjin Subway Station 天神地下鉄駅	42	ANA
49	Hotel Centraza & Gourmet City ホテルセントラーザ	15	Tenjin Core Building 天神コア	43	JAS
50	Sun Life Hotel 2 サンライフホテル2	16	Iwataya Department Store 天神岩田屋	44	British Consulate 英国領事館
51	Hotel Clio Court ホテルクリオコート	17	NHK	45	Fukuoka Kōtsū Bus Centre 福岡交通バスセンター
PLACES TO EAT		18	NTT	52	NTT
4	Nanak's Restaurant ナナク	19	Solaria Plaza ソラリアプラザ		

KYŪSHŪ

Hotels There are numerous business hotels around the city centre, particularly around JR Hakata station. The *Green Hotel 1* and *Green Hotel 2* (☎ 092-451-4111) are two of about 10 hotels directly behind the railway station. They both have singles/doubles from ¥5900/7800.

Other hotels behind the station include two *Sun Life* hotels – No 1 (☎ 092-473-7111) and No 2 (☎ 092-473-7112). Both are standard business hotels with rooms from ¥6700/10,000. The *Hotel Clio Court* (☎ 092-472-1111) is a glossier and more

expensive hotel with singles from ¥7000 to ¥9000, doubles and twins from ¥14,000. Facing the Clio Court is the *Hotel Centraza Hakata* (☎ 092-461-0111) which is also in the more expensive category: prices here are from ¥9500/19,000 for singles/doubles.

The *Mitsui Urban Hotel* (☎ 092-451-5111), five blocks from JR Hakata station along Daihaku-dōri, has singles/doubles from ¥7200/13,000; the rooms are typically minute. Next door is the similarly priced *Chisan Hotel Hakata* (☎ 092-411-3211). The smaller *Hakata Business Hotel* (☎ 092-

431-0737) has singles/doubles from ¥6000/
9000 and the *Business Hotel Royal* (☎ 092-
411-3300), near the Chisan and Mitsui
Urban hotels, has singles/doubles from
¥4800/6800.

The *ANA Hotel Hakata* (☎ 092-471-7111)
on the left as you leave JR Hakata station, is
one of the best places in town, with
singles/doubles from ¥12,000/21,000. A little
beyond it, close to the Sumiyoshi-jinja Shrine,
is the *Hokke Club Hakata* (☎ 092-271-3171),
a member of the popular Hokke Club business
hotel chain; rooms without bathroom are
¥4800/8500 including breakfast.

Places to Eat
As the western terminus of the shinkansen
line from Tokyo, the busy JR Hakata station
offers a great number of places to eat including a full assortment of fast-food restaurants,
department stores and other places offering
eating possibilities. The station itself has two
underground restaurant malls, both with a
bewildering array of restaurants with some
great lunch time bargains.

Behind the railway station under the Hotel
Centraza is *Gourmet City* with two basement
floors of restaurants offering Chinese, Japanese and European food and desserts. At
lunch time there are lots of teishoku bargains
and it's open until 11 pm. The Green Hotel's
Ginroku restaurant is good value while the
Hotel Clio Court has a series of restaurants
known as the *Clio Seven*. There are plenty of
restaurants, bars, shops and bakeries around
the Suehiro Inn.

The underground shopping mall at Tenjin
has numerous eating places. Try *Art Coffee*
for a ¥200 cup of coffee, a good ¥380 setto
(set breakfast) or a great selection of hot dogs
or sandwiches from ¥250 to ¥450. Entrances
from the mall lead into various department-
store food basements. In particular, the
Daimaru basement has a fantastic selection
of food including sandwiches, pizza slices,
bentō (boxed lunches) or whatever else you
fancy. You can take your fast food across the
road and eat it in the Kego Park beside the
Kego-jinja Shrine. Once night falls, lots of
little roadside noodle vendors set up shop on
Shōwa-dōri and Watanabe-dōri. They are
cheap and lively places for a bite to eat.

The Nakasu Island entertainment district,
between Hakata and Tenjin, has many restaurants and a variety of fast-food outlets
including a *McDonald's* and a huge *Mister
Donut*. Along the western bank of the island
at night, you'll find a collection of snack
stands offering noodles, kebabs and other
quick meals which you can enjoy while
watching the lights across the Naka-gawa
River.

One of the best areas for restaurant
hunting is the Oyofuku-dōri area. Almost
opposite Mr Donut is *Taiwan Yatai*, a small
but friendly place where they do authentic
Taiwanese food at very reasonable prices.
Just up the road from here is *Taj*, an Indian
restaurant whose Japanese sign announces
essuniku kāri senmon, or the 'ethnic curry
specialist'. *Nanak's* is another Indian restaurant on the corner of Shōwa-dōri; look out
for English sign inviting you to 'enjoy nice
dishes'.

Entertainment
Nakasu Island is one of the busiest entertainment districts in Japan with several thousand
bars, restaurants and clubs, but it's not really
the place to go unless you are on a company
expense account or are into sleazy strip
shows. The gaijin set gravitate towards
Oyofuku-dōri, just down from the Nishitetsu
Grand Hotel. There's plenty happening here
on most nights of the week, although naturally the weekends are when the place comes
to life.

It may not be the place for a few drinks, but it's still
worth taking an evening stroll through the Nakasu
Island entertainment district. Many of the buildings
sport extensive backlit menus of the activities available inside. They are likely to leave you with the
impression that half of Fukuoka's female population
is employed in pouring drinks for and being fondled
by sozzled Japanese businessmen.

The *Tennis Club*, with its picture of a pretty hostess
in tennis whites executing a graceful backhand volley,
looked like it might make for an interesting evening
out, even if the racket-swinging hostesses pose the
risk of the damage at the end of the evening being
more than financial.

Back on Oyofuku-dōri, good places to meet locals are *Umie*, which is on the main drag just down from a palatial Mr Donut, and *New York 30's*, which is just a few doors further down the road. Umie is hard to miss, as the outside has been done up with a colourful paint job. It's more popular with eccentric local Japanese and the music is mainly early '80s new wave. New York 30's is probably the best place in Fukuoka to meet resident locals – it seems that they manage to squeeze every foreigner in town in here on weekends. Between 10.30 pm and 4.30 am on Saturday nights, *Bollox*, just around the corner from the main post office, has a really happening disco with a good mix of Japanese and gaijin. There's a ¥2000 cover charge, which gets you two 'free' drinks.

During the summer evenings from mid-April to August, rooftop beer gardens are popular, and you'll see a number of them on buildings lining the Naka-gawa River. There's also one on the Izutsuya department store above JR Hakata station.

Things to Buy
Clay Hakata dolls depicting women, children, samurai and geisha are a popular Fukuoka craft. Hakata *obi*, the silk sashes worn with a kimono, are another typical craft of the region. Try the Iwataya department store in Tenjin for these and other items.

Getting There & Away
Air Fukuoka is an international gateway to Japan with flights to and from Australia, Hong Kong, South Korea, the Philippines, Taiwan and the USA. There are also internal flights to other centres in Japan including more than 20 flights a day to Tokyo (¥25,350, one hour and 45 minutes); almost all of these go to Haneda Airport rather than Narita International Airport. Flights to Osaka (¥14,400) take just over an hour.

Train & Bus JR Hakata station is the western terminus of the 1177 km Tokyo-Osaka-Hakata shinkansen service. There are approximately 15 services a day to/from Tokyo (¥21,300, six to seven hours), 30

to/from Osaka (¥14,310, three to four hours) and 50 to/from Hiroshima (¥8530, 1½ to two hours).

JR lines also fan out from Hakata to other centres in Kyūshū. The Nippō line runs through Hakata, Beppu, Miyazaki and Kagoshima; the Kagoshima line through Hakata, Kumamoto, Yatsushiro and Kagoshima; and both the Nagasaki and Sasebo lines from Hakata to Saga and Sasebo or Hakata to Nagasaki. From Tenjin railway station the Nishitetsu Omuta line operates through Tenjin, Dazaifu, Kurume, Yanagawa and Omuta. You can also travel by road or train to Karatsu and continue from there to Nagasaki by train.

Buses depart from the Kōtsū bus centre near JR Hakata station and from the Tenjin bus centre. There are buses to Tokyo (15 hours), Osaka, Nagoya and many destinations around Kyūshū.

Ferry The Hakata-Nagasaki Holland Village boat service would be an interesting way to get to Nagasaki (see the Nagasaki Holland Village section later), but it doesn't come cheap (¥6800).

There are also services from Fukuoka to Okinawa, to Iki-shima Island and other islands off Kyūshū. Ferries operate between the Tokyo ferry terminal and Kokura harbour, taking around 36 hours, and also between Osaka and Shinmonshi harbour, taking around 12 hours.

Fukuoka also offers an international ferry connection, with a high-speed hydrofoil service connecting the city with Pusan in Korea daily. The hydrofoil is run by JR Kyūshū (☎ 095-281-2315); tickets cost ¥12,400 one way, ¥21,500 return; and the journey takes just under three hours. The Camellia line (☎ 092-262-2323) also runs a ferry service to Pusan, but it takes around 15 hours. Tickets range from ¥8500 to ¥18,000.

Getting Around
To/From the Airport Fukuoka Airport is conveniently close to the city centre, a complete contrast with the airport in Tokyo. Airport buses take about 15 minutes to JR

Hakata station (¥240) or 30 minutes to Tenjin (¥270). Transfer tickets on to the subway system can be bought from ticket-vending machines at the airport. The airport bus departs from platform No 12 at the Kōtsū bus centre (next to JR Hakata station). Taxis between the airport and city centre cost from around ¥1000. The airport has three terminals – No 3 is for international flights, No 2 is for JAL and JAS flights to Tokyo (both Haneda and Narita airports) and to Okinawa, and No 1 is for all other domestic flights.

Train There are two subway lines in Fukuoka. Line No 1 (Ichi-go) operates from JR Hakata station through Tenjin and out to Meinohama; from there trains continue west on the JR Chikuhi line. Line No 2 (Ni-go) operates from the Nakasu-Kawabata station (the junction subway station between Tenjin and Hakata) out to Kawabata and Kaizuka.

Bus City and long-distance bus services operate from the Kōtsū bus centre at JR Hakata station and the Tenjin bus centre at Tenjin. The Nishitetsu bus company covers most tourist attractions around the city within its ¥150 fare zone and you can get a ¥700 one-day pass.

DAZAIFU 太宰府
Dazaifu, with its superb shrine and interesting temples, is almost close enough to be a suburb of Fukuoka. You could take a day trip to Dazaifu or even stay there and skip Fukuoka altogether.

Dazaifu was the governmental centre of Kyūshū during the Kofun period (300-710) and through the Heian period (794-1185). Dazaifu was also important as the chief port for commercial and cultural contacts with China. It diminished in importance from the 16th century, and is now dwarfed by its huge neighbour Fukuoka.

Information
The information office outside Nishitetsu Dazaifu station, near the entranceway to the Tenman-gū Shrine, has helpful staff and an excellent English brochure and map.

Tenman-gū Shrine 天満宮
The poet and scholar Sugawara-no-Michizane was an important personage in the Kyoto court until he fell foul of political intrigue and was exiled to distant Dazaifu where he died two years later. Subsequent disasters which struck Kyoto were blamed on his unfair dismissal and he became deified as Tenman Tenjin or Kankō, the god of culture and scholars. His great shrine and burial place attracts countless visitors.

The brightly painted orange shrine is entered via a picturesque arched bridge and behind the shrine building is the Kankō Historical Museum (entry ¥200) with dioramas showing events in Tenjin's life. The treasure house has artefacts connected with his life and the history of the shrine. The shrine's Honden (Main Hall) was rebuilt in 1583.

Kōmyō-ji Temple 光明寺
In this small temple the Ittekikaino-niwa Garden is a breathtakingly beautiful example of a Zen garden and a peaceful contrast to the crowds and hype in the nearby shrine.

Kaidan-in & Kanzeon-ji Temples
戒壇院・観世音寺
Now a Zen Buddhist temple, the Kaidan-in dates from 761 AD and was one of the most important monasteries in Japan. The adjacent Kanzeon-ji Temple dates from 746 AD but only the great 697 AD bell, said to be the oldest in Japan, remains from the original construction.

Kanzeonji Treasure Hall
This treasure hall has a wonderful collection of statuary, most of it of wood, dating from the 10th to 12th centuries and of impressive size. The style of some of the pieces is more Indian or Tibetan than Japanese. The display is open from 9 am to 5 pm and entry is ¥400.

Other Attractions
The **Dazaifu Exhibition Hall** displays finds from local archaeological excavations and is open daily from 9 am to 4.30 pm except Monday. Nearby are the **Tofurō Ruins**,

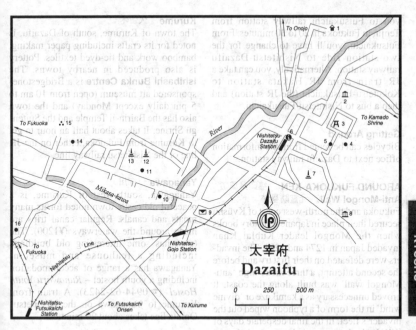

太宰府
Dazaifu

0   250   500 m

1	Dazaifu Youth Hostel 太宰府ユースホステル
2	Kankō Historical Museum 観光歴史資料館
3	Tenman-gū Shrine 天満宮
4	Treasure House 宝物殿
5	Five-Arched Bridge 五孔橋
6	Bicycle Rental & Tourist Information レンタサイクル
7	Kōmyō-ji Temple & Garden 光明寺
8	Kyūshū Historical Museum 九州歴史資料館
9	Post Office 郵便局
10	Dazaifu City Office 市役所
11	Treasure House 宝蔵
12	Kanzeon-ji Temple 観世音寺
13	Kaidan-in Temple 戒檀院
14	Dazaifu Exhibition Hall 太宰府展示館
15	Tofurō Ruins 都府楼跡
16	Enoki-sha 榎社

foundations of the buildings from the era when Dazaifu governed all of Kyūshū. Enoki-sha is where Sugawara Michizane died and from here his body was transported to its burial place, now the shrine, on the ox cart which appears in so many local depictions. The **Kyūshū Historical Museum** near the shrine is open from 9.30 am to 4.30 pm daily except Monday; admission is free.

Places to Stay

The *Dazaifu Youth Hostel* (☎ 092-922-8740) is actually in one of the Dazaifu temples; it has only 24 beds and charges ¥2400 per night. Ryokan and other accommodation can be found in the nearby town of Futsukaichi Onsen.

Getting There & Away

Train & Bus A Nishitetsu line train will take

you to Futsukaichi railway station from Tenjin in Fukuoka in 20 to 30 minutes. From Futsukaichi, you'll have to change for the two-station ride to Nishitetsu-Dazaifu railway station. Alternatively, you can take a JR train from JR Hakata station to Kokutetsu-Futsukaichi (the JR station) and then a bus to Nishitetsu-Futsukaichi.

Getting Around
Bicycles can be rented from the information office next to Dazaifu railway station.

AROUND FUKUOKA-KEN 福岡県周辺
Anti-Mongol Wall 元寇防塁跡
Fukuoka and the north-west coast of Kyūshū secured their place in Japanese history books when the Mongol leader Kublai Khan invaded Japan in 1274 and 1281. The invaders were defeated on their first try and before the second attempt, a three metre high 'anti-Mongol wall' was built along the coast. It proved unnecessary as a kamikaze or 'divine wind' in the form of a typhoon wiped out the invader's fleet. In the final desperate days of WW II, the Japanese tried to create their own divine wind with kamikaze suicide pilots.

The wall extended for 20 km and some short stretches have been excavated at the Genkō fort north of Imajuku near Imazu-wan Bay. To get to the wall, take a Nishinoura bus from the Fukuoka Kōtsū bus centre and get off at Midōrimachi; the wall is known as *boheki*. Other stretches of anti-Mongol wall can be seen at Iki-no-Matsubara, back towards the city near the Odo Yacht Harbour, and at Nishijin, closer again towards the city centre.

Genkai Quasi-National Park
The Genkō fort wall at Imajuku is in the Genkai Quasi-National Park and the nearby Obaru beach offers surprisingly good swimming although there are even better beaches further west. **Keya-no-Oto** (Great Cave of Keya) is at the western end of the Itoshima Peninsula. It's a popular tourist attraction and buses run there directly from the Kōtsū bus centre in Hakata, taking about 1½ hours.

Kurume 久留米
The town of Kurume, south of Dazaifu, is noted for its crafts including paper making, bamboo work and tie-dyed textiles. Pottery is also produced in nearby towns. The **Ishibashi Bunka Centre** is a Bridgestone-sponsored art museum (open from 10 am to 5 pm daily except Monday) and the town also has the Bairin-ji Temple and the Suitengū Shrine. It takes about half an hour to get to Kurume from Fukuoka, either on the JR line or the Nishitetsu railway line.

Yanagawa 柳川
Yanagawa, south-west of Kurume, is a peaceful old castle town noted for its many moats and canals. Regular canal trips are made around the waterways (¥1200). The town has some interesting old buildings including a teahouse and museum. Yanagawa has a range of accommodation including a youth hostel – *Runowaru Youth Hostel* (☎ 0944-62-2423). A train from Kurume to Yanagawa on the Nishitetsu-Omuta line takes about 20 minutes.

Saga-ken 佐賀県

KARATSU 唐津
The small town of Karatsu (population 80,000) has a reconstructed castle and superb display of the floats used in the annual Karatsu Okunchi Festival. Only 50 km west of Fukuoka, it makes a good jumping-off point for visits to the picturesque Higashi-Matsuura-hantō Peninsula. Potters in Karatsu turn out primitive but well-respected pottery with clear connections to the Korean designs first introduced into Japan. The sandy beach east of Karatsu at Niji-no-Matsubara draws crowds in summer.

Karatsu-jō Castle 唐津城
Although it's just a modern reconstruction, the castle looks great, perched on a hill overlooking the sea. Inside, there's a museum with archaeological and pottery displays;

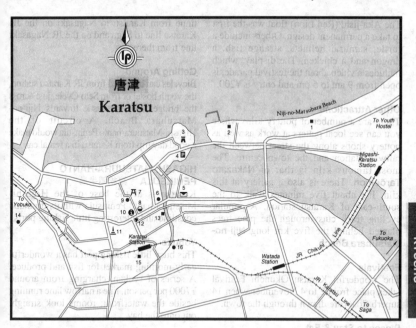

唐津
Karatsu

Niji-no-Matsubara Beach

To Youth
Hostel

Migashi-
Karatsu
Station

To
Yobuko

To
Fukuoka

Karatsu
Station

Watada
Station

JR Chikuni Line

JR Karatsu Line

To
Saga

PLACES TO STAY

1 Kokuminshukusha
   Niji-no-Matsubara

2 Ryokan Yoyokaku
   旅館洋洋閣

13 Karatsu Green Hotel
    唐津グリーンホテル

15 Karatsu City Hotel
    唐津シティホテル

PLACES TO EAT

12 France's Bakery
    フランスベーカリー

OTHER

3 Karatsu-jō Castle
   唐津城

4 Car Park
   駐車場

5 Main Post Office
   中央郵便局

6 NTT

7 Karatsu Shrine
   唐津神社

8 Showa Bus Station
   昭和バスセンター

9 Yama Festival Float
   Exhibition Hall
   曳山展示場

10 Tourist
    Information Centre
    観光案内所

11 Kinsho-ji Temple
    近松寺

14 Kojiro Kiln
    小次郎窯

16 Nakazato
    Tarōemon Kiln
    中里太郎右衛門窯

opening hours are from 9 am to 5 pm and
admission is ¥300.

Okunchi Festival Floats 曳山展示場
The 14 floats used in the Karatsu Okunchi
Festival are displayed in the Yama Festival

Float Exhibition Hall beside the Karatsu-
jinja Shrine. The festival is believed to have
started in the 1660s with floats from each of
the 17 areas of the city. From 1819, the
design of the floats was standardised; previously a new float had been built each year.

The Aka-jishi (Red Lion) float was the first to take a permanent design. Others include a turtle, samurai helmets, strange fish, a dragon and a chicken. The display, which includes a video about the festival parade, is open from 9 am to 5 pm and entry is ¥200.

Other Attractions
There are a number of pottery kilns where you can see local potters at work as well as pottery shops along the street between the railway station and the town centre. The most famous kiln is that of **Nakazato Tarōemon**. There is also a gallery at this kiln. It's about five minutes walk to the south-east of Karatsu station. A popular cycling track cuts through the pine trees planted behind the five km long **Niji-no-Matsubara Beach**.

Festivals
The wonderful Karatsu Okunchi Festival takes place from 2 to 4 November when 14 superb floats are drawn through the town.

Places to Stay & Eat
The *Niji-no-Matsubara Youth Hostel* (☎ 0955-72-4526) is near the popular beach resort just west of the town. There are 56 beds at ¥1840 or ¥1990 depending on the season.

The *Karatsu City Hotel* (☎ 0955-72-1100) is a big, modern hotel right behind the railway station. Singles/doubles start from ¥6600/12,000. Most other hotels and ryokan are along the Niji-no-Matsubara Beach and are fairly expensive. One that isn't is a kokuminshukusha (people's lodge): *Niji-no-Matsubara Hotel* (☎ 0955-72-5181) has rooms from ¥5500. North of here on the beachfront, the expensive *Ryokan Yōyōkaku* (☎ 0955-72-7181) has rooms ranging from ¥15,000 to ¥40,000.

Getting There & Away
From Fukuoka take the No 1 (Ichi-go) subway line from Hakata or Tenjin to the end of the line and continue on the JR Chikuhi line. It takes about one hour 20 minutes to reach Karatsu and costs ¥950. You can continue from Karatsu to Nagasaki on the JR Karatsu line to Saga and on the JR Nagasaki line from there.

Getting Around
Bicycles can be rented from JR Karatsu station, the youth hostel or from Seto Cycle, just across the bridge from the castle towards Niji-no-Matsubara Beach. A circuit of the Higashi-Matsuura-hanto Peninsula would make a good day trip from Karatsu in a rental car.

HIGASHI-MATSUURA-HANTŌ PENINSULA   東松浦半島
Karatsu is at the base of the Higashi-Matsuura-hantō Peninsula with its dramatic coastline and interesting little fishing ports.

Yobuko   呼子
This busy little fishing port has a wonderful early-morning market for fish and produce. A series of ryokan, charging from around ¥7000 per person, line a narrow lane running beside the waterfront; rooms look straight out onto the bay.

Hatomizaki Underwater Observatory   玄海海中公園
A pier leads out to this underwater observatory where you can see different species of local fish attracted to the observatory by regular feeding. Near by is a government-run kokuminshukusha (people's lodge) with rooms from around ¥4200 per person.

Nagoya Castle   名護屋城址
It was from this now ruined castle that Hideyoshi launched his unsuccessful invasions of Korea.

POTTERY TOWNS   焼物の町
Imari and Arita are the major pottery towns of Saga-ken. From the early 1600s, pottery was produced in this area using captive Korean potters. The work was done in Arita and nearby Okawachiyama and the Korean experts were zealously guarded so that the secrets of their craft did not slip out. Pottery from this area, with its brightly coloured glazes, is still highly esteemed in Japan.

Imari 伊万里

Although Imari is the name commonly associated with the pottery from this area, it is actually produced in Okawachiyama and Arita. Okawachiyama, where 20 pottery kilns operate today, is a 15-minute bus ride from JR Imari station. The nearby **Nabeshima Hanyō-kōen Park** shows the techniques and living conditions in a feudal-era pottery. Imari is about an hour by bus from Karatsu, a little less by train on the JR Chikuhi line.

Arita 有田

It was at Arita that kaolin clay was discovered in 1615, permitting the manufacture of fine porcelain for the first time. It's a sprawling town, less interesting than Imari, but you can visit the **Kyūshū Ceramic Art Museum** (open from 9 am to 4.30 pm daily except Monday, ¥200) and Korean potter Ri Sanpei's original kaolin quarry. The **Rekishi Minzoku Shiryōkan** (Folk History Museum) is by the quarry and the **Arita Tōji Bijutsukan** (Arita Ceramic Art Museum) is also near by; both have the same opening hours as the Kyūshū Ceramic Museum. Pottery connoisseurs will find the **Imaizumi Imaemon Gallery** (open from 9 am to 5 pm daily except Sunday), the **Sakaida Kakiemon Kiln** (open from 9 am to 5 pm) and the Genemon Kiln (open Monday to Saturday from 8 am to 5.30 pm) very interesting.

Arita is about 25 minutes from Imari on the Matsuura line. Alternatively, there are direct buses running from the Tenjin bus centre in Fukuoka. There are 10 services a day, taking one hour 55 minutes and costing ¥1800.

Islands off Kyūshū's North-West Coast
九州北西岸の島々

Five larger and many smaller islands lie to the north-west of Kyūshū and are accessible from Fukuoka, Sasebo and Nagasaki. Tsushima Island, the largest of the group, is in the strait midway between Japan and Korea and is actually closer to Pusan than to Fukuoka. These are islands strictly for those who want to get far away from it all; foreign visitors are very rare. Some of the islands are part of Saga-ken, others part of Nagasaki-ken.

Places to Stay

There are youth hostels and many minshuku and ryokan on Tsu-shima, Hirado-shima and Fukue-jima islands.

Getting There & Away

Air There are a number of local air services to the islands. ANK flies between Fukuoka and Iki-shima Island for ¥5210, Fukuoka and Tsu-shima Island for ¥7960, Fukuoka and Fukue-jima Island for ¥10,430 and Nagasaki and Fukue-jima Island for ¥6410.

Ferry Ferry services operate from Fukuoka to Tsu-shima (¥3500) and Iki-shima islands, from Yobuko to Iki-shima Island (¥1400), from Sasebo to Nakadōri Island (¥2000) and from Nagasaki to Nakadōri and Fukue-jima islands (¥2000).

TSU-SHIMA ISLAND   対馬

The mountainous island of Tsu-shima, 682 sq km in area, is actually two islands; the narrow neck of land connecting the two parts was channelled through during the 16th century. The port of **Izuhara** is the island's main town and has a fort originally built by Toyotomi Hideyoshi during an expedition to Korea in 1592. The island has seen a more recent conflict when the Czar's fleet was utterly routed by the Japanese during the Russo-Japanese War in 1905. The conflict took place in the Tsushima Straits, between Tsu-shima and Iki-shima islands.

Tsu-shima has a number of small towns and a road runs most of its length. **Aso-wan Bay**, the almost totally enclosed bay between the north and south islands, has many islets and inlets.

IKI-SHIMA ISLAND   壱岐

Iki-shima, with an area of 138 sq km, is south

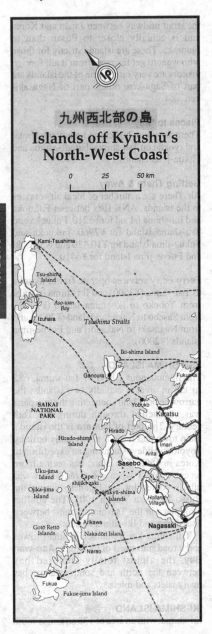

KYŪSHŪ

九州西北部の島

Islands off Kyūshū's North-West Coast

0   25   50 km

Kami-Tsushima

Tsu-shima Island

Izuhara

Aso-wan Bay

Tsushima Straits

Iki-shima Island

Gonoura   Fukuoka

SAIKAI NATIONAL PARK   Yobuko

                                           Karatsu

Hirado-shima Island   Hirado

                           Arita   Imari

Uku-jima Island   Sasebo

Cape shijiki-zaki

Ojika-jima Island   Kyūjūkyū-shima Islands

                                    Holland Village

Gotō Rettō Islands   Arikawa

                      Nakadōri Island   Nagasaki

                      Narao

Fukue

Fukue-jima Island

---

of Tsu-shima and much closer to Fukuoka. Iki-shima is an attractive island with fine beaches; it's also relatively flat and a good place for cycling. **Gonoura** is the main port and Toyotomi Hideyoshi also built a fort there.

HIRADO-SHIMA ISLAND 平戸島

The island of Hirado-shima, close to Sasebo and actually joined to Kyūshū by a bridge from Hirado-guchi, has had an interesting European history. Portuguese ships first landed on Hirado-shima in 1549 and, a year later, St Francis Xavier paid a visit to the island (after his expulsion from Kagoshima).

It was not until 1584 that the Portuguese formally established a trading post on the island but they were soon followed by the Dutch (in 1609) and the British (in 1613). Relations between the British and Dutch became so acrimonious that in 1618, the Japanese had to restore law and order on the island. In 1621, the British abandoned Japan and turned their full attention to India. Things were not easy for the Europeans during the anti-Christian period in Japan and today there is very little trace of the European trading operations. The main town, **Hirado**, was burnt down in 1906.

Hirado-shima has some older buildings including a **museum** in the residence of the Matsuura, who ruled the island from the 11th to the 19th centuries. There are fine views over the Gotō Rettō Islands from **Cape Shijiki-zaki** and the western coast of the island is particularly attractive. From Kashimae, half an hour by bus from Sasebo, regular boats operate to Hirado-shima via the Kyūjūkyū-shima Islands.

GOTŌ RETTŌ ISLANDS 五島列島

The two main islands in the Gotō Rettō group are **Fukue-jima** and **Nakadōri** are near by, but there are three other medium-sized islands, squeezed between the two large ones, plus over 100 small islands and islets. At one time, the islands were a refuge for Japanese Christians fleeing the Edo government's anti-Christian repression;

A	B	C
D	E	F
G	H	I

Temples & Pagodas

A: Pagoda, Miyajima (TW)
B: Pagoda, Yamaguchi (TW)
C: Pagoda, Hase-dera Temple (John Wright)
D: Pagoda, Mt Haguro-san (CT)

E: Tennō-ji, Onomichi (TW)
F: Pagoda, Kyoto (CT)
G: Ninna-ji, Kyoto (TW)
H: Kōsani-ji, Setoda (TW)
I: Kōjō-ji, Setoda (TW)

A	B	C
D	E	F
G	H	I

Castles
A: Nagoya Castle (RI)
B: Himeji-jō, Western Honshū (CT)
C: Kumamoto-jō, Kyūshū (TW)
D: Osaka-jō, Kinki District (CT)

E: Momotarō (Peach Boy) statue (TW)
F: Karatsu-jō, Kyūshū (TW)
G: Matsuyama-jō, Shikoku (TW)
H: Kōchi-jō, Shikoku (TW)
I: Takamatsu-jō, Shikoku (TW)

today the main attraction is the natural beauty of the mountainous islands.

Fukue, the fishing port on the island of the same name, is the main town in the group. The **Ishida-jō Castle** in the town was burnt down in 1614 and rebuilt in 1849. Along with Hirado-shima and a strip of the Kyūshū coast, the Gotō Rettō Islands are part of the Saikai National Park.

KYŪJŪKYŪ-SHIMA ISLANDS 九十九島
Between Hirado-shima and the Kyūshū coast are the 170-odd Kyūjūkyū-shima Islands; the name actually means '99 islands'. Cruise boats operate around the islands from Sasebo.

Nagasaki-ken 長崎県

NAGASAKI 長崎
Nagasaki is a busy and colourful city (population 450,000) but its unfortunate fate as the second atomic bomb target obscures its fascinating early history of contact with the Portuguese and Dutch. Even after Commodore Perry's historic visit to Japan, Nagasaki remained one of the major contact points with the West. Despite the popular image of Nagasaki as a totally modern city rising from an atomic wasteland, there are many reminders of its earlier history and European contact. The bomb actually missed its intended target towards the south of the city and scored a near direct hit on the largest Catholic church in Japan.

History
Nagasaki has the most varied history of any city in Japan, much of it tied up with the dramatic events of the 'Christian Century'. The accidental arrival of an off-course Portuguese ship at Tanega-shima Island in 1542 signalled the start of Nagasaki's long period as Japan's principal connection with the West.

The first visitors were soon followed by the great missionary St Francis Xavier in 1560 and although his visit was also brief,

these Portuguese contacts were to have far-reaching effects. The primitive guns introduced by the Portuguese soon revolutionised warfare in Japan, forcing the construction of new and stronger castles and bringing to an end the anarchy and chaos of the 'Country at War' century.

Among the first Japanese to be converted to Christianity by the visitors was a minor daimyō (regional lord) in north-western Kyūshū. As a result of his conversion, the daimyō's new port of Nagasaki, established in 1571, soon became the main arrival point for Portuguese trade ships. Although the Portuguese principally acted as intermediaries between China and Japan, the trade was mutually profitable and Nagasaki quickly became a fashionable and wealthy city.

The growing influence of Christianity soon began to worry the Japanese and by 1587, Hideyoshi had decided to kick out the troublesome Jesuit missionaries and take direct control from Kyoto. By the end of the century, there were so many Christians in Japan and so much fear that their allegiance might lie outside the country that persecution became a serious business. The crucifixion of 26 European and Japanese Christians in Nagasaki in 1597 epitomised this new attitude and in 1614 the religion was completely banned. Suspected Christians were rounded up, tortured and killed; the Japanese wives and children of foreigners were deported; and the Catholic Portuguese and Spanish traders were expelled in favour of the Protestant Dutch, who were perceived as being more interested in trade and less in religion.

Finally, a bloody rebellion in 1637 brought the 'Christian Century' to a dramatic close and ushered in Japan's two centuries of near complete isolation from the West. On the Shimabara-hantō Peninsula near Nagasaki, the peasantry rose up against the oppressive nobility and ran rings around the local armies. The peasantry held out for 80 days in a siege of Hara-jō Castle, but were finally wiped out by the local armies who had called in the support of the Dutch.

The shōgun then banned all foreigners

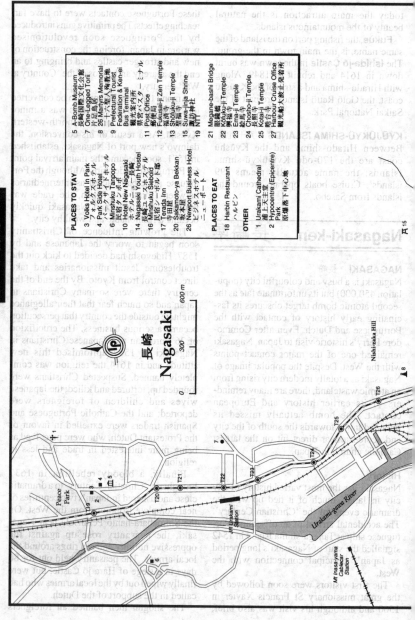

PLACES TO STAY

3 Voks Hotel In Park
フォールズスホテル
4 Park Side Hotel
パークサイドホテル
6 Minshuku Tanpopo
民宿タンポポ
10 Hotel New Nagasaki
ホテルニュー長崎
14 Nagasaki Youth Hostel
民宿ニューボルト館
16 Minshuku Siebold
民宿シーボルト館
17 Terada Inn
寺田屋
26 Sakamoto-ya Bekkan
坂本屋
26 Newport Business Hotel
ニューポート

PLACES TO EAT

18 Harbin Restaurant
ハルピン

OTHER

1 Urakami Cathedral
浦上天主堂
2 Hypocentre (Epicentre)
原爆落下中心地
5 A-Bomb Museum
長崎国際文化会館
7 One-Legged Torii
片足鳥居
8 26 Martyrs Memorial
二十六聖人殉教地
9 Prefectural Tourist
Federation & Ken-ei
Bus Terminal
県営バスターミナル
11 Post Office
郵便局
12 Fukusai-ji Zen Temple
福済寺
13 Shōfuku-ji Temple
聖福寺
15 Suwa-jinja Shrine
諏訪神社
19 NTT

21 Megane-bashi Bridge
眼鏡橋
22 Kōfuku-ji Temple
興福寺
23 Enmei-ji Temple
延命寺
24 Chosho-ji Temple
長照寺
25 Kotai-ji Temple
皓台寺
27 Harbour Cruise Office
観光船下大波止発着所

長崎

Nagasaki

0   300   600 m

Nishi-zaka Hill

Urakami-gawa River

JR Urakami Station

Mt Inasa-yama Cablecar Station

Peace Park

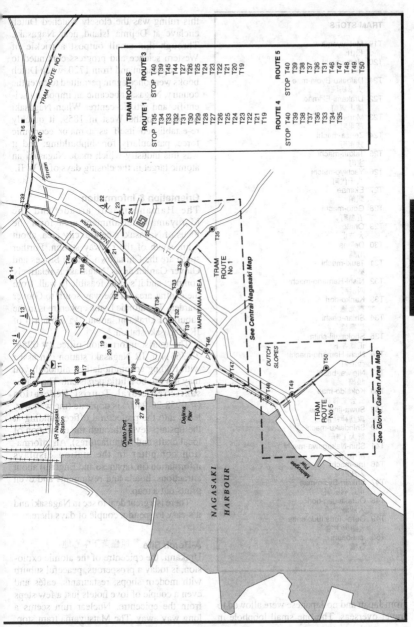

TRAM ROUTES

ROUTE 1	ROUTE 3	ROUTE 5	ROUTE 4
STOP	STOP T40	STOP T40	STOP T40
T35	T39	T39	T39
T34	T45	T38	T38
T33	T44	T37	T37
T32	T27	T36	T36
T31	T26	T31	T33
T30	T25	T46	T35
T29	T24	T47	
T28	T23	T48	
T27	T22	T49	
T26	T21	T50	
T25	T20		
T24	T19		
T23			
T22			
T21			
T19			

TRAM ROUTE No 4

Nishama-zawa

Stream

TRAM ROUTE No 1

MARUYAMA AREA

See Central Nagasaki Map

DUTCH SLOPES

See Glover Garden Area Map

TRAM ROUTE No 5

JR Nagasaki Station

Ohato Port Terminal

Dejima Pier

NAGASAKI HARBOUR

TRAM STOPS

T19 Matsuyama
    松山
T20 Hamaguchi
    浜口
T21 Daigaku-Byoin-mae
    大学病院前
T22 Urakami-Ekimae
    浦上駅前
T23 Mori-machi
    茂里町
T24 Zenza-machi
    銭座町
T25 Takari-machi
    宝町
T26 Yachiyo-machi
    八千代町
T27 Ekimae
    駅前
T28 Gotō-machi
    五島町
T29 Ohato
    大波止
T30 Dejima
    出島
T31 Tsuki-machi
    築町
T32 Nishi-Hamano-machi
    西浜町
T33 Kanko-dori
    観光通
T34 Shian-bashi
    思案橋
T35 Shokakuji-shita
    正覚寺下
T36 Nishi-Hamano-machi
    西浜町
T37 Nigiwai-bashi
    眼橋
T38 Kokaido-mae
    公会堂前
T39 Suwa-jinja-mae
    諏訪神社前
T40 Shindaiku-machi
    新大工町
T41 Shin-Nakagawa-machi
    新中川町
T46 Irie-machi
    入江町
T47 Shimin-Byoin-mae
    市民病院前
T48 Ōurakaigan-dori
    大浦海岸通
T49 Ōura- Tenshudo-shita
    大浦天主堂下
T50 Ishi-bashi
    石橋

from Japan and no Japanese were allowed to travel overseas. The one small loophole in this ruling was the closely watched Dutch enclave at Dejima Island near Nagasaki. Through this small outpost a trickle of Western science and progress continued to filter into Japan and from 1720, when Dutch books were once again permitted to enter the country, Nagasaki became an important scientific and artistic centre. When Nagasaki reopened to the West in 1859, it quickly re-established itself as a major economic force, particularly for shipbuilding, and it was this industry which made Nagasaki an atomic target in the closing days of WW II.

Orientation & Information

The Hamano-machi arcade and the Maruyama entertainment area form the focus of Nagasaki's central city area, about a km south of the railway station. Further south are the Chinatown, Dutch Slopes and Glover Garden areas. Nagasaki is relatively compact and it's quite feasible to walk from the central area all the way south to Glover Garden. The atomic bomb epicentre is in the suburb of Urakami, about 2½ km north of JR Nagasaki station.

The tourist information office (☎ 0958-23-3631) in JR Nagasaki station can assist with finding accommodation, although you may have to be a little persistent. The Nagasaki Prefectural Tourist Federation (☎ 0958-26-9407) is opposite (the walkway leads into the prefectural office building at the upstairs level, through the exhibition of local crafts and manufactures). An information computer in the station displays information (in Japanese and English) about attractions, hotels and restaurants and even prints out a map.

There is a great deal to see in Nagasaki and it's easy to spend a couple of days there.

A-Bomb Site   原爆落下中心地

Urakami, the epicentre of the atomic explosion, is today a prosperous, peaceful suburb with modern shops, restaurants, cafés and even a couple of love hotels just a few steps from the epicentre. Nuclear ruin seems a long way away. The Matsuyama tram stop, the eighth stop north of JR Urakami station on tram routes 1 or 3, is near the site.

The Epicentre The Hypocentre Park has a black stone column marking the exact point above which the bomb exploded. Near by are bomb-blasted relics including a section of the wall of the Urakami Cathedral and a buckled water tower.

A-Bomb Museum The Kokusai Bunka Kaikan (International Cultural Hall) as the museum is curiously named, is an ugly and badly designed building overlooking the Hypocentre Park. The four floors of photographs, reports, equipment and displays telling the story of the blast are quite enough to leave most visitors decidedly shaken. Entry to the museum is ¥50 and it is open from 9 am to 6 pm (April to October) and from 9 am to 5 pm (November to March). Behind the museum is the Nagasaki Municipal Museum; entry is ¥100.

Peace Park North of the Hypocentre Park is the Heiwa-kōen (Peace Park) presided over by the Nagasaki Peace Statue. At the time of the explosion, the park was the site of the Urakami Prison and every occupant of the prison – prisoners and warders – was killed instantly. An annual antinuclear protest is held at the park on 9 August.

Urakami Cathedral The original Urakami Cathedral, the largest church in the East, was completed in 1914 and flattened in 1945. Relics from the cathedral are displayed in the Hypocentre Park. The replacement cathedral was completed in 1959.

Other Relics The 'One-legged Torii' is 850 metres south-east of the epicentre. The blast knocked down one side of the entrance arch to the Sanno Shintō-gū Shrine but the other leg still stands to this day.

Dr Nagai Takashi devoted himself to the treatment of bomb victims until he himself died in 1951 from the bomb aftereffects; his small hut is preserved as a memorial.

Nagasaki Railway Station Area
長崎駅周辺
26 Martyrs Memorial A few minutes' walk from JR Nagasaki station on Nishizaka Hill is a memorial wall with reliefs of the 26 Christians crucified in 1597. In this, Japan's most brutal crackdown on Christianity, six of those crucified were Spanish friars, the other 20 were Japanese and the two youngest were boys aged 12 and 13. The memorial dates from

The Atomic Explosion
When the USAF B-29 bomber *Bock's Car* set off from Tinian in the Marianas on 9 August 1945 to drop the second atomic bomb on Japan, the target was Kokura on the north-eastern coast of Kyūshū. Fortunately for Kokura it was a cloudy day and, despite flying over the city three times, the bomber's crew could not sight the target, so a course was set for the secondary target, Nagasaki.

The B-29 arrived over Nagasaki at 10.58 am but again visibility was obscured by cloud. When a momentary gap appeared in the cloud cover, the Mitsubishi Arms Works, not the intended Mitsubishi shipyard, was sighted and became the target. The 4.5 ton 'Fat Man' bomb had an explosive power equivalent to 22 kilotons of TNT, far more than the 13 kilotons of Hiroshima's 'Little Boy'. Afterwards, the aircraft turned south and flew to Okinawa, arriving there with its fuel supply almost exhausted.

The explosion took place at 11.02 am, at an altitude of 500 metres, completely devastating the Urakami suburb of northern Nagasaki and killing 75,000 of Nagasaki's 240,000 population. Another 75,000 were injured and it is estimated that that number again have subsequently died as a result of the blast. Anybody out in the open within two km of the epicentre suffered severe burns from the heat of the explosion; even four km away exposed bare skin was burnt. Everything within a one km radius of the explosion was destroyed and the resultant fires burnt out almost everything within a four km radius. A third of the city was wiped out. ■

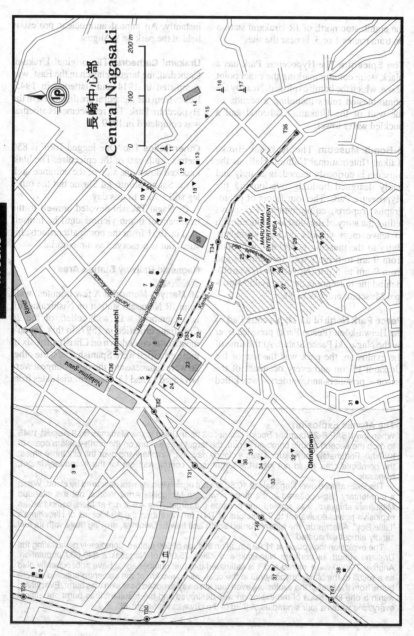

長崎中心部
Central Nagasaki

0   100   200 m

MARUYAMA
ENTERTAINMENT
AREA

Chinatown

Hamanomachi

Kanko-dori Arcade

Hamano-dori Arcade

Nakajima-gawa

River

Shianbashi-dori

Kankō-dōri

Nishi-hama

River

Note: See pages 675 & 676 for tram stops and routes.

1962 and behind it is an interesting museum with displays about Christianity in the area; entry is ¥250. The museum is open from 9 am to 6 pm (closes an hour earlier from December to February).

Fukusai-ji Zen Temple Although the Fukusai-ji Temple is not on any list of architectural or cultural gems, this unique construction, also known as the Nagasaki Kannon Universal Temple shouldn't be missed. In fact you can't miss it, since the temple building is in the form of a huge turtle, carrying on its back an 18 metre high figure of the goddess Kannon. It faces JR Nagasaki station from near the 26 Martyrs Memorial. Inside, a Foucault Pendulum (a device which demonstrates the rotation of the earth on its tilted axis) hangs from near the top of the hollow statue. Only Leningrad and Paris have larger examples of these pendulums.

The original temple was built in 1628 but was completely burnt down by the A-bomb fire. The replacement, totally unlike the original of course, was built in 1979. A bell tolls from the temple at 11.02 am daily, the exact time of the explosion. Entry is ¥200.

Shōfuku-ji Temple The Shōfuku-ji, not to be confused with the Sōfuku-ji Temple, is near the Nagasaki Youth Hostel and JR Nagasaki station. The temple gardens are particularly pleasant and contain an arched stone gate dating from 1657 and moved here from the old Jingū-ji Temple outside the city in 1886. The main building, of typical Chinese style, was reconstructed in 1715. Almost adjacent to the temple is the Kanzan-ji Temple with the biggest camphor tree in Nagasaki.

Suwa-jinja Shrine 諏訪神社
The Okunchi Festival (7-9 October) with its dragon dance, is Nagasaki's most important

annual celebration and is centred at this shrine. The Suwa-jinja Shrine was originally established in 1555, and although it is mostly new, its wooded hilltop setting is attractive. Tram lines 3, 4 and 5 all run to the Suwa-jinja-mae stop, close to the shrine.

Sōfuku-ji Temple　崇福寺

An Obaku Zen temple, and one of Nagasaki's most important, the Sōfuku-ji dates from 1629 and has a fine gateway which was built in China and brought to Japan for reassembling in 1696. Inside the temple, you can admire a great bell from 1647 and a huge cauldron used to prepare food for victims of a famine in 1680. The temple is open from 8 am to 5 pm and entry is ¥150.

Temple Row

The path between Sōfuku-ji to Kōfuku-ji temples is lined with a series of lesser temples which you can visit en route between the two major temples. Just down the road from the Sōfuku-ji, steep steps lead up to the Daijo-ji, behind the huge Kowloon Restaurant. The entrance is the most interesting part; it's now used as a preschool.

Almost at the bottom of the road, turn right a few steps to the Hosshin-ji Temple bell; cast in 1483, it's the oldest temple bell in Nagasaki. Climb up the stairs to the large Kuroganemochi tree at the entrance to the Daion-ji Temple. Follow the road to the left of the temple to the grave of Matsudaira Zushonokami. He had been magistrate of Nagasaki for a year when, in 1808, the British warship HMS *Phaeton* sailed into Nagasaki Harbour and seized two Dutch hostages. The British and Dutch were on opposite sides in the Napoleonic War at that time. Unable to oppose the British, Zushonokami capitulated to their demands for supplies, then committed seppuku.

A short distance further on, turn down the path to the Kotai-ji Temple; it's a favourite with local artists and has a notable bell dating from 1702. Again, the grounds are used by a preschool. Continuing towards the Kōfuku-ji, you come to the Chosho-ji and the Ema-ji temples, both pleasant escapes from the hustle of modern Japan. Nagasaki's temple

row does not end with the Kōfuku-ji, there are several temples beyond it. Only the major temples at the beginning and end of the row charge admission.

Kōfuku-ji Temple　興福寺

The final temple along the temple-row walk dates from the 1620s and has always had strong Chinese connections. The temple is noted for its lawns and cycad palms and for the Chinese-influenced architecture of the main hall. Like the Sōfuku-ji, it is an Obaku Zen temple and entry is ¥200; opening hours are from 8 am to 5 pm.

Megane-bashi Bridge　眼鏡橋・中島川

Parallel to the temple row is the Nakajima-gawa Stream, crossed by a picturesque collection of bridges. At one time, each bridge was the distinct entranceway to a separate temple. The best known of the bridges is Megane-bashi (Spectacles Bridge) so called because if the water is at the right height, the arches and their reflection in the water together create a 'spectacles' effect. The double arched stone bridge was built in 1634 but in 1982 a typhoon flood washed away all the bridges along the stream. The Megane-bashi has been meticulously rebuilt.

Maruyama Area　丸山周辺

The Shian-bashi tram stop marks the site of the Shian-bashi Bridge over which pleasure seekers would cross into the Maruyama quarter. The bridge and the elegant old brothels are long gone but this is still the entertainment area of Nagasaki. During Japan's long period of isolation from the West, the Dutch – cordoned off at their Dejima trading post – were only allowed contact with Japanese trading partners and courtesans. It's said that fortunes were made as much from smuggling as from the world's oldest profession!

In between the bars, restaurants and clubs, Maruyama still has a few reminders of those old days. A walk up from Shian-bashi to where the first road forks, leads to Fukusaya, an old *kasutera* (sponge cake) shop where the cake recipe is said to have come from the

Portuguese. An elegantly wrapped package of this traditional Nagasaki delicacy costs from ¥600.

Turn left at this junction, pass the police post and you come to the driveway entrance to Kagetsu, now an elegant and expensive restaurant, but at one time an even more elegant and expensive brothel.

Dejima Museum　出島資料館

The old Dutch trading enclave is long gone, swallowed up by new buildings and land reclamation to the point where it is now well inland from the sea. From the mid-1600s until 1855, this small isolated community was Japan's only contact with the Western world and fortunes were made by traders here in the exchange of Japanese crafts for Western medicine and technology. The small museum near the old site of Dejima has exhibits on the Dutch and other foreign contact with Nagasaki. It's open from 9 am to 5 pm daily except Monday; entry is free. Across the road in the museum yard is an outdoor model of Dejima. Attempts to reconstruct the trading post have fallen foul of local landowners.

Chinatown Area　新地

Theoretically, during Japan's long period of seclusion, Chinese traders were just as circumscribed in their movements as the Dutch, but in practice, they were relatively free to come and go from their compound. Only a couple of buildings remain from the old area, but Nagasaki has an energetic Chinese community which has had a great influence on Nagasaki's culture, festivals and cuisine.

Dutch Slopes　オランダ坂

The gently inclined flagstoned streets known as the Dutch Slopes or 'Oranda-zaka' were once lined with wooden Dutch houses. To reach them, take a tram to the Shimin-Byōin-mae stop or walk there from the Dejima Museum or Glover Garden.

Confucian Shrine & Museum of China
孔子廟・中国歴代博物館

Behind the gaudily coloured Confucian Shrine is the Historical Museum of China with exhibits on loan from the Beijing Museum of History. The original building dates from 1893 but was destroyed in the fires following the A-bomb explosion. The shrine, near the Dutch Slopes, is also known as the Kōshi-myō-tojinkan; entry is ¥515.

Glover Garden　グラバー園

At the southern end of Nagasaki, a number of the former homes of the city's pioneering Meiji-period (1868-1912) European residents have been reassembled in this hillside garden. The series of moving stairways up the hill, plus the fountains, goldfish and announcements, give it the air of a cultural Disneyland but the houses are attractive, the history is interesting, and the views across Nagasaki are superb.

The garden takes its name from Thomas Glover (1838-1911), the best known of the expatriate community. This amazingly energetic Scot seemed to have time to dabble in half a dozen fields at once. Glover's arms-importing operations played an important part in the Meiji Restoration; he built the first railway line in Japan and he even helped establish the first modern shipyard from which Nagasaki's Mitsubishi shipyard is a direct descendant.

The best way to explore the hillside garden is to take the walkways to the top and then walk back downhill. At the top of the park is the Mitsubishi No 2 Dock building with displays about the city's important shipyard. Going down the hill you come to the Walker House, the Ringer and Alt houses and finally the Glover House.

Halfway down the hill, above the Glover House, is the renowned statue of the Japanese opera singer Miura Tamaki. The statue is often referred to as Madame Butterfly although, of course, she was a purely fictitious character. Puccini, the Italian composer of *Madame Butterfly*, is also honoured here with a relief made, so the inscription goes, of Italian marbles. You exit the garden through the Nagasaki Traditional Performing Arts Museum with a display of dragons and floats used in the colourful Okunchi Festival.

Entry is ¥600 and the park is open from

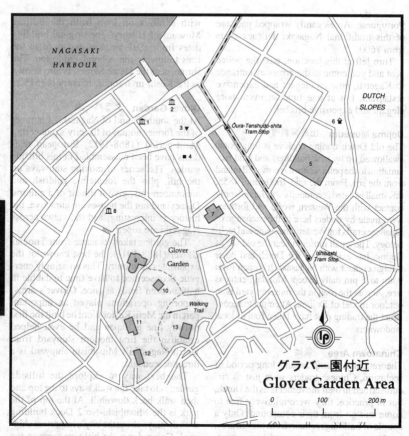

グラバー園付近
Glover Garden Area

0   100   200 m

1	History Museum 歴史民俗資料館	6	Oranda-zaka Youth Hostel オランダ坂ユースホステル	11	Ringer House リンガ邸
2	Telegraph Office Museum Annexe 郵便局資料館	7	Ōura Catholic Church 大浦天主堂	12	Alt House オルト邸
3	Shikai-rō Restaurant 四海楼	8	Nagasaki Traditional Performing Arts Museum 十六番館	13	Mitsubishi No 2 Dock Building 旧三菱第二ドックハウス
4	Nagasaki Tōkyū Hotel 長崎東急ホテル	9	Glover House グラバー邸		
5	Confucian Shrine & Historical Museum of China	10	Walker House ワーカ邸		

8 am to 6 pm (March to November) and from 8.30 am to 5 pm (December to February). Glover Garden, the Historical Museum of China and the Oura Church are all near the end of tram Route 5, get off at the Oura-Ten-shudo-shita tram stop.

Ōura Catholic Church 大浦天主堂
Just below Glover Garden is this prettily situated church, built between 1864 and 1865 for Nagasaki's new foreign community. Soon after its opening, a group of Japanese came to the church and announced that Christianity had been maintained among the Urakami community throughout the 250 years it had been banned in Japan. Unfortunately, despite Japan's newly opened doors to the West, Christianity was still banned for the Japanese and when this news leaked out, thousands of Urakami residents were exiled to other parts of Japan, where many of them died before Christianity was finally legalised in 1872. The church is dedicated to the 26 Christians crucified in 1597 and has beautiful stained-glass windows. It's open from 8 am to 5.45 pm (8.30 am to 4.45 pm in winter) and entry is ¥250.

Jūrokuban-kan Mansion 十六番館
The Jūrokuban-kan Mansion near the garden has displays of Nagasaki's Dutch and Portuguese history in an 1860 building used by the first US diplomatic mission to the city. It's open from 8.30 am to 5 pm and entry is ¥500.

Historical Museum 歴史民俗資料館
Housed in the 1908 Hong Kong & Shanghai Bank building near the Ōura Church, this museum has a mildly interesting collection of historical items. Some of them relate to telegraph lines, a subject of limited interest to the average punter. The old bank was the point from which Japan was first linked with the outside world by telegraph, via Shanghai, in 1871.

Mt Inasa-yama Lookout 稲佐山展望台
From the western side of the harbour, a cablecar (ropeway) ascends to the top of the 332 metre Mt Inasa-yama offering superb

views over Nagasaki, particularly at night. The round trip costs ¥800 and the cablecar operates every 20 minutes from 9 am to 10 pm in summer and from 9 am to 5 pm in winter. Bus Nos 3 or 4 leave from outside JR Nagasaki station; get off at the Ropeway-mae stop. For the return trip, take a No 30 or No 40 bus.

Siebold House シーボルト邸
Near the Shin-Nakagawamachi tram stop is the site of Dr Siebold's house. The doctor is credited with being an important force for the introduction of Western medicine and scientific learning to Japan between 1823 and 1829.

Nagasaki Aquarium 長崎水族館
Nagasaki Aquarium vies with its Shimonoseki counterpart for the title 'largest aquarium in the Orient'. Opening hours are from 9 am to 5.30 pm, closing half an hour earlier from December to February. It's 12 km out from the city centre, about half an hour by bus from JR Nagasaki station.

Harbour Cruises
Cruises around Nagasaki's interesting harbour and by the huge Mitsubishi shipyard are particularly popular. There are up to five cruises per day starting at around 8 am and costing ¥770. In the evening, there's a 1½ hour harbour cruise for ¥1030.

Festivals
Nagasaki's major annual event is the Okunchi Festival (7-9 October), featuring Chinese-influenced dragon dances and parades. The festival centres around the Suwa-jinja Shrine (although tourists are not allowed in there) and there are displays concerning the festival at the Glover Garden.

Places to Stay
Nagasaki has a wide range of accommodation possibilities, from the love hotels clustered around the A-bomb site to the more up-market hotels of the Glover Garden area.

Youth Hostels There are four youth hostels in Nagasaki. The *Nagasaki Youth Hostel* (☎ 0958-23-5032) has 132 beds at ¥2300 and is within walking distance of JR Nagasaki station; it's well signposted in English.

The *Oranda-zaka Youth Hostel* (☎ 0958-22-2730) is south of the centre on the hilly Dutch Slopes street and can be reached by tram No 5; get off at the Shimin-Byōin-mae stop. Beds are ¥2200.

The other two youth hostels are inconveniently located about 20 minutes by bus from JR Nagasaki station. They are the *Nanpōen Youth Hostel* (☎ 0958-23-5526) in Hamahira-chō, which costs ¥2300, and the *Uragami-ga-Oka Youth Hostel* (☎ 0958-47-8473) in Miyoshimachi, also ¥2300.

Minshuku & Ryokan Central Nagasaki, obviously the best place to be based, has a couple of affordable ryokan. *Miyuki-sō* (☎ 0958-21-3487), five minutes north of the Maruyama entertainment district, has singles/doubles for ¥3300/7000. Slightly more expensive, but still a great deal, the clean and friendly *Fukumoto Ryokan* (☎ 0958-21-0478) has singles/doubles for ¥4000/8000.

Minshuku Tanpopo (☎ 0958-61-6230), a Japanese Inn Group member, is north of JR Nagasaki station and near the A-bomb site. Get off at the Matsuyama tram stop or JR Urakami station, cross the river, and walk to the street with a petrol station. Follow that street, turn left at the first junction and take the right side of the fork. Rooms are ¥4000 (singles) or ¥3500 per person in double or triple rooms.

Minshuku Siebold (☎ 0958-22-5623) is a small place with just five rooms from ¥3500 per person without meals. To get there, take tram No 3 from JR Nagasaki station, beyond the Suwa-jinja-mae stop to Shindaiku-machi. Follow the road left from the tram stop and take the first right.

More expensive options include the *Terada Inn* (☎ 0958-22-6178), five minutes walk south of JR Nagasaki station; it has rooms from ¥7000. To get there, take the first left after Gotō-machi tram stop, turn left

again and look out for it on the left. South of JR Nagasaki station in the central city area, the *Sakamoto-ya Bekkan* (☎ 0958-26-8211) is an old and very well-kept place costing from ¥14,000 to ¥44,000 per person including meals.

Hotels Some of the hotels found in the following areas are:

North of the Station The *Park Side Hotel* (☎ 0958-45-3191) is at 14-1 Heiwa-machi right beside the A-Bomb Museum and overlooking the Hypocentre Park. It's a pleasantly quiet location with singles/doubles from ¥6300/10,500. In summer there's a beer garden on the roof.

Just below the Park Side Hotel and beside the Hypocentre Park are three discreet love hotels. Somehow the idea of making love only metres away from the epicentre seems a little curious but, as usual with love hotels, if you can wait until late (which usually means 10 pm) you can get an interesting room for the night from around ¥7000. The hotels in this cluster are the *Volks Hotel In Park* (☎ 0958-43-2900), the *Hotel Seagull* (☎ 0958-48-0008) and the *Hotel Palette*.

Nagasaki Station Area There are less business hotels around the station area than you generally find in other Japanese cities. The expensive *Hotel New Nagasaki* (☎ 0958-26-8000) has singles from ¥14,000 to ¥20,000, doubles and twins from ¥22,000 to ¥42,000. Opposite the station, the *Nishikyūshū Dai-Ichi Hotel* (☎ 0958-21-1711) charges from ¥5800/9000 for singles/doubles. For a cramped cheapie, directly behind the Nishikyūshū Dai-Ichi Hotel is the *Capsule Inn Nagasaki* (☎ 0958-21-1099). A capsule for the night is ¥2800.

Central Nagasaki Near the Maruyama entertainment area, the *Holiday Inn* (☎ 0958-28-1234) has singles/doubles from ¥9800/15,500. The *Nagasaki Grand Hotel* (☎ 0985-23-1234) is also close to the central entertainment and business areas and has singles from ¥8000 to ¥8700, doubles and twins from ¥13,000 to ¥16,500 as well as a very popular beer garden.

A little further back towards the harbour is the *Harbour Inn Nagasaki* (☎ 0958-27-1111). This is a comfortable modern business hotel with singles/doubles from ¥5830/9020. Next door is the *Hotel Ibis* (☎ 0958-24-2171), another economical business hotel with singles/doubles at ¥5200/8800. Closer again to the harbour and overlooking the harbour cruise dock, is the *Newport Business Hotel* (☎ 0958-21-0221) with singles from ¥5000, doubles and twins from ¥9000. Reception is on the 4th floor.

South of the Holiday Inn, where the entertainment area merges into the Chinatown area, is the *Nagasaki Washington Hotel* (☎ 0958-28-1211). Rooms cost from ¥7500 to ¥15,600 in this more expensive business hotel. Just around the corner, a more economical alternative is the *Terminal Hotel* (☎ 0958-21-4111), with singles/doubles at ¥5200/8200. Also close by is the smaller but even more economical *Shinchi Business Hotel* (☎ 0958-27-1123), where singles range from ¥4430 and twins from ¥8240.

Glover Garden Area South of the centre, below the Dutch Slopes, is the *Hotel New Tanda* (☎ 0958-27-6121). It has singles from ¥7800 to ¥9700, doubles from ¥13,000 and twins from ¥15,500; it has a popular rooftop beer garden in summer.

Nagasaki Tōkyū Hotel (☎ 0958-25-1501), just below Glover Garden, is typical of the more expensive hotels in the Tōkyū chain. Singles cost from ¥10,500 to ¥12,000, doubles from ¥19,000 to ¥30,000.

Places to Eat
Nagasaki's local speciality is *shippoku*, a multi-dish meal which illustrates the city's diverse Chinese, European and Japanese influences. You generally need a group of two or more people to try shippoku. Another local speciality is the thick Chinese noodle known as *champon*, usually served as a soup. 'Sara-udon' is like a drier version of this noodle dish.

Nagasaki's European influence can be seen in a number of excellent Western restaurants.

The railway station area has a selection of restaurants with plastic meal displays and fast-food places but Nagasaki's restaurant centre is around the Hamano-machi arcade and Maruyama entertainment area. For a cheap, quick breakfast in the railway station try the *Train D'Or* bakery.

Closing days for Nagasaki restaurants seem to vary, so check first.

Hamano-machi There are a number of restaurants along the Hamano-machi arcade itself including the popular *Tivoli Restaurant*, which serves vaguely Italian food. The excellent *Garde Pizza House*, a block north of the arcade, has no less than 54 varieties of pizza on offer – all at ¥700/1050/1400 for small/medium/large. Pasta and other dishes are also available. The restaurant has an English menu and is open daily from 11 am at 9 pm.

Not far from Garde Pizza is *Bharata Restaurant*, an upstairs Indian restaurant in the Yasaka St building. It can be a little hard to find although the name is in English outside. It offers excellent South Indian thalis for ¥1250 or tandoori and curry dishes from ¥800. Bharata is closed on Monday. Back on Kankō-dōri, opposite a Kentucky Fried Chicken, is *Nanak's* (☎ 0958-27-7900), another fine Indian restaurant with friendly Indian staff. Their Bombay Course, a combination of tandoori, curry, butter naan, salad and a drink is a good deal at ¥2300.

Near by, on Kajiya-machi, is *Ginrei Restaurant*, a relatively expensive Western-style restaurant, instantly identifiable from its ivy-covered frontage. It specialises in steaks and a variety of dishes are illustrated at the entrance.

The *Hamakatsu Restaurant* serves a variety of local specialities including a relatively inexpensive shippoku, although that still means a cost of about ¥4500 per person. There's an illustrated menu and the downstairs area is cheaper than upstairs. A little further up the street is the huge Chinese *Kowloon Restaurant*.

There are plenty of fast-food places in this area as well. There are a couple of *Mister Donut*, one at the Kajiya-machi end of the Hamano-machi arcade, while along Kankō-dōri you can choose from *Kentucky Fried Chicken*, *McDonald's* and *Lotteria*.

Maruyama If you cross Kankō-dōri by the Shian-bashi tram stop, you enter the Maruyama entertainment area. In among the pachinko parlours and bars along Shianbashi-dōri you'll find an *Italian Tomato* pasta specialist (dishes from ¥1000) and the *Yagura-chaya* robatayaki next to Kento's nightclub.

At the end of Shianbashi-dōri the road forks; turn left, walk past the police post and at the far end of the square is the entrance road to *Kagetsu Restaurant*, a shippoku restaurant with a history stretching back over 300 years. At one time it was a high-class brothel and today its prices are as high as its history is long; count on ¥20,000 per person!

Take the other fork at the end of Shianbashi-dōri and you'll find the *Obinata Restaurant* at 3-19 Funadaiku-machi with an interesting and imaginative Western menu, a wide selection of wines and fairly reasonable prices.

Chinatown During Japan's long period of isolation from the West, Nagasaki was a conduit not only for Dutch trade and culture but also for the trade and culture of the Chinese. Today that influence can be seen in the city's many Chinese-style temples and Chinese restaurants. The food is not exactly authentic, but it's still good. Unfortunately, Nagasaki's Chinatown reputation means that a lot of the dishes are overpriced; a bowl of noodles you'd pay ¥500 for elsewhere will probably set you back around ¥800 here.

Popular Chinese restaurants around the Nagasaki Washington Hotel include *Saiko*, *Kyōka-en*, *Chūka-en* and *Kōzan-rō*. These places tend to be on the pricey side, so if you're trying to keep your costs down look out for some of the smaller restaurants operating in the Chinatown area.

The *Shikai-rō Restaurant* at 4-5 Matsugae-

chō is a Nagasaki institution; it's a huge building which is able to accommodate over 1000 diners on five floors. The restaurant claims to be the creator of the popular champon noodles. There's an English menu but last orders are taken at 8 pm.

Other Areas There are a number of interesting possibilities in other areas of the city particularly between Hamano-machi and JR Nagasaki station. *Zac's*, upstairs in the building by the Megane-bashi Bridge, suggests that by eating there you can 'produce a fashionable life'. You can choose from no less than 60 varieties of pizza from ¥730 to ¥880, though choosing can be tricky as the menu board is all in Japanese. At lunch time a small pizza, salad and drink costs ¥580.

If you'd like a change from Japanese food then *Harbin Restaurant* is a wonderful place to make your escape. This Russian/French restaurant has a menu in English, white tablecloths, heavy cutlery, dark wood and excellent food. At lunch time you can select from a long menu offering a starter, main course, bread and butter and tea or coffee all for ¥1300 to ¥1600 – a real bargain. At night, main courses cost from ¥1700 to ¥5000.

The *Sakamoto-ya Bekkan* at 2-13 Kanaya-machi, also between the JR Nagasaki station and central areas, is a good place for traditional shippoku dishes.

Entertainment
There are plenty of bars, clubs and pachinko parlours around the Maruyama entertainment area. Try *Kento's* on Shianbashi-dōri; It specialises in live '50s and '60s pop music, everything from *Peppermint Twist* and *Hippy Hippy Shake* to *Hound Dog* and *Johnny Angel*! There's a ¥1500 entry charge plus you must buy at least one drink and one food item from their reasonably priced menu – good fun from around ¥3000. Just east of the Hamano-machi arcade are a couple of Japanese live houses, including *Live House Nina*.

There are plenty of other bars, pubs and clubs in this very busy area. *With Nagasaki*, just across Kankō-dōri, is a nine storeyed building completely devoted to clubs and bars. On Kajiya-machi, above the Juraka Restaurant, *Goody Goody* has excellent live jazz and a ¥2000 entry charge. The beer garden at the *Nagasaki Grand Hotel* is a popular place for a drink in summer. The *Hotel New Tanda*, near the Dutch Slopes, has a rooftop beer garden.

Things to Buy
There are displays of local crafts and products directly opposite JR Nagasaki station on the same floor as the prefectural tourist office. You'll find lots of shops along the busy Hamano-machi shopping arcade. For Japanese visitors, the Portuguese-influenced kasutera sponge cake is *the* present to take back from Nagasaki and Fukusaya is the place to buy it – see Maruyama in Nagasaki's Places to Eat section for details.

Please ignore Nagasaki's tortoise-shell crafts: turtles need their shells more than humans do.

Getting There & Away
Air There are flights between Nagasaki and Kagoshima, Tokyo (Haneda Airport), Osaka and Okinawa as well as flights to and from a variety of lesser locations.

Train By local train, it takes about 2½ to three hours from Hakata to Nagasaki on the JR Nagasaki line for ¥2470; add ¥1650 if you want to travel by limited express (tokkyū). Kyoto to Nagasaki takes about six hours (with a change at Hakata, the terminus for the shinkansen). To get to Kumamoto from Nagasaki, take a JR Nagasaki main line train north to JR Tosu station (two hours) and a Kagoshima main line train from there (one hour).

Bus Regular buses operate between Nagasaki and Kumamoto, the three hour trip costs ¥3600 but note the following section about the interesting route via the Shimabara-hantō Peninsula. From the Ken-ei bus terminal opposite JR Nagasaki station, buses go to Unzen from stand No 3 (express buses from stand No 2), Shimabara from stand No 5,

Sasebo from stand No 2, Fukuoka from stand No 8, Kumamoto and Kokura (Kitakyūshū) from stand No 6 and sightseeing buses from stand No 12.

Night buses for Osaka, Kōbe and Nagoya leave from both the Kei-ei bus terminal and the Nagasaki Highway bus terminal next to the Irie-machi tram stop. There are also buses running to Sasebo and the Holland Village from here.

Hitching Hitching out of Nagasaki is easier if you take a train or bus to Isahaya and start from there.

Getting Around
To/From the Airport Nagasaki's airport is about 40 km from the city and is situated on an artificial island. Buses to the airport (one hour, ¥1150) operate from stand No 4 in the Ken-ei bus terminal opposite JR Nagasaki station.

Bus Buses cover a greater area (reaching more of the sights) but are, of course, much harder to decipher than the trams. Nagasaki is compact enough to explore on foot.

Tram The best way of getting around Nagasaki is on the excellent and easy to use tram service. There are four colour-coded routes numbered 1, 3, 4 and 5 (there's no No 2 for some reason). Most stops are signposted in English. It costs ¥100 to travel anywhere in town or you can get a ¥500 all-day pass for unlimited travel. The passes are available from the shop beside the station information counter, from the prefectural tourist office across the road or from major hotels. On a one-ride ticket you can only transfer to another line at the Tsukimachi stop. The trams stop around 11 pm at night.

AROUND NAGASAKI 長崎周辺
Huis ten Bosch ハウステンボス
An hour north of Nagasaki, near the town of Sasebo, the development that began as the Biopark and grew into Nagasaki Holland Village has now expanded into Huis ten Bosch, an environment-friendly Dutch town

covering 158 hectares. It's easy to scoff at sights like this, which whiff ever so slightly of the Japanese theme park obsession, but anyone who makes the effort and forks out the money (it's not cheap) is likely to come away feeling it was worthwhile.

The idea itself is fascinating: the developers wanted to create an 'eco-city' with a Dutch theme, and in a combination of Dutch and Japanese skills came up with a town that looks (down to every small detail) like it was magically transported to Kyūshū from the Netherlands. Beneath the skin of the town, however, is a round-the-clock computer controlled energy conservation and waste recycling system. Like 40% of the Netherlands, the town is built on reclaimed land, and Dutch expertise was employed in building dykes and creating the six km of canals whose waters are continually renewed and cleansed using locks in combination with the ocean tides.

Huis ten Bosch (pronounced 'house-ten-bosh') means House in the Woods, the name of the Dutch royal family's residence, a complete replica of which is the centrepiece of the town. Although this *is* a theme park – and you could easily spend a couple of days going through all the place has to offer – there are at present 250 Dutch-style homes in town with price tags from US$570,000 to US$3,570,000; by 1998 the developers plan to have accommodation for 10,000 people. The town also has banks, travel agencies, a post office, hospital and a university (with 20 Dutch foreign-exchange students studying Japanese).

As a day trip from Nagasaki, it's worth setting off early. It's easy to spend a couple of hours wandering around looking at the buildings and taking a boat ride through the canal system, before even beginning to dip into the sights.

The town divides into a number of areas: Breukelen, with its windmills, castle and the East-India Company attraction; Nieuwstad, with its amazing Mysterious Escher building complete with a 3D movie using MC Escher graphics and, among other attractions, the Horizon Theatre, which recreates a Dutch fairy tale about the sea (avoid the front row if you don't want to get wet); Museumstad, which has five museums (check out Animation World); Binnenstad, which is the shopping and entertainment area, and even has a cheese market; Utrecht, the restaurant area with a plaza with the 105 metre Domtoren, a replica of the Netherland's tallest church tower; Spakenburg, with its Great Voyage Theatre, Tall Ship Museum and Porcelain Museum along with some fine restaurants; and finally Paleis Huis ten Bosch and the Forest Park.

Note the palace gardens, which were designed back in the 1720s but never came to fruition because of the expense it would have involved – it took modern Japan to come up with the money 270 years later.

Nagasaki Holland Village is still running, and it's a 40 minute shuttle cruiser ride (¥600 including entry to the village) from Huis ten Bosch. If you are just planning to take a wander around the latter, it would be possible to visit both in one day; if you want to take in the attractions of Huis ten Bosch though you'd have to move fairly quickly. Don't underestimate the size of the place.

Five minutes by bus from Holland Village is the Biopark, which is open from 9 am to 5.30 pm (6.30 pm during the summer) and costs ¥1250. It's run by the same organisation as Huis ten Bosch and Holland Village and is billed as the 'zoo of the future'; you get to wander around with the animals (nothing savage in here), pet them and so on. It would make a good combination day outing with Holland Village, but it would be too much to try and squeeze in Huis ten Bosch as well.

Costs Huis ten Bosch is a very special theme park (less thrills, but more interesting than Tokyo Disneyland in our opinion), but it doesn't come all that cheap. If you just want to wander around and take a look at the place, a general 'passport' (and it actually looks like a passport) costs ¥3900. This will get you into some of the free attractions, but there aren't too many of these. A Prince 10 passport gives you 10 'stars' (as a gauge, the

Horizon Theatre costs four stars, while the Mysterious Escher costs two stars) and costs ¥4800. A King 30 gives you 30 stars, which would cover just about everything, and costs ¥5600. Finally, the Great Voyage passport gives you 35 stars, and a cruise shuttle ride and entry to Holland Village for ¥6200.

Places to Stay It's actually possible to stay in Huis ten Bosch – if you have the money. There's talk of having a camping ground available by the time it is completely finished in 1998, but in the meantime, the town's four hotels are probably out of the price range of most travellers. The hotels are *Hotel Europe*, with standard double rooms from ¥32,000, *Hotel Den Haag*, with economy doubles from ¥22,800, *Hotel Amsterdam*, with standard triples from ¥37,000, and *Forest Villa*, with four person cottages from ¥50,000. All of the accommodation follows the Dutch theme with no compromises and bookings can be made by ringing NHV Hotels (☎ 0956-27-0270).

Places to Eat There's an enormous range of places to eat in Huis ten Bosch, making it almost impossible to make recommendations. Possibilities range from burgers to excellent Italian, Indian and Dutch (!) cuisine. *Patisserie*, in Utrecht, is devoted to cheesecakes and there's also the *Chocolate Shop*.

Getting There & Away There's a Huis ten Bosch information office at JR Nagasaki station, which will be able to tell you when the next train or bus to the town run. Both trains and buses take a little over an hour, leave around approximately once an hour, and cost around ¥1300 one way or ¥2400 return. Buses run from the Kei-en bus terminal opposite the railway station. There are also buses running direct from Kumamoto and Fukuoka, as well as a special Huis ten Bosch train from Fukuoka. The *Beetle*, a high-speed hovercraft, does the trip twice daily to and from Fukuoka (8.25 am and 1.45 pm) for ¥6800, taking two hours 20 minutes. It departs from the harbour just to the north of Nakasu Island.

Getting Around Well, it's not *that* big – you can walk. But there are also boats cruising the canals, 'classical buses' trundling the streets, taxis idling along and horse carts cantering backwards and forwards, as well as the possibility of bicycle hire for ¥1000 per day. The tandem bicycles are the same cost and look like lots of fun.

Shimabara-hantō Peninsula
島原半島

A popular route to or from Nagasaki is to travel via the Shimabara-hantō Peninsula and take the regular car ferry service between Shimabara and Misumi, south of Kumamoto. Bus services connect with the ferry, and tour buses (No 262) also operate directly between Nagasaki and Kumamoto. The major attractions on the peninsula are Unzen with its hot springs and walks in the nearby Unzen National Park and Shimabara itself.

It was the uprising on the Shimabara

Shimabara-hantō Peninsula
島原半島

Peninsula (1637-38) which led to the suppression of Christianity in Japan and the country's subsequent two centuries of seclusion from the West. The peasant rebels made their final valiant stand against overwhelming odds (37,000 versus 120,000) at Hara-jō Castle, almost at the southern tip of the peninsula. The warlords even chartered a Dutch man-of-war to bombard the hapless rebels who held out for 80 days but were eventually slaughtered. Little remains of the castle.

In June 1991, 1369 metre Mt Unzen-dake erupted after laying dormant for 199 years. The explosion left at least 38 people dead. Nearby villages were evacuated and the lava flow reached the outskirts of the town of Shimabara.

UNZEN 雲仙
The Japanese enthusiasm for hot springs runs riot once again in this onsen town. Unfortunately the bubbling and spurting 'hells' or *jigoku* are rather spoilt by the spaghetti tangle of pipes running back and forth, taking the hot water to the various hotels and spas. (Jigoku are hot springs for looking at rather than bathing in.) A few centuries ago, the boiling hot water was put to a much more sinister use: in the era when Christianity was banned, dropping Christians into a boiling pool was a favourite method of execution.

Later, Unzen was a popular resort for Western visitors from Hong Kong and Shanghai and its much acclaimed golf course dates from that time. From the town there are popular walks to Mt Kinugasa, Mt Takaiwa and Mt Ya-dake. Outside the town, reached via the Nita Pass, is Mt Fugen-dake, part of the Unzen-dake range, with its popular hiking trail.

Information
There's a tourist information office with displays about the vicinity and a tourist information office opposite the post office.

Places to Stay
Unzen has numerous hotels and ryokan (most of them very pricey) and two kokuminshukusha with nightly costs from around ¥5600 including dinner and breakfast. They are the *Seiun-sō* (☎ 0957-73-3273) and the *Yurin-sō* (☎ 0957-73-3355). *Lodge Unzen* (☎ 0957-73-2141) is about the only economical alternative to these, with singles/doubles for ¥5700/6800.

Getting There & Away
Bus Direct buses between Nagasaki and Unzen take less than 2½ hours and cost ¥1700. Buses run more frequently from the town of Isahaya, which is 40 minutes by train (¥560) from Nagasaki on the Nagasaki line. From Isahaya, buses take 1½ hours and cost (¥1150). From Unzen, it takes another 50 minutes by bus to Shimabara. The bus to Nita Pass, the starting point for the Mt Fugen walk, operates regularly from the Unzen bus terminal (¥300, half an hour). There's a ¥700 toll fee for cars. The No 262 Nagasaki-Kumamoto tour bus goes via Unzen.

MT FUGEN WALK 普賢岳
The circular walk to Mt Fugen starts with the cablecar ascent of 1333 metre Mt Myoken. Ask for a one-way (*katamichi*) ticket for ¥500, though nearly everybody gets a return (*ōfuku*). From the summit, it's a 20 minute ridge walk to 1347 metre Mt Kunimi, the final stretch leaves the Mt Fugen path and scrambles steeply to the summit.

After returning to the main trail, the path drops steeply down the ridge line to a saddle between Mt Kunimi and Mt Fugen. From there, you can continue around the northern side of Mt Fugen to Kazāma and Watoana or around the southern side through the Azami Valley. For the full experience, continue the ascent for another half an hour to the 1359 metre summit. This is a good place for lunch and there are superb views all the way to Mt Aso on a clear day.

The descent on the eastern side is more gradual and eventually meets the circular trail just a couple of minutes south of the Fugen Pond or north of the Fugen Shrine. From the shrine, the trail drops again, cutting across the southern side of the mountain. Ignore the south-east turn-off and you'll eventually reach the Azami Valley trail junc-

普賢岳
Mt Fugen Walk

0   0.5   1 km

Other Attractions
In the Teppochō district, north-west of the castle, is **Bukeyashiki**, a small stretch of samurai walled street. Just south of the town centre, near the Shimamtetsu bus station, are carp streams with lots of colourful goldfish. Also south of the town centre in the Koto-ji Temple is the **Nehan Zō** or 'Nirvana Statue', the longest reclining Buddha statue in Japan, though by Thai or Burmese reclining-Buddha standards, eight metres isn't all that long.

Places to Stay
Shimabara has the *Shimabara Youth Hostel* (☎ 0957-62-4451/6107) which costs ¥2300 per person. There's also a variety of hotels. The *Ajisai Inn* (☎ 0957-64-1101) has rooms from ¥5500.

Getting There & Away
Train & Bus You can reach Shimabara from Nagasaki by bus via Unzen or by rail via Isahaya. The JR trains on the Nagasaki line run to Isahaya, where you connect with the private Shimabara Tetsudō railway line to Shimabara. Trains from Isahaya take one hour and cost ¥1090. Shimabara Tetsudō railway station is a few hundred metres to the east of the castle.

tion where you'll find a trail map, bird chart, entrance torii and benches for a final sit and relax. From there, it's an easy stroll back to the base of the cablecar run. The walk takes 2½ to three hours at an easy pace. Another possibility is to follow the trail in a counter-clockwise direction, finishing up at the top of the cablecar run – from there you could take the cablecar back down or simply walk on the trail beneath it.

SHIMABARA 島原
Shimabara is the port for ferries to Misumi, south of Kumamoto, and has a rebuilt castle and other attractions. The ferry terminal has an information desk.

Shimabara-jō Castle 島原城
The castle, originally built in 1624, played a part in the Shimabara Rebellion in 1637 and was rebuilt in 1964 during Japan's nation-wide spate of castle reconstruction. It houses a museum of items connected with the Christian uprising. There's also a small sculpture museum in the watch tower with works by Seibo Kitamura who sculpted the Nagasaki Peace Statue. Entry is ¥300.

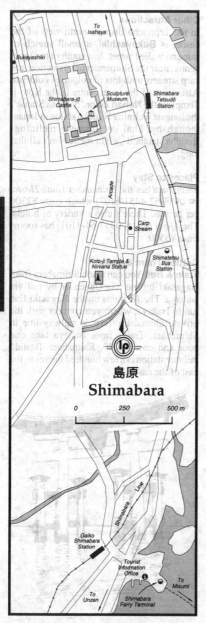

島原
Shimabara

0   250   500 m

To Isahaya

Bukeyashiki

Shimabara-jō Castle

Sculpture Museum

Shimabara Tetsudō Station

Arcade

Carp Stream

Koto-ji Temple & Nirvana Statue

Shimatetsu Bus Station

Shimabara Line

Gaiko Shimabara Station

Tourist Information Office

To Unzen

Shimabara Ferry Terminal

To Misumi

Ferry Ferries run 13 to 17 times a day to Misumi and take about an hour. The fare is ¥830 per person or ¥2370 to ¥4840 for a car and driver. From Misumi it's 50 minutes by train or 1½ hours by bus to Kumamoto. Ferries also run to the Amakusa Islands from Shimabara.

Kumamoto-ken 熊本県

KUMAMOTO 熊本
Kumamoto (population 565,000) has one of Japan's finest reconstructed (as opposed to original) castles plus a contender for Japan's 'best garden' title. Add a few lesser temples and shrines, a very active entertainment area and a convenient location whether you're travelling up, down or across the island and a pause in Kyūshū's third-largest city becomes a very worthwhile proposition.

Orientation & Information
The JR station is some distance south of Kumamoto's concentrated town centre where you'll find not only offices, banks, hotels, restaurants and the entertainment area but also the big Kumamoto Kōtsū bus centre, the castle and other attractions.

The tourist information office is on the ground floor of the station building. The staff speak very little English and are not particularly helpful, but they have a good English-language map and brochure, in which you'll find information about Kumamoto's unique Kobori swimming style – 'the art of swimming in the standing posture attired in armor and helmet'! Kinokuniya and Nagasaki Books are good bookshops in the central arcades. The Nippon Telegraph & Telephone (NTT) office, for long-distance phone calls, is beside the Kumamoto Kōtsū bus centre.

Kumamoto-jō Castle 熊本城
Kumamoto's castle dominates the centre of town and, like many other castles in Japan, it looks superb at night. Although Kumamoto-jō is a modern reproduction, the

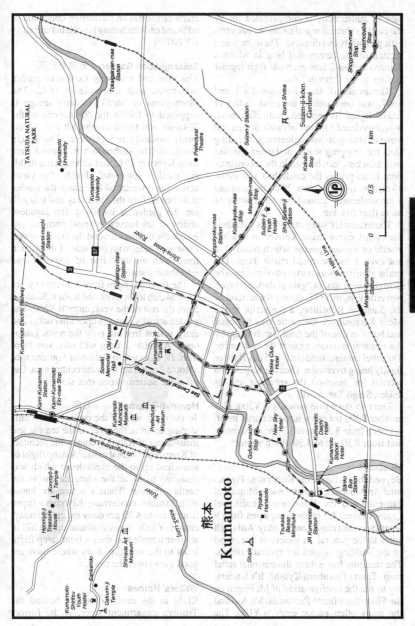

KYŪSHŪ

1 km

0.5

0

Tokaigakuen-mae Station

Shogyokyu-mae Stop

Hatchobaba Stop

TATSUDA NATURAL PARK

Kumamoto University

Izumi Shrine

Suizen-ji-koen Gardens

Prefectural Theatre

Kumamoto University

Suizen-ji Station

Suizen-ji-koen

Kurokami-machi Station

57

Shira-kawa River

Misotenjin-mae Stop

Kokubu Stop

Kotsukyoku-mae Stop

Danpokyoku-mae Station

Suizen-ji Youth Hostel

Shin Suizen-ji Station

JR Hōhi line

Fujisaki-gu-mae Station

3

Minami-Kumamoto Station

Kumamoto Electric Railway

Kami-Kumamoto Station

Kami-Kumamoto Eki-mae Stop

Soseki Memorial Old House

Kumamoto Castle

See Central Kumamoto Map

Hokke Club Hotel

3

New Sky Hotel

Kumamoto Daiichi Hotel

Kumamoto Municipal Museum

Prefectural Art Museum

JR Kagoshima Line

Gofuku-machi Stop

Kumamoto Station Hotel

Kommyō-ji Temple

Honmyō-ji Treasure House

Kurokami-machi Stop

Kuro-kawa River

Isri-i-gawa

Pyokan Hanasoto

Tsukasa Besso Minshuku

Sanko Station

Tassaibashi-dori

JR Kumamoto Station

Shimada Art Museum

熊本

Kumamoto

Stupa

Gakurin-ji Temple

Kumamoto Shritsu Youth Hostel

Sankeido

lack of authenticity is compensated for by the castle's sheer size and its numerous interesting exhibits and displays. These include a section of the ceremonial boat in which a daimyō and his followers made their regular voyage to the court of Edo.

Kumamoto-jō, built between 1601 and 1607, was once one of the great castles of feudal Japan. Its architect, Kato Kiyomasa, was considered a master of castle design and some of his ingenious engineering, including slots for dropping stones and other missiles onto attackers, can be seen in the reconstruction. In its prime, the castle had 120 wells, 49 turrets, 18 turret gates, 29 castle gates and a circumference around the outer walls of more than five km.

The extremely steep outer walls with their backward curve were known as *musha-gaeshi* or *nezumi-gaeshi*, which meant that not even a mouse could climb them. The main donjon was entered through the *kuragari mon ato*, or 'gate of dark passage'. Nevertheless, in 1877, during the turmoil of the Satsuma Rebellion, a postscript to the Meiji Restoration, the castle was besieged and burnt in one of the final stands made by the samurai warriors against the new order. The rebel samurai held out for 55 days before finally being overcome. (See the Kagoshima section for more on the rebellion and its leader, Saigō Takamori.)

Entry to the castle grounds is ¥200, plus another ¥300 for entry into the castle itself. It's open from 8.30 am to 5.30 pm in summer and from 8.30 am to 4.30 pm in winter.

Museums

Beyond the castle are the Kumamoto Prefectural Art Museum, the Kumamoto Municipal Museum and the Kumamoto Traditional Crafts Centre. All of them are open from 9 am to 5 pm and closed on Monday. Although entry to the general art gallery is free, most of the building is used for special exhibits. The museum has a three-dimensional relief map of part of southern Kyūshū. It's interesting to see the configuration of Mt Fugen on the Shimabara-hantō Peninsula, Mt Aso and the many other peaks; entry is ¥100. The

crafts centre has an interesting collection of odds and ends including porcelains and entry is ¥190.

Suizenji-kōen Garden   水前寺公園

This fine and relatively expansive garden originated with a temple in 1632. The Momoyama or 'stroll' garden's design is supposed to follow the 53 stations of the Tōkaidō, and the miniature Mt Fuji is certainly instantly recognisable. The Kokin Denju-no-Ma Teahouse was moved here from Kyoto in 1912 and although the building itself is somewhat shoddy, the views across the ornamental lake show the garden at its finest. Turn the other way and you will see the garden at its worst: the Japanese ability to see beauty in small portions and ignore the ugliness around the corner is well illustrated here, with one side of the garden lined with an ugly line of souvenir and refreshment stalls.

The garden is open from 7.30 am to 6 pm from March to October and from 8.30 am to 5 pm the rest of the year; entry is ¥200. The garden actually remains open after hours and entry is then free but only the north gate is open. A Route 2 tram will take you there from JR Kumamoto station or you can take a Route 2 or 3 tram from the central area. Get off at the Suizenji-kōen-mae stop.

Honmyō-ji Temple   本妙寺

To the north-west of the centre, on the hills sloping up from the river, is the temple and mausoleum of Kato Kiyomasa, the architect of Kumamoto's great castle. A steep flight of steps lead up to the mausoleum which was designed to be at the same height as the castle's donjon. There's a treasure house with exhibits concerning Kiyomasa (open from 9 am to 4.30 pm daily except Monday; entry is ¥300). Steps continue up the hill to another temple and then a final steep flight leads to the very top, from where there are good views over the town.

Writers' Homes

Right in the centre of town, behind the Tsuruya department store, is the former home of writer Lafcadio Hearn (Koizumi Yagumo). Entry is free but it's not as interesting as his first Japanese residence in Matsue (see Matsue in the Western Honshū chapter). The Meiji-era novelist Natsume Soseki's former home is preserved as in the Soseki Memorial Hall. It's just north of the castle and the Traditional Crafts Centre.

Tatsuda Nature Park　立田自然公園
The Tatsuda Nature Park with the 1646 Taisho-ji Temple and a famous teahouse is north-east of the centre. The grave of Hosokawa Gracia (1563-1600) is in the temple grounds. She was an early convert to Christianity but her husband had her killed to prevent his enemies from capturing her. To get there, take a Kusunoki-danchi-Musashigaoka-danchi line bus from platform 28 at the Kotsū bus centre to the Tatsuda Shizen-kōen-iriguchi stop.

The International Folk Art Museum is half an hour by bus from central Kumamoto or 15 minutes beyond the Tatsuda Park and displays crafts from all over the world.

Other Attractions
Continue up the hill beyond the cheap ryokan and minshuku near JR Kumamoto station, past the large collection of love hotels and you eventually reach the **pagoda** topping the hill. The effort of the climb is rewarded with superb views over the town. Also on this side of town, north of the pagoda and south of the Honmyō-ji Temple, is the privately owned **Shimada Art Museum** (open from 9 am to 5 pm daily except Wednesday).

Places to Stay
Accommodation in Kumamoto is scattered: you'll find places around the railway station, the town centre and many others between the two locales.

Youth Hostels
Kumamoto has two hostels. The *Suizen-ji Youth Hostel* (☎ 096-371-9193) is about halfway between the town centre and Suizen-ji Garden and costs ¥2300 per night. The Misotenjin-mae stop on tram Routes 2 or 3 is close by. The *Kumamoto-Shiritsu Youth Hostel* (☎ 096-352-2441) is west of town, across the Iseri-gawa River, and costs ¥1600 or ¥1800 depending on the time of year. A bus from platform 36 at the Kumamoto Kōtsū bus centre will take you there.

Ryokan & Minshuku A 10 minute walk north of the station (crossing the railway lines, walking up the hill and taking the right fork in the road twice) brings you to *Ryokan Hanasato* (☎ 096-354-9445), which costs ¥5300 per person for a Japanese-style room with toilet and washbasin. The road continues beyond the ryokan up the hill to the pagoda at the top and passes a varied collection of love hotels on the way. Generally, the hotels cost between ¥2800 and ¥4000 for a short 'rest' (a strange description for what is supposed to go on there!) or ¥4500 to ¥7000 for overnight 'lodging'. The *Minshuku Higogi* (☎ 096-352-7860/354-9812), also along the road, costs ¥3500 for a room or ¥5600 with two meals.

The Japanese Inn Group's representative in Kumamoto has become ridiculously expensive, although the Japanese-style rooms and the location are both very good. The *Maruko Hotel* (☎ 096-353-1241) is in the town centre, north-east of the castle, and has 46 rooms, nearly all of them Japanese style, at ¥13,000/25,000 for singles/doubles with bathroom. From JR Kumamoto station, take a Route 2 tram and get off at the Tetori-Honcho stop. There's a prominent sign from the covered arcade. One block north of the Maruko Hotel is the pleasant *Ryokan Saekya* (☎ 096-353-5181), where singles/doubles cost ¥7000/14,000.

Hotels The *Kumamoto Station Hotel* (☎ 096-325-2001) is about two minutes walk from the station, just across the first small river. It's a typical modern business hotel with Japanese and Western-style rooms from ¥5800/10,200 for singles/doubles.

The *Hokke Club Hotel* (☎ 096-322-5001), between the railway station and the centre, is another typical business hotel with singles from ¥5800 to ¥6200 and doubles or twins

KYŪSHŪ

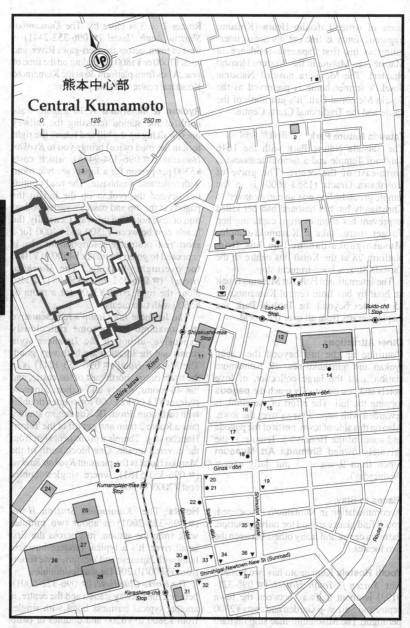

熊本中心部

Central Kumamoto

0 125 250 m

PLACES TO STAY		20	Deutsche Hand-Made Sausage	11	Municipal Office/City Hall 市役所
1	Ryokan Saekya 栄屋旅館	29	Lotteria ロッテリア	12	Parco Department Store パルコ
2	Maruko Hotel 丸小旅館	32	Yōrōnotaki Restaurant 養老の滝	13	Tsuruya Department Store 鶴屋
5	Kumamoto Castle Hotel 熊本ホテルキャッスル	33	Higokko Robatayaki 肥後っ子	14	Lafcadio Hearn House 小泉八雲旧居
7	Tsukasa Honten Hotel 司本店ホテル	34	Kyōya Noodle Shop 京屋ラーメン	18	Kinokuniya Bookshop 紀伊国屋書店
24	Kumamoto Kankō Hotel 熊本観光ホテル	35	Sanesu Steakhouse さねすステーキハウス	21	Kento's Nightclub
27	Kumamoto Kōtsū Centre Hotel 熊本交通センターホテル	36	McDonald's マクドナルド	22	Suntory Shot Bar
31	Kumamoto Tōkyū Inn 熊本東急イン	37	Kentucky Fried Chicken	23	JAL
				25	NTT
PLACES TO EAT		**OTHER**		26	Kumamoto Kōtsū Bus Centre 熊本交通バスセンター
8	Mr Donut ミスタードーナツ	3	Traditional Crafts Centre 伝統工芸館		
15	Swiss Restaurant スイスレストラン	4	Kumamoto-jō Castle 熊本城	28	Iwataya Isetan Department Store 岩田屋伊勢丹
16	Maharao Restaurant まはらおレストラン	6	Nagasaki Books 長崎書店	30	Oldies Shot Bar
17	Yatai Restaurant 自由市場	9	Rock Balloon (bar)		
19	Blue Seal Ice Cream	10	Post Office 郵便局		

from ¥7800. The *Kumamoto Kōtsū Centre Hotel* (☎ 096-354-1111) is centrally located right above the Kumamoto Kōtsū bus centre and has singles from ¥7500. Reception is on the 3rd floor. Also in the centre of town, the *Kumamoto Tōkyū Inn* (☎ 096-322-0109) is part of the popular Tōkyū chain and has singles/doubles from ¥6800/9800.

More expensive hotels include the *New Sky Hotel* (☎ 096-354-2111) about midway between the railway station and the town centre. This efficiently run and well-equipped modern hotel has both Japanese and Western-style rooms which cost from ¥8800/15,000 for singles/doubles. Overlooking the castle, the *Kumamoto Castle Hotel* (☎ 096-326-3311) has singles from ¥8500 to ¥10,500 and doubles from ¥12,500 to ¥13,500.

Places to Eat

The station area is not particularly good for restaurants, but if you're out this way the best selection is in the station itself. The 2nd floor has a good range of tempura, rāmen and generic Western-style restaurants, all with plastic replicas gracing the window spaces. Over in the central part of town, the best advice is to strike off into the side streets that run off the arcades. This whole area is brimming with everything from slurp-'em-down-and-run noodle shops to top-class restaurants. For the unadventurous, the central arcades carry all the old familiars: *McDonald's, Kentucky Fried Chicken, Mister Donut, Lotteria* and even *Blue Seal Ice Cream.*

Just off the Shinshigai Arcade is the *Higokko Robatayaki* where you can sit at the bar and select from a wide range of kebabs. The chef will grill the kebabs right in front of you and pass them over the counter on a long paddle, rather like the one used for removing pizzas from a pizza oven. Each spit costs around ¥300 to ¥500. On the corner of the arcade and Sakae-dōri is *Kyōya*, a small place with an wide and inventive selection of cheap soba dishes.

Just south of these two places is *Yōrōnotaki*, a link in a huge and very successful robatayaki chain. It has an excellent illustrated menu with everything from pizza to sushi, and prices are very reasonable. This place often has specials on its draught beer to attract customers.

Back down the Shimotori Arcade, the *Maharao Restaurant* offers a variety of curry and rice dishes from ¥800 to ¥2000, while opposite it the *Swiss Restaurant* serves coffee, cakes, ice cream and light lunches. Next door to the Swiss Restaurant is *Kōrantei*, an excellent Chinese restaurant with some good teishoku deals at lunch time. Try the roast-pork noodle soup *(chashū men)* for ¥600 and see just how good rāmen can be. Not far from here is the *Yatai Restaurant* (the kanji announce it as the 'free market'), a really lively place with reggae music and a wide range of inexpensive Japanese food. The restaurant itself has a garden appearance to it.

For the gourmet, Kumamoto's local specialities are raw horsemeat *(ba-sushi)* and fried lotus root *(karashi-renkon)*, both of which can be sampled at Yōrōnotaki.

Entertainment

Like most Japanese cities, the central area has a mind-boggling array of bars and clubs. Many of these places are horribly expensive, so take care. The old Kumamoto Nightlife Information Board has disappeared, but most of the hotels stock a pamphlet called *Kumamoto Music Street*, which lists all the bars with live music, and also includes approximate prices. Most of the places in the pamphlet look indescribably dull. On the street, places like *Big Fat Mama*, *Psychopath* and *Bikini Club* sounded promising, and playboy types with unlimited funds might possibly have a very interesting time of it in Kumamoto.

For a quiet drink at affordable prices there's a *Suntory Shot Bar* just off Ginza-dōri. Down towards Shinshigai is the *Oldies Shot Bar* (the name refers to the music not the clientele), which has a ¥700 cover charge. The popular foreigners' hangout is *Rock Balloon*, a basement bar plastered with graffiti and frequented by a good mix of local foreign residents and Japanese. The music here is good but loud; draught beers cost ¥500 and there's no cover charge.

The *Kumamoto Castle Hotel* operates a beer garden from May to August, while the *Kumamoto Kōtsū Centre Hotel* on top of the bus station has a popular rooftop beer garden which also serves snacks like French fries, chicken kebabs, sushi and so on for ¥200 to ¥1000. You order and pay for food as you enter and there's a display cabinet showing what's available. A big mug of beer is ¥600.

Things to Buy

The Traditional Crafts Centre displays local crafts and shows how they're made. *Higo zōgan*, black steel with silver and gold inlaid patterns wrought into a chrysanthemum-like shape, is a renowned local craft. These items range from around ¥5000, though what you'd do with one it's hard to say. Another curious local product is the *ohanake kintai*, which is a tiny red head with a little red protruding tongue, the whole affair topped with a black dunce's cap – don't travel without one. Entry to the crafts centre's downstairs shop area is free but it costs ¥160 to see the upstairs exhibits. The tourist office map identifies the centre as the *Industrial Art Museum*; it's just north of the Kumamoto Castle Hotel.

Getting There & Away

There are flights to Kumamoto from Tokyo, Osaka, Nagoya and Naha (Okinawa). The JR Kagoshima line between Hakata and Nishi-Kagoshima runs through Kumamoto and there is also a JR line to Miyazaki on the south-eastern coast. Buses depart from the Kōtsū bus centre for Hakata, taking just over 1½ hours. The cost is ¥1850 for the basic futsū (local train) fare, add ¥1750 for limited express service.

See the Shimabara-hantō Peninsula

section for details on travel to Nagasaki via Misumi, Shimabara and Unzen. Kumamoto is a popular gateway to Mt Aso (see that section for transport details and the Beppu section for travel across Kyūshū via Mt Aso to Beppu).

Getting Around
To/From the Airport The airport bus service takes nearly an hour between the airport and JR Kumamoto station.

Tram Kumamoto has an effective tram service which will get you to most places of interest. On boarding the tram you take a ticket with your starting tram stop number, when you finish your trip a display panel at the front indicates the fare for each starting point. From the railway station to the castle/town centre costs ¥140. Alternatively you can get a ¥500 one-day pass for unlimited travel.

There are two tram routes. Route 2 starts from near JR Kumamoto station, runs through the town centre and out past the Suizen-ji-kōen Garden. Route 3 starts to the north, near Kami-Kumamoto station and merges with Route 2 just before the centre. Services are frequent, particularly on Route 2.

MT ASO AREA 阿蘇山周辺
In the centre of Kyūshū, halfway from Kumamoto to Beppu, is the gigantic Mt Aso volcano caldera. There have been a series of eruptions over the past 30 million years but the explosion which formed the outer crater about 100,000 years ago must have been a big one. Depending on who is doing the measuring it's 20 km to 30 km across the original crater from north to south, 15 km to 20 km east to west and 80 km to 130 km in circumference. Inside this huge outer crater there are towns, roads, railways, farms, 100,000 people and a number of smaller volcanoes, some of them still active.

Orientation & Information
Highway Routes 57, 265 and 325 make a circuit of the outer caldera and the JR Hōhi line runs across the northern section. Aso is the main town in the crater but there are other towns including Takamori on the southern side. All the roads running into the centre of the crater and to the five 'modern' peaks within the one huge, ancient, outer peak, are toll roads. There's a very helpful and informative tourist office at JR Aso station.

Five Mountains of Aso
Aso-gogaku (Five Mountains of Aso) are the five smaller mountains within the outer rim. They are Mt Eboshi-dake (1337 metres), Mt Nishima-dake (1238 metres), Mt Naka-dake (1216 metres), Mt Neko-dake (1408 metres) and Mt Taka-dake (1592 metres). Mt Naka-dake is currently the active volcano in this group. Mt Neko-dake, furthest to the east, is instantly recognisable from its craggy peak but Mt Taka-dake, between Neko-dake and Naka-dake, is the highest.

Mt Naka-dake 中岳
Recently Mt Naka-dake has been very active indeed. The cablecar to the summit of Naka-dake was closed from August 1989 to March 1990 due to eruptions and it had only been opened for a few weeks when the volcano erupted again in April '90, spewing dust and ash over a large area to the north.

In 1958, when a totally unexpected eruption killed 12 onlookers, concrete 'bomb shelters' were built around the rim for sightseers to take shelter in an emergency. Nevertheless, an eruption in 1979 killed three visitors over a km from the cone in an area which was thought to be safe. This eruption destroyed the cablecar which used to run up the north-eastern slope of the cone, and, although the supports still stand, the cablecar has never been replaced.

When Mt Naka-dake is not misbehaving, the cablecar whisks you up to the summit in just four minutes (¥410 one way or ¥820 return). There are departures every eight minutes. The walk to the top takes less than half an hour. The 100 metre deep crater varies in width from 400 metres to 1100 metres and there's a walk around the southern edge of the crater rim.

阿蘇山

Mt Aso

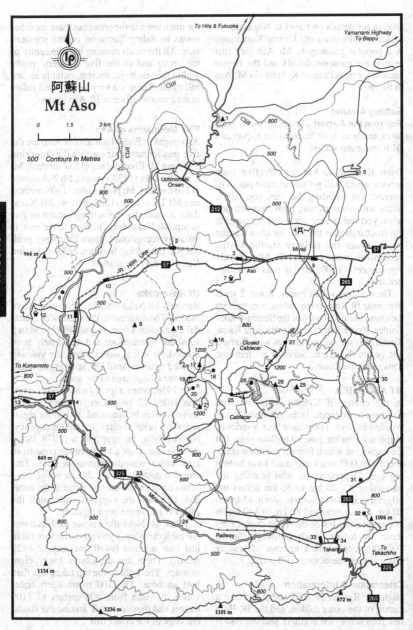

0   1.5   3 km

500 Contours In Metres

To Hita & Fukuoka

Yamanami Highway
To Beppu

Cliff

Cliff

800

500

Uchinomaki
Onsen

500

212

500

JR Hohi Line

964 m

500

57

57

265

9

10

57

8

15

16

1200

27

1200

30

26   28

29

12

11

17

19   18

20

21

1200

25

Cablecar

Closed
Cablecar

To Kumamoto

800

13   14

57

500

500

500

22

849 m

325

23

Minamiaso

Railway

24

500

800

800

500

31

265

800

32   1006 m

33   34

To
Takachiho

1154 m

1236 m

1101 m

872 m

325

265

KYŪSHŪ

1	Mt Daikanbo & Lookout 大観峰	13	Tateno Station 立野駅
2	JR Uchinomaki-onsen Station 内牧温泉駅	14	Tochinoki Pension Village とちのきペンション村
3	JR Aso Station 阿蘇駅	15	Mt Komezuka 米塚
4	Aso-jinja Shrine 阿蘇神社	16	Mt Ojo-dake 往生岳
5	Lookout 展望台	17	Mt Nishima-dake 二島岳
6	JR Miyaji Station 宮地駅	18	Ski Field スキー場
7	Aso Youth Hostel 阿蘇ユースホステル	19	Aso Volcanic Museum 阿蘇火山博物館
8	Mt Janoo 蛇ノ尾	20	Kusasenri Meadow 草千里
9	Akamizu Hot Springs 赤水温泉	21	Mt Eboshi-dake 烏帽子岳
10	JR Ichinokawa Station 市川駅	22	Choyo Station ちょよ駅
11	JR Akamizu Station 赤水駅	23	Aso-shimoda Station 阿蘇下田駅
12	YMCA & Youth Hostel Aso Camp	24	Nakamatsu Station 中松駅
25	Aso-nishi Cablecar Station 阿蘇西ロープウェイ乗り場		
26	Mt Naka-dake Crater 岳火口		
27	Sensui-kyō 仙酔峡		
28	Mt Naka-dake 中岳		
29	Mt Taka-dake 高岳		
30	Mt Neko-dake 根子岳		
31	Takamori Pension Village 高森ペンション村		
32	Pagoda 塔		
33	Takamori Station 高森駅		
34	Murataya Ryokan Youth Hostel むらたや旅館 ユースホステル		

KYŪSHŪ

Mt Aso Walks

There are plenty of interesting walks around Mt Aso. You can walk all the way to the Aso-nishi cablecar station from the Aso Youth Hostel in about three hours. From the top of the cablecar run you can walk around the crater rim to the peak of Mt Naka-dake and on to the top of Mt Taka-dake. From there you can descend either to Sensui-kyō, the bottom station of the old cablecar run on the north-eastern side of Naka-dake, or to the road which runs between Taka-dake and Neko-dake. Either road will then take you to Miyaji, the next railway station east from Aso. The direct descent to Sensui-kyō is very steep, so it's easier to continue back from Taka-dake to the Naka-dake rim and then follow the old cablecar route down to Sensui-kyō.

Allow four or five hours from the Aso-nishi cablecar station to Sensui-kyō. Buses down to Miyaji are irregular and the down-hill walk takes about 1½ hours.

Shorter walks include the interesting ascent of Mt Kijima-dake from the Aso Vol-

canic Museum. From the top you can descend to the top of the ski lift on the ski field just east of the museum. You can also climb to the top of Mt Eboshi-dake and any of these peaks offer superb views over the whole Aso area. The outer rim of the ancient crater also gives good views from a number of points. Shiroyami-tempodai, a lookout on the Yamanami Highway as it leaves the crater, is one good point; Daikanbo near Uchinomaki Onsen is another.

Aso Volcanic Museum 阿蘇火山博物館

Despite the usual shortage of non-Japanese labelling, the Aso Volcanic Museum will undoubtedly fill a few gaps in the average person's knowledge of volcanoes. There are displays, models and natural history exhibits. An entertaining selection of videos shows various volcanoes around the world strutting their stuff while another film shows what the Aso volcano can do along with scenes of the Aso region through the seasons and local festivals. The museum is open from 9 am to 5 pm daily and admission is ¥820.

Kusasenri & Mt Komezuka
草千里・米塚山

In front of the museum is the Kusasenri meadow (literally 'a thousand km of grass'), a grassy meadow in the flattened crater of an ancient volcano. There are two lakes in the meadow. Just off the road which runs from the museum down to the town of Aso is the perfectly shaped small cone of Mt Komezuka, another extinct volcano. The name means 'rice mound', because that's exactly the shape it is.

Aso-jinja Shrine 阿蘇神社

Aso-jinja Shrine is a 20 minute walk north of JR Miyaji station and is dedicated to the 12 gods of Mt Aso.

Places to Stay & Eat

There are over 50 places to stay around Mt Aso including a youth hostel, a collection of places (many of them pensions) at Uchinomaki Onsen, north of Aso, and pensions at Tochinoki Onsen (to the west of the caldera) and the village of Takamori (to the south).

Aso The *Aso Youth Hostel* (☎ 0967-34-0804) is a 15 to 20 minute walk or a three minute bus ride from JR Aso station and costs ¥1800 or ¥1950 depending on the time of year. There's a camping ground further along the road from the hostel. *Aso No Fumoto* (☎ 0967-32-0264) is a good minshuku, conveniently close to JR Aso station, which costs ¥5600 per person. There are a large number of pensions around Aso, most of them around ¥7000 per person. The interestingly named *Pension Windy Umbrella* (☎ 0967-32-3951) has rates from ¥7500. There's also a good little restaurant with an English menu in the station.

Takamori The *Murataya Ryokan Youth Hostel* (☎ 0967-62-0066) costs ¥2200 and is right in Takamori. The *Minami Aso Kokumin Kyūkamura* (☎ 0967-62-2111), a national vacation village, costs ¥7500 per person with two meals, and from ¥5200 without; it's crowded in July and August.

Just outside Takamori, on the southern side of the ancient crater, is a *pension mura* (pension village) with prices around ¥7500 per person including dinner and breakfast. Pensions include the *Wonderland* (☎ 0967-62-3040), *Cream House* (☎ 0967-62-3090) and *Flower Garden* (☎ 0967-62-3021). (The others don't have their names in English but they're all in one convenient little clump.)

Just out of Takamori towards the kokumin kyūkamura is *Dengaku-no-Sato* an old farmhouse restaurant where you cook your own kebab-like *dengaku* on individual hibachi barbecues. The restaurant closes at 7.30 pm and the set meal teishoku is good value for around ¥1600.

Other Places The *YMCA/Youth Hostel Aso Camp* (☎ 0967-35-0124) is near JR Akamizu station, the third stop west of JR Aso station. The cost per night is ¥2000. *Minami Aso Kokuminshukusha* (☎ 0967-67-0078) is near the Aso-shimoda private railway station, the third stop west of Takamori. Rooms cost from ¥3600 without meals.

Getting There & Away

The JR Hōhi line operates between Kumamoto and Beppu via Aso. From JR Aso station there are buses to the Aso-nishi cablecar station. From Kumamoto to Aso, local trains take 1½ hours (¥930), while limited express trains take one hour and cost ¥1650. The Beppu-Aso limited express service costs ¥2800 and takes 2½ hours. To get to Takamori on the southern side of the crater, transfer from the JR Hōhi line to the Minamiaso private railway line at Tateno.

From March to November the *Aso Boy* steam train makes a daily run from Kumamoto to Aso, terminating at Miyaji railway station. The one-way fare is ¥1730.

Bus No 266 starts from the Sankō bus terminal at JR Kumamoto station, stops at the Kumamoto Kōtsū bus centre then continues right across Kyūshū with an excursion to the Aso volcanic peaks and then along the Yamanami Highway to Beppu. The trip takes seven hours including a short photo stop at the Kusasenri meadow in front of the Aso

Volcanic Museum and costs from ¥7500. Buses from Beppu to Aso take 2½ to three hours and cost ¥3000, plus another ¥1100 for the services that continue to the Aso-nishi cablecar station.

From Takamori, buses continue south to the mountain resort of Takachiho, a 1½ hour trip along a very scenic route.

Getting Around

Buses operate approximately hourly from JR Aso station via the Aso Youth Hostel to the Aso-nishi cablecar station on the slopes of Mt Naka-dake. The trip takes 40 minutes up, 30 minutes down and costs ¥600. There are less frequent services between Miyaji and Sensui-kyō on the northern side of Mt Naka-dake.

Buses also operate between Aso and Takamori. Cars can be rented at Aso and at Uchinomaki Onsen, one stop west from JR station.

SOUTH OF KUMAMOTO　熊本の南部

Yatsushiro　八代

The castle town of Yatsushiro, directly south of Kumamoto, was where Hosokawa Tadoki retired. The powerful daimyō is chiefly remembered in Japan for having his Christian wife killed to stop her falling into the hands of his enemies. Near the castle ruins is the 1688 Shohinken house and garden. The town's Korean-influenced Koda-yaki pottery is admired by pottery experts.

Hinagu & Minamata　日奈久・水俣

Further south along the coast at Hinagu there are fine views out towards the Amakusa Islands. South again is the port of Minamata which became infamous in the late '60s and early '70s when it was discovered that the high incidence of illness and birth defects in the town were caused by mercury poisoning. A local factory had dumped waste containing high levels of mercury into the sea and this had contaminated the fish eaten by local residents. The company's ruthless efforts to suppress the story focused worldwide attention on the town.

Hitoyoshi　人吉

Directly south of Yatsushiro towards the Kirishima volcano chain, the town of Hitoyoshi is noted for the 18 km boat trip down the rapids of the Kuma-gawa River. There are a variety of trips taking from about 2½ hours, ending at Osakahama and costing ¥2370 per person. The boat trips shut down between November and February, and even for the rest of the year there are only three to four services a day on weekdays. The weekends are more lively, with seven to eight services daily. The boat departure point is about 1½ km south-east of the railway station, directly across the river from the ruins of Hitoyoshi Castle. Ask for *kuma-gawa kudari*.

Getting There & Away From Kumamoto it's half an hour on the JR Kagoshima line to Yatsushiro then one hour on the JR Hisatsu line to Hitoyoshi. From Hitoyoshi, it's a little over 1½ hours on the Hisatsu line and then the JR Kitto line to Kobayashi, from where buses run to Ebino in the Kirishima National Park.

AMAKUSA ISLANDS　天草諸島

South of the Shimabara-hantō Peninsula are the Amakusa Islands. The islands were a stronghold of Christianity during Japan's Christian Century and the grinding poverty here was a major factor in the Shimabara Rebellion in 1637. It's still one of the more backward regions of Japan.

Hondo is the main town on the islands and has a museum relating to the Christian era. Tomioka, where the Nagasaki ferries berth, has castle ruins and a museum. This west coast area is particularly interesting.

There are ferry services from various places in Nagasaki-ken (including Mogi near Nagasaki and Shimabara on the Shimabara Peninsula) and from the Kumamoto-ken coast (including Yatsushiro and Minamata). In addition, the Amakusa Five Bridges link the island directly with Misumi, south of Kumamoto.

Kagoshima-ken
鹿児島県

Kyūshū's southernmost prefecture has the large city of Kagoshima, overlooked by the ominous, smoking volcano of Sakurajima across Kinkō-wan Bay. South of Kagoshima is the interesting Satsuma-hantō Peninsula while to the north is the Kirishima National Park with its superb volcanoes.

KIRISHIMA NATIONAL PARK
霧島国立公園

The day walk from the village on the Ebino-kōgen Plateau to the summits of a string of volcanoes is one of the finest volcanic hikes in Japan. It's about 15 km from the summit of Mt Karakuni-dake to the summit of Mt Takachiho-no-mine and there's superb scenery all the way. If your time or energy is limited there are shorter alternatives such as a pleasant lake stroll on the plateau or a walk up and down Mt Karakuni-dake or Mt Takachiho. The area is also noted for its spring wildflowers and has fine hot springs

and the impressive 75 metre Senriga-taki Waterfall.

Orientation & Information
There are tourist information offices with maps and some information in English at Ebino-kōgen Village and at Takachiho-gawara, the two ends of the volcano walk. There are restaurant facilities at both ends of the walk as well, but Ebino-kōgen has most of the hotels, camping facilities and the like. Kobayashi to the north and Hayashida, just to the south, are the main towns near Ebino-kōgen.

Ebino-kōgen Walk えびの高原
The Ebino-kōgen lake circuit is a pleasantly relaxed stroll around a series of volcanic lakes – Lake Rokkannon Mi-ike has the most intense colour, a deep blue-green. Across the road from Lake Fudou, at the base of Mt Karakuni-dake, is a steaming jigoku (hot spring). From there you can make the stiff climb to the 1700 metre summit of Mt Karakuni-dake, skirting the edge of the volcano's deep crater before arriving at the high point on the eastern side. There are good

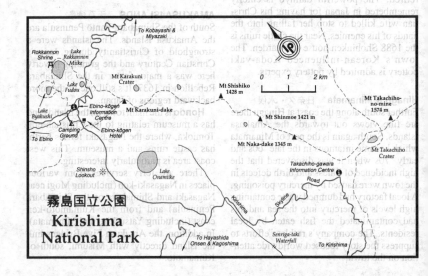

Left: Boats, Hiroshima River (TW)
Right: Cemetery, Onomichi (TW)
Bottom: Taga-jinja phallus, Uwajima (TW)

Top: Ueno-kōen Park, Tokyo (TW)
Middle: Sensō-ji Temple, Asakusa, Tokyo (TW)
Bottom: Paper cranes, Peace Memorial Park, Hiroshima (TW)

views back over Ebino-kōgen Plateau, but the view to the south is superb, taking in the perfectly circular caldera lake of Onamiike, the rounded Mt Shinmoe-dake and the perfect cone of Mt Takachiho-no-mine. On a clear day, you can see right down to Kagoshima and the smoking cone of Sakurajima.

Longer Walks

The views across the almost lunar landscape from any of the volcano summits is otherworldly. If you have time you can continue from Mt Karakuni-dake to Mt Shishiko, Mt Shinmoe-dake, Mt Naka-dake and Takachiho-gawara, from where you can make the ascent of Mt Takachiho-no-mine. Close up, Takachiho is a decidedly ugly looking volcano with a huge, gaping crater. Legends relate that Ninigi-no-mikoto, a descendant of the sun goddess, arrived in Japan on the summit of this mountain.

Places to Stay

Ebino-kōgen Village has a good choice of accommodation including the expensive *Ebino-kōgen Hotel* (☎ 0984-33-1155), with rooms from ¥12,500 and a kokuminshukusha, *Ebino Kōgen-sō* (☎ 0984-33-0161), with accommodation from ¥5700 per person including two meals. Just north-east of the centre is the *Ebino-kōgen Rotemburo* with basic but cheap huts around a popular series of open-air hot-spring baths. There's also a camping ground. More accommodation can be found at Hayashida Onsen, between Ebino-kōgen and the Kirishima-jingū Shrine.

Getting There & Away

JR Kobayashi station to the north of Ebino-kōgen and Kirishima-jinja station to the south are the main railway junctions. From Miyazaki or Kumamoto take a JR Ebino-go limited express train to Kobayashi on the JR Kitto line, from where buses operate to Ebino. From Kagoshima (around one hour) or Miyazaki (1½ hours) you can take a JR Nippō limited express to Kirishima-jinja railway station. From there buses operate to

Takachiho-gawara (about 45 minutes) and Ebino-kōgen.

A direct bus to Ebino-kōgen is probably the best way to go. The two main approaches are Kagoshima and Miyazaki, though there are also direct buses from Fukuoka (4½ hours, ¥5000). Buses arrive and depart from Ebino-kōgen (the village on the Ebino-kōgen Plateau, not to be confused with the town of Ebino down on the plains). You can arrive there from Kobayashi to the north, Miyazaki to the east or Kagoshima to the south and continue on another service. From Nishi-Kagoshima railway station in Kagoshima, buses depart for Kirishima-jingū Shrine and Hayashida Onsen at least hourly and some continue on to Ebino-kōgen. It takes about two hours 10 minutes to Hayashida Onsen and costs ¥1200.

There are good views of the volcano scenery from buses driving along the Kirishima Skyline road.

KIRISHIMA-JINGŪ SHRINE　霧島神宮

The bright orange Kirishima-jingū Shrine is colourful and beautifully located, with fine views down towards Kagoshima and the smoking cone of Sakurajima, but otherwise is not of great interest. It originally dates from the 6th century although the present shrine was built in 1715 and is dedicated to Ninigi-no-mikoto, who made his legendary landing in Japan on the summit of Mt Takachiho.

The shrine can be visited en route to the park from Kagoshima or Miyazaki; see the preceding Kirishima National Park section for transport details. The shrine is about 15 minutes by bus from Kirishima-jingū railway station and it's another 50 minutes by bus to the Ebino-kōgen Plateau.

KAGOSHIMA　鹿児島

Known to the Japanese as the Naples of Japan, Kagoshima (population 536,000) is the southernmost major city in Kyūshū and a warm, sunny and relaxed place – at least as long as Kagoshima's very own Vesuvius, Sakurajima, is behaving itself and the wind is blowing in the right direction. Only a

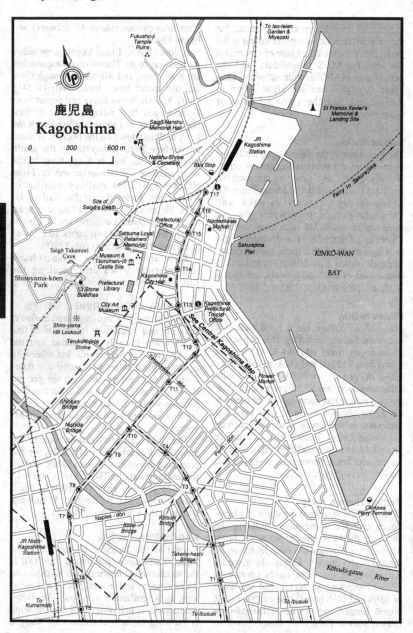

KYŪSHŪ

鹿児島
Kagoshima

0   300   600 m

To Iso-teien
Garden &
Miyazaki

Fukushō-ji
Temple
Ruins

St Francis Xavier's
Memorial &
Landing Site

Saigō Nanshu
Memorial Hall

JR
Kagoshima
Station

Nanshu Shrine
& Cemetery

Bus Stop

T17

Site of
Saigō's Death

T16

Prefectural
Office

Namerikawa
Market

T15

Satsuma Loyal
Retainers
Memorial

Ferry to Sakurajima

Saigō Takamori
Cave

Museum &
Tsurumaru-jō
Castle Site

T14

Sakurajima
Pier

KINKŌ-WAN
BAY

Shiroyama-kōen
Park

13 Stone
Buddhas

Prefectural
Library

Kagoshima
City Hall

Shiro-yama
Hill Lookout

City Art
Museum

T13

Kagoshima
Prefectural
Tourist
Office

Terukuni-jinja
Shrine

T12

See Central Kagoshima Map

Tenmonkan-
dōri

T11

Flower
Market

Shinkan
Bridge

Nishida
Bridge

T10

T9

T4

Perm - dōri

Okinawa
Ferry Terminal

T8

T3

T7

Naples - dōri

Kōtei
Bridge

Kōtsuki
Bridge

JR Nishi-
Kagoshima
Station

Takeno-hashi
Bridge

T2

Kōtsuki-gawa
River

To
Kumamoto

T6

T1

T5

To Ibusuki

To Ibusuki

TRAM STOPS

Route 1

T1 Kōtsū-kyoku
交通局

T2 Takenohashi
竹の橋

T3 Shinyashiki
新屋敷

T4 City Hospital
市立病院前

Route 2

T5 Nakasu-dōri
中洲通り

T6 Miyako-dōri
都通り

T7 Nishi Kagoshima Station
西鹿児島駅前

T8 Takamibashi
高見橋

T9 Kajya-machi
加治屋町

Route 1 & 2

T10 Takami-baba
高見馬場

T11 Tenmonkan-dōri
天文館通り

T12 Izuro-dōri
いづろ通り

T13 Asahi-dōri
朝日通り

T14 City Hall
市役所前

T15 Prefectural Office
県庁前

T16 Sakurajima Sanbashi-dōri
桜島桟橋通り

T17 Kagoshima Station
鹿児島駅前

stone's throw away from Kagoshima, across Kinkō-wan Bay, is Sakurajima's huge cone. When this very active volcano spits out great clouds of dust and ash, and the wind carries it across the bay and dumps it on the streets of Kagoshima, the city is not so sunny and relaxed at all. 'Dustfall' brings out the umbrellas just as frequently as rainfall.

History

Kagoshima's history has been dominated by a single family, the Shimazu clan, who held sway there for 29 generations and nearly 700

years until the Meiji Restoration. The Kagoshima region, known as Satsuma, was always receptive to outside contact and for many years was an important centre for trade with China. St Francis Xavier first arrived here in 1549, making Kagoshima one of Japan's earliest contact points with Christianity and the West.

The Shimazu family's interests were not confined to trade, however. In the 16th century their power extended throughout Kyūshū and they also gained control of the islands of Okinawa, where they treated the people so oppressively that the Okinawans have regarded the mainland Japanese with suspicion ever since.

During the 1800s, as the Tokugawa Shogunate increasingly proved its inability to respond to the challenge of the industrialised West, the Shimazu were already looking further afield: in the 1850s, the Shimazu established the country's first Western-style manufacturing operation. Then, in 1865, the family smuggled 17 young men out of the country to study Western technology firsthand in the UK. In conjunction with the Mori clan of Hagi (see the Hagi section in the Western Honshū chapter) the Shimazu played a leading part in the Meiji Restoration.

Orientation & Information

Kagoshima sprawls north-south along the bayside and has two major JR stations, Nishi-Kagoshima to the south and Kagoshima to the north. The town centre is between the two stations, and accommodation is evenly distributed between here and the Nishi-Kagoshima station area. The Iso-teien Garden, the town's principal attraction, is north of Kagoshima station but most other things to do are around the centre, particularly on the hillside that forms a backdrop to the city. While these hills provide one clear landmark, the city's other great landmark, the smoking Sakurajima volcano, is even more evident.

The tourist information office (☎ 0992-53-2500) in the Nishi-Kagoshima station car park is open from 8.30 am to 5 pm and has a surprising amount of information in English,

KYŪSHŪ

if you ask for it. Also in front of the station is the curious stepped column with 17 people perched on it, commemorating the 17 Kagoshima students who defied the 'no going overseas' rules. The main post office is right beside the station.

The Tenmonkan-dōri tram stop, where the lively Tenmonkan-dōri shopping and entertainment arcade crosses the tram lines, marks the town centre. There's another tourist office (☎ 0992-22-2500) at JR Kagoshima station, and the Kagoshima Prefectural Tourist Office (☎ 0992-23-5771), 4th floor Sangyo Kaikan Building, 9-1 Meizan-chō, is between the centre and JR Kagoshima station. Kagoshima Airport also has a tourist office that can make hotel reservations, though in many ways it's better to just head into central Kagoshima and look around for a place.

Iso-teien Garden 磯庭園

The Shimazu family not only dominated Kagoshima's history, they also left the city its principal attraction, the beautiful bayside Iso-teien Garden. The 19th Shimazu lord laid the garden out in 1660 incorporating one of the most impressive pieces of 'borrowed scenery' to be found anywhere in Japan – the fuming cone of Sakurajima.

Although the garden is not as well kept and immaculate as tourist literature would have you believe, it is pleasant to wander through. Look for the stream where the 21st Shimazu lord once held poem parties – the participants had to compose a poem before the next cup of sake floated down the stream to them.

The garden contains the Shimazu Villa, the family home of the powerful Shimazu clan. Above the garden and reached by a cablecar (¥280 one way) is the Isoyama recreation ground, which has great views over the city. Look for the large rock on the hillside overlooking the garden, into which are carved two Chinese characters proclaiming it 'a huge rock'.

The garden is north of the centre (10 minutes by Hayashida line bus No 11 from the stop outside JR Kagoshima station) and

open from 8.30 am to 5.30 pm, except in winter, when it closes half an hour earlier. Entry is ¥800.

Shōko Shūseikan Museum

This museum, adjacent to Iso-teien Garden, shows items relating to the Shimazu family and is housed in the building established in the 1850s as Japan's first factory. At one time the factory employed 1200 workers. Exhibits relate to the Shimazu family and to the factory's activities but only a few items are labelled in English. Entry is included in the garden admission fee and opening hours are the same.

Other Museums

The City Art Museum (Kagoshima Shiritsu Bijutsukan) has a small permanent collection principally dedicated to the works of local artists but also including paintings by European impressionists along with regular special exhibitions. Entry is ¥200, and the museum is open from 9 am to 4.30 pm, closed on Monday. , the Kagoshima Prefectural Museum of Culture (Reimeikan) is on the former site of Tsurumaru-jō Castle: the walls and the impressive moat are all that remain of the 1602 castle. The museum has displays on Kagoshima's history with special emphasis on the Satsuma period and entry is ¥260. The gallery and the museum are both open from 9 am to 4.30 pm daily except Monday.

The Kagoshima Prefectural Museum covers natural history and science and has an interesting exhibit on the Sakurajima volcano, tracing its history and eruptions. Entry is ¥200.

Saigō Takamori 西郷隆盛

There are numerous reminders of Saigō Takamori's importance in Kagoshima including the large statue of him near the City Art Museum. In true Japanese fashion, there's a sign showing you where to stand in order to get yourself and the statue in the same photograph. The cave where he hid and the place where he eventually committed suicide are on Shiro-yama Hill. Further north there is the Nanshū Shrine, the Saigō Nanshū Memorial Hall (entrance ¥100; closed on Monday), where displays tell of the failed rebellion, and the Nanshu-bochi Cemetery, which contains the graves of more than 2000 of Saigō's followers.

St Francis Xavier   フランシスザビエル
There are a number of memorials to St Francis Xavier around the city, including a church and a memorial park near the city centre. Near the waterfront, north of JR Kagoshima station and towards the Iso-teien Garden, is a memorial at his supposed landing spot.

Kōtsuki-gawa River   甲突川
Kagoshima enjoys twin-city status with Naples in Italy and Perth in Australia. The street running perpendicular to the Nishi-Kagoshima station starts as Naples-dōri and changes to Perth-dōri after it crosses the Kōtsuki-gawa River. There's a very pleasant riverside walk from near the station. Start at the attractive 18th century stone Nishida Bridge and walk south; there are four other attractive bridges along the way.

The statue of Ōkubo Toshimichi, another important local personage in the events of the Meiji Restoration (he became the prime minister in the new government) is by the tramline road. Further south is the site of Saigō's home and the 'Statue of Hat', appropriately named after the statue's only item of apparel.

Morning Market   朝市
Kagoshima's *asa ichi*, or morning market,

operates daily (except Sunday) in front of the Nishi Kagoshima station from 6 am to around noon. It's a raucous, lively event and worth taking a look at. There's another morning market up at the main JR station, but the Nishi-Kagoshima station market is the better one to visit.

Other Attractions
Behind the prefectural museum is the **Ter-ukuni-jinja Shrine**, dedicated to Shimazu Nariakira, the 28th Shimazu lord who was responsible for building Japan's first factory and introducing modern Western technology to the area. He also designed Japan's rising sun flag. Continue up the hillside behind the shrine and you eventually reach the lookout in **Shiroyama-kōen Park**, which has fine views over the city and across to Sakurajima. An alternative route up the hill from behind the Reimeikan Museum starts from beside the Satsuma Loyal Retainers' Memorial.

North of the memorial are the remains of the **Fukusho-ji Temple**, once the Shimazu family temple. Iso-hama Beach, near the Iso-teien Garden, is the town's popular summer getaway. The **Ijinkan** or 'foreigners' residence', also near Iso Garden, was used by British engineers brought to Japan to help set up the factory at Shōko Shuseikan. **Tagayama Park**, between Iso Garden and Kagoshima station, has a noted statue of Admiral Togo, who defeated the Czar's fleet in the Russo-Japanese war of 1905.

Some distance south of Kagoshima is the **Hirakawa Zoological Park**, which has a koala collection. It's open daily, except

Saigō Takamori
Although the Great Saigō had played a leading part in the Meiji Restoration in 1868, in 1877 he changed his mind, possibly because he felt the curtailment of samurai power and status had gone too far, and led the ill-fated Satsuma or Seinan Rebellion. Kumamoto's magnificent castle was burnt down during the rebellion but when defeat became inevitable, Saigō eventually retreated to Kagoshima and committed seppuku. Despite his mixed status as both a hero and villain of the restoration, Saigō is still a great figure in Satsuma's history and indeed in the history of Japan. His square-headed features and bulky appearance are instantly recognisable and Kagoshima has a famous Saigō statue, as does Ueno-kōen Park in Tokyo. ■

KYŪSHŪ

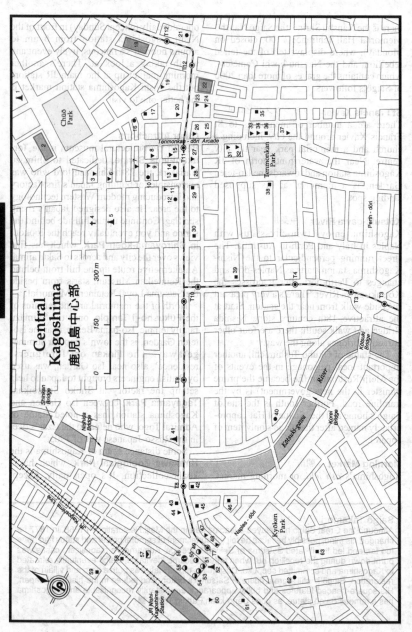

Central
Kagoshima
鹿児島中心部

Chūō
Park

Tenmonkan - dōri Arcade

Tenmonkan
Park

Perth - dōri

Kōtsuki-gawa
River

Kōtsuki
Bridge

Kōrei
Bridge

Kyōken
Park

Naples - dōri

Shinkan
Bridge

Nishida
Bridge

JR Kagoshima line

JR Nishi-
Kagoshima
Station

0   150   300 m

PLACES TO STAY

13 Kagoshima
Hayashida Hotel
かごしま林田ホテル

17 Business Hotel
Nichisenren
ビジネスホテル日専連

29 New Central
Hotel/ANA
ニューセントラルホテル

30 Kagoshima
Washington Hotel

35 Business Hotel
Satsuma
ビジネスホテル薩摩

36 Kagoshima Kankō
Hotel

38 City Hotel Tenmonkan
シティホテル天文館

39 Hokke Club
Kagoshima
法華クラブ鹿児島

42 Kagoshima Tōkyū Inn
鹿児島東急イン

43 Hotel Taisei Annexe
ホテルタイセイアネックス

45 Station Hotel New
Kagoshima
ステーションホテルニューカゴシマ

46 Kagoshima Gasthof
鹿児島ガストフ

58 City Hotel Kagoshima
シティホテル鹿児島

59 Union Hotel

61 Business Hotel Suzuya
ビジネスホテルすずや

63 Silk Inn Kagoshima
シルクイン鹿児島

PLACES TO EAT

3 Kumasotei Restaurant
くまそ亭

6 Le Ciel de Paris
Patisserie
ルシエルドゥパリ

7 Casa Salone
Restaurant
カーササローネ

8 Roman Yakata
Restaurant
ロマンヤカタ

9 Wakana Restaurant
吾愛人

11 Kentucky Fried
Chicken
ケンタッキーフライドチキン

15 Zabon Rāmen
Restaurant
ざぼんラーメン

19 Dom Dom Hamburgers
ドムドム

20 Mr Donut
ミスタードーナッツ

23 Kentucky
Fried Chicken
ケンタッキーフライドチキン

24 McDonald's
マクドナルド

25 Häagen Dazs
Icecream

26 Toit-vert Patisserie
天文館トワベール

27 Lotteria
ロッテリア

28 Vie de France Bakery
ヴィドゥフランス

31 Boulangerie
ブランジェリー

32 Mujaki Restaurant
天文館むじゃき

33 Seafood
Restaurant Paeriya
巴絵里屋

34 Bali Bali Yakiniku
House
バリバリ焼肉ハウス

37 Akachōchin
Robatayaki
あかちょうちん

44 Italian Tomato
Restaurant
イタリアントマト

47 Satsuma Restaurant
薩摩レストラン

48 Mr Donut
ミスタードーナッツ

60 Vesuvio Restaurant
ヴェスヴィオ

OTHER

1 Saigō Takamori Statue
西郷隆盛銅像

2 Kagoshima
Prefectural Museum
県立博物館

4 St Francis Xavier
Church
ザビエル教会

5 St Francis Xavier
Memorial
ザビエル記念碑

10 Namusete Bar
ナマセテ

12 JAL
日本航空

14 JTB
日本交通公社

16 T-Bone Bar
Tボーン

18 Yamakataya
Department Store &
Bus Terminal
山形屋

21 Izuro (Stone Lantern)
石灯籠

22 Mitsukoshi
Department Store
三越

40 Site of Saigo House
西郷旧居

41 Statue of Ōkubo
Toshimichi
大久保利通生地

49 Hayashida Sangyo
Kōtsū (Kirishima),
Minami Kyūshū
Kosoku (Miyazaki)
林田産業交通 (至霧島)

50 City Bus
(Kagoshima City)
シティバス (鹿児島市)

51 Kagoshima Kōtsū
(Chiran, Ibusuki)
鹿児島交通

52 17 Young Pioneers
Statues
若き薩摩の群像

53 Hayashida
Sangyo Kōtsū
(Ebino, Kirishima)
林田産業交通 (至えびの)

54 JR Bus (Sakurajima)
JRバス (至桜島)

55 Kagoshima
Kōtsū & City Bus
(Sightseeing Buses)
鹿児島交通 (観光バス)

56 Tourist
Information Office
観光案内所

57 Post Office
郵便局

62 Morning Market
朝市

Tuesday, from 9 am to 5 pm (the koala section closes at 4 pm) and costs ¥200 entry.

Festivals

One of Kagoshima's more unusual events is the late July umbrella burning festival. Boys burn umbrellas on the banks of the Kōtsuki-gawa River in honour of the Soga brothers, though why they do this isn't exactly clear.

Places to Stay

The only youth hostel close to Kagoshima is the *Sakurajima Youth Hostel*. To get there you have to take the ferry across the bay (see the following Sakurajima section for details). If you are not in the market for youth hostel accommodation, it is difficult to find inexpensive alternatives in Kagoshima. The Nishi-Kagoshima station area is a good hunting ground for business hotels, but the cheapest places in town are over the river in central Kagoshima.

Nishi-Kagoshima Station Area The cheapest hotel in the area (only 22 singles) is the *Business Hotel Suzuya* (☎ 0992-58-2385), which has singles ranging from ¥3900 to ¥4300. One of the better value lower end station-area hotels is the *Silk Inn Kagoshima* (☎ 0992-58-1221), where singles/doubles/twins cost from ¥5000/5500/8500. Alternatively, turn left immediately out of the station, pass the post office and take the first left across the railway tracks to the *Union Hotel* (☎ 0992-53-5800). It's a friendly place with rooms at ¥5200/ 9000 but definitely at the tatty and worn-out end of the business hotel spectrum and for emergency accommodation only. Nearby is the *City Hotel Kagoshima* (☎ 0992-58-0331), with rooms starting at ¥4944.

Close to each other are the *Hotel Taisei* (☎ 0992-56-6111) and the *Hotel Taisei Annexe* (☎ 0992-57-1111). They are both modern business hotels, and the main hotel has singles from ¥5500 to ¥6000 and doubles at ¥8500, while the annexe has singles at ¥5300 and doubles at ¥8500. North of these is another relatively inexpensive place; the *Kagoshima Dai-Ichi Hotel* (☎ 0992-55-

0256). It has singles from ¥5000 and doubles at ¥8000.

More up-market options include the *Kagoshima Gasthof* (☎ 0992-52-1401), which has singles/twins for ¥6500/15,000; the *Station Hotel New Kagoshima* (☎ 0992-53-5353), with singles/doubles at ¥6000/ 11,000; and the *Kagoshima Tōkyū Inn* (☎ 0992-53-3692), with singles/doubles from ¥7400/13,000.

Central Kagoshima Probably the cheapest business hotel in town is right in the centre, close to a McDonald's and a Dom Dom Hamburger (so you can spend the money you've saved on junk food). The *Business Hotel Nichisenren* (☎ 0992-25-6161) has singles from ¥3000 and twins for ¥5500, but don't expect anything more than the basics. There are no bathrooms in the rooms, so you'll have to seek out the local sento.

Another cheapie is just south of the Mitsukoshi department store. The *Business Hotel Satsuma* (☎ 0992-26-1351) has singles with/without bath for ¥4100/3500 and twins for ¥6400/7400. Moving back down towards the Nishi-Kagoshima station area, the *Hokke Club Kagoshima* (☎ 0992-26-0011) has singles/twins from ¥3400/ 7400.

By the tramline and close to the Ten-monkan-dōri shopping arcade, the *Kagoshima Hayashida Hotel* (☎ 0992-24-4111) is an important central meeting point and has singles/doubles from ¥6800/9500. The hotel features a large central garden atrium. Across the road is the *New Central Hotel* (☎ 0992-24-5551), where singles/ doubles range from ¥5700/9300 – it comes complete with a bunny-girl bar on the top floor. Another central option, right in the heart of all the entertainment action, is the *City Hotel Tenmonkan* (☎ 0992-23-7181), which has singles at ¥5100 and doubles at ¥10,000.

Places to Eat

For the greatest variety of eating options, just take a stroll around the Tenmonkan area. There's everything from fast-food barns to rowdy robotayaki to hole-in-the wall rāmen shops where red-faced salarymen slurp back a quick bowl of noodles. Probably the best place to start looking is the Tenmonkan-dōri arcade. This place is thick with bakeries and restaurants with plastic meal displays. *Häagen Dazs* is *the* place for ice creams; there are a couple of good patisseries (*Toit Vert* and *Boulangerie*); and for colourful plastic food displays check out *Mujaki*, a huge place with five floors of dining at reasonable prices. Diagonally opposite Mujaki is the *Seafood Restaurant Paeriya*, where main courses start at around ¥1600.

Further down the arcade, *Akachochi* is a robatayaki of wildly exaggerated cheerfulness – the welcomes are bawled out so loudly that new arrivals reel back at the door. The menu is in Japanese only, though some dishes are illustrated and most are in the ¥250 to ¥500 range. Look for the octopus over the entrance. There's another branch of this popular robatayaki near the Nishi-Kagoshima station.

The area to the south-west of the arcade features a number of the town's more interesting restaurants including *Kumasotei* (☎ 0992-22-6356), which is a favourite for its Satsuma cuisine. There is an English menu (although English-speaking visitors seem to be so infrequent that the owners often have trouble finding it!) which offers a variety of set lunches from ¥2000 to ¥5000, and set dinners from ¥3000 to ¥20,000 (including tax and service). The ¥4000 dinner gives you a taste of all the most popular Satsuma specialities.

Other places in this central area include *Casa Salone* for good value Italian fare, *Wakana* with a variety of meals (all with plastic versions on display), *Roman Yakata* for Italian dishes, *La Sei* for French dishes and *Le Ciel de Paris*, a pleasant little patisserie/coffee bar.

Kagoshima is renowned for its rāmen, the soup stock for which is made with a secret recipe. You can try it at *Zabon Rāmen*, which is just around the corner from the Kagoshima Hayashida Hotel. A bowl of Kagoshima's famous noodles will set you back ¥700. Generally you buy a ticket for your meal at the vending machine just inside the door, but the friendly staff will do it for you if you look confused. Zabon rāmen is the No 2 button. Further down the same street is another famous noodle shop – *Kuruiwa Rāmen*.

Although the Tenmonkan area reigns supreme, there are also a few restaurants around the Nishi-Kagoshima station area, including an old railway carriage converted into a restaurant called the *Vesuvio* (an appropriate name, given the Naples-Vesuvius versus Kagoshima-Sakurajima connections). Pizza and spaghetti feature heavily on the menu. There are also a few fast-food places like *Mr Donut* in this area.

Entertainment

There's a lot happening in the Tenmonkan area – shot bars, discos, bunny bars, peep shows, karaoke boxes and hide-away coffee shops, but much of it is very Japanese and not particularly accessible to visiting gaijin. For a quiet drink that isn't going to clear out your wallet, try *Namusete*, a basement reggae bar around the corner from the Kagoshima Hayashida Hotel. It's run by a couple of laid-back Japanese guys who sell Nepalese T-shirts and jewellery on the side

Satsuma

Kagoshima's cuisine speciality is known as Satsuma, the food of the Satsuma region. Satsuma dishes include *tonkotsu*, which is pork ribs seasoned with miso and black sugar then boiled until they're on the point of falling apart; *kibinago*, a sardine-like fish which is usually prepared as sashimi with vinegared miso sauce; *satsuma-age*, a fried fish sausage; *satsuma jiru*, a chicken miso soup; *torisashi*, which is raw chicken with soy sauce; *katsuo no tataki*, which is sliced bonito; *katsuo no shioka*, which is salted bonito intestines; and *sakezushi*, a mixed seafood sushi.

Kagoshima rāmen is the region's renowned noodle dish. *Shōchū*, the Kagoshima firewater, comes in many forms, including *imo-shōchū*, made from sweet potatoes. There's also a local sweet-potato ice cream. ■

KYŪSHŪ

(the owner sold his jacket to a drunken customer when we were there), and the place is popular with Kagoshima's small foreign community. Another place worth checking out is *T-Bone*, a small blues bar with all kinds of blues related paraphernalia on the walls.

Things to Buy

Satsuma specialities that Japanese like to buy when they are in Kagoshima include a Satsuma variation on the *ningyō* (Japanese doll), cards printed with inks produced from Sakurajima volcanic ash, Satsuma *kiriki* (cut glass) and nifty little wooden fish on wheels. The latter sounds like a decidedly odd item, but are a traditional toy and look good in a rough-hewn, colourful way. All these things can be bought in the Kagoshima specialities store (☎ 0992-25-6120) north of the Tenmonkan area.

Local crafts are also displayed in the same building as the Kagoshima Prefectural Tourist Office (see Orientation & Information in this for its location). Mitsukoshi, Yamakataya and Takashimaya are the main department stores, and all are good places to seek out souvenir items.

Getting There & Away

Air Kagoshima's airport has overseas connections with Hong Kong and Seoul, as well as domestic flights to Tokyo, Osaka, Nagoya and a variety of other places in Honshū and Kyūshū. Kagoshima is the major jumping-off point for flights to the South-West Islands and also has connections with the Kagoshima-ken islands and Naha on Okinawa. (See the Okinawa & the South-West Islands chapter for more details.)

Train Both the Nishi-Kagoshima and JR Kagoshima stations are arrival and departure points for other areas of Japan. While the Nishi-Kagoshima station is close to a greater choice of accommodation, the JR Kagoshima station is closer to Iso-teien Garden and the Sakurajima ferry. The stations are about equal distance north and south of the town centre.

It takes about 4½ hours by train from Fukuoka/Hakata via Kumamoto to Kagoshima on the JR Kagoshima line. The local train fare is ¥5150; add ¥2560 for the limited express service. The JR Nippō line connects Kagoshima with Kokura on the north-eastern tip of Kyūshū for ¥7210, plus ¥2780 for limited express. Nippō line trains operate via Miyazaki and Beppu.

Trains also run south from Kagoshima to the popular hot-spring resort of Ibusuki, taking about one hour 10 minutes.

Bus Hayashida buses to Kirishima and Ebino-kōgen go from the Takashimaya department store in the centre. A good way of exploring Chiran and Ibusuki, south of Kagoshima, is by rented car, but you can also get there by bus from bus stop No 10 at Nishi-Kagoshima station. Buses also run from Nishi-Kagoshima railway station to other places near and far, including the following:

Destination	Bus Stop	Duration	Fare
Miyazaki	No 8	2½ hours	¥2700
Kumamoto	No 17	3½ hours	¥3600
Fukuoka	No 16	4½ hours	¥5300
Osaka	No 8	12½ hours	¥12,000
Kyoto	No 16	13½ hours	¥12,600
Nagoya	No 16	14½ hours	¥14,000

There are also daily tours to Ibusuki and Chiran, among other places, from bus stop No 4. Most of the tours will be unlikely to be of interest to most Western visitors but, as an example of what's on offer, at 10.10 am daily a bus heads off to Chiran, whizzes you around the sights and then does the same thing in Ibusuki, ending the day with a soak in a hot spring (which you'll probably need after all that running around). All this for a mere ¥3950.

Ferry Ferries shuttle across the bay to Sakurajima but also operate further afield. There are car ferry services from Kagoshima to Osaka on Honshū and to a number of the South-West Islands, including Okinawa. For Osaka, ferries take 15½ hours and a 2nd class ticket costs ¥9270; contact the Blue Highway Line (☎ 0992-22-4511). For ferries to Okinawa, bookings can be made with travel agents, but you can also contact the Queen Coral Marikku Line (☎ 0992-25-1551), which has daily ferries to Okinawa via Amami Ō-shima, Tokuno-shima, Okino-Erabu-jima and Yoron-jima. The trip takes around 25 hours and costs ¥11,840 in 2nd class. The Akebono Maru company (☎ 0992-46-4141) does exactly the same routing daily for the same price.

Getting Around
To/From the Airport Buses operate between Nishi-Kagoshima station (bus stop No 7) and the airport every 20 minutes, stopping off at Tenmonkan on the way; the 40 km trip takes a bit less than an hour and costs ¥1100.

Bus City bus tours operate twice daily at 9.05 am and 1.45 pm from the Nishi-Kagoshima station (No 4 bus stop) and cost ¥2200. There is also a comprehensive city bus network, though you won't need it for most of Kagoshima's sights. For information on the one-day unlimited travel pass, see the Tram entry.

Tram As in Nagasaki and Kumamoto, the tram service in Kagoshima is easy to understand, operates frequently and is the best way of getting around town. You can pay by the trip (¥160) or get a one-day unlimited travel pass for ¥500. The pass can also be used on city buses, and can be bought at the Nishi-Kagoshima station tourist information booth.

There are two tram routes. Route 1 starts from Kagoshima station, goes through the centre and on past the suburb of Korimoto to Taniyama. Route 2 follows the same route through the centre, then diverges at Takamibaba to Nishi-Kagoshima station and terminates at Korimoto.

SAKURAJIMA 桜島
Dominating the skyline from Kagoshima is the brooding cone of this decidedly over-active volcano. In fact, Sakurajima is so active that the Japanese differentiate between its mere eruptions (since 1955 there has been an almost continuous stream of smoke and ash) and real explosions, which have occurred in 1914, 1915, 1946, 1955 and 1960. The most violent erruption was in 1914, during which the volcano poured out over three billion tonnes of lava, overwhelming numerous villages and converting Sakurajima from an island to a peninsula. The flow totally filled in the 400 metre wide and 70 metre deep strait which had separated the volcano from the mainland and extended the island further west towards Kagoshima.

Sakurajima actually has three peaks – Kita-dake (1117 metres), Naka-dake (1060 metres) and Minami-dake (1040 metres) – but at present only Minami is active. While some parts of Sakurajima are covered in deep volcanic ash or crumbling lava, other places have exceptionally fertile soil and huge *daikon* (radishes) weighing up to 35 kg are grown. Sakurajima is also known for its tiny oranges, only three cm in diameter, but at ¥500 each even the Japanese find them expensive.

Sakurajima Visitors' Centre
桜島ビジターセンター
The tourist information office near the ferry terminal has a variety of exhibits about the volcano, its eruptions and its natural history. The working model showing the volcano's growth over the years is the centre's main attraction. The centre is open from 9 am to 5 pm daily except Monday and entry is free.

Lookouts 展望台
Although visitors are not permitted to climb the volcano there are several good lookout points. The Yunohira lookout is high on the side of the volcano and offers good views up the forbidding, barren slopes and down across the bay to Kagoshima. The Arimura lava lookout is east of Furusato Onsen; there are walkways across a small corner of the immense lava flow and the lookout points

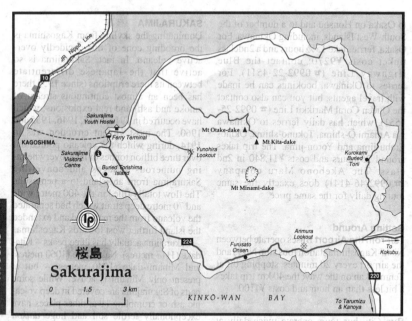

桜島
Sakurajima

0   1.5   3 km

KINKŌ-WAN BAY

offer a glimpse of the immense outpouring that linked the island to the mainland in 1914. The An-ei lava flow lies to the west, the 1914 Taisho lava flow to the east.

Other Attractions

A complete circuit of the volcano is 38 km. Just south of the tourist information office is **'buried Torishima Island'**, where the 1914 Taisho lava flow totally engulfed the small island which had been half a km offshore. On the way down the mountainside the lava swallowed three villages and destroyed over 1000 homes.

Continuing anticlockwise around the island, you come to the monument to writer Hayashi Fumiko, the hot springs at Furusato Onsen and then the **Arimura lava lookout**. At the **Kurokami buried torii**, only the top of a shrine's entrance torii emerges from the volcanic ash – another reminder of the 1914 eruption.

Organised Tours

Three-hour sightseeing bus tours operate several times daily from the ferry terminal and cost ¥1700. JR buses operate from the Sakurajima ferry terminal up to the Arimura lookout for ¥330.

Places to Stay

The *Sakurajima Youth Hostel* (☎ 0992-93-2150) is near the ferry terminal and tourist information office and has beds at ¥1850 or ¥2050, depending on the season. The ferry service is so quick that it's possible to stay here and commute to Kagoshima.

Getting There & Away

The passenger and car ferry service shuttles back and forth between Kagoshima and Sakurajima. The trip takes 15 minutes and costs ¥150 per person, payable at the Sakurajima end. From Kagoshima station or the Sakurajima Sanbashi-dōri tram stop, the ferry terminal is a short walk through the Nameriwaka market area.

Getting Around

Getting around Sakurajima without your own transport can be difficult. You can rent bicycles from near the ferry terminal but a complete circuit of the volcano would be quite a push, even without the climbs to the various lookouts.

Satsuma-hantō Peninsula & Cape Sata-misaki
薩摩半島・佐多岬

The Satsuma-hantō Peninsula, south of Kagoshima, has fine rural scenery, an unusual kamikaze pilots' museum, the hot-spring resort of Ibusuki, the conical peak of Mt Kaimon, and Chiran, with its well-preserved samurai street. On the other side of Kinkō-wan Bay is Cape Sata-misaki, the southernmost point on the main islands of Japan.

GETTING AROUND

Using public transport around the region is time-consuming although it is possible to make a complete loop of the peninsula by train and bus through Kagoshima, Chiran, Ibusuki, Mt Kaimon-dake, Makurazaki, Bōnotsu, Fukiage-hama and back to Kagoshima. The Ibusuki-Makurazaki JR line runs south from Kagoshima to Ibusuki then turns west to Makurazaki. You can continue on from there by bus and eventually make your way back to Kagoshima.

This is, however, a place where renting a car can be useful. Alternatively, there are tour buses which operate from Kagoshima via Chiran to Ibusuki and from Ibusuki back to Kagoshima via Chiran and Tarumizu on the opposite side of the bay. There's a Yamakawa-Nijeme ferry service across the southern end of the bay.

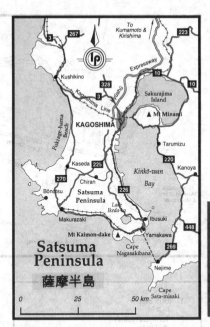

CHIRAN   知覧

South of Kagoshima, Chiran is a worthwhile place to pause en route to Ibusuki. This interesting little town has a well-preserved samurai street with a fine collection of samurai houses and gardens, plus a fascinating memorial and museum to WW II's kamikaze pilots. Chiran was one of the major bases from which the hapless pilots made their suicidal and less than totally successful attacks on Allied shipping.

Samurai Street   武家屋敷街

The seven houses along Chiran's samurai street are noted for their finely preserved gardens, where you'll find all the standard features of formal garden design. Look for the use of 'borrowed scenery', particularly in No 6 (the houses are numbered on the brochure you pick up at the street entry point) where the garden is not so impressive but the 'borrowed' hill is focused wonderfully. Notice how each garden features a 'mountain',

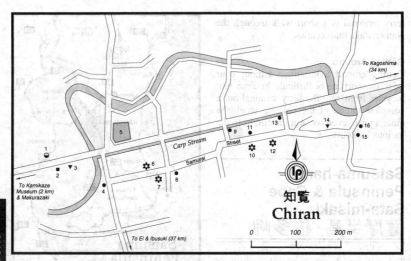

知覧
Chiran

1	Bus Stop バス停
2	Tomiya Ryokan 富屋旅館
3	Noodle Shop ラーメン
4	Ticket Entrance クーポン券取扱所
5	Town Hall 役場
6	Saigō Keiichirō Garden 西郷恵一郎庭園
7	Hirayama Soyo Garden 平山ソヨ
8	Hirayama Ryōichi 平山亮一
9	Ticket Entrance クーポン券取扱所
10	Sata Tamiko Garden 佐多民子庭園
11	Sata Mifune 佐多美舟氏庭園
12	Sata Naotada Garden 佐多直忠氏庭園
13	Ticket Entrance クーポン券取扱所
14	Taki-An Restaurant 多喜庵レストラン
15	Mori Shigemitsu House 森重堅氏庭園
16	Ticket Entrance クーポン券取扱所

backed by a tall hedge and always in the left corner when viewed with the house to your back; this feature is particularly evident in Nos 1, 4 and 5.

Traditionally, the outhouses were placed just inside the front gate, where an occupant could eavesdrop on comments from passersby. House No 3 has a good example of this. The water features are always imitated by sand or gravel except in No 7, the Mori Shigemitsu House, where real water is used. The Mori Shigemitsu House is particularly well preserved and dates from 1741.

Between houses No 3 and No 4/5 is the thatched-roof building of Futatsuya Minke, now used as a souvenir stand. Along the main road, parallel to the samurai street, is a well-stocked carp stream.

Entry to the samurai street houses is ¥310, payable at one of the entry points. The houses and gardens are open from 9 am to 5.30 pm.

Kamikaze Museum　特攻平和会館
A more modern version of the samurai are commemorated in the Tokko Heiwa Kaikan (Kamikaze Museum) at the western end of town. There's a distinctly weird feeling to

this comprehensive collection of aircraft, models, mementoes and photos of the young, fresh-faced pilots who enjoyed the dubious honour of flying in the Special Attack Corps. Unfortunately, there's hardly a word in English, apart from the message that they did it for the dream of 'peace and prosperity'. Crashing your aircraft into a battleship seems a strange way of ensuring peace and prosperity but the bare statistics indicate that, far from achieving the aim of 'a battleship for every aircraft', only minor ships were sunk at the cost of over 1000 aircraft and, of course, their pilots. The museum is open from 9 am to 4.30 pm and entry is ¥310.

Chiran History Museum
The exhibits at the history museum relate mainly to the samurai homes and, but for the absence of English explanations, would probably be a very educational experience. It's open daily from 9 am to 5 pm and entry is ¥205.

Places to Stay & Eat
Most visitors take a day trip to Chiran or stop there en route between Kagoshima and Ibusuki. If you want to stay overnight, the *Tomiya Ryokan* (☎ 0993-83-4313) is on the main street opposite the bus stop, and has rooms from ¥8000. Also opposite the bus stop is a noodle shop which is good for a cheap lunch. *Taki-An* on the samurai street is a rather more traditional place with a nice garden where you can sit on tatami mats to eat a bowl of pleasantly up-market soba noodles at ¥650. The menu is all in Japanese but there are plenty of fellow diners whose meals you can point at.

Getting There & Away
Kagoshima Kōtsū buses to Chiran and Ibusuki run from stop No 10 at the Nishi-Kagoshima station or from the Yamakataya bus terminal at the Yamakataya department store in central Kagoshima. Chiran is 35 km from Kagoshima, the bus takes about one hour 20 minutes and the fare is ¥800.

IBUSUKI 指宿
At the south-western end of the Satsuma-

hantō Peninsula, 50 km from Kagoshima, is the hot-spring resort of Ibusuki, a good base from which to explore other parts of the peninsula. The staff at the JR Ibusuki station information counter are very helpful.

Hot Springs
For onsen connoisseurs, Ibusuki has two renowned hot springs. On the beach in front of the Ginsho Hotel you can pay ¥510 for the somewhat dubious pleasure of being buried up to your neck in hot sand produced by steam rising up through the beach from somewhere in the bowels of the earth.

You pay at the entrance (the fee includes a yukata and towel), change in the changing rooms then wander down to the beach where the burial ladies are waiting, shovel in hand. Those unused to real onsen heat may find the experience too hot to bear and quickly retreat to the baths to wash the sand off. You can take part in this ritual between 8.30 am and 9 pm from April to October and between 8.30 am and 8 pm from November to March.

The other unusual hot spring is the huge Jungle Bath at the Ibusuki Kankō Hotel, which is actually a host of different hot-spring pools surrounded by tropical vegetation. The Jungle Bath costs ¥620 and operates from 6 am to 10 pm.

Other Attractions
The town's modern art gallery is also next to the Kankō Hotel and is open from 8 am to 5.30 pm daily. There are fine views over Ibusuki and along the coast from the 214 metre summit of Mt Uomi-dake.

Places to Stay & Eat
Ibusuki has two hostels. The *Ibusuki Youth Hostel* (☎ 0993-22-2758/2271) is just north of the station and costs ¥1900 or ¥2100, depending on the season. The ryokan-style *Tamaya Youth Hostel* (☎ 0993-22-3553) at 5-27-8 Yunohama is near the sand baths and costs ¥2200 or ¥2300.

Minshuku Marutomi (☎ 0993-22-5579) is a small but popular place, close to the town centre and just a stone's throw from the sand baths. The cost per person, including two

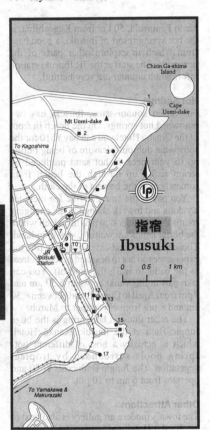

meals, is ¥5500. *Minshuku Sakura-sō*
(☎ 0993-23-3590) is 2½ km from town,
directly below Mt Uomi-dake, and costs
¥7000 per person including two meals. The
owner speaks good English, the rooms are
comfortable, the food is good and there's an
outdoor bath.

On the other side of Uomi-dake is the
Kokumin Kyūka Mura (☎ 0993-22-3211), a
large people's lodge that charges ¥7500 for
rooms with two meals.

More expensive hotels and ryokan include
Ryokan Syūsuien (☎ 0993-23-4141), which
has a restaurant with a very high reputation

and rooms from ¥24,000 to ¥100,000, and
the *Ginsho Hotel*, which charges ¥13,000
upwards with two meals. Although many
visitors eat at the ryokan's restaurant,
Ibusuki has many other restaurants to choose
from, especially around the JR station. There
is also a good supermarket on the road
leading straight out from the station.

Getting There & Away
Ibusuki is about 1½ hours from Kagoshima
by bus; see the Chiran section for details.
Trains operate from Nishi-Kagoshima

station on the Makurazaki line. They take one hour 15 minutes and cost ¥800.

OTHER SATSUMA-HANTŌ PENINSULA ATTRACTIONS

Lake **Ikeda-ko**, west of Ibusuki, is a beautiful volcanic caldera lake inhabited by giant eels weighing up to 15 kg. Heading west along the coast you come to **Cape Nagasakibana** from where the offshore islands, including the smoking cone of Iwo-jima, can be seen on a clear day. **Mt Kaimon-dake**'s beautifully symmetrical 922 metre cone can be climbed in about two hours from the Kaimondake bus stop.

At the south-western end of the peninsula is **Makurazaki**, a busy fishing port and the terminus of the railway line from Kagoshima. Just beyond Mazurazaki is **Bōnotsu**, a pretty little fishing village which was an unofficial trading link with the outside world via Okinawa during Japan's two centuries of seclusion. North of Bōnotsu is **Fukiage-hama**, where the long beach is used for an annual summer sand castle construction competition. The *Fukiage-hama Youth Hostel* (☎ 0992-92-3455) costs ¥1900 or ¥2100, depending on the season.

CAPE SATA-MISAKI   佐多岬

The southernmost point on the main islands of Japan is marked by the oldest lighthouse in Japan. You can reach Cape Sata-misaki from the Kagoshima side of Kinkō-wan Bay either by going around the northern end of the bay, taking the ferry from Kagoshima to Sakurajima or by taking the ferry from Yamakawa, south of Ibusuki, to Nejime, near Cape Sata-misaki. An eight km bicycle track leads down to the end of the cape.

Miyazaki-ken   宮崎県

OBI   飫肥

Only five km from the coast, the pretty little castle town of Obi has some interesting buildings around its old castle site. From 1587, the wealthy Ito clan ruled from the

castle for 14 generations, surviving the 'one kingdom one castle' ruling in 1615. The clan eventually moved out in 1869 when the Meiji Restoration ended the feudal period.

Obi Castle   飫肥城

Although only the walls of the actual castle remain, the grounds contain a number of interesting buildings. The ¥300 entry fee includes all these buildings and Yoshokan House just outside the castle entrance. Opening hours are from 9.30 am to 5 pm.

Yoshokan House When the Obi lord was forced to abandon his castle after the Meiji Restoration, he moved down the hill to the Yoshokan, formerly the residence of the clan's chief retainer. It stands just outside the castle entrance and has a large garden incorporating Mt Atago as 'borrowed scenery'. Beyond this house you enter the castle proper through the impressive Ote-mon Gate.

Obi Castle Museum The castle museum has a collection relating to the Ito clan's long rule over Obi and includes everything from weapons and armour to clothing and household equipment.

Matsuo-no-Maru House Matsuo-no-Maru, the lord's private residence, has been reconstructed and there's an excellent descriptive leaflet of this quite extensive house. There's even a room with a window specifically placed for comfortable viewing of the autumn moon. When the lord visited the toilet at the far end of the house, he was accompanied by three pages – one to lead the way, one to carry water for the lord to wash his hands and one to fan him during the summer months! Look for the English sign on the toilet itself which requests 'no urinating!', the absence of a Japanese equivalent implying that gaijin are capable of atrocities that no well brought up Japanese would even consider.

Merchant's Museum   商家資料館
In the Honmachi area of the town, tradition-

KYŪSHŪ

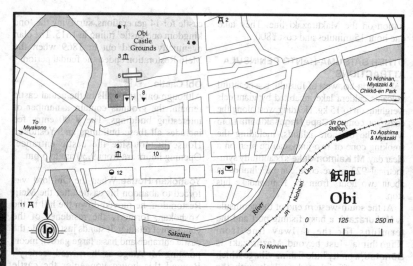

Obi

1	Matsuo-no-Maru House 松尾の丸
2	Tanoue Hachiman-jinja Shrine 田上八幡神社
3	Obi Castle Museum 資料館
4	Shintokudo School 振徳堂
5	Ote-mon Gate 大手門
6	Yoshokan House 豫章館
7	Ōtemon Chaya Restaurant 大手門茶屋
8	Obi-ten Restaurant オビテン　レストラン
9	Merchant's Museum 商家資料館
10	Carp Stream 鯉遊泳
11	Ioshi-jinja Shrine いおし神社
12	Bus Station バスターミナル
13	Post Office 郵便局

ally the merchants' quarters, there's a carp stream alongside a section of one street (see map). When the main road through Obi was widened in 1980, many of the town's old merchant houses were demolished but one fine building, dating from 1866, has been rebuilt as a merchant's museum which gives an excellent idea of what a shop of that era would have been like. It's open from 9.30 am to 5 pm and entry is ¥100.

Other Attractions
The **Shintōkudo**, adjacent to the castle, was established as a samurai school in 1801. Up the hill behind the Shintōkudo is the **Tanoue Hachiman-jinja Shrine**, shrouded by trees and reached by a steep flight of steps. On the western side of the river, the **Ioshi-jinja Shrine** has a pleasant garden and the Ito family mausoleum. The **Chikkō-en Park** is on the eastern side of town, near the railway station.

Places to Eat
The entranceway to the castle is flanked by the *Obi-ten Restaurant* to the right, with up-market Japanese cooking featuring mountain vegetables, and the *Ōtemon Chaya* to the left, a friendly and unassuming noodle shop. Featured on the menu of the latter are *tsukimi soba* (literally 'moon-viewing soba') and curry udon. If neither of the latter appeal

to you, resort to the plastic replicas just inside the entrance.

Getting There & Away
The JR Nichinan line runs through Obi and Aoshima to Miyazaki. Miyazaki to Obi costs ¥800 and takes around an hour. Route 222 from Miyakono to Obi and Nichinan on the coast is a superb mountain road, twisting and winding as it climbs over the hills.

CAPE TOI-MISAKI & NICHINAN-KAIGAN COAST
都井岬・日南海岸
Like Cape Sata, the views over the ocean from Cape Toi-misaki are superb. The cape is also famed for its herds of wild horses although the word 'wild' has to be treated with some suspicion in Japan! There's a good beach at Ishinami-kaigan where, during the summer only, you can stay in old farmhouse minshuku. The tiny island of Kō-jima, just off the coast, has a group of monkeys which were the focus for some interesting anthropological discoveries. Further north, the beautiful 50 km stretch of coast from Nichinan to Miyazaki offers stunning views, pretty little coves, interesting stretches of 'washboard' rocks and, at holiday times, heavy traffic.

Udo-jingū Shrine   鵜戸神宮
The coastal shrine of Udo-jingū is brightly painted in orange and has a wonderful setting. If you continue through the shrine to the end of the path, you'll find yourself in an open cavern overlooking some weird rock formations at the ocean's edge. A popular sport is to buy five round clay pebbles for ¥100 and try to get them into a shallow depression on top of one of the rocks. Succeeding at this task is supposed to make your wish come true. Generally wishes are concerned with marriage and childbirth because, as a Japanese pamphlet explains, 'Udo is the god of marriage and easy childbirth'; the god is probably not too good at granting less domestic wishes. Buses bound for Nichinan from the Miyazaki Kōtsu bus station take

around one hour 10 minutes to get the shrine and cost ¥1240.

Aoshima   青島
This popular beach resort, about 10 km south of Miyazaki, is a real tourist trap famed for the small island covered in betel palms, fringed by 'washboard' rock formations and connected to the mainland by a causeway. Due to the prevailing warm currents, the only place you'll find warmer water in Japan is much further south in the Okinawa Islands.

The island itself has the attractive **Aoshima-jinj Shrine**. Other attractions include the **Tropical Botanical Garden** and **Children's World** (¥600). Aoshima is on the Nichinan railway line, and can be reached from Miyazaki in around 30 minutes. The island shrine is connected to the mainland by a bridge and is only around five minutes walk from Aoshima station.

Places to Stay The *Aoshima Youth Hostel* (☎ 0985-65-1657) is near the railway tracks and costs ¥1900 or ¥2200, depending on the season. The *Aoshima Kokuminshukusha* (☎ 0985-65-1533) has Japanese-style rooms starting from ¥6000 with two meals. Aoshima also has a wide variety of hotels, most of them aimed at Japanese tourists with lots of money to throw around.

Getting There & Away Aoshima is on the JR Nichinan-Miyazaki line and less than half an hour away from JR Miyazaki station by train.

MIYAZAKI   宮崎
Miyazaki (population 290,000) is a reasonably large city with an important shrine and a pleasant park. Due to the warm offshore currents, the town has a balmy climate. The area around Miyazaki played an important part in early Japanese civilisation and some interesting excavations can be seen in Saitobaru, 27 km north.

Orientation & Information
JR Miyazaki station is immediately to the east of the town centre and the restaurant and

KYŪSHŪ

Miyazaki
宮崎

0   0.5   1 km

Heiwadai-kōen Park
Haniwa Garden
To Saito & Nobeoka
Prefectural Museum
Miyazaki-jingū Shrine
Miyazaki-jingū Station
See Miyazaki Station Area Map
JR Miyazaki Station
Oyodo-gawa River
Miya-ko City
Bus Station
Minami-Miyazaki Station
To Aoshima & Nichinan
To Airport

KYŪSHŪ

entertainment area. Most hotels and the youth hostel are reasonably close to the station and even the more expensive hotels (mainly along the riverside) are still quite close to the station area. The main bus station is south of the Oyodo-gawa River while the town's two principal attractions – the Miyazaki-jingū Shrine and the Heiwadai-kōen Park – are several km north.

There's a tourist information office in JR Miyazaki station that can help with finding accommodation and one in the prefectural office where you will also find a display of local products. The prefectural tourist office

is just off Tachibana-dōri, the main street through town.

Miyazaki-jingū Shrine & Museum
宮崎神宮・宮崎県総合博物館
The Miyazaki Shrine is dedicated to the Emperor Jimmu, the semimythical first emperor of Japan and founder of the Yamoto court. At the northern end of the shrine grounds is the Miyazaki Prefectural Museum with displays relating to local history and archaeological finds. Entry to the museum is ¥155 and it's open from 9 am to 4.30 pm daily except Monday. Also worth a look is the Minka-en, with its collection of traditional-style kyūshū homes. It's also closed on Monday.

The shrine is about 2½ km north of JR Miyazaki station or a 15 minute walk from the Miyazaki-jingū station, one stop north. From the station, the shrine is easy to find. Just look out for the big torii gate. Bus No 1 also runs to the shrine.

Heiwadai-kōen Park 平和台公園
The *heiwa* or 'peace' park has as its centrepiece a 36 metre high tower constructed in 1940, a time when peace in Japan was about to disappear. Standing in front of the tower and clapping your hands produces a strange echo.

The Haniwa Garden in the park is dotted with reproductions of the curious clay *haniwa* figures which have been excavated from burial mounds in the region. You can buy small and large examples of these often rather amusing figures from a shop in the Haniwa Garden or from the park's main shopping complex. Small figures cost as little as ¥800 but the large ones are in the ¥10,000 to ¥20,000 bracket.

The Haniwa Garden is about 1½ km north of the Miyazaki Shrine but the museum, in the northern corner of the shrine grounds, is only a couple of minutes walk from the southern corner of the park. Bus No 8 runs to the park from outside JR Miyazaki station.

Festivals
On 3 April there is a samurai horse riding event at Miyazaki-jingū Shrine. Mid-April's

Furusato festival has around 10,000 participants in traditional attire dancing to local folksongs; you can see it on Tachibana-dōri. A similar event takes place in late July, with mikoshi (portable shrines) being carried through the streets. In late July, Miyazaki is host to Kyūshū's largest fireworks show. Most locals seem to rate the major event of the year as the Dunlop Phoenix Golf Tournament, which is held in mid-November and attracts golfers from all over the world.

Places to Stay

The *Fujin Kaikan Youth Hostel* (☎ 0985-24-5785) is within walking distance of Miyazaki station and costs ¥2300. There are only 23 beds in the hostel, so it would be wise to book ahead.

Apart from youth hostel accommodation, the cheapest accommodation around is in the *Business Hotel Family* (☎ 0985-27-991, which has singles from ¥3500. Another reasonably inexpensive alternative is the *Shinshū Ryokan* (☎ 0982-24-4008), just across the road from the station, a few doors down on the right in the arcade. There's no English sign, but you can't miss it. Rooms without meals are ¥4500.

A cheap option for the fairly desperate can be provided by the tourist information office in Miyazaki station. They have discount tickets for *Supāru 21 Kenkō Rando* (in English 'Spa 21 Health Land') (☎ 0985-47-2100), where you can spend the night on a designer lounge for ¥2100. It's a bit of a hike out of town, but the information office will give you the lowdown on how to find the place.

Across the road from the station, the *Miyazaki Oriental Hotel* (☎ 0985-27-3111) is a straightforward business hotel with singles from ¥5500 to ¥8700 and doubles and twins at ¥9500.

Hotel Bigman (☎ 0985-27-2111) (what a great name!) is further west along the road from the youth hostel. It has singles/doubles from ¥5400/9400. When it comes to good names, the proprietors didn't stop at the hotel title; the Bigman also has the *Realips Coffee Bar*! Just around the corner from the Bigman

is the *Business Hotel Tachibana* (☎ 0985-27-6868), another low-cost business hotel with singles at ¥5100 and doubles and twins from ¥8400 to ¥9400.

Most of the more expensive hotels are clustered along the riverside between the Tachibana Bridge and the Oyodo-ōhashi Bridge. The *Miyazaki Plaza Hotel* (☎ 0985-27-1111/2727) has doubles/twins from ¥13,500/14,000. Next to it is the *Miyazaki Kankō Hotel* (☎ 0985-27-1212) with singles at ¥10,000 and doubles and twins from ¥11,000 to ¥120,000. Other riverside hotels include the *Kandabashi Hotel* (☎ 0985-25-5511), an expensive place with doubles and twins from ¥16,000. One place outside the riverside hotel strip is the *Miyazaki Washington Hotel* (☎ 0985-28-9111) which is in the town centre and entertainment area and has singles/twins from ¥7500/12500.

Places to Eat

In the station area, the best place is in the arcade, where there are dozens of rāmen shops with plastic displays outside. There are also a few fast-food options, like *Italian Tomato* and *Mister Donut*, dotted around, but by no means as many as you might expect of such a large town. Head right up the arcade and into the entertainment area for the best range of restaurants.

Suginoko (☎ 0985-22-5798) specialises in Miyazaki cuisine with its emphasis on locally grown vegetables. Although the menu is in Japanese only, there is a brief description in English posted downstairs and simply asking for the teishoku (the set meal of the day) will get you something interesting. A lunch-time 'hanashobu course' (mainly tempura) is ¥1500, a 'hamayu course' (mainly sushi) is ¥2500. At night the set meals cost from ¥3800 to ¥6000. In the heart of the entertainment district, look out for *Meiji-ya*, a lively robatayaki with a locomotive exterior. You'll hear it as you come down the street; speakers outside the restaurant blast out the puffing and whistling sounds of a labouring little steam train.

The Hotel Oriental has good quality Chinese restaurant on its ground floor. It

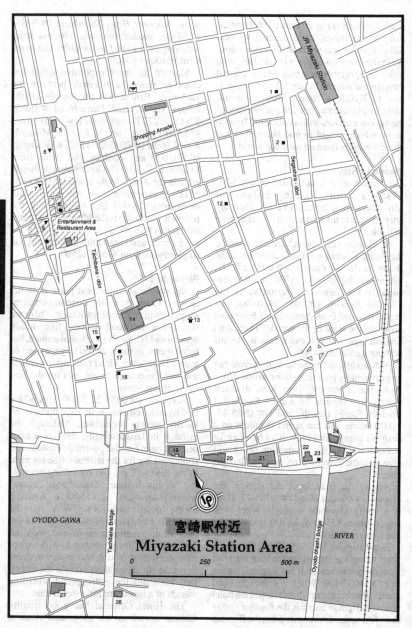

OYODO-GAWA

Tachibana Bridge

Oyodo-obashi Bridge

RIVER

宮崎駅付近
Miyazaki Station Area

0   250   500 m

JR Miyazaki Station

Segashira-dōri

Shopping Arcade

Entertainment &
Restaurant Area

Tachibana - dōri

PLACES TO STAY		21	Miyazaki Kankō Hotel 宮崎観光ホテル	9	Meijiya Restaurant 明治屋
1	Shinshū Ryokan 新洲旅館	22	Ronkotei Hotel ホテル臨江亭	15	Mos Burgers モスバーガー
2	Miyazaki Oriental Hotel 宮崎オリエンタルホテル	23	KKR Hotel ＫＫＲホテル	16	Suginoko Restaurant 杉の子
11	Miyazaki Washington Hotel 宮崎ワシントンホテル	24	Miyazaki Grand Hotel 宮崎グランドホテル	**OTHER**	
12	Business Hotel Family ビジネスホテルファミリー	25	Phoenix Hotel ホテルフェニックス	3	NTT
13	Fujin Kaikan Youth Hostel 婦人会館ユースホステル	26	Kōnan-sō Hotel ホテル江南荘	4	Main Post Office 中央郵便局
17	Hotel Bigman ホテルビッグマン	27	Sun Route Hotel サンルートホテル	5	ANA/JAS
18	Business Hotel Tachibana ビジネスホテル橘	**PLACES TO EAT**		8	Loose Bar ルース
19	Kandabashi Hotel ホテル神田橋	6	Italian Tomato Restaurant イタリアントマト	10	Suntory Shot Bar/ Time (bar)
20	Miyazaki Plaza Hotel 宮崎プラザホテル	7	Mr Donut ミスタードーナツ	14	Prefectural Office 宮崎県庁

even serves dim sum, which is fairly rare in this part of the world. The riverside *Phoenix Hotel* has a rooftop beer garden with good views over the city. The Miyazaki station is known for its *shiitake ekiben*, a boxed lunch featuring a mushroom dish.

Entertainment

Locals claim that Miyazaki has some 3500 bars and, after taking a stroll through the entertainment area, you won't find this too difficult to believe; it's packed with boozing establishments from basement level upwards. For a quiet, inexpensive beer head over to the *Suntory Shot Bar*, where a draught beer costs ¥380. *Time*, next door and upstairs, looks promising and is actually quite pleasant, with its laid-back music played to a background of swishing waves and hawking seabirds, but it's pretty expensive.

Places popular with local expats (and there's a surprisingly large number of them) include *Loose*, just around the corner from the Suntory Shot Bar, and *Studio 505*. You really need to be in these places on a Friday or Saturday night if you want to meet people though. Studio 505 is about 50 metres on the

right-hand side after the arcade ends; it's on the 5th floor. It has a ¥2500 cover charge that includes four drinks.

Getting There & Away

Air Miyazaki is connected with Tokyo (¥27,550), Osaka (¥16,300), Okinawa (¥22,850) and other centres by air.

Train The JR Nippō line runs from Kokura (5½ hours, ¥5360) in the north through Miyazaki to Kagoshima (2½ hours, ¥2160) in the west. If you're coming from Kagoshima, you may have to change trains in Kokubo. There are also train connections to Kumamoto (4½ hours, ¥5460), Fukuoka (Hakata) (5½ hours, ¥8860) and south through Obi to Nichinan.

Bus The Miyazaki Kōtsu city bus station is south of the Oyodo-gawa River near JR Minami-Miyazaki station, and this is where most buses originate. There is also a second bus station opposite the Miyazaki railway station that has buses to Saitobaru. Take a bus No 10 down the coast to Aoshima and Nichinan or a Cape Toi Express for Cape Toi-misaki. Buses also go from here to

Ebino-kōgen in the Kirishima National Park, taking about two hours 15 minutes, to Fukuoka, Kagoshima and other centres. You can connect with many of the bus services along Tachibana-dōri, but figuring out just which stop you're meant to be standing at is not that easy, and if you don't read Japanese you'll probably save yourself some frustration by heading down to the south bus station.

It is also possible to get long-distance buses from the Miyazaki bus station to Kagoshima (2½ hours, ¥2700), Fukuoka (five hours, ¥6000) and to Osaka (12½ hours, ¥11,500). Osaka buses run only once a day and do the trip by night.

Boat There are ferry services linking Miyazaki with Osaka, Kōbe and Kawasaki. To Osaka, it takes around 16½ hours and 2nd-class tickets cost ¥8230. To Kōbe, it takes 14 hours and 2nd-class tickets cost ¥7260. To Kawasaki, it takes 20 hours and 2nd-class tickets cost ¥17,710. For reservations in Miyazaki, contact Seacom (☎ 0985-29-8311). Seacom can also be reached in Osaka (☎ 06-311-1533) and in Kawasaki (☎ 044-266-3281).

Getting Around
To/From the Airport Miyazaki's airport is conveniently situated only about 20 minutes by bus from JR Miyazaki station. Buses run every 20 minutes from the Miyazaki Kōtsu bus station opposite the main railway station and head to the airport via the south bus station.

Bus Although bus services start and finish at the Miya-kō city bus station near JR Minami-Miyazaki station, many of them run along Tachibana-dōri in the centre, including No 1 to the Miyazaki-jingō Shrine and No 8 to Heiwadai-kōen Park. Miyazaki-Eigyosho, the other bus terminal, is near JR Miyazaki station.

Tours from the Miya-kō city bus station are operated by the Miyazaki Kōtsū Bus Company and cover not only the sights in town but sights along the coast to Aoshima and the Udo-jingō Shrine. The all-day tours cost about ¥5000.

SEAGAIA

By the time you have this book in your hands, the Seagaia Ocean Dome will have opened. Whether you're interested in paying the place a visit will depend a lot on how you feel about hi-tech theme parks. The theme in this case is water and, if the promotional material is anything to go by, you'll spend most of the time being squirted with it, dumped in it and floating around in it. Hyped as a 'paradise within a paradise', the sponsors had best come up with the goods or many people will be put off by the ¥4200 entry charge. Buses will run from JR Miyazaki station out to the dome.

SAITOBARU 西都原

If the haniwa pottery figures in Miyazaki piqued your interest in the region's archaeology, then head north 27 km to the **Saitobaru Burial Mounds Park**, where several sq km of fields and forest are dotted with over 300 burial mounds (kofun). The 4th to 7th century AD mounds range from insignificant little bumps to hillocks large enough to appear natural creations. They also vary in shape, some being circular, some square, others a curious keyhole shape. Many are numbered with small signs, though any information is in Japanese. There's an interesting small museum with displays about the burial mounds and the finds that have been made, including swords, armour, jewellery, haniwa pottery figures and much more. Another exhibit shows items from the 18th century Edo period.

Entry to the museum is ¥155 and it is open from 9 am to 4.30 pm daily except Monday. The park area is always open. Buses run to Saitobaru from the Miyazaki Kōtsu bus station next to Miyazaki railway station, and the one hour trip costs ¥950. If you want to explore the mound-dotted countryside you're either going to need your own transport or plan to walk a lot. Saitobaru is just outside the town of Saito.

西都原古墳群

Saitobaru
Burial Mounds

0   250   500 m

TAKACHIHO 高千穂
The mountain resort town of Takachiho is about midway between Nobeoka on the coast and Mt Aso in the centre of Kyūshū. It's famed for its beautiful gorge and for a number of interesting shrines. There's a helpful tourist information counter by the tiny railway station.

Takachiho-kyō Gorge 高千穂峡
Takachiho's beautiful gorge, with its waterfalls, overhanging rocks and sheer walls, is the town's major attraction. There's a one km walk alongside the gorge, or you can inspect it from below in a rowboat, rented for a pricey ¥1000 for 40 minutes. The gorge is about two km from the centre, a ¥700 ride by taxi. Buses run to the gorge for ¥210, but they are not frequent.

Takachiho-jinja Shrine 高千穂神社
The Takachiho-jinja shrine, about a km from JR Takachiho station, is surrounded by won-

derful tall trees. The local Iwato Kagura dances are performed from 8 to 9 pm each evening, and entry is ¥300.

Amano Iwato-jinja Shrine 天岩戸神社
The Iwato-gawa River splits the Amano Iwato-jinja Shrine into two parts. The main shrine, Nishi Hongu, is on the west bank of the river; while on the east bank is Higashi Hongu, at the actual cave where the sun goddess hid and was lured out by the first performance of the Iwato Kagura dance. From the main shrine it's a 15 minute walk to the cave. The shrine is eight km from Takachiho. Buses leave every 45 minutes from the bus station and cost ¥340 while a taxi would cost around ¥1500.

Amano Yasugawara Cave 天安河原洞
A beautiful short walk from the Amano Iwato-jinja Shrine alongside a picture-postcard stretch of stream takes you to the Amano Yasugawara cave. There, it is said, the gods conferred on how they could persuade the sun goddess to leave her hiding place and thus bring light back to the world. Visitors pile stones into small cairns all around the cave entrance.

Takachiho Legends
Ninigi-no-mikoto, a descendant of the sun goddess Amaterasu, is said to have made landfall in Japan on top of Mt Takachiho in southern Kyūshū. Or at least that's what's said in most of Japan; in Takachiho the residents insist that it was in their town that the sun goddess' grandson arrived, not on top of the mountain of the same name.

They also lay claim to the sites for a few other important mythological events, including Ama-no-Iwato, the 'boulder door of heaven'. Here Amaterasu hid and night fell across the world. To lure her out another goddess performed a dance so comically lewd that the sun goddess was soon forced to emerge from hiding to find out what was happening. That dance, the Iwato Kagura, is still performed in Takachiho today. ■

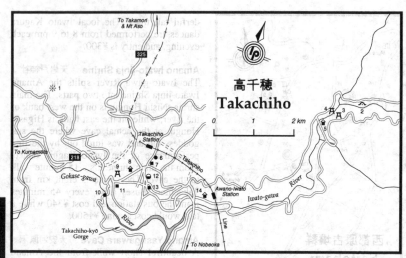

高千穂
Takachiho

0   1   2 km

PLACES TO STAY

5 Iwato Furusato Youth Hostel
   岩戸ふるさとユースホステル
7 Business Hotel Kanaya
   かなやホテル
8 Yamatoya Ryokan & Youth Hostel
   旅館大和屋ユースホステル
11 Kokuminshukusha Takachiho-sō
   国民宿舎高千穂荘
13 Folkcraft Ryokan Kaminoya
   民芸旅館上ノ屋
14 Takachiho Youth Hostel
   高千穂ユースホステル

OTHER

1 Kunimigaoka Lookout
   国見が丘
2 Amano Yasugawara Cave
   天安川原
3 Amano Iwato-jinja
   Shrine - Higashi Hongu
   天岩戸神社東本宮
4 Amano Iwato-jinja
   Shrine - Nishi Hongu
   天岩戸神社西本宮
6 City Hall
   市役所
9 Takachiho-jinja Shrine
   高千穂神社
10 Takachiho-kyō Gorge Bridge
   高千穂大橋
12 Bus Station
   バスターミナル

Kunimigaoka Lookout 国見ヶ丘

From the 'land surveying bluff' overlooking Takachiho, the gods are said to have gazed across the countryside. Today tourists can drive up there to admire the superb view.

Festivals

Important Iwato Kagura festivals are held on 3 May, 23 September and 3 November at the Amano Iwato-jinja Shrine. There are also all-night performances in farmhouses from the end of November to early February and a visit can be arranged by inquiring at the shrine. A short dance performance takes place every night at the Takachiho-jinja Shrine.

Places to Stay

Takachiho has plenty of places to stay: the list at JR Takachiho station information counter includes more than 20 hotels, ryokan and pensions and another 20 minshuku. Despite this plethora of accommodation, every place in town can be booked out at peak holiday periods.

There are three youth hostels in the area, each costing ¥2300 a night. Right in the town centre, the *Yamatoya Ryokan & Youth Hostel*

(☎ 0982-72-2243/3808) is immediately recognisable by the huge figure painted on the front. The *Takachiho Youth Hostel* (☎ 0982-2-5152) is a couple of km from the centre, near the JR Amano-Iwato station. The *Iwato Furusato Youth Hostel* (☎ 0982-74-8254/8750) is near the Amano Iwato-jinja Shrine. Nightly costs at all three are ¥2300.

The *Folkcraft Ryokan Kaminoya* (☎ 0982-72-2111) is a member of the Japanese Inn Group and just down from the bus station, right in the centre of Takachiho. The friendly owner speaks good English and rooms range from ¥4000 or ¥6500 with two meals; rates are cheaper without the meals.

The *Business Hotel Kanaya* (☎ 0982-72-3261), on the corner of the station road and the main road through town, has singles from ¥4500. The ryokan part of the *Yamatoya Ryokan & Youth Hostel* costs from ¥9500 to ¥14,000, including meals. The *Iwato Furusato Youth Hostel* also has a ryokan section, which costs from ¥6000.

The minshuku all cost from ¥5000 a night – bookings can be made at the JR station information counter. A reliable one is the *Kokuminshukusha Takachiho-sō* (☎ 0982-72-3255), where rooms with two meals are ¥5000.

Places to Eat

Many people will eat in their ryokan or minshuku but Takachiho has plenty of restaurants with plastic meal displays as well as other, up-market restaurants. If you need a meal you could definitely do worse than *Kencha's*, a cheerful little yakitori (grill restaurant specialising in chicken dishes) marked by a bamboo frontage, banners, flags, signs, lanterns and a cavepeople cartoon across the top. It's opposite the Folkcraft Ryokan, near the bus station.

Getting There & Away

The JR Takachiho line runs inland from Nobeoka on the coast, taking just over 1½ hours and costing ¥1300. Alternatively, there are bus services to Takachiho: buses take about three hours 15 minutes from Kumamoto, 3½ hours from Fukuoka (¥3910), 1½ hours

from Nobeoka (¥1650) or less than an hour from Takamori near Mt Aso.

Getting Around

Although you can walk to the gorge and the Takachiho-jinja Shrine, the other sites are some distance from town and public transport is a problem. Regular tours leave from the bus station: the 'A Course' (¥1100) covers everything, while the 'B Course' (¥750) misses the Amano Iwato-jinja Shrine.

Ōita-ken　　大分県

The Ōita Prefecture offers an insight into the Japanese onsen (hot-spring) mania at both its best (Yufuin) and worst (Beppu). The region also bears traces of Japan's earliest civilisations, particularly on the Kunisaki Peninsula and around Usuki.

BEPPU　別府

Beppu (population 140,000) is the Las Vegas of spa resort towns, a place where bad taste is almost a requisite. Many Kyūshū travellers gravitate to Beppu and most come away disappointed. Beppu is not only onsen fever at its worst, it's also Japanese tourism at its most kitsch. If you're trying to develop an appreciation and understanding of the Japanese onsen mania for onsen, you are not going to find it here. Beppu can be fun – just don't take it seriously.

Information

The JR Beppu station concourse has a tourist information counter with maps and other information, but Beppu also has a Foreign Tourist Information Office (☎ 0977-23-1119) a few blocks from the station on the 3rd floor of the Kitahama Centre building. The office has information sheets, maps and other useful material in English and usually has helpful personnel on hand who can speak English.

The JR Beppu station area is very convenient for visitors: facilities include a choice of accommodation, restaurants, banks, travel

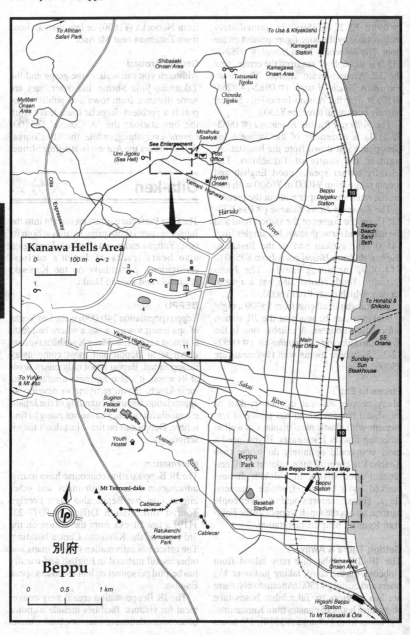

To African
Safari Park

To Usa & Kitakyūshū

Kamegawa
Station

Shibaseki
Onsen Area

Tatsumaki
Jigoku

Kamegawa
Onsen Area

Myōban
Onsen
Area

Takachiho-jinja Shrine

Chinoike
Jigoku

Minshuku
Saekya

Umi Jigoku
(Sea Hell)

See Enlargement

Post
Office

Hyotan
Onsen

Yamani Highway

Beppu
Daigaku
Station

Haruki

River

Expressway

Ōita

Beppu
Beach
Sand
Bath

10

Kanawa Hells Area

0   100 m

1

3

8

5

6   9   10

4

7

Yamani Highway

11

To Honshū &
Shikoku

SS
Oriana

Main
Post Office

Sunday's
Sun
Steakhouse

To Yufuin
& Mt Aso

Sakai

River

10

Suginoi
Palace
Hotel

Youth
Hostel

Asami

River

Beppu
Park

See Beppu Station Area Map

Beppu
Station

Baseball
Stadium

別府
Beppu

Mt Tsurumi-dake

Cablecar

Ratukenchi
Amusement
Park

Cablecar

Hamawaki
Onsen Area

0   0.5   1 km

Higashi Beppu
Station

To Mt Takasaki & Ōita

1	Yama Jigoku (Mountain Hell) 山地獄
2	Kamado Jigoku (Oven Hell) かまど地獄
3	Oniyama Jigoku (Devils' Mountain Hell) 鬼山地獄
4	Shiraike Jigoku (White Pond Hell) 白池地獄
5	Kinryū Jigoku (Golden Dragon Hell) 金龍地獄
6	Hotel Ashiya ホテルあしや
7	Hinokan Sex Museum 秘宝館
8	Rakurakuen Ryokan 楽々園旅館
9	Kamenoi Bus Terminal (Buses to Chinoike Jigoku) 亀の井バスターミナル（至血の池地獄）
10	Kamenoi Bus Terminal (Buses to Beppu Station) 亀の井バスターミナル（至別府駅）
11	Oishi Hotel 大石ホテル

agencies and, of course, the railway station and other transport facilities. Beppu is, however, a sprawling town and the hot-spring areas are spread out, often some distance from the town centre. The adjacent town of Ōita is virtually contiguous with Beppu, and although it lacks any notable attractions, it could be an alternative place to stay.

Hot Springs

Beppu has two sorts of hot springs and there are lots of statistics about the more than 100 million litres of hot water they pump out every day. The jigoku are hot springs for looking at. The onsen are hot springs for bathing in.

The Hells Beppu's most hyped attraction is the 'hells' or jigoku, a collection of hot springs where the water bubbles forth from underground, often with unusual results. Admission to each hell is ¥300, or you can get a booklet of tickets for ¥1500 which covers all except one hell. The only real reason to visit all of them would be if you had a passion to see Japanese tourism at its absolute worst – car parks overflowing with

tour buses, enthusiastic flag-waving visitors, souvenir stands, the full panopoly of delights. If this doesn't interest you, save your money: Rotorua in New Zealand has equally interesting and much less spoilt thermal activity. Jigoku tour buses depart regularly from the JR Beppu station bus stop and cost ¥2700.

The hells are in two groups: seven at Kannawa, about eight km north-west of the station, and two more several km away. In the Kannawa group, the Umi Jigoku (Sea Hell), with its large expanse of gently steaming blue water, and the Shiraike Jigoku (White Pond Hell) are quite pleasant. Kinryū Jigoku (Golden Dragon Hell) and Kamado Jigoku (Oven Hell) have a dragon figure and a demon figure overlooking the pond...big deal. Skip the Oniyama Jigoku (Devil's Mountain Hell) where crocodiles are kept in miserable concrete pens, and the Yama Jigoku (Mountain Hell), where a variety of animals are kept under miserable conditions.

The smaller group has the Chinoike Jigoku (Blood Pool Hell) with its photogenically red water, and the Tatsumaki Jigoku (Waterspout Hell), where a geyser performs regularly. The former is worth a visit, but the latter can be skipped (there's too much concrete and too little natural beauty). The final hell, and the one not included in the group admission ticket, is the Hon Bōzu Jigoku (Monk's Hell). It has a collection of hiccupping and belching hot mud pools and is up the long hill from the main group of hells.

From the bus stop at JR Beppu station, bus Nos 16, 17, 41 and 43 go to the main group of hells at Kannawa. There are half a dozen buses an hour but the round trip costs virtually the same as an unlimited travel day pass. The No 26 bus continues to the smaller Chinoike/Tatsumaki group and returns to the station in a loop.

Onsen Ostensibly, it's sitting back and relaxing in the warm spring water that's Beppu's main attraction (though who can tell how many visitors are also drawn by the hype), and scattered around the town are eight onsen areas. Onsen enthusiasts will spend their time in Beppu moving from one bath to another. Costs range from ¥200 to ¥600, although some are cheaper and others more expensive. Bring your own soap and towel.

The Beppu onsen area is in the town centre area near JR Beppu station. Among the popular onsen is the Takegawara Onsen (¥600), which dates from the Meiji era and includes a sand bath. Here, the heat from the spring rises up through the sand and patrons lie down in a shallow trench and are buried up to their necks in the super-heated sand.

In the south-western part of town, near the road to Oita, is the Hamawaki onsen area with the popular old Hamawaki Koto Bath. North of the town, the Kannawa onsen area (near the major group of hells) is one of the most popular onsen areas in Beppu. There are also many ryokan and minshuku in this area.

The quieter Shibaseki onsen area is near the smaller group of hells, close to a mountain stream. Also north of JR Beppu station, near Kamegawa station, is the Kamegawa onsen area where the Hamada Bath is particularly popular. The Beppu Municipal Beach Sand Bath (¥600) is two km south of the Kamegawa onsen area. In the hills north-west of the town centre is the Myōban onsen area.

Suginoi Palace Any tour of Beppu's onsen eventually has to make its way to the Suginoi Palace. On a hill overlooking Beppu, very close to the youth hostel, is the large, deluxe Suginoi Hotel, a favourite of tour groups. The adjacent Suginoi Palace has games, night-time entertainment, a museum, swimming pool, bowling hall and two huge fantasyland baths, one for males and one for females, which are switched each day so patrons can try both over a two day period.

Bus Nos 4 and 14 go to the Suginoi Palace. Bus No 4 leaves from the western exit of Beppu railway station and continues to Kannawa. The palace is open from 8 am to 11.30 pm and costs ¥1800 entry.

Hinokan Sex Museum　秘宝館

All that lolling around in hot water must have some sort of sensual side to it, so a sex museum seems just the thing for Beppu. It's in among the Kannawa hells, beside the large Indian temple relief opposite the Ashiya Hotel. Inside you'll find a bizarre collection ranging from 'positions' models and illustrations to a large collection of wooden phalluses (some very large indeed).

Erotic art on display ranges from Papua New Guinean fertility figures to Tibetan Tantric ones. There are life-size models which plunge into copulatory action at the press of a button, including one of Snow White having a lot of fun with the Seven Dwarfs. Another button lights up the windows of a model apartment building to reveal something happening in every room, including one room with tiny figures of Popeye and Olive Oil on a rotating bed. Entry costs a hefty ¥1500 and opening hours are from 9 am to 11 pm.

Mt Takasaki Monkey Park 高崎山自然動物園

A couple of km beyond Beppu towards Ōita, tribes of monkeys descend to the park at the foot of Mt Takasaki for a daily feed. It's said that the monkeys got into the habit of appearing for a free meal in the 1950s when a local farmer decided that feeding them was more economical than allowing them simply to take his crops. The monkeys are in three distinct tribes: the largest with about 1000 members, the other two with 500 and 400. Each tribe has its own appointed feeding time during the day.

Admission to the park is ¥500 and Ōita Kōtsū buses from the Kitahama bus station operate to the Mt Takasaki park entrance (shared with the Marine Palace Aquarium) every 20 minutes.

The SS Oriana オリアナ号

In the pre-jet era, the British ocean liner SS *Oriana* operated regularly between England and Australia. Later, as the ocean-liner era ground to a halt, the *Oriana* became a popular cruise ship. Today the 41,000

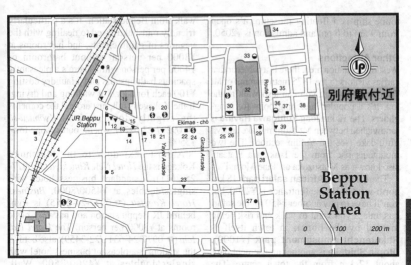

別府駅付近

**Beppu
Station
Area**

KYŪSHŪ

| 0 | 100 | 200 m |

PLACES TO STAY

1 Kamenoi Hotel
   亀の井ホテル
3 Business Hotel
   Kagetsu
   ビジネスホテル花月
6 New Hayashi Hotel
   ニュー ハヤシ ホテル
10 Hotel Dai-Ichi
   ホテル第一
13 Kiyomizu-sō Hotel
   清水荘
14 Minshuku Kokage
   民宿こかげ
17 Hotel New Kimekiya
   ホテル ニュー きめきや
22 Green Hotel
   グリーン ホテル
37 Hanabishi Hotel
   花菱ホテル
38 Seifu Hotel
   清風ホテル

PLACES TO EAT

4 Kentucky
   Fried Chicken
   ケンタッキーフライドチキン
7 Bentō Shop
   吉四六弁当
11 Jūtoku-ya Restaurant
   十徳屋

12 Italian Tomato
   Restaurant
   イタリアントマト
15 Sundelica Bakery
   France-kan
   さんでりか フランス館
21 Marui Shokudō
   Restaurant
   丸井食堂
23 Kani Ryōri Restaurant
   カニ料理屋
25 Tairitsu Honten
   Noodle Shop
   大陸本店
39 Royal Host Restaurant
   ロイヤルホースト

OTHER

2 Foreign Tourist
   Information Office
   外国人旅行者観光案内所
5 Laundry
   コインランドリー
8 Beppu Station
   Bus Stop
   別府駅バス停
9 Car Rental Office
   駅前レンタカー
16 Kintetsu
   Department Store
   近鉄百貨店
18 Scala-za Cinema
   スカラ座

19 Iyo Bank
   伊予銀行
20 Beppu Shinyo Bank
   別府信用金庫
24 Fukuoka City Bank
   福岡市銀行
26 Cinema
   別府オスカー
27 Takegawara Onsen
   竹瓦温泉
28 JTB

29 Robatayaka
   & Beer Pub
   ろばたやきビールパブ
30 Post Office
   郵便局
31 Ōita Bank
   大分銀行
32 Cosmopolitan
   Shopping
   Centre/Tokiwa
   Department Store
   コスモピア/常盤百貨店
33 Airport Bus Stop
   空港バス停
34 Beppu Tower
   別府タワー
35 Kamenoi Bus Station
   亀の井バス停
36 Kitahama Bus Station
   北浜バス停

tonne ship is a floating museum; it's open from 9 am to 6 pm and admission is ¥2050.

Other Attractions

West of the station area, there is a cablecar that carries visitors to the 1375 metre summit of **Mt Tsurumi-dake** but you can also walk to the top. It's a popular launching point for hang-gliders. The 12 km long **Yufugawa Ravine** is sandwiched between Mt Tsurumi-dake and Mt Yufu-dake (see the Yufuin section). The two mountains rise from the Tsukahara Plateau, also known as Matsuzuka or 'Pine Mound'.

There's a large **African safari park** 18 km north-west of Beppu (entrance is ¥2200, but you'll have to pay another ¥450 for the safari bus unless you want to walk and risk being mauled by the lions); in town itself is **Rakutenchi amusement park** (¥1000). **Utopia Shidaka** is another amusement park about 12 km from the town centre. The **Marine Palace Aquarium** (¥1050) is by the seafront, sharing the same car park as the monkey park at Mt Takasaki. There's fun galore in Beppu!

Places to Stay

Although places to stay are scattered around Beppu, they are concentrated on the Suginoi Palace hill, around JR Beppu station and in the Kannawa hot-springs area.

Around Suginoi The huge *Suginoi Hotel* (☎ 0977-24-1141), overlooks Beppu from its hillside location but you'll pay for the view; rooms range from ¥20,000 to ¥30,000. Near by is the *Beppu Shōwa-en Hotel* (☎ 0977-22-3211), which is even more expensive at ¥50,000 for the cheapest rooms.

The *Beppu Youth Hostel* (☎ 0977-23-4116) costs ¥2500 a night and is very close to the Suginoi Hotel. To get to the hostel, take a No 4 bus (departing hourly, from Beppu station's western exit) or a No 14 bus (departing half hourly) and get off at the Kankaiji-bashi bus stop.

Around Beppu Station The *Minshuku Kokage* (☎ 0977-23-1753), a member of the Japanese Inn Group, is just a few minutes walk from Beppu station. It's a particularly friendly minshuku, used to dealing with the vagaries of gaijin clients, and has rooms at ¥3000 per person without bathroom or ¥4000 per person with. There's a pleasantly spacious bath upstairs and a laundry costing ¥100 each for a load of washing and drying. If the Kokage is full, just around the corner is the slightly down at heel *Kyōmizu-sō* (☎ 09277-23-0221), where rooms range from ¥3500.

Almost next door to the Minshuku Kokage is the *Hotel New Kimekiya* (☎ 0977-25-2611), a standard business hotel with singles/doubles at ¥4500/8000. *Business Hotel Kagetsu* (☎ 0977-24-2355) is right behind JR Beppu station and has very basic rooms at ¥3000 per person. The *Hotel Dai Ichi* (☎ 0977-24-6311/22-3459), also behind the station, is a pleasant business hotel with singles/doubles at ¥4200/7500. Walk straight out from the station and along Ekimae-chō a short distance to the *New Hayashi Hotel* (☎ 0977-24-5252). This is a straightforward business hotel where singles/doubles cost ¥4200/7500. A bit further down the same street is the *Green Hotel* (☎ 0977-25-2244), with singles/doubles at ¥4500/8000. South of the station is the larger *Kamenoi Hotel* (☎ 0977-22-3301), with rooms from ¥12,000. There are a number of hotels along Route 10 through town, at the bottom of the station road. The beach area is also crowded with hotels but most of them are very expensive.

Kannawa Jigoku Area There are a number of minshuku and ryokan around the Kannawa hot springs, including the big *Hotel Ashiya* (☎ 0977-67-7711), which is right in among the jigoku.

Also close to the Kannawa jigoku is the *Rakurakuen Ryokan* (☎ 0977-67-2682) which costs from ¥6000 to ¥9000 per person and has a variety of baths to try. Up the road from the jigoku, behind the small post office, is *Minshuku Sakaeya* (☎ 0977-66-6234). It costs ¥3600 per person (room only) or ¥7000 with breakfast and dinner. This popular minshuku is in an interesting old building and your food is cooked using hot-springs heat.

Places to Eat

Beppu is renowned for its freshwater fish, for its fugu (globefish) and for the wild vegetables grown in the mountains further inland. *Morisawa* is a good restaurant for local specialities.

One of the best places for a meal in the station area is *Jūtoku-ya*, an izakaya with an enormous range of dishes on its illustrated menu, all at very reasonable prices. It's also a good place for a couple of beers with snacks.

The area around the Minshuku Kokage is good for yakitori restaurants; most of them have dishes ranging from ¥200 to ¥400 as well as beer on tap. Just off the Yayoi arcade, look out for *Kani Ryōri*, which specialises in crab but also has other, less expensive items on its menu. You can't miss this place as it has an enormous crab suspended over the doorway. Back on Ekimae-chō, between the two arcades, there's an excellent little rāmen shop, and on the same side of the road, closer to the station, is the *Marui Shokudō*, a good place for inexpensive tonkatsu and katsudon (pork cutlet dishes).

In the station you'll find a *Lotteria*, a *Little Mermaid* (bakery) and a *Kentucky Fried Chicken*. Elsewhere in Beppu you'll find a *McDonald's*, a *Mos Burger*, a *Sunday's Sun* (steakhouse) and other fast-food restaurants. Finally, the Beppu station area seems to be overflowing with that indigenous variation of the fast-food barn, the bentō (boxed lunch) shop. There must be around a dozen of them scattered along Ekimae-chō, all of them serving excellent-value take-away meals

Getting There & Away

Air There are flights to Ōita Airport from Tokyo, Osaka, Nagoya, Kagoshima and Okinawa.

Train From Fukuoka/Hakata via Kokura in Kitakyūshū it takes about 2½ hours on the JR Nippō line to Beppu. The basic futsū fare is ¥3190, while the limited express service

costs an additional ¥2150. The line continues on down the coast to Miyazaki. The shinkansen from Tokyo runs to Kokura and on to Fukuoka/Hakata. The JR Hōhi line runs from Beppu to Kumamoto via Mt Aso; it takes about 2½ hours to Aso and another hour down to Kumamoto.

Bus The Yamanami Highway bus No 266 links Beppu and Kumamoto with a side trip to Mt Aso. The journey between Beppu and Mt Aso takes about three hours, another hour from Mt Aso to Kumamoto.

Ferry The Kansai Kisen ferry service (☎ 0977-22-1311) does a daily run between Beppu and Osaka (¥5870, 17 hours), stopping en route at Kōbe (¥5870, 14 to 15 hours), Hiroshima (¥3600, 5½ to 8½ hours), Takamatsu (¥4700, 11 hours), Matsuyama (¥2400, 4½ hours), Uwajima (¥1900, three hours) and Yawatahama (¥1750, three hours). Late evening boats to Western Honshū should pass through the Inland Sea during daylight hours the next morning.

If you just want to get to Shikoku, Uwajima Unyū (☎ 0977-21-2364) runs five services a day to Yawatahama (¥2370) and one service to Uwajima (¥2880).

There's a convenient ferry service from Saganoseki, which travels around the southern side of the bay towards Usuki then on to Misaki on Shikoku. The trip, which takes a little over one hour and costs ¥600, is a very convenient route. Other Shikoku services operate from Usuki to Yawatahama (¥1300, two hours) and from Saiki to Sukumo (¥1650, three hours).

Getting Around

To/From the Airport Hovercraft run from Ōita and Beppu to Ōita Airport, which is 40 km around the bay from Beppu. The airport bus service takes about an hour (¥1300) and leaves from the stop outside the Cosmopolitan shopping centre.

Bus There are four local bus companies, of which Kamenoi is the largest. Most buses are numbered, but Ōita Kōtsū buses for the

KYŪSHŪ

Mt Takasaki monkey park and Ōita are not. An unlimited travel 'My Beppu Free' pass for Kamenoi buses is not free at all; the 'mini pass' version covers all the local attractions, including the hells, for ¥800. A 'wide pass' goes further afield: ¥1400 for one day or ¥2200 for two. The passes are available at the JR Beppu station information counter and at the Beppu Youth Hostel.

A variety of bus tours operate from the Kitahama bus station including tours to the Kannawa hot springs, the African safari park and other attractions.

USUKI 臼杵
About five km from Usuki is a collection of superb 10th to 13th century **Buddha images**. There are more than 60 images in a series of niches in a ravine. Some are complete statues while others have only the heads remaining, but many are in wonderful condition, even with paintwork still intact. The **Dainichi Buddha head** is the most impressive and important of the Usuki images. There are various other stone Buddha images at sites around Ōita Prefecture such as Motomachi, Magari and Takase but the Usuki ones are the most numerous and most

interesting. Entry to the ravine is ¥520 and it's open from 8.30 am to sunset. There's a choice of restaurants at the site. The town of Usuki is about 40 km south-east of Beppu; trains take a little under one hour and cost ¥1400. It's then a 20 minute bus ride to the ravine site; alternatively, you could walk the few km from the Kami-Usuki station.

YUFUIN 湯布院
If Beppu is the hot-spring resort scene at its glitzy worst, then Yufuin is its smaller, more refined relation. About 25 km inland from Beppu, Yufuin makes a pleasant stop between Beppu and Mt Aso and has an interesting variety of baths to sample, including some fine *rotemburo* (open-air baths).

Information
The tourist information office in front of the railway station has some information in English. Change money in Beppu, as there's no place to do it readily in Yufuin. There are onsen festivals in April and May.

Things to See & Do
As in Beppu, making a pilgrimage from one onsen to another is a popular activity in

Yufuin. The difference is that in Yufuin it's rural peace which is on offer, not city hype. The Kinrinko and Makinote rotemburo are special attractions. **Lake Kinrin-ko** is fed by hot springs, so it's warm all year round.

The town has a number of interesting temples and shrines including the **Kozenin-ji**, **Bussan-ji** and **Bukko-ji** temples. Yufuin is also noted for its arts and handicrafts, which can be seen at the **Mingei-mura Folk Art Village** and in a number of shops and galleries.

The double-peaked 1583 metre **Mt Yufu-dake** volcano overlooks Yufuin and takes about two hours to climb. Take a bus from the Kamenoi bus station to Yufu Tozanguchi, about 20 minutes away on the Beppu-Yufuin bus route.

Places to Stay & Eat

Yufuin has many minshuku, ryokan and pensions, including the popular *Pension Yufuin* (☎ 0977-85-3311), which costs from ¥8600 per person, including two meals. It's a typically Japanese 'rural Western' guesthouse fantasy! *Yufuin Sansō Guest House* (☎ 0977-84-2105) is a kokuminshukusha which costs from ¥5800 per person, including two meals. Most of the ryokan around town are high-class places with very high costs.

Getting There & Away

Bus Nos 36 and 37 go to Yufuin from the JR Beppu station bus stop every hour and the one hour trip costs ¥900. The JR Kyūdai line runs to Yufuin from Ōita. Continuing beyond Yufuin is not always easy. Kyūshū Kokusai Kankō (KKC) buses go to Mt Aso and Kumamoto but not year round.

BEPPU TO MT ASO
別府から阿蘇山方面へ

Yamanami Highway やまなみハイウェイ

The picturesque Yamanami Highway extends 63 km from the Mt Aso region to near Yufuin; from there, the Ōita Expressway runs to Beppu on the east coast. There's a ¥1850 toll to drive along this scenic road but tour buses operating between Kumamoto, Aso and Beppu, or the reverse,

also use this route. The road crosses a high plateau and passes numerous mountain peaks, including **Mt Kujū-san** (1788 metres), the highest point in Kyūshū.

Taketa 竹田

South of Yufuin, near the town of Taketa, are the **Oka-jō Ato Castle ruins**, which have a truly magnificent ridge-top position. The ruins are about two km from JR Bungo-Taketa station; take a bus there and walk back into town. There are some interesting old buildings, reminders of the Christian period and a museum. Bungo-Taketa is on the JR Hōhi line between Ōita and Mt Aso. From Mt Aso to Taketa, it takes just under an hour by train or bus; from there it's just over an hour by train to Ōita – a little longer by bus.

KUNISAKI-HANTŌ PENINSULA
国東半島

Immediately north of Beppu, the Kunisaki-hantō Peninsula bulges eastwards from the Kyūshū coast. The region is noted for its early evidence of Buddhist influence, including some rock-carved images which are related to the better known ones at Usuki.

Usa 宇佐

In the early post-WW II era, when 'Made in Japan' was no recommendation at all, it's said that companies would register in Usa so they could proclaim that their goods were 'Made in USA'! The town is better known for its bright orange **Usa-jinja Shrine**, the original of which dated back over 1000 years. The current shrine is much newer and connected with Hachiman, the god of war.

Other Attractions

The Kunisak-hantō Peninsula is said to have more than half of all the stone Buddhas in Japan. The 11th century **Fuki-ji Temple** in Bungotakada is the oldest wooden structure in Kyūshū and one of the oldest wooden temples in Japan. Right in the centre of the peninsula, near the summit of Mt Futago-san, is the **Futago-ji Temple**, dedicated to Fudomyo-o, the god of fire.

KYŪSHŪ

国東半島

Kunisaki-hantō
Peninsula

Carved into a cliff behind the Taizo Temple, two km south of **Maki Ōdō**, are two large Buddha images: the six metre high figure of the Dainichi Buddha and an eight metre high figure of Fudō-Myō-o. These are known as the **Kumano Magaibutsu** and are the largest Buddhist images of this type in Japan. Other stone statues, thought to be from the Heian period of 1000 to 1100 AD, can be seen in **Maki Ōdō**.

Getting Around

The easiest way to tour the peninsula is on the daily five to seven-hour bus tours from Beppu or Nakatsu. Beppu's Ōita Airport is on (or rather off!) the peninsula, about 40 km from Beppu.

NORTHERN ŌITA-KEN
大分県の北部
Nakatsu 中津

In the far north of Ōita-ken on the JR Nippō line is Nakatsu, a small town that is noted

most of all for its picturesque castle. Like most, **Nakatsu-jō Castle**, originally dating back from 1588, is a modern reconstruction but it still looks good. There are exhibitions of samurai armour and weapons in the castle, and you can easily browse through the place in a couple of hours. The castle is open from 9 am to 5 pm daily, and entrance is ¥250.

There's a tourist information booth at the station, and the castle is about a one km walk to the north-west. There's some accommodation in Nakatsu, but it's probably more of a quick stopover en route between Fukuoka and Beppu. The *Hotel Sunroute* (☎ 0979-24-7111) is just behind the station, and has singles/doubles from ¥4810/9560. The *Hiyoshi Ryokan* (☎ 0979-22-07310) is north of the station and has rooms from ¥6000.

Yaba-kei Gorge 耶馬渓

From Nakatsu, Route 212 turns inland and runs through the picturesque Yaba-kei Gorge. The gorge extends for about 10 km, beginning about 16 km from Nakatsu. The **Ao-no-Dōmon** (Ao Tunnel), at the start of the gorge, was originally cut over a 30 year period by a hard-working monk in order to make the Rankan-ji Temple more accessible.

Smaller gorges join the main one, and there are frequent buses up the gorge road from Nakatsu. A 35 km cycling track follows a now disused railway line. You can rent bicycles and stay at the *Yabakei Cycling Terminal* (☎ 0979-54-2655), which costs ¥4900 with two meals. There's also the *Yamaguniya Youth Hostel* (☎ 0979-52-2008), which costs ¥2400 per night.

From Nakatsu station there are Ōita-kōtsu buses doing the 40 minute trip to Ao-no-Dōmon for ¥490. For the cycling terminal Ōita Kōtsu Hida-bound buses do the trip in around 55 minutes and cost ¥890.

Hita Area 日田・その周辺

Further inland from the Yaba-kei Gorge is Hita, a quiet country town and onsen resort where cormorant fishing (ukai) takes place in the river from May to October. You can view the operation from tourist boats during the season. Just across the prefectural border in Fukuoka-ken you can also see cormorant fishing in **Harazura**, another hot-spring resort.

North of Hita, towards Koishiwara, is **Onta**, a small village renowned for its curious pottery. The **Onta-yaki Togeikan Museum** has a display of the local product. Koishiwara also

has a pottery tradition dating back to the era when Korean potters were first brought to Kyūshū.

Hita is on the JR Kyūdai line between Ōita (two hours) and Kurume (one hour). By bus it takes about 45 minutes to travel from Hita to Onta.

Okinawa & the South-West Islands
沖縄・南西諸島

The South-West Islands, or Nansei-shotō as they are known in Japanese, meander for more than 1000 km in the direction their name suggests from the southern tip of Kyūshū to Yonaguni-jima Island, just a strenuous stone's throw (a little over 100 km) from the east coast of Taiwan.

The northern half of the Nansei-shotō group falls within Kagoshima-ken and includes the Osumi-shotō Islands and the Amami-shotō Islands.

The four island groups which form the southern half of the Nansei-shotō Islands comprise Okinawa-ken. Of these, the most important islands – and those that attract the most visitors – are the Okinawa (or Ryūkū) Islands to the north and the Yaeyama Islands to the south.

Okinawa, the hub of the island chain, is referrred to as the *hontō* and its key role in the closing months of WW II holds a continuing fascination for visitors. However, for an insight into Okinawan culture and to enjoy the least spoilt natural aspects of the islands, you must continue on to the *ritō* or 'outer islands'. Kume-jima, for example, is famed for its unspoilt beauty; Taketomi-jima is a tiny island with a picture-postcard village; and Iriomote-jima is Japan's last wilderness, cloaked in dense tropical jungle. Prime scuba-diving sites are found around the Kerama-rettō Islands and around Iriomote-jima Island.

In between the Okinawa Islands and the Yaeyama Islands are the Miyako Islands, while 350 km to the east of Okinawa are the isolated Daito Islands.

A warm climate, fine beaches, excellent scuba diving and traces of traditional culture are the prime attractions for visitors to Nansei-shotō. But don't think of these islands as forgotten backwaters with a mere handful of visitors – both ANA and JAL fly tourists to Okinawa from mainland Japan by

the 747-load and even the local flights from Okinawa to other islands in the chain are by 737s. Despite having survived centuries of mainland exploitation and then horrific destruction during the closing months of WW II, the traditional ways of these islands may not survive the onslaught of mass tourism.

HISTORY

The islands of the Nansei-shotō chain look like stepping stones from Japan to Taiwan, and they have long been a bridge between Japanese and Chinese culture. For the often unfortunate residents of the islands this has sometimes resulted in being squeezed and pulled from both sides. More recently Okinawa was the scene for some of the most violent and tragic action in the closing months of WW II.

For centuries, the islands formed a border zone between Chinese and Japanese suzerainty. In the 14th century the Chinese influence was felt most strongly in the Okinawa Islands, and the islands' kingdoms maintained strong links with China for 500 years. In the 15th century the whole island of Okinawa was united under the rule of the Shō dynasty, and the capital shifted from Urasoe to Shuri, where it was to remain until the Meiji Restoration. The period from 1477 to 1525 is remembered as a golden age of Okinawan history. By the 17th century, however, Japanese power was on the ascendancy and the Okinawans found themselves under a new ruler when the Satsuma kingdom of southern Kyūshū invaded in 1609; the islands were controlled with an iron fist and taxed and exploited greedily. In 1879 the islands were formally made a prefecture under Meiji rule.

After being treated as foreign subjects by the Satsuma regime, the Okinawans were pushed to become 'real' Japanese. They

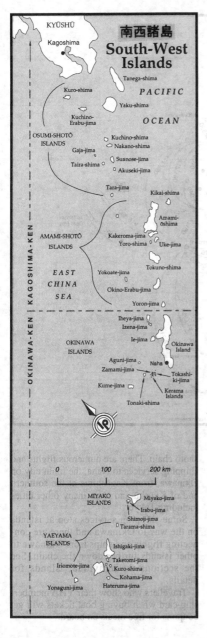

KYŪSHŪ

Kagoshima

南西諸島
**South-West
Islands**

Tanega-shima

Kuro-shima

PACIFIC

Yaku-shima

Kuchino-
Erabu-jima

OCEAN

OSUMI-SHOTŌ
ISLANDS

Kuchino-shima
Nakano-shima

Gaja-jima

Suanose-jima

Taira-shima

Akuseki-jima

Tara-jima

Kikai-shima

Amami-
Ōshima

AMAMI-SHOTŌ
ISLANDS

Kakeroma-jima
Yoro-shima   Uke-jima

*EAST
CHINA
SEA*

Yokoate-jima

Tokuno-shima

Okino-Erabu-jima

Yoron-jima

Iheya-jima
Izena-jima

Ie-jima

Okinawa
Island

OKINAWA
ISLANDS

Aguni-jima

Naha

Zamami-jima

Tokashi-
ki-jima

Kume-shima

Kerama
Islands

Tonaki-shima

KAGOSHIMA-KEN   OKINAWA-KEN

0   100   200 km

MIYAKO
ISLANDS

Miyako-jima

Irabu-jima

Shimoji-jima

Tarama-shima

YAEYAMA
ISLANDS

Ishigaki-jima

Taketomi-jima
Kuro-shima

Iriomote-jima

Kohama-shima

Yonaguni-jima   Hateruma-shima

payed a heavy price for this new role when they were trapped between the relentless US hammer as it smashed down upon the fanatically resistant Japanese anvil in the closing stages of WW II.

The war arrived in Okinawa with a fury in October 1944 when US bombing commenced, and on 1 April 1945, US troops landed on the island. The Japanese were prepared to make an all-out stand and it took 82 horrendous days for the island to be captured. Not until 22 June was the conquest complete, by which time 13,000 US forces and, according to some estimates, a quarter of a million Japanese had died. Many of the Japanese deaths were of civilians, and there are terrible tales of mass suicides by mothers clutching their children and leaping to their deaths off cliff tops to avoid capture by the foreigners whom, they had been led to believe, were barbarians.

The Japanese commanders committed seppuku (ritual suicide) but a final horror remained. The underground naval headquarters at Tomigusuku were so well hidden they were not discovered until three weeks after the US victory. The underground corridors contained the bodies of 4000 naval officers and men, all of whom had committed suicide.

Following the victory over the Japanese and the subsequent US occupation, Okinawa became a major US military base during the cold war. Sovereignty of the island was finally returned to Japan in 1972, but even today a strong US military presence persists on Okinawa.

Among the inhabitants of the islands there's a trace of mistrust towards mainland Japan. Under Satsuma control the Okinawans were exploited by the mainland and were looked upon as expendable during WW II. The region is still economically backward compared to the mainland and to many main-island Japanese, it is now viewed principally as a place for a beach vacation.

CLIMATE

The climate of the Nansei-shotō Islands is much warmer than that of the Japanese main

OKINAWA & SOUTH WEST ISLANDS

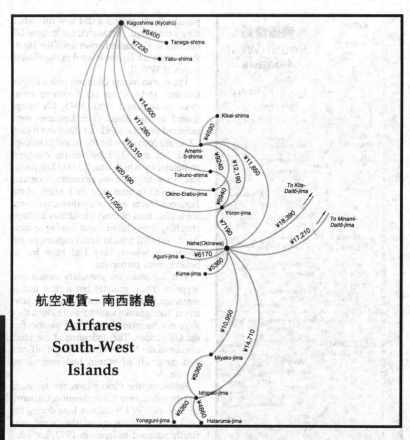

Kagoshima (Kyūshū)
¥6400
¥7230 • Tanega-shima
• Yaku-shima

¥14,600
¥17,280
¥19,310
• Kikai-shima
¥4590

Amami-
ō-shima ¥9240 ¥12,190 ¥11,850

Tokuno-shima

¥20,490
Okino-Erabu-jima ¥6940

¥21,050
Yoron-jima

To Kita-
Daitō-jima

Naha (Okinawa)
¥7190
¥18,390

To Minami-
Daitō-jima
¥17,210

Aguni-jima • ¥6170

¥5360
Kume-jima •

航空運賃 – 南西諸島
**Airfares
South-West
Islands**

¥10,950
¥14,710

¥5360
Miyako-jima

Ishigaki-jima
¥5360 ¥4860
Yonaguni-jima •   • Hateruma-jima

islands, and Okinawa is virtually a tropical getaway. November to April is considered to be the best season; May and June can bring heavy rain; July to August is not only very hot but also very crowded; while September and October is the typhoon season. Although the winter months (November to March) are cooler, the crowds are lighter, and for divers, underwater visibility is at its best.

GETTING THERE & AWAY

Okinawa is the travel hub of the Nansei-

shotō chain. There are numerous flights and shipping services to Naha, the main city on Okinawa, from Kagoshima at the southern end of Kyūshū and from many other cities including Tokyo.

Some shipping services stop at islands on the way to Okinawa and there are connecting flights and ships from Okinawa to other islands further down the chain. See the sections on individual islands for details.

Travellers who show their YHA membership card when buying boat tickets will get coupons for free meals on board.

Osumi-shotō Islands
大隅諸島

The northernmost island group of the Nansei-shotō chain is the Osumi-shotō Islands. Tanega-shima and Yaku-shima, the two main islands of the group, are less than 100 km from Kagoshima at the southern end of Kyūshū. The islands, one flat and long, the other high and round, are about as different as two islands could be. South of these two main islands are the smaller, scattered Tokara Islands.

GETTING THERE & AWAY
Ferry services and JAS flights connect Kagoshima with the two main islands – 3½ hours by ferry to Tanega-shima, 4½ to Yaku-shima. Boats operate between Cape Shimama-zaki at the southern end of Tanega-shima Island and Kamiyaku on Yaku-shima Island.

TANEGA-SHIMA ISLAND 種子島
Tanega-shima Island's low-lying terrain is mainly devoted to agriculture. The island is about 55 km long and the port of **Nishino-omote** (population 26,000) is the main town. The island has an important place in Japanese history, for this was where a Portuguese ship first made landfall in Japan in 1543. The introduction of modern European firearms from this first contact played an important part in bringing the disastrous 'Country at War' or Muromachi period to a close.

YAKU-SHIMA ISLAND 屋久島
In contrast to Tanega-shima's flatness, volcanic Yaku-shima Island rises to the 1935 metre high peak of **Mt Miyanoura-dake**, the highest point in southern Japan. Mt Kuromi, the island's second-highest peak, is only

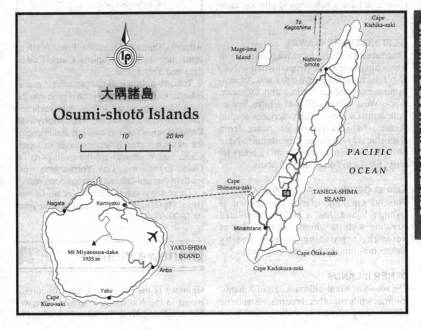

大隅諸島
Osumi-shotō Islands

slightly lower at 1836 metres. The island is just 25 km in diameter, but the towering terrain catches every inbound rain cloud, giving the island one of the wettest climates in Japan.

Kamiyaku, on the north-east coast, is the main port; a road runs around the island, passing through Ambo and Yaku. From Ambo you can take a taxi up the slopes of the mountain and walk past a waterfall and through an ancient cedar forest.

Amami-shotō Islands
奄美諸島

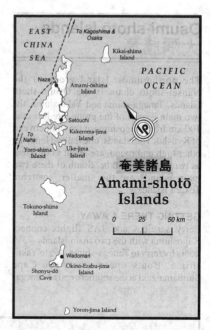

There are five main islands in the Amami-shotō group. From Kagoshima to Amami-ōshima, the largest island in the group, is about 180 km. The islands are predominantly agricultural (producing bananas, papayas, pineapples and sugar cane) and have a sub-tropical climate, clear water and good beaches.

GETTING THERE & AWAY
There are JAS flights from Kagoshima to all five main islands. Air Nippon Koku (ANK) also flies between Kagoshima and Amami-ōshima and Amami-ōshima and Okinawa. South-West Airlines (SWAL) links Yoron-jima with Okinawa. Ferry services stop at Amami-ōshima Island en route from Kagoshima to Okinawa. Kagoshima to Naze on Amami-ōshima takes about 12 hours by ferry; Osaka to Naze takes 25 hours.

AMAMI-ŌSHIMA ISLAND 奄美大島
This 40 km long island, also known as Oshima Island, has a highly convoluted coastline with the almost enclosed Bay of Setouchi separating it from nearby Kakeroma-jima. Naze is the main port.

OTHER ISLANDS
The island of **Kikai-shima** is east of Amami-ōshima, while the other three main islands lie like stepping stones in a direct line from

Amami-ōshima to Okinawa. From north to south they are Tokuno-shima, Okino-Erabu-jima and Yoron-jima.

Tokuno-shima is the largest after Amami-ōshima but **Okino-Erabu-jima** is probably the most interesting island, with its coral reefs and thatched-roof rice barns. The **Shonyu-dō Cave** stretches for over two km and is one of the most important limestone caves in Japan. China and Wadomari are the main ports on Okino-Erabu-jima. Tiny **Yoro-shima**, just south of Amami-ōshima, also has coral reefs.

There are youth hostels on Okino-Erabu-jima (☎ 09979-2-2024) and Yoron-jima (☎ 0997-97-2273).

Okinawa Island 沖縄

Okinawa is the largest and most important island in the Nansei-shotō chain. Okinawa had developed distinct cultural differences to mainland Japan, particularly in architecture, but the destruction of WW II obliterated almost every trace of the old architecture. The USA retained control of Okinawa after the war, handing it back to Japan in 1972. The 26 years of US occupation did a pretty effective job of wiping out any remaining traces of the old Okinawan ways, but for good measure the Japanese have turned the island into a major tourist resort. Okinawa still has the biggest US military base in Japan, with 50,000 military and non-military personnel and dependents.

Okinawa's wartime history may have some interest for foreign visitors, but the islands further south will probably offer a more interesting insight into the history of ancient Ryūkyū.

NAHA 那覇

Naha (population 304,000) is the capital of Okinawa; it was flattened in WW II and little trace remains of the old Ryūkū culture. Today Naha is chiefly a gateway to other places but there are a number of interesting things to see in this colourful modern town.

Orientation & Information

Kokusai-dōri (International Blvd), Naha's main street, is 1½ busy km of hotels, bars, restaurants and shops. The airport is only three km west of Naha while a similar distance east is Shuri, the most interesting remains of 'old' Naha. Shuri was the Okinawan capital prior to the Meiji Restoration when Naha took on the role.

The tourist information counter at the airport is not open for all flights. Unfortunately, there are no other tourist information offices in town, though the larger hotels have maps available. If you in desperate need of some tourism-related help, try ringing the Naha City Tourism Section (☎ 862-3276).

If you're intending to explore Okinawa and other islands, particularly with a rented car, get a copy of *Okinawa by Road* (Kume Publishing, 1989, ¥1550) which should be available at some bookshops in Naha. Don't confuse the English edition with the similar-looking and more readily available Japanese-language version.

You can quickly get your fill of the US forces radio on 648 kHz AM – the ads are amazingly awful.

Central Naha 那覇中心部

Kokusai-dōri, with its curious mix of restaurants, army-surplus stores, nightclubs and hotels, makes an interesting walk day or night. It's very much the heart of Naha. Turning south off Kokusai-dōri opposite the Mitsukoshi department store leads you to the Heiwa-dōri shopping arcade, which has the distinct flavour of an Asian market.

If you continue to the east end of Kokusai-dōri, a right turn takes you towards Shuri, while a left turn quickly brings you to the reconstructed gates of **Sōgen-ji Temple**. These stone gates once led to the 16th century temple of the Ryūkyū kings, but like almost everything else in Naha, it was destroyed in WW II. Continue beyond the gates and almost at the waterfront is the **Commodore Perry Memorial**, commemorating his 1853 landing in Naha (prior to his arrival in Tokyo). Near by is a foreigners' cemetery.

OKINAWA & SOUTH WEST ISLANDS

Habu Snakes

Any discussion of the South-West Islands eventually gets around to 'deadly *habu* snakes'. Perhaps it's a reflection of Japan's severe shortage of real dangers, but you could easily get the impression that the poor habu is the world's most dangerous snake and that they're waiting behind every tree, shrub, bush or bar stool on the islands. They're neither so deadly nor so prolific; in fact the most likely place to see one is at a mongoose versus habu fight put on for tourists. Nevertheless, it's probably not a good idea to go stomping through the bushes barefoot. Do stomp though, the vibrations will scare any snakes away. ■

EAST CHINA SEA

Cape Hedo-misaki

Oku

Ie-jima Island
Mt Gusuku
Ie

Okinawa
Memorial
Park

Kouri-jima
Island

Nakijin
Castle   Nakijin
Motobu
Motobu-hantō
Peninsula

Shioya
Bay

Okuma
Beach

Hentona

Kijoka

Ogimi

Aha

Minna-jima
Island

Sesoko-jima
Island

Yagaji-jima
Island

Taira

Nago

Okinawa
Submarine
Park

Manza
Beach

Onna

Ginoza

Moon
Beach

Okinawa

Expressway

Kin

Ryūkyū
Village

Cape
Zanpa-
misaka

Ishikawa

Ikei
Island

South-East
Botanical
Gardens

Gushikawa

Henza & Miyagi
Islands

Kadena
Air Force
Base

Okinawa

Hamahiga Island

Nakamura House
Nakagusuku Castle

Tsuken
Island

沖縄

Urasoe

Shuri

Underground Naval
Headquarters

Okinawa Island

0   10   20 km

Naha

Naha
Airport

Yonabaru

Baten

Chinen Marine Centre

Gyokusen-dō
Cave

Kudaka
Island

Itoman

Buckner
Memorial

Komaka
Island

Ō-jima Island

PACIFIC

Himeyuri-no-Tō Memorial

Mabuni Hill
Konpaku-no-Tō Memorial

OCEAN

Nashiro
Beach

Cape Kiyan-saki

OKINAWA & SOUTH-WEST ISLANDS

Tsuboya Area　壺屋

Continue along the Heiwa-dōri shopping arcade, taking the left fork at the junction, and a short walk beyond the arcade will bring you to the Tsuboya pottery area. If you miss it simply continue in the same direction until you hit the big Himeyuri-dōri and Tsuboya is across the road from McDonald's.

About 20 traditional pottery workshops still operate in this compact area, a centre for ceramic production since 1682. You can peer into many of the small workshops and there are numerous shops selling popular Okinawan products such as the *shiisā* (lion roof guardians) or the containers for serving *awamori*, the local firewater. The **Tsuboya Pottery Centre** (Tsuboya Toki Kaikan) is open from 9 am to 6 pm and has items from all the kilns.

Waterfront Temples

Kume-dōri runs from Kokusai-dōri straight to the waterfront, where the hilltop Naminoue-gū Shrine and the Gokoku-ji and Kōshi-byō temples are picturesquely sited overlooking the sea and the red-light district! The buildings are unexceptional modern reconstructions and the neat little bay they overlook has been totally ruined by the highway flyover which runs straight across it. Okinawan road building often seems to make no concessions for natural features. The Tsuji entertainment area was once a brothel quarter; now it features clubs, bars and some noted restaurants, together with a collection of colourful love hotels and US-style steakhouses. As Japanese red-light areas go, it's decidedly lacking in atmosphere.

Shuri Area　首里

Prior to the Meiji Restoration, Shuri was the capital of Okinawa; that title passed to Naha in 1879. Shuri's temples, shrines, tombs and castle were all destroyed in WW II. Some reconstructions and repairs have been made but it's a pale shadow of the former city.

Shuri is about 2½ km from the east end of Kokusai-dōri. Bus Nos 12, 13, 14 and 17 run directly to the entrance (*shurijō kōen*

iriguchi) of the park for ¥170. At the park entrance is a building with a restaurant and information booth.

Prefectural Museum

The museum's displays are connected with Okinawan lifestyle and culture and include some exhibits on the Battle of Okinawa and a large model of the Shuri Castle. Entry to the museum is ¥200 and it's open from 9 am to 5 pm except Monday. The Ryūtan Pond across the road was built in 1427 and was used for dragon-boat races.

Shurijō-kōen Park

Most of what's left of the old Ryūkyū royal capital can be found in this park area. Entrance to the park itself is free, but there's a hefty entry charge for Shuri Castle.

Just up from the entrance to the park is the reconstructed old residence of the Okinawan royal family, **Shuri Castle**. The original was destroyed in the WW II Battle of Okinawa. The castle was only opened in early 1993, so don't expect much in the way of historical atmosphere. All the same, the reconstruction work has been carried out with meticulous attention to detail, and there are several exhibition halls with interesting historical displays. The result is undoubtedly Naha's prime tourist attraction. The castle is open from 9 am to 5 pm, and entry is a rather steep ¥800.

The castle's walls have numerous gates that are of minor interest. The pick of them is the Chinese-influenced **Shureino-mon Gate**. The ceremonial entrance to Shuri Castle, it was originally built nearly 500 years ago and was rebuilt in 1958. It's considered to be *the* symbol of Okinawa, so there's a constant stream of tour groups and school parties lining up to be photographed in front of it. A couple of young women in traditional Okinawan costume stand ready to make guest appearances in the photos, for a suitable fee.

Also worth checking out is the 15th-16th century Kankai-mon Gate with its traditional Okinawan design. It was rebuilt right after the war. The Kyukei-mon Gate, built in

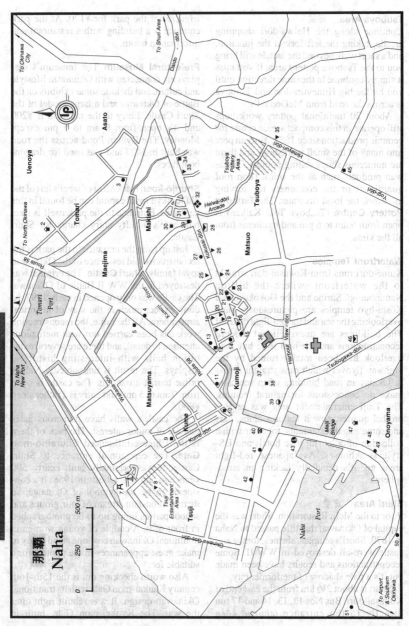

OKINAWA & SOUTH-WEST ISLANDS

那覇
Naha

OKINAWA & SOUTH WEST ISLANDS

1508, has also been restored. The third large gate, the Keisei-mon, was originally built in 1546.

There are a couple of temples on the park grounds, but don't expect too much from them – they look a little the worse for wear. The **Benzaiten-dō Temple** is in the middle of Enkan Pond, just down from Shuri Castle. It was originally built in 1502, rebuilt in 1609 after being destroyed, and rebuilt again in 1968 after being burnt out during WW II. Cross the road to the rather bedraggled remnants of the **Enkaku-ji Temple**. This temple

dates from 1492, but it too was destroyed in the Battle of Okinawa. The outer gate, a bridge leading over a lotus pond, and the steps beyond the pond leading to the main gate are all that remain. Engaku-ji has an entrance fee of ¥160.

In the far west of the park, the wartime destruction also did not spare the **Tamaudōn Tombs** (also known as Gyokuryo), which date from 1501, but have been restored. Traditionally, bodies were first placed in the central chamber. When the flesh had decayed the bones were removed,

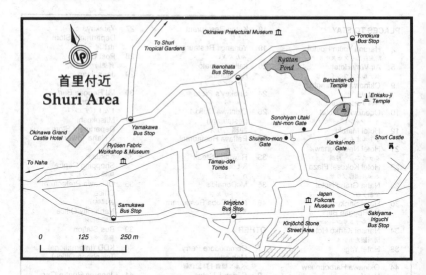

首里付近
Shuri Area

To Shuri Tropical Gardens

Okinawa Prefectural Museum

Tonokura Bus Stop

Ryūtan Pond

Ikanohata Bus Stop

Benzaiten-dō Temple

Enkaku-ji Temple

Yamakawa Bus Stop

Okinawa Grand Castle Hotel

Sonohiyan Utaki Ishi-mon Gate

Ryūsen Fabric Workshop & Museum

To Naha

Shureino-mon Gate

Kankai-mon Gate

Shuri Castle

Tamau-dōn Tombs

Samukawa Bus Stop

Kinjōchō Bus Stop

Japan Folkcraft Museum

Kinjōchō Stone Street Area

Sakiyama-Iriguchi Bus Stop

0   125   250 m

cleaned and permanently interred – kings and queens to the left, princes and princesses to the right. Stone lion figures look down on the courtyard from the central tower and both sides. Entry is ¥200 and opening hours are from 8.30 am to 6 pm in summer and from 8.30 am to 5.30 pm in winter.

Kinjōchō Stone St At one time the 15th century Kinjōchō-no-ishitatamimichi ran for 10 km from Shuri to the port at Naha. Now there's just one stretch of a couple of hundred metres plus a few side lanes, but the steep and narrow path with its old stone walls and ornate gateways is very picturesque.

Other Attractions The **Shuri Kannon-dō Temple** dates from 1618; it is on the Naha side of Shuri. The **Sueyoshi-gū Shrine** originally dates from the mid-15th century; it is well to the north of Shuri, in Sueyoshi Park. The **Shuri Tropical Gardens**, with over 400 varieties of tropical plantlife, may be worth a look, but the ¥1030 entry charge will no doubt deter most potential visitors.

Housed in a building brought from Ishigaki, the **Japan Folkcraft Museum** displays traditional crafts and has a collection

of photographs of pre-war Okinawa. The museum is open daily except Tuesday. There are a number of factories in the Shuri area producing Bingata, the most famous of the traditional fabrics of Okinawa. The **Ryūsen Fabric Workshop & Museum** specialises in Ryūsen, an expensive material rather similar to Bingata.

Festivals

Popular local festivals include the colourful Geisha Horse Festival (Jiriuma) during which young women ride wooden horses in a parade starting from the Teahouse of the August Moon in the Tsuji entertainment district. The festival usually takes place in March. The Hārii dragon boat races take place in early May, particularly in Itoman and Naha. In August the Tsunahiki Festival takes place in various locations but particularly in Itoman, Naha and Yonabaru – huge teams contest a tug-of-war using a gigantic rope (up to a metre thick).

Places to Stay

The information desk at Naha Airport has a map and hotel list in English and the staff will book accommodation. Okinawa's hotels tend to be scattered around Naha, although there are many along Kokusai-dōri, which is probably the best area to be based.

Youth Hostels Naha has two youth hostels. The *Naha Youth Hostel* (☎ 0988-57-0073) is the largest, with room for 80 people at ¥2400 a night. It's in Onoyama, south of the Meiji Bridge, near the road to the airport. It's closed from 21 to 30 January. From the airport you can take No 101 or 24 bus and get off at the Kōen-mae stop.

The *Harumi Youth Hostel* (☎ 0988-67-3218/4422), is north of the city, near Route 58. It accommodates 38 people at ¥2400 a night.

Hotels Just off Kokusai-dōri is *Hotel Sankyo* (☎ 0988-67-0105), a basic but comfortable enough business hotel with rooms from ¥4000. In an alley just around the corner from the Sankyo are a couple of ryokan with cheaper rates. If you are walking from the Sankyo, they are on the left and have flourescent signs (no English) outside. The second place has basic rooms for ¥2500.

The *Air Way Hotel* (☎ 0988-61-1122) is another fairly cheap business hotel. It's on Route 58 at 2-3-6 Matsuyama and has singles/doubles at ¥5500/9500. *Hotel Maruki* (☎ 0988-62-6135) is next to the JAL office, overlooking the Kumoji River near Kokusai-dōri. Singles/doubles start at ¥5000/9000. *Hotel Yagi* (☎ 0988-62-3008) is near the bus station at 1-16-5 Izumizaki and is similarly priced.

There are plenty of moderately priced places along Kokusai-dōri, including the *Hotel Kokusai Plaza* (☎ 0988-62-4243), where singles/doubles cost ¥6500/12,000. Right behind it is the similarly priced *Naha Grand Hotel* (☎ 0988-62-6161), with singles from ¥6000 to ¥7000 and doubles for ¥12,000. Next door to the Grand is the *Hotel New Okinawa* (☎ 0988-67-7200), with rooms from ¥6000.

Other possiblities include the *Okinawa Washington Hotel* (☎ 0988-69-2511), which is away from the city centre, halfway between Kokusai-dōri and the waterfront at 2-32-1 Kume. This popular chain hotel has

singles/doubles from ¥6300/12,000. The *Nansei Kankō Hotel* (☎ 0988-62-7144) at 3-13-23 Makishi is right on Kokusai-dōri and has rooms from ¥6500 per person. The big and glossy *Oceanview Hotel* (☎ 0988-53-2112) is on Route 58 and prices start from ¥9700/14,000 for singles/twins – no doubles available.

The red-light area near the waterfront has numerous love hotels including the *Wake Hotel* which has a huge mermaid perched on the roof and the imaginatively named *Hotel Joy Box*.

Places to Eat
Perhaps due to the US military presence, Naha has just about every variety of fast-food restaurant available in Japan, many of them in duplicate or triplicate. Along Kokusai-dōri alone you'll find *McDonald's, Kentucky Fried Chicken, Mos Burger, Lotteria, Mister Donut, Shakey's Pizza, A&W Burgers, Dom Dom Hamburger* and probably a few others. Shakey's offers unlimited quantities of pizza from 10 am to 3 pm for ¥520.

Among the restaurants along Kokusai-dōri, it used to be hard to pass by *Rawhide*, with its sign outside announcing 'Stake & Robster', but they've now corrected the spelling without doing anything about the food, which is just average. Okinawa is said to have the best-priced steaks in Japan (which is not saying a great deal), and there are plenty of steakhouses along Kokusai-dōri, although the best of them are in the Tsuji area, near the Naminoue-gū Shrine. Here you can choose from *Restaurant George, Jackie's Steakhouse, Restaurant Stateside, Restaurant Texas, Restaurant 88* and others. These restaurants offer steaks from around ¥1300 up; they also have delicacies like pizza and tacos. The Tsuji area also has some fine traditional restaurants like the *Teahouse of the August Moon*.

Back on Kokusai-dōri the *Italian Tomato* offers good pasta from ¥800 to ¥1200; it's a real OL (office ladies) hangout, the salarymen clearly don't bother with it. Just opposite is *Oriibunoki Spaghetti*, another

Italian-style place that does excellent lunch sets for ¥750. Look for the sign announcing 'Spaghetti' next door to a Doutor coffee shop.

Just off Kokusai-dōri is *Yūnangii*, a pleasant red-lantern (aka-chōchin) bar – cheerful, crowded and friendly. There is a great selection of awamori (the local firewater) for ¥500 a glass or ¥2500 a bottle. You can eat well here for around ¥1000; simply asking for the local specialities works fine. It's closed on Sunday.

For home-cooked style Okinawan cuisine, a restaurant regarded highly by locals is *Kotori* (☎ 0988-61-8787). It's on a side street off Kokusai-dōri, and cooking is done behind the counter, which makes ordering less of a strain. It's closed on Sunday. For a smorgasbord of Okinawan and Japanese cuisine in a lively setting, you can't do better than *Okinawa Qulio*. It's in the basement opposite *Shakey's Pizza*, and is an excellent combination of atmosphere and economical prices. The photo menu even comes with English transliterations of the Japanese names. It's open daily until 1 am.

An interesting, though slightly more expensive alternative to Okinawan and Japanese fare can be found in *Bazāru*, a place specialising in *mukokuseki ryōri*, or 'no nationality cuisine'. The food here is a combination of Chinese, Korean, Indonesian and Thai dishes, and you can order main courses for around ¥1800. It's open from 6 pm to around 1 pm, and is closed Sunday. For straight Thai cuisine without the international touch, check out *Pattaya* on Kokusai-dōri. It has reasonably inexpensive lunch sets.

Entertainment

Naha is a laid-back kind of place and it has a less lively nightlife than many other Japanese cities. Still, it's worth heading out for a drink or two in the evening; the locals are friendly and it's easy to make friends.

Right next to the Hotel Sankyo is the *I&I Reggae Bar*. Struggle up a dingy flight of stairs and you'll get to a dingy little bar. On a lively night, though, this place really gets

hopping, with a good range of reggae and Okinawan music. It's popular with 'alternative' type locals. Just around the corner, on Kokusai-dōri, is *Jean Jean*, a live performance house with different live acts every night. Many of the performers are Okinawan, and this is a good place to catch a glimpse of the lively local music scene. Entry ranges from ¥1000 to ¥2500, depending on the reputation of the act, and you need to get there early; most performances start around 7 pm and finish around 9.30 pm.

If you happen to be in Naha on the 8th of any month, head to the 5th floor of the *Javy Building*. Once a month Kina Shōkichi, the doyen of the Okinawan music scene, holds a performance, usually in combination with local dance performers. It's an excellent show; the music, a kind of electric/traditional crossover is haunting, and the local devotees are keen to chat to visiting foreigners about Okinawan music and culture. The concert costs ¥2500.

Finally, for a night out dancing, there's a branch of the '50's dance club *Kento's* north of Kokusai-dōri, and a massive disco with a capacity for 1000 sweaty bodies called *Disco Plaza*. The latter is opposite Mitsukoshi department store on Kokusai-dōri and has an entry charge of ¥3000 for women and ¥4000 for men, a common Japanese practice.

Things to Buy

Okinawa is renowned for its pottery and its fabrics. Tsuboya pottery owes its origins to Chinese influences, as opposed to the Korean techniques which form the basis of most other Japanese pottery. Much of the pottery is in the form of storage vessels but look for the *shiisa* (guardian lion figures) which can be seen perched on the rooftops of many traditional Okinawan buildings. Shiisa usually come in pairs, one with the mouth open, the other with the mouth closed.

Okinawa also has its own distinctive textiles, particularly the brightly coloured Bingata fabrics made in Shuri. Other fabrics made on Okinawa or other islands in the chain include Bashōfu (from northern Okinawa), Jōfu (from Miyako), Kasuri (from southern Okinawa), Minsā (from Taketomi), Ryūsen and Tsumugi (from Kume). Another popular Okinawan product is awamori which has an alcohol content of 30-60%. Drink with care! Real daredevils might want to look out for the version that comes with a small habu snake coiled in the bottom of the bottle. The I&I Reggae Bar generally has an opened bottle tucked away if you want try a glass.

Getting There & Away
Air Direct flights to Okinawa include Northwest Orient from the USA, Continental from Guam, JAL from Hong Kong and China Airlines from Taipei. JAL, ANA, ANK, JAS and South-West Airlines (SWAL) connect major cities on the main Japanese islands with Naha, including Fukuoka (1½ hours, ¥23,100), Kagoshima (1½ hours, ¥21,050), Nagoya (two hours ¥32,750), Osaka (two hours, ¥29,100), Hiroshima (two hours ¥26,600), Tokyo (2½ hours, ¥34,900) and a number of other centres. SWAL have the most connections to the other South-West Islands. See the South-West Islands Airfares chart for details.

Airlines with offices in Naha include ANA or ANK (☎ 0988-66-5111), JAS (☎ 0988-67-8111), JAL (☎ 0988-62-3311) and SWAL (☎ 0988-57-4961). All the offices can be found in the city centre except for SWAL which is across the Meiji Bridge towards the airport. There are plenty of travel agencies in central Naha, particularly on Kokusai-dōri, which can handle bookings.

Sea Various operators have shipping services to Naha from Tokyo, Osaka, Kōbe, Kagoshima and other ports. The schedules are complex and there is a wide variety of fares. From Tokyo it takes about 50 hours (¥20,000 to ¥50,000), from Osaka about 36 hours (¥15,000 to ¥40,000), from Kōbe about 40 hours (¥15,000 for ¥40,000) and from Kagoshima about 24 hours (¥12,000 to ¥30,000). Shipping companies include Arimura Sangyo, Kansai Kisen, Oshima Unyu, Ryūkyū Kaiun (RKK) and Terukuni Yusen. The frequency of services varies from

eight to 10 a month from Tokyo to more than 30 a month from Kagoshima.

From Naha Port ferries head south to Ishigaki-jima and Miyako-jima islands, north to Yoron-jima Island and Kagoshima. From Naha New Port there are ferries to Fukuoka/Hakata, Kagoshima, Kōbe, Osaka and Tokyo and also to Miyako and Ishigaki islands. From the Tomai Port, ferries operate to a number of the smaller islands including Kume, Aguni and the Daito Islands.

The Arimura Sangyo shipping company (☎ 0988-64-0087 in Naha, 03-3562-2091 in Tokyo), operates a weekly ferry service between Okinawa and Taiwan. Boats depart from Naha Port on Thursday or Friday and from Keelung (or sometimes Kaohsiung) in Taiwan on Sunday. The service generally operates directly between Naha and either Keelung or Kaohsiung, but it occasionally (check beforehand) stops at Miyako and Ishigaki. The trip takes about 16-19 hours and costs range between ¥15,600 (economy class) and ¥24,300 (1st class).

Getting Around
To/From the Airport The busy Naha Airport is only three km from the town centre – 10 minutes by taxi for ¥800 to ¥1100 or 12 minutes by bus No 24 or 102 for ¥170. The buses run three to six times an hour (7 am to 10 pm) via the main bus station and then down Kokusai-dōri. The airport has three widely spaced terminals: international, domestic 1 (for mainland Japan) and domestic 2 (for the South-West Islands).

Bus The bus system is relatively easy to use. For local town buses, you simply dump ¥170 into a slot next to the driver as you enter. For longer trips you collect a ticket showing your starting point as you board and pay the appropriate fare as you disembark; a board at the front shows the various starting numbers and the equivalent fares. Buses run from Naha to destinations all over the island.

There are many bus tours around the island, particularly to the war sites in the south.

Car & Motorcycle Okinawa is a good place to get around in a rented vehicle since the traffic is not too heavy and the northern end of the island is lightly populated and has poor public transport. There are numerous rental companies in Naha with cars from around ¥5000 per day plus ¥1500 insurance. Convertibles are very popular. Try Japaren (☎ 0988-61-3900), Nippon Rent-a-Car (☎ 0988-68-4554) or Toyota Rent-a-Car (☎ 0988-57-0100), among others.

A number of places rent scooters and motorcycles. A 50 cc scooter costs from ¥1500 for three hours to ¥3000 for a day; a 250 cc motorcycle ¥4000 to ¥8000. Try Sea Rental Bikes (☎ 0988-64-5116) or Trade (☎ 0988-63-0908).

SOUTHERN OKINAWA   沖縄の南部

The area south of Naha was the scene of some of the heaviest fighting during the closing days of the Battle of Okinawa. There are a number of reminders of those terrible days as well as some other places of interest in this densely populated part of the island.

The initial US landing on Okinawa took place north of Naha at Kadena and Chatan beaches on 1 April 1945. By 20 April US forces had captured the northern part of the island and the area south of their landing place to Naha. The rest of the island was not captured until 21 June.

Underground Naval Headquarters
旧海軍司令部壕

About five km directly south of Naha is the underground naval headquarters (described in one Japanese tourist brochure as the 'shelter of the defunct Japanese naval headquarters') where 4000 men committed suicide as the battle for Okinawa drew to its prolonged and bloody conclusion. Only 200 metres of the 1.5 km of tunnels is open but you can wander through the maze of corridors, see the commander's final words on the wall of his room and inspect the holes and scars in other walls from the grenade blasts which killed many of the men. In Japanese the headquarters are known as *kyū kaigun shireibugō*, though the sign from the main road simply reads 'Kaigungo Park'. Entry is ¥410 and it's open from 8.30 am to 6 pm (5 pm in the winter). To get there take bus No 33 or 101 from the Naha bus station to the Tomigusuku-kōen-mae stop, a 10 minute walk from the site.

Nearby is the Tomigusuku-kōen Park with

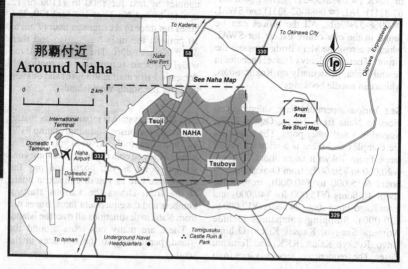

那覇付近
Around Naha

0   1   2 km

To Kadena
To Okinawa City
Naha New Port
See Naha Map
International Terminal
Domestic 1 Terminal
Naha Airport
Domestic 2 Terminal
Tsuji
NAHA
Tsuboya
Shuri Area
See Shuri Map
Okinawa Expressway
58
330
332
331
329
To Itoman
Underground Naval Headquarters
Tomigusuku Castle Ruin & Park

The War & Okinawa

The Battle of Okinawa is still a controversial subject. The Okinawans had long felt they'd got a tough deal from mainland Japan. Back in the Satsuma days they were exploited and looked down upon by the mainlanders. In the struggle for Okinawa during WW II they were expendable, a people to be used in order to delay the barbarian invasion of the mainland. The Okinawans paid a terrible price for that delay, as far more Okinawan civilians died than mainland military personnel.

Masahide Ota's *The Battle of Okinawa* (Kume Publishing, 1984) gives some interesting insights into the relentless ferocity of the struggle, but I came out of the underground naval headquarters pondering the sheer idiotic futility of it all. What I felt was anger at the stupidity, rather than sorrow for the deaths. If you're searching for reasons why the decision was made to nuke Nagasaki and Hiroshima, perhaps what happened in Okinawa will supply some answers.

Tony Wheeler

pleasant views of Naha, though there is very little trace of Tomigusuku Castle, after which the park was named.

Itoman Area 糸満

The fisherfolks' Hakugin-dō Shrine is in this port town, 12 km south of Naha. You can also check out the Kōchi family tombs here, while just south is Nashiro Beach and the Lieutenant General Buckner Memorial, in memory of the US commander who was killed here by stray shrapnel in the final days of the Battle of Okinawa. The site of Gushikawa Castle at Cape Kiyan-saki is now popular with hang gliders, but in the closing days of the Battle of Okinawa many civilians jumped to their death from the cliffs. Itoman can be reached by bus No 33, 34 or 35 from Naha bus station.

War Sites

Around the southern end of the island are a series of sites connected with the final days of the Battle of Okinawa. On 19 June 1945 at **Himeyuri-no-Tō**, 200 schoolgirls and their teachers committed suicide in the school grounds rather than fall into the hands of the US military. The memorial to this event is now one of the most popular tourist attractions in Okinawa. Directly south on the coast is the **Konpaku-no-Tō Memorial** to 35,000 unknown victims of the fighting who were subsequently buried here.

At **Mabuni-no-Oka** (Mabuni Hill), the remaining Japanese forces were virtually pushed into the sea. In their underground hideaway the commanders committed seppuku (ritual suicide) on 23 June 1945, while above ground the US forces already had complete control of the island. Memorials from every prefecture in Japan dot the hillside and the **Peace Memorial Museum** tells the gruesome story of the struggle. One reader recommended looking out in particular for the 'brooding half-grey sphere' that is a memorial to the Korean labourers and comfort women who lost their lives in the war. The hill area is open daily from 9 am to 4.30 pm except Monday; entry is ¥100. Also at this extensive site is the **Peace Hall** (¥520), a seven sided tower built in 1978 and housing a 16 metre high Buddha statue. Behind the hall is a **Peace Art Museum**.

Taking public transport to the sites is time consuming. Bus Nos 82, 83 and 85 go there from Itoman; get off at the Komesu stop for Konpaku-no-Tō or the Kenji-no-Tō stop for Mabuni Hill. There are frequent bus tours from Naha, which cost about ¥4000.

Gyokusen-dō Cave 玉泉洞

Japan has plenty of limestone caves but for those who can't get enough of stalactites and stalagmites there are more here. Nearly a km of the cave is open to visitors from 9 am to 5, 5.30 or 6 pm (depending on the time of year). Entry is ¥730. When you leave the cave you can continue straight in to the Gyokusendō Habu Park (¥620) and see the unfortunate 'deadly' habu suffering the traditional 'deadly' defeat by a mongoose. Bus No 54 from Naha bus station takes 50 minutes to

OKINAWA & SOUTH WEST ISLANDS

reach the cave; bus Nos 51 and 52 drop you further from the cave (15 minutes walk versus five minutes) but depart from Naha much more frequently.

Other Attractions
Just beyond the Mabuni Hill memorials is the **Okinawa Coral Museum**. Coral is much nicer where it belongs – underwater. Continuing north on Route 15, you'll find **Himeyuri Park**, which specialises in cactus. Turn east on Route 76 to reach **Tomori-no-Ojishi**, where a large stone shiisā (lion) overlooks a reservoir. This particular shiisā dates back to at least 1689; a popular image from the Battle of Okinawa shows a US soldier sheltering behind it while watching with binoculars.

Tiny **Ō-jima Island** is linked to the main island by bridge and has good beaches, as has Nibaru Beach a little further north. The island can be reached directly by bus from the Naha bus station by taking No 52, which takes around one hour and costs ¥500.

North of Ō-jima is the **Chinen Marine Leisure Centre**. This place is popular with Japanese tourists for the glass-bottomed boat cruises, although 'cruise' is perhaps too grand a term; for ¥720 you get exactly 15 minutes to peer underwater, while ¥1030 will get you 25 minutes. There are also boats from here to **Kudaka Island** and minute **Komaka Island**, which is encircled by fine beaches. The leisure centre can be reached by bus Nos 37 and 38 from the Naha bus station for ¥610.

CENTRAL OKINAWA 沖縄中央部
Central Okinawa (north of Naha through Okinawa City to Ishikawa City) is heavily populated, but beyond this area the island is much less crowded. The US military bases are principally in the southern part of central Okinawa, the resorts in the northern part. Dotted around this stretch of Okinawa is an amazing number of artificial tourist attractions where many thousands of yen could be squandered on entry fees.

Urasoe 浦添
Urasoe, eight km north of Naha, was the early capital of the Rūkyū kingdom, and today its two main attractions are the **Yōdore Royal Tombs**, dating back to the 13th century, and **Jōseki-kōen Park**. The latter contains the ruins of the original castle residence of the Okinawan royal family and costs ¥310 entry. The tombs date back to the 13th century and are about 20 minutes walk from the park; ask for Urasoe Yōdore. The No 56 Bus runs to Urasoe Jōseki-kōen Park from the Naha bus station for ¥310.

Nakagusuku Castle 中城城跡
The hilltop ruins of **Nakagusuku Castle** have a wonderful position overlooking the coast. The castle was built in 1448, preceding stone construction of this type on the mainland by 80 years. It's much better stonework than that found on the mainland. The castle was destroyed in 1458 in a bizarre episode of feudal manoeuvring known as the Amawari Rebellion. When Gosamaru, the Nakagusuku lord, heard that Amawari, another Okinawan lord, was plotting a rebellion against the king he mobilised his troops. The scheming Amawari then convinced the king that it was Gosamaru who was planning to revolt, so the hapless Nakagusuku ruler committed suicide.

There's no sign pointing out the castle site and an earlier 'pass' sign down the road is a red herring. Look for the entrance gate with a field in front of it and the inevitable tourist activity. To get there by public transport from Naha, take a bus to Futenma and from there bus No 58. It's open from 8.30 am to 5.30 pm and entry is ¥500.

Nakamura House 中村家
A half km up the road from the castle is probably the best preserved traditional Okinawan house on the island. The Nakamura family's origins in the area can be traced back to the 15th century, but the foundations of this house date from around 1720. The construction is typical of a well-off farming family's residence at that time. Originally, the roof would have been thatched but it was later roofed with traditional red tiles. As you explore this interesting and surprisingly

comfortable-looking home, notice the substantial stone pig pens, the elevated storage area (to deter rats) and the trees grown as typhoon windbreaks. The house is open from 9 am to 5.30 pm and entry is ¥300. It's a 10 minute walk up from Nakagusuku Castle; bus No 58 passes by the house.

Okinawa City 沖縄市
Okinawa City is the US military centre on Okinawa, centred around the Kadena Air Force Base which was the initial target of the US invasion. The pre-war village has mushroomed to a population of over 100,000. The city has all the hallmarks of American influence, from pizzerias to army surplus stores. There's even an *A&W Burgers* outlet where you can order from your car over an intercom and your food is brought out to you – shades of American drive-ins of the '50s. The Tuttle Bookstore at the Plaza House shopping mall is the best English-language bookshop on Okinawa.

Attractions around Okinawa City, some of them decidedly artificial, include the **Moromi Folkcraft Museum**, the **Koza-yaki Pottery Factory**, **Okinawa Children's Land**, the Tonan or **South-East Botanical Gardens** and the Agena and Katsuren Castle sites. Bullfights, where one bull tries to push another out of a ring, are held on Sunday at **Gushikawa**, near Okinawa Children's Land.

Bus Nos 21, 22, 23, 24, 25, 26, 31, 63, 77 and 90 all run to Okinawa City from Naha in a little over one hour.

Okinawa City to Nago 沖縄市から名護へ
The South-East Botanical Gardens are popular with Japanese tourists, but are a hassle to get to by public transport from Naha. Buses run from Okinawa City, and the Gardens are open from 9 am to 6 pm; entry is ¥720. Enthusiasts of castle ruins can find more of them at the Iha Castle site near Ishikawa and at the Zakimi Castle site on the west coast, north of Kadena. In the Zakimi Castle Park the **Yomitan Museum** displays local farming equipment.

The Okinawan resort strip starts from **Zanpa Beach** on Cape Zanpa-misaki. The **Ryūkyū Village** offers yet another opportunity to see a re-creation of Okinawan farming life, and yet another snake park where, for the amusement of tourists, those 'deadly' habu lose out (once again) to those plucky mongooses. More beach life can be found at the Ramada Renaissance Resort, Moon Beach and Manza Beach, while just before Nago is the **Okinawa Submarine Park**, which has an underwater observatory.

As well as the expensive resort hotels along this coast, there is also the *Maeda-misaki Youth Hostel* (☎ 09896-4-2497) near the Ryūkyū Village. Bus No 20 from Naha runs along the west coast past all these sites to Nago. It takes about one hour 20 minutes to get to the Ryūkyū Village or Moon Beach; one hour 40 minutes to Manza Beach and two hours to the submarine park.

NAGO 名護
If you're spending a couple of days exploring Okinawa then Nago (population 51,000) is a good overnight stop; it's about two-thirds of the way up the island. There are fine views over the town and the coast from the **castle hill**, although little trace remains of the castle itself. In spring the cherry blossoms on the

OKINAWA & SOUTH WEST ISLANDS

Bullfighting
Battles between opposing bulls, where one tries to push the other out of the ring (rather like sumō wrestlers) are known as *tōgyū* in Japan. The custom is found in a long sweep of islands all the way from Indonesia to Japan. There are about a dozen tōgyū stadiums in Okinawa, the most important ones being the Agena Stadium in Gushikawa and the Kankō Stadium in Okinawa City. The most important fights are held in May and November, but they take place a couple of times a month year-round. The bulls for Okinawa tōgyū events are bred on Kuro-shima Island, near Iriomote. ■

名護
Nago

0   100   200 m

To Cape Hedomisaki

To Okinawa Memorial Park

To Nago Castle Hill

Route 58

To Naha

PLACES TO STAY

1   Nago Castle Hotel
    ホテル名護キャッスル
11 Hotel Okura
    ホテルおおくら
12 Shiroyama Hotel
    ホテル城山
13 Futubase Hotel
    ホテル双葉荘

PLACES TO EAT

2   Restaurant
    レストラン
4   Dom Dom
    ドムドムレストラン
10 Shinzan Shokudō Restaurant
    新山食堂
16 A & W Burgers
    A & Wバーガース
17 McDonald's
    マクドナルド

OTHER

3   Oki-Mart Supermarket & Bus Stop
    おきマートスーパー／バス停
5   Market
    市場
6   NTT
7   Nago Cross Roads
    名護十字路
8   Bowling Alley
    北ボーリング場
9   Banyan Tree
    バンヤンの樹
14 Post Office
    郵便局
15 Museum
    名護博物館

hill are particularly good. A fine old banyan tree, the **Hinpun Gajumara**, is a useful landmark in the centre of town. You can find out all about traditional farming (which is fast-disappearing on Okinawa) at the **Nago Museum**. The museum is close to the banyan tree and is open from 10 am to 6 pm; entry is ¥100.

Places to Stay & Eat

The *Nago Castle Hotel* (☎ 0980-52-5954) is a clean, pleasant place close to the centre of town, with singles for ¥4200 and breakfast available for ¥500. The fancier *Hotel Okura*

(☎ 0980-52-2250) has singles at ¥5000 and doubles at ¥8700. Both hotels have popular restaurants; the latter does Okinawan specialities while the former has a sign announcing 'pizza'. Another accommodation possibility is the *Hotel 21st Century* (☎ 0980-53-2655), which has singles from ¥5500. It's further north up Route 58.

Shinzan Shokudō is a famous Nago noodle shop that has been running for 60 years. It's near the Okura Hotel. Nago has many fast-food outlets – a *McDonald's* and *A&W Burgers* mark the entry to town. There's also the usual plethora of bars, snack bars and so on in the entertainment area. Two blocks south-east of the Nago Castle Hotel is a big, bright, friendly and busy restaurant (see the Nago map); there's nothing in English, but enough food comes over the bar for the 'point and ask' routine to afford success, and you can eat well for ¥1000.

Getting There & Away
Nago is the junction town for buses to northern Okinawa or the Motobu-hantō Peninsula. From Okinawa City bus station bus Nos 20 and 21 make the 62 km trip in about 2½ hours for ¥1600.

MOTOBU-HANTŌ PENINSULA
本部半島
Jutting out to the north-west of Nago, the hilly Motobu-hantō Peninsula has several points of interest as well as ferry services to nearby Ie-jima Island.

Okinawa Memorial Park
海洋博覧会記念公園
The site of the 1975 International Ocean Exposition has a cluster of tourist attractions, most of which can be bypassed without any great sacrifice. Entry to the park itself is free, but the individual attractions charge entry fees. The aquarium (¥620) is claimed to be one of the largest in the world and the sharks and rays in the big tank, particularly the huge whale shark, are indeed impressive, although the tank is very crowded.

Aquapolis (¥510) is a rusting and faded vision of a floating city of the future where

the main news is that there will still be a demand for tacky souvenirs. There's also the Oceanic Culture Museum (¥160), the Museum of Okinawa (¥150), the Native Okinawan Village (free), the Tropical Dream Centre, with orchid and other flower displays around the curious circular spiral tower (¥620), and a dolphin show (free). The park also has a beach and an amusement park.

The park is open from 9.30 am to 5.30, 6 or 7 pm depending on the season; it's closed on Thursday. Individual attractions close half an hour earlier. On Sunday and holidays, three No 93 buses run directly from Naha to the park; on other days you will have to take a bus to Nago, and from there take a No 70 bus on the Motobu Peninsula Bise line (¥700). Shuttle buses run around the surprisingly sprawling park and cost ¥100.

Nakijin Castle Site   今帰仁城跡
Winding over a hilltop, the 14th century walls of Nakijin Castle may not be as neat as Nakagusuku but they look terrific. From the summit of the hill there are superb views out to sea. Entry is ¥150; bus No 66 operates from Nago for ¥810, and bus No 65 from the Okinawa Memorial Park. The castle site is open daily from 8 am to 6 pm.

Other Attractions
The **Yambaru Wildlife Park** and **Izumi Pineapple Garden** are other peninsula sites. There are also two islands connected to the peninsula by road. To the south is **Sesoko-jima**, which has good beaches on the western side as well as camping facilities. Bus No 76 takes around 55 minutes from Nago and costs ¥610. From the bus stop it's around 20 minutes' walk to the west side beaches (the island is only eight sq km). To the north of the peninsula is Yagaji-jima, which has little in the way of interest.

Three km west of Sesoko-jima is tiny Minna-jima Island (0.56 sq km), with fabulous beaches (again, like Sesoko-jima, the best ones are to the west). The only drawback of this island is that you can expect it to be packed with day-trippers from the expensive resorts in the high season, and out of season it's difficult to get to. Ferries run from Motobu Port just south of the Sesoko bridge.

Ie-jima Island

North-west of the Motobu-hantō Peninsula, Ie-jima Island has a wonderful view from the top of **Mt Gusuku**. It's around a 45 minute walk from the pier. The truly indolent might consider a taxi, which should cost around ¥600. Around five minutes walk to the south of the pier is a monument to the American war correspondent Ernie Pyle, who was killed on the island during the early days of the Battle of Okinawa. Also possibly worth checking out is the **Jimamuraya Sightseeing Park**, not far to the north of the Ernie Pyle monument. It has an entry charge of ¥300.

Those planning a longer stay on the island can hire tents at the *Iejima Seishōnen Ryokō Mura* (Youth Travel Village). Alternatively, the *Marco Polo Pension*, around 300 metres to the north of the pier has rooms for ¥6000 with two meals included. The *Hill Top Hotel*, a nondescript white building, is around 15 minutes walk in the same direction and has similar rates. Ferries make the 40 minute trip to the island from Motobu Port four times daily for ¥570. Buses around the eight km by three km island are irregular, but bicycles, scooters and cars can be rented.

NORTHERN OKINAWA 沖縄の北部

The northern part of Okinawa is lightly populated and comparatively wild and rugged. A road runs around the coast, making this an interesting loop trip, but buses are infrequent and do not continue all the way along the east coast.

West Coast to Cape Hedo-misaki
西海岸から平戸岬へ

Route 58 north from Nago has virtually converted Shioya Bay into an enclosed lake. The village of **Kijoka** is noted for its traditional houses and for the production of the very rare cloth known as Bashōfu. You should make an advance appointment if you want to visit the Kijoka Bashōfu Weaving Workshop. Further north there's an expensive resort at **Okuma Beach** (rates range from ¥14,000),

while the town of Hentona has shops, minshuku and other facilities.

Cape Hedo-misaki marks the northern end of Okinawa. The rocky point is liberally sprinkled with cigarette ends and soft-drink cans. Nevertheless, it's a scenic spot backed by hills, with rocks rising from the dense greenery. Bus No 67 (¥870) travels along the coast from Nago, but you have to continue north from Hentona on No 68 or 69 (¥470).

East Coast 東海岸

From Cape Hedo-misaki, the road continues to **Oku**, the termination point for buses travelling up the west coast via the cape. The English sign 'Hotel' at the beginning of the village leads you, 50 metres further on, to the cheap and cheerful *Oku Ryokan*. Then, 200 metres further along, another sign 'Wellcomes' you to *Lodging Okuyanbaruso*.

There are good beaches around Oku. For the next 15 km the road stays very close to the coastline, with more fine-looking beaches but frequent warnings of current and tide dangers for swimmers, divers and snorkellers. **Aha** is a picturesque village which still has some traditional thatched-roof houses.

ISLANDS AROUND OKINAWA
沖縄周辺の島々

Apart from the islands just a stone's throw from the Okinawan coast, there are three other island groups a little further away.

Iheya-jima & Izena-jima Islands
伊平屋島・伊是名島

North of Okinawa, these two islands have good beaches and snorkelling and a number of hotels and minshuku. A daily ferry runs from Motobu's port to Izena (1½ hours) and to Iheya (another 20 minutes).

Kerama-rettō Islands 慶良間諸島

There are about 20 islands in this group west of Okinawa, only four of them inhabited. The islands have fine beaches, some good walks, great lookouts and some of the best scuba diving in Japan. Ferries from Naha take one to 1½ hours; flights are also available.

Kume-jima Island　久米島

Further west of the Kerama-rettō Islands is beautiful Kume-jima Island, with its superb scenery, excellent beaches and the long curving sweep of sandbank at **Sky Holiday Reef**, just east of the island. The Uezu House is a samurai-style home dating from 1726.

There are ryokan and minshuku on the island, particularly near **Eef Beach** where there is also a small resort hotel. Day trips can be made from Eef Beach to Sky Holiday Reef.

From Naha, ferries to the island take approximately 3½ hours, and SWAL has regular daily flights, taking 35 minutes at a cost of ¥5360.

You can get around the island by rented car, scooter or bicycle.

Miyako Islands
宮古列島

About 300 km south-west of Okinawa, directly en route to the Yaeyama Islands, is the small Miyako group, comprising Miyako itself and, a few km to the west, Irabu-jima and Shimoji-jima Islands, plus a scattering of smaller islands.

MIYAKO-JIMA ISLAND　宮古島

Like the other Okinawa-ken islands, Miyako offers beaches and diving, and, since it escaped the destruction rained down upon Okinawa itself during WW II, some traces of Ryūkū culture and architecture remain. One thing it does not offer is the poisonous habu snake which seems to engender so much fear and loathing throughout the South-West Islands. Miyako is the Ireland of the Nansei-shotō chain – no snakes here!

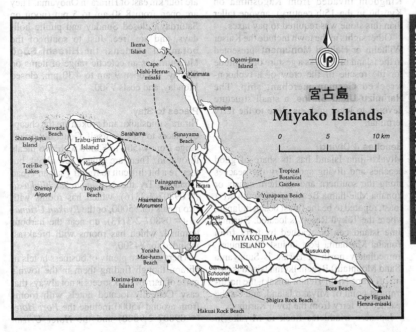

OKINAWA & SOUTH WEST ISLANDS

Orientation & Information

Hirara, the main town on Miyako-jima Island, is compact and easy to get around. Each year the very low spring tide reveals the huge Yaebishi reef, north of Ikema Island.

Hirara 平良

There are a few minor attractions in Hirara (population 33,000), but the operative word is indeed 'minor'. They are hardly worth the effort on a hot sticky day. Near the waterfront, just north of the ferry terminal, is the **Nakasone Toimiyā**, a large mausoleum to a 15th century Miyakoan hero who not only conquered the Yaeyama Islands to the south but also prevented an invasion from the north. There's another impressively large mausoleum cut into the hillside just beyond it.

Continuing north along the coast road you'll find the **Jintōzeiseki**, a 1.4 metre high stone more or less plonked down in someone's front garden. During the heavy-handed rule of the Satsumas (the Satsuma Kingdom invaded from Kagoshima on Kyūshū in the 15th century), anyone taller than this stone was required to pay taxes.

Other sights in the town include the Kaiser Wilhelm or **Hakuai Monument**, presented to the island in 1878 as a gesture of gratitude for the rescue of the crew of a typhoon-wrecked German merchant ship. The **Harimizu Utaki Shrine**, a small structure devoted to local gods, is close to the ferry terminal.

Beaches & Diving

Miyako-jima Island has its share of good beaches and diving spots. Try the beaches along the southern and northern coasts or Yonaha Mae-hama Beach on the south-west coast, reputed to be the finest beach in Japan, where the Tōkyū Resort is located. Kurima-jima Island can be reached by ferry from Yonaha Maehama Port in just 10 minutes. Immediately north of Hirara is Sunayama (Sand Mountain) Beach. Ikema Island is two km off Cape Nishi-Henna-misaki, the northernmost point of Miyako Island, and can be reached by ferry from the town Karimata.

Japanese triathletes flock to Miyako in

April each year for the Strongman Challenge, which involves a three km swim, a 136 km bicycle race and a 42 km marathon. Miyako is also a popular scuba-diving centre and there are a number of dive operators on the island.

Cape Higashi-Henna-misaki 東平安名岬

At the south-eastern end of the island this long, narrow and quite spectacular peninsula ends with a picturesquely placed lighthouse overlooking the rocky coastline.

Other Attractions

The **Hisamatsu-goyushi Monument** in the village of Hisamatsu, a few km south-west of Hirara, commemorates the fishermen who spotted the Russian fleet steaming north during the Russo-Japanese War of 1904-05. Admiral Tōgō was able to intercept them north of Kyūshū (see the Tsu-shima Island section in the Kyūshū chapter).

The **Hirara Tropical Botanical Gardens** are four km east of Hirara in Onoyama. They are open from 8.30 am to 5 pm (noon on Saturday), closed Sunday and public holidays, and are free. Just to south of the botanical gardens, the **Hirashi Sōgō Museum** has an eclectic range of items on display. It's open 9 am to 4.30 pm, closed Monday, and costs ¥300.

Places to Stay

Hirara's minshuku and ryokan are the cheapest places to base yourself. Generally prices range from ¥4500 to ¥5000 with two meals thrown in. There are quite a few about, but they're a bit difficult to find if you can't read Japanese. Try the *Minshuku Shichifuku-sō* (☎ 09807-2-2316), which has rooms with two meals for ¥5000, or the *Ryokan Uruma-sō* (☎ 09807-2-3113), up near the harbour terminal, which has rooms with breakfast included for ¥4500.

There are also plenty of business hotels in Hirara, though finding them in the town's maze of narrow backstreets is not always that easy. Centrally located hotels with rooms from around ¥5000 include the *Port Hotel* (☎ 09807-2-9820) and the *Hotel Urizun*

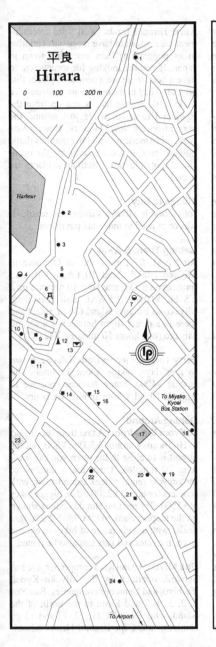

平良
Hirara

0   100   200 m

Harbour

To Miyako
Kyoei
Bus Station

To Miyako
Kyoei
Bus Station

To Airport

PLACES TO STAY

5   Hotel Kyowa
    ホテル共和
8   Ryokan Uruma-sō
    旅館うるま荘
9   Port Hotel
    ポート観光ホテル
11 Hotel Urizun
    ホテルうりずん
14 Grand Hotel
    グランドホテル
17 New Marakatsu Hotel
    ホテルニュー丸勝
21 Minshuku Shichifuku-sō
    民宿七福荘

PLACES TO EAT

15 Tsubohachi Restaurant
    つぼ八
16 Mos Burger
    モスバーガー
19 Nomura Restaurant
    野村レストラン

OTHER

1   Tax Stone
    人頭税石
2   Mausoleum
    和利真良豊見親之墓
3   Nakasone Toimiyā Mausoleum
    仲宗根豊見見之墓
4   Harbour Terminal
    平良港ターミナル
6   Harimizu Utak Shrine
    張水御嶽神社
7   Yachiyo Bus Station
    八千代バスターミナル
10 Jammin' Reggae Bar
    じゃみんレゲエバー
12 Kaiser Wilhelm Monument
    ドイツ皇帝博愛記念碑
13 Post Office
    郵便局
18 Sankyū Rent-a-Bike
    サンキューレンタバイク
20 Tomihama Motorcycle Rental
    とみはまモーターサイクルレンタル
22 New York Bar
    ニューヨークバー
23 Market
    平良市公設市場
24 Marutama Motorcycle Rental
    まるたまモーターサイクルレンタル

OKINAWA & SOUTH WEST ISLANDS

(☎ 09807-2-4410). The slightly pricier *Grand Hotel* (☎ 09807-2-3351), where rooms start at ¥5500, is also right in the centre of town. The new *Hotel Kyowa* is near the waterfront, overlooking the Harimizu Utaki Shrine, but rooms here are more expensive again, ranging from ¥6500.

The *New Marakatsu Hotel* (☎ 09807-2-9936) is a rambling, slightly tatty place down an entrance alley from the main road in Hirara. There's no sign in English but look for the big letter 'K' in a circle at the top of the hotel sign. Singles are ¥6500 and doubles are ¥9000.

Elsewhere on the island is the expensive *Tōkyū Resort* (☎ 09807-6-2109), on the beautiful Yonaha Mae-hama Beach, where prices range from ¥16,000 to ¥93,000. There are a few places to stay on neighbouring Irabu-jima Island, including the *Minshoku Katera-sō* (☎ 09807-8-3654), close to Toguchi Beach. It has rooms with breakfast from ¥4000.

Places to Eat
Tsubohachi is a very modern robatayaki (grilled food restaurant); the sign outside proclaims it's a 'Casual House'. Not only does the full-colour menu show all the possibilities, but it also lists the calories for each one! (Not for the beer, thank goodness.) Most dishes are ¥300 to ¥500.

Just down the road from Tsubohachi (toward the Kentucky Fried Chicken) are a couple of sushi places that are popular with locals. Look out for the blue nori curtains outside and the blonde wood exteriors. Just behind the Ryokan Uruma-sō is *Rakkii* (☎ 09807-2-7928), a sushi place with a good local reputation, where you can eat from around ¥1000.

Fast-food places around the centre of town include a *Mos Burger*, next door to Tsubohachi, and a *Kentucky Fried Chicken* just down the road from it. There are also lots of red-lantern bars and 24-hour coffee shops, the latter good for a set breakfast or 'morning service'.

The people of Miyako have a reputation for being outgoing and friendly – to the point where Hirara's Izzatu (west side) entertainment area is said to have more bars (relative to its population) than any other town in Japan. If you are looking for somewhere to have a beer, there are a couple of places that aren't too bad in the central area. *Jammin'*, a funky little reggae bar, is just up from the Ryokan Uruma-sō, while just around the corner from the New Marakatsu Hotel is *New York*, an 'American-style' bar that has darts, billiards and, if you are unlucky, the occasional spot of karaoke. Both these places are open late.

Things to Buy
Jōfu fabric is Miyako's traditional textile. It was once used to make tax payments.

Getting There & Away
Air SWAL fly from Naha on Okinawa to Miyako Island about 10 times daily (45 minutes on a 737, one hour 10 minutes on a YS-11, ¥10,950). SWAL also flies from Miyako to Ishigaki Island (35 minutes) and there is a direct flight between Tokyo and Miyako (two hours 50 minutes, ¥42,070).

Ferry There are ferries from Naha every two to five days, taking about 13 hours and costing ¥4000. Some services continue to Ishigaki Island, taking another six hours.

Getting Around
To/From the Airport A taxi from the airport to Hirara costs around ¥500 to ¥600, but the airport is so close to the town you can walk it in 20 minutes. There are a number of motorcycle rental places around town with scooters for hire at ¥2500 a day, bigger bikes at ¥5500. Try the two Honda dealers shown on the map, or Sankyū (☎ 09807-2-2204), a dealer with a wide range of bikes to choose from. Bicycles and cars can also be rented.

Bus Miyako Island has a comprehensive bus network operated by the Miyako Kyoei, Yachiyo, and Ueno bus companies. Bus Nos 1, 2, 3, 4, 7 and 8 run to the north of the island; while Nos 10, 11, 12, 13 and 15 go south towards Cape Higashi-Henna-misaki.

IRABU-JIMA & SHIMOJI-JIMA ISLANDS
伊良部島・下地島

If you fly over Shimoji-jima Island (between Okinawa and Ishigaki) have a look at the airport runway. It seems to be out of all proportion to the size of the island and the number of flights it gets. This is because JAL and ANA use it for 747 pilot training.

Irabu and Shimoji, linked by six bridges, are pleasantly rural islands with fields of sugar cane. **Sawada** and **Toguchi** are two good beaches. On Shimoji-jima Island the **Tōri-ike Lakes** are linked to the sea by hidden tunnels.

Getting There & Away
SWAL have a daily flight from Naha on Okinawa to Shimoji but most visitors arrive on the regular 15 minute, ¥450 ferry crossing between Hirara on Miyako-jima Island and Sarahama on Irabu-jima Island. There are two agencies selling tickets for boats in the ferry terminal.

Yaeyama Islands
八重山列島

At the far south-western end of the Nansei-shotō chain are the islands of the Yaeyama group, consisting of two main islands (Ishigaki-jima and Iriomote-jima) and a scattering of smaller islands between and beyond the two main ones. There are some fine dive sites around the islands, particularly on Yonaguni-jima Island, the westernmost point in Japan, and Hateruma-jima Island, the southernmost point. Although there are many Japanese visitors to the islands, most of them, in true Japanese fashion, are daytrippers. Come nightfall on Iriomote or Taketomi most of the tourists will have scuttled back to their hotels on Ishigaki.

ISHIGAKI-JIMA ISLAND   石垣島
Ishigaki-jima is the major flight destination for the Yaeyama island group, and boat services fan out from its harbour to the other islands. There are a few sights in the town of Ishigaki itself, and for most visitors it's mainly of interest as a jumping-off point to the other islands. Ishigaki-jima is about 400 km south-west of Okinawa Island.

Orientation & Information
For Japan, Ishagiki town is an incredibly torpid little place. Don't expect much in the way of excitement. The town's focus is its busy harbour. As for the rest of town – you can stroll around it in a few minutes. Parallel to the main street are two shopping arcades. If you plan to take supplies to the outer islands you'll find a better choice in the arcades than at the places around the harbour. There are several interesting places to visit outside Ishigaki town itself, such as Mt Omoto-dake and the Tamatorizeki-tenbōai Viewing Platform.

Miyara Dōnchi House
Although the South-West Islands never really had samurai, this is essentially a samurai house. It dates from 1819 and is the only one left in the whole island chain. The building itself is run down and the garden is poorly maintained, but it's still nice to see. Entry is ¥100; it's closed on Tuesday.

Torin-ji Temple
Founded in 1614, this Zen temple is the most important on the island. 'Sentry' boxes flank the gates and statues dating from 1737 (said to be the guardian deities of the islands) can be seen in the dim interiors. Immediately adjacent to the temple is the 1787 Gongen-dō Shrine. The original shrine was built in 1614 but destroyed in a flood in 1771. Every month, from the 15th to the 19th, if you get up very early, you can see Zen meditation being practised here from 5.30 am to 6.30 am. The temple is about a 15 minute walk from the harbour.

Mt Omoto-dake
Mt Omoto-dake (526 metres) in the centre of the island is the highest point in Okinawa Prefecture. Mt Banna-dake, five km from town, is only 230 metres high but has fine

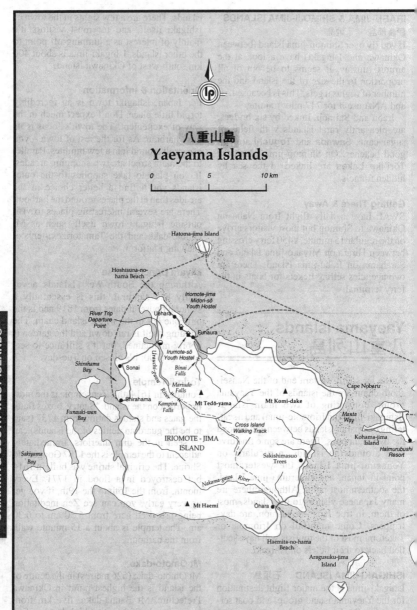

八重山島
Yaeyama Islands

0   5   10 km

Hatoma-jima Island

Hoshisuna-no-
hama Beach

Iriomote-jima
Midori-sō Youth Hostel

Uehara

Funaura

River Trip
Departure
Point

Irumote-sō
Youth Hostel

Shinhama
Bay

Sonai   Binai
                       Falls

Shirahama   Mariudo
                       Falls

Funauki-wan   Kampira
Bay   Falls

Sakiyama   Mt Tedō-yama   Mt Komi-dake
Bay

                       IRIOMOTE - JIMA
                       ISLAND

                                          Cross Island
                                          Walking Track

                                                          Sakishimasuō
                                                          Trees

                                   Nakama-gawa River

            Mt Haemi

                                          Ōhara

                       Haemita-no-hama
                       Beach

Cape Nobaru

Manta
Way

Kohama-jima
Island

Haimurubushi
Resort

Aragusuku-jima
Island

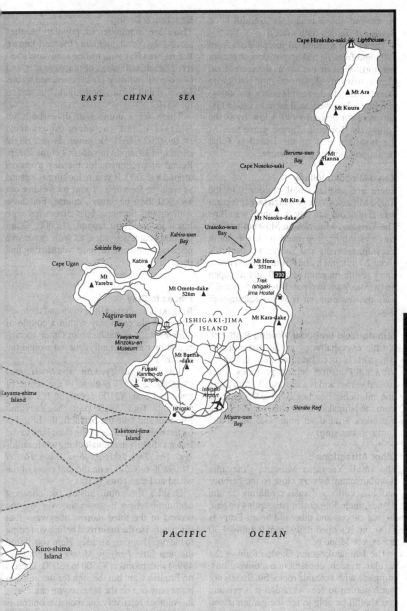

views and the Banna-dake Shinlin-kōen Botanical Garden (entry free).

The Fusaki Kannon-dō Temple dates from 1701 and from its hilltop position, about six km north-west of the town, there are good views towards Taketomi and Iriomote islands. Entry to the temple is free, but unless you hire a bicycle you'll have to take a taxi out there for around ¥990. Close by is the Tōjin-baka Tomb, a Chinese grave site. At the northern end of the island is Cape Hirakubo-saki and a lighthouse.

Kaiyo Minzoku Village

There are several small museums in the Kaiyo Minzoku Village which faces Nagura-wan Bay about halfway to Kabira-wan Bay. The Yaeyama Minzoku-en Museum will tell you everything you need to know about Yaeyama weaving and Yaeyama pottery. It's about 20 minutes by bus from Ishigaki town. Entry to the museum is ¥500 and it's open daily from 9 am to 6 pm. Bus Nos 5, 6 and 7 pass the museum en route to Kabira-wan Bay.

Tamatorizeki-tenbōdai Viewing Platform

A little over halfway up the east coast of Ishigaki is the Tamatorizeki-tenbōdai Viewing Platform which provides great coastal views, and is a short walk from some fine untouched beaches. Bus No 9 goes there from the Ishigaki bus terminal for ¥710. The trip takes around an hour. Get off at the Tamatori bus stop.

Other Attractions

The small Yaeyama Museum (Yaeyama Hakubutsukan) is very close to the harbour and has various displays relating to the islands, including coffin palanquins or *gau*, dugout canoes and other old boats. Entry is ¥100 and it's open daily from 9 am to 4.30 pm except Monday.

The Ishigakike-teien Garden follows the regular garden construction conventions, complete with volcanic rocks, but there's not much garden to see. Although it is private, you should be able to see the garden if you ask politely.

Beaches & Diving

There are a number of popular beaches around the island, including the well-known Kabira-wan Bay with its fine sandy and sheltered beach, collection of places to stay and black-pearl industry. It can be reached by bus Nos 5, 6 and 7 from the Ishigaki bus station for ¥510.

There are a number of dive shops on Ishigaki Island, including Aquamarine (☎ 09808-2-0863). However, as you might expect, in Japan diving doesn't come cheap. Rental of equipment for the day averages around ¥15,000. If you're looking at lessons as well (in Japanese), count on forking out ¥80,000 for a beginner's course. For those with diving licences, boat dive trips with lunch included are around ¥12,000. Other popular beach activities, all with expensive price tags on them, include windsurfing and para-sailing.

Places to Stay

Ishigaki is a compact little town and there are plenty of places to stay within a couple of minutes walk of the harbour. Other accommodation can be found scattered around the island.

The *Yaesu Ryokan Youth Hostel* (☎ 09808-2-3157) is close to the centre of town and costs ¥2100 per night. It's a little tricky to find. Walk past the Yaeyama Museum and take the first left; the hostel is on the right-hand side of the third lane to the left in a slightly decrepit looking white building. The *Trek Ishigaki-jima Youth Hostel* (☎ 09808-6-8257) is on the east coast of the island and also costs ¥2100.

Besides the youth hostel, the cheapest accommodation in town is over on the second of the three narrow alleyways that run parallel to the main road before you come to the two shopping arcades. Here you'll find the neat little *Pension Mitake* (☎ 09808-2-4993) with rooms at ¥3500 to ¥5000. There's no English sign, but the sign for the pension is the only one on the lane, so you can't miss it. Another relatively inexpensive option is the *Minshuku Yaeyama-sō* (☎ 09808-2-

石垣島
Ishigaki

0   125   250 m

To Kabira

To Airport

Inter-Island Harbour

Arcades

PLACES TO STAY	
5	Hotel Marina City ホテルマリナシティ
6	Hotel Miyahira ホテルミヤヒラ
10	Ō-Hara Hotel 大原ホテル
11	Pension Mitake ペンションみたけ
14	Grand Hotel グランドホテル
18	Minshuku Yaeyama-sō 民宿八重山荘
20	Yaesu Ryokan Youth Hostel 八重洲旅館 ユースホステル

PLACES TO EAT	
4	Mizushi Restaurant 三寿司
8	Pekin Ryōri Restaurant 北京料理
9	Taimon Restaurant 大門レストラン

12	A&W Burgers A ＆ W バーガーズ
15	Mos Burger モスバーガー
16	Iso Restaurant レストラン磯

OTHER	
1	Ishigakike-teien Garden 石垣氏庭園
2	Torin-ji Temple 桃林寺
3	Gongen-dō Shrine 権現堂
7	Bus Station バスターミナル
13	Ferry Company Offices フェリー事務所
17	Post Office 郵便局
19	Yaeyama Museum 八重山博物館

3231). It's a pleasant place with singles from ¥5000 with two meals.

On the business hotel front, the *Ō-Hara Hotel* (☎ 09808-2-3380) is a quiet, well kept place with singles for ¥6000. The Japanese-style rooms here are very nice, and cost only an extra ¥150. Incidently, the hotel's name comes from the town on Iriomote, not from some wayward Irishman.

More expensive hotels include the *Ishigaki Grand Hotel* (☎ 09808-3-6161) right across from the harbour, with rooms from ¥10,000. Also near the harbour are the *Hotel Miyahira* (☎ 09808-2-6111) (¥9000 to

¥12,000) and the *Hotel Marina City* (☎ 09808-2-0088), which has rooms from ¥6500. The top hotel in town (and the only place which has an international telephone) is the *Hotel Nikkō Yaeyama* (☎ 09808-3-3311), where singles/doubles start at ¥10,000/18,000. It's way up in the north of town, around 25 minutes walk from the harbour.

Places to Eat

Ishigaki is an unusual Japanese town in that you have walk around a bit to find somewhere to eat. There isn't a restaurant

OKINAWA & SOUTH WEST ISLANDS

beckoning you in on every corner. Even the fast-food chains are poorly represented in this neck of the woods, with a *Mos Burger* and an *A&W Burgers* both seemingly struggling to make ends meet.

The *Iso Restaurant* (☎ 09808-2-7721) serves good food in a bright and cheerful setting; you can even see in from outside! Set meals featuring local specialities are available from ¥1000 to ¥2000 (you can eat well for ¥1500); beers cost ¥600. Right across the narrow road from Iso is the pleasant *Ishigaki-sen* (☎ 09808-2-8084), a local red-lantern bar.

Other possibilities include a couple of Chinese restaurants, both close to the Ō-Hara Hotel: the *Pekin Ryōri Restaurant* and the *Taimon Restaurant*. The former is a tiny place opposite the docks, and the Taimon is a bigger place with a sign outside in English proclaiming 'Chinese Restaurant'. *Mizushi* (☎ 09808-2-3708) is a counter-style sushi restaurant with a good local reputation. It's up the road from the Ō-Hara Hotel, and is open from 5 pm till midnight, except Wednesday.

Getting There & Away
Air SWAL has more than 10 flights a day between Naha (Okinawa Island) and Ishigaki (one hour, ¥14,710) and three between Miyako and Ishigaki islands (30 minutes, ¥5360). ANK operate less frequent services between Naha and Ishigaki. SWAL fly from Ishigaki to the tiny Yonaguni-jima and Hateruma-jima islands. There are controversial plans to extend the Ishigaki Airport runway which would result in the destruction of the beautiful coral reefs in the adjacent bay at Shiraho.

Ferry There are ferry services every two to five days directly beween Naha and Ishigaki (13 hours, ¥5500) or via Miyako Island. Miyako to Ishigaki takes about six hours and costs ¥2000. The Okinawa to Taiwan ferry service occasionally operates via Ishigaki, but not very often (see Naha, Getting There & Away for details).

Ishigaki is the centre for all the Yaeyama

Islands' ferry services and the small harbour is a hive of activity. The ferry company offices are along the two sides of the harbour and there are often several operators, at a variety of prices, to a given destination.

Getting Around
A taxi between the airport and town costs about ¥700; there is no convenient bus service. Bus services fan out from Ishigaki town, the station is across the road from the harbour. A bus to Kabira costs ¥510, to the top end of the island costs ¥950. Car rental is available at the airport and in town, and bicycles can also be rented in town; the going rate is ¥500 per hour or ¥1500 per day. For motorcycle rental contact Sankyū (☎ 09808-2-5528), an established agent with a good selection of bikes from ¥2500 per day.

TAKETOMI-JIMA ISLAND 竹富島
Only a 10 minute boat ride from Ishigaki is the popular but relaxed little island of Taketomi. It's noted for its beaches and the pretty little flower-bedecked village in the centre of the island. Even if you only come over for a day trip, don't forget to bring a towel and your bathing costume. There's excellent swimming at Koindo-hama beach, around 20 minutes' walk from the harbour area.

Orientation & Information
Taketomi-jima is a pancake-flat island with its village smack in the middle. From Taketomi Village, the roads fan out to various places around the edge. A perimeter road following the 10 km coastline is on the drawing board and a section has already been constructed around the north-western quadrant. The tourist information office has a coral and shell display.

Taketomi Village 竹富村
Akayama Oka is a tiny lookout atop an even tinier hillock but, on this otherwise flat island, it offers good views over the red-tiled roofs. Look for the walls of coral and rock and the angry guardian lion figures (shiisā) on the rooftops. The other observation point

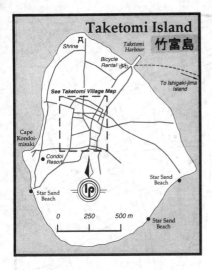

Taketomi Island
竹富島

Shrine

Taketomi Harbour

Bicycle Rental 🚲

To Ishigaki-jima Island

See Taketomi Village Map

Cape Kondoi-misaki

Kondoi Resort

Star Sand Beach

Star Sand Beach

Star Sand Beach

0   250   500 m

is the Nobukuru lookout, at the northern end of the village, on top of someone's house. It costs ¥100.

The **Kihōin Shūshūkan** is a small private museum with a diverse collection of local items and a ¥300 entry price. **Taketomi Mingeikan** is a local craft centre where you can see the island's Minsā belts and other local textiles being produced. Opposite the craft centre is the **Nishitō Utaki Shrine**, dedicated to a 16th century ruler of the Yaeyama Islands.

Beaches

Most of the island is fringed with beach, but the water is generally very shallow. At several places you can look for star sand (*hoshisuna*), tiny grains of sand with a distinctive star shape. They're actually the dried skeletons of tiny creatures. Although you are requested not to souvenir more than a few grains (where do you put them?), it's sold by the bucketful at shops and at Ishigaki Airport. The map shows good star-sand hunting points. Around Cape Kondoi-misaki on the western side of the island you'll find star sand and the best swimming spot on the island.

Places to Stay & Eat

The *Takana Ryokan & Youth Hostel* (☎ 09808-5-2151) is opposite the post office. Costs per night are ¥2100 for the hostel and from ¥5500 with two meals for the ryokan section. The *Nohara-sō* is cheaper, however, with rooms for ¥4000 with two meals. Close by, the *Shinda-sō* offers similar standards for ¥4500. Accommodation is not difficult to find on Taketomi, as many of the traditional houses around the island are minshuku or ryokan.

There are also a few restaurants and coffee bars scattered around, though the island is by no means a gourmet paradise. *Chirorin-mura*, a rustic little snack bar, is a good place for a lunch-time bowl of noodles for ¥500. Both beer barrels and tree stumps are used as stools at the tables and bar.

Getting There & Away

The best deal for getting to the island is with the Yaeyama Kankō travel service, whose boats do the 10 minute run from Ishigato-jima Island approximately every 20 minutes for ¥570. Shinzato Kankō also runs ferries from Ishigaki and back every half hour between 8.30 am and 5.30 pm, but they cost ¥1030 (well, it's a better class of boat).

Getting Around

The island is small enough to get around most of it on foot if the weather isn't too muggy. Otherwise, there are numerous bicycle rental places on the island including one near the docks. Bikes cost ¥200 an hour, ¥1000 a day and are great for exploring the tiny island's sandy roads. You can also hire tandem bicycles and motor scooters. For Japanese visitors, a popular activity is taking a tour of the island in a cart drawn by water buffalo. It actually looks like it might be fun. The cost is ¥1000 for 50 minutes, which is about what it takes to trundle around the island's points of interest.

IRIOMOTE-JIMA ISLAND   西表島

Dense jungle blankets much of Iriomote-jima, an island which could well qualify as Japan's last frontier. Trekking through the

OKINAWA & SOUTH WEST ISLANDS

1 Tourist Information
    観光案内所
2 Kihōin Shūshūkan
    Museum
    喜宝院蒐集館
3 Akayama Oka Lookout
    赤山丘展望台
4 Nishitō Utaki Shrine
    西塘御嶽神社
5 Taketomi Mingeikan
    (Craft Centre)
    竹富民芸館
6 Takana Ryokan &
    Youth Hostel
    高那旅館及び
    ユースホステル
7 Post Office
    郵便局
8 NTT
9 Oxcart Rides
    水牛カート乗り場
10 Nobukuru Lookout
    のぶくる展望台
11 Chirorin-mura
    Snack Bar
    スナックバー
    ちろりん村
    Bicycle Hire
    Ryokan

竹富村
Taketomi Village

To Taketomi
Harbour

To Cape
Kondoi-misaki

OKINAWA & SOUTH-WEST ISLANDS

interior, you may find leeches, which in Japan is probably good enough for the 'wilderness' tag. The island's major attractions are fine beaches, rivers and waterfalls, and the Iriomote wildcat. Similar in size (and appearance) to a domestic cat, the Iriomote wildcat is nocturnal and rarely seen. The picturesque road signs alerting drivers of its possible presence are, however, quite common.

Much easier to find are the curious sakishimasuo trees with their twisting, ribbon-like root buttresses. You will find them all over the island but particularly

along the coast about five km north of Ōhara. The Iriomote National Park includes about 80% of the island, plus a number of neighbouring islands.

Orientation & Information

Iriomote-jima has several tiny towns – Funaura, Uehara and Shirahama in the north and Ōhara in the south – and a perimeter road runs about halfway around the coast from just beyond Ōhara to Shirahama. No roads run into the interior, which is virtually untouched. There's a tourist information office at the top of the car park by the docks near Funaura; the staff will book accommodation for you.

River Trips

Iriomote-jima's number one attraction and the principal goal for the many day-trippers is the trip up the Urauchi-gawa River to the **Mariudo Falls**. The winding brown river is indeed a lot like a tiny stretch of the Amazon and, from where the boat stops, you have about a 1½ hour round-trip walk to the Mariudo Falls and on to the long, rapids-like **Kampira Falls**. There are some good swimming places around the falls. From the falls a walking track continues right across the island. The river trip costs ¥1440. Boats operate from 8.30 am to 5 pm, but they need a minimum of four passengers to set off. There will probably be less waiting around if you get here in the morning, when most of the day trippers turn up.

From close to the Ōhara docks it is also possible to take river cruises up Iriomote's second-largest river, the **Nakama-gawa River**. The cruises last for around one hour and 20 minutes through lush jungle-like vegetation and cost ¥1240.

Beaches & Diving

There are some fine beaches around the island and star sand can be found at Hoshisuna-no-hama (Star Sand Beach). Sonai, beyond the Urauchi-gawa River towards Shirahama, also has a pleasant beach and some good places to stay. Haemita-no-hama Beach, south of Ōhara, is said to be the best beach on the island.

Diving around Iriomote-jima certainly isn't cheap, but there are some fine sites like the famed Manta Way in the straits between Iriomote and Kohama, where you are almost certain to come across manta rays. A day's diving typically costs ¥10,000 for the boat and ¥5000 for the gear.

Walks

There are some great walks in Iriomote's jungle-clad interior. The **Binai Falls** on the hills behind the lagoon are visible from boats coming into Funaura. To get to the falls you wade across the shallow lagoon from the causeway, plod through the mangroves behind the lagoon and then follow the river up to the base of the falls. A path branches off from the river and climbs to the top of the falls, from where there are superb views down to the coast. The walk takes 1½ to two hours and the falls are great for a cooling dip, but bring salt or matches to get rid of leeches.

From the Kampira Falls at the end of the Urauchi-gawa River trip you can continue on the cross-island trail to **Ōhara**. The walk takes about eight hours and is particularly popular in the spring, when the many trekkers manage to lay a confusing network of false trails.

Places to Stay & Eat

Iriomote-jima has many ryokan, minshuku and pensions, each one lining up its minibus to meet incoming boats at Funaura. The staff at the Funaura Harbour information office will make bookings. The best places are found along the coast west of the harbour towards the Hoshisuna-no-hama Beach or further west near the Urauchi-gawa River. There's also some good accommodation in the small village of Sonai, where the *Hoshisuna-sō Minshuku* (☎ 09808-5-6411) is particularly good.

The *Irumote-sō Youth Hostel* (☎ 09808-5-6255) has a great hillside location near Funaura Harbour, good facilities, great food and a dive shop. The nightly cost is ¥2400. Continuing west along the coast from Funaura you soon come to the *Iriomote-jima Midori-sō Youth Hostel* (☎ 09808-5-6526/6253), which costs ¥1700 per night.

If you don't want a youth hostel and you want to be close to Funaura Harbour, *Funaura House* (09808-5-6715) is a pleasant place with rooms for ¥5000 to ¥7500 including two meals. Plonked in between Ōhara and Haemita Beach, the best rated strip of sand on the island, is the *Minshuku Hae-sō* (☎ 09808-5-6513), with rooms from ¥4000 to ¥8000. Almost directly opposite is the *Minshuku Iketaya* (☎ 09808-5-5255), where rooms are ¥5000 with two meals. *Robinson's Inn* is a pleasant coffee bar on the main junction in Uehara, a km along the road from Funaura Harbour. Next to it is the *Minshuku Akebo-no-kan* (☎ 09808-5-6151), with rooms for ¥4500 with two meals.

Getting There & Away

A variety of boats operate between Ishigaki and Iriomote, most to Funaura, which is the place to get the Urauchi-gawa River Cruise, rather than Ōhara. Occasionally there are services to Shirahama. The fares vary from around ¥1750 to ¥2400 and the trip typically takes from 40 minutes to one hour on the faster craft. The slower and less frequent ferries are cheaper.

Boats run out to Funaura from the Shinzato Kankō travel service four times a day at 8.30 and 11 am and 1.30 and 4.00 pm. The same boat returns from Funaura at 9.20 am, noon and 2.30 and 5 pm. Tickets cost ¥1800. The Yaeyama Kankō travel service offers the same deal for ¥2060.

Getting Around

Many of the minshuku and the youth hostels rent bicycles (¥200 per hour, ¥1200 per day) and scooters (¥600, ¥3000). Cars can also be rented: try Iriomote Rent-a-Car (☎ 09808-5-5303). There's a regular bus service between Ōhara and Shirahama at the two ends of the island's single road. A bus all the way from one end to the other takes nearly an hour and costs ¥960; a bus from Funaura Harbour to the Urauchi-gawa River costs ¥220.

ISLANDS AROUND IRIOMOTE

西表島周辺の島々

Directly north of Iriomote, clearly visible from Funaura, tiny **Hatoma-jima Island** has a handful of minshuku and some very fine beaches and snorkelling.

Close to the east coast of Iriomote-jima, the small island of **Kohama-jima** has a sprinkling of minshuku, the expensive Haimurubushi Resort (where rates start at ¥21,200) and superb scuba diving, particularly in **Manta Way**. Boats operate there from Ishigaki. Minshukus on the island are generally around ¥4500 with two meals included. Clustered together in the center of

the island are three such places: the *Minshuku Ufudaki-sō* (☎ 09808-5-3243); the *Kayama-sō* (☎ 09808-5-3236); and the *Nagata-sō* (☎ 09808-5-3250). From the Ishigaki harbour there are four operators, including Yaeyama Kankō (see the Ishigaki map) offering seven boats a day to the island for ¥1000. The trip takes 25 to 30 minutes.

There are also regular services to the smaller Kuro-shima Island, directly south of Kohama. It's renowned as the place where bulls are raised for Okinawa's bullfights (*tōgyū*), but it's also got good diving and a couple of pensions and minshuku. The *Minshuku Kuroshima* (☎ 09808-5-4251) is south-east of the harbour and has rooms from ¥4500 with two meals. The Yaeyama Kankō travel service has five ferries a day from Ishigaki for ¥1100 and, as the trip only takes around 40 minutes, it's possible to do it as a day trip. The Shinzato Kankō ticket office has four boats a day to Kuro Island. Boats leave at 9 am, noon, and 2 and 4.30 pm. They return at 9.40 am and 12.40, 4.40 and 5.10 pm. Tickets cost ¥1500.

YONAGUNI-JIMA ISLAND 与那国島

Yonaguni-jima Island is 100 km west of Iriomote-jima and Ishigaki-jima islands and only 110 km from the east coast of Taiwan. The hilly island is just 11 km long and there are fine views from the top of 231 metre **Mt Urabu**. It's said that on a clear day you can see the mountains of Taiwan from Yonaguni. The island is renowned for its strong sake and its jumbo-sized moths known as *yonagunisan*. Traditional houses on the island have thatched roofs, but tiled roofs are becoming the norm.

All things considered, there's not a lot to see in Yonaguni, but it has a reputation among some young Okinawans as being a mysterious place, perhaps because it's so far from the mainland and so close to Taiwan. The coastline is marked with some great rock formations, much like those on the east coast of Taiwan. The most famous of these is **Tachigami-iwa Rock** (literally the 'standing-god rock') on the south-east coast. Another famous rock formation is the

Sanninu-dai (or Gunkan-iwa) Rock on the south-west coast. For Japanese this rock is famously evocative of virility and other masculine qualities (one in particular). Of interest mainly to Japanese on tours of the island is the **Iri-saki Rock**, a rock carved with an inscription proclaiming it the westernmost point of Japan.

Yunaguni Island's airport is about 10 minutes by taxi from the main town of **Sonai**. There's not a great deal of interest in town, but you might want to check out the **Yunaguni Minzoku Shiryōkan**, with its cluttered displays of items from Yunaguni's history. It's free and open daily from 8.30 am to 6 pm. Also worth checking out is the **Yunaguni Traditional Crafts Centre** in the east of town, where you can see locals working on traditional looms, probably for the benefit of the occasional tourist.

Places to Stay

There are a few hotels and minshuku in Sonai and a couple of places over near Japan's westernmost rock. In terms of both economy and atmosphere, No 1 is *Minshuku Omori* (☎ 09808-7-2419), an interesting little place with rooms for ¥4000 with two meals. It's just south of the Minzoku Shiryōkan. Just up the road from the Minzoku Shiryōkan is the *Hotel Irifune* (☎ 09808-7-2311), which even sports an English sign outside. It has rooms with two meals for ¥6000. There are plenty of other places besides these if you care to look around.

Getting There & Away

SWAL fly to Yonaguni-jima Island from Ishigaki twice daily; the 40 minute flight costs ¥5360 one way, ¥9640 return. The Fukuyama ferry service (☎ 09808-7-2555) has two boats a week from Ishigaki to Yunaguni at a cost of ¥3500. The trip takes 6½ hours.

Getting Around

Don't expect much in the way of public transport in this neck of the woods. Basically there isn't any, although the island is rumoured to have four public buses running somewhere everyday. Fortunately there are bikes for hire at an average cost of ¥2500 per day. A four-hour taxi romp around the island will set you back a cool ¥15,000. Car hire is also available at the airport and in Sonai.

HATERUMA-JIMA ISLAND　ハテルマ島

Directly south of Iriomote-jima Island is tiny Hateruma-jima Island, only five km long and the southernmost point of Japan. Hateruma means 'the end of the coral'. Like the westernmost rock on Yunaguni-jima Island, Hateruma-jima Island sports a **southernmost rock** (have your photo taken in front of both of them and really impress the folks back home!). There are a few minshuku on the island, but you can also visit as a day tripper. The Shinzato Kankō company on the harbour in Ishigaki has at least three boats a day at 8.40 and 11 am and 3.40 pm. The same boat heads back to Ishigaki at 9.50 am, 12.40 and 4.50 pm. Of course you can always spend a lot more money and around the same amount of time (by the time you've got out to the airport and mucked about with check-in) by taking a SWAL flight from Ishigaki, which takes 20 minutes and costs ¥4860.

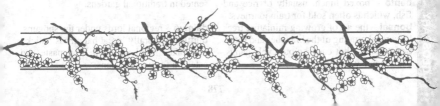

Glossary

abecu – from *avec*, the French word for 'with' and used by the Japanese to refer to a courting couple. Love Hotels were called *Abecu Hoteru* but this has now fallen out of use and the English is more commonly used.

aimai – ambiguous and unclear talk, not coming to the point.

Ainu – the original people of Japan, recognisable by their rounded eyes, hirsute appearance and wavy hair; only isolated pockets of pure Ainu remain, in the northern extremes of Hokkaidō.

aka-chōchin – red-lantern bar; working man's pub.

akirame – to relinquish; resignation.

amakudari – 'descent from heaven'; a retiring civil servant who then goes to work for a private corporation which he formerly dealt with.

annaijo – information office.

Arahitogami – living god, the emperor.

arubaito – from the German *arbeit*, meaning 'to work', adapted into Japanese to refer to part-time work.

ayu – sweetfish caught during *ukai* (cormorant fishing).

baito – from *arbeit*, the German word for 'work'; a part time job or an illegal immigrant worker.

bangasa – rain umbrella made from oiled paper.

banzai – literally '10,000 years', *banzai* means 'hurrah' or 'hurray'; in the West this exclamation is mostly associated with WW II, although its modern use is quite peaceful.

basho – *sumō* wrestling tournament.

basho-gara – literally 'the character of a place', fitting to the particular conditions or circumstances.

bentō – boxed lunch, usually of rice and fish, which is often sold for train journeys.

bonsai – the art of growing miniature trees by careful pruning of the branches and roots.

boso-zoku – hot car or motorcycle gangs, usually noisy but harmless.

bottle keep – system where you buy a whole bottle of liquor in a bar and they keep it for you to drink on subsequent visits. Real entertainers may have bottles stored at numerous bars around town.

bugaku – dance pieces played by court orchestras in ancient Japan.

bunraku – classical puppet theatre using huge puppets to portray dramas similar to *kabuki*.

burakumin – literally 'village people', the *burakumin* were traditionally outcastes associated with lowly occupations such as leather work.

bushidō – 'Way of the Warrior', set of values followed by the samurai.

butsudan – Buddhist altar in Japanese homes.

carp – carp *(koi)* are considered to be a brave, tenacious and vigorous fish and the *koinobori* carp windsocks are flown in honour of sons whom it is hoped will inherit a carp's virtues. Many towns and villages have carp ponds or channels teeming with colourful ornamental *nishiki-goi* carp.

chaniwa – tea garden.

chanoyu – tea ceremony.

charm – small dish of peanuts or other snack food served, often unrequested, with a drink at a bar – and charged for.

chizu – map.

chō – city area (for large cities) between a ward *ku* and *chōme* in size; also a street.

chōme – city area of a few blocks.

chōchin – paper lantern.

chōnan – oldest son.

chu – loyalty.

crane – cranes are a symbol of longevity and are often reproduced in *origami* and represented in traditional gardens.

daimyō – regional lords under the shōguns.

daifuku – literally 'great happiness'; sticky rice cakes filled with red bean paste and eaten on festive occasions.

danchi – public apartments.
dantai – a group (such as the ubiquitous Japanese tourist group).
deru kui wa utareru – 'the nail that sticks up gets hammered down'; popular Japanese proverb which is more or less the opposite of the Western 'the squeaky wheel gets the oil'!
donko – name for local trains in country areas.

eboshi – black, triangular samurai hat.
eki – railway station.
ekiben – *bentō* lunch box bought at a railway station.
ema – small votive plaques hung in shrine precincts as petitions for assistance from the resident deities.
engawa – traditional veranda from a Japanese house overlooking the garden.
enka – often referred to as the Japanese equivalent of country & western music, these are folk ballads about love and human suffering that are popular among the older generation.
enryō – individual restraint and reserve.
ero-guro – erotic and grotesque *manga*.

fu – urban prefecture.
fude – brush used for calligraphy.
fugu – poisonous blowfish or pufferfish.
fundoshi – loincloth or breechcloth; traditional male garment consisting of a wide belt and a cloth drawn over the genitals and between the buttocks. Now usually seen only at festivals or on *sumō* wrestlers.
furigana – Japanese script used to give pronunciation for *kanji*.
furii kippu – one day open ticket.
futon – traditional quilt-like mattress which is rolled up and stowed away during the day.
fusuma – sliding screen.
futsū – literally 'ordinary'; a basic stopping-all-stations train.

gagaku – music of the imperial court.
gaijin – literally 'outside people'; foreigners.
gaman – to endure.
gasshō-zukuri – 'hands in prayer' architectural style.
gei-no-kai – the 'world of art and talent';

usually refers to TV where there's not much of either.
geisha – not a prostitute but a 'refined person'; a woman versed in the arts and dramas who entertains guests.
genkan – foyer area where shoes are removed or replaced when entering or leaving a building.
geta – traditional wooden sandals.
giri – a person's social obligations.
giri-ninjō – combination of social obligations and one's personal values; the two are often in conflict.
go – board game in which players alternately place white and black counters down, with the object of surrounding the opponent and making further moves impossible; probably originating in China, where it is known as *weiqi*.

hachimaki – headband worn as a symbol of resolve; *kamikaze* pilots wore them in WW II, students wear them to exams.
haiku – 17 syllable poems.
haitaku – a hired taxi.
hakurai – literally 'brought by ship'; foreign or imported goods.
hanami – cherry blossom viewing.
haniwa – earthenware figures found in Kofun period tombs.
hanko – stamp or seal used to authenticate any document; in Japan your *hanko* carries much more weight than your signature.
harakiri – belly cutting; common name for *seppuku* or ritual suicide.
hara-kyū – acupuncture.
hashi – chopsticks.
heiwa – peace.
henro – pilgrims on the Shikoku 88 Temple Circuit.
higasa – sunshade umbrella.
hiragana – phonetic syllabary used to write Japanese words.

ichi-go – square wooden sake 'cups' holding 180 ml.
ijime – bullying or teasing.
ikebana – art of flower arrangement.
irezumi – a tattoo or the art of tattooing. Japanese tattoos are usually much more

complex and artistic than their Western counterparts. Traditionally they are worn by *yakuza* (Japanese Mafia members), but carpenters and labourers are just as likely to be tattooed.

itadakimasu – before-meals expression; literally 'I will receive'.

ittaikan – feeling of unity, of being one type.

izakaya – Japanese version of a pub; beer and sake and lots of snacks available in a rustic, boisterous setting.

jiage-ya – specialists used by developers to persuade recalcitrant landowners to sell up.

jika-tabi – split-toe boots traditionally worn by Japanese carpenters and builders, which have recently become fashionable attire.

jigoku – 'hells' or hot springs for looking at.

jikokuhyō – the book of timetables.

jitensha – bicycle.

jujitsu – martial art from which *judō* was derived.

juku – cramming schools.

kabuki – form of Japanese theatre based on popular legends and characterised by elaborate costumes, stylised acting and the use of male actors for all roles.

kachi-gumi – the 'victory group' who refuse to believe Japan lost WW II.

keigo – honorific language used to show respect to elders.

kaikan – hotel-style accommodation sponsored by government; literally 'meeting hall'.

kaiseki – Japanese cuisine which obeys very strict rules of etiquette for every detail of the meal and the diner's surroundings.

kaisha – a company, firm.

kaisoku – rapid train.

kaisūken – discount bus tickets.

kakizome – New Year's resolutions.

kami – Shintō gods; spirits of natural phenomena.

kamidana – Shintō altar in Japanese homes.

kamikaze – 'divine wind'; typhoon that sunk Kublai Khan's 13th century invasion fleet and the name adopted by suicide pilots in the waning days of WW II.

kampō – Chinese herbal medicines that were

dominant in Japan until the 19th century, when Western pharmaceuticals were introduced.

kana – the two phonetic syllabaries, *hiragana* and *katakana*.

kanban-musume – 'shop sign girl'; girl who stands outside a shop or business to lure customers in.

kanbu – management.

kanji – literally 'Chinese script'; Chinese ideographic script used for writing Japanese.

Kannon – Buddhist Goddess of Mercy, adopted by the underground Christians as a substitute Virgin Mary during Japan's long period of isolation from the West.

kannushi – chief priest of a Shintō shrine.

kanpai – 'Cheers!'

karakasa – oiled paper umbrella.

karaoke – bars where you sing along with taped music (usually mournful folk ballads); literally 'empty orchestra'.

karōshi – 'death by overwork'; the recently recognised phenomenon of overworked businessmen falling dead on urban streets.

kasa – umbrella.

kasekininrui – 'fossil breed'; ancient form of *kyujinrui*.

katamichi – one-way ticket.

katana – Japanese sword.

katakana – phonetic syllabary used to write foreign words.

ken – prefecture.

kendō – oldest martial art; literally 'the way of the sword'.

ki – life force, will.

kimono – brightly coloured, robe-like traditional, outer garment.

kin-en-sha – nonsmoking carriage.

kissaten – coffee shop.

kōban – police box; the officers in this local police station keep a careful eye on their district.

koinobori – carp banners and windsocks; the colourful fish pennants which wave over countless homes in Japan in late April and early May are for Boys' Day, the final holiday of Golden Week. These days Boys' Day has become Children's Day and the windsocks don't necessarily simply fly in honour of the household's sons.

kokki – Japanese national flag.

kokumin-kyūka-mura – national vacation villages; a form of inexpensive accommodation set up by the government to ensure that all citizens have access to low-cost holiday accommodation.

kokuminshukusha – peoples' lodges; an inexpensive form of accommodation.

kokutetsu – Japanese word for Japan Railways (JR); literally, 'national line'.

komeitō – clean party government; third-largest political party.

kone – personal connections.

kotatsu – heated table with a quilt or cover over it to keep the legs and lower body warm.

koto – 13-stringed instrument that is played flat on the floor.

kura – mud-walled storehouses.

kyakuma – drawing room of a home, where guests are met.

kyōiku mama – education mother; a woman who pushes her kids through the Japanese education process.

kyujinrui – 'old breed'; opposite of *shinjuru*.

kyūkō – ordinary express train (faster than a *futsū*, only stopping at certain stations).

live house – nightclub or bar where live music is performed.

machi – city area (for large cities) between a *ku* (ward) and *chōme* (area of a few blocks) in size; also street or area.

maiko – apprentice *geisha*.

mama-san – woman who manages a *water trade* bar or club.

maneki-neko – beckoning cat figure frequently seen in restaurants and bars; it's supposed to attract customers and trade.

manga – Japanese comics (contents often include soft porn).

māningu sābisu – see *morning service*

matsuri – festival.

meinichi – the 'deathday' or anniversary of someone's death.

meishi – business card; very important in Japan.

mentsu – face.

miai kekkon – arranged marriage; now rare.

mibun – social rank.

miko – shrine maidens.

mikoshi – portable shrines carried around by hordes of sweaty, half-naked salarymen during festivals.

minshuku – the Japanese equivalent of a B&B; family-run budget accommodation.

misoshiru – bean-paste soup.

mitsubachi – accommodation for motorcycle tourers.

mizu-shōbai – see *water trade*.

mochi – pounded rice made into cakes and eaten at festive occasions.

mōfu – blanket.

morning service – *māningu sābisu*; a light breakfast served until 10 am in many *kissaten*; often simply referred to as *māningu* by customers.

mukō – 'over there'; anywhere outside Japan.

mura – village.

nagashi – folk singers and musicians who wander from bar to bar.

nagashi somen – flowing noodles.

nengajo – New Year cards.

new humans – the younger generation, brought up in more affluent times than their parents and consequently less respectful of the frugal values of the postwar generation.

Nihon or **Nippon** – Japanese word for Japan; literally 'source of the sun'.

nihonga – term for Japanese-style painting.

ningyō – Japanese doll.

ninja – practitioners of *ninjutsu*.

ninjō – debt; fellow feeling; that which is universally right.

ninjutsu – 'the art of stealth'.

nō – classical Japanese drama performed on a bare stage.

noren – cloth hung as a sunshade, typically carrying the name of the shop or premise; indicates that a restaurant is open for business.

norikae – to change buses or trains; make a connection.

norikaeken – transfer ticket (trams and buses).

o- – prefix used to show respect to anything it is applied to. See *san*.

obāsan – grandmotherly type; an old woman.

obi – sash or belt worn with a kimono.

o-cha – tea.

ofuku – return ticket.

o-furo – traditional Japanese bath.

ol – 'office lady'; female employee of a large firm; usually a clerical worker.

omake – an extra bonus or premium when you buy something.

omiai – arranged marriage; rare in modern Japan.

omiyage – the souvenir gifts which Japanese must bring back from any trip.

on – favour.

onbu – 'carrying on the back'; getting someone else to bear the expense, pick up the tab. Also the custom of carrying a baby strapped to the back.

onnagata – male actor playing a woman's role (usually in *kabuki*).

onsen – mineral bath/spa area, usually with accommodation.

origami – art of paper folding.

oshibori – hot towels provided in restaurants.

otsumami – bar snacks or *charms*.

oyabun/kobun – teacher/pupil or senior/junior relationship.

pachinko – vertical pinball game which is a Japanese craze (estimated to take in over ¥6 trillion a year) and a major source of tax evasion, yakuza funds, etc.

puripeido kādo – 'prepaid card'; a sort of reverse credit card: you buy a magnetically coded card for a given amount and it can be used for certain purchases until spent. The prepaid phonecards are the most widespread but there are many others such as Prepaid Highway Cards for use on toll roads.

pinku saron – 'pink saloon'; seedy hostess bars.

rakugo – Japanese raconteurs, kind of stand-up comics.

robatayaki – *yakitori* with a deliberately rustic, friendly, down home atmosphere; see also *izakaya*.

romaji – Japanese roman script.

rōnin – 'masterless samurai'; students who must resit university entrance exams.

rotemburo – open-air baths.

ryokan – traditional Japanese inn.

saisen-bako – offering box at Shintō shrines.

sakazuki – sake cups.

sakoku – Japan's period of national seclusion.

sakura – cherry blossoms.

salaryman – standard male employee of a large firm.

sama – even more respectful suffix than *san* (see below); used in instances such as *o-kyaku-sama* – the 'honoured guest'.

samurai – warrior class.

san – suffix which shows respect to the person it is applied to; see also *o*, the equivalent prefix. Both can occasionally be used together as *o-kyaku-san*, where *kyaku* is the word for guest or customer.

san-sō – mountain cottage.

satori – Zen concept of enlightenment.

seku hara – sexual harassment.

sembei – soy-flavoured crispy rice biscuits often sold in tourist areas.

sempai – one's elder or senior at school or work.

sensei – generally translates as 'teacher' but has wider reference. Politicians are *sensei* through their power rather than their teaching ability.

sentō – public baths.

seppuku – ritual suicide by disembowelment.

setto – set breakfast.

shamisen – three-stringed banjo-like instrument.

shi – city (to distinguish cities with prefectures of the same name).

shiken-jigoku – 'examination hell'; the enormously important and stressful entrance exams to various levels of the Japanese education system.

shikki – lacquerware.

shinjū – double suicide by lovers.

shinjinrui – 'new species'; young people who do not believe in the standard pattern of Japanese life. Opposite of *kyujinrui*.

shinkansen – ultra fast 'bullet' trains; literally 'new trunk line', since new railway lines were laid for the high speed trains.

shitamachi – low-lying, less affluent parts of Tokyo.

shodō – Japanese calligraphy; literally the 'way of writing'.

shōgi – an Oriental version of chess in which each player has 20 pieces and the object is to capture your opponent's king.

shōgun – military ruler of old Japan.

shōji – sliding rice-paper screens.

shōjin ryōri – vegetarian meals (especially at temple lodgings).

shūji – the 'practice of letters'; a lesser form of *shodō*.

shukubō – temple lodgings.

shunga – explicit erotic prints; literally 'spring pictures', the season of spring being a popular Chinese and Japanese euphemism for sexuality.

shuntō – spring labour offensive; an annual 'strike'.

shūyū-ken – excursion train ticket.

soba – noodles.

soapland – Japanese euphemism for bathhouses that offer sexual services.

sōgō shōsha – integrated trading houses, like the old *zaibatsu*.

sokaiya – yakuza who specialise in ensuring that company general meetings go smoothly.

soroban – an abacus.

sukebe – lewd in thought and deed; can be a compliment in the right context (among male drinking partners for example), but generally shouldn't be used lightly; English equivalent would be something like 'sleaze bag'.

sumi-e – black-ink brush paintings.

sumō – Japanese wrestling.

Suzuki – the most common Japanese family name, equivalent to Smith in English.

tabi – split-toed Japanese socks used when wearing *geta*.

tachishōben – men urinating in public are a familiar sight in Japan. It's the cause of some academic discussion over Japanese concepts of private places (strict rules apply) and public ones (anything goes); insiders (your friends don't care) and outsiders (whether they care doesn't matter); and even rural environments (we're all farmers at heart) versus urban ones (even in the city).

tadaima – 'now' or 'present'; a traditional greeting called out when one returns home.

tako – kites.

tanin – outsider, stranger, someone not connected with the current situation.

tanka – poems of 31 syllables.

tanuki – racoon or dog-like folklore character frequently represented in ceramic figures.

tarento – 'talent'; referring to musical performers generally notable for their lack of it.

tatami – tightly woven floor matting on which shoes are never worn. Traditionally, room size is defined in the number of tatami mats.

tatemae – 'face'; how you act in public, your public position.

teikiken – discount commuter passes.

teishoku – set lunch.

tekitō – suitable or appropriate.

tennō – heavenly king, the emperor.

to – metropolis.

tokkuri – sake flask.

tokkyū – limited express; faster than an ordinary express (kyūkū) train.

tokonoma – alcove in a house in which flowers may be displayed or a scroll hung.

torii – entrance gate to a shintō shrine.

tsukiai – after work socialising by salarymen.

tsunami – huge 'tidal' waves caused by an earthquake.

uchi – literally 'one's own house' but has other meanings relating to 'belonging' and 'being part of'.

ukai – fishing with trained cormorants.

ukiyo-e – wood-block prints; literally 'pictures of the floating world'.

umeboshi – pickled plums; thought to aid digestion and often served with rice in bentō lunch sets.

wa – harmony, team spirit; also the old *kanji* used to denote Japan, and still used in

Chinese and Japanese as a prefix to indicate things of Japanese origin; see *wafuku*.

wabi – enjoyment of peace and tranquillity.

wafuku – Japanese-style clothing.

waka – 31 syllable poem.

wanko – lacquerware bowls.

waribashi – lacquered chopsticks.

warikan – custom of sharing the bill (among good friends).

washi – Japanese paper.

water trade – entertainment, bars, prostitution, etc.

yakitori – chicken kebabs.

yakitori-ya – restaurant specialising in *yakitori*.

yakuza – Japanese mafia.

yamabushi – mountain priests (Shugendō Buddhism practitioners).

yama-goya – mountain huts.

yamato – a term of much debated origins that refers to the Japanese world, particularly in contrast to things Chinese.

yamato damashii – Japanese spirit, a term with parallels to the German *Volksgeist*; it was harnessed by the militarist government of the '30s and '40s and was identified with unquestioning loyalty to the emperor.

yamato-e – traditional Japanese-style painting.

yaoya – Zen vegetable shops.

yatai – festival floats.

yenjoy girl – unmarried woman with time and cash to spare.

yōfuku – Western-style clothing.

yomiuri giants – *the* Japanese baseball team; although there are 12 big league teams over 50% of the population back the Giants.

yukata – rather like a dressing gown, worn for lounging or casual use; standard issue for bathing in ryokan.

zabuton – small cushions for sitting on (used in *tatami* rooms).

zaibatsu – industrial conglomerates; the term arose prior to WW II but the Japanese economy is still dominated by huge firms like Mitsui, Marubeni or Mitsubishi which are involved in many different industries.

Index

MAPS

TEXT

Map references are in **bold** type.

Castles

Gardens

Shrines

Temples

THANKS

Thanks to all the following travellers and others (apologies if we've misspelt your name) who took time to write to us about their experiences in Japan.

To those whose names have been omitted through oversight – apologies – your time and efforts are appreciated.

Thomas Ackermann (D), Kevin Adams (USA), Sebastian Allon, Katherine Anning, Alexander Arensberg (D), Miri Ariki (C), Robert Aronoff (USA), Andy Bain, Rene Bakker (NL), Cynthia Balaberda (C), Steven Bammel (USA), Dale Bay, Niels Bentzon (D), Jocelyn, Paul Bertheau (C), Staphane Biehler (F), Enrique Bisset (Sp), Sophie Blackmore (USA), Dick Blankenship (USA), Mr/Ms Blitstein, Jorn Borup (Dk), Marcia Breen (Aus), Deirdre Brennan (Aus), Nina Broberg (Aus), David Brooks (C), Chris Caley (Aus), Chris Calogeras (Aus), Eli Charne (USA), Severine Charon (F), Linda Ciano (USA), Matthre Clancy, Clare Clark, Peter Clark, Dorothy Cohen, Sue Collis (Aus), Jacky Copson, Del & Trish Corachi (USA), Lewis Cornwell (Aus), Frederick Court (Aus), William Cox (USA), P Cunningham (Aus), Sebastien de Laporte (F), Diana Delonis, Mike Doria (USA), Allison Dowd, Martin DuDemaine, Mark Elliott, Jim Ellison (J), Leslie Elmslie (I), Geert Embrechts, John Eriksen (Dk), David Evans (UK), Leonardo H Fernandez (Sp), J Mason Florence, John Eggers Fohlmann (Dk), Mrs F Fukuyama (USA), Chieko Furusawa (Jap), Linda Gano, Sean Garrity, Michael Geist (C), Hezi Gildor (Isr), Francine Govers (NL), Steve Graf (CH), Marti Griera (Sp), Marc Grutering (B), V Hamill (NZ), Sune Olofsson, Hansen (Dk), Kurt Hanson, Shannon Hanzek, Jane Harland (UK), John Harris (Aus), Brian Harrison, Alix Harrower (UK), Maria Heffner (USA), Roland Hellmann (F), Dean Henderson (USA), Kerstin Hendriks (D), Steve Hill (UK), Danya Hill, Michael Hoer, Hugh Hoffmann UK), Vanessa Holford, Sarah Hopkins, Sandy Howard (USA), Catherine Howard (Aus), Scott Howe, Clare Hudson (USA), Tsipi & Chanan Itai (Isr), Jo Jacobson, Cameron Johnson, Hisao Kato (Jap), Miyata Kazuaki (Jap), Ron Keehn (USA), Kenneth D Keith(USA), Kristian Kirchheiner, Heather Knox (NZ), Andrea Kreiner (D), S E Kuhn (USA), Gregg LaMarsh (C), D Laurence (F),

Dr Hugh Lavery (Aus), James Lawson (Aus), Adam Lebuwitz, Jennifer Ledwidge, Winnie Leung, Dr William Linnard (UK), Vauda Loaies, Patrick Logan (USA), Karen Lunde, Inge Mander (D), Dale Martin, Robert Mason (UK), Dudley McConnell, Heather McDougal (USA), Michele McFarland, P McLaren, Lee Meagher (Aus), Alan Mierch (USA), John Milanese (Aus), Sotaro Mimura (J), Nicole Miran (Isr), Kazuaki Miyata (J), Benjamin Moeling, Peter Moloney (Aus), Lieuwe Montsma (NL), Timothy Morey (UK), Joy Sachie Mori, Yasuko Morikawa (J), Barbara Mueller (J), Dale Myers (USA), Kay Nellins (UK), Kate Neuss (Aus), Adele Nevill (UK), Pamela Neville (C), D E Newkirk (USA), George Ng (HK), James Nickel (USA), Anthony Ogden, Jens Otto, Irene Otto (D), Danilo Palermo (Bra), Graham Pascoe (Aus), Nit Patan (Isr), Melissa Patrick (Aus), M G Payne (UK), Peter Payne, Neil Pearson, John Piedmont (USA), Ronald Popma (NL), C Price, Scott Pulizzi, Vanessa Quinn, D Michelle Raglannd, Katy Rhodes (UK), Jonathan Richmond (USA), Malcolm Roxburgh (UK), Julian Ryall, Jennifer Saal (USA), Toshi Sakai (USA), Gabi Sasaki (CH), Miss J A Saunders (Aus), Ro – Scheffers (NL), Uwe Schlokat (A), Thomas Schmidt (USA), Markus Schmieg (D), Britt Sexton (USA), Safia Shaw (UK), Brad Shields, Bernard & Edith Sigg (F), Stephen Simms, Tania Sironic (Aus), Brian Smith (Aus), Simon Sostaric (Aus), Andrew Stables, Mark Stamp (USA), I Steinwads (D), Todd Stradford (USA), Cooper Suzanne, Robert Swiderski (UK), Mary D Syseskey (USA), Kei Tanaka (J), Martin Taylor, Stephen Till, Masao Torii (J), Stephan Tschudi (CH), John Tully (USA), – Turner (USA), M van den Broek, Andre van der Berg (D), Mrs C van der Hulst (NZ), Michael Vandeman (USA), Ceci Vander, Tom & Virginia Verberne (Aus), Angie-Marie Vick (UK), Sandra Vogel (CH), Ben Walker (Aus), Annette Warrick (UK), Niki Willcott, Amanda Willcox (UK), Christopher Wilmott (UK), Roberto Wolnowicz, Garth Wooler, Sandy Yamada (J), Be-san Yeo (J), Erwin Ysewijn (J), Andrea Zanichelli (I), Daniel Zucker (USA)

A – Austria, Aus – Australia, B – Belgium, Bra – Brazil, C – Canada, CH – Switzerland, D – Germany, Dk – Denmark, F – France, HK – Hong Kong, I – Italy, Isr – Israel, J – Japan, NL – Netherlands, NZ – New Zealand, S – Sweden, Sp – Spain, UK – United Kingdom, USA – United States of America

LONELY PLANET TV SERIES & VIDEOS

Lonely Planet travel guides have been brought to life on television screens around the world. Like our guides, the programmes are based on the joy of independent travel, and look honestly at some of the most exciting, picturesque and frustrating places in the world. Each show is presented by one of three travellers from Australia, England or the USA and combines an innovative mixture of video, Super-8 film, atmospheric soundscapes and original music.

Videos of each episode – containing additional footage not shown on television – are available from good book and video shops, but the availability of individual videos varies with regional screening schedules.

Video destinations include:

Alaska; Australia (Southeast); Brazil; Ecuador & the Galapagos Islands; Indonesia; Israel & the Sinai Desert; Japan; La Ruta Maya (Yucatan, Guatemala & Belize); Morocco; North India (Varanasi to the Himalaya); Pacific Islands; Vietnam; Zimbabwe, Botswana & Namibia.

Coming in 1996:

The Arctic (Norway & Finland); Baja California; Chile & Easter Island; China (Southeast); Costa Rica; East Africa (Tanzania & Zanzibar); Great Barrier Reef (Australia); Jamaica; Papua New Guinea; the Rockies (USA); Syria & Jordan; Turkey.

The Lonely Planet television series is produced by:
Pilot Productions
Duke of Sussex Studios
44 Uxbridge St
London W8 7TG
United Kingdom

Lonely Planet videos are distributed by:
IVN Communications Inc
2246 Camino Ramon, San Ramon
California 94583, USA

107 Power Road, Chiswick
London W4 5PL, UK

For further information on both the television series and the availability of individual videos please contact Lonely Planet.

THE LONELY PLANET TRAVEL ATLAS

Tired of maps that lead you astray?

Sick of maps that fall apart after a few days' travel?

Had enough of maps that get creased and torn in all the wrong places?

**Lonely Planet is proud to announce the solution to all these problems –
the Lonely Planet travel atlas!**

Produced in conjunction with Steinhart Katzir Pub-
lishers, a range of atlases designed to complement
our guidebooks is now available to travellers
worldwide.

Unlike other maps and road atlases, which look
good on paper but often lack accuracy, LP's travel
atlases have been thoroughly checked on the road
by Lonely Planet's experienced team of authors. All
details are carefully checked to ensure that the atlas
conforms with the equivalent Lonely Planet
guidebook.

The handy book format means that the atlas can
withstand months of rigorous travelling adventures. So whether you're struggling through an
Icelandic gale or packed like a sardine on a back-
country bus in Asia, you'll find it easier to get where
you're going with a Lonely Planet travel atlas. (Ideal
for armchair travellers too!)

- full colour
- travel information in English, French, German, Spanish and Japanese
- place names keyed to LP guidebooks; no confusing spelling differences
- one country - one atlas. No need to buy five maps to cover large countries
- multilingual atlas legend
- comprehensive index

Available now:
Thailand; India; Zimbabwe, Botswana & Namibia and Vietnam

Coming soon:
Israel; Turkey; Laos and Chile

PLANET TALK
Lonely Planet's FREE quarterly newsletter

We love hearing from you and think you'd like to hear from us.

When...is the right time to see reindeer in Finland?
Where...can you hear the best palm-wine music in Ghana?
How...do you get from Asunción to Areguá by steam train?
What...is the best way to see India?

For the answer to these and many other questions read PLANET TALK.

Every issue is packed with up-to-date travel news and advice including:

- *a letter from Lonely Planet founders Tony and Maureen Wheeler*
- *travel diary from a Lonely Planet author - find out what it's really like out on the road*
- *feature article on an important and topical travel issue*
- *a selection of recent letters from our readers*
- *the latest travel news from all over the world*
- *details on Lonely Planet's new and forthcoming releases*

To join our mailing list contact any Lonely Planet office.

Also available: Lonely Planet T-shirts. 100% heavyweight cotton (S, M, L, XL)

LONELY PLANET PUBLICATIONS
Australia: PO Box 617, Hawthorn 3122, Victoria
tel: (03) 9819 1877 fax: (03) 9819 6459 e-mail: talk2us@lonelyplanet.com.au

USA: Embarcadero West, 155 Filbert St, Suite 251, Oakland, CA 94607
tel: (510) 893 8555 TOLL FREE: 800 275-8555 fax: (510) 893 8563
e-mail: info@lonelyplanet.com

UK: 10 Barley Mow Passage, Chiswick, London W4 4PH
tel: (0181) 742 3161 fax: (0181) 742 2772 e-mail: 100413.3551@compuserve.com

France: 71 bis rue du Cardinal Lemoine – 75005 Paris
tel: 1 46 34 00 58 fax: 1 46 34 72 55 e-mail: 100560.415@compuserve.com

World Wide Web: http://www.lonelyplanet.com/

Guides to North-East Asia

Beijing - city guide
Beijing is the hub of a vast nation. This guide will help travellers to find the best this ancient and fascinating city has to offer.

North-East Asia on a shoestring
Concise information for independent low-budget travel in China, Hong Kong, Japan, Macau, North Korea, South Korea, Taiwan and Mongolia.

China - a travel survival kit
This book is the recognised authority for independent travellers in the People's Republic. With essential tips for avoiding pitfalls, and comprehensive practical information, it will help you to discover the real China.

Hong Kong, Macau & Canton - a travel survival kit
This practical guide has all the travel facts on these three close but diverse cities, linked by history, culture and geography.

Korea - a travel survival kit
South Korea is one of the great undiscovered destinations, with its mountains, ancient temples and lively modern cities. This guide also includes a chapter on reclusive North Korea.

Mongolia - a travel survival kit
Mongolia is truly a destination for the adventurous. This guide gives visitors the first real opportunity to explore this remote but newly accessible country.

Seoul - city guide
It is easy to explore Seoul's ancient royal palaces and bustling market places with this comprehensive guide packed with vital information for leisure and business travellers alike.

Taiwan - a travel survival kit
Traditional Chinese ways survive in prosperous Taiwan. This guide has Chinese script and pinyin throughout.

Tibet - a travel survival kit
The fabled mountain-land of Tibet is slowly becoming accessible to travellers. This guide has full details on this remote and fascinating region, including the border crossing to Nepal.

Tokyo - city guide
Tokyo is a dynamic metropolis and one of the world's leading arbiters of taste and style. This guide will help you to explore the many sides of Tokyo, the modern Japanese miracle rolled into a single fascinating, sometimes startling package.

Also available:
Cantonese phrasebook, *Mandarin Chinese* phrasebook, *Korean* phrasebook, *Tibet* phrasebook, and *Japanese* phrasebook.

Lonely Planet Guidebooks

Lonely Planet guidebooks cover every accessible part of Asia as well as Australia, the Pacific, South America, Africa, the Middle East, Europe and parts of North America. There are six series: *travel survival kits*, covering a country for a range of budgets; *shoestring guides* with compact information for low-budget travel in a major region; *walking guides*; *city guides*, *travel atlases* and *phrasebooks*.

Australia & the Pacific

Australia
Australian phrasebook
Bushwalking in Australia
Islands of Australia's Great Barrier Reef
Outback Australia
Fiji
Fijian phrasebook
Melbourne city guide
Micronesia
New Caledonia
New South Wales & the ACT
New Zealand
Tramping in New Zealand
Papua New Guinea
Bushwalking in Papua New Guinea
Papua New Guinea phrasebook
Queensland
Rarotonga & the Cook Islands
Samoa
Solomon Islands
Sydney city guide
Tahiti & French Polynesia
Tonga
Vanuatu
Victoria
Western Australia

North-East Asia

Beijing city guide
China
Cantonese phrasebook
Mandarin Chinese phrasebook
Hong Kong, Macau & Canton
Japan
Japanese phrasebook
Korea
Korean phrasebook
Mongolia
Mongolian phrasebook
North-East Asia on a shoestring
Seoul city guide
Taiwan
Tibet
Tibet phrasebook
Tokyo city guide

Middle East

Arab Gulf States
Egypt & the Sudan
Arabic (Egyptian) phrasebook
Iran
Israel
Jordan & Syria
Middle East
Turkey
Turkish phrasebook
Trekking in Turkey
Yemen

South-East Asia

Bali & Lombok
Bangkok city guide
Cambodia
Indonesia
Indonesian phrasebook
Ho Chi Minh City city guide
Jakarta city guide
Java
Laos
Lao phrasebook
Malaysia, Singapore & Brunei
Myanmar (Burma)
Burmese phrasebook
Philippines
Pilipino phrasebook
Singapore city guide
South-East Asia on a shoestring
Thailand
Thailand travel atlas
Thai phrasebook
Thai Hill Tribes phrasebook
Vietnam
Vietnam travel atlas
Vietnamese phrasebook

Africa

Africa on a shoestring
Central Africa
East Africa
Trekking in East Africa
Kenya
Swahili phrasebook
Morocco
Arabic (Moroccan) phrasebook
North Africa
South Africa, Lesotho & Swaziland
West Africa
Zimbabwe, Botswana & Namibia
Zimbabwe, Botswana & Namibia travel atlas

Mail Order

Lonely Planet guidebooks are distributed worldwide. They are also available by mail order from Lonely Planet, so if you have difficulty finding a title please write to us. US and Canadian residents should write to Embarcadero West, 155 Filbert St, Suite 251, Oakland CA 94607, USA ; European residents should write to 10 Barley Mow Passage, Chiswick, London W4 4PH; and residents of other countries to PO Box 617, Hawthorn, Victoria 3122, Australia.

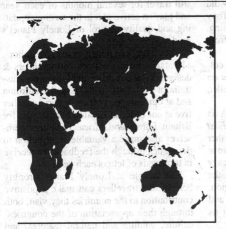

Indian Subcontinent
Bangladesh
India
India travel atlas
Hindi/Urdu phrasebook
Trekking in the Indian Himalaya
Karakoram Highway
Kashmir, Ladakh & Zanskar
Nepal
Trekking in the Nepal Himalaya
Nepali phrasebook
Pakistan
Sri Lanka
Sri Lanka phrasebook

Central America & the Caribbean
Baja California
Central America on a shoestring
Costa Rica
Eastern Caribbean
Guatemala, Belize & Yucatán: La Ruta Maya
Mexico

North America
Alaska
Backpacking in Alaska
Canada
Hawaii
Honolulu city guide
Pacific Northwest USA
Rocky Mountain States
Southwest USA
USA phrasebook

Europe
Baltic States & Kaliningrad
Baltics States phrasebook
Britain
Central Europe on a shoestring
Central Europe phrasebook
Czech & Slovak Republics
Dublin city guide
Eastern Europe on a shoestring
Eastern Europe phrasebook
Finland
France
Greece
Greek phrasebook
Hungary
Iceland, Greenland & the Faroe Islands
Ireland
Italy
Mediterranean Europe on a shoestring
Mediterranean Europe phrasebook
Poland
Prague city guide
Russia, Ukraine & Belarus
Russian phrasebook
Scandinavian & Baltic Europe on a shoestring
Scandinavian Europe phrasebook
Slovenia
Switzerland
Trekking in Greece
Trekking in Spain
Vienna city guide
Western Europe on a shoestring
Western Europe phrasebook

South America
Argentina, Uruguay & Paraguay
Bolivia
Brazil
Brazilian phrasebook
Chile & Easter Island
Colombia
Ecuador & the Galápagos Islands
Latin American Spanish phrasebook
Peru
Quechua phrasebook
Rio de Janeiro city guide
South America on a shoestring
Trekking in the Patagonian Andes
Venezuela

Indian Ocean
Madagascar & Comoros
Maldives & Islands of the East Indian Ocean
Mauritius, Réunion & Seychelles

The Lonely Planet Story

Lonely Planet published its first book in 1973 in response to the numerous 'How did you do it?' questions Maureen and Tony Wheeler were asked after driving, bussing, hitching, sailing and railing their way from England to Australia.

Written at a kitchen table and hand collated, trimmed and stapled, *Across Asia on the Cheap* became an instant local bestseller, inspiring thoughts of another book.

Eighteen months in South-East Asia resulted in their second guide, *South-East Asia on a shoestring*, which they put together in a backstreet Chinese hotel in Singapore in 1975. The 'yellow bible' as it quickly became known to backpackers around the world, soon became *the* guide to the region. It has sold well over half a million copies and is now in its 8th edition, still retaining its familiar yellow cover.

Today there are over 140 Lonely Planet titles in print – books that have that same adventurous approach to travel as those early guides; books that 'assume you know how to get your luggage off the carousel' as one reviewer put it.

Although Lonely Planet initially specialised in guides to Asia, they now cover most regions of the world, including the Pacific, South America, Africa, the Middle East and Europe. The list of *walking guides* and *phrasebooks* (for 'unusual' languages such as Quechua, Swahili, Nepali and Egyptian Arabic) is also growing rapidly.

The emphasis continues to be on travel for independent travellers. Tony and Maureen still travel for several months of each year and play an active part in the writing, updating and quality control of Lonely Planet's guides.

They have been joined by over 50 authors, 110 staff – mainly editors, cartographers & designers – at our office in Melbourne, Australia, at our US office in Oakland, California and at our European office in Paris; another five at our office in London handle sales for Britain, Europe and Africa. Travellers themselves also make a valuable contribution to the guides through the feedback we receive in thousands of letters each year.

The people at Lonely Planet strongly believe that travellers can make a positive contribution to the countries they visit, both through their appreciation of the countries' culture, wildlife and natural features, and through the money they spend. In addition, the company makes a direct contribution to the countries and regions it covers. Since 1986 a percentage of the income from each book has been donated to ventures such as famine relief in Africa; aid projects in India; agricultural projects in Central America; Greenpeace's efforts to halt French nuclear testing in the Pacific; and Amnesty International.

Lonely Planet's basic travel philosophy is summed up in Tony Wheeler's comment, 'Don't worry about whether your trip will work out. Just go!'.